Smith and Keenan's
ENGLISH LAW

Tenth edition

Denis Keenan

LLB(Hons), FCIS, DMA, CertEd

of the Middle Temple, Barrister-at-Law
Formerly Head of Department of Business Studies and Law
Mid-Essex Technical College and School of Art
(now Anglia Polytechnic University)

PITMAN
PUBLISHING

Pitman Publishing Limited
128 Long Acre, London WC2E 9AN

A Division of Longman Group UK Limited

© Kenneth Smith and Denis Keenan, 1963, 1966
© Denis Keenan and Mrs K Smith, 1969, 1973, 1975, 1979, 1982
© Denis Keenan, 1986
© Denis Keenan,1989
© Denis Keenan, 1992

Tenth edition first published in Great Britain 1992
Reprinted 1993, 1994

A CIP catalogue record for this book is available from
the British Library.

ISBN 0 273 03729 3

Typeset by Avocet Typesetters, Bicester, Oxon
Printed in England by Clays Ltd, St Ives plc

Contents

Preface   xiv

Table of Statutes   xvi

Table of Cases   xxii

1 The nature and development of English law   1

Classification of English law   1
The development of English law – generally   3
The common law   4
Equity   7
Defects of the common law   7
Relationship of law and equity   10
Legislation   12
Delegated legislation   13
Custom   14
Canon law   15
Legal treatises   16

2 The courts of law   18

The Supreme Court of Judicature   18
The courts today   19
Magistrates' courts   19
Youth courts   27
The County Court   28
The Crown Court   33
The Central Criminal Court   34
The High Court – generally   35
The Commercial Court   36
The Companies' Court   37
The Bankruptcy Court   37
The Court of Protection   38
The Restrictive Practices Court   38
The Court of Appeal – generally   39
The Civil Division   39
The Criminal Division   40
Assistance for transaction of judicial business
   in the Supreme Court   42
The House of Lords   43
The Judicial Committee of the Privy Council   44
Removal and retirement of judges   45
Arbitration   45
Conciliation   46
Tribunals   46

The Court of Justice of the European Communities 46
The role of the European Court at Luxembourg 48
The European Court of Human Rights 49

3 Other courts and tribunals and legal services 51

Administrative tribunals 52
Employment tribunals 53
Administrative inquiries 55
Advantages of tribunals 56
The Tribunals and Inquiries Acts 56
Legal aid 57
Domestic tribunals 57
Judicial control over inferior courts and tribunals 59
Other controls on decision making 65
Coroners' courts 68
Legal services – provision of 70
Payment for legal services 73
The main legal professions 73
Some important judicial officers 78

4 Criminal procedure 82

Criminal procedure – generally 82
The prosecutor 83
The Director of Public Prosecutions 85
Prosecuting fraud 85
Getting the person accused into court 86
Summary trial before magistrates
  (other than in a Youth Court) 91
Proceedings relating to children and young persons 95
Trial on indictment in the Crown Court 99
Legal aid 99
Reporting of committal proceedings 99
Alibi 101
Place and time of trial 101
The offence and indictment 102
Arraignment 103
Jury trial 104
Committal to the Crown Court for sentence 112
Appeals in criminal cases 112
Contempt of Court Act, 1981 112
Sentencing 112

5 Civil procedure 122

Bringing a civil action to trial 122
The trial 129
Appeals 132
Enforcing a judgment 132

6 The law-making process I – the UK Parliament   **135**

Legislation   135
Delegated legislation   140
Interpretation of statutes by the judiciary   145

7 The law-making process II – case law and the legislative organs of the European Community   **151**

Case law or judicial precedent   151
EC law   163
Law reform   167

8 Persons and the Crown   **168**

Natural persons   168
Juristic persons   187
Unincorporated associations   191
The Crown   196

9 Law of contract – making the contract I   **201**

The essentials of a valid contract   201
Classification of contracts   202
The formation of contract   204
Agreement   204
Offer and invitation to treat   204
Acceptance – generally   206
Termination of offer   212

10 Law of contract – making the contract II   **216**

Consideration   216
Consideration in relation to formation of a contract – generally   217
Consideration viewed in relation to the discharge or variation of a contract   223
Common law – the rule of accord and satisfaction   223
Equity – the rule of promissory estoppel   224
Discharge of contract by performance – relevance of the *High Trees* case   226
Equitable estoppel – other applications   226
Intention to create legal relations   226

11 Law of contract – making the contract III   **230**

Formalities   230
Capacity to contract   232
Minors   233
Consequences of the defective contracts of minors   234
Mental disorder and drunkenness   236
Corporations   236

12 Law of contract – reality of consent I   241

Introduction   241
Agreement mistake in general   241
Documents mistakenly signed   242
Unilateral mistake   242
Bilateral identical (or common) mistake   243
Non-identical bilateral (or mutual) mistake   246

13 Law of contract – reality of consent II   247

Misrepresentation   247
Meaning of representation   247
Types of actionable misrepresentation and remedies
   in general   251
Compensation under the Financial Services Act, 1986   252
Agent's breach of warranty of authority   253
Negligence at common law   253
Remedy of rescission   255
Contracts *uberrimae fidei* (utmost good faith)   256
Duress   257
Undue influence and associated equitable pleas   259
Economic duress   260
Unconscionable bargains   262
No general rule that all contracts must be fair   262

14 Law of contract – contractual terms   263

Inducements and terms generally   263
Inducements and terms distinguished   263
Conditions and warranties   267
Innominate terms   268
Implied terms – generally   268
Implied terms in consumer law – sale of goods   270
Title   270
Sales by description   272
Implied conditions as to fitness   273
Merchantable quality   275
Fitness and merchantability   278
Sale by sample   280
Implied terms in consumer law – the supply of goods
   and services   280
Supply of goods other than by sale   280
Contracts for the transfer of property in goods   281
Contracts for work and materials   282
The terms implied   282
Remedies   284
Exchange and barter   285
Contracts for the hire of goods   285
The terms implied   286

Exclusion clauses   288
The supply of services   288
Exclusion clauses   290

15 Law of contract – exclusion clauses   291

Exclusion clauses – the issue of communication   291
Construction of exclusion clauses   294
The doctrine of fundamental breach   295
The approach of Parliament to exclusion clauses   295
Exclusion clauses applicable if reasonable   297
Reasonableness   298
Provisions against evasion of liability   301

16 Law of contract – illegality and public policy   303

Introduction   303
Public policy – the contribution of the judiciary:
    illegal contracts   304
Consequences   305
Public policy and the judiciary – void contracts   307
Contracts in restraint of trade generally   308
Voluntary contractual restraints of trade on employees
    generally   309
Contractual restraints on employees through the period
    of notice   309
Non-contractual restraints on employees: confidential
    information   310
Employee restraints arising from agreements between
    manufacturers and traders   311
Restraints imposed on the vendor of a business   311
Restrictions on shareholder-employees   311
Restrictions accepted by distributors of merchandise   312
Involuntary restraints of trade   312
Consequences where the contract is contrary to public
    policy: severance   312
Public policy: the contribution of Parliament   313
Wagering contracts: insurance and dealing in
    differences   315
Contracts affected by the Restrictive Trade Practices
    Act, 1976   316
The Resale Prices Act, 1976   317
The Fair Trading Act, 1973   317
The Competition Act, 1980   318
The European Community approach to restrictive
    practices   319

17 Law of contract – discharge of contract   322

Discharge by agreement   322

Discharge by performance generally   323
Construction of the contract as entire   323
Substantial performance   323
Acceptance of partial performance   324
Full performance prevented by the promisee   324
Time of performance   325
Tender   325
Appropriation of payments   326
Discharge by frustration generally   327
Contracts for personal service   327
Government interference   328
Destruction of the subject matter of the contract   328
Non-occurrence of an event   328
Commercial purpose defeated   329
Situations in which the doctrine does not apply   329
The Law Reform (Frustrated Contracts) Act, 1943   330
Discharge by breach   331
Anticipatory breach and supervening events   332
Effect of breach on contract   332
Other matters relevant to breach   332

18 Law of contract – remedies and limitation of actions 334

Damages generally   334
Liquidated damages   334
Unliquidated damages   335
Mitigation of loss   336
Provisional damages for personal injuries   337
Interest on debt and damages   337
Equitable remedies   337
Claims for restitution: quasi-contract   339
Limitation of actions   340

19 Law of contract – employment protection   342

Recruitment and selection of employees   342
Protection during employment   344
The contract of employment   344
Pay   345
Equal treatment in terms and conditions of
    employment as between men and women
    in the same employment   346
Discrimination in the treatment of employees   347
Disclosure of information   348
Guarantee payments   348
Suspension from work on medical grounds   349
Maternity provision   349
Time off   352
Insolvency of employer   352

Health and safety at work   352
Trade union membership and activities   354
Termination of the contract of employment   354
Discriminatory dismissal   365
Redundancy   365
Written statement of reasons for dismissal   370

20 The law of torts – general principles   **371**

The nature of a tort   371
Damage and liability   372
Parties in the law of torts   374
Corporations   378
Unincorporated associations and trade unions   379
Vicarious liability   382
Who is a servant or employee?   382
Nature of vicarious liability   387
Liability for torts of independent contractors   392
General defences   394
Remedies   402
Damages – generally   402
Nervous shock   408
Damage after successive accidents   409
Cessation of liability   411

21 The law of torts – specific torts   **415**

Torts affecting the person   415
Arrest and the tort of trespass to the person   418
Remedies available against false imprisonment   419
Torts affecting property   420
Wrongful interference with goods   424
Recaption   428
Replevin   428
Nuisance   428
Public nuisance   429
Private nuisance   429
Negligence – generally   434
The duty of care – generally   435
The duty of care – economic loss   437
Negligence – product liability   445
Statutory product liability – claims against the
   manufacturer   446
Negligence – professional liability   448
Negligence – occupiers' liability   455
Highway authorities   459
Defective Premises Act, 1972   459
Negligence – of employers   460
Torts against business interests   461

Defamation   463
Publication   463
The rule in *Rylands* v *Fletcher*   476

22 The law of property   **480**

The nature of property   480
Ownership   481
Possession   482
Bailment   485
Land law   491
Equitable interests   492
Co-ownership   494
A leasehold or a term of years   496
Servitudes   500
Restrictive covenants   505
The transfer of land   507
Personal property   508
Mortgages of land   509
Registration of land charges   517
Mortgages of personal chattels   520
Mortgages of choses in action   521
Other forms of security   521
Lien   521
Assignments of choses in action   525

23 Criminal law   **528**

Crime and civil wrongs distinguished   528
Terminology and outcome of criminal and civil
  proceedings   528
Nulla poena sine lege   529
Constituent elements of a criminal offence   530
The *actus reus*   530
Omissions or failures to act   531
The *mens rea* – generally   532
Mens rea in statutory offences   535
The mental element – corporations   537

24 Criminal law – specific offences   **540**

Homicide   540
Murder   540
Manslaughter   541
Voluntary manslaughter   541
Involuntary manslaughter   543
Causing death by dangerous driving   544
Violent crimes which are not fatal   544
Assault and battery   545
Statutory offences against the person   546
Sexual offences   548

25 Criminal law – age and responsibility: general defences — 550

Liability of minors	550
Insanity	551
Automatism	553
Drunkenness and drugs	554
Duress	555
Necessity	557
Mistake	557
Self-defence	558
Preventing crime	559

Cases and materials — 561

The nature and development of English law	561
Other courts and tribunals and legal services	563
Criminal procedure	
The law-making process I – the UK Parliament	574
The law-making process II – case law and the legislative organs of the European Community	580
Persons and the Crown	581
Law of contract – making the contract I	587
Law of contract – making the contract II	607
Law of contract – making the contract III	630
Law of contract – reality of consent I	635
Law of contract – reality of consent II	647
Law of contract – contractual terms	660
Law of contract – exclusion clauses	674
Law of contract – illegality and public policy	684
Law of contract – discharge of contract	698
Law of contract – remedies and limitation of actions	709
Law of contract – employment protection	716
Law of torts	724
The law of torts – specific torts	763
The law of property	809
Criminal law – general principles	828
Criminal law – specific offences	841
Criminal law – age and responsibility: general defences	847

Glossary of commonly used legal words and phrases	857
Index	859

Preface to the tenth edition

In this tenth edition the book has undergone its most major revision since it was first published in 1963. The aim has been to produce a more readable text and also to respond to a questionnaire kindly completed by lecturers in polytechnics and colleges before work on the tenth edition began.

Basically they wanted an expansion of the criminal law chapter and this has been done – indeed, there are now three chapters on criminal law covering the major topics which appeared in the earlier editions of the book. Negotiable instruments and banking could be left out, they said, being more commonly covered at later stages under the heading of business law.

The Appendix of cases and materials should be retained according to the answers to the questionnaires and it has been, and once again each case or sometimes a group of cases has introductory material which makes it possible to more effectively study the cases along with or separately from the text. The intention is that this publication should continue as in effect a text and casebook combined. The major case summaries contain, as before, appropriate extracts from important judgments.

Formerly the cases were quoted in the text in italics with a number reference to the summary in the Appendix. Unfortunately, with the increase in the number of important cases, this began to somewhat disturb the flow of the text. Now essential cases appear in a box following an undisturbed section of relevant text. The number reference to the Appendix is retained and the box contains a few words to assist recall of the facts of the case at, say, a revision stage prior to an examination.

Again it has been necessary to substantially rewrite certain sections of the book and naturally to update it since the law never stands still. The amendments are necessary if the book is to continue to be useful to those categories of students who have used it over the years. These include students on BA Business Studies and other degree courses as well as students taking BTEC HND and CIB Foundation and very many other non-lawyers both here and abroad taking law in a wide variety of business and other courses.

In the preparation of this edition the Publishers and I have once again received the valuable assistance of my wife in terms of the preparation of the indexes, together with the organisation of sources of new material since the last edition.

I must also express my thanks to Simon Lake and Pat Bond of Pitman Publishing for their general support of the publication and also to Giovanna Ceroni, the Editorial Co-ordinator at Pitman who organised the editing of the book. Thanks also to those who designed, set and printed this very different edition.

For the errors and omissions, in terms of the level at which the book aims, I am of course responsible.

Denis Keenan
Maenan
March 1992

Table of Statutes

Abortion Act, 1967 *540*
Acts of Parliament Numbering and
   Citation Act, 1962 *139*
Acquisition of Land (Assessment of
   Compensation) Act, 1919 *562*
Administration of Estates Act, 1925
   4, 147, 491
Administration of Justice Act, 1960
   37, 157
Administration of Justice Act, 1970
   37, 512, 513
Administration of Justice Act, 1973
   512, 513
Administration of Justice Act, 1982
   *19, 42, 80, 105, 337, 376, 380,
   381, 382, 402, 727*
Administration of Justice Act, 1985
   72, 77, 476, 508
Adoption Act, 1976 *171*
Agricultural Marketing Act, 1958
   569
Air Guns and Shot Guns Act, 1962
   729
Animals Act, 1971 *422, 750*
Appellate Jurisdiction Act, 1876 *19,
   43, 151*
Attachment of Earnings Act, 1971
   32

Bail Act, 1976 *89, 90*
Banking Act, 1979 *195*
Baths and Wash-houses Acts,
   1846–78 *563*
Betting and Loans (Infants) Acts,
   1892 *233*
Bill of Rights, 1689 *471*
Bills of Exchange Act, 1882 *15, 163,
   219, 221, 525, 614*
Bills of Sale Acts, 1878–82 *520,*
526, 827
Bristol and Exeter Railways Act, 1836
   574
British Nationality Act, 1948 *562*
British Nationality Act, 1981 *176*
British Railways Act, 1968 *574*
Building Societies Act, 1986 *513*

Carriage by Air Act, 1961 *413*
Carriage of Goods by Sea Act, 1971
   391
Celluloid and Cinematograph Film
   Act, 1922 *576*
Charging Orders Act, 1979 *133*
Children Act, 1989 *20, 25, 26, 31,
   95, 96, 169, 170, 171*
Children and Young Persons Act,
   1933 *97, 98, 838*
Children and Young Persons Act,
   1963 *550*
Children and Young Persons Act,
   1969 *25, 98, 170*
Cinematograph Act, 1909 *565, 566*
Civil Aviation Act, 1949 *767*
Civil Aviation Act, 1971 *569*
Civil Aviation Act, 1982 *420, 767*
Civil Liability (Contribution) Act,
   1978 *198, 379*
Coinage Act, 1971 *325*
Companies Act, 1948 *625*
Companies Act, 1985 *85, 146, 168,
   188, 189, 195, 203, 238, 239, 240,
   378, 455, 526, 607, 625, 790*
Companies Act, 1989 *188, 238, 240*
Company Directors Disqualification
   Act, 1986 *172*
Competition Act, 1980 *318, 319*
Congenital Disabilities (Civil Liability)
   Act, 1976 *374, 375*

Consumer Arbitration Agreements Act, 1988 45
Consumer Credit Act, 1974 *32, 185, 231, 270, 318, 511*
Consumer Protection Act, 1987 *446, 447, 448, 589, 668, 669, 672*
Consumer Safety Act, 1978 *447*
Consumer Safety (Amendment) Act, 1986 *447*
Contempt of Court Act, 1981 *100, 111, 112*
Copyright Act, 1956 *608*
Copyright, Designs and Patents Act, 1988 *32, 608*
Coroners Act, 1988 *68, 69, 132*
County Courts Act, 1846 *28*
County Courts Act, 1984 *28, 289, 32, 33, 40, 132*
Courts Act, 1971 *6, 33, 37, 45*
Courts and Legal Services Act, 1990 *20, 21, 27, 28, 29, 31, 34, 35, 43, 52, 53, 66, 67, 69, 70, 71, 72, 73, 75, 76, 77, 78, 81, 83, 179, 377, 508*
Criminal Appeal Act, 1968 *41, 42*
Criminal Damage Act, 1971 *834, 835, 851*
Criminal Justice Act, 1925 *557*
Criminal Justice Act, 1967 *89, 101, 564*
Criminal Justice Act, 1972 *41, 120*
Criminal Justice Act, 1982 *23, 89, 91, 96, 97, 109*
Criminal Justice Act, 1987 *85*
Criminal Justice Act, 1988 *41, 42, 84, 85, 89, 91, 96, 106, 119, 120, 121, 725*
Criminal Justice Act, 1991 *25, 28, 84, 96, 97, 98, 114, 115, 116, 117, 118*
Criminal Justice (Amendment) Act, 1981 *100*
Criminal Law Act, 1967 *167, 559, 856*
Criminal Law Act, 1977 *22, 24, 423, 424, 529*
Criminal Procedure (Insanity) Act, 1964 *551*
Criminal Procedure (Insanity and Unfitness to Plead) Act, 1991 *551*
Criminal Procedure (Right of Reply) Act, 1964 *109*
Crown Proceedings Act, 1947 *196,*

198, 199, 200, 377, 810
Crown Proceedings (Armed Forces) Act, 1987 *199*
Currency Act, 1983 *325*
Currency and Bank Notes Act, 1954 *325*

Dangerous Drugs Act, 1965 *836*
Data Protection Act, 1984 *372*
Defamation Act, 1952 *399, 465, 466, 468, 469, 471, 473, 474, 801*
Defective Premises Act, 1972 *149, 458, 459, 460*
Directors' Liability Act, 1890 *651*
Domicile and Matrimonial Proceedings Act, 1973 *174, 175*
Domestic and Appellate Proceedings (Restriction of Publicity) Act, 1968 *473*
Dramatic and Musical Performers Protection Act, 1925 *838*
Drug Trafficking Offences Act, 1986 *119, 333*

Education Act, 1944 *570, 571*
Employers' Liability (Compulsory Insurance) Act, 1969 *382, 461*
Employers' Liability (Defective Equipment) Act, 1969 *461*
Employment Act, 1980 *342, 348, 349, 351, 357, 358, 775*
Employment Act, 1982 *193, 342*
Employment Act, 1988 *193, 342, 354*
Employment Act, 1989 *342, 343, 356, 366, 368, 370*
Employment Act, 1990 *193, 194, 354, 356*
Employment Protection Act, 1975 *55, 348*
Employment Protection (Consolidation) Act, 1978 *46, 54, 198, 322, 342, 344, 345, 347, 348, 349, 351, 352, 354, 355, 356, 357, 365, 366, 367, 370, 717*
Enduring Powers of Attorney Act, 1985 *186*
Environmental Protection Act, 1990 *434*
Equal Pay Act, 1970 *182, 184, 346, 718*

European Assembly Elections Act, 1978 *165*

European Communities Act, 1972 *13, 166*

European Communities (Amendment) Act, 1986 *48, 164, 165*

Exchange Control Act, 1947 *687*

Explosive Substances Act, 1883 *856*

Extradition Act, 1989 *26*

Fair Trading Act, 1973 *38, 317*

Family Law Reform Act, 1969 *168, 169, 233*

Fatal Accidents Act, 1976 *380, 381, 382, 442*

Finance Act, 1964 *561*

Financial Services Act, 1986 *58, 85, 121, 188, 189, 248, 254, 257, 316, 649, 651*

Firearms Act, 1968 *729*

Food Safety Act, 1990 *534*

Foreign Compensation Act, 1950 *144*

Gaming Act, 1845 *315*

Geneva Conventions Act, 1957 *561*

Health and Safety at Work Act, 1974 *342, 349, 352, 353, 720, 721*

Health and Social Services and Social Security Adjudications Act, 1983 *52*

Highways Act, 1980 *459, 795*

Highways (Miscellaneous Provisions) Act, 1961 *795*

Homicide Act, 1957 *541, 542*

Housing Act, 1925 *562*

Housing Act, 1961 *818*

Housing Act, 1980 *51*

Housing Act, 1988 *30*

Human Fertilisation and Embryology Act, 1990 *36, 374*

Immigration Act, 1971 *119, 173, 567, 577*

Immigration Act, 1988 *173*

Immigration Appeals Act, 1969 *574*

Industrial Training Act, 1964 *575*

Income and Corporation Taxes Act, 1988 *583*

Infant Life (Preservation) Act, 1929 *540*

Infants Relief Act, 1874 *233*

Innkeepers Act, 1878 *523*

Insolvency Act, 1986 *30; 31, 172, 621*

Interpretation Act, 1889 *575*

Interpretation Act, 1978 *145, 576*

Judgments Act, 1838 *337*

Judicature Acts, 1873–1875 *11, 18, 19, 151, 646*

Judicial Pensions Act, 1959 *45*

Judicial Proceedings (Regulation of Reports) Act, 1926 *473*

Juries Act, 1974 *104, 105, 106, 110, 111, 132*

Juries (Disqualification) Act, 1984 *104, 106, 111*

Justices of the Peace Act, 1979 *19, 20, 377*

Land Charges Act, 1925 *491, 515, 517*

Land Charges Act, 1972 *517, 518*

Land Drainage Act, 1930 *752*

Landlord and Tenant Act, 1954 *816*

Landlord and Tenant Act, 1988 *499*

Land Registration Act, 1925 *491, 508, 517, 518, 519, 657, 825, 826*

Land Registration Act, 1988 *518*

Latent Damage Act, 1986 *412, 413*

Law Commissions Act, 1965 *167*

Law Officers Act, 1944 *79*

Law of Property Act, 1925 *139, 163, 169, 230, 325, 491, 492, 494, 495, 498, 502, 506, 507, 509, 510, 512, 514, 525, 526, 601, 602, 617, 657, 819, 821*

Law of Property Act, 1969 *506, 507, 517*

Law of Property (Miscellaneous Provisions) Act, 1989 *202, 230, 231, 507, 593*

Law Reform (Contributory Negligence) Act, 1945 *442, 446, 478*

Law Reform (Frustrated Contracts) Act, 1943 *330, 699, 707*

Law Reform (Husband and Wife) Act, 1962 *376, 379*

Law Reform (Married Women and Tortfeasors) Act, 1935 *376, 379*

Law Reform (Miscellaneous Provisions) Act, 1934 *380, 381*

Law Reform (Miscellaneous Provisions) Act, 1970   229, 380, 404, 613
Law Reform (Personal Injuries) Act, 1948   162, 403
Leasehold Reform Act, 1967   499, 516, 517
Legal Aid Act, 1988   21, 90
Licensing Act, 1872   837, 839
Licensing Act, 1921   841
Licensing Act, 1961   840
Life Peerages Act, 1958   135
Limitation Act, 1980   219, 255, 326, 340, 341, 381, 412, 413, 428, 459, 460, 476, 484, 485, 715, 763
Limited Partnerships Act, 1907   195
Local Land Charges Act, 1975   503

Magistrates' Courts Act, 1980   22, 23, 24, 25, 27, 84, 86, 91, 92, 93, 99, 100, 101, 564, 573
Magna Carta, 1215   4
Malicious Damage Act, 1861   42, 835
Marine Insurance Act, 1906   231, 655
Maritime Conventions Act, 1911   413
Married Women's Property Act, 1882   221, 376, 816
Matrimonial and Family Proceedings Act, 1984   31
Matrimonial Causes Act, 1975   29
Matrimonial Homes Act, 1967   518
Matrimonial Homes Act, 1983   518, 519, 826
Mental Health Act, 1983   38, 236, 552
Mercantile Law Amendment Act, 1856   232
Merchant Shipping Act, 1970   699
Merchant Shipping Act, 1988   581
Merchant Shipping (Amendment) Act, 1862   767
Merchant Shipping (Oil Pollution) Act, 1971   767
Minors' Contracts Act, 1987   233, 235, 633
Misrepresentation Act, 1967   251, 252, 253, 254, 263, 298, 650, 654, 661, 681
Municipal Corporations Act, 1882   568

Murder (Abolition of Death Penalty) Act, 1965   113, 136

National Health Service (Amendment) Act, 1986   199
National Assistance Act, 1948   612
New Zealand Workers' Compensation Act, 1922   734
Nuclear Installations Act, 1965   375, 413

Occupiers' Liability Act, 1957   455, 456, 458, 741, 743, 793
Occupiers' Liability Act, 1984   455, 456, 457
Offences against the Person Act, 1861   102, 103, 109, 111, 120, 417, 533, 540, 546, 547, 550, 554, 833, 837, 844, 845

Parliament Act, 1911   138
Parliament Act, 1949   138
Parliamentary and Health Service Commissioners Act, 1987   66, 67
Parliamentary Commissioner Act, 1967   66
Parliamentary Commissioner (Consular Complaints) Act, 1981   66
Parliamentary Constituencies Act, 1986   143
Parliamentary Papers Act, 1840   471
Partnership Act, 1890   133, 194, 195
Pharmacy and Poisons Act, 1933   589
Poisons Act, 1972   589
Police Act, 1964   377
Police and Criminal Evidence Act, 1984   21, 82, 86, 87, 88, 416, 418, 419, 421, 766
Policies of Assurance Act, 1867   526
Post Office Act, 1953   572
Post Office Act, 1969   229, 377, 412
Powers of Criminal Courts Act, 1973   2, 91, 114, 117, 118, 119, 120
Prescription Act, 1832   503, 504, 822
Proceedings against Estates Act, 1970   380
Prosecution of Offences Act, 1879   85
Prosecution of Offences Act, 1985   83, 84, 85

Protection from Eviction Act,
1977   724, 769
Protection of Birds Act, 1954   589
Provisions of Oxford, 1258   8
Public Health Act, 1875   751
Public Health Act, 1936   575
Public Order Act, 1986   177, 182,
423
Public Trustee Act, 1906   191

Race Relations Act, 1976   177, 178,
179, 180, 181, 182, 184, 185, 342,
347, 364, 365, 368, 583
Railway Fires Act, 1905   751
Real Property Act, 1845   617
Recorded Delivery Service Act,
1962   601
Representation of the People Act,
1983   175
Refreshment Houses Act, 1860   578
Rehabilitation of Offenders Act, 1974
121, 470
Resale Prices Act, 1976   38, 221,
304, 314, 315, 316, 317, 318, 615
Reservoirs Act, 1975   478
Restrictive Trade Practices Act, 1956
38, 796
Restrictive Trade Practices Act, 1976
38, 304, 316, 317, 318, 319, 796
Rights of Light Act, 1959   503
Rivers (Prevention of Pollution) Act,
1951   837
Road Traffic Act, 1930   849
Road Traffic Act, 1972   398, 544
Road Traffic Act, 1988   91, 92, 93,
532
Road Traffic Act, 1991   544
Road Traffic Offenders Act, 1988
94, 765
Royal Assent Act, 1967   139
Rules of the Supreme Court (Crown
Proceedings) Act, 1947   196

Sale of Goods Act, 1893   163
Sale of Goods Act, 1979   15, 139,
163, 205, 226, 233, 236, 270, 271,
272, 273, 274, 275, 276, 277, 278,
279, 280, 281, 282, 283, 284, 285,
286, 287, 288, 289, 290, 296, 297,
299, 301, 302, 324, 327, 340, 445,
446, 509, 523, 596, 642, 665, 666,

667, 668, 669, 670, 671, 672, 673,
674, 685, 726
Settled Land Act, 1925   491, 493,
494
Sex Discrimination Act, 1975   146,
182, 184, 342, 584, 719
Sex Discrimination Act, 1986   182,
183, 342, 343, 346, 347, 355, 364,
365, 368
Sexual Offences Act, 1956   549
Sexual Offences (Amendment) Act,
1976   846, 847
Short Titles Act, 1896   139
Slander of Women Act, 1891   465,
798
Social Security Act, 1975   52
Social Security Act, 1985   345
Social Security Act, 1986   349, 350
Social Security Act, 1989   403
Social Security Act, 1990   68
Social Security and Housing Benefit
Act, 1982   345
Social Security Pensions Act, 1975
68
Statute of Frauds, 1677   231, 232,
630, 631
Statute of Westminster, 1285   6, 8
Statutory Instruments Act, 1946   141,
142, 144
Statutory Sick Pay Act, 1991   345
Supply of Goods (Implied Terms) Act,
1973   270, 281, 287, 296, 297
Supply of Goods and Services Act,
1982   270, 281, 288, 289, 290,
297, 299, 340, 784
Supreme Court Act, 1981   6, 11, 19,
34, 35, 36, 39, 40, 42, 61, 64, 80,
81, 84, 102, 131, 337, 339, 561
Supreme Court of Judicature
(Consolidation) Act, 1925   19

Tattooing of Minors Act, 1969   169
Telecommunications Act, 1984   377
Theatres Act, 1968   465, 475
Theft Act, 1968   86, 97, 119, 120
Torts (Interference with Goods) Act,
1977   424, 425, 426, 427, 523
Town and Country Planning Act,
1990   52
Trade Descriptions Act, 1968   149
Trade Union and Labour Relations
Act, 1974   193, 194, 229, 775
Transport Act, 1981   751

Transport (London) Act, 1969 *564*
Trial of Lunatics Act, 1883 *551*
Tribunals and Inquiries Act, 1958 *56*
Tribunals and Inquiries Act, 1971
  56, 62, 63
Truck Act, 1831 *346*

Unfair Contract Terms Act, 1977
  *288, 290, 293, 295, 296, 297, 298,
  299, 300, 301, 302, 454, 456, 457,
  489, 652, 655, 674, 675, 680, 681,
  683, 684, 743*

Unsolicited Goods and Services Act,
  1971 *209, 487*
Unsolicited Goods and Services
  (Amendment) Act, 1975 *209, 487*

Wages Act, 1986 *346*
Waterworks Clauses Act, 1874 *788*
Weeds Act, 1959 *807*
Wildlife and Countryside Act, 1981
  168
Wireless Telegraphy Act, 1949 *570*

Table of Cases

Note The number of the case in the Appendix is printed in **bold** type; the page on which the case is cited is printed in *italic* type.

Abbatt *v* Treasury Solicitor (1969) *192*

Abbey National *v* Cann (1990) *826*

Adams *v* Lindsell (1818) **66,** *212*

Adams *v* Ursell (1913) **375,** *430*

Adamson *v* Jarvis (1827) *379*

Agreement between the Members of ABTA (1983) *316*

Ailsa Craig Fishing Co. Ltd *v* Malvern Fishing Co. Ltd (1983) *681, 683*

Ajayi *v* R.T. Brisco (Nigeria) Ltd (1964) *623*

Alan (W.J.) Co. *v* El Nasr Export Import Co. (1972) **98,** *226*

Alcock *v* Chief Constable of South Yorkshire (1991) *760*

Alexander *v* Mercouris (1979) *148*

Alexander *v* N.E. Railway Co. (1865) **438,** *469*

Alexander *v* Railway Executive (1951) **182,** *294, 683*

Alexander *v* Rayson (1936) *685*

Alidair *v* Taylor (1978) *357*

Allcard *v* Skinner (1887) *149, 259, 260*

Allen *v* Greenwood (1979) *504*

Allen *v* Sir Alfred McAlpine & Sons Ltd (1968) *125*

Alpenstow Ltd *v* Regalian Properties plc (1985) *592*

Alphacell *v* Woodward (1972) **524,** *535, 538*

Amalgamated Investment & Property *v* John Walker & Sons (1976) *706*

American Express Co. *v* British Airways Board (1983) *377*

Anandarajah *v* Lord Chancellor's Department (1984) *158*

Anderson Ltd *v* Daniel (1924) *314*

Anisminic Ltd *v* Foreign Compensation Commission (1969) *144*

Anns *v* Merton London Borough Council (1977) *436, 437, 450, 451, 453, 790*

Ansell *v* Thomas (1973) *415*

Appleson *v* Littlewood Ltd (1939) *629*

Archbolds (Freightage) Ltd *v* Spanglett Ltd (1961) *314*

Argy Trading Development Co. Ltd *v* Lapid Developments Ltd (1977) **392,** *435*

Arnold *v* National Westminster Bank plc (1990) **33,** *161*

Ashbury Railway Carriage and Iron Co. *v* Riche (1875) **116,** *237, 238, 239*

Ashby *v* Tolhurst (1937) **462,** *486*

Ashby *v* White (1703) *373*

Ashton *v* Turner (1980) *401*

Associated Provincial Picture Houses Ltd *v* Wednesbury Corporation (1947) *60*

Atkinson *v* Denby (1862) *687*

Atkinson *v* Newcastle Waterworks Co. (1877) **411,** *444*

Atlantic Baron, The (1978) *261*

Atlas Express *v* Kafco (1989) *261*

Attia *v* British Gas plc (1987) *760*

Attica Sea Carriers Corporation *v* Ferro-Staal Poseidon Bulk Reederei GmbH (1976) *708*

Attorney General *v* Corke (1933) **451**, *477, 778*

Attorney General *v* Fulham Corporation (1921) **6**, *60, 61*

Attorney General *v* Gastonia Coaches (1976) **371**, *429*

Attorney General of the Duchy of Lancaster *v* G.E. Overton (Farms) (1982) *70*

Attorney General for Northern Ireland *v* Gallagher (1963) **557**, *555*

Attorney General's Reference (No 4 of 1980) (1981) *531*

Attorney General's Reference (No 2 of 1982) (1984) *41*

Attorney General's Reference (No 2 of 1983) (1984) **568**, *559*

Attwood *v* Lamont (1920) *313*

Avery *v* Bowden (1855) **235**, *332*

B & S Contracts & Design *v* Victor Green Publications (1984) *261*

B.P. Exploration Co. (Libya) *v* Hunt (No 2) (1982) *330*

Baker *v* Hopkins (1959) **307**, *397*

Baker *v* James (1921) **303**, *396*

Baker *v* Willoughby (1969) **346**, *411, 761*

Baldry *v* Marshall (1924) **168**, *275*

Balfour *v* Balfour (1919) **101**, *228, 627*

Bannerman *v* White (1861) **152**, *266*

Banque Keyser Ullmann SA *v* Skandia (UK) Insurance Co. (1989) *256*

Barker *v* Addiscott (1969) *493*

Barnett *v* Chelsea and Kensington Hospital Management Committee (1968) **331**, *407*

Barnett *v* French (1981) *199*

Bartlett *v* Sydney Marcus Ltd (1965) *670*

Barton *v* Armstrong (1975) *258*

Basildon District Council *v* J.R. Lesser (Properties) Ltd (1985) *332*

Bass *v* Gregory (1890) **486**, *501*

Baster *v* London and County Printing Works (1899) *370*

Bates (Thomas) & Son *v* Wyndhams (Lingerie) (1981) **131**, *245, 637*

Beach *v* Freeson (1971) **442**, *472*

Beach *v* Reed Corrugated Cases Ltd (1956) **238**, *335*

Beale *v* Taylor (1967) **161**, *272, 273*

Beaman *v* A.R.T.S. (1949) **348**, *414*

Beard *v* London General Omnibus Co. (1900) *736*

Beaulieu *v* Finglam (1401) *5*

Bebee *v* Sales (1916) **271**, *375*

Beckwith *v* Philby (1827) **318**, *400*

Bell *v* Lever Bros Ltd (1932) **125**, *244, 715*

Bell Houses Ltd *v* City Wall Properties Ltd (1966) *238*

Belvoir Finance Co. Ltd *v* Stapleton (1970) *686*

Bentley (Dick) Productions Ltd *v* Harold Smith (Motors) Ltd (1965) *661*

Berg *v* Sadler and Moore (1937) **202**, *307*

88 Berkeley Road, London, NW9: Rickwood *v* Turnsek, re (1971) *496*

Bernstein *v* Skyviews & General (1977) **360**, *421*

Berry, re (1936) *562*

Best *v* Samuel Fox & Co. Ltd (1952) **265**, *373, 376*

Beswick *v* Beswick (1967) **89**, *160, 220, 337, 338, 578, 616*

Bettini *v* Gye (1876) **155**, *264, 267, 324, 332*

Billings *v* Riden (1958) *777*

Bigos *v* Bousted (1951) **197**, *306*

Binions *v* Evans (1972) **482**, *497*

Bird *v* Jones (1845) **352**, *418*

Birkett *v* James (1977) *125*

Birkmyr *v* Darnell (1704) *631*

Bissett *v* Wilkinson (1927) *249*

Bliss *v* Hall (1838) **375**, *430*

Blyth *v* Birmingham Waterworks Co. (1856) *439*

Bodley *v* Reynolds (1846) *428*

Bolam *v* Friern Barnet Hospital Management Committee (1957) *454*

Bollinger *v* Costa Brava Wine Co. Ltd (1959) *462*

Bolton *v* Mahadeva (1972) **215**, *323*

Bolton *v* Stone (1951) *772*

Bolton (H.L.) (Engineering) Ltd *v* Graham (1956) *538*

Bone *v* Seale (1975) **382**, *431*

Bourhill *v* Young (1943) **343**, *409, 435*

Bower *v* Peate (1876) **296**, *393*

Bowes v Shand (1877) **219,** *325*

Bowmakers Ltd v Barnett Instruments
Ltd (1944) **194,** *306*

Boychuk v H.J. Symons (Holdings)
Ltd (1977) **258,** *358*

Boys v Blenkinsop (1968) **5,** *17*

Braband v King (1895) **472,** *489*

Brace v Calder (1895) **244,** *336*

Bradbury v Morgan (1862) **72,** *215*

Bradford Corporation v Pickles (1895)
267, *373, 433, 776*

Bratty v Attorney General for
Northern Ireland (1963) *553*

Brew Bros v Snax (Ross) (1969) **388,**
192, 432

Bridges v Hawkesworth (1851) *769*

Brinkibon v Stahag Stahl (1982) *600*

British Car Auctions v Wright (1972)
588, 590

British Celanese v Hunt (1969) **380,**
431, 434, 477

British Crane Hire Corporation v
Ipswich Plant Hire (1974) *293,
297*

British Labour Pump Co. v Byrne
(1979) *369*

British Reinforced Concrete Co. v
Schelff (1921) **209,** *311*

British Railways Board v Herrington
(1972) *456*

British Railways Board v Pickin (1974)
21, *139*

British Steel Corporation v Granada
Television (1980) *200*

British Sulphur v Lawrie (1987) *358*

British Transport Commission v
Gourley (1955) *402*

Britt v Galmoye (1928) **288,** *390,
392*

Brogden v Metropolitan Railway
(1877) **51,** *207*

Bromley London Borough Council v
Greater London Council (1982)
564

Brown (BS) & Son Ltd v Craiks Ltd
(1970) **169,** *277*

Brunsden v Humphrey (1884) *411*

Bryant v Lefever (1879) *819*

Buckinghamshire County Council v
Moran (1989) *485*

Building Employers' Confederation
Application (1985) *317*

Bulmer v Bollinger (1974) *48*

Bunker v Charles Brand & Son
(1969) **417,** *456*

Burmah Oil Ltd v The Governor of
the Bank of England (1981) *262*

Burnett v British Waterways Board
(1973) **301,** *395, 396*

Burnley Borough Council v England
(1978) **23,** *145*

Buron v Denman (1848) **319,** *400*

Butler Machine Tool Co. v Ex-Cell-O
Corporation (England) (1979) **55,**
208

Butt v Cambridgeshire and Isle of Ely
County Council (1969) **273,** *375*

Byrne v Boadle (1863) **406,** *441*

Byrne v Deane (1937) **427,** *463*

Byrne v Van Tienhoven (1880) **68,**
211, 213

C. & P. Haulage v Middleton
(1983) *711*

Caldwell v Sumpters (1972) **504,**
522, 523, 827

Cambridge Water Co. v Eastern
Counties Leather plc (1991) *479*

Campbell v Paddington Borough
Council (1911) **278,** *379, 772*

Campbell v Tameside Metropolitan
Borough Council (1982) *127*

Candler v Crane, Christmas
(1951) *448, 789*

Caparo Industries plc v Dickman
(1988) **413,** *437, 453*

Capper Pass v Lawton (1976) **252,**
347

Carlill v Carbolic Smoke Ball Co.
(1893) **46,** *204, 207, 209, 210,
213, 218, 227, 598, 677*

Carmarthen County Council v Lewis
(1955) **272,** *375*

Casey's Patents, re, Stewart v Casey
(1892) **85,** *220*

Cassell & Co. Ltd v Broome (1972)
404

Cassidy v Daily Mirror Newspapers
Ltd (1929) **429,** *467*

Cassidy v Ministry of Health (1951)
282, *385*

Castle v St Augustine's Links (1922)
372, *429*

Cavalier v Pope (1906) *458*

Cavendish-Woodhouse v Manley
(1984) *277, 667*

Cehave N.V. *v* Bremer Handelgesellschaft mbH—*The Hansa Nord* (1975) **156,** *268*

Cellulose Acetate Silk Co. Ltd *v* Widnes Foundry Ltd (1933) **237,** *335*

Central Asbestos Co. *v* Dodd (1972) *159*

Central London Property Trust *v* High Trees House Ltd (1947) **96,** *11, 225, 226, 620, 622, 624, 701, 780*

Centrovincial Estates *v* Merchant Investors Assurance (1983) *212*

Century Insurance Co. *v* Northern Ireland Road Transport Board (1942) **285,** *389*

Chadwick *v* British Railways Board (1967) *339, 409*

Chancery Lane Safe Deposit & Offices Co. Ltd *v* Inland Revenue Commissioners (1966) *579*

Chandler *v* D.P.P. (1964) **515,** *533*

Chandler *v* Webster (1904) **231,** *330*

Chapelton *v* Barry U.D.C. (1940) **178,** *292, 675, 678*

Chaplin *v* Hicks (1911) *711*

Chaplin *v* Leslie Frewin (Publishers) (1965) *631*

Chapman *v* Lord Ellesmere (1932) **446,** *475*

Chappell *v* Nestlé (1959) **76,** *217*

Chappell *v* National Car Parks (1987) *811*

Charge Card Services, *re* (1988) *326*

Charing Cross Electricity Supply Co. *v* Hydraulic Power Co. (1914) **450,** *477*

Chasemore *v* Richards (1859) *728*

Cheney *v* Conn (1968) **2,** *13*

Cheshire *v* Bailey (1905) *737*

Cheshire Banking Co., Duff's Executors Case, *re* (1886) **73,** *215*

Chess (Oscar) Ltd *v* Williams (1957) **153,** *251, 267*

Chief Constable of West Midlands *v* Gillard (1985) *24*

Chillingworth *v* Esche (1923) *207*

Christie *v* Davey (1893) **378,** *373, 430, 776*

Christie *v* Leachinsky (1947) **355,** *419*

Churchward *v* R. (1865) *197*

City Index Ltd *v* Leslie (1990) *316*

Cityland and Property (Holdings) Ltd *v* Dabrah (1967) **499,** *511*

Clark *v* Lindsay (1903) *329*

Clarke *v* Dickson (1858) **144,** *256*

Clarke *v* Dunraven (1897) *607*

Clay *v* Yates (1856) *689*

Clayton's Case (1816) *327, 702*

Clea Shipping Corporation *v* Bulk Oil International—*The Alaskan Trader* (1983) *336, 708*

Cleveland Petroleum Co. Ltd *v* Dartstone (1969) **213,** *312*

Clifford Davies Management *v* W.E.A. Records (1975) *262*

Clifton *v* Palumbo (1944) *590*

Cobb *v* Great Western Railway (1894) **334,** *407*

Cochrane *v* Willis (1865) **124,** *244*

Coggs *v* Bernard (1703) *610*

Cohen *v* Daily Telegraph (1968) *471*

Colchester Estates (Cardiff) *v* Carlton Industries (1984) *160*

Coldman *v* Hill (1919) **475,** *489*

Coldunell Ltd *v* Gallon (1986) *40*

Coleman *v* Skyrail Oceanic Ltd (1981) **254,** *348*

Collins *v* Godefroy (1831) **80,** *219*

Colvilles *v* Devine (1969) *442*

Combe *v* Combe (1951) **99,** *226, 625*

Commission for Racial Equality *v* Dutton (1988) *177, 180*

Commission for Racial Equality *v* Imperial Society of Teachers of Dancing (1983) **38,** *180*

Condon *v* Basi (1985) *741*

Congreve *v* Home Office (1976) *570*

Conway *v* Rimmer (1968) *200*

Cook *v* Alexander (1973) **443,** *473*

Cook *v* Broderip (1968) **416,** *456*

Cooper *v* Firth Brown Ltd (1963) *710*

Cooper *v* Phibbs (1867) **127,** *245, 643*

Cope *v* Rowlands (1836) *314*

Cope *v* Sharp (1912) **317,** *399*

Cornish *v* Midland Bank (1985) *659*

Corpe *v* Overton (1833) *634*

Corporation of London *v* Appleyard (1963) *770*

Cotman *v* Brougham (1918) *237, 238*

Couturier *v* Hastie (1856) **123,** *244*

Cowan v Milbourn (1867) **201,** *307*

Cowan v O'Connor (1880) *211*

Crabb v Arun District Council (1975) *502, 625*

Craig Dec'd, *re* (1970) *259*

Cramer v Cramer (1987) *175*

Craven-Ellis v Canons Ltd (1936) **247,** *340*

Cresswell v Sirl (1948) **316,** *399*

Cricklewood Property and Investment Trust Ltd v Leighton's Investment Trust Ltd (1945) **230,** *329*

Crofter Hand Woven Harris Tweed Co. Ltd v Veitch (1942) **426,** *462*

Crompton (Alfred) Amusement Machines v Customs and Excise Commissioners (1973) **45,** *200*

Crow v Wood (1970) **487,** *501, 502*

Crown Suppliers (P.S.A.) v Dawkins (1991) *177*

Crowther v Shannon Motor Co. (1975) **167,** *275, 277*

Cuckmere Brick Co. Ltd v Mutual Finance (1971) *513*

Cundy v Le Coq (1884) **525,** *535*

Cundy v Lindsay (1878) **119,** *243, 638*

Curran v Northern Ireland Co-Ownership Housing Association (1987) *437*

Currie v Misa (1875) *216*

Curtis v Chemical Cleaning and Dyeing Co. (1951) **176,** *291*

Customs and Excise Commissioners v Ap S. Samex (1983) *48, 49*

Cutler v United Dairies (1933) **308,** *397*

Cutsford v Mansfield Inns (1986) *320*

Cutter v Powell (1795) *698*

Czarnikow v Koufos (*The Heron II*) (1967) **241,** *336, 406*

D. v N.S.P.C.C. (1977) *200*

D. & C. Builders Ltd v Rees (1965) *93, 224, 225, 619*

D. & L. Caterers Ltd v D'Anjou (1945) **276,** *379, 465*

D.P.P. v K. (1990) **540,** *546*

D.P.P. v Kent & Sussex Contractors Ltd (1944) *538*

D.P.P. v Majewski (1976) **554,** *554*

D.P.P. v Morgan (1975) **546,** *549, 558*

D.P.P. for Northern Ireland v Lynch (1975) *156*

Daily Mirror Newspapers v Gardner (1968) **425,** *462*

Daniels v White and Sons (1938) **397,** *439, 784*

Dann v Curzon (1911) **188,** *305, 306*

Dann v Hamilton (1939) **304,** *396, 398*

Darlington (Peter) Partners Ltd v Gosho Co. Ltd (1964) *279*

Davey v Harrow Corporation (1957) **453,** *478*

Davie v New Merton Board Mills (1958) *461*

Davies v Benyon-Harris (1931) *633*

Davies v. Collins (1945) **476,** *490*

Davies v Liverpool Corporation (1949) **333,** *407*

Davis v Johnson (1978) *148, 157*

Davis Contractors Ltd v Fareham U.D.C. (1956) *327*

Davis v Rubin (1967) **447,** *476*

Davis v Whitby (1974) **494,** *503*

Davstone Estates Ltd, *re* (1969) *690*

Dawsons Ltd v Bonin (1922) **145,** *257*

Deacons v Bridge (1984) *693*

Dearle v Hall (1828) *516*

De Barnardy v Harding (1853) **218,** *324*

Deeley v Lloyds Bank Ltd (1912) **221,** *327*

Denithorne v Davies (1967) *632*

Denmark Productions v Boscobel Productions (1967) *632*

Derry v Peek (1889) **141,** *252*

Deyong v Shenburn (1946) **464,** *486*

Dickinson v Del Solar (1930) **275,** *378*

Dickinson v Dodds (1876) **69,** *213, 215*

Dickson v Combermere (1863) *198*

Diment v N.H. Foot (1974) **493,** *503*

Dimes v Grand Junction Canal (1852) **10,** *63*

Director General of Fair Trading v Smiths Concrete (1991) *382*

Dixons Ltd v J.L. Cooper Ltd (1970) *403*

Dolphin's Conveyance, *re* (1970) *506*

Donaldson *v* McNiven (1952) **270,** *375*

Donoghue *v* Stevenson (1932) **264,** *155, 160, 296, 372, 435, 436, 437, 445, 449, 450, 460, 487, 668*

Dooley *v* Leyland Vehicles Ltd (1986) *368*

Doorman *v* Jenkins (1843) **471, 489**

Dowouna *v* John Lewis Partnership plc (1987) *362*

Draper *v* Hodder (1972) *753*

Draper's Conveyance, re (1967) **480,** *496*

Dulieu *v* White & Sons (1901) **338,** *408*

Dunlop *v* New Garage and Motor Co. Ltd (1915) *710*

Dunlop *v* Selfridge (1915) **87,** *217, 220, 271, 314, 707*

Dunton *v* Dover District Council (1977) **377,** *430*

Durham Fancy Goods Ltd *v* Michael Jackson (Fancy Goods) Ltd (1968) **100,** *226*

Dymond *v* Pearce (1972) **374,** *429*

Eaglehill Ltd *v* J. Needham (Builders) Ltd (1972) *212*

Earl of Oxford's Case (1615) **1,** *11*

Easson *v* L.N.E. Railway Co. (1944) **404,** *441*

Eastbourne Herald Case, The (1973) **20,** *101*

East Suffolk Rivers Catchment Board *v* Kent (1940) *444*

Edgington *v* Fitzmaurice (1885) **135,** *250, 254*

Edler *v* Auerbach (1950) **195,** *306*

Edwards *v* Newland (1950) **477,** *490*

Edwards *v* Skyways Ltd (1964) *228, 629*

Egger *v* Viscount Chelmsford (1964) **445,** *474*

Electrochrome Ltd *v* Welsh Plastics Ltd (1968) **266,** *373*

Eley *v* Bedford (1971) *403*

Ellenborough Park, re (1956) **488,** *501*

Elliot *v* Richard Stump Ltd (1987) *724*

Elliott *v* C. (1983) *834*

Elvin and Powell *v* Plummer Roddis Ltd (1933) **370,** *426, 812*

Elwes *v* Brigg Gas Co. (1886) *770*

Emanuel *v* Greater London Council (1970) **448,** *477*

Enderby Town Football Club Ltd *v* The Football Association Ltd (1971) *62*

Entores Ltd *v* Miles Far East Corporation (1955) **63,** *210*

Errington *v* Errington (1952) *213*

Esso Petroleum Co. Ltd *v* Commissioners of Customs & Excise (1976) *589*

Esso Petroleum Co. Ltd *v* Harper's Garage (Stourport) Ltd (1967) **212,** *312, 511, 697*

Esso Petroleum *v* Mardon (1976) *254*

Evans *v* Merzario (1976) **180,** *266, 293*

Faccenda Chicken Ltd *v* Fowler (1986) *310*

Factortame Ltd *v* Secretary of State for Transport (1989) **34,** *64, 167*

Fagan *v* Metropolitan Police Commissioner (1968) **350,** *417, 535, 545*

Farringdon *v* Leigh (1987) *802*

Felthouse *v* Bindley (1862) **61,** *210*

Fender *v* Mildman (1937) *303, 304, 305*

Fercometal Sarl *v* Mediterranean Shipping Co. Ltd (1988) *709*

Ferguson *v* John Dawson & Partners (1976) **283,** *385*

Ferguson *v* Weaving (1951) **532,** *536*

Ferguson *v* Welsh (1987) *793*

Fielding and Platt Ltd *v* Najjar (1969) **200,** *307*

Filby *v* Hounsell (1896) *592*

Financings Ltd *v* Stimson (1962) **71,** *214*

Firm of Solicitors, re a (1991) *77*

Fitch *v* Dewes (1921) **207,** *309*

Fitter *v* Veal (1701) *411*

Fitzleet Estates Ltd *v* Cherry (Inspector of Taxes) (1977) *579*

Flemyng *v* Hector (1836) *191*

Fletcher *v* Budgen (1974) *149*

Fletcher's Application, re (1970) *67*

Foakes *v* Beer (1884) **92,** *224*

Foley *v* Classique Coaches Ltd (1934) **58,** *209*

Ford Motor Co. (England) Ltd *v* Armstrong (1915) **236,** *335*

Forsikrings Vesta *v* Butcher (1988) *332*

Forster & Sons Ltd *v* Suggett (1918) **205,** *309, 310*

Foster *v* Driscoll (1929) *685*

Foster *v* Mackinnon (1869) *636*

Fouldes *v* Willoughby (1841) **368,** *426*

Fowler *v* Lanning (1959) **351,** *418, 425*

Fox *v* Stirk (1970) *175*

Fraser *v* Thames Television Ltd (1983) *664*

Freeman *v* Home-Office (1984) *416*

Froom *v* Butcher (1975) *442, 443*

Frost *v* Aylesbury Dairy Co. Ltd (1905) *274*

Fulham *v* Newcastle Chronicle & Journal (1977) **433,** *467*

Fuller *v* Stephanie Bowman (1977) **260,** *367*

G.K.N. Bolts & Nuts Ltd Sports & Social Club, Leek and Others *v* Donkersley and Others (1982) *192*

Garden Cottage Foods Ltd *v* Milk Marketing Board (1983) *320, 321, 338*

Gardiner *v* Sevenoaks R.D.C. (1950) **25,** *148*

Garrard *v* Southey (1952) **279,** *384*

Gateway Hotels Ltd *v* Stewart (1988) *723*

Gaumont British Distributors *v* Henry (1939) **526,** *536*

Geddling *v* Marsh (1920) **170,** *279*

Gier *v* Kujawa (1971) *674*

Gibson *v* Manchester City Council (1979) *591*

Gilbert *v* Stone (1647) *399*

Gilberthorpe *v* News Group Newspapers (1989) *40*

Gilchrist Watt and Sanderson Pty *v* York Products Pty (1970) **79,** *218*

Giles *v* Walker (1890) **452,** *434, 478*

Gilford Motor Co. Ltd *v* Horne (1933) **42,** *188*

Gill *v* El Vino Co. Ltd (1983) **39,** *184, 185*

Gill & Duffus SA *v* Société pour L'exportation des Sucres SA (1985) *264, 662*

Glasbrook Bros Ltd *v* Glamorgan County Council (1925) **82,** *219*

Global Dress Co. *v* Boase (1966) **470,** *488*

Goddard *v* O'Brien (1880) *620*

Godley *v* Perry (1960) **174, 280,** *446*

Goldsmith *v* Burrow Construction Ltd (1987) *823*

Goldsoll *v* Goldman (1915) *313*

Goldsworthy *v* Brickell (1987) *658*

Good *v* Cheesman (1831) **94,** *224*

Goode *v* Harrison (1821) *633*

Goodinson *v* Goodinson (1954) **203,** *307*

Gordon *v* Dickson, McFarlane and Robinson (1982) *452*

Gordon *v* Gordon (1819) **146,** *257*

Gordon *v* Selico Co. Ltd (1986) *248*

Gorely *v* Codd (1966) *729*

Gorris *v* Scott (1874) **412,** *444*

Gosling *v* Anderson (1972) **140,** *252*

Gough *v* National Coal Board (1954) **419,** *458*

Gould *v* Gould (1969) *227, 628*

Gouriet *v* Union of Post Office Workers (1977) **19,** *80*

Graff *v* Panel on Take-overs and Mergers (1980) *472*

Grant *v* Australian Knitting Mills Ltd (1936) **165,** *274, 445*

Grappelli *v* Derek Block (Holdings) (1981) **434,** *467*

Great Northern Railway *v* Witham (1873) **56,** *208*

Greaves & Co. *v* Baynham Meikle & Partners (1974) **399,** *439*

Greenock Corporation *v* Caledonian Railway (1917) **454,** *478*

Griffiths *v* Liverpool Corporation (1966) **422,** *459*

Griffiths *v* Peter Conway Ltd (1939) **164,** *274, 668*

Griffiths *v* Studebakers (1924) **529,** *536*

Grigsby *v* Melville (1972) **490,** *501*

Grist *v* Bailey (1966) *643*

H. *v* Chief Constable of South Wales (1986) *550*

H. *v* H. (1983) *305*

H. *v* Ministry of Defence (1991) *131*

Hadley *v* Baxendale (1854) **240,** *336*

Hair *v* Prudential Assurance (1983) 655

Hale *v* Jennings Bros (1938) *806*

Haley *v* London Electricity Board (1964) **401,** *440*

Halifax Building Society *v* Clark (1973) *512*

Hall *v* Brooklands Auto-Racing Club (1933) **300,** *395*

Hambrook *v* Stokes (1925) **341,** *409*

Hannah *v* Peel (1945) *769*

Hansa Nord, The (1975) **156,** *268*

Harakas *v* Baltic Mercantile & Shipping Exchange Ltd (1982) *476*

Harbutt's Plasticine Ltd *v* Wayne Tank and Pump Co. Ltd (1970) *680*

Hargreaves *v* Bretherton (1958) **262,** *372*

Harlingdon Ltd *v* Hull Fine Art Ltd (1990) *666*

Harper *v* National Coal Board (1974) *159*

Harris *v* Birkenhead Corporation (1975) *795*

Harris *v* James (1876) **386,** *432*

Harris *v* Nickerson (1873) **47,** *205*

Harris *v* Sheffield United Football Club (1987) *612*

Harrison *v* British Railways Board (1981) *397*

Harrison *v* Michelin Tyre Company (1985) *735*

Hart *v* O'Connor (1985) *634*

Hartley *v* Hymans (1920) *701*

Hartley *v* Ponsonby (1857) *610*

Harvey *v* Facey (1893) **50,** *206*

Haynes *v* Harwood (1935) *746*

Hayward *v* Challoner (1967) **458,** *484*

Hayward *v* Thompson (1981) *801*

Heasmans *v* Clarity Cleaning (1987) *738*

Hedley Byrne *v* Heller and Partners (1963) **142,** *254, 255, 288, 301, 449, 450, 649, 650, 660, 781, 789*

Hegarty *v* Shine (1878) *401*

Hemmings *v* Stoke Poges Golf Club (1920) **363,** *422*

Henthorn *v* Fraser (1892) *211*

Herd *v* Weardale Colliery (1915) **353,** *418*

Herne Bay Steam Boat Co. *v* Hutton

(1903) **227,** *328*

Heron II, The (1967) **241,** *336, 406*

Hewitt *v* Bonvin (1940) *383*

Hewson *v* Downes (1969) *403*

Heydon's Case (1584) *146*

Hickman *v* Maisey (1900) *420*

Higgins *v* Northampton Corporation (1927) **118,** *243*

High Trees Case (1947) **96,** *11, 225, 226, 620, 622, 624, 701, 780*

Hill *v* Baxter (1958) **551,** *530, 553*

Hill *v* J. Crowe (1977) **398,** *439*

Hill *v* Tupper (1863) **485,** *500*

Hillas *v* Arcos (1932) **57,** *209*

Hillesden Securities Ltd *v* Ryjack Ltd (1983) *428*

Hinz *v* Berry (1970) **340,** *409, 760*

Hochster *v* De La Tour (1853) **232,** *331, 332*

Hodgson *v* Marks (1970) **150,** *260*

Hoenig *v* Isaacs (1952) **216,** *324*

Hollier *v* Rambler Motors Ltd (1972) *292, 294, 676*

Hollywood Silver Fox Farm *v* Emmett (1936) **381,** *431*

Holwell Securities Ltd *v* Hughes (1974) **65,** *212*

Home Counties Dairies Ltd *v* Skilton (1970) **206,** *309*

Home Office *v* Dorset Yacht Co. Ltd (1970) *436*

Home Office *v* Harman (1982) *128*

Honeywill & Stein Ltd *v* Larkin Bros Ltd (1934) *393*

Horne *v* Midland Railway Co. (1873) **242,** *336*

Horrocks *v* Low (1972) **444,** *474*

Horton *v* Horton (1961) **78,** *218*

Hotel and Catering Industry Training Board *v* Automobile Proprietary Ltd (1969) **22,** *143*

Houghland *v* R. Low (Luxury Coaches) Ltd (1962) **469,** *488*

Hounslow London Borough *v* Twickenham Garden Developments (1970) **362,** *422*

Household Fire Insurance Co. *v* Grant (1879) **64,** *154, 212*

Howatson *v* Webb (1908) *636*

Hubbard *v* Pitt (1975) **379,** *430*

Huddersfield Police Authority *v* Watson (1947) *157*

Hughes *v* Liverpool Victoria Friendly

Society (1916) **196,** *306*
Hughes *v* Lord Advocate (1963) **326,** *406*
Hughes *v* Metropolitan Railway (1877) *224, 622, 625*
Hulton & Co. *v* Jones (1910) **435,** *468*
Humming Bird Motors *v* Hobbs (1986) *251, 651*
Huth *v* Huth (1915) *464*
Hutton *v* Esher U.D.C. (1973) **24**
Hutton *v* Warren (1836) **157,** *14, 146, 268*
Hyde *v* Wrench (1840) **53,** *208*
Hyett *v* G.W. Railway (1948) **309,** *397*
Hyman *v* Nye (1881) **467,** *488*

I. *v* D.P.P. (1989) *550*
ICI Ltd *v* Shatwell (1964) **306,** *397*
IRC *v* Bullock (1976) **35,** *173, 175, 583*
IRC *v* Federation of Self-Employed and Small Businesses Ltd (1981) **8,** *61*
Imperial Loan Co. *v* Stone (1892) **114,** *236*
Ingram *v* Little (1961) **121,** *159, 243*
Interfoto Picture Library Ltd *v* Stiletto Visual Programmes Ltd (1988) *292*
International Sales & Agencies Ltd *v* Marcus (1982) *239*
Irvine, *re* (1928) *606*

Jackson *v* Horizon Holidays (1975) **88,** *220, 617*
Jackson *v* Rotax Motor and Cycle Co. Ltd (1910) *277*
Jackson *v* Union Marine Insurance Co. Ltd (1874) **228,** *329*
Jaggard *v* Dickson (1980) *851*
James *v* Chief Constable of Kent (1986) *26*
James *v* Eastleigh Borough Council (1990) *584*
James *v* Smee (1955) **530,** *536*
Janov *v* Morris (1981) *125*
Jarvis *v* Swans Tours (1973) **239,** *335*
Jarvis *v* Williams (1955) **367,** *426*
J.E.B. Fasteners Ltd *v* Marks Bloom & Co. (1981) *450, 790*

Jenkin *v* Pharmaceutical Society (1921) **43,** *190*
Jeune *v* Queens Cross Properties Ltd (1973) *499*
Jobling *v* Associated Dairies (1980) **345,** *411*
John *v* Mendoza (1939) **191,** *305*
John Michael Design *v* Cooke (1987) *691*
Johnson *v* Timber Tailors (Midlands) (1978) **249,** *344*
Johnstone *v* Pedlar (1921) **321,** *400*
Jones *v* Boyce (1816) *444*
Jones (A.E.) *v* Jones (F.W.) (1977) *496*
Jones *v* Lawrence (1969) **409,** *443*
Jones *v* National Coal Board (1957) *131*
Jones *v* Northampton Borough Council (1990) *192*
Jones *v* Padavatton (1969) **104,** *228*
Jones *v* Vernons Pools Ltd (1938) **106,** *229*
Jorden *v* Money (1854) *225*
Joscelyne *v* Nissen (1970) **129,** *245*
Julian *v* Furby (1982) *627*
Junior Books Ltd *v* Veitchi Co. Ltd (1982) **396,** *438, 445, 727, 783, 784*

Karflex Ltd *v* Poole (1933) *270*
Kearley *v* Thompson (1890) **199,** *306*
Keene *v* Muncaster (1980) **26,** *148*
Kelly *v* Barrett (1924) **495,** *506*
Kelson *v* Imperial Tobacco Co. (1957) **358,** *421*
Kennaway *v* Thompson (1980) **390,** *433, 773*
Kennedy *v* de Trafford (1897) *513*
Kerr *v* Kennedy (1942) *465*
King's Norton Metal Co. Ltd *v* Edridge, Merrett & Co. Ltd (1897) *638*
Kirkham *v* Anderton (1990) *742*
Kitchen *v* Royal Air Force Association (1958) *763*
Klein *v* Calnori (1971) **295,** *392*
Kleinwort Benson Ltd *v* Malaysian Mining Corporation, Berhand (1989) **105,** *229*
Knight *v* Marquis of Waterford (1844) *18*

Knightsbridge Estates Trust Ltd *v* Byrne (1939) **496,** *511, 825*

Knupffer *v* London Express Newspaper Ltd (1944) **436,** *468, 802*

Kodeeswaran *v* A.G. of Ceylon (1970) *198*

Kong Chuek Kwan *v* The Queen (1985) *544*

Koppel *v* Koppel (1966) **502,** *520*

Kores Manufacturing Ltd *v* Kolok Manufacturing Co. Ltd (1959) **208,** *311*

Kowalski *v* The Berkeley Hotel (1985) *722*

Kreglinger *v* New Patagonia Meat and Cold Storage Co. (1914) **498,** *511, 825*

Krell *v* Henry (1903) **226,** *328*

Kruse *v* Johnson (1898) *145*

Laker Airways *v* Department of Trade (1977) **16,** *65*

Lamb *v* Camden London Borough Council (1981) *434*

Lambert *v* Lewis (1981) **173,** *279*

Lancashire Loans Ltd *v* Black (1934) **148,** *259*

Lane *v* Holloway (1967) *401*

Lane *v* London Electricity Board (1955) **27,** *148, 788*

Larner *v* Fawcett (1950) **505,** *523*

Latimer *v* A.E.C. Ltd (1953) **403,** *440*

Law *v* National Greyhound Racing Club Ltd (1983) *58*

Leaf *v* International Galleries (1950) **126,** *244, 255, 666, 715*

Leaman *v* R. (1920) *198*

Learoyd Bros *v* Pope (1966) **478,** *490*

Lee *v* Lee's Air Farming Ltd (1960) **284,** *385*

Lee *v* Showmen's Guild of Great Britain (1952) *58*

Leesh River Tea Co. *v* British India Steam Navigation Co. (1966) *737*

Leigh *v* Gladstone (1909) *399, 417*

Lens *v* Devonshire Club (1914) *228*

L'Estrange *v* Graucob Ltd (1934) **175,** *291*

Letang *v* Cooper (1964) *425, 764*

Lewis *v* Averay (1971) **120,** *159, 243*

Lewis *v* Clay (1898) *636*

Lewis *v* Daily Telegraph Ltd (1964) *256, 463*

Limpus *v* London General Omnibus Co. (1862) **286,** *389*

Littledale *v* Liverpool College (1900) **459,** *484*

Liverpool City Council *v* Irwin (1977) *269, 664*

Lloyd *v* Grace, Smith & Co. (1912) *391, 737*

Lloyd *v* Singleton (1953) *563*

Lloyds *v* Harper (1880) *605, 616*

Lloyds Bank *v* Bundy (1974) **151,** *260, 262, 620*

Lobb (Alec) (Garages) Ltd *v* Total Oil Ltd G.B. (1985) *697*

Lockett *v* A & M Charles Ltd (1938) *726*

London and Northern Bank, *ex parte* Jones, *re* (1900) *601*

London Artists *v* Littler (1969) **439,** *470*

London Association for the Protection of Trade *v* Greenlands (1916) **440,** *472*

London Street Tramways *v* London County Council (1898) *155*

Long *v* Lloyd (1958) **143,** *256*

Lumbe *v* Allday (1831) *466*

Lumley *v* Gye (1853) **424,** *462*

Luna, The (1920) *674*

Lynn *v* Bamber (1930) **248,** *341*

McArdle, *re* (1951) **84,** *220*

McCall *v* Abelesz (1976) *724*

McCarthy and Stone *v* Julian S. Hodge & Co. (1971) *516*

McC. *v* Runeckles (1984) *550*

McKean *v* Rayner Bros Ltd (Nottingham) (1942) *390*

McKew *v* Holland and Hannan and Cubitts (Scotland) Ltd (1969) **336,** *408*

McLoughlin *v* O'Brian (1982) **342,** *409*

McManus *v* Fortescue (1907) *205*

McNerny *v* Lambeth Borough Council (1989) *458, 460*

Malas (Hamzeh) *v* British Imex (1958) *222*

Malone *v* Laskey (1907) **383,** *432*

Mandla *v* Dowell Lee (1983) *177*

Mapes *v* Jones (1974) *252*

Mareva Compania Naviera SA *v* International Bulk Carriers SA (1975) *339*

Maritime National Fish Ltd *v* Ocean Trawlers Ltd (1935) **229**, *329*

Marriage *v* East Norfolk River Catchment Board (1950) **324**, *401*

Martindale *v* Duncan (1973) **328**, *407*

Mash and Murrell *v* Joseph I Emmanuel (1961) *277*

Massey *v* Crown Life Insurance (1978) **257**, *355*

Mathew *v* Bobbins (1980) *259*

Matthews *v* Baxter (1873) **115**, *236*

Maynard *v* Osmond (1977) *62*

Meah *v* McCreamer (1986) *754*

Mears *v* L.S.W. Railway (1862) *483*

Mears *v* Safecar Security (1982) **251**, *269, 345*

Meering *v* Grahame White Aviation Co. (1919) **354**, *418*

Meikle *v* McPhail (Charleston Arms) (1983) **259**, *361, 362, 369*

Mercantile Union Guarantee Corporation Ltd *v* Ball (1937) **111**, *233*

Mercer *v* Denne (1905) *14*

Merritt *v* Merritt (1970) **102**, *228*

Mersey Docks and Harbour Board *v* Coggins and Griffiths (Liverpool) Ltd (1947) **280**, *384*

Microbeads A.C. *v* Vinhurst Road Markings (1975) *271*

Midland Bank plc *v* Perry (1987) *660*

Miliangos *v* George Frank (Textiles) Ltd (1975) **31**, *156, 160*

Millard *v* Serck Tubes (1969) **423**, *461*

Millensted *v* Grosvenor House Ltd (1937) *126*

Miller *v* Jackson (1977) *772, 773*

Mills *v* Fowkes (1839) *326*

Mint *v* Good (1951) **385**, *432*

Mirehouse *v* Rennell (1833) *151*

Mitchell (George) (Chesterhall) Ltd *v* Finney Lock Seeds Ltd (1983) **187**, *300, 454*

Moffat *v* Kazana (1968) **457**, *484*

Moorcock, The (1889) **158**, *269*

Moore *v* Bresler Ltd (1944) *538*

Moore *v* R. Fox & Sons (1956) *442*

Moore & Co. *v* Landauer & Co. (1921) **162**, *272*

Morgan *v* Odhams Press (1971) **430**, *467*

Morgan *v* T. Wallis (1974) **329**, *407*

Morgan Crucible Co. plc *v* Hill Samuel (1990) **414**, *453*

Morgans *v* Launchbury (1972) **293**, *392*

Morris *v* C.W. Martin & Sons Ltd (1965) **289**, *391, 489*

Morris *v* Murray (1990) *744*

Morriss *v* Marsden (1952) **274**, *376*

Moses *v* Winder (1980) *554, 850*

Mountford *v* Scott (1974) *603, 608*

Mountstephen *v* Lakeman (1871) **108**, *232*

Mourton *v* Poulter (1930) **420**, *458*

Muir *v* Keay (1875) **29**, *148*

Murphy *v* Brentwood District Council (1990) *437, 453, 579*

Murray *v* Harringay Arena Ltd (1951) **299**, *395*

Napier *v* National Business Agency (1951) **193**, *305*

Nash *v* Inman (1908) **109**, *233*

Nash *v* Sheen (1953) *416*

National Carriers *v* Panalpina (Northern) (1981) *706*

National Coal Board *v* Evans (1951) *314, 398, 425*

National Coal Board *v* Galley (1958) *370*

National Provincial Bank Ltd *v* Ainsworth (1965) *518*

National Westminster Bank plc *v* Morgan (1985) *659*

Nathan *v* Ogdens Ltd (1905)

Navy, Army and Air Force Institutes *v* Varley (1977) **253**, *347*

Net Book Agreement 1957 (1962) *221, 315, 317*

Nettleship *v* Weston (1971) **312**, *398, 440*

Neuwirth *v* Over Darwen Industrial Co-operative Society (1894) **466**, *487*

Newman *v* Bourne & Hollingsworth (1915) **465**, *487*

New Zealand Shipping Co. Ltd *v*

Satterthwaite (1974) **181,** *215,*
293, 294, 391, 587, 613
Niblett Ltd *v* Confectioners' Materials
Co. Ltd (1921) **160,** *271*
Nichol *v* Godts (1854) *273*
Nichols *v* Marsland (1876) **315,**
399, 478, 808
Nicholson *v* Secretary of State for
Energy (1977) *62*
Nicolene *v* Simmonds (1953) **60,** *209*
Nissan *v* Attorney General
(1967) **320,** *400*
Noakes *v* Rice (1902) **497,** *511*
Nordenfelt *v* Maxim Nordenfelt Guns
and Ammunition Co. (1894) **210,**
311
Norris *v* Southampton City Council
(1982) **223,** *328*
North East Coast Ship Repairers *v*
Secretary of State for Employment
(1978) *723*
North Ocean Shipping Co. Ltd *v*
Hyundai Construction Co. Ltd, *The*
Atlantic Baron (1978) *261*
Northumberland & Durham District
Banking Co., *ex parte* Bigge
(1859) *250*
Norwich Pharmacal Co. *v*
Commissioners of Customs and
Excise (1973) **44,** *200*
Nottingham *v* Aldridge (1971) *292,*
392

Oakley *v* Lyster (1931) **369,** *426*
O'Brien *v* Robinson (1973) **484,** *499*
O'Connell *v* Jackson (1971) *442*
Office Angels Ltd *v* Rainer-Thomas
and O'Connor (1991) *691*
O'Leary *v* Islington London Borough
Council (1983) *778*
O'Reilly *v* Mackman (1983) *64*
Oliver *v* Ashman (1962) *402*
Oliver *v* Birmingham Bus Co. (1932)
410, *443*
Olley *v* Marlborough Court Ltd
(1949) **179,** *293*
Omnium D'Entreprises *v* Sutherland
(1919) **233,** *331, 332*
Orman *v* Saville Sportswear Ltd
(1960) *717*
Ormrod *v* Crosville Motor Services
(1953) **290,** *392*
Osborn *v* Thos Boulter & Son (1930)

441, 472
Ough *v* King (1967) *504*
Overseas Tankship (UK) Ltd *v* Morts
Dock and Engineering Co. Ltd (*The*
Wagon Mound) (1961) **325,** *156,*
405, 406
Overseas Tankship (UK) Ltd *v* Miller
Steamship Property Ltd (*The Wagon*
Mound (No. 2)) (1966) *433, 753*
Owen (Edward) Engineering *v*
Barclays Bank Int. (1977) *222*
Owens *v* Brimmell (1976) *744*
Owens *v* Liverpool Corporation
(1939) **344,** *409*

Padfield *v* Min of Agriculture,
Fisheries and Food (1968) *569*
Page Motors *v* Epsom and Ewell
Borough Council (1981) *434, 779*
Paine *v* Colne Valley Electricity
Supply Co. Ltd (1938) *461*
Panesar *v* Nestlé & Co. Ltd
(1980) *716*
Pannett *v* McGuinness & Co. (1972)
421, *458*
Pao On *v* Lan Yiu Long (1979) *258*
Paris *v* Stepney Borough Council
(1951) **400,** *440*
Parker *v* British Airways Board (1982)
365, *425, 484*
Parkinson *v* The College of
Ambulance Ltd and Harrison (1925)
192, *305, 306*
Parsons Bros *v* Shea (1965) *330, 331*
Partridge *v* Crittenden (1968) **49,**
205, 588
Pauley *v* Kenaldo Ltd (1953) *385*
Payne *v* Cave (1789) *212*
Pearce *v* Brain (1929) **113,** *205,*
234, 235
Pearce *v* Brooks (1866) **189,** *305,*
306
Pearce *v* Merriman (1904) *227*
Pearson *v* North Western Gas Board
(1968) **408,** *442*
Peck *v* Lateu (1973) *228*
Peco Arts Inc. *v* Hazlitt Gallery Ltd
(1983) *715*
Peek *v* Gurney (1873) **137,** *250, 649*
Penny *v* Northampton Borough
Council (1974) *795*
Penny *v* Wimbledon U.D.C. (1899)
323, *401*

Perera v Vandiyar (1953) **261,** *372*
Performance Cars Ltd v Abraham (1961) **347, 411**
Performing Rights Society Ltd v Mitchel and Booker (Palais de Dance) Ltd (1924) *383*
Peters v Prince of Wales Theatre (Birmingham) Ltd (1943) **456,** *478*
Pharmaceutical Society of Great Britain v Boots Cash Chemists Ltd (1953) *48, 205*
Pharmaceutical Society of Great Britain v Dickson (1968) **214,** *58, 312*
Philco Radio Corporation v Spurling (1949) **337,** *408*
Phipps v Pears (1964) **489,** *501*
Photo Production Ltd v Securicor Transport Ltd (1980) **185,** *295, 683*
Pickard v Smith (1861) *393*
Pickett v British Rail Engineering Ltd (1979) *402*
Pinnel's Case (1602) *223, 224*
Pirelli General Cable Works Ltd v Oscar Faber & Partners Ltd (1983) *412*
Pitts v Hunt (1990) *744*
Plowman v Ash (1964) *691*
Plummer v I.R.C. (1988) *175*
Poland v John Parr & Sons (1927) *389*
Polemis and Furniss Withy & Co, re (1921) *156*
Polkey v A.E. Dayton Services Ltd (1987) *360, 369*
Pollock & Co. v Macrae (1922) **183,** *295*
Porcelli v Strathclyde Regional Council (1986) *347*
Portec (UK) Ltd v Mogensen (1976) *158*
Posner v Scott-Lewis (1986) *338*
Post Office v Union of Post Office Workers (1974) *354*
Poulton v L. & S.W. Railway (1867) **277,** *379*
Poussard v Spiers and Pond (1876) **154,** *264, 267, 324, 327, 332*
Powell v Gelstone (1916) *464*
Powell v Lee (1908) *599*
Price v Civil Service Commission (1977) **255,** *348*

Pride of Derby and Derbyshire Angling Assn v British Celanese (1952) *410, 751*
Pridham v Hemel Hempstead Corporation (1970) *795*
Priest v Last (1903) **163,** *274*
Priestley v Fowler (1837) *162*
Prince of Hanover v Attorney General (1957) *3, 13, 577*
Proffit v British Railways Board (1984) *457*
Provident Financial Group plc v Whitegates Estate Agency (1989) *310*
Puhlhofer v Hillingdon London Borough Council (1986) *61*
Purnell v Shields (1973) *442*
Pursell v Horn (1838) *416*

Quinn v Leatham (1901) *159*
Quinn v Williams Furniture Ltd (1981) **40,** *184*

R. v Bailey (1800) **566,** *558*
R. v Bedwellty UDC (1943) *64*
R. v Belfon (1976) **543,** *547*
R. v Bird (Debbie) (1985) *856*
R. v Birmingham City Council, ex parte Equal Opportunities Commission (1989) *183*
R. v Board of Visitors of the Maze Prison, ex parte Hone and McCarten (1988) *62*
R. v Brighton Justices, ex parte Robinson (1973) **7,** *61*
R. v Burgess (1991) *848*
R. v Caldwell (1981) **518,** *534, 544, 545, 547, 844*
R. v Camplin (1978) **534,** *542*
R. v Chapman (1976) *105*
R. v Cheshire (1991) *830*
R. v Church (1966) **539,** *543*
R. v Clarke (1972) **549,** *552*
R. v Commission for Racial Equality, ex parte Prestige Group plc (1983) *171*
R. v Commissioner of Police of the Metropolis, ex parte Blackburn (1973) **14,** *65, 84*
R. v Cunningham (1957) **517,** *534, 546, 547, 839, 844, 845*
R. v Curley (1909) **510,** *531*

R. *v* D.P.P., *ex parte* Hallas (1988) 84

R. *v* Dairy Product Quota Tribunal for England and Wales, *ex parte* Caswell (1989) 65

R. *v* Dickie (1984) *551*

R. *v* Drew (1985) *103*

R. *v* Dudley and Stephens (1884) **564**, *557*

R. *v* Dyson (1908) **533**, *540*

R. *v* Eccles Justices, *ex parte* Fitzpatrick (1989) 20

R. *v* Exeter Crown Court, *ex parte* Beattie (1974) 74

R. *v* Fairbanks (1986) *111*

R. *v* Ford (1989) *106*

R. *v* Fotheringham (1988) *554*

R. *v* Gittins (1984) **538**, *543*

R. *v* Gotts (1991) **559**, *555*

R. *v* Gould (1968) **32**, *157*

R. *v* Graham (1982) *556*

R. *v* Greater Manchester Coroner, *ex parte* Tal (1984) *157*

R. *v* Guildford Crown Court, *ex parte* Siderfin (1989) *104*

R. *v* Hammersmith Coroner, *ex parte* Peach (1980) 68

R. *v* Hancock (1968) *833*

R. *v* Hardie (1984) **555**, *554*

R. *v* Hayward (1908) **509**, *530*

R. *v* Hazletine (1967) *103*

R. *v* Henn (1980) 49

R. *v* Hennessy (1989) **548**, *552*

R. *v* Highbury Corner Magistrates' Court, *ex parte* Di Matteo (1990) *119*

R. *v* Howe (1981) *156*

R. *v* Howe (1987) *555*

R. *v* Hudson (1971) **560**, *556*

R. *v* ICR Haulage Ltd (1944) *538*

R. *v* Immigration Appeal Adjudicator, *ex parte* Crew (1982) **28**, *148*

R. *v* Immigration Appeal Tribunal, *ex parte* Joyles (1972) *574*

R. *v* Inspector of Taxes, *ex parte* Kissane (1986) *564*

R. *v* Instan (1893) **512**, *532*

R. *v* Ishmael (1970) 42

R. *v* Johnson (1989) **535**, *542*

R. *v* Jordan (1956) *830*

R. *v* Kemp (1956) **547**, *552*

R. *v* Kimber (1983) **565**, *558*

R. *v* Latimer (1886) **519**, *534*

R. *v* Lawrence (1981) *834*

R. *v* Le Brun (1991) *836*

R. *v* Leeds Justices, *ex parte* Sykes (1983) *100*

R. *v* Lewisham Borough Council, *ex parte* Shell U.K. (1988) *64*

R. *v* Lipman (1969) **553**, *554*

R. *v* Liverpool City Justices, *ex parte* Topping (1983) *566*

R. *v* Lloyd (1989) *741*

R. *v* Local Commissioner for Administration for the South, the West Midlands, etc. (1988) *67*

R. *v* London County Council, *ex parte* Entertainments Protection Association (1931) **9**, *63*

R. *v* Lord Chancellor's Department, *ex parte* Naugle (1991) *198*

R. *v* Lowe (1973) **527**, *536, 543*

R. *v* McInnes (1971) **567**, *559*

R. *v* M'Naghton (1843) *551, 552, 553*

R. *v* Maguire (1991) *41*

R. *v* Malcharek (1981) *830*

R. *v* Mara (1986) **256**, *353*

R. *v* Marlborough Street Stipendiary Magistrate, *ex parte* Bouchereau (1977) *27*

R. *v* Martin (1881) **541**, *546*

R. *v* Martin (1989) **563**, *556, 557*

R. *v* Mason (1980) *106*

R. *v* Maxwell (1990) *111*

R. *v* Miller (1983) **514**, *532*

R. *v* Moloney (1985) **515**, *533*

R. *v* Morris (1991) *105*

R. *v* Mulvihill (1990) *566*

R. *v* Nedrick (1986) *833*

R. *v* Northumberland Compensation Appeal Tribunal, *ex parte* Shaw (1952) *62*

R. *v* O'Grady (1987) **556**, *554*

R. *v* Panel on Take-overs (1987) *58, 59*

R. *v* Parmenter (1991) **542**, *546, 547, 844*

R. *v* Pembliton (1874) **520**, *534*

R. *v* Pittwood (1902) **513**, *532*

R. *v* Quick (1973) **552**, *553*

R. *v* R. (1991) **544**, *548*

R. *v* Reading Crown Court, *ex parte* Bello (1990) *90*

R. *v* Rose (1884) **569**, *559*

R. *v* Samuel (1988) *87*

R. *v* Sangha (1988) *835*

R. *v* Savage (1991) *533*

R. *v* Secretary of State for Foreign and Commonwealth Office (1984) *568*

R. *v* Secretary of State for Home Department, *ex parte* Hosenball (1977) **12**, *63, 162*

R. *v* Secretary of State for Home Department, *ex parte* Smart (1991) *113*

R. *v* Secretary of State for Social Services, *ex parte* Grabasky (1972) **15, 65**

R. *v* Seers (1984) *543*

R. *v* Shepherd (1988) **562**, *556*

R. *v* Smith (1959) **511, 531**

R. *v* Spratt (1991) *546, 844*

R. *v* Sullivan (1970) *101*

R. *v* Sullivan (1983) *847*

R. *v* Swaysland (1987) *130*

R. *v* Tandy (1987) **537**, *543*

R. *v* Thornton (1991) **536**, *542*

R. *v* Tolson (1889) **523**, *535*

R. *v* Tonner (1985) *107*

R. *v* Towers (1874) **508**, *530*

R. *v* Uxbridge Justices, *ex parte* Smith (1985) *20, 94*

R. *v* Watson (1988) *109*

R. *v* Wandsworth Justices, *ex parte* Read (1942) *27*

R. *v* Wear Valley District Council, *ex parte* Binks (1985) *62, 567*

R. *v* West Yorkshire Coroner, *ex parte* Smith (1982) *68*

R. *v* Wheat and Stocks (1921) *580*

R. *v* Williams (1923) **545, 549**

R. *v* Windle (1952) **550**, *553*

R. *v* Wirral Magistrates Courts, *ex parte* Meikle (1990) *100*

R & B Customs Brokers Co. Ltd *v* United Dominions Trust Ltd (1987) *296*

Race *v* Ward (1955) *14*

Raffles *v* Witchelhaus (1864) **133**, *246*

Ralux NV/SA *v* Spencer Mason CA (1989) *123*

Rambarran *v* Gurrucharran (1970) **294**, *392*

Ramsgate Victoria Hotel Co. *v* Montefiore (1866) **70**, *214*

Ratcliffe *v* Evans (1892) *465*

Rayfield *v* Hands (1958) **74**, *215,*

678

Rayner *v* Mitchell (1877) *390*

Read *v* Coker (1853) *415*

Read *v* Lyons (1947) **449**, *477*

Reardon Smith Line *v* Hansen-Tangen (1976) *663*

Rederiaktiebolaget Amphitrite *v* R. (1921) *197*

Redgrave *v* Hurt (1881) **138**, *250*

Reed *v* Dean (1949) **468**, *488*

Regazzoni *v* K.C. Sethia Ltd (1958) **190**, *305*

Rees-Hough Ltd *v* Redland Reinforced Plastics Ltd (1984) *301*

Reilly *v* R. (1934) *197*

Resolute Maritime Inc. *v* Nippon Kaijji Kyokai (1983) *650*

Reynolds *v* Atherton (1922) *606*

Rhodes *v* Moules (1895) *427*

Rickards *v* Lothian (1913) **455**, *478*

Rickards (Chas) Ltd *v* Oppenhaim (1950) **220**, *226, 325*

Ridge *v* Baldwin (1963) **13**, *63*

Rigby *v* Chief Constable of Northampton (1985) *750*

Roake *v* Chadha (1983) *506, 618*

Robb *v* Green (1895) *310*

Robert Petroleum *v* Bernard Kenny (1983) *152*

Roberts *v* Church Commissioners for England (1971)

Roberts *v* Gray (1913) **110**, *233*

Robertson *v* Ridley (1989) *192*

Robins *v* Gray (1895) **503**, *522*

Robinson *v* The Post Office (1973) **332**, *407*

Roe *v* Minister of Health (1954) **405**, *375, 441, 753*

Rogers *v* Parish (Scarborough) Ltd (1987) *278*

Rogers, Sons & Co. *v* Lambert & Co. (1891) **479**, *490*

Rolled Steel Products *v* British Steel Corporation (1985) *239*

Rondel *v* Worsley (1967) **18**, *76, 440*

Rookes *v* Barnard (1964) *404, 405*

Roscorla *v* Thomas (1842) *614*

Rose *v* Pim (1953) **130**, *245*

Rose *v* Plenty (1976) **287**, *389*

Rose and Frank Co. *v* Crompton and Brothers Ltd (1925) **107**, *229*

Ross *v* H.M. Advocate (1991) **558**, *555*

Rothermere *v* Times Newspapers (1973) *131*

Routledge *v* Grant (1828) **67, *213***

Routledge *v* McKay (1954) *266*

Rowland *v* Divall (1923) **159,** *270, 340*

Roy *v* Prior (1969) **263,** *372*

Royal Trust Co. of Canada *v* Markham (1975) *512*

Rylands *v* Fletcher (1868) *393, 476, 478, 479, 749, 766, 775, 778, 781, 806, 807, 808, 809*

SCM (UK) Ltd *v* Whittall & Son Ltd (1970) **394,** *438*

Saif Ali *v* Sydney Mitchell & Co. (1978) *572*

St. Stephen Walbrook, *re* (1987) *16*

Salmon *v* Seafarer Restaurants Ltd (1983) *793*

Salomon *v* Salomon (1897) **41,** *188, 539, 734*

Salsbury *v* Woodland (1969) **297,** *394*

Saunders *v* Anglia Building Society (1970) **117,** *242*

Saunders (Mayfair) Furs *v* Davies (1965) **474,** *489*

Sauter Automation *v* Goodman (HC) (Mechanical Services) (1960) *594*

Sayers *v* Harlow U.D.C. (1958) **335,** *408*

Scammell *v* Ouston (1941) **59,** *209, 598*

Schloimovitz *v* Clarendon Press (1973) **437,** *468*

Schorsch Meier GmbH *v* Hennin (1975) **30,** *156, 579*

Schuler (L) AG *v* Wickham Machine Tool Sales (1973) *265*

Scott *v* London & St Katherine Docks Co. (1865) **407,** *441*

Scott *v* Phillips (1973) *176*

Scott *v* Shepherd (1773) **330,** *407*

Secretary of State for Education and Science *v* Tameside Metropolitan Council (1976) **17,** *65*

Sedleigh-Denfield *v* O'Callaghan (1940) **389,** *432*

Shadwell *v* Shadwell (1860) **83,** *219, 678*

Shah *v* Barnet London Borough Council (1983) *149*

Shaw *v* D.P.P. (1961) **507,** *529*

Sheldon *v* West Bromwich Corporation (1973) *818*

Shell-Mex *v* Manchester Garages (1971) **481,** *496*

Shenton *v* Smith (1895) *198*

Shine *v* General Guarantee Corporation (1988) *278*

Shipton, Anderson & Co. and Harrison Brothers Arbitration, *re* (1915) **224,** *328*

Short *v* J.W. Henderson Ltd (1946) *384*

Siboen (The) and *The Sibotre* (1976) *258*

Sidaway *v* Bethlem Royal Hospital Governors (1984) **394,** *416*

Sigsworth, *re* (1935) *147*

Sim *v* Stretch (1936) **432,** *467*

Simaan General Contracting Co. *v* Pilkington Glass Ltd (1988) *783*

Simms *v* Leigh Rugby Football Club (1969) **298, *395, 417***

Simpkins *v* Pays (1955) **103,** *228*

Simpson *v* London & North Western Rail Co. (1876) *712*

Simpson *v* Simpson (1988) *259*

Sisley *v* Britannia Security Systems (1983) **250,** *344*

Skeate *v* Beale (1840) *258*

Slazengers Ltd *v* Gibbs (C) & Co. (1916) *463*

Smirk *v* Lyndale Developments Ltd (1974) **460,** *485*

Smith *v* Baker (1891) **305,** *396*

Smith *v* Bush (1987) **454,** *652*

Smith *v* Chadwick (1884) **139,** *251*

Smith *v* Land and House Property Co. (1884) **136,** *250, 254*

Smith *v* Leech Braine & Co. Ltd (1962) **327,** *407*

Smith *v* Mawhood (1845) *314*

Smith *v* Morgan (1971) *209*

Smith *v* Scott (1972) **387,** *432, 807*

Smith and Snipes Hall Farm *v* River Douglas Catchment Board (1949) **90,** *222*

Smith *v* South Wales Switchgear (1978) *294*

Solle *v* Butcher (1949) **128,** *11, 242, 245, 642, 706*

Somerset *v* Wade (1894) **528,** *536*

Southport Corporation *v* Esso

Petroleum Co. (1954) *357, 421, 477*

South Staffordshire Water Co. *v* Sharman (1896) **366,** *425, 484, 486*

South Western General Property Co. Ltd *v* Marton (1982) *682*

Spartan Steel & Alloys Ltd *v* Martin & Co. Ltd (1972) **395,** *438, 732*

Spencer *v* Harding (1870) *208, 590*

Spooner and Others, *ex parte* (1987) *537, 539*

Spurling *v* Bradshaw (1956) *676*

Stag Line Ltd *v* Tyne Ship Repair Group Ltd (1984) *301*

Stanley *v* International Harvester (1983) *152*

Stanley *v* Powell (1891) **313,** *398*

Stansbie *v* Troman (1948) *757*

Steinberg *v* Scala (1923) **112,** *234*

Steiner *v* Inland Revenue Commissioners (1973) **37,** *175*

Stephen (Harold) & Co. Ltd *v* Post Office (1978) *377*

Stevenson *v* McLean (1880) **54,** *208, 603*

Stilk *v* Myrick (1809) **81,** *219*

Stocks *v* Wilson (1913) *234*

Stone *v* Taffe (1974) *455*

Storey *v* Ashton (1869) *390*

Storey *v* Challands (1837) *466*

Storey *v* Fulham Steel Works (1907) **222,** *328*

Stubbings *v* Webb (1991) *417*

Sturges *v* Bridgman (1879) **391,** *433*

Sumpter *v* Hedges (1898) **217,** *324*

Sweet *v* Parsley (1969) **522,** *535, 536*

Sybron Corporation *v* Rochem Ltd (1983) *641*

Sykes (F. & S.) (Wessex) *v* Fine-Fare (1967) *596*

Systems Reliability Holdings plc *v* Smith (1990) **211,** *311*

Tai Hing Cotton Mill Ltd *v* Liu Chong Hing Bank Ltd (1985) *158*

Tarry *v* Ashton (1876) **373,** *429, 741*

Taylor *v* Bowers (1876) **198,** *306*

Taylor *v* Caldwell (1863) **225,** *328*

Tee *v* Tee (1973) **36,** *175*

Tehidy Minerals *v* Norman (1971)

492, 503, 504, 505

Tetley *v* Chitty (1986) *777*

Thabo-Meli *v* The Queen (1954) **521,** *535*

Thomas *v* Thomas (1842) **75,** *217*

Thomas National Transport (Melbourne) Pty Ltd and Pay *v* May and Baker (Australia) Pty Ltd (1966) **184,** *295*

Thompson *v* L.M.S. Railway (1930) **177,** *292*

Thompson *v* Lohan (1987) *296, 297*

Thornton *v* Shoe Lane Parking Ltd (1971) *676*

Tinn *v* Hoffman (1873) *211*

Tolley *v* Fry & Sons (1931) **431,** *467*

Tomlin *v* Standard Telephones and Cables Ltd (1969) *207*

Tool Metal Mfg Co. Ltd *v* Tungsten Electric Co. Ltd (1955) **97,** *225, 226, 623*

Treloar *v* Nute (1977) *485*

Trenbart (John) Ltd *v* National Westminster Bank Ltd (1979) *767*

Tsi Kwong Lam *v* Wong Chit Sen (1983) *514*

Tubantia, The (1924) **364,** *425*

Tulk *v* Moxhay (1848) **91,** *222, 505, 707*

Turbervell *v* Savage (1669) **349,** *416*

Tweddle *v* Atkinson (1861) **86,** *220*

Twine *v* Bean's Express Ltd (1946) *389, 736*

Twomax Ltd and Goode *v* Dickson, McFarlane and Robinson (1982) *452*

UCB Leasing Ltd *v* Holtam (1987) *287*

Ultzen *v* Nichols (1894) **463,** *486*

United Dominions Trust *v* Western (1975) *636*

United Railways of Havana, *re* (1960) *578, 579*

Universe Tankships Inc of Monrovia *v* International Transport Workers' Federation (1982) *261*

Vandyke *v* Fender (1970) **291,** *392*

Vane *v* Yiannopoullos (1965) **531,** *536*

Van Lynn Developments Ltd *v* Pelias

Construction Co. Ltd (1968) *525*

Varley *v* Whipp (1900) *273*

Vaughan *v* Taff Vale Railway (1860) **322**, *401*

Vauxhall Estates Ltd *v* Liverpool Corporation (1932) *4, 13*

Victoria Laundry Ltd *v* Newman Industries Ltd (1949) **243**, *336*

Videan *v* BTC (1963) **310**, *398*

Vitol SA *v* Esso Australia (1988) *703*

Vizetelly *v* Mudie's Select Library Ltd (1900) *464*

Wadley *v* Eager Electrical (1986) *359*

Wagon Mound, The (1961) **325**, *156, 405, 406*

Wagon Mound, The (No 2) (1966) *433, 753*

Waldron-Kelly *v* British Railways Board (1981) *289, 300*

Walker *v* Boyle (1982) **186**, *298*

Wallis's Caton Bay Holiday Camp *v* Shell-Mex & BP (1974) *485*

Walsh *v* Lonsdale (1882) **483, 498**, *510*

Ward *v* Byham (1956) *612*

Ward *v* Kirkland (1966) **491**, *502*

Ward *v* Tesco Stores (1976) *787*

Warlow *v* Harrison (1859) *205*

Warner Bros *v* Nelson (1937) **245**, *338*

Warren *v* Henlys Ltd (1948) *388, 389*

Warren *v* Mendy (1989) *714*

Watt *v* Hertfordshire County Council (1954) **402, 440**

Webster *v* Cecil (1861) **122**, *243*

Welby *v* Drake (1825) **95**, *224*

Welch *v* Cheesman (1974) **147**, *258*

Weller & Co. *v* Foot & Mouth Disease Research Institute (1965) **393, 438, 477, 782**

Wembley Park Estate Co. Ltd's Transfer, re (1968) *506*

Wenman *v* Ash (1853) *464*

Western Bank *v* Schindler (1976) *512*

West Midland Co-operative Society Ltd *v* Tipton (1986) *360*

Wheat *v* E. Lacon & Co. Ltd (1966) **415**, *455*

Wheatley *v* Lodge (1971) **356**, *419*

Whitbread & Co. plc *v* Mills (1988) *359*

White *v* Blackmore (1972) **302**, *396*

White *v* Bluett (1853) **77**, *217, 612*

White *v* City of London Brewery Co. (1889) **500**, *512*

White & Carter (Councils) Ltd *v* McGregor (1961) **234, 331, 336**

Whitehouse *v* Jordan (1981) *439*

Whiteley *v* Chappell (1868-9) *147*

Whitwood Chemical Co. *v* Hardman (1891) **246**, *338*

Wilchik *v* Marks (1934) **384**, *432*

Wilkie *v* London Passenger Transport Board (1947) *206*

Wilkinson *v* Downton (1897) **268**, *373, 408*

Williams *v* Compair Maxam (1982) *361, 369*

Williams *v* Fawcett (1985) *157*

Williams *v* Humphrey (1975) **269**, *375*

Williams *v* Roffey Bros and Nicholls (Contractors) Ltd (1990) *611*

Williams & Glyn's Bank Ltd *v* Boland (1980) **501**, *513, 519*

Wilson *v* Brett (1843) **473**, *489*

Wilson *v* Maynard Shipping Consultants A.B. (1978) *158*

Wilson *v* Pringle (1986) *416*

Wilson *v* Rickett Cockerell & Co. Ltd (1954) **171**, *279*

Wilsons and Clyde Coal Co. *v* English (1938) *460*

Winkfield, The (1902) **461**, *486*

Winn *v* Bull (1877) **52**, *207*

Winter Garden Theatre *v* Millenium Productions Ltd (1948) **361**, *422*

With *v* O'Flanagan (1936) **134**, *248*

Wood *v* Lectric (1932) *227, 588*

Wood *v* Scarth (1858) **132**, *18, 246*

Woodar *v* Wimpey (1980) *616*

Woodford *v* Smith (1970) *192*

Woodman *v* Photo Trade Processing Ltd (1981) *289, 299, 300*

Woodworth *v* Conroy (1976) *523*

Woolridge *v* Sumner (1962) **311**, *398*

Woolerton and Wilson Ltd *v* Richard Costain (Midlands) Ltd (1969) **359**, *421*

Woolmington *v* D.P.P. (1935) **506**, *83, 529*

Wormell *v* RHM Agriculture (East) Ltd (1986) **172**, *279*

Wren *v* Holt (1903) **166,** *274*
Wright *v* Tyne Improvement
   Commissioners (1968) **281,** *384*
Wyatt *v* Kreglinger and Fernau
   (1933) **204,** *308*
Wybot *v* Faure (1986) *471*

Yachuk *v* Oliver Blais & Co. Ltd
   (1949) **418,** *458*
Yates Building Co. *v* R.J. Pulleyn &
   Son (York) (1975) **62,** *210*
Yianni *v* Edwin Evans & Sons (1981)
   443
Young *v* Bristol Aeroplane Co. (1944)
   156
York (1748) *550*
Youssoupoff *v* M.G.M. Pictures
   (1934) **428,** *465*
Yuen Kun Yen *v* A.G. of Hong Kong
   (1987) *437*

1
The nature and development of English law

Classification of English law

The following are the main classifications of English law with which this book deals. The areas of law mentioned will be considered in more detail as relevant in the chapters which follow. They are given here merely as an overview of what is to come.

PRIVATE AND PUBLIC LAW

Private law is concerned with the legal relationships of ordinary persons in everyday transactions. It is also concerned with the legal position of corporate bodies and associations of persons the first of which are given a special form of legal personality. Private law includes contract and commercial law, the law of tort, family law, e.g. divorce, adoption and guardianship, trusts and the law of property which involves a consideration of the rights which can exist in property and how property can be transferred from one person to another.

Public law is concerned with the constitution and functions of the many different kinds of governmental organisations, including local authorities, such as county and district councils, and their legal relationship with the citizen and each other. These relationships form the subject matter of constitutional and administrative law. Public law is also concerned with crime which involves the State's relationship with the power of control over the individual.

There is also a division into *criminal and civil law*. Criminal law is concerned with legal rules which provide that certain forms of conduct shall attract punishment by the State, e.g. homicide and theft. Civil law includes the whole of private law and all divisions of public law except criminal law.

In order to understand the various branches of substantive private law which are considered in detail later, it is necessary to be able in particular to distinguish the following –

CONTRACT

A contract is an agreement made between two or more persons which is intended to have legal consequences. Thus, if there is a breach of contract, the parties can go to court and obtain a remedy. We shall see in the chapters on contract which agreements the courts will enforce, under what conditions they are enforceable, and what remedies are available to injured parties. It should be noted that the parties to a contract enter voluntarily into their obligations; the function of the law is merely to act in an impartial way in order to settle any disputes which may arise between the parties to the contract.

TORT

A tort, on the other hand, is a civil wrong independent of contract. It arises out of a duty imposed by law, and a person who commits a tortious act does not voluntarily undertake the liabilities which the law imposes on him. There are many kinds of tort with a common characteristic: injury of some kind inflicted by one person on another. Nuisance, trespass, slander and libel are well-known civil wrongs. The typical remedy in this branch of the law is an action for damages by the injured party against the person responsible for the injury. Such damages are designed not to punish the wrongdoer but to compensate the injured party.

CRIME

A crime is in a different category. It is difficult to define a crime, but it is a public offence against the State, and, while an individual may be injured, the object of a criminal charge is to punish the offender, not to compensate the victim, though under the provisions of the Powers of Criminal Courts Act, 1973, compensation orders can now be made. Criminals are prosecuted, usually by a Crown Prosecutor, and if found guilty receive the appropriate punishment.

Crimes and civil wrongs distinguished

The distinction does not lie in the *nature of the act* itself. For example, if a railway porter is offered a reward to carry A's case and runs off with it, then the porter has committed a crime, that of theft, and two civil wrongs, i.e. the tort of conversion and a breach of his contract with A. Again, a railway signalman who carelessly fails to operate the signals so that a fatal accident occurs will have committed one crime, i.e. manslaughter, if persons are killed, and two civil wrongs, the tort of negligence in respect of those who die and those who are merely injured and a breach of his contract of service with British Rail in which there is an implied term to take due care. It should also be noted that in this case the right of action in tort and the right of action in contract would be brought by different persons.

The distinction does depend on the *legal consequences* which follow the act. If the wrongful act is capable of being followed by what are called criminal proceedings that means that it is regarded as a *crime*. If it is capable of being followed by civil proceedings that means that it is regarded as a *civil wrong*. If it is capable of being followed by both it is both a crime and a civil wrong. Criminal and civil proceedings are usually easily distinguishable; they are generally brought in different courts, the procedure is different, the outcome is different and the terminology is different.

Terminology and outcome of criminal and civil proceedings

In *criminal proceedings* a prosecutor *prosecutes* a defendant. If the prosecution is successful it results in the conviction of the defendant. After the conviction the court may deal with the defendant by giving him a custodial sentence, e.g. prison; or a non-custodial sentence, e.g. probation. In rare cases the court may discharge the defendant without sentence.

As regards *civil proceedings,* a plaintiff *sues* (brings an action against) a defendant. If the plaintiff is successful this leads to the court entering judgment ordering the defendant to pay a debt owed to the plaintiff or money damages. Alternatively, it may require the defendant to transfer property to the plaintiff or to do or not to do something (injunction) or to perform a contract (specific performance). Some of these remedies are legal and others equitable. The matter of remedies for breach of contract and for torts will be dealt with in more detail in the chapters on those topics.

TRUSTS

A trust arises where one or more persons holds property, e.g. shares, for the benefit of other persons. People often wish to provide for their children or grandchildren when they die. They may leave some of their property on trust, particularly where, as in the case of grandchildren, they are minors, i.e. under the age of 18 years. They can appoint trustees who will take over the ownership of the property but they will not themselves benefit from that ownership since the capital and/or income of the trust will be used for the benefit of the children or grandchildren who are called the beneficiaries. Trusts may also be set up by living persons. The characteristics of a trust are that the trustees own the trust property but the beneficiaries get the benefits.

The development and sources of English law – generally

Our present legal system began, for all practical purposes, in the reign of Henry II (1154–1189). When he came to the throne justice was for the most part administered in local courts, i.e. by local lords to their tenants in the feudal courts, and by the County Sheriffs, often sitting with the Earl and the Bishop, in the courts of the Shires and Hundreds. They administered the law in their respective areas and decided the cases which came before them on the basis of local custom. Many of these customary rules of law were the same or similar in all parts of the country, but there were some differences. For instance, primogeniture, the right of the eldest son to inherit the whole of his father's land where there was no will, i.e. on intestacy, applied almost universally throughout England; but in Kent there existed a system of land-holding called gavelkind tenure whereby on intestacy all the sons inherited equally; while in Nottingham and Bristol, under the custom of Borough-English, the property passed to the youngest son. These customs were finally abolished by s. 1 and Part IV of the Administration of Estates Act, 1925, and replaced by the rule that land vests in those administering the deceased's estate for distribution to near relatives – in most cases spouse and children.

A Royal Court existed called the Curia Regis (King's Council) but this was in general available only to high-ranking persons to whom the King had granted interests in large estates.

In addition, the Curia Regis followed the person of the King and those wishing to complain to the court had to incur the expense, delay and frustration of pursuing the King in his constant movements about the country and abroad. It seems that one plaintiff followed the King through England and France for five years before his case was heard.

However, s. 17 of the Statute of 1215, Magna Carta, provided that what is now the High Court should not follow the King but should be held 'in some certain place'. This turned out to be Westminster and so what is now the High Court became centred in London. It is now in the Strand.

Steps were also taken to ensure that royal justice would go out to the shires and be open to all. This began with the General Eyre which also was instrumental in unifying the law. This is considered below.

The common law

The administrative ability of the Normans began the process destined to lead to a unified system of law which was nevertheless evolutionary in its development. The Normans were not concerned to change English customary law entirely by imposing Norman law on England. Indeed, many charters of William I giving English boroughs the right to hold courts stated that the laws dispensed in those courts should be laws of Edward the Confessor, which meant that English customary law was to be applied.

Attempts were made to ensure a greater uniformity in English law and the chief means by which this was achieved was the introduction of the General Eyre (which simply means 'a journey') whereby representatives of the King were sent from Westminster on a tour of the Shires for the purpose of checking on the local administration. During the period of their visit they would sit in the local court and hear cases, and gradually they came to have a judicial rather than an administrative function.

Henry II took steps to formalise the jurisdiction of the General Eyre by the Assize of Clarendon (1166) and the Assize of Northampton (1176). These provided that in relation to the criminal law there should be twelve men in every county to be responsible for presenting to the sheriff those suspected of serious crimes. The accused were then brought before the General Eyre when it arrived in the area. As regards the civil law, a new civil remedy called the Assize of Novel Disseisin was offered to persons who complained that their land had been wrongly seized. From this remedy grew a range of civil actions which were brought before the General Eyre. Thus royal and more uniform justice began to come to the country as a whole.

The General Eyre disappeared in the reign of Richard II (1377–99), but a system of circuit judges from what is now the High Court took its place, the first circuit commission being granted in the reign of Edward III (1327–77). By selecting the best customary rulings and applying these outside their county of origin, the circuit judges gradually moulded existing local customary laws into one uniform law 'common' to the whole kingdom. Thus, customs originally local ultimately applied throughout the whole of the realm. Even so, there was no absolute unification even as late as 1389, and in a case in what is now the High Court in that year, a custom of Selby in Yorkshire was admitted to show that a husband was not in that area liable for his wife's trading debts, though the common law elsewhere regarded him as liable.

Furthermore, the right to make a will of personal property, e.g. jewellery, was not universal in England until 1724 when it finally extended to the City of London. Before that time half of the personalty, 'the dead man's part', went to the church and the other half to the wife and children. Land could still not be left by will but descended to the heir at law, though it later became possible, as it is today, to leave land by will.

However, many new rules were created and applied by the royal judges as they went on circuit and these were added to local customary law to make one uniform body of law called 'common law'. Thus the identity between custom and the common law is not historically true, since much of the common law in early times was created by the judges, who justified their rulings by asserting they were derived from the 'general custom of the Realm'. Thus, in *Beaulieu* v *Finglam* (1401) Y.B. 2 Hen. 4, f. 18, pl. 6, it was said that a man who by his negligence failed to control a fire so that it spread to his neighbour's house was liable in damages according to 'the law and custom of the realm', though it is not easy to see which customary rule the court based its decision on.

THE ROYAL COMMISSIONS

The circuit judges from what is now the Queen's Bench Division came eventually to derive their authority from Royal Commissions, the granting of which marked the real beginning of the assize system. The Commissions were –

Commission of oyer and terminer

This commission, which dates from 1329, directed the judges to 'hear and determine' all complaints of grave crime within the jurisdiction of the circuit.

General gaol delivery

This commission, which dates from 1299, gave the judges power to clear the local gaols and try all prisoners within the jurisdiction of the circuit.

Other criminal cases were heard by Justices of the Peace either summarily or sitting in quarter sessions (now abolished) and the circuit judges were also made Justices of the Peace so as to increase their jurisdiction.

Commission of Assize for Civil Actions

Civil actions were usually heard at Westminster but under the Statute of Westminster II, 1285, the circuit judges heard *civil cases* under provisions known as *nisi prius* which required the local sheriff to send a jury to London *unless before* the appointed time the royal justices came to hear the case locally, which in practice they always did. Thus civil cases were opened in London, tried by circuit judge and jury in the locality and the verdict recorded in London. This lasted until the nineteenth century when a Commission of Assize for Civil Actions was granted.

THE COURTS ACT, 1971

The system, which lasted for many years, was brought to an end by the Courts Act, 1971, s. 1(2) which provided that all courts of assize were abolished and commissions to hold any court of assize would not be issued. This section, having achieved its purpose, was repealed by Sch. 7 of the Supreme Court Act, 1981.

STARE DECISIS

Initially the system was held together by the doctrine of *stare decisis*, or standing by previous decisions. Thus when a judge decided a new problem in a case brought before him, this became a new rule of law and was followed by subsequent judges. In later times this practice crystallised into the form which is known as the binding force of judicial precedent, and the judges felt bound to follow previous decisions instead of merely looking to them for guidance. By these means the common law earned the status of a system. Indeed it was possible for Bracton, Dean of Exeter and a Justice Itinerant of Henry III, to write the first exposition of the common law before the end of the thirteenth century – *A Treatise on the Laws and Customs of England*. There was also an earlier treatise ascribed to Ranulph de Glanvill in 1187, but this was not so comprehensive as the work of Bracton. Nevertheless, the number of writs which Bracton describes as being available in the Royal Courts is much in excess of those described by Glanvill and shows the rapid growth of the system in its first 100 years.

To sum up, the common law is a judge-made system of law, originating in ancient customs, which were clarified, *much* extended and universalised by the judges, although that part of the common law which concerned the ownership of land was derived mainly from the system of feudal tenures introduced from Europe after the Norman Conquest. It is perhaps also worth noting that the term 'common law' is used in four distinct senses, i.e. as opposed to (*a*) local law; (*b*) Equity; (*c*) statute law; and (*d*) any foreign system of law.

Equity

The growth of the common law was rapid in the thirteenth century but in the fourteenth century it ceased to have the momentum of earlier years. As a legal profession came into existence the judges came to be chosen exclusively from that profession instead of from a wider variety of royal officials as had been the case in the thirteenth century. The common law courts became more self-conscious about what they were doing and attempted to become more systematic. There was much talk about the proper way of doing things, of not being able to do this or that and much clever reasoning. Reports of cases in the Year Books, the nearest we have to law reports at this time, show a considerable concern with procedural points and niceties, a reluctance to depart from what had become established, a close attention to the observance of proper forms and much less concern with what the circumstances of a particular case demanded if it was to be settled in an appropriate way.

Defects of the common law

As a result of this hardening up of the system complaints were made by large numbers of people about the inadequacy of the service provided by the courts and the defects of the common law. The main defects were as follows –

THE WRIT SYSTEM

Writs were issued by the clerks in the Chancellor's office, the Chancellor being in those days a clergyman of high rank who was also the King's Chaplain and Head of Parliament. In order to bring an action in one of the King's courts, the party wishing to do so had to obtain from the Chancery a writ for which he had to pay. A writ was a sealed letter issued in the name of the King, and it ordered some person, Lord of the Manor, Sheriff of the County or the defendant, to do whatever the writ specified.

The old common law writs began with a statement of the plaintiff's claim, which was prepared in the Royal Chancery (or office) and not by the plaintiff's advisers as is the statement of claim today. Any writ which was new, because the plaintiff or his advisers had tried to draft it to suit the plaintiff's case, might be abated, i.e. thrown out by the court. Thus, writs could only be issued in a limited number of cases, and if the complaint could not be fitted within one of the existing standard writs, no action could be brought.

For example, the writ of trespass to land was available. However, trespass is a *direct* wrong, e.g. actually being on the land. *Indirect* activity affecting enjoyment of land was not covered, e.g. nuisance from smelly pigs or smoky bonfires. There was *at that time* no writ to deal with this type of indirect harm. The common law came to expand its writs to cover an action for damages in this situation, but in the meantime equity had carved out a jurisdiction and had an ideal remedy to deal with nuisance, i.e. the issue of an injunction requiring the defendant to cease the activity or pay a fine or be imprisoned for contempt of court. Moreover, writs were expensive, and their cost could deprive a party of justice. In some cases the cost of the writ was more than the amount of the plaintiff's claim so he did not bother to sue.

However, a practice grew up under which the clerks in Chancery provided new writs even though the complaint was not quite covered by an existing writ, thus extending the law by extending the scope of the writ system. This appeared to Parliament to be a taking away of its powers as the supreme lawgiver. Further, it took much work away from the local courts into the Royal Courts, thus diminishing the income of the local barons who persuaded Parliament to pass a statute called the Provisions of Oxford in 1258, forbidding in effect the practice of creating new writs to fit new cases. This proved so inconvenient that an attempt to remedy the situation was made by the Statute of Westminster II in 1285 which empowered the clerks in Chancery to issue new writs *in consimili casu* (in similar cases), thus adapting existing writs to fit new circumstances. The common law began to expand again, but it was still by no means certain that a writ would be forthcoming to fit a particular case, because the clerks in Chancery used the Statute with caution at first.

PROCEDURE

Other difficulties arose over the procedure in the common law courts, because even the smallest error in a writ would avoid the action. If X complained of the trespass of Y's mare, and in his writ by error described the mare as a stallion, his action could not proceed and he would have to start again. Furthermore, some common law actions were tried by a system called 'wager of law', and the plaintiff might fail on what was really a good claim if a defendant could bring more people to say that the claim was false than the plaintiff could get to support it.

The system worked well in local courts where the witnesses (called 'oath helpers') knew the parties and circumstances of the case. However, in cases brought at Westminster it fell into disrepute because 'oath helpers' who would support any case could be hired outside court for a few pence a head.

DEFENCES AND CORRUPTION

In common law actions the defendant could plead certain standard defences known as *essoins* which would greatly delay the plaintiff's claim. For example, the defendant might say that he was cut off by floods or a broken bridge. He might also plead the defence of sickness which could delay the action for a year and a day. In early times these defences were checked by sending four knights to see the defendant, but at a later stage there was no checking and the defences were used merely to delay what were often good claims. There were also complaints about the bribery, corruption or oppression of juries, the bias of sheriffs in favour of the powerful and the inability of a successful claimant to enforce a judgment or recover property from his more powerful neighbour.

REMEDIES

The common law was also defective in the matter of remedies. The only remedy the common law had to offer for a civil wrong inflicted on a plaintiff was damages, i.e. a payment of money, which is not in all cases an adequate compensation.

For example, if A trespasses each day on B's land, B is unlikely to be satisfied with damages. He would rather stop A from trespassing which equity could do by its remedy of injunction. The common law could not compel a person to perform his obligations or cease to carry on a wrong, though it is not true to say that the common law was entirely lacking in equitable principles, and even in early times there were signs of some equitable development; but generally the rigidity of the writ system tended to stifle justice.

TRUSTS AND MORTGAGES

Furthermore, the common law did not recognise the 'concept of the trust or use' and there was no way of compelling the trustee to carry out his obligations under the trust. Thus if S conveyed property to T on trust for B, T could treat the property as his own and the common law would ignore the claims of B. In addition, the main right of a borrower (or mortgagor) is the right to redeem (or recover) the land he has used as a security for the loan. Originally at common law the land became the property of the lender (or mortgagee) as soon as the date decided upon for repayment had passed, unless during that time the loan had been repaid. However, equity regarded a mortgage as essentially a security, and gave the mortgagor the right to redeem the land at any time on payment of the principal sum, plus interest due to the date of payment. What is more important, this rule applied even though the common law date for repayment had passed. This rule, which still exists, is called the Equity of Redemption.

Many people, therefore, unable to gain access to the King's courts, either because they could not obtain a writ, or because the writ was defective when they got it, or because they were caught in some procedural difficulty, or could not obtain an appropriate remedy, began to address their complaints to the King in Council. For a time the Council itself considered such petitions, and where a petition was addressed to the King in person, he referred it to the Council for trial. Later the Council delegated this function to the Chancellor, and eventually petitions were addressed to the Chancellor alone.

The Chancellor began to judge such cases in the light of conscience and fair dealing. He was not bound by the remedies of the common law and began to devise remedies of his own. For example, the Chancellor could compel a person to perform his obligations by issuing a decree of *specific performance* or could stop him from carrying on a wrong by the issue of an *injunction*. The Chancellor also recognised interests in property which were unknown to the common law, in particular the concept of the trust (as it became known) under which persons might be made the legal owners of property for the use or benefit of another or others. As we have seen, the common law did not recognise the interests of the beneficiaries under a trust, but allowed the legal owner to deal with the property as if no other interests existed. Equity, however, enforced the beneficial interests.

In order to bring persons before him the Chancellor issued a form of summons, called a *subpoena*, which did not state a cause of action but merely told the recipient to appear in Chancery. There were no rules of evidence and the Chancellor's Court did not sit in a fixed place; some hearings were even held in the Chancellor's private house. Equity was thus not cramped by anything like the writ system or the excessive formality of the common law. Eventually as new Chancellors took over, and Vice-Chancellors were appointed to cope with the increasing volume of work, uncertainty crept into the system, and conflicting decisions were common.

At this stage in its development equity adopted the practice of following previous decisions (or *stare decisis*) which had proved so powerful a force in unifying the diverse systems of local custom under the common law. This was precipitated by the Reformation and by the appointment in 1530 of Sir Thomas More as Chancellor. More was a common lawyer and not a cleric. From then on non-clerical Chancellors were drawn from the ranks of the common lawyers and naturally followed the system of precedent which they had seen used in the common law courts. Lord Ellesmere (1596–1617) began to apply the same principles in all cases of the same type, and later, under Lord Nottingham (1673–82), Lord Hardwicke (1736–56) and Lord Eldon (1807–27), Equity developed in scope and certainty.

Relationship of law and equity

Although law and equity eventually operated alongside each other with mutual tolerance, there was a period of conflict between them. This arose out of the practice of the Court of Chancery which issued 'common injunctions' forbidding a person on threat of imprisonment from bringing an action in the common law courts, or forbidding the enforcement of a common law judgment if such a judgment had been obtained.

Thus, if X by some unfair conduct, such as undue influence (see further p. 259), had obtained an agreement with Y, whereby Y was to sell X certain land at much below its real value, then, if Y refused to convey the land, X would have his remedy in damages at common law despite his unfair conduct. However, if Y appealed to the Chancellor, the latter might issue a common injunction which would prevent X from bringing his action at common law unless he wished to suffer punishment for defiance of the Chancellor's injunction. Similarly, if X had already obtained a judgment at common law, the Chancellor would prevent its enforcement by ordering X, on threat of imprisonment, not to execute judgment on Y's property.

However, the common law courts retaliated by waiting for the Chancellor to imprison the common law litigant for defiance of the injunction, and then the common law would release him by the process of *habeas corpus*, which is a type of writ used to obtain the release of a person who has been unlawfully detained in prison or elsewhere (see further p. 419).

This period of rivalry culminated in the *Earl of Oxford*'s case in 1615 when Lord Coke, representing the common law courts offered a direct challenge to the Court of Chancery's jurisdiction. The challenge was taken up and James I, on the advice of Lord Bacon, then his Attorney-General and later Lord Chancellor, gave a firm decision that where common law and Equity were in conflict Equity should prevail. This principle now appears in s. 49 of the Supreme Court Act, 1981, having appeared in a number of earlier Judicature Acts.

After that the two systems settled down and carved out separate and complementary jurisdictions. Equity filled in the gaps left by the common law, and became a system of case law governed by the binding force of precedent. However, it also lost much of its earlier freedom and elasticity. It is certainly no longer a court of conscience.

Many reforms were still to come. Equitable and legal remedies had to be sought in different courts, but this in due course was rectified by the Judicature Acts, 1873–75, which brought about an amalgamation of the English Courts. Since then both common law and equitable remedies have been available to a litigant in the same action and in the same court.

Before leaving the topic, a final charcteristic of equity should be noted which is that equity never says the common law is wrong but merely provides alternative solutions to legal problems. This is illustrated by certain cases in the Law of Contract. For example, the decisions in *Central London Property Trust Ltd* v *High Trees House Ltd* (1947) (see p. 224) and *Solle* v *Butcher* (1950) (see p. 245) show how modern equity sometimes adopts a different solution from that provided by the common law. Equity is not, therefore, a complete system of law. It complements the rules of the common law but does not replace them.

> **ESSENTIAL CASE LAW AND COMMENT**
>
> The *Earl of Oxford*'s Case, 1615 – Relationship of law and equity (1)

Legislation

In early times there were few statutes and the bulk of law was case law, though legislation in one form or another dates from AD 600. The earliest Norman legislation was by means of Royal Charter, but the first great outburst of legislation came in the reign of Henry II (1154–89). This legislation was called by various names: there were Assizes, Constitutions, and Provisions, as well as Charters. Legislation at this time was generally made by the King in Council, but sometimes by a kind of Parliament which consisted in the main of a meeting of nobles and clergy summoned from the shires.

In the fourteenth century parliamentary legislation became more general. Parliament at first asked the King to legislate, but later it presented a bill in its own wording. The Tudor period saw the development of modern procedure, in particular the practice of giving three readings to a bill.

From the Tudor period onwards Parliament became more and more independent and the practice of law making by statute increased. Nevertheless statutes did not become an important source of law until the last two centuries, and even now, although the bulk of legislation is large, statutes form a comparatively small part of the law as a whole. The basis of our law remains the common law, and if all the statutes were repealed we should still have a legal system of sorts, whereas our statutes alone would not provide a system of law but merely a set of disjointed rules.

Parliament's increasing involvement with economic and social affairs increased the need for statutes. Some aspects of law are so complicated or so novel that they can only be laid down in this form; they would not be likely to come into existence through the submission of cases in court. A statute is the ultimate source of law, and, even if a statute is in conflict with the common law or equity, the statute must prevail. It is such an important source that it has been said – 'A statute can do anything except change man to woman', although in a purely legal sense even this could be achieved. No court or other body can question the validity of an Act of Parliament.

Statute law can be used to abolish common law rules which have outlived their usefulness, or to amend the common law to cope with the changing circumstances and values of society. Once enacted, statutes, even if obsolete, do not cease to have the force of law, but common sense usually prevents most obsolete laws from being invoked. In addition, statutes which are no longer of practical utility are repealed from time to time by Statute Law Repeal Acts. Nevertheless, a statute stands as law until it is specifically repealed by Parliament. This may take place by implication as where an earlier Act is repealed by a later one which is inconsistent with it.

An Act of Parliament is absolutely binding on everyone within the sphere of its jurisdiction (but see p. 166), but all Acts of Parliament can be repealed by the same or subsequent parliaments; and this is the only exception to the rule of the absolute sovereignty of Parliament – it cannot bind itself or its successors.

ESSENTIAL CASE LAW AND COMMENT

Cheney v *Conn.*, 1968 – The court cannot declare a statute to be invalid **(2)**

Prince of Hanover v *Attorney-General*, 1957 – A statute remains law until repealed **(3)**

Vauxhall Estates Ltd v *Liverpool Corporation*, 1932 – Repeal by implication **(4)**

REPEAL OF STATUTES AND THE EUROPEAN COMMUNITY

As regards the power of Parliament to abolish or alter statute law by a later Act an interesting situation arises in connection with our membership of the European Community.

The obligation of the British Parliament on entry to the European Community was to ensure that Community law was paramount. The view of the European Court is that Community law overrides English law where the latter is inconsistent with it. Section 3 of the European Communities Act, 1972 binds our courts to accept this principle and talks of applying the principles of Community law with the idea that it prevails. Section 2(4) of the 1972 Act states that a UK statute should be construed so as to be consistent with Community law. However, many authorities on constitutional law see this obligation as a dilemma in the sense that Community law cannot be paramount when like the rest of our law it is at the mercy of any future Act of Parliament which must, under the fundamental rule of our constitution, prevail over any pre-existing law whatsoever. In other words, Community law is paramount as the result of the European Communities Act, 1972, which could be repealed by a future Act of Parliament. It would seem to be the duty of our courts to accept that repeal.

Delegated legislation

Many modern statutes require much detailed work to implement and operate them, and such details are not normally contained in the statute itself, but are filled in from some other source. For example, much of our social security legislation gives only the general provisions of a complex scheme of social benefits, and an immense number of detailed regulations have had to be made by civil servants in the name of, and under the authority of, the appropriate Minister. These regulations, when made in the approved manner, are just as much law as the parent statute itself. This form of law is known as delegated or subordinate legislation.

Custom

In early times custom was taken by the judges and turned into the common law of England, and it is still possible, even today, to argue the existence of a local or trade custom before the courts. Local customs consist in the main of customary rights vested in the inhabitants of a particular place to use, for various purposes, land held in the private ownership of another. For example, to take water from a spring (*Race* v *Ward* (1855) 24 L.J.Q.B. 153) and for fishermen to dry their nets on private land (*Mercer* v *Denne* [1905] 2 Ch. 538). A local custom can also affect the terms of a contract as is illustrated by *Hutton* v *Warren*, 1836. (See p. 663.) As a present-day source of law, however, custom is of little importance.

THE LAW MERCHANT

Mercantile law, or *lex mercatoria*, is based upon mercantile customs and usages, and was developed separately from the common law. The Royal Courts did not have a monopoly of the administration of justice and certain local courts continued to hear cases long after the Royal Courts were established. One notable area was that involving mercantile and maritime disputes. Disputes between merchants, local and foreign, which arose at the fairs where most important commercial business was transacted in the fourteenth century, were tried in the courts of the fair or borough, and were known as 'courts of pie powder' (*pieds poudrés*) after the dusty feet of the traders who used them.

These courts were presided over by the mayor or his deputy or, if the fair was held as part of a private franchise, the steward appointed by the franchise holder. The rules applied were the rules of the European law merchant developed over the years from the customary practices of merchants and the jury was often made up of merchants. The fair or borough courts were supplemented for a time by 'Staple Courts' which sat in the staple towns. These towns, which were designated by Edward III (1327–77) as the exclusive centres of trade for such commodities as wine, wool, leather and tin, were required to hold courts to decide the trading disputes of merchants and again the customary practices of merchants were used.

Maritime disputes were heard by maritime courts sitting in major ports such as Bristol. These, too, applied a special European customary law developed from the customary practices of seamen.

The common law courts were slow to show an interest in dealing with commercial matters. In part this was due to the idea that their jurisdiction had a geographical limit and was restricted to matters which had arisen in England between English citizens. Foreign matters, and many of these commercial disputes did involve either a foreign merchant or a contract made or to be performed abroad, were left to some other body, especially if it could raise questions about the relations between the King and foreign sovereigns where the King's Council might be a more appropriate body. To some extent also it was due to the fact that the common law courts and the common law had come into existence at a time when land was the most important commodity and the procedures and concerns of the common law courts were adapted to problems arising from disputes about the possession and ownership of land. They were formal, slow and ill-adapted to the needs of merchants who required a speedier justice administered according to rules with which they were familiar.

When the Court of Admiralty developed, it took over much of the work of the merchants' courts, but from the seventeenth century onwards the common law courts began to acquire the commercial work, and many rules of the law merchant were incorporated into the common law. This was achieved partly by fiction. For example, to get over the fact that technically it still lacked jurisdiction over matters arising abroad the Court accepted allegations that something that had occurred abroad had in fact occurred in England within its jurisdiction, e.g. by using the fiction that Bordeaux was in Cheapside.

Lord Mansfield and Lord Holt played a great part in this development, in particular by recognising the main mercantile customs in the common law courts without requiring proof of them on every occasion. Perhaps the most important mercantile customs recognised were that a bill of exchange was negotiable and that mere agreements should be binding as contracts. In this way the custom of merchants relating to negotiable instruments and contracts including the sale of goods became part of the common law, and later, by codification, of statute law in the Bills of Exchange Act, 1882, and the Sale of Goods Act, 1979.

Canon law

A brief mention should be made of the ecclesiastical or church courts since prior to 1857 they dealt not only with offences against church doctrine and morality but also with other matters such as matrimonial causes, legitimacy and the inheritance of property when a person died. Many of the rules laid down by these courts were derived from Roman Law and were inherited by the civil courts to which these matters were eventually transferred. In 1970 the civil courts concerned were amalgamated into the Family Division of the High Court (see p. 36).

The present position is that the church courts remain to deal with disciplinary and moral offences committed by the clergy and certain of the laity, e.g. parish clerks and churchwardens, of the Church of England, and certain other matters, e.g. decoration, alteration and use of churches.

The court of first instance is that of the diocesan chancellor, called a Consistory Court. He must be a member of the Church of England and is usually a practising barrister. Appeal lies from him to the Court of Arches in the province of Canterbury, and to the Chancery Court of York in the northern province. On matters concerning conduct, there is a further appeal to the Judicial Committee of the Privy Council and on other matters, e.g. the suitability of a Henry Moore altar in a Wren church (*Re St. Stephen Walbrook* [1987] 2 All E.R. 578), there may be an appeal to the Court of Ecclesiastical Cases Reserved. The church courts are not courts of common law and the prerogative orders (see p. 60) – which operate as a valuable check on the abuse of power by other courts and tribunals – do not apply to them.

Legal treatises

One last source remains to be considered, namely legal treatises. Throughout the centuries great English jurists have written books, some in the nature of legal textbooks, which have helped to shape the law and inform the legal profession.

We have already mentioned Bracton whose *Treatise on the Laws and Customs of England* was written in the thirteenth century and was probably based on the decisions of Martin de Pateshull, who was Archdeacon of Norfolk, Dean of St. Pauls and an Itinerant Justice from 1217 to 1229, and on those of William de Raleigh who was the Rector of Bratton Fleming in Devon and an Itinerant Justice from 1228 to 1250.

Sir Edward Coke, who lived from 1552 to 1634, is a celebrated name. His *Institutes* covered many aspects of law. For example, his *First Institute*, published in 1628, was concerned with land law. His *Second Institute*, published in 1642, was concerned with the principal statutes. The *Third Institute*, published in 1644, dealt with Criminal Law, while the *Fourth Institute*, also published in 1644, was concerned with the Jurisdiction and History of the Courts, this work containing bitter attacks on the Court of Chancery. During his lifetime Coke occupied the offices of Recorder of London, Solicitor-General, Speaker of the House of Commons, Attorney-General, and finally Chief Justice of Common Pleas.

Sir William Blackstone, who lived from 1723 to 1780, published his *Commentaries* in 1765. These are concerned with various aspects of law and are based on his lectures at Oxford. He was a Judge of the Common Pleas and was also the first Professor of English Law to be appointed in any English university.

In addition to older treatises such as those mentioned above, the works of modern writers, sufficiently eminent in the profession, are sometimes quoted when novel points of law are being argued in the Courts.

ESSENTIAL CASE LAW AND COMMENT

Boys v *Blenkinsop*, 1968 – Textbooks as a source of law **(5)**

2
The courts of law

The Royal Courts of Westminster developed out of the *Curia Regis* (or the King's Council). The Court of Exchequer was the first court to emerge from the *Curia Regis* and dealt initially with disputes connected with royal revenues. The Court of Common Pleas was set up in the time of Henry II to hear disputes between the King's subjects. The Court of King's Bench was last to emerge and initially was closely associated with the King himself, hearing disputes between subjects and the King.

As the system developed the Court of Chancery was added and there was also a Court of Admiralty. The Court of Probate and the Divorce Court developed from the old ecclesiastical courts which formerly dealt with these matters. Each of these courts had its own jurisdiction, sometimes overlapping and sometimes conflicting. This was particularly true with regard to the common law courts and the Court of Chancery. For example, in *Knight* v *Marquis of Waterford* (1844) 11 Cl. & Fin. 653, the appellant was told by the House of Lords after 14 years of litigation in Equity, that he had a good case but must begin his action again in a common law court. It is useful to refer at this point to *Wood* v *Scarth*, 1858 (see p. 646). This case is a further illustration of the delays which resulted from the administration of law and equity in separate courts. Anyway, this was how the English legal system entered the nineteenth century and it was this inheritance that the Victorians set out to rationalise into the form with which we are familiar.

The Supreme Court of Judicature

In order to rationalise the system the Supreme Court of Judicature was established. Under the Judicature Acts, 1873–1875 the High Court was divided into five divisions: Queen's Bench, Common Pleas, Exchequer, Chancery, and Probate, Divorce and Admiralty, the number being reduced to three by an Order in Council in 1881 when the Common Pleas and Exchequer Divisions were merged into the Queen's Bench Division. The Court of Appeal was given jurisdiction over appeals.

THE HOUSE OF LORDS

The House of Lords was not included in the Supreme Court of Judicature by the Judicature Acts because of Parliament's opposition to its hereditary character. Its jurisdiction as a final court of appeal was established by the Appellate Jurisdiction Act, 1876 which also provided the House with trained judges, i.e. Life Peers with legal training. The Judicature Acts, 1873–1875 were consolidated in the Supreme Court of Judicature (Consolidation) Act, 1925. This Act is now repealed by the Supreme Court Act of 1981, s. 1 of which reaffirms the previous position by providing that the Supreme Court of England and Wales shall consist of the Court of Appeal, the High Court of Justice and the Crown Court, and that the Lord Chancellor shall be the President of the Supreme Court. The Restrictive Trade Practices Court and the Employment Appeal Tribunal are not included even though they are staffed in part by High Court judges and appeals lie to the Court of Appeal.

The courts today

In recent times far-reaching changes have been made in the structure and jurisdiction of the civil and criminal courts by various reforming statutes. The present system of courts exercising both civil and criminal jurisdiction is set out on pp. 22 and 23.

Magistrates' courts

Although, as we shall see, the Crown Court tries the most serious criminal cases (all those in fact which are tried on indictment with a jury), the great bulk of the criminal work of the country is performed in the magistrates' courts.

TYPES OF MAGISTRATES

Magistrates may be of several kinds as follows –

(*a*) *Lay magistrates*. These are appointed by the Lord Chancellor on behalf of, and in the name of, the Queen. (See s. 6(1), Justices of the Peace Act, 1979, as amended by s. 65 of the Administration of Justice Act, 1982.) The Lord Chancellor is advised by a local advisory committee. Some persons, e.g. the spouses of police officers, cannot be appointed.

(*b*) *Stipendiary magistrates*. These are full-time magistrates who sit in certain commission areas. The area to which an appointment is made is entirely a matter for the Lord Chancellor. They are appointed by the Queen on the recommendation of the Lord Chancellor and must have a seven-year general advocacy qualification within the meaning of s. 71 of the Courts and Legal Services Act, 1990. Section 27 of this Act governs rights of audience before the courts. It preserves the existing rights of barristers and the more limited existing rights of solicitors but otherwise provides that a right of audience in relation to any proceedings exists only if granted by an authorised body. The General Council of the Bar and the Law Society are made authorised bodies by s. 27 of the 1990 Act but others may be designated by Order in Council. Section 27 takes away the power of judges to determine rights of audience and introduces a machinery under which practitioners who are not barristers may obtain rights of audience previously enjoyed exclusively by barristers. A seven-year general qualification means that the person concerned has had a right of audience in any part of the Supreme Court or all proceedings in county or magistrates courts for seven years. At the present time there are 16 stipendiary magistrates in the provinces, appointments having been made, e.g. in West Midlands, Greater Manchester, and Merseyside. Metropolitan stipendiary magistrates are the counterpart in London of the stipendiary magistrates in the provinces and are appointed in the same way. Currently there are 46 such magistrates, not including the Chief Metropolitan Magistrate, working, for example, in courts such as Bow Street and Tower Bridge.

(c) *Ex-officio magistrates.* Persons can become magistrates by holding another office. For example, the Lord Mayor and aldermen of the City of London are ex-officio magistrates.

THE CLERK

Each bench of lay magistrates has a salaried clerk, who is usually employed whole time. He assists the magistrates on questions of procedure and law whenever the magistrates ask for his help, though he can, as in *R v Uxbridge Justices, ex p. Smith* [1985] Crim. L.R. 670, offer advice on *law* unasked and may leave the court to give it to the magistrates after they have retired to consider their decision, though he cannot lawfully advise on the *decision*. However, when magistrates wish the clerk to retire with them to give advice they should request him to do so clearly in open court (*R v Eccles Justices, ex p. Fitzpatrick, The Times,* 28 February 1989). The clerk and his magistrates are responsible for the administration of the court.

Certain functions of the magistrates may be delegated to the clerk. For example, s. 28 of the Justices of the Peace Act, 1979, gives power to make rules delegating to the clerk the functions of a single justice. This includes issuing summonses and granting legal aid. Section 28 is amended by s. 117 of the Courts and Legal Services Act, 1990 which allows rules to be made to allow delegation of the duties and powers of the clerk to deputy or assistant clerks. The power is of general application but will be of particular use in the handling of family proceedings under the Children Act, 1989. The clerk is appointed by the Magistrates' Courts Committee for the relevant area from persons having a five-year magistrates' court qualification within the meaning of the Courts and Legal Services Act, 1990, i.e. a right of audience in relation to all proceedings in magistrates' courts for five years, though some clerks hold office by reason of a length of service qualification, i.e. having regularly acted as a court clerk for not less than five years prior to 1 January 1980.

THE DUTY SOLICITOR

Under s. 1 of the Legal Aid Act, 1988 the Legal Aid Board has responsibility for Duty Solicitor Schemes in all magistrates' courts. Local solicitors attend on a rota basis to advise defendants who have no solicitor of their own. The duty solicitor, who is entitled to be paid under the Legal Aid Scheme specifically for acting as such, can advise on the plea, i.e. guilty or not guilty. If the plea is not guilty he can apply for bail and ask for an adjournment to apply for legal aid and prepare a defence. If the plea is guilty he can put in a 'plea in mitigation' (see further p. 94) in the hope of influencing the magistrates to give a lighter sentence.

The role of the duty solicitor was made more important when s. 58 of the Police and Criminal Evidence Act, 1984 gave persons held in custody at a police station a right of access to legal advice. Since then duty solicitors have been available on a 24 hour basis to go to police stations to give advice paid for by legal aid.

COMMISSION AREAS

The Commission areas for which magistrates sit are metropolitan districts, metropolitan counties, non-metropolitan counties, London Commission Areas and the City of London. Of these, metropolitan districts and non-metropolitan counties may be divided into petty sessional areas or divisions.

MAGISTRATES' COURTS COMMITTEES

These are appointed for the various Commission areas. The functions of these committees are limited to making recommendations to the Home Secretary regarding proposed Petty Sessional Area or Divisional Boundary changes, the provision of courthouses, the appointment of justices' clerks and their staff, and the training of magistrates, which is compulsory, and their clerks' staff under the supervision of the Judicial Studies Board. This Board also supervises the training of judicial chairmen and members of tribunals. It also provides training on matters such as the reviewing of sentencing cases and the drug problem for assistant recorders, circuit judges, and district judges, assistant district judges and deputy district judges who also hear family and civil cases in the county court.

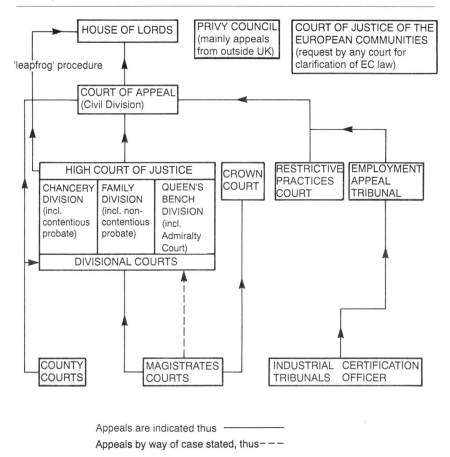

Appeals are indicated thus ─────────
Appeals by way of case stated, thus ─ ─ ─

Fig. 2.1 System of courts exercising civil jurisdiction

CLASSIFICATION OF CRIMINAL OFFENCES

Before discussing the powers of magistrates in regard to criminal prosecutions it is necessary to classify criminal offences for procedural purposes. Proceedings are regulated by the Magistrates' Courts Act, 1980. Criminal jurisdiction falls into three classes of offence listed in the Criminal Law Act, 1977 as –

(*a*) offences triable only on indictment before a jury, e.g. murder and manslaughter;

(*b*) offences triable only summarily by the magistrates, e.g. most road traffic offences, such as, for example, driving or attempting to drive a vehicle when unfit to drive through drink or drugs;

(*c*) offences triable either way, e.g. theft or handling stolen goods.

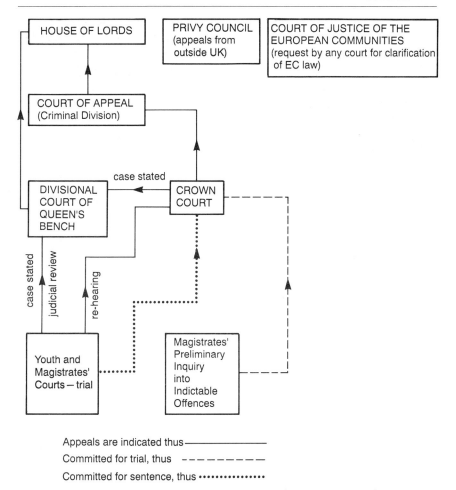

Appeals are indicated thus ————————
Committed for trial, thus — — — — — — —
Committed for sentence, thus ················

Fig. 2.2 System of courts exercising criminal jurisdiction

There is, under the 1980 Act, a single procedure applying to all cases where a person who has attained the age of 17 appears before a magistrates' court. This is as follows –

(*a*) if the offence is triable only on indictment then the magistrates will carry out a preliminary investigation. This can be carried out by one magistrate but it is usual for at least two to sit. The object of the investigation is to see whether the prosecution can establish a *prima facie* case. If so, the defendant is committed to the Crown Court for trial and if not, the case is dismissed, though such dismissals are extremely rare.

Under s. 6 of the Magistrates' Courts Act, 1980, and s. 61 of the Criminal Justice Act, 1982, provided that all the evidence for both prosecution and defence consists of written statements, and the defendant and his lawyer agree, the magistrates may commit him for trial in the Crown Court without even considering the evidence. The great majority of committals are now done in this way. Comparatively few go through the old style committal procedure which involves a full hearing of the prosecution's evidence, though some defendants exercise their right to test the case against them by requiring the prosecution witnesses to give their evidence and be cross-examined. If this does happen, reporting of that evidence is restricted. (See further p. 99.)

(*b*) If the offence is triable only summarily the magistrates will actually try the offence and not merely investigate the prosecutor's case.

(*c*) Where the offence is triable either way the procedure is as follows

   (i) the magistrates must begin by considering whether the offence is more suitable for summary trial or for trial on indictment;

  (ii) if the magistrates consider that the offence is more suitable for summary trial the accused must be asked whether he consents to be tried summarily or wishes to be tried by a jury. If he consents to be tried summarily the court proceeds with summary trial; if he does not so consent the court proceeds as examining justices.

 (iii) If the court considers that the offence is more suitable for trial on indictment the accused must be given an opportunity to make representation that he should be tried summarily and the court is then to decide whether to proceed to summary trial or as examining justices.

        A Practice Note issued in October 1990 is designed to encourage magistrates to try cases where the defendant has consented to a summary trial. There has been inconsistency in the past as between courts. Some magistrates' courts have always committed certain 'triable either way' cases to the Crown Court, e.g. burglary and offences of violence against the person. The guidance given to magistrates by the Practice Note should mean that they will try more cases of burglary, theft, reckless driving, indecent assault, fraud, criminal damage, handling stolen property, social security frauds, and offences involving violence and public disorder.

 (iv) Where the magistrates have begun to try a case summarily and the offence in question is triable either way the court may at any time before the conclusion of the prosecution evidence change from summary trial to committal proceedings. Similarly, if the court has begun to inquire into the information as examining justices, it may, after representations by the prosecution or accused and having regard to all the circumstances of the case, change to summary trial.

However, once it has been decided that the matter is suitable for a summary trial and the defendant has elected for this and pleaded guilty, the magistrates cannot, according to the decision of the House of Lords in *Chief Constable of West Midlands Police* v *Gilliard* [1985] 3 All E.R. 634, subsequently commit the defendant for trial in the Crown Court but can only commit for sentence under s. 38 of the Magistrates' Courts Act, 1980.

As regards offences triable either way, SI 1985/601 introduces rules under s. 48 of the Criminal Law Act, 1977 requiring advance disclosure of the prosecution's case to defendants. This was not a requirement before the passing of the Statutory Instrument.

The rules apply *in either way cases only* and under the rules a prosecutor may withold information if he thinks that it could lead to the intimidation of a witness or to an interference with the course of justice.

The rules do not oblige the police to take statements from witnesses but merely to disclose any which they have. The purpose of the disclosure requirements is that advance knowledge of the case for the prosecution will often reveal its strength and lead to more guilty pleas. Some of the busiest courts have independently introduced various forms of pre-trial review which also lead to an increase in the number of guilty pleas when the strength of the case against the defendant is reviewed.

SENTENCING

The maximum custodial penalty which the magistrates may impose for any offence is in most cases six months' imprisonment. The general maximum fine for any one offence is £5000. In addition the magistrates can make compensation orders requiring a defendant to compensate the victim of his crime, up to a maximum figure of £5000 per offence. There are also restitution orders under which the defendant can be required to return stolen property and, in addition, the magistrates may make probation orders and supervision orders which operate to some extent like probation, and which were introduced by s. 11 of the Children and Young Persons Act, 1969 to replace probation for juvenile offenders (see now Children Act, 1989 Part IV), and community service orders under which the defendant may be required to carry out some useful service within the community. Also under the Criminal Justice Act, 1991 magistrates have power to combine community service and probation and to impose curfews enforced by electronic tagging. In addition, it should be noted that if the magistrates are trying an indictable offence summarily and feel that the circumstances are such that the defendant should be given a greater sentence than can be given in a Magistrates' Court, they may commit the defendant to the Crown Court for sentence under s. 38 of the Magistrates' Court Act, 1980. Further details are given at the sentencing section which appears at p. 113.

Bail, remand and administration

In addition to committals, trials and sentencing, magistrates also make vital decisions on whether to grant bail to the defendant or remand him to prison to await his trial. They also issue summonses and warrants to arrest persons and search premises.

Civil jurisdiction

The magistrates also have a limited civil jurisdiction which includes what are known as family proceedings for the maintenance of children and applications for matrimonial relief such as separation orders and maintenance orders made by women who do not initially opt for divorce on breakdown of marriage. They can also deal with questions regarding the adoption of children and so far as parents and other relatives are concerned they can decide the place of residence of a child and rights of contact with him or her. There is also power to order a violent spouse to leave the home in order to protect the other spouse and children (if any). They may also consent to the marriage of a minor of 16 or 17 years of age who is not a widow or widower, where other relevant consents, e.g. those of parents, are not forthcoming. These family matters are dealt with in separate branches of the magistrates' court known as the family proceedings court and family panels (see s. 92 and Sch. 11 of the Children Act, 1989). The magistrates also deal with matters relating to the licensing of pubs, restaurants, betting shops and casinos and the enforcement of the Council Charge. Where a foreign state wants an alleged criminal living in England and Wales to be returned the request for extradition is heard under the provisions of s. 9 of the Extradition Act, 1989 by a Metropolitan stipendiary magistrate.

APPEALS

Appeals from the magistrates in family proceedings are to the Divisional Court of the Family Division. As regards criminal offences, appeal may be to the Crown Court or to the Divisional Court of Queen's Bench as follows –

(a) *Crown Court.* An appeal to the Crown Court may be made by the accused only, provided he did not plead guilty. The appeal may be against conviction or sentence on law or fact and no permission is required. If he pleaded guilty he may appeal against sentence only. An appeal against conviction takes the form of rehearing in the Crown Court and although the Crown Court may give greater punishment than the magistrates in fact gave, it is, in general terms, limited to a prison sentence of not more than six months or a fine of not more than £5000. When the Crown Court is reviewing sentence it must hear the antecedents of the person making the appeal and consider all the relevant reports on him together with affording him an opportunity to address the court in mitigation.

(b) *Divisional Court of Queen's Bench.* An appeal to the Divisional Court of Queen's Bench may be made by either the accused or the prosecution by means of *case stated*. This means that the magistrates must set out in writing their findings of fact together with the arguments put forward by the parties and their decision and the reasons for it. The appeal questions the decision of the magistrates on the ground that it is wrong in *law*. Issues of *fact* should not be appealed against by way of case stated (*James* v *Chief Constable of Kent*, *The Times*, 7 June 1986). It is available to a person who has pleaded guilty. If the Divisional Court or the House of Lords gives leave, there may be a further appeal to the House of Lords but the Divisional Court must certify that the case raises a matter of law of public importance.

(c) *Judicial review.* Whenever a court, including, obviously, a magistrates' court, acts without jurisdiction, or fails to observe the rules of natural justice, (see further p. 61) or makes an important procedural error, any person affected, and obviously a defendant, may apply to the High Court to review the decision of the magistrates and issue an order of *certiorari*. (See further p. 61.) These types of defects in a magistrates' court must be challenged by judicial review and not by case stated. (*R v Wandsworth Justices, ex parte Read* [1942] 1 All E.R. 56.)

Under ss. 108 and 109 of the Courts and Legal Services Act, 1990 magistrates who act beyond their jurisdiction may be sued for damages and costs by persons affected but only if they act in bad faith. However, s. 53 of the Justices of the Peace Act, 1979 provides for their indemnification out of local funds.

(*d*) *The European Court.* The magistrates may refer matters to the European Court. Thus in *R v Marlborough Street Stipendiary Magistrate, ex parte Bouchereau* [1977] 3 All E.R. 365, the magistrate indicated that he proposed making a recommendation for the deportation of B, but it was said that the magistrate had no such power since B was a migrant worker protected by Article 48 of the Treaty of Rome. The magistrate decided to refer the matter to the European Court under Article 177 of the Treaty and this was held to be in order by a Divisional Court which decided also that legal aid legislation allows a magistrates' court to order legal aid for the purposes of proceedings before the European Court of Justice.

(*e*) *Rectification of mistakes by the magistrates themselves.* Section 142 of the Magistrates' Courts Act, 1980 provides an alternative to appeal to the Crown Court or Divisional Court. The section gives magistrates the power to re-open a case to rectify their mistake but only if the defendant has been found guilty, not if he has been acquitted. The power may be used, e.g. to deal with a sentence passed in excess of the court's powers and also where the defendant asks for a review of his sentence on the grounds that it is too harsh. The prosecution or the defence may institute a review and it would seem that the magistrates may do so of their own volition.

Youth courts

The magistrates also have a part to play in regard to children over ten but under 14 and young persons who are over 14 but have not attained the age of 18. Criminal proceedings cannot be brought against a person under the age of ten. For this purpose the magistrates sit as a youth court. This court must sit in a different building or room from that in which other courts are held or else must sit on a different day. The court consists of three magistrates who are drawn from a special panel of persons who need no longer be under 65 years of age and it is usual for one or more female magistrates to be present. The public is excluded from these courts and there are strict controls on press reports. Youth courts have a range of sentences at their disposal including custodial measures. (See further p. 113.) The Criminal Justice Act, 1991 provides that the youth court in each area shall hold at least one sitting fortnightly outside the times at which the court normally sits, e.g. in the evening or on Saturday morning if in the opinion of the court this is justified by the number of cases where to require a parent or guardian to attend the court at the times at which it normally sits would jeopardise the employment of the parent or guardian or would be undesirable for any other reason.

The County Court

The magistrates' courts deal with most of the less serious criminal matters in this country. At something like the same level, but dealing exclusively with civil cases, is the county court. County courts were created by the County Courts Act, 1846, to operate as the chief lower courts for the trial of civil disputes, and a large number of cases are heard in these courts annually. They are now governed by the County Courts Act, 1984. Section references are to that Act unless otherwise stated.

A county court is presided over by a circuit judge appointed by the Crown on the advice of the Lord Chancellor (s. 5 and see p. 34). The judge usually sits alone, though, under ss. 66 and 67, there is provision for a trial by a jury of eight persons in some cases, e.g. where fraud, libel, slander, malicious prosecution, or false imprisonment is alleged. Under s. 77 appeal lies direct to the Court of Appeal (Civil Division). The judge is assisted by a district judge who acts as clerk of the court and may try certain cases, e.g. where the defendant fails to appear at the hearing or admits the claim and where the sum claimed or the amount involved does not exceed £5000 and if the judge gives leave and with the consent of the parties any other action or matter. The Lord Chancellor may, with the agreement of the Treasury as to numbers and salaries, appoint such assistant district judges as he considers necessary for carrying out the work of the court. He may also appoint deputy district judges as a temporary measure to dispose of business in the county court. An assistant district judge and a deputy district judge have the same powers as the district judge. District judges, assistant district judges and deputy district judges are appointed from persons who have a seven-year general advocacy qualification within the meaning of the Courts and Legal Services Act, 1990. (See ss. 6–9 (as amended by the Courts and Legal Services Act, 1990).)

JURISDICTION

Regarding the jurisdiction of the court a plaintiff in a default action may sue out of any county court he wishes regardless of the defendant's place of residence or business or where the cause of action arose. A default action is one where the *only* relief claimed is the payment of money, e.g. a liquidated sum such as a debt for goods sold but not paid or an unliquidated sum such as a claim for damages for personal injuries. However, if in a liquidated claim the defendant files a defence this will generally result in the case being transferred to the defendant's home court and the defendant has a right to apply for a transfer to his home court in unliquidated claims. In actions in which there is a claim for relief other than the payment of money, e.g. a possession order for land or the recovery of goods or an injunction to restrain a nuisance, the general rule is that the plaintiff must bring his action in the court of the district where the defendant dwells or carries on business, or that for the district in which the cause of action wholly or mainly arose, and where land is involved, the action is generally brought in the court of the district in which the land is situated. Under s. 3 of the Courts and Legal Services Act, 1990 the county court has the same jurisdiction as the High Court to grant an injunction or a declaratory judgment setting out the rights of the parties, in respect of, or relating to, any land or the possession, occupation, use or enjoyment of any land. This jurisdiction applies only where the capital value of the land or interest in land does not exceed £30,000.

Apart from this, a county court can give the same remedies as the High Court although the orders of *mandamus, certiorari* and prohibition are available only in the High Court (see further p. 60). County courts are also prohibited – patent court apart – from granting an Anton Piller order or a Mareva injunction (see further p. 338) though the Mareva jurisdiction under s. 37 of the Matrimonial Causes Act, 1973 remains so that the court can grant such an injunction to a wife whose husband is about to remove his property abroad to defeat her claim for financial relief against him.

The general jurisdiction of county courts and the procedure therein are governed by the County Courts Act, 1984, the Courts and Legal Services Act, 1990 and the High Court and County Courts Jurisdiction Order, 1991 (SI 1991/724 (L5)) and the County Court Rules. The latter are in the form of delegated legislation and are set out in an annual volume known as the County Court Practice. In general terms, the extent of the jurisdiction is as follows –

(*a*) *Actions founded on contract and tort.* Here the position is as follows –

- (i) Claims for damages in respect of personal injuries and death must be commenced in a county court unless the claim is for £50,000 or more.
- (ii) Other actions (except libel and slander which are exclusive to the High Court) of which the value is less than £25,000 will be tried in a county court unless –
  (1) criteria set out in SI 1991/724 (L5) para. 7(5) lead the county court to believe that the case should be transferred to the High Court and the High Court agrees; or
  (2) the action is commenced in the High Court and the High Court believes that in view of the relevant criteria it ought to try the action.

(iii) An action of the value of £50,000 or more is to be tried in the High Court unless –

(1) it is commenced in the county court and the county court having had regard to the relevant criteria does not think it should be tried in the High Court; or

(2) it is commenced in the High Court which having regard to the criteria thinks it ought to transfer it to the county court for trial.

The criteria referred to above are –

(1) whether the claim is really of the alleged value, including the value of any counterclaim which the defendant may be making;

(2) whether the action is otherwise important and in particular whether it raises questions of importance to persons who are not parties or questions of general public interest. In which case presumably there would be a tendency to trial in the High Court;

(3) the complexity of the facts, legal issues, remedies or procedures involved are such that it might be better tried in the High Court;

(4) whether transfer is likely to result in a more speedy trial of the action. This would tend towards a trial in the county court in many cases but it should be noted that the 1991 Order makes it clear that no transfer shall be made on the grounds of (4) alone.

Statement of value. The value of the action appears on what is called a Statement of Value sent to a Master for High Court claims or to a District Judge for county court claims by the solicitor acting for the plaintiff or by a party acting in person. The solicitor for the defendant or the defendant in person can also submit one and in a dispute the relevant court officer must decide where the hearing will take place.

(*b*) *Equity matters*, e.g. mortgages and trusts where the amount involved does not exceed £30,000, unless the parties agree to waive the limit. Under this heading would be found requests for repossession orders by building societies against mortgage defaulters.

(*c*) *Actions concerning title to land, and actions for recovery of possession of land*, where the capital value of the land or interest in land does not exceed £30,000. There is unlimited jurisdiction in cases involving residential tenancy security issues (see e.g. s. 40 of the Housing Act, 1988), or by agreement between the parties.

(*d*) *Bankruptcies.* Here there is unlimited jurisdiction, but not all county courts have bankruptcy jurisdiction. The Lord Chancellor is empowered by s. 374 of the Insolvency Act, 1986 to exclude any county court from having such jurisdiction. Bankruptcy cases in the London insolvency district are heard in the Bankruptcy Court of the High Court. Appeal from the county court in bankruptcy matters is to the Divisional Court of the Chancery Division.

(*e*) *Company winding up.* Where the paid-up share capital of the company does not exceed £120,000, the county court of the district in which the company's registered office is situated has concurrent jurisdiction with the High Court provided that the relevant county court has a bankruptcy jurisdiction (ss. 117 and 416 of the Insolvency Act, 1986).

(*f*) *Probate proceedings*, where the value of the deceased's estate is estimated to be £30,000 or less.

(*g*) *Admiralty matters*. Some county courts in coastal areas have Admiralty jurisdiction which is limited to £5000 except in salvage cases where the limit is £15,000. The parties may by agreement waive these limits.

(*h*) *Matrimonial and Family proceedings*. The jurisdiction of county courts in matrimonial causes is derived from s. 33 of the Matrimonial and Family Proceedings Act, 1984, and the Children Act, 1989.

A county court designated by the Lord Chancellor as a 'divorce county court' has jurisdiction in certain matters relating to any undefended matrimonial cause, but may *try* such a cause only if further designated as a court of trial. Every matrimonial cause must be commenced in a divorce county court and is to be heard and determined there, unless transferred to the High Court, e.g. under s. 39 of the 1984 Act, i.e. on the application of a party or on the court's own motion.

Thus the divorce process generally takes place in the divorce county court. Divorce county courts are now divided into two, i.e. the divorce county court and the Family Hearing Centre. If in a divorce case where the parties have children an application is made for an order under s. 8 of the Children Act, 1989 (e.g. a Residence Order settling the arrangements to be made as to the person with whom the child is to live), then the s. 8 application must be dealt with at a family hearing centre by a nominated circuit judge.

As regards cases concerning children the coming into force of the Children Act, 1989 has reinforced the philosophy that children cases should be heard by a judiciary who by reason of their experience and training are specialists in family work. Accordingly the Lord Chancellor has, under the Courts and Legal Services Act, 1990 with the agreement of the President of the Family Division, nominated certain circuit judges to deal with family proceedings and child care cases. There are special arrangements in London where jurisdiction is given to nominated district judges of the Family Division.

(*i*) *Small claims*. If the amount claimed does not exceed £1000 the case is referred for arbitration by the district judge or, if a party applies, by the circuit judge or an outside arbitrator upon receipt by the court of a defence to the claim. If there is a reference to arbitration the parties will be encouraged to conduct the case without legal representation. In addition the hearing is informal and in private. In general the strict rules of evidence are dispensed with so that e.g. hearsay evidence may be allowed. This is evidence which has not been obtained from personal experience but from someone else, e.g. 'John told me that Harry was drunk'. In addition each side pays its own costs.

Rules to be made under s. 7 of the Courts and Legal Services Act, 1990 will give the arbitrator, usually the district judge or an assistant or deputy district judge, a more interventionist role under which he can if necessary take control of the questioning to ensure that each party has a fair hearing.

(*j*) *Pre-trial review*. It should also be noted that a *pre-trial review* by the district judge is now a regular feature of ordinary actions in the county court and also in default actions, i.e. cases in which a fixed sum of money, such as a debt, is claimed. A major advantage of the pre-trial review is that the parties may compromise the claim and settle, thus saving time and money involved in going to trial. However, if there is no compromise then at the conclusion of the review the date of trial is fixed or the action is adjourned for the hearing to be fixed at a later date. If the defendant does not attend the review the plaintiff may be given a judgment if adequate documentary evidence is presented by him.

(*k*) *Patents county court*. Part VI of the Copyright, Designs and Patents Act, 1988 provides for the setting up of patents county courts with a countrywide jurisdiction to hear and determine proceedings relating to patents and designs and matters ancillary thereto. Concern about the high cost of resolving patent disputes in the High Court led the Oulton Committee in its report of November 1987 to recommend the creation of specialist county courts as a solution to the problem. SI 1990/1489 designated the Edmonton County Court as the first patents county court.

(*l*) *Miscellaneous matters*. The county court derives an important part of its jurisdiction from social legislation, e.g. adoption of children, guardianship of infants, legitimacy, race relations, and the enforcement of legislation concerning landlord and tenant.

Although in many matters the county court has concurrent jurisdiction with the High Court, there are certain matters over which the county courts have *exclusive* jurisdiction so that actions concerning them cannot be commenced in the High Court, e.g. regulated consumer credit agreements or hire agreements where the fixed sum credit does not exceed £15,000 or, in a running account, the credit limit does not exceed £15,000 (s. 141 Consumer Credit Act, 1974). The court's jurisdiction in proceedings relating to extortionate credit agreements under s. 139 of the Consumer Credit Act, 1974, is unlimited. Furthermore, where the lender on mortgage is seeking to take possession of land and the mortgage includes a dwelling house and no part of the land is in Greater London, the county court has exclusive and unlimited jurisdiction. (S. 21, County Courts Act, 1984 as amended.) In addition, the Attachment of Earnings Act, 1971, s. 1 gives the county court alone the power to order attachment of earnings for ordinary civil debt.

ENFORCEMENT OF JUDGMENTS

As regards the enforcement of judgments the Order of 1991 provides that county court judgments for the payment of sums of money of £5000 or more *must* be enforced, e.g. by procedures leading to execution on property, in the High Court and *may* be enforced in the High Court if they are for £2000 or more. Below that they *must* be enforced in the county court.

CONCILIATION

The Bar Council and other groups of lawyers are seeking to develop conciliation procedures in the county court to resolve disputes outside of the courtroom and out of court hours, e.g. between 5 pm and 8 pm. The district judge would identify cases suitable for settlement by this method which could then be used if the parties agreed. However, refusal to accept the recommendation of the district judge could lead to a failure to recover all proper costs if a trial were to proceed in spite of that recommendation, because of the refusal of a party to accept it.

The parties would provide the conciliator with summaries of their case, their pleadings and essential documents. The conciliator would be a lawyer with at least seven years' experience of litigation. He would put the parties in separate rooms and move between them discussing the merits of each case and suggesting a settlement. This may result in an acceptance of a settlement by the parties. If not the conciliator will bring them together and give them his assessment of the probable result of a trial. This is not binding on the parties but may lead to a last minute settlement. If not there will have to be a trial. This procedure has been used with great success in the United States and in Australia, New Zealand and Canada. Its development here seems likely.

APPEAL

Appeal from a decision of a county court judge lies direct to the Court of Appeal (Civil Division). (S. 77, County Courts Act, 1984.) As regards the small claims procedure a party may apply to the circuit judge to set aside the arbitrator's award.

The Crown Court

The Crown Court is a superior court of record created by the Courts Act, 1971. The Crown Court system replaced Courts of Assize and Quarter Sessions. It deals in the main with criminal work, though appeals from magistrates' courts in matters concerning betting, gaming, and licensing now lie to the Crown Court.

CONSTITUTION

The jurisdiction and powers of the Crown Court are exercised by the following –

(a) *High Court judges.* Certain cases are not appropriate for trial in a Crown Court by a circuit judge or recorder but are reserved for trial in that court by a High Court judge. All offences have been divided for the purpose of trial into four classes and, for example, Class 1 offences must be tried by a High Court judge. These include murder and treason. On the other hand, offences such as wounding or causing grievous bodily harm would normally be tried by a circuit judge or recorder.

(*b*) *Circuit judge.* Circuit judges are appointed by the Queen on the recommendation of the Lord Chancellor from persons who have a ten-year Crown Court or ten-year County Court advocacy qualification within the meaning of s. 71 of the Courts and Legal Services Act, 1990; or are Recorders; or have held as a full-time appointment for at least three years one of the offices listed in Part 1A of Sch. 2 of the 1990 Act, e.g. chairman of an industrial tribunal; or a Master of a division of the High Court (see p. 80); or a district judge; or a Stipendiary Magistrate. A Crown Court or County Court qualification means that the person concerned has a right of audience in regard to all proceedings in the Crown Court or County Court as the case may be, and in this case has had it for at least ten years. Unlike High Court judges who are *invited* to take appointment, those wishing to become circuit judges *apply* to the Lord Chancellor.

(*c*) *Recorder and Assistant Recorder.* These are part-time appoints made by the Queen on the recommendation of the Lord Chancellor from persons with a ten-year Crown Court or County Court advocacy qualification. Again, those who wish to become Recorders apply to the Lord Chancellor.

(*d*) *Magistrates.* When the Crown Court is hearing an appeal or a committal for sentence from the Magistrates' Court, between two and four justices sit with the judge or recorder. Where a judge of the High Court, Circuit Judge, or Recorder, sits with Justices of the Peace, he presides and –

(i) the decision of the Crown Court may be a majority decision; and
(ii) if the members of the court are equally divided, the judge of the High Court, circuit judge, or recorder shall have a casting vote. (S. 73(3), Supreme Court Act, 1981.)

JURISDICTION

All indictable offences are triable in the Crown Court. An indictment is a formal statement of a serious crime prepared for a trial by jury. The Court also hears appeals from magistrates and committals for sentence from the magistrates. It also hears appeals from youth courts and for this purpose forms a youth appeals court. This consists of a circuit judge plus two magistrates drawn from the youth court panel.

The Central Criminal Court

Before leaving the subject of the Crown Court special mention should be made of the Central Criminal Court, otherwise referred to as the 'Old Bailey'. This court continues as a Crown Court sitting in the City of London, though its constitution is slightly different in that the Lord Mayor and any alderman of the City may sit with any judge of the High Court or any circuit judge or recorder.

The High Court – generally

Under s. 4(1)(e) of the Supreme Court Act, 1981, the High Court is staffed by a maximum of 85 judges (when all posts are filled) known as *puisne* judges (pronounced 'puny'). The *puisne* judges of the High Court are styled 'Justices of the High Court'. The number of *puisne* judges may be increased by Order in Council. Appointment is by the Queen on the advice of the Lord Chancellor from persons with a ten-year High Court qualification, i.e. from those who have had a right of audience (or advocacy) in relation to all proceedings in the High Court for at least ten years. Also eligible are Circuit judges who have held that office for at least two years (s. 10 (3) of the 1981 Act as amended by s. 71 of the Courts and Legal Services Act, 1990).

The Queen's Bench Division has the largest staff, currently 54 *puisne* judges. The Court is presided over by the Lord Chief Justice. As regards jurisdiction, every type of common law civil action, e.g. contract and tort, can be heard by the Queen's Bench Division at the Royal Courts of Justice in the Strand. In addition, the judges of this division staff the Crown Court and sit in the Court of Appeal (Criminal Division) as well as the Divisional Court of Queen's Bench and the Central Criminal Court. Admiralty business is now assigned to a separate court called the Admiralty Court within the Queen's Bench Division. The same is true of commercial business which is heard by a separate court called the Commercial Court within the Queen's Bench Division. The Commercial Court also provides an arbitration service. (See p. 36.)

The Chancery Division currently has 13 *puisne* judges and is presided over by the Lord Chancellor. However, he is nominal head only and does not try cases. A Vice-Chancellor is now appointed to perform organisational and administrative functions as deputy to the Lord Chancellor. The Vice-Chancellor also hears cases. Under s. 10(3)(a) of the Supreme Court Act, 1981, the appointment is by the Queen from persons qualified to be a Lord Justice of Appeal. (See p. 39.) Company business is assigned to a separate court called the Companies Court within the Chancery Division. Apart from company work the Chancery Division deals with partnership matters, mortgages, trusts, revenue matters, rectification of deeds and documents, the administration of estates of deceased persons and contentious probate. The bulk of the bankruptcy work of the Chancery Division is performed by Registrars in Bankruptcy who deal with cases arising in the London insolvency district, provincial bankruptcies being dealt with by the local county court. The Patents Court forms part of this Division and deals with cases which are outside the jurisdiction of the patents county court (see p. 32).

The Family Division has 16 *puisne* judges and is presided over by the President of the Division. The Court deals with all aspects of family law including family property and children in terms for example of adoption, guardianship and wardship. A more recent acquisition of jurisdiction arises under the Human Fertilisation and Embryology Act, 1990 where the Family Division may e.g. make an order providing for a child to be treated in law as the child of the parties to a marriage if the child has been carried by a woman other than the wife as a result of the placing in her of an embryo (s. 20).

DIVISIONAL COURTS

Each of the three divisions of the High Court has divisional courts. These are constituted by not less than two judges.

(*a*) *Divisional Court of Queen's Bench*. This hears appeals on points of law on cases stated by magistrates and the Crown Court. It also has a supervisory jurisdiction under which it exercises the power of the High Court to discipline inferior courts and to put right their mistakes by means of judicial review through the orders of *mandamus*, *certiorari*, and *prohibition*. It can also deal with the writ of *habeas corpus* and *election petitions*.

(*b*) *Divisional Court of the Chancery Division*. This court hears appeals in bankruptcy cases from county courts outside London, the Bankruptcy Court of the Chancery Division hearing bankruptcy appeals from London.

(*c*) *The Divisional Court of the Family Division*. This court hears appeals from magistrates' courts in family proceedings.

The Commercial Court

Since 1964 the High Court has operated a Commercial Court. Section 6 of the Supreme Court Act, 1981 now constitutes, as part of the Queen's Bench Division, a Commercial Court for the trial of causes of a commercial nature, e.g. insurance matters. The judges of the Commercial Court are such High Court Judges as the Lord Chancellor may from time to time nominate to be Commercial Judges. They are, in practice, drawn from those who have spent their working lives in the commercial field.

They combine the general work of a Queen's Bench Judge with priority for commercial cases. The Act merely continues formal independence to the Commercial Court. Commercial litigation has since 1895 been dealt with in the Queen's Bench Division on a simplified procedure and before a specialist judge, the intention being to overcome the reluctance of commercial men, who prefer the privacy of arbitration, to resort to the machinery of the courts.

Two specific steps were proposed in the Administration of Justice Bill, 1970 to attract such customers: first a power was to be taken to allow the court to sit in private and to receive evidence which would not normally be admissible in an ordinary court, and secondly High Court judges were to be allowed to sit as arbitrators. The first of these proposals was rejected by the House of Commons at the Report Stage but the second was passed into law and s. 4 of the Administration of Justice Act, 1970 enables a judge of the Commercial Court to take arbitrations. Before doing so he must obtain clearance from the Lord Chief Justice that the pressure of work in the High Court and Crown Court will enable him to be made available for this purpose, but in practice this is unlikely to cause difficulty.

Thus, although in theory the Court has no wider power than other courts of the Queen's Bench Division, there is, in practice, a general discretion for departures in procedure and admission of evidence where the parties consent or where the interests of justice demand it or where it is necessary to expedite business. The power to hold hearings in private is restricted but s. 12 of the Administration of Justice Act, 1960 gives a power which could be used if, for example, trade secrets were involved. Commercial cases may be tried by a judge alone, or by a judge and a jury. It was once a special jury in that it consisted of persons who had knowledge of commercial matters. An ordinary jury is now used since s. 40 of the Courts Act, 1971 abolished special juries. All actions in the Commercial Court are tried in the City of London.

Where a judge of the Commercial Court is acting as an arbitrator he sits in private and in any place convenient to the parties. There is no requirement for such arbitrations to take place in the Law Courts. The conduct of the hearing should be as informal as any other arbitration. In addition, the award is made privately to the parties and not published like a judgment.

There is also the Commercial Court of the Northern Circuit based on courts sitting in Liverpool and Manchester. This court is modelled on and in general follows the procedures of the Commercial Court in London. Its range of work is, however, wider and includes sale of goods, hire purchase, agency, banking, guarantees, carriage of goods and insurance. Designated circuit judges conduct the hearings.

The Companies' Court

This is really a court of the Chancery Division where company matters are tried before a single judge whose special concern is with company work. The work of the court is divided into company liquidation proceedings, and other company matters.

The Bankruptcy Court

The bulk of the bankruptcy work of the Chancery Division is performed by Registrars in Bankruptcy who deal with cases arising in the London insolvency district, provincial bankruptcies being dealt with by those county courts with bankruptcy jurisdiction.

The Court of Protection

This court is concerned to protect and administer the property and effects of those who are by reason of mental disorder not able to manage these matters for themselves.

Part VII of the Mental Health Act, 1983 deals with Court of Protection matters. The judges of the Chancery Division are nominated under s. 93(1) to act. There is also a Master and Assistant Master nominated under s. 93(4). Very little work is in practice referred to a nominated judge.

The usual remedy is to appoint a receiver to look after the patient's property and affairs. It is usual for a near relative, e.g. a spouse, to apply and be appointed.

The Restrictive Practices Court

This superior court of record was set up by the Restrictive Trade Practices Act, 1956. Following a consolidation of restrictive trade practices legislation the registration and judicial investigation of restrictive trading agreements is now covered by the Restrictive Practices Court Act, 1976, the Restrictive Trade Practices Act, 1976 and the Resale Prices Act, 1976. These Acts, which are further discussed in the chapters on the law of contract (see p. 316), are designed to prevent manufacturers entering into agreements which restrict free competition and tend to fix prices in regard to *goods*. The court investigates agreements which may be of this nature to see whether they are contrary to the public interest.

The court has power to enforce its rulings by injunction, but in practice business men do not try to implement an agreement which the court has not sanctioned. The court also deals with the question of resale price maintenance agreements under the Resale Prices Act, 1976 (see p. 317) and acquired an additional jurisdiction under the Fair Trading Act, 1973 (see now Restrictive Trade Practices Act, 1976) to consider restrictive agreements in regard to *services* (see p. 316). In addition, as we are a member of the EC, the competition rules laid down in the Treaty of Rome have been since 1 January 1973 part of our own law. Two Articles of the Treaty of Rome provide for common rules of competition (Articles 85 and 86) and the court may be rquired to consider these from time to time. Under s. 5 of the Restrictive Trade Practices Act, 1976 the Restrictive Practices Court may postpone or defer taking decisions under the provisions of the Restrictive Trade Practices Act, 1976, where this would conflict with Community law.

The court consists of the following judges, one of whom is appointed by the Lord Chancellor to be President of the Court: three *puisne* judges of the High Court nominated by the Lord Chancellor; one judge of the Court of Session of Scotland nominated by the President of that Court; one judge of the Supreme Court of Northern Ireland nominated by the Lord Chief Justice of Northern Ireland. The judges are assisted by up to ten laymen appointed by the Queen on the recommendation of the Lord Chancellor, as being persons with knowledge of, or experience in, industry, commerce or public affairs. The court may sit in divisions, each division being constituted by one judge and two laymen. The judges decide matters of law but matters of fact are decided by a majority of the members of the court. Where the proceedings involve only issues of law the court may consist of a single member, that member being a judge.

The Court of Appeal – generally

The Court of Appeal consists of two divisions –

(*a*) *the Civil Division* which exercises the jurisdiction formerly exercised by the former Court of Appeal, and
(*b*) *the Criminal Division* which exercises the jurisdiction formerly exercised by the Court of Criminal Appeal.

The Civil Division

The work of the Civil Division is carried out by a maximum of 28 Lords Justices of Appeal. This number can be increased by Statutory Instrument. The Court is presided over by the Master of the Rolls, who is appointed by the Prime Minister who is in turn advised by the Lord Chancellor. A normal court consists of three judges but there may on occasion be a full court of five or seven. The qualification for a Lord Justice of Appeal is a ten-year High Court qualification, i.e. having had a right of audience in relation to all proceedings in the High Court for at least ten years or having been a *puisne* judge. (S. 10(3)(b), Supreme Court Act, 1981 as amended.) They are appointed by the Queen on the advice of the Prime Minister and the Master of the Rolls. It should be noted that also included in the judiciary in the Civil Division are the Lord Chancellor, ex-Lord Chancellors, Law Lords, the Lord Chief Justice, and the President of the Family Division. The Lord Chancellor may also request judges of the High Court to sit. However, under s. 56 of the Supreme Court Act, 1981 a judge may not sit on an appeal to the Court of Appeal if he sat at the hearing of the case in the lower court. This applies to both civil and criminal cases.

As regards jurisdiction, the Civil Division hears appeals from any division of the High Court and from the County Court (but not in bankruptcy cases) and from orders of Judges in Chambers or Masters in Chambers regarding pre-trial matters and from a number of tribunals, e.g. the Employment Appeal Tribunal and the Lands Tribunal (see further p. 53). The court may on appeal uphold or reverse the lower court or substitute a new judgment. Exceptionally, it may order a new trial as it did e.g. in *Gilberthorpe* v *News Group Newspapers*, *The Independent*, 15 June 1989 where fresh evidence had become available.

The Supreme Court Act, 1981 made changes in the organisation of the business of the Court of Appeal, Civil Division. The object was to speed up the rate at which appeals are heard and prevent a long backlog.

First, it created the office of Registrar of Civil Appeals. (S. 88 and Sch. 2.) The Registrar relieves the judges of the need to deal with some judicial matters, e.g. applications for leave to serve notice of appeal out of time. He also deals with administrative matters, e.g. he ensures that the parties to an appeal and their advisers have given the court all the necessary documents so that there will be no confusion or delay when the appeal comes on for hearing. (See s. 58.)

Secondly, it allows appeals in cases prescribed by the Lord Chancellor with the agreement of the Master of the Rolls to be heard by a two-judge court. If they do not agree the case must be re-argued before a court of at least three judges. (S. 54.) While fullest use of the two-judge court will be made, it will sometimes be in the public interest that three judges should sit, as where the issues are complex. In such cases counsel should apply to the registrar for the hearing to take place before a court of three (*Coldunell Ltd.* v *Gallon* [1986] 1 All E.R. 429.

Finally, county court legislation has been amended and under s. 77(2) of the County Courts Act, 1984 the Lord Chancellor may, by order, prescribe classes of proceedings in the county court, e.g. according to the amount of the claim, in which there is no right of appeal without leave of the judge of the county court or of the Court of Appeal or where there is no appeal from a district judge (or a deputy or assistant) beyond the county court (circuit) judge.

The Criminal Division

The work of the Criminal Division is carried out by the Lord Chief Justice and the same 28 Lords Justices of Appeal, as a maximum, who also sit in the Civil Division. It should also be noted that the Lord Chief Justice may ask any judge of the High Court to sit in the Criminal Division. The normal court consists of three judges but sometimes a full court of five or seven will sit if the case is a difficult one. Under s. 55 of the Supreme Court Act, 1981 a court of two may sit to deal with appeals against sentence. A single judge may carry out some functions, e.g. grant leave to appeal against conviction or sentence. (S. 31, Criminal Appeal Act, 1968). The success rate in terms of the ordinary prisoner seeking leave to appeal against *conviction* is negligible, though thousands of appeals against *sentence* are heard annually.

JURISDICTION

The Criminal Division hears appeals from the Crown Court against conviction and sentence and may dismiss or allow the appeal or order a new trial. In addition the Home Secretary may refer a case to the Criminal Division under s. 17(1)(a) of the Criminal Appeal Act, 1968. A recent example is to be found in *R v Maguire, The Times*, 28 June 1991. All the appellants had, following an IRA bomb attack on a Birmingham pub, been convicted of knowingly having in their possession or under their control an explosive substance namely nitro-glycerine, under such circumstances as to give rise to a reasonable suspicion that it was in their possession or control for an unlawful object. Following a reference to the Court of Appeal by the Home Secretary the convictions were quashed, on the grounds that they were unsafe and unsatisfactory because the possibility of innocent contamination of the appellants' hands could not be excluded. An expert prosecution witness had failed to disclose this at the trial.

Furthermore, the Attorney-General may refer for an opinion on a point of law arising from a charge which resulted in an acquittal (s. 36(1), Criminal Justice Act, 1972). An example is to be found in *Attorney-General's Reference (No. 2 of 1982)* [1984] 2 W.L.R. 447, where two directors, A and B were alleged to have committed theft of the company's property leaving it without funds to pay its creditors. They were also the only shareholders. Since theft requires a taking from some other person without that person's consent, the trial judge held that the offence of theft had not been committed and A and B were acquitted. On the reference of the Attorney-General the Court of Appeal held that since a company was a separate person at law (see further p. 187), A and B could steal from it. Furthermore, although the consent of the directors would often be imputed to the company, it was irrational to do so here when A and B were alleged to be acting dishonestly in relation to the company. The Court of Appeal was of the opinion that A and B could be legally charged with theft. It should be noted that the Court of Appeal's opinion has no effect upon the outcome of the original trial. The acquittal stands.

POWER TO INCREASE SENTENCE

Section 36 of the Criminal Justice Act, 1988 allows the Attorney-General to refer a case for increased sentence if it appears that the judge in the Crown Court has been too lenient. The Court of Appeal must give leave before the reference can be heard and has power on hearing the reference to give any sentence which the original court could have given. Thus the sentence may be increased or reduced. The section is an attempt to deal with public disquiet over lenient sentences.

NEW TRIALS

The court may order a new trial under s. 7 of the Criminal Appeal Act, 1968 as amended by s. 54 of the Criminal Justice Act, 1988. The power is quite extensive and a retrial can be ordered if the Court of Appeal is satisfied that it is in the interests of justice to do so. It is intended in the main to prevent unmeritorious defendants from escaping justice because of some technical mistake at the original trial.

There is also a power to order a new trial at common law where there has been a fundamental defect in the trial so that it was a nullity. Thus, in *R v Ishmael* [1970] Crim. L.R. 399, the accused had been sentenced to life imprisonment having pleaded guilty at his trial to an offence under s. 3 of the Malicious Damage Act, 1861 (arson of buildings, punishable by life imprisonment) thinking he was charged with an offence under s. 7 of the 1861 Act (arson of goods, punishable by 14 years' imprisonment). The Court of Appeal held that he must be tried again.

Vice-presidents

Under s. 3(3) of the Supreme Court Act, 1981, the Lord Chancellor may appoint one of the ordinary judges of the Court of Appeal as Vice-President of both Divisions of that court, or one of those judges as Vice-President of the Criminal Division and another of them as Vice-President of the Civil Division. The Vice-President will preside in the absence, for example, of the Lord Chief Justice or the Master of the Rolls.

Assistance for transaction of judicial business in the Supreme Court

Section 9 of the Supreme Court Act, 1981 brings together a number of provisions enabling assistance to be given by judges, former judges and deputy judges in terms of the business of the Supreme Court.

A judge of the Court of Appeal is competent to act on request in the High Court and the Crown Court. A person who has been a judge of the Court of Appeal is competent to act in the Court of Appeal, the High Court and the Crown Court. A *puisne* judge of the High Court is competent to act in the Court of Appeal. A person who has been a *puisne* judge of the High Court is competent to act in the Court of Appeal, the High Court and the Crown Court. A circuit judge is competent to act in the High Court.

By reason of s. 58 of the Administration of Justice Act, 1982 a Recorder is competent to act in the High Court.

Under s. 9(4) of the Supreme Court Act, 1981, if it appears to the Lord

Chancellor that it is expedient as a temporary measure to make an appointment in order to facilitate the disposal of business in the High Court or the Crown Court, he may appoint a person qualified for appointment as a *puisne* judge of the High Court to be a deputy judge of the High Court during such period or on such occasions as the Lord Chancellor thinks fit.

The House of Lords

CONSTITUTION

The court is constituted by the Lord Chancellor and Lords of Appeal in Ordinary (or Law Lords). There are at any one time between nine and eleven Law Lords, two of whom normally come from the Scottish judiciary. The Law Lords are life peers and each of them is appointed by the Queen on the Prime Minister's advice, who is in turn advised by the Lord Chancellor, from among persons who have a Supreme Court qualification, i.e. a right of audience in relation to all proceedings in the Supreme Court. No number of years is stated. (See s. 6, Appellate Jurisdiction Act, 1876 as amended by the Courts and Legal Services Act, 1990, Sch. 10.) Normally the appointments are made from the Lords Justices of Appeal. A minimum of three law lords is required to constitute a court but in practice five normally sit to hear an appeal. The decision is by majority judgment.

JURISDICTION

(a) *Civil.* On the civil side the House of Lords hears appeals from the Court of Appeal (Civil Division), the Court of Session in Scotland, when one or two Scottish Law Lords sit, and the Supreme Court of Northern Ireland when a Law Lord from Northern Ireland sits. In all cases the lower court must certify that a point of law of general public importance is involved and either the lower court or the Appeal Committee of the House of Lords consisting of three Law Lords must give leave. In addition, there is a direct appeal from the High Court or Divisional Court to the House of Lords by what is referred to as the 'leapfrogging method'. This phrase is used because the appeal goes straight to the House of Lords and not through the Court of Appeal. All parties must consent and the appeal must raise a point of law of public importance relating wholly or mainly to a statute or statutory instrument. The trial judge must certify the importance of the case and the House of Lords must give leave. This 'leapfrogging' procedure is most likely to be used in revenue appeals and patent matters where construction of statutes is often very involved.

(b) *Criminal.* On the criminal side the Court hears appeals from the Court of Appeal (Criminal Division) and the Divisional Court of Queen's Bench. In both cases the lower court must certify that a point of law of general public importance is involved and either the lower court or the Appeal Committee of the House of Lords must give leave. The House of Lords is not a final appellate tribunal for Scotland in criminal matters, but the Scottish Court of Criminal Appeal is.

The proceedings in the House of Lords are surprisingly informal. The Law Lords are not robed but sit in dark suits generally in panels of five at a table in one of the committee rooms in the Houses of Parliament at Westminster.

The Judicial Committee of the Privy Council

The Privy Council is a lineal descendant of the ancient King's Council, and was originally a sort of cabinet advising the Crown. The Judicial Committee, which is not part of the Supreme Court, is a final court of appeal in civil and criminal matters from the courts of some Commonwealth and Colonial territories, but the changes which have taken place in the Commonwealth have restricted the number of cases coming before it, many Commonwealth countries preferring to hear appeals within their own judicial systems. However, some aspects of this jurisdiction survive. For example, Malaysia and New Zealand have retained the Privy Council as a final appeal court in spite of their constitutional independence. The Australia Act Commencement Order of 1986 abolished appeals to the Privy Council from Australia.

The court is still the final court of appeal on criminal and civil matters from the Channel Islands and the Isle of Man, and also from those islands and colonies, such a Gibraltar, Hong Kong and Belize, whose independence is not a viable proposition. There is strictly speaking no right of appeal, but it is customary to petition the Crown for leave to appeal. It is also the final court of appeal from English ecclesiastical courts, and here it is assisted by the Archbishops of Canterbury and York who, as assessors, advise on ecclesiastical matters. In wartime it hears appeals from the Admiralty Court on matters concerning prize. It also hears appeals from disciplinary bodies for dentists, opticians, and professions relating to medicine.

The Judicial Committee (or the Board as it is called) is comprised of the Lord Chancellor, the Lords of Appeal in Ordinary, and all Privy Councillors who have held high judicial office in the United Kingdom, together with Commonwealth judges who have been appointed members of the Privy Council. It does not actually decide cases, but advises the Crown which implements the advice by an Order in Council. This advice used to be unanimous, but since March, 1966, dissenting members of the Privy Council who were present at the hearing of the appeal may express their dissent, giving reasons therefor. The Court is not bound by its own previous decisions.

Removal and retirement of judges

Section 17(4) of the Courts Act, 1971 contains the only formal power to remove a judge. The power relates to circuit judges and states that the Lord Chancellor may, if he thinks fit, remove a circuit judge from office on the ground of incapacity or misbehaviour. Recorders, Assistant Recorders, and Magistrates are governed by similar provisions. Other judges can only be removed by a motion approved by both Houses of Parliament.

As regards retirement, the Judicial Pensions Act, 1959 provides for retirement at 75 years of age except in the case of circuit judges and recorders where the age is 72, but the Lord Chancellor may extend this to 75.

Arbitration

ARISING FROM CONTRACT

Not uncommonly commercial contracts, for example contracts of insurance, contain a provision under which the parties agree to submit disputes arising under the contract to an arbitrator who need not be a lawyer but might in, say, a building dispute, be a surveyor who has knowledge and experience of the subject matter of the dispute.

Arbitration proceedings are better than court proceedings in only two main ways: first, they are private in that there need be no publicity (e.g. a public hearing followed by a law report), and second, the arbitrator will have special experience of the particular trade or business which a judge would not have. Privacy is usually the determining factor in the choice by the parties of commercial arbitration rather than litigation.

Arbitration is no longer cheap since experienced arbitrators can command daily fees of several hundred pounds, and the lawyers who appear before the arbitrators charge the same fees as for litigation in the courts. There is no guarantee of a quick resolution because it may be several months before the parties can agree upon the identity of the arbitrator(s) and also the parties are dependent in arranging the arbitration on the availability of the arbitrator, whose diary may be as full as the waiting lists in the ordinary courts.

The Consumer Arbitration Agreements Act, 1988, ss. 1 and 4 prevent the abuse of arbitration clauses which businesses may put into their contracts with consumers. The Act provides that such clauses cannot be enforced against a non-consenting consumer, who may therefore use the civil court system, where the amount involved is within the jurisdiction of the small claims court, i.e. £1000. Where the claim does not fall within the small claims limit the court may allow the arbitration clause to operate if, in the circumstances, this would not be detrimental to the consumer's interests.

OTHER ARBITRATIONS

Arbitration also occurs under Codes of Practice prepared by various Trade Associations with the assistance of the Office of Fair Trading. The arbitration service for a particular code of practice is usually provided by the Chartered Institute of Arbitrators. The Trade Associations concerned, e.g. the Association of British Travel Agents and the Motor Agents Association, make a substantial contribution to the cost of administration but the consumer has to pay a fee. This is normally refunded if the consumer is successful.

ARBITRATION IN THE HIGH COURT AND COUNTY COURT

These arbitrations have already been considered at p. 31.

Conciliation

Sometimes a dispute is settled following an initiative by an outside agency. For example the Advisory, Conciliation and Arbitration Service (ACAS) is, under the Employment Protection (Consolidation) Act, 1978, given a role in settling matters which are, or could be, the subject of proceedings before an industrial tribunal.

When a complaint or claim is presented to an industrial tribunal, say for equal pay or sex discrimination, a copy is sent to the conciliation officer. It is his duty to try to settle the dispute so that it need not go to an industrial tribunal. He can do this if asked to by the person making the complaint or the person against whom it is made, or even on his own initiative where he thinks there is a good chance of a settlement.

During the course of conciliation the parties can speak freely with the conciliation officer because anything which is said to the conciliation officer during the course of an attempted settlement is not admissible in evidence if the matter goes to an industrial tribunal unless the person who made the statement agrees.

Tribunals

These are considered in detail in Chapter 3 which is concerned with tribunals and legal services.

The Court of Justice of the European Communities

This court, which is often referred to as the European Court, sits in Luxembourg, and is charged with ensuring that Community law is observed in regard to the interpretation and implementation of the Treaties. Its decisions must be accepted by the courts of member states and there is no right of appeal. Matters before the court are disposed of in front of all the judges, though some preliminary (or interlocutory) matters can be dealt with by a division of three judges.

The court consists of a President of the whole court, a First Advocate-General, the Presidents of the First, Second, Third, Fourth and Fifth Chambers (three persons in all) together with nine judges, five Advocates-General, and a Registrar; 20 persons in all. There is no requirement of professional law practice and the court consists of professional judges, academic lawyers and public servants. A judge may be removed only by unanimous decision of the other judges.

PROCEDURE

There is more emphasis upon submissions in writing (pleadings) rather than oral argument. The proceedings are more inquisitorial and the judges play a more active role in terms of asking questions during hearings.

As we have seen, there is a First Advocate-General and five Advocates-General. They assist the court and they give an independent view of the proceedings *at the end of the case.*

The court gives a single judgment and no dissenting views are given. Enforcement of judgments is through the national courts of member states. The language in which the case is heard is a matter for the plaintiff, except where the defendant is a member state when it will be in the language of that state.

An important function of the court is under Art. 177 of the Treaty of Rome to hear references from national courts for a ruling on the interpretation of provisions of Community law. The court is mainly concerned with actions alleging failure to fulfil the obligations of the Treaty by member states in terms of the free movement of goods, equal pay and sex discrimination, and free movement of persons, which includes recognition of professional qualifications and diplomas obtained in one state of the EC as entitling the holder to practise a profession in another.

Under various other Articles of the Treaty of Rome the court may deal with the following types of actions –

(*a*) actions by the Commission against member states for failure to fulfil Treaty obligations (Art. 189);

(*b*) actions by one member state against another for failure to fulfil Treaty obligations (Art. 170);

(*c*) actions by a member state or an individual or company against the Council or Commission for acting in breach of the Treaty (Art. 173);

(*d*) actions by a member state against the Council or Commission for failure to act (Art. 176).

COURT OF FIRST INSTANCE

The European Communities (Amendment) Act, 1986 was the UK Parliament's ratification of the Single European Act under which a new court of first instance was set up by a decision of the Council of Ministers of the EC in 1988. It consists of a president and eleven judges and deals with certain categories of case to relieve pressure on the Court of Justice, in particular appeals against Commission Decisions in competition cases (see further, p. 319) and disputes between the Community and its employees. Appeal is to the European Court on a point of law only.

The role of the European Court at Luxembourg

It was decided by the Court of Appeal in *Bulmer* v *Bollinger* [1974] 2 All E.R. 1226 that the High Court and the Court of Appeal have a jurisdiction to interpret Community law and that they are not obliged to grant a right of appeal to the European Court of Justice. However, if the case goes to the House of Lords on appeal, the House of Lords is bound to refer the matter to the European Court of Justice if either or both of the parties wishes this. The decision in *Bulmer* was based upon an interpretation of Article 177 of the Treaty, which provides, in effect, that although any court or tribunal of a member state *may* ask the European Court to give a ruling, only the final court of appeal, in our case the House of Lords, is *bound* to ask for a ruling if a party requests it.

In the case Bulmers had marketed products for many years under the name of 'Champagne Cider' and 'Champagne Perry'. Bollingers claimed that this was contrary to an EC regulation which restricted the use of the word 'champagne' to wine produced from grapes grown in the Champagne district of France. The Court of Appeal decided that since cider was made from apples and perry was made from pears, there was no infringement of the regulation. The court also refused to refer the matter to the European Court.

In the course of his judgment Lord Denning, M.R., laid down certain guidelines to assist judges in deciding whether to refer a case to the European Court or not. The main guidelines are as follows –

(*a*) *The time to get a ruling.* The length of time which may elapse before a ruling can be obtained from the European Court should always be borne in mind. It is important to prevent undue protraction of proceedings. The English judge should always consider this delay and the expense to the parties. However, in *Customs & Excise Commissioners* v *A.P.S. Samex* [1983] 1 All E.R. 1042, Bingham, J., while accepting that a reference should not be made in, say, the High Court, simply because if it was not made one of the parties would go on making appeals, it might be that if the High Court did make the reference, thus preventing further appeals to English courts, it would be cheaper for the parties in the long run.

(*b*) *The European Court must not be overloaded.* In this connection it should be borne in mind that all the judges must sit on a reference from a national court and they cannot split up into divisions of, say, three or five judges. Thus, if there are too many references, the court would not be able to get through its work.

(c) *The reference must be on a question of interpretation only of the Treaty.* It is a matter for the national courts to find the facts and apply the Treaty, though the way in which the national court has interpreted the Treaty can then be a matter for reference.

(d) *The difficulty of the question of Community law raised.* Lord Denning was of opinion that unless the point raised was 'really difficult and important' it would be better for the English judge to decide it himself. However, in *A.P.S.Samex* (above) Bingham, J. took the view that in some cases, even though the point raised might not be of great difficulty, the European Court should receive a reference because it was in a better position, among other things, to make the sort of decision which would further the orderly development of the Community. These statements by Bingham, J. in this case are to be welcomed because they show a greater willingness in the judiciary to take matters to Luxembourg and not to make too many decisions themselves thus to some extent shutting out the European Court.

In regard to criminal matters, a circuit judge presiding over a criminal trial on indictment has a discretion conferred on him by Article 177 of the Treaty of Rome to refer any question of interpretation of the Treaty to the European Court. It was held by the House of Lords in *R v Henn* [1980] 2 All E.R. 166 that it can seldom be a proper exercise of the presiding judge's discretion to seek a preliminary ruling before the facts of the alleged offence have been ascertained, since this could result in proceedings being held up for several months. It is generally better, said the House of Lords, that the judge should interpret the Treaty himself in the first instance and his interpretation can be reviewed thereafter if necessary through the hierarchy of the national courts, any of which may refer to the European Court.

In general terms, therefore, the House of Lords has an obligation to make a reference under Art. 117. Lower courts *may* do so but if they think that the relevant community law is sufficiently clear to be applied to the case straightaway they will not refer. This is known as the doctrine of *acte clair*.

The European Court of Human Rights

This Court, which sits in Strasbourg, was set up by the Convention for the Protection of Human Rights and Fundamental Freedoms to ensure the observance of the engagements undertaken by contracting states under the Convention. The United Kingdom is one of the states which have accepted the Court's jurisdiction. The jurisdiction of the Court in contentious matters extends to all cases concerning the interpretation and application of the Convention. It cannot be approached directly. All alleged breaches of the

Convention must go first to the European Commission of Human Rights. Since its creation in 1959 it has dealt with a wide variety of problems, including compulsory sex education in state primary schools in Denmark, where it was found that there was no violation of the Convention, and punishment by birching in the Isle of Man, where one or more breaches of the Convention were found to exist. More recently, the Court decided against Britain by regarding the caning of schoolchildren against the wishes of their parents as a breach of the Convention. The Court has power to grant 'just satisfaction' of a pecuniary nature to the injured party.

3
Other courts and tribunals and legal services

All of the famous writers on constitutional theory have drawn attention to the dangers of any system which takes away from the citizen, in his dealings with government and other officials, the protection of the law functioning in its traditional setting, i.e. the courts of law, which were considered in a previous chapter.

However, one of the most significant developments of this century is the considerable increase in what might be called broadly administrative justice dispensed in special courts outside of the ordinary system.

This has arisen from the great extension in the functions of government which has taken place, particularly in the last forty years. For example, the government pays pensions to various classes of persons, and a wide variety of social security benefits and in order to further schemes of social welfare, it is often necessary for a public body to acquire land by compulsory purchase.

Obviously disputes arise between individuals and the State. A person may claim a benefit to which the State suggests he is not entitled, and landowners are often aggrieved by the compulsory purchase of their land and the compensation offered for it. The settlement of such disputes might have been given over to the ordinary courts of law, but instead increasing use has been made of an administrative court of one kind or another.

Lord Denning, in *Freedom under the Law*, has said of these tribunals –

> They are a separate set of courts dealing with a separate set of rights and duties. Just as in the old days there were ecclesiastical courts dealing with matrimonial cases and the administration of estates and just as there was the Chancellor dealing with the enforcement and administration of trusts so in our day there are the new tribunals dealing with the rights and duties between man and the State.

It should not be assumed, however, that all administrative tribunals are concerned with disputes between man and the State. Some deal with disputes between individuals. The Rent Assessment Committees which when acting to resolve disputes are known as Rent Tribunals (see s. 72, Housing Act, 1980) set up to deal with rent and other questions arising under statutory provisions relating to the letting of houses, are an example of a situation in which the government has provided a specialised court to deal with certain disputes between landlord and tenant rather than give the particular jurisdiction to the ordinary courts of law.

Furthermore, administrative justice is not always meted out in a permanent independent tribunal. For example, the local planning authority may grant planning permission with or without conditions or may refuse permission or fail to notify their decision within the period laid down. In the case of a grant with conditions, or a refusal to grant, or delay in notification, the applicant may appeal to the Secretary of State through the Department of the Environment. The decision of the Secretary of State is final, though there may be an appeal by the authority or the applicant to the High Court on the grounds set out in s. 288(1) of the Town and Country Planning Act, 1990, e.g. that the order is not within the provisions of that Act.

We shall now consider in more detail the way in which certain of these tribunals work.

Administrative tribunals

It is not appropriate in a book of this nature to deal with all the tribunals in this field but consideration will be given to some important ones as examples.

SOCIAL SECURITY TRIBUNALS

The procedure is governed by Sch. 8 of the Health and Social Services and Social Security Adjudications Act, 1983 and the Social Security Act, 1975 (as amended by the 1983 Act). Where a person wishes to make a claim for benefit under social security legislation, including unemployment benefit, the claim must in the first instance be made to a local officer attached to the local Social Security office who may authorise payment, or refuse payment, or refer the claim to a local tribunal.

If payment is refused, application can be made to the local adjudication officer to review his decision. If payment is still not made the person claiming can appeal to a local Social Security Appeal Tribunal which has three members, two non-lawyers, one drawn from a panel of persons representing employers and the self-employed, and one drawn from a panel of persons representing employees. The third member is usually a lawyer, for example a local solicitor appointed by the Secretary of State to be chairman.

If the tribunal allows the appeal the adjudication officer may appeal against that decision to a Social Security Commissioner. The same route of appeal is given to the person making the claim where the tribunal does not decide in his favour. Leave to appeal is required in all cases.

Social Security Commissioners are appointed by the Crown from amongst persons having a ten-year general qualification within s. 71 of the Courts and Legal Services Act, 1990. There is an appeal from a Commissioner to the Court of Appeal with leave of the Commissioner or the Court of Appeal and ultimately to the House of Lords. This procedure effectively supersedes the former one whereby an application could be made by the DSS or the claimant to the High Court for judicial review.

VALUATION AND USE OF LAND TRIBUNALS

Another important tribunal is the *Lands Tribunal* which deals with disputes arising over the valuation and compensation payable on compulsory acquisition of land by public authorities under a variety of statutes, together with appeals from local valuation courts on the value of property for various purposes. The tribunal has a President, who is either a person who has held high judicial office or a person who holds a seven-year general qualification within s. 71 of the Courts and Legal Services Act, 1990, and other members, of the same standing, or persons experienced in the valuation of land. The jurisdiction of the tribunal may be exercised by any one or more of its members. Procedure is governed by rules made by the Lord Chancellor, and these are published by Statutory Instrument. The tribunal ordinarily sits in public and travels round the country, and there is a right of audience and legal representation. The decisions of the tribunal are written and reasoned, and appeal lies to the Court of Appeal on points of law. Either party can require the tribunal to state a case for consideration by the Court of Appeal. Legal aid, and by implication legal representation, is available in respect of proceedings in the Lands Tribunal.

Employment tribunals

These consist of industrial tribunals from which there is an appeal to the Employment Appeal Tribunal.

INDUSTRIAL TRIBUNALS

The jurisdiction of these tribunals includes, for example, disputes arising out of the contract of employment or unfair dismissal, redundancy, equal pay and sex discrimination. (See further p. 342.)

The chairman of each tribunal is a person with a seven-year general qualification within s. 71 of the Courts and Legal Services Act, 1990, appointed by the Lord Chancellor and he sits with two other members selected by the President of Industrial Tribunals who is himself appointed by the Lord Chancellor. The selection is made from a panel of persons compiled by the Secretary of State for Employment on the basis of knowledge or experience of employment problems in industry or commerce. The tribunals sit at suitable centres throughout the United Kingdom.

If a sum of money awarded by a tribunal is not paid over to the claimant he can apply to the county court for a warrant of execution (see p. 133).

Legal aid is not available for a lawyer to represent a claimant before a tribunal but legal advice may be given in respect of employment matters. This can include the drafting of documents in relation to the proceedings and assistance with the way in which the case is to be presented to the tribunal. A legal aid lawyer can attend the tribunal hearing with his client but cannot speak or argue on his behalf. If legal representation is required at the hearing, the party concerned must take responsibility for payment subject to recovery of costs, which are only exceptionally awarded. (See below.)

Written applications for the case to be heard by an industrial tribunal are made on an originating notice of application form available from local Job Centres. The person against whom the claim is made will receive a copy of the application from the tribunal secretariat and if he wishes to defend the claim he should enter an appearance through the secretariat within 14 days of receiving the originating application.

Industrial tribunals have power to request the parties to give each other further particulars of the grounds which are relied upon and to grant discovery of documents.

Hearings before industrial tribunals normally take place in public though there may be a private hearing where, in the opinion of the tribunal, this would be appropriate, as where evidence is to be presented which relates to national security.

As regards costs, an industrial tribunal does not make an award but may do so where in its opinion a party to any proceedings has acted frivolously or vexatiously, as where, for example, an employer refuses to take any part in the proceedings.

The decision is made by a majority and is given orally at the meeting or, if necessary, reserved and given at a later date. In any case it is recorded in a document which is signed by the chairman and contains reasons for the decision. The parties each receive a copy. It should also be noted that where an employee has died tribunal proceedings may be started or continued by his personal representatives.

An industrial tribunal can review and change its decision afterwards where, for example, new evidence has become available which could not have been known of or foreseen at the original hearing.

THE EMPLOYMENT APPEAL TRIBUNAL

Appeal from an industrial tribunal lies only on questions of law. The determination of the facts by an industrial tribunal cannot be challenged on appeal and it is therefore most important that the facts are properly presented to the tribunal at the hearing. Under s. 136(3) of the Employment Protection (Consolidation) Act, 1978 it will also hear an appeal from the ACAS Certification Officer by a trade union aggrieved by his refusal to issue it with a certificate that it is independent. The major legislative privileges are given to those trade unions which are independent of the employer and not, for example, to employer-dominated staff associations. The Certification Officer adjudicates upon the matter of independence under s. 8 of the Employment Protection Act, 1975.

The Employment Appeal Tribunal is a superior court of record with an official seal. Although the central office of the tribunal is in London, it may sit at any time and in any place in Great Britain. It may also sit in one or more divisions.

Appeals are usually heard by a judge of the High Court or a judge of the Court of Appeal and either two or four appointed members who do not belong to the judiciary but have special knowledge or experience of industrial relations, either as representatives of employers or workers. The reason why the judge will sit with either two or four appointed members is so that in either case there are an equal number of persons whose experience is as representatives of employers and of workers. The decision need not be unanimous but may be by a majority. Each member of the court, including the judge, has a vote so that the judge could be outvoted, but this is extremely rare. Exceptionally, if the parties to the proceedings consent, a case may be heard by a judge and one appointed member.

Appeals to the Employment Appeal Tribunal are commenced by serving on the tribunal within 42 days of the date on which the document recording the decision or order appealed against was sent to the person appealing, a notice of appeal. The appropriate form is set out in the Employment Appeal Tribunal Rules.

The hearing will normally take place in public but the tribunal may sit in private to hear evidence where, for example, it relates to national security or could cause substantial injury to an organisation appearing before it, as where a company's trade secrets might be revealed. Legal aid is available for proceedings in the Employment Appeal Tribunal.

The Employment Appeal Tribunal may review and change any order made by it on a similar basis to the provisions already mentioned in regard to industrial tribunals. Appeal lies on any question of law, decision, or order of the Employment Appeal Tribunal, either with leave of the Tribunal or of the Court of Appeal to the Court of Appeal. Legal aid would be available on such appeal according to the usual rules. There may then be a further appeal to the House of Lords under the usual rules.

Administrative inquiries

As we have seen in some areas of administrative action, e.g. planning, there is in general no right of appeal from the initial decision of the government or a local authority to an independent tribunal. The relevant Acts of Parliament normally provide for an opportunity to put a case against the decision at a public inquiry conducted before an inspector who is normally a Ministry official. The inspector makes a report to the Ministry concerned and the decision is made by the Minister himself or a senior civil servant on his behalf.

Advantages of tribunals

As a method of deciding disputes tribunals and administrative inquiries have advantages. For example, the tribunals and inquiries generally specialise in a particular field, and can thus acquire a detailed knowledge of disputes in that field. The procedure of tribunals is simple and informal, and it is often suggested that this puts those appearing before them at ease so that they are better able to present their case. Certainly such justice is cheaper and there are in general no court fees and costs, though if the assistance of a lawyer is required he will have to be paid and there is as yet no legal aid in this field except in the Lands Tribunal and the Employment Appeal Tribunal.

However, appellants who are not represented by lawyers may take full advantage of the rights of appeal given, though sometimes this results in references to tribunals which are frivolous by nature. Generally speaking, administrative tribunals and inquiries give quick decisions, and appellants are not subjected to the delays which are sometimes met with in ordinary courts of law. Tribunals and inquiries are usually local by nature; they are therefore able to acquaint themselves with local conditions, and can carry out inspections of property and sites where this would assist them in their decision.

The Tribunals and Inquiries Acts

Criticism of administrative tribunals led to the setting up of a Committee on Administrative Tribunals and Inquiries under the chairmanship of Sir Oliver Franks which reported in 1957. The main areas of disquiet were that tribunals did not give reasons for their decisions and furthermore that those decisions were not subject to appeal to the High Court on a point of law.

The majority of the proposals of the Franks Committee were accepted by Parliament and enacted in the Tribunals and Inquiries Act, 1958. This Act, together with certain changes and additions in subsequent legislation has been re-enacted as the Tribunals and Inquiries Act, 1971.

The implementation of Franks led to the following main changes –

(*a*) A Council on Tribunals now gives advice to the Lord Chancellor on the working of tribunals and reports to Parliament from time to time on its work.

(*b*) The chairmen of the various tribunals are selected by the ministers in whose fields they work from a panel of persons appointed by the Lord Chancellor. The chairmen are usually lawyers.

(*c*) A tribunal must normally allow a party who wants it to have a lawyer to represent him.

(*d*) All material facts are disclosed to all parties before a tribunal hearing and the hearing is in public unless e.g. public security is involved.

(*e*) Reasons for decisions are given if requested.

(*f*) Appeals lie from most tribunals to the Divisional Court of Queen's Bench.

Unfortunately, governments have often set up new tribunals without proper consultation with the Council on Tribunals to see whether an existing tribunal might take on the work. This has resulted in a proliferation of tribunals with a bewildering multiplicity of separate jurisdictions. That apart, the implementation of most of the Franks' Committee recommendations means that there are no longer any major reasons for dissatisfaction with the powers and duties of tribunals.

There are those who continue to argue for appeal to a special Administrative Division of the High Court. Such a division has not been set up. However, a special panel of judges of the Queen's Bench Division has been created to sit in the Divisional Court when a case involving administrative law is taken before it. This goes some way to meet the arguments of those who advocate a special Administrative Division.

Legal aid

Legal aid in tribunals has been reviewed from time to time but it has been felt appropriate to recommend that it should be available only for proceedings in the Lands Tribunal and the Employment Appeal Tribunal. Many still regard the present position as unreasonable.

In particular it is felt that legal aid is appropriate in cases heard before e.g. the Social Security Commissioners. In addition there is no reason why legal aid should not be extended to some of the domestic tribunals, e.g. in respect of hearings before the Disciplinary Committee of the Institute of Chartered Accountants in England and Wales (see below).

Domestic tribunals

Another area in which persons or groups of persons or other public agencies exercise judicial or quasi-judicial functions over others is to be found in the system of domestic tribunals. These are, in general, disciplinary committees concerned with the regulation of certain professions and trades, some having been set up by statute and others merely by contract between members and the association concerned. Examples of tribunals regulating professions are what might be referred to broadly as the disciplinary committees of the General Medical Council, Architects' Registration Council, The Law Society, the UK Central Council for Nursing, Midwifery and Health Visiting, and the Inns of Court. As regards the regulation of the investment industry and the City of London, there is the Securities and Investments Board set up by the Financial Services Act, 1986 and the Panel on Take-Overs and Mergers, together with recognised investment exchanges, e.g. The London Stock Exchange.

There are also certain trade organisations which are corporate bodies set up under statute. They represent the producers and distributors of particular commodities, and they control the production and sale of those commodities mainly by fixing prices. They are able to enforce their instructions by levying fines on members or excluding them from the scheme, and are mainly concerned with agriculture. Each Board has a Disciplinary Committee which has a chairman who is generally a lawyer. The parties are normally entitled to an oral hearing in public, and the Committee may subpoena witnesses and take evidence on oath. One of the most important Boards is the Milk Marketing Board.

Because domestic tribunals are not *public* authorities but *private associations based on contract* the courts cannot control the decisions which these tribunals make by the process of judicial review leading to the issue of a prerogative order, e.g. *certiorari* or *mandamus* (*Law* v *National Greyhound Racing Club Ltd* [1983] 3 All E.R. 300) (and see p. 64).

At one time members were bound by the rules of these tribunals no matter how unreasonably or unfairly they might operate. For example, if the rules allowed expulsion there was no remedy against this even though a person so expelled might be unable to work if he was not a member of the association.

The breakthrough came in the decision of the Court of Appeal in *Lee* v *Showmen's Guild of Great Britain* [1952] 1 All E.R. 1175 which brought domestic tribunals under the control of the courts. Mr Lee ran a roundabout. He occupied the same pitch each year at Bradford Summer Fair. Another Guild member, Mr Shaw, claimed the pitch and a committee of the Guild found that Mr Shaw was entitled to have it and that Mr Lee was guilty of unfair competition. They fined Mr Lee £100. He then brought an action claiming a declaration that the committee's decision was invalid. The Court of Appeal upheld Mr Lee's claim in the main because it was at last accepted that the contract associations could not by that contract rule out the jurisdiction of the court because no contract intended to bind the parties to it could oust that jurisdiction (see further p. 307).

Since that time the courts have intervened to see that the rules of these associations are correctly interpreted and that the principles of natural justice (see further p. 61) are observed. They have developed a jurisdiction to redress wrongful expulsion; wrongful refusal to admit to membership; refusal to admit women and restrictive activities in terms of what members can do. Thus in *Pharmaceutical Society of Great Britain* v *Dickson* [1968] 2 All E.R. 686 the House of Lords decided that the Society could not by its rules restrict chemists in terms of what they sold in their shops.

In *R* v *Panel on Take-Overs ex p. Datafin plc* [1987] 1 All E.R. 564, the Court of Appeal decided that having regard to the *public* consequences of non-compliance with the code, e.g. that a bid by one company for another could be declared invalid if the procedures of the code were infringed, application for judicial review of Panel decisions would be available in an appropriate case. This represents a considerable extension of the law to allow judicial review of domestic bodies where their decisions have effect upon the non-member public. However, it is doubtful whether the *Datafin* decision could be extended to purely domestic tribunals, e.g. the UK Central Council for Nursing, Midwifery and Health Visiting whose proceedings affect only their members and not to any significant effect the public who are not members.

A person aggrieved by the decision of a domestic tribunal can, however, ask the court for the remedy of a *declaration* of his rights or an *injunction*. These have proved quite powerful remedies as a means of controlling purely domestic tribunals.

Judicial control over inferior courts and tribunals

We must now consider what *control* the ordinary courts of law have over administrative action as expressed in the decisions of tribunals and inquiries and what *methods* are used to exercise that control.

Control by the judiciary is exercised as follows –

(*a*) by statutory rights of appeal from the tribunal;

(*b*) by application of the doctrine of *ultra vires*;

(*c*) by the use of the principal administrative law remedies, i.e. injunctions, declarations, and the prerogative orders of *certiorari*, prohibition, and *mandamus*, through an application under the Rules of the Supreme Court for judicial review.

These methods of control will now be considered in more detail.

STATUTORY RIGHT OF APPEAL

Where, as in the case of the Lands Tribunal, the Act of Parliament setting up or controlling the tribunal gives a right of appeal to the ordinary courts of law, the courts are entitled to re-hear the whole case and are not limited to a consideration of the reasons given by the tribunal for its decision. The court can consider the whole matter afresh, and can substitute a new decision for that of the tribunal.

ULTRA VIRES

No public authority may lawfully make a decision and take action on it unless it is authorised by law to do so or the act is construed as being reasonably incidental to its authorised activities. An act which does not conform with the above is treated by the courts as void under the doctrine of *ultra vires* (beyond the powers of).

The doctrine applies to bodies and individuals such as ministers exercising judicial, quasi-judicial, legislative or administrative functions, including local authorities, tribunals, government departments and other public authorities, though Parliament's legislative powers are unlimited. (See p. 12.)

Typically, the *ultra vires* method of control is used where the decision taken is unauthorised by the powers given to the authority. However, even when the authority acts within its powers, the court can review the decision if it is unreasonable to a high degree (*Associated Provincial Picture Houses Ltd* v *Wednesbury Corp.* [1947] 2 All E.R. 680).

ESSENTIAL CASE LAW AND COMMENT

Attorney-General v *Fulham Corporation,* 1921 – The *ultra vires* method of control (6)

PREROGATIVE ORDERS AND JUDICIAL REVIEW

Where no right of appeal is given it may be possible to challenge the decision of an inferior court or public tribunal by having recourse to the supervisory jurisdiction of the High Court.

This jurisdiction is exercised by the Queen's Bench Division of the High Court by means of the prerogative orders known as *certiorari*, prohibition, and *mandamus*. These orders, which are not available as of right but at the discretion of the court, were formerly prerogative writs, which a subject might obtain by petitioning the Crown.

The Sovereign has no such power today, the control being exercised by the Queen's Bench Division, the former writs being now called orders. (S. 29, Supreme Court Act, 1981.)

A person cannot normally invoke the supervisory jurisdiction of the High Court if other more appropriate procedures for appeal exist.

Order 53 of the Rules of the Supreme Court introduces a comprehensive system of judicial review. A statutory basis for this procedure also appears in s. 31 of the Supreme Court Act, 1981. It allows an application to cover under one umbrella, as it were, all the remedies of *certiorari*, *mandamus*, and prohibition, and also declaration and injunction. There is no need to apply for one of these remedies individually. Any combination of them is available under the one claim for judicial review. Damages may also be claimed on an application for judicial review. (S. 31(4), 1981 Act.) No application for judicial review may be made without leave. Application is made for this to a single judge.

There have been difficulties in the past as to whether a person had the necessary *locus standi*, i.e. interest, to bring an action for one of the administrative remedies. *Locus standi* is dealt with in Order 53 and s. 31(3), 1981 Act, which lay down a simple test which is that the applicant must have 'a sufficient interest in the matter to which the application relates'. The test is, of course, rather vague, but Lord Denning, in discussing the remedy of judicial review in *The Discipline of Law* states:

> The court will not listen to a busybody who is interfering in things which do not concern him, but it will listen to an ordinary citizen who comes asking that the law should be declared and enforced, even though he is only one of a hundred, or one of a thousand, or one of a million who are affected by it. As a result, therefore, of the new procedure, it can I hope be said that we have in England an *actio popularis* by which an ordinary citizen can enforce the law for the benefit of all – as against public authorities in respect of their statutory duties.

However, it should not be assumed that judicial review is available to redress any decision which might be regarded in a broad sense as 'unfair'. The House of Lords made it clear in *Puhlhofer* v *Hillingdon L.B.C.* [1986] 1 All E.R. 467 – an attempt to challenge a decision not to house the applicant – that persons seeking judicial review must base their case on one of the accepted principles of review, e.g. *ultra vires* or procedural irregularity.

ESSENTIAL CASE LAW AND COMMENT

R v *Brighton Justices, ex parte Robinson*, 1973 – Judicial review not available where appropriate procedures for appeal exist **(7)**

I.R.C. v *National Federation of Self-Employed and Small Businesses Ltd*, 1981 – Judicial review: the need for *locus standi* **(8)**

Grounds on which *certiorari* lies

The only grounds on which *certiorari* lies are as follows –

(*a*) *Want or excess of jurisdiction.* This exists where the inferior court or body has adjudicated on a matter which it had no power to decide, i.e. where it is acting beyond its powers (*ultra vires*).

Certiorari is not the only remedy which may be used to control *ultra vires* acts. Note, for example, the use of an injunction in the *ultra vires* situation seen in *A.-G.* v *Fulham Corporation*, 1921 at p. 563.

(*b*) *Denial of natural justice.* The principle is that, although a tribunal should not be required to conform to judicial standards, but should be free to work out its own procedures, nevertheless it must observe the rules of natural justice, i.e. there must be no bias and both sides should be heard.

(i) *Bias.* This may be pecuniary bias but other forms of bias are relevant as where, for example, the chairman of magistrates states that he always prefers the evidence for the prosecution given by the police.

(ii) *The right to be heard.* There is no inherent right to an oral hearing; written evidence may be acceptable. However, the right to be heard (*audi alteram partem*) implies that notice of the hearing or other method of stating one's case must be given together with notice of the case which is to be met (see *R* v *Wear Valley D.C. ex p. Binks* (1985) and *R* v *Board of Governors of London Oratory School ex p. R* (1988) at p. 567). In addition, though the law is not entirely free from doubt, it is the better view that a reasonable opportunity to cross-examine witnesses is part of the *audi alteram partem* principle. Thus in *Nicholson* v *Secretary of State for Energy* (1977) 76 L.G.R. 693, the right of cross-examination at a public inquiry into the siting of an opencast mine was upheld on the basis that the denial of that right was a breach of natural justice.

Legal representation is also part of the *audi alteram partem* principle. Public tribunals under the Tribunals and Inquiries Act, 1971 will normally allow a party who wants it to have a lawyer to represent him. As regards a domestic tribunal, the Court of Appeal in *Enderby Town Football Club Ltd* v *The Football Association Ltd* [1971] 1 All E.R. 215 laid down the following broad principles –

(1) If the rules of the organisation say nothing about it the matter is basically within the discretion of the tribunal.

(2) If the case involves difficult points of law it is better for the parties to use the ordinary courts and get a declaratory judgment setting out their rights. If, however, a tribunal is used legal representation should be allowed and the court will intervene on the grounds of public policy to see that it is.

(3) A rule forbidding legal representation altogether is probably invalid. A tribunal should always be given a discretion.

However, it seems that in *disciplinary cases* where it is necessary to reach decisions quickly, it might well be appropriate to refuse legal representation. Thus, in *Maynard* v *Osmond* [1977] 1 All E.R. 64, the Court of Appeal held that natural justice did not require that a police constable should have legal representation at a hearing before the chief constable on a disciplinary matter involving an allegation that a sergeant had falsely stated that P.C. Maynard had been asleep while on duty. Furthermore the House of Lords decided in *R* v *Board of Visitors of the Maze Prison ex p. Hone and McCarten* [1988] 1 All E.R. 321 that a prisoner charged with a disciplinary offence is not entitled, as of right, to legal representation at the disciplinary hearing.

Whether a decision is judicial, quasi-judicial or administrative, or disciplinary, the rules of natural justice need not necessarily be applied if national security is involved.

(c) *Effect of failure to comply with rules.* In recent times the courts have made it clear that anything done by a tribunal in breach of natural justice (or *ultra vires*) is void. If action has been taken on the decision of a tribunal which is void that action is also void. If the decision was merely voidable action taken on it prior to the court quashing it would be valid.

(*d*) *Error of law on the face of the record. Certiorari* lies to quash a decision the record of which discloses an error of law. According to Lord Denning in *R v Northumberland Compensation Appeal Tribunal, ex parte Shaw* [1952] 1 All E.R. 122, the record consists of 'the document which initiates the proceedings, the pleadings (if any), and the adjudication, but not the evidence or the reasons unless the tribunal chooses to incorporate them.' As we have seen, the Tribunals and Inquiries Act, 1971 requires reasoned decisions in cases coming before tribunals and inquiries so that there should now normally be a record giving reasons which will assist the High Court in exercising its supervisory jurisdiction. In addition, if a reasoned decision is required by the 1971 Act the order of *mandamus* lies to compel the tribunal or inquiry to give one.

However, the above provisions do not apply to magistrates' courts. If an order of a magistrates' court does not contain reasons for the making of the order, then, provided the magistrates have stayed within their jurisdiction and observed the rules of natural justice, *certiorari* does not lie on the order under this heading.

ESSENTIAL CASE LAW AND COMMENT

R v London County Council, ex parte Entertainments Protection Assoc. Ltd, 1931 – *Certiorari* and *ultra vires* **(9)**
Dimes v Grand Junction Canal, 1852 – Monetary bias **(10)**
R v Bingham Justices, ex parte Jowitt, 1974 – Other bias **(11)**
R v Secretary of State for Home Department, ex parte Hosenball, 1977 – Natural justice and national security **(12)**
Ridge v Baldwin, 1963 – Effect of failure to comply with rules of natural justice and *ultra vires* **(13)**

Prohibition lies to prevent an inferior tribunal from exceeding its jurisdiction, or infringing the rules of natural justice. It is governed by similar principles to *certiorari*, except that it does not lie when once a final decision has been given (*certiorari* is then the appropriate order). The object of prohibition is to prevent an inferior tribunal from hearing and deciding a matter which is beyond its jurisdiction. Prohibition and *certiorari* are available against the Crown and public authorities but not against private persons or bodies, e.g. the big industrial conglomerates and trade unions.

Applications for *certiorari* and prohibition are often brought together, e.g. to quash a decision already made by a tribunal, and to prevent it from continuing to exceed or abuse its jurisdiction.

The order of *mandamus* may be issued to any person or body (not necessarily an inferior court, since it might be issued to a local authority). It commands him or them to carry out some public duty. Once again, it is not available against private persons or bodies.

It might be used to compel an administrative tribunal to hear an appeal which it is refusing to hear, or to compel a local authority to carry out a duty lying upon it, e.g. to produce its accounts for inspection by a council tax payer. (*R* v *Bedwellty U.D.C.* [1943] 1 K.B. 333.) *Mandamus* lies to compel the exercise of a duty and of a discretionary power, though in the case of the latter not in a particular way.

It is not available against the Crown itself; but it may issue against Ministers or other Crown servants to enforce a personal statutory duty.

The High Court has power to issue prerogative orders under s. 29(3) of the Supreme Court Act, 1981 in respect of all decisions of the Crown Court (with the exception of matters relating to trial on indictment) where such orders are normally appropriate, e.g. where an error of law appears on the face of the record in, say, a licensing decision as where the Crown Court appears to have misinterpreted the licensing provisions. (*R* v *Exeter Crown Court, ex parte Beattie* [1974] 1 All E.R. 1183.) Appeals from trials on indictment are to the Court of Appeal, Criminal Division.

INJUNCTION AND DECLARATORY JUDGMENT

The High Court can also exercise control over the decisions of inferior tribunals by granting, at its discretion, an injunction to prevent, for example, the implementation of a decision made by an inferior tribunal which does not observe the rules of natural justice. The remedy is not available against the Crown. (*Factortame Ltd* v *Secretary of State for Transport* [1989] 2 All E.R. 692.) Defiance of an injunction amounts to contempt of court. In many ways the remedy is like prohibition. However, it is rarely used against public tribunals. It is more commonly brought into play against domestic tribunals.

A *declaratory judgment* may be asked for by a person aggrieved by the decision of an inferior tribunal so that the High Court can state the legal position of the parties. Defiance of a declaratory judgment is not a contempt of court and there is no method by which it can be enforced, but parties usually observe it. However, disobedience could lead to a later action for an injunction or damages in which the law would already have been decided leaving only the facts to be proved. A declaration by the court that an administrative act was *ultra vires* will make it void and of no effect. It is particularly useful in respect of complaints against the actions of government departments and ministers.

DAMAGES

Although a public authority has acted unlawfully in the sense of being *ultra vires*, a person affected, such as Shell U.K. in *R* v *Lewisham B.C. ex parte Shell U.K.* (see p. 564), cannot recover damages against the wrongdoer unless he can base his claim on breach of contract, or a tort or alleges infringement of a property right (*O'Reilly* v *Mackman* [1983] 2 AC 237).

ESSENTIAL CASE LAW AND COMMENT

R v *Commissioner of Police of the Metropolis, ex parte Blackburn,*
1973 – *Mandamus* and discretionary powers **(14)**
R v *Secretary of State for Social Services, ex parte Grabaskey,*
1972 – *Mandamus* may be issued against Ministers **(15)**
Laker Airways v *Department of Trade,* 1977 – Declaratory
judgments: actions of government departments and Ministers **(16)**

JUDICIAL REVIEW – DELAY

It was decided in *R* v *Dairy Produce Quota Tribunal for England and Wales ex parte Caswell* [1989] 3 All E.R. 205 that if application for judicial review was not made promptly or within three months at the latest as prescribed by Order 53 of the Rules of the Supreme Court (see p. 60) the judge had to refuse leave to continue an action unless the applicant had a good reason for the delay.

Other controls on decision making

MINISTERS OF THE CROWN AND THE COURTS

Sometimes an Act of Parliament places a minister in a supervisory role over, for example, the decisions of local authorities, and where this is so he must act judicially and not administratively in respect of that supervisory role. If he does not exercise the supervisory role in the way envisaged by the Act which gave it to him, the Minister's directions are themselves subject to review by the court. This is of course in addition to the parliamentary question and the rule of ministerial responsibility to Parliament.

ESSENTIAL CASE LAW AND COMMENT

Secretary of State for Education and Science v *Tameside*
Metropolitan Borough Council, 1976 – Courts can examine
executive action **(17)**

THE OMBUDSMAN

It has become a popular idea to give the citizen safeguards against maladministration which are in addition to the traditional ones of application to a court or tribunal, by the setting up in various areas of administration of Ombudsmen, so called because the system is modelled upon the Scandinavian office of ombudsman. Some examples appear below.

The Parliamentary Commissioner for Administration and other Commissions

A further check on abuse of power by government departments was created by the appointment of the Parliamentary Commissioner for Administration (or 'Ombudsman') under the provisions of the Parliamentary Commissioner Act, 1967. The Commissioner is appointed by the Crown and has the same security of tenure as a judge of the Supreme Court. He is also a member of the Council on Tribunals. His function is to investigate complaints relating to the exercise of administrative functions. However, investigation of Central Government departments is made only at the request of a Member of Parliament and a citizen who wishes to have a complaint investigated must first bring it to the notice of an M.P.

Unfortunately, the Commissioner is very often limited to a consideration of the *administrative procedures* followed and is powerless to act if the correct procedure has been followed even though the decision is bad. Furthermore, he cannot investigate personnel matters. Nevertheless, each year sees a steady rise in the number of complaints referred to him, though the Commissioner and his functions are still not well enough known and he is at the present time less effective than his counterparts in other countries. In fact Britain is alone among the countries with national Ombudsmen in not allowing the Ombudsman to initiate his own investigations. Most of the complaints involve government departments in constant contact with the public, more complaints being levied against the Department of Social Security, followed by the Inland Revenue, than any other department.

The Commissioner's jurisdiction under the Act of 1967 is limited to certain aspects of Central Government administration but the Parliamentary Commissioner (Consular Complaints) Act, 1981 extends the jurisdiction of the Parliamentary Commissioner to complaints about the conduct of United Kingdom consular officers abroad. The Parliamentary and Health Service Commissioners Act, 1987 extends the jurisdiction of the Parliamentary Commissioner to non-departmental bodies etc. listed in Sch. 1, e.g. the Data Protection Registrar.

More recently s. 110 of the Courts and Legal Services Act, 1990 has extended the jurisdiction of the Commissioner to administrative acts of the administrative staff of courts and tribunals. This does not include review of the acts of the judiciary or tribunal members.

There is now a Health Service Commissioner for England and Wales to investigate complaints about certain aspects of the National Health Service. The Commissioner is the present Parliamentary Commissioner who therefore combines the two offices.

In addition, there are two Commissions for Local Administration in England and Wales each consisting of Local Commissioners appointed by the Secretary of State plus the Parliamentary Commissioner. A Local

Commissioner may investigate a written complaint made by a member of the public who claims to have sustained injustice in consequence of maladministration in connection with action taken by or on behalf of a local authority, joint board, police authority or water authority, being action taken in the exercise of administrative functions. The complaint will normally be made in writing either through a member of the local authority complained against *or* with evidence that a member has been asked to refer it but has not done so. Furthermore, it must be made within a time limit of twelve months. Any one of the Local Commissioners has the same powers as the High Court to require the attendance of witnesses and production of documents when he is conducting an investigation. He must report the results of any investigation to the person who referred the complaint to him, to the complainant and to the authority concerned which must make copies available for public inspection. If he finds that injustice has been caused, the authority concerned must consider his report and notify him of what action they have taken. The greatest number of complaints relates to activities of local housing and planning authorities. Certain matters, such as the conduct of legal proceedings, action taken to prevent crime, or action concerning the giving of instruction or discipline in schools, are excluded from the jurisdiction of a Local Commissioner.

Under the Act of 1967 the Parliamentary Commissioner is given discretion whether to investigate a complaint or not. In consequence, the order of *mandamus* will not issue to him since he has no duty to hear a complaint (*Re Fletcher's Application* [1970] 2 All E.R. 527). Furthermore, there is no way of enforcing the findings of the Ombudsman and there are those who feel that it would improve matters if the courts had power to enforce these findings. However, judicial review is available against the decisions of local commissioners (see R v *Local Commissioner for Administration for the South, the West, the West Midlands etc.* [1988] 3 All E.R. 151.

Legal ombudsman

Sections 21–26 of the Courts and Legal Services Act, 1990 set up the office of Legal Ombudsman. The object is to help people who have a genuine cause for complaint against members of the legal profession but have not been able to sort their problems out. The Ombudsman has power to investigate the handling of complaints by the Law Society, the Bar and the Council for Licensed Convenyancers, reinvestigate the complaints and recommend remedies including the payment of compensation. He reports annually to the Lord Chancellor and Parliament.

Other ombudsmen

A Banking Ombudsman, an Insurance Ombudsman and a Building Society Ombudsman have been appointed to deal, on a limited basis, with disputes in those industries. The Council of the Stock Exchange has also appointed an Ombudsman to mediate in disputes between investors and stockbrokers. In addition s. 43 of the Courts and Legal Services Act, 1990 provides for a Conveyancing Ombudsman (see further p. 72).

Section 12 and Sch. 3 of the Social Security Act, 1990 insert new sections into the Social Security Pensions Act, 1975 to establish a Pensions Ombudsman to adjudicate in disputes between an individual and a pension scheme or provider. In addition the Institute of Chartered Accountants in England & Wales has recently proposed the appointment of an Ombudsman to review complaints against its members. There is also the Investment Referee who investigates disputes against those in the investment business.

Coroners' courts

These courts, which commenced in 1194, are amongst the oldest English courts still in existence. Their chief function is to inquire into cases of violent, unnatural or suspicious death, together with cases of sudden death without apparent cause. They also inquire into deaths in prison and deaths by handling – which is still a possible punishment, for example, for the crime of treason.

A coroner has jurisdiction to hold an inquest on a body lying within his jurisdiction even though the death and cause of death has not occurred in England and Wales. Thus in *R* v *West Yorkshire Coroner, ex parte Smith* [1982] 3 All E.R. 1098 the Court of Appeal decided that the coroner was obliged under what is now s. 8 of the Coroners Act, 1988 to hold an inquest into the death of a nurse who had died in Saudi Arabia but whose body had been brought back to this country. However, the coroner faces special difficulties in such a case because he cannot summon witnesses from abroad or request the production of documents. (See further p. 127.)

The procedure is that of an inquest or inquiry; it is not a trial. The object is to find out the identity of the deceased, the cause of his death, and where the death took place. The coroner's officer, a serving police officer, collects evidence before the inquest begins. All witnesses are under oath, but the rules of evidence are not applied as strictly as they are in other courts. The coroner decides what constitutes relevant and admissible evidence, and has much discretion at all stages of the investigation.

THE CORONER'S JURY

In cases such as suspected murder or death in prison, the coroner may summon a jury of from seven to eleven persons, and he may accept the verdict of the majority so long as there are not more than two dissentients. He is required to summon a jury under s. 8(3) of the Coroners Act, 1988 where the death with which he is concerned occurred in circumstances the continuance or possible recurrence of which is prejudicial to the health or safety of the public or any section of the public. An example from earlier legislation is the decision of the Court of Appeal in *R* v *Hammersmith Coroner, ex parte Peach* [1980] 2 All E.R. 7, where it was held that the suspicious or unauthorised use by a police officer of a lethal weapon was a matter coming within s. 8, and acordingly it was compulsory to have a jury. Section 8(3) also requires a coroner to summon a jury where the deceased was in police custody or death resulted from an injury caused by a police officer in the purported exercise of his duty.

Section 9 of the 1988 Act provides that a person is not qualified to serve as a juror at an inquest held by a coroner unless he is for the time being qualified to serve as a juror in the Crown Court, the High Court, and the county court. (See further p. 104.) The Act also provides criminal penalties for evasion of service on a coroner's jury.

The coroner can require a *post mortem*, and the attendance of medical and other witnesses who may be examined on oath.

If the court finds that a death was a result of murder, manslaughter or infanticide, this does not operate to convict the person said to be responsible, and a coroner can in no case charge a person with those offences.

It may happen that before the end of the inquest a person is charged with an offence, e.g. murder or manslaughter, in connection with the death of the deceased. On being informed of this by e.g. a clerk to magistrates the coroner must adjourn the inquest until after the conclusion of the relevant criminal proceedings and if he has summoned a jury he may, if he thinks fit, discharge them. This is to prevent inquests turning into, in effect, murder trials as they sometimes did in the 1920s.

After the conclusion of the relevant criminal proceedings the coroner may resume the adjourned inquest if, in his opinion, there is sufficient cause to do so. If he does resume an inquest then the finding of the inquest as to the cause of death must not be inconsistent with the outcome of the relevant proceedings (s. 16(7) Coroners Act, 1988).

Under s. 1 of the Coroners Act, 1988 coroners are appointed for each coroner's district in a Metropolitan County or Greater London and for each Non-Metropolitan County and for the City of London by the relevant Councils. Appointment is from persons with a five-year general qualification within s. 71 of the Courts and Legal Services Act, 1990 or legally qualified medical practitioners who have had at least five years in practice.

Section 6 of the 1988 Act provides that every coroner *must* appoint a deputy coroner and *may* appoint an assistant deputy provided in each case that the approval of the Chairman of the relevant Council is obtained. This is to ensure continuity in the office where a coroner dies or retires. The qualifications for a deputy or assistant deputy are as for a coroner himself. All the appointments referred to above are generally part time and there can be dismissal for inability or misbehaviour. The Lord Chief Justice and the judges of the High Court are by reason of holding that office also coroners *ex officio* as it is referred to.

TREASURE TROVE

Under s. 30 of the 1988 Act the coroner also retains jurisdiction in treasure trove. Treasure trove is money, coin, manufactured gold, silver plate or bullion deliberately hidden in the earth or other private place, the owner being unknown. Such property belongs to the Crown. The coroner is concerned to establish that the property was deliberately hidden because, if it was not, but merely lost, the finder, not the Crown, acquires a good title to it, except as against the true owner. However, if the finder makes prompt report of his discovery of treasure trove, the present practice of the Crown is to restore the article to him, or if it is required for a museum, to pay him its value. Nevertheless, the Crown has no prerogative right to treasure trove if the objects are not of gold or silver, and in *Attorney-General of the Duchy of Lancaster* v *Overton (G.E.) (Farms)* [1982] 1All E.R. 524, the Court of Appeal held that 7811 third century Roman coins of debased silver, containing only 0.2% to 18% silver found in a field at Coleby, Lincs, were not treasure trove and therefore not the property of the Crown.

REFORM

The coroner's court has a number of major weaknesses, particularly where the death has occurred in controversial circumstances. It cannot subpoena witnesses and those witnesses who attend voluntarily cannot be compelled to answer questions under oath, nor can they be made to submit to cross-examination. Furthermore, there is no power of discovery of documents. This has led to suggestions that, at least in controversial cases, there should be a tribunal of inquiry headed by a High Court judge with the usual rules of evidence and procedure available so that the truth of the matter may be better arrived at.

Legal services – provision of

The question of who is allowed to provide legal services and the type of service which particular persons can provide is dealt with in Part II of the Courts and Legal Services Act, 1990 (ss. 17–70). Section references are to that Act unless otherwise indicated.

GENERAL PRINCIPLES

As regards the achievement of the objectives and general principles of the Act, i.e. the development of legal services, Part II places duties on certain persons. The Lord Chief Justice, the Master of the Rolls, the President of the Family Division and the Vice-Chancellor – called Designated Judges – plus the Lord Chancellor are required to agree on training regulations and rules of conduct for those supplying legal services. They are also required to decide whether to grant an application from a professional or other organisation to be given the right to confer on their members rights of audience before the courts and also the right to conduct litigation, i.e. pre-trial work.

In practice applications are considered by the Lord Chancellor's Advisory Committee on Legal Education and Conduct which has a lay majority. Advice can also be received from the Director General of Fair Trading in terms e.g. of possible restrictive practices in rules of entry or other matters leading to a lack of competition.

RIGHTS OF AUDIENCE

Section 27 sets out a statutory framework to deal with rights of audience before courts and tribunals. The Advisory Committee has a most important advisory role in relation to applications by professional and other bodies to be permitted by the Lord Chancellor and the four Designated Judges to grant rights of audience or rights to conduct litigation. The first specific matter for consideration by the Advisory Committee was an application by the Law Society for permission to grant further rights of audience to solicitors whose rights had before the Act been very limited.

The granting of rights of audience for the future depends solely upon whether practitioners who wish to be advocates can demonstrate that they have the necessary education and training and are subject to appropriate codes of conduct. This is a matter for what are called 'authorised bodies', which initially include the General Council of the Bar and the Law Society, but other bodies may be designated by Order in Council by application to the Lord Chancellor under s. 29. There is machinery for revoking an authorisation made under s. 29 again by Order in Council. This does not apply to the General Council of the Bar or the Law Society who are designated by s. 27 not s. 29. Existing rights of audience which the law formally gave to barristers and solicitors are preserved by ss. 31 and 32. Finally those who act as advocates but are not entitled to do so commit an offence under s. 70(1).

RIGHTS TO CONDUCT LITIGATION

Section 28 sets out a statutory framework to deal with the right to conduct litigation, e.g. the right to issue writs and generally conduct pre-trial work. The new rules displace the virtual monopoly which solicitors have had over pre-trial proceedings. Existing rights of solicitors to conduct this work are preserved but for the future rights to conduct litigation will depend solely upon whether the persons concerned can demonstrate that they have the necessary education and training and are bound by an appropriate code of conduct. This is again a matter for authorised bodies which initially include the Law Society but other bodies may make an application to the Lord Chancellor under s. 29 for designation by Order in Council which again may be revoked by Order in Council. This does not apply to the Law Society which is designated under s. 28 not s. 29. Those who act as authorised litigators when not entitled to do so commit an offence under s. 70(1).

CONVEYANCING SERVICES

Sections 34–52 are concerned to develop legal services by providing a wider choice of persons who may practise conveyancing which involves the preparation of the document (conveyance) which transfers a freehold interest in land after sale and the necessary documentation involved.

A sole regulatory body is set up by the 1990 Act. It is called the Authorised Conveyancing Practitioners Board and it is given the task of authorising, supervising and disciplining practitioners authorised for conveyancing work. Previously such work was restricted to solicitors, barristers and licensed conveyancers. They now face competition from authorised conveyancing practitioners.

A conveyancing ombudsman scheme to investigate complaints against authorised practitioners is set up and rules regulating the scheme are to be made by the Board. The ombudsman can make compensation orders against practitioners including sums of money to represent inconvenience and distress as well as loss.

There is also the Council for Licensed Conveyancers which was set up under the Administration of Justice Act, 1985, Part II to grant licences and regulate practitioners of conveyancing services. This continues but s. 53 of the 1990 Act extends the powers of the Council so that if it becomes an authorised or approved body it can extend the licences given to licensed conveyancers to allow them to undertake probate work, i.e. to get formal proof of a will which must be applied for when the person making the will dies or to get letters of administration to wind up the estate when there is no will, and to grant some rights of audience and rights to conduct litigation.

PROBATE SERVICES

Formerly it was an offence for any person other than a solicitor or barrister to draft or prepare *for payment* the papers leading to a grant of probate or letters of administration. However, under ss. 54 and 55 there is machinery under which bodies may apply for approved status under which their members could become 'probate practitioners' (s. 55) as can the employees of banks, building societies, and insurance companies under s. 54.

ADMINISTRATION OF OATHS AND THE TAKING OF AFFIDAVITS

It is sometimes necessary for a person to make a statement on oath as to the truth of what is said in a document. If the statement in the document is false to the knowledge of the person giving the oath that person commits the crime of perjury and can be prosecuted and may be fined or imprisoned. Every solicitor with a practising certificate can administer oaths and take affidavits but now s. 113 provides that in the interests of competition authorised litigators and advocates may do so and may use the title 'Commissioner for Oaths'.

Payment for legal services

CONTINGENCY FEES

In the past any form of contingency fee arrangement between a lawyer and a client, e.g. to give the lawyer a share of the damages if successful but nothing on failure, was unenforceable in English law. However, s. 58 permits written conditional fee agreements between advocates or litigators and their clients. The contents of such agreements are limited to provisions under which the advocate or litigator receives normal fees plus an uplift in the event of success but no fees in the event of failure. The uplift must be set out in the agreement and the Lord Chancellor is given power after consultation with the General Council of the Bar, the Law Society and other authorised bodies to regulate the percentage of uplift to be allowed. Such agreements are not permitted in criminal proceedings and in certain others, e.g. proceedings in adoption. The greatest scope for the use of these agreements will be in cases of personal injury and defamation. Agreements other than those in line with s. 58, e.g. agreements for a percentage of the damages awarded, remain unenforceable.

PAYMENT OF SOLICITORS BY HOURLY RATES

Section 98 provides for agreements between a solicitor and client relating to the hourly rate which the solicitor will charge. The agreement must be in writing and the Court may set it aside if it is unfair or unreasonable. The intention here is to widen the number of situations in which a solicitor will agree the terms of business in advance with a client.

LEGAL AID

The availability of State-funded legal aid for litigation and legal advice in criminal and civil proceedings is considered in the chapters on Procedure.

The main legal professions

Although the changes in the provision of legal services effected by the Courts and Legal Services Act, 1990 are immense the *main* participants in such provision will continue to be barristers and solicitors, the latter being assisted by legal executives. The nature of these professions is considered in outline below.

BARRISTERS

Barristers conduct cases in court, and generally draft the pleadings which outline the manner in which the case is to be conducted. They also give opinions on difficult legal problems.

There is, of course, nothing to stop a party presenting his own case, though when it comes to an appeal to the House of Lords, unless leave has been granted by the Court of Appeal, it is necessary for two Queen's Counsel to certify that it is reasonable to bring the case to appeal.

Call to the English Bar is the prerogative of the four Inns of Court – Lincoln's Inn, Gray's Inn, the Inner Temple and the Middle Temple. The Inns of Court are unincorporated societies governed by Masters of the Bench, who are judges or senior barristers, and Call to the Bar is by the Benchers.

Council of Legal Education

The Council of Legal Education is responsible for the education and examination of students at later stages of qualifying and holds lectures which are conducted by leading academic and practising lawyers.

Once a student has passed the examinations and 'kept terms' by dining in the hall of his Inn a set number of times, he must (if he wishes to practise generally), become a pupil of a senior barrister, often referred to as a pupil master, for a period of twelve months. A barrister must then find chambers from which to practise. Since 1981 it has been possible to follow a commercial pupillage, i.e. a period spent in employment under the guidance of an approved barrister in industry or commerce which will count towards the compulsory period of pupillage which barristers must undergo before practising on their own. In addition a barrister who is employed e.g. by a company or local authority and who has completed pupillage or has been an employed barrister for five years can appear in court for his employer. This has enabled barristers to compete rather better with solicitors for posts in industry, commerce and local government.

Circuits

After call, a barrister intending to practise generally will join a circuit and he will then practise within that circuit though he may take cases on others. There are six circuits in England and Wales, i.e. Midland and Oxford; North Eastern; Northern; South Eastern; Wales and Chester; and Western.

There are no partnerships at the Bar, and one barrister cannot employ another, but it is usual though not essential for counsel to group together in chambers and employ a clerk who is responsible for the administration of the chambers, fees, appointments and instructions. There is, however, no objection to what is called 'purse-sharing' under which a particular chambers pools all its fees and each barrister draws the same monthly 'salary'. Some of what remains can go to make payments to pupil barristers, and indeed the Bar Council has approved a scheme of payment for trainees of at least £6000 a year and chambers which find this difficult may apply for help to the Bar Council support fund.

Under a Bar Council code of conduct barristers are allowed to advertise, work without clerks and open chambers where they like. They are no longer restricted to setting up chambers in or near the Inns of Court.

Queen's Counsel

Experienced barristers may apply to the Lord Chancellor to 'take silk', i.e. to become Queen's Counsel which gives the entitlement to wear a silk gown in court. The Lord Chancellor recommends suitable applicants to the Queen who makes the appointment. After appointment as Queen's Counsel a barrister will not in general appear without a junior, i.e. another barrister who is not a Q.C., and his practice henceforth tends to be restricted to the more important cases requiring two counsel, i.e. a junior to deal with less difficult but time-consuming procedural matters and the drafting of pleadings, leaving the Q.C. to concentrate on advocacy.

Until 1977 the rules of conduct laid down by the Bar *prevented* a Q.C. from working without a junior. The rule was dropped following a report by the Monopolies Commission that the practice was contrary to the public interest. However, most Q.C.s still claim that they need the assistance of a junior, and the scheme to avoid duplication of service appears to have failed.

Briefing and negligence

A barrister will not normally deal directly with a client and will usually be briefed by a solicitor, and he cannot sue for his fees, though a solicitor who fails to pay over to counsel fees received from a client is liable to disciplinary action, and indeed under an arrangement between the Law Society and the Bar a briefing solicitor is personally liable, except in legal aid cases, to pay counsel's fees even if the solicitor has not received them from the client. However, s. 61 of the Courts and Legal Services Act, 1990 now allows a barrister to enter into a contract with a client for the provision of services and payment of fees. More recently the Bar Council has approved proposals which allow direct access to barristers by other professions, e.g. accountants, for opinions but not if litigation is involved. Thus the usual route through a solicitor need not always be followed.

As regards fees, barristers are entitled to a 'brief fee' which covers preparation of the case plus the first day of the trial (if any). Added to this is a sum called a 'refresher' payable for the second and each subsequent day of the trial for however long it continues. The costs of one side for a week in court on, say, a contested personal injury case with a Q.C. can run into several thousands of pounds on top of which fees are also payable to the firm of solicitors involved in preparatory work.

As a result of decisions of the House of Lords it may be said that as regards professional negligence, a barrister has immunity in terms of his conduct and management of litigation. However, a barrister may be sued for advice given or work done negligently before a case comes to trial, and it is only where the pre-trial work is so intimately connected with the conduct of the case in court that it can fairly be said to be a preliminary decision affecting the way the case is to be conducted at the actual hearing that a barrister can claim immunity.

In this connection s. 62 of the Courts and Legal Services Act, 1990 gives the same common law immunity in negligence but no more to authorised advocates and also to authorised litigators who do from time to time appear in court for a client. In addition no claim can be brought by a client in contract for which immunity would be given in tort and the Legal Services Ombudsman cannot intervene in this particular area either.

ESSENTIAL CASE LAW AND COMMENT

Rondel v *Worsley*, 1967 – Advocates: immunity in negligence **(18)**

Conduct

In matters of conduct, counsel is under an obligatory duty to pursue his case in a proper manner. He must inform the court of all the relevant statutes and precedents, and, where a legal authority is against his argument, he must not suppress it, though he may attempt to distinguish or criticise it. He must also ensure that his client has a fair hearing. If a prosecuting counsel in a criminal case is aware of facts which support the case for the accused, or lessen the gravity of the offence, he must state them. Counsel may not plead guilty for a client, but may persuade him to do so if it is in the client's interest.

In addition barristers are required to act for any client whether legally aided or not in any field in which they profess to practise. This is called the 'cab-rank' rule which is referred to in s. 17(3)(c) of the Courts and Legal Services Act, 1990 as a matter for consideration in approving an application by e.g. a professional body for authorisation of its members as advocates.

SOLICITORS

The profession of solicitor is derived from three former branches of the legal profession. The early stages of litigation in the King's Bench and Common Pleas was conducted by *attorneys*; in the Court of Chancery by *solicitors*, so called because cases in Chancery could go on for years and the only way of getting the case moving was to employ a person to *'solicit'* or cajole the court into action, and in the Ecclesiastical Courts and Admiralty by *proctors*. These three branches fused in 1831 to form the Law Society, though their functions were not fused under the one name of solicitor until 1875. The Law Society is responsible for prescribing the qualifications and setting the examinations, issuing practising certificates and preserving minimum standards of behaviour. It also runs a compensation fund for those who have suffered from the wrongful acts and defaults of solicitors, supervises the charges made by solicitors for their work and provides a complaints system.

Today a solicitor is in some respects a business man who advises his clients on legal, financial and other matters. His work is not all of a legal nature, but most of it requires legal training. Much of the work of a solicitor is concerned with property. He investigates title to land, prepares contracts of sale, conveyances and wills, and often acts as executor and trustee. He also assists promoters in company formation. As we have seen since the passing of the Administration of Justice Act, 1985 and the Courts and Legal Services Act, 1990 practising solicitors no longer have a monopoly of conveyancing which may now be done also by licensed conveyancers and authorised conveyancers who need not be qualified as solicitors.

There is a Practice Rule forbidding a solicitor from acting for both parties to a transaction though there are exceptions, e.g. where both parties are established clients. In addition it was decided by the Court of Appeal in *Re a firm of Solicitors* (1991) 141 N.L.J. 746 that a firm of solicitors will not be allowed to act for a present client against a former client if it was reasonable to anticipate that there was a danger that information gained by the firm while acting for a former client would be used against that former client.

In future the distinction between solicitors and barristers in the matter of advocacy in court will not be so marked as it has been in the past. As we have seen under arrangements set up by the Courts and Legal Services Act, 1990 solicitors, who wish to do so, will undoubtedly be able to acquire wider rights of advocacy before our courts. However, many will continue to follow their traditional role as litigators involved in pre-trial work where their functions will be to prepare the case, ascertain the facts, arrange for the presence of the necessary witnesses and any documents which may be required, and conduct any disputes over costs which have been awarded after judgment.

In order to qualify as a solicitor it is necessary to complete the examinations of the Law Society as appropriate and serve a period under training with a solicitor. After this application must be made to the Law Society for admission as a solicitor, and admission must be approved by the Master of the Rolls, since a solicitor is an officer of the court. A person may then practise alone, or as a member of a partnership, and every practising and some employed solicitors must take out an annual practising certificate. Section 9 of the Administration of Justice Act, 1985 will, when brought into force, allow solicitors to form incorporated practices. A number of solicitors are employed in local and central government departments and by commercial firms.

LEGAL EXECUTIVES

The Institute of Legal Executives which was established in 1963 gives professional status to the unadmitted staff employed e.g. in solicitors' offices. There are two examinations: the first leads to Associate membership of the Institute and the second, which is of higher standard, leads to Fellowship. Legal executives frequently carry heavy responsibilities in connection with the business of the firm. A great deal of the routine work in connection with e.g. conveyancing also falls on them. Under arrangements put in place by the Courts and Legal Services Act, 1990 legal executives will be able to acquire wider rights in terms of (*a*) audience in our courts, and (*b*) pre-trial work.

NOTARY PUBLIC

A notary public is an officer of the law who is appointed by the Court of Faculties of the Archbishop of Canterbury. He is a civil lawyer empowered to verify e.g. the signature of documents and authenticate the contents of documents. He may also administer oaths and declarations. In other words his main function is to substantiate evidence of human activities. A notary will often also be a solicitor but this is not essential since there is a separate professional body called The Notaries Society.

LAW CENTRES

Since 1970 when the North Kensington law centre was set up there has been a growth in such centres which are sources of legal advice. They employ lawyers and some supporting lay staff and are funded by the local authority for the area in which they are situated and by legal aid income and sometimes by private donations. They work mainly in the fields of housing, employment and immigration. In recent times they have been desperately under funded and some have closed. Nevertheless where they do exist they provide a vital legal service in some of our poorer communities.

INFORMATION AND ADVICE FROM NON-LAWYERS

Those in business can obtain information and advice on legal maters from non-lawyers. Accountants are highly competent in the law of taxation and also in company law. In addition firms of accountants will undoubtedly obtain recognition under the Courts and Legal Services Act, 1990 to carry out probate services and some will obtain rights of audience. Government departments can be helpful – for example the Department of Employment is prepared to advise on employment legislation, as the Inland Revenue is on tax, and as the Customs and Excise are on VAT regulations. There are also government sponsored organisations which provide information and advice such as the Equal Opportunities Commission on sex discrimination. Those in business may also obtain useful information and advice from a relevant trade association and of course from their own professional institutes and associations. Advice on social matters such as rent reduction, security of tenure or property and social benefits can be obtained from Citizens' Advice Bureaux.

Some important judicial officers

THE LORD CHANCELLOR

The Lord Chancellor is the Speaker of the House of Lords and the ultimate head of the Judiciary in that he is the chief judge in the country, and controls the administration of the courts of law. He is also the Chairman of the Judicial Committee of the Privy Council. He advises the Crown on the appointment of High Court judges, and circuit judges. He is responsible for the appointment of Justices of the Peace, and advises on the appointment of recorders, stipendiary magistrates and Metropolitan stipendiaries. He is also the custodian of the Great Seal, which represents the signature of the Crown in its corporate capacity. Unlike the Speaker of the House of Commons, he may take part in debates and may vote in all divisions, but has no casting vote. The office is political, and the holder is usually a Cabinet Minister. However, the Prime Minister could appoint as Lord Chancellor a person who was not a politician. The one essential requirement is that he must be a lawyer. His position serves to support the contention that there is no separation of judicial, legislative and executive powers in the British Constitution.

THE ATTORNEY-GENERAL AND THE SOLICITOR-GENERAL

The Attorney-General and the Solicitor-General are known as the Law Officers. The appointments are political and change with the government. As a rule the Law Officers are not members of the Cabinet.

The Attorney-General

The Attorney-General is appointed by Letters Patent under the Great Seal, and is usually a member of the House of Commons. He represents the Crown in civil matters and can prosecute in important criminal cases. He is the Head of the English Bar, and points of professional etiquette are referred to him. He also advises government departments on legal matters, and advises the court on matters of parliamentary privilege. He can institute litigation on behalf of the public, e.g. to stop a public nuisance or the commission of a crime and to enforce or regulate public charitable trusts, because he acts on behalf of the public as a whole. Individuals do not have sufficient interest (or *locus standi*) to bring actions in these cases.

Where a person does not have sufficient *locus standi* to initiate proceedings himself, he may ask the Attorney-General to take proceedings. If the Attorney-General does act at the relation of a private individual, the action is known as a 'relator action' and the relator is responsible for the costs incurred. If the Attorney-General refuses to act no court can compel him to do so.

The Solicitor-General

The Solicitor-General is the subordinate of the Attorney-General, and sometimes gives a joint opinion with him when asked by government departments. In spite of his title he is a member of the Bar and he need not, strictly speaking, be in the House of Commons. His duties are similar to those of the Attorney-General and he is in many ways his deputy. Both Law Officers are precluded from private practice. The Law Officers Act, 1944, provides that any functions authorised or required to be discharged by the Attorney-

General may be discharged by the Solicitor-General, if the office of Attorney-General is vacant, or if the Attorney-General is unable to act because of absence or illness, or where the Attorney-General authorises the Solicitor-General to act in any particular matter.

ESSENTIAL CASE LAW AND COMMENT

Gouriet v *Union of Post Office Workers,* 1977 – Law Officers: Attorney-General's enforcement of the law in the public interest **(19)**

MASTERS

Many matters arise for decision between the time of issue of the writ and the trial of the action, e.g. what documents must be shown by one side to the other; what time should be allowed for putting in statements of claim and defences; what is the most convenient and proper place for the trial to be held. These will usually be dealt with by a master, but sometimes by a judge.

Queen's Bench and Chancery Masters

These are salaried officials of the High Court, the former being appointed from among persons having a seven-year general advocacy qualification.

Taxing Masters

These are salaried officers of the Supreme Court, being persons who have a seven-year general advocacy qualification. They fix the costs which one party is directed to pay to the other. In most important provincial towns there is a District Registry under the supervision of a *District Registrar* who performs the same functions as a master in London.

OFFICIAL REFEREES

Cases which involve detailed examination of books and documents, e.g. lengthy building disputes, are referred separately for trial, and are known as Official Referee's Business. Under s. 68 of the Supreme Court Act, 1981, as amended by s. 59 of the Administration of Justice Act, 1982, the Lord Chancellor has currently nominated seven circuit judges to carry out Official Referee's Business. Much of their work is heavy and protracted and they work from courts and chambers adjacent to the Royal Courts of Justice in London.

THE OFFICIAL SOLICITOR

The Official Solicitor is an officer of the Supreme Court who acts in litigation to protect the interests of persons suffering under mental disability. He is also concerned to protect the interests of children in adoption matters and those of persons imprisoned for contempt of court.

In future the Official Solicitor must have a ten-year general advocacy qualification but the right to act as a litigator is preserved by s. 90(3A) of the Supreme Court Act, 1981 (as inserted by the Courts and Legal Services Act, 1990). Section 54 of the 1990 Act also makes clear that the Official Solicitor can apply for probate.

CIRCUIT ADMINISTRATORS

The Royal Commission on Assizes and Quarter Sessions (Beeching Commission) recommended the appointment of a Circuit administrator in each of the six Circuits into which England and Wales was divided. A legal qualification is not essential. Their function is to a large extent managerial and they took over from Clerks of Assize, Clerks of the Peace, and other officers of the numerous different courts who previously had to try to provide the public and the legal profession with a court service. There is now one person at each High Court and Crown Court Centre to whom all involved can turn in respect of administrative problems.

Circuit administrators must as far as possible ensure prompt hearings for civil and criminal cases at their centres. Their function in the High Court and Crown Court Centres is to decide whether cases should be heard by High Court judges or Circuit judges.

PRESIDING JUDGES

Under s. 72 of the Courts and Legal Services Act, 1990 the Lord Chief Justice with the agreement of the Lord Chancellor appoints two High Court judges known as Presiding Judges who are assigned to each of the six Circuits in England and Wales. They take it in turn to spend substantial periods of time in the area and have general responsibility for the local High Court and Crown Court Centre. They see to the convenient and efficient distribution of judges in the area, and give support and guidance to the Circuit administrator on these matters.

Under the same section the Lord Chief Justice also appoints a Lord Justice as a Senior Presiding Judge to oversee all the Circuits. His function is to provide the Presiding Judges with a Senior Lord Justice to whom they can turn for advice rather than to the Lord Chief Justice himself, and to relieve the Lord Chief Justice of some of the administrative work in which he would otherwise be involved both in and out of London.

4
Criminal procedure

Having described the system of major criminal courts and tribunals existing in England and Wales, we shall now consider the procedure in the major courts which leads to a prosecution and conviction for crime.

Criminal procedure – generally

The system of trial in this country is accusatorial in that a trial is a contest between two persons. As regards crime, these persons are normally the Queen (on behalf of the community) and the person accused of the crime.

Advocates representing the prosecution and the defence each put forward evidence to the court so that a decision may be made on the question before the court which is, did the accused commit the offence with which he is charged?

It should also be noted in particular that a person accused of crime is presumed innocent until proved guilty and is given certain protections in regard to the proof of his guilt as follows –

(*a*) *The Code of Practice for the Detention, Treatment and Questioning of Persons by the Police.* This Code is prepared by the Home Office under powers given by s.66 of the Police and Criminal Evidence Act, 1984. The latest revised Code came into force on 1 April 1991 and ensures that a person cannot be trapped by questioning into an admission of guilt. The main safeguard of the Code is that once an investigating police officer has grounds to believe that the person being questioned has committed an offence, whether he has admissible evidence to that effect or not, questioning *about the offence* can continue, but only after the suspect has been 'cautioned'. This involves telling the suspect that he need not say anything but that, if he does, what he says may be written down and given in evidence. At any subsequent trial anything said by the person while a suspect may be used for or against his case.

If questioning is interrupted the Code states that the caution should be given afresh each time questioning is resumed. It also provides that a person who is not under arrest when he is cautioned, e.g. a person cautioned over a minor traffic offence, should be so informed.

Under the revised Code it is not now generally permissible to conduct interviews and questioning except at a police station *once a decision to arrest has been taken*. If an interview is conducted at a place other than a police station which it may be on the grounds of 'necessity' the suspect must be asked to verify the notes of the interview 'unless it is impracticable'. The police also have a duty to keep a record of any unsolicited comments and ask the suspect to verify these as well. The suspect should write his agreement on the relevant record as soon as is practicable. Where legal advice has been requested verification should await the arrival of a solicitor.

(*b*) *The burden of proof.* Once in court the prosecution must prove its case beyond all reasonable doubt. The magistrates or jury need not be *certain* of the accused's guilt, but they must in effect be *sure* that he has committed the crime. (And see *Woolmington* v *DPP*, 1935 at p. 828.)

The prosecutor

The Prosecution of Offences Act, 1985 establishes a national prosecution service for England and Wales. The service separates the *prosecution* of offences from the police service which is concerned with *detection and investigation*.

The police continue to decide whether to prosecute, caution, or take no further action in the first instance. However, if they do decide to prosecute, the case is handed over to the Crown Prosecutors. The Crown Prosecution Service has power to advise the police at this stage. However, Crown Prosecutors have no right to be informed of cases and cannot insist that any advice they give is accepted until the police decide to prosecute. This is a major weakness in the Act.

The Director of Public Prosecutions (see further p. 85) is in charge of the Crown Prosecution Service under the general superintendence of the Attorney-General. The Service conducts all police prosecutions except minor motoring matters. Thus Crown Prosecutors are able to take the decision to continue or drop a case without consulting the police and may in that sense override the wishes of the police. However, withdrawal of charges in court is another matter. A Crown Court judge may refuse to allow a case to be dropped. (*R* v *Broad* (1978), 68 Cr. App. R. 281.) However, s. 23 of the 1985 Act allows Crown Prosecutors to discontinue any proceedings in the magistrates' courts (before the opening of a contested trial) without the prior permission of the court. The situation in the Crown Court remains unchanged.

The staff of the Crown Prosecution Service, called Crown Prosecutors, are appointed by the DPP and must have a general advocacy qualification under the Courts and Legal Services Act, 1990. The senior prosecuting officer in the various areas is called a Chief Crown Prosecutor. The DPP may, however, employ pesons with a general advocacy qualification who are not members of the Crown Prosecution Service.

The Act also gives the Secretary of State power to set limits on the time for the opening of criminal proceedings and under it cases must be brought to court within time limits to be specified in regulations made under s. 22 of the 1985 Act. Regulations have been made and are now extended to the whole country. Under them if a defendant is remanded in custody, which under the Criminal Justice Act, 1991, Sch. 12, para. 35 includes local authority accommodation for children and young persons, his summary trial must begin within 56 days, or his committal for trial in the Crown Court within 70 days of his first appearance in the dock. From the date of committal to pleading guilty or not guilty before the Crown Court the limit is 112 days. If the limits are not met the defendant must be released on bail but the court can extend the time limit if it is satisfied that there is good and sufficient cause and that the prosecution has acted as quickly as it could.

As regards court appearances during the above periods relating to the time of trial, s. 155 of the Magistrates' Courts Act, 1980 – as inserted by the Criminal Justice Act, 1988 – allows magistrates to remand in custody *without the consent of the defendant* for up to 28 days in one go. The defendant must be age 17 or over and have been previously remanded for up to eight days on the same offence and be before the court. Representations by the parties must be allowed and the defendant's right to apply for bail is not prejudiced.

The right of persons to institute private prosecutions is retained and under s. 6 the DPP may take over the prosecution at any time and, if he wishes, effectively stop it by not offering any evidence. Amendments to the Supreme Court Act of 1981 control and restrict vexatious proceedings, whether civil or criminal.

Private prosecutions are only instituted where the police are reluctant to be involved, as in an assault summons between neighbours. However, there have been more spectacular cases, e.g. the prosecution of *Gay News* for blasphemy by Mrs Mary Whitehouse. It is unfortunate, however, that a Queen's Bench Divisional Court decided in *R v D.P.P., ex parte Hallas* (1988) 87 Cr. App. R. 340 that a private citizen trying to set up a prosecution has no right of access to police statements, reports or photographs held by the Crown Prosecution Service. Mrs Hallas was trying to set up a prosecution for causing death by reckless driving against the allegedly drunk driver of the car which had killed her son. Section 6 gives no right to these materials. Disclosure can however be ordered by the court once the private prosecution has begun. (*R v Pawsey* [1989] Crim. L.R. 152.)

A private individual who is of opinion that the police are failing to prosecute in a particular case may ask the High Court to compel them to do so. (See *R v Commissioner of Police of the Metropolis, ex parte Blackburn*, 1973, at p. 568.)

Government departments, such as the Inland Revenue, also employ a staff of prosecutors to bring prosecutions for offences in connection with the department's activities, for example fraudulent tax evasion.

The Director of Public Prosecutions

The Director of Public Prosecutions may also become involved. The office of Director of Public Prosecutions was created by the Prosecution of Offences Act, 1879 (see now Prosecution of Offences Act, 1985). He is appointed by the Home Secretary from among persons with a ten-year general advocacy qualification but acts under the superintendence of the Attorney-General, who is formally answerable to Parliament for his actions. The Director prosecutes through his own staff and on some occasions through Treasury Counsel.

Sometimes an offence *must* be referred to the Director before prosecution. For example, under ss. 329 and 732 of the Companies Act, 1985 (as amended by the Financial Services Act, 1986) a company whose shares are quoted on a recognised investment exchange, e.g. the London Stock Exchange, is required to inform that Exchange of the purchase of shares in the company by its own directors. Failure to give such information can lead to the prosecution of the company and its directors but such a prosecution can only be brought with the consent of either the Secretary of State for Trade and Industry or the Director of Public Prosecutions.

Even if the offence is not one which must be referred to the Director, his advice through the Crown Prosecution Service is often sought by police authorities where, for example, they are not sure whether there is sufficient evidence to warrant the institution of criminal proceedings in a particular case.

Prosecuting fraud

The Criminal Justice Act, 1987 (as amended by the Criminal Justice Act, 1988) reforms the law relating to trials for fraud following the Report of the Roskill Committee on Fraud Trials, 1986.

Section 1 sets up a Serious Fraud Office under a Director, who is supervised by the Attorney-General, to investigate and prosecute complex and/or serious frauds. Sections 4–6 which are aimed at simplifying fraud trials allow a case of alleged fraud to be transferred to the Crown Court without the need for committal proceedings in front of magistrates if the prosecution gives notice of transfer. However, the magistrates retain certain powers, e.g. to grant bail and legal aid. Also the defendant may at this stage apply to the Crown Court for the charge against him to be dismissed on the grounds that the evidence of the prosecution does not disclose a *prima facie* case against him, i.e. that the evidence is not strong enough for him to be required to answer to it. Sections 7–11 reinforce the simplifying theme by providing for Preparatory Hearings before a judge sitting alone to be held when the trial first begins in the Crown Court so as to simplify the issues which will eventually go to the jury. This is in effect a pre-trial review at which points of law may be decided and also questions relating to the admissibility of evidence. These decisions are binding at subsequent stages of the trial.

INVOLVEMENT OF ATTORNEY-GENERAL

In some cases the consent of the Attorney-General is required before prosecution. This applies, for example, in the case of prosecutions under the Official Secrets Acts. The Attorney-General can therefore prevent prosecution by refusing his consent.

Getting the person accused into court

All persons accused of crime appear first in the magistrates' court. The appearance of the person accused is obtained by a summons or charge following arrest without a warrant. Arrest under a warrant signed by a magistrate under s. 1 (1) of the Magistrates' Courts Act, 1980 is not common today. The main use of warrants is to arrest those who, having been bailed, do not turn up for trial.

To get a summons the prosecutor must give a short account of the alleged offence, usually in writing, to the magistrates or their clerk (a process called laying an information). The information may be substantiated by a police officer swearing as to its truth before a magistrate and must be so substantiated if it is used as the basis for a warrant for arrest. A summons setting out the offence is then issued and served upon the person accused either in person or, for minor offences, through Recorded Delivery or Registered post.

Arrest without warrant occurs where a police officer arrests a person whom he reasonably suspects has committed, or is committing, or is about to commit, for example, an arrestable offence under s. 24 of the Police and Criminal Evidence Act, 1984 (PACE). This is e.g. an offence punishable with a maximum of five years' imprisonment or more. Most crimes of theft under the Theft Act 1968 are arrestable offences. Powers of arrest without warrant under the 1984 Act are more fully considered on p. 418.

Under s. 30 of PACE a person who has been arrested should be taken to a police station as soon as practicable unless his presence is required elsewhere for the effective investigation of crime. Under s. 34(1) of PACE, a person arrested for an offence may be held at a police station only if certain detention conditions apply. He must be released if they cease to apply.

The relevant conditions are set out in ss. 37 and 38 of PACE. Before a person is charged there is only one condition which is that there are reasonable grounds for believing that the detention is necessary to secure or preserve evidence of, or relating to, the offence for which the person was arrested, or to obtain such evidence by questioning him. (S. 37(2).) After charge there are a number of detention conditions, e.g. that the defendant's name and address are not known, or it is reasonably thought that he may have given a false name and address, or that he may not be long enough at his address for a summons to be served. (S. 38(1).) Under s. 36 of PACE, every police station must have a custody officer who is reponsible for supervising the detention and proper treatment of the detained person. Section 40 of PACE provides for periodic review of the validity of the detention, the first to be made within six hours of detention. Subsequent reviews must be at intervals of not more than nine hours.

Sections 41 and 42 of PACE provide that holding a suspect for more than 24 hours without a charge requires the approval of a person of the rank of superintendent (or above) for a further 12 hours and after that of a magistrates' court. The magistrates can approve any period provided it is not longer in total than 96 hours after which time the suspect must be charged or released. If the magistrates' permission is refused the suspect must be either charged or released at that point in time. There may, of course, be a duty to release earlier if there are not reasonable grounds under s. 37(2) of PACE for detention. There are some exceptional cases where the above rules do not apply. These are set out in s. 51 of PACE, and include terrorist offences.

Section 56 of PACE provides that when a suspect arrives at a police station he is entitled to have someone informed that he is under arrest. This is expressed to be one friend or relative, or other person who is known to him or who is likely to take an interest in his welfare. Such person must be told of the arrest without delay and of the whereabouts of the suspect.Under s. 58 of PACE a person held in custody is entitled, if he so requests, to consult a solicitor privately. However, under ss. 56 and 58, if a suspect is alleged to have committed a serious arrestable offence e.g., rape or drug trafficking, a superintendent may postpone the above rights for 36 hours. It was decided by the Court of Appeal in *R v Samuel* [1988] 2 All E.R. 135 that the right to see a *particular* solicitor can be refused if the police officer concerned has reason to believe that the solicitor will e.g. alert other suspects. Obviously this will be rare and even when it occurs the detainee must be allowed to see a different solicitor.

The latest Code of Practice under s. 66 of PACE which came into force on 1 April 1991 spells out procedures to be followed to comply with PACE. The Code states that on arrival at a police station a detained person is entitled to receive two notices of his or her rights and is entitled to see in the charging room of the police station a poster telling him or her of his or her right to legal advice.

The Notice to Detained Persons lists the three basic rights as follows –

(*a*) to speak to an independent solicitor free of charge;
(*b*) to have someone told that they have been arrested;
(*c*) to consult the Codes of Practice.

The Code makes it clear that the above are continuing rights and do not cease to exist if they are not demanded immediately upon arrival at the police station. The Notice of Entitlements summarises the provisions of Code C (Detention, Treatment and Questioning) and Code D (Identification). It also sets out entitlement to visits, a reasonable standard of physical comfort, adequate food and drink and washing facilities. The Notice also advises vulnerable groups such as juveniles and mentally disordered persons of their right to have present at e.g. interview (except in urgent cases), charging, cautioning and review an 'appropriate adult', e.g. a parent or brother. In addition there are two boxes on the custody record one of which requests a solicitor immediately and the other which has to be signed by the person in custody to say that he or she does not require a solicitor at that time. If legal advice is requested the custody officer must act immediately to get such advice for the suspect. The Code also provides that someone other than the suspect, e.g. a parent, may ask a solicitor to attend. The request for legal advice need not therefore come from the suspect.

Under s. 46 of PACE, a person who has been charged and is being held in custody must be brought before magistrates as soon as practicable, and in any event not later than the first sitting after he is charged with the offence (s. 46(2)). If no sitting is due on the day of the charge or the next day, the custody officer must inform the clerk to the justices for the area of the situation. (S. 46(3).) The clerk must then arrange for the court to sit not later than the day following the day on which he was charged. (S. 46(6).)

BAIL

(a) *By police.* Under s. 47 of PACE the custody officer (see above) must, after charges have been laid, consider whether the detention conditions (see above) apply. If not, he must order the release of the accused on bail in accordance with the Bail Act, 1976 (see below) or without bail. An accused who is not released must be brought before the magistrate as soon as practicable. (See above.)

(b) *By magistrates.* When an accused person comes before magistrates, e.g. on a preliminary hearing, the magistrates have to decide at the end of the hearing whether to remand the accused in custody, in one of the remand prisons for persons awaiting trial, or release him on bail.

Under s. 154 of the Criminal Justice Act, 1988 the magistrates are obliged to consider bail on each successive remand but *are not obliged to hear argument* in support of a bail application unless there are new circumstances or circumstances not previously brought before them. They are not obliged to review matters previously considered. They are, however, obliged to hear argument in support of bail at the first hearing and at the next if they have refused bail at the first.

A remand in custody before sentence can be for a maximum of eight days. However, under s. 59 and Sch. 9 of the Criminal Justice Act, 1982 there is no need for a court appearance every time a remand is necessary. With the consent of an accused person of 17 or over, for whom a solicitor is acting, up to three remands in custody may be made in his absence. He must be present at the fourth remand when if he consents the whole procedure can start again. The custody time limits before trial have already been considered (see p. 84).

The granting of bail is covered by the Bail Act, 1976, which is applied also to those in customs detention by s. 150 of the Criminal Justice Act, 1988. Section 4 of the 1976 Act contains a statutory presumption in favour of granting bail, though this does not apply in breach of bail cases. Under the section a person accused of crime must be granted bail unless –

(*a*) he is charged with, or convicted of, an offence which is punishable with imprisonment and the court is satisfied there are good grounds for believing that, if released on bail, he would fail to appear at a subsequent hearing or commit an offence while on bail or obstruct the course of justice by intimidating witnesses: or

(*b*) the court is satisfied that he ought to remain in custody for his own protection, or if he is a juvenile, for his own welfare; or

(*c*) there has not been enough time to obtain information about the defendant for the court to reach a decision; or

(*d*) the defendant has been convicted of an imprisonable offence and remanded for enquiries or, say, a medical report, and it seems to the court that it is not practical to complete the enquiries or make the report unless the defendant is kept in custody.

Where the defendant is charged with, or convicted of, an offence which is not punishable with imprisonment, the grounds for refusing bail are much more restricted. However, such a person can be refused bail if he has previously failed to answer bail and if the court believes, in view of that failure, that he will again fail to surrender to custody if released on bail. Conditions may be imposed on the granting of bail, e.g. the handing in of a passport or regular reporting to the police.

Section 153 of the Criminal Justice Act, 1988 provides that when the prosecution opposes bail, the court will have to give reasons for granting it where a person is charged with murder, attempted murder, manslaughter, rape or attempted rape.

As regards appeals, an unconvicted defendant can, under s. 22 of the Criminal Justice Act, 1967, appeal to a High Court judge against a refusal by the magistrates to grant bail. Under s. 60 of the Criminal Justice Act, 1982 he may, as an alternative to the High Court judge, go to a Crown Court judge in chambers for bail. Section 29 of the 1982 Act gives the Crown Court power to grant bail pending an application to the Court of Appeal for leave to appeal against sentence, or pending an appeal to that court against conviction or indictment.

Section 3 of the 1976 Act imposes a duty upon a person granted bail to surrender to custody. This duty is enforceable by the creation of the offence of absconding in s. 6. Security for surrender into custody and sureties may not be required nor conditions imposed on the grant of bail except as provided by s. 3. Thus security may be required of a defendant only if it appears likely that he will leave Great Britain. The court may ask for sureties other than the defendant to provide an additional guarantee to secure the defendant's surrender to custody. As regards conditions, the section makes it plain that these are only to be imposed to ensure the defendant's surrender to custody, that he does not commit a further offence while on bail, that he does not interfere with the course of justice, as by intimidating witnesses, and that he makes himself available for the purposes of enabling enquiries or a report to be made. The section also provides for the parent or guardian of a juvenile to stand as surety in a sum not exceeding £50 to ensure that the juvenile complies with the requirements attached to the grant of bail.

Section 6 also creates the offence of failing, without reasonable cause, to surrender at the time and place appointed. The offence is punishable in a magistrates' court by a maximum of three months' imprisonment and/or a fine, and in a superior court, such as a Crown Court, with twelve months' imprisonment and/or a fine. Section 7 provides for the arrest of a defendant who fails to surrender himself to custody at the appointed time and place or who breaches any of the conditions attched to the grant of bail.

If the court requires sureties under s. 3, then s. 8 provides for the first time in statutory form some matters which should be taken into account in deciding the suitability of sureties. The list, which is neither mandatory nor exhaustive, relates to the financial resources, character (including previous convictions) and proximity to the defendant (in terms of blood relationship, dwelling, or otherwise) of the proposed surety. In addition, the section enables a person who is not accepted as a surety to apply to a court to have the matter reconsidered. Section 9 creates the offence of agreeing at any time and regardless of whether or not a person in fact becomes a surety, to indemnify that person against his liability as a surety. Thus, if A asks B to stand as a surety for C and tells B that he (A) will pay to B any sum which B has to pay into court because C absconds, then A commits this s. 9 offence. The penalties for this offence are the same as those for the offence of absconding. No proceedings may be instituted under this section without the consent of the Director of Public Prosecutions.

Where a person who has stood surety for a defendant's bail cannot be blamed for his failure to surrender, as where the surety has not been told when the defendant was required to appear, then the surety should not forfeit his recognisance (*R* v *Reading Crown Court ex p. Bello.*, *The Times*, 10 December 1990).

Section 19 of the Legal Aid Act, 1988 provides for the granting of legal aid for defendants who wish to be represented in actions relating to whether they are entitled to bail or not.

The three major weakneses of the Act are as follows –

(*a*) it does not place any duty on the court to find out the defendant's personal circumstances so that there continues to be the risk that the court will hear only the police view on the bail/custody issue.

(*b*) it does not deal with the duration of remands in custody. Remands in custody are frequently made because of a police objection to bail on the basis that there are further police enquiries to be made. There are those who think that this should not stand as a distinct ground for refusing bail and that the court should question the police more closely when they object to bail on these grounds. However, the Act makes no reference to this problem.

(*c*) that the court is not required to hear argument in favour of bail at each remand hearing (see further p. 88).

Before leaving the subject of bail, the provision of bail hostels is worthy of consideration. These hostels, which are provided by the probation service, give an accused person an address so that he need not necessarily be remanded in custody because he has no fixed abode, which is still a ground under s. 1(4) of the Magistrates' Courts Act, 1980, though persons of no fixed abode are not bound to be refused bail. The Secretary of State is given power to approve bail hostels and to provide a system of inspection under s. 49 of the Powers of Criminal Courts Act, 1973 (as amended by the Criminal Justice Act, 1982, Schs. 11 and 16). Before this statutory measure there were only a limited number of such hostels provided by voluntary organisations.

On granting bail the court may impose a condition that the defendant reside at a bail hostel and abide by its rules so that a remand in custody can result if the defendant misbehaves (s. 131, Criminal Justice Act, 1988, amending s. 3 of the Bail Act, 1976).

Summary trial before magistrates (other than in a Youth Court)

Since the majority of summary trials before magistrates relate to motoring offences, such an offence has been chosen as an example of the form of summary trial.

THE ALLEGED OFFENCE

Let us suppose that on 29 March 1992, Freda Jones was driving her car along George Road, Barchester and that her attention was distracted by the sun so that she ran into the back of a stationary delivery van which was parked at the kerbside in an area where there were no parking restrictions.

THE SUMMONS

The police are intending to bring a prosecution against Freda under the Road Traffic Act, 1988, for careless and inconsiderate driving. Freda will receive a summons as follows.

BARCHESTER MAGISTRATES' COURT

To Freda Jones

12 Acacia Avenue, Barchester, Barchestershire.

You are hereby summoned to appear on 7 June 1992 at 2.00 p.m. before the Magistrates' Court at 14 High Street, Barchester to answer to the following information laid on 29 March 1992 that you at George Road, Barchester, did drive a motor vehicle without due care and attention contrary to s. 3 and Schs. 1 and 2 of the Road Traffic Act, 1988.

Informant	Police Constable Peter Green
Address	Barchester Police Station
Date	3 April 1992
Signed	J. Bloggs
	Justices' Clerk

STATEMENT OF FACTS

IF YOU INFORM THE CLERK of the Court that you wish to plead guilty to the offence set out in the summons above, without appearing before the Court, and the Court proceeds to hear and dispose of the case in your absence under s. 12 of the Magistrates' Courts Act, 1980, the following Statement of Facts will be read out in open Court before the Court decides whether to accept your plea. If your plea of guilty is accepted the Court will not, unless it adjourns the case after convicting you and before sentencing you, permit any other statement to be made by or on behalf of the prosecutor with respect to any facts relating to the offence.

On 29 March 1992 at 10.00 hours you were the driver of Mini Metro FEY 856Y travelling north on George Road, Barchester. On approaching the junction with Marks Road you collided with a Ford delivery van C113 PJC which was parked at the kerbside. When asked by the Police Reporting Officer what had happened you said: 'I had the sun in my eyes. I did not see the van.'

Signed Peter Green
(on behalf of the Prosecutor)

Freda will be advised that under s. 7 of the Road Traffic Act, 1988 her driving licence must be at the Court by the date of the hearing and that failure to comply could lead to the suspension of the licence and a fine.

Freda is unlikely to get legal aid for a lawyer to defend her. Many magistrates are reluctant to give legal aid in motoring offences. This contrasts with persons pleading not guilty in the Crown Court. They are likely to get legal aid whatever the offence.

THE TRIAL

Freda could plead guilty by letter since the offence is summary only and the maximum sentence is not more than three months' imprisonment (s. 12,

Magistrates' Courts Act, 1980). In fact it is punishable only by a fine. If Freda does plead guilty by letter she must under s. 8 of the Road Traffic Act, 1988 give notification of her date of birth and sex. However, on the assumption that Freda is to attend court and plead not guilty, the main aspects of the procedure is as set out below.

The charge. Freda appears in answer to the summons and the first thing that happens is that the Clerk to the Magistrates identifies Freda as the defendant and then reads out the offence with which she is charged.

Election to trial by jury. This does not arise in Freda's case because the offence of careless and inconsiderate driving under s. 3 of the Road Traffic Act, 1988 cannot be tried on indictment before a jury. If, however, the police had decided to charge her with reckless driving under s. 2 of the Road Traffic Act, 1988, the question of trial on indictment would have arisen because the offence is triable either way.

Attendance of defendant. We shall assume that Freda having refused to plead not guilty by letter will actually attend court to plead not guilty. If she does not and has not given a reasonable explanation for her absence the matter may be heard without her attending. If there is a reasonable explanation the case is adjourned.

Freda's plea. Since Freda's case will be dealt with summarily by the magistrates, the clerk will ask her whether she pleads guilty or not guilty. If Freda pleads guilty such a plea in itself constitutes a conviction and the magistrates have the power to sentence her without hearing evidence, though they also have the power to decide that even on a guilty plea it is desirable in the circumstances to hear evidence on oath.

The prosecution's case. Since we know that Freda will plead not guilty, the prosecution will have to prove its case. If the prosecution opens the case the prosecutor will give a brief outline of the facts and a brief summary of the law particularly if a technical defence is expected. He will then call his witnesses and ask questions of them (called examination-in-chief). It is then open to Freda or her solicitor to cross-examine the witnesses for the prosecution and the prosecution may re-examine them.

The defence. When the case for the prosecution has been presented the defence may –

(*a*) submit that there is no case to answer; or
(*b*) proceed to open the case for the defence.

The choice in (*a*) above could be taken where, for example, the prosecution has failed to establish a main ingredient of the offence, or where the prosecution's evidence is so weak that the court could not reasonably convict Freda on it. Freda's solicitor may support his submission of no case to answer by a speech in which he may draw the attention of the court to inconsistencies and omissions in the prosecution's case. Since these are matters of law the prosecution may reply.

The court will then consider the submission and may retire in order to do so. Should the court accept the submission the case is dismissed. If they find that there is a case to answer then the defence proceeds. On the assumption that the court does not accept the submission of no case to answer, oral evidence is given by witnesses for the defence and by the defendant, who are in turn examined by the prosecution and may be re-examined by the defence. The defence may make the closing speech provided that the defence has not opened the case which the defence rarely does because then the right to make a closing speech is lost. The prosecution does not make a closing speech as such but may reply on disputed points of law raised by the defence in the closing speech.

Decision and sentence. When the case for the defence is closed the court must consider whether to convict the defendant or dismiss the information. The court decides by a majority and lay justices do not normally give reasons for their findings, though some stipendiaries do. There is no need for unanimity and if magistrates are equally divided a new trial is ordered. The justices may ask their clerk to give them advice privately on matters of law (and see *R* v *Uxbridge Justices ex p. Smith,* 1985 at p. 20), but they must not ask for or listen to the views of the clerk on issues of fact, and it is certainly improper for them to ask the clerk to retire with them when no issues of law arise in the case.

If the magistrates decide to convict they will then enquire whether the accused has any previous convictions or breaches of court orders recorded against her and may hear both the prosecution and the defence as to her character. The defendant may ask the court to take into account other offences with which he has not been charged but wishes to confess to and be sentenced for. This does not arise in Freda's case. The defence may also address the court in what is called mitigation. This could consist, for example, of an address outlining the defendant's domestic stress, perhaps in Freda's case, that her boyfriend had recently been severely injured in a road accident. The court will then decide upon the sentence and announce it. Once the court has done this, or has dismissed the summons, it will not normally change its decision. However, as we have seen, magistrates' courts are given the power to re-open a case to rectify a mistake in any order they have made within 14 days. The court on the second occasion must be constituted in the same way as it was on the first occasion or with a majority of the same justices. This procedure could be used, for example, where the magistrates had omitted to order the endorsement of a defendant's driving licence. (See also p. 27.)

If Freda's defence has failed, the magistrates can fine her. They have a discretion as to whether to disqualify her from driving, though an endorsement of her licence is obligatory (Road Traffic Offenders Act, 1988, Sch. 2). Freda may also be ordered to make a contribution to the legal costs.

Proceedings in relation to children and young persons

Those aged ten and under 17 *who are charged with a criminal offence* appear before a youth court as either a child (if aged ten to 14) or a young person (if over 14 and under 18). Minors under ten years of age are by presumption of law incapable of any crime (see further p. 550).

In addition to criminal proceedings in youth courts, there are *care proceedings* which may be brought in Family Proceeding Courts (see also p. 26) by the officers of a local authority or other authorised persons, for example, an inspector of the National Society for the Prevention of Cruelty to Children.

CARE AND SUPERVISION PROCEEDINGS

These may be brought because a minor of any age up to 17 is thought to be in some sort of trouble, as where he is e.g. beyond the control of parents or guardians.

Care orders

Section 31 of the Children Act, 1989 makes provision for care and supervision orders (see below) replacing earlier statutory provisions. There is now one ground for the making of such orders in a Family Proceedings Court or other court (see below). It is that the child concerned is suffering or is likely to suffer significant harm and that the harm is attributable to the care being given to the child that care not being what it would be reasonable to expect a parent to give him; or that the child is beyond parental control. An order may be made on its own or as part of any family proceedings in the High Court, the County Court or a Magistrates' Court. No care or supervision order may be made in regard to a child who has reached 17 or 16 if the child is married.

Section 33 sets out the effect of a care order. In particular the local authority is given parental responsibility but cannot e.g. agree to an adoption or impose a change of religion. Section 23 puts a duty on the local authority to provide accommodation and to maintain the children in its care.

Under s. 34 the local authority must allow the child reasonable contact with its parents or guardian. This may be refused for up to seven days if it is necessary to safeguard or promote the child's welfare.

Supervision orders

Where a supervision order is made, s. 35 sets out the duties of the supervisor while the order is in force. There is, in particular, a duty to advise, assist and befriend the child. Schedule 3, Parts I and II contain further provisions including the duration of the order. Initially this is one year but this may be extended by the court on the application of the supervisor to give up to a total of three years from the date it was made. Children will in the main be supervised by local authority social workers.

Education supervision orders

Section 36 allows the court to make an education supervision order on the application of a local education authority where a child is not being properly educated. This means that he is not receiving efficient full-time education suitable to his age, ability and aptitude including any special educational needs he may have. These orders which put the child under the supervision of the local education authority are the usual order for non-attendance at school. They cannot be made in regard to a child in the care of a local authority. Schedule 3, Part III provides that the duration of these orders is initially one year. They may be extended by the court on the application of the supervisor but *each* extension is limited to a maximum of three years. The order expires when the child ceases to be of compulsory school age or a care order is made in respect of him.

Interim orders

The court may under s. 38 make interim care or supervision orders where it feels that the problems currently affecting the child will be overcome in the near future. An interim order lasts for a maximum of eight weeks but the court may make further orders *each* for a maximum of four weeks.

Discharge of orders

Section 39 allows the court to discharge or vary care and supervision orders.

Care and supervision orders in criminal proceedings

Section 90 abolishes care orders in criminal proceedings but allows supervision orders to be made with a requirement that the child reside in local authority accommodation for a maximum of six months.

CRIMINAL PROCEEDINGS

Under the Criminal Justice Acts, 1982 and 1988, persons under 21 years of age found guilty of a criminal offence in a youth court if under 18, or in a magistrates' or Crown Court if between 18 and 21, *cannot be sent to prison for any offence.* The possibilities open to the court are fines and the following –

(*a*) *A community sentence* by means of a community order. This includes a probation order, a curfew order, a supervision order and an attendance centre order (see further p. 117).

(*b*) *A custodial sentence.* Subject to what is said at (*d*) below, there is only one custodial sentence for young offenders, i.e. detention in a Young Offenders Institution. The sentence is available for males and females who are under 21 but not less than 15. (Criminal Justice Act, 1991, s. 62.) The minimum period of detention is, for males and females under 21 but not less than 18, a period of 21 days, and in the case of males and females under 18, a period of two months. A court cannot pass a custodial sentence exceeding twelve months on an offender aged 15, 16 or 17, and if the offence committed attracts a sentence of more than that the excess is to be treated as remitted (s. 62, 1991 Act). In general terms a court should not impose this custodial sentence unless it is satisfied that in the circumstances there is no other way of dealing with the offender.

(*c*) *Attendance centre orders.* These require a young offender to spend a specific number of hours (up to a maximum of 24 in all) at an attendance centre, usually on a Saturday afternoon. The regime is one of vigorous exercise and instruction in recreational activities.

(*d*) *Crimes attracting imprisonment for life.* Under s. 8 of the Criminal Justice Act, 1982 a person under 21 who is convicted of an offence for which the sentence is fixed by law as imprisonment for life such as murder and manslaughter must be sentenced to custody for life, though a child or young person under 18 who is convicted of murder must be detained during Her Majesty's pleasure. (Children and Young Persons Act, 1933, s. 53(1).) A person aged 18 or over but under 21 who is convicted of any other offence carrying up to life imprisonment, e.g. robbery under s. 8 of the Theft Act, 1968, may be sentenced to custody for life.

A criminal trial of a person under 21 in a youth court or a magistrates' or higher court, as appropriate, proceeds in the usual way with the prosecution opening its case and witnesses being examined-in-chief and cross-examined. Then the case for the defence is presented and the magistrates retire to make a decision. If they decide that the young person is guilty his previous convictions, if any, are made known to the court.

However, as is the case with all custodial sentences the court must first obtain and consider a pre-sentence report (see further p. 115).

There are statutory powers to fine young offenders and to order payment by a parent or guardian, unless e.g. it would be unreasonable to do so, as where the offender's finances are better than those of the parent or guardian.

APPEARANCE IN ADULT COURTS

Sometimes a person under 18 may appear in an adult court. The circumstances are as follows –

(*a*) when the young person is charged jointly with a person over 18 and the magistrates think they should be tried together, as where they are members of a gang;

(*b*) when a child or young person is charged, for example, with murder or some other serious offence, he will be sent for trial to the Crown Court. Possible sentences have already been considered.

RESPONSIBILITIES OF PARENTS AND GUARDIANS

Where a child or young person is charged with an offence or is for any other reason brought before a court the court may in any case and must in the case of a child or young person under the age of 16 require a person who is a parent or guardian of his to attend at the court during all stages of the proceedings unless the court is satisfied that it would be unreasonable to require such attendance in the circumstances of the case (s. 34A Children and Young Persons Act, 1933 as inserted by the Criminal Justice Act, 1991 s. 55).

Under s. 55 of the Children and Young Persons Act, 1933 (as amended by the Criminal Justice Act, 1991) the court has a power to order a parent or guardian to pay a fine instead of the child or young person.

Under s. 57 of the 1991 Act where the offender has not reached the age of 16 years the court has a *duty* to exercise its *power* to require the offender's parent or guardian to enter into a recognisance (i.e. be bound over) to take proper care of him. The parent or guardian's consent is required but if this is unreasonably refused the parent or guardian can be ordered to pay a fine not exceeding £1000. The amount of the recognisance which is forfeited if the recognisance is broken is limited to £1000. The undertaking lasts for a maximum of three years or until the offender reaches 18 if this is sooner. The parent or guardian has an appeal to the Crown Court from a magistrates' order or to the Court of Appeal from a Crown Court order. The court also has power to vary or revoke the order on the application of the parent or guardian. The court has power (not a duty) to carry out the above procedures where the offender is 16 or over. If it does not exercise its duty in regard to offenders under 16 it must state in open court why it has not.

DETENTION PENDING TRIAL AND REMANDS

Sections 58 and 59 of the Criminal Justice Act, 1991 make amendments to PACE and the Children and Young Persons Act, 1969 under which in general terms arrested juveniles should be detained in secure local authority accommodation rather than a police station pending trial and if remanded should be remanded to local authority secure accommodation and not to a prison.

SUPERVISION OF YOUNG OFFENDERS AFTER RELEASE

Under s. 64 of the Criminal Justice Act, 1991 where a person is released from a term of detention in a young offenders institution or under s. 53 of the Children and Young Persons Act, 1933 (see p. 97) he must come under the supervision of a probation officer or a social worker of a local authority social services department if he is under the age of 22 years. The supervision period ends three months after release or on reaching 22 whichever is the sooner.

Trial on indictment in the Crown Court

Persons appearing in the Crown Court for trial on indictment have committed rather serious offences. They will have appeared before a magistrates' court and been committed for trial by that court after a preliminary hearing in which the prosecution has made out a *prima facie* case against the person accused. That is, the prosecution has shown that there is sufficient evidence against the accused to make a full trial necessary.

Before the preliminary hearing the accused will no doubt have appeared before the magistrates and may have been remanded. Issues of bail or no bail will have been decided and the accused will have been instructed how to apply for legal aid and given the necessary form. The usefulness of the duty solicitor at this stage has already been described. (See p. 21.)

Legal aid

Legal aid in criminal proceedings is given only to those charged with offences and is not available to persons wishing to bring a prosecution.

The criteria for granting legal aid include cases involving complex points of law or where the defendant has language difficulties. The most important, however, is whether a defendant is at serious risk of losing his liberty, his job, or his reputation. A very large percentage of those appearing before the Crown Court get legal aid. Many of those who appear before magistrates are not legally represented.

Reporting of committal proceedings

In general, the only evidence given at committal proceedings is by the prosecution, the accused merely reserving his defence for the actual trial. If full reporting of committal proceedings was allowed, the accused could be prejudiced because by the time his trial occurred the general public, including probably the jury, would have read only one side of the case and might have reached the conclusion that the accused was guilty. However, this need not happen because under s. 8(4) of the Magistrates' Courts Act, 1980, newspaper, television and radio reports of committal proceedings are restricted to the following matters –

(*a*) the name of the court and the names of the justices;
(*b*) the names, addresses, ages and occupations of the prosecutor, defendants, and witnesses;
(*c*) the offences under consideration;
(*d*) the names of the advocates;

(e) the decision of the court;

(f) where a committal is ordered, the charges involved;

(g) the name of the higher court to which the committal is ordered;

(h) in the case of an adjournment, the date and place to which the hearing is adjourned;

(i) any order as to bail and whether or not legal aid was granted.

On conviction for an offence against the above provisions, editors and publishers of newspapers and periodicals, together with their counterparts in the field of broadcasting, are liable to a maximum fine not exceeding £5000. (Magistrates' Courts Act, 1980, s. 8(5)(c).)

Under s. 8(2) of the Magistrates' Courts Act, 1980, as amended by the Criminal Justice (Amendment) Act, 1981, where there are two or more accused and one objects to the making of an order by the magistrates lifting the reporting restrictions, then the magistrates must hear representations which any of the accused may wish to make and will make an order lifting the restrictions if, and only if, satisfied that it is in the interests of justice to do so. In fact when an application is made to lift reporting restrictions all the co-defendants should be present and allowed to make representations. (R v Wirral Magistrates' Court ex parte Meikle, The Times, 30 May 1990.) In general terms, the reasons for lifting reporting restrictions must have some relevance to the issue to be considered at the trial, such as the prejudice of the police against the accused and not, as in R v Leeds Justices, ex parte Sykes [1983] 1 All E.R. 460, because an accused person wishes to give publicity to the conduct of the police who at first said they would not bring charges for conspiracy to rob but later decided to do so. There was no evidence of police prejudice in that conduct.

There is no restriction on reporting if the magistrates decide not to commit for trial. After the trial of the defendant (or the last if there is more than one defendant) reporters can mention in detail matters raised in committal proceedings.

When a preliminary hearing changes into a summary trial reporters can report fully the committal proceedings which took place before the summary trial.

Liability may be incurred under the Magistrates' Courts Act, 1980, where a report of committal proceedings contains *any* details other than those permitted by s. 8(4) (above), and quite irrespective of whether or not the details are potentially prejudicial in nature. This distinguishes the s. 8(4) offence from the offence of contempt of court under the Contempt of Court Act, 1981. If there is to be a contempt, the material published must be likely to be prejudicial to a fair trial. The reporting of *trials*, as distinct from *committal proceedings*, is governed by the Contempt of Court Act, 1981. (See further p. 112.) However, s. 4 of the Contempt of Court Act, 1981 makes it clear, for the avoidance of doubt, that no action for contempt can be brought against those who comply with s. 8 of the 1980 Act.

> **ESSENTIAL CASE LAW AND COMMENT**
>
> *The Eastbourne Herald Case*, 1973 – Criminal proceedings:
> excessive reporting **(20)**

Alibi

Section 11 of the Criminal Justice Act, 1967, is designed to prevent the use of 'sprung' or late alibis which were once so widespread in criminal trials. The section provides that, in general, notice of alibi must be given in advance of a trial on indictment. This is not required in summary trials because of the ease with which the prosecution can ask for an adjournment where the defendant 'springs' an alibi on the prosecution at the last moment.

The following warning (or one similar to it) must be given during the course of committal proceedings, usually by the clerk.

> You must understand that at your trial you will not be allowed to give evidence in support of an alibi which means that you were somewhere else when the offence was committed unless you have given notice to the solicitor for the prosecution giving the particulars of the alibi. You can either give those particulars now or send them to the solicitor for the prosecution within the next seven days. The solicitor for the prosecution is (name).

Although this warning need not be given if it seems unnecessary having regard to the nature of the offence charged, it should as a general rule be given where there is any doubt, because the Act provides that failure to give it will allow the defendant to introduce a last-minute alibi at his trial. Where an unrepresented defendant does not appear to understand what is meant by 'alibi', the word must be explained to him.

There is a discretion in the trial judge to allow alibi evidence to be heard even though particulars of it were not given within seven days, provided the prosecution has been given time to investigate the alibi before the trial started. (*R v Sullivan* [1970] 2 All E.R. 681.) It is unusual for the defence to give notice of an alibi at the committal proceedings.

Place and time of trial

Under s. 7 of the Magistrates' Courts Act, 1980, a magistrates' court committing a person to trial on indictment to the Crown Court has to specify the Crown Court centre at which he is to be tried and in selecting that centre must have regard to –

(*a*) the convenience of the defence, the prosecution and the witnesses;

(*b*) the expediting of the trial;

(*c*) any directions regarding the distribution of Crown Court business given by the Lord Chief Justice or by an officer of the Crown Court with the concurrence of the Lord Chancellor under the Supreme Court Act, 1981.

Under s. 76 of the Supreme Court Act, 1981 the Crown Court may alter the place of any trial on indictment by varying the decision of the magistrates or a previous decision on the matter made by the Crown Court. Under the 1981 Act the defendant or the prosecutor, if dissatisfied with the place of trial as fixed by the magistrates or by the Crown Court, may apply to the Crown Court to vary the place of trial. The Crown Court may deal with the application as it sees fit. An application under the 1981 Act must be heard in open court by a High Court judge.

The above provisions are designed to bring an accused person to trial as quickly as possible. However, the prosecutor and the accused and his advisers must be given time in which to prepare the case properly. Accordingly, s. 77 of the Supreme Court Act, 1981 (as amended) provides for the laying down under Crown Court Rules of the minimum period from the date of committal when the trial shall commence. These minimum periods cannot be *shortened* without the consent of the accused and the prosecutor or *lengthened* without an order of the Crown Court.

The offence and indictment

Let us suppose that Jim Green has recently and successfully objected to the granting of planning permission to Fred Brown, his neighbour, which has prevented Fred from using part of his land for car-breaking. Let us also suppose that on the evening of 25 February 1992, Jim left home for work and shortly afterwards in a lane not far from his home he was attacked by Fred who was wearing a black balaclava over his head. Fred attacked Jim with a knife. Jim suffered serious injuries requiring five stitches in his cheek, six on his right hand, and 16 in his stomach. Jim was detained in hospital for several days.

Fred is now to be tried on indictment for the offence. An indictment is a printed accusation of crime made at the suit of the Queen and read out to the accused at the trial. In Fred's case the main contents of the indictment will state the court of trial and set out the following –

Fred Brown is charged as follows –

Statement of Offence – WOUNDING contrary to s. 18 of the Offences Against the Person Act, 1861.

Particulars of Offence – Fred Brown on 25 February 1992, in the

County of Barchestershire, wounded Jim Green with intent to cause grievous bodily harm.

In this case there is only one offence but if there had been more each would have appeared in a separate paragraph. Each paragraph is referred to as a 'count'.

There may be a motion by the defence to quash the indictment. This is quite rare because such a motion is appropriate only where there is an error apparent on the face of the indictment. A possible ground to quash the indictment is that a count set out in it is bad for duplicity, as where assault and theft are charged in the same count.

Arraignment

When the day of Fred's trial arrives the clerk of the court will confirm Fred's identity, read out the indictment and ask Fred whether he is guilty or not guilty. This is called the arraignment.

If Fred pleads guilty counsel for the prosecution will give the court a summary of the evidence together with details of Fred's background and record. The defence will put in a plea for mitigation of sentence and sentence will then be passed.

Fred may, while intending to plead 'not guilty' to the s. 18 offence, be prepared to plead 'guilty' to a lesser offence which is not on the indictment. In this case Fred may be prepared to plead guilty to unlawful wounding under s. 20 of the Offences Against the Person Act, 1861. This carries a maximum period of five years' imprisonment, whereas the s. 18 offence carries a maximum term of imprisonment for life. This change of plea may arise because of a bargain reached between Fred's lawyer and the prosecution's lawyer, often with the judge's approval. This is known as 'plea-bargaining'.

If the prosecution refuses to accept the plea to the lesser offence then the trial will continue and if Fred is acquitted he cannot be sentenced on the basis of his guilty plea to the lesser offence (*R* v *Hazeltine* [1967] 2 All E.R. 671) which is regarded as withdrawn if not accepted by the prosecution. It should be noted that a trial judge may allow a defendant to change his plea to not guilty at any time before sentence is passed, even though a formal verdict of guilty has been returned by the jury on the direction of the judge after the trial has begun (*R* v *Drew* [1985] 1 WLR 914).

Some persons may of course be too mentally disordered to plead at all. This is referred to as 'unfitness to plead' and is further considered at p. 551.

We will assume that Fred pleads not guilty and in this case a jury must be sworn in.

Jury trial

THE MEMBERSHIP OF THE JURY

Under the Juries Act, 1974, a person is eligible for jury service if he or she is not less than 18 and not more than 70 and is included on the Register of Electors for parliamentary and/or local government elections, and has been resident in the United Kingdom, the Channel Islands, or the Isle of Man for at least five years since the age of 13. As regards exemptions and qualifications, these include members of the judiciary, those concerned with the administration of justice, such as barristers and solicitors, police and prison officers, the clergy, and persons receiving treatment for mental illness. The 1974 Act makes it an offence for anyone in these categories to serve as a juror. In addition, penalties are imposed upon persons who are eligible and have been duly summoned but fail to attend or are unfit through drink or drugs. Under the Juries Act, 1974, anyone imprisoned for more than three months and up to five years is disqualified for jury service for ten years, and anyone imprisoned for a term of over five years or for life is disqualified for life. Nevertheless, under the 1974 Act criminals could sit on juries. For example, those put on probation were not barred. However, the Juries (Disqualification) Act, 1984 disqualifies from jury service anyone who has served a custodial sentence of any kind or has had such a sentence suspended, or has been put on probation or placed under a community service order. The disqualification period is ten years, but only five years for those placed on probation. Those punished by fines can, of course, still sit on a jury.

Certain persons, although not ineligible for jury service, can if asked to serve, claim to be excused 'as of right'. These include members of Parliament, full-time serving members of H.M. Forces, those in medical or similar professions and persons between the ages of 65 and 70. In addition, the 1974 Act provides that a person summoned for jury service may be excused for good reasons whether he is in one of the special classes or not. For example a potential juror may appeal to the court to be excused on the basis of a conscientious objection to serving on a jury (*R* v *Guildford Crown Court ex parte Siderfin* [1989] 3 All E.R. 73).

The Act also provides for exemptions to be granted administratively for prior jury service; previously only the trial judge could grant exemption. Under s. 5 of the Juries Act, 1974 the defence has a right to see the names, and in London the addresses as well, of the jury panel. This could assist 'jury nobbling' but it remains a right at the present time.

As regards summoning and excusal, each summons for jury service is accompanied by details of the provisions for eligibility, disqualifications, and excusals as of right. A person receiving a summons will be asked to complete a form telling the court whether he or she is qualified for jury service and, if so, whether it is the person's wish to be excused either 'as of right' or for any other reason, e.g. because of personal circumstances, such as a mother with very young children, or a person running a one-man business. Much depends upon the Clerk of the Court; some are more difficult than others in terms of the acceptance of personal reasons for not serving.

Under s. 61 of the Administration of Justice Act, 1982 questions may be put to a prospective juror to ascertain whether he is qualified for jury service *at any time,* and not just when he attends following a jury summons. If a juror refuses without reasonable excuse to answer, or knowingly or recklessly gives a false answer to the questions which are customarily set out in the jury summons, he will commit an offence punishable with a fine. This applies also to a juror who pretends to have a disqualification which he does not have in order to try to avoid jury service.

As regards disabilities, the 1974 Act provides that the court may also exclude anyone from jury service because physical disability or insufficient understanding of English makes his ability to act effectively as a juror doubtful. However, s. 18 provides that no judgment after verdict should be reversed by reason, amongst other things, that any juror was unqualified or unfit to serve. Thus in *R* v *Chapman* (1976) 63 Cr. App. R. 75 where, after a trial at which both defendants had been found guilty by a unanimous verdict, it was discovered that one juror had been deaf so that he was unable to follow the proceedings, it was held that that did not make the verdict unsafe or unsatisfactory and was a situation covered by the Juries Act, 1974, s. 18. However, a judge has a discretion *to discharge* a juror *during the trial,* e.g. for bias, as where on a charge of shoplifting from a store a juror reveals that she is employed by that store (*R* v *Morris, The Times,* 24 January 1991).

Under s. 3 of the 1974 Act the responsibility for summoning jurors is placed upon the Lord Chancellor, though the court's administration at each centre acts as summoning officer. Juries are paid travelling and subsistence allowances and are compensated for loss of earnings and other expenses.

ADVANTAGES AND DISADVANTAGES OF JURY TRIAL

Some take the view that the verdict of a jury is more acceptble to the public than the verdict of a judge, and certainly the jury system gives ordinary persons a part to play in the administration of justice. It is perhaps better that lay men and women should decide matter of fact and the credibility of witnesses. The jury system also tends to clarify the law, in that the judge has to explain the more important points arising at the trial in clear and simple terms, so that the jury may arrive at a proper verdict.

On the other hand, juries may be too easily swayed by experienced advocates and the random method of selection sometimes produces a jury which is not as competent in intellectual terms as it might be in weighing the evidence and following the arguments presented. It has been suggested that trial by (say) three judges would be better, particularly where difficult issues are involved.

All indictable offences are triable before a jury of twelve persons. A panel of more than twelve jurors is brought into court and the clerk will select twelve jurors by a ballot.

CHALLENGE

The names of the jury as selected by the clerk's ballot are called out on selection and each person goes into the jury box to be sworn. Under s. 110 of the Criminal Justice Act, 1988 the right to challenge jurors without cause (reasons), in proceedings for the trial of a person on indictment, is abolished.

Now a challenge must be supported by reasons. The defence may, before a potential juror is sworn, say 'Challenge for cause' in order e.g. to challenge the inclusion of a man who has published anti-semitic articles where the defendant is of the Jewish faith. The cause should not be stated in the presence of the potential juror and the other potential jurors who are waiting to be sworn: they should be excluded from the court while the matter is argued before the judge. Jurors may also be challenged because they know the defendant.

The prosecution can also challenge for cause. However, they have, in effect, a right to challenge without cause under the 'stand by' procedure. The prosecution may call on a juror to 'stand by for the Crown', i.e. to be excluded unless it is impossible for a jury to be empanelled without calling on him. In practice they are not called again. This right should not be used to ensure a pro-prosecution jury.

JURY VETTING

Following judicial decisions, particularly perhaps that of the Court of Appeal in R v Mason [1980] 3 All E.R. 777, that it was not only lawful but necessary and a 'commonsense' precaution, for the police to vet jurors' criminal records and pass information to the prosecution so that challenge could be made, the Attorney-General has issued guidelines on jury checks. In the first place the guidelines state that a person will in general be disqualified or ineligible for a jury only as provided by the Juries Act, 1974 and the Juries (Disqualification) Act, 1984. However, where the case involves national security and part of the evidence is likely to be heard *in camera* (i.e. the court closed to the public and the news media), or in terrorist cases, extra precautions may be necessary. However, no check on the records of police special branches will be made except on the authority of the Attorney-General following a recommendation from the D.P.P. Furthermore, checks involving so-called strong political motives will not be made except in terrorist cases or where national security is involved and the court is expected to sit *in camera*. There is, of course, no reason why routine police checks on criminal records for the purpose of ascertaining whether or not a jury panel includes any person disqualified under the Juries Act, 1974 should not continue.

It was held in R v Ford [1989] 3 All E.R. 445 that fairness in the composition of a jury was best achieved by random selection and a trial judge had no power to interfere with the make up of a jury in order to get a racially mixed jury on the trial of a black defendant charged with reckless driving.

THE OATH

The twelve persons who survive the selection procedure are then sworn, by each holding a Bible in his right hand and reading the following oath –

I swear by Almighty God that I will faithfully try the defendant and give a true verdict according to the evidence.

The affirmation which jurors may select if non-Christian is as follows –

I do solemnly, and sincerely and truly declare and affirm that I will faithfully try the defendant and give a true verdict according to the evidence.

All jurors must take the oath in the presence of each other. The jury is then addressed by the clerk who explains the charges and tells them that having heard the evidence they must decide whether the defendant is guilty or not, and the trial begins officially at this point (*R* v *Tonner* [1985] 1 All E.R. 807).

JUROR PERSONATION

It may be that a person who receives a jury summons will get someone to stand in for them. This is known as juror personation and there are legal consequences. A notice is included in all jury summonses. It says –

Impersonation of Jurors: It is an offence for any person to impersonate a juror and serve on a jury on his or her behalf. As a matter of routine, court staff may need to verify the identity of a juror. Those attending for jury service are therefore requested to have with them some form of personal identification.

THE JUDGE

Criminal offences are divided into four classes for the purpose of trial in a Crown Court. In broad terms the position is that *Class 1* offences, e.g. murder, treason and spying, are tried by a High Court judge. *Class 2* offences, e.g. manslaughter, rape, infanticide and sexual intercourse with a girl under 13, are tried by a High Court judge unless a particular case is released as suitable for a circuit judge by or on the authority of the Circuit Presiding Judge (see p. 81) as where the circumstances of the offence are not of unusual gravity. *Class 3* offences, i.e. all indictable offences other than those in Classes 1, 2 and 4, e.g. arson, perjury, corruption of Government or local government officers, may be tried by a High Court judge or a circuit judge or recorder. *Class 4* offences are all offences which are triable summarily or on indictment, e.g. reckless driving, plus certain others, e.g. causing death by reckless driving, burglary and wounding or causing grievous bodily harm with intent. These may be tried by a High Court judge but will normally be listed for trial by a circuit judge or recorder, or assistant recorder.

Thus it is likely that Fred will be tried by a circuit judge or recorder, or assistant recorder.

TRIAL AND EVIDENCE

The advocate appearing for the prosecution will make an opening speech outlining the case to the Court and will then call witnesses to confirm the facts. However, before doing so he must tell the jury that the burden of proof rests on the prosecution to establish that the defendant is guilty beyond a reasonable doubt. A witness will first take the oath appropriate to his religion or affirm if he has no religious belief. The Christian oath is most often used. It is: 'I swear by Almighty God that the evidence I shall give shall be the truth, the whole truth and nothing but the truth'. Contrary to popular belief it does not end with 'so help me God'.

During the examination-in-chief, counsel for the prosecution must not lead his witnesses, i.e. must not suggest a particular answer to his question. Thus counsel for the prosecution cannot ask one of his witnesses, say, a police officer, 'Did the defendant punch you when you arrested him?' He must instead say, 'What happened when you arrested the defendant?'

Also, in examination-in-chief counsel must not contradict his own witness by referring to a prior inconsistent statement made in, say, committal proceedings, unless the witness becomes 'hostile', i.e. as where he is now showing bias against the person calling him. In addition hearsay evidence is not admissible. A witness must give evidence only as to what he himself saw or heard. Thus evidence given by a witness either for the prosecution or the defence in the form: 'Alice told me that she saw Bill in the pub on Wednesday' would be inadmissible.

After counsel for the prosecution has carried out his examination-in-chief of a witness counsel for the defence can cross-examine the witness. In this situation he can lead and say, for example, 'My client was upset by the circumstances of his arrest, wasn't he? There was no need to have called him a lying swine, was there?' Counsel for the prosecution can also refer to prior inconsistent statements of the witness.

When the prosecution has called all its witnesses the defence will present its case and call witnesses to support it. These witnesses are examined-in-chief, cross-examined, and sometimes re-examined. More rarely, defence counsel may, before calling his witnesses, try to bring the trial to an end by endeavouring to persuade the judge that there is no case to answer, e.g. that the prosecution has not produced sufficient evidence to warrant the trial proceeding. This argument takes place without the jury. If the judge agrees with defence counsel he will call the jury back and tell them to give a formal acquittal. Otherwise the trial proceeds.

The defendant may give evidence on oath or by affirmation on his own behalf, though he is not obliged to give evidence at all. Section 72 of the Criminal Justice Act, 1982 abolishes the right of an accused person to make an unsworn statement from the dock without being subject to cross-examination. However, the accused may address the court or jury if he has no legal representation and may make a statement in mitigation of sentence without being sworn. If he gives evidence on oath in the ordinary way he may be cross-examined but there can be no cross-examination where a mere statement is made, though the making of a statement in this way often leads to the suggestion that the defendant has something to hide.

After the defence witnesses have been heard the prosecution makes its closing speech, followed by the defence, which always has the last word. (Criminal Procedure (Right of Reply) Act, 1964.)

SUMMING UP

The judge will then explain his role to the jury. He will say that he will tell them what the law is and that the law is a matter for him but that they are the only judges of the facts in the case. He will repeat that it is for the prosecution to prove guilt. The judge will then sum up the evidence on both sides and will define the law of the offence. If he misleads the jury on this the accused may well have grounds for a successful appeal. The judge will also explain that although Fred is charged under s. 18 of the Offences Against the Person Act, 1861 of wounding with intent to cause grievous bodily harm, the jury may acquit him of that offence and yet find him guilty of the lesser offence of unlawful wounding under s. 20 of the Offences Against the Person Act, 1861. The judge may then explain to the jury that they must endeavour to reach a unanimous verdict (but see below), though whether he does so or not is a matter of discretion (*R* v *Watson* [1988] 1 All E.R. 897). The judge will then leave the court and the jury, escorted by a bailiff, will retire to a jury room where they must stay until they reach a verdict. If a verdict is not reached on the day the jury retire they will be taken to a hotel to spend the night.

THE VERDICT

If the jury is unanimous in finding Fred guilty they will tell the jury bailiff that they are ready to come back into court. The judge and counsel return and the jury files in. A court usher will ask the foreman of the jury what their verdict is. We assume that they have found Fred guilty of the s. 18 offence; the foreman says so.

At this stage Fred's previous convictions, if any, will be handed to the judge who may refer to some of them openly in court. Counsel for the defence will then normally put in a plea in mitigation, saying, perhaps, that Fred has not been in trouble before or at least not for some time, according to his record, in the hope that this plea will lead to a lighter sentence.

The judge will then address the defendant and pass sentence, which in view of the violence involved in Fred's case, is likely to be a term of imprisonment.

MAJORITY VERDICTS

The Juries Act, 1974, provides for majority verdicts of juries in criminal proceedings. Section 17 provides that the verdict of the jury in criminal proceedings need not be unanimous if –

(a) in a case where there are not less than *eleven* jurors, *ten* of them agree on the verdict. In the case of an ordinary jury of twelve this means that the judge can accept a verdict of eleven to one or ten to two; and

(b) in a case where there are *ten* jurors, *nine* of them agree on the verdict. If there are only nine jurors the verdict must be unanimous (see further p. 111).

A court must not accept a majority verdict of guilty unless the foreman of the jury has stated in open court the number of jurors who respectively agreed to and dissented from the verdict. No such statement is required if the verdict is one of not guilty so that it will not be known that a verdict of not guilty was by a majority.

Furthermore, a court must not accept a majority verdict unless it appears to the court that the jury have had not less than two hours' deliberation or such longer period as the court thinks reasonable, having regard to the nature and complexity of the case.

The judge cannot accept a majority verdict after less than two hours' deliberation and if the jury is not unanimous after two hours he should send them back, at least once more, to try to reach unanimity. If they still cannot he should send them back to see if they can reach a decision by the necessary majority, having directed them on the law relating to majority verdicts.

When the jury returns to the courtroom the judge will ask whether the required majority has agreed on a verdict. If they have, the verdict is accepted *provided*, according to a Practice Direction made on 11 May, 1970, that at least two hours and *ten minutes* have elapsed between the time at which the last juror left the jury box to go to the jury room and the time when the judge asked whether the jury had reached a verdict by the required majority.

Before the judge asks whether the jury has reached a majority verdict the senior officer of the court present must announce the deliberation time which the jury has had. The extra ten minutes was added in order to reduce the number of appeals made to the Court of Appeal on the ground that majority verdicts had been accepted although the deliberation time had been less than two hours, as for example where the jury had returned to put a question to the court during the deliberation period.

The majority provision is, of course, a controversial one because the principle of the unanimous decision was an old and much-respected feature of English law, indeed the requirement for a jury to be unanimous first appeared in a case in 1367. The main reason for the change was the growing problem of deliberate corruption or intimidation of jurors to secure an acquittal. The majority of ten to two was chosen because it was felt that it would be difficult to find more than one or two who were susceptible to bribery or intimidation, particularly in view of the fact that those with criminal records are excluded from jury service under the Juries Act, 1974 and the Juries (Disqualification) Act, 1984. It should be noted that what happens in a jury room is not supposed to be disclosed. This is now reinforced by s. 8 of the Contempt of Court Act, 1981. This makes it an offence for a juror to reveal the discussions in the jury room and for a newspaper or any other organisation or person to try to find out by interviewing a juror.

ALTERNATIVE VERDICTS

The common law, as restated by s. 6(3) and (4) of the Criminal Law Act, 1967, provides for alternative verdicts, which means that a jury can convict an accused of an offence other than the one with which he is charged. Although the wording of s. 6 appears wider than the common law rule, subsequent cases seem to indicate that a jury cannot convict of an offence different in *character* from the offence charged. The power is limited to a conviction for an offence involving *the same criminal act* but with a lesser degree of aggravation. As we have seen, in Fred's case it would have been possible for the jury to bring in a verdict of unlawful wounding under s. 20 of the Offences Against the Person Act, 1861 although the charge was wounding with intent to cause grievous bodily harm under s. 18, of the 1861 Act.

Where there exists an alternative and less serious offence to the one charged, the judge *must* direct the jury on the lesser offence if there is evidence to support it (*R v Fairbanks* [1986] 1 WLR 1202), but not apparently if the main offence is very serious and the alternative offence is trifling. So in a case of robbery the judge is not bound to direct the jury on the alternative offence of theft (*R v Maxwell* [1990] 1 All E.R. 801).

NUMBER OF JURORS

The number of jurors will normally be twelve unless the number has been reduced in accordance with s. 16 of the Juries Act, 1974. The section provides for the continuation of criminal trials where a juror dies or is discharged by the court, whether through illness or for any other reason.

If the number of members of the jury is not reduced below nine, the trial may proceed and the verdict may be given accordingly.

However, in a trial for any offence punishable with death, e.g. treason, this rule only applies if assent in writing is given by or on behalf of both the prosecution and the accused, or each of the accused if there is more than one.

Moreover, the court has discretion in any criminal trial to discharge the jury if it sees fit to do so when its numbers are depleted.

Committal to the Crown Court for sentence

As we have seen, there are times when the Crown Court sits to sentence persons convicted of offences before the magistrates. This happens where the magistrates have found a particular defendant guilty and then have had access to his previous convictions showing, shall we say, a very bad record, and feel that the defendant should receive a greater sentence than they can give. In such a situation they will commit the defendant to the Crown Court for sentence.

The Crown Court may sit solely for the purpose of sentencing and if so consists of a judge (either a High Court judge or circuit judge or recorder) and not less than two nor more than four magistrates. The decision as regards the sentence is by a majority and if there is an equality of voting the judge has a casting vote.

Appeals in criminal cases

A person who has been convicted and sentenced by a criminal court has rights of appeal. These have already been considered in Chapter 2 (see p. 41).

Contempt of Court Act, 1981

Under s. 4 of the 1981 Act the trial judge may make an order imposing restrictions on the reporting of a trial in e.g. newspapers. The section gives the court power to order the postponement of publication of reports of a trial or part of a trial where it appears necessary to avoid a substantial risk of prejudicing that trial or other proceedings pending or imminent, as where witnesses or potential witnesses might be intimidated.

Section 11 gives the court power to prohibit the publication of any name or other matter in connection with the proceedings where the court has allowed the name or other matter to be withheld from the public when the proceedings were before the court.

Sentencing

Before considering the range of sentences a criminal court can now give, it may be advantageous to state in broad terms the purposes which are, or were, behind certain types of sentence. These are as follows –

(a) *The philosophy of retribution.* This is based on the idea of atonement. Retribution emphasises the position of the social group against which the criminal offends rather than that of the criminal himself. By imposing punishment society exacts retribution. The science of criminal law has gradually moved away from this philosophy.

(b) *The philosophy of deterrence.* This emphasises the social objective. Punishment must be designed so as to deter, as far as possible, the commission of similar offences in terms of deterring both an actual offender and other members of society who have not yet committed crimes. This philosophy still prevails in modern criminology.

(c) *The philosophy of reformation.* This involves the use of, for example, educational methods, either in addition to, or in substitution for, punishment proper. In general terms the increasing attempt to understand the social and psychological causes of crime has led to a growing emphasis on this philosophy.

Underlying all of the above philosophies is, of course, the need to protect society from the criminal and this leads on occasions to sentences which are *preventive* in aim such as, for example, long prison sentences and disqualification from driving.

(d) *Reparation.* In modern times the principle of requiring the criminal to make reparation to his victim and/or to the community is increasingly the motive behind sentencing policy. The principle is expressed, for example, in sentences involving compensation orders and community service orders.

TYPES OF SENTENCE

The death penalty is still available for those aged 18 or over for treason and piracy with violence but the Murder (Abolition of Death Penalty) Act, 1965, abolished the death penalty for murder. The sentence which the judge *must* give is now life imprisonment but he may recommend a minimum period for which the convicted person should be detained before the Home Secretary considers release on licence. However, the Home Secretary is the sole judge of how long a person convicted of murder should spend in custody – the judiciary may only make recommendations. (*R* v *Secretary of State for the Home Department ex parte Smart, The Times*, 22 January 1991.) There is no power to administer corporal punishment upon an offender. Sentences which are available are set out below.

(a) *Custodial sentences.* The punishment for most crimes is laid down by Acts of Parliament. The usual provision lays down a maximum fine and/or imprisonment, leaving the court to decide what sentence to give up to that maximum.

Persons who are serving life imprisonment may be released on licence by the Home Secretary at any time. Others are entitled to a reduction of sentence of up to one-third for good behaviour. In addition, those who have served one-third of their sentences, provided that this has involved at least six months in prison, may be released on licence or parole. The licence may be revoked by the Home Secretary, e.g. for failure to co-operate with the supervising officer, or by the Crown Court or a Magistrates' Court if there is a conviction of crime. The sentences available to the magistrates in youth courts have already been considered (see p. 95).

The Powers of Criminal Courts Act, 1973 provides for the system of suspended sentences. The essential features of the system are as follows –

(i) Any court which passes a sentence of imprisonment for a term of not more than two years *may* order the sentence as a suspended sentence and announce the *operational period*, i.e. the length of the term of suspension, i.e. 'nine months suspended for two years'. The maximum operational period is two years and the minimum one year. (S. 22(1).) If the offender commits another offence within the stated period the original sentence can, at the discretion of the court, be activated and the offender made to serve it after any sentence imposed for the subsequent offence.

(ii) Under s. 22(2) (as amended by the Criminal Justice Act, 1991 which restricts the right to impose custodial sentences) a court *must not* give a suspended sentence unless it feels (a) that the case is one in which a sentence of imprisonment would have been appropriate even if there had been no power to suspend it, i.e. the court would have been prepared to see the offender go to prison, and (b) that the sentence and suspension are justified in the exceptional circumstances of the case. The court must also consider whether in addition to the suspended sentence a fine or compensation order (see p. 119) should be imposed on the offender.

It was held in *R v Dobbs* (1983) 5 Cr. App. R. (S) 378 that the courts have no power to suspend a sentence of what is now detention in a young offenders institution, either in whole or in part.

As regards custodial sentences the following provisions of the Criminal Justice Act, 1991 (CJA 91) are relevant.

(i) A court is not to pass a custodial sentence unless it feels –
    (1) that the offence or a combination of the offence and one other associated with it is so serious that only a custodial sentence will do; or
    (2) if the offence is a violent or sexual offence that a custodial sentence is necessary to protect the public.
    However, in spite of what is said above the court can pass a custodial sentence on those offenders who refuse to consent to a community sentence (see below) s. 1).
    Where a court does give a custodial sentence it must state which of reasons (1) or (2) above have influenced it and explain to the offender in ordinary language why a custodial sentence is being passed.

(ii) The same rules as to disclosure of reasons (1) or (2) above apply to any custodial sentence *which is longer* than is on the face of it warranted by the offence (s. 2).

(iii) Before passing a custodial sentence the court must obtain and consider a pre-sentence report by a probation officer or a local authority social worker (s. 3). Similarly a medical report by an approved medical practitioner in the field is required before a court may pass a custodial sentence on a mentally disordered offender (s. 4).

(*b*) *Fines* – generally these are available for every offence except murder and treason. Any criminal court may order the payment of a sum of money by an offender, in general up to a maximum laid down by statute. In general terms this is up to a maximum of £5000 in a magistrates' court, and unlimited in a Crown Court. Failure to pay can lead to imprisonment but the court will first enquire into the offender's ability to pay.

The fine is a most appropriate sentence to give against a corporation, and company legislation often provides for default fines on registered companies and their officers, e.g. for failure to file returns with the Registrar of Companies.

(*c*) *Unit fines.* Under the CJA 91, ss. 17–24, fines in magistrates' courts are decided by multiplying units representing the seriousness of the offence by the weekly disposable income of the offender up to but not exceeding the maximum fine for the offence. In the past problems have occurred in that offenders have been sent to prison for failing to pay fines which were always unaffordable because of the offender's financial circumstances.

Units of seriousness are as follows –

(i) 2 units in the case of a level 1 offence;
(ii) 5 units in a level 2 offence;
(iii) 10 units in a level 3 offence;
(iv) 25 units in a level 4 offence; and
(v) 50 units in a level 5 offence.

A level 1 offence is one which is punishable by a maximum fine of £200, after that the position is as follows –

– level 2 a maximum fine of £500;
– level 3 a maximum fine of £1000;
– level 4 a maximum fine of £2500;
– level 5 a maximum fine of £5000.

On conviction an offender can be required to provide evidence of means before he is sentenced. A simplified form is used asking only some twelve questions. There are penalties for giving false information. The bottom and top limits of disposable income have been fixed *initially* at £4 and £100 respectively with a reduction to 80p and £20 in the case of those under 18.

Consequently the maximum fine for adults for the most serious level 5 offences will be 50 units at £100 per week, i.e. £5000. There are provisions designed to prevent it from being more profitable e.g. to pay a fine than to buy a TV licence.

Default in payment of unit fines will result in imprisonment based upon the 'seriousness' formula as follows –

- not more than 2 units, 7 days;
- more than 2 units but not more than 5 units, 14 days;
- more than 5 units but not more than 10 units, 28 days;
- more than 10 units but not more than 25 units, 45 days;
- more than 25 units, 3 months.

Where at the time of imprisonment a part of the fine has been paid there will be a proportionate reduction in the prison sentence, e.g. if say half has been paid the sentence will be cut by half and so on. Fines may be deducted from income support if the court applies to the Secretary of State under s. 24.

Unit fines are compulsory in magistrates' courts but they do not apply where the magistrates are fining a corporate body and the method does not apply in the Crown Court where fines are in general higher. It does mean that offenders will be fined differently for the same offence. Suppose we take a level 3 offence where the maximum fine is £1000. Let us also assume that Mr Bloggs and Mr Snooks have committed the same level 3 offence at level of seriousness 2. If the weekly disposable income of Mr Bloggs is £10 he will be fined £10 per week for five weeks, i.e. a total fine of £50. If Mr Snooks' weekly disposable income is say £40 he will pay £40 per week for five weeks, i.e. £200. The deterrent effect would be about the same given their respective income levels.

(d) *Community sentences.* The CJA 91 states that a court shall not pass a community sentence, i.e. impose a community order, on an offender unless it feels that the offence or a combination of that offence and another offence associated with it is serious enough to require it (s. 6). A 'community order' means any one of the following –

- (i) a probation order;
- (ii) a community service order;
- (iii) a combination order, i.e. an order combining probation and community service;
- (iv) a curfew order;
- (v) a supervision order; and
- (vi) an attendance centre order (s. 6).

The court must obtain a pre-sentence report (as already described) before imposing certain community orders, e.g. a probation order which contains requirements as to residence and/or restricts activities and/or requires the offender to take treatment for drug or alcohol dependency (s. 7).

We can now have a look at the various community sentences in a little more detail as follows.

(1) *Probation orders*. When a court convicts a person of or over the age of 16 years of an offence – not being an offence for which the sentence is fixed by law as is life imprisonment for murder – it may make a probation order if it feels that this is desirable to achieve the rehabilitation of the offender or to prevent him committing *any* further offences, e.g. petty theft, or to protect the public as where any further offences are likely to be violent. The offender will then come under the supervision of a probation officer. Before the order is made the court must explain to the offender in simple language what the effect of the order is including any additional requirement such as undergoing treatment for drug abuse and what will happen if the order is not complied with, e.g. that a fine not exceeding £1000 maybe imposed on him and that in some cases attendance at an attendance centre may be required (Sch. 2, 1991 Act). The court has power under Sch. 2 to review the order on the application of the probation officer or the offender and in any case the court cannot make the order unless the offender is willing to comply with it (s. 2, Powers of Criminal Courts Act, 1973 (PCCA) as substituted by s. 8 of the 1991 Act).

(2) *Community service orders*. Where the offender is 16 or over and with his consent the court may make a 'Community Service Order' to be performed at given times but not interfering with educational or work routines. A report by a probation officer or by a local authority social worker must be considered. In addition the court must be satisfied that the offender is a suitable person to carry out the work proposed in the community and that suitable work is available for the offender to do in the area in which he lives or will live. The offender must also keep in touch as required with the supervising officer and notify that officer of any change of address (s. 14, PCCA as amended by the CJA 91, s. 10).

The total number of hours is between 40 and 240 to be served within a year. In the case of those aged 16 but not 17 the hours are 40 to 120. The service is prescribed by the Home Secretary and consists of such things as building playgrounds, gardening, helping elderly or disabled people or repairing vandalised property. The Community Service Order may be made for breach of probation or instead of committal to prison for failure to pay a fine (Sch. 2, CJA 91). Proceedings for breach of a Community Service Order may be initiated by probation officers through the supervising magistrates' court either by summons or warrant.

(3) *Combination orders*. A court which convicts a person of or over 16 of an offence punishable with imprisonment may, if the sentence is not fixed by law (see above) and the offender consents, make a combination order requiring the offender to (a) be under the supervision of a probation officer for not less than twelve months nor more than three years, i.e. a probation order, and (b) perform unpaid work in the community for the number of hours specified in the order being in this case a total of not less than 40 hours

and not more than 100, i.e. a community service order (s. 11, CJA 91).

(4) *Curfew orders.* When a court convicts a person of or over 16 of an offence whether imprisonable or not – provided it is not an offence for which the punishment is fixed by law (see above) – the court may with the consent of the offender make a curfew order requiring him to remain for periods specified in the order at a place also specified therein. The maximum period for curfew is six months from the date of the order. The periods must be not less than two hours nor more than twelve hours in any one day.

Also the order must as far as practicable avoid any conflict with religious beliefs in terms e.g. of attendance at services or of any other community order or with work or education. The effect of the order and the consequences of failure to comply with it must be explained to the offender and the court may review the order in the same way as other community sentences (see above). The court must obtain and consider information about the place where the offender is to be during curfew and the effect this will have on other persons who will be in the same place (s. 12, CJA 91).

A curfew order may also include a requirement for electronic monitoring of the offender provided arrangements exist in the area for doing so. The Home Secretary can make orders as to persons who may be recognised for the monitoring, e.g. the police (s. 13, CJA 91).

(5) *Supervision and attendance centre orders.* These have already been considered in the section concerned with criminal proceedings in relation to children and young persons (see p. 95).

(6) *Miscellaneous sentences.* These include binding over to keep the peace with the sanction that a sum of money will be forfeited if there is a breach; endorsement of driving licence and disqualification from driving.

(7) *Absolute and conditional discharge.* A court may give an absolute discharge where the accused is in breach of the law but the court considers that there are mitigating factors, e.g. no previous criminal record and sometimes unemployment or old age. Or it may give a conditional discharge which means that the court will not pass sentence on the offender unless he commits another offence during a specified period not exceeding three years, in which case he can be sentenced also for the original offence.

OTHER MATTERS RELEVANT TO SENTENCING

(a) If the accused is a 'first offender' and is not legally represented at a summary trial, he must not be sentenced to imprisonment, or detention as a young offender, unless either he failed in his application for legal aid on the ground that he had sufficient means, or he refused or failed to apply for legal aid (PCCA s. 21).

(b) Crown Courts and magistrates' courts are given power to defer sentence for six months to see how the offender behaves after conviction, e.g. whether he has made any reparation for his offence. The consent of the offender is required before sentence can be deferred (PCCA, s. 1).

(*c*) The court has power to order forfeiture of *any* property in the offender's possession which was used or intended for use for the purpose of committing or facilitating the commission of *any* offence. There is no restriction as to the type of offence to which it may apply (PCCA, s. 43A). This section is intended to cover property such as motor vehicles and radio equipment as well as the traditional tools of the criminal's trade. The only requirement is that the property must have played an integral part in the crime. Thus when sentencing for the offence of driving while disqualified the court has power to order forfeiture of the car. (*R* v *Highbury Corner Magistrates' Court, ex p. Di Matteo, The Times*, 18 December 1990). The court may order the sale of forfeited property and the payment of the proceeds to the victim of the crime. This provides a useful addition to a compensation order (see below).

(*d*) On a conviction similar to that set out in (*c*) above the court may order the offender to be disqualified from driving if a vehicle was used for the purpose of committing or facilitating the commission of an offence. (PCCA, s. 44.) The person disqualified need not have been the driver.

(*e*) Under s. 3 of the Immigration Act, 1971 both a Crown Court and a magistrates' court may recommend deportation of non-patrials given that certain conditions regarding notice have been fulfilled.

(*f*) Under s. 1 of the Drug Trafficking Offences Act, 1986 the Crown Court, when sentencing for any drug trafficking offence, may make a confiscation order. The Court is required to determine whether the defendant has benefited from drug trafficking and, if so, how much is to be ordered by way of confiscation. The maximum order will be the value of the defendant's proceeds of drug trafficking or the amount of his realisable property whichever is the greater.

(*g*) As we have seen under ss. 35–36 of the Criminal Justice Act, 1988 the Attorney-General may refer to the Court of Appeal cases in which it appears to him that the sentence has been too lenient. The Court of Appeal may then pass such sentence as it thinks appropriate and which it was in the power of the lower court to pass.

COMPENSATORY AWARDS

In order to avoid the need for a victim of crime to bring an action in a civil court for compensation there is some power in criminal courts to give monetary compensation. Sections 35 to 38 of the Powers of Criminal Courts Act, 1973 provide for reparation by the offender. *Compensation orders* are available for any 'personal injury, loss or damage resulting from' an offence of which the offender is convicted or which he asks to have taken into consideration in sentence. Where property which is the object of an offence under the Theft Act, 1968 is damaged the offender may be ordered to pay compensation however and by whomsoever the damage was caused, i.e. even if not by himself. Compensation for victims of theft and burglary has been the main use of s. 35.

Magistrates' courts are limited to a total of £5000 in respect of one conviction, i.e. the offence of which the person is convicted and any other offences which he asks to have taken into consideration. In making an order the court must consider the offender's means. There is no limit to the amount which a Crown Court can order. However, the amount should not be so great that the offender has no hope of paying it, or that it will take too long to pay, say more than two years. These compensation orders operate alongside the scheme for compensation for criminal injuries out of public funds (see below). Amendments to the PCCA made by the Criminal Justice Act, 1988, ss. 104 and 105 have extended the scope of compensation orders to cover funeral expenses and payments for bereavement to close relatives where death is caused in road traffic offences. The court must now give reasons why it has not made a compensation order when it could have done so. Payment is also postponed until the offender has exhausted all rights of appeal. In addition the making of a compensation order does not prevent a claim for damages at civil law. However, the amount of any compensation order which has been paid must be deducted from the damages and if the damages are less than the order the court can reduce the amount of the order but there is no provision for a refund if it has been fully paid.

RESTITUTION ORDERS

Restitution orders may also be made in regard to property which is the object of an offence under s. 28(1)(c) or (3) of the Theft Act, 1968 and under s. 6 of the Criminal Justice Act, 1972. Restitution orders may also be made in respect of an offence which the accused asks to have taken into consideration. A restitution order and a compensation order may be made in respect of the same goods if recovered in a damaged condition.

CRIMINAL INJURIES COMPENSATION BOARD

The compensatory awards set out above are ineffective if the offender is never caught or if when caught he has no money or property with which to pay compensation. In consequence there is, under ss. 108–117 and Schs. 6 and 7 of the Criminal Justice Act, 1988, a scheme of state compensation operated by the Criminal Injuries Compensation Board.

The Board may make discretionary payments to those suffering personal injury which is attributable to certain criminal offences, e.g. rape and assault under s. 47 of the Offences Against the Person Act, 1861. Payments are not made for offences against property unless it was a physical aid to the victim, e.g. glasses, a hearing aid or a wheelchair. Dependants of a person who dies as a result of a relevant crime may claim. There are rights of appeal. The Board can, having made an award, seek to reimburse itelf by a claim against the offender. Those who cannot show the need for this sort of compensation may, of course, make an application under s. 35 of the Powers of Criminal Courts Act, 1973 if possible. (See p. 119.) Compensation is not available if the award for injuries is less than the minimum prescribed by statutory instrument under s. 114 of the 1988 Act (currently £550).

REHABILITATION OF OFFENDERS ACT, 1974 – NON-DISCLOSURE OF SENTENCE

The provisions of this Act are an attempt to give effect to the principle that when a person convicted of crime has been successful in living down that conviction and has avoided further criminal activities, common justice demands that his efforts should not be prejudiced by the unwarranted disclosure of that earlier conviction.

All sentences are subject to rehabilitation except imprisonment for life and custodial sentences of more than 30 months. After the expiry of certain defined periods the offender is rehabilitated. For example, if it was a custodial sentence for a term exceeding six months but not exceeding 30 months, rehabilitation is after ten years; if for a term not exceeding six months, it is seven years, or if the sentence was a fine, it is five years. In the case of those who were under 18 at the date of conviction, the rehabilitation periods are halved.

So far as the employment of persons with previous convictions is concerned, it should be noted that any questions seeking information as to a person's previous convictions shall be treated as not relating to spent convictions and any obligation on any person to disclose matters shall not require him to disclose a spent conviction, and a spent conviction or failure to disclose a spent conviction is not a proper ground for dismissing or excluding a person from or prejudicing him in any occupation or employment. There is an exception (see SI 1986/1249) where the employment allows contact with persons under 18, e.g. in care, leisure and recreational activities. Here questions can be asked designed to reveal spent convictions particularly those with a sexual connotation. Such spent convictions are a ground for dismissal which will not, for that reason alone, be unfair.

Another exception occurs under the Financial Services Act, 1986. One of the primary purposes of the Act is to protect the public from the activities of unscrupulous and dishonest people who may find their way into the investment business. For example those who are authorised to conduct investment business are under a duty to take reasonable care not to employ or continue to employ unsuitable persons. In this connection s. 189 of the 1986 Act provides that the 1974 Act does not apply to a spent conviction for fraud or dishonesty or to an offence under companies legislation such as insider dealing or under legislation relating to building societies, friendly societies, insurance, banking or other financial services, insolvency, consumer credit or consumer protection.

5
Civil procedure

In this chapter we shall consider the way in which a civil action is brought and concluded in the High Court.

For the purposes of our High Court action we shall deal with a case of breach of contract under which John, a miller operating as a sole trader, was to sell to Nature Foods Ltd 1000 tons of special high quality stone-ground flour in accordance with a sample shown to an agent of Nature Foods at the time, the price being £60 per ton. John claims that flour in accordance with the sample was delivered and that he has not been paid.

It appears that Nature Foods have not paid because the flour had defects in terms of quality not revealed by a reasonable examination of the sample. They will counterclaim for damages for breach of contract by John.

Bringing a civil action to trial

Reference should be made at this point to p. 28 which sets out the monetary limits on the jurisdiction of the County Court from which it will be seen that John's claim might in some circumstances be brought before the County Court. However, we shall assume that in this case the claim is to be made in the High Court. If John is wealthy no problems arise in terms of his ability to pay for the service of lawyers. If he is not wealthy then his position is much more difficult. If the claim against Nature Foods proceeds to trial and John is successful then he will receive most of his costs from Nature Foods. However, if he fails in his claim he may have to pay his own and most of Nature Foods' costs.

LEGAL AID

It is unlikely that John will be able to claim legal aid because legal aid in civil proceedings is only for persons of very limited means. The qualifying capital and income limits are revised at intervals but John is unlikely to qualify. However, the provisions are useful to persons of very limited means in some instances, say employment disputes, since legal aid is available, for example, for proceedings before the Employment Appeal Tribunal. In civil proceedings a person of limited means can get two kinds of legal aid: advice and assistance from a litigator, e.g. a solicitor, and legal aid for civil court proceedings. There is also, as we have seen, criminal legal aid which provides for payments to lawyers to represent a person charged before the court with a criminal offence.

ATTEMPT TO SETTLE

On the assumption that John has sufficient funds to proceed and has duly consulted a solicitor, the next step is to attempt an early settlement, and the solicitors of each party will correspond on this. If this fails then John's solicitor must consider going to court (or litigation) and whether or not an action by John would be successful.

On this issue John's solicitor may rely on his own view but in a difficult case will usually consult counsel. Counsel will give a written opinion and on the assumption that this is favourable, proceedings are commenced.

Nevertheless, in view of the costs of litigation, John's solicitor will continue, even after service of the writ and before trial, to seek a settlement. A number of cases are settled on the steps of the court itself on the day of the trial to avoid further costs.

THE WRIT

The first step is to issue a writ (the equivalent in the County Court is called a summons). The writ is drafted by John's solicitor or counsel and filed in the court office where it is also sealed and returned to the plaintiff. The writ is then served on the defendant, or his solicitors, but in the case of Nature Foods, which is a corporation, service will be at its registered office or solicitors, personally by the plaintiff or his agent or by ordinary first class mail. There is currently no specific provision in the Rules of the Supreme Court for general service by fax but in *Ralux NV/SA* v *Spencer Mason CA, The Times,* 19 May 1989 the Court of Appeal said that a legible fax which could be proved to have come into the hands of the other party could be good service.

The writ tells the defendants, Nature Foods, that the plaintiff, John, has a claim against them. It calls on Nature Foods to satisfy the claim or return to the Central Office of the Supreme Court, or a District Registry if the writ was issued by a District Registry, the accompanying Acknowledgement of Service.

ACKNOWLEDGEMENT OF SERVICE

On the assumption that Nature Foods wish to contest John's case, their solicitor will inform the court that this is so. This is done by completing and returning the form of Acknowledgement of Service received with the writ.

This should be done within 14 days of service of writ. If Nature Foods do not give notice of intention to defend John will be entitled to judgment. John is claiming a liquidated sum, i.e. £60,000, and if Nature Foods fail to give notice of intention to defend John may enter *final* judgment for that sum plus interest (see p. 337) and costs. However, if John's action had been for an unliquidated sum, e.g. damages for negligence, *final* judgment could not have been obtained because the damages would have to be assessed. In such a case John would have obtained an interlocutory judgment, the amount of damages being then assessed by a Master (see p. 80). The defendant may attend the hearing before the Master in person or by solicitor or counsel to dispute the amount of damages. After this procedure has been followed the plaintiff may enter *final* judgment.

STATEMENT OF CLAIM

If Nature Foods give notice of intention to defend, then John, through his lawyers, must deliver a 'statement of claim'. This may have been done with the writ but if not, it is delivered separately. In this case it would seem to have been reasonable to endorse the statement of claim on the writ. However, in a more complex case it might be reasonable to serve a separate statement of claim.

The statement of claim sets out in detail the facts which the plaintiff alleges support his claim and the relief sought and the defendant receives a copy. All material facts must be set out and the plaintiff will not be allowed at the trial to introduce material of which the defendant has not been given notice.

The evidence supporting John's claim need not be stated and there need be no mention that the facts set out reveal an alleged breach of contract because this is obvious, both to the court and Nature Foods' lawyers.

The facts must be given in sufficient *detail* to enable the defendants to prepare a defence. Places and dates must be given so that the defendant may try to show that the event did not happen or, if it did, to give a different version of it.

STRIKING OUT

If a statement of claim is alleged to disclose no cause of action, e.g. a claim in negligence where the defendant alleges no duty of care (see p. 435), or is too vague or so full of irrelevant matter as to prejudice a proper defence at the trial, the defendant can apply to a Master (see p. 80) in what are known as interlocutory proceedings to have it 'struck out'. If the application is successful the plaintiff must deliver a new statement of claim.

In addition, a plaintiff's claim may be struck out under the Rules of the Supreme Court. Examples are for failing to serve a statement of claim or to comply with requirements relating to further and better particulars, discovery of documents (see p. 127), and interrogatories (see p. 128).

However, the court has an inherent power to strike out a claim if, as the Court of Appeal decided in *Allen* v *Sir Alfred McAlpine & Sons Ltd* [1968] 1 All E.R. 543, there has been inordinate and inexcusable delay which gives rise to a substantial risk that a fair trial is not possible. These principles were approved by the House of Lords in *Birkett* v *James* [1977] 2 All E.R. 801. Furthermore, it was held by the Court of Appeal in *Janov* v *Morris* [1981] 3 All E.R. 780 that in an appropriate case of delay the court may even strike out a second claim made by a second writ within the limitation period, thus effectively preventing the plaintiff from ever receiving the relief claimed.

FURTHER AND BETTER PARTICULARS

A statement of claim which merely fails to give sufficient detail will not be struck out but the defence may ask for 'further and better particulars', and the plaintiff must then supply the details required of the allegations he has made. He may not allege totally new matters.

The request for particulars is made initially by letter but if the plaintiff fails to give the necessary details, either properly or at all, the defendant may apply to a Master who may order the plaintiff to comply with the request. Failure to comply with these requirements may result in the striking out of the plaintiff's claim.

THE DEFENCE

When the defence is satisfied that it understands the allegations in the statement of claim and the detail given in the particulars, then it must put forward its version of the dispute. The document in which this is done is called a 'defence'.

The defence answers the facts relied on by the plaintiff and sets out any new facts on which the defence relies. If an allegation in the statement of claim is denied, the defence must say so. If it is not denied the court will assume that it is admitted.

A defence which is vague or irrelevant may be struck out, and one which does not give sufficient detail gives the right to the plaintiff to ask for further and better particulars of it.

REPLY

If the plaintiff merely wishes to deny the defendant's allegations he need do nothing more. If, however, he wants to raise further allegations in order to answer a point in the defence, he pleads these in a further document called a 'reply'. This process may continue, replies being exchanged, until each party has raised every point which is considered relevant.

COUNTERCLAIM

In many cases only a statement of claim and a defence are necessary. However, sometimes the defendant says that not only is the plaintiff's claim unfounded, but that it is he who has a claim against the plaintiff. Where this is so the defendant sets out his claim in a separate part of his defence, called a 'counterclaim'. This is, in effect, a reverse statement of claim to which the plaintiff will deliver a reply containing a 'defence to counterclaim'. Nature Foods will deliver a counterclaim in regard to the alleged breach of contract by John.

PAYMENT INTO COURT

A payment in, as it is usually called, is a sum of money which the defendant pays into the Pay Office of the Central Office of the Supreme Court in London or a District Registry in a city outside London. A note of the payment is sent to the plaintiff, or to the defendant in the case of a payment in by a plaintiff in respect of a counterclaim by a defendant, and to any co-defendants or co-plaintiffs, as the case may be. A payment in, which is allowed in all actions for debt and damages, may be made at any time, even after service of writ and during the trial, but not after the judge has started to sum up.

A payment in, e.g. by a defendant, is intended to put pressure on the plaintiff. If Nature Foods were to pay in a sum of money less than £60,000, say, £45,000 representing what they thought to be a fair settlement of the claim, John must decide either to take the sum paid in or go on to trial or with the trial if it has commenced.

The snag is that if John refuses the offer and the judge at the trial awards less, even a penny less, than the £45,000 paid in, John will have to pay his own costs *and* those of Nature Foods incurred after payment in, and may be left with little, if anything, of whatever sum the judge has awarded him. Normally, as a winning plaintiff, John would have had his costs paid by Nature Foods.

The judge is not told that there has been a payment in until *all* questions of liability and the amount of debt or damages to be awarded have been decided. If the judge is, e.g. by some mistake by a solicitor for a party, made aware of a payment in, he has, according to *Millensted* v *Grosvenor House Ltd* [1937] 1 K.B. 717, a discretion whether to continue to try the case or to order a retrial by another judge.

THE PLEADINGS

The pleadings consist of the statement of claim, the defence, a counterclaim by the defence, various replies, and further and better particulars and requests therefor. Thus, in our case the statement of claim will allege that on a given date the parties signed a written contract under which John was to supply 1000 tons of flour in accordance with a sample at a price of £60 per ton; that the flour was duly delivered but the price has not been paid.

Nature Foods will admit the contract and the non-payment but say that the flour did not conform with the sample. In addition, because of John's failure to perform the contract properly, Nature Foods were unable to bake sufficient high quality bread to fulfil all their contracts with health food shops. Nature Foods, having become liable to pay damages to their customers, counterclaim for those damages plus compensation for loss of goodwill. John then delivers a reply denying the allegations made in the defence and saying that he delivered flour which did conform with the agreed sample.

When the plaintiff and the defendant do not wish to plead any additional facts, the pleadings are said to be closed.

The precise matters now in dispute are clear to both sides so that they can now prepare their evidence accordingly. In addition, a judge will see clearly from the pleadings the matters which he is called upon to decide.

DRAFTING THE PLEADINGS

All the documents forming the pleadings are usually drafted by counsel so that papers, e.g. letters, must be sent to counsel and returned after drafting and delivery to the other party. All of this takes time and leads to the delays which occur before trial.

DISCOVERY

When the pleadings are closed the case has reached the discovery of documents stage. Although every fact relied upon by a party must be disclosed to the other, the evidence which will be used to prove those facts in court need not be disclosed until it confronts the other party at the trial.

To this there is a major exception which is that each party can be required to disclose to the other the *documentary evidence* which he has whether it *assists or impedes his case.* The opponent may take copies of the documents which may include any kind of writing, however informal, e.g. bills and rent books. The method of exchanging documents after close of pleading is called 'discovery'. Discovery is available only against a party to an action and not against a witness.

There may be objections to disclosure. If so, the court can, if it thinks fit, order production. However, a person cannot be required to produce privileged documents, e.g. confidential communications passing between a client and his solicitor where the purpose is to enable legal advice to be given.

During recent years there have been a number of cases on *public interest immunity* where the issue has been the necessity for the proper administration of public services for public authorities to refuse to disclose documents.

It appears that the court will uphold public interest immunity unless disclosure is fundamental to a particular litigant's case. Thus in *Campbell v Tameside Metropolitan Borough Council* [1982] 2 All E.R. 791 the Court of Appeal decided that C, who had been seriously assaulted by an 11-year-old child at the school where she was a teacher, could have discovery of the local authority reports on the child by teachers and psychiatrists to assess the local authority's knowledge of his previous violent behaviour which was vital as a ground for her claim against the authority.

A party to civil litigation and his solicitors who have obtained by discovery documents belonging to the other party must not use them for any purpose of their own apart from the action as a result of which discovery was granted.

In *Home Office* v *Harman* [1982] 1 All E.R. 532 the House of Lords held that it was a civil contempt of court for the solicitor of a litigant in an action against the Home Office for alleged unlawful confinement in a prison 'control unit' isolated from the rest of the prison system, to allow a journalist access to documents obtained by discovery to write an article highly critical of the Home Office and the control unit. This was civil contempt, said the House of Lords, even though the documents concerned had been read out at the trial.

ADVICE ON EVIDENCE

The next step is to ask counsel to use his ability and experience to decide how to use the rules of procedure before trial to get John into the best possible position and what evidence should be called at the trial.

This stage is most important because cases are often won or lost by the way in which the evidence is prepared and presented.

INTERROGATORIES

If a fact essential to success cannot be proved by a party because those facts are peculiarly within the knowledge of his opponent, the problem may be overcome by the use of 'interrogatories'.

These are questions which one side may require the other to *answer on oath*. The answer may then be read at the trial. Whether a particular question may or may not be asked is a matter to be decided by a Master on the hearing of a Summons for Directions.

Remember that particulars are designed to make clear the opponent's allegations which, if he fails to prove them, will lose him his case. Discovery and interrogatories are concerned with evidence. If they fail to provide the evidence required then other methods of proof may be used. However, each party is tied to the pleadings and if he cannot establish the facts there set out no other facts will do, unless, of course, in his pleadings he sets out two fact situations on which he may rely.

Thus, Nature Foods may be asked for particulars as to why the delivery of flour failed to conform with the sample, but not whether there is any record in, say, a stock book. That should have been dealt with on discovery. Nor may Nature Foods be asked for particulars relating to whether they told one of their customers by telephone prior to delivery of the flour that they did not want it. Such a question might be asked as an interrogatory.

NOTICE TO ADMIT

A party faced on the pleadings with the problem of proving a particulr fact, e.g. that a letter was in fact written by the person whose signature it appears to bear, may serve a notice on his opponent requiring him to admit that fact in order to save the expense of producing the necessary evidence.

If the other party refuses to admit then, when costs are being considered, the party asking for the admission may try to convince the judge or Master that refusal to admit was unreasonable and that his opponent must pay the cost of proving that point, whatever the result of the case.

NOTICE TO PRODUCE A DOCUMENT

If either party wishes at the trial to refer to a document which is in his opponent's possession he must serve on his opponent a Notice to Produce the Document. This notice does not make the opponent produce it at the trial but it gives him warning that its contents may be brought into question so that he has a reasonable opportunity of bringing the document to the trial in order to prove his own version of what it contains.

SETTING DOWN FOR TRIAL

The case may now be 'set down' to wait for a time for hearing.

There is much criticism of the time taken to get a case into court and reforms may be desirable. However, the procedure outlined above is important because the most costly part of any civil action is the actual proceedings in court so that it is vital that the pre-trial procedure should ensure that the precise issues at stake are clear and that no time in court will be wasted on irrelevant matters. Also, it would be most unjust if pre-trial procedure did not ensure that both parties had fair warning of the case which each has to meet and of the facts and documents which will be put in question.

EVIDENTIAL DOCUMENTS AND LAW

It is necessary to assemble the evidential documents in advance of the trial in chronological order in what is called a bundle. The bundle is usually prepared by those acting for the plaintiff.

If the legal argument is likely to be complex a party may serve an outline submission in writing (called a skeleton argument) on all the parties and the court in advance of the trial. The Court of Appeal generally *requires* skeleton arguments.

The trial

The parties and their witnesses will assemble for the trial. If a witness refuses to appear a 'subpoena' may be issued. This is a summons to appear and give evidence on condition that reasonable expenses are offered by the party calling the witness. Those who ignore a subpoena are in contempt of court and may be punished by fine or imprisonment.

Often the case will not be heard at the time stated in the list. The court must not be kept waiting and so cases are listed in such a way as to cope, for example, with actions which, as we have seen, are settled out of court at the last moment. If this does not happen, however, there is a trial and others are kept waiting.

When the action is 'called on' counsel for the plaintiff begins. He explains the matters in dispute to the judge, goes through the pleadings and outlines the plaintiff's case, indicating how it will be supported by evidence. Then he calls his witnesses.

The court requires that evidence be given on oath (or affirmation by a person who objects to swearing on the Bible). Documentary evidence such as a letter is not normally admissible and the writer must be called and give evidence on oath unless it is difficult or impossible to call him.

As in a criminal trial counsel for the plaintiff cannot ask his own witnesses 'leading questions' nor is hearsay evidence admissible. After the examination-in-chief the witnesses for the plaintiff may be cross-examined by counsel for the defence, the object being to discredit their evidence. After cross-examination counsel for the plaintiff may re-examine a witness.

Sometimes a witness will give an account of events which is totally different from that which he told to the plaintiff's solicitors; counsel for the plaintiff is not allowed to discredit his own witness unless the judge gives leave as he may do if he feels that the witness is prejudiced against the person who called him. Such a witness is called a hostile witness and his examination-in-chief is more like a cross-examination since it is designed to discredit his evidence.

At the end of the plaintiff's case it is the turn of counsel for the defence to produce evidence to refute it. The plaintiff does not have to prove his case beyond a reasonable doubt, as the prosecution in a criminal trial does, but must show that what he alleges is probably the right version, i.e. proof on a balance of probabilities. The court must be satisfied that it is more likely than not (or more probable than not) that the relevant fact is established. (*R* v *Swaysland*, *The Times*, 15 April 1987.)

The defence need not necessarily produce evidence. If the plaintiff's case is weak the defence may submit to the judge that there is no case to answer. If the judge agrees the action is finished and judgment is given for the defence. However, if the judge does not accept the submission of no case to answer he will immediately give judgment for the plaintiff, so counsel for the defendant will not easily take this course of action.

If there is no submission of no case to answer the defence will call its witnesses who will be examined, cross-examined and re-examined.

Counsel for the defence then makes a closing speech showing how in his view the plaintiff's case has failed. The plaintiff's counsel then presents his view. Both will give an indication of what they think the damages should be. Either party may make a final Response as it is called. This is on a matter of law only and may be with leave of the judge or by his invitation. Thus a party may say, 'My learned friend referred to the case of *Bloggs* v *Snooks* on which I have not addressed you. I would be grateful if you would allow me to address you on that point.' Sometimes the judge will say to a party, 'What do you say about [a point raised by the other party in closing his case] Mr Taylor [counsel]?'

The judge will have remained largely silent during the trial, though he may have asked for an obscure point to be clarified. In fact a judge should not be too 'active' and interfering and if he is his decision may be overturned in an appeal court. The classic statement of the trial judge's function was given by Lord Denning in a civil appeal, *Jones* v *National Coal Board* [1957] 2 All E.R. 155 where he said,

> The judge's part in all this is to hearken to the evidence, only himself asking questions of witnesses when it is necessary to clear up any point that has been overlooked or left obscure; to see that the advocates behave themselves seemly and keep to the rules laid down by law; to exclude irrelevancies and discourage repetition; to make sure by wise intervention that he follows the points the advocates are making and can assess their worth; and at the end to make up his mind where the truth lies.

The statement is not confined to civil trials though in a criminal trial 'the truth' is a matter for the jury.

After the closing speeches the judge considers the evidence and will then give judgment stating the grounds on which it is based, though if a judge requires more time to consider the case he may reserve judgment and give it at a later date. The judge will also decide the amount of damages unless there is a jury as there may be in an action for defamation (see below).

CIVIL JURY

Section 69 of the Supreme Court Act, 1981 gives the court discretion with regard to juries in civil cases, though a jury must be empanelled at the request of the defendant where fraud is alleged, or at the request of either party in cases of libel, slander, malicious prosecution and false imprisonment. If the trial is likely to involve long and detailed examination of documents or accounts or scientific evidence, the court has the discretion to refuse a jury trial even in these cases.

However, libel actions involving issues or persons of national importance should be tried with a jury, even if complex documents are involved. (*Rothermere* v *Times Newspapers* [1973] 1 All E.R. 1013.) The percentage of jury trials in civil actions is very small and outside of the above areas the court is not likely to exercise its discretion to allow a jury. In *H* v *Ministry of Defence, The Times,* 1 April 1991, for example, the Court of Appeal held that it was normally inappropriate to order trial by jury for the assessment of damages in actions for personal injuries since the damages were based on consideration of conventional scales of damages known to the judiciary but not to a jury.

Juries are not used in Admiralty cases but there is a power to summon a jury in the Chancery Division. This power is, in practice, neglected.

A civil jury consists of twelve persons, though the parties may, in a particular case, agree to proceed with less. There is a right, under s. 66 of the County Courts Act, 1984, to ask for a jury of eight persons in a County Court, where the case is an appropriate one, as where, for example, fraud, or malicious prosecution, or false imprisonment are alleged. These rights are rarely exercised. In addition, a coroner must, under s. 8(3) of the Coroners Act, 1988, summon a jury of seven to eleven persons in some cases, e.g. where the deceased was in police custody, or death was the result of an injury caused by a police officer in the purported execution of his duty, and may accept the verdict of the majority if the dissentients are not more than two. Where there is no jury the judge determines the facts as well as the law.

Apart from a coroner's jury a civil jury had formerly to be unanimous. However, under s. 17 of the Juries Act, 1974, the verdict of the jury in civil proceedings in the High Court need not be unanimous if –

(a) where there are not less than eleven jurors, ten of them agree on the verdict; and
(b) where there are ten jurors, nine of them agree on the verdict.

The verdict of a jury of eight persons in a county court need not be unanimous if seven of them agree on the verdict. The two hours deliberation necessary for a jury before a majority verdict is permissible is not required for a civil jury. It is enough if it appears to the court that the jury had such period of time for deliberation as the court thinks reasonable, having regard to the nature and complexity of the case. In civil cases the court may accept a verdict by *any* majority so long as both parties consent. (S. 17(5) of the 1974 Act.)

Appeals

Consideration has already been given in Chapter 2 to the rights of appeal in civil cases (and see p. 22).

Enforcing a judgment

Let us assume that the judge has given judgment for John on his claim and to Nature Foods on their counterclaim for sums of money thought appropriate in the circumstances of the case. Let us suppose that neither party is prepared to pay these sums. How can a party to an action get the money the court has awarded him? Some of the more important methods available to *judgment* creditors are set out below.

(a) *The writ of fi fa (fieri facias).* A plaintiff can ask the High Court for this writ which orders the sheriff of the county in which the debtor's goods are located to seize through bailiffs the defendant's goods and sell them if necessary in order to pay the plaintiff. In the County Court there is a similar procedure but it is based upon a warrant of execution.

(b) *The charging order.* The court may make such an order over, say, the defendant's land or other property such as shares. If the money is not paid the plaintiff can have the property sold and recover his damages from the proceeds of sale. The Charging Orders Act, 1979 defines the type of property in respect of which a charging order may be made. The 1979 Act widened the scope of property which may be made the subject of an order so that, for example, a charging order may now be made over a debtor's beneficial interest under a trust.

(c) *The garnishee order.* If the creditor knows that the debtor is owed money by a third party – where, for instance, there is a credit balance on the debtor's bank account – the creditor may wish to divert the payment away from the debtor to himself. This can be done by applying to the court for a garnishee order *nisi*. The order is addressed to the third party, e.g. the bank, forbidding it to pay the debt to the debtor and requiring a representative to attend before the court to show why the money (or part of it) should not be paid over to the judgment creditor.

The order is served at least seven days before the next court hearing on the matter and if at that hearing no cause has been shown as to why payment should not be made to the judgment creditor, the court can make a garnishee order absolute, requiring payment by the bank to the judgment creditor.

(d) *Attachment of earnings.* Where the defendant is in employment the plaintiff can obtain an attachment of earnings order through the County Court. Under such an order the defendant's employer is required to deduct a specified sum from the defendant's wages or salary and pay the money into court for the plaintiff. Attachment is not available against the profits of the self-employed.

(e) *Equitable execution.* The court may appoint a *receiver* where, for example, the defendant owns property. The receiver can take over income such as rent and apply it in order to pay the plaintiff. The judgment creditor of a person who is a partner can, under s. 23 of the Partnership Act, 1890, obtain an order charging that partner's interest in the partnership property and profits with payment of the judgment debt. If the judgment creditor feels that he will experience difficulty in getting the firm to pay over, e.g. the profit share of the partner concerned, he can ask for the appointment of a receiver.

The enforcement of a non-money judgment, such as an injunction, is by means of the offence of contempt of court. If a defendant fails to obey an injunction he is in contempt of court and the court may, if the plaintiff applies, punish him. It may make, for example, an order for committal under which if the defendant still refuses to comply with the injunction, he may be imprisoned. Alternatively, the court may issue a write of sequestration. This writ, which is directed by the court to commissioners, usually four in number, commands them to enter the lands and take the rents and profits and seize the goods of the person against whom it is directed. Thus the court can in effect take control of the defendant's property until the plaintiff has complied with the court's order.

(f) Where as here the debt exceeds £750, bankruptcy or company insolvency proceedings could be considered. This would at least ensure that an insolvency practitioner (generally an accountant) would be put in charge of the debtor's assets and ensure a fair and legal distribution of the assets between creditors as well as effectively preventing the debtor from dealing with them.

6
The law-making process I – the UK Parliament

The word 'source' has various meanings when applied to law. One may treat the word 'source' as referring to the *historical or ultimate origins of law* and trace the *development* of the common law, equity, legislation, delegated legislation, custom, the law merchant, canon law and legal treatises, as we have done in Chapter 1. But on the other hand one may treat the word 'source' as referring to the *methods by which laws are made or brought into existence,* and consider the current processes of legislation, delegated legislation, judicial precedent and, to a limited extent, custom. In this chapter we shall be concerned with the *methods by which laws are made,* i.e. the *active* or *legal* souces of law and in particular the laws which are made by the UK Parliament and how they are interpreted by the judiciary.

Legislation

It is common knowledge that much of our law is contained in Acts of Parliament. Parliament consists of two chambers – the House of Commons and the House of Lords. The House of Commons contains 651 members, each of whom represents a geographical area in the country called a constituency. Members of Parliament (M.P.s) are elected at general elections. Casual vacancies, occurring e.g. through the death of a member, are filled separately at by-elections. The House of Lords, on the other hand, consists in the main of hereditary peers, though under the provisions of the Life Peerages Act, 1958, there has been added a number of distinguished people from various walks of life who hold life peerages, but whose descendants will have no right to a seat when the life peers are dead. In addition to the Lords Temporal there are also the Lords Spiritual, e.g. the Archbishops of Canterbury and York, and certain other bishops. Over 1000 people are eligible to sit in the House of Lords but many do not exercise their right to do so.

An Act of Parliament begins as a Bill, which is the draft of a proposed Act.

TYPES OF BILLS

A session of Parliament normally lasts for one year commencing in October or November. During that time, a large number of Bills become law, most of which are *Government Bills*. The government is formed by the parliamentary party having an overall majority, or at least the greatest number, of members in the House of Commons, or more rarely by a formal coalition of, or more informal arrangement between, two or more parties who between them can command such a majority. The government is led by a Prime Minister who appoints a variety of other Ministers such as the Chancellor of the Exchequer, the Home Secretary, the Foreign Secretary, and others to manage various departments of State. A small group of these Ministers, called the Cabinet, meets frequently under the chairmanship of the Prime Minister and formulates the policy of the government. An important part of this policy consists of presenting Bills to Parliament with a view to their becoming law in due course. Such Bills are usually presented by the Minister of the department concerned with their contents.

The legislative intentions of the government are given in outline to Parliament at the commencement of each session in the Queen's Speech. This is read by the Queen but is prepared by the government of the day. Most Government Bills are introduced in the House of Commons, going later to the House of Lords and finally for the Royal Assent. However, some of the less controversial Government Bills are introduced in the House of Lords, going later to the Commons and then for the Royal Assent. Money Bills, i.e. those containing only provisions relating to finance and taxation, e.g. the annual Finance Bill, and other Bills with financial clauses must start in the Commons.

Members of either House whether government supporters or not have a somewhat restricted opportunity to introduce *Private Members' Bills*. Such Bills are not likely to become law unless the government provides the necessary parliamentary time for debate. Some, however, survive to become law, for example, the Murder (Abolition of Death Penalty) Act, 1965. Those that are lost usually fail to be debated fully because influential and anonymous objectors work behind the scenes to ensure that they are taken towards the end of the session when parliamentary time is at a premium. In addition, the severe restriction of debating time for Private Members' Bills makes such time as is available an ideal stamping ground for the determined filibuster who wishes to talk the bill out. In spite of all this many more Private Members' Bills have reached the statute book in recent times.

A session of Parliament is brought to an end by the Monarch by prorogation and a Bill which does not complete the necessary stages and receive the Royal Assent in one session will lapse. It can be introduced in a subsequent session but must complete all the necessary stages again. Bills also lapse when Parliament is dissolved prior to a General Election. The above provisions do not apply to *Private Bills* (see below) which because of the costs involved in promotion can complete their remaining stages in a new session. The sittings of Parliament within a session are divided by periods of 'recess'. Bills do not lapse when Parliament goes into recess.

Bills are also divided into *Public* and *Private* Bills. *Public Bills,* which may be Government or Private Members' Bills, alter the law throughout England and Wales and extend also to Scotland and Northern Ireland unless there is a provision to the contrary. A *Private Bill* does not alter the general law but confers special local powers. These Bills are often promoted by local authorities, where a new local development requires compulsory purchase of land for which a statutory power is needed. Enactment of these Bills is by a different parliamentary procedure.

The Speaker of the House of Commons rules whether a Bill is public or private if there is doubt as where e.g. the Bill might affect areas beyond that of the local authority concerned, as would be the case if a seaport authority forbade the export of live animals from the port.

ENACTMENT OF BILLS

A Public Bill and a Private Members' Bill follow the same procedure in Parliament. These Bills may be introduced in either House; though, as we have seen, a money Bill, which is a public Bill certified by the Speaker as one containing provisions relating to taxation or loans, must be introduced in the Commons by a Minister and not a Private Member. The following procedure relates to a Public or Private Members' Bill introduced in the Commons.

On its introduction the Bill receives a purely formal first reading. Only the title of the Bill is read out by the Clerk of the House. The purpose of this stage is to tell Members that the Bill exists. It is then printed and published. Later it is given a second reading, at which point its general merits may be debated, but no amendments are proposed to the various clauses it contains. There is an alternative procedure for the second reading stage of *Public Bills in the Commons,* which is designed to save parliamentary time. A Minister may move that the Bill be referred to a Standing Second Reading Committee of between 30 and 80 M.P.s. They report to the Commons recommending with reasons whether or not the Bill should be read a second time. The report of the Committee must be put to the House for a vote without debate or amendment. This procedure does not apply if 20 Members rise in their seats to object. Private Members' Bills are automatically referred to the Second Reading Committee.

The Second Reading Committee procedure has saved a lot of parliamentary time and assisted the passing of many non-controversial Bills for which the government would otherwise have had to find debating time. There is also a rule limiting speeches in second reading debates in the Commons to ten minutes which also saves time.

Having survived the second reading, the Bill passes to the Committee stage. Here details are discussed by a Standing Committee of 15 to 20 members chosen in proportion to the strength of the parties in the House of Commons.

Amendments to the clauses are proposed, and, if not accepted by the Government, are voted on, after which the Bill returns to the House at the Report stage. The Committee mentioned may be a Committee of the Whole House, if the legislation is sufficiently important. Certain Bills in the Commons may be sent to a Special Standing Committee which is given power to hear evidence from outsiders, thus following to some extent the procedure for Private Bills. (See below.)

At the Report stage the amendments may be debated, and the Bill may in some cases be referred back for further consideration. It is then read for the third time, when amendments may strictly speaking be moved but in practice only verbal alterations are taken.

After passing the third reading, the Bill is said to have 'passed the House'. It is then sent to the House of Lords where it goes through a similar procedure and must pass through all stages successfully *in the same session of Parliament*. If the Lords propose amendments, the Bill is returned to the Commons for approval. At one time the House of Lords had the power to reject Bills sent up by the Commons. Now, under the provisions of the Parliament Acts, 1911 and 1949, this power amounts to no more than an ability to delay a Public Bill (other than a money Bill) for a period of one year; a money Bill may be delayed for one month only. The supremacy of the Commons stems from the fact that it is an elected assembly, responsible to its electors and coming periodically at intervals of not more than five years before the public for re-election. The Lords may veto a Private Bill and have retained the power to reject a Bill which attempts to extend the duration of Parliament beyond five years.

PRIVATE BILLS – A JUDICIAL STAGE

The main difference between the enactment of a *Private Bill* and a *Public Bill* is that the committee stage of a Private Bill may be judicial. Any person whose interests are specifically affected by the Bill, normally in relation to property or business interests, may lodge a petition against the Bill in accordance with the procedure set out in Standing Orders. In such a situation the Bill is referred to an Opposed Committee consisting of four M.P.s of all parties appointed by the House. They must be entirely disinterested in a material sense, in the matters with which the Bill is concerned. The Committee hears both the petitioner and the promoter, who usually appear by counsel. If the petition succeeds the Bill is amended to take account of it. There is no appeal against the decision of the Committee. Since this is a somewhat lengthy procedure, some statutes allow ministers to grant special powers to local authorities by what is called a Provisional Order. Such an order does not take effect unless and until it is embodied (usually along with others) in a Provisional Order Confirmation Bill which is passed by Parliament and given the Royal Assent. There are also radical proposals to change the Private Act of Parliament procedure because the parliamentary timetable is becoming clogged up by the number of these Bills, many of which are concerned with new powers for railways and harbours. The suggestion is that power of approval be given to local authorities and/or public inquiries followed by a parliamentary debate only. This could well be an improvement since public inquiries are more accessible than the Private Bill procedure.

ROYAL ASSENT

When a Bill has passed through both the Commons and the Lords, it requires the Royal Assent. It is not customary for the Monarch to consent in person and in practice consent is given by a committee of three peers, including the Lord Chancellor. The Royal Assent Act, 1967 provides that an Act is duly enacted and becomes law if the Royal Assent is notified to each House of Parliament, sitting separately, by the Speaker of that House or the acting Speaker.

The former Bill is then referred to as an Act or a Statute, and may be regarded as a *literary* as well as a *legal* source of law. However, an Act may specify a future date for its coming into operation, or it may be brought into operation piecemeal by ministerial order. The courts have no power to examine proceedings in Parliament in order to determine whether the passing of an Act or delegated legislation has been obtained by means of any irregularity or fraud.

ESSENTIAL CASE LAW

British Railways Board v *Pickin*, 1974 – The courts and
  parliamentary proceedings **(21)**

SHORT TITLE – NUMBERING AND CITATION

It should be noted that, as well as having a title setting out what its objects are, each Act has, under the provisions of the Short Titles Act, 1896, a short title to enable easy reference to be made. Each Act has also an official reference. The Law of Property Act, 1925, is the short title of an Act whose official reference is 15 & 16 Geo.5, c. 20, which means that the Law of Property Act, 1925, was the twentieth statute passed in the session of Parliament spanning the fifteenth and sixteenth years of the reign of George the Fifth.

The Acts of Parliament Numbering and Citation Act, 1962 provides that chapter numbers assigned to Acts of Parliament passed in 1963 and after shall be assigned by reference to the calendar year and not the session in which they are passed. For example, the official reference of the Sale of Goods Act, 1979 is 1979, c. 54.

STATUTE LAW AND CASE LAW DISTINGUISHED

The essential differences between statute law and case law are apparent from the definition of a statute. It is –

an express and formal laying down of a rule or rules of conduct to be observed in the future by the persons to whom the statute is expressly or by implication made applicable.

Thus a statute openly creates new law, whereas a judge would disclaim any attempt to do so. Judges are, they say, bound by precedent and merely select existing rules which they apply to new cases. (But see p. 159.) A statute lays down general rules for the guidance of future conduct; a judgment merely applies an existing rule to a particular set of circumstances. A judgment gives reasons and may be argumentative; a statute gives no reasons and is imperative.

Delegated legislation

Modern statutes may require much detailed work to implement and operate them. In such a case the Act is drafted so as to provide a broad framework, the details being filled in by ministers by means of delegated legislation. For example, much of our Social Security legislation gives only the general provisions of a complex scheme of social benefits and an immense number of detailed regulations have had to be made by civil servants in the name of and under the authority of the appropriate minister. These regulations when made in the approved manner are just as much law as the parent statute itself. This form of law is known as *delegated* or *subordinate* legislation.

ADVANTAGES

A number of advantages are claimed for delegated legislation as follows.

(*a*) *It saves Parliamentary time* in that ministers are left, with the civil service, to make the detailed rules, Parliament concerning itself solely with the broad framework of the legislation.

(*b*) *Speed.* The Parliamentary procedure for enacting bills is slow whereas rules and orders can be put more rapidly into law, particularly in a time of national emergency.

(*c*) *Parliament cannot foresee all the problems* which may arise after an Act has become law. Delegated legislation can deal with these if and when they arise.

(*d*) *Delegated legislation is less rigid* in that it can be withdrawn quickly by another statutory instrument if it proves impracticable.

(e) *The aptitude of the legislature is limited* and experts in the Departments of State can better advise a minister on the technicalities of a certain branch of law. It would be difficult to give this kind of advice to the Lords or Commons as a whole.

DISADVANTAGES

However, there are disadvantages as follows.

(a) *Parliamentary control over legislation is undoubtedly reduced.* However, the power to make delegated legislation must be given by an Act of Parliament (sometimes referred to as the enabling statute) and so Parliament is to that extent in broad control because it must pass the enabling statute.

Beyond that much depends upon what the enabling statute says about reference to Parliament when instruments are made. There are different requirements and the inclusion of one rather than another in an enabling statute does not appear to be based upon any detectable principle.

The enabling Act may require –

(i) that the instrument be merely laid before Parliament. Where this is so M.P.s and Peers have no right to change it but laying before Parliament does, at least, inform them that the instrument exists. In some cases the instrument is already in force. However, Members may ask Parliamentary questions about instruments laid for information only;

(ii) that Parliament may annul the instrument, e.g. within 40 days of laying. Where this is so a resolution of either House to annul the instrument is effective, but if there is no such resolution the instrument passes into law. However, whether there is a debate leading to a resolution to annul the instrument is entirely dependent upon the initiative of an M.P. or Peer to engineer the debate since the Government is not obliged to find time for it;

(iii) that each House of Parliament must pass a resolution approving the instrument. Where this is so the Government must obviously find time for a debate and a resolution approving the instrument must be made in each House, otherwise it will not become law;

(iv) that the instrument be laid in draft before Parliament and may only be issued if an affirmative resolution is passed by each House in its favour;

(v) that the instrument be laid in draft without reference to affirmative resolutions, in which case by s. 6 of the Statutory Instruments Act of 1946 it may be made law after a period of 40 days if no resolutiion is passed during that period by either House against it.

It should be noted that if it is essential that an instrument come into operation before copies of it can be laid before Parliament, then it may do so provided notification is sent to the Lord Chancellor and the Speaker of the House of Commons explaining why copies could not be laid before the instrument came into operation.

There are also other controls both by the judiciary and by Parliament itself. (See below.)

(*b*) *It is said that there is too much delegated legislation* so that it is difficult to know what the law is, particularly in view of the fact that little publicity is given to statutory instruments whereas most important Acts of Parliament are referred to at one time or another in the Press. The difficulty is that a defendant's *ignorance of the law is no excuse,* though s. 3(2) of the Statutory Instruments Act of 1946 protects a person in respect of a crime contained in a statutory instrument *if the instrument has not been published,* unless it is proved that reasonable steps have been taken for the purpose of bringing the content of the instrument to the notice of the public or of persons likely to be affected by it or the person in fact charged. The section does not protect if the instrument has been published but a particular defendant does not know of its existence.

(*c*) *The dangers of sub-delegation are on occasions quite real.* One can find in some cases a pedigree of four generations of instrument emanating from a statute as follows –

    (i) regulations made under the statute;
    (ii) orders made under the regulations;
    (iii) directions made under the orders;
    (iv) licences issued under the directions.

When this happens it does reduce very seriously the control by Parliament of the making of new laws since Parliament would only see the parent statute and the first set of regulations.

TYPES OF DELEGATED LEGISLATION

In modern statutes delegated powers are exercisable by four main vehicles as follows –

(*a*) *Statutory instruments.* Most powers conferred on ministers in modern statutes are exercisable by ministerial or departmental regulations or orders, called collectively statutory instruments.

(*b*) *Orders in Council.* Powers of special importance relating to constitutional issues, e.g. emergency powers, are conferred on the Queen in Council. These powers are in fact exercised by the Cabinet who are all Privy Councillors by means of an order in council.

(*c*) *Bye-laws of Local Authorities.* These are made by local authorities under powers given to them in Acts of Parliament and require the approval of the appropriate Minister.

(*d*) *Rules of the Supreme Court and County Court.* These are made by

Rules Committees set up by statute specifically to make rules concerning the practice and procedure of the courts. The Rules Committees are made up of judges and senior members of the legal profession.

JUDICIAL CONTROL

Delegated legislation takes effect as if it were part of the enabling statute. Therefore it has statutory force and, as we have seen, the courts cannot declare a statute *ultra vires*. However, delegated legislation does not acquire statutory force unless it is *intra vires,* i.e. properly made in accordance with the terms of the enabling Act. The courts can declare delegated legislation *ultra vires* in this sense. There are two approaches to the *ultra vires* rule as regards delegated legislation as follows –

(*a*) *Substantive ultra vires.* This means that the Minister has exceeded the powers given to him in the parent statute. If a Minister is authorised to make regulations as to road traffic, clearly if he purports to make regulations under the same parent statute concerning rail traffic, they would be held by the courts to be *ultra vires* and invalid.

(*b*) *Procedural ultra vires.* This means that the instrument is invalid because the minister has failed to follow some mandatory procedural requirement specified in the parent Act. For example, much Social Security legislation requires the minister to consult various advisory bodies before making rules and orders. If a rule or order was made without the necessary consultation, then it would be *ultra vires* in procedural terms and invalid.

ESSENTIAL CASE LAW AND COMMENT

Hotel and Catering Industry Training Board v *Automobile Proprietary Ltd,,* 1969 – Delegated legislation and *ultra vires* **(22)**

HENRY VIII (OR OUSTER) CLAUSES

Sometimes a section of an Act will give a minister or the Queen in Council very wide powers so that it is difficult to say that any instrument made or decision taken under it is *ultra vires*. These are referred to as 'Henry VIII Clauses' after the way in which that monarch used to legislate in arbitrary fashion by a proclamation. A more modern expression is an 'ouster clause', i.e. a clause attempting to prevent a decision being reviewed by the court. For example, s. 4(7) of the Parliamentary Constituencies Act, 1986 provides that 'The validity of any Order in Council purporting to be made under this Act – shall not be called in question in any legal proceedings whatsoever.' It was at one time thought that the courts were powerless to intervene to review any order made under such a provision. However, in more recent times the courts have taken power to overcome ouster clauses by saying, in effect, that if the exercise of such a power is not in accordance with the law, as where it is e.g. *ultra vires* or made by misinterpreting the power given, the minister or tribunal has lost jurisdiction and the court can intervene. In other words the jurisdiction is to decide correctly but not incorrectly. An illustration is provided by the decision of the House of Lords in *Anisminic Ltd* v *Foreign Compensation Commission* [1969] 1 All E.R. 208. A Ltd applied to the Commission for compensation for property seized by Egypt in 1956 at the time of the Suez crisis relating among other things to the blocking of the Suez canal. The Foreign Compensation Act, 1950 was relevant. It said that decisions of the Commission 'shall not be called into question in any court of law'. The Commission decided that A Ltd was not entitled to compensation but in doing so misinterpreted the statute. This said the House of Lords made the decision *ultra vires* and void. It was therefore not a 'decision' and the court could question it. Being merely asked to say what the law was the court gave a declaratory judgment that the decision was void.

PARLIAMENTARY CONTROL

The main Parliamentary control is through a Joint Committee on Statutory Instruments between the House of Commons and the House of Lords. The Joint Committee is appointed to consider statutory instruments with a view to determining whether the special attention of Parliament should be drawn to the legislation on various grounds. The grounds, briefly, are as follows; that the legislation –

(*a*) imposes a tax on the public;

(*b*) is made under an enactment containing specific provisions excluding it from challenge in the courts;

(*c*) purports to have retrospective effect where there is no express authority in the enabling statute;

(*d*) has been unduly delayed in publication or laying before Parliament;

(*e*) has come into operation before being laid before Parliament and there has been unjustifiable delay in informing the Speaker of the delay under s. 4(1) of the Statutory Instruments Act, 1946;

(*f*) may be beyond the powers given by the parent statute or makes some unusual or unexpected use of those powers;

(*g*) calls for better explanation as to its meaning.

As regards law coming from the European Community there is also a system of three standing committees consisting of 10 M.P.s to examine the proposals of the Community in terms of legal matters and to question Ministers about them. There are also Commons debates before the twice-yearly EC summit meetings to give M.P.s a chance to air their views on the agendas for the summit meetings.

BYE-LAWS OF LOCAL AUTHORITIES

These must be *intra vires*, i.e. within the powers given to the local authority in the enabling statute, and also reasonable. Thus, in *Kruse* v *Johnson* [1898] 2 Q.B. 91 a local authority bye-law making it an offence to sing within 50 yards of a dwelling house was upheld but the court decided that unreasonableness could be a ground for invalidating bye-laws.

ESSENTIAL CASE LAW AND COMMENT

Burnley Borough Council v *England*, 1978 – Bye-laws: challenge in court **(23)**

Interpretation of statutes by the judiciary

The main body of the law is to be found in statutes, together with the relevant statutory instruments, and in case law as enunciated by judges in the courts. But the judges not only have the duty of declaring the common law, they are also frequently called upon to settle disputes as to the meaning of words or clauses in a statute.

Parliament is the supreme lawgiver, and the judges must follow statutes. (But see p. 581.) Nevertheless there is a considerable amount of case law which gathers round Acts of Parliament and delegated legislation since the wording sometimes turns out to be obscure. Statutes were at one time drafted by practising lawyers who were experts in the particular branch of law of which the statute was to be a part. Today, however, statutes are drafted by parliamentary counsel to the Treasury, and, although such persons are skilled in the law, the volume of legislation means that statutes are often obscure and cases continue to come before the courts in which the rights of the parties depend upon the exact meaning of a section of a statute. When such a case comes before a judge, he must decide the meaning of the section in question. Thus even statute law is not free from judicial influence.

The judges have certain recognised *aids to interpretation*, and these are set out below.

STATUTORY AIDS

Judges may get some guidance from statute law.

(*a*) The Interpretation Act, 1978, which is itself a statute, defines terms commonly used in Acts of Parliament, e.g. that 'person' includes a corporation as well as a human being.

(*b*) A complex statute will normally contain an interpretation section, defining the terms used in the particular Act, e.g. ss. 735–44A of the

Companies Act, 1985 define, among other things, 'accounts' and 'director', and the judges have recourse to this.

(c) Every Act of Parliament used to have what was known as a preamble, which set out at the beginning the general purpose and scope of the Act. The preamble was often quite lengthy and assisted the judge in ascertaining the meaning of the statute. Modern public Acts do not have this type of preamble, but have instead a long title which is not of so much assistance in interpretation. For example, the Sex Discrimination Act, 1975, which contains 87 sections and a number of schedules, says merely: 'An Act to render unlawful certain kinds of sex discrimination and discrimination on the grounds of marriage, and establish a Commission with the function of working towards the elimination of such discrimination and promoting equality of opportunity between men and women generally; and for related purposes.' All private Acts must have a preamble setting out the objects of the legislation, and this preamble must be proved by the promoters at the Committee stage in the House of Lords. So far as private Acts are concerned the preamble may be of considerable assistance.

ESSENTIAL CASE LAW AND COMMENT

Hutton v Esher U.D.C., 1973 – Statutory interpretation and the Interpretation Act **(24)**

GENERAL RULES OF INTERPRETATION EVOLVED BY JUDGES

There are a number of generally recognised rules or canons of interpretation, and some of the more important ones are now given.

The mischief rule

This was set out in *Heydon's* case (1584), 3 Co. Rep. 7a. Under this rule the judge will look at the Act to see what was its purpose and what mischief in the common law it was designed to prevent.

Broadly speaking, the rule means that where a statute has been passed to remedy a weakness in the law the interpretation which will correct that weakness is the one to be adopted.

The literal rule

According to this rule, the working of the Act must be construed according to its literal and grammatical meaning whatever the result may be. The same word must normally be construed throughout the Act in the same sense, and in the case of old statutes regard must be had to its contemporary meaning if there has been a change with the passage of time.

The Law Commission, in an instructive and provocative report on the subject of interpretation (Law Com. 21), said of this rule that 'to place undue emphasis on the literal meaning of the words of a provision is to assume an unattainable perfection in draftsmanship'.

The rule, when in operation, does not always achieve the obvious object and purpose of the statute. A classic example is *Whiteley* v *Chappell* (1868–9), 4 L.R.Q.B. 147. In that case a statute concerned with electoral malpractices made it an offence to personate 'any person entitled to vote' at an election. The defendant was accused of personating a deceased voter and the court, using the literal rule, found that there was no offence. The personation was not of a person entitled to vote. A dead person was not entitled to vote, or do anything else for that matter. A deceased person did not exist and could therefore have no rights. It will be seen, however, that the literal rule produced in that case a result which was clearly contrary to the object of Parliament.

The golden rule

This rule is to some extent an extension of the literal rule and under it the words of a statute will as far as possible be construed according to their ordinary plain and natural meaning, unless this leads to an absurd result. It is used by the courts where a statutory provision is capable of more than one literal meaning and leads the judge to select the one which avoids absurdity, or where a study of the statute as a whole reveals that the conclusion reached by applying the literal rule is contrary to the intentions of Parliament.

Thus, in *Re Sigsworth* [1935] Ch. 89 the court decided that the Administration of Estates Act, 1925, which provides for the distribution of the property of an intestate amongst his next of kin, did not confer a benefit upon the person (a son) who had murdered the intestate (his mother), even though the murderer was the intestate's next of kin, for it is a general principle of law that no one can profit from his own wrong.

The *ejusdem generis* rule

This is a rule covering things of the same genus, species or type. Under it, where general words follow particular words, the general words are construed as being limited to persons or things within the class outlined by the particular words. So in a reference to 'dogs, cats, and other animals,' the last three words would be limited in their application to animals of the domestic type, and would not be extended to cover animals such as elephants and camels which are not domestic animals in the UK.

Expressio unius est exclusio alterius

(The expression of one thing implies the exclusion of another.) Under this rule, where specific words are used and are not followed by general words, the Act applies only to the instances mentioned. For example, where a statute contains an express statement that certain statutes are repealed, there is a presumption that other relevant statutes not mentioned are not repealed.

Noscitur a sociis

(The meaning of a word can be gathered from its context.) Under this rule words of doubtful meaning may be better understood from the nature of the words and phrases with which they are associated.

ESSENTIAL CASE LAW AND COMMENT

Gardiner v *Sevenoaks R.D.C.*, 1950 – The mischief rule **(25)**
Keene v *Muncaster*, 1980 – The golden rule **(26)**
Lane v *London Electricity Board*, 1955 – The *ejusdem generis* rule **(27)**
R v *Immigration Appeals Adjudicator, ex parte Crew*, 1982 – The rule of *expressio unius* **(28)**
Muir v *Keay*, 1875 – The rule of *noscitur a sociis* **(29)**

OTHER CONSIDERATIONS AND PRESUMPTIONS

In addition to the major rules of interpretation, there are also several other considerations which the judge will have in mind. He will concern himself only with the wording of the Act, and will not go to *Hansard* to look up reports of the debates during the passage of the Act.

There is here some conflict with the mischief rule, since it might be thought there is no better way to ascertain what mischief the Act was designed to prevent than by reference to the Parliamentary debates in Hansard. Nevertheless, the Law Commission in their deliberations on the matter of statutory interpretation decided against the use of Hansard since they doubted the reliability of statements made in Parliamentary debates.

The House of Lords decided in *Davis* v *Johnson* [1978] 1 All E.R. 1132 that it is now permissible for the court to refer to reports by such bodies as the Law Commission and committees or commissions appointed by the Government or by either House of Parliament from which the reform of the law stems.

However, according to the judgments, e.g. that of Lord Diplock, 'Where legislation follows on a published report of this kind the report may be used as an aid to identify the mischief which the legislation is intended to remedy but not for the purpose of construing the enacting words . . .'. In other words the relevant report can assist in terms of what the legislation was designed to do but not whether the words it uses achieve it.

A statute is presumed not to alter the existing law unless it expressly states that it does. There is also a presumption against the repeal of other statutes and that is why statutes which are repealed are repealed by specific reference.

In the absence of any express indication to the contrary, a construction which would exclude retrospective effect is to be preferred to a construction which would not. Thus in *Alexander* v *Mercouris* [1979] 3 All E.R. 305, where the plaintiff sued the defendant for alleged defective workmanship in the conversion of two flats, the plaintiff tried to bring his case under the

Defective Premises Act, 1972 (see further p. 459) which came into force on 1 January 1974. However, it appeared that the defendant commenced the work in November 1972 and it was held by the Court of Appeal that no claim could be brought under the Act as the Act could not be construed as having retrospective effect. Some Finance Acts do have retrospective effect in terms of taxation.

When a statute deprives a person of property, there is a presumption that compensation will be paid. Unless so stated it is presumed that an Act does not interfere with rights over private property. There is a rebuttable presumption against alteration of the common law. Any Act which presumes to restrict private liberty will be very strictly interpreted, though the strictness may be tempered in times of emergency. It is presumed that an Act does not bind the Crown on the ground that the law, made by the Crown on the advice of the Lords and Commons, is made for subjects and not for the Crown. Furthermore, as we have seen, the courts lack the power to examine proceedings in Parliament in order to determine whether the passing of an Act has been obtained by means of any irregularity of fraud. (See *British Railways Board* v *Pickin*, 1974 at p. 574.)

However, the Law Commissioners have recommended that more emphasis should be placed on the importance of interpreting a statute in the light of the general purposes behind it and the intentions of Parliament. This is referred to as a purposive interpretation. Thus in *Fletcher* v *Budgen* [1974] 2 All E.R. 1243 the Divisional Court of Queen's Bench decided that under the Trade Descriptions Act, 1968, a buyer of goods, in this case a car dealer, could be guilty of the offence of falsely describing goods when he told a private seller that his car was almost worthless, bought it, repaired it and sold it at a considerable profit. Lord Widgery, C.J. said that although he had never thought of the Act as applying to buyers of goods, it was necessary in the public interest that it should, at least in the case of expert buyers, and that in his view such decision 'is not in any sense illogical and is not likely to run counter to any intention which Parliament may have had'.

However, as Lord Scarman said in *Shah* v *Barnet London Borough Council* [1983] 1 All E.R. 226 at p. 238: 'Judges may not interpret statutes in the light of their own views as to policy. They may, of course, adopt a purposive interpretation if they can find in the statute read as a whole or in material to which they are permitted by law to refer as aids to interpretation an expression of Parliament's purpose or policy.'

Rules of interpretation tend to some extent to cancel each other. Thus by using one or other of these rules judges can be narrow, reformist, or conservative. In fact Pollock, in his *Essays in Jurisprudence and Ethics,* suggests –

English judges have often tended to interpret statutes on the theory that Parliament generally changes the law for the worse and that the business of the judges is to keep the mischief of its interference within the narrowest possible bounds.

It must be said that this comment applies particularly to judicial interpretation of welfare law where they have sometimes been reluctant to fill in gaps in order to make the law work, whereas if the Act is in the field of 'lawyers' law then they have been prepared to do precisely this in order, for example, to convict a guilty person of crime. This is, however, not surprising since judges are the product of a legalistic training and are clearly ill-equipped to pronounce upon welfare law, whereas in crime, for example, they are dealing with rules which they better understand so that they feel less reluctant to fill in gaps.

7
The law-making process II – case law and the legislative organs of the European Community

We are concerned in this chapter to explain the methods by which the judiciary become involved in the law-making process and the effect of European Community legislation – how it is made and interpreted, together with the official bodies involved in law reform.

Case law or judicial precedent

Case law still provides the bulk of the law of the country, although Parliament is becoming much more active in making new laws and statute law may come to dominate the common law. This trend is, of course, encouraged by the existence of the Law Commission which is constantly putting forward proposals to codify the law by statute. Some case law states the law itself, and some is concerned as we have seen with the interpretation of statutes. We will examine here case law which is law in its own right. Case law is built up out of precedents, and a precedent is a previous decision of a court which may, in certain circumstances, be binding on another court in deciding a similar case. This practice of following previous decisions is derived from custom, but it is a practice which is generally observed. As Park, C.J. said in *Mirehouse* v *Rennell* (1833) 1 Cl. & Fin. 527, 'Precedent must be adhered to for the sake of developing the law as a science.' In more modern times attention to precedent is essential because without it no lawyer could safely advise his client and every quarrel would lead to a law suit. Even in early times the itinerant judges adopted the doctrine of *stare decisis*, and this doctrine has been developed in modern times so that it means that a precedent binds, and must be followed in similar cases, subject to the power to distinguish cases in certain circumstances.

The modern doctrine of the binding force of judicial precedent only fully emerged when there was (*a*) good law reporting, and (*b*) a settled judicial hierarchy. By the middle of the nineteenth century law reporting was much more efficient, and the Judicature Acts, 1873–1875, created a proper pyramid of authority which was completed when the Appellate Jurisdiction Act, 1876, made the House of Lords the final Court of Appeal. Judicial precedents may be divided into two kinds –

(1) Binding Precedents
(2) Persuasive Precedents

but before we explain the precise meaning of these terms, we have still to find out where these precedents are to be found. The answer is in the law reports; and as we have seen the doctrine of judicial precedent depends upon an accurate record being kept of previous decisions.

LAW REPORTS

Since 1865 law reports have been published under the control of what is now called the Incorporated Council of Law Reporting, which is a joint committee of the Inns of Court, The Law Society, and the Bar Council. They are known simply as the Law Reports, and they have priority in the courts because the judge who heard the case sees and revises the report before publication. Nevertheless private reports still exist, and of these the All England Reports, published weekly and started in 1936, are the only *general* reports existing in the private sector. These reports are now revised by the judge concerned with the case. In 1953 the Incorporated Council began to publish reports on a weekly basis and these are known as the Weekly Law Reports. *The Times* newspaper publishes summarised reports of certain cases of importance and interest on the day following the hearing, as do other newspapers e.g. the *Financial Times,* the *Independent* and the *Guardian*, and there are also certain specialised series of reports covering, for example, the fields of taxation, shipping, company law and employment law. In a Practice Direction in 1990 (see *The Times,* 7 December 1990) the Master of the Rolls stated that in the House of Lords and the Court of Appeal the general rule was that the Law Reports published by the Incorporated Council of Law Reporting should be cited in preference to other reports where there was a choice. It is not absolutely essential that a case should have been reported in order that it may be cited as a precedent, and occasionally oral evidence of the decision by a barrister who was in court when the judgment was delivered may be brought.

The issue of the citation of unreported cases was raised by Lord Diplock in the House of Lords in *Roberts Petroleum* v *Bernard Kenny* [1983] 1 All E.R. 564, and Sir John Donaldson, M.R. in *Stanley* v *International Harvester, The Times,* 7 February 1983. These have become readily available since the Lexis Computer Retrieval System came into use. Lexis records, for example, 3000 Court of Appeal decisions a year. Of these only some 350 are reported in any of the major series such as All England, and Weekly Law Reports. These, as we have seen, are edited by the judge(s). Both judges seemed determined to discourage the growing resort by counsel to unreported cases. Indeed, in the *Stanley* case the view was that counsel should beware of citing to the courts cases which are of no great novelty or authority, but which are supplied in unnecessary profusion by computers.

Decided cases are usually referred to as follows: *Smith* v *Jones*, 1959. This means that, in a court of first instance, Smith was the plaintiff, Jones the defendant, and that the case was published in the set of reports of 1959, though it may have been heard at the end of 1958. This is called the Short Citation. A longer citation is required if the report is to be referred to, and might read as follows: *Smith* v *Jones* [1959] 1 Q.B. 67 at p. 76. The additional information means that the case is to be found in the First Volume of the Reports of the Queen's Bench Division, the report commencing on page 67, the number 76 being used to indicate the page on which an important statement is to be found. Where the date is cited in square brackets it means that the date is an essential part of the reference, and without the date it is very difficult to find the report in question. For many years now the Incorporated Council's reports have been written up in a certain number of volumes each year. It will be seen that a mere reference to Vol. 1 of the Queen's Bench Division will not be sufficient unless the year is also quoted. The same procedures are followed in the All England Reports.

The early reports by the Incorporated Council and other collections did not use the year as a basic item of the citation, but continued to extend the number of volumes regardless of the year. So a case may be cited as follows: *Smith* v *Jones,* 17 Ch. D. 230. It can be found by referring to Vol. 17 of the Chancery Division reports, and it is not necessary to know the year in which the report was published, though this will be ascertained when the report is referred to. Where the date is not an essential part of the citation it is quoted in round brackets. The abbreviations used in the Official Reports for the various divisions are: Q.B. for Queen's Bench; Ch. for Chancery; P. for Probate, etc.; Fam. for Family; and A.C. for the House of Lords and Privy Council (Appeal Cases). The reports of decisions of the Court of Appeal appear under the reference of the division in which they were first heard. As regards the case title petitions for leave to appeal and appeals to the Court of Appeal carry the same title as that which obtained in the court of first instance. This results in the plaintiff being shown first in the title whether he or she be the petitioner/appellant or respondent in the Court of Appeal. Since a Practice Note of 1974 ([1974] 1 All E.R. 752), this is now true of the House of Lords so that appeals to the House of Lords now carry the same title as that which obtained in the court of first instance, though in the Official Reports the reference A.C. is still used in House of Lords and Privy Council cases.

PRECEDENT – GENERALLY

We are now in a position to refer to a decided case but we still have to find out where the precedent is to be found, since the whole of the case is reported, and the judge may have said things which are not strictly relevant to the final judgment. We must know what to take as precedent, and what to ignore, so that we can find what is called the *ratio decidendi*. The doctrine of precedent declares that cases must be decided in the same way when their *material* facts are the same. The *ratio* is therefore defined as the *principle* of law used by the judge to arrive at his *decision* together with his *reasons* for doing so. To take an example from contract law, in *Household Fire Insurance Company* v *Grant* (1879) (see p. 600) the court *decided* that a letter of acceptance took effect when it was posted, the *reason* behind this *principle* being that the Post Office was the common agent of the parties.

The *ratio decidendi* of a decision may be narrowed or widened by a subsequent judge before whom the case is cited as an authority. Although a judge will give reasons for his ruling, he is neither concerned nor obliged to formulate *all* the possibilities which may stem from it. Thus the eventual and accepted *ratio decidendi* of a case may not be the *ratio decidendi* that the judge who decided the case would himself have chosen, but the one which has been approved by subsequent judges. This is inevitable, because a judge, when deciding a case, will give his reasons but will not usually distinguish in his remarks, in any rigid or unchangeable way, between what we have called the *ratio decidendi* and what are called *obiter dicta*. The latter are things said in passing, and they do not have binding force. Such statements of legal principle are, however, of some persuasive power, particularly the *dicta* of cases heard in the House of Lords.

The reason why *obiter dicta* are merely persuasive is because the prerogative of judges is not to make the law by formulating it and declaring it (this is for the legislature) but to make the law by applying it to cases coming before them. A judicial decision, unaccompanied by judicial application, is not of binding authority but is *obiter*. A judge does sometimes indicate which of his statements are *obiter dicta*. For example he may say: 'If it were necessary to decide the further point, I should be inclined to say that . . .'. What follows is said in passing.

It may therefore be said that the *ratio decidendi* of any given case is an abstraction of the legal *principle* from the *material* facts of the case, and, the *decision* which the judge made thereon together with his *reasons* for so doing. Of course, the higher the level of abstraction, the more circumstances the *ratio decidendi* will fit. Let us take the following fact situation: 'At 12 noon on a Saturday A, a woman aged 30, drove a car through the centre of Manchester at 80 mph. She mounted the pavement and injured B, an old man of 90. B sued A and the judge found that she was liable.' If a subsequent judge feels that the principle in *B* v *A* should be restricted he will tend to retain many of the facts of the case as material. If he feels that the principle should be extended he will not regard many of the facts of the situation as material and so produce a broad principle of wide application. Thus, a very narrow *ratio* would be as follows: 'If a woman aged 30 by the negligent driving of a car injures an old man of 90, she is liable to compensate him in damages.' However, the law of negligence is a much wider principle and the *ratio* is: 'If A, by negligence injures B, A is liable to compensate B in damages.'

The same principles of abstraction apply when a judge chooses to follow *obiter dicta*. This is well illustrated by the way in which the decision of the House of Lords in *Donoghue* v *Stevenson,* 1932 was developed to produce the modern doctrine of negligence. (See further p. 435.)

BINDING FORCE – GENERALLY

It is now necessary to examine which precedents are binding, and this depends also upon the level of the court in which the decision was reached. It would be useful to consider again at this point the diagrams on pp. 22 and 23 which deal with the structure of the civil and criminal courts.

THE HOUSE OF LORDS

Starting with the highest authority, the House of Lords, we find that this body was bound by its own decisions (*London Street Tramways* v *London County Council* [1898] A.C. 375), except, for example, where the previous decision had been made *per incuriam*, i.e. where an important case or statute was not brought to the attention of the court when the previous decision was made. However, in July 1966, the House of Lords abolished the rule that their own decisions on points of law were absolutely binding upon themselves. The Lord Chancellor announced the change on behalf of himself and the Lords of Appeal in Ordinary in the following statement –

> Their Lordships regard the use of precedent as an indispensable foundation upon which to decide what is the law and its application to individual cases. It provides at least some degree of certainty upon which individuals can rely in the conduct of their affairs, as well as a basis for orderly development of legal rules.
>
> Their Lordships nevertheless recognize that too rigid adherence to precedent may lead to injustice in a particular case and also unduly restrict the proper development of the law. They propose therefore to modify their present practice and, while treating former decisions of this House as normally binding, to depart from a previous decision when it appears right to do so.
>
> In this connexion they will bear in mind the danger of disturbing retrospectively the basis on which contracts, settlements of property and fiscal arrangements have been entered into and also the special need for certainty as to the criminal law.
>
> This announcement is not intended to affect the use of precedent elsewhere than in this House.

A practice direction issued in March 1971 by the Appeal Committee of the House of Lords requires lawyers concerned with the preparation of cases of appeal to state clearly in a separate paragraph of the case any intention to invite the House to depart from one of its own decisions.

The declaration was not used for over 20 years to overrule decisions in the field of criminal law. It has now been used in the context of crime. For example, in *R* v *Howe* [1987] 2 W.L.R. 568, the House of Lords overruled its previous decision in *D.P.P. for Northern Ireland* v *Lynch* [1975] 1 All E.R. 913 which had decided that duress could be a defence in a prosecution for murder. *R* v *Howe* removes the defence of duress from the law relating to murder altogether so that the defence is now never available to any participant in murder.

ESSENTIAL CASE LAW AND COMMENT

Schorsch Meier Gmbh v *Hennin*, 1975 – A case leading to the use of the 1966 declaration **(30)**

Miliangos v *George Frank (Textiles) Ltd*, 1975 – The declaration applied **(31)**

THE COURT OF APPEAL

On the next rung of the hierarchy there is the Court of Appeal (Civil Division), and this court is bound by its own previous decisions, as well as by those of the House of Lords. (*Young* v *Bristol Aeroplane Co.* [1944] 2 All E.R. 293.) There are, however, two main exceptions to the above rule.

(*a*) If there are two conflicting decisions of its own on the case before it the Court may choose which one to follow.

(*b*) The Court will not follow a decision of its own if that decision is inconsistent with a decision of the House of Lords or the Judicial Committee of the Privy Council. Thus *Re Polemis* [1921] 3 K.B. 560, a Court of Appeal decision which said that in negligence all *direct* harm was actionable even if not foreseeable was disapproved of by the Privy Council in *The Wagon Mound*, 1961 (see p. 325) and was not subsequently followed by the Court of Appeal.

The decisions of the Court of Appeal (Civil Division) are binding on the lower civil courts, i.e. the High Court and the County Court.

On the criminal side, the Court of Appeal (Criminal Division) is bound by the decisions of the House of Lords and normally by its own decisions and those of the former Court of Criminal Appeal and the earlier Court for Crown Cases Reserved. However, an ordinary court of three judges in the Criminal Division may deviate from previous decisions more easily than the Civil Division because different considerations apply in a criminal appeal where the liberty of the accused is at stake and in any case a full court of the Criminal Division can overrule its own previous decisions. A full court generally consists of five judges instead of three as is usual in an ordinary sitting. A decision of the Civil Division is not binding on the Criminal Division and vice versa. Decisions of the Criminal Division are binding on lower criminal courts, i.e. the Crown Court and Magistrates' Courts.

It is perhaps worth noting that Lord Denning in *Davis v Johnson* [1978] 1 All E.R. 841 took the view that the Court of Appeal should take for itself guidelines similar to those taken by the House of Lords in 1966 to depart from a previous decision of its own where that decision was clearly wrong. However, Lord Denning does not appear to have received sufficient support for this view and a declaration on the lines he suggests has not been made.

However, it was decided in *Williams v Fawcett* [1985] 1 All E.R. 787 that the Court of Appeal could depart from one of its own previous decisions where that decision was felt to be wrong in law and there was unlikely to be an appeal to the House of Lords by a person whose liberty was at stake.

ESSENTIAL CASE LAW AND COMMENT

R v Gould, 1968 – Precedent in criminal appeals **(32)**

DIVISIONAL COURTS

Divisional Courts are, in civil cases, bound by the decisions of the House of Lords, the Court of Appeal (Civil Division) and generally by their own previous decisions. However, a Divisional Court of Queen's Bench decided in *R v Greater Manchester Coroner ex parte Tal* [1984] 3 All E.R. 240 that a Divisional Court would normally follow a previous decision of another Divisional Court but could in rare cases exercise its power to refuse to follow a previous Divisional Court decision if the court was convinced that the previous decision was wrong. In criminal cases there is, under ss. 12–15 of the Administration of Justice Act, 1960, an appeal from the Divisional Court of the Queen's Bench Division straight to the House of Lords, and the Divisional Court is not bound by the decisions of the Criminal Division of the Court of Appeal. The decisions of Divisional Courts are binding on judges of the High Court sitting alone and on Magistrates' Courts but not on Crown Courts (see below).

THE HIGH COURT

At the next lower stage, a High Court judge, although bound by the decisions of the Court of Appeal and the House of Lords is not bound by the decisions of another High Court judge sitting at first instance. (*Huddersfield Police Authority v Watson* [1947] 2 All E.R. 193.) Nevertheless such a judge will treat previous decisions as of strong persuasive authority. If a judge of the High Court refuses to follow a previous decision on a similar point of law the Law Reports will contain two decisions by judges of equal authority and the cases will remain in conflict until the same point of law is taken to appeal before a higher tribunal whose decision will resolve the position (and see the statement of Nourse, J. in the *Colchester Estates* case at p. 160).

THE CROWN COURT

A judge sitting in the Crown Court, the jurisdiction of which is largely confined to criminal cases, is bound by decisions made in criminal matters by the House of Lords and Court of Appeal (Criminal Division) but not apparently by decisions of the Divisional Court of the Queen's Bench Division. (*R* v *Colyer* [1974] Crim. L.R. 243.) A judge sitting in the Crown Court and exercising a civil jurisdiction, e.g. licensing, is bound by the decisions of the House of Lords, Court of Appeal and the High Court.

MAGISTRATES' COURTS AND COUNTY COURTS

These courts are bound by the decisions of the higher courts. Their own decisions are not reported officially and have no binding force on other courts at the same level.

THE EMPLOYMENT APPEAL TRIBUNAL

As regards this Tribunal only the decisions of the Court of Appeal and the House of Lords on matters of law are binding, though the decisions of the earlier Industrial Relations Court and the High Court in England are of great persuasive authority and the Tribunal would not lightly differ from the principles which are to be found in those decisions. (*Per* Bristow, J. in *Portec (UK) Ltd* v *Mogensen* [1976] 3 All E.R. 565 at p. 568.) These remarks remain valid even though the *Portec* case was overruled in terms of its decision by *Wilson* v *Maynard Shipbuilding Consultants A.B.* [1978] 2 All E.R. 78. Nevertheless, Wait, J., who as President of the EAT presided in *Anandarajah* v *Lord Chancellor's Department* [1984] I.R.L.R. 131, ruled that no assistance could be derived from precedent in deciding whether a dismissal was unfair. (See further p. 354.)

THE JUDICIAL COMMITTEE OF THE PRIVY COUNCIL

The decisions of the Judicial Committee of the Privy Council are not binding, either on the Committee itself or on other English courts save the Ecclesiastical and Prize Courts. Its decisions are technically only of persuasive authority in English law, and this derives from the fact that the Judicial Committee hears appeals from overseas territories. Thus, when it hears an appeal from Hong Kong, it may not apply a rule of law used (say) in a previous appeal from the Channel Islands.

As regards the relationship of the Judicial Committee and the House of Lords, where the law applicable to the case is English, the Committee will feel bound to follow a relevant decision of the House of Lords but not otherwise (*Tai Hing Cotton* v *Liu Chong Bank* [1985] 2 All E.R. 947).

GENERAL EXCEPTIONS TO THE RULE OF BINDING PRECEDENT

Having examined the relationship of the above courts with regard to the rule of binding precedent, it should be noted that a court is not always bound to follow a precedent which according to the rules outlined above ought to be binding on it. It is by avoiding the following of precedents that judges can, and do, make law.

Thus, when the court in question is invited to follow a binding precedent, it may refuse to do so, for example:

(a) by *distinguishing* the case now before it from the previous case *on the facts*. A case is *distinguished* when the court considers that there are important points of difference between the facts of the case now before it and a previous decision which it is being invited to follow. As Lord Halsbury said in *Quinn* v *Leatham* [1901] A.C. 495 –

> Every judgment must be read as applicable to the particular facts proved, or assumed to be proved, since the generality of the expressions which may be found there are not intended to be expositions of the whole law but govern and are qualified by the particular facts of the case in which such expressions are found.

This process of narrowing down the implications of the *ratio decidendi* of a previous case by 'distinguishing' is a device often used by a court which does not wish to follow an earlier decision which would otherwise be binding on it.

If a court feels that an earlier case was wrongly decided but cannot overrule it because the *ratio decidendi* of the case now before it does not cover all the matters raised in the earlier case, it may, by way of *obiter dictum, disapprove* the earlier case which is then to some extent affected as a precedent. Examples of distinguishing are to be found by comparing the decisions in *Ingram* v *Little*, 1961 and *Lewis* v *Averay*, 1971 (see pp. 638–9);

(b) by refusing to follow the previous case because its *ratio* is *obscure*. Thus in *Harper* v *NCB* [1974] 2 All E.R. 441 the Court of Appeal refused to follow the decision of the House of Lords in *Central Asbestos Co* v *Dodd* [1972] 2 All E.R. 1135 because the majority of three to two judges who found for Dodd left behind no discernible *ratio*. It was unclear whether the decision that Mr Dodd, who brought an action against his employers because he contracted an industrial disease in the course of his employment after the time limit of three years had elapsed, succeeded (i) because he knew that the injury arose from his employment but did not know that he could sue; or (ii) that he knew he could sue but not that the disease arose from his employment;

(c) by declaring the previous case to be in *conflict with a fundamental principle of law*, as where, for example, the court in the previous case has not applied the doctrine of privity of contract (see *Beswick* v *Beswick*, 1967, p. 616);

(*d*) by finding the previous decision to be *per incuriam*, i.e. where an important case or statute was not brought to the attention of the court or ignored (see view of Bristow, J. in *Miliangos* at p. 579) when the previous decision was made;

(*e*) because the previous decision is one of several *conflicting decisions* at the same level. In this connection the comments of Nourse, J. in *Colchester Estates (Cardiff)* v *Carlton Industries* [1984] 2 All E.R. 601 are of interest. He said that as a general rule, a judge faced with two conflicting authorities of judges of the same rank should feel himself bound by the later of them. This would not, however, be the rule if it appeared to the judge deciding the case that the later judgment was wrong in not following the first, as for example, where some other binding authority had not been cited to the earlier judge or judges;

(*f*) because the *previous decision* had been *overruled by statute.*

Cases heard in the County Court and in the Magistrates' Courts are not generally reported, and for this reason do not create binding precedents. It would not be desirable to report such cases, for English law already possesses such a large number of reported cases that decisions are sometimes made in which relevent precedents are not cited or considered, and may therefore be *per incuriam.* Some judges feel that this position is exacerbated by unreported cases stored in computers. (See p. 152.)

PERSUASIVE PRECEDENTS

These consist of decisions made in lower courts, and in the Judicial Committee of the Privy Council of *obiter dicta* at all levels and also decisions of Irish, Scottish, Commonwealth, and United States courts, the reason being that these nations also base their law on the common law of England, though some parts of the law of Scotland are derived from Roman law. Cases coming to the House of Lords from Scotland do not bind English courts. They are only persuasive unless the legal principles involved are the same in both systems of law. The House of Lords normally gives a direction as to the binding nature of such decisions; for example, *Donoghue* v *Stevenson*, 1932 (see p. 725), which is a fundamental case on the law of negligence, is binding on both jurisdictions, although it was an appeal from the Scottish Court of Session.

In the absence of any persuasive authority from the above sources the court may turn to textbooks and sometimes to Roman law. The weight which a court will give to persuasive authority may depend upon the standing of the judge whose decision or dictum it was and whether it was a reserved judgment, i.e. a case in which the court took time to consider the judgment. Reserved judgments are highly regarded. Undefended cases in which the issues have not been fully argued on both sides do not carry great weight.

DECLARATORY AND ORIGINAL PRECEDENTS

One further classification of precedents must be noted. They may be either 'declaratory' or 'original' –

A *declaratory precedent* is one which is merely the application of an existing rule of law.

An *original precedent* is one which creates and applies a new rule. Original precedents alone develop the law; declaratory precedents are merely further evidence of it. Thus, if a judge says: 'The matter before us is not covered by authority and we must decide it on principle . . .' an original precedent is indicated.

REVERSING, OVERRULING AND *RES JUDICATA*

It often happens that when a case has been decided in (say) the High Court, a decision is taken to appeal to an appellate court, in this case the Court of Appeal. The Court of Appeal will re-examine the case and, if it comes to a different conclusion from the judge in the High Court, it reverses his decision. Reversal, therefore, applies to a decision of an appellate court in the same case. Sometimes, however, the case which comes before the appellate court has been decided by following a previously decided case, the judge having followed precedent. In this case, if the appellate court decides to differ from the decision reached in the lower court, it is said to overrule the case which formed the basis of the precedent.

Reversal affects the parties, who are bound by the decision of the appellate court, and it affects precedent because lower courts will in future be bound to follow the decision. *Overruling affects precedent*, but does not reach back to affect the parties in the original case now regarded as wrongly decided, and it is not necessary, for example, for a successful plaintiff to return his damages. Furthermore, the case could not be tried again because the rule of *res judicata* would apply. So the rule of *res judicata* (a matter which has been adjudicated on) protects defendants against a multiplicity of actions in regard to the same issues.

The rule of *res judicata* can in modern law be divided into what is called cause of action estoppel and issue estoppel. Cause of action estoppel prevents a party to an action from suing again on the same matter in order to try to overturn the earlier decision. The earlier decision must stand once all rights of appeal have been exhausted or abandoned. Issue stoppel is different and the court may in some cases allow an issue which was dealt with in an earlier action between the parties to be litigated again in a later claim between them.

ESSENTIAL CASE LAW AND COMMENT

Arnold v *National Westminster Bank plc*, 1990 – Cause of action and issue estoppel **(33)**

ADVANTAGES AND DRAWBACKS OF CASE LAW

The system of judicial precedent has several *advantages*. Up to a point it can claim the *advantage of certainty*, since it is possible to predict the ruling of a court because judicial decisions tend to be consistent. Nevertheless judges have a habit of distinguishing cases on the facts and, as we have seen, avoiding the following of cases in a variety of other ways. This means that the claim to certainty has to be taken with reservations. Another claim put forward in favour of case law is its *power of flexibility and growth*. New decisions are constantly being added as new cases come before the courts. In this way the law tends to keep pace with the times and can adapt itself to changing circumstances. Judicial precedent covers a *wealth of detail*. There is a case in point for every rule, and there is a *practical character* to judicial rulings. Legal rules are made only as the need arises, and the law is not made in advance on the basis of theory. When a case arises, a decision is taken and the ruling is usually recorded, so that when a similar case arises again the law will be there to be applied.

Case law has certain *drawbacks*. These drawbacks are in some cases merely the converse aspects of the advantages. For example, Jeremy Bentham criticised *the principle of the 'law following the event'*, and applied the epithet 'dog's law' to the system. 'It is', he says, 'the judges that make the common law. Do you know how they make it? Just as a man makes laws for his dog. When your dog does something you want to break him of, you wait till he does it then beat him. This is the way you make laws for your dog: this is the way the judges make law for you and me.'

A further criticism is that *the binding force of precedent limits judicial discretion*. It has been said that judges are engaged in 'forging fetters for their own feet'. This can be illustrated by the doctrine of common employment, which was laid down by the House of Lords in *Priestley* v *Fowler* (1837), 3 M. & W. 1. This doctrine said that if an employee was injured by a fellow employee whilst both were acting within the scope of their employment, their employer was not liable vicariously for that negligence. The rule operated in a most unjust fashion during the period of great industrial development, but it continued to bind judges for over a century until it was finally abolished by the Law Reform (Personal Injuries) Act, 1948. All the judges could do in the meantime was to try to limit its scope.

Limiting the scope of a decision may lead to the court's making *illogical distinctions*. Judges and counsel pay attention to differences in cases which are fundamentally similar, in order to uphold the doctrine of precedent and still not feel bound to follow an inconvenient rule. Often these distinctions have real substance, but occasionally they are illogical and serve to complicate the law.

Difficulties of the kind outlined above may not now arise in such an acute form because, as we have seen, the House of Lords is no longer bound by its own decisions, though this tends to detract from the element of certainty.

A further criticism must be noted – that of *bulk and complexity*. The number of reported cases is so large that the law can be ascertained only by searching through a large number of reports. This search has been eased somewhat where case law has been codified by statute in order to produce a rational arrangement. The Bills of Exchange Act, 1882, the Sale of Goods Act, 1893 (now 1979), and the Law of Property Act, 1925 have to a large extent produced order in what might have been called chaos, but case law still tends to develop even around a codifying statute, and its sections soon have to be read in the light of interpretative cases.

Finally, it is a major criticism of our system of case law that only the House of Lords gives the ultimate authoritative judicial ruling on a matter. However, whether this happens depends upon the litigants footing the bill to get to the House of Lords or the Legal Aid Fund doing so. It would be an improvement if we had a system under which the High Court or Court of Appeal could refer a question of law to the House of Lords at public expense, rather on the lines of Art. 177 of the EC Treaty which allows reference to the Court of Justice by domestic courts on matters involving Community Law.

PRECEDENT IN THE EUROPEAN COURT

In line with the normal Continental approach, there is no doctrine of binding precedent, though the body of decisions which the court is making in the interpretation of the Treaty are having strong persuasive influence. These decisions are cited before the court in argument and are also quoted in judgments. In terms of the interpretation of legislation, the European Court has much broader powers than those which English courts have. There is no question of being restricted, for example, to the words of the Treaty or regulations. The Court may consider the reasons for enactment and the general objectives and policy of the Communities. It can have regard to *travaux préparatoires*, i.e. statements and publications made prior to enactment and *doctrine*, i.e. views of learned writers as to what the law should be.

EC law

On 1 January 1973 the United Kingdom became a member of the European Community and in consequence subject to an additional source of law.

Membership of the EC

At the time of writing the membership of the European Community is France, Germany, Italy, Belgium, The Netherlands, Luxembourg, United Kingdom, Republic of Ireland, Denmark, Greece, Spain and Portugal. The most recent development came in the Single European Act which is designed to remove any remaining barriers to the achievement of a truly 'common' market. It creates within the EC an area without internal frontiers which allows the free movement of goods, services, people and capital. The target date for implementation is the end of 1992 by which time all impediments should have been removed. The Single European Act needed ratification by the parliaments of the member states. In the UK this was achieved by the European Communities (Amendment) Act, 1986.

THE INSTITUTIONS OF THE COMMUNITY

There are four main institutions dealing with the functions of the EC. The Commission proposes legislation, the Parliament advises, the Council of Ministers enacts while the Court of Justice has jurisdiction over the interpretation and implementation of Community Law.

The Commission

This consists of commissioners nominated by member states. A president is appointed from the commissioners. The Commission is charged with implementing the Treaty, with bringing to the Council proposals for furthering the aims of the Community, and with supervising the adherence to the Treaty by the member states.

The term of office of commissioners is four years, though they may resign or be compulsorily retired for misconduct by the Court of Justice before that period expires. In addition, a vote of censure carried by a two-thirds majority in the European Parliament results in the compulsory retirement of the whole Commission. Commissioners must not take instructions from their national governments but must act independently in the interests of the communities. Individual commissioners have special responsibilities, e.g. for agriculture and transport.

The Commission consists of 17 members. France, Germany, Italy, the United Kingdom and Spain are allowed to appoint two commissioners each while the other member states appoint one each.

The Commission initiates most Community legislation and in some areas the Commission can enact legislation itself where the Council of Ministers has delegated power to it to do so. An example is agriculture. As to procedure, either on the suggestion of the Council of Ministers or because some pressure group or other has demonstrated a need, a draft of legislation is thrashed out at the Commission's headquarters in Brussels. The draft Directive is submitted to the European Parliament which sends it to one of its 19 committees where a member is appointed Rapporteur. Such a person must have a measure of political balance because his or her task is to obtain a majority vote. The Committee states its view to Parliament and any member can move amendments. Parliament then asks the Commission whether it will accept the amendments and in recent times the Commission has been required to go to greater lengths than previously to ensure agreement with the Parliament. This is a result of the Single European Act which set up what is called the Co-operation Procedure. Finally the proposal for legislation is submitted by the Commission to the Council of Ministers which may enact the Draft within days or sometimes delay for years, as has been the case with some of the social reform Directives.

As an additional function the Commission can bring any member state or commercial undertaking before the Court of Justice where it feels community obligations are not being carried out and in the case of breach of restrictive practices and anti-monopoly provisions, the Commission operates quasi-judicially and can issue a decision on the matter and impose a fine.

Council of Ministers

The council which has its permanent offices in Brussels is composed of one representative from each of the member states. The representative is usually the Foreign Secretary but others may attend where a matter of importance in a particular field is involved, e.g. if agriculture, the Minister of Agriculture.

There is a Committee of Permanent Representatives consisting of the various ambassadors to the member states which assists the Council in preliminary discussions designed to clarify issues before they reach the Council.

The Council enacts legislation on proposals from the Commission. The representatives of the larger countries have more votes than others and in most cases more than a simple majority is required. Thus for the admission of a new member state the Council must approve unanimously.

However, under the European Communities (Amendment) Act, 1986 which implements the Single European Act, 1986 and is designed to speed up decision making within the Community, more matters will be decided by a simple majority vote with less need than before for unanimity.

European Parliament

This represents the peoples of the member states, and sits in either Luxembourg or Strasbourg. Seats are allocated to member states on the basis of population. The members, who tend to act in political rather than national groups, are elected by the electorate of the state which they represent. In the UK the relevant legislation is the European Assembly Elections Act, 1978.

The Parliament does not legislate, but advises. However, it is invariably consulted on proposals for legislation. It provides a place where community problems can be discussed and questions put to the Council and Commission. As we have seen, an important power is to remove the Commission members from office by a vote of censure passed by a majority of two-thirds. This is a sanction which the Parliament has if the Commission fails to propose what Parliament has advised. In addition, it has power to veto the annual Community budget which in effect freezes the activities of the Community.

TYPES AND SOURCES OF COMMUNITY LAW

There are three principal types of Community legislation. *Regulations* are of general application in the member countries and, under Art. 189 of the

Treaty of Rome, in theory become part of domestic law without the need for UK legislation to implement them. In practice, however, some may give rise to consequential subordinate legislation or require the repeal or amendment of existing Acts. *Decisions* are of more particular application, and are also immediately operative. Decisions may be addressed to a state or to an individual or a corporation and an example of a decision would be a Commission ruling that a company was adopting restrictive practices in its operations within the Market contrary to Arts 85/86 of the Treaty. (See p. 319.) Such a decision could also impose a fine. Decisions have the force of law but affect the recipient only. *Directives* are under Art. 189 binding in principle, but is it left to the member countries to decide upon the means of giving them legal and administrative effect usually within a given time scale. In Britain this is dealt with by s. 2 of the European Communities Act, 1972, and the most common method of incorporating directives into British law will be by statutory instruments, subject to annulment by 'negative' resolution of Parliament. (See p. 141.) However, the UK's response to the many Directives on Company Law is included in various sections of the Companies Act, 1985. (See p. 188.) Nevertheless, fundamental obligations in a directive, such as free movement of workers, which are not subject to any exception or conditions may have immediate effect without the need for legislation in the UK.

As regards the *provisions of the Treaty of Rome itself*, these are enforceable in the High Court under s. 2 of the European Communities Act, 1972, provided the High Court can find out from the words of the Treaty itself what right has been infringed. If this is not possible, as where a person claims relief against sex discrimination generally on the basis of an article of the Treaty which deals merely with discrimination on the grounds of pay, no 'enforceable Community right' is created.

There is also the additional problem that many articles of the Treaty are expressed in general terms making it difficult to judge precisely what rights are conferred, so that in many cases the Treaty provides only the bones of suggested rights and is not enforceable in the absence of a UK Act of Parliament which expresses clearly the *detailed* rights conferred in the UK as a response to the *general* requirements of the Treaty. In any case an industrial tribunal cannot take into account an 'enforceable Community right' since it was set up by a UK Act of Parliament to administer only UK Acts of Parliament dealing with specific industrial matters.

APPLICATION OF EC LAW IN UK CASES

Section 3 of the European Communities Act, 1972 requires our courts to take note of the provisions of the Treaty of Rome (among others) and also the decisions of the European Court.

Although arguments about the subject rage on there can be little doubt now that EC law is supreme and that the sovereignty of the UK Parliament is thereby reduced.

ESSENTIAL CASE LAW AND COMMENT

Factortame Ltd v *Secretary of State for Transport (No. 2)*, 1991 –
Supremacy of EC law **(34)**

Law reform

It should be noted that a number of official bodies exist to consider and make proposals for *law reform*, and the work of these bodies can have a considerable influence on the development of statute law. The most important of these bodies is the Law Commission, which was set up by the Law Commissions Act, 1965. Section 1 of the Act establishes the Commission to promote the reform of English law and deals with the constitution of the Commission. The Lord Chancellor appoints the members of the Commission, on a full-time basis, from among persons holding judicial office, experienced barristers and solicitors and university teachers of law. Section 3 states the duty of the Commission to be to keep under review the whole of English law with a view to its systematic development and reform, including the codification of such law, the elimination of anomalies, the repeal of obsolete enactments and generally the simplification and modernisation of the law. The present programme of the Law Commission includes the codification of the law of contract. The Criminal Law Act, 1967, which abolished the distinction between felonies and misdemeanours and certain obsolete crimes, resulted from proposals made by the Commission.

In arriving at its programme the Commission consults with the chairmen of the Criminal Law Revision Committee and the Law Reform Committee, which are bodies set up on a part-time basis by the Home Secretary to consider specific matters of law reform which he may refer to them in the fields of criminal and civil law respectively. The work of the Commission and the Committees may be regarded as a source of law in that it is a *historical source* of the law contained in the statute which implements its proposals. Thus the proposals of the Law Commission may be regarded as a historical source of the Criminal Law Act, 1967.

8
Persons and the Crown

In law a *person* possesses certain rights and owes certain duties. There are two categories of persons as follows –

(*a*) *Natural persons.* These are human beings who are referred to as natural persons. An adult human being has in general terms a full range of rights and duties. However, even in regard to human beings, the law distinguishes between certain classes and gives to them a *status* which may carry with it a more limited set of rights and duties than are given to the normal adult. These classes include minors, persons of unsound mind, bankrupts and aliens, and the significance of belonging to these categories will be more fully examined in connection with the chapters on substantive law, such as contract, tort and crime. Non-human creatures are not legal persons and do not have the full range of rights and duties which a human being acquires at birth. However, animals may be protected by the law for certain purposes, e.g. conservation. (See Wildlife and Countryside Act, 1981.)

(*b*) *Juristic persons.* Legal personality is not restricted to human beings. In fact various bodies and associations of persons can, by forming a corporation to carry out their functions, create an organisation with a range of rights and duties not dissimilar to many of those possessed by human beings. In English law such corporations are formed by charter, statute or registration under the Companies Act, 1985 or previous Acts; there is also the common law concept of the Corporation Sole.

Natural persons

Here we shall consider some of the more important general principles of law relating to minors, persons of unsound mind, bankrupts and aliens together with the rules governing a natural person's domicil and nationality and the general principles of law preventing discriminatiion against natural persons.

MINORS

The Family Law Reform Act, 1969, s. 1(1) reduced the age of majority from 21 to 18 years. There is also a provision in the Act which states that a person attains a particular age, i.e. not merely the age of majority, at the first moment of the relevant birthday, though this rule is subject to any contrary provision in any instrument (i.e. a deed) or statute. (S. 9.)

Section 1(2) provides that the age of 18 is to be substituted for 21 wherever there is a reference to 'full age', 'infancy', 'minor', 'minority' in –

(*a*) any statutory provision made *before or after* 1 January 1970;

(*b*) any deed, will or other instrument made *on or after* that date.

This sub-section draws a distinction between *statutory provisions* and *private dispositions*. In the case of the former the new age of 18 is substituted. Thus, in s. 164 of the Law of Property Act, 1925 which uses the word 'minority' to deal with restrictions on the accumulation of income in a trust as where the income is reinvested and not given to a beneficiary, references to 'minority' will be construed as applying to persons under 18 years of age. However, in the case of private dispositions such as deeds, wills and settlements the Act does not apply retrospectively. Accordingly, if in a deed made before 1 January 1970, a person X is to take property 'on attaining his majority', he will take it at age 21 years. If the deed was on or after 1 January 1970, he would take it at 18 years. The reasons for this rule is that where persons in the past have arranged their affairs in reliance on the law as it stood, it would be unjust to interfere. The following general matters relating to minors can be considered at this point.

(*a*) A minor cannot contract a valid marriage under the age of 16 years and requires the consent of his parents or if the parents are divorced or separated, the one with custody, or if one parent is dead, the survivor (or on failure that of a magistrates' court) to marry under 18 years of age.

(*b*) A person under 18 years cannot vote at elections and must be 21 before he can sit in Parliament or be a member of the council of a local authority.

(*c*) With regard to civil litigation, a minor sues through a 'next friend', i.e. an adult who is liable for the costs (if any) awarded against the minor in the action, though the minor must indemnify him. A minor defends an action through a 'guardian *ad litem*' who is not liable for costs. The minor's father or mother usually acts as 'next friend' or 'guardian *ad litem*'.

(*d*) A person of 16 or over can give valid consent to medical treatment and it is not necessary as before to obtain the consent of a parent or guardian. (Family Law Reform Act, 1969 (s. 8).)

(*e*) The Tattooing of Minors Act, 1969, makes it an offence, punishable by fine, for a person other than a duly qualified medical practitioner to tattoo a person under the age of 18. The person charged with the offence will have a defence if he can show that at the time he had reasonable cause to believe that the person tattooed was 18 years of age or over.

THE PROTECTION OF CHILDREN

The Children Act, 1989 introduced a new regime to ensure the safety and protection of children. Of major importance are two new orders provided for by Part V of the Act. The first is an Emergency Protection Order which replaces the old 'Place of Safety Order' under the Children and Young Persons Act, 1969. These safety orders were much criticised in the alleged child abuse cases which led to the Cleveland Report into alleged abuse in that area and the Orkney affair. Amongst other things it was thought that the safety order was too easy to get and could lead to children being taken into the custody of the relevant local authority even in the absence of hard evidence of abuse.

Under s. 44 an Emergency Protection Order will only be made if the court which is asked to grant it is satisfied that –

(*a*) there is reasonable cause to believe that the child is likely to suffer significant harm; or

(*b*) enquiries are being made by the relevant local authority and these are being frustrated by denial of access to the child where such access is urgently required; or

(*c*) the applicant is an authorised person such as a local authority or the National Society for the Prevention of Cruelty to Children and the applicant has reasonable cause to suspect that a child is suffering or likely to suffer significant harm and the enquiries of the authorised person are being frustrated by lack of access.

It will be seen that an Emergency Protection Order will be granted only on the basis of hard evidence.

However, s. 43 provides for Child Assessment Orders and these allow a local authority or authorised person to apply to the court to take the child away from home, if necessary, for assessment in cases which are not necessarily emergencies. Here the court must be satisfied that the child is suffering or is likely to suffer 'significant harm' and that an assessment is needed which would not otherwise be likely to take place. This order is not designed for absolute emergencies but could be asked for following a case conference of interested professionals which had considered a case where a child had e.g. suddenly ceased to attend a day nursery in suspicious circumstances or where neighbours had reported repeated screaming.

Also of importance is the new concept of 'parental responsibility' introduced by ss. 2, 3 and 12 of the 1989 Act. Parental responsibility involves maintenance of the child and seeing to its education and providing accommodation, medical attention and so on. This is no longer a matter for the natural parents. Parental responsibility is now held by others, e.g. grandparents and even the local authority. It can be held by several people concurrently. Every person who has parental responsibility can act *alone* in most cases to ensure the welfare of the child. In many cases therefore there will be a small army of persons including relatives and the local authority who will be able to intervene legally if the natural parents are found wanting in terms e.g. of the welfare of the child.

ADOPTION – THE EFFECT OF

An adopted child qualifies as a child of the adoptive parents' marriage. (S. 39 of the Adoption Act, 1976.) This principle applies in interpreting wills, settlements made during lifetime and intestacies which take effect on or after 1 January 1976. Where questions of seniority arise s. 42 of the 1976 Act provides that the adopted child is deemed to have been born on the date of the adoption and if adoptive parents adopt two or more children on the same day they are regarded as born on that day in the order of the actual dates of their births. For example, we may take a gift in the will of a testator 'to the eldest son of X'. Suppose that X had a natural child (A) in 1975 and in 1976 adopted a child (B) then aged 10, it appears that the natural child (A) takes the gift although B is biologically the elder.

However, the above rules do not affect a document where there is reference to the age of a child. (S. 42(2)(b) of the 1976 Act.)

Thus if a testator gave his estate 'to the children of X at 25' it is clear that an adopted child would take the gift when he in fact attained that age and not 25 years after his adoption. It also seems that a gift to 'the first son of X to attain 25' would go to an adoptive child if he attained 25 before X's natural born children, although, as we have seen, he would not take as X's 'eldest son' in the example given above.

Adopted persons may, on reaching the age of 18, have a copy of their birth certificate as of right and not as formerly only by leave of the court. (Ss. 51 and 51A of the Adoption Act, 1976.)

Under amendments made by the Children Act, 1989, Sch. 10, when information such as a birth certificate is supplied the registration authorities must tell the applicant that counselling services are available and from whom, e.g. a local authority. The Registrar must also maintain a register of relatives of adopted persons who wish to make contact. A person supplied with information about his natural parents may have access to this register if he wishes.

PERSONS SUFFERING FROM MENTAL DISORDER

We shall be giving fuller consideration to the position of mentally disordered persons in contract, tort and crime in the chapters which follow. However, the following general points can be noted now.

If a person suffering from mental disorder goes through a ceremony of marriage but cannot understand the nature of marriage, i.e. the responsibilities and change of status involved, the marriage will be void.

In connection with mental disorder, it is of interest to note the existence of the Court of Protection which is concerned with proper management of a mental patient's property. The Court operates through receivers who are, in many cases, close relatives of the patient. The Court can administer the patient's property and make a will for the patient or make lifetime gifts of that property on the application of the patient's receiver.

UNDISCHARGED BANKRUPTS

Bankruptcy procedure is set out in the Insolvency Act, 1986. Bankruptcy proceedings which involve asking the court to make a bankruptcy order may be taken against a debtor by his creditor(s). The debtor's afairs will then be taken over by an insolvency practitioner who is an accountant in practice though in the case of many bankruptcies the estate is too small for this and a state official called the Official Receiver does the work. A petition to the court for a bankruptcy order is most usually presented by a creditor who must be owed £750 or more. Two or more creditors (none of whom is owed as much as £750) may present a joint petition if they are together owed £750 or more by the debtor as where creditor A is owed £280 and creditor B is owed £600.

As regards the disabilities of an undischarged bankrupt he is disqualified from being an M.P. and cannot be a member of a local authority council. Under s. 360 of the 1986 Act he is guilty of an offence if either alone or jointly with another person he obtains credit of £250 or more unless he tells the person giving it that he is an undischarged bankrupt − in general he will not then get the credit. Under s. 11 of the Company Directors Disqualification Act, 1986 it is an offence for an undischarged bankrupt to act as a company director or to promote or form or manage a company without the permission of the court which made the bankruptcy order.

These disabilities come to an end on discharge of the bankrupt. This occurs automatically and without application to the court three years after the bankruptcy order was made unless the Official Receiver feels that the debtor is not complying with his obligations as where he is concealing assets. Where this is so the Official Receiver can ask the court to rescind the automatic discharge provisions. There is automatic discharge subject to the above rules after two years where the debts owed were less than £20,000 (s. 279(2)), Insolvency Act, 1986).

Any money owed by the debtor which has not been paid at the date of discharge is no longer payable at law by the debtor who can then go back into business legally free of his old debts and with no restrictions on obtaining credit.

ALIENS

An alien cannot acquire property in a British ship or aircraft, save as a member of a limited liability company if the company itself is British, nor can he become the master of a British ship. Aliens cannot vote at elections or become Members of Parliament. They also require work permits if they wish to take up employment here and may be deported if convicted of certain crimes. Citizens of the Republic of Ireland are not treated as aliens and may vote at elections and become Members of Parliament.

Powers of internment and deportation are provided for by statute (see *R v Secretary of State for Home Department ex parte Hosenball*, 1977 at p.

567). There is also legislation to control immigration to the United Kingdom. These provisions were considerably strengthened by the Immigration Acts of 1971 and 1988. Aliens who are here for more than six months are required to register with the police.

DOMICIL – GENERALLY

The basis of jurisdiction and the law to be applied in many matters coming before English courts, e.g. wills, matrimonial causes and taxation, may depend on the domicil of the parties. A person's domicil is the country which he regards as his permanent home, and thus contains a dual element of actual residence in a country and the intention of remaining there. Where a country has within its national boundaries several jurisdictions, the person's domicil must be determined with reference to a particular jurisdiction, e.g. there is no such thing as domicil in the United States of America, though a person may be domiciled in a particular State. England and Wales, Scotland, Northern Ireland, the Channel Islands, and the Isle of Man are distinct jurisdictions within the British Isles. A person must always have a domicil, and he can only have one domicil at a time. It should be noted that the concepts of domicil and nationality are, as appropriate, applied to corporate bodies.

ESSENTIAL CASE LAW AND COMMENT

I.R.C. v *Bullock*, 1976 – Domicil and taxation **(35)**

DOMICIL OF ORIGIN

The domicil of origin of a child is that of its father at the date of the child's birth if the father is alive at that date and is married to the child's mother, i.e. if the child is legitimate (for example, the Nova Scotia domicil of Mr Bullock in *I.R.C.* v *Bullock*, 1976). If the child is illegitimate or, though legitimate, the father is not alive when it is born, it takes its domicil of origin from that of its mother at the date of the child's birth. Foundlings take their domicil of origin from the place where they were found.

DEPENDENT DOMICIL

The concept of dependent domicil applies as follows –

Minors (i.e. persons under the age of 18 years)

(a) *At common law*. The domicil of a legitimate, legitimated or adopted child is dependent on, and changes with, that of its father or adoptive father, and after the father's death with that of its mother or adoptive mother. The domicil of an illegitimate child depends on, and changes with, that of its mother.

(*b*) *Under statute.* Sections 3 and 4 of the Domicile and Matrimonial Proceedings Act, 1973 are concerned with the domicil of minors. Where previously the domicil of a minor had to follow that of his father until the age of majority, a minor can under the Act acquire an independent domicil at the age of 16, or under that age if he marries before then. This latter principle cannot of course apply to any marriages in this country, but it may apply to those in this country, e.g. Nigerians, who may be married under 16 according to their domiciliary law. The provision referred to above, which is in s. 3 of the Act, avoids the previous possibility of a father leaving this country and establishing a domicil elsewhere, thus changing the domicil of his minor son who had remained in this country. Furthermore, it had always been uncertain whether, after the divorce of the parents, a child's domicil continued to follow his father's or followed that of his mother with whom the child was living. Now s. 4(2) of the 1973 Act provides that the child's domicil where he is under 16 or has not set up an independent domicil and his father and mother are alive but living apart shall be that of his mother if −

(*a*) he then has his home with her and has no home with his father; or
(*b*) he has at any time had her domicil by virtue of (*a*) above and has not since had a home with his father.

The section also deals with other possible situations, for example where the mother is dead and the child has not returned to his father, he will keep the domicil he acquired under s. 4(2).

Married women

By s. 1 of the Domicile and Matrimonial Proceedings Act, 1973, the domicil of a married woman is not bound to be determined by that of her husband, as was the case at common law. She is capable of acquiring a separate domicil in exactly the same manner as her husband. By s. 1(2) of the 1973 Act a married woman is treated as retaining the domicil of her husband (as a domicil of choice if it is not one of origin) at the coming into force of the Act unless and until it is changed in accordance with common law rules for determining such change.

Certain consequences regarding jurisdiction in divorce proceedings follow from the general principles enacted by the above section. As a wife can now acquire a separate domicil from that of her husband, jurisdiction is now based upon the domicil of either party in England and Wales at the time of the proceedings or on the ground that either party was habitually resident in those countries for one year before the proceedings commenced. The court has power to stay proceedings where courts in two countries have jurisdiction. This would prevent, for example, divorce proceedings being taken in an English court and a Scottish court contemporaneously as where the husband had an English domicil but his wife had acquired one in Scotland.

DOMICIL OF CHOICE

A person, other than a minor under 16, can change his domicil of his own volition. To do so he must be in the new country, and have a 'fixed and settled intention' to abandon his domicil of origin or choice, and to settle instead in the new country.

A person retains his domicil of origin until he acquires a domicil of choice, and since a person must always have a domicil, there can be no abandonment of the domicil of origin unless a domicil of choice is acquired instead. However, having acquired a domicil of choice, a person who abandons it without acquiring a fresh domicil of choice, reverts to his domicil of origin.

The country in which a person resides is on the face of it the country of his domicil. Where it is claimed that a domicil of origin has been changed for one of choice, the onus of proof is on the party claiming that such a change has taken place. Examples of evidence which suggest a change of domicil are oral or written declarations to this effect, letters, wills as in *I.R.C. v Bullock*, the adoption of a new name, as where a German living in England changes his name to Richmond from Reichman, an application for naturalisation, the purchase of land, or a grave, or of a home or a business in the new country. It was decided in *Plummer v I.R.C.* [1988] 1 All E.R. 97 that it is not enough merely to express an intention *eventually* to live and work in the new country. Furthermore it was held in *Cramer v Cramer* [1987] 1 F.L.R. 116 that domicil is not established by an *intention to marry* a person resident in the new country at some time in the future even where the intention to marry is reciprocated by the other party.

ESSENTIAL CASE LAW AND COMMENT

Tee v Tee, 1973 – Reverting to domicil of origin **(36)**
Steiner v I.R.C., 1973 – Evidence of change of domicil **(37)**

RESIDENCE

The residence of a person is important for certain purposes, e.g. liability for income tax, and a person who is not domiciled in the UK may nevertheless be liable to UK tax if he is regarded as resident here in the year of assessment. Furthermore the jurisdiction of magistrates in matrimonial matters is based on the residence of the parties and not their domicil, as is the right to vote in a particular constituency at an election under s. 1(1) of the Representation of the People Act, 1983. On the other hand the jurisdiction of the High Court in matrimonial proceedings is based either on domicil or habitual residence for one year. (S. 5, Domicile and Matrimonial Proceedings Act, 1973.) Domicil must, therefore, be distinguished from residence.

The term residence imports a certain degree of permanence, and must not be casual or merely undertaken as a traveller. In *Fox v Stirk* [1970] 3 All

E.R. 7, the Court of Appeal decided that two undergraduates were resident at their universities and entitled to have their names on the electoral register for that constituency although their parental homes were elsewhere. On the other hand in *Scott* v *Phillips* 1973 S.L.T. (Notes) 75 it was held that the plaintiff, who lived mainly at his house in Inveresk but had a cottage on lease in Berwickshire in which he spent 3½ months each year, was not resident in Berwickshire and therefore not entitled to have his name included on the electoral roll for that county. Obviously, residence can be changed at any time by moving to a new home. Temporary absences abroad while on holiday or on business do not create a gap in the period of residence, which is determined on the facts of the case.

NATIONALITY

The main importance of nationality today is in the realm of public law, since aliens and nationals are treated similarly in most matters of civil law. However, matters such as allegiance and the right to vote at elections and sit in Parliament are governed by the nationality of the person concerned. A wholesale reform of nationality was brought into effect by the British Nationality Act, 1981. The broad general principles relating to the acquisition of British citizenship are set out below.

British citizenship

A child born in the United Kingdom will be a British citizen if the father or mother is a British citizen and is settled in the UK which implies an entitlement to stay here *indefinitely*.

Citizenship by descent

A mother or father can transmit his or her British citizenship to a child born outside the UK. However, under s. 2(1)(a) of the 1981 Act this applies to one generation only. Where the parent himself or herself is a British citizen by descent further requirements of registration and residence must be complied with by the child. (See s. 3(2), 1981 Act.)

Registration

Certain persons, e.g. British Dependent Territories' citizens who are those living in the remaining colonies, e.g. Belize, and British overseas citizens, e.g. a citizen of a former British colony who retained British citizenship on independence, are entitled to be *registered* as a British citizen if they are settled in the UK and have been resident here for five years. (S. 4, 1981 Act.)

Naturalisation

This is available to anyone and continues to be at the Home Secretary's discretion on the basis of five years' residence with requirements of knowledge of the English language, good behaviour and intention to live in the UK. (S. 6, 1981 Act.)

British citizens have full rights of entry into the UK and to residence here.

DISCRIMINATION

We shall now consider the rules of law which are designed to prevent discrimination against natural persons. Discrimination in employment is dealt with in Chapter 19.

RACIAL DISCRIMINATION

The Race Relations Act, 1976 and the Public Order Act, 1986 are designed to deal with discrimination on racial grounds and with relations between different racial groups. It should be noted before considering the main provisions of the Acts that under s. 72 of the 1976 Act a term in a contract which purports to exclude or limit any provisions of that Act is unenforceable by any person in whose favour the term would operate.

THE RACE RELATIONS ACT, 1976

Discrimination to which the Act applies

Section 1 provides that it is *direct discrimination* to treat a person less favourably on racial grounds and *indirect discrimination* where there is some requirement or condition, e.g. of employment, which, although it applies to all potential employees, is discriminatory since a smaller proportion (or none) of black applicants can comply with it than white. Thus a rule insisting that bus conductors wear company caps could be *indirect discrimination* against Sikh applicants, who were held to be a protected ethnic group by the House of Lords in *Mandla* v *Dowell Lee* [1983] 1 All E.R. 1062.

Section 2 deals with *discrimination by way of victimisation* of a person who has, for example, brought or given evidence in proceedings under the Act against a discriminator or alleged discriminator. Thus if A brings proceedings against his employer, B, for alleged discrimination and as a consequence A's landlord, C, will not allow A to use a goods lift provided for common use in the block of flats where A lives, then C could be guilty of victimisation under s. 2. Under s. 3, 'racial grounds' means colour, race, nationality, or ethnic or national origins, and 'racial group' means a group of persons defined by reference to colour, race, nationality, or ethnic or national origin.

For example in *Commission for Racial Equality* v *Dutton, The Times,* 29 July 1988, the Court of Appeal held that gypsies were a racial group for the purposes of the Act. They were not, however, synonymous with 'travellers' so that a notice in a public house saying 'sorry, no travellers' did not directly discriminate against them. It did, however, indirectly discriminate against them. However, in *Crown Suppliers (P.S.A.)* v *Dawkins* [1991] I.R.L.R. 327, the Employment Appeal Tribunal decided that Rastafarians are not a group defined by ethnic origin within the meaning of the 1976 Act. Therefore a van driver who was turned down for a job because he would not cut his hair had not been discriminated against. Rastafarians were a religious sect not an ethnic group. The Act still permits discrimination on grounds of religious belief unless that constitutes racial discrimination, as it would if the religion was Jewish but not if it was Catholic or Protestant since the last two named are not matters of race.

Areas of racial discrimination not relating directly to the contract of employment appear below.

Partnerships

Section 10 of the 1976 Act extends protection against discrimination to partnerships as regards failure to offer a partnership or the terms on which it is offered, including benefits, facilities and services. Thus discrimination would exist if a partner was refused a cheap loan for house purchase under the firm's scheme or was refused the use of a firm's car. The section applies only to firms of six or more partners, though there is a power in s. 73 to reduce this number but this has not yet been done. The provision as it stands will allow discrimination in the majority of medical practices but not e.g. in the larger firms of accountants and solicitors. The section also covers discrimination in cases where persons are preparing to form themselves into a partnership.

Trade unions etc.

Section 11 renders unlawful discriminatory practices by trade unions, employers' associations and professional trade bodies. Surprisingly, individual discriminatory action by shop stewards is not covered by the Act. Thus if a shop steward discriminates with the authority of his union, the union will be liable, but if he acts without authority, no one is liable. This appears to be a defect in the Act since it is well known that white organised labour has in several areas of the country held back black development in employment.

Qualifying bodies

Section 12 provides that it is unlawful for an authority or body which can confer an authorisation or qualification which is needed for, or facilitates employment in, a particular trade or profession, e.g. the General Medical Council, to discriminate against a person in terms of conferring that authorisation or qualification.

Discrimination in education

Sections 17–19 make it unlawful for responsible bodies, e.g. governing bodies of educational establishments including both State and private schools, to discriminate on racial grounds as regards, for example, allocation of places.

Discrimination in provision of goods, facilities or services

Under s. 20, discrimination by, for example, shops, hotels, boarding houses and banks is outlawed as is discrimination in clubs which have 25 or more members. When membership of a club reaches 25 or more a licence to serve intoxicating liquor must be sought. Clubs with membership of less than 25 members are excluded and may discriminate.

Discrimination in the disposal or management of premises

Section 21 states that discrimination on racial grounds by a seller of property in terms of the buyer or by, say, a brewery in terms of who shall manage a public house, is unlawful. The section does not apply to owner-occupiers of houses who sell the property without employing an estate agent or advertising it for sale. (S. 21(3).) There is also an exemption for the letting of accommodation in premises where the occupier or a near relative of his resides and intends to continue to reside on the premises which are 'small premises' under s. 22(2), e.g. where there is not room for more than six persons in addition to the occupier and members of his household. Section 23 provides for exemptions allowing discrimination where a person takes into his home and treats as a member of his family a child, an elderly person or a person requiring a special degree of care and attention. Thus discrimination on racial grounds in the choice of foster children is not unlawful. Section 24 provides that where a tenant requires the licence or consent of the landlord to assign or sublet to another person it is unlawful for that licence or consent to be withheld in a discriminatory way, as where a landlord will not allow a tenant to assign to a black tenant.

As we have seen, discrimination in clubs with 25 or more members is unlawful but s. 26 provides an exemption for organisations whose main object is to confer benefits on ethnic or national groups and does not exclude others. Thus the London Welsh Club is still a lawful association but must not exclude black Welshmen.

By s. 27 the Act applies only to benefits, facilities and services in Great Britain. However, it does extend outside Great Britain in some cases. For example, discrimination in Great Britain in regard to the provision of facilities for travel is unlawful even though the facilities are to be supplied outside Great Britain.

Discrimination in the legal profession

The Race Relations Act, 1976 did not make unlawful discrimination on the grounds of race either by or within barristers' chambers or by solicitors in relation to barristers approached to take on cases. The Courts and Legal Services Act, 1990 inserts a new section, s. 26A, into the 1976 Act making it unlawful for a barrister or a barrister's clerk to discriminate against current or prospective pupils or members of chambers on the grounds of race. It also makes it unlawful to discriminate on the grounds of race in regard to the giving or withholding of instructions to a barrister.

Discriminatory practices

Under s. 28 there may be a discriminatory practice, even where there is no victim. Thus a factory which has discriminatory recruiting procedures may be regarded as discriminating even during a recession when there has been no recruitment for some time. However, proceedings under s. 28 can be brought only by the Commission for Racial Equality.

Advertisements

Section 29 makes discriminatory advertisements unlawful, as in *Commission for Racial Equality* v *Dutton*, 1988 (see p. 177), unless, as in an employment advertisement, there is, for example, a GOQ (genuine occupational qualification), e.g. being Chinese is a GOQ for employment in a Chinese restaurant, but not a take-away.

Instructions, pressure or inducement to discriminate

Under ss. 30 and 31 it is unlawful to instruct a person to discriminate or to put pressure on a person to discriminate in a way which the 1976 Act makes *unlawful*. The act must be unlawful so instructions by a landlord to his tenant not to take black foster children would not be unlawful. Under s. 32 an employer is vicariously liable (see p. 382) together with the offending employee for any act done by the employee in course of employment, whether the act was done with the knowledge or approval of the employer or not. Similarly, principals will be liable for the *authorised* acts of their agents but in neither case does vicarious liability extend to criminal proceedings. An employer (not a principal) is given a defence if he can show that he took such steps as were reasonably practicable to prevent his employee doing discriminatory acts. Under s. 33 those who assist others to do unlawful acts are also liable.

ESSENTIAL CASE LAW AND COMMENT

The Commission for Racial Equality v *Imperial Society of Teachers of Dancing*, 1983 – Inducement to discriminate **(38)**

Charities

Section 34 makes it clear that any provision in an existing or future charitable instrument, e.g. a trust, which confers benefits on persons of a different colour is void. Further, it is unlawful to do any act in Great Britain to give effect to such a provision.

General exceptions

Certain general exceptions from liability are set out in Part IV of the Act. Under s. 35 acts done to meet the special needs of racial groups with regard, for example, to education, training and welfare, such as special language training for groups whose first language is not English, are not unlawful. Sections 37 and 38 allow positive discrimination in favour of particular racial groups by training bodies, employers and trade unions, employers' associations, and professional and trade associations, by encouraging members of those groups to take work by giving special talks and guided tours of factories and premises. Under s. 39 the selection of sports teams on the basis of nationality, place of birth, and length of residence is exempted from the provisions of the Act. Thus a county cricket club may, if that is a rule, continue to select teams from among those born in the county but cannot refuse to select a person otherwise willing and able who was born in the county of, say, Pakistani parents.

The Commission for Racial Equality

Section 43 sets up the Commission (CRE) which is to work towards the elimination of discrimination; to promote equality of opportunity; good relations between different racial groups and to keep under review the working of the Act. Under s. 47 the CRE has issued codes of practice giving guidance on ways of achieving equality of opportunity and eliminating discrimination in the employment field and in housing including rented housing. Sections 48–52 give the CRE power to conduct formal investigations, for example into alleged discriminatory employment practices, in order to carry out its duties. The court may prevent such an investigation going ahead on the grounds e.g. that the concern to be investigated has not been given an opportunity to make representations of its own position. (*R v Commission for Racial Equality, ex parte Prestige Group plc* [1983] I.R.L.R. 408.)

Enforcement

The enforcement provisions which are set out in Part VIII are of two types –

(*a*) *Complaints by an individual* who is the subject of unlawful conduct other than 'discriminatory practices', advertising or pressures or instructions to discriminate. In employment cases the complaint goes to an industrial tribunal (s. 54) (see below). Complaints of discrimination in education and in the provision of goods, facilities and services and in housing may be made to the county court (s.57). Complaints that a responsible body in an educational establishment has discriminated must be notified to the Secretary of State for Education who must be given a maximum of two months to consider the matter before court proceedings can be commenced (s. 57(5)). It should be noted that an individual is now given direct access to courts and tribunals in race relations matters; under previous legislation only the Race Relations Board (now abolished) could institute proceedings.

(*b*) *Enforcement by the CRE*. This involves : (i) the issuing of a non-discrimination notice (s. 58); (ii) proceedings in the county court or industrial tribunal where there are discriminatory practices, advertisements or pressures or instructions to discriminate (s. 63); (iii) proceedings in the county court for an injunction where there has been persistent discrimination (s. 62); (iv) assisting individual complainants in certain matters of principle or complexity or other special considerations (s. 66).

It should be noted that a non-discrimination notice will require a person not to commit any further discriminatory acts and, where in order to comply with this it is necessary to change practices or arrangements, to inform the

CRE that the changes have been effected and bring these changes to the attention of other persons concerned. There is a right of appeal within six weeks against such a notice to an industrial tribunal which may modify or quash the notice (s. 59). If an appeal against a notice is dismissed, the notice becomes final and is entered on the CRE's Register of Notices (s. 61).

THE PUBLIC ORDER ACT 1986

Part III of the Act makes it an offence to stir up racial hatred by use of words or behaviour or display of written material (s. 18); by publishing or distributing written material (s. 19); by the public performance of plays (s. 20); by distributing, showing or playing a recording (s. 21); by radio or television broadcasting or including a programme in a cable or satellite service (s. 22); by possessing racially inflammatory material (s. 23). There are powers of police entry and search of premises to discover material (s. 24) and a power of forfeiture under s. 25. Nothing in the Act applies to fair and accurate reports of Parliamentary proceedings, nor to law reports (s. 26).

Institution of proceedings requires the consent of the Attorney-General. The maximum sentence is two years' imprisonment and/or an unlimited fine (s. 27). If a corporation is found guilty any director or other officer who consented to or connived at the offence is also guilty (s. 28).

SEX DISCRIMINATION

The three main Acts of Parliament involved here are the Sex Discrimination Acts, 1975 and 1986 and the Equal Pay Act, 1970, to which amendments have been made by the Equal Pay (Amendment) Regulations, 1983. Some provisions of the above legislation relate to the field of employment and are dealt with in Chapter 19.

Sex Discrimination Act, 1975

The form of drafting used in the Race Relations Act, 1976, was based on the Sex Discrimination Act, 1975, and the reader will recognise many similar features.

Under the Act of 1975 it is unlawful to treat anyone, on the grounds of sex, less favourably than a person of the opposite sex is or would be treated in the same circumstances. Once again, a term in a contract which purports to exclude or limit any provision of the Act is unenforceable by any person in whose favour the term would operate (s. 73(3)).

Sex discrimination defined

There are two kinds of discrimination as follows −

(a) *Direct* discrimination which involves, for example, treating a woman less favourably than a man because she is a woman *or because of marital status;*

(*b*) *Indirect* discrimination which occurs where conditions are applied which favour, quite unjustifiably, one sex more than the other, as where a firm advertises for clerical workers who must be six feet tall.

It should be noted that although the Act is written in terms of discrimination against women, it applies equally to discrimination against men either because they are men *or because of marital status.*

AREAS OF DISCRIMINATION

Areas of sexual discrimination not relating directly to the contract of employment appear below.

(*a*) *Partnerships.* The sex discrimination provisions were extended to all partnerships regardless of the number of partners by the Sex Discrimination Act 1986. The provisions cover failure to offer a person a partnership on grounds of sex or to offer it but on worse terms or to refuse benefits or give inferior benefits, facilities and services to a partner on the grounds of sex.

(*b*) *Trade unions and qualifying bodies.* The provisions relating to sex discrimination are applied as they are for racial discrimination with the necessary changes being made.

(*c*) *Education.* Co-educational schools, colleges, and universities may not discriminate in the provision of facilities or in their admissions. Thus it would be unlawful to refuse a girl admission to a metalwork class because she is a girl. In addition, the Careers Service must not discriminate in the advice and assistance offered to girls and boys, though single-sex schools are still permissible.

Local education authorities are required to provide secondary education without discriminating on the grounds of sex. In *R v Birmingham City Council ex parte Equal Opportunities Commission* [1989] 1 All E.R. 769 it appeared that the Council provided considerably fewer grammar school places for girls than for boys. The House of Lords approved a declaration that the Council's arrangements were unlawful.

(*d*) *Housing, goods, facilities and services.* In general, no one providing housing, goods, facilities or services to the public may discriminate because of sex. There are some exceptions where discrimination will not be unlawful; these include, for example, situations where it is necessary to preserve decency and privacy, e.g. public lavatories.

Discrimination must not be used in the buying or renting of accommodation and a hotel, boarding house or restaurant may not refuse accommodation or refreshment on the grounds of sex.

In addition, a bank, building society, finance house or other credit business must offer credit, a mortgage or loan on the same terms that it would offer the facilities to someone of the opposite sex.

ESSENTIAL CASE LAW AND COMMENT

Gill v *El Vino Co Ltd*, 1983 – Sex discrimination: facilities and services **(39)**

Quinn v *Williams Furniture Ltd*, 1981 – Sex discrimination: credit **(40)**

(*e*) *Advertising.* Advertisements with job descriptions such as 'salesgirl, waiter, stewardess, postman' are deemed to discriminate unless they contain an indication that both men and women are eligible, though it should be noted that only the Equal Opportunities Commission (EOC) can bring proceedings in matters to do with advertising.

Victimisation

The provisions here are similar to those set out in the Race Relations Act, 1976, so that the law will protect a person if they are victimised for bringing a complaint under the Sex Discrimination Act, 1975.

The Equal Opportunities Commission

The Equal Opportunities Commission was set up to ensure effective enforcement of the Sex Discrimination Act and the Equal Pay Act (see Chapter 19) and to promote equal opportunity between the sexes. The Commission has power to hold formal investigations, and if satisfied that practices are unlawful, can issue non-discrimination notices requiring that they cease. When holding a formal investigation, either on its own initiative or because it has been asked to do so by the Secretary of State, the Commission has power to require any person to furnish information and to attend hearings to give evidence.

The Commission has power to help individuals in the preparation and conduct of complaints in both courts and tribunals, and as well as investigating areas of inequality between the sexes, the Commission has a duty to make recommendations to the Government about the operation of existing law. It is also empowered to undertake or assist others to undertake research and educational work and generally to advise people as to their rights.

The Race Relations Act, 1976, made minor amendments in the Sex Discrimination Act. In particular, the EOC was given power to issue codes of practice giving practical guidance on equality of opportunity and the elimination of discrimination between men and women, i.e. powers matching those given to the CRE. This was achieved by adding s. 56A to the Sex Discrimination Act, 1975.

A code of practice 'for the elimination of sex and marriage discrimination and the promotion of equality of opportunity in employment' was issued and came into force on 30 April 1985. Breach of the Code does not make a person liable to proceedings but its provisions may be taken into account by tribunals.

Enforcement

The provisions, which are similar to those of the Race Relations Act, 1976, are as follows –

(a) *Individuals' rights.* Complaints in the employment field may be made to industrial tribunals (see further p. 53).

Complaints in all other fields may be made to a county court and if the court finds in favour of the complainant it may award: (i) an order declaring the rights of the parties as e.g. in *Gill* v *El Vino Co. Ltd* 1983 at p. 583; (ii) an injunction; or (iii) damages which may include loss of earnings and also compensation for injured feelings.

(b) *The Equal Opportunities Commission.* The functions of the EOC in regard to enforcement are as follows –

    (i) the Commission may conduct formal investigations into any matter in order to carry out its duties and where it discovers conduct which contravenes the Sex Discrimination Act or the Equal Pay Act it is empowered to issue a non-discrimination notice. The result of issuing such a notice is the same as that under the Race Relations Act, 1976 (see p. 181);

    (ii) the Commission can institute legal proceedings in respect of persistent discrimination, including judicial review (*R* v *Birmingham City Council ex parte E.O.C.* (1989) – see p. 183);

    (iii) the Commission has the sole right to institute legal proceedings in respect of discriminatory practices in advertisements, and instructions and pressure to discriminate;

    (iv) the Commission has power to assist individual complainants in preparing their case on e.g. difficult aspects of the law.

(c) *Qualifying bodies.* Where a qualifying body is required by law to satisfy itself as to the good character of an applicant for the authorisation or qualification it can confer, it must have regard, in deciding whether or not to issue, renew, or extend the authorisation or qualification, to any evidence tending to show that the applicant, or any of his past or present employees or agents has practised unlawful discrimination in, or in connection with, the carrying on of any profession or trade. Discrimination by persons who require such authorisations or qualifications to carry on their profession or trade may therefore be drawn to the attention of the appropriate qualifying body, e.g. the Law Society. An additional example would be an allegation against a person in the consumer credit or hire business, for which a licence from the Director-General of Fair Trading is required. Such an allegation may be referred to the Director-General who is required to have regard to evidence of discrimination when considering the fitness of a person to hold a licence under the Consumer Credit Act, 1974.

PERSONS AND LEGAL RELATIONSHIPS

The law recognises and defines certain common relationships. The following, in particular, have relevance to the various branches of substantive law dealt with in later chapters.

Agency

It is quite common to find parties having the relationship of principal and agent. Sometimes a person (the principal) wishes to have certain tasks carried out – he may wish to sell a house or buy shares in a company. He therefore employs an estate agent or a stockbroker to carry out his purposes. Sometimes an agent is a specialist who carries out a limited range of duties, e.g. an auctioneer who sells a wardrobe put into an auction. Sometimes he has wider powers, and may even be able to bind the principal in all the ways the principal could bind himself, as where the agent has a power of attorney.

An agent may be specifically appointed as such, but in some cases an agent acquires his status without specific authority being given to him, and such an agent may bind his principal by what is called usual authority. If P appoints A to be the manager of a hotel, A may be able to bind P in a contract although he had no actual authority to make it, for the law is not solely concerned with the actual authority of an agent but regards him as having the usual powers of an agent of his class. It follows that the usual powers of a hotel manager will be relevant in deciding the sort of agreement which A can make on behalf of P. The doctrine of usual authority does not apply where the third party knows that the agent has no authority to make the contract.

An agent's powers may also be extended in an emergency. If A is a carrier of perishable goods for P, he may be able to sell them on behalf of P is the goods are deteriorating and he cannot get P's instructions with regard to disposal. A becomes an agent of necessity for the purpose of sale, though his actual authority is to carry the goods. Agency may also arise out of conduct resulting in apparent authority. If a husband pays the debts which his wife incurs with the local dressmaker, he may be liable to pay for an expensive article of clothing which she buys without his consent, because the husband has, by his conduct, led the dressmaker to believe that the wife has power to bind her husband in contracts of this nature. This type of agency is not peculiar to the relationship of husband and wife and could arise wherever P holds out A as having authority to make contracts on P's behalf. It is also possible in certain circumstances for a principal to ratify, i.e. adopt, the contracts of his agent, even though the agent had no actual authority when making the contract.

At one time, if a person appointed an agent to manage his or her affairs, the appointment became invalid when the person making the appointment lost mental capacity. However, under the Enduring Powers of Attorney Act, 1985 it is possible to enter into an agency agreement which does not terminate on the principal's loss of mental capacity.

Bailment

A bailment arises when one person (the bailor) hands over his property to the care of another (the bailee). The reasons for such a situation are many. The bailee may have the custody of the property by way of loan or for carriage. The article may be pledged, or left with another to be repaired or altered. Sometimes the bailee has the mere custody of the goods; sometimes he may use the property, as when he 'purchases' a radio set under a hire-purchase (or consumer credit) agreement or borrows a lawn mower. In all cases of bailment, the property or ownership remains with the bailor; the possession with the bailee.

A bailment is an independent legal transaction and need not necessarily originate in a contract. When X hands his goods to Y under a bailment Y has certain duties in regard to the care of the goods even though the bailment is not accompanied by a contract. Thus Y may be held liable for negligent damage to the goods even though he had not been promised any money or other benefit for looking after them. Bailment is considered in more detail on p. 486.

Lien

A lien is a right over the property of another which arises by operation of law and can be independent of any contract. In its simplest form it gives a creditor, such as a watch repairer, the right to retain possession of a debtor's property, in this case his watch, until he has paid or settled the debt, incurred in this case as a result of repairing the watch. Lien is considered in more detail on p. 521.

Juristic persons

As we have seen, the concept of personality is not restricted to human beings and we shall now consider corporate personality in terms of the nature and types of corporations.

THE REGISTERED JOINT STOCK COMPANY

The enormous increase in industrial activity during the industrial revolution of the last century made necessary and inevitable the emergence of the registered joint stock company and the concept of limited liability. For the first time it was possible for the small investor to contribute to the capital of a business enterprise with the assurance that, in the event of its failure, he could lose no more than the amount he had contributed or agreed to contribute. The principles of 'legal entity' and 'perpetual succession' apply, whereby the joint stock company is deemed to be a distinct legal person, able to hold property and carry on business in its own name, irrespective of the particular persons who may happen to be the owners of its shares from time to time.

The concept of corporate personality is capable of abuse and where, for example, the concept has been used to evade legal obligations, the courts have been prepared to investigate sharp practice by individuals who are trying to hide behind a corporate mask or front.

ESSENTIAL CASE LAW AND COMMENT

Salomon v *Salomon & Co*, 1897 – The concept of legal personality **(41)**

Gilford Motor Company v *Horne*, 1933 – Looking behind corporate personality **(42)**

Joint Stock Companies are formed by registration under the Companies Act, 1985 or previous Acts. The main current controlling statute is the Companies Act, 1985. It provides for two types of registered companies: the Public Limited Company and the Private Company. A registered company is fully liable for its debts but the liability of the members may be limited either to the amount unpaid on their shares, i.e. *a company limited by shares*, or to the amount they have agreed to pay if the company is brought to an end (wound up), i.e. *a company limited by guarantee*. Some companies are *unlimited* and the members are fully liable for the unpaid debts of the company if, and only if, the company goes into liquidation.

The allotted capital of a public limited company, which must before it can trade or borrow money be at least £50,000 with 25% of the nominal value and the whole of any premium paid up, is usually raised by the public subscribing for its shares, which are issued with varying rights as to dividends, voting powers, and degrees of risk. Shares are freely transferable and are almost invariably listed on a recognised investment exchange such as the London Stock Exchange. When making a public issue of shares, the company is under a statutory obligation to publish full particulars of the history, capital structure, loans, profit record, directors, and many other matters calculated to assist the intending shareholder to assess the possibilities of the company. Such a document is called a Prospectus, and the directors are liable to penalties for fraud, misrepresentation or failure to disclose the material information as required by Part IV (Listed Securities) and Part V (Unlisted Securities) of the Financial Services Act, 1986, together with the rules of a recognised investment exchange such as the London Stock Exchange.

The minimum number of members is two (but see p. 189) but there is no upper limit. Incorporation is achieved by lodging with the Registrar of Companies certain documents of which the following are the most important –

(*a*) *The Memorandum of Association* is a document which defines the constitution of the company, and sets out in the Objects Clause the powers of the company. Since the passing of the Companies Act, 1989 this clause no longer entirely governs the activities into which the company can legally enter (but see p. 236). In the memorandum one also finds the company's name, together with a statement that the liability of the members is limited (where this is the case); the situation of its Registered Office, i.e. England or Wales or Scotland (this governs the company's nationality and domicile); the amount of its Authorised Capital; and an Association Clause in which the subscribers ask for incorporation and agree to take at least one share. Under s. 1 of the Companies Act, 1985 the memorandum of a public limited company has a clause stating that that is what it is.

(*b*) *The Articles of Association* contain the regulations governing the relationship between the company and its members, and thus cover the internal or domestic affairs of the company. Such matters as alteration of shareholders' rights, powers of directors, conduct of meetings, and resolutions, are contained in the Articles.

The directors of a company stand in the fiduciary position of agents towards the company whose money they control, and many of the provisions of the Companies Act, 1985 are framed to ensure the maximum possible degree of disclosure by the directors of information calculated to keep the members acquainted with the affairs of the company.

The Memorandum and Articles of Association are public documents which must be deposited with the Registrar of Companies at Companies Registration Office in Cardiff and are open to public inspection along with other records relating to charges on the company's property, and copies of important resolutions. Each year the company's Annual Return, giving particulars of share capital, debentures, mortgages and charges, list of members, particulars of directors and secretary, is sent by the Registrar of Companies to the company for checking, and if necessary, alteration if there have been changes, before return to the Registrar. In addition, the company's accounts and the directors' and auditors' reports are filed with the Registrar within ten months (private company) and seven months (public company) of the end of the accounting period to which they relate. Any person may inspect the Register of Members at the Registered Office of the company.

The private company, which has a minimum of two members and no maximum number, is now a firmly established feature of the present day business world. The private company is barred by s. 170 of the Financial Services Act, 1986 from going to the general public for subscriptions for its securities. An EC Directive allowing private limited companies to have only one member is due to be brought into force in the UK by 1 January 1992. The Registrar will have to be informed if all the shares are held by one member.

Dissolution of a registered company usually takes place by the company being put into liquidation, as a result of the process of winding up.

OTHER TYPES OF CORPORATION

Incorporation may also be achieved by a *Royal Charter* granted by the Crown. The procedure is for the organisation desiring incorporation to address a petition to the Privy Council, asking for a grant of a charter and outlining the powers required. If the Privy Council consider that the organisation is an appropriate one, the Crown will be advised to grant a charter. Charter companies were formerly used to further the development of new countries, e.g. the East India Company and the Hudson Bay Company, but now they are usually confined to non-commercial corporations, e.g. the Institute of Chartered Accountants in England and Wales and the Institute of Chartered Secretaries and Administrators. Universities are also incorporated in this way. It is possible for the liability of members to be limited, and a chartered company, sometimes known as a 'Common Law Corporation', has the same powers as an individual person in spite of limitations in its charter. However, it is said that the Crown may forfeit the charter if the company pursues *ultra vires* activities, and certainly a member can ask the court to grant an injunction preventing the company from carrying out *ultra vires* activities.

ESSENTIAL CASE LAW AND COMMENT

Jenkin v *Pharmaceutical Society*, 1921 – Charter companies: acts inconsistent with charter **(43)**

Companies have also been created by special Act of Parliament, and governed by their special Acts and also by Acts which apply to statutory companies generally, which are known as 'Clauses Acts'. These Acts together define and limit their activities. The purpose of statutory companies was to promote undertakings of the nature of public utility services, e.g. gas and electricity, where monopolistic powers and compulsory acquisition are essential to proper functioning. The liability of members could be limited. Many of the former statutory public utility companies were nationalised by other statutes and operate on a national basis, e.g. British Coal. In more recent times many of these undertakings have been privatised and run as public limited companies, e.g. gas and electricity.

All the forms of incorporation which we have discussed have one feature in common, i.e. they produce corporations aggregate having more that one member. However, English law recognises the concept of the *Corporation Sole*, i.e. a corporation having only one member. A number of such corporations were created by the common lawyers. They were concerned because land did not always have an owner, and there could be a break, however slight, in ownership. Church lands for example were vested in the vicar of the particular living, and at higher levels in other church dignitaries, such as the bishop of the diocese. When such persons died, the land had no legal owner until a successor was appointed, so the common lawyers created the concept of the corporation sole whereby the office of Vicar or Bishop was a corporation, and the present holder of the office the sole member of that corporation. The death of the office holder had thereafter no effect on the corporation, which never dies, and each successive occupant of the office carries on exactly where his predecessor left off. The Bishop of London is a corporation sole, and the present holder of the office is the sole member of the corporation. The Crown is also a corporation sole.

It does not seem likely that any further corporations sole will be created by the common law, but they may still be created by statute. For example, the Public Trustee Act, 1906, sets up the office of Public Trustee as a corporation sole. The Public Trustee is prepared to act as executor or trustee, when asked to do so, and much property is vested in him from time to time in the above capacities. It would be most inconvenient to transfer this property to the new holder of the office on the death or retirement of the current one, and so the person who holds the office of Public Trustee is the sole member of a corporation called the Public Trustee, and the property over which he has control is vested in the corporation, and not in the individual who is the holder of the office.

Unincorporated associations

Having considered juristic personality, we will now turn to organisations which have no personality separate and distinct from the members. Many groups of people and institutions exist which carry on their affairs in much the same way as incorporated associations, but which are in fact non-charitable unincorporated associations. Examples are cricket clubs, tennis clubs, and societies of like kind. Such associations have no independent legal personality, and their property is treated as the joint property of all the members. The main areas of legal difficulty arising in regard to these associations are as follows –

Liability of members in contract. This rests on the principles of the law of agency. Thus a member who purports to make a contract on behalf of his club is usually personally liable. The other members will only be liable as co-principals if they had authorised the making of the contract. This would be the case if, for example, the rules of the club so provided. Alternatively, the members may ratify the contract after it is made. However, it appears that no member has authority to make a *purchase on credit* (*Flemyng* v *Hector* (1836) 2 M. & W. 172) unless he is specifically authorised to do so. Membership of a club usually involves payment of an annual subscription and nothing more. Consequently it is expected that everything needed by the club will be paid for from existing funds. If more money is needed a meeting of members should be called so that subscriptions might be raised rather than pledge the credit of the members.

Liability of members in tort. A person is liable if he committed the tort and in addition may be liable vicariously for the tort of his employee (see p. 382). These principles have been applied to clubs in two main types of case, viz. –

(*a*) Where a person has been injured as a result of the dangerous condition of the club premises. The Court of Appeal held in *Robertson* v *Ridley* [1989] 2 All E.R. 474 that at common law membership of the committee of a members' club did not of itself carry with it any duty of care towards the members. However, this rule could be changed by the rules of the club which could create a duty of care in the committee in regard to the safety of club premises. It was, however, held in *Jones* v *Northampton Borough Council, The Times*, 21 May 1990 that if a member of a club or of its committee is given a task to do on behalf of the other members he owes them a duty of care to warn them of any circumstances of which he becomes aware which give rise to the risk of injury. In this case A who was the chairman of a sports club booked accommodation for a six-a-side football match in premises which to his knowledge had a leaking roof making the floor slippery. He was held liable to a member of the team who was injured because of this.

(*b*) Where a person has been injured as a result of the negligence of an employee of the club. The tendency here is to find that the employee is employed by the officer or committee or trustees who appointed him. (*Bradley Egg Farm Ltd* v *Clifford* [1943] 2 All E.R. 378.)

Rights of members in the assets of the association. While a club is functioning the individual members have no separate rights in its property. They do, however, acquire realisable rights when the club is dissolved. On dissolution the general rule is that the assets are sold and after liabilities have been discharged any surplus is divided equally among those persons who are members at the time of dissolution regardless of length of membership or of subscriptions paid (*Re GKN Bolts & Nuts Ltd Sports & Social Club, Leek and Others* v *Donkersley and Others* [1982] 2 All E.R. 855), subject, of course, to any contrary provision in the rules of the club. It should be noted that a club is not dissolved simply because it changes its name and constitution with the express or implied consent of the members. (*Abbatt* v *Treasury Solicitor* [1969] 3 All E.R. 1175.)

Rights of members under the rules. The rules of an unincorporated association constitute a contract between the members of the association and the court will grant an injunction to a member who is denied a right given under the rules, e.g. the right to vote at meetings (*Woodford* v *Smith* [1970] 1 All E.R. 1091), or if he is expelled either where there is no power of explusion under the rules, or if the power exists it has not been exercised properly as where the principles of natural justice (see p. 61) have not been observed.

Procedure. If only a few of the members are liable no problems arise since they can all be sued personally. If, however, it is intended to allege that all the members are liable this procedure is impracticable since all would have the right to be individually defended and represented. In this sort of case a representative action is available. Under the Rules of the Supreme Court and the county court rules the plaintiff may ask for a *representative order* to be made against certain members of the association and sue them. If he is successful these members will be liable to pay the damages but may also be entitled to an indemnity from the funds of the association, and in this way the plaintiff is in effect paid from the association's funds. Similarly some members of an unincorporated association can sue for wrongs done to the association by means of the representative order procedure.

TRADE UNIONS

As regards the status of trade unions, s. 2(1) of the Trade Union and Labour Relations Act, 1974 provides that a trade union shall not be treated as if it were a body corporate but it is capable of making contracts; the property of the trade union is vested in trustees on trust for the union; it is capable of suing and being sued in its own name, whether in proceedings relating to property or founded on contract or tort or any other cause of action whatsoever; proceedings for any offence alleged to have been committed by it or on its behalf may be brought against it in its own name and any judgment made in proceedings of any description brought against a trade union are enforceable, e.g. by way of execution against the property held in trust for the union as if the union were a body corporate.

Section 3(1) of the 1974 Act extends the identical provisions to an employers' association where it is unincorporated. However, an employers' association may be a body corporate.

Under s. 15 of the Employment Act, 1982 (as amended by the Employment Act, 1990) the liability of trade unions is as follows:

Industrial action against the employer of its members (primary action)

In an official strike the union is liable for torts committed during the dispute. The most usual tort is interfering with contracts of employment by organising the strike. There may be other torts, e.g. damage to the employer's property.

A trade union has immunity in regard to the tort of interference with contracts of employment only if the industrial action is preceded by a ballot of members and the action is commenced within four weeks of the ballot taking place, unless under s. 8 of the 1990 Act the union was prevented from calling action during that period by e.g. a court injunction. The majority of those voting must vote in favour of the action. Under the Employment Act, 1988 the ballot must be secret and there must be separate ballots for each place of work. An official scrutineer must supervise the way in which voting papers are drawn up and sent to members to prevent ballot-rigging. Under s. 5 of the Employment Act, 1990 balloting is extended to self-employed members of a trade union. Section 7 of the 1990 Act requires the voting papers for industrial action ballots to say who can call for such action if there is a vote in favour. The statutory immunity of the trade union will not apply unless the action is called by the specified person.

If there is no ballot the union can be sued for an injunction and damages which are limited according to the number of members it has.

Action which is not against the employer (secondary action)

Under s. 4 of the 1990 Act virtually all forms of secondary action are unlawful and the union is liable for torts including interfering with contracts of employment and there is no immunity by reason of a ballot. An injunction and damages may be awarded and again the damages are limited according to the memberhip of the union involved.

Unofficial industrial action

Section 6 of the 1990 Act makes a trade union legally responsible for the acts of its committees and officials including shop stewards and other officials regardless of whether they are authorised by the rules of the union to act on its behalf. This means that a trade union is potentially liable for industrial action organised by any of its officials or committees unless the union takes steps to repudiate the call for action. Section 6 contains a requirement that the union must 'do its best' to give individual written notice to the members involved.

Contracts made by a trade union are normally enforceable in accordance with the general principles of the law of contract. However, under s. 18 of the Trade Union and Labour Relations Act, 1974 collective agreements, i.e. with an employer in regard to wages, hours and conditions of work of a group of workers, are presumed *not* to be intended to be legally enforceable *unless* they are in writing and contain a provision to that effect.

THE PARTNERSHIP

A partnership is defined in s. 1 of the Partnership Act, 1890, as 'the relationship which subsists between persons carrying on a business in common with a view of profit'. It will be noted that there must be a business; that it must be carried on in common by the members (whether by all of them, or by one or more of them acting for the others, will depend on the agreement subsisting between them); and that there must be the intention to earn profits. An association of persons formed for the purpose (say) of promoting some educational or recreational object to which the whole of the funds of the association shall be devoted, and from which no advantage in the nature of a distribution of a profit shall accrue to the members, is not a partnership.

Participation in the profits of a business may be regarded as *prima facie* evidence of a partnership, but it is not conclusive – the intention of the parties must be examined. Thus, an employee whose remuneration is based on a share of profits, or the widow or child of a deceased partner receiving an annuity in the form of a share of profits, would not legally be deemed to be partners. Neither does the common ownership of property constitute a partnership (see further p. 494), nor the lending of money in consideration of an agreement to pay the interest, or to repay the capital, as a share or percentage of profits as they accrue. (But in such a case the lender should take the precaution of having the agreement embodied in writing, signed by all the parties, and setting out clearly the fact that he is not to be considered a partner.)

The question of citation as a partner is of great importance because the existence of a partnership, if such is proved, will involve all parties cited as partners in unlimited liability for the debts of the firm. Partners are agents for the firm, and can bind the other partners in contracts concerning the business of the firm whether they are specifically authorised to make them or not.

Two or more persons can combine to form a partnership, which can be brought into existence in a highly formal or a very casual manner. *No legal formalities are essential*, but it is desirable and usual for the rights and liabilities of the partners to be defined in a formal Deed of Partnership, or at least in a written Partnership Agreement. On the other hand, a mere oral agreement is equally binding, and in extreme cases a relationship of partnership may be inferred from the conduct of the parties. The partners are at liberty to vary the arrangements made between them, and where the conduct of the parties has for a lengthy period been inconsistent with the terms as originally agreed, it will be presumed that they intend that the new arrangements shall be binding on them The Partnership Act makes provisions as to contribution of capital, division of profits, rights of partners to participate in active management, and so on, but these only apply in so far as they are not varied by agreement between the partners.

Section 716 of the Companies Act, 1985, prohibits the formation of a partnership consisting of more than 20 persons for the purpose of carrying on any business for gain. The Banking Act of 1979, s. 51(2) and Sch. 7 applies the usual limit of 20 to banking partnerships.

However, certain partnerships of solicitors, accountants and stockbrokers are exempted from this prohibition by s. 716 of the Companies Act, 1985. Regulations made by the Department of Trade and Industry exempt from the prohibition in s. 716 of the Act of 1985 certain other partnerships, e.g. patent agents and also certain partnerships of surveyors, auctioneers, valuers, estate agents and town planners.

There is no limitation on the activities of partners provided these are legal; nor is there any limit to the liability of the individual partners for the debts of the firm, each partner being liable to the full extent of his personal estate for any deficiencies of the partnership. However, provision is made for the introduction of limited partners whose liability is limited to the amount of capital they have introduced, though there must always be at least one general partner who is fully liable for the debts of the firm. Such a partnership must be registered as a limited partnership under the Limited Partnerships Act, 1907.

The partnership was the normal form of business organisation for operations on a fairly large scale before the advent of the joint stock company, but it is now largely restricted to the type of enterprise requiring intimate personal collaboration between the members, or where incorporation is not possible or desirable, as among doctors, solicitors and accountants, though the increasing control over companies including, in particular, private companies, may see some revival of the partnership as a more general business organisation. However, in the legal and accounting professions particularly, negligence liability is encouraging a move towards incorporation of firms to achieve limited liability.

One of the defects of the partnership is its lack of continuity. On the death of a partner the continuing partners must account to his personal representatives for the amount of his interest in the firm. This difficulty may be met to some extent by providing funds out of the proceeds of an insurance policy on the deceased partner's life, or by arranging for the balance of his capital account to be left in the business as a loan, but failing these measures the sudden withdrawal of a large amount of capital may well cause serious dislocation of the smaller business, or even end its operations. The most serious defect of a partnership, however, is the difficulty of providing additional funds for expansion, and this may induce partners to admit new members for the sake of their capital, regardless of their fitness for taking an active part in controlling the business.

A *partnership firm is not a* persona *at law*; a partnership is an aggregate of its members. In the matter of procedure the Rules of the Supreme Court make it possible for the firm to sue and be sued in its own name, but this does not confer upon it a legal personality as is possessed by a corporation. This makes the holding of property more difficult in the partnership. For example, land cannot be conveyed to the firm. Instead it is conveyed to some or all of the partners as legal owners who declare a *trust for sale* for all the partners in equity.

The Crown

The Crown consists of the Monarch and her Ministers, together with the Central Government departments staffed by civil servants, the armed forces, and the Privy Council which retains some powers, e.g. to arrange for the coronation of the Monarch. The police are not servants of the Crown, nor are the nationalised industries, e.g. British Coal, part of the Crown.

Until 1947 the Crown was not liable for the tortious acts of its servants, and was liable only to a limited extent in contract, though the person who did the wrongful act could be sued and the Crown often stood behind him and paid the damages against him. Actions in contract could only be started by an awkward procedure known as a Petition of Right, with the consent of the Crown given on the advice of the Attorney-General.

The rather anomalous position at common law which has been outlined above arose out of the ancient maxim, 'The King can do no wrong', which was extended to cover the activities of the Departments of State and their servants. The Crown Proceedings Act, 1947, and the Rules of the Supreme Court (Crown Proceedings) Act, 1947, which were required to support the

Act in the matter of procedure, came into force together on 1 January 1948, to rectify the matter.

The general effect of this legislation is to abolish the rule that the Crown is immune from legal process, though s. 40 preserves the immunity of the Monarch in a personal capacity from any liability in law, and to place the Crown as regards civil proceedings in the same position as a subject. Proceedings by Petition of Right are abolished, and all claims which might before the Act have been enforced by Petition of Right can be brought by ordinary action in accordance with the Act.

CONTRACTUAL CLAIMS

The Crown is now liable in contract where a Petition of Right could have been brought before, and also in tort. Regarding contractual claims, there are some limitations upon the rights of the other party, viz. –

Executive necessity

In *Rederiaktiebolaget Amphitrite* v R [1921] 3 K.B. 500, a neutral shipowner's vessel was detained in England although the British Legation in Stockholm had given an undertaking that it would not be. The basis of Rowlatt, J.'s decision for the Crown was that the Government cannot by contract hamper its freedom of action in matters which concern the welfare of the State. This statement has been regarded as much too wide and is probably of very limited application.

The main result of the ruling of Rowlatt, J. is that contracts with the Government normally contain cancellation clauses which provide for compensation. In practice the Crown does not invoke the *Amphitrite* rule to avoid liability for such compensation.

Parliamentary funds

In *Churchward* v R [1865] 1 Q.B. 173, a contract to carry mail for eleven years was terminated by the Crown in the fourth year. Shee, J., in deciding for the Crown, held that it was a condition precedent of the contract that Parliament would allocate funds and if they chose not to there was no claim. This decision came under criticism in subsequent cases and the better view is that it is limited to cases where Parliament has *expressly* refused to grant the necessary funds.

This rule does, of course, cause hardship to contractors with the Government but it must be continued if the control of Parliament over public expenditure is to be maintained.

Freedom to legislate

In *Reilly* v R [1934] A.C. 176, a barrister who was employed by the Canadian Government had his contract terminated by legislation. The Privy Council found for the Crown on the ground that the Crown cannot by contract restrict its right to legislate.

Contracts of employment

Here the position is as follows –

(*a*) *Military personnel.* Military employees cannot successfully claim against the Crown for breach of contract (*Dickson* v *Combermere* (1863) 3 F. & F. 527) nor can they claim arrears of pay (*Leaman* v *R* [1920] 3 K.B. 663).

(*b*) *Civil servants.* It was the position at common law that civil servants were dismissible at pleasure (*Shenton* v *Smith* [1895] A.C. 229) but could claim arrears of pay (*Kodeeswaran* v *A.G. of Ceylon* [1970] 2 W.L.R. 456). The general rule that those in Crown service might be dismissed at the Crown's pleasure could be varied by legislation. A well-known example is the provision under which judges of the High Court and the Court of Appeal hold their offices during good behaviour (s. 11(3), Supreme Court Act, 1981).

However, in *R* v *Lord Chancellor's Department ex parte Nangle* [1991] I.R.L.R. 343 a Divisional Court of Queen's Bench held that a civil servant is employed under a contract of service based upon the Civil Service Pay and Conditions of Service Code. This sets out conditions regarding e.g. pay, pensions, holidays and so forth. Admittedly para. 14 of the Code says that a civil servant does not have a contract of employment enforceable in the courts but the court held in this case that para. 14 must be seen in context. It could not be said that all the carefully prepared terms and conditions of service in the Code were to be regarded as purely voluntary. Mr Nangle could sue for damages for breach of contract if as he alleged his employers the Crown had failed to follow a code of practice when transferring him to another department with a loss of a salary increment following allegations that he had assaulted and sexually harassed a female colleague. The provisions of the Employment Protection (Consolidation) Act, 1978 which protect employees against e.g. unfair dismissal apply to civil servants but not to forces personnel.

Actions in tort will lie against the Crown for the torts of its servants or agents committed in the course of their employment; for breach of duty owed at common law by an employer to his servants; for breach of the duties attaching to the ownership, occupation, possession or control of property; and for breach of statutory duties, e.g. breaches of the duty of fencing dangerous machines under factory legislation.

The law as to indemnity and contribution under the Civil Liability (Contribution) Act, 1978 applies to Crown cases, so if the Crown is a joint tortfeasor, it can claim a contribution from fellow wrongdoers, which may, under s. 2(2) of the 1978 Act be a complete indemnity, so that where the Crown is led into publishing a libel, it may claim an indemnity against the party responsible. (See further p. 379.) The Law Reform (Contributory Negligence) Act, 1945 also applies to Crown cases. (See further p. 446.)

Under s. 10 of the Crown Proceedings Act, 1947 both the Crown and any member of the Armed Forces were immune from liability in tort in respect of the death of, or personal injury to another member of the Armed Forces on duty, provided that the death or injury arose out of service which ranked for the purpose of pension. This section was repealed in regard to acts or omissions causing injury after 15 May 1987 (see Crown Proceedings (Armed Forces) Act, 1987).

Actions under the Act may be brought in the High Court or a county court, and under ss. 17 and 18 of the 1947 Act the Treasury is required to publish a list of authorised government departments for the purposes of the Act, and of their solicitors. Actions by the Crown will be brought by the authorised department in its own name, or by the Attorney-General. Actions against the Crown are to be brought against the appropriate department, or, where there is doubt as to the department responsible or appropriate, against the Attorney-General.

In any civil proceedings by or against the Crown, the court can make such orders as it can make in proceedings between subjects, except that no injunction or order for specific performance can be granted against the Crown. The court can, in lieu thereof, make an order declaratory of the rights of the parties in the hope that the Crown will abide by it. No order for the recovery of land, or delivery up of property, can be made against the Crown, but the court may instead make an order that the plaintiff is entitled as against the Crown to land or to other property or to possession thereof. No execution or attachment will issue to enforce payment by the Crown of any money or costs. The procedure is for the successful party to apply for a certificate in the prescribed form giving particulars of the order. This is served on the solicitor for the department concerned, which is then required to pay the sum due with interest if any. The above exceptions show that, in spite of the Act, the rights of the subject against the Crown are still somewhat imperfect.

For historic, constitutional and procedural reasons also, the Crown cannot be prosecuted for crime. Once again a nominated defendant is put forward; e.g. for a road traffic offence, such as using a lorry with a defective tyre, the principal transport officer of the Department concerned would probably be nominated. Unfortunately, this practice results in the officer concerned acquiring a long record of motoring convictions in a personal capacity. Accordingly, in *Barnett* v *French* [1981] 1 W.L.R. 848, the Court of Appeal suggested the use of the name 'John Doe' for the nominated defendant who, for the purpose of criminal records, would be shown as having a date of birth 'circa 1657'. The name 'John Doe' was used in civil actions from about that time onwards as part of a very elaborate procedure to prove the title to land. The procedure is no longer in use.

The general rule that statutes do not bind the Crown unless by express words or necessary implication is contained in s. 40 of the 1947 Act. It produced an absurd result when it was decided that public health and hygiene legislation did not apply to National Health Service hospital kitchens. This anomaly was abolished by the National Health Service (Amendment) Act, 1986 though the general immunity in other areas given by s. 40 was preserved.

CROWN PRIVILEGE IN CIVIL PROCEEDINGS

As we have seen, either party to a civil action can, amongst other things, ask the court to order the other party to produce any relevant documents for inspection. (See p. 127.) Under s. 28 of the Crown Proceedings Act, 1947, this right lies against the Crown though the Crown could refuse to obey the order if production of the document(s) would be injurious to the public interest. It had been felt for some time that ministers whose departments were involved in civil litigation had abused this right. Undoubtedly, some plaintiffs failed in an action against the Crown because even the judge could not obtain access to documents necessary to support the claim. As a result of a number of cases of this kind, the House of Lords decided, in *Conway* v *Rimmer* [1968] 1 All E.R. 874, that even though a minister certifies that production of a particular document would be against the public interest the judge may nevertheless see it and decide whether the minister's view is correct. If the judge cannot accept the minister's decision he may overrule him and order disclosure of the document to the party concerned. Thus the decision of the minister is no longer conclusive though it is unlikely that a judge would order disclosure if there was a danger of real prejudice to the national interest.

However, despite *dicta* in *Conway* v *Rimmer* that claims to privilege on grounds of confidentiality could not expect sympathetic treatment, the courts vary in their interpretation of this view.

ESSENTIAL CASE LAW AND COMMENT

Norwich Pharmacal Co v *Commissioners of Customs and Excise*,
  1973 – Crown or public interest privilege: documents **(44)**
Alfred Crompton Amusement Machines v *Customs and Excise*
  Commissioners (No. 2), 1973 – Non-disclosure of documents:
  privilege **(45)**

PRIVILEGE IN CIVIL PROCEEDINGS – THE PUBLIC INTEREST GROUND

Privilege extends beyond cases against the Crown. Thus in *D* v *NSPCC* [1977] 1 All E.R. 589 the House of Lords held that the NSPCC or a local authority is entitled to privilege from disclosing the names of its informants in relation to child neglect or ill-treatment.

The House of Lords decided in *British Steel Corporation* v *Granada Television* [1980] 3 W.L.R. 774 that the information media and their journalists do not have immunity from the obligation to disclose their sources of information when disclosure is necessary in the interests of justice. Their Lordships went on to say, however, that the remedy is equitable and may be withheld in the public interest.

Public interest privilege has really replaced the older Crown privilege. However, the latter has been included as a separate head of privilege to show the historical development.

9
Law of contract – making the contract I

A contract may be defined as an *agreement*, enforceable by the law, between two or more persons to do or abstain from doing some act or acts, their intention being to create *legal relations* and not merely to exchange mutual promises, both having given something, or having promised to give something of *value as consideration* for any benefit derived from the agreement.

The definition can be criticised in that some contracts turn out to be unenforceable and, in addition, not all legally binding agreements are true contracts. For example, a transaction by deed derives its legally binding quality from the special way in which it is made rather than from the operation of the laws of contract, e.g. a deed is enforceable even in the absence of valuable consideration. In consequence, transactions by deed are not true contracts at all. Nevertheless, the definition at least emphasises the fact that the basic elements of contracts are (i) an agreement, (ii) an intention to create legal relations, and (iii) valuable consideration.

The essentials of a valid contract

The essential elements of the formation of a valid and enforceable contract can be summarised under the following headings –

(a)   There must be an offer and acceptance, which is in effect the agreement.
(b)   There must be an intention to create legal relations.
(c)   There is a requirement of written formalities in some cases.
(d)   There must be consideration (unless the agreement is by deed).
(e)   The parties must have capacity to contract.
(f)   There must be genuineness of consent by the parties to the terms of the contract.
(g)   The contract must not be contrary to public policy.

In the absence of one or more of these essentials, the contract may be void, voidable, or unenforceable.

Classification of contracts

Before proceeding to examine the meaning and significance of the points set out above the following distinctions should be noted.

VOID, VOIDABLE AND UNENFORCEABLE CONTRACTS

A *void* contract has no binding effect at all and in reality the expression is a contradiction in terms. However, it has been used by lawyers for a long time in order to describe particular situations in the law of contract and its usage is now a matter of convenience. A *voidable* contract is binding but one party has the right, at his option, to set it aside. An *unenforceable* contract is valid in all respects except that it cannot be enforced in a court of law by one or both of the parties should the other refuse to carry out his obligations under it. Contracts of guarantee are unenforceable unless evidenced in writing (see further p. 231).

EXECUTED AND EXECUTORY CONTRACTS

A contract is said to be *executed* when one or both of the parties have done all that the contract requires. A contract is said to be *executory* when the obligations of one or both of the parties remain to be carried out. For example, if A and B agree to exchange A's scooter for B's motor cycle and do it immediately, the *possession* of the goods and the *right* to the goods are transferred *together* and the contract is *executed*. If they agree to exchange the following week the *right* to the goods is transferred but not the *possession* and the contract is *executory*. Thus an *executed* contract conveys a *chose in possession* (see p. 481), while an *executory* contract conveys a *chose in action* (see p. 481).

SPECIALTY CONTRACTS

Specialty contracts are also called deeds.

The general law of contract *requires* a deed in the case of a lease of more than three years, which must be under seal if it is to create a legal estate. In addition a transfer of property, e.g. a conveyance, which imposes covenants (or agreements) in regard, for example, to the use of the land, is a contract and must also be by deed. In addition, a conveyance is an *agreement* by the vendor of land to convey his title or ownership and the *agreement* of the purchaser to take it.

As regards the *form* of a deed the Law of Property (Miscellaneous Provisions) Act, 1989 is now relevant. Section 1 requires, as before, that a deed must be in writing but gets rid of the requirement for sealing where a deed is entered into by an individual. The signature of the individual making the deed must be witnessed and attested. Attestation consists of a statement that the deed has been signed in the presence of a witness.

The section also provides that it must be made clear on the face of the document that it is intended to be a deed. The usual form to satisfy this requirement and attestation is: 'signed as a deed by AB in the presence of XY'.

As far as companies are concerned s. 36A of the Companies Act, 1985 provides that while a company may continue to execute documents by putting its common seal on them it need not have such a seal. Any document signed by a director and the secretary of the company or by two directors and said to be executed by the company will be regarded as if the seal had been put on it. Once again it must be made clear on the face of the document that it is intended to be a deed and the form here could be as follows: 'signed as a deed: AB director and CD secretary (or another director) – for and on behalf of Boxo Ltd'.

A deed has certain characteristics which distinguish it from a simple contract –

(*a*) *Merger*. If a simple contract is afterwards embodied in a deed made between the same parties, the simple contract merges into, or is swallowed up by the deed, for the deed is the superior document. But if the deed is only intended to cover part of the terms of the previous simple contract, there is no merger of that part of the simple contract not covered by the deed.

(*b*) *Limitation of actions*. The right of action under a specialty contract is barred unless it is brought within twelve years from the date when the cause of action arises in it, i.e. when the deed could first have been sued upon. Time does not run from the date of making the deed. A similar right of action is barred under a simple contract after only six years. (See further p. 340.)

(*c*) *Consideration is not essential* to support a deed, though specific performance will not be granted if the promise is gratuitous. (See p. 337.) Simple contracts must be supported by consideration.

(*d*) *Estoppel*. Statements in a deed tend to be conclusive against the party making them, and although he might be able to prove they were not true, the rule of evidence called 'estoppel' will prevent him from doing this by excluding the very evidence which would be needed. In modern law, however, a deed does not operate as an estoppel where one of the parties wishes to bring evidence to show fraud, duress, mistake, lack of capacity or illegality.

Simple contracts form the great majority of contracts, and are sometimes referred to as parol contracts. This class includes all contracts not by deed, and for their enforcement they require consideration. Simple contracts may be made orally or in writing, or they may be inferred from the conduct of the parties; but no simple contract can exist which does not arise from a valid offer and a valid acceptance supported by some consideration. When these elements exist, the contract is valid in the absence of some vitiating element such as lack of capacity of one of the parties, lack of reality of consent, or illegality or impossibility of performance.

The formation of contract

In order to decide whether a contract has come into being it is necessary to establish that there has been an *agreement* between the parties. In consequence it must be shown that an *offer* was made by one party (called the offeror) which was *accepted* by the other party (called the offeree) and that *legal relations* were intended.

Agreement

A contract is an agreement and comes into existence when one party makes an offer which the other accepts. The person making the offer is called the offeror, and the person to whom it is made is called the offeree. An offer may be express or implied. Suppose X says to Y – 'I will sell you this watch for £5', and Y says – 'I agree'. An express offer and acceptance have been made; X is the offeror and Y the offeree. Alternatively Y may say to X: 'I will give you £5 for that watch'. If X says: 'I agree', then another express offer has been made, but Y is the offeror and X is the offeree. In both cases, the acceptance brings a contract into being. In order to find out who makes the offer and who the acceptance, it is necessary to examine the way in which the contract is negotiated.

Offer and invitation to treat

An offer is an undertaking by the offeror that he will be bound in contract by the offer if there is a proper acceptance of it. An offer may be made to a specific person or to any member of a group of persons, and in cases of an offer embracing a promise for an act designed to produce a unilateral contract, to the world at large.

> **ESSENTIAL CASE LAW AND COMMENT**
>
> *Carlill* v *Carbolic Smoke Ball Co*, 1893 – Offer: the unilateral situation **(46)**

INVITATION TO TREAT – AUCTIONS

Problems relating to contractual offers have risen in the case of *auction sales* but the position is now largely resolved. An advertisement of an auction is not an offer to hold it. At an auction the bid is the offer; the auctioneer's request for bids is merely an invitation to treat. The sale is complete when the hammer falls, and until that time any bid may be withdrawn. (*Payne* v *Cave* (1789) 3 Term Rep. 148.)

Where an auction is expressly advertised as subject to a 'reserve price' the above rules are not applied and there is no contract unless and until the reserve price is met and this is so even if the auctioneer knocks the goods down below the reserve price by mistake (*McManus* v *Fortescue* [1907] 2 K.B. 1). The auctioneer is not liable for a breach of warranty of authority to sell at the price knocked down because the sale is advertised as being subject to a reserve and this indicates to those attending the sale that the auctioneer's authority is limited.

The position when the auction is without reserve is not absolutely certain because it has never been clearly decided whether an advertisement to sell articles by auction without any reserve price constitutes an offer to sell to the highest bidder. It is at any rate clear that s. 57(2) of the Sale of Goods Act, 1979 prevents any *contract of sale* coming into existence if the auctioneer refuses to accept the highest bid. There remains the possibility once the auction of an item has begun that the auctioneer may be liable in damages on the basis of a breach of warranty that he has authority to sell, and will sell, the goods to the highest bidder. This device appears to be sanctioned by the decision of the Court of Exchequer Chamber in *Warlow* v *Harrison* (1859) 1 E & E 309.

ESSENTIAL CASE LAW AND COMMENT

Harris v *Nickerson*, 1873 – Invitation to treat: the auction situation
(47)

INVITATION TO TREAT – PRICE INDICATIONS: PRICE LISTS AND CATALOGUES

If I expose in my shop window a coat priced £50, this is not an offer to sell. It is not possible for a person to enter the shop and say: 'I accept your offer; here is the £50.' It is the would-be buyer who makes the offer when tendering the money. If by chance the coat has been wrongly priced, I shall be entitled to say: 'I am sorry; the price is £100', and refuse to sell. An invitation to treat is often merely a statement of the price and not an offer to sell.

The same principles have been applied to prices set out in price lists, catalogues, circulars, newspapers and magazines.

ESSENTIAL CASE LAW AND COMMENT

Pharmaceutical Society of Great Britain v *Boots Cash Chemists (Southern) Ltd*, 1953 – Price indications **(48)**
Partridge v *Crittenden*, 1968 – Magazines and circulars **(49)**

COMPANY PROSPECTUSES/ADVERTISEMENTS IN CONNECTION WITH SALE OF SECURITIES

A prospectus/advertisement issued by a company in order to invite the public to subscribe for its shares (or debentures) is an invitation to treat, so that members of the investing public offer to buy the securities when they apply for them and the company, being the acceptor, will only accept the proportion of public offers which matches the shares or debentures which the company wishes to issue. If there are more offers than shares the issue is said to be over-subscribed. Some applicants then get no shares at all or only a proportion of what they applied for. The conditions of issue also allow the company to make a binding contract by a *partial* acceptance in this way. Normally acceptance must be absolute and unconditional. (See p. 207.)

OTHER SITUATIONS

In other cases, such as automatic vending machines, the position is doubtful, and it may be that such machines are invitations to treat. However, it is more likely that the provision of the machine represents an implied offer which is accepted when a coin is put into it. However, it does seem that if a bus travels along a certain route, there is an *implied offer* on the part of its owners to carry passengers at the published fares for the various stages, and it would appear that when a passenger puts himself either on the platform or inside the bus, he makes an *implied acceptance* of the offer, agreeing to be bound by the company's conditions and to pay the appropriate fare: *per* Lord Greene *obiter* in *Wilkie* v *London Passenger Transport Board* [1947] 1 All E.R. 258.

NEGOTIATIONS FOR THE SALE OF LAND

With regard to negotiations for the sale of land the same principles are again applied, with perhaps this difference that in a case involving the sale of land where *specific performance is a possible remedy* the court may be reluctant to grant that remedy unless the intention to contract is very clear.

ESSENTIAL CASE LAW AND COMMENT

Harvey v *Facey*, 1893 – Offers and the sale of land **(50)**

Acceptance – generally

Once the existence of an offer has been proved, the court must be satisfied that the offeree has accepted the offer, otherwise there is no contract. An agreement may nevertheless be inferred from the conduct of the parties.

The person who accepts an offer must be aware that the offer has been made. Thus if B has found A's lost dog and, not having seen an advertisement by A offering a reward for its return, returns it out of goodness of heart, B will not be able to claim the reward. He cannot be held to accept an offer of which he is unaware. However, as long as the acceptor *is aware* of the making of the offer, his motive in accepting it is immaterial. (See *Carlill* v *Carbolic Smoke Ball Co.*, 1893 at p. 588.)

It should be noted that an acceptance brings the offer to an end because the offer then merges into the contract.

ESSENTIAL CASE LAW AND COMMENT

Brogden v *Metropolitan Railway*, 1877 – Acceptance by conduct **(51)**

CONDITIONAL ASSENT

An acceptance must be absolute and unconditional. One form of conditional assent is an acceptance 'subject to contract'. The law has placed a special significance on these words, and they are usually construed as meaning that the parties do not intend to be bound until a formal contract is prepared.

In other cases of conditional assent, i.e. where the words 'subject to contract' are not used, the attitude of the court is not so predictable, but it would seem that if the court decides that the further agreement of the parties is not a condition precedent to the formation of the contract, but is merely part of the performance of an already binding agreement, the court will enforce the contract.

A potential purchaser can generally recover any deposit paid if he does not continue with a 'subject to contract' purchase. (*Chillingworth* v *Esche* [1923] All E.R. 97.)

The effect of the use of the words 'without prejudice' in letters forming the basis of negotiations between parties to a contract was considered by the court in *Tomlin* v *Standard Telephones and Cables Ltd* [1969] 3 All E.R. 201. It was decided that the words meant 'without prejudice to the position of the writer of it if the terms which he proposed therein were not accepted'. If the terms were accepted a binding contract was established.

ESSENTIAL CASE LAW AND COMMENT

Winn v *Bull*, 1877 – Conditional acceptances **(52)**

COUNTER-OFFER

A counter-offer is a rejection of the original offer and in some cases has the effect of cancelling it. Where the counter-offer *introduces a new term*, the original offer is cancelled, though the counter-offer may be accepted either expressly or by implication. However, a simple request for information where the offeree merely *tries to induce a new term* may not amount to an actual counter-offer.

ESSENTIAL CASE LAW AND COMMENT

Hyde v *Wrench*, 1840 – Effect of counter-offer **(53)**
Stevenson v *McLean*, 1880 – Request for information **(54)**
Butler Machine Tool Co v *Ex-Cell-O Corporation*, 1979 –
    Accepting a counter-offer **(55)**

Acceptance in the case of tenders

In the case of an invitation to submit tenders for the purchase of specific goods, as in *Spencer* v *Harding*, 1870 (see p. 590), the person or company which asks for the tender will usually be regarded as making an invitation to treat. The tender is the offer and the person who asks for it may accept it or reject it as he thinks fit. If tenders are asked for an indefinite amount of goods, e.g. 'coal as required during 1992 not exceeding 100,000 tonnes' the 'acceptance' of such a tender results in a standing offer by the supplier to supply the goods set out in the tender as and when required by the person accepting it. Each time the buyer orders a quantity, there is a contract confined to that quantity; but if the buyer does not order any of the goods set out in the tender, or a smaller number than the supplier quoted for, there is no breach of contract. Conversely, if the person submitting the tender wishes to revoke his standing offer, he may do so, except in so far as the buyer has already ordered goods under the tender. These must be supplied or the tenderer is in breach of contract.

ESSENTIAL CASE LAW AND COMMENT

Great Northern Railway v *Witham*, 1873 – The tender as a
    standing offer **(56)**

INCOMPLETE (OR INCHOATE) AGREEMENTS

A contract will not be enforced unless the parties have expressed themselves with reasonable clarity on the matter of essential terms. A situation may therefore exist in which the parties have gone through a form of offer and acceptance but this has left some terms unclear so that if either party wishes to avoid the contract he may claim to do so on the basis that he does not know precisely what to do in order to perform his part of it. The concept of the inchoate contract normally arises as a defence to an action for breach of contract.

In such a case it may be possible for the court to complete the contract by reference to a *trade practice* or *course of dealing* between the parties. Sometimes the agreement itself may provide a method of completion as where it contains an arbitration clause. However, if the court cannot obtain assistance from these sources, it will not usually complete the contract for the parties, and the contract, being *inchoate*, cannot be enforced. However, a covenant in a conveyance that the purchaser should be given 'the first option of purchasing . . . at a price to be agreed upon' certain adjoining land imposes an obligation on the vendor at least to offer the land to the purchaser at a price at which he is willing to sell or in other words give him first refusal (*Smith* v *Morgan* [1971] 2 All E.R. 1500).

However, it is necessary to distinguish between a term which has yet to be agreed by the parties and a term on which they have agreed but is in the event meaningless or ambiguous. In the first case, no contract exists unless the deficiency can be made good by the methods outlined above. In the second case, it may be possible to ignore the term and enforce the contract without it. However, if the term is still being negotiated the contract will be inchoate and unenforceable. In addition, the term must be *clearly* severable from the rest of the contract, i.e. it must be possible to enforce the contract without it.

ESSENTIAL CASE LAW AND COMMENT

Hillas & Co. Ltd v *Arcos Ltd*, 1932 – Inchoate agreements: a course of dealing **(57)**
Foley v *Classique Coaches Ltd*, 1934 – Inchoate agreements: an arbitration clause **(58)**
Scammell v *Ouston*, 1941 – Where the agreement is inchoate **(59)**
Nicolene v *Simmonds*, 1953 – A meaningless term is ignored **(60)**

COMMUNICATION OF ACCEPTANCE

An acceptance may be made in various ways. It may be made in writing or orally, or at an auction by the fall of the hammer, but it must in general be communicated and communication must be made by a person authorised to make it. Silence cannot amount to acceptance except sometimes where there is the prior consent of the offeree which is, for example, implied in circumstances such as those in *Carlill*'s case (see p. 587). Thus if P says to Q: 'If I do not hear from you before noon tomorrow, I shall assume you accept my offer', he will find he is unable, at least without Q's consent to this method of making a contract, to bind Q in this way, and Q need take no action at all.

This rule of the common law goes some way towards preventing inertia selling, though protection is now given by the Unsolicited Goods and Services Acts, 1971 and 1975. The Acts provide for fines to be made on persons making demands for payment for goods which they know are unsolicited. If the demand is accompanied by threats a higher scale of fines applied. Furthermore, under s. 1 of the 1971 Act, unsolicited goods may be kept by the recipient without payment *after a period of 30 days* provided the recipient gives notice to the sender asking that they be collected, or *after six months* even if no such notice has been given.

> **ESSENTIAL CASE LAW AND COMMENT**
>
> *Felthouse* v *Bindley*, 1862 – Silence does not amount to acceptance **(61)**

WAIVER OF COMMUNICATION

There are some cases in which the offeror is deemed to have waived communication of the acceptance. This occurs in the case of *unilateral contracts* such as promises to pay money in return for some act to be carried out by the offeree. Performance of the act operates as an acceptance, and no communication is required, (*Carlill* v *Carbolic Smoke Ball Co.*, 1893, see p. 587.) In addition acceptance need not necessarily be communicated if the post is used (see below).

MODE OF COMMUNICATION PRESCRIBED BY OFFEROR

The offeror may stipulate the mode of acceptance, e.g. to be by letter so that there will be written evidence of it. In such a case, however, the offeror could still waive his right to have the acceptance communicated in a given way and agree to the substituted method.

In addition, an acceptance made in a different way may be effective if there is no prejudice to the offeror, as where the method used is as quick and reliable as the method prescribed.

Thus although the method of communication may be prescribed by the offeror very clear words are required to make the court treat that method as essential.

> **ESSENTIAL CASE LAW AND COMMENT**
>
> *Yates Building Co* v *R. J. Pulleyn & Sons (York)*, 1975 – Prescribed mode of acceptance: the matter of prejudice **(62)**

ORAL ACCEPTANCES

If the offeror has not stipulated a method of acceptance, the offeree may choose his own method, though where acceptance is by word of mouth it is not enough that it be spoken, it must actually be heard by the offeror. In this connection an interesting development occurs with the use of the telephone and teleprinter. Since these are methods of instantaneous communication, it is held that the contract is not complete unless the apparent communication takes place.

> **ESSENTIAL CASE LAW AND COMMENT**
>
> *Entores Ltd* v *Miles Far Eastern Corporation*, 1955 – Acceptance by telex and telephone **(63)**

USE OF POST AND TELEMESSAGES IN OFFER AND ACCEPTANCE

If the post is the proper method of communication between the parties then acceptance is deemed complete immediately the letter of acceptance is posted, even if it is delayed or is lost or destroyed in the post so that it never reaches the offeror. Nevertheless, the letter of acceptance must be properly addressed and properly posted and the court must be satisfied that it was within the contemplation of the parties that the post might be used as a method of communicating acceptance. Thus in *Henthorn v Fraser* [1892] 2 Ch. 27 the post was the proper method of accepting an offer, which the offeror had, in fact, handed to the offeree, because the parties lived in different towns.

The rule relating to acceptance by post is a somewhat arbitrary one seeming to favour the offeree and is in practice kept within narrow confines. For example if the statements of the parties appear to exclude the rule then the court will not apply it. Where there is a misdirection of a letter containing an offer, then the offer is made when it actually reaches the offeree, and not when it would have reached him in the ordinary course of the post.

In contrast with the rule regarding acceptance by post, a letter of revocation is not effective until it actually reaches the offeree, whereas a letter of acceptance is effective when it is posted. (*Byrne v Van Tienhoven*, 1880 at p. 603.) A telemessage is effective as an acceptance when it is given to the Telecom operator. (*Cowan v O'Connor* (1880) 20 Q.B.D. 640 decided this was so with the telegram, which was the predecessor of the telemessage.)

The better view is that, in English law, an acceptance cannot be recalled once it has been posted even though it has not reached the offeror. Thus, if X posted a letter accepting Y's offer to sell goods, X could not withdraw the acceptance by telephoning Y and asking him to ignore the letter of acceptance when it arrived, and Y could hold X bound by the contract if he wished to do so. This is obvious, the rules being what they are, since otherwise Y would be bound when the letter was posted, and X would be reserving the right to withdraw his acceptance during the transit of the letter even though Y was still bound.

There is some controversy as to whether agreement can result from *identical cross-offers*. For example, suppose X by letter offers to sell his bicycle to Y for £50, and Y, by means of a second letter, which crosses X's letter in the post, offers to buy X's bicycle for £50. Can there be a contract? The matter was discussed by an English court in *Tinn v Hoffman* (1873) 29 L.T. 271, and the court's conclusion was that no contract could arise, though this is regarded as too strict a view of the position. The matter is still undecided by the judges and it is possible to hold the view that today a contract would come into being where it appears that the parties have intended to create a legally binding agreement on the same footing.

ESSENTIAL CASE LAW AND COMMENT

Household Fire Insurance Co v *Grant*, 1879 – Effect of posting an
   acceptance **(64)**
Holwell Securities Ltd v *Hughes*, 1974 – The post rule of
   acceptance excluded **(65)**
Adams v *Lindsell*, 1818 – A misdirected offer **(66)**

Termination of offer

We shall now consider the ways in which an offer may be terminated.

REVOCATION – GENERALLY

The general rule is that *an offer may be revoked at any time before* it is
accepted. (*Payne* v *Cave* (1789) 3 Term Rep. 148.) Once an offer has been
accepted it cannot be withdrawn merely because the offeror made a mistake,
provided the offeree was not aware of that mistake. Thus in *Centrovincial
Estates* v *Merchant Investors Assurance, The Times,* 8 March 1983 it was
held by the Court of Appeal that a landlord who offered to grant a tenancy
at a stated rent of £65,000, which the tenant accepted, could not withdraw
the offer merely because he made a mistake in the offer and had intended
to ask for a rent of £126,000. If the offeree knows that the offeror is mistaken
the contract may be void for unilateral mistake. (See p. 242.)

Sometimes there is what is known as an option attached to the offer, and
time is given to the offeree in which to make the decision whether to accept
the offer or not. If the offeror agrees to give seven days, then the offeree may
accept the offer at any time within seven days, or he need not accept at all.
However, the offeror need not keep the offer open for seven days but can
revoke it unless the offeree has given some consideration for the option.

Revocation, to be effective, must be communicated to the offeree before
he has accepted the offer. The word 'communication' merely implies that
the revocation must have come to the knowledge of the offeree.

Presumably the offeree cannot ignore facts suggesting an attempt to
communicate a revocation. If A offers B a car and before B accepts A posts
a letter of revocation which B receives but, recognising A's handwriting, does
not open until he has written and posted a letter of acceptance, it would seem
unfair to regard A as bound in contract and he would probably not be. In
addition, it appears from statements made in the House of Lords in *Eaglehill
Ltd* v *J. Needham (Builders) Ltd* [1972] 3 All E.R. 895, where their Lordships
were discussing notice of dishonour of a bill of exchange, that an offer would
be revoked when the letter of revocation 'was opened in the ordinary course
of business or would have been so opened if the ordinary course of business
was followed'.

Communication may be made directly by the offeror or may reach the offeree through some other reliable source. Suppose X offers to sell a car to Y and gives Y a few days to think the matter over without actually giving him a valid option. If, before Y has accepted, X sells the car to Z and Y hears from P that X has in fact sold the car, it will be of no avail for Y to purport to accept and try to enforce the contract against X, provided P is a reliable source.

ESSENTIAL CASE LAW AND COMMENT

Routledge v *Grant*, 1828 – Revocation where there is an option **(67)**
Byrne v *Van Tienhoven*, 1880 – Communication of revocation **(68)**
Dickinson v *Dodds*, 1876 – Communication of revocation by third parties **(69)**

REVOCATION – UNILATERAL CONTRACTS

Where the offer consists of a promise in return for an act, as where a reward is offered for the return of lost property, the offer, although made to the whole world, can be revoked as any other offer can. It is thought to be enough that the same publicity be given to the revocation as was given to the offer, even thought the revocation may not be seen by all the persons who saw the offer.

A more difficult problem arises when an offer which requires a certain act to be carried out is revoked after some person has begun to perform the act but before he has completed it. If, for example, X offers £1000 to anyone who can successfully swim the Channel, and Y, deciding he will try to obtain the money, starts his swim from Dover, can X revoke his offer from a helicopter when Y is half-way across the Channel? One view is that he cannot on the grounds that an offer of the kind made by X is two offers in one, namely (i) to pay £1000 to a successful swimmer and (ii) something in the nature of an option to hold the offer open for a reasonable time once performance has been embarked upon, so that the person trying to complete the task has a reasonable time in which to do so.

Other lawyers reach the same conclusion by distinguishing between the acceptance of the offer and the consideration necessary to support it. As regards the latter, the completion of the act involved is necessary before the offeror can be required to pay any money because until the act is completed the necessary consideration has not been supplied. However, acceptance may be assumed as soon as the offeree has made a beginning on the performance of the contract and proof of the fact that he has made a beginning makes revocation impossible. The problem could have arisen in *Carlill*'s case (at p. 587) if the company had tried to revoke its offer after Mrs Carlill had started to perform the contract by using the Smoke ball.

The matter also came before the Court of Appeal in *Errington* v *Errington* [1952] 1 All E.R. 149. In that case a father bought a house for his son and daughter-in-law to live in. He paid the deposit but the son and daughter-in-law made the mortgage payments after the father gave the building society book to the daughter-in-law, saying, 'Don't part with this book. The house will be your property when the mortgage is paid.' The son left his wife who continued to live in the house. It was held by the Court of Appeal that neither the father nor the plaintiff, his widow, to whom the house was left by will, could eject the daughter-in-law from the property. As Lord Denning said: 'The father's promise was a unilateral contract – a promise of the house in return for their act of paying the instalments. It could not be revoked by him once the couple entered on the performance of the act . . . .' The Court went on to decide that the son and daughter-in-law would be fully entitled to the house once they had made all the mortgage repayments.

LAPSE OF TIME

If a time for acceptance has been stipulated, then the offer lapses when the time has expired. If no time has been stipulated, then the acceptance must be within a reasonable time. What is reasonable is a *matter of fact* for the judge to decide on the circumstances of the case.

> **ESSENTIAL CASE LAW AND COMMENT**
> *Ramsgate Victoria Hotel Co* v *Montefiore*, 1866 – Offer and lapse of time **(70)**

CONDITIONAL OFFERS

An offer may terminate on the happening of a given event if it is made subject to a condition that it will do so, e.g. that the offer is to terminate if the goods offered for sale are damaged before acceptance. Such a condition may be made expressly in the contract as where e.g. a seller offers to sell goods by tender from time to time subject to a condition that the seller can himself obtain adequate supplies. It may also be implied from the circumstances.

> **ESSENTIAL CASE LAW AND COMMENT**
> *Financings Ltd* v *Stimson*, 1962 – Conditional offers **(71)**

EFFECT OF DEATH OF A PARTY

The effect of death would appear to vary according to the type of contract in question, whether the death is that of the offeror or the offeree, and whether death takes place before or after acceptance.

Death of offeror before acceptance

It would seem that if the contract envisaged by the offer is not one involving the personality of the offeror, the death of the offeror may not, until notified to the offeree, prevent acceptance. However, there is a contrary point of view based on the judgment of Mellish, L.J. in *Dickinson* v *Dodds*, 1876 (at p. 603) where he said, 'it is admitted law that, if a man who makes an offer dies, the offer cannot be accepted after he is dead . . .'. If the contract envisaged by the offer does involve a personal relationship, such as an offer to act as agent, then the death of the offeror certainly prevents acceptance.

Death of offeree before acceptance

Once the offeree is dead, there is no offer which can be accepted. His executors cannot, therefore, accept the offer in his stead. The offer being made to a living person can only be accepted by that person and assumes his continued existence. The rule would seem to apply *whether the proposed contract involves a personality relationship or not.*

Death of parties after acceptance

Death after acceptance has normally no effect unless the contract is for personal services, when the liability under the contract ceases. Thus, if X sells his car to Y and before the car is delivered X dies, it would be possible for Y to sue X's personal representatives for breach of contract if they were to refuse to deliver the car. But if X agrees to play the piano at a concert and dies two days before the performance, one could hardly expect his personal representatives to play the piano in his stead.

ESSENTIAL CASE LAW AND COMMENT

Bradbury v *Morgan*, 1862 – Where the offeror dies before acceptance **(72)**
Re Cheshire Banking Co, 1886 – Where the offeree dies before acceptance **(73)**

OFFER AND ACCEPTANCE NOT IDENTIFIABLE

Sometimes the usual processes of offer and acceptance are not easily identifiable and yet a contract is deemed to exist. (See *The New Zealand Shipping Co. Ltd* v *A.M. Satterthwaite & Co. Ltd*, 1974 at p. 677.) There are also situations of collateral contract. These derive from another main contract, and for purposes of illustration reference should be made to the essential case law and comment as indicated below.

ESSENTIAL CASE LAW AND COMMENT

Rayfield v *Hands*, 1958 – The concept of the collateral contract **(74)**

10
Law of contract – making the contract II

In this chapter we continue the study of those elements of contract law which go to making a mere agreement into a contract which is at least potentially binding on the parties. Consideration and intention to create legal relations are looked at here.

Consideration

DEFINITION AND RELATED MATTERS

Consideration, which is essential to the formation of any contract not made under seal, was defined in *Currie* v *Misa* (1875) L.R. 10 Ex 153 as –

> Some right, interest, profit or benefit accruing to one party, or some forbearance, detriment, loss or responsibility given, suffered or undertaken by the other.

Paying (or promising to pay) money in return for the supply of goods or services constitutes the most common form of consideration.

Consideration may be *executory*, where the parties exchange promises to perform acts in the future, e.g. C promises to deliver goods to D and D promises to pay for the goods; or it may be *executed*, where one party promises to do something in return for the act of another, rather than for the mere promise of future performance of an act. Here the performance of the act is required before there is any liability on the promise. Where X offers a reward for the return of his lost dog, X is buying the act of the finder, and will not be liable until the dog is found and returned.

The definition in *Currie* v *Misa* suggests that consideration always refers to the type called executed consideration since it talkes of 'benefit' and 'detriment', whereas in modern law executory contracts are enforceable. Perhaps the definition given by Sir Frederick Pollock is to be preferred –

> An act of forbearance of one party, *or the promise thereof*, is the price for which *the promise* of the other is bought, and *the promise* thus given for value is enforceable.

This definition which was adopted by the House of Lords in *Dunlop* v *Selfridge*, 1915 (see p. 615), fits executory consideration as well as executed. The 'promise for a promise' concept really means that consideration can consist in a promise to act in the future, e.g. to deliver goods or to pay for goods.

Consideration in relation to formation of a contract – generally

There are a number of general rules governing consideration in terms of the *formation* of a contract –

(*a*) *Simple contracts must be supported by consideration.* This has a long history, but in practical terms it is the common law's way of limiting the number of agreements which can be brought before the courts for enforcement. Other legal systems have required e.g. part performance by one or other of the parties or some kind of formality. The effect of the consideration rule is that in English law an agreement, even if the parties intend legal relations, is not a contract unless it is supported by consideration or made by deed.

(*b*) *Consideration need not be adequate, but must have some value, however slight.* The courts do not exist to repair bad bargains, and though consideration must be present, the parties themselves must attend to its value. However, where the consideration for a transaction is of very small value, it may raise a suspicion of fraud, duress or undue influence on the part of the person gaining the advantage. However, what is offered by way of consideration must be capable of expression in terms of economic value or at least the giving up of some right. That apart, acts or omissions even of a trivial nature may be sufficient to support a contract.

ESSENTIAL CASE LAW AND COMMENT

Thomas v *Thomas*, 1842 – Adequacy of consideration **(75)**
Chappel & Co Ltd v *Nestlé Co Ltd*, 1959 – Adequacy: a
   commercial application **(76)**
White v *Bluett*, 1853 – Economic value required **(77)**

Although there were once arguments to the contrary, it is now accepted that forbearance to sue may be adequate consideration. It is not necessary to show that the action would have succeeded but merely that if it had been brought to trial it might have done. Thus the court would be unlikely to accept that a bookmaker could supply consideration by forgoing a claim against a client for stake money. Such an action, being based on an illegal transaction, could have no hope of success.

ESSENTIAL CASE LAW AND COMMENT

Horton v *Horton*, 1961 – Implied forbearance to sue **(78)**

A self-seeking act in itself may not suffice, and in the case of *Carlill* v *Carbolic Smoke Ball Co.*, 1893, see p. 587, the consideration was provided not by using the smoke ball to cure influenza, but by the unpleasant method of its use. A gift promised conditionally may be binding, if the performance of the condition causes the promisee trouble or inconvenience, e.g. 'I will give you my old car if you will tow it away.' So too may a gift of property with onerous obligations attached to it, e.g. a promise to give away a lease would be binding, if the donee promised to perform the covenants to repair and pay rent. A promise to give away shares which were partly paid up would be good, if the donee promised to pay the outstanding calls.

(*c*) *Bailment.* The concept of *bailment* gives rise to problems because a person may be held liable for negligent damage to or loss of goods in his care, although he received no money or other consideration for looking after them. However, confusion can best be avoided by regarding bailment as an independent transaction, which has characteristics of contract and tort but is neither. It seems that when X hands his goods to Y under a bailment Y has certain duties in regard to the care of the goods, whether the bailment is accompanied by a contract or not.

Of course the court may be invited to refuse a claim on the contract by a person who has given inadequate consideration by invoking the doctrine of inequality of bargaining power. (See further p. 260.) However, at the present time the basis of this doctrine, which has been applied in particular by Lord Denning, is somewhat vague and has not, as yet, received much direct judicial support.

ESSENTIAL CASE LAW AND COMMENT

Gilchrist Watt and Sanderson Pty v *York Products Pty*, 1970 – Bailment and consideration **(79)**

(*d*) *Consideration must be sufficient.* Sufficiency of consideration is not the same thing as adequacy of consideration. The concept of sufficiency arises in the course of deciding whether the acts in question *amount to consideration at all*. This situation arises where the consideration offered by the promisor is an act which he is already bound to carry out. Thus, the discharge of a *public duty* imposed by law is not consideration nor is the performance of a *contractual duty* already owed to the defendant. However, where the contractual duty is not precisely coincident with the public duty but is in excess of it, performance of the contractual duty may provide consideration and the actual performance of an outstanding contractual obligation may be sufficient to support a promise of a further payment by a third party.

ESSENTIAL CASE LAW AND COMMENT

Collins v *Godefroy*, 1831 – Sufficiency and public duties **(80)**
Stilk v *Myrick*, 1809 – Sufficiency and contractual duties **(81)**
Glasbrook Bros Ltd v *Glamorgan County Council*, 1925 –
  Sufficiency: public duty exceeded **(82)**
Shadwell v *Shadwell*, 1860 – Sufficiency: payments by third parties
  (83)

(*e*) *Consideration must be legal.* An illegal consideration makes the whole contract invalid. (See further p. 304.)

(*f*) *Consideration must not be past.* Sometimes the act which one party to a contract puts forward as consideration was performed before any promise of reward was made by the other. Where this is so, the act in question may be regarded as *past consideration* and will not support a contractual claim. This somewhat technical rule seems to be based on the idea that the act of one party to an alleged contract can only be regarded as consideration if it was carried out in response to some promise of the other. Where this is not so, the act is regarded as gratuitous, being carried out before any promise of reward was made.

However, there are exceptions to this rule –

(i) Where services are rendered at the express or implied request of the promisor in circumstances which raise an implication of a promise to pay. This exception is not entirely a genuine one since the promisor is assumed to have given an implied undertaking to pay at the time of the request, his subsequent promise being regarded as deciding merely *the actual amount to be paid*. In this situation the act, which follows the request but precedes the settling of the reward, is more in the nature of *executed consideration* which, as we have seen, will support a contract.

(ii) A debtor or his duly authorised agent can make a written acknowledgement of the debt to the creditor or his agent (s. 29, Limitation Act, 1980). Time begins to run again from the date of acknowledgement. However, once a debt is statute barred it cannot be revived in this way (s. 29(7) of the 1980 Act). (See further p. 340.) Again, this exception is not wholly genuine since the Limitation Act, 1980, does not provide that past consideration will support the subsequent acknowledgement of debt. The Act simply states that *no consideration of any kind* need be sought.

(iii) Section 27 of the Bills of Exchange Act, 1882, provides that an antecedent debt or liability will support a bill of exchange or cheque. This genuine exception was probably based on a pre-existing commercial custom. This is essential particularly in the case of cheques many of which are based on a form of past consideration. Thus if S sells goods to B a debt comes into being payable in legal tender (i.e.

bank notes or coins – see further p. 325) when the contract is made. So when B decides to pay S by cheque, which he may do provided S is agreeable, the cheque is based upon a previous or antecedent debt or liability and is for past consideration. Nevertheless this type of consideration will support the cheque should an action be brought on it.

ESSENTIAL CASE LAW AND COMMENT

Re McArdle, 1951 – Consideration must not be past **(84)**
Re Casey's Patents, Stewart v *Casey*, 1892 – The effect of a
    previous request **(85)**

(*g*) *Consideration must move from the promisee*, i.e. the person to whom the promise is made (the promisee) must give some consideration for it to the promisor. From this arises the doctrine of privity of contract which is considered below.

PRIVITY OF CONTRACT

This means that in general third parties cannot sue for the carrying out of promises made by the parties to a contract. Thus, if a contract between A and B requires B to benefit C, the privity rule prevents C from suing B. However, A may sue B if B breaks the contract, and the court may award A damages or may grant a decree of specific performance under which B must perform the contract for the benefit of C. If A and C are, in fact, both parties to the contract with B then C still cannot sue B unless he has provided some consideration. Merely being a party to the contract is not enough. Even though C may be named in the document, if any, which records and constitutes the contract between A and B, or may be a party to their oral deliberations, if he does not undertake anything in return for a promise from A or indeed from B, then he is not participating in a bargain with A and/or B and is not a party to the contract. This view is based upon the belief that the 'privity' rule is merely an aspect of the rule that 'consideration must move from the promisee'. The position is different if A, B and C are parties to a deed. C can then sue B for damages if B fails to carry out his promises in the deed. Deeds do not require consideration.

ESSENTIAL CASE LAW AND COMMENT

Tweddle v *Atkinson*, 1861 – Privity of contract illustrated **(86)**
Dunlop v *Selfridge*, 1915 – Privity: a further application **(87)**
Jackson v *Horizon Holidays*, 1975 – Remedies of the promisee:
    damages **(88)**
Beswick v *Beswick*, 1967 – Remedies of the promisee: specific
    performance **(89)**

MAIN EXCEPTIONS TO THE PRIVITY RULE

There are cases in which a person is allowed to sue upon a contract to which he is not a party as follows.

Agency

A principal, even if undisclosed, may sue on a contract made by an agent. This exception is perhaps more apparent than real, because in fact the principal is the contracting party who has merely acted through the instrumentality of the agent.

Cheques and other bills of exchange

The holder for value of a cheque or other bill of exchange can sue prior parties. Thus if A buys goods from B and pays by cheque which B then indorses over to C his son as a birthday present then C can sue A even though no consideration has moved from him to A. C cannot sue B because as between immediate parties absence of consideration makes a successful claim impossible. These rules are to be found in the Bills of Exchange Act, 1882 in s. 27.

Price restrictions

Under the Resale Prices Act, 1976, s. 26, the supplier of goods is given a statutory cause of action, so that he may enforce against a person not a party to the contract of sale a condition as to a minimum resale price. However, the resale price agreement must have been approved under the provisions of the Resale Prices Act, 1976, otherwise there can be no enforcement of it. (See p. 317.) Books are one of the few items approved for this purpose. (See *Net Book Agreement*, 1957 [1962] 3 All E.R. 751.) Under s. 26 a *maximum* resale price can be enforced against a third party without the approval of the court provided the third party receives the goods with notice of the restriction.

Insurance

Section 11 of the Married Women's Property Act, 1882, provides that if a man insures his life for the benefit of his wife and/or children, or a woman insures her life for the benefit of her husband and/or children, a trust is created in favour of the objects of the policy, who, although they are not parties to the contract with the insurance company, can sue upon it. In addition the policy moneys are not liable for the deceased's debts.

Bankers' commercial credits and performance bonds

As regards bankers' commercial credits, it is common commercial practice for an exporter, E, to ask the buyer of the goods, B, to open, with his banker, a credit in favour of E, the credit to remain irrevocable for a specified time. B agrees with his banker that the credit should be opened and, in return, promises to repay the banker, and usually gives him a lien over the shipping documents. The banker will also require a commission for his services. B's banker then notifies E that a credit has been opened in his favour, and E can draw upon it on presentation of the shipping documents.

It will be seen that E and B's banker are not in privity of contract. It might be thought that this could give rise to problems in the unlikely event that the banker did not pay. However, this is not so. In fact the buyer/customer of the bank cannot stop payment. In *Malas (Hamzeh)* v *British Imex* [1958] 1 All E.R. 262 the plaintiffs, who were buyers of goods, applied to the court for an injunction restraining the sellers (who were the defendants in the case) from drawing under a credit established by the buyer's bankers. The Court of Appeal refused to grant this injunction and Jenkins, L.J. said: 'The opening of a confirmed letter of credit constitutes a bargain between the banker and the vendor of the goods which imposes on the banker an absolute obligation to pay . . .'. Sellers, L.J. said that there could well be exceptions where the court could exercise a jurisdiction to grant an injunction, as where there was a fraudulent transaction. However, in other situations the binding nature of the banker's commercial credit is an exception to the doctrine of privity of contract.

There have been similar developments making performance bonds enforceable by commercial custom so that where a bank guarantees performance of an export contract by the supplier a claim may be made against the bank if the contract is not performed. The leading authority for this is *Edward Owen Engineering Ltd* v *Barclays Bank International Ltd*, *The Times*, 1 July 1977.

Assignment

If A owes B £10 B may assign the right to receive the money to C and provided that assignment is a legal assignment (as distinct from an equitable one) C may sue A without the assistance of B as a party to the claim. The matter of assignment is considered more fully at p. 525.

Land law

The position in land law is that benefits and liabilities attached to or imposed on land may in certain circumstances follow the land into the hands of other owners.

ESSENTIAL CASE LAW AND COMMENT

Smith and Snipes Hall Farm Ltd v *River Douglas Catchment Board*, 1949 – Exceptions to the privity rule: passing of benefits **(90)**
Tulk v *Moxhay*, 1848 – The passing of burdens **(91)**

Consideration viewed in relation to the discharge or variation of a contract

All that has so far been said in regard to consideration relates to the *formation* of a contract. As we have seen there must be consideration in order to bring a contract into existence, deeds apart. The rules are rather different where a contract is to be *discharged* or *varied*. There are a number of ways in which a contract may be discharged, all of which will be dealt with later. However, the one with which we are now concerned is *discharge by agreement* under which contract A is to be discharged or varied by a new contract, B, the question being to what extent does contract B require consideration? The attitude of the common law is different from that of equity, as we shall see.

Common law – the rule of accord and satisfaction

At common law if A owes B £10 and wishes to discharge that obligation by paying B £9 he must –

(*a*) obtain the agreement (accord) of B; and

(*b*) provide B with some consideraton (satisfaction) for giving up his right to £10 unless the release is by deed.

This is the common-law rule of accord and satisfaction. The rule is an ancient one and an early example of it is to be found in the judgment of Brian, C.J. in *Pinnel's* case (1602) 5 Co. Rep., 117a. Pinnel sued Cole in debt for what would now be £8.50 which was due on a bond on 11 November 1600. Cole's defence was that at Pinnel's request he had paid him £5.12 on 1 October and that Pinnel had accepted this payment in full satisfaction of the original debt. Although the court found for Pinnel on a technical point of pleading, it was said that –

(*a*) payment of a lesser sum on the due day in satisfaction of a greater sum cannot be any satisfaction for the whole; but

(*b*) payment of a smaller sum at the creditor's request before the due day is good consideration for a promise to forgo the balance for it is a benefit to the creditor to be paid before he was entitled to payment and a corresponding detriment to the debtor to pay early.

The first branch of the rule in *Pinnel's* case was much criticised but was eventually approved by the House of Lords and the doctrine then hardened because of the system of binding precedent.

Exceptions to the rule

The practical effect of the rule is considerably reduced under common law by the following exceptions which have been made to it –

(*a*) Where there is a dispute as to the sum owed. If the creditor accepts less than he thinks is owed to him the debt will be discharged. For example, A says that B owes him £11. B says it is only £9. A agrees to take £10. Then, even if it can be proved that A was owed £11, he cannot recover the £1. He has compromised his claim.

(*b*) Where the creditor agrees to take something different in kind, e.g. a chattel, the debt is discharged by substituted performance. Thus, if A gives B a watch worth £5 and B is agreeable to taking it, then the debt of £10 will be discharged. The legal theory here seems to be that the article given may be worth more than the balance of the debt and the court is not prepared to be a valuer. In this connection it should be noted that a cheque for a smaller sum no longer constitutes substituted performance.

(*c*) The payment of a smaller sum before the larger is due gives the debtor a good discharge. This is the second branch of the rule in *Pinnel's* case.

(*d*) If a debtor makes an arrangement with his creditors to compound his debts, e.g. by paying them 85p in the £1, he is satisfying a debt for a larger sum by the payment of a smaller sum. Nevertheless, it is a good discharge, the consideration being the agreement by the creditors with each other and with the debtor not to insist on their full rights.

(*e*) Payment of a smaller sum by a third party operates as a good discharge.

ESSENTIAL CASE LAW AND COMMENT

Foakes v *Beer*, 1884 – Pinnel's case: House of Lords approves **(92)**
D. & C. Builders v *Rees*, 1965 – Cheque not substituted
   performance: extinguishing rights **(93)**
Good v *Cheesman*, 1831 – Compositions with creditors **(94)**
Welby v *Drake*, 1825 – Payments by third parties **(95)**

Equity – the rule of promissory estoppel

There has always been some dissatisfaction with the common-law rule of accord and satisfaction. After all, if A owes B £10 and B agrees to take £9, as he must before there can be any question of discharging the obligation of A to pay £10, why should B be allowed afterwards to break his promise to take £9 and succeed in an action against A simply because A gave him no consideration?

It was to deal with this sort of situation that the equitable doctrine of promissory estoppel was propounded, first by Lord Cairns in *Hughes* v *Metropolitan Railway* (1877) 2 App. Cas. 439 and later by Denning, J. (as

he then was) in the *High Trees* case, 1947 (see below) and later by the House
of Lords in *Tool Metal Manufacturing Co. Ltd* v *Tungsten Electric Co. Ltd*,
1955 (see below).

The doctrine of estoppel is basically a rule of evidence under which the
court, surprisingly enough, is not prepared to listen to the truth.

It occurs at common law out of physical conduct. Suppose A and B go
into a wholesaler's premises and A asks for goods on credit. The wholesaler,
who knows that B is creditworthy, but has no knowledge of A, is not prepared
to give credit until A says, 'do not worry, you will be paid, B is my partner'.
If B says nothing and A receives the goods on credit and does not pay, then
B could be sued for the price, even though he can produce evidence that he
was not in fact A's partner. This evidence will not be admitted because the
wholesaler relied on a situation of partnership created by B's conduct and
the statement is concerned with *existing fact* which is essential at common
law (see *Jorden* v *Money* (1854) 5 H.L. Cas. 185) or a statement about *future
conduct* is not enough at common law.

INGREDIENTS OF PROMISSORY ESTOPPEL

The doctrine of promissory estoppel has the following ingredients –

(*a*) It arises from a promise made with the intention that it should be acted
upon.

(*b*) It was once thought that the person who had received the promise must
do something to show that he had relied on it. If A, a landlord, said B could
pay only half his usual rent while he was unemployed, it was thought that
B would have to show, for example, that he had spent what should have
been the rent money on travelling expenses to find work in the district.
Reliance upon the promise in this way is not, it would appear, a necessary
requirement. All that would seem to be necessary is that the debtor has made
the part-payment; he need not do anything else.

(*c*) It relates only to variation of a contract by agreement and does not
affect the requirement of consideration on formation of contract.

(*d*) So far as the rule has been developed in cases, it merely *suspends* rights
but does not totally discharge them because it does not preclude enforcement
of the original contract after reasonable notice has been given. Thus it does
not create a binding variation for the future. (See *Tool Metal Manufacturing
Co. Ltd* v *Tungsten Electric Co. Ltd* at p. 622.)

(*e*) The promise must be freely given and not extorted by threats. (See
D. & C. Builders v *Rees*, 1965 at p. 619.)

(*f*) Of considerable importance is a *dictum* by Lord Denning in *D. & C.
Builders* v *Rees*, 1965 (see p. 619) that the rule could be developed to the
point at which it operated, not merely to suspend rights, but to preclude
enforcement of them. If this point is reached, then if A owes £10 and B agrees
to take £9, A will be discharged from his obligation to pay £10 without the
need for consideration.

Discharge of contract by performance – relevance of the *High Trees* case

The rule of equitable estoppel has relevance in discharge of a contract by performance. (See p. 325.) Although the agreed date of delivery must usually be complied with in a contract of sale, the buyer may waive the condition relating to the date of delivery and accept a later date. Such a waiver may be binding on him whether made with or without consideration. It was held by Lord Denning in *Charles Rickards Ltd* v *Oppenhaim*, 1950 (see p. 701) that the binding nature of a waiver without consideration might be based on the *High Trees* case (i.e. a promissory estoppel to accept a later delivery date). Alternatively, the seller may rely on s. 11(2) of the Sale of Goods Act, 1979, which states: 'Where a contract of sale is subject to any condition to be fulfilled by the seller, the buyer may waive that condition.'

Equitable estoppel – other applications

The principle of Equity on which promissory estoppel is based is one of general application and may be applied whenever the court feels it is necessary in the interests of justice to do so.

Intention to create legal relations

The law will not necessarily recognise the existence of a contract enforceable in a court of law simply because of the presence of mutual promises. It is necessary to establish also that both parties made the agreement with the intention of creating legal relations so that if the agreement was broken the party offended would be able to exercise legally enforceable remedies. The subject can be considered under two headings as follows.

CASES WHERE THE PARTIES HAVE NOT EXPRESSLY DENIED THEIR INTENTION TO CREATE LEGAL RELATIONS

Advertisements

Most advertisements are statements of opinion and as such are not actionable. Thus unless the advertisement makes false statements of specific verifiable facts, which is rare, the court will not enforce the claims made for the product on a contractual basis. However, where a company deposits money in the bank against possible claims then the court is likely to hold that legal relations were contemplated (*Carlill* v *Carbolic Smoke Ball Co* (1893)), though a deposit is not essential (*Wood* v *Lectric Ltd* (1932) – see p. 588).

Family agreements

Many of these cannot be imagined to be the subject of litigation but some may be. The question is basically one of construction and the court looks at the words and the surrounding circumstances. The two basic divisions of family agreements are set out below.

(*a*) *Husband and wife.* With regard to agreements between husband and wife, it is difficult to draw precise conclusions. However, the following situations have appeared in decided cases.

   (i)   Where husband and wife were living together in amity when the agreement was made, then the agreement is not enforceable as a contract because legal proceedings are an inappropriate method of settling purely domestic disputes.

  (ii)   Where husband and wife were living together but not in amity or were separated altogether when the agreement was made, the court may enforce it.

 (iii)   If the words used by the parties are uncertain, then the agreement will not be enforced, the uncertainty leading to the conclusion that there was no intention to create legal relations. Thus in *Gould* v *Gould* [1969] 3 All E.R. 728 a contractual intention was negatived where a husband on leaving his wife undertook to pay her £15 per week 'so long as I can manage it'. The uncertainty of this term ruled out a legally binding agreement.

Agreements of a non-domestic nature made between husband and wife are enforceable, e.g. in *Pearce* v *Merriman* [1904] 1 K.B. 80 it was held that a husband may be his wife's tenant and as such could be made to pay the rent.

(*b*) *Other family and personal relationships.* The question of intention to create legal relations arises for consideration here as well but it seems that the less close the relationship between the parties the more likely it is that the court *will presume* that legal relations were intended. However, in these cases also *uncertainty* as to the terms of the agreement normally leads to the conclusion that there was no contractual intention.

Other cases

There may well be other areas where intention to create legal relations is doubtful but which have not been the subject of cases in court. Again, the matter is one of fact for the court. However, in the case of clubs and societies many of the relationships which exist and promises which are made are enforceable only as moral obligations. They are merely *social agreements*. For example, the decision in *Lens v Devonshire Club*, *The Times*, 4 December 1914, would suggest that if a person competes for a prize at a local golf club and is the winner, he or she may not be able to sue for the prize which has been won if it is not otherwise forthcoming.

However, in *Peck v Lateu*, *The Times*, 18 January 1973, two ladies attended bingo sessions together and had an arrangement to pool their winnings. One of them won an additional 'Bonanza' prize of £1107 and claimed it was not covered by the sharing arrangements. Pennycuick, V.C. held that there was an intention to create legal relations and to share all prizes won. The plaintiff was entitled to a share in the prize.

It should also be borne in mind that quotations and estimates may be passed from one person to another without any intention that they should be legally binding *at that stage*.

ESSENTIAL CASE LAW AND COMMENT

Balfour v *Balfour*, 1919 – Husband and wife living in amity **(101)**
Merritt v *Merritt*, 1970 – Effect of separation **(102)**
Simpkins v *Pays*, 1955 – Intention in family relationships **(103)**
Jones v *Padavatton*, 1969 – Family relationships and uncertainty
  (104)

CASES WHERE THE PARTIES EXPRESSLY DENY ANY INTENTION TO CREATE LEGAL RELATIONS

By contrast with family arrangements, agreements of a commercial nature are *presumed* to be made with contractual intent. Furthermore, the test applied by the court is an *objective* one so that a person cannot escape liability simply because *he did not* have a contractual intention. The presumption is a strong one and it was held in *Edwards v Skyways Ltd* [1964] 1 All E.R. 494 that the use of the words *ex gratia* in regard to an airline pilot's contractual redundancy payment did not displace the presumption, so that the airline had to make the payments and did not have a discretion whether to make them or not.

However, the Court of Appeal has held more recently that a court need not necessarily presume intention to create legal relations just because the parties are in business.

ESSENTIAL CASE LAW AND COMMENT

Kleinwort Benson Ltd v *Malaysian Mining Corporation, Berhand,* 1989 – Business contracts: intention not always assumed **(105)**

Some agreements where the court would normally assume an intention to create legal relations may be expressly taken outside the scope of the law by the parties agreeing to rely on each other's honour. This is a practice which appears to be allowable to pools companies who are especially subject to fraudulent entries but should not be allowed to spread into other areas of *standardised* contracts, i.e. contracts where the consumer has no choice of supplier as where he requires electrical services laid on which can only be provided by a monopoly corporation.

There is no such objection where business men reach agreements at arm's length, and if the parties expressly declare, or clearly indicate, that they do not wish to assume contractual obligations, then the law accepts and implements their decision.

ESSENTIAL CASE LAW AND COMMENT

Jones v *Vernon's Pools Ltd,* 1938 – Business agreements: contractual intent may be excluded **(106)**
Rose and Frank Co v *Crompton (J.R.) & Bros. Ltd,* 1925 – An honourable pledge clause **(107)**

STATUTORY PROVISIONS

Sometimes an Act of Parliament renders an agreement unenforceable. Thus under s. 1 of the Law Reform (Miscellaneous Provisions) Act, 1970, a contract of engagement, which is, in effect, an agreement to marry, is not enforceable at law since there is a statutory presumption that there was no intention to create legal relations. Thus actions for breach of promise are no longer possible.

In addition, under s. 29 of the Post Office Act, 1969, the acceptance of ordinary letters and packets for transmission does not give rise to a contract between the post office and the sender.

Finally, under s. 18 of the Trade Union and Labour Relations Act, 1974, collective agreements between trade unions and employers (or employers' associations) concerning industrial conditions such as hours, wages, holidays, procedures in disputes and so on, are presumed *not* to be intended to be legally enforceable unless they are in writing and contain a provision to that effect.

11
Law of contract – making the contract III

In this chapter we shall conclude the study of those elements of contract law which go to making a *mere agreement* into *a binding contract*. *Formalities* (*or the need for writing*) and the requirement that the parties must have *capacity in law* to make the contract are considered here.

Formalities

In most cases a contract made orally (or by parol, which is an alternative expression) is usually just as effective as a written one. Exceptionally, however, written formalities are required as follows.

CONTRACTS WHICH MUST BE MADE BY DEED

A lease of more than three years should be made by deed otherwise no legal estate is created (see s. 52 and s. 54, Law of Property Act, 1925). If there is no deed then there is in equity a contract for a lease. This is an estate contract under s. 2(3), Law of Property Act, 1925. It is enforceable against third parties who acquire the freehold from the landlord only if it has been registered at the Land Registry. Registration gives notice to the whole world. Failure to register makes the contract void against a later purchaser of the freehold from the landlord for a consideration, even though in fact the purchaser *knows* the lease exists (s. 199(1), Law of Property Act, 1925). The purchaser could turn out the tenant if the lease was not registered. However, where it is registered the tenant is protected.

As regards the form of a deed the Law of Property (Miscellaneous Provisions) Act, 1989 is now relevant and is considered at p. 202.

CONTRACTS WHICH MUST BE IN WRITING

For example, the following simple contracts are required by statute to be in writing otherwise they are affected in various ways:

(*a*) Regulated consumer credit agreements, including hire-purchase agreements, under which the amount of credit does not exceed £15,000 and the customer is not a company (Consumer Credit Act, 1974, s. 61). If these agreements are not in appropriate written form they cannot be enforced by the dealer, unless the court thinks it is fair in the circumstances to allow him to enforce the contract.

(*b*) Contracts of marine insurance, which must be embodied in a written policy otherwise the contract is not effective, being inadmissible in evidence unless embodied in a written policy signed on behalf of the insurer (Marine Insurance Act, 1906, s. 22).

(*c*) Contracts for the sale or other disposition of land are required by statute to be in writing otherwise they are invalid, i.e. there is no contract. Section 2(1) of the Law of Property (Miscellaneous Provisions) Act, 1989 provides that a contract for the sale or other disposition of an interest in land can only be made in writing and only by incorporating all the terms which the parties have expressly agreed in one document or, where contracts are exchanged, in each contract. The document must be signed by each party.

There are some exeptions to the above requirements as follows:

(i) leases for three years or less where the tenant takes possession can be granted orally;

(ii) sales at public auctions are excluded and the contract is regarded as made when the auctioneer's hammer falls. There is thus no requirement of writing at all at auction sales.

Since the document must now contain all the terms agreed by the parties and be signed by both parties solicitors and conveyancers are no longer at risk that pre-contract correspondence signed by only one party might amount to a contract itself as was a possibility before. The practice of heading correspondence 'subject to contract' can now be brought to an end.

CONTRACTS WHICH MUST BE EVIDENCED IN WRITING

Here we are concerned with contracts of guarantee where the Statute of Frauds, 1677 requires writing which, though not essential to the formation of the contract, is needed as evidence if a dispute about it comes before a court. The court will not enforce the guarantee in the absence of written evidence.

The provision in the Statue of Frauds applies to guarantees and not to indemnities. It is therefore necessary to distinguish between these two. In a contract of indemnity the person giving the indemnity makes himself primarily liable by using such words as 'I will see that you are paid'.

In a contract of guarantee the guarantor expects the person he has guaranteed to carry out his obligations and the substance of the wording would be: 'If he does not pay you, I will'. An indemnity does not require writing because it does not come within the Statute of Frauds: a guarantee requires a memorandum.

An additional distinction is that it is an essential feature of a guarantee that the person giving it is totally unconnected with the contract except by reason of his promise to pay the debt. Thus a *del credere* agent who, for an extra commission, promises to make good losses incurred by his principal in respect of the unpaid debts of third parties introduced by the agent, may use the guarantee form 'if they do not pay you I will' but no writing is required. Such a promise is enforceable even if made orally because even where a person does promise to be liable for the debt of another that promise is not within the Statute of Frauds where it is, as here, an incident of a wider transaction, i.e. agency.

ESSENTIAL CASE LAW AND COMMENT

Mountstephen v *Lakeman*, 1871 – guarantee and indemnity distinguished **(108)**

The memorandum in writing to satisfy the court need not exist when the contract is made but must be in existence when an action, if any, is brought for breach of the guarantee. A guarantee cannot be proved orally – writing is required as evidence. The memorandum must identify the parties, normally by containing their names. The material terms must be included, e.g. that it is a guarantee of a bank overdraft facility limited to £50,000. The memorandum must also contain the signature of the party to be charged or his agent properly authorised to sign. However, the law is not strict on this point and initials or a printed signature will do. The 'party to be charged' is the proposed defendant and there may be cases where one party has a sufficient memorandum to commence an action whereas the other may not since the memorandum does not contain the other party's signature. This could happen where the memorandum was in a letter written by Bloggs to Snooks. The letter would presumably be signed by Bloggs but not by Snooks. It would therefore be a good memorandum for an action by Snooks but not by Bloggs. Section 3 of the Mercantile Law Amendment Act, 1856 dispenses with the need to set out the consideration in the memorandum but it must exist. It is normally the extension of credit by A to B in consideration of C's guarantee of B's liability if B fails to pay.

Capacity to contract

Adult citizens have full capacity to enter into any kind of contract but certain groups of persons and corporations have certain disabilities in this connection. The most important groups for our purposes are dealt with below.

Minors

The Family Law Reform Act, 1969, s. 1, reduced the age of majority from 21 to 18 years. Contracts made by minors were governed by the common law (including parts of sale of goods legislation) as amended by the Infants Relief Act, 1874 and the Betting and Loans (Infants) Act, 1892. The Minors' Contracts Act, 1987 repealed the relevant parts of the 1874 and 1892 Acts so that minors' contracts are now governed by the rules of common law (including the Sale of Goods Act, 1979) as amended by the Minors' Contracts Act, 1987.

VALID CONTRACTS

These are as follows:

(*a*) *Executed contracts for necessaries.* These are defined in s. 3(3) of the Sale of Goods Act, 1979 as 'Goods suitable to the condition in life of the minor and to his actual requirements at the time of sale and delivery.' If the goods are deemed necessaries the minor may be compelled to pay a reasonable price which will usually, but not necessarily, be the contract price. The minor is not liable if the goods, though necessaries, have not been delivered. This, together with the fact that he is only required to pay a reasonable price, illustrates that a minor's liability for necessaries is only quasi-contractual.

(*b*) *Contracts for the minor's benefit.* These include contracts of service, apprenticeship and education.

However, trading contracts of minors are not enforceable no matter how beneficial they may be to the minor's trade or business. The theory behind this rule is that when a minor is in trade his capital is at risk and he might lose it, whereas in a contract of service there is no likelihood of capital loss.

ESSENTIAL CASE LAW AND COMMENT

Nash v *Inman*, 1908 – What are necessaries? **(109)**
Roberts v *Gray*, 1913 – Contracts which are beneficial **(110)**
Mercantile Union Guarantee Corporation v *Ball*, 1937 – Trading contracts not 'beneficial' **(111)**

CONTRACTS NOT BINDING UNLESS RATIFIED

These are as follows:

(*a*) *Loans.* These are not binding on the minor unless he ratifies the contract of loan after reaching 18 which he may now legally do. No fresh consideration is now required on ratification.

(*b*) *Contracts for non-necessary goods.* Again, these are not binding on the minor unless he ratifies the contract after reaching 18 as he may now legally do. Once again, no fresh consideration is required on ratification.

It should be noted that in spite of the fact that the contracts in (*a*) and (*b*) above are not enforceable against the minor, he gets a title to any property which passes to him under the arrangement and can give a good title to a third party as where, for example, he sells non-necessary goods on to someone else (who takes in good faith and for value). This was decided in *Stocks* v *Wilson* [1913] 2 K.B. 235. Furthermore, any money or property transferred by the minor under the contract can only be recovered by him if there has been a total failure of consideration (see below).

CONTRACTS BINDING UNLESS REPUDIATED

These are usually contracts by which the minor acquires an interest of a permanant nature in the subject-matter of the contract. Such contracts bind the minor unless he takes active steps to avoid them, either during his minority or within a reasonable time thereafter. Examples of voidable contracts are shares in companies, leases of property and partnerships.

ESSENTIAL CASE LAW AND COMMENT

Steinberg v *Scala (Leeds) Ltd*, 1923 – Minors: voidable contracts
(112)

Consequences of the defective contracts of minors

We must now have a look at what happens where there has been some performance of a contract with a minor which is either not binding unless ratified or binding unless repudiated.

RECOVERY BY MINOR OF MONEY PAID

Where a minor has paid money under these defective contracts he cannot recover it unless total failure of consideration can be proved, i.e. that the minor has not received any benefit at all under the contract. The court is reluctant to say that no benefit has been received. This can be seen in the context of a contract not binding unless ratified in *Pearce* v *Brain* (see below) and in the context of a contract binding unless repudiated in *Steinberg* v *Scala* (see above).

> **ESSENTIAL CASE LAW AND COMMENT**
>
> *Pearce* v *Brain*, 1929 – Recovery of money paid or property transferred **(113)**

EFFECT OF PURCHASE BY MINOR OF NON-NECESSARY GOODS

As we have seen, the minor acquires a title to the goods and can give a good title to a third party who takes them bona fide and for value (*Stocks* v *Wilson* [1913] 2 K.B. 235). The tradesman who sold the goods to the minor cannot recover them from the third party.

However, as regards recovery from the minor, if he still has the property, s. 3 of the Minors' Contracts Act, 1987 provides that the court can order restitution, for example, of non-necessary goods to the tradesman, where the minor is refusing to pay for them. As we know, he cannot be sued for the price.

The question of recovery in any particular case is left to the court which must regard it as just and equitable to allow recovery, though a restitution order can be made whether the minor is fraudulent, as where he obtained the goods by overstating his age, *or not*. Fraud is no longer a requirement for restitution. Money will be virtually impossible to recover because it will normally be mixed with other funds and not identifiable. However, the minor could be made under s. 3 to offer up any goods acquired in exchange for the non-necessary goods. The tradesman recovers the goods in the state he finds them and cannot ask for compensation from the minor if they are, for example, damaged.

Thus if Ann, a minor, buys a gold necklace and does not pay for it the seller can recover the necklace from Ann. If Ann exchanges the necklace for a gold bangle the seller can recover the gold bangle from Ann. If Ann sells the necklace for £500 it is not clear whether the seller can get restitution of the money unless it has been kept separate from Ann's other funds or can be identified in a fund containing other money of Ann's, for example, a bank account into which she has paid her salary. Section 3 says that the seller can recover the article passing under the contract 'or any property representing it'. It is at least arguable that Ann's general funds do not solely represent the necklace in the way that the bangle does. Judicial interpretation is required.

GUARANTEES

Section 2 of the Minors' Contracts Act, 1987 provides that a guarantee by an adult of a minor's transaction shall be enforceable against the guarantor even though the main contractual obligation is not enforceable against the minor. Thus if a bank makes a loan to a minor or allows a minor an overdraft and an adult gives a guarantee of that transaction, then although the loan or overdraft cannot be enforced against the minor, the adult guarantor can be required to pay.

Mental disorder and drunkenness

Where the property and affairs of a mental patient are placed under the management of the court by order under Part VII of the Mental Health Act, 1983, the mental patient has no capacity to contract as regards that property. However, the other party is bound should the patient's representatives wish to regard him as bound.

Apart from the above, the position is governed by the common law as follows:

(*a*) A contract made by a person who by reason of mental disease or drunkenness is incapable of understanding what he is doing is valid unless he can prove:
   (i)   that he did not understand the nature of the contract; and
   (ii) that the other party knew this to be the case.
(*b*) A contract made by such a person is binding on him if he afterwards ratifies it at any time when the state of his mind is such that he can understand what he is doing.
(*c*) Where necessaries are sold and delivered to a person who by reason of mental incapacity or drunkenness is incompetent to contract, he is bound to pay a reasonable price (Sale of Goods Act, 1979, s. 3(2)).
(*d*) Necessaries are 'goods suitable to the condition in life of such person and to his actual requirements at the time of the sale and delivery' (s. 3(3), 1979 Act). Therefore the principle of 'necessaries' is applied to persons with mental incapacity and drunkards in the same way as it is to minors.

ESSENTIAL CASE LAW AND COMMENT

Imperial Loan Co v *Stone*, 1892 – Contract and mental disorder **(114)**
Matthews v *Baxter*, 1873 – Contracts with drunkards **(115)**

Corporations

We have seen that regardless of the method by which it is formed, a company on incorporation becomes a *legal person*, acquires an identity quite separate and distinct from its members, and carries on its activities through agents (see p. 187). In carrying out those activities and making contracts companies and their agents are to some extent restrained by the *ultra vires* rule. *Ultra vires* acts are those which are *beyond the powers of* the company. Our concern here is to look at that rule as it affects registered companies.

ULTRA VIRES RULE – STATUTORY AND REGISTERED COMPANIES

The powers of statutory corporations are contained in the statute setting them up and these powers are sometimes increased by subsequent statutes or by delegated legislation. Acts beyond these powers are *ultra vires* and *void*, i.e. of no effect.

The powers of registered companies are determined by the objects clause of the memorandum of association and an act in excess of the powers given in this clause is *at common law ultra vires* and *void*, i.e. of no effect.

ESSENTIAL CASE LAW AND COMMENT

Ashbury Railway Carriage & Iron Co v *Riche*, 1875 – The *ultra vires* rule before the intervention of Parliament **(116)**

By way of explanation of the decision in the *Ashbury* case it should be said that the *ultra vires* rule was brought in by the courts in earlier times to protect shareholders. It was thought that if a shareholder X bought shares in a company which had as its main object publishing and allied activities then X would not want the directors of that company to start up a different kind of business because he wanted his money in publishing.

In more recent times it has been noted that shareholders are not so fussy about the kind of business the directors take the company into so long as it makes money to pay dividends and raises the price of the company's shares on the stock market thus giving a capital gain. In these days of the conglomerates it is doubtful whether any investor invests in a company because of only one facet of its trading.

The people most affected by the *ultra vires* rule in more recent times were those who had supplied goods or services to a company for a purpose not covered by its objects clause. If the company was solvent no doubt such creditors would be paid but if it went into insolvent liquidation they would not even be able to put in a claim. Other creditors might get some part of their debts paid, say 20p in the £1 if the company had any funds, but the *ultra vires* suppliers would get nothing. For this reason it became usual to put in the objects clause of the memorandum a large number of objects and powers, and to include a special clause stating that each clause of the objects clause contained a separate and independent object which could be carried on separately from any of the others. The House of Lords decided in *Cotman* v *Brougham* [1918] A.C. 514 that this type of clause was legal, and this greatly relieved the problem of *ultra vires* by giving the directors legitimate access to many kinds of business listed in the objects clause.

Also the decision of the Court of Appeal in *Bell Houses* v *City Wall Properties Ltd* [1966] 2 All E.R. 674 states that the objects clause can be drafted in such a way as to allow the company to carry on any additional business which the members or directors choose.

In this way the limitations which are placed by the common law on a company's business activities by the *ultra vires* rule have been much reduced, though of course the control over the activities of the directors by the members has also been lessened. In fact with a large number of clauses in the objects clause as one finds in the typical memorandum, and with sub-clauses such as those approved in *Cotman* and *Bell Houses*, the modern company's contractual capacity approaches that of a natural person. The *ultra vires* rule as a method of controlling the activities of the boards of companies has been largely abandoned as the twentieth century has progressed. In addition there has been massive statutory intervention by Parliament to make the *ultra vires* rule ineffective (see below).

COMPANIES ACT, 1985

Section 35, as inserted by the Companies Act, 1989, now represents the United Kingdom's response to Article 9 of the First Directive (No. 68/151) issued by the European Community for the harmonisation of company law in the member states of the EC. It is intended largely to eliminate the effect of the *ultra vires* rule on the claims of creditors, though it has perhaps less impact today since fewer transactions are likely to be *ultra vires* at common law.

However, on the assumption that the narrow scope of a particular company's objects clause may lead to a transaction being *ultra vires* at common law a review of the provisions is worthwhile.

The company's capacity

Section 35(1) of the Companies Act, 1985 states: 'The validity of an act done by a company shall not be called into question on the ground of lack of capacity by reason of anything in the company's memorandum.' The immediate effect of this would be to put right the sort of problem which was raised in *Ashbury*. Something in its memorandum, i.e. its objects clause, confined it to making things for railways but not a whole railway system. Mr Riche's action would now have been successful and he would have got a remedy from the court, i.e. damages for breach of contract. In addition the drafting techniques approved in *Cotman* and *Bell Houses* will continue to be useful in converting long objects clauses into a series of independent objects and allowing the members or directors to choose new businesses for the company. These clauses will undoubtedly continue in use for many years to come.

Exceptions to s. 35(1)

(*a*) A shareholder may ask for an injunction to prevent the directors entering into an *ultra vires* contract, but if the contract has been made the court cannot grant an injunction to stop it proceeding. In addition no injunction can be granted if the members have ratified the contract by special resolution.

(*b*) Directors are as before placed under a specific duty to observe the limitations on their powers in the memorandum and the articles and can be sued by the company for any loss caused by a transaction which is outside the company's constitution (s. 35A(5)). However, the *ultra vires* act can be ratified by a special resolution of the members, and if it is desired to exempt the directors from liability for damage then another special resolution is required. It was not possible for the members to ratify in this way before the present legislation (see the *Ashbury* decision).

(*c*) Where the transaction is with a director of the company or its holding company or a person connected with him, e.g. a spouse, then it is voidable (i.e. the company can have it set aside). However, the members may ratify it by special resolution where the problem is that the transaction is beyond the company's capacity.

Power of the directors to bind the company

Section 35A(1) of the Companies Act, 1985 states: 'In favour of a person dealing with a company in good faith, the power of the board of directors to bind the company, or authorise others to do so shall be deemed to be free of any limitation under the company's constitution.'

Actual knowledge of the contents of the memorandum or articles is not in itself bad faith. Those who have read these documents but have misinterpreted them will be all right. If we look at the *Ashbury* situation it would have been possible for business men to misinterpret the objects clause which actually allowed the company to enter into 'general contracting' but the court took a restrictive view and said that this covered only general contracting in the field of making things for railways. Those who have actual knowledge of the company's or directors' lack of authority and act in bad faith will not be all right as in *International Sales and Agencies Ltd* v *Marcus* [1982] 3 All E.R. 551 where a sole effective director used the company's power to draw cheques to issue cheques to pay the private loan of a director who had died insolvent. He was aided and abetted by the lender who knew all about the circumstances and who along with the sole effective director was acting contrary to the company's interests. The cheques were held to be invalid and could not be enforced against the company.

Exceptions to s. 35A(1)

(*a*) If the act of the directors is illegal. Thus it would not authorise the issue of shares at a discount because this is forbidden by the Companies Act, 1985.

(*b*) It would not help in a situation in which the directors had used their powers for an improper purpose provided this is known to the other party. Thus in *Rolled Steel Products (Holdings) Ltd* v *British Steel Corporation* [1985] 3 All E.R. 401 a managing director and major shareholder of a company called Scottish Sheet Steel gave a guarantee of that company's debts to British Steel. British Steel wanted additional security and the managing director gave one on behalf of Rolled Steel which was another company of which he was managing director and major shareholder. The companies were not connected in any way and British Steel knew that the managing director was not acting for the benefit of Rolled Steel and that therefore he was using his legitimate power to give guarantees on behalf of Rolled Steel for an improper purpose. The guarantee by Rolled Steel was not enforceable against it. If British Steel had not been aware of the improper purpose, it would have been.

(*c*) The company cannot sue on the transaction but only the third party. The section says: 'In favour of a person dealing with a company . . .'. However, the members can ratify the transaction by special resolution if the company's lack of capacity is the problem or by an ordinary resolution if only the directors' powers are in issue.

(*d*) As before if the party dealing with the company is a director of the company or its holding company or connected person, e.g. a spouse, the director concerned cannot rely on s. 35A. The transaction is voidable by the company, but as already mentioned the company can ratify it by special or ordinary resolution as the case may be.

The single line clause

Section 3A of the Companies Act, 1985 states that a company may alter its objects (or be registered with objects) which merely state that the company is to 'carry on business as a general commercial company'. This means that it can carry on any trade or business whatsoever. All necessary powers will be implied.

If a company does register with or change its objects clause to this new formula it will have effectively opted out of the *ultra vires* rule even for internal purposes of shareholder injunctions.

Rule of constructive notice

At one time knowledge of the contents of a company's constitution was assumed by the courts to be in the minds of all of us even if we had not seen or read it. This was because the memorandum and articles are registered with the Registrar of Companies and the register can be inspected.

Under more recent provisions added by the Companies Act, 1989 to the Companies Act, 1985 the rule of constructive notice of the contents of the company's memorandum and articles and also company documents kept by the Registrar is abolished.

12
Law of contract – reality of consent I

In this chapter we begin a study of the various factors which can affect an agreement once it has been formed. We begin by dealing with the law relating to mistake which affects the true consent of one or both parties so that one or both of them may be asked to be released from their contractual obligations.

Introduction

A contract which is regular in all respects may still fail because there is no real consent to it by one or both of the parties. There is no *consensus ad idem* or meeting of the minds. Consent may be rendered unreal by mistake, misrepresentation, duress and undue influence. There are also instances of inequality of bargaining power where it would be inequitable to enforce the resulting agreement.

It is particularly important to distinguish between mistake and misrepresentation because a contract affected by mistake is void, whereas a contract affected by misrepresentation is only voidable. As between the parties themselves, this makes little difference since in both cases goods sold and money paid can be recovered. However, the distinction can be vital so far as third parties are concerned. If A sells goods to B under circumstances of mistake and B resells them to C, then C gets no title and A can recover the goods from him or sue him for damages in conversion. If, on the other hand, the contract between A and B was voidable for misrepresentation, then if B sold the goods to C who took them bona fide and for value before A had rescinded his contract with B, then C would get a good title and A would have a remedy only against B.

Agreement mistake in general

Mistake, to be operative, must be of *fact* and not of *law*. Furthermore, the concept has a technical meaning and does not cover, for example, errors of judgment as to value. Thus, if A buys an article thinking it is worth £100 when in fact it is worth only £50, the contract is good and A must bear the loss if there has been no misrepresentation by the seller. This is what is meant by the maxim *caveat emptor* (let the buyer beware). An interesting example of how the judiciary can interpret what some might think to be mistakes of law as mistakes of fact is provided by *Solle* v *Butcher* at p. 642.

The various categories of mistake will now be considered, beginning with the rather special case where a document is signed by mistake.

Documents mistakenly signed

If a person signs a contract in the mistaken belief that he is signing a document of a different nature, there may be a mistake which avoids the contract. He may be able to plead *non est factum* ('it is not my deed'). This is a defence open to a person who has signed a document by mistake. Originally it was a special defence to protect those who could not read who had signed deeds which had been incorrectly read over to them. At one time the defence was available only where the mistake referred to the *kind* of document it was and not merely its contents. Now the defence is available to a person who has signed a document having made a *fundamental* mistake as to the kind of document it is or as to its contents. Furthermore, the defendant must prove that he made the mistake despite having taken all reasonable care. If he is negligent he will not usually be able to plead the defence.

ESSENTIAL CASE LAW AND COMMENT

Saunders v *Anglia Building Society*, 1970 – Documents mistakenly signed: the legal effect **(117)**

Unilateral mistake

Unilateral mistake occurs when one of the parties, X, is mistaken as to some fundamental fact concerning the contract and the other party, Y, knows, or ought to know, this. This latter requirement is important because if Y does not know that X is mistaken the contract is good.

The cases are mainly concerned with mistake by one party as to the *identity* of the other party. Thus a contract may be void for mistake if X contracts with Y thinking that Y is another person, Z, and if Y knows that X is under that misapprehension. Proof of Y's knowledge is essential but since in most cases Y is a fraudulent person, the point does not present great difficulties.

ESSENTIAL CASE LAW AND COMMENT

Higgins (W) Ltd v Northampton Corporation, 1927 – Relevance of
  knowledge of the mistake **(118)**
Cundy v Lindsay, 1878 – Mistake as to identity **(119)**

There were difficulties where the parties contracted face to face because
in such a case the suggestion could always be made that whatever the
fraudulent party was saying about his identity, the mistaken party must be
regarded as intending to contract with the person in front of him, whoever
he was. Thus in this situation, the court might find on the facts of the case
that the contract was voidable for fraud or sometimes void for mistake.

However, the position is now a little clearer as a result of the decision in
Lewis v Averay (1971) (see below) where it was said that if the parties
contracted face to face the contract will normally be voidable for fraud but
rarely void for mistake. However, much depends upon the facts of the case
and if the court is convinced on the evidence that identity was vital then even
a 'face to face' contract will be regarded as void for mistake, as *Ingram v
Little* (1961) (see below) shows.

ESSENTIAL CASE LAW AND COMMENT

Lewis v Averay, 1971 – Mistake as to identity when the parties are
  face to face **(120)**
Ingram v Little, 1961 – Another approach **(121)**

EFFECT OF UNILATERAL MISTAKE IN EQUITY

If the plaintiff is asking for an equitable remedy, such as rescission of the
contract or specific performance of it, then equitable principles will apply.
As far as unilateral mistake is concerned, equity follows the principles of the
common law and regards a contract affected by unilateral mistake as void
and will therefore rescind it or refuse specific performance of it. Rectification
of the contract is also available (see p. 245).

ESSENTIAL CASE LAW AND COMMENT

Webster v Cecil, 1861 – Unilateral mistake: the equitable
  approach **(122)**

Bilateral identical (or common) mistake

This occurs where both parties are mistaken and each makes the same
mistake. There is no general rule that common mistake affects a contract

and in practice only common mistakes as to the existence of the subject matter of the contract or where the subject matter of the contract already belongs to the buyer will make the contract void at common law. The principles applied are considered below.

(*a*) *Cases of* res extincta. Here there is a common mistake as to the existence of the subject matter of the contract. Thus, if S agrees to sell his car to B and unknown to both the car had at the time of the sale been destroyed by fire, then the contract will be void because A has innocently undertaken an obligation which he cannot possibly fulfil. It should be noted that the goods may actually exist but the rule of *res extincta* applies if they are not in the condition envisaged by the contract.

(*b*) *Cases of* res sua. These occur where a person makes a contract about something which already belongs to him. Such a contract is void at common law.

ESSENTIAL CASE LAW AND COMMENT

Couturier v *Hastie*, 1856 – An example of *res extincta* **(123)**
Cochrane v *Willis*, 1865 – *Res sua* illustrated **(124)**

(*c*) *Other cases – mistakes as to quality.* These occur when the two parties have reached agreement but have made an identical mistake as to some fact concerning the quality of the subject matter of the contract. Suppose, for example, that X sells a particular drawing to Y for £5000 and all the usual elements of agreement are present, including offer and acceptance and consideration, and the agreement concerns an identified article. Nevertheless, if both X and Y think that the drawing is by a well-known Victorian artist when it is in fact only a copy worth £25, then the agreement is made in circumstances of common mistake.

At common law a mistake of the kind outlined above has no effect on the contract and the parties would be bound in the absence of fraud or misrepresentation. The case law shows how reluctant the courts have been to establish a general rule of common mistake.

ESSENTIAL CASE LAW AND COMMENT

Bell v *Lever Bros Ltd*, 1932 – Mistakes as to quality **(125)**
Leaf v *International Galleries*, 1950 – Quality mistakes: a further
   illustration **(126)**

EFFECT OF IDENTICAL BILATERAL (OR COMMON) MISTAKE IN EQUITY

The position in equity is as follows.

(*a*) *Cases of* res extincta *and* res sua. Equity treats these in the same way as the common law, regarding the agreement as void. The equitable remedy of specific performance is not available for such an agreement which may also be rescinded.

(*b*) *Other cases*. Equity will apparently regard an agreement affected by common mistake as voidable even though the case is not one of *res extincta* or *res sua*. This is the only situation in which the equitable approach differs from that of the common law. The court may order that the contract be set aside on terms, i.e. the court may require the parties to consider first conditions imposed by the court to achieve a fairer solution to the problem. If this is not acceptable the court will rescind the contract.

ESSENTIAL CASE LAW AND COMMENT

Cooper v *Phibbs*, 1867 – Equity and *res sua* **(127)**
Solle v *Butcher*, 1950 – Mistake as to quality: the equitable
  approach **(128)**

(*c*) *Rectification*. If the parties are agreed on the terms of their contract but because, for example, of drafting or typing errors certain terms are set out incorrectly, the court may order equitable rectification of the contract so that it properly represents what the parties agreed. Thus if A orally agrees to give B a lease of premises for 99 years and in the subsequent written contract the term is expressed as 90 years by mistake, then if A will not co-operate to change the lease, B may ask the court to rectify it by substituting a term of 99 years for 90 years. In order to obtain rectification it must be proved:

(i) that there was complete agreement on all the terms of the contract or at least continuing intention to include certain terms in it which in the event were not included. It is not necessary to show that the term was intended to be legally binding prior to being written down;

(ii) that the agreement continued unchanged until it was reduced into writing. If the parties disputed the terms of the agreement then the written contract may be taken to represent their final position;

(iii) that the writing does not express what the parties had agreed. If it does then there can be no rectification.

(iv) Rectification is available for both common and unilateral mistake.

ESSENTIAL CASE LAW AND COMMENT

Joscelyne v *Nissen*, 1970 – Rectification: no need for previous
  binding agreement **(129)**
Frederick Rose (London) Ltd v *William Pim & Co Ltd*, 1953 –
  Rectification where writing is what the parties agreed **(130)**
Thomas Bates & Sons Ltd v *Wyndham's (Lingerie) Ltd*, 1981 –
  Rectification available for unilateral mistake **(131)**

Non-identical bilateral (or mutual) mistake

If X offers to sell car A and Y agrees to buy, thinking X means car B, there is a bilateral mistake which is non-identical. It will be remembered that in the previous category the mistake was bilateral but both parties had made an identical mistake. Confusion of this non-identical bilateral kind generally exists in the mind of one party only and may therefore have no effect on the contract (see below).

EFFECT OF NON-IDENTICAL BILATERAL (OR MUTUAL) MISTAKE AT COMMON LAW

The contract is not necessarily void because the court will try to find the 'sense of promise'. This usually occurs where, although the parties are at cross purposes, the contract actually *identifies* their agreement.

If the parties are at cross purposes and the contract does *not identify* their agreement it is void.

EFFECT OF NON-IDENTICAL BILATERAL (OR MUTUAL) MISTAKE IN EQUITY

Equity also tries to find the sense of the promise as identified by the contract, thus following the law. However, equitable remedies are discretionary and even where the sense of the promise as identified by the contract can be ascertained equity will not necessarily grant specific performance if it would cause hardship to the defendant.

ESSENTIAL CASE LAW AND COMMENT

Wood v *Scarth*, 1858 – The sense of the promise: the hardship rule **(132)**

Raffles v *Wichelhaus*, 1864 – Where there is no sense of the promise **(133)**

13
Law of contract – reality of consent II

In this chapter we continue a study of further situations in which a contract can be affected by lack of proper consent. Topics considered to complete the study of consent problems are misrepresentation, duress, undue influence, economic duress and unconscionable bargains.

Misrepresentation

Misrepresentation is an expression used to describe a situation in which there is no genuineness of consent to a contract by one of the parties. The effect of misrepresentation on a contract is less serious than that of mistake because the contract becomes *voidable and not void*. This means that the party misled can ask the court to rescind the contract, i.e. to put the parties back into the positions they held before the contract was made. Thus in a sale of goods the goods would be returned to the seller and the money to the buyer.

However, the effect on third parties is more fundamental because if A sells goods to B under circumstances of misrepresentation by B and before A has a chance to rescind the contract B sells the goods to C, who takes them for value without notice of the misrepresentaion, C has a good title and A cannot recover the goods or sue him in conversion. His remedy is against B and the type of remedy available will depend upon the nature of B's misrepresentation, i.e. whether it was fraudulent, negligent or innocent.

Meaning of representation

A representation is an inducement only and its effect is to lead the other party merely to make the contract. A representation must be a statement of some specific existing and verifiable fact or past event. It becomes a misrepresentation, of course, when it is false.

Thus there are five ingredients as follows.

THERE MUST BE A STATEMENT

In consequence silence or non-disclosure has no effect except in the following circumstances.

(*a*) *Failure to disclose a change in circumstances.* Where the statement was true when made but became false before the contract was made there is a duty on the party making the statement to disclose the change and if he does not do so his silence can amount to an actionable misrepresentation.

(*b*) *Where the contract is* uberrimae fidei (of utmost good faith), such as a contract of insurance (see further p. 256).

(*c*) *Where there is a confidential or fiduciary relationship between the parties*, as where they are solicitor and client. Here the equitable doctrine of constructive fraud may apply to render the contract voidable.

Although this branch of the law is closely akin to undue influence, which will be considered later, there is a difference in the sense that in undue influence the person with special influence, such as a solicitor over his client, is often the prime mover in seeking the contract. Constructive fraud, however, could apply where the client was the prime mover in seeking a contract with his solicitor. In such a case if the solicitor remains silent as regards facts within his knowledge material, say, to the contract price, then the client could rescind the contract for constructive fraud.

(*d*) *Where statute requires disclosure*, as does the Financial Services Act, 1986 under which a number of specified particulars must be disclosed in an advertisement/prospectus issued by a company to invite the public to subscribe for shares or debentures. The particulars must give all such information as investors and their professional advisers would reasonably require and reasonably expect to find in the advertisement/prospectus for the purpose of making an informed assessment as to whether to buy the securities.

(*e*) *In cases of concealed fraud*, following the case of *Gordon v Selico Co Ltd*, *The Times*, 26 February 1986. In that case a flat in a block of flats which had recently been converted by a developer was taken by the plaintiff on a 99-year lease. Soon after he moved in dry rot was discovered. Goulding, J., who was later upheld by the Court of Appeal, decided that deliberate concealment of the dry rot by the developer could amount to fraudulent misrepresentation whereupon damages were awarded to the plaintiff. Silence can, therefore, amount to misrepresentation in the case of concealed fraud.

ESSENTIAL CASE LAW AND COMMENT

With v *O'Flanagan*, 1936 – Where circumstances change **(134)**

SPECIFIC EXISTING AND VERIFIABLE FACT OR PAST EVENT

The representation must be a statement of some specific, existing and verifiable fact or past event, and in consequence the following are excluded.

(*a*) *Statements of law.* Everyone is presumed to know the law which is equally accessible to both parties and on which they should seek advice and not rely on the statements of the other party. Thus, if A has allowed B, a tradesman, to have goods on credit and C has agreed orally to indemnify A in respect of the transaction, then if A enters into a second contract with B under which A is to receive two-thirds of the price of the goods from B in full settlement on B's representation that C's indemnity is unenforceable at law because it is not in writing, then the second contract would be good because A cannot deny that he knows the law because of the maxim 'ignorance of the law is no excuse'.

(*b*) *Statement as to future conduct or intention.* These are not actionable, though if the person who makes the statement has no intention of carrying it out, it may be regarded as a representation of fact, i.e. a misrepresentation of what is really in the mind of the maker of the statement.

(*c*) *Statements of opinion.* Again these are not normally actionable unless it can be shown that the person making the statement held no such opinion whereupon the statement may be considered in law to be a misstatement of an existing fact as to what was in the mind of the maker of the statement at the time. However, in *Bissett* v *Wilkinson* [1927] A.C. 177 it was held that a vendor of land was not liable for stating that it could support 2000 sheep, because he had no personal knowledge of the facts, the land having never been used for sheep farming. The buyer knew this so that it was understood by him that the seller could only be stating his opinion.

Nevertheless the expression of an opinion may involve a statement of fact. Suppose A writes a reference for B to help B get a house to rent and A says to C, the prospective landlord: 'B is a very desirable tenant'. A is doing two things: first he is giving his opinion of B, but also he is making a statement of fact by saying that he *believes* B to be a very desirable tenant. If in fact therefore A actually believes B to be a bad tenant he is lying as to what is in his mind.

(*d*) *Sales talk, advertising, 'puffing' (or what is called these days 'hype').* Not all statements in this area amount to representations. The law has always accepted that it is essential in business that a seller of goods or services should be allowed to make some statements about them in the course of dealing without necessarily being bound by everything he says. Thus, if a salesman confines himself to statements of opinion such as 'This is the finest floor polish in the world' or 'This is the best polish on the market', there is no misrepresentation. However, the nearer a salesman gets to a statement of specific verifiable fact, the greater the possibility that there may be an action for misrepresentation. Thus a statement such as 'This polish has as much wax in it as Snooks' wax polish' may well amount to a misrepresentation if the statement is not in fact true.

ESSENTIAL CASE LAW AND COMMENT

Edgington v *Fitzmaurice*, 1885 – Statements as to future conduct or intention **(135)**

Smith v *Land and House Property Corporation*, 1884 – Opinion may be construed as fact **(136)**

THE STATEMENT MUST INDUCE THE CONTRACT

It must therefore:

(*a*) have been relied upon by the person claiming to have been misled who must not have relied on his own skill and judgment;

(*b*) have been material in the sense that it affected the plaintiff's judgment;

(*c*) have been know to the plaintiff. The plaintiff must always be prepared to prove that an alleged misrepresentation had an effect on his mind, a task which he certainly cannot fulfil if he was never aware that it had been made.

Thus in *Re Northumberland and Durham District Banking Co ex parte Bigge* (1858) 28 L.J. Ch. 50 a person who bought shares in a company asked to have the purchase rescinded because the company had published false reports as to its solvency. Although these reports were false, the claimant failed because, among other things, he was unable to show that he had read any of the reports or that anyone had told him what they contained;

(*d*) have been addressed to the person claiming to have been misled.

ESSENTIAL CASE LAW AND COMMENT

Peek v *Gurney*, 1873 – The statement must induce the contract: the common law approach **(137)**

KNOWLEDGE THAT STATEMENT IS UNTRUE

If the person to whom the false statement was made knew that it was untrue then he cannot sue in respect of it because he has not been misled. However, it is not an acceptable defence to an action for misrepresentation that the representee was given the means of discovering that the statement was untrue.

ESSENTIAL CASE LAW AND COMMENT

Redgrave v *Hurd*, 1881 – No need to check on a statement **(138)**

DID THE STATEMENT INFLUENCE THE REPRESENTEE'S DECISION?

The law requires that a misrepresentation must have operated on the mind of the representee. If it has not, as where the representee was not influenced by it, there is no claim.

ESSENTIAL CASE LAW AND COMMENT

Smith v *Chadwick*, 1884 – Was the statement material? **(139)**

Types of actionable misrepresentation and remedies in general

INNOCENT MISREPRESENTATION

A purely innocent misrepresentation is a false statement made by a person who had reasonable grounds to believe that the statement was true, not only when he made it but also at the time the contract was entered into. As regards reasonable grounds, the representer's best hope of proving this will be to show that he himself had been induced to buy the goods by the same statement, particularly where he is not technically qualified to verify it further (see *Humming Bird Motors Ltd* v *Hobbs* (1986) and *Oscar Chess Ltd* v *Williams* (1957), pp. 651 and 660). The party misled can ask the court to rescind the contract but has no right to ask for damages. However, the court may at its discretion award damages instead of rescission, provided the remedy of rescission is still available and has not been lost, e.g. by delay (Misrepresentation Act, 1967, s. 2(2)). Rescission in effect cancels the contract and the court may in some cases regard this as a drastic remedy, particularly where there has been misrepresentation on a trivial matter, such as the quality of the tyres on a car. Suppose the seller of a car in a private sale says: 'the previous owner fitted new tyres at 26,000 miles'. If that statement is false but the seller was told this by the previous owner, then the court could award damages instead of rescission, thus leaving the contract intact but giving the party misled monetary compensation. Statements by dealers, however, are often taken to be terms of the contract (see p. 266).

NEGLIGENT MISREPRESENTATION

A negligent misrepresentation is a false statement made by a person who had no reasonable grounds for believing the statement to be true. The party misled may sue for rescission (see below) and/or damages and the requirement to prove that the statement was not made negligently but that there were reasonable grounds for believing it to be true is on the maker of the statement (or representer) (Misrepresentation Act, 1967, s. 2(1)).

The sub-section recognises only a claim for damages and says nothing about rescission. However, in *Mapes* v *Jones* (1974) 232 E.G. 717 a property dealer contracted to lease a grocer's shop to the plaintiff for 21 years but in fact did not have sufficient interest in the property himself to grant such a lease, the maximum period available to him being 18 years. Despite constant requests no lease was supplied as originally promised and the plaintiff shut the shop and elected to treat the contract as repudiated. Willis, J. held that the plaintiff was entitled to rescission for misrepresentation under s. 2(1) of the 1967 Act. He also found that the defendant's delay in completion was a breach of condition which *also* allowed the plaintiff to repudiate the contract.

ESSENTIAL CASE LAW AND COMMENT

Gosling v *Anderson*, 1972 – Negligent misrepresentation illustrated **(140)**

FRAUDULENT MISREPRESENTATION

A fraudulent misrepresentation is a false representation of a material fact made knowing it to be false, or believing it to be false, or recklessly not caring whether it be true or false. Mere negligence is not enough. An element of dishonesty is required. For example, if Mr Tidbury in the *Gosling* case had *known* that there was no planning permission for the garage but had nevertheless gone on to state that there was, then the element of dishonesty would have been present and he would have been guilty of fraud. The party misled may sue for rescission and/or damages. As regards the action for damages, the plaintiff sues not on the contract but on the tort of deceit.

ESSENTIAL CASE LAW AND COMMENT

Derry v *Peek*, 1889 – Fraudulent misrepresentation defined **(141)**

Compensation under the Financial Services Act, 1986

Under this Act, where the directors of a company publish an advertisement or prospectus containing false statements made innocently they may have to pay a form of damages called compensation.

There are a number of special defences available under the Act. For example, a director may deny responsibility for the prospectus, as where he ceased to be a director before it was issued. Assuming, however, that he does admit responsibility for the prospectus, the defences are that:

(a) he had reasonable grounds for believing the statement to be true;

(b) the statements were made on the authority of an expert who was thought to be competent;

(c) the statements were a copy of an official document; or

(d) he published a correction or took reasonable steps to see that one was published and he reasonably believed it had been.

Experts, such as accountants, are also liable under the Act for false statements in their reports which are included in the prospectus. Again, the defence of lack of responsibility is available, as where the expert has not consented to the inclusion of his report in the prospectus. However, given that he accepts responsibility for the inclusion of his report, he has a defence if he can show that he had reasonable grounds for believing the statement to be true. Presumably, he could sustain this defence by showing, amongst other things, that the false statement came from an official document. Furthermore, whether or not a professional person has reasonable grounds will almost always depend upon the steps taken to *verify* the statement. If these are reasonable the professional person will not be liable even if the statement is wrong.

Agent's breach of warranty of authority

Under the law of agency where an agent misrepresents himself as having authority he does not possess, the third party will not obtain a contract with the principal and if he suffers loss as a consequence he may sue the agent for breach of warranty of authority, the action being for damages and brought in *quasi-contract*. Quasi-contract is based on the idea that a person should not obtain a benefit or unjust enrichment or cause injury to another with impunity merely because there is no obligation in contract or another established branch of law which will operate to make him account. The law may in these circumstances provide a remedy by implying a *fictitious promise* to account for the benefit of the enrichment or to compensate for damage caused.

Negligence at common law

THE TORT REMEDY IN GENERAL

Where the parties concerned were not in a *pre-contractual relationship* when the statement was made, s. 2(1) of the Misrepresentation Act, 1967 will not apply. However, an action for damages for negligence will lie in tort, provided the false statement was made negligently. The law relating to tortious negligent misstatements is considered in more detail at p. 448. However, the leading case is looked at now.

ESSENTIAL CASE LAW AND COMMENT

Hedley Byrne & Co Ltd v *Heller & Partners*, 1963 – Negligent misstatements: the tort remedy **(142)**

USE OF THE TORT REMEDY IN CONTRACT CASES

In *Esso Petroleum* v *Mardon* [1976] 2 All E.R. 5 the court held that the principle in *Hedley Byrne* could apply even where the parties concerned were in a pre-contractual relationship and in addition that the person who had made the statement need not necessarily be in business to give advice, provided it is reasonable for one party to rely on the other's skill and judgment in making the statement. Mr Mardon was awarded damages for a negligent misstatement by a senior sales representative of Esso in regard to the amount of petrol he could expect to sell per year from a petrol station which he was leasing from Esso. The facts of *Mardon* pre-dated the 1967 Act and the court could not use it. The decision is obviously important but where the facts have occurred since 1967 the Misrepresentation Act is likely to prove more popular to plaintiffs who have been misled *into making contracts*, since they can ask the representer to show he was not negligent. In *Hedley Byrne* claims the burden of proof is on the plaintiff to prove negligence.

There is a very obvious use, however, for the tort of negligence claim even where the careless misstatement has induced a contract. The tort claim allows an action for a misleading *opinion or falsely stated intention*, whereas misrepresentation in all its forms requires a misstatement of *fact*, not opinion or intention. The use of *Hedley Byrne* would today make the legal gymnastics seen in *Edgington* v *Fitzmaurice* (1885) (see p. 647) and *Smith* v *Land and House Property Co* (1884) (see p. 647) unnecessary.

USE OF TORT REMEDY FOR INACCURATE COMPANY SECURITIES ADVERTISEMENTS

As regards actions against directors and experts in respect of statements in an advertisement for the sale of securities or in a prospectus, there is as we have seen a statutory claim under the Financial Services Act, 1986 and under *Hedley Byrne* at common law. The claim against directors under *Hedley Byrne* is specifically preserved by the Financial Services Act, 1986 in s. 150(4). A claim under the Misrepresentation Act, 1967 is against 'the other party to the contract', i.e. the company or issuing house, and not against directors or agents.

It will be recalled in *Esso Petroleum Co Ltd* v *Mardon* (1976) (see above) that the court held that it was too restrictive to limit the duty in *Hedley Byrne* to persons who carried on or who held themselves out as carrying on the *business* of giving information or advice. The acceptance of these views means that the duty can apply more widely and brings in company directors in terms that they could be liable on a personal basis for negligence.

In any case, it is a requirement as part of admission of the shares to a full Stock Exchange listing or USM (Unlisted Securities Market) quotation that the advertisement or prospectus shall state that the directors have taken reasonable care to ensure that the facts stated in it are true and accurate, that there are no misleading omissions and that, accordingly, all the directors take responsibility for the prospectus.

In view of this statement, it is likely that a duty of care is owed only by the individuals involved in the making of the statements and not by the company as such. If this is so, no claim can be made against the company. This would accord with the general principle of capital maintenance inherent in the prospectus remedies, i.e. it is difficult to get one's money back from the company and easier to get compensation from directors or experts, leaving capital contributed with the company.

In view of this it would seem that an action for rescission of the contract (see below) against the company will not in the company law context be a likely remedy. In any case it is very quickly lost as we shall see.

Remedy of rescission

As we have seen, this remedy is available to a party misled by innocent, negligent or fraudulent misrepresentation. It restores the status quo, i.e. it puts the parties back to the position they were in before the contract was made. However, the remedy may be lost:

(a) *By affirmation.* If the injured party affirms the contract he cannot rescind. He will affirm if with full knowledge of the misrepresentation he expressly affirms the contract by stating that he intends to go on with it or if he does some act from which an implied intention may properly be deduced. In the company situation this could, for example, be attending a company meeting to complain about an inaccurate prospectus.

(b) *By lapse of time.* This is a form of implied affirmation and applies as follows:

(i) In innocent and negligent misrepresentation the position is governed by equity and the passage of a reasonable time, even without knowledge of the misrepresentation, may prevent the court from granting rescission: *Leaf* v *International Galleries* (1950) – see p. 641.

(ii) In fraudulent misrepresentation the position is governed by s. 32 of the Limitation Act, 1980 and lapse of time has no effect on rescission where fraud is alleged as long as the action is brought within six years of the time when the fraud was, or with reasonable diligence could have been, discovered.

(c) *Where status quo cannot be restored.* Rescission is impossible if the parties cannot be restored to their original positions as where goods sold under a contract of sale have been consumed.

(d) *Where a third party has acquired rights in the subject matter of the contract.* Thus if X obtains goods from Y by misrepresentation and pawns them with Z, Y cannot rescind the contract on learning of the misrepresentation in order to recover the goods from Z. Nor can he sue Z in conversion (*Lewis* v *Averay* (1971) – see p. 638).

ESSENTIAL CASE LAW AND COMMENT

Long v *Lloyd*, 1958 – Application of the affirmation rule **(143)**
Clarke v *Dickson*, 1858 – Inability to restore status quo **(144)**

Contracts *uberrimae fidei* (utmost good faith)

Silence does not normally amount to misrepresentation. However, an important exception to the rule occurs in the case of certain contracts where from the circumstances of the case one party alone possesses full knowledge of all the material facts and in which therefore the law requires him to show utmost good faith. He must make full disclosure of all the material facts known to him otherwise the contract may be rescinded. The contracts concerned are as follows.

AT COMMON LAW

Contracts of insurance provide the only true example of a contract *uberrimae fidei*. There is a duty on the person taking up the insurance to disclose to the insurance company all facts of which he is aware which might affect the premium or acceptance of the risk. Failure to do so renders the contract voidable at the option of the insurance company. This could happen, for example, where a person seeking insurance did not disclose that he had been refused insurance by another company. Where there is a failure to disclose the insurance company is not required by law to meet the claim but must return the premiums. In other words the contract is rescinded. A recent decision that this is so is *Banque Keyser Ullmann SA* v *Skandia (UK) Insurance Co* [1989] 3 W.L.R. 25.

In addition, most proposals for insurance require the proposer to sign a declaration in which he warrants that the statements he has made are true and agrees that they be incorporated into the contract as terms. Where this is so any false statement which the proposer makes will be a ground for avoidance of the contract by the insurance company, even though the statement was not material in terms of the premium.

ESSENTIAL CASE LAW AND COMMENT

Dawsons Ltd v *Bonin*, 1922 – The contract may widen the duty of disclosure **(145)**

BY STATUTE

As regards contracts to take shares in a company, there is a duty on the directors or its promoters, under the Financial Services Act, 1986, to disclose various matters essential to an informed assessment as to whether an investor should purchase the securities. These provisions, and those in earlier statutes which preceded them, had to be put into law by Parliament because the judiciary had always refused to regard the sale of securities by a company as a contract *uberrimae fidei*. They did not, therefore, require the advertisement or prospectus under which the shares were issued necessarily to disclose all the material facts.

IN EQUITY-FIDUCIARY RELATIONSHIPS

In contracts between members of a family, partners, principal and agent, solicitor and client, guardian and ward, and trustee and beneficiary, the relationship of the parties requires that the most ample disclosure should be made. The duties of disclosure arising from the above fiduciary relations recognised by equity are not situations of *uberrimae fidei*. In contracts *uberrimae fidei* it is the nature of the contract, i.e. insurance, which requires disclosure regardless of the relationship of the parties. In the fiduciary situation it is the relationshp of parties and not the particular contract which gives rise to the need to disclose.

ESSENTIAL CASE LAW AND COMMENT

Gordon v *Gordon*, 1819 – Disclosure in a family situation **(146)**

Duress

Duress will affect all contracts and gifts procured by its use. Duress, which is a common-law concept, means actual violence or threats of violence to the person of the contracting party or those near and dear to him. The threats must be calculated to produce fear of loss of life or bodily harm.

THREATS OF VIOLENCE

A contract will seldom be procured by actual violence but threats of violence are more probable. The threat must be illegal in that it must be a threat to commit a crime or tort. Thus to threaten an imprisonment, which would be unlawful if enforced, constitutes duress, but not, it is said, if the imprisonment would be lawful. However, the courts are unlikely to look with favour on a contract obtained by threatening to prosecute a criminal. A contract procured by a threat to sue for an act which was not a crime, e.g. trespass, would not be affected by duress.

ESSENTIAL CASE LAW AND COMMENT

Welch v *Cheesman*, 1973 – Duress by threats of violence **(147)**

THREATS TO PROPERTY

In *Skeate* v *Beale* (1840) 11 Ad. & E.L. 983 a tenant owed £19 10s. in old money and agreed to pay £3 7s. 6d. immediately and the remaining £16 2s. 6d. within a month if his landlord would withdraw a writ of distress under which he was threatening to sell the tenant's goods. The tenant later disputed what he owed and the landlord tried to set up the agreement and sued for the remaining £16 2s. 6d. It was held that the landlord was entitled to £16 2s. 6d. under the agreement which was not affected by duress since the threat was to sell the tenant's goods. However, more recently the courts have been moving away from the view that threats to property cannot invalidate contracts. In *The Siboen and The Sibotre* [1976] Lloyd's Rep. 293 it was said that duress could be a defence if a person was forced to make a contract by the threat of having a valuable picture slashed or his house burnt down.

DURESS PROBABLY RENDERS A CONTRACT *VOIDABLE*

This, at least, is the view expressed in Cheshire & Fifoot's *Law of Contract* (a leading text on contract law), though other writers have argued that the effect of duress is to render a contract void. However, the judgments of the Privy Council in *Barton* v *Armstrong* [1975] 2 All E.R. 465 and *Pao On* v *Lau Yiu Long* [1979] 3 All E.R. 65 suggest that duress has the same effect as fraud, i.e. it renders a contract voidable. The issue is an important one for third parties, since if B procures goods from A by duress and sells the goods to C, who has no knowledge of the duress, A will be able to recover the goods from C if the contract is void, but will not be able to do so if it is voidable. On the authorities to date, therefore, A would have no claim against C.

Undue influence and associated equitable pleas

The doctrine of undue influence was developed by equity. The concept of undue influence is designed to deal with contracts *or gifts* obtained without free consent by the influence of one mind over another.

If there is no special relationship between the parties undue influence may exist, but must be proved by the person seeking to avoid the contract.

Where a confidential or fiduciary relationship exists between the parties, the party in whom the confidence was reposed must show that undue influence was not used, i.e. that the contract was the act of a free and independent mind. It is desirable, though not essential, that independent advice should have been given.

There are several confidential relationships which are well established in the law, namely parent and child, solicitor and client, trustee and beneficiary, guardian and ward and religious adviser and disciple. In these cases there is a presumption of undue influence by the parent, the solicitor, the trustee and so on. There is no presumption of such a relationship between husband and wife, nor, according to the Court of Appeal in *Mathew* v *Bobbins* (1980) 256 E.G. 603 between employer and employee. However, a presumption of undue influence may be made between husband and wife where there are special circumstances such as the lack of sufficient mental capacity in either party to resist the influence of the other leading to gifts of property which are quite out of character with the donor's normal inquiring disposition when disposing of property (*Simpson* v *Simpson*, *The Times*, 11 June 1988). The fiduciary relationship between parent and child ends usually, but not necessarily, on reaching 18 or on getting married.

ESSENTIAL CASE LAW AND COMMENT

Lancashire Loans Ltd v *Black*, 1934 – Undue influence: parent and child **(148)**

Allcard v *Skinner*, 1887 – Undue influence: religious adviser and disciple **(149)**

However, there may be a presumption of undue influence even though the relationship between the parties is not in the established categories outlined above. In *Re Craig Dec'd* [1970] 2 All E.R. 390 Ungoed-Thomas, J. ruled that presumption of undue influence arose on proof:

(*a*) of a gift so substantial or of such a nature that it could not on the face of it be accounted for on the grounds of the ordinary motives on which ordinary men acted, and

(*b*) of a relationship of trust and confidence such that the recipient of the gift was in a position to exercise undue influence over the person making it.

ESSENTIAL CASE LAW AND COMMENT

Hodgson v *Marks*, 1970 – Undue influence: outside the special categories **(150)**

EFFECT OF UNDUE INFLUENCE ON THIRD PARTIES

A contract between A and B procured by undue influence cannot be avoided by rescission against third parties who acquire rights for value without notice of the facts. Where this has happened the party suffering the undue influence, say, A, will have to rely on tracing the proceeds of sale into the original purchaser's, i.e. B's, assets. The contract may be avoided and the property recovered from third parties for value with notice of the facts and also against volunteers (i.e. persons who have given no consideration) even though they were unaware of the facts.

EFFECT OF UNDUE INFLUENCE ON THE PARTIES TO THE CONTRACT

Undue influence renders the contract voidable so that it may be rescinded. However, since rescission is an equitable remedy, there must be no delay in claiming relief after the influence has ceased to have effect. Delay in claiming relief in these circumstances may bar the claim since delay is evidence of affirmation. This is illustrated by the case of *Allcard* v *Skinner* at p. 656.

Economic duress

Apart from the old concepts of duress and undue influence, the courts are developing in modern times wider rules to protect persons against improper pressure and inequality of bargaining power as it affects contracts. This development was perhaps best described by Lord Denning in *Lloyds Bank* v *Bundy* [1974] 3 All E.R. 757 where he said, having discussed duress and various forms of undue pressure in contract:

> Gathering all together, I would suggest that through all these instances there runs a single thread. They rest on 'inequality of bargaining power'. By virtue of it, the English law gives relief to one who, without independent advice, enters into a contract on terms which are very unfair or transfers property for consideration which is grossly inadequate, where his bargaining power is grievously impaired by reason of his own needs or desires, or by his own ignorance or infirmity coupled with undue influence or pressures brought to bear on him by or for the benefit of the other.

Economic duress is within this concept. Suppose A agrees to build a tanker for B by an agreed date at an agreed price and B enters into a contract with

C under which the tanker is to be chartered to C from the agreed completion date or shortly afterwards. If A then threatens not to complete the contract by the agreed date unless B pays more and B makes an extra payment because he does not want to be liable in breach of contract to C, then the agreement to pay more is affected by economic duress. (See the judgment of Mocatta, J. in *North Ocean Shipping Co Ltd* v *Hyundai Construction Co Ltd, The Atlantic Baron* [1978] 3 All E.R. 1170.)

The decision of the House of Lords in *Universe Tankships Inc of Monrovia* v *International Transport Workers' Federation* [1982] 2 All E.R. 67 is instructive in that it affirms the existence of the doctrine of economic duress. In that case a ship called the *Universe Sentinel*, which was owned by Universe Tankships, was 'blacked' by the respondent trade union, the ITF, which regarded the ship as sailing under a flag of convenience. ITF was against flag-of-convenience ships and refused to make tugs available when the ship arrived at Milford Haven to discharge her cargo. The blacking was lifted after Universe Tankships had made an agreement with ITF regarding improvements in pay and conditions of the crew and had paid money to ITF which included a contribution of $6480 to an ITF fund known as The Seafarers' International Welfare Protection and Assistance Fund. Universe Tankships sued for the return of the $6480 on the basis of economic duress, and the House of Lords held that they were entitled to recover it. It appears from the judgments that the effect of economic duress is to make the contract voidable and to provide a ground for recovery of money paid as money had and received to the plaintiff's use – a form of quasi-contractual claim.

The decision in *Universe Tankships* was applied by the Court of Appeal in *B. & S.Contracts & Design* v *Victor Green Publications* [1984] I.G.R. 419 where A agreed to erect stands for B who was doing a presentation at Olympia. A's employees threatened to strike unless they received extra money which they had demanded and to which they were not entitled. A said that the contract could not proceed unless these extra sums were paid by B as an increase in the contract price. B paid the extra sums to get the work done and then recovered them in this action. The money was paid under economic duress.

It should also be noted that where extra contractual payments have been arranged under circumstances of economic duress they cannot be recovered in a claim before a court. Thus in *Atlas Express* v *Kafco* [1989] 1 All E.R. 641 Atlas, a national road carrier, made a contract to deliver cartons of basketware to Woolworths stores for Kafco who were a small company importing and distributing the basketware. A price of £1.10 per carton was agreed but the first load had fewer cartons than had been anticipated and Atlas told Kafco that they would not carry any more without a minimum payment per trip regardless of the number of cartons carried. Kafco could not find another carrier quickly and, being worried about their contract with Woolworths if the latter did not get their supplies, Kafco agreed to the new terms but later refused to pay the new rate, only the per carton rate. The High Court held that the claim of Atlas for the minimum rate must be dismissed. The circumstances amounted to economic duress and there was no proper consent by Kafco.

Unconscionable bargains

The court will, in what it regards as an appropriate case, set aside a contract which is affected by improper pressure by one party or where there is inequality of bargaining power. However, mere inequality is not in itself enough: the court will look at all the circumstances of the case.

ESSENTIAL CASE LAW AND COMMENT

Lloyds Bank v *Bundy*, 1974 – Unconscionable bargains illustrated (151)

Further examples of inequality of bargaining power may be found in *Clifford Davis Management* v *WEA Records* [1975] 1 All E.R. 237 where A, an experienced manager, obtained a contract with a pop star, B, who had little or no business experience, under which B gave A the copyright in all his compositions for a period of years. It was held that B could avoid the contract because A had exploited his superior bargaining power.

No general rule that all contracts must be fair

There is no rule of law which states that a fair price must be paid in *all* transactions and some unfair contracts will be held binding provided the parties were of equal bargaining strength. In *Burmah Oil Ltd* v *The Governor of the Bank of England*, *The Times*, 4 July 1981, Burma was in financial difficulties and sold a large holding of shares which it had in British Petroleum to the government at a price below the Stock Exchange price. Burma then brought an action to set the contract aside. The court refused to do so. Although there was authority to set aside a transaction where one party had acted without independent advice, or where the bargaining strength of one party was grievously impaired, neither of those situations existed in this case. The relationship was purely commercial and the contract for the sale of shares must stand.

14
Law of contract – contractual terms

We shall now consider the contents of the contract by explaining the types of terms express or implied which may be found in a contract.

Inducements and terms generally

Even where it is clear that a valid contract has been made it is still necessary to decide precisely what it is the parties have undertaken to do in order to be able to say whether each has performed or not performed his part of the agreement.

In order to decide upon the terms of the contract it is necssary to find out what was said or written by the parties. Furthermore, having ascertained what the parties said or wrote, it is necessary to decide whether the statements were mere inducements (or representations) or terms of the contract, i.e. part of its actual contents. The distinction in diagrammatic form together with an indication of remedies appears in Fig. 14.1 at p. 264.

The distinction is less important than it was since the passing of the Misrepresentation Act, 1967. Before the Act became law there was often no remedy for a misrepresentation which was not fraudulent, and in such a case the plaintiff's only hope of obtaining a remedy was to convince the court that the defendant's statement was not a mere inducement but a term of the contract of which the defendant was in breach and for which damages might be obtained. As we have seen, under the Misrepresentation Act, 1967 the new form of negligent misrepresentation which did not exist before will now give rise in many cases to an action for damages even in respect of a mere misrepresentation or inducement.

Inducements and terms distinguished

Nevertheless, it is still necessary to consider the main tests applied by the courts in order to distinguish between a mere misrepresentation and a term

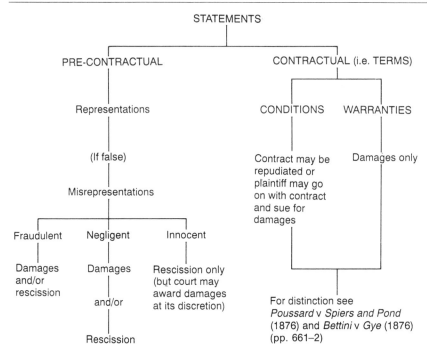

Fig. 14.1

of the contract, bearing in mind always that the question whether a statement is an inducement or a term and, if a term, whether a condition or warranty *is a matter of fact for the judge*. Fact decisions of this sort vary widely according to the circumstances of each case, so that it is virtually impossible to predict with absolute accuracy what the outcome of a particular case will be. However, by way of illustration the following headings contain the major guidelines which are applied.

THE STATEMENTS AND INTENTIONS OF THE PARTIES

The court will always be concerned to implement the intentions of the parties as they appear from statements made by them. Thus in *Gill & Duffus SA v Société pour l'Exportation des Sucres SA* [1985] 1 Lloyd's Rep. 621 the defendants agreed to sell sugar to Gill. A term of the contract (not specified as a condition or warranty) said that the defendants were to name a port at which the sugar was to be loaded by 14 November 'at latest'. The defendants did not nominate a port by that time and so Gill refused to take any sugar from the defendants and regarded the contract as cancelled. The defendants then tried to make a nomination of a port but Gill refused to accept it saying that they had repudiated the contract because of the defendants' breach of condition (or repudiatory breach). Following a decision unfavourable to them at arbitration, Gill appealed. Leggatt, J. said that there were no words in the English language by which a deadline could be appointed more concisely, more precisely, or with more finality than 'at latest'. They meant what they said and the judge had no doubt that the intention of the parties as gathered from the contract itself would be best carried out by treating the promise not as a mere warranty but as a condition precedent by the failure to perform which the other party was relieved of liability. Gill's contention was accepted. There was a repudiatory breach of condition. Where in a contract the parties have indicated that a particular undertaking is to be a term of the contract, the courts will in general abide by the wishes of the parties. However, the court will not slavishly follow the parties' statements and where, for example, the parties appear to have regarded a trivial matter as a vital term of the agreement, the court may still take the view that it is not.

Thus so far as a written contract is concerned, the court may disregard a statement by the parties that a particular undertaking is a condition and say instead that it is a warranty. So far as wholly oral contracts are concerned, the court may ignore the statements of the parties and decide that a particular undertaking is a condition, a warranty, or a mere inducement.

Thus in *L. Schuler AG* v *Wickham Machine Tool Sales* [1973] 2 All E.R. 39 the plaintiffs entered into a contract for four years with the defendants giving them the sole right to sell panel presses in England. A clause of the contract provided that it should be a condition of the agreement that the defendants' representative should visit six named firms each week to solicit orders. The defendants' representatives failed on a few occasions to do so and the plaintiffs claimed to be entitled to repudiate the agreement on the basis that a single failure was a breach of condition giving them an absolute right to treat the contract as at an end. The House of Lords said that such minor breaches by the defendants did not entitle the plaintiffs to repudiate. The House of Lords construed the clause on the basis that it was so unreasonable that the parties could not have intended it as a condition giving Schuler a right of repudiation, but rather as a warranty. Thus Schuler were themselves in breach of contract leaving Wickham with a claim for damages against Schuler.

This case is also an example of the court trying to give redress in regard to an unconscionable bargain and to correct unscrupulous commercial conduct.

THE NATURE OF THE STATEMENT

A statement is likely to be an inducement rather than a term if the person making the statement asks the other party to check or verify it, e.g. 'The car is sound but I should get an engineer's report on it'.

In addition a statement is likely to be a term rather than a mere inducement if it is made with the intention of preventing the other party from looking for defects and succeeds in doing this, e.g. 'The car is sound, you need not look it over'.

THE IMPORTANCE OF THE STATEMENT

If the statement is such that the plaintiff would not have made the contract without it, then the statement will be a term of the contract and not a mere inducement.

ESSENTIAL CASE LAW AND COMMENT

Bannerman v *White*, 1861 – Representations and terms: a vital undertaking **(152)**

THE TIMING OF THE STATEMENT

A statement made during preliminary negotiations tends to be an inducement. Where the interval between the making of the statement and the making of the contract is distinct then the statement is almost certain to be an inducement. Thus in *Routledge* v *McKay* [1954] 1 All E.R. 855 the plaintiff and the defendant were discussing the possible purchase and sale of the defendant's motor cycle. Both parties were private persons. The defendant, taking the information from the registration book, said, on 23 October, that the cycle was a 1942 model. On 30 October a written contract of sale was made. The actual date of the cycle was later found to be 1930. The buyer's claim for damages for breach of warranty failed in the Court of Appeal. In this case the interval between the negotiations and the contract was well marked and the statement was not a term. However, the interval is not always so well marked and in such cases there is a difficulty in deciding whether the statement is an inducement or term.

ORAL STATEMENTS LATER PUT INTO WRITING

If the statement was oral and the contract was afterwards reduced to writing, then the terms of the contract tend to be contained in the written document and all oral statements tend to be pre-contractual inducements. Even so the court may still consider the apparent intentions of the parties and decide that they had made a contract which was part oral and part written (see *Evans* v *Merzario* (1976) at p. 676).

SPECIAL SKILL AND KNOWLEDGE OR LACK OF SAME

Where one of the parties has special knowledge or skill with regard to the subject matter of the contract, then the statements of such a party will normally be regarded as terms of the contract. In addition it will be difficult for an expert to convince the court that a person with no particular knowledge or skill in regard to the subject matter has made statements which constitute terms of the contract.

> **ESSENTIAL CASE LAW AND COMMENT**
>
> *Oscar Chess Ltd* v *Williams*, 1957 – Effect of special skill and knowledge **(153)**

Conditions and warranties

Having decided that a particular statement is a term of the contract and not a mere inducement, the court must then consider the importance of that statement in the context of the contract as a whole. Not all terms are of equal importance. Failure to perform some may have a more serious effect on the contract than failure to perform others. The law has applied special terminology to contractual terms in order to distinguish the vital or fundamental obligations from the less vital, the expression *condition* being applied to the former and the expression *warranty* to the latter. A condition is a fundamental obligation which goes to the root of the contract. A warranty on the other hand is a subsidiary obligation which is not so vital that a failure to perform it goes to the root of the contract.

This distinction is important in terms of remedies. A breach of condition is called a repudiatory breach and the injured party may elect either to repudiate the contract or claim damages and go on with the contract.

It should be noted that the plaintiff must go on with the contract and sue for damages if he has affirmed the contract after knowledge of a breach of condition. He may do this expressly as where he uses the goods, or by lapse of time as where he simply fails to take any steps to complain about the breach for what in the court's view is an unreasonable period of time. A breach of warranty is not repudiatory and the plaintiff must go on with the contract and sue for damages.

Whether a term is a condition or warranty is basically a matter for the court which will be decided on the basis of the commercial importance of the term. As we have seen, the words used by the parties are, of course, relevant, but are not followed slavishly by the court which may still decide differently from the parties on the basis of the commercial importance of the term.

It should be noted that the word *warranty* is sometimes used in a different way, e.g. by a manufacturer of goods who gives a *warranty* against faulty workmanship offering to replace parts free. The term *warranty* is used by the manufacturer as equivalent to a guarantee. We are concerned here with its use as a term of a contract.

> **ESSENTIAL CASE LAW AND COMMENT**
>
> *Poussard* v *Spiers and Pond*, 1876 – Condition: a vital commercial undertaking **(154)**
> *Bettini* v *Gye*, 1876 – Warranty: a collateral undertaking **(155)**

Innominate terms

In modern law there are also terms which the parties call conditions and where the breach has *in fact* had a serious result on the contract. The court will then agree that the breach should be treated as a breach of condition and the contract can be repudiated. There are also terms which the parties call warranties and where the breach has *in fact* not been serious. The court will then agree that the breach shall be treated as a breach of warranty and the contract cannot be repudiated. The parties must go on with it though the person injured by the breach has an action for damages.

There are also what are called *innominate terms*. The effect of these on the contract will depend upon how serious the breach has turned out to be *in fact*. If the breach has turned out to be serious the court will then treat the term as a condition, so that the contract can be repudiated. If *in fact* the breach has not had a serious effect on the contract the court will treat it as a breach of warranty, so that the parties must proceed with the contract, though the injured party will have an action for damages.

Thus if Dodgy Motors advertises a car for sale as having done 32,000 miles this statement is likely to be a warranty giving an action for damages only if in fact the car has done, say, 34,000 miles. If, however, the car had done 60,000 miles the court would be likely to regard the statement as a condition allowing repudiation of the contract.

ESSENTIAL CASE LAW AND COMMENT

The Hansa Nord, 1975 – The innominate term illustrated **(156)**

Implied terms – generally

Before leaving the topic of the contents of the contract it must be appreciated that in addition to the express terms inserted by the parties, the contract may contain and be subject to implied terms. Such terms are derived from custom or statute, and in addition a term may be implied by the court where it is necessary in order to achieve the result which in the court's view the parties obviously intended the contract to have.

CUSTOMARY IMPLIED TERMS

A contract may be regarded as containing customary terms not specifically mentioned by the parties.

ESSENTIAL CASE LAW AND COMMENT

Hutton v *Warren*, 1836 – A contract containing a customary term **(157)**

JUDICIAL IMPLIED TERMS

Implication according to parties' intentions

The court may imply a term into a contract whenever it is necessary to do so in order that the express terms decided upon by the parties shall have the effect which was presumably intended by them. This is often expressed as the giving of 'business efficacy' to the contract, the judge regarding himself as doing merely what the parties themselves would *in fact* have done in order to cover the situation if they had addressed themselves to it.

ESSENTIAL CASE LAW AND COMMENT

The Moorcock, 1889 – When the court implies a term **(158)**

Implication as a matter of law

Sometimes, however, the courts imply a term which is quite complex so that the parties would not, *in fact*, have addressed themselves to it. Here the judge is saying *as a matter of law* how the contract should be performed. This is illustrated by *Liverpool City Council* v *Irwin* [1977] A.C. 239 where the House of Lords held that it was an implied term of a lease of a maisonette in a block of properties owned by the Council that the landlord should take reasonable care to keep the common parts of the block in a reasonable state of repair, although the obligation to do so would *not* have been accepted by the landlord.

When *Irwin*'s case was in the Court of Appeal, Lord Denning, in deciding that there should be an implied term regarding maintenance, rejected the business efficacy test as the only test, saying that the court could imply a term whenever it was *just and reasonable* to do so, whether or not the term was strictly *necessary* to the performance of the contract or not. Although the House of Lords implied a term relating to maintenance, they did not go along with the view of Lord Denning that the test should be reasonableness regardless of necessity. The Court of Appeal returned to the 'necessary' approach in *Mears* v *Safecar Security* [1982] 2 All E.R. 865 and refused to imply a term into a contract of service that payment should be made to an employee during sickness. Stephenson, L.J. was of opinion that the term could not be implied because, although it might be *reasonable* to imply a term relating to sick-pay, it was not *necessary* in a contract of employment. The term relating to maintenance in *Irwin* was in a sense not absolutely vital to performance of the contract in that the tenants could have walked up the stairs, even in the dark, to their flats if lift and light maintenance had not been carried out, but it was much closer to being necessary to performance of the contract than was the sick-pay term in *Mears*.

Implied terms in consumer law – sale of goods

In a contract for the sale of goods or hire-purchase the Sale of Goods Act, 1979 and the Supply of Goods (Implied Terms) Act, 1973, ss. 8–11 (as amended by Sch. 4, Part 1, para. 35 the Consumer Credit Act, 1974, and s. 17 of the Supply of Goods and Services Act, 1982), deal with the matter of implied terms.

A major method by which Parliament has sought to protect the consumer in the area of contract is by passing statutes which imply protective terms into contracts. The main implied terms in contracts of sale of goods are considered below.

Title

The rules governing title are as follows.

IMPLIED CONDITION AS TO TITLE

Section 12(1) provides that, unless the circumstances show a different intention, there is an implied condition on the part of the seller that in the case of a sale he has the right to sell the goods, and that in the case of an agreement to sell, he will have the right to sell the goods at the time when the property is to pass.

ESSENTIAL CASE LAW AND COMMENT

Rowland v *Divall*, 1923 – S. 12 and total failure of consideration
(159)

The decision in *Rowland*, which has been applied in subsequent cases (see *Karflex Ltd* v *Poole* [1933] 2 K.B. 251), produces an unfortunate result in that a person who buys goods to which the seller has no title is allowed to recover the whole of the purchase price even though he has had some use and enjoyment from the goods before he is dispossessed by the true owner. It is thus difficult to suggest that there has been total failure of consideration. The Law Reform Committee (see 1966 Cmnd. 2958, para. 36) has recommended that, subject to further study of the law relating to restitution, an allowance in respect of use and enjoyment should be deducted from the purchase price and the balance returned to the plaintiff. It should be noted that the 1979 Act does not deal with this matter.

Section 12(1) might be construed as meaning that the seller must have the power to give ownership of the goods to the buyer, but if the goods can only be sold by infringing a trade mark, the seller has no right to sell for the purposes of s. 12(1).

ESSENTIAL CASE LAW AND COMMENT

Niblett Ltd v *Confectioners' Materials Co Ltd*, 1921 – A sale which infringed a registered mark **(160)**

IMPLIED WARRANTIES AS TO TITLE

Section 12(2) provides that there is:

> An implied warranty that the goods are free, and will remain free until the time when the property is to pass, from any charge or encumbrance not disclosed or known to the buyer before the contract is made, and that the buyer will enjoy quiet possession of the goods except so far as it may be disturbed by the owner or other person entitled to the benefit of any charge or encumbrance so disclosed or known.

This does not apply where a limited interest is sold, but ss. 12(4) and (5) do and contain similar provisions (see below).

It is not easy to see what rights this sub-section gives over those in s. 12(1). The law does not recognise encumbrances over chattels unless the person trying to enforce them is in possession of the goods or in privity of contract with the person who is in possession (*Dunlop* v *Selfridge* (1915) – see p. 651). Thus if A uses his car as security for a loan from B then –

(*a*) if B takes the car into his possession the charge will be enforceable if necessary by a sale of the vehicle;

(*b*) the charge is equally enforceable against the car while it is still in A's possession, though if A sells it to C then B will be prevented by lack of privity of contract from enforcing any remedies against the vehicle once it is in the possession of C.

Thus if situation (*a*) above applied the sub-section is unnecessary since A could not deliver the vehicle even if he sold it and would therefore be liable in damages for non-delivery to C. If situation (*b*) above applied then the encumbrances would not attach to the vehicle once C had taken possession. C would not, therefore, require a remedy.

However, the usefulness of s.12(2) is illustrated by the decision of the Court of Appeal in *Microbeads AC* v *Vinhurst Road Markings Ltd* [1975] 1 All E.R. 529. In this case A sold road-marking machines to B. After the sale C obtained a patent on the machines so that their continued use by B was in breach of that patent and C was bringing an action against B in respect of this. In a claim by A against B for the purchase price, B wished to include in their defence breach of ss. 12(1) and (2). It was held by the Court of Appeal that they could include breach of s. 12(2) but not breach of s. 12(1). There had been no breach of s. 12(1) at the time of the sale so that A had not infringed that sub-section but since B's quiet possession had been disturbed after sale, A was in breach of s. 12(2).

SALES UNDER A LIMITED TITLE

Under s. 12(3), the sale of a limited interest is now possible. Where the parties intend only to transfer such a title as the seller may have, there is an implied warranty that all charges or encumbrances known to the seller and not known to the buyer have been disclosed to the buyer before the contract is made (s. 12(4)), and an implied warranty that the buyer's quiet possession will not be disturbed (s. 12(5)). There is an action by the buyer for breach of these warranties if, for example, he is dispossessed by the true owner. Furthermore, the seller is not able to contract out of this liability.

Sales under a limited title are common where the sale is of goods taken in execution by the bailiffs to satisfy a judgment debt.

Sales by description

Section 13(1) provides that, where there is a contract for the sale of goods by description, there is an implied condition that the goods shall correspond with the description.

(a) A sale is by description where the purchaser is buying on a mere description having never seen the goods. A classic example occurs in the case of mail-order transactions.

(b) A sale may still be by description even though the goods are seen or examined or even selected from the seller's stock by the purchaser, as in a sale over the counter, because most goods are described if only by the package in which they are contained. Therefore a sale in a self-service store would be covered by s. 13 though no words were spoken by the seller.

ESSENTIAL CASE LAW AND COMMENT

Beale v *Taylor*, 1967 – Application of s. 13 where the goods are seen **(161)**

If s. 13 applies it is enforced strictly, and every statement which forms part of that description is treated as a condition giving the buyer the right to reject the goods, even though the misdescription is of a minor nature. There is no such thing as a 'slight breach' of condition.

Buyers have been allowed to reject goods on seemingly trivial grounds, e.g. misdescriptions of how the goods are packed, and regardless of the fact that no damage has been suffered.

ESSENTIAL CASE LAW AND COMMENT

Moore & Co v *Landauer & Co*, 1921 – Packaging is part of the description **(162)**

However, if the defect is a matter of quality and/or condition of the goods rather than an identifying description, s. 14 (see below) rather than s. 13 applies. Although the Sale of Goods Act applies in the main to sales by dealers, s. 13 applies even where the seller is not a dealer in the goods sold (*Varley* v *Whipp* [1900] 1 Q.B. 513).

There can be no contracting out of s. 13 at all where a business sells to a consumer or the contract is between persons in a private capacity. In a non-consumer sale contracting out is allowed to the extent that it is 'fair or reasonable' (see further p. 298).

Where the sale is by sample as well as by description, s. 13(2) provides that the bulk must correspond with both the sample and the description. Thus in *Nichol* v *Godts* (1854) 10 Ex. 191 a purchaser bought by sample 'foreign refined rape oil'. It was held that the goods must not only correspond with the sample, which they did, but also be in fact 'foreign refined rape oil' and not a mixture of rape and hemp oil which was inferior.

SALE BY DESCRIPTION AND MISREPRESENTATION DISTINGUISHED

It should be noted that the description must be an identifying description to come under s. 13 as in *Beale* v *Taylor* (above). Statements regarding the state of a car's tyres, e.g. 'they were fitted 5000 miles ago', are concerned more with quality and/or condition of the goods and s. 13 probably does not apply, the claim being for misrepresentation. If s. 13 did apply, then every trivial statement about the goods would be a breach of condition and the law relating to misrepresentation would have no place – a rather unlikely situation.

Statements such as the one above do not identify the goods. Suppose I were to say to a student: 'The notes you require are in the boot of my car. Here are the keys. My car is the one which had new tyres fitted 5000 miles ago.' How would the student find the car? Not easily: the statement does not identify the vehicle!

Implied conditions as to fitness

Section 14(3) lays down the following conditions.

Where the seller sells goods in the course of a business and the buyer (or debtor in a credit sale) expressly, or by implication, makes known: (a) to the seller, or (b) to the dealer in a credit sale any particular purpose for which the goods are being bought, there is an implied condition that the goods supplied under the contract are reasonably fit for that purpose whether or not that is a purpose for which such goods are commonly supplied, except where the circumstances show that the buyer (or debtor) does not rely, or that it is unreasonable for him to rely, on the skill or judgment of that seller or dealer.

There is no need for the buyer to specify the particular purpose for which the goods are required when they have in the ordinary way only one purpose, e.g. a hot-water bottle. If ordinary goods in everyday use are required for a particular purpose this must be made known to the seller.

ESSENTIAL CASE LAW AND COMMENT

Priest v *Last*, 1903 – Where the goods have only one purpose **(163)**
Griffiths v *Peter Conway Ltd*, 1939 – Where the goods must cope
  with the plaintiff's abnormalities **(164)**

FITNESS FOR THE PURPOSE: MEANING OF RELIANCE

Reliance on the seller's skill and judgment will be readily implied even to the extent of saying that, at least in sales to the general public as consumers, the buyer has gone to the seller because he relies on the seller having selected his stock with skill and judgment. The buyer must show that he has made known the purpose for which the goods are being bought. Reliance will then be presumed, unless it can be disproved, or if the seller can show that reliance was unreasonable.

The court has to decide what amounts to 'unreasonable reliance'. However, presumably the seller can disclaim responsibility. For example, suppose B goes into S's general stores and sees some tubes of glue. If he then asks whether the glue will stick metal to plastic and S says: 'I am not expert enough to say', then if B buys the glue and it does not stick metal to plastic it would surely be unreasonable for B to suggest that he relied on S's skill and judgment.

There will in general be no implication of reliance where the buyer knows that the seller deals in only one brand of goods, e.g. where a public house sells only one brand of beer.

ESSENTIAL CASE LAW AND COMMENT

Grant v *Australian Knitting Mills Ltd*, 1936 – Reliance on seller's
  skill and judgment readily implied **(165)**
Wren v *Holt*, 1903 – Position where seller obliged to sell only one
  product **(166)**

FITNESS: APPLICATION TO NON-MANUFACTURED GOODS

The rules relating to fitness for the purpose under s. 14(3) apply also to non-manufactured goods. Thus in *Frost* v *Aylesbury Dairy Co Ltd* [1905] 1 K.B. 608 the defendants who were retailers of milk were held liable under s. 14(3) when they sold milk containing germs which caused the plaintiff's wife to die of typhoid fever.

FITNESS: SECOND-HAND GOODS

In deciding the matter of fitness for the purpose in the case of second-hand goods the buyer must expect that defects are likely to emerge sooner or later. However, if defects occur fairly quickly after sale this is strong evidence that the goods were not reasonably fit at the time of sale.

ESSENTIAL CASE LAW AND COMMENT

Crowther v *Shannon Motor Company*, 1975 – Fitness and second-hand goods **(167)**

FITNESS AND MERCHANTABLE QUALITY DISTINGUISHED

Before proceeding to consider merchantable quality, we must distinguish the two heads of liability, i.e. fitness and merchantable quality. Under s. 14(2) an article is regarded as not merchantable because of a manufacturing defect so that a perfect article would have served the purpose, or in other words it is the right article but it is faulty. Under s. 14(3) an article is regarded as not fit for the purpose because of its design or construction. It may be perfect in terms of its manufacture but its construction or design does not allow it to fit the purpose and consequently no amount of adjustment or repair will ever make it right. In other words, it is a perfect article but the wrong article for the purpose.

ESSENTIAL CASE LAW AND COMMENT

Baldry v *Marshall*, 1924 – Where goods not fit but merchantable **(168)**

Merchantable quality

By s. 14(2) *where the seller sells goods in the course of a business* there is an implied condition that the goods supplied under the contract are of merchantable quality, except that there is no such condition:

(*a*) as regards defects specifically drawn to the buyer's attention before the contract is made; or

(*b*) if the buyer examines the goods before the contract is made, as regards defects which that examination ought to reveal.

If the seller does not normally deal in goods of the type in question, there is no condition as to fitness (nor as to merchantability unless the sale is by sample which is dealt with below). The *only* condition in such a case is that the goods correspond with the description. This arises because s. 14(1) provides that except as provided by s. 14 and s. 15 (sale by sample), and subject to any other enactment, there is no implied condition or warranty about the quality or fitness for any particular purpose of goods supplied under a contract of sale. If, therefore, S (who is not a dealer) sells a car to B with no express terms as to quality and fitness, the court is prevented by s. 14 from implying conditions or warranties, even though S seems, from the circumstances, to have been warranting the car in good order.

The s. 14 provision regarding merchantable quality applies where the sale is by a dealer who does not ordinarily sell goods of precisely the same description. Thus if B ordered an 'X' brand motor bike from S who has not formerly sold that make, s. 14 applies if the motor bike is unfit or unmerchantable.

There is no need under s. 14(2) for the buyer to show that he relied on the seller's skill and judgment, and the seller is liable for latent defects even though he is not the manufacturer and is merely marketing the goods as a wholesaler or retailer. Such a seller can, however, obtain an indemnity from the manufacturer if the buyer successfully sues him for defects in the goods.

SALES THROUGH AN AGENT

Section 14(5) is concerned with the problem of a private seller who sells through an agent. The sub-section provides that the implied conditions of fitness and merchantability operate if the agent is selling in the ordinary course of business unless the principal is not acting in the course of business and the buyer is aware of this, or reasonable steps have been taken to bring it to his notice. Thus, for example, an auctioneer acting for a private seller could exclude these sections by making it clear that the principal was a private seller.

EXAMINATION OF THE GOODS

The buyer is not obliged to examine the goods but if he does do so he will lose the protection of s. 14(2) if he fails to notice obvious defects, at least in respect of such defects as where a new washing machine is examined and the buyer misses a rather obvious scratch on the front of the machine. The buyer can also lose his right to complain where the seller actually points out the defects.

THE PRICE PAID

The interpretation of the word 'merchantable' has often been discussed in the courts. Section 14(6) provides: goods of any kind are of merchantable quality within the meaning of this Act if they are as fit for the purpose or purposes for which goods of that kind are commonly bought as it is reasonable to expect having regard to any description applied to them, the price (if relevant) and all the other relevant circumstances.

The price paid by the buyer is therefore a factor to be taken into account. Goods (provided they are not defective) are not unmerchantable simply because their resale price is slightly less than that which the buyer paid, though they may be if the difference in purchase and resale price is substantial.

ESSENTIAL CASE LAW AND COMMENT

B. S. Brown & Son Ltd v *Craiks Ltd*, 1970 – Merchantability and the resale price **(169)**

HOW WERE THE GOODS DESCRIBED?

As regards the description applied to the goods, old cars or other mechanical items which are sold and described as scrap need not be merchantable. Furthermore, 'shop-soiled', 'fire-damaged', 'flood-salvage' and so on might imply non-merchantable lines. In addition, old items, such as antiques and curios would not presumably be required to be in perfect working order. However, as we have seen it was held in *Cavendish-Woodhouse* v *Manley* (1984) 82 L.G.R. 376 that the phrase on an invoice 'bought as seen' merely confirms that the purchaser has seen the goods. It does not exclude any implied terms as to quality or fitness.

DURATION OF MERCHANTABLE QUALITY

As regards the time during which the goods must be merchantable, the law is not clear. So far as perishable goods are concerned, the decision in *Mash and Murrell* v *Joseph I. Emmanuel* [1961] 1 All E.R. 485 is relevant. In that case potatoes, though sound when loaded in Cyprus, were rotten by the time the ship arrived in Liverpool, though there was no undue delay. It was held by Diplock, J. that the sellers were liable under s. 14(2) because the goods should have been loaded in such a state that they could survive the normal journey and be in merchantable condition when they arrived. In addition, the seller is liable for defects inherent in the goods when they are sold and will not escape merely because the defects do not become apparent until a later time. Circumstances such as those seen in *Crowther* v *Shannon Motor Co* (1975) (at p. 669) provide an illustration of this situation.

GOODS PARTIALLY DEFECTIVE

Where part only of the goods are unmerchantable it seems to depend on how much of the consignment is defective. In *Jackson* v *Rotax Motor and Cycle Co Ltd* [1910] 2 K.B. 937 the plaintiffs supplied motor horns to the defendants and one consignment was rejected by the defendants who alleged they were unmerchantable. Half the goods were dented and scratched because of bad packing and the Court of Appeal held that the buyers were entitled to reject the consignment.

MERCHANTABLE QUALITY: AN UNSATISFACTORY TEST

The test of merchantable quality in s. 14(6) is now regarded as somewhat unsatisfactory. A buyer of goods has no rights at all where there are a number of minor defects such as small scratches and dents in a new car. The car is not necessarily unmerchantable because of these defects, nor is it unfit for the purpose. The Law Commission in Working Paper 85 suggest a new test as follows: 'The goods should be of such quality as would in all the circumstances of the case be fully acceptable to a reasonable buyer who had full knowledge of their condition, quality and characteristics.'

However, recent cases show a more helpful interpretation even of existing law by the judiciary. In *Shine* v *General Guarantee Corporation* [1988] 1 All E.R. 911 the Court of Appeal held that a second-hand car was not of merchantable quality where the manufacturers' rust warranty had been terminated because, unknown to the buyer, the car had been involved in an accident and had been submerged in water. The plaintiff brought his action on learning this, though he had only minor problems with the car. Bush, J. said: 'Irrespective of its condition, it was a car which no member of the public knowing the facts would touch with a barge pole unless they could get it at a substantially reduced price to reflect the risk they were taking.' He went on to add that a car was not just a form of transport it was also an investment and those who bought cars must have in mind their eventual saleability and in the case of Mr Shine, and no doubt others, pride in what was a specialist car (a Fiat X19 Bertoni-bodied sports car) for the enthusiast.

Again, in *Rogers* v *Parish (Scarborough) Ltd* [1987] 2 All E.R. 232 the Court of Appeal decided that a new Range Rover was not of merchantable quality or fit fo the purpose although it was capable of being driven and the defects repaired. Mustill, L.J. made clear that it was not enough to consider whether a car was roadworthy and driveable. There were other relevant factors. These were: 'The appropriate degree of comfort, ease of handling and reliability and, one may add, a pride in the vehicle's outward and interior appearance . . . The buyer was entitled to value for his money.' These cases do begin to extend the concept of merchantability more into line with what most consumers would think it should be.

Fitness and merchantability

PRIVATE SALES

The rules as to fitness for purpose and merchantable quality do not apply to private sales of second-hand goods and there is still a fairly wide application of the maxim *caveat emptor* (let the buyer beware). In practice only manufacturers, wholesalers, retailers and dealers in new or second-hand goods will be caught by the implied conditions. The courts cannot imply conditions and warranties into private contracts similar to those implied by the Act into sales by dealers, because, as we have seen, s. 14(1) forbids it.

EXTENSION TO ITEMS SUPPLIED WITH GOODS

The implied terms relating to fitness and merchantable quality extend also to other items supplied under the contract of sale of goods, e.g. containers, foreign matter and instructions for use.

ESSENTIAL CASE LAW AND COMMENT

Geddling v *Marsh*, 1920 – Fitness and merchantability: returnable bottles **(170)**

Wilson v *Rickett, Cockerell & Co Ltd*, 1954 – Where foreign matter is supplied with the goods **(171)**

Wormell v *R.H.M. Agriculture (East) Ltd*, 1986 – Application to instructions for use **(172)**

INJURY TO THIRD PARTY, PURCHASER'S INDEMNITY

It should be noted that if a retailer sells goods which are faulty and in breach of s. 14 he is obliged to indemnify the purchaser if the faulty goods injure a third party to whom the purchaser is found liable. However, no such indemnity is payable if the purchaser has continued to use the goods having become aware that they are faulty and dangerous.

ESSENTIAL CASE LAW AND COMMENT

Lambert v *Lewis*, 1981 – Where goods are used by the buyer after knowledge of defects **(173)**

USAGE OF TRADE

Section 14(4) provides that an implied warranty or condition as to quality or fitness for a particular purpose may be attached to a contract of sale by usage. Where the transaction is connected with a particular trade, the customs and usages of that trade give the context in which the parties made their contract and may give a guide as to their intentions. Thus in a sale of canary seed in accordance with the customs of the trade it was held that the buyer could not reject the seed delivered on the grounds that there were impurities in it. A custom of the trade prevented this but allowed instead a rebate on the price paid (*Peter Darlington Partners Ltd* v *Gosho Co Ltd* [1964] 1 Lloyds Rep. 149).

Sale by sample

Section 15(1) states that a contract of sale is a contract of sale by sample where there is a term in the contract, express or implied, to that effect. The mere fact that the seller provides a sample for the buyer's inspection is not enough: to be such a sale either there must be an express provision in the contract to that effect, or there must be evidence that the parties intended the sale to be by sample.

There are three implied conditions in sale by sample.

(*a*) *The bulk must correspond with the sample in quality* (s. 15(2)(a)).

(*b*) *The buyer shall have a reasonable opportunity of comparing the bulk with the sample* (s. 15(2)(b)). The buyer will not be deemed to have accepted the goods until he has had an opportunity to compare the bulk with the sample, and will be able, therefore, to reject the goods, even though they have been delivered, if the bulk does not correspond with the sample. He is not left with the remedy of damages for the breach of warranty.

(*c*) *The goods shall be free from any defect, rendering them unmerchantable, which would not be apparent on reasonable examination of the sample* (s. 15(2)(c)).

The effect of s. 15(2)(c) is to exclude the implied condition of merchantability if the defect could have been discovered by reasonable examination of the sample whether or not there has in fact been any examination of the sample. This is presumably based upon the premise that the seller is entitled to assume that the buyer will examine the sample. The provision is in contrast with s. 14(2) where the implied condition of merchantability is not excluded unless an examination has actually taken place (see p. 276).

A reasonable examination for the purpose of a sale by sample is such an examination as is usually carried out in the trade concerned.

ESSENTIAL CASE LAW AND COMMENT

Godley v *Perry*, 1960 – When a sale is by sample **(174)**

Implied terms in consumer law – the supply of goods and services

Having looked at the implied terms in a contract of sale of goods we can now move on to consider the law relating to contracts for work and material, e.g. car repairs where goods and services are supplied *together* and the goods are used or supplied in such a process as distinct from being *sold on their own* (which would be a sale of goods), and for the supply of services and the implied terms therein.

Supply of goods other than by sale

As regards the rights of those who purchase goods, we have seen that the Sale of Goods Act, 1979 applies and that ss. 12–15 of that Act imply terms to which a buyer may resort if the goods are faulty, defective or unsuitable. Those who take goods on hire-purchase are similarly protected by ss. 8–11 of the Supply of Goods (Implied Terms) Act, 1973.

As regards contracts for work and materials, the supply of goods (or the materials used) is governed by Part I of the Supply of Goods and Services Act, 1982. The services supplied (or the work element) are governed by Part II of the 1982 Act.

Contracts of exchange or barter, hire, rental or leasing are governed by Part I of the 1982 Act, while contracts for services only, e.g. a contract to carry goods or advice from an accountant or solicitor, are governed by Part II of the 1982 Act. The relevant provisions of the Act are dealt with in detail below. Section references are to the 1982 Act unless otherwise indicated.

Contracts for the transfer of property in goods

The contracts concerned are dealt with in s. 1(1) which provides that a contract for the transfer of goods means a contract under which one person transfers, or agrees to transfer to another, the property in goods, unless the transfer takes place under an excluded contract. These excluded contracts are set out in s. 1(2). They are contracts for the sale of goods, hire-purchase contracts, and those where the property in goods is transferred on a redemption of trading stamps. (These are governed by the Trading Stamps Act, 1964.) Transfer of property rights in goods by way of mortgage, pledge, charge or other security are excluded, as are gifts.

There must be a contract between the parties. If not, the statutory implied terms cannot be relied upon if the goods supplied prove to be defective. Thus a chemist supplying harmful drugs under a National Health Service prescription will not come within the Act. This is because the patient does not provide consideration. The chemist collects the prescription charge for the government and not for himself. The payment to the chemist does not come from the patient unless it is a private prescription where the patient has paid the full amount. Otherwise an action against the chemist would have to be framed in the tort of negligence.

As regards promotional free gifts, e.g. the giving away of a radio to a purchaser of a television set, the free gift may not be within the 1982 Act. The matter is not free from doubt, but s. 1(2)(d) excludes contracts for the supply of goods which are enforceable only because they are made by deed which would seem to exclude other gifts. Furthermore, the Law Commission Report (No. 95 published in 1979) on which the Act is based concludes that gifts are outside the scope of the Act.

Contracts for work and materials

It is impossible to provide a complete list of contracts for work and materials but they fall under three broad heads as follows.

(a) *Maintenance contracts.* Here the organisation doing the maintenance supplies the labour and spare parts as required. An example would be a maintenance contract for lifts.

(b) *Building and construction contracts.* Here the builder supplies labour and materials. An example would be the alteration of an office or workshop involving the insertion of new windows and extending the central heating system.

(c) *Installation and improvement contracts.* Here the contractor does not have to build or construct anything but, for example, fits equipment into an existing building or applies paint to it. Examples are the fitting of an air-conditioning system, or painting and decorating an office or workshop.

The terms implied

TITLE

Section 2 implies terms about title. Under s. 2(1) there is an implied condition that the supplier has a right to transfer the property in the goods to the customer. Under s. 2(2) two warranties are implied:

(a) that the goods are free from any charge or encumbrance which has not been disclosed to the customer; and

(b) that the customer will enjoy quiet possession except when disturbed by the owner or other person whose charge or encumbrance has been disclosed.

The customer would have an action here if he suffered loss as a result of the true owner reclaiming or suing in conversion where the materials fitted had been stolen. Sections 2(3), (4) and (5) are concerned with sales under a limited title. If under the contract the supplier is to give only such title as he may possess, s. 2(1) does not apply but warranties are implied that the supplier will disclose all charges and encumbrances which he knows about and that the customer's quiet possession of the goods will not be disturbed by, for example, the supplier or the holder of an undisclosed charge or encumbrance.

Cases involving bad title have occurred not infrequently in the sale of goods but the problem seems to have arisen only rarely in contracts for work and materials.

DESCRIPTION

Under s. 3 there is an implied condition that where a seller transfers property in goods by description, the goods will correspond with the description. If the goods are supplied by reference to a sample as well as a description they must correspond with the sample as well as the description. Section 3 applies even where the customer selects the goods.

Section 3 will operate, for example, where a person is having his house or business premises extended and agrees with the contractor a detailed specification which describes the materials to be installed. It will not operate in some types of maintenance contract where the materials to be replaced are unknown until the maintenance is carried out. The materials fitted in the course of such a contract will not be described *before* the contract is made but probably only in an invoice *after* it has been made, which is too late to apply s. 3. It should be noted that ss. 2 and 3 apply to supplies in the course of a business *and* to a supply by a person other than in the course of a business, e.g. a milkman 'moonlighting' by doing the odd decorating job, provided there is a contract. They would not apply to a mere friendly transaction without consideration.

QUALITY AND FITNESS

The first implied term in this area is in s. 4 and it relates to *merchantable quality* (s. 4(2)). Merchantability is defined in s. 4(9) which states that the goods must be as fit for the purpose for which they are commonly supplied as it is reasonable to expect, having regard to their description, price and other relevant circumstances. This condition of merchantable quality does not apply to defects:

(*a*) drawn to the customer's attention before the contract is made; or
(*b*) which any prior examination the customer *has actually made* ought to have revealed.

Thus if the materials used are dangerous, unsafe, defective or faulty, and will not work properly under normal conditions, the supplier is in breach of s. 4(2).

However, if the materials are described as 'seconds' or 'fire-damaged' the customer cannot complain if the materials are of lower quality than goods not so described.

As regards defects which ought to have been revealed where the customer has examined the goods, it is not likely that materials used in a contract for work and materials will be identified before the contract or that the customer will examine them. If they are examined the customer should ensure that it is done properly so that obvious defects are seen and the goods rejected.

The second implied term in s. 4 relates to *fitness for the purpose* (s. 4(5)). Where a customer makes known, either expressly or by implication, to the supplier any particular purpose for which the goods are being acquired, there is an implied condition that the goods are reasonably fit for the purpose. This condition does not apply where the customer does not rely on, or it is not reasonable for him to rely on, the skill or judgment of the supplier.

If, for example, a factory process requires a lot of water supplied under high pressure, e.g. to clean special equipment, and the factory owners ask for the installation of a system of pressure hoses and a pump, revealing to the contractor precisely what the requirements are, then the contractor will be in breach of s. 4(5) if the pressure is inadequate. This will be so even though the pressure hoses and pump are perfectly merchantable and would have been quite adequate for use in a different type of installation.

Of course, the way out of the fitness problem for the supplier is for him to make it clear to the customer that he has no idea whether the equipment will be suitable for the customer's special requirements. In such a case he will not be liable, though he may put some customers off by his unhelpful attitude.

SAMPLE

If under the contract there is a transfer of the property in goods by reference to a sample, then under s. 5 there is an implied condition that:

(*a*) the bulk will correspond with the sample in quality;

(*b*) the customer will have a reasonable opportunity of comparing the bulk with the sample; and

(*c*) there will not be any defect making the goods unmerchantable which would not have been apparent on a reasonable examination of the sample.

Except as provided by ss. 4 and 5, no conditions or warranties as to quality or fitness are to be implied into contracts for the transfer of goods. Sections 4 and 5 apply only to a supply of goods in the course of a business, and not to a supply by those such as the moonlighting decorator.

Remedies

In so far as the implied terms are conditions and are broken by the supplier, then the customer can treat the contract as repudiated. The customer is discharged from his obligation to pay the agreed price and may recover damages. The breach of implied warranties gives the customer only the right to sue for damages.

Exchange and barter

The most likely transactions to emerge here are the exchange of goods for vouchers and coupons as part of promotional schemes. Part I of the 1982 Act applies and the retailer who supplies the goods under a contract to the customer is the one who is liable if they are in breach of, for example, the implied terms of fitness and/or merchantable quality. The manufacturer will be liable to the retailer, of course.

An exchange transaction in which goods are simply exchanged is not a sale but is covered by the 1982 Act. Where part of the consideration is money, as in a part-exchange of an old car for a new one with a cash difference, the contract is presumably a sale of goods because money is at least part of the consideration. It does not really matter now whether it is a sale or a supply, because the implied terms are almost identical.

Often where there has been a sale of faulty goods the seller exchanges them for other goods of the same type, although he is under no legal duty to do so unless a particular contract expressly provides. What happens if the other goods are faulty? The substitute goods must comply with the implied terms as to title, description, quality and fitness, and there is no longer any point in going into legal niceties as to whether the exchange is a sale or supply.

THE TERMS IMPLIED

The implied terms in exchange or barter are the same as those implied in a contract for work and materials, i.e. s. 2 (title), s. 3 (description), s. 4(2) (merchantable quality), s. 4(5) (fitness) and s. 5 (sample).

Contracts for the hire of goods

The main areas of hiring (or renting or leasing) are as follows:

(a) *office equipment*, e.g. office furniture and a variety of machines, including telephones;
(b) *building and construction plant and equipment*, e.g. cranes and JCBs;
(c) *consumer hiring*, e.g. cars, televisions and videos.

Under s. 6(1) a contract for the hire of goods means a contract under which one person bails, or agrees to bail, goods to another by way of hire. There must be a contract, so that when the next-door neighbour makes a free loan of his lawnmower the Act does not apply. Also excluded are hire-purchase agreements. A contract is a contract of hire whether or not services are also provided. This would be the case where a supplier rented a television to a customer and also undertook to service it.

The terms implied

TITLE

Section 7 deals with title. It reflects s. 2 except that being a contract of hire it makes provision only for the transfer of possession and not for the transfer of ownership. There is an *implied condition* on the part of the supplier that he has the right to transfer possession of the goods to the customer by hiring for the appropriate period. There is also a *warranty* that the customer will enjoy quiet possession of the goods except where it is disturbed by the owner or other person entitled to the benefit of any charge or encumbrance disclosed to the customer before the contract was made.

If, for example, the undisclosed true owner retakes possession so that the supplier is in breach of s. 7, then the customer will have an action for damages. These will reflect the value he had had under the contract before the goods were taken from him. Thus if C pays S £120 for the year's rent of a television but the undisclosed true owner takes it back after, say, two months, the damages would, on the face of it, be £100.

Neither of the terms in s. 7 prevents the supplier from taking the goods back himself provided the contract allows this, as where it provides *expressly* for the repossession of the goods on failure to pay the rental or the court is prepared to *imply* that it does.

DESCRIPTION

Section 8 is the equivalent of s. 3. Where the supplier hires or agrees to hire the goods by description there is an implied condition that the goods will correspond with the description. If the goods are hired by reference to a sample as well as by description, they must correspond with the description as well as the sample. Section 8 applies even where the customer selects the goods. If the goods do not match the description the customer will be able to reject them and recover damages for any loss.

QUALITY AND FITNESS

Section 9 enacts the same provisions for hiring contracts as s. 4 does for contracts of work and materials and exchange and barter. Except as provided by ss. 9 and 10 (hire by sample), there are no implied terms regarding quality or fitness for any purpose of goods hired.

There are two terms in s. 9 as follows.

(a) *An implied condition that the goods hired are of merchantable quality.* There is no such condition where a particular defect has been drawn to the customer's attention before the contract was made or to defects which he should have noticed *if he actually examined* the goods.

(b) *An implied condition that the goods hired are reasonably fit for any purpose to which the customer is going to put them.* The purpose must have been made known to the supplier, expressly or by implication. The condition does not apply if the customer does not rely on the skill of the seller or if it is unreasonable for him to have done so.

Once again, where goods are to be hired for a special purpose, the supplier should make it clear that the customer must not rely on him if he wishes to avoid the implied condition of fitness. This has rather special application to those who supply DIY equipment on hire. A supplier in this area should certainly not overestimate the capacity of, for example, power tools, in order to get business. If he does he certainly faces s. 9 liability.

Where the goods are leased by a finance house, it is responsible for breach of the implied terms in the hiring contract. It is in effect the supplier. This is also true of hire-purchase where the implied terms of the Supply of Goods (Implied Terms) Act, 1973 apply against the finance company.

As regards fitness for the purpose, it is enough to involve the finance company in liability if the customer has told the distributor of the purpose. Generally, of course, the finance house will have an indemnity against the distributor under which it may recover any damages it has to pay, so it will all get back to the distributor in the end.

The above conditions relate to the state of the goods at the beginning of the hiring and for a reasonable time thereafter. It does not impose upon the supplier a duty to maintain and repair. This must be provided for separately in the contract.

Thus in *UCB Leasing Ltd* v *Holtom* (1987) 137 N.L.J. 614 the Court of Appeal decided that where a car was the subject of a long leasing agreement, the owner was not under an obligation to provide a vehicle which was fit for the purpose during the whole period of the leasing. Instead, rather like a sale of goods, the obligation is to provide a vehicle which is fit at the outset of the agreement. If it is not, the hirer must rescind quickly if he wishes to return the car. If he does not do so he cannot return the vehicle but is entitled to damages only.

SAMPLE

Section 10 applies and is in line with s. 5 (above). Section 10 states that in a hiring by sample there is an implied condition that the bulk will correspond with the sample in quality; that the customer will have a reasonable opportunity to compare the bulk with the sample; and that there will be no defects in the goods supplied rendering them unmerchantable which would not have been apparent on a reasonable examination of the sample.

As with ss. 4 and 5 (above) the terms of ss. 9 and 10 are implied only into contracts for hiring entered into in the course of a business. Thus if there is a hiring for value with a private owner, or a mere friendly lending without consideration, s. 9 of the Act would not apply. Incorrect and express statements by a private owner would be actionable in the comon law of contract provided that there was consideration. In a friendly lending there could be an action for negligent misstatements made by the owner about the goods if they cause damage (see *Hedley Byrne* v *Heller & Partners* (1963), p. 652).

Exclusion clauses

Section 11 of the 1982 Act applies the provisions of the Unfair Contract Terms Act, 1977 to exclusion clauses in work and materials barter and exchange, and hiring contracts. The effect of this is set out below.

(a) *Consumer transactions.* In a contract covered by Part I of the Act, the rights given by the implied terms under ss. 3–5 and ss. 8–10 of the 1982 Act cannot be excluded or restricted. The circumstances in which a person deals as a consumer are described at p. 295.

(b) *Business contracts.* In these circumstances the supplier can only rely on an exclusion clause if it is reasonable. However, the obligations relating to title in s. 2 of the 1982 Act cannot be excluded in a business dealing relating to work and materials and barter and exchange any more than they can in a consumer dealing (see s. 7, Unfair Contract Terms Act, 1977, as amended by s. 17(2) of the 1982 Act).

However, the term in s. 7 relating to the right of possession in the case of a hiring can be excluded in a consumer or business contract if reasonable.

The supply of services

The main areas of complaint in regard to services have been the *poor quality of service*, e.g. the careless servicing of cars; *slowness in completing work*, where complaints have ranged over a wide area from, for example, building contractors to solicitors; *the cost of the work*, i.e. overcharging. Part II of the Act is concerned to deal with these matters.

THE CONTRACTS COVERED

Under s. 12(1) a contract for the supply of a service means a contract under which a person agrees to carry out a service. A contract of service (i.e. an employment contract) or apprenticeship is not included, but apart from this no attempt is made to define the word 'service'. However, the services provided by the professions, e.g. accountants, architects, solicitors, and surveyors, are included.

Section 12(4) gives the Secretary of State for Trade and Industry power to exempt certain services from the provisions of Part II. Of importance here is the Supply of Services (Exclusion of Implied Terms) Order, 1982 (SI 1982/1771) which retains the common-law liability in negligence of lawyers by exempting barristers and solicitors when acting as advocates before various courts and tribunals. It also exempts services rendered by a director to his company, thus retaining existing common-law liability in this area too. This is largely because more time is needed to consult the relevant interests and decide what sort of liability there should be in the areas referred to.

Part II applies *only to contracts*. If there is no contract there cannot be implied terms. This will exclude work done free as a friendly gesture by a friend or neighbour. If, however, injury is caused to a person who is not in a contractual relationship with a supplier as a result of the negligence of the supplier, there may be an action in the tort of negligence at common law (see p. 434).

DUTY OF CARE AND SKILL

This duty applies to contracts which are purely for service, e.g. advice from an accountant or solicitor, and also to the service element of a contract for work and materials. Section 13 provides that where the supplier of a service is acting in the course of a business there is an implied term that the supplier will carry out that service with reasonable skill and care. This means that the service must be performed with the care and skill of a reasonably competent member of the supplier's trade or profession. In other words, the test is objective, not subjective. Thus an incompetent supplier may be liable even though he has done his best. A private supplier of a service, e.g. a moonlighter, will not have this duty.

There is no reference to conditions and warranties in regard to this implied term. Generally, therefore, the action for breach of the term will be damages. In a serious case repudiation of the contract may be possible. This is rather like the intermediate term concept discussed at p. 268.

Cases such as *Woodman* v *Photo Trade Processing Ltd* and *Waldron-Kelly* v *British Railways Board*, which were brought on the basis of the common-law tort of negligence, would now be brought under the 1982 Act (see further p. 300).

TIME FOR PERFORMANCE

Section 14 provides that a supplier who acts in the course of a business will carry out the service within a reasonable time. This term is only implied where the time for performance is not fixed by the contract, but left to be fixed in a manner agreed by the contract, or determined by the dealings of the parties. Section 14 states that what is a reasonable time is a question of fact. A plaintiff can claim damages for unreasonable delay. Of course, if a time for performance is fixed by the contract, it must be performed at that time and the question of reasonableness does not arise. Time is of the essence in commercial contracts unless the parties expressly provide otherwise or there is a waiver (see further p. 325).

THE CHARGES MADE FOR THE SERVICE

Under s. 15 the customer's obligation is to pay 'a reasonable charge' which is again a matter of fact. This matter is not implied where the charge for the service is determined by the contract, left to be determined in a manner agreed by the contract, or determined by the dealings of the parties. The section in essence enacts the common-law rule of *quantum meruit* (see p. 339); it protects both the supplier and the customer, and applies to a supply in the course of a business and to a supply by a moonlighter.

Exclusion clauses

Section 16 of the 1982 Act applies the provisions of the Unfair Contract Terms Act, 1977 to exclusion clauses in regard to services. Section 2 of the 1977 Act is concerned with liability for negligence. There can be no exclusion of liability if death or personal injury is caused. In other cases an exclusion clause may apply if reasonable.

Section 3 of the 1977 Act is concerned with liability for breach of contract. Broadly speaking, there can be no exclusion of liability for breach of contract, or a different performance or non-performance, unless reasonable (see further p. 298). The terms implied by the 1982 Act cannot be excluded in a consumer transaction. They can in a non-consumer deal if reasonable. The criteria relating to bargaining power and so on apply only to the exclusion of implied terms in a non-consumer transaction relating to goods, but they will no doubt be applied by analogy to contracts under the 1982 Act.

15
Law of contract – exclusion clauses

In this chapter we shall look at the rules which decide whether an exclusion clause which purports to exclude liability for breach of contract and other civil damage is valid.

Exclusion clauses – the issue of communication

A contract may contain express terms under which one or both of the parties excludes or limits liability for breach of contract or negligence. Although such express terms are permissible, both the courts and Parliament have been reluctant to allow exclusion clauses to operate successfully where they have been imposed on a weaker party, such as an ordinary consumer, by a stronger party, such as a person or corporation in business to supply goods or services.

The judges have protected consumers of goods and services against the effect of exclusion clauses in two main ways, i.e. by deciding that the exclusion clause never became part of the contract, and by construing (or interpreting) the contract in such a way as to prevent the application of the clause.

WAS THE CLAUSE PART OF THE CONTRACT?

The court will require the person wishing to rely on an exclusion clause to show that the other party agreed to it at or before the time when the contract was made, otherwise it will not form part of the agreement. In this connection:

(a) *Where a contract is made by signing a written document* the signer will in general be bound by everything which the document contains, even if he has not read it, unless the signature was induced by misrepresentation as to the effect of the document. An exception is the rule of *non est factum* provided the signer is not negligent.

ESSENTIAL CASE LAW AND COMMENT

L'Estrange v *Graucob (F)*, 1934 – Where the document containing the clause is signed **(175)**

Curtis v *Chemical Cleaning and Dyeing Co*, 1951 – Where the plaintiff was misled as to the extent of the clause **(176)**

(*b*) *Where the terms are contained in an unsigned document*, the person seeking to rely on an exclusion clause must show that the document was an integral part of the contract which could be expected to contain terms. However, if the document is contractual in the sense outlined above the clause will apply even though the plaintiff did not actually know about the exclusion clause in the sense that he had not read it. Communication may be constructive so long as the document adequately draws the attention of a reasonable person to the existence of terms and conditions.

ESSENTIAL CASE LAW AND COMMENT

Thompson v *L.M.S. Railway*, 1930 – A constructive communication **(177)**

Chapelton v *Barry U.D.C.*, 1940 – Where the document is not contractual **(178)**

This rule of constructive communication will not necessarily be applied if the term in the contract is particularly burdensome for the other party. In such a case the law may require that the burdensome clause is actually brought to the attention of the other party. This results from the decision of the Court of Appeal in *Interfoto Picture Library Ltd* v *Stiletto Visual Programmes Ltd* [1988] 1 All E.R. 348. In that case Interfoto sent some transparencies to Stiletto for them to make a selection. The delivery note, which is a contractual document, contained a clause that if the transparencies were not returned within 14 days Stiletto would pay £5 per day for each transparency retained after that. Stiletto delayed returning the transparencies for some three weeks and ran up a bill of some £3783. When they were sued for this sum the court said that it could not be recovered by Interfoto because the clause was not specifically drawn to the attention of Stiletto. The court awarded damages of £3.50 per transparency per week but would not apply the clause.

(*c*) *As regards previous dealings*, where the defendant has not actually given the plaintiff a copy of conditions or drawn his attention to them when making a particular contract, the doctrine of constructive notice will not apply, at least in consumer transactions, in order to enable the defendant to rely on previous communications in previous dealings, unless, perhaps, the dealings have been frequent. Thus in *Hollier* v *Rambler Motors* [1972] 1 All E.R. 399 it appeared that the plaintiff had had his car repaired five times in five years (i.e. infrequently) by the defendants and had signed a form containing a clause stating 'the company is not responsible for damage caused by fire to customers' cars on the premises'. On the occasion in question the plaintiff was not required to sign a form when leaving his car for repair. In the event the car was damaged by fire caused by the defendants' negligence. In an action by the plaintiff the defendants pleaded the cause. It was held by the Court of Appeal that the plaintiff succeeded and that the clause did not apply. Previous dealings were not incorporated and in any case as a matter of construction the wording was not sufficiently plain to exclude negligence.

However, where the parties are, for example, large corporations, terms used in previous dealings between the parties themselves *or in the trade generally* may be incorporated.

Thus in *British Crane Hire Corporation Ltd* v *Ipswich Plant Hire Ltd* [1974] 1 All E.R. 1059 the defendants hired a crane from the plaintiffs who were the owners. The agreement was an oral one, though after the contract was made the defendants received a printed form from the plaintiffs containing conditions. One of these was that the hirer of the crane was liable to indemnify the owner against all expenses in connection with its use. Before the defendants signed the form the crane sank into marshy ground, though this was not the fault of the defendants. The plaintiffs were put to some cost in repairing the crane and now sued the defendants for an indemnity under the contract. The defendants argued that the indemnity had not been incorporated into the oral contract of hire. It was held that the bargaining power of the defendants was equal to that of the plaintiffs and the defendants knew that printed conditions in similar terms to those of the plaintiffs were *in common use in the business*. The conditions had therefore been incorporated into the oral contract on the basis of the common understanding of the parties and the plaintiffs' claim for an indemnity succeeded.

(*d*) *Any attempt to introduce an exclusion clause after the contract has been made is ineffective* because the consideration for the clause is then past.

(*e*) *An exclusion clause may be made ineffective by an inconsistent oral promise.*

ESSENTIAL CASE LAW AND COMMENT

Olley v *Marlborough Court Ltd*, 1949 – Belated notice of an exclusion clause **(179)**

J. Evans & Son (Portsmouth) Ltd v *Andrea Merzario Ltd*, 1976 – An inconsistent promise **(180)**

(*f*) *The rule of privity of contract may also prevent the application of an exclusion clause.* Thus, if A, the owner of a road haulage company, excludes his own and his employees' liability for damage to the goods of his business customers by a properly communicated clause, an employee who causes damage to the goods will be liable, although his employer will not be, provided the clause is reasonable under the Unfair Contract Terms Act, 1977, because the employee has not supplied consideraton for the contract which is between his employer and the customers.

Reference should, however, be made to the case of *NZ Shipping* v *A. M. Satterthwaite* (see below) where by application of the rules relating to acceptance in unilateral contracts and the performance of existing contractual duties owed to a third party the court was able to hold that a stevedore could take the benefit of an exclusion clause in the shipping company's contract of carriage.

> **ESSENTIAL CASE LAW AND COMMENT**
>
> *The New Zealand Shipping Co Ltd* v *A. M. Satterthwaite & Co Ltd*, 1974 – An exclusion clause avoids privity rule **(181)**

Construction of exclusion clauses

Rules of construction (i.e. interpretation) of contract may, when applied, prevent the application of an exclusion clause. The major rules of construction are as follows.

THE *CONTRA PROFERENTEM* RULE

Under this rule if there is any ambiguity or room for doubt as to the meaning of an exclusion clause the courts will construe it in a way unfavourable to the person who put it into the contract. An example of the application of this rule is to be seen in *Hollier* v *Rambler Motors* (p. 292) because the Court of Appeal, having decided that previous dealings were not incorporated, went on to use the rule by saying that the wording in the form was not sufficiently plain to exclude negligence. That ambiguity had therefore to be construed against the defendants who put it into the contract. Those who wish to exclude liability for negligence must use clear words, said the House of Lords in *Smith* v *South Wales Switchgear* [1978] 1 All E.R. 18.

> **ESSENTIAL CASE LAW AND COMMENT**
>
> *Alexander* v *Railway Executive*, 1951 – The *contra proferentem* rule **(182)**

THE REPUGNANCY RULE

This rule says in effect that the exemption clause is in direct contradiction to the main purpose of the contract and is therefore repugnant to it. Where such repugnancy exists the exemption clause can be struck out. Thus, if A makes a contract to supply oranges to B but includes a clause which allows him to supply any sort of fruit, the clause is repugnant to the main purpose of the contract and could be struck out. Thus, A would be liable in breach of contract if he supplied B with apples and could not rely on the clause to excuse his breach of contract.

THE FOUR CORNERS RULE

Under this rule exemption clauses only protect a party when he is acting within the four corners of the contract. Thus he is liable for damage which occurs while he is deviating from the contract and he would not be protected by the exclusion clause.

ESSENTIAL CASE LAW AND COMMENT

Pollock v *Macrae*, 1922 – Where the clause is repugnant **(183)**
Thomas National Transport (Melbourne) Pty Ltd v *May and Baker (Australia) Pty Ltd*, 1966 – The four corners rule **(184)**

The doctrine of fundamental breach

This doctrine was usually invoked where a plaintiff sought a remedy on a contract containing exemption clauses which had been adequately communicated. The doctrine said, in effect, that where one party had fundamentally broken his contract, i.e. done something fundamentally different from what he had contracted to do, an exclusion clause could not protect him, and that this was a *rule of law* and *not a rule of construction*, so that the court had no discretion in the matter.

After some years of differing judicial opinion regarding this the House of Lords eventually affirmed that there was no rule by which exclusion clauses had become inapplicable to exclude liability for a fundamental breach of contract. It was in each case a question of construction whether in fact the clause covered the breach which had taken place.

ESSENTIAL CASE LAW AND COMMENT

Photo Production Ltd v *Securicor Transport Ltd*, 1980 – The end of fundamental breach **(185)**

The approach of Parliament to exclusion clauses

Parliament has tried to prevent the widespread use of exclusion clauses by the passing of various statutes, the main one being the Unfair Contract Terms Act, 1977.

The strongest protection is given by the Act to persons who deal as consumers (C), though those dealing otherwise than as consumers, e.g. where the goods are bought for use in a business, are covered. To be a consumer one must be dealing as a *private buyer* with a *person in business* (B). Thus a contract between a *private buyer* and a *private seller* is not a consumer deal.

However, in *R. & B. Customs Broker Co Ltd* v *United Dominions Trust*

Ltd [1988] 1 All E.R. 847 the Court of Appeal decided that when a business buys goods it may still take advantage of consumer law applying to an ordinary member of the public if the transaction concerned is not a regular one. The facts of the case were that R & B Customs bought a car for the use of a director. The contract excluded an implied term under s. 14(3) of the Sale of Goods Act, 1979 that the goods be fit for the purpose. Such an exclusion does not operate if the sale is between a person in business and a consumer. It was held that R & B Customs must be treated as a consumer. The purchase of the car was not a frequent transaction and unless regularity could be established the transaction could not be regarded as an integral part of the business and was not therefore in the course of business.

CLAUSES RENDERED INEFFECTIVE BY THE UNFAIR CONTRACT TERMS ACT

These are as follows:

(*a*) *Any exclusion clause contained in a contract or notice* by which B tries to exclude or restrict his liability for death or personal injury resulting from negligence is wholly ineffective (ss. 2 and 5). However, in *Thompson* v *Lohan* [1987] 2 All E.R. 631 A hired plant together with operatives to B. The contract contained a clause stating that B was liable for the negligence of the operatives who were A's employees. This clause was held by the Court of Appeal not to be contrary to s. 2 of the Unfair Contract Terms Act. It was not designed to restrict or exclude liability to those who might be injured by the negligence of the operatives but merely decided whether A or B was to bear the liability.

(*b*) A *manufacturer's guarantee* cannot exclude or restrict the manufacturer's liability for loss or damage arising from defects in goods if used by a consumer which results from negligence in manufacture or distribution (s. 5). The section is concerned with actions either in negligence or on the collateral contract (see further p. 215) which the guarantee can create against the manufacturer who is not the seller of the goods to the customer. The section is not concerned with a contractual relationship between the seller and the customer which is covered by ss. 6 and 7. Thus a manufacturer's twelve-month guarantee for a vacuum cleaner which said that the goods would, if defective, be replaced or repaired free of charge but ended with a phrase such as: 'This guarantee is in lieu of, and expressly excludes, all liability to compensate for loss or damage howsoever caused' would not prevent a claim by the purchaser against the manufacturer if he/she was electrocuted by the cleaner (see *Donoghue* v *Stevenson* (1932), p. 725).

(*c*) A *clause under which B tries to exclude his liability*, whether by guarantee or otherwise, to C for breach of the implied terms in the Sale of Goods Act, 1979 (on a sale) or the Supply of Goods (Implied Terms) Act, 1973 (as amended) (on a hire-purchase transaction), e.g. that the goods are fit for the purpose or of merchantable quality, is wholly ineffective, as is a clause which tries to exclude against the consumer the implied terms in the Supply of Goods and Services Act, 1982 in a contract of pure hiring, e.g. of a car, or a contract for work and materials, as in the repair of a car (ss. 6(2) and 7(2), Unfair Contract Terms Act, 1977).

Section 6 also applies to non-business liability. However, since the implied terms requiring merchantable quality and fitness for the purpose do not apply to non-business transactions, only s. 13, Sale of Goods Act, 1979 (sale by description) can be implied. However, s. 13 cannot be excluded in a non-business transaction with a consumer.

Exclusion clauses applicable if reasonable

GENERAL

These are as follows:

(*a*) Any clause by which B tries to exclude or restrict his liability for loss arising from negligence other than death or personal injury (s. 2(2)).

(*b*) Any clause by which B tries to exclude or restrict his liability to a non-consumer for breach of the implied terms in the Sale of Goods Act, 1979, the Supply of Goods (Implied Terms) Act, 1973, and the Supply of Goods and Services Act, 1982 relating, for example, to contracts of hiring and work and materials (ss. 6(3) and 7(3)).

(*c*) Any clause by which B tries to exclude his liability for breach of contract if the contract is with a consumer or, in the case of a non-consumer contract, the agreement is on B's written standard terms (s. 3(1) and (2)(a)). There is no definition of 'written standard terms' in the 1977 Act, but it obviously covers cases in which the seller requires that all (or nearly all) of his customers purchase goods on the same terms with no variation from one contract to another. This section applies also to cases where the clause purports to allow B to render a substantially different performance, as where a tour operator tries to reserve the right to vary the accommodation or itinerary or reserves the right to render no performance at all (s. 3(2)(b)).

(*d*) As regards *indemnity clauses in consumer transactions*, B may agree to do work for C only if C will indemnify B against any liability which B may incur during performance of the contract, e.g. an injury to X caused by B's work (s. 4). B may, for example, be a builder who takes an indemnity from C, the owner of a property on which B is to do work in regard to any injuries which B's work might cause to third parties. Such an indemnity will be unenforceable by B unless reasonable. Such clauses are unlikely to be found reasonable and B will have to cover himself by insurance. The section does not cover non-consumer situations and the indemnity found in *British Crane Hire* (see p. 293) would still be enforceable (and see *Thompson* v *Lohan* (1987) at p. 296).

INDUCEMENT LIABILITY

Any clause purporting to exclude liability for misrepresentation applies only if reasonable, whether the transaction is with a consumer or a non-consumer (s. 3, Misrepresentation Act, 1967, as substituted by s. 8(1) of the Unfair Contract Terms Act, 1977). Thus an estate agent would not be able to exclude his liability for falsely representing the state of a house unless the court felt that it was reasonable for the agent to exclude his liability, as it might be if the property was very old and there had been no survey.

Section 3 also applies to non-business liability. A private seller cannot exclude his liability for misrepresentation unless he can show that the exclusion clause concerned satisfied the test of reasonableness.

ESSENTIAL CASE LAW AND COMMENT

Walker v *Boyle*, 1982 – When liability for misrepresentation cannot be excluded **(186)**

Reasonableness

THE BURDEN OF PROOF

The burden of proving that the clause is reasonable lies upon the party claiming that it is – usually B, the person in business (s. 11(5)).

MEANING OF REASONABLENESS

Although the matter is basically one for the judge, the following guidelines appear in the 1977 Act.

(*a*) *The matter of reasonableness* must be decided on the circumstances as they were when the contract was made (s. 11(1)).

(*b*) *Where a clause limits the amount payable* regard must be had to the resources of the person who included the clause and the extent to which it was possible for him to cover himself by insurance (s. 11(4)). The object of this rule is to encourage companies to insure against liability in the sense that failure to do so will go against them if any exclusion clause which they have is before the court. However, in some cases it may be right to allow limitation of liability, e.g. in the case of professional persons such as accountants where monetary loss may be caused to a horrendous amount following negligence and be beyond their power to insure against.

(*c*) *Where the contract is for the supply of goods*, i.e. under a contract of sale, hire-purchase, hiring, or work and materials, the criteria of reasonableness are laid down by s. 11(2) and Sch. 2 of the 1977 Act. They are:

(i) strength of the bargaining position of the parties. Thus if one party is in a strong position and the other in a weaker in terms of bargaining power, the stronger party may not be allowed to retain an exclusion clause in the contract;

(ii) availability of other supplies. Again, if a seller is in a monopolistic position so that it is not possible for the buyer to find the goods readily elsewhere, the court may decide that an exclusion clause in the contract of a monopolistic seller shall not apply;

(iii) inducements to agree to the clause. If the goods have been offered for sale at £10 without an exemption clause but at £8 with the inclusion of the clause, the court may see fit to allow the clause to apply at the lower price because there has been a concession by the seller in terms of the price;

(iv) buyer's knowledge of the extent of the clause. If the clause had been pointed out to the buyer and he is fully aware that it reduces the liability of the seller, then this will be relevant in deciding whether the seller should be allowed to rely on the clause. If a buyer is reasonably fully informed and aware of the seller's intentions as regards exclusion of liability, then the buyer may have to accept the clause;

(v) customs of trade and previous dealings. If, for example, exclusion clauses are usual in the trade or have been used by the parties in previous dealings, then the court may decide that an exclusion clause should apply. It should be noted that previous dealings do not seem relevant in consumer transactions, unless quite regular, but they are in this area where one is considering a non-consumer situation;

(vi) whether the goods have been made, processed or adapted to the order of the buyer. Obviously if the seller has been required by the buyer to produce goods in a certain way, then it may well be fair and reasonable for the seller to exclude his liability in respect of faults arising out of, for example, the buyer's design which he insisted was used. It would probably be reasonable to exclude the implied term under the Sale of Goods Act, 1979 that the goods were fit for the purpose (see further p. 273).

Although the above criteria are strictly speaking confined to exclusion of statutory implied terms in, for example, the Sale of Goods Act, 1979, they are being applied in other situations. For example, Judge Clarke in the *Woodman* case (see below) felt it was right to use them where what was at issue was a negligent service. The Supply of Goods and Services Act, 1982 has not changed the law regarding the exclusion of liability of a supplier of services. Services are not specifically mentioned in the 1977 Act but they fall within the ambit of ss. 2 and 3 which deal with negligence and breach of contract respectively.

> **ESSENTIAL CASE LAW AND COMMENT**
>
> *Mitchell (George) (Chesterhall) Ltd* v *Finney Lock Seeds Ltd*, 1983
> – Reasonableness: the tests to be applied **(187)**

REASONABLENESS – OTHER CASE LAW

The following is a selection of other case law on the 1977 Act to illustrate its application.

Section 2(2) came up for consideration in two County Court cases which were brought under the Act. In *Woodman* v *Photo Trade Processing Ltd*, heard in the Exeter County Court in May 1981, Mr Woodman took to the Exeter branch of Dixons Photographic for processing a film which carried pictures of a friend's wedding. The film was of special value because Mr Woodman had been the only photographer at the wedding, and he had said he would give the pictures as a wedding present. Unfortunately, the film was lost and when Dixons were sued they relied on an exclusion clause which, it appeared, was standard practice throughout the trade and had been communicated. The clause read as follows: 'All photographic materials are accepted on the basis that their value does not exceed the loss of the material itself. Responsibility is limited to the replacement of film. No liability will be accepted consequently or otherwise, however caused.' His Honour Judge Clarke found in the County Court that the customer had no real alternative but to entrust his film to a firm that would use such an exclusion clause and that, furthermore, Dixons could have foreseen that the film might be irreplaceable and although they could argue that the exclusion clause enabled them to operate a cheap mass-production technique, it could not be regarded as reasonable that all persons, regardless of the value of their film, should be required to take their chance of the system losing them. The judge therefore granted compensation of £75 to Mr Woodman and held that the exclusion clause was unreasonable.

In *Waldron-Kelly* v *British Railways Board*, which was heard in the Stockport County Court in 1981, the plaintiff delivered a suitcase to Stockport railway station so that it could be taken to Haverfordwest station. The contract of carriage was subject to the British Railways Board general conditions 'at owner's risk' for a price of £6.00. A clause exempted the Board from any loss, except that if a case disappeared then the Board's liability was to be assessed by reference to the weight of the goods, which in this case was £27.00 and not to their value, which in this case was £320.00. The suitcase was lost whilst it was in the control of British Rail. In the County Court Judge Brown held that the plaintiff succeeded in his contention that the exclusion clause was unreasonable and therefore of no effect. The judge held that in the case of non-delivery of goods the burden of proof to show what had happened to the goods was on the bailee. British Rail had failed to show that the loss was not their fault, and in any case the fault and loss were not covered by the exclusion clause because it did not satisfy the test of reasonableness.

Further, in *Stag Line Ltd* v *Tyne Ship Repair Group Ltd* [1984] 2 Lloyd's Rep. 211 Staughton, J., in finding that exclusion clauses inserted into the contract by the defendants were not fair and reasonable, said:

> The courts would be slow to find clauses in commercial contracts made between parties of equal bargaining power to be unfair or unreasonable, but a provision in a contract, which deprived a ship owner of any remedy for breach of contract or contractual negligence unless the vessel were returned to the repairer's yard for the defect to be remedied would be unfair and unreasonable because it would be capricious; the effectiveness of the remedy would depend upon where the ship was when the casualty occurred and whether it would be practical or economic to return the vessel to the defendants' yard.

Also in *Rees-Hough Ltd* v *Redland Reinforced Plastics Ltd* [1984] Construction Industry Law Letters, His Honour Judge Newey QC decided that it was not fair and reasonable for the defendants to rely on an exclusion clause in their standard terms and conditions of sale. They had sold pipes to the plaintiffs which were not fit for the purpose for which the defendants knew they were required, nor were they of merchantable quality under the Sale of Goods Act, 1979 (see further pp. 273 and 275) and the clause excluded liability for this. Clearly, then, it is difficult to apply exclusion clauses which try to prevent liability for supplying defective goods.

Where there is no contract, as in the *Hedley Byrne* situation where a bank used a 'without responsibility' disclaimer, s. 2(2) of the Act applies the reasonable test to the disclaimer (see further p. 454).

Provisions against evasion of liability

GENERAL

If an attempt is made to exclude or restrict liability in contract X by a clause in a secondary contract Y, then the clause in Y is ineffective (s. 10). For example, C buys a television set from B. There is an associated maintenance contract. The sale of a television would be within s. 6 of the 1977 Act and so there could be no exclusion of B's implied obligations. Any attempt to exclude or restrict these obligations in the maintenance contract would also fail. If the transaction was a non-consumer one the 'reasonable' test would have to be applied.

Nor can the Act be excluded by a clause which states that the contract is to be governed by the law of another country which does not outlaw exclusion clauses, at least if it is part of an evasion scheme, or if the contract is with a United Kingdom consumer and the main steps in the making of the contract took place in the UK (s. 27).

The Act does not apply to insurance contracts, nor to contracts for the transfer of an interest in land (s. 1(2) and Sch. 1, para. 1(a) and (b)). House purchase is therefore excluded though inducement liability cannot be excluded unless reasonable (see p. 298). Nor does it apply to certain contracts involving the supply of goods on an international basis because these are covered by conventions. Furthermore, it should be noted that a written arbitration agreement will not be treated as excluding or restricting liability for the purposes of the 1977 Act and such an agreement is valid (s. 13(2)).

FAIR TRADING ACT, 1973

Under s. 13 of this Act the Director-General of Fair Trading can in the course of investigating consumer trade practices deal in particular with 'terms and conditions on which or subject to which goods or services are supplied'. This, of course, concerns exemption clauses being used in consumer transactions. If after investigation the Director-General feels that a particular practice in terms of exemption clauses should cease he will make a report to the Minister who may introduce a statutory instrument to stop the practice. For example, the Consumer Transactions (Restrictions on Statements) Order, 1976 (No. 1813) as amended by SI 1978/127 makes it a criminal offence to sell or supply goods and purport that the implied terms in sale of goods and hire-purchase legislation can be excluded in a consumer sale since this might suggest to the customer that he has no rights so that he will not bother to try to enforce them.

16
Law of contract – illegality and public policy

In this chapter we are concerned to describe the effect of illegality and public policy on the freedom of contract. The more commercial aspects of restraint of trade and restrictive practices are treated in greater depth.

Introduction

Freedom of contract must always be subject to overriding considerations of public policy.

Public policy has been ascertained as follows –

(*a*) *At common law by the judiciary.* At one time the judiciary had wide powers of discretion in the matter of creating new categories of public policy but this view is now unacceptable. In *Fender* v *Mildmay* [1937] 3 All E.R. 402 the House of Lords declared against the extension of the heads of public policy, at least by the judiciary. However, up to 1938 the judiciary had created a number of categories of public policy. These fell into two areas as follows –

  (i) *Illegal contracts.* These involve some degree of moral wrong and contracts to commit crimes or to defraud the Revenue fall into this category.

  (ii) *Void contracts.* In these cases there is not in any strict sense blameworthy conduct; the contracts are rendered void because if enforced by the courts they could produce unsatisfactory results on society. Examples are contracts in restraint of trade, e.g. an agreement under which an employee covenants with his employer that on the termination of his contract he will not work for a rival firm or start a competing business, and contracts prejudicial to marriage, e.g. a contract under which a person promises not to marry at all.

(*b*) *By Parliament.* Parliament expresses its view as to what is public policy by Acts of Parliament and rules and orders made by ministers under Acts of Parliament. Again, statute law in this area falls into two categories as follows –

  (i) *The creation of illegal contracts.* This happens where the Act of Parliament actually makes the contract *unlawful*. Thus s. 1 of the

Resale Prices Act, 1976, declares unlawful all *collective* agreements between suppliers of goods to 'blacklist' retailers who sell below the minimum resale price agreed by the suppliers.

(ii) *The creation of void contracts.* Here there is no suggestion that the contract is unlawful in the strict sense or that moral blame attaches. There are two main areas as follows –

(1) Wagering contracts, which will be dealt with later, and

(2) The prevention of restrictive practices. Thus agreements by suppliers to fix prices or restrict supplies are void under the Restrictive Trade Practices Act, 1976, unless the parties can prove to the Restrictive Practices Court that their agreement is beneficial and in the public interest.

Public policy – the contribution of the judiciary: illegal contracts

ILLEGAL CONTRACTS

These contracts involve some form of moral weakness which society in general seeks to control. They are as follows –

(*a*) *Contracts to commit crimes or civil wrongs.* Thus a contract between an agent and his client whereby the agent was to receive a double commission would be illegal because it has as its object the commission of a fraud on the principal, since if the agent takes a double commission there is a conflict of interest.

(*b*) *Contracts involving sexual immorality.* Agreements for future illicit cohabition are void, because the promise of payment might encourage immoral conduct in a person who otherwise would not have participated. However, a contract under which a person promises to pay another money in return for past illicit cohabitation is not illegal because it does not necessarily encourage future immorality between the parties. Such a contract will, however, be unenforceable unless made under seal because it is for past consideration. Furthermore, contracts which are on the face of it legal may be affected if *knowingly* made to further an immoral purpose. Immorality seems to refer only to extra-marital sexual intercourse.

It may be asked whether legally enforceable rights of maintenance may be created by a contract between cohabitants, i.e. persons who live together as husband and wife though unmarried. Certainly, a contract could be made, but its enforceability is doubtful. It was the view of the House of Lords in *Fender* v *St. J. Mildmay* [1937] 3 All E.R. 402 that the courts could not enforce an immoral promise between a man and a woman such as the payment of money or some other consideration in return for an immoral association. However, much depends upon the view a court would now take of this. The older cases, such as *Fender*, tended to regard the payment of money as a reward for and to induce the sexual aspect of the relationship. It may be that the courts would enforce a maintenance agreement which was entered into as part of a stable relationship between cohabitants, and which could not be seen as mere payment for a sexual relationship.

Nevertheless, in *H v H*, *The Times*, 22 April 1983, the court refused to enforce maintenance support provisions in what was in effect a wife-swapping contract intended by the four parties to be permanent. Thus the matter of enforceable maintenance by contract must remain doubtful in terms that it may be contrary to public policy. In addition, the court may not enforce it on the basis that the parties did not intend to create legal relations, a concept which may affect contracts between members of a family or friends.

(*c*) *Contracts prejudicial to good foreign relations.* This category includes contracts to carry out acts which are illegal by the law of a foreign and friendly country, since to enforce such contracts would encourage disputes.

(*d*) *Contracts prejudicial to the administration of justice.* Thus, a contract tending to defeat the bankruptcy laws is illegal at common law.

(*e*) *Contracts tending to corruption in public life.* A contract to procure a title or honour is illegal under this head.

(*f*) *Contracts to defraud the Revenue.* This applies to frauds in connection with national taxes or local business rates.

ESSENTIAL CASE LAW AND COMMENT

Dann v Curzon, 1911 – A contract to commit a crime **(188)**
Pearce v Brooks, 1866 – The prostitute's carriage **(189)**
Regazzoni v K. C. Sethia, 1958 – A contract to avoid apartheid sanctions **(190)**
John v Mendoza, 1939 – An attempt to avoid a bankruptcy **(191)**
Parkinson v College of Ambulance, 1925 – Buying a title **(192)**
Napier v National Business Agency Ltd, 1951 – A tax fiddle that failed **(193)**

Consequences

The consequences of illegality in the above cases depend upon whether the contract was unlawful on the face of it, i.e. there was no way in which lawful performance could be achieved, or whether the contract was lawful on the face of it, i.e. it could have been performed in a lawful manner.

(*a*) *Contract unlawful on face of it.* This includes all the categories mentioned above except some contracts involving sexual immorality. The consequences where the contract is unlawful on the face of it are as follows –

 (i) The contract is void and there is no action by either party for debt (see *Dann* v *Curzon*, 1911), damages, specific performance or injunction.

 (ii) Money paid or property transferred to the other party under the contract is irrecoverable. (See *Parkinson* v *College of Ambulance*, 1925.) Unless –

   (1) The plaintiff is relying on rights other than those which are contained in the contract. Thus if A leases property to B for five years and A knows that B intends to use the property as a brothel, then A cannot recover rent or require any covenant to be performed without pleading the illegal lease. However, at the end of the term A can bring an action for the return of his property as *owner* and not as a landlord under an illegal lease. In addition, if the action is to redress a wrong which, although in a sense connected with the contract, can really be considered independent of it, the law will allow the action.

   (2) The plaintiff is not *in pari delicto* (of equal wrong). Where the contract is unlawful on the face of it, equal guilt is presumed but this presumption may be rebutted if the plaintiff can show that the defendant was guilty of fraud, oppression or undue influence.

   (3) The plaintiff repents provided that the repentance is genuine and performance is *partial* and not *substantial*.

ESSENTIAL CASE LAW AND COMMENT

Bowmakers Ltd v *Barnet Instruments Ltd*, 1944 – Where the plaintiff sues as owner **(194)**

Edler v *Auerbach*, 1950 – An action independent of the illegal contract **(195)**

Hughes v *Liverpool Victoria Legal Friendly Society*, 1916 – A contract induced by fraud **(196)**

Bigos v *Bousted*, 1951 – Where repentance is not genuine **(197)**

Taylor v *Bowers*, 1876 – A partial performance **(198)**

Kearley v *Thomson*, 1890 – A substantial performance: no redress **(199)**

 (*b*) *Contract lawful on face of it.* The result here is as follows –

 (i) Where both parties intended the illegal purpose. There is no action by either party for debt, damages, specific performance or injunction (see *Pearce* v *Brooks*, 1866) or to recover money paid or property transferred under the contract.

 (ii) Where one party was without knowledge of the illegal purpose. The innocent party's rights are unaffected and he may sue for debt, damages, specific performance, or injunctions or to recover money paid or property transferred.

(iii) The party who would have performed the contract in an unlawful manner has no action on it nor can he recover property delivered to the other party under the contract.

ESSENTIAL CASE LAW AND COMMENT

Fielding and Platt Ltd v *Najjar*, 1969 – An action by an innocent party **(200)**

Cowan v *Milbourn*, 1867 – Where the plaintiff intended unlawful performance **(201)**

Berg v *Sadler and Moore*, 1937 – Unlawful performance: no recovery of money or property **(202)**

Public policy and the judiciary – void contracts

These contracts do not involve any type of moral weakness but are against public policy because they are inexpedient rather than unprincipled. The contracts concerned are contracts to oust the jurisdiction of the courts, contracts prejudicial to the status of marriage and contracts in restraint of trade. These are dealt with individually below.

CONTRACTS TO OUST THE JURISDICTION OF THE COURTS

A contract which has the effect of taking away the right of one or both of the parties to bring an action before a court of law is void, though it may be possible to *sever* the offensive part of the contract and enforce the rest. This rule does not make void honourable pledge clauses because in such cases the parties do not intend to be bound by the contract at all. If the contract is to be binding, however, then the parties cannot exclude it from the jurisdiction of the courts. Furthermore, arbitration clauses are not affected. Many commercial contracts contain an arbitration clause, the object being to provide a cheaper or more convenient remedy than a court action. An arbitration clause in a contract is not void if the effect of it is that the parties are to go to arbitration *first* before going to court. An arbitration clause which denies the parties access to the courts completely is, of course, invalid.

ESSENTIAL CASE LAW AND COMMENT

Goodinson v *Goodinson*, 1954 – Severing an unlawful promise **(203)**

CONTRACTS PREJUDICIAL TO THE STATUS OF MARRIAGE

A contract in absolute restraint of marriage, i.e. one in which a person promises not to marry at all, is void. Partial restraints, if reasonable, are said to be valid, e.g. a contract not to marry a person of certain religious faith, or not to marry for a short period of time. However, there are no recent cases and it may be that even a partial restraint would be regarded as void today. Marriage brokage contracts, i.e. contracts to introduce men and women with a view to their subsequent marriage, are also void on the grounds that third parties should not be free to reap financial profit by bringing about matrimonial unions.

As regards separation agreements, these are invalid if made for the future, as where a husband promises that he will make provision for his wife if she should ever live apart from him, unless the agreement is made as part of a reconciliation arrangement. In this case the agreement is valid, although it may make provision for a renewed future separation. If the parties are not living in amity or are actually separated, then a separation agreement is valid. Once it is apparent that the parties cannot live together in amity it is desirable that a separation which has become inevitable should be concluded upon reasonable terms.

CONTRACTS IN RESTRAINT OF TRADE

Originally all contracts in restraint of trade were regarded as void but in the seventeenth century the courts began to allow certain of them to operate if reasonable, apparently because of the reluctance of masters to train apprentices unless they were able to restrain those apprentices in some way on the completion of the apprenticeship.

Because of the obvious importance of this area of the law together with restrictive practices generally the remainder of this chapter will be devoted to this subject.

Contracts in restraint of trade generally

Such contracts are *prima facie* void and will only be binding if reasonable. Thus the contract must be reasonable between the parties which means that it must be no wider than is necessary to protect the interest involved in terms of the area and time of its operation. It must also be reasonable as regards the public interest. Finally, the issue of reasonableness is a matter of law for the judge on the evidence presented to him which would include, for example, such matters as trade practices and customs.

ESSENTIAL CASE LAW AND COMMENT

Wyatt v *Kreglinger and Fernau*, 1933 – Restraint of trade and the public interest **(204)**

Voluntary contractual restraints of trade on employees generally

Here the contract is entered into voluntarily by the parties and as regards employees it should be noted that there are only two things an employer can protect:

(*a*) *Trade secrets*. A restraint against competition is justifiable if its object is to prevent the exploitation of trade secrets learned by the employee in the course of his employment. In this connection it should be noted that the area of the restraint must not be excessive. Furthermore, a restraint under this heading may be invalid because its duration is excessive.

(*b*) *Business connection*. Sometimes an employer may use a covenant against *solicitation* of persons with whom the employer does business. The problem of area is less important in this type of covenant, though its duration must be reasonable. The burden on the employer increases as the duration of the restraint is extended, though in rare situations a restraint for life may be valid.

ESSENTIAL CASE LAW AND COMMENT

Forster & Sons Ltd v *Suggett*, 1918 – A restraint in regard to trade secrets **(205)**

Home Counties Dairies v *Skilton*, 1970 – A restraint preventing customer solicitation **(206)**

Fitch v *Dewes*, 1921 – A client restraint for life **(207)**

Contractual restraints on employees through the period of notice

In recent times the court has had to consider the validity of contracts of service with restrictively long periods of notice which have sometimes been given to able and ambitious executives. Typically such contracts provide that if the employee leaves he must give notice of, say, one year and during that time the employer can suspend him from work but agrees to give him full pay and other benefits. The contract will normally also provide that the employer may exclude the employee from the workplace so that he cannot after serving his notice obtain any further information which might be of benefit to the new employer nor can he work for the new employer during the period of notice without being in breach of contract. He can either do nothing or pursue his hobbies. This is why the period of notice has been called 'garden leave'.

Such a contract was considered by the Court of Appeal in *Provident*

Financial Group plc v *Whitegates Estate Agency* [1989] I.R.L.R. 84. The court did not decide that such a contract was void but said it would be cautious about granting an injunction to stop an employee from working for the new employer during the period of notice. However, the court would be prepared to hear a claim for damages by the employer.

Non-contractual restraints on employees: confidential information

The position is different where the employee has no restraint of trade clause in his contract. Thus in *Faccenda Chicken Ltd* v *Fowler* [1986] 1 All E.R. 617, Mr Fowler was sales manager for Faccenda Chicken Ltd for seven years and set up a van sales operation whereby refrigerated vans travelled around certain districts offering fresh chicken to retailers and caterers. He left the company and set up his own business selling chickens from refrigerated vans in the same area. Eight of the company's employees went to work for him. Each of the salesmen in the company knew the names and addresses of the customers, the route and timing of deliveries, and the different prices quoted to different customers.

The company unsuccessfully brought an action for damages in the High Court, alleging wrongful use of confidential sales information and were also unsuccessful in a counterclaim for damages for breach of contract by abuse of confidential information in Mr Fowler's action against them for outstanding commission.

It is generally the case that rather more protection in terms of preventing an employee from approaching customers can be obtained by an express term which is reasonable in terms of its duration. In the absence of an express term, it is clear from this decision of the Court of Appeal that confidential information of an employer's business obtained by an employee in the course of his service may be used by that employee when he leaves the job unless, as the Court of Appeal decided, it can be classed as a trade secret or is of such a confidential nature that it merits the same protection as a trade secret. For example, there would have been no need for a term in the contract of service in *Forster* (see p. 690). The court could have prevented use of the secret process for a period without this. It should, however, be noted that in *Faccenda* the Court of Appeal did say that if the employees had written down lists of customers, routes, etc., as distinct from having the necessary information in their memories, and presumably being unable to erase it, short of amnesia, they might have been restrained for a period from using the lists. This follows the case of *Robb* v *Green* [1895] 2 Q.B. 315 where the manager of a firm dealing in live game and eggs copied down the names of customers before leaving and then solicited these for the purposes of his own business after leaving the employment of the firm. He was restrained from soliciting the customers.

Employee restraints arising from agreements between manufacturers and traders

The courts are concerned to prevent an employer from obtaining by indirect means restraint protection which he could not have obtained in an express contract with the employee.

ESSENTIAL CASE LAW AND COMMENT

Kores Manufacturing Co Ltd v *Kolok Manufacturing Co Ltd*, 1958 – Employee restraints between employers **(208)**

Restraints imposed on the vendor of a business

Such a restraint will be void unless it is required to protect the business sold and not to stifle competition.

It should be noted, however, that the protection of the business sold may in rare situations involve a world-wide restraint.

ESSENTIAL CASE LAW AND COMMENT

British Reinforced Concrete Co v *Schelff*, 1921 – Restraints against mere competition not allowed **(209)**
Nordenfelt v *Maxim Nordenfelt Guns and Ammunition Co*, 1894 – An exceptional world-wide restraint **(210)**

Restrictions on shareholder-employees

The courts will generally allow wider restraints in the case of vendors of businesses than in the case of employees. However, what is the position where the employee is also a shareholder and therefore also a proprietor of the business?

ESSENTIAL CASE LAW AND COMMENT

Systems Reliability Holdings plc v *Smith*, 1990 – Where the employee is also a shareholder in the employing company **(211)**

Restrictions accepted by distributors of merchandise

A manufacturer or wholesaler may refuse to make merchandise available for distribution to the public unless the distributor accepts certain conditions restricting his liberty of trading. This is the main purpose of the solus agreement used by petrol companies. Such agreements are void unless reasonable.

There is an important distinction here between a garage proprietor who borrows money on mortgage of his own property from a petrol company and agrees to sell only that company's products for a period of time. The rule relating to unreasonable restraints of trade applies to the mortgage. However, if the petrol company is the owner of the land and garage premises and grants a lease to a tenant who will run the garage then the rule relating to unreasonable restraints of trade does not apply to an agreement in the lease to take the petrol company's products.

ESSENTIAL CASE LAW AND COMMENT

Esso Petroleum Co Ltd v *Harper's Garage (Stourport) Ltd*, 1967 –
Restraint in a mortgage **(212)**
Cleveland Petroleum Co Ltd v *Dartstone Ltd*, 1969 – A restraint in a lease **(213)**

Involuntary restraints of trade

We have so far considered, subject to an exception in the case of confidential information, restrictions against trading contained in contracts. However, the doctrine is not confined to these voluntary restraints. It extends to involuntary restraints imposed by trade associations or professional bodies upon their members. Such restraints are void unless reasonable.

ESSENTIAL CASE LAW AND COMMENT

Pharmaceutical Society of Great Britain v *Dickson*, 1968 –
Restraints imposed by a professional body **(214)**

Consequences where the contract is contrary to public policy: severance

Where a contract is rendered void by the judiciary it is enforceable only in so far as it contravenes public policy. Thus lawful promises may be severed and enforced. A contract of service which contains a void restraint is not wholly invalid and the court will sever and enforce those aspects of it which do not offend against public policy. Thus an employee who has entered into a contract of service which contains a restraint which is too wide can recover his wages or salary.

The court will not add to a contract or in any way redraft it but will merely strike out the offending words. What is left must make sense without further additions otherwise the court will not sever the void part in order to enforce what is good. For example, A agrees 'not to set up a competing business within ten miles' in a covenant when he sells his business. If we suppose that five miles would be reasonable the court will not in fact substitute 'five' and then enforce the covenant because this would mean making a contract for the parties.

It is important also to note that the court will not delete the invalid part of a restraint clause if it is the major part of the restraints imposed.

Thus in *Attwood* v *Lamont* [1920] 3 K.B. 571 the heads of each department in a business of a general outfitter were required to sign a contract agreeing, amongst other things, after leaving the business not to be engaged in 'the trade or business of a tailor, dressmaker, general draper, milliner, hatter, haberdasher, gentlemen's, ladies' or children's outfitters, at any place within a radius of ten miles of the employers' place of business at Regent House, Kidderminster . . .'. Lamont, who was employed as cutter and head of the tailoring department, left and began to compete, doing business with some of his former employer's customers. The employer then tried to enforce the above restraint which was drawn too wide in terms of the various departments covered, since Lamont had never been concerned with departments other than the tailoring department. The court refused to sever the tailoring covenant from the rest because that would have meant severing almost the whole of the restraint in order to leave the restraint regarding tailoring.

A contrast is provided by *Goldsoll* v *Goldman* [1915] 1 Ch. 292. In that case the defendant sold imitation jewellery and when he sold his business he agreed 'not for two years to deal in real or imitation jewellery in any part of the United Kingdom'. The court was prepared to sever the words 'real or' in order to make the restraint valid and restrict the defendant from competing in imitation jewellery. Only two words needed to be deleted and this was a very small part of the restraint as a whole.

Public policy: the contribution of Parliament

Some contracts are prohibited by statute in terms that they are illegal, the words 'unlawful' being used in the statute concerned. In this context 'statute' includes the orders, rules and regulations that ministers of the Crown and other persons are authorised by Parliament to issue.

The statutory prohibitions with which we are concerned may be express or implied.

IMPLIED STATUTORY PROHIBITION

In these cases the statute itself does not say expressly that contracts contravening its provisions are necessarily illegal. The statute may affect the formation of a particular contract as where a trader does business without taking out a licence. In some cases the statute may affect the manner of performance of the contract as where a trader is required to deliver to a purchaser a written statement such as an invoice containing, for example, details of the chemical composition of the goods.

In either case whether failure to comply with a statutory provision renders the contract illegal is a matter of construction of the statute and is for the judge to decide.

If, in the opinion of the judge, the Act was designed to protect the public then the contract will be illegal. Thus in *Cope* v *Rowlands* (1836) 2 M. & W. 149 and unlicensed broker in the City of London was held not to be entitled to sue for his fees because the purpose of the licensing requirements was to protect the public against possibly shady dealers. Furthermore, in *Anderson Ltd* v *Daniel* [1924] 1 K.B. 138 a seller of artificial fertilisers was held unable to recover the price of goods which he had delivered because he had failed to state in an invoice the chemical composition of the fertilisers which was required by Act of Parliament.

On the other hand, if in the opinion of the judge the purpose of the legislation was mainly to raise revenue or to help in the administration of trade, contracts will not be affected. Thus in *Smith* v *Mawhood* (1845) 14 M. & W. 452 it was held that a tobacconist could recover the price of tobacco sold by him even though he did not have a licence to sell it and had not painted his name on his place of business. The purpose of the statute involved was not to affect the contract of sale but to impose a fine on offenders for the purpose of revenue. In addition, in *Archbolds (Freightage) Ltd* v *Spanglett Ltd* [1961] 1 Q.B. 374 a contract by an unlicensed carrier to carry goods by road was held valid because the legislation involved was only designed to help in the administration of road transport.

EXPRESS STATUTORY PROHIBITION

In a book of this nature it would be inappropriate to deal in detail with all statutes which render contracts illegal but a modern example is found in the Resale Prices Act, 1976, s. 1. One particular type of agreement, namely an agreement between a number of manufacturers for the collective enforcement of conditions regulating the price at which goods may be sold, is prohibited and made unlawful.

Such agreements were not usually regarded as illegal at common law but the doctrine of privity of contract prevented enforcement of the resale price agreement by a manufacturer against a retailer (see, for example, *Dunlop* v *Selfridge* (1915), p. 615). Consequently, manufacturers not having access to the ordinary courts of law often brought the retailer before a secret and possibly unjust trade association tribunal which might put the retailer quite unreasonably on a stop list so that he was denied supplies.

Under Part 1 of the Resale Prices Act 1976 *collective* agreements by two or more persons regulating the price at which goods may be resold are unlawful. There is no criminal penalty but the Crown may institute civil proceedings in the High Court and obtain, for example, an injunction to prevent the practice.

It is important to note that *individual* agreements between one manufacturer and his retailers are sanctioned by s. 26 of the Resale Prices Act 1976 so that such a manufacturer now has access to the ordinary courts of law to enforce his agreement. The action may be for damages or an injunction, though it is important to note that s. 26 only applies if the resale price agreement has been approved by the Restrictive Practices Court under the Resale Prices Act 1976. In fact very few such agreements have been approved, although an example is the *Net Book Agreement* [1962] 3 All E.R. 751 under which publishers can enforce resale price maintenance agreements in respect of books.

In that case the court thought that abolition of resale price maintenance would lead to fewer stockholding booksellers (because, for example, supermarkets would stock and sell more cheaply the best-selling books) and fewer new titles, particularly of slow-selling but useful books on specialist topics which would not be stocked by supermarkets. All of this the court thought would be detrimental to the public interest. The case was decided under earlier legislation before there was a separate Act concerned with retail price maintenance.

Wagering contracts: insurance and dealing in differences

In essence for a wager to exist it must be possible for one party to win and one party to lose and there must be two persons or two groups opposed to each other in their views as to a future event. Thus, where S, Y and Z each put £5 into a fund to be given to the party whose selected horse wins a given race, there is no wager. The only commercial importance of the concept of wagering and the only reason why it is introduced in a book of this nature relates to insurance and dealing in differences (see below). A contract is not a wager if the person to whom the money is promised on the occurrence of the event has an interest in the non-occurrence of that event, e.g. where a person has paid a premium to insure his house against destruction by fire. Such an interest is called an *insurable interest* and is not a wager. However, to insure someone else's property would be a wager and not a valid contract of insurance.

The Gaming Act 1845 renders wagering contracts void so that there is no action for the bet or for the winnings. However, it should be noted that if the bet or the winnings have actually been paid over they cannot be recovered. Payment operates as waiver of the Act and the payment over of the money confers a good title to that money upon the person to whom it is paid.

It has become more common in recent times for persons to deal in differences, i.e. to bet on the future rises or falls in selected stock exchange indexes. No securities are bought or sold, the only transaction being the payment by one party to the other of the eventual difference in the indexes according to the accuracy or otherwise of the gambler's predictions.

It was decided in *City Index Ltd* v *Leslie, The Times*, 3 October 1990, that such a contract was validated by s. 63 of the Financial Services Act, 1986 so long as it was made 'by way of business'. The plaintiffs offered clients a differences service and recovered £34,580 plus interest from the defendant whose predictions of rise and fall had not been successful.

Contracts affected by the Restrictive Trade Practices Act, 1976

Under the Act of 1976 collective agreements between two or more persons designed to fix prices and/or regulate supplies of *goods* must be registered with the Director General of Fair Trading. They are then presumed void unless the parties can prove to the Restrictive Trade Practices Court that the agreement is in the public interest. This might be done, for example, where the parties can show that the agreement is designed to maintain the export trade. If the parties attempt to operate the agreement in spite of the fact that it has not been approved by the Restrictive Practices Court, the Director General of Fair Trading may ask for an injunction to prevent the operation of the agreement. However, it is rare that such action has to be taken because in most cases the firms concerned have not attempted to operate an agreement if it has been rejected by the court.

This Act also allows the Director General of Fair Trading to investigate restrictive practices in regard to services. If necessary the matter can be brought before the Restrictive Trade Practices Court which has a jurisdiction in respect of restrictive agreements relating to services.

An example is provided by *Agreement between the Members of the Association of British Travel Agents, The Times*, 25 June 1983. In that case it appeared that under the ABTA agreement no tour operator could sell foreign package tours through a non-ABTA agent. The Director General of Fair Trading thought that that was contrary to the public interest under the Restrictive Trade Practices Act of 1976 and took the agreement to the Restrictive Practices Court. However, the court decided that the agreement was valid because (a) the accounting discipline imposed by ABTA in terms of financial statements and returns from their agents and operators was valuable in terms of the public interest, and (b) there were ABTA arrangements under which members of the Association would cope with those who had booked holidays with an operator or agent who had collapsed because of insolvency. This again was very much in the public interest.

The Restrictive Practices Court may approve modifications to a registered agreement or may make an order under s. 4(1) of the Restrictive Trade Practices Act, 1976 on the application of the Director General of Fair Trading, allowing the Director to approve modifications where the variation is not a substantial one (see re *Building Employers' Confederation's Application* [1985] I.C.R. 167).

The Resale Prices Act, 1976

This Act is concerned with arrangements (or agreements) under which a supplier *imposes* upon a buyer a restriction in regard to the price at which the buyer must resell the goods he has bought under that arrangement or agreement.

Resale price maintenance agreements are presumed void under the 1976 Act unless the supplier can prove to the Restrictive Practices Court that the restriction is in the public interest. This might be done, for example, by showing that after-sales service would be reduced or non-existent unless the resale price maintenance agreement was enforced (and see the *Net Book Agreement* (1962) at p. 315). We have already seen that if a minimum resale price maintenance agreement is approved by the Restrictive Practices Court it can be enforced regardless of the doctrine of Privity of Contract under s. 26 of the Resale Prices Act, 1976.

A *maximum* resale price can be enforced under s. 26 against a third party if the goods have been acquired by that third party with notice of the restriction. Maximum resale price arrangements do not require the approval of the court.

The Fair Trading Act, 1973

This Act gives wide powers to the Office of Fair Trading under the Director General of Fair Trading by reason of which it can deal with monopolies, mergers, restrictive practices, and the protection of consumers against trading practices which are considered unfair. A recent example is a report by the Director on the 'timeshare' industry which reveals that undesirable techniques are used by some organisations to induce people to buy and make unduly hasty decisions about this. The report contains recommendations to the government for changes in the law to control these matters. The Office of Fair Trading is perhaps best known for its duty to vet mergers between parties having a large share of the relevant market and to recommend to the Department of Trade and Industry whether they should be referred to the

Monopolies and Mergers Commission. The government is not bound to take the advice of the Office of Fair Trading regarding reference. The Office of Fair Trading has, however, a much wider brief under the following main pieces of legislation: the Consumer Credit Act, 1974; the Competition Act, 1980 (see below); and, as we have seen, the Restrictive Trade Practices Act, 1976 and also the Resale Prices Act, 1976.

As regards consumer protection and surveillance of traders it works with local Trading Standards Consumer Protection departments and advice agencies and gives information on consumer rights. It can obtain assurances of future obedience of the law from traders under the Fair Trading Act, 1973 and under the Consumer Credit Act, 1974 it vets the fitness of traders offering credit and resolves disputes over the accuracy of information on people which is given by credit reference agencies.

The competition legislation brings monopolies and mergers and other trade practices which restrict, distort or prevent competition in the UK under the surveillance and control of the Office of Fair Trading.

The Competition Act, 1980

The main significance of this Act is that it brings within the scope of investigation the practices of single firms which are neither monopolies in a statutory sense nor in collusion with other enterprises for the purposes of the Restrictive Trade Practices Act, 1976.

The Act provides a two-stage inquiry process. First of all the Director General of Fair Trading can, under s. 3 of the Act, initiate a preliminary inquiry into a practice of a firm or firms and is required to report publicly his findings as to whether it constitutes an anti-competitive practice and if so, whether he feels it is right to refer the matter for investigation to the Monopolies and Mergers Commission. A company may volunteer undertakings in regard to the abandonment of its restrictive or monopolistic practices to the Director General at this stage and he may accept them instead of taking the matter to the Monopolies and Mergers Commission.

If the matter goes to the Commission, the Commission must assess and report whether the practice is anti-competitive and, in addition, whether it has operated or may be expected to operate against the public interest. Where the conclusion of the Commission is adverse the Secretary of State may make an order under s. 10 requiring the company to desist from or amend the practice concerned, or ask the Director General of Fair Trading to seek undertakings from the company.

A number of s. 3 investigations have been made by the Office of Fair Trading. For example, there was an investigation into certain practices within the Raleigh Group. The report of the Director General found certain anti-competitive practices by the company regarding the supply of their products to discount stores. These operated against the public interest. Accordingly, the company gave the Director General an undertaking not to refuse to supply certain makes of bicycle to discount stores and certain other retail outlets.

Section 13 provides for prices to be investigated by the Director General at the direction of the Secretary of State if the price is a matter of 'major public concern'. There are no follow-up powers by which any recommendations could be enforced.

Section 11 allows public bodies to be referred to the Monopolies and Mergers Commission for a review of efficiency and costs, sometimes known for short as an efficiency audit. Section 12 allows the relevant minister to order the body concerned to prepare a plan to put matters right. A number of reports have been published, e.g. one dealing with the London and South Eastern commuter services of British Rail. A further example was the investigation into the efficiency of London Underground Ltd. A recent example was a reference under s. 11 to the Monopolies and Mergers Commission to conduct an efficiency audit or review into the services provided by the Commonwealth Development Corporation.

The European Community approach to restrictive practices

Under Articles 85 and 86 of the Treaty of Rome all agreements between firms which operate to prevent or restrict competition in the Market are void. Under s. 5 of the Restrictive Trade Practices Act, 1976 the Director General of Fair Trading and the Restrictive Practices Court are to take Articles 85 and 86 into account (a) on the issue of registration of a particular agreement; and (b) if the agreement comes before the court for adjudication.

RESTRICTIVE TRADING AGREEMENTS AND THE TREATY OF ROME GENERALLY

We have already considered the position under English domestic law with regard to restrictive trading agreements. Some consideration must now be given to the position under Community law.

Policy and source law

The provisions of the Treaty, which have been part of our law since January 1973, are based, as UK law is, on the protection of the public interest. The basis of the competition policy is to be found in Articles 85 and 86 of the Treaty. These ban practices which distort competition between members of the Community (Art. 85), and prohibit the abuse of a monopolistic position by an organisation within the Market (Art. 86). There is an additional aim of raising living standards.

Relationship with UK law

On the matter of relationship, national legislation on restrictive trade practices and monopolies applies alongside Community law unless it conflicts with Community law as interpreted by the Commission or the European Court of Justice. Therefore, if a restrictive agreement or merger threat affects only the UK market, the matter will remain subject exclusively to UK legislation. If such agreement affects trade between two or more Member States then to that extent national law is excluded by Community law. Furthermore, if there is an overlap between Community and national law, Community law predominates. Therefore, once an agreement with inter-Market effect has been exempted by the Commission under Art. 85, it will from then on be immune from attack under UK restrictive practices or resale prices legislation. If the agreement had already been regarded as invalid under that legislation the invalidation will cease to be effective if the Commission exempts it under Art. 85. Additionally, if the restrictive practice has been approved by a UK court its approval will lapse if the agreement turns out to infringe the provisions of Art. 85. This is why it is important for UK restrictive practices courts to decline or postpone exercising jurisdiction where the Treaty applies and the Commission has already initiated proceedings.

APPLICATION OF ARTICLES 85 AND 86, TREATY OF ROME

It is perhaps inappropriate in a non-specialist book of this nature to go through the many illustrative cases on the above articles of the Treaty of Rome which have been heard by the European Court of Justice. However, by way of illustration and to show the application of the Articles in English cases before English courts we can consider the following.

Article 85

Of interest here is the case of *Cutsforth* v *Mansfield Inns* [1986] 1 All E.R. 577. C supplied coin-operated machines to 57 Humberside public houses owned by Northern County Breweries. M acquired Northern and requested all the tenants of the old Northern public houses to operate equipment supplied by M's list of nominated suppliers. M refused to put C on that list. This was held to be an infringement of Art. 85 and an injunction was granted preventing M from interfering with C's agreements with the tenants of the 57 public houses and from taking any action to limit the freedom of those tenants to order machines from C. M was not infringing Art. 86 because they were not in a dominant position in the market.

Article 86

An illustration of the use of Art. 86 in an English court of law is provided by *Garden Cottage Foods Ltd* v *Milk Marketing Board* [1982] 2 All E.R. 292. Garden Cottage (the company) was a middle-man transferring butter from the Board to traders in the bulk market in Europe and the UK taking a cut of the price. In March 1982 following some packaging problems which the company appeared to have overcome, the Board refused to supply direct. It said that supplies must be obtained from one of four independent distributors nominated by the Board.

These distributors were the company's competitors. The company would have to pay more to them for its supplies than if it bought direct from the Board. Therefore it could not compete on price, and would be forced out of business.

The company alleged that the Board was in breach of Art. 86 of the Treaty of Rome. This provides: 'Any abuse by one or more undertakings of a dominant position when in the Common Market or in a substantial part of it, shall be prohibited as incompatible with the Common Market in so far as it may affect trade between Member States . . .'.

The Court of Appeal, and later the House of Lords (see *Garden Cottage Foods Ltd* v *Milk Marketing Board* [1983] 2 All E.R. 770), decided that there had been a breach of Art. 86.

As regards remedies the court was asked to grant an injunction restraining the Board from refusing to maintain normal business relations contrary to Art. 86. The case was dealt with on that basis. However, the House of Lords was of the opinion that the remedy of damages was available for breach of the Treaty but there is still some uncertainty about this. UK courts have not as yet clarified precisely what remedies are available in this area.

17
Law of contract – discharge of contract

In this chapter we shall consider the four methods by which a contract can be discharged or terminated.

The discharge of a contract means in general that the parties are freed from their mutual obligations. A contract may be discharged in four ways: *lawfully* by agreement, by performance or by frustration, and *unlawfully* by breach.

Discharge by agreement

Obviously, what has been created by agreement may be ended by agreement. Discharge by agreement may arise in the following ways.

OUT OF THE ORIGINAL AGREEMENT

Thus the parties may have agreed at the outset that the contract should end automatically on the expiration of a fixed time. This would be the case, for example, with a lease of premises for a fixed term. Alternatively, the contract may contain a provision entitling one or both parties to terminate it if they wish. Thus a contract of employment can normally be brought to an end by giving reasonable notice. This area of the law is, of course, subject to statutory minimum periods of notice laid down by s. 49 of the Employment Protection (Consolidation) Act, 1978. They are one week after one month's service, two weeks after two years' service and an additional week for each year of service up to twelve weeks after twelve years' service. Section 49 provides that the employee must, once he has been continuously employed for one month, give at least one week's notice to his employer to terminate his contract of employment. This is regardless of the number of years of service. Individual contracts may provide for longer periods of notice both by employer and employee.

OUT OF A NEW CONTRACT

If the contract is *executory*, i.e. a promise for a promise, and there has been no performance, the mutual release of the parties provides the consideration and is called bilateral discharge. The only difficulty here is in relation to the form of the release. The position is as follows:

(*a*) written contracts may be rescinded or varied by oral agreement;
(*b*) deeds may be rescinded or varied orally;
(*c*) contracts required to be evidenced in writing may be totally discharged by oral agreement but variations must be in writing.

If the contract is executed as where it has been performed or partly performed by one party, then the other party who wishes to be released must provide consideration for that release unless it is effected by deed. This is referred to as unilateral discharge. In other words, the doctrine of accord and satisfaction applies. This matter has already been dealt with and is really an aspect of the law relating to consideration (see p. 223).

Discharge by performance generally

A contract may be discharged by performance, the discharge taking place when both parties have performed the obligations which the contract placed upon them. Whether performance must comply exactly with the terms of the contract depends on the following.

Construction of the contract as entire

According to the manner in which the court construes the meaning, the contract may be an entire contract. Here the manner of performance must be complete and exact.

> **ESSENTIAL CASE LAW AND COMMENT**
> *Bolton* v *Mahadeva*, 1972 – Where the contract is entire **(215)**

There is obviously some hardship when the entire contract rule is applied because some work is done by A for B which B does not pay for and certain other approaches have been worked out by the judiciary as follows.

Substantial performance

If the court construes the contract in such a way that precise performance of every term by one party is not required in order to make the other party liable to some extent on it, then the plaintiff may recover for work done, though the defendant may, of course, counterclaim for any defects in performance. In this connection it should be noted that in construing a contract to see whether a particular term must be fully performed or whether substantial performance is enough, the court will refer to the difference between conditions and warranties. A condition must be wholly performed whereas substantial performance of a warranty is often enough. (*Poussard* v *Spiers and Pond* (1876) and *Bettini* v *Gye* (1876) – see pp. 661–2.)

ESSENTIAL CASE LAW AND COMMENT

Hoenig v *Isaacs*, 1952 – Where there is substantial performance (216)

Acceptance of partial performance

If, for example, S agrees to deliver three dozen bottles of brandy to B and delivers two dozen bottles only, then B may exercise his right to reject the whole consignment. But if he has accepted delivery of two dozen bottles he must pay for them at the contract rate (s. 30(1), Sale of Goods Act, 1979).

However, the mere conferring of a benefit on one party by another is not enough; there must be evidence of acceptance of that benefit by the party upon whom it was conferred. The acceptance must arise following a genuine choice.

ESSENTIAL CASE LAW AND COMMENT

Sumpter v *Hedges*, 1898 – Has partial performance been accepted? **(217)**

Full performance prevented by the promisee

Here the party who cannot further perform his part of the contract may bring an action on a *quantum meruit* against the party in default for the value of work done up to the time when further performance was prevented.

ESSENTIAL CASE LAW AND COMMENT

De Barnardy v *Harding*, 1853 – Where full performance is prevented **(218)**

Time of performance

Section 41 of the Law of Property Act, 1925 provides that stipulations as to the time of performance in a contract are not construed to be of the essence of the contract and therefore need not be strictly complied with, unless equity would have regarded them as such. There are the following exceptional situations in which time was of the essence even in equity.

(*a*) The contract fixes a date and makes performance on that date a condition.

(*b*) The circumstances indicate that the contract should be performed at the agreed time. Thus, in the sale of a business, equity will generally take the view that the contract should be completed on time so that uncertainties regarding a change of owner should not be prolonged and affect adversely the goodwill of the business. Commercial contracts, such as contracts for the sale of goods where a time is fixed for delivery, are also in this category.

(*c*) Where the time of performance was not originally of the essence of the contract or has been waived but one party has been guilty of undue delay, the other party may give notice requiring that the contract be performed within a reasonable time.

ESSENTIAL CASE LAW AND COMMENT

Bowes v *Shand*, 1877 – Sale of goods: time is of the essence **(219)**
Chas Rickards Ltd v *Oppenhaim*, 1950 – Waiver of time of
  delivery **(220)**

Tender

With regard to the manner of performance, the question of what is good tender arises. Tender is an offer of performance which complies with the terms of the contract. If goods are tendered by the seller and refused by the buyer the seller is freed from liability, given that the goods are in accordance with the contract as to quantity and quality. As regards the payment of money, this must comply with the following rules.

(*a*) It must be in accordance with the rules relating to legal tender. By s. 1(2) and (6) of the Currency and Bank Notes Act, 1954 a tender of a note or notes of the Bank of England expressed to be payable to bearer on demand is legal tender for the payment of any amount. A tender of notes of a bank other than the Bank of England is not legal tender, though the creditor may waive his objection to the tender if he wishes. As regards coins, s. 2 of the Coinage Act, 1971, as amended by the Currency Act, 1983, provides that coins made by the Mint shall be legal tender as follows:

(i) Certain gold coins for payment of any amount. We are referring here to the gold sovereign. These are legal tender if struck after 1837. Even though the sovereign contains just under ¼ ounce of gold it is valid only for £1 although it is worth much more as a collector's item.

(ii) Coins of cupro-nickel or silver of denominations of more than 10 pence, i.e. 20p, 50p, £1 and £2 coins are legal tender for payment of any amount not exceeding £10.

(iii) Coins of cupro-nickel or silver of denominations of not more than 10 pence (in practice, the 5p and 10p coins) are legal tender for payment of any amount not exceeding £5.

(iv) Coins of bronze, i.e. the 2p and 1p coins, are legal tender for payment of any amount not exceeding 20 pence.

There is power of proclamation to call in coins which then cease to be legal tender or to make other coins legal tender.

(*b*) There must be no request for change.

(*c*) Tender by cheque or other negotiable instrument or by charge card or credit card is not good tender unless the creditor does not object. It should be noted that if a proper tender of money is refused the debt is not discharged, but if the money is paid into court the debtor has a good defence to an action by his creditor and the debt does not bear interest.

In connection with payment by credit card or charge card the consumer normally discharges his obligation to the seller by payment in this way. If the card company cannot pay the seller as where that company is insolvent the seller has no redress against the consumer subject always to the terms of the contract (*Re Charge Card Services* [1988] 3 All E.R. 702).

Appropriation of payments

In connection with performance it is important to consider the rules governing appropriation of payments. Certain debts are barred by the Limitation Act, 1980 and money which has been owed for six years under a simple contract or twelve years under a specialty contract without acknowledgment may not be recoverable by an action in the courts. Where a debtor owes several debts to the same creditor and makes a payment which does not cover them all, there are rules governing how the money should be appropriated. These are as follows.

(*a*) The debtor can appropriate either expressly by saying which debt he is paying or by implication as where he owed £50 and £20 and sends £20.

(*b*) If the debtor does not appropriate the creditor can appropriate to any debt, *even to one which is statute-barred* (see further p. 340). However, if the statute-barred debt is £50 and the creditor appropriates a payment of £25 to it the balance of the debt is not revived and cannot be sued for (*Mills v Fowkes* (1839) 5 Bing. N.C. 455).

(c) Where there is a current account there is a presumption that the creditor has not appropriated payments to him to any particular item. The major example is a bank current account. Appropriation here is on a chronological basis, i.e. the first item on the debit side of the account is reduced by the first item on the credit side: a first in first out principle. This follows from the rule in *Clayton's Case* (1816) 1 Mer. 572.

ESSENTIAL CASE LAW AND COMMENT

Deeley v *Lloyds Bank*, 1912 – Clayton's case applied **(221)**

Discharge by frustration generally

If an agreement is impossible of performance from the outset it is void. This is at the root of s. 6 of the Sale of Goods Act, 1979 which provides that where there is a contract for the sale of specific goods and the goods, without the knowledge of the seller, have perished at the time when the contract is made, it is void. However, some contracts are possible of performance when they are made but it subsequently becomes impossible to carry them out in whole or in part and they are then referred to as frustrated.

The judges developed the doctrine of discharge by frustration, which applies, as the House of Lords decided in *Davis Contractors Ltd* v *Fareham U.D.C.* [1956] 2 All E.R. 145, in the restricted set of circumstances where there has been such a change in the significance of the obligation that the thing undertaken would, if performed, be a different thing than that contracted for. The subject is considered under the following heads.

Contracts for personal service

Such a contract is discharged by the death of the person who was to perform it; thus if A agrees to play the piano at a concert and dies before the date on which the performance is due, his personal representatives will not be expected to go along and play in his stead.

Incapacity of a person who has to perform a contract may discharge it. However, temporary incapacity is not enough unless it affects the contract in a fundamental manner (*Poussard* v *Spiers and Pond* (1876) – see p. 661).

The doctrine of frustration will usually only apply where there is no fault by either party. Where performance of the contract is prevented by the fault of one party, that party is in breach of contract and that is the proper approach to the problem.

ESSENTIAL CASE LAW AND COMMENT

Storey v *Fulham Steel Works*, 1907 – Illness did not frustrate the contract **(222)**

Norris v *Southampton City Council*, 1982 – Frustration and breach in a personal service contract **(223)**

Government interference

In times of national emergency the government may often requisition property or goods in the national interest. This will have the effect of frustrating relevant contracts.

ESSENTIAL CASE LAW AND COMMENT

Re Shipton, Anderson & Co and Harrison Bros' Arbitration, 1915 – Frustration by government action **(224)**

Destruction of the subject matter of the contract

Physical destruction of the subject matter of the contract operates to frustrate it.

ESSENTIAL CASE LAW AND COMMENT

Taylor v *Caldwell*, 1863 – A fire at a concert hall **(225)**

Non-occurrence of an event

Where the taking place of an event is vital to the contract its cancellation or postponement will, in the absence of a contrary provision, frustrate it. However, if the main purpose of the contract can still be achieved there will be no frustration.

ESSENTIAL CASE LAW AND COMMENT

Krell v *Henry*, 1903 – A coronation is cancelled **(226)**

Herne Bay Steamboat Co v *Hutton*, 1903 – Cancellation of a naval review **(227)**

Commercial purpose defeated

Physical destruction of the subject matter is not essential to frustration. It extends to situations where although there is no physical destruction the essential commercial purpose of the contract cannot be achieved – a rule referred to as 'frustration of the common venture'.

ESSENTIAL CASE LAW AND COMMENT

Jackson v *Union Marine Insurance Co*, 1874 – A ship is stranded **(228)**

Situations in which the doctrine does not apply

It is now necessary to consider the three situations where the application of the rules relating to frustration are limited.

EXPRESS PROVISION IN THE CONTRACT

In such a case the provisions inserted into the contract by the parties will apply. Thus in some of the coronation seat cases, e.g. *Clark* v *Lindsay* (1903) 19 T.L.R. 202, the contracts provided that if the procession was postponed the tickets would be valid for the day on which it did take place or that the parties should get their money back with a deduction for the room owner's expenses. These took effect to the exclusion of the principles of frustration.

SELF-INDUCED EVENTS

The rules relating to frustration did not apply where the event making the contract impossible to perform was the voluntary act of one of the parties.

LEASES AND CONTRACTS FOR THE SALE OF LAND

Judicial opinion has been divided as to whether leases and contracts for the sale of land can be frustrated since these create an interest in land which survives any frustrating event.

ESSENTIAL CASE LAW AND COMMENT

Maritime National Fish Ltd v *Ocean Trawlers Ltd*, 1935 – Effect of a self-induced frustration **(229)**

Cricklewood Property and Investment Trust Ltd v *Leighton's Investment Trust Ltd*, 1945 – Frustration where a title to land is acquired **(230)**

The Law Reform (Frustrated Contracts) Act, 1943

This important statute has laid down the conditions which will govern the rights and duties of the parties when certain contracts are frustrated.

BEFORE 1943

The common-law doctrine of frustration did not make the contract void *ab initio* (from the beginning) but only from the time when the frustrating event occurred. Thus money due and not paid could be claimed and money paid before the frustrating event was not recoverable.

ESSENTIAL CASE LAW AND COMMENT

Chandler v *Webster*, 1904 – A startling application of the common-law rules **(231)**

AFTER 1943

The position under the Act is as follows:

(*a*) Money paid is recoverable.

(*b*) Money payable ceases to be payable.

(*c*) The parties may recover expenses in connection with the contract or retain the relevant sum from money received, if any.

(*d*) It is also possible to recover on a *quantum meruit* (a reasonable sum of money as compensation) where one of the parties has carried out acts of part performance before frustration, provided the other party has received what the Act calls 'a valuable benefit' under the contract other than a money payment 'before the time of discharge', i.e. to the time of the frustrating event. There are difficulties in regard to the expression 'valuable benefit', particularly where the work is destroyed, since the Act is not clear as to whether a sum can be recovered by the person conferring the benefit where there has been destruction of his work. In *Parsons Bros* v *Shea* (1965) 53 D.L.R. (2d) 86 a Newfoundland court, in dealing with an identical provision under the Newfoundland Frustrated Contracts Act, 1956, held that the carrying out of modifications to a heating system in a hotel subsequently destroyed by fire could not be regarded as conferring any 'benefits' upon the owner. However, in *BP Exploration* v *Hunt (No. 2)* [1982] 1 All E.R. 125 the plaintiffs were engaged to develop an oil field on the defendant's land and were to be paid by oil from the wells. After the wells came on stream but before BP had received all the oil which the development contract provided they should have, the wells were nationalised by the Libyan government which gave the defendant some compensation. The contract was obviously frustrated but Goff, J., who was later affirmed by the Court of Appeal and the House of Lords, gave BP a sum of 35 million dollars as representing the 'benefit' received by the defendant prior to the frustrating event.

Clearly, here there was a surviving benefit conferred before the frustrating event and at the time of it, e.g. the value of the oil already removed by Mr Hunt before nationalisation and, of course, his claim for compensation against the Libyan government. None of these things would have been available to him before BP's discovery and extraction of oil on his land. Since the benefit conferred up to the time of frustration clearly survived the frustrating event, i.e. the nationalisation, the case does not resolve the problems posed by *Parsons Bros* v *Shea* (above) where the benefit did not survive the frustrating event.

However, it is the better view that there is no need for the benefit conferred to survive the frustrating event. The court can make an award provided benefit was once conferred. The fact that it did not survive the frustrating event can be taken into account by the court when assessing (and probably reducing) how much it gives to the plaintiff.

Discharge by breach

This occurs where a party to a contract fails to discharge it lawfully but instead breaches one or more of the terms of the contract. There are several forms of breach of contract as follows:

(*a*) Failure to perform the contract is the most usual form as where a seller fails to deliver the goods by the appointed time or where, although delivered, they are not up to standard as to quality or quantity.

(*b*) Express repudiation which arises where one party states that he will not perform his part of the contract.

(*c*) Some action by one party which makes performance impossible.

Any breach which takes place before the time for performance has arrived is called an *anticipatory breach*. Thus the situations described in (*b*) and (*c*) above are anticipatory breaches.

Where the breach is anticipatory the aggrieved party may sue at once for damages. Alternatively, he can wait for the time for performance to arrive and see whether the other party is prepared at that time to carry out the contract.

ESSENTIAL CASE LAW AND COMMENT

Hochster v *De la Tour*, 1853 – An express repudiation **(232)**

Omnium D'Enterprises and Others v *Sutherland*, 1919 – An implied repudiation **(233)**

White and Carter (Councils) Ltd v *McGregor*, 1961 – Anticipatory breach: where a party carries on with the contract **(234)**

Anticipatory breach and supervening events

It may be dangerous to wait for the time of performance to arrive since the contract may, for example, have become illegal, thus providing the party who was in anticipatory breach with a good defence to an action.

ESSENTIAL CASE LAW AND COMMENT

Avery v *Bowden*, 1855 – Anticipatory breach: where the second breach was excused **(235)**

Effect of breach on contract

Not every breach entitles the innocent party to treat the contract as discharged. It must be shown that the breach affects a vital part of the contract, i.e. that it is a breach of condition rather than a breach of warranty (contrast *Poussard* v *Spiers* (see p. 661) with *Bettini* v *Gye* (see p. 662)) or that the other party has no intention of performing his contract as in *Hochster* v *De la Tour* (see above) or has put himself in a position where it is impossible to perform it as in *Omnium D'Enterprises and Others* v *Sutherland* (see above).

Other matters relevant to breach

Two further points arise in connection with breach of contract. The first is that the concept of contributory negligence does not apply. In *Basildon District Council* v *J. E. Lesser (Properties) Ltd* [1985] 1 All E.R. 20 the plaintiff sued for breach of contract in regard to the building of dwellings which had become unfit for habitation without repair. There was a defence that the damages payable should be reduced on the basis that the council's officers were guilty of contributory negligence. It was said that they should have noticed the lack of appropriate depth in foundations on seeing the building contractors' original drawings. It was decided by the High Court that the defence of contributory negligence did not apply in contract but only in tort.

It should be noted, however, that the obligation in the above case was entirely contractual. If the plaintiff could have sued, either in contract or in tort, as where the damage arises from a breach of contract and a tort, then even if the injured party decides to sue for breach of contract only the damages can be reduced if he is contributorily negligent (see *Forsikrings Vesta* v *Butcher*) [1988] 2 All E.R. 43.

Secondly, the Drug Trafficking Offences Act, 1986, in s. 24 brings in what is called a 'laundering' offence under which anyone knowingly assisting with the retention, control or investment of drug-trafficking proceeds could be liable to a maximum of 14 years' imprisonment. Banks, building societies, accountants, solicitors and other advisers are given protection by the Act if they disclose their suspicions about their client's finances if these seem to be connected with drug trafficking. However, the Act ensures that they cannot be sued for breach of contract if they pass on to the appropriate authorities their suspicions that any funds or investments may be connected with drug trafficking.

18
Law of contract – remedies and limitation of actions

In this chapter we shall consider the various remedies which exist both in common law and equity to deal with losses arising from contractual relationships and the rules which govern the recovery of money compensation through damages together with the time limits which are placed on the bringing of claims.

Damages generally

This is the main remedy for breach of contract and the rules of law relating to an award of damages are considered below.

Liquidated damages

In some cases the parties foreseeing the possibility of breach may attempt in the contract to assess in advance the damages payable. Such a provision for *liquidated* damages will be valid if it is a genuine pre-estimate of loss and not a *penalty* inserted to make it a bad bargain for the defendant not to carry out his part of the contract. The court will not enforce a penalty but will award damages on normal principles used in the assessment of unliquidated damages (see below).

Certain tests are applied in order to decide whether or not the provision is a penalty. Obviously, extravagant sums are generally in the nature of penalties. Where the contractual obligation lying on the defendant is to pay money then any provision in the contract which requires the payment of a larger sum on default of payment is a penalty because the damage can be accurately assessed. Where the sum provided for in the contract is payable on the occurrence of any one of several events it is probably a penalty for it is unlikely that each event can produce the same loss. If the sum agreed by the parties is regarded as liquidated damages it will be enforced even though the actual loss is greater or smaller.

> **ESSENTIAL CASE LAW AND COMMENT**
>
> *Ford Motor Co (England) Ltd* v *Armstrong*, 1915 – No genuine pre-estimate of loss **(236)**
>
> *Cellulose Acetate Silk Co Ltd* v *Widnes Foundry Ltd*, 1933 – Liquidated damages where the loss is smaller **(237)**

Unliquidated damages

ASSESSMENT

Unliquidated damages are intended as compensation for the plaintiff's loss and not as punishment for the defendant. Thus where no loss has been suffered, as where a seller fails to deliver the goods but the buyer is able to purchase elsewhere at no extra cost, the court will award *nominal* damages, i.e. an award of a small sum, e.g. £2, to reflect the view that any loss or damage is purely technical.

Exemplary or punitive damages which exceed the actual loss suffered by an amount intended to punish the offending party are not awarded for breach of contract. The intention is that the plaintiff should be placed in the same situation as if the contract had been performed.

Thus in an action by an employee for wrongful dismissal the court will base its award on 'net' wages, i.e. after deduction of income tax and national insurance contributions. An award based on 'gross' wages or salary would make the employee better off than if the contract had continued.

> **ESSENTIAL CASE LAW AND COMMENT**
>
> *Beach* v *Reed Corrugated Cases Ltd*, 1956 – Damages are compensatory **(238)**

TYPE OF LOSS RECOVERABLE

Damages can include compensation for financial loss, personal injury and damage to property. Also there may be included a sum by way of compensation for disappointment, vexation and mental distress.

> **ESSENTIAL CASE LAW AND COMMENT**
>
> *Jarvis* v *Swans Tours Ltd*, 1973 – Damages for mental distress **(239)**

REMOTENESS

Apart from the question of *assessment*, the matter of *remoteness of damage* arises. The consequence of a breach of contract may be far reaching and the law must draw a line somewhere and say that damages incurred beyond a certain limit are too remote to be recovered. Damages in contract must therefore be proximate.

The modern law regarding remoteness of damage in contract is based upon the case of *Hadley* v *Baxendale* (see below), as further explained in *The Heron II* (see below). These cases are authority for the statement that damages in contract will be too remote to be recovered unless they arise naturally, i.e. in the usual course of things, or if they do not arise naturally they are such that the defendant, as a reasonable man, *ought* to have had them in contemplation as likely to result. Damage which does not arise naturally and which would not have been in the contemplation of the reasonable man can only be recovered if the defendant was made aware of it *and* agreed to accept the risk of the loss.

ESSENTIAL CASE LAW AND COMMENT

Hadley v *Baxendale*, 1854 – Where damages are too remote **(240)**
The Heron II, 1967 – Where damages are in contemplation **(241)**
Horne v *Midland Railway Co*, 1873 – Has the defendant agreed to be liable for the loss? **(242)**
Victoria Laundry Ltd v *Newman Industries Ltd*, 1949 – Where loss arises naturally from the breach **(243)**

Mitigation of loss

The injured party has a duty to *mitigate* or minimise his loss, i.e. he must take all reasonable steps to reduce it. Thus a seller whose goods are rejected must attempt to get the best price for them elsewhere and the buyer of goods which are not delivered must attempt to buy as cheaply as possible elsewhere. Loss arising from failure to take such steps cannot be recovered.

ESSENTIAL CASE LAW AND COMMENT

Brace v *Calder*, 1895 – There must be a mitigaton of loss **(244)**

However, the plaintiff is not under a duty to mitigate his loss before there has been a breach of contract which the plaintiff has accepted as a breach. No doubt this is logical but it can produce startling results (see *White and Carter (Councils) Ltd* v *McGregor* (1961), p. 707). More recently the requirement of a 'legitimate interest' in keeping the contract going has made the position more equitable (see, for example, *Clea Shipping*, p. 708).

Provisional damages for personal injuries

The Administration of Justice Act, 1982 makes provision for a court to award provisional damages for contractual claims for personal injuries. Thus in an action for a fracture to the hip caused to a passenger in an accident involving a negligently driven bus the court can make an order for damages payable at once for the fracture and an award of provisional damages in case in the future chronic arthritis affects the injured passenger. If it does, but not otherwise, the provisional damages may also be recovered without another visit to the court to prove the damage.

Interest on debt and damages

Under the provisions of s. 15 and Sch. 1 of the Administration of Justice Act, 1982, which inserted s. 35A of the Supreme Court Act, 1981, the court has power to award interest on debt or damages at the end of the trial or where judgment is obtained in default, i.e. where there is no defence and no trial. Interest may also be awarded where the defendant settles after service of writ but before judgment. Interest is not available where a person settles *before* service of writ no matter how long he has kept the other party waiting. The interest payable is at such rate as the court thinks fit or as rules of court may provide. The rate currently payable on judgment debts under s. 17 of the Judgments Act, 1838 which is likely to be a guideline is 15% per annum (SI 1985/437). The interest is tax-free (s. 74, Administration of Justice Act, 1982).

Equitable remedies

Damages are the common law remedy for breach of contract. However, in some situations equity will provide more suitable remedies and these will now be considered.

A DECREE FOR SPECIFIC PERFORMANCE

This is an equitable remedy which is sometimes granted for breach of contract, where damages are not an adequate remedy or where specific performance is regarded by the court as a more appropriate remedy (see *Beswick* v *Beswick* (1967), p. 616). It is an order of the court and constitutes an express instruction to a party to a contract to perform the actual obligations which he undertook in a contract. For all practical purposes the remedy is now confined to contracts for the sale of land, though it may be a more appropriate remedy in the case of a contract to pay an annuity because the exact value of the annuity will depend on how long the annuitant lives and this cannot be known at the time of the breach (see *Beswick* v *Beswick* (1967), p. 616). It is not normally granted in the case of contracts for the sale of goods because other goods of a similar kind can be purchased and the difference assessed in money damages. In addition, it should be noted that specific performance will not be granted if the court cannot adequately supervise its enforcement. Thus contracts of a personal nature, such as employment, which rely on a continuing relationship between the parties will not generally be specifically enforced because the court cannot supervise performance on the day-to-day basis which would be necessary. However, if constant supervision by the court is not required, a decree of specific performance may be made of a personal service undertaking. Thus in *Posner* v *Scott-Lewis* [1986] 3 All E.R. 51 Mervyn-Davies, J. decided that the tenants of a block of flats could enforce by specific performance an undertaking in their leases that the defendant landlords would employ a resident porter to keep the communal areas clear. The court had only to ensure that the appointment was made. The plaintiffs were not asking the court to supervise the porter's day-to-day work. Furthermore, specific performance will not be awarded either to or against a minor because a minor's contracts cannot in general be enforced against him and those which can, i.e. beneficial contracts (see p. 233), are in the nature of contracts of personal service. Equity requires equality or mutuality as regards its remedies and this does not exist in the case of minors' contracts.

AN INJUNCTION

This is an order of the court used in this context to direct a person not to break his contract. The remedy has a somewhat restricted application in the law of contract and will be granted to enforce a negative stipulation in a contract where damages would not be an adequate remedy. Being an equitable remedy it is only ordered on the same principles as specific performance, so that it will not normally be awarded where damages are an adequate remedy (but see *Garden Cottage Foods Ltd* v *Milk Marketing Board* (1982), p. 321). Its main use in the contractual situation has been as an indirect means of enforcing a contract for personal services but a clear negative stipulation is required. The court will not imply one.

ESSENTIAL CASE LAW AND COMMENT

Warner Brothers Pictures Incorporated v *Nelson*, 1937 – Enforcing a negative stipulation **(245)**
Whitwood Chemical Co v *Hardman*, 1891 – A negative stipulation will not be implied **(246)**

THE MAREVA INJUNCTION

This remedy, which can be of assistance to a party suing for breach of contract, has developed considerably over recent times. In general terms a court will not grant an injunction to prevent a person disposing of his property merely to assist a person suing, for example, for a debt, to recover his money. However, the Mareva injunction is an exception to that general rule and is granted to restrict removal of assets outside the jurisdiction, often by a foreign defendant, where this is a real and serious possibility. The injunction takes its name from the second case in which it was awarded, i.e. *Mareva Compania Naviera SA* v *International Bulk Carriers SA* [1975] 2 Lloyds Rep. 509. However, the power of the High Court to issue Mareva injunctions is now recognised by s. 37 of the Supreme Court Act, 1981 which makes it clear that the power applies to domestic as well as foreign defendants. It is clearly a valuable addition to existing contractual remedies, particularly when business is now so often conducted on an international scale.

RESCISSION

This is a further equitable remedy for breach of contract. The rule is the same when the remedy is used for breach as it is when it is used for misrepresentation. If the contract cannot be completely rescinded it cannot be rescinded at all; it must be possible to restore the status quo.

REFUSAL OF FURTHER PERFORMANCE: A SELF-HELP REMEDY

If the person suffering from the breach desires merely to get rid of his obligations under the contract, he may refuse any further performance on his part and set up the breach as a defence if the party who has committed the breach attempts to enforce the contract against him.

Claims for restitution: quasi-contract

Quasi-contract is based on the idea that a person should not obtain a benefit or an unjust enrichment as against another merely because there is no obligation in contract or another established branch of the law which will operate to make him account for it. The law may in these circumstances provide a remedy by implying a fictitious promise to account for the benefit or enrichment. This promise then forms the basis of an action in quasi-contract.

In practice the following two areas are important.

CLAIMS ON A *QUANTUM MERUIT*

This remedy means that the plaintiff will be awarded as much as he has earned or deserved. The remedy can be used contractually or quasi-contractually as follows.

(a) *Contractually*. Here it may be used to recover a reasonable price or remuneration where there is a contract for the supply of goods or services but the parties have not fixed any precise sum to be paid. This area is also covered by statute law in the case of a sale of goods by s. 8 of the Sale of Goods Act, 1979, and in the case of a supply of goods, e.g. a new distributor in a car repair contract, or the mere supply of a service by s. 15 of the Supply of Goods and Services Act, 1982.

(b) *Quasi-contractually*. A claim on this basis may be made where, for example, work has been done under a void contract. The plaintiff cannot recover damages for breach because no valid contract exists, but he may in some circumstances recover on a *quantum meruit*.

ESSENTIAL CASE LAW AND COMMENT

Craven-Ellis v *Canons Ltd*, 1936 – A claim on a *quantum meruit* **(247)**

TOTAL FAILURE OF CONSIDERATION: ACTIONS FOR MONEY HAD AND RECEIVED

Of particular importance here is the action for total failure of consideration. A total failure will result in the recovery of all that was paid. A common reason for total failure of consideration arises where A, who has no title, sells goods to B and B has to give up the goods to the true owner. B can then recover the whole of the consideration from A, his action being based upon the quasi-contractual claim of money had and received.

It should be noted that the action is based on failure of consideration and not its absence. Thus money paid by way of a gift cannot be recovered in quasi-contract. As we have seen the decision in *Rowland* v *Divall*, 1923 would appear to have been based on total failure of consideration (see p. 665).

Limitation of actions

Contractual obligations are not enforceable for all time. After a certain period the law bars any remedy in the main because evidence becomes less reliable with the passage of time. Time is the greatest enemy of the truth. The Limitation Act, 1980 lays down the general periods within which an action may be brought. They are as follows.

(a) An action on a simple contract may be brought within six years from the date when the cause of action accrued.

(b) An action upon a contract made by deed may be brought within twelve years from the date when the cause of action accrued.

Where the plaintiff's claims include a claim for damages in respect of personal injuries, the period is three years.

A person may suffer personal injury the extent of which only comes to light more than three years after the breach of contract which caused it. For example, A is a passenger on B's coach and B's careless driving causes an accident as a result of which A suffers injury consisting of bruising of the face. Four years later A goes blind as a result of the accident. Under the Limitation Act, 1980, A has three years from his knowledge of the blindness to sue B and the court's permission is not required. The court may extend this period at its discretion, though in this case application must be made to the court for the extension.

A right of action 'accrues' from the moment when breach occurs, not from the date when the contract was made. Thus if money is lent today for four years the creditor's right to recover it will not expire until ten years from today.

If when the cause of action accrues the plaintiff is under a disability by reason of minority or unsoundness of mind, the period will not run until the disability is ended or until his death, whichever comes first. Once the period has started to run subsequent insanity has no effect.

If the plaintiff is the victim of fraud or acts under a mistake, the limitation period will not begin to run until the true state of affairs is discovered or should with reasonable diligence have been discovered.

ESSENTIAL CASE LAW AND COMMENT

Lynn v *Bamber*, 1930 – Limitation of actions where there is fraud
(248)

The Limitation Act does not truly discharge a contract, which is why it has been dealt with separately here. The Act merely makes the contract unenforceable in a court of law and if the defendant does not plead the statutes of limitation, the judge will enforce the contract. In addition, where the contractual claim is not for damages but for a debt or other liquidated (i.e. ascertained) demand, time for making a claim can be extended by a subsequent payment of money not appropriated by the debtor, because, as we have seen, the creditor can appropriate it, or by the debtor or his duly authorised agent making a written acknowledgment of the debt to the creditor or his agent. Time begins to run again from the date of the acknowledgment. However, once a debt is statute-barred it cannot be revived in this way (s. 29, Limitation Act, 1980).

Equitable remedies, i.e. specific performance or an injunction, are not covered by the ordinary limitation periods but will usually be barred much earlier under general equitable rules. An equitable remedy must be sought promptly and, according to the nature of the contract, a short delay of weeks or even days may bar the remedy.

19
Law of contract – employment protection

An ever-increasing feature of contract law is the way in which particular contracts are controlled by legislation to which the general principles of contract law yield; nowhere is this more obvious than in the contract of employment. Accordingly, the main features of this legislation, which are so important in all walks of business life, are given below. The major statutes concerned are abbreviated for convenience so that the Employment Protection (Consolidation) Act, 1978 becomes the EPCA; the Sex Discrimination Act, 1975 the SDA; the Sex Discrimination Act, 1986 the SDA 86; the Race Relations Act, 1976 the RRA; the Health and Safety at Work Act, 1974 the HASAWA; the Employment Act, 1980 the EA 80; the Employment Act, 1982 the EA 82; the Employment Act, 1988 the EA 88; the Employment Act, 1989 the EA 89 and the Employment Act, 1990 the EA 90.

Recruitment and selection of employees

Here the employer must take account of race relations and sex discrimination legislation. The RRA establishes a Commission for Racial Equality with a duty to work towards the elimination of discrimination on the grounds of race. Its powers are much the same as those of the Equal Opportunities Commission set up under the SDA. It is unlawful for an employer to discriminate between applicants for jobs on the grounds of colour, race, nationality or ethnic or national origins. It is also unlawful to publish an advertisement which could be interpreted as discriminatory. Thus job descriptions such as 'waiter' and 'salesgirl' have largely disappeared from our newspapers. However, one still sees advertisements which are clearly intended to attract female employees which are nevertheless within the law, e.g. 'publishing director requires sophisticated PA/secretary with style and charm who can remain cool under pressure'.

Under the SDA it is unlawful for a person to discriminate against another on grounds of sex or marital status when determining who will be offered a job and in regard to the terms and conditions of the job. There are exceptions where the sex or marital status of the person required is a genuine occupational qualification (GOQ), e.g. for reasons of physiology (as in the employment of a model) or for reasons of decency or privacy (as in the case of single-sex establishments such as schools and prisons) or where the job is one of two held by a married couple.

It should be noted that it is unlawful for a firm of six or more partners to discriminate on the grounds of race in regard to the selection of new partners and benefits, facilities, or services given to partners, unless a GOQ applies. Sex discrimination is unlawful in partnerships of all sizes and in companies and by sole traders, no matter how small the workforce (s. 1, Sex Discrimination Act, 1986).

EXCEPTIONS

There are some major exceptions as follows –

(a) *Private households.* Race discrimination is *not* unlawful where the employment is in a private household. Sex and marital discrimination is now in general unlawful even in private households except where the work involves e.g. intimate contact of a physical kind (SDA 86).

(b) *Work outside Great Britain.* Discrimination legislation does not apply to work which is done wholly or mainly outside Great Britain.

(c) *Under s. 5 of the EA 89.* Under these provisions the appointment of head teachers in schools and colleges may be restricted to members of a religious order where such a restriction is contained in a trust deed or other relevant instrument setting up the school or college.

ENFORCEMENT

As regards enforcement, those who believe they have been discriminated against may complain to an industrial tribunal within three months of the date of the act complained of. A conciliation officer of the Advisory Conciliation and Arbitration Service will try to settle the complaint without the need for a tribunal hearing. If this is not possible and the matter goes to a tribunal the tribunal may make an order declaring the rights of the parties in relation to the complaint. In addition, it may make an order for compensation which could cover loss of prospective earnings and injured feelings. It may also recommend that the employer take, within a specified period, action which appears to the tribunal to be practicable for the purpose of obviating or reducing the adverse effect of any act of discrimination on which the complaint is based. Proceedings (relating for example to discriminatory advertisements and instructions to discriminate) may only be instituted by the Commission for Racial Equality or the Equal Opportunities Commission, as the case may be.

ESSENTIAL CASE LAW AND COMMENT

Johnson v *Timber Tailors (Midlands)*, 1978 – Racial discrimination
(249)
Sisley v *Britannia Security Systems*, 1983 – A matter of decency
(250)

Protection during employment

Once an employee has taken up employment there are the following safeguards.

The contract of employment

The EPCA provides that an employee is entitled to one week's notice after four weeks' service. After two years' service, the minimum notice is increased to two weeks, and for each year of service afterwards it is increased by one week, to a maximum of twelve weeks after twelve years' service. The statutory minimum period of notice which an employee must give is one week, irrespective of the period of employment, provided he has been employed for at least four weeks.

In addition, an employer must give his employee written information about the terms of employment not later than 13 weeks after the employment has commenced. This statement must contain the names of the employer and the employee; the date when the employment began; whether employment with a previous employer is to be counted as part of the employee's 'continuous period of employment' and, where this is so, the date on which it began (this is important to the employee, for example, in terms of redundancy payments); the title of the job; the scale or rate of remuneration or the method of calculating remuneration; the intervals at which remuneration is paid; any terms and conditions relating to the hours worked, entitlement to holidays and holiday pay, sickness or injury and sick pay, pensions and length of notice; there must also be a note specifying any disciplinary rules, the name of a person to whom the employee can apply in case of any disciplinary decision or grievance; and the disciplinary and grievance procedures, where these are laid down. The rules for calculating continuous employment, normal hours and a week's pay are in the EPCA.

An employee who does not receive written particulars or who wants to dispute their accuracy or sufficiency may refer the matter to an industrial tribunal. The tribunal may then make a declaration that the employee has a right to a statement and what particular should be included in it or amended with it. The statement approved by the tribunal is then deemed to have been given by the employer to the employee and will form the basis of his rights.

Pay

Under the EPCA, an employee is entitled to an itemised pay statement, containing the gross amount for wages or salary; the amounts of any variable and fixed deductions and the reasons for them; and the net amount of wages or salary payable. As only gross and net amounts and deductions are required, it is apparently unnecessary for workers to be informed as to details of their basic rates, overtime payments or shift premiums. The fixed deductions can be aggregated so long as the employee is issued with a statement of fixed deductions which is reissued every twelve months, and he is notified of any alterations when they are made. If an employee does not receive a pay statement or if he receives one that is inadequate, he may refer the matter to an industrial tribunal. The industrial tribunal will make a declaration which will include answers to questions relating to the employer's failure to give particulars or his failure to give accurate amounts. The declaration then determines these matters. Where there have been unnotified deductions from pay during the previous 13 weeks, the tribunal may order the employer to pay to the employee a sum not exceeding the total unnotified deductions.

There is no presumption that a contract of employment contains an implied term that sick pay will be paid.

ESSENTIAL CASE LAW AND COMMENT

Mears v *Safecar Security*, 1982 – No presumption about sick pay (251)

STATUTORY SICK PAY

Employers are required to provide what is called *statutory sick pay* (SSP) on behalf of the government. The law is to be found in the main in the Social Security and Housing Benefit Act, 1982, the Social Security Act, 1985 and the Statutory Sick Pay Act, 1991. It is not necessary in a book of this nature to go into detail in regard to the scheme but the main principles are that when an employee falls sick he or she gets a weekly amount from the employer and not from the Department of Social Security. The employer partially recovers the amount paid as statutory sick pay by deducting 80% of the gross amount of SSP from the total amount of employees' (primary) and employers' (secondary) Class I NI contributions due to the Collector of Taxes in respect of all employees for the tax month in which the SSP was paid or from contributions due from subsequent months. Since 6 April 1985 employees have also been authorised to deduct from contributions a sum equivalent to the employers' NIC due on SSP. This was ended by the Statutory Sick Pay Act, 1991.

SSP goes on for 28 weeks and since the vast majority of employees are not sick for anything like as long as this, employee sickness benefit is, in effect, now paid by the employer. It is not possible to avoid the SSP provisions and any clause in a contract of employment which sets out to do this is void.

METHOD OF PAYMENT AND DEDUCTIONS FROM PAY

Under the Wages Act, 1986 employees no longer have a right to be paid in cash. The Truck Acts 1831–1940, which used to give this right, were repealed by the 1986 Act. Payment may still, of course, be made in cash, but an employer can if he wishes pay the employee, for example, by cheque or by crediting the employee's bank account. It should be noted, however, that if a worker was paid in cash before the 1986 Act came into force the method of payment may only be changed if the worker agrees to a variation of the contract of service.

Deductions from pay are unlawful unless they are (a) authorised by Act of Parliament, such as income tax and National Insurance deductions; or (b) contained in a written contract of employment. As regards (b) deductions from the wages of workers in the retail trade, e.g. petrol station cashiers, for stock and cash shortages are limited to 10% of the gross wages payable on any pay day but deductions may be made by instalments and no limit is placed on the amount which may be deducted from a final pay packet when employment is terminated. These provisions are enforceable by the employee against the employer in industrial tribunals.

Equal treatment in terms and conditions of employment as between men and women in the same employment

The Equal Pay Act, 1970, as amended by the SDA, implies a term into women's contracts of employment which requires equal treatment in terms of pay, holidays, sick pay and hours of work.

The Equal Pay Act, 1970 provides that the contracts of employment of all women are regarded as containing an equality clause which operates on pay when a woman is employed on 'like work' or on work 'rated as equivalent' to that of a man, e.g. by a job evaluation study.

Under the Equal Pay (Amendment) Regulations, 1983, there is a further instance when equality is to have effect, i.e. where a woman is employed on work which is, in terms of the demands made on her, for instance under such headings as effort, skill and 'decision', of equal value to that of a man in the same employment. In addition, under the Regulations a complaint may go before an industrial tribunal, even if the two jobs under comparison have already been shown to be unequal in a job evaluation study. However, there will have to be reasonable grounds for saying that the evaluation study discriminated on the grounds of sex.

A woman who believes she is not being treated equally may complain to an industrial tribunal, which may award arrears of remuneration or damages.

ESSENTIAL CASE LAW AND COMMENT

Capper Pass v *Lawton*, 1976 – An equal pay claim succeeds **(252)**
Navy, Army and Air Force Institutes v *Varley*, 1977 – An equal pay claim fails **(253)**

Discrimination in the treatment of employees

Under the SDA and RRA, it is unlawful to discriminate against a person on grounds of race, sex or marital status as regards opportunities for promotion, training or transfer, or in the provision of benefits, facilities or services or by dismissal or any other disadvantages. However, the EPCA allows women to receive special treatment when they are pregnant, and employers have in the past been able to provide different retiring ages based on sex. There is no discrimination where the sex or marital status of the employee is a genuine occupational qualification.

As regards retirement, ss. 2 and 3 of the SDA 86 provide that employers will no longer be able to have policies which set different compulsory retirement dates for men and women in comparable positions.

If an unlawful act of discrimination is committed by an employee, such as a personnel officer, the employer is held responsible for the act along with the employee unless the employer can show that he took all reasonable steps to prevent the employee from discriminating. If he can do this only the employee is responsible. It was decided in *Porcelli* v *Strathclyde Regional Council* [1986] I.C.R. 564 that sexual harassment which affects a woman's working conditions is contrary to ss. 1(1) and 6(2)(b) of the SDA under the general heading of subjection to 'any other detriment'.

ENFORCEMENT

As regards enforcement by employees, those who believe that they have been discriminated against may make a complaint to an industrial tribunal within three months of the date of the act complained of. It is then the duty of a conciliation officer to see whether the complaint can be settled without going to a tribunal. If, however, a tribunal hears the complaint, it may make an order declaring the rights of the employee and employer in regard to the complaint, the intention being that both parties will abide by the order for the future. The tribunal may also give the employee money compensation, and may additionally recommend that the employer take, within a specified period, action appearing to the tribunal to be practicable for the purpose of obviating or reducing discrimination.

ESSENTIAL CASE LAW AND COMMENT

Coleman v *Skyrail Oceanic Ltd*, 1981 – A direct discrimination **(254)**

Price v *The Civil Service Commission*, 1977 – An indirect discrimination **(255)**

Disclosure of information

The Employment Protection Act, 1975 requires employers to disclose information necessary for the purpose of collective bargaining and for purposes of good industrial relations to representatives of trade unions. The Advisory Conciliation and Arbitration Service (ACAS) has published a code of practice indicating the sort of information that should be disclosed.

If a union representative asks for information for collective bargaining purposes and the employer fails to disclose it, a complaint may be made to the Central Arbitration Committee. Conciliation may be attempted at this stage. If it fails, or is not attempted, the Committee will hear the complaint and may make a declaration upholding it and pass on the necessary information obtained from the employer to the union representative. If the employer continues to fail to disclose information, a further complaint may be lodged, and if this is upheld after another hearing, it allows the Committee to force arbitration on an employer if the union presents a claim.

Guarantee payments

Employees with not less than four weeks' continuous service are entitled to a guarantee payment if they are not provided with work on a normal working day (EPCA). The amount of the guarantee payment is reviewed from time to time by statutory instrument and is currently £14.10 per day. This guarantee is, under the EA 80, limited to five days in any three-month period. The provisions do not apply if the failure to provide work is due to a trade dispute, or if the employee has been offered suitable alternative work but has refused it.

An employee may present a complaint to an industrial tribunal that his employer has failed to pay the whole or any part of a guarantee payment to which the employee is entitled. The industrial tribunal may make an order to pay the employee the amount of guarantee payment which it finds is due to him.

Suspension from work on medical grounds

An employee with not less than four weeks' continuous service who is suspended from work under the provisions of an Act of Parliament (e.g. the HASAWA) or a code of practice, not because he is ill but because he is exposed to a health hazard at his work and may become ill if he continues at work, is entitled to be paid normal wages while suspended for up to 26 weeks (EPCA).

An employee may present a complaint to an industrial tribunal that his employer has failed to pay the whole or any part of remuneration to which he is entitled on suspension, and the tribunal may order the employer to pay the employee the remuneration due to him.

Maternity provision

FOR ANTE-NATAL CARE

Under the EPCA, as amended by the EA 80, a pregnant employee who has, on the advice of her doctor or midwife or health visitor, made an appointment to get ante-natal care must have time off to keep it and she must also be paid. Except for the first appointment the employer can ask for proof of the appointment in the form, for example, of an appointment card. An employer who does not give the employee these rights can be taken to a tribunal by the employee but this must normally be during the three months following the employer's refusal. Compensation may be given to the employee, both where the employer has failed to give time off and also where he has given time off but has failed to pay the employee. In either case the compensation will be the amount of pay to which she would have been entitled if time off with pay had been given as the law requires. Part-time employees are entitled to this time off and it does not make any difference how many hours they work each week.

FOR STATUTORY MATERNITY PAY

The Social Security Act, 1986 made major alterations to the maternity payments scheme. Prior to the Act a woman who qualified received maternity pay from which was deducted the state maternity allowance. Maternity pay was then recouped by the employer from the Maternity Pay Fund.

(a) *As regards the amount and time for which it is paid*, under the Social Security Act of 1986 statutory maternity pay (SMP) is payable through the employer who recoups it from National Insurance contributions. To qualify the woman must have worked for her present employer for at least 26 weeks ending with the week immediately preceding the 14th week before the expected week of confinement, and her normal weekly wage must not be less than the lower limit for payment of national insurance contributions, currently £54. If so, she is entitled to a payment at the lowest rate of statutory maternity pay, currently £46.30 for 18 weeks. Women who have been with the employer for two years or more, if normally employed for 16 or more hours per week, or five years or more if normally employed for eight hours or more but less than 16 hours a week will receive SMP of nine-tenths of earnings for the first six weeks of the maternity leave. The flat rate, currently £46.30, is paid for the rest of the period.

The period of 18 weeks can commence anywhere between the beginning of the eleventh week before the expected week of confinement and the sixth week before the expected week of confinement and must end no later than eleven weeks after the expected week of confinement.

(*b*) *Non-payment – remedies.* If the employer does not make payments of SMP, to which the employee thinks she is entitled, she may under the Social Security Act, 1986:

(i) Require the employer to supply her, within a reasonable time, with a written statement of his position in the matter. This will indicate why he feels that there is no entitlement, or a smaller entitlement.

(ii) If this does not resolve the dispute the employee, or the Department of Social Security, may refer the matter to an adjudication officer. An appeal from him lies to the Social Security Appeal Tribunal and from that tribunal to a Social Security Commissioner.

An employer who refuses to pay after a final decision has been made that he should pay commits a criminal offence.

If the employee cannot obtain payment from the employer, as where he is insolvent, she may apply to the Department of Employment for payment. If the Department of Employment makes the payment it may recover from the employer as by proving in the insolvency.

THE RIGHT TO RETURN TO WORK

The employee must comply with certain formalities in order that she may have the right to return to work. These are that she must give her employer at least 21 days written notice before her absence begins:

(*a*) giving the reason why she will be absent and the expected week of confinement; and

(*b*) of her intention to return to work if this is what she is going to do.

The employer may require the employee to produce a medical certificate giving the expected date of confinement.

Although a woman gives notice of her intention to return to work she is not forced to do so. This leaves the employer in a state of some uncertainty.

The 1978 Act, as amended by the Employment Act, 1980, allows the employer to check what the situation is. The employer is allowed to make a request for information from the employee. The employer cannot do this until seven weeks have passed from the beginning of the week of confinement. The employer's request must be in writing and will ask the employee to confirm her intention to return. The request must also contain a warning to the employee of the consequences of failure to comply.

An employee intending to return must confirm the fact in writing within 14 days of receiving the request or as soon as reasonably practicable, otherwise the right to return is lost. However, confirmation does not oblige the employee to return.

In order actually to get back to work, the woman must give written notice to the employer at least 21 days before the notified date of return, that date being not later than 29 weeks after the beginning of the week in which the birth occurred.

The return to work can be postponed by either the employer or the employee by up to four weeks from the date notified. The employer can postpone it for any reason so long as those reasons are notified to the employee. The employee can only postpone if she is ill and cannot work and has a medical certificate to that effect.

If there is, for example, industrial action, so that the woman cannot return on the date notified, then she may return when the interruption is over or as soon as is reasonably practicable afterwards.

If the employee carries out all the formalities for return to work but the employer refuses to allow her to return, she will be regarded as dismissed and the employer will have to show that this was not unfair dismissal (see further p. 361).

If, because of a reorganisation in the firm during the woman's absence, her job is no longer available, the employer must offer her suitable alternative employment. If there is such employment and it is not offered to her she can claim unfair dismissal. If no such work is available she is redundant and can claim a redundancy payment. If she refuses to take suitable alternative work she will have no claim on the employer.

Small employers are specially protected because they cannot easily cope with a long absence by an employee. So, if there are not more than five employees counted together with those of an 'associated employer' (e.g. in a holding and subsidiary company situation the employees in the holding company are counted together with those of the subsidiary company in deciding whether the figure is five or less), at the time when the employee left, and it is not reasonably practicable for the employer to take the employee back or to offer alternative work, then the employer is not liable if he does not take the employee back.

It should also be noted that an employee who has been absent on maternity leave must be given, on return, any pay rises granted to her grade of employment during her absence and there must be no loss of seniority or pension rights.

Time off

Time off with pay must be granted by employers to trade union officials to carry out their trade union duties and to receive training both on and off the premises (EPCA). Employees are also entitled to unpaid time off to take part in union activities (other than industrial action). The Advisory Conciliation and Arbitration Service has issued a Code of Practice as to what is reasonable. Reasonable unpaid time off must also be given to employees who hold certain public offices, e.g. as JPs or local councillors. Redundant employees must be given reasonable paid time off to look for work or arrange training for a job.

In addition the Health and Safety Commission has approved a Code of Practice to govern the exercise of the right of safety representatives appointed by recognised trade unions to have time off with pay to undergo training in health and safety matters. Furthermore, as we have seen, under the EA 80, there is a right for pregnant employees to take time off to attend ante-natal clinics. Unreasonable refusal to allow time off or to pay for time taken off gives the employee grounds to complaint to an industrial tribunal.

Insolvency of employer

An employee whose employer becomes insolvent is entitled to obtain payment of certain debts owed to him from the National Insurance Fund (E A 90). The legal rights and remedies in respect of the debts covered are transferred to the Secretary of State for Employment so that he can try to recover from the assets of the insolvent employer the cost of any payments made. Employees must apply for payment to the employer's representative, e.g. administrative receiver or liquidator, who, if unable to pay the claim in the near future, will submit the application to the Secretary of State for payment from the National Insurance Fund (formerly the Redundancy Fund) which remains in existence for this purpose. Debts included are arrears of pay up to £205 per week for a period not exceeding eight weeks, holiday pay up to £205 per week with a limit of six weeks in the last twelve months of employment; payment in lieu of notice for the minimum statutory period, up to £205 per week; any outstanding payment in regard to an award by an industrial tribunal of compensation for unfair dismissal; reimbursement of the fees of an apprentice or articled clerk.

It should be noted that the above amounts are reviewed annually by ministerial order.

Health and safety at work

The HASAWA lays down certain general duties of employers to their employees in the field of health and safety. There is a general duty on employers to ensure as far as is reasonably practicable the health, safety and welfare of all employees while at work. However, in particular, the employer must provide and maintain plant and equipment and safe systems of work; avoid risks to safety and health in handling, storing and transporting articles and substances; provide and maintain safe premises and safe means of entering and leaving them; provide and maintain adequate welfare facilities and arrangements; provide information, training and supervision as required in order to ensure the safety and health of employees; prepare and / or revise policy statements on the safety and health of employees and give proper publicity to these; consult in these matters with safety representatives appointed by trade unions; establish safety committees where union representatives ask for this.

An employer must also conduct his undertaking in such a way that so far as is reasonably practicable those who are not his employees are not exposed to risk. Additionally, an employer must ensure so far as is reasonably practicable that premises which are open to others not employed by him are safe. There is also a duty to use the best practical methods to prevent noxious or offensive substances going into the atmosphere.

Directors are required to set out in their annual reports what their companies are doing in safety and health matters, and regulations will be issued specifying the classes of company that will have to comply with this provision and the kind of information which should be included.

Employees must take reasonable care of their own and other people's health and safety and co-operate with the employer in the carrying out of his duties. The Act also states that no person shall intentionally or recklessly interfere with or misuse anything which is provided in the interests of health, safety and welfare, e.g. safety equipment, and no employer may charge any employee for anything done or provided to comply with the employer's statutory duties.

Finally, those who design, manufacture, import or supply equipment, machinery and plant must ensure that the design and construction is safe.

Enforcement is in the hands of the inspectorate of the Health and Safety Executive set up by the Act. Inspectors may issue a prohibition notice if there is a risk of serious personal injury. This operates to stop the activity concerned until remedial action specified in the notice has been taken. They may also issue an improvement notice if there is a contravention of any of the relevant statutory provisions, under which the employer must remedy the fault within a specified time. They may prosecute any person contravening the relevant statutory provision instead of or in addition to serving a notice. Failure to comply with a prohibition notice could lead to imprisonment, though there is an appeal to an industrial tribunal.

ESSENTIAL CASE LAW AND COMMENT

R v Mara, 1986 – Health and safety: the duty to non-employees
(256)

Trade union membership and activities

Under the EPCA employers have a duty not to take action against employees just because they are members of, or take part in at an appropriate time, the activities of a trade union which is independent of the employer. According to the decision in *Post Office* v *Union of Post Office Workers* [1974] 1 All E.R. 229 this includes activities on the employer's premises.

Under the provisions of s. 11 of the EA 88 dismissal for failing to join a trade union is always automatically unfair even if there is a closed shop situation within the industry concerned. This provision greatly weakens the maintenance by trade unions of closed shops.

If action is taken against employees they may complain to a tribunal which can award money compensation or make an order saying what the trade union rights of the employee are so that the employer can grant them in the future. If the employee has been dismissed then the unfair dismissal remedies apply (see further p. 358).

In addition ss. 1−3 of the EA 90 gives job seekers a new right not to be refused employment or the services of an employment agency on the grounds that they are or are not trade union members. The Act also protects people who will not agree to become or cease to be union members or to make payments in lieu of membership subscriptions. This means that it is no longer lawful to operate any form of closed shop. Any individual who believes that he or she has been unlawfully refused employment or the service of an employment agency because of union or non-union membership can complain to an industrial tribunal within three months of the refusal. If the case is made out the tribunal can award compensation up to the current maximum of £10,000.

The compensation will generally be paid by the employer or employment agency concerned but in cases where a trade union is joined as a party and the tribunal decides that the unlawful refusal resulted from pressure applied by the union it may order the union to pay some or all of the compensation.

The tribunal can also recommend that the prospective employer or employment agency should take action to remedy the adverse effect of their unlawful action on the complainant.

Termination of the contract of employment

UNFAIR DISMISSAL: GENERALLY

Before a person can ask an industrial tribunal to consider a claim that another has unfairly dismissed him or her it is once again essential to establish that the relationship of employer and employee exists between them. In this connection the EPCA provides that an employee is a person who works under a contract of service or apprenticeship, written or oral, express or implied.

ESSENTIAL CASE LAW AND COMMENT

Massey v Crown Life Insurance Co, 1978 – Unfair dismissal claims and the self-employed **(257)**

In addition to showing that he is an employee the claimant must comply with an *age requirement.* The unfair dismissal provisions do not apply to the dismissal of an employee from any employment if the employee has on or before the effective date of termination attained the age which, in the undertaking in which he is employed, was the normal retiring age for an employee holding the position which he held, or for both men and women aged 65 (SDA 86).

However, such persons are not excluded where the dismissal is automatically unfair, e.g. for taking part in trade union ativities (see further p. 358).

As regards the period of employment, the unfair dismissal provisions do not apply to the dismissal of an employee from any employment if the employee has not completed one year's continuous employment ending with the effective date of termination of employment unless the dismissal is automatically unfair. For those who started work on or after 1 October 1980 the total length of employment must exceed two years provided that during that period there were no more than 20 employees in the same firm, together with any associated employer. Again, this does not apply if the dismissal is automatically unfair and, clearly, companies within a group are associated employers. Those who started work on or after 1 June 1985 must also complete at least two years' service regardless of the size of the firm unless the dismissal is automatically unfair.

In addition, the EPCA states that no account should be taken of employment during any period when the hours of employment are normally less than 16 hours per week. After five years' employment the figure is reduced to eight hours. Again, the requirement of having worked 16 or eight hours, as the case may be, does not apply to dismissals which are automatically unfair.

As regards persons ordinarily employed outside Great Britain, the EPCA states that an employee has no protection against unfair dismissal if he is engaged in work wholly or mainly outside Great Britain. The following are also ineligible and cannot claim.

(*a*) Those on fixed contracts of two years or more if they have agreed in writing, either in the contract or during its duration, to forgo the right to compensation. If the contract was made on or after 1 October 1980 the period of the fixed term is reduced to one year.

(*b*) Any employee dismissed while taking unoffocial strike or other industrial action is unable to complain of unfair dismissal (s. 9, EA 90).

(c) Women who are dismissed because of pregnancy if they have not been employed for two years prior to the eleventh week before the expected week of confinement.

(d) Certain other categories are excluded by the EPCA, e.g. members of the armed forces and of the police.

It should also be noted that s. 16 of the EA 89 allows regulations to be made to test the strength of the case of each party before a full hearing proceeds. Pre-hearing reviews are introduced at which the chairman of the tribunal may sit alone without the two lay assessors. The chairman may, at his discretion and following an application by one of the parties, or of his own motion, require a deposit of up to £150 from the other party as a condition of proceeding further if it is considered that his or her case has no reasonable prospect of success, or that to pursue it would be frivolous, vexatious or otherwise unreasonable.

Industrial Tribunal Regulations also provide for pre-hearing assessments, and if a party to the proceedings before an industrial tribunal considers that an application, or a particular contention, is unlikely to succeed or be accepted he can ask for a pre-hearing assessment to be made. A tribunal can make such an assessment of its own volition. Following the pre-hearing assessment, at which the parties may submit written representations and put forward oral argument but not evidence, the tribunal may indicate its opinion that if the party who is unlikely to succeed carries on with the application or persists in the contention an order for costs may be made against him. The opinion is placed before the tribunal which conducts the full hearing if it takes place. No member of the tribunal which gave the opinion may be a member of the tribunal which takes the full hearing.

DISMISSAL – MEANING OF

An employee cannot claim unfair dismissal unless there has first been a dismissal recognised by law. We may consider the matter under the following headings.

Actual dismissal

This does not normally give rise to problems since most employees recognise the words of an actual dismissal, whether given orally or in writing.

A typical letter of dismissal appears below.

> Dear Mr Bloggs,
> I am sorry that you do not have the necessary aptitude to deal with the work which we have allocated to you. I hope that you will be able to find other work elsewhere which is more in your line. As you will recall from your interview this morning, the company will not require your services after the 31st of this month.

Constructive dismissal

This occurs where it is the employee who leaves the job but is compelled to do so by the conduct of the employer. In general terms the employer's conduct must be a fundamental breach so that it can be regarded as a repudiation of the contract. Thus, if a male employer were to sexually assault his female secretary then this would be a fundamental breach entitling her to leave and sue for her loss on the basis of constructive dismissal.

Fixed-term contracts

When a fixed-term contract expires and is not renewed there is a dismissal. However, where a contract is for two years or more the employee may have waived his right to complain of unfair dismissal. If the contract is made on or after 1 October 1980 the period of the fixed term is reduced to one year.

DISMISSAL – GROUNDS FOR

If an employer is going to escape liability for unfair dismissal he must show that he acted *reasonably* and, indeed, the EPCA requires the employer to give his reasons for dismissal to the employee in writing.

It should be remembered that the question whether a dismissal is fair or not is a matter of *fact* for the particular tribunal hearing the case and one cannot predict with absolute accuracy what a particular tribunal will do on the facts of a particular case. Basically, when all is said and done, the ultimate question for a tribunal is – 'was the dismissal fair and reasonable' in fact.

The EA 80 amended the EPCA by including in the test of reasonableness required in determining whether a dismissal was fair, the 'size and administrative resources of the employer's undertaking'. This was included as a result of fear that the unfair dismissal laws were placing undue burdens on small firms and causing them not to engage new workers. The EA 80 also removed the burden of proof from the employer in showing reasonableness so that there is now no 'presumption of guilt' on the employer and the tribunal is left to decide whether or not the employer acted reasonably.

Reasons justifying dismissal

These are as follows.

(*a*) *Lack of capability.* This would usually arise at the beginning of employment where it becomes clear at an early stage that the employee cannot do the job in terms of lack of skill or mental or physical health. It should be remembered that the longer a person is in employment the more difficult it is to establish lack of capability.

By way of illustration we can consider the case of *Alidair* v *Taylor* [19788] I.R.L.R. 82. The pilot of an aircraft had made a faulty landing which damaged the aircraft. There was a board of inquiry which found that the faulty landing was due to a lack of flying knowledge on the part of the pilot who was dismissed from his employment. It was decided that the employee had not been unfairly dismissed, the tribunal taking the view that where, as in this case, one failure to reach a high degree of skill could have serious consequences, an instant dismissal could be justified.

However, it was decided in *British Sulphur* v *Lawrie* [1987] I.R.B. 338 that the dismissal of an employee who was alleged to be unwilling or incompetent to do a particular job could still be unfair if the employee was not provided with adequate training.

(*b*) *Conduct.* This is always a difficult matter to deal with and much will depend upon the circumstances of the case. However, incompetence and neglect are relevant, as are disobedience and misconduct, e.g. by assaulting fellow employees. Immorality and habitual drunkenness could also be brought under this heading and, so it seems, can dress where this can be shown to affect adversely the way in which the contract of service is performed.

ESSENTIAL CASE LAW AND COMMENT

Boychuk v *H. J. Symons (Holdings) Ltd*, 1977 – A dismissal for conduct **(258)**

(*c*) *Redundancy.* Genuine redundancy is a defence. Where a person is redundant his employer cannot be expected to continue the employment, although there are safeguards in the matter of *unfair selection for redundancy* (see p. 361).

(*d*) *Dismissals which are union related.* An employee will be regarded as automatically unfairly dismissed if the principal reason for the dismissal was that he was, or proposed to become, a member of a trade union which was independent of the employer; that he had taken part or proposed to take part in the activities of such a union at an appropriate time, i.e. outside working hours or within working hours with the consent of the employer; that he was not a member of any trade union or of a particular one or had refused or proposed to refuse to become or remain a member. Under the relevant provisions of the EA 80 all closed shop dismissals are now automatically unfair.

The position in regard to job applicants under the EA 90 has already been considered (see p. 354).

(*e*) *Statutory restriction placed on employer or employee.* If, for example, the employer's business was found to be dangerous and was closed down under Act of Parliament or ministerial order, the employees would not be unfairly dismissed. Furthermore, a lorry driver who was banned from driving for twelve months could be dismissed fairly.

(*f*) *Some other substantial reason.* An employer may on a wide variety of grounds which are not specified by legislation satisfy an industrial tribunal that a dismissal was fair and reasonable.

Crime and suspicion of crime may be brought under this heading, though if dismissal is based on suspicion of crime, the suspicion must be reasonable and in all cases the employee must be told that dismissal is contemplated and in the light of this information be allowed to give explanations and make representations against dismissal.

Where an employee has been charged with theft from the employer and is awaiting trial, the best course of action is to suspend rather than dismiss him, pending the verdict. Investigations which the employer must make, as part of establishing a fair dismissal, could be regarded as an interference with the course of justice. It is best, therefore, not to make them, but to suspend the employee. The case of *Wadley* v *Eager Electrical* [1986] I.R.L.R. 93 should be noted. In that case husband and wife worked for the same firm. The wife was convicted for stealing £2000 from the company whilst employed as a shop assistant. The husband was a service engineer with the firm. Husband and wife were dismissed and it was held that the husband's dismissal was unfair. He was a good employee of 17 years' standing and no misconduct had been made out against him.

The matter of fair or unfair dismissal depends also upon the terms of the contract. If the difficulty is that a particular employee is refusing to do work which involves him, say, spending nights away from home, then his dismissal is likely to be regarded as fair if there is an *express term* in his contract requiring this. Of course, the nature of the job may require it, as in the case of a long-distance lorry driver where such a term would be implied, if not expressed.

Employees who are in breach of contract are likely to be regarded as fairly dismissed. However, this is not an invariable rule. Thus a long-distance lorry driver who refused to take on a particular trip because his wife was ill and he had to look after the children would be unfairly dismissed (if dismissal took place) even though he was, strictly speaking, in breach of his contract.

Grievance and disciplinary procedures

These are usually part of the contract. The employer must comply with them if he wishes to avoid liability. If a series of oral and written warnings is laid down, the procedure should be observed. However, reasonableness will always prevail.

No matter how good the employer's reason for dismissal may be there may still be a claim by the employee for unfair dismissal if the dismissal was 'unfair in all the circumstances'.

In *Whitbread & Co plc* v *Mills* [1988] I.R.L.R. 43 the President of the Employment Appeal Tribunal (EAT), Mr Justice Wood, gave guidance on the issue of whether an employer had acted reasonably as the law requires. In applying the guidance let us assume that the main reason for dismissal is the acceptable one of incompetence as in the case of a senior member of a publisher's staff who commissions books without proper market research so that they do not sell and the publisher is caused loss.

Having reached the conclusion that the incompetence is established the employer must according to Mr Justice Wood satisfy a tribunal on four other matters, otherwise the dismissal might still be unfair, though the employee's compensation might be reduced for contributory fault (see below). The four matters are:

(a) Can the employer satisfy a tribunal that he complied with the pre-dismissal procedures which a reasonable employer could and should have applied in the circumstances of the case? If the tribunal finds that the employer has not acted reasonably in this regard, at the date of dismissal, then according to the decision in *Polkey* v *A. E. Dayton Services Ltd* [1988] I.C.R. 564 it is not open to the tribunal to say that the procedures do not matter since it is clear that the employee was incompetent. The unfairness of the dismissal could still give the employee a successful claim.

(b) Where there is a contractual appeal process the employer must have carried it out in its essentials. A minor departure may sometimes be ignored but a total or substantial failure entitles a tribunal to find that the dismissal was unfair. Even though no contractual appeal process exists it may nevertheless be reasonable, as was decided in *West Midland Co-operative Society Ltd* v *Tipton* [1986] I.C.R. 192, for some sort of appeal to be arranged since this is encouraged by the Code of Practice issued by ACAS.

(c) Where conduct is the main reason the employer must show, on a balance of probabilities, that at the time of the dismissal he believed the employee was guilty of misconduct and that in all the circumstances of the case it was reasonable for him to do so.

(d) During the disciplinary hearings and the appeal process the employer must have been fair to the employee. In particular the employee must have been heard and allowed to put his case properly or, if he was not at a certain stage of the procedures, this must have been corrected before dismissal.

Thus if an employee commits an armed robbery on his employer's premises he could, and would, be dismissed quite fairly without going through a warning procedure. There would be no need to tell him that if he robbed the premises again he was in danger of losing his job!

Employee's contributory fault

This can reduce the compensation payable to the employee by such percentage as the tribunal thinks fit. Suppose an employee is often late for work and one morning his employer, who can stand it no more, sacks him. The dismissal is likely to be unfair in view of the lack of warning but a tribunal would very probably reduce the worker's compensation to take account of the situation.

Principles of natural justice also apply; it is necessary to let the worker state his case before a decision to dismiss is taken. Furthermore, reasonable inquiry must be made to find the truth of the matter before reaching a decision. Failure to do this will tend to make the dismissal unfair.

Unacceptable reasons for dismissal

These are as follows.

(*a*) *Dismissal in connection with trade unions*. This has already been considered on p. 354.

(*b*) *Unfair selection for redundancy*. An employee dismissed for redundancy may complain that he has been unfairly dismissed if he is of the opinion that he has been unfairly selected for redundancy, as where the employer has selected him because he is a member of a trade union or takes part in trade union activities, or where the employer has disregarded redundancy selection arrangements based, for example, on 'last in, first out'. Ideally, all employers should have proper redundancy agreements on the lines set out in the Department of Employment booklet, *Dealing with Redundancies*.

However, even though there is in existence an agreed redundancy procedure, the employer may defend himself by showing a 'special reason' for departing from that procedure, e.g. because the person selected for redundancy lacks the skill and versatility of a junior employee who is retained.

There is, since the decision of the EAT in *Williams* v *Compair Maxam* [1982] I.C.R. 156, an overall standard of fariness also in redundancy arrangements. The standards laid down in the case require the giving of maximum notice; consultation with unions, if any; the taking of the views of more than one person as to who should be dismissed; a requirement to follow any laid down procedure, i.e. last in, first out; and finally, an effort to find the employees concerned alternative employment within the organisation. However, the EAT stated in *Meikle* v *McPhail (Charleston Arms)* (1983) (see p. 722) that these guidelines would be applied less rigidly to the smaller business.

(*c*) *Industrial action*. The position in this context has already been considered at p. 358.

(*d*) *Dismissal of pregnant employee*. A woman who is dismissed because she is pregnant will be treated as having been unfairly dismissed unless certain circumstances apply, for example that she is unable to do her job and cannot be offered, or has refused, suitable alternative work. Even in these cases where the dismissal would be regarded as fair, the woman is nevertheless entitled to maternity pay and may claim reinstatement after confinement.

Refusal to take a woman back after pregnancy is also unfair dismissal. If at the start of the absence due to pregnancy there are five employees or less (including those employed by an associated company) the employer may show that it is not reasonably practical to offer the worker her old job back or another one substantially similar in terms and there is no unfair dismissal. In larger firms than this, as we have seen above, the employee's rights can be curtailed only if the employer can show that it is not reasonably practical to give the old job back and that a suitable alternative has been offered and unreasonably refused. Failure by the employer to comply with the obligations placed on him by law can result in the employee obtaining an order that she can be taken back or, if this is refused or is not practical, an order for compensation on the grounds of unfair dismissal.

An employee who delays her return to work beyond the appropriate date may be dismissed and if she is the dismissal will not be unfair (*Dowouna* v *John Lewis Partnership plc* [1987] I.R.L.R. 310.

(*e*) *Pressure on employer to dismiss unfairly.* It is no defence for an employer to say that pressure was put upon him to dismiss an employee unfairly. So, if other workers put pressure on an employer to dismiss a non-union member so as, for example, to obtain a closed shop, the employer will have no defence to a claim for compensation for the dismissal if he gives in to that pressure. If an employer alleges that he was pressurised into dismissing an employee and that pressure was brought on him by a trade union or other person by the calling, organising, procuring or financing of industrial action, including a strike, or by the threat of such things, and the reason for the pressure was that the employee was not a member of the trade union, then the employer can join the trade union or other person as a party to the proceedings if he is sued by the dismissed worker for unfair dismissal. If the tribunal awards compensation it can order that a person joined as a party to the proceedings should pay such amount of it as is just and equitable, and if necessary this can be a complete indemnity so that the employer will recover all the damages awarded against him from the union.

(*f*) *Transfer of business.* The Transfer of Undertakings (Protection of Employment) Regulations, 1981 apply to transfers of businesses which take place on or after 1 May 1982. Under the Regulations if a business or part of it is transferred and an employee is dismissed because of this, the dismissal will be treated as automatically unfair. However, the person concerned is not entitled to the extra compensation given to other cases of automatically unfair dismissal (see p. 365).

If the old employer dismissed before transfer, or the new employer dismissed after the transfer, either will have a defence if he can prove that the dismissal was for 'economic, technical or organisational' reasons requiring a change in the workforce and that the dismissal was reasonable in all the circumstances of the case.

ESSENTIAL CASE LAW AND COMMENT

Meikle v *McPhail (Charleston Arms)*, 1983 – A dismissal for economic reasons **(259)**

UNFAIR DISMISSAL AND FRUSTRATION OF CONTRACT

In cases appearing before industrial tribunals there is a certain interplay between the common-law rules of frustration of contract (see p. 327) and the statutory provisions relating to unfair dismissal. At common law a contract of service is frustrated by incapacity, e.g. sickness, if that incapacity makes the contract substantially impossible of performance at a particularly vital time, or by a term of imprisonment. If a contract has been so frustrated then a complaint of unfair dismissal is not available because the contract has been discharged on other grounds, i.e. by frustration. Thus termination of a contract of service by frustration prevents a claim for unfair dismissal.

REMEDIES FOR UNFAIR DISMISSAL

These are as follows.

Conciliation

An industrial tribunal will not hear a complaint until a conciliation officer has had a chance to see whether he can help. A copy of the complaint made to the industrial tribunal is sent to the conciliation officer and if he is unable to settle the complaint, nothing said by the employer or employee during the process of conciliation will be admissible in evidence before the tribunal.

Other remedies

An employee who has been dismissed may:

(a) seek reinstatement or re-engagement; or
(b) claim compensation.

The power to order (a) above is discretionary and in practice rarely exercised. However, reinstatement means taken back by the employer on exactly the same terms and seniority as before; re-engagement is being taken back but on different terms.

Calculation of compensation

The compensation for unfair dismissal is in four parts as follows.

(a) *The basic award* (maximum: £5160). This award is computed as a redundancy payment (see p. 367 before reading on) except there is no maximum age limit. Contributory fault of the employee is taken into account.

Example: Fred, a 35-year-old lorry driver employed for ten years earning £140 per week (take home £120) is unfairly dismissed. He did his best to get a comparable job but did not in fact obtain one until two weeks after the tribunal hearing. Fred had a history of lateness for work and his contributory fault is assessed at 25 per cent.

Fred's basic award: Fred is in the category 22 years of age but under 41 years of age for redundancy which allows one week's pay for every year of service:

10 × £140	£1400		
Less: 25%	£350		
	£1050	=	basic award

If Fred's dismissal had been automatically unfair, e.g. for union membership, the minimum award is £2700. This may be reduced for contributory fault.

(b) *Compensatory award* (maximum: £10,000). This consists of:

(i) estimated loss of wages, net of tax and other deductions to the date of the hearing less any money earned between date of dismissal and the hearing;
(ii) estimated future losses;
(iii) loss of any benefits such as pension rights and expenses;
(iv) loss of statutory rights. It is rare to get an award under this heading but it can be given for loss of minimum notice entitlement. For example, Fred has been continuously employed for ten years. He was entitled to ten weeks' notice which he did not get. He now has a new job but it will take him time to build up that entitlement again. A tribunal can award something for this. Once again contributory fault is taken into account.

Fred's compensatory award:

			£
The loss up to the hearing	10 × £140		1400
Loss up to time of getting new job	2 × £140		280
			1680
Less: 25%			420
		£	1260
Loss of statutory rights: a nominal figure of		100	
Less: 25%		25	75
			£1335

Fred's total award is therefore:

	£
Basic	1050
Compensatory	1335
	£2385

If Fred has lost anything else, e.g. use of firm's van at weekends and/or pension rights, these would be added to the compensatory award subject to 25% discount for contributory fault.

Additional award. This is available in addition to the above where an employer fails to comply with an order for reinstatement or re-engagement unless it was not practicable for him to do so.

(i) If the original dismissal was unlawful under the RRA or SDA, it is not less than 26 weeks' pay nor more than 52 weeks' pay with a maximum of £205 per week, and an overall maximum of £10,000.
(ii) In other cases (not where dismissal is automatically unfair – see below), it is not less than 13 weeks' pay nor more than 26 weeks' pay calculated as in (i) above.

(c) *A special award.* This is payable where the dismissal is automatically unfair and the employee has asked for reinstatement or re-engagement but the tribunal has refused to make such an order. It can make a special award instead. The compensation is a week's pay but without limit as to amount, multiplied by 104 weeks with a minimum amount of £13,400 and a maximum of £26,800. However, if a tribunal does make an order for reinstatement or re-engagement and the employer does not comply but cannot show that it was reasonably impracticable for him to do so, the compensation is increased to a week's pay (no limit) multiplied by 156 with a minimum of £20,100 and no maximum. In all cases a deduction will be made for contributory fault, if any, of the employee.

Any unemployment or supplementary benefits received by the employee are deducted from any award made by a tribunal. However, the employer must pay the amount(s) in question direct to the DSS.

(d) *Time limits.* A claim for compensation against an employer must reach the tribunal within three months of the date of termination of employment. The period in regard to dismissal in connection with a strike or other industrial action is six months. A worker can claim while working out his notice but no award can be made until employment ends.

A tribunal can hear a claim after three months if the employee can prove that:

(i)   it was not reasonably practicable for him to claim within three months;

(ii) he did so as soon as he could in the circumstances.

Discriminatory dismissal

In addition to legislation relating to unfair dismissal generally, the SDA and the RRA deal with complaints to industrial tribunals for dismissal on the grounds of sex, marital status or race. The nature and scope of these provisions have already been considered and it is only necessary to add here that there are provisions in the EPCA which prevent double compensation being paid, once under sex discrimination legislation or race discrimination legislation, and once under the general unfair dismissal provisions of the EPCA.

Redundancy

The EPCA gives an employee a right to compensation by way of a redundancy payment if he is dismissed because of a redundancy.

MEANING OF REDUNDANCY

Under the EPCA redundancy is *presumed* to occur where the services of employees are dispensed with because the employer ceases, or intends to cease carrying on business, or to carry on business at the place where the employee was employed, or does not require so many employees to do work of a certain kind. Employees who have been laid off or kept on short time without pay for four consecutive weeks (or for six weeks in a period of 13 weeks) are entitled to end their employment and to seek a redundancy payment if there is no reasonable prospect that normal working will be resumed.

ELIGIBILITY

In general terms, all those employed under a contract of service as employees are entitled to redundancy pay, including a person employed by his/her spouse. Furthermore, a volunteer for redundancy is not debarred from claiming. However, certain persons are excluded by statute or circumstances. The main categories are listed below:

(*a*) a domestic servant in a private household who is a close relative of the employer. The definition of 'close relative' for this purpose is father, mother, grandfather, grandmother, stepfather, stepmother, son, daughter, grandson, granddaughter, stepson, stepdaughter, brother, sister, half-brother, or half-sister;

(*b*) an employee who has not completed at least two years of continuous service since reaching the age of 18;

(*c*) men and women who have reached retirement age. In this connection s. 16 of the EA 89 removes a previous discriminatory feature which was that men could receive statutory redundancy payments up to age 65 but women only up to age 60. This anomaly remained even though the SDA 86 removed the right of employers to set discriminatory retiring ages. Where there is a 'normal retiring age' for the job in question which is below 65 and is the same for men and women, i.e. non-discriminatory, the entitlement of both sexes is restricted to that age. In all other cases women's entitlement is extended to age 65 in line with that of men.

(*d*) part-time workers who normally work less than 16 hours per week. After five years' employment the figure is reduced to eight hours;

(*e*) where in the case of a fixed term contract of two years or more the employee has agreed in writing in the contract or at any stage of the contract to forgo his right to claim redundancy payment;

(*f*) employees who normally work outside Great Britain under their contract;

(*g*) workers on strike can generally be dismissed by their employers without liability to make a redundancy payment. This applies even though the employer was short of work at the time of the strike so a redundancy situation did exist. Where the strike takes place after a redundancy notice has been given, the employee concerned may still get part or all of his redundancy pay by applying to a tribunal which has a power under the EPCA to make an award which is 'just and equitable', the amount being arrived at by the tribunal.

An employee who accepts an offer of suitable alternative employment with his employer is not entitled to a redundancy payment. Where a new offer is made, there is a trial period of four weeks following the making of the offer, during which the employer or the employee may end the contract while retaining all rights and liabilities under redundancy legislation.

ESSENTIAL CASE LAW AND COMMENT

Fuller v *Stephanie Bowman*, 1977 – Unreasonable refusal of alternative employment **(260)**

AMOUNT OF REDUNDANCY PAYMENT

Those aged 41 to 65 (or retiring age if lower) receive one and a half weeks' pay (up to a maximum of £205 per week) for each year of service up to a maximum of 20 years. In other age groups the above provisions apply except that the week's pay changes, i.e. for those aged 22, but under 41, it is one week's pay, and for those 18, but under 22, it is a half week's pay.

For example, a man of 52 who is made redundant having been continuously employed for 18 years and earning £120 per week as gross salary at the time of his redundancy would be entitled to a redundancy payment as follows:

34 to 41 years = 7 years at one week's pay	= 7 weeks
41 to 52 years = 11 years at one and a half week's pay	= 16½ weeks
	23½ weeks

It follows, therefore, that the redundancy payment would be 23½ weeks × £120 = £2820.

Employees over 64 (both men and women) have their redundancy payment reduced progressively so that for each complete month by which the age exceeds 64 (or 59) on the Saturday of the week on which the contract ends, the normal entitlement is reduced by one-twelfth. Thus a man (or woman) aged 64 years and three months would have three-twelfths of the award deducted. The tapering provisions set out above do not apply if the normal retiring age is 64 or lower. Complaints by employees in respect of the right to a redundancy payment or questions as to its amount may, as we have seen, be made to an industrial tribunal which will make a declaration as to the employee's rights which form the basis on which payment can be recovered from the employer.

REBATES FOR EMPLOYERS

Section 13 of the EA 89 abolished the scheme under which employers with less than ten employees could claim a rebate from the government towards the cost of payment.

PROCEDURE FOR HANDLING REDUNDANCIES

A good starting-point is to ask for voluntary redundancies. If this does not provide enough persons then any agreed formula must be followed, e.g. last in, first out. Selection procedures may also be based on poor work performance or attendance record and there is no requirement on the employer to determine reasons for this (*Dooley* v *Leyland Vehicles Ltd* [1986] I.R.L.R. 36). If there is no agreed procedure the employer must decide after considering the pros and cons in each case. Everyone should, as far as possible, be allowed to express his or her views, e.g. through elected representatives, if any. An attempt to relocate a redundant worker should be considered. Failure to do so can result in a finding of unfair dismissal unless, of course, there was no chance of finding suitable alternative work.

Selecting, say, a white single girl, or a West Indian single man to go, rather than a married white man with two children and a mortgage might appear to be humane. However, unless the decision is made on the basis of competence, experience, reliability and so on, the dismissal is likely to be unfair and also a breach of the SDA and/or the RRA.

Under the Employment Protection Act 1975 where an employer proposes to dismiss as redundant *any* employee where there is an independent trade union recognised by that employer in regard to the class of the employee concerned, the employer has a duty to consult with representatives of that union. This means there must be consultation even for one dismissal. However, where 100 or more workers are to be dismissed within 90 days or less, the employer must consult at least 90 days before the first dismissal takes place. If the proposal is to dismiss ten or more workers within 30 days at one establishment he must consult at least 30 days before the first dismissal.

Failure to do this gives the union(s) a right to go to a tribunal which, unless it finds that the employer could not reasonably consult because of circumstances, may make a declaration of non-compliance and possibly grant *protective awards*. These are awards of remuneration for a protected period for those employees dismissed without proper consulation. The maximum period where 100 or more workers are dismissed is 90 days; 10 or more, 30 days; less than 10, 28 days.

The employer must also inform the Department of Employment if dismissing 100 or more employees within 90 days or less, or 10 or more within 30 days or less. The DoE must be informed of this intention at least 90 days or 30 days respectively, before the first dismissal is to take place. There is no need to notify if it is proposed to make less than ten employees redundant. Failure to notify can mean a fine on conviction by the court. Notification to the DoE applies whether or not there is a recognised trade union.

General standards of fairness for redundancy were laid down by the Employment Appeal Tribunal in *Williams* v *Compair Maxam* [1982] I.C.R. 156. These were the giving of maximum notice; consultation with unions, if any; the taking of the view of more than one person as to who should be dismissed; the requirement to follow any laid down procedure, e.g. last in, first out; and, finally, an effort to find the employees concerned alternative employment within the organisation. It should be noted that in *Meikle* v *McPhail (Charleston Arms)* [1983] I.R.L.R. 351 the EAT stated that these guidelines would be applied less rigidly to the smaller business.

As we have seen, when a worker is to be made redundant, the ACAS Code of Practice and the decision in *Williams* v *Compair Maxam* (1982) (above) both stress the importance of consultation.

However, as the result of the EAT's decision in *British Labour Pump Co* v *Byrne* [1979] I.R.L.R. 94 mere failure to consult on the employer's part was not in itself enough to make a dismissal for redundancy automatically unfair. Under the *British Labour Pump* principle a failure to consult was not to be regarded as unreasonable if consultation would have made no difference in the end, as where, for example, the company was insolvent and its state so grave that redundancy was probably inevitable anyway.

However, the House of Lords decided to overrule the *British Labour Pump* principle in *Polkey* v *A. E. Dayton Services Ltd* [1987] I.C.R. 142. The House of Lords decided that where an employer failed to consult or warn an employee it was not right for an industrial tribunal to ask in considering whether the employee had been unfairly dismissed whether he would nevertheless have been dismissed even if he had been consulted or warned. The correct question was whether the employer's action in regarding his reason for dismissing the employee as sufficient had been reasonable or unreasonable *at the time of dismissal*. That the facts subsequently showed that redundancy had been inevitable was not the point.

While the *British Labour Pump* case reigned supreme, the consultation procedures of Codes of Practice and judicial decisions were much weakened. Subsequent events might justify a redundancy without consultation so that the employer could say that he would not have acted differently in the event even if there had been consultation with employees. The House of Lords in *Polkey* was clearly concerned to re-establish good industrial relations practice which involves consultation except, perhaps, where the employer's situation is so totally hopeless that there would be no point in consultation. However, in other cases consultation is not only a courtesy, it can sometimes produce solutions leading to the retention of employees.

Collective agreements on redundancy

The Secretary of State may, on the application of the employer and the unions involved, make an order modifying the requirements of redundancy pay legislation if he is satisfied that there is a collective agreement which makes satisfactory alternative arrangements for dealing with redundancy. The provisions of the agreement must be 'on the whole at least as favourable' as the statutory provisions, and must include, in particular, arrangements allowing an employee to go to an independent arbitration or to make a complaint to an industrial tribunal.

Written statement of reasons for dismissal

At common law an employer is not required to give his employee any reasons for dismissal. However, the EPCA provides that where an employee is dismissed, with or without notice, or by failure to renew a contract for a fixed term, he must be provided by his employer on request, within 14 days of that request, with a written statement giving particulars of the reasons for his dismissal. This provision applies only to employees who have been continuously employed for a period of two years (EA 89, s. 11). The written statement is admissible in evidence in any proceedings relating to the dismissal and if an employer refuses to give a written statement the employee may complain to an industrial tribunal. If the tribunal upholds the complaint it may make a declaration as to what it finds the employer's reasons were for dismissing the employee and must make an award of two weeks' pay without limit as to amount to the employee.

EMPLOYEE'S BREACH OF CONTRACT

An employer may sue his employees for damages for breach of the contract of service by the employee. Such claims are potentially available, for example, for damage to the employer's property, as where machinery is damaged by negligent operation, as was the case in *Baster* v *London and County Printing Works* [1899] 1 Q.B. 901, or for refusal to work resulting in damage by lost production, as was the case in *National Coal Board* v *Galley* [1958] 1 All E.R. 91. Such claims are rare and impractical because of the fact that the employee will not, in most cases, be able to meet the claim, and also, perhaps more importantly, because they lead to industrial unrest. In these circumstances we do not pursue the matter further here.

20
The law of torts – general principles

It is difficult to give a satisfactory definition of a tort. According to Professor Winfield 'tortious liability arises from a duty primarily fixed by law: this duty is towards persons generally and its breach is redressible by an action for unliquidated damages'.

The nature of a tort

It is a matter of dispute whether there should be a law of tort or a law of torts: there are two schools of thought. One maintains that there should be a law of tort, i.e. that all harm should be actionable in the absence of just cause or excuse. If there was merely a law of specific torts, then no new new torts could be created by the courts and the categories of tortious liability would be closed. It is urged that under the flexibility of case law new torts have come into being, and in no case has an action been refused simply because it was novel. This is called the *general principle of liability theory*. The other view is that there should be a law of torts – that there should be only specific torts and unless the damage suffered can be brought under a known or recognised head of liability, there should be no remedy. This view is supported by modern cases where an attempt has been made, unsuccessfully, to establish a purported tort of eviction and a tort of perjury. Thus the courts have refused to create new torts even when given the opportunity. This is particularly unfortunate in the case of perjury. Perjury is not merely an offence against the State, as it has been traditionally regarded by the courts. It can cause an individual great loss or hardship and many feel that the victim should have a civil remedy in damages.

In addition, there is a danger in modern society of a serious invasion of privacy resulting from the increasing availability and use of electronic and other devices as a means of surreptitious surveillance and the accumulation of personal information about individuals in data banks, computers and credit registers. Apart from e.g. the law of defamation which protects against the publication of falsehoods, the common law of tort does not appear to be capable of extending to a remedy for invasion of privacy as such.

There is, yet, no general legislation on the matter of privacy, but the Data Protection Act, 1984 deals with information stored on computers. The details of the Act are beyond the scope of a book of this nature but the job of safeguarding the privacy of the individual in terms e.g. of the information kept on him and the uses to which it is put falls under the Act to the Data Registrar who is appointed by the Crown. He supervises a central register on which all data users must enter details of data banks and their purposes. The Registrar and 'data subjects', the latter through the courts, have access to records on computers.

Hence we may conclude that at the present there is no general principle of liability in tort. Nevertheless, if judges have not created new torts, they have applied old-cases to new situations. This has resulted in an extension of the old torts and there is a tendency to expand the area of liability, particularly in the field of negligence (see p. 435). If this continues, the law may reach a stage approximating to a general liability for wrongful acts, for, as Lord Macmillan said in *Donoghue* v *Stevenson*, 1932, 'the categories of negligence are never closed'.

ESSENTIAL CASE LAW AND COMMENT

Perera v *Vandiyar*, 1953 – No tort of eviction **(261)**
Hargreaves v *Bretherton*, 1958 – No tort of perjury **(262)**
Roy v *Prior*, 1969 – No tort of perjury reaffirmed **(263)**
Donoghue v *Stevenson*, 1932 – The categories of negligence can
  be expanded **(264)**

Damage and liability

The law distinguishes between two concepts – (1) *Damnum*, which means the damage suffered, and (2) *Injuria*, which is an injury having legal consquences. Sometimes, but not always, these two go together. For instance, if I negligently drive a car and injure a person, he suffers *damnum* (the hurt) and *injuria* (because he has a right of action to be compensated). There are, however, cases of *damnum sine injuria* (damage suffered without the violation of a legal right), and *injuria sine damno* (the violation of a legal right without damage).

The mere fact that a person has suffered damage does not entitle him to maintain an action in tort. Before an action can succeed, the harm suffered must be caused by an act which is a violation of a right which the law vests in the plaintiff or injured party. Damage suffered in the absence of the violation of such legal right is known as *damnum sine injuria*. Furthermore a person who suffers *damnum* cannot receive compensation on the basis of *injuria* suffered by another. The concept of *damnum sine injuria* is not the same as that concerning whether there is a law of tort or a law of torts because under the concept of *damnum sine injuria* a person may suffer harm and have no claim even though the harm was suffered *as a result of a known tort*.

ESSENTIAL CASE LAW AND COMMENT

Best v *Samuel Fox & Co Ltd*, 1952 – No proprietary right in a spouse **(265)**

Electrochrome Ltd v *Welsh Plastics Ltd*, 1968 – Loss but no damage to the plaintiff's property **(266)**

MALICE

The fact that the defendant acts with malice, i.e. with the intention of injuring his neighbour, does not give rise to a cause of action unless a legal right of the plaintiff is infringed. On the other hand, whenever there is an invasion of a legal right, the person in whom the right is vested may bring an action and recover damages (though these may be nominal) or, what may be more important, obtain an injunction, although he has suffered no actual harm. For example, an action will lie for an unlawful entry on the land of another (trespass) although no actual damage is done. Furthermore, in *Ashby* v *White* 1703), 2 Ld. Raym. 938, it was held that an elector had a right of action, for a form of nuisance or distrubance of rights, when his vote was wrongly rejected by the returning officer although the candidate for whom he tried to vote was elected. This is known as *injuria sine damno*.

MOTIVE

It is important to be clear on the mental element or the question of malice in tort. The law of torts is concerned more with the effects of injurious conduct than with the motives which inspired it. Hence, just as a bad intention will not necessarily make the infliction of damage actionable, so an innocent intention is usually no defence. However, there are circumstances in which malice is important. Thus where a person puts in motion the criminal law against another, this is actionable if malice is shown to be present and is known as the tort of malicious prosecution. Furthermore, the question of malice may be raised when certain *defences* are pleaded. Thus in the law of defamation the defences of qualified privilege and fair comment are allowed only where the defendant has not been malicious. Finally, in regard to the tort of nuisance, certain acts which would not necessarily be a nuisance may be regarded as such if they are exercised unreasonably. Malice is sometimes regarded as evidence of conduct which is unreasonable. (See *Christie* v *Davey*, 1893, p. 774.)

ESSENTIAL CASE LAW AND COMMENT

Bradford Corporation v *Pickles*, 1895 – Effect of bad intention **(267)**

Wilkinson v *Downton*, 1897 – Effect of innocent intention **(268)**

Parties in the law of torts

It is now necessary to consider certain categories of persons whose capacity in connection with tortious acts is limited.

MINORS

A minor can sue in tort as a plaintiff in the ordinary way except that, as in contract, he must sue through an adult as next friend. He cannot compromise his action except by leave of the court, unlike an adult, who does not require such permission.

At common law there was a doubt as to whether a child had a cause of action for personal injuries caused before its birth. The matter is now covered by the Congenital Disabilities (Civil Liability) Act, 1976. Section 1 establishes civil liability where a child is born disabled in consequence of the intentional act or the negligence or the breach of statutory duty of some person before the child's birth. There can be no liability unless the child is born alive. Section 44 of the Human Fertilisation and Embryology Act, 1990 extends the 1976 Act to cover children conceived following infertility treatments.

It was held in *C v S* [1987] 1 All E.R. 123 that a foetus has no right of action unless it is subsequently born alive. If it is stillborn the parents might have an action, e.g. for nervous shock. Causation must be proved which may be difficult in the case of pre-natal injuries. A mother cannot be liable under s. 1 for causing injury to her child by her own negligence, except where the injury is caused by the mother's negligence in driving a motor vehicle when she knows, or ought reasonably to know, that she is pregnant. Barristers and judges, among others, have been strongly opposed to children being given a cause of action against their mothers, recognising the danger of inter-family disputes, and, subject to what has been said about motor vehicle liability where the action is in effect against an insurance company and not really against the mother, their view has prevailed in the Act. The liability of a father is not, however, excluded and he can be liable to his child for injuries caused by his own negligence.

The section also distinguishes between matters arising *before* conception (where the injury can be to *either* parent) and matters arising when the child's mother is pregnant or during the actual process of childbirth (where the injury can *only* be to the mother). Thus the injury could result, for example, from irradiation which damages the progenitive capacity of the father. It also covers physical damage to the child during childbirth as by the negligent handling of instruments by those attending the mother. The injuries must be caused during the pregnancy and there could be problems in dating the beginning of this in some cases. The defendant is presumed to take the mother as he finds her and thus cannot say that he did not know she was pregnant nor that the damage to her child was not foreseeable.

The common-law defence of *volenti non fit injuria* is applicable and in this sense if the mother is *volenti* so is the child. It is recognised that this may penalise the child but it was thought that any other solution would prejudice the position of women in society because organisations worried that a woman might be pregnant may refuse to enter into a wide variety of contracts with her. Incidentally, so far as the consent which the child is deemed to give results from an exemption clause in a contract made by the mother, then s. 1 creates a new exception to the doctrine of privity of contract. Section 1 also provides that the child's damages awarded against the defendant are to be reduced by any contributory negligence of the mother. Finally, s. 1 provides that professional persons, such as doctors, are under no liability for treatment or advice given according to prevailing professional standards of care. This codifies the common-law rule in *Roe* v *Minister of Health*, 1954 (see p. 786).

Section 3 clarifies the compensation provisions of the Nuclear Installations Act, 1965, where damage results from a nuclear incident and provides for compensation under the Act in the case of a child born subsequently with disabilities attributable to the incident.

A minor is liable as defendant for all his torts except in a limited number of instances. Where the tort alleged requires a mental ingredient, the age of the minor (in cases of extreme infancy) may show an inability to form the necessary intent. In cases of negligence, a very young child cannot be expected to show the same standard of care as an older person.

Basically children are liable for their own torts, but a father may be liable vicariously, if the relationship of employer and employee exists between him and the child or if there is the relationship of principal and agent. Simply as a father he is not liable unless the injury is caused by his negligent control of the child and so when he is liable, it is really for his own tort, i.e. negligence in looking after the child. Such a liability may extend to other persons (not being parents) who have control of children, e.g. teachers and education authorities, and, if such persons or authorities act negligently, they may be held responsible for the harm caused by children under their care or control. Nevertheless, the basis of the action is negligent control or supervision.

ESSENTIAL CASE LAW AND COMMENT

Williams v *Humphrey*, 1975 – A minor is sued for negligence **(269)**
Donaldson v *McNiven*, 1952 – Parental control: no negligence **(270)**
Bebee v *Sales*, 1916 – Where a parent is negligent **(271)**
Carmarthenshire County Council v *Lewis*, 1955 – Negligent control by a local authority **(272)**
Butt v *Cambridgeshire and Ely County Council*, 1969 – A local authority is not negligent **(273)**

PERSONS SUFFERING FROM MENTAL DISORDER

In criminal law a person of unsound mind has considerable exemption from criminal liability (see p. 551), but these rules have never been applied to civil injuries. This is understandable if it is borne in mind that the aim of the law of torts is to compensate the injured party, not to punish the offender. In the light of this, any exemptions accorded to a person of unsound mind should be narrow, and he should be liable unless his state of mind prevents him having the necessary intent (where a mental ingredient is part of the tort) and in extreme cases where no voluntary act is possible.

ESSENTIAL CASE LAW AND COMMENT

Morriss v *Marsden*, 1952 – Mental patients in tort **(274)**

HUSBAND AND WIFE

The rule used to be that a married woman was liable for her torts only to the extent of her separate property and that beyond this the husband was fully liable. Since the Law Reform (Married Women and Tortfeasors) Act, 1935, the wife is fully liable for her torts and the husband as such is no longer held responsible, unless, as in the case of a minor, there is a relationship of employer and employee or principal and agent.

The old common-law rule whereby one spouse could not sue the other in tort has now been altered. The Law Reform (Husband and Wife) Act, 1962, provides that each of the parties to a marriage shall have the like right of action in tort against the other as if they were not married, but where the action is brought by one of the parties to the marriage against the other during the subsistence of the marriage, the court may stay the action if it appears –

(*a*) that no substantial benefit would accrue to either party from the continuation of the proceedings; or

(*b*) that the question or questions in issue could more conveniently be disposed of on an application made under s. 17 of the Married Women's Property Act, 1882. (This provides for the determination of questions between husband and wife regarding title to or possession of property by a summary procedure.)

It should also be noted that under s. 2(a), Administration of Justice Act, 1982 a husband has no right of action against a person who by a tortious act deprives him of the society and services of his wife, i.e. loss of consortium. A wife has no such right by reason of case law in respect of loss of consortium. (See *Best* v *Samuel Fox & Co. Ltd*, 1952 at p. 726.)

THE CROWN AND ITS SERVANTS

Prior to 1947 the Crown had considerable immunity in the law of tort and contract stemming from the common-law maxim: 'The King can do no wrong.' We have already seen that, by the Crown Proceedings Act, 1947, the Crown is, in general, now liable in the same way as a subject. (See further p. 196.)

The Crown is not liable for torts committed by the police nor is the local authority which appoints and pays them. However, the Police Act, 1964, s. 48(1), provides that the chief officer of police for any police area is liable for the torts of police officers, e.g. wrongful arrest. The Act also provides that any damages and costs awarded against the chief officer shall be payable out of police funds.

POSTAL AND TELECOMMUNICATIONS AUTHORITIES

The Post Office is a public authority but is not an agent of the Crown. It is liable, subject to limitations set out in the Post Office Regulations, for loss of or damage to inland registered postal packets (s. 30, Post Office Act, 1969). Apart from this, neither the Post Office nor any of its servants, officers, or sub-postmasters is liable for anything done or omitted to be done in regard to anything in the post or for failure to collect the post (s. 29(1) and (2)). Thus in *Harold Stephen & Co. Ltd v Post Office* [1978] 1 All E.R. 939, the Court of Appeal refused to grant an injunction against the Post Office to companies in the Cricklewood area of London whose businesses were in jeopardy because they were receiving no mail through the Post Office closing the local sorting office and suspending post office workers who refused to handle mail in support of workers employed in the private sector.

Persons engaged in the carriage of mail or their servants, agents or sub-contractors, are not liable for loss or damage in regard to the post (s. 29(3)). Thus in *American Express Co. v British Airways Board* [1983] 1 All E.R. 557, the plaintiffs gave a postal packet containing travellers' cheques to the Post Office for delivery abroad. The Post Office gave it to the defendants and it was stolen by one of their employees. The plaintiffs claimed damages for breach of bailment. Lloyd, J. held that the defendants were not liable; they were exempted by s. 29(3) of the 1969 Act.

Since the enactment of the Telecommunications Act, 1984, British Telecom provides its telecommunications service under standard service contracts and is liable in the ordinary way for breach. However, the contracts concerned have exclusion clauses, e.g. in the case of failure to repair equipment during an industrial dispute.

JUDICIAL IMMUNITY

A judge has absolute immunity for acts in his judicial capacity. Section 44 of the Justices of the Peace Act, 1979 (inserted by s. 108 of the Courts and Legal Services Act, 1990) extends this immunity to magistrates and their clerks, the intention being that they should be put in the same position as other judges. Counsel and witnesses have immunity in respect of all matters relating to the cases in which they are concerned. This is mainly of importance in connection with possible actions for slander.

FOREIGN SOVEREIGNS AND AMBASSADORIAL STAFFS

These persons have immunity from actions in both contract and tort. However, it should be noted that if they remain in this country after finishing their duties, they may become liable even if the tort was committed before. They may, of course, voluntarily submit to the jurisdiction of our courts, since immunity is from suit and not from liability.

ESSENTIAL CASE LAW AND COMMENT

Dickinson v *Del Solar*, 1930 – Ambassadorial staff are immune from suit not liability **(275)**

ALIENS

Enemy aliens, including British subjects who voluntarily reside or carry on business in an enemy state, cannot bring an action in tort, although they themselves can be sued. Other aliens have neither disability nor immunity.

CORPORATIONS

A corporation can, as a plaintiff, sue for all torts committed against it. Obviously certain torts, such as assault, cannot by their nature be committed against corporations, but a corporation can maintain an action for injury to its business. Section 35 of the Companies Act, 1985 does not apply to tortious activities and in cases where the corporation is the defendant we must consider separately tortious acts which are *intra vires* (within its powers) and *ultra vires* (outside its powers). In this connection the contents of the company's objects clause will be relevant in terms of what it can and cannot do. However, where a company has adopted the single line clause permitted by s. 3A of the Companies Act, 1985 its capacity to commit torts is virtually the same as that of a human being.

(*a*) *Intra vires activities*. Where a servant or agent of the corporation commits a tort while acting in the course of his employment in an *intra vires* activity, then the corporation is liable. Although it has been said that any tort committed on behalf of a corporation must be *ultra vires* (since Parliament does not authorise corporations to commit torts) this view is fallacious, since a corporation can have legal liability without legal capacity. A corporation is liable under the principles of vicarious liability for the torts of its employees or agents committed on *intra vires* activities.

(*b*) *Ultra vires activities*. Here we have to distinguish between express and non-express authority. A corporation will not be liable if a servant engages in an *ultra vires* activity without express authority. Thus, if a corporation has not got authority and has not given it, you cannot infer it. On the other hand, where a tortious action is *ultra vires* but has been expressly authorised, the courts have taken the view that the *ultra vires* doctrine is irrelevant, and the corporation is liable for it.

ESSENTIAL CASE LAW AND COMMENT

D. & L. Caterers Ltd and Jackson v *D'Anjou,* 1945 – An action by a company **(276)**

Poulton v *London and South Western Railway Co.,* 1867 – An *ultra vires* act **(277)**

Campbell v *Paddington Borough Council,* 1911 – Is *ultra vires* relevant if act authorised? **(278)**

UNINCORPORATED ASSOCIATIONS AND TRADE UNIONS

These have already been considered in Chapter 8 and their position in tort is set out on pp. 193 and 194.

JOINT TORTFEASORS

Formerly there was no right of contribution between joint tortfeasors, but under the Law Reform (Married Women and Tortfeasors) Act, 1935, it was laid down that, if one joint tortfeasor was sued and paid damages, he could claim a contribution from fellow wrongdoers. The relevant provisions are now contained in the Civil Liability (Contribution) Act, 1978. However, there can be no contribution where the person claiming it is liable to *indemnify* the person from whom it is claimed. For example, an auctioneer is entitled to be indemnified by a client who has instructed him to sell goods to which, as it subsequently appears, the client does not have a title. (*Adamson* v *Jarvis* (1827) 4 Bing. 66.) Therefore if the true owner sues the client for wrongful interference and the client pays the damages, he has no right to a contribution against the auctioneer although the auctioneer is also liable for wrongful interference because the auctioneer is a person whom the client would have had to indemnify if the true owner had chosen to sue the auctioneer. The amount of the contribution is settled by the court on the basis of what is just and equitable given the responsibility of each party for the injury and may be the full amount of the damages originally awarded against the person claiming the contribution.

In connection with the right of contribution the Law Reform (Husband and Wife) Act, 1962, has an important effect. Where a spouse A is injured by the joint negligence of the other spouse B and of a third party C, e.g. in a car accident, if C is sued by A, he can now claim a contribution from the negligent spouse B, since B is now a person liable for the purposes of the Act of 1978.

EXECUTORS AND ADMINISTRATORS

General effect of death

Section 1(1) of the Law Reform (Miscellaneous Provisions) Act, 1934 (as amended by the Law Reform (Miscellaneous Provisions) Act, 1970) provides that all causes of action subsisting against or vested in a person at the time of his death shall survive against, or as the case may be, for the benefit of his estate.

This does not apply to actions for defamation. Furthermore, damages, recoverable in an action by the representatives of the deceased shall not include exemplary damages (see further p. 404). The right of a person to claim for bereavement under s. 1A of the Fatal Accidents Act, 1976 (see below) does not survive for the benefit of his estate (s. 4(1), Administration of Justice Act, 1982, amending s. 1(2)(a) of the Act of 1934). No damages may be awarded for loss of income in respect of any period after the death of an injured person (s. 4(2)(b), Administration of Justice Act, 1982, amending s. 1(2)(a) of the Act of 1934).

Under the Proceedings Against Estates Act, 1970 all actions against the personal representatives of a deceased person, whether founded in contract or tort, are now subject to the normal three-year (personal injuries) or six-year (other injuries) limitation period.

Fatal accident

If, as a result, e.g. of negligence, a person is killed, there are two sorts of claim against the person responsible. The executors of the deceased may wish to go ahead with any claim *which the deceased would have had if he had lived*. There may also be relatives who wish to claim because they have suffered as a result of the death.

(*a*) *Claims by the estate.* As we have seen, under the Law Reform (Miscellaneous Provisions) Act, 1934, most causes of action in tort subsisting at the time of a person's death survive for (or against) his estate.

As regards a fatal accident, the estate can claim damages for the period between the injury and death, e.g. for pain and suffering and loss of amenity, as where an arm is amputated before death. Damages may be awarded for earnings lost and medical expenses incurred up to the time of death.

There is no claim for loss of expectation of life (s. 1(1)(a), Administration of Justice Act, 1982), nor is there a claim for lost earnings in respect of the period between the actual death and the cessation of notional working life (i.e. the lost years). Section 4(2) of the 1982 Act now states that no damages may be awarded for loss of income after death.

If the injured person died immediately the estate has no claim except for funeral expenses (s. 1(2)(c), of the 1982 Act). If, e.g. a relative, pays the funeral expenses but was not dependent on the deceased and so has no general claim under the Fatal Accidents Act, 1976, that dependent may claim those funeral expenses under the 1976 Act.

(*b*) *Claims by dependants.* These are brought under the Fatal Accidents Act, 1976. The claim is independent of the one made by the estate under the 1934 Act (as amended). Two awards of damages may therefore be made, one for the executors on behalf of the estate, and the other to the executors collectively for the dependants.

Under the provisions of the Fatal Accidents Act, 1976 a person whose negligence has caused the death of another may be liable to certain relatives of the deceased who have suffered financial loss because of the death. The following persons are entitled to claim *but only if they were dependent on the deceased* – husband, wife, children, grandchildren, parents, grandparents, brothers, sisters, aunts, and uncles, and their issue; the relationship may be traced through step-relatives, adoption, or illegitimacy, and relatives by marriage have the same rights as the deceased's own relatives. However, dependency ceases on adoption (*Watson* v *Willmott* [1990] 3 W.L.R. 1103). Under s. 1(3)(b) of the 1976 Act, as amended by the Administration of Justice Act, 1982, any person who was living with the deceased in the same household for two years or more before the death and was living for all of the time as the husband or wife of the deceased may claim. This allows unmarried cohabitants to claim.

A single action must be brought on behalf of all eligible dependants and the total damages apportioned according to their dependancy. The action may be brought by the personal representatives of the deceased, but if there are none, or they fail to bring the action within six months of the death, the dependants may bring it.

If the deceased was guilty of contributory negligence or was a volunteer (see p. 394), the damages awarded will be reduced or extinguished, according to the degree to which the deceased was at fault or was a volunteer. Ordinarily, also, if more than three years have elapsed between injury and death, no Fatal Accidents Act claim can be brought (s. 11(1), Limitation Act, 1980). However, it is open to the personal representatives to ask the court to exercise the discretionary provisions of s. 33 of the Limitation Act, 1980 to override the limitation period. (See further p. 412.) Furthermore, if the plaintiff dies before the limitation period has expired, a new limitation period runs under s. 11(5) of the Limitation Act, 1980. This period is three years from either the date of death or the date of the personal representative's knowledge that there is a cause of action, whichever is the later.

The probability of pecuniary loss is a matter for the plaintiff to prove and the court to decide as a matter of fact. However, it should be noted that the object of the Fatal Accidents Act is to provide maintenance for relatives who have been deprived of maintenance by the death.

There is also now an award of £7500 for bereavement (s. 1A(3), Fatal Accidents Act, 1976, as amended by the Administration of Justice Act, 1982). This sum will be increased as appropriate by statutory instrument. It is in favour of a wife or husband or the parents of the deceased but in the case of parents only if he or she was under 18 at the time of death and unmarried, or the mother of a child under 18 at the time of death and unmarried who was illegitimate (s. 1A(2)(b), Fatal Acidents Act, 1976). No proof of dependency is required.

Section 4 of the Fatal Accidents Act, 1976 as amended by the Administration of Justice Act, 1982, provides that in assessing damages any benefits which have arisen, or will arise, or may arise to any person as a result of the death are to be disregarded. Thus friendly society or trade union benefits, pensions, or gratuities accruing to a relative would be ignored, even though the penuniary loss was in a sense thereby reduced.

PARTNERS, PRINCIPALS AND AGENTS GENERALLY

Partners are jointly and severally liable for the torts of other partners committed in the ordinary course of business, or with the authority of co-partners. A principal is liable for the torts of his agent committed within the scope of his authority, whether by prior authority or subsequent ratification.

Vicarious liability

While the person who is actually responsible for the commission of a tort is always liable, sometimes another person may be liable although he has not actually committed it. In such a case both are liable as joint tortfeasors. This is the doctrine of vicarious liability, and the greatest area of this type of liability is that of master and servant. A master (employer) is liable for the torts of his servant (employee) committed in the course of his employment, and so wide is the risk that it is commonly insured against. Under the Employers' Liability (Compulsory Insurance) Act, 1969, an employer *must* insure himself in respect of vicarious liability for injuries caused by his employees to their colleagues. Insurance is not compulsory in respect of injuries to persons other than employees.

There is a comparison to be made with contract because whether an employer is bound as a party to a contract made by the employee depends upon whether the employee has the *authority to make the contract* on behalf of the employer and not simply whether the employee was *acting within the course of employment* which is the basic tort test (*Director General of Fair Trading* v *Smiths Concrete, The Times,* 26 July 1991).

Who is a servant or employee?

According to Salmond on Torts, a servant may be defined as 'any person employed by another to do work for him on the terms that he, the servant, is to be subject to the control and direction of his employer in respect of the manner in which his work is to be done.' This definition was approved by the court in *Hewitt* v *Bonvin* [1940] 1 K.B. 188. In most cases the relationship is established by the existence of a *contract of service*, which may be express or implied and is usually evidenced by such matters as, for example, the power to appoint, the power of dismissal, the method of payment, the payment of National Insurance by the employer, the deduction of tax under PAYE, and membership of pension schemes (if any).

THE CONTROL TEST

However, in deciding whether the relationship of employer and employee exists, the courts have not restricted themselves to cases in which there is an ordinary contract of service but have often stated that the right of *control* is the ultimate test. In *Performing Right Society Ltd* v *Mitchel and Booker (Palais de Danse) Ltd* [1924] 1 K.B. 762 at p. 767, McCardie, J., said –

> The nature of the task undertaken, the freedom of action given, the magnitude of the contract amount, the manner in which it is paid, the powers of dismissal, and the circumstances under which payment of the reward may be withheld, all these bear on the solution of the question. But it seems clear that a more guiding test must be secured . . . It seems . . . reasonably clear that the final test, if there be a final test, and certainly the test to be generally applied, lies in the nature and degree of detailed control over the person alleged to be a servant. This circumstance is, of course, one only of several to be considered but it is usually of vital importance.

The learned judge then went on to decide that the defendants, who employed a dance band under a written contract for one year, were liable for breaches of copyright, which occurred when members of the band played a piece of music without the consent of the holder of the copyright, because the agreement gave the defendants 'the right of continuous, dominant and detailed control on every point, including the nature of the music to be played'.

The existence of the control test means that where an employer (X) lends out his employee (Y) to another employer (Z), then Z may be liable for the wrongs of Y even though there is no contract of service between Y and Z, though such liability is rare.

An employer also owes certain duties to his employees, e.g. to provide proper plant, equipment and premises, and this is a further reason for deciding whether Z has become the master by virtue of the control test. There is a presumption that control remains with X and the onus is upon him to prove that control has passed to Z. The burden is a heavy one and the temporary employer will not often become liable. Nevertheless, transfer of control may be more readily inferred where an employee is lent on his own without equipment or where he is unskilled.

Transfer of control is often a convenient method of making the temporary employer liable to, and for, the employee and does not affect the contract of service. A contract of service is a highly personal one and it cannot be transferred from one employer to another without the consent of the employee. However, where there is a contract for hire of plant and the loan of an employee to operate it, the contract of hiring may provide that the hirer shall indemnify the owners for claims arising in connection with the operation of the plant by the employee.

ESSENTIAL CASE LAW AND COMMENT

Garrard v *Southey*, 1952 – The control test: a transfer of employer **(279)**

Mersey Docks and Harbour Board v *Coggins and Griffiths*, 1947 – A situation of no transfer **(280)**

Wright v *Tyne Improvement Commissioners*, 1968 – Effect of contractual indemnity **(281)**

The control test was an appropriate one in the days when a master could be expected to be superior to his servant in knowledge, skill and experience. However, in modern times it is unreal to say that all employers of skilled labour can tell employees *how* to do their work. Accordingly the test has been modified in recent cases, the court tending to look for the power to control in incidental or collateral matters, e.g. hours of work and place of work. The existence of this sort of control enables the court to decide whether a person is part of the *organisation* of another, and it might be called a '*when and where*' test.

The control test also gives rise to difficulties in the case of the employees of companies. Subordinate employees are controlled by superior employees and some control is obviously present if the management is regarded as 'the company'. However, when one considers the position of directors and top management it is difficult to see how the company, being inanimate, can exercise control. In the case of 'one-man' companies, where the managing director is also virtually the sole shareholder, the reality of the situation is that the servant controls the company and not vice versa. Nevertheless, directors of companies, even 'one-man' companies, are regarded as employees, presumably because the usual incidents of a contract of service are present and despite the absence of genuine control.

Although control is the ultimate test in establishing the relationship of master and servant, it is also necessary to deal briefly with other circumstances which may be taken as evidence of the existence of the relationship. In *Short* v *J. W. Henderson Ltd* (1946) 62 T.L.R. 427, Lord Thankerton regarded the power to select or appoint, the power to dismiss, and the payment of wages, as relevant in establishing the existence, or otherwise, of a contract of service.

ESSENTIAL CASE LAW AND COMMENT

Cassidy v *Ministry of Health*, 1951 – An organisation test **(282)**
Ferguson v *John Dawson & Partners*, 1976 – A 'when and where' test **(283)**
Lee v *Lee's Air Farming Ltd*, 1960 – Directors and senior employees **(284)**

THE POWER TO SELECT OR APPOINT

The absence of a power to select or appoint may prevent the relationship of employer and employee arising. Thus, in *Cassidy* v *Ministry of Health* [1951] 2 K.B. 343 Denning, L.J., as he then was, made it clear that a hospital authority is not liable for the negligence of a doctor or surgeon who is *selected* and *employed* by the patient himself. The employer need not make the appointment himself, and an appointee may be an employee even though the employer *delegated* the power of selection to another employee, or even an independent contractor, such as a firm of management consultants, or was *required by law to accept* the employee, e.g. Ministers of State often have power to appoint members of statutory bodies who become the employees of those bodies.

THE POWER TO DISMISS

An express power of dismissal is strong evidence that the contract is one of service. Many public bodies have a restricted power of dismissal in the sense that rights of appeal are often provided for, but such rights do not prevent a contract of service from arising, nor does the fact that these authorities cannot dismiss certain of their employees without the approval of the Crown or a Minister.

PAYMENT OF WAGES OR SALARY

A contract of service must be supported by consideration which usually consists of a promise to pay wages, or a salary. Where the amount of remuneration or the rate of pay is not fixed in advance, this suggests that the contract is not one of service, but is for services. The employer usually pays his employees directly, but in *Pauley* v *Kenaldo Ltd* [1953] 1 All E.R. 226, at p. 228, Birkett, L.J., said 'a person may be none the less a servant by reason of the fact that his remuneration consists solely of tips'.

An employee may be employed on terms that his remuneration is to consist wholly or partly of commission which the employer pays directly, the commission being a method of assessment of the amount of the remuneration.

Salaries are paid to people who are certainly not employees, e.g. Members of Parliament, whereas payment of wages generally indicates a contract of service. However, little, if anything, turns on the distinction between wages and salaries, and we may conclude that the terms used to describe the way in which a person is paid have little bearing on the relationship between himself and the person who pays him.

In addition to the above indications of a contract of service the following matters have also been regarded as relevant in deciding difficult cases of relationship.

DELEGATION

In the normal contract of service the employee performs the work himself, and *power to delegate performance of the whole contract* to another is some indication that there is no contract of service. However, the fact that delegation is forbidden does not show *conclusively* that the contract is one of service, for agreements with independent contractors may forbid delegation.

EXCLUSIVE SERVICE

The fact that an employer can demand the *exclusive services of another* is a material factor leading to the inference of a contract of service and in some cases it has been the deciding factor. However, in the absence of an express contractual provision an employer cannot usually require the exclusive services of his employee, and cannot complain if the employee works for someone else in his spare time. This being so, an employee and an independent contractor are usually both able to work for more than one person, and the exclusive service test may not help in deciding difficult cases of relationship. However, it is true to say that the typical employee works for one person, and the typical independent contractor works for many.

PLACE OF WORK

If the services are always rendered on the *employer's premises* this is some evidence of the existence of a contract of service, though it is not conclusive. Similarly, the fact that a person works at his home or other premises is some evidence of a contract for services.

It may also be a material factor whether the services are rendered by a person having a *recognised trade or profession*, e.g. a surveyor or a consulting engineer, which he is exercising in a business because such persons tend to be independent contractors rather than employees and persons not exercising a particular calling may more easily be regarded as the employees of those who employ them.

PLANT AND EQUIPMENT

Provision of large-scale plant and equipment by the employer is an indication of the existence of a contract of service and a person who supplies his own large-scale plant and equipment is often an independent contractor. However, provision of minor equipment, such as tools, carries little weight as a test of relationship, for many employees provide their own tools.

OBLIGATION TO WORK

A contract of service and one for services usually *impose an obligation to do the work concerned* and an obligation to work is not helpful in the matter of relationships. However, persons such as salesmen who are paid entirely by commission, and who are not obliged to work at all, are probably not working under a contract of service.

HOURS OF WORK AND HOLIDAYS

The right to control the *hours of work and the taking of holidays* is also regarded as evidence of the existence of a contract of service. Further an independent contractor is usually engaged for a specific job, whereas an employee is usually employed for an indefinite time.

EMPLOYEES AND INDEPENDENT CONTRACTORS

An employee is a person whose work is at least *integrated* into the employer's business organisation, whereas an independent contractor merely *works for* the business but is *not integrated* into it. Thus, firms of builders, architects, and estate agents are usually regarded as independent contractors, while factory and office workers are usually regarded as employees.

An employee works under a contract of service, whereas an independent contractor's contract is said to be one 'for services' under which he is to carry out a particular task or tasks. Although he may be sued for breach of contract if he fails to carry out his contract properly, the purchaser of his services has no other control over the manner of his work.

Nature of vicarious liability

The doctrine seems at first sight unfair because it runs contrary to two major principles of liability in tort, viz –

(a) that a person should be liable only for loss or damage caused by his *own acts or omissions*; and

(b) that a person should only be liable where he was at *fault*.

The doctrine of vicarious liability is a convenient one in the sense that employers are, generally speaking, wealthier than their employees and are better able to pay damages, though the doctrine is often justified on the grounds that an employer *controls* his employee. However, it should be noted that control is not in itself a ground for imposing vicarious liability, e.g.

parents are not vicariously liable for the torts of their children. It is also said that vicarious liability is a just concept because the employer profits from the employee's work and should therefore bear losses caused by the employee's torts. Again, the employer *chooses* his employee and there are those who say that if he chooses a careless employee he ought to compensate the victims of the careless employee's torts. Further, employer and employee are often identified in the sense that the act of the employee is regarded as the act of his employer and this theory that an employer and his employee are part of a *group* in much the same way as other associations of persons, e.g. companies, is expressed in the often quoted maxim *qui facit per alium facit per se* (he who does a thing through another does it himself). However, in practice the employer does not really suffer loss because he commonly insures against the possibility of vicarious liability and usually the cost of this insurance is put on to the goods or services which he sells. This has the effect of spreading the loss over a large section of the community in much the same way as welfare state benefits.

COURSE OF EMPLOYMENT

In order to establish vicarious liability it is necessary to show that the relationship between the defendant and the wrongdoer is that of employer and employee, and that when the employee committed the wrong he was in the *course of his employment.* It is sometimes difficult to decide whether a particular act was done during the course of employment, but the following matters are relevant.

ACTS PERSONAL TO THE EMPLOYEE

Some acts done by an employee while at work are so personal to him that they cannot be regarded as being within the scope of employment. Employees do not generally have authority to use violence against third parties, and the use of such violence will usually be beyond the scope of employment, and the employer will not be liable. Thus in *Warren v Henlys Ltd* [1948] 2 All E.R. 935, the employer of a petrol pump attendant was held not liable for the latter's assault on a customer committed as a result of an argument over payment for petrol. However, where such authority exists, e.g. in the case of door-keepers at dance halls, the employer will be liable if the employee ejects a troublemaker but uses excessive force.

IMPROPER PERFORMANCE OF ACTS WITHIN SCOPE OF EMPLOYMENT

The employer may be liable where the tort committed by the employee is not a personal or independent act but is merely an improper way of performing an act which is within the scope of employment.

The tortious acts for which an employer may be liable must arise out of the employee's employment, but the employer may be liable in such circumstances even if the act is one which he has expressly forbidden his employee to do. The point has arisen in cases in which employees have given lifts to third parties in the employer's vehicle. In *Twine* v *Bean's Express Ltd* [1946] 1 All E.R. 202, a driver employed by the defendants gave a lift to a third person who was killed by reason of the employee's negligent driving. Instructions that employees were not to give lifts were displayed in the van. The court held that the employers were not liable because in giving a lift to the third person the driver went *beyond the scope of his employment.*

However, if the express prohibition only affects the *way* in which the employee is to perform his work and is not regarded as affecting the *scope* of his employment, the employer may be liable.

ESSENTIAL CASE LAW AND COMMENT

Century Insurance Co Ltd v *Northern Ireland Road Transport Board*, 1942 – An improper act in course of employment **(285)**
Limpus v *London General Omnibus Co*, 1862 – A race for passengers **(286)**
Rose v *Plenty*, 1976 – Helping the milkman **(287)**

EMERGENCIES

Where the employee takes emergency measures with the intention of benefiting his employer in cases where the latter's property appears to be in danger, the employer will tend to be liable even though the acts of the employee are excessive. Thus in *Poland* v *John Parr & Sons* [1927] 1 K.B. 236, a boy was injured by a carter who knocked the boy off the back of his cart to protect his employer's property from theft. It was held that the carter's action was within his implied authority and his employers were liable. If, however, the employee's act is not merely *excessive* but *outrageous* as in *Warren* v *Henlys Ltd* [1948] 2 All E.R. 935, the employer will not be liable.

EMPLOYEE MIXING EMPLOYER'S BUSINESS WITH HIS OWN

The cases under this heading have arisen largely out of the use of motor vehicles, and since it is clear that there can be no vicarious liability if the employee's wrong is not the result of his carrying out his contract of service, the employer will not be liable if he lends his vehicle to his employee entirely for the employee's own purpose.

However, a more difficult situation arises where the activity is basically an authorised one but the employee deviates from it in order to execute some business of his own. The mere fact of deviation will not prevent the employer being liable and this was made clear in the judgment of Cockburn, C.J., in *Storey* v *Ashton* (1869), L.R. 4 Q.B. 476, when he said –

> I am very far from saying that, if the servant when going on his master's business took a somewhat longer road, that, owing to his deviation he would cease to be in the employment of the master so as to divest the latter of all liability; in such cases it is a question of degree as to how far the deviation could be considered a separate journey. Such a consideration is not applicable to the present case, because here the carman started on an entirely new and independent journey which had nothing to do with his employment.

However, if the journey is unauthorised the employee does not render his employer liable merely by performing some small act for his employer's benefit during the course of it. Thus in *Rayner* v *Mitchell* (1877), 2 C.P.D. 257, a brewer's vanman, without permission, took a van from his employer's stables for personal reasons, namely to deliver a coffin to a relative's house. On the way back he picked up some empty beer barrels and then was involved in an accident injuring the plaintiff. It was held that the brewer was not liable.

ESSENTIAL CASE LAW AND COMMENT

Britt v *Galmoye*, 1928 – An accident while not on the employer's business **(288)**

EMPLOYEE USING HIS OWN PROPERTY ON EMPLOYER'S BUSINESS

The mere fact that an employee is using his own property in carrying out his employer's business will not prevent the employer from being liable for torts arising out of the use of the employee's property. The decided cases are largely concerned with methods of travel, and in *McKean* v *Rayner Bros Ltd (Nottingham)* [1942] 2 All E.R. 650, an employee who was told to deliver a message by using the firm's lorry was held to be in the course of his employment when he performed the task by driving his own car, contrary to his instructions. However, if the employee's act is unreasonable, as where an employee who is authorised to travel by car charters an aeroplane and flies it himself, then the act will be unauthorised and the employer will not be liable if the employee, or a third party, is injured.

EFFECT OF CONTRACTUAL EXCEPTIONS CLAUSES

Cases may arise in which the employer has attempted to exempt himself from the wrongs of his employee by means of an exemption clause in a contract with a third person who is injured. Such clauses will be effective to exempt the employer from liability if they are properly communicated to the third person. However, they will not protect the employee against his personal liability at common law because he has not usually given any consideration to the third person and is not in privity of contract with him. Statute may extend the protection of an exemption clause in the employer's contract to his employees.

For example, the Carriage of Goods by Sea Act, 1971 provides that an employee or agent of a carrier by sea, but not an independent contractor, shall be entitled to avail himself of the same defences and limits of liability as the carrier. As regards an independent contractor, note *New Zealand Shipping Co.* v *A.M. Satterthwaite & Co.* 1974 at p. 677 where stevedores, who were independent contractors, took the benefit of an exemption clause in a contract between the carrier and the owner of the goods. However, the principle of privity will apply in other situations, e.g. to an employee of a carrier of goods by road who would not be protected by an exclusion clause in the contract between his employer and the owner of the goods being carried.

FRAUDULENT AND CRIMINAL ACTS

In early law the courts would not accept the principle of vicarious liability in fraud but gradually the concept was extended, first to cases in which the employee's fraud was committed for his employer's benefit, and later even to cases where the fraud was committed by the employee entirely for his own ends. The leading case is *Lloyd* v *Grace, Smith & Co.* [1912] A.C. 716. The defendants were solicitors and employed a clerk in their conveyancing department. The clerk fraudulently induced the plaintiff to transfer some property to him and later sold that property at a profit for his own purposes. Nevertheless, the defendants were held liable for the plaintiff's loss. The liability, however, still depends upon the employee having actual or apparent authority to undertake work or carry out duties of the sort which have enabled him to commit fraud, and obviously if the fraud is committed outside the course of employment then the employer will not be liable.

Criminal conduct on the part of an employee may be regarded as being in the course of his employment so that the employer will be liable at civil law for any loss or damage caused to a third person by the employee's criminal act.

ESSENTIAL CASE LAW AND COMMENT

Morris v *C. W. Martin & Sons Ltd*, 1965 – Vicarious liability for civil aspects of crime **(289)**

CASUAL DELEGATION

If Y lends his car to X for X's own purposes, then Y is not liable, even if in a general way X is his employee. (See *Britt* v *Galmoye* 1928 at p. 736.) Nevertheless, if Y has a purpose and X also has a purpose, and X is driving a car of Y's partly for his own and partly for Y's purposes, then Y would apparently be liable if X committed a tort. This is known as a case of casual delegation of authority. In these cases of casual delegation, the courts are guided by the doctrine of the *de facto* employee, and by using this doctrine they have extended the vicarious liability of the employer into the area of principal and agent. In fact the person actually committing the wrong is often called the agent. The result is to extend the area of operation of the doctrine of vicarious laibility since it is easier to find the relationship of principal and agent than it is to establish the relationship of employer and employee.

However, merely giving permission to use the vehicle is not enough to make the owner liable, nor is he liable merely because he is the owner and there will, of course, be no vicarious liability in the owner where he did not consent to the taking of the vehicle.

ESSENTIAL CASE LAW AND COMMENT

Ormrod v *Crosville Motor Services Ltd*, 1953 – A casual delegation **(290)**

Vandyke v *Fender*, 1970 – Employer and employee or principal and agent? **(291)**

Nottingham v *Aldridge*, 1971 – A trainee returning to work **(292)**

Morgans v *Launchbury*, 1972 – Mere permission to drive is not enough **(293)**

Rambarran v *Gurrucharran*, 1970 – Ownership alone does not produce liability **(294)**

Klein v *Calnori*, 1971 – No liability if vehicle driven without owner's consent **(295)**

Liability for torts of independent contractors

An independent contractor is by definition a person whose methods and modes of work are not controlled by the person who employs him, and this being so it would be unfair to give an employer general liability for the torts of such a contractor. However, there are circumstances in which a person may be liable for the torts of an independent contractor employed by him and these are set out below. However, it should be borne in mind that the circumstances listed below are not truly examples of vicarious liability. Instead they are based on the idea that the employer himself is in breach of a primary duty which he owes the plaintiff, as where e.g. he undertakes hazardous operations.

(*a*) *Where the employer authorises or ratifies the torts of the contractor.*

If, for example, an employer authorises, or afterwards, with knowledge, approves the conduct of an independent contractor in tipping the employer's industrial waste material on another's land, both the employer and the contractor will be liable in trespass as joint tortfeasors.

(*b*) *Where the employer is negligent himself*, as where he selects an independent contractor without taking care to see, as far as he can, that he is competent to do the work required, or gives a competent contractor imperfect instructions or information, as where, for example, he knows that his land is liable to subsidence and fails to tell a contractor who erects something on the land which slips and causes damage to another.

(*c*) *Where liability for the tort is strict, so that responsibility cannot be delegated.* Thus, an employer is liable for injuries to workmen resulting from failure to fence dangerous machinery securely. This duty is laid down by safety legislation, and it is no defence that the employer has delegated the task of fencing to an independent contractor who has failed to do the job properly. Moreover, liability under the rule in *Rylands* v *Fletcher*, 1868 (see p. 476) cannot be avoided by employing an independent contractor. It seems also that liability is strict where there is interference with an easement of support.

ESSENTIAL CASE LAW AND COMMENT

Bower v *Peate*, 1876 – Where an independent contractor interferes with an easement of support **(296)**

(*d*) Finally there is a *miscellaneous group of cases* in which an employer has been held liable for the torts of an independent contractor and the principle which seems to run through them all is that the work which the employer has instructed the independent contractor to undertake is extra hazardous. Thus, work *on or under* the highway is attended with some risk if due precautions are not taken, though work *near* the highway is not for that reason alone regarded as extra hazardous. In *Pickard* v *Smith* (1861) 10 C.B., N.S. 470, the defendant who was the tenant of a refreshment room at a railway station was held liable when a coal merchant's servant left the coal cellar flap open while delivering coal to the defendant and a passenger on railway premises fell into the cellar and was injured. Again in *Honeywill & Stein Ltd* v *Larkin Bros Ltd* [1934] 1 K.B. 191, the plaintiffs had received permission from the theatre owner to take photographs in a theatre on which the plaintiffs had recently done work. A firm of photographers was employed by the plaintiffs and in order to take indoor photographs had, in those days, to use magnesium flares with the result that the theatre curtains caught fire and much damage was caused. The plaintiffs paid for the damage, and sued the photographers for an indemnity to which the court said they were entitled. It also emerged that the plaintiffs would have been liable if they had been sued by the theatre owner.

Where an employer is held liable to a third person for the torts of an independent contractor he will, in most cases, be able to claim an indemnity from the contractor. It should also be noted that an employer is not liable for what are called the *collateral* wrongs of his contractor, but only for wrongs which necessarily arise in the course of the contractor's employment. Thus, if A employs B, an independent contractor, to do some excavation work on his land, A will be liable if, say, his neighbour's greenhouse is damaged by the excavations but A will not be liable for loss caused by B's servants making off with the plants.

ESSENTIAL CASE LAW AND COMMENT

Salsbury v *Woodland*, 1969 – Work on or near the highway **(297)**

General defences

Some torts have special defences which can be raised in a particular action, but there are certain general defences which can be raised in any action in tort if they seem to be appropriate.

VOLENTI NON FIT INJURIA

(To one who is willing no harm is done.) This is alternatively called the doctrine of the assumption of risk. There are two main aspects of this defence –

(*a*) Deliberate harm.
(*b*) Accidental harm.

In the first case the plaintiff's assent may prevent his complaining of some deliberate conduct of the defendant which would normally be actionable. If A takes part in a game of rugby football, he must be presumed to accept the rough tactics which are a characteristic and *normal* part of the game, and any damage caused would not give rise to an action although if the same tactics were employed in the street, an action could be sustained. Similarly, although to stick a knife into a person would normally be actionable, if a surgeon does it with the consent of the patient it is not so.

In this connection cases have come before the courts in recent times in which the issue of *informed consent* has been raised. For example, in *Sidaway* v *Bethlem Royal Hospital Governors* [1984] 1 All E.R. 1018, the plaintiff gave her consent for an operation to relieve pain in her neck. The surgeon did not tell her of the possibility of damage to the spinal cord, which was in any case remote. However, there was such damage to the plaintiff's spinal cord and she sued the surgeon regarding her consent as nullified because not all possible risks had been disclosed to her before she gave it. Her claim failed in the Court of Appeal. The risk of spinal cord injury was in any case too remote to found a claim in negligence. As regards the doctor's duty of disclosure prior to a valid consent, Sir John Donaldson, M.R. said it was 'giving or withholding information as is reasonable in all the circumstances . . ., including the patient's true wishes, with a view to placing the patient in a position to make a rational choice'. This test was satisfied here and the plaintiff's consent was valid.

ESSENTIAL CASE LAW AND COMMENT

Simms v *Leigh Rugby Football Club*, 1969 – Effect of consent in sports **(298)**

IMPLIED CONSENT

The plaintiff may *impliedly* consent to run the risk of accidental harm being inflicted upon him. Thus one of the risks incidental to watching an ice-hockey match is that the puck may strike and injure a spectator, or in attendance at a motor race, that cars may run off the track for various reasons, injuring spectators. These are possible hazards unless spectators are to be so fenced or walled in that they cannot see the sport and the maxim *volenti non fit injuria* would apply.

ESSENTIAL CASE LAW AND COMMENT

Murray v *Harringay Arena*, 1951 – Watching ice-hockey **(299)**
Hall v *Brooklands Auto-Racing Club*, 1933 – Watching motor sport **(300)**

NOTICE

In addition, the plaintiff may be *expressly* put on notice that he undertakes a particular activity at his own risk. However, it is essential for the defendant to show as a matter of fact that the plaintiff agreed to *accept* the risk. This means, for one thing, that he must have had a choice and if a contract, e.g. of employment, forces him to accept the risk, there is no true assent.

ESSENTIAL CASE LAW AND COMMENT

Burnett v *British Waterways Board*, 1973 – No true consent **(301)**

CONTRACTUAL CONSENT

If a person's assent to harm being inflicted upon him is purely contractual, it can only operate within the limits allowed by the law of contract; the doctrine of privity of contract applies. Thus if a carrier by road puts an exclusion clause in the contract with the customer excluding liability for damage to the goods, the customer could sue the driver if his negligence caused damage to the goods. The driver could not raise the exclusion clause in his defence because he was not a party to the contract in which it was contained. Sometimes a non-contractual agreement excluding liability for negligence has been upheld.

ESSENTIAL CASE LAW AND COMMENT

White v *Blackmore*, 1972 – A non-contractual assent **(302)**

DEFENDANT'S KNOWLEDGE OF RISK

The defendant must show that the plaintiff knew of the risk. (See *White* v *Blackmore*, 1972.) He must then go on to show that the plaintiff agreed to accept the risk. It does not follow that because a person has knowledge of a potential danger he assents to it. The rule applies equally to cases of *implied volenti* and to cases of *express volenti*. (See *Burnett* v *British Wterways Board*, 1973.) This principle, i.e. that knowledge is not assent, is most often exemplified in the employer and employee cases and in rescue cases, and has restricted the application of the defence.

ESSENTIAL CASE LAW AND COMMENT

Baker v *James Bros*, 1921 – Knowledge is not assent : a defective motor car **(303)**
Dann v *Hamilton*, 1939 – A drunken driver **(304)**
Smith v *Baker*, 1891 – Stone which fell from a crane **(305)**

INHERENT DANGER

Where the danger is inherent in the job, as in the case of a test pilot, the maxim applies; but where the danger is not inherent, then the defence will rarely succeed. (See *Smith* v *Baker*, 1891.) In instances where an employee expressly assumes a risk, and is even paid extra for doing so, the harm resulting will hardly ever be laid at the door of the employer, unless there is evidence that the employer was negligent and created a risk which was not normally present even in a job inherently dangerous.

STATUTORY DUTIES

The doctrine of *volenti non fit injuria* cannot be pleaded by an employer in an action for damages based on breach of a statutory duty, e.g. to fence machinery under safety legislation. The reason is that the object of the statute, to protect workmen, cannot be defeated by a private agreement between employer and employee.

However, where an employee is in breach of a statutory duty and the employer is not, then if the party injured by the breach of statutory duty seeks to make the employer vicariously liable for the tort of the employee, the employer can plead the defence if the circumstances are appropriate.

ESSENTIAL CASE LAW AND COMMENT

ICI v *Shatwell*, 1964 – *Volenti* and breaches of statutory duty **(306)**

THE RESCUE CASES

A different situation arises in what are known as *rescue cases*. In these the plaintiff is injured while intervening to save life or property put in danger by the defendant's negligence. If the intervention is a reasonable thing to do for the saving of life or property, then this does not constitute the assumption of risk, nor does the defence of contributory negligence apply, but if it is not reasonable then the defences of *volenti* and contributory negligence could apply. A person may take greater risks in protecting or rescuing life than in the mere protection of property, though even in protecting property reasonable risks may be taken.

ESSENTIAL CASE LAW AND COMMENT

Baker v *Hopkins*, 1959 – An attempted rescue **(307)**
Cutler v *United Dairies*, 1933 – An unnecessary intervention **(308)**
Hyett v *Great Western Railway*, 1948 – Preserving property **(309)**

DUTY TO RESCUERS

The duty of care owed to a rescuer is an original one and is not derived from or secondary to any duty owed to the rescued person by another. Thus a rescuer may recover damages even though no duty was owed to the person rescued. In addition, the person rescued may be liable in negligence to the rescuer. In *Harrison* v *British Railways Board* [1981] 3 All E.R. 679, Mr Harrison, a guard, jumped off his train as it left the platform to rescue a fellow-employee, A, who was negligently trying to board the moving train, but had slipped and was hanging on to a carriage door. The driver, who was unaware of the incident, was not in any way negligent but A was held liable to Mr Harrison in negligence in regard to the injuries which Mr Harrison sustained when he jumped off the train in order to rescue A.

Furthermore, it is important to remember that the question whether the plaintiff has assented to the possibility of harm being inflicted upon him does not arise until it has been shown that the defendant has committed a tort against the plaintiff. If the harm is not tortious the defence is irrelevant.

Finally, Parliament has in s. 148(3) of the Road Traffic Act, 1972 legislated to prevent exclusion of liability to passengers in motor vehicles on the basis of *volenti*. This certainly covers cases of express *volenti* where a person is given a lift in a car in which there is a notice saying that passengers are at their own risk. Whether it covers cases of implied *volenti* such as *Dann* v *Hamilton*, 1939 (see p. 743) is more doubtful. A passenger who knows that a driver is under the influence of drink or drugs may, if he is injured, be barred from recovering damages on the grounds of *public policy* since he is aiding and abetting a criminal offence. For this reason there is doubt as to the correctness of the decision in *Dann* v *Hamilton*, 1939 where the public policy principle was not considered.

Section 148 of the 1972 Act does not prevent the driver from pleading contributory negligence if this is appropriate.

ESSENTIAL CASE LAW AND COMMENT

Videan v *British Transport Commission*, 1963 – Where no duty is owed to the person rescued **(310)**

Wooldridge v *Sumner*, 1962 – Has the defendant committed a tort? **(311)**

Nettleship v *Weston*, 1971 – Matters of public policy **(312)**

INEVITABLE ACCIDENT

The mere fact that the damage caused is accidental cannot itself be a defence if there is a duty to avert the particular consequences, but there are occasions where the defence of inevitable accident can be raised. Such an accident would be one which was not avoidable by any precautions a reasonable man could have been expected to take. It should be noted, however, that most so-called accidents have a cause, and this defence is of comparatively rare occurrence.

ESSENTIAL CASE LAW AND COMMENT

Stanley v *Powell*, 1891 – An inevitable accident **(313)**

National Coal Board v *Evans*, 1951 – Cutting a cable **(314)**

ACT OF GOD

This is something which occurs in the course of nature, which was beyond human foresight, and against which human prudence could not have been expected to provide. It is something in the course of nature so unexpected in its consequences that the damage caused must be regarded as too remote to form a basis for legal liability. It arises always from the course of nature and has no human causation. This distinguishes it from inevitable accident.

ESSENTIAL CASE LAW AND COMMENT

Nichols v *Marsland*, 1876 – An Act of God **(315)**

NECESSITY

This defence is put forward when damage has been intentionally caused, either to prevent a greater evil or in defence of the realm. Such damage is justifiable if the act was reasonable. Thus where a whole area is threatened by fire, the destruction of property not yet alight with a view to stopping the spread of the flames would be damage intentionally done but reasonable in the circumstances. Furthermore, in *Leigh* v *Gladstone* (1909) 26 T.L.R. 139 the forcible feeding of a suffragette in prison was held justified by the necessity of preserving her life. This decision, which has been much criticised, means that it is not an assault for prison officials to take reasonable steps to preserve the health and life of those in custody.

However, duress does not appear to be a defence and in *Gilbert* v *Stone* (1647), Aleyn 35, the defendant was held liable for trespass although he entered the plaintiff's house only because twelve armed men had threatened to kill him if he did not do so.

ESSENTIAL CASE LAW AND COMMENT

Cresswell v *Sirl*, 1948 – Necessity: when dogs worry sheep **(316)**
Cope v *Sharpe*, 1912 – Necessity: a heath fire **(317)**

MISTAKE

It is normally no defence in tort to say that the wrongful act was done by mistake. Even if the consequences of an act were not fully appreciated, everyone is presumed to intend the probable consequences of his acts. A mistake of law is no excuse, and this is usually true of a mistake of fact, unless it is reasonable in the circumstances, e.g. in a case of wrongful arrest.

However, the defence of unintentional defamation under s. 4 of the Defamation Act, 1952 is to some extent based on mistake. (See further p. 474.)

> **ESSENTIAL CASE LAW AND COMMENT**
>
> *Beckwith* v *Philby*, 1827 – A mistaken arrest **(318)**

ACT OF STATE

Sometimes the State finds it necessary to protect persons from actions in tort when they have caused damage whilst carrying out their duties. This defence cannot be raised in respect of damage done anywhere to British subjects or where the court holds that damage has been done to a friendly alien.

> **ESSENTIAL CASE LAW AND COMMENT**
>
> *Buron* v *Denman*, 1848 – Act of State and a slave trader **(319)**
> *Nissan* v *Attorney-General*, 1967 – Defence not available against
>   British subjects **(320)**
> *Johnstone* v *Pedlar*, 1921 – Damage to a friendly alien **(321)**

STATUTORY AUTHORITY

The acts of public authorities, e.g. local authority councils, are often carried out under the provisions of a statute. This statutory authority to act may give the public authority concerned a good defence if an action in tort arises as a result. However, much depends upon the wording of the relevant statute. *Statutory authority may be absolute* in which case the public authority concerned has a *duty* to act. Alternatively, *statutory authority may be conditional*, in which case the public authority concerned has the *power* to act but is not bound to do so.

If the authority given is *absolute*, then the body concerned is not liable for damage resulting from the exercise of that authority provided it has acted reasonably and there is no alternative way of performing the act.

On the other hand, if the authority given is *conditional*, the body concerned may carry out the relevant act only if there is no interference with the rights of others.

Whether statutory authority is *absolute* or *conditional* is a matter of construction of the statute concerned, though statutory powers are usually conferred in *conditional* or permissive form. The basic rules of construction in these cases appear to be as follows –

(*a*) Is the authorised act of such public importance as to override private interests?

(*b*) If it is not, statutory powers are probably conferred subject to common-law rights.

In addition, the matter of statutory compensation may be relevant. If the statute provides for compensation for loss resulting from an authorised act there may be no other claim even though the maximum compensation allowed by the statute is less than the actual loss. On the other hand, if there is no provision for compensation in the statute there is a presumption that private rights remain and that an action in respect of any infringement of these rights may be brought.

It should be noted that the above principles also apply where the act done is authorised by delegated legislation.

ESSENTIAL CASE LAW AND COMMENT

Vaughan v *Taff Vale Railway*, 1860 – An absolute authority **(322)**
Penny v *Wimbledon U.D.C.*, 1899 – A conditional authority **(323)**
Marriage v *East Norfolk Rivers Catchment Board*, 1950 – Statutory compensation **(324)**

JUSTIFICATION OR SELF DEFENCE

Where a person commits a tort in defence of himself or his property, he will not be liable provided the act done in such defence is reasonable or proportionate to the harm threatened, though no provocation by words can justify a blow. (*Lane* v *Holloway* [1967] 3 All E.R. 129.) The defence extends to acts in defence of the members of one's family and probably to acts in defence of persons generally.

ILLEGALITY

It would appear that an action in tort may be defeated on the ground that the plaintiff was committing an illegal or immoral act when the tort occurred. Thus in *Ashton* v *Turner* [1980] 3 All E.R. 870 three men committed a burglary after an evening's drinking and sought to escape in a car owned by one of them. The car crashed and a passenger was injured. He claimed damages alleging negligence against the driver and the car owner. It was held by Ewbank, J., dismissing the claim, that as a matter of public policy the law might not recognise a duty of care owed by one participant in a crime to another for acts done in the course of that commission, and in any case *volenti non fit injuria* was a defence open to the driver. Again in the Irish case of *Hegarty* v *Shine* (1878) 4 L.R. Ir. 288 the plaintiff, an unmarried woman, brought an action for trespass on the grounds that she had contracted venereal disease following her relationship with the defendant over a period of some two years. Palles, C.B. denied her a remedy, saying 'the cause of an action here is a *turpis causa* incapable of being made the foundation of an action. The cause of action is the very act of illicit sexual intercourse'. It would appear, therefore, that the maxim *ex turpi causa* is not confined solely to contract. (For the contractual application see p. 305.)

Remedies

The remedies available to a person who has suffered injury or loss by reason of the tort of another are *damages*, the granting of an *injunction*, and in some cases an order for *specific restitution* of land or chattels of which the plaintiff has been dispossessed.

Damages – generally

Usually the damages awarded are *compensatory* and the underlying principle is that of *restitutio in integrum*, i.e. the damages awarded are designed to put the plaintiff in the position he would have been in if he had not suffered the wrong.

In the case of *personal injuries*, e.g. loss of a limb, damages obviously cannot restore the plaintiff to his previous position. However, damages for personal injuries may be awarded under the following heads –

(*a*) pain and suffering;
(*b*) loss of enjoyment of life, or of amenity, as where brain damage causes permanent unconsciousness;
(*c*) loss of earnings, both actual and prospective.

As regards earnings, *Oliver* v *Ashman* [1962] 2 Q.B. 210 decided that where a tortious act had reduced the life expectancy of the plaintiff he could recover a sum representing loss of earnings for the reduced number of years for which he was likely to live but not for the lost years. In *Pickett* v *British Rail Engineering Ltd* [1979] 1 All E.R. 774, the House of Lords overruled *Oliver* and decided that earnings during the lost years should be taken into account, less, of course, taxation (see *Gourley* below) and the deduction of an estimated sum to represent the victim's probable living expenses during those years. Thus if A, aged 30, is injured by negligence and would have lived to 70 before but since the accident only to 50, then earnings from ages 30 to 50 and 50 to 65 (the lost years) must now be taken into account.

Although s. 1(1)(a) of the Administration of Justice Act, 1982 has abolished the claim for *damages* for loss of expectation of life, it leaves unchanged the right to claim *income* for the 'lost' years.

DEDUCTIONS – TAX

The House of Lords decided in *British Transport Commission* v *Gourley* [1955] 3 All E.R. 796, that the fact that the plaintiff would have paid tax on his earnings must be taken into account so as to reduce the damages awarded in regard to earnings. The money is not paid to the Revenue so it is a benefit either to the defendant or to his insurance company. However, the rule has some logic on the grounds that damages are *compensatory*, and gross salary must be reduced to net salary to achieve true compensation.

DEDUCTIONS – COLLATERAL BENEFITS

The Law Reform (Personal Injuries) Act, 1948, s. 2 (as amended by the Social Security Act, 1989, s. 22) requires full deduction of the value of certain Social Security benefits, e.g. benefits payable for sickness and/or disablement received by the plaintiff or likely to accrue to him for five years after the accident occurred, though if the plaintiff did not know that he had a right to a particular form of national insurance benefit, and had not acted unreasonably in failing to claim it, the sum which he might have received will not be deducted from the damages awarded. (*Eley* v *Bedford* [1971] 3 All E.R. 285.)

Many cases have come before the courts on the matter of deduction of a wide variety of collateral benefits. In general the policy is one of non-deduction and sums received from other forms of insurance are not taken into account, nor is a disability or state retirement pension (*Parry* v *Cleaver* [1969] 1 All E.R. 555 and *Hewson* v *Downes* [1969] 3 All E.R. 193).

CLASSIFICATION OF DAMAGES

It is possible to classify damages under a number of headings, and this classification applies to both contract and tort.

Ordinary damages

These are damages assessed by the court for losses arising naturally from the breach of contract, and in tort for losses which cannot be positively proved or ascertained, and depend upon the court's view of the nature of the plaintiff's injury. For example, the court may have to decide what to award for the loss of an eye, there being no scale of payments; and this is so whether the action is in tort or for breach of contract.

Special damages

These are awarded in tort for losses which can be positively proved or ascertained, e.g. damage to clothing; garage bills, where a vehicle has been damaged; doctor's fees; and so on. However, where it is difficult to determine the exact proportions of a claim for special damages, e.g. loss of profit not supported by accurate figures, the court must do its best to arrive at a fair valuation. (*Dixons Ltd* v *J. L. Cooper Ltd* (1970), 114 S.J. 319.) In contract, the term covers losses which do not arise naturally from the breach, so that they will not be recoverable unless within the contemplation of the parties as described at p. 336.

Exemplary and aggravated damages

The usual object of damages both in contract and tort is to compensate the plaintiff for loss which he has incurred arising from the defendant's conduct. The object of *exemplary (or punitive) damages* is to punish the defendant, and to deter him and others from similar conduct in the future. Thus, it was at one time thought that, if the court had arrived at a sum of money which would sufficiently compensate the plaintiff, it could award a further sum, not as compensation for the plaintiff, but as a punishment to the defendant, the exemplary damages being in the nature of a fine. An award of exemplary damages had always confused the functions of the civil and criminal law, and it would appear that since the judgment of Lord Devlin in *Rookes* v *Barnard* [1964] 1 All E.R. 367, an award of exemplary damages should only be made in certain special cases as follows –

(*a*) *Where there is arbitrary or unconstitutional action by servants of the State*, e.g. an unreasonable false imprisonment or detention by State authorities.

(*b*) *Where the defendant's conduct has been calculated by him to make a profit for himself which may well exceed the compensation payable to the plaintiff.* Thus a newspaper may decide that the increased sales of the paper containing a libel will more than compensate for any damages which may have to be paid to the person libelled. In such a case exemplary damages may be awarded to the plaintiff, though the intention to profit must be proved. It is not enough that the newspaper has been sold and some profit necessarily made. An example of the application of this head is to be seen in *Cassell & Co. Ltd* v *Broome* [1972] 1 All E.R. 801 where the House of Lords upheld an award of £25,000 exemplary damages against defendants who published a book containing defamatory passages where the right circumstances appeared to exist and a defence, if raised, would have failed.

(*c*) *Where exemplary damages are expressly authorised by statute.*

Exemplary or punitive damages were sometimes awarded in contract for breach of promise of marriage, particularly where a female plaintiff had allowed the defendant to have sexual intercourse with her on the promise of marriage. This action is now abolished by the Law Reform (Miscellaneous Provisions) Act, 1970, s. 1 and examples of exemplary damages would seem in the main to be confined to actions in tort.

Aggravated damages, on the other hand, can be awarded (generally only in tort) where the defendant's conduct is such that the plaintiff requires more than the usual amount of damages to *compensate him* for the unpleasant method in which the tort was committed against him. However, an award of aggravated damages is still *compensatory*.

The state of the law may perhaps be illustrated by taking a hypothetical case. Suppose a tenant T is evicted from his flat by the landlord L before T's term has expired, and that in order to evict T the landlord uses excessive violence. The court may decide that in an ordinary case of trespass and assault

T would be adequately compensated by an award of damages of (say) £750. However, if the court considers that L used particularly violent and unpleasant methods to achieve this eviction, it may award a further sum (say) £150 as aggravated damages because, on the facts of the case, this is necessary to compensate T. It would appear that the court cannot since *Rookes'* case go on and make a further award to T in order to punish and deter L.

Nominal damages

Sometimes a small sum (say £2) is awarded where the plaintiff proves a breach of contract, or the infringement of a right, but has suffered no actual loss.

Contemptuous damages

A farthing was sometimes awarded to mark the court's disapproval of the plaintiff's conduct in bringing the action. Such damages may be awarded where the plaintiff has sued for defamation of character in spite of the fact that he has engaged in defamatory activities against the defendant. Since farthings are no longer legal tender, the decimal penny would now be used.

Liquidated damages

These are damages agreed upon by the parties to the contract, and only a breach of contract need be proved; no proof of loss is required. Damages in tort are not normally liquidated.

Unliquidated damages

Where no damages are fixed by the contract it is left to the court to decide their amount. In such a case the plaintiff must produce evidence of the loss he has suffered, as is normal in the case of tort.

Liquidated and unliquidated damages have already been considered in more detail (see p. 334).

REMOTENESS OF DAMAGE

The consequences of a defendant's wrongful act or omission may be endless. Even so a plaintiff who has established that the defendant's wrong caused his loss may be unable to recover damages because his loss is not sufficiently connected with the defendant's wrong to make the latter liable. In other words, the loss is too remote a consequence to be recoverable. The decision of the Judicial Committee of the Privy Council in *Overseas Tankship (UK) Ltd* v *Morts Dock and Engineering Co. Ltd*, 1961 (see below) (generally referred to as *The Wagon Mound*) laid down the modern test for remoteness of damage in tort which is as follows –

(*a*) *Regarding culpability or responsibility for the harm.* The test is an objective test rather than a subjective one, because the law substitutes for the defendant a hypothetical reasonable man, and then proceeds to make the defendant only responsible for the damage which the reasonable man would have foreseen as a likely consequence of his act.

(*b*) *Regarding liability to compensate the plaintiff.* The law now requires the defendant to compensate the plaintiff only for the foreseeable result of his act. The defendant is not liable for all the direct consequences of his act, but only for those which, as a reasonable man, he should have foreseen. However, it appears from more recent decisions that the *precise* nature of the injury suffered need not be foreseeable: it is enough if the injury was of a *kind* that was foreseeable even though the form it took was unusual.

ESSENTIAL CASE LAW AND COMMENT

The Wagon Mound, 1961 – The test for remoteness of damage **(325)**

Hughes v *Lord Advocate*, 1963 – Precise chain of events need not be foreseen **(326)**

Status of *The Wagon Mound*

Certain problems were raised by the decision in *The Wagon Mound*.

(*a*) Being a decision of the Judicial Committee of the Privy Council, it was not binding on English courts but was persuasive only.

In the event the House of Lords in *Hughes* v *Lord Advocate*, 1963 (see above) treated the decision in *The Wagon Mound* as a correct statement of the law, subject in *Hughes'* case to an additional principle that the precise chain of circumstances need not be envisaged if the consequence turns out to be within the general sphere of contemplation and not of an entirely different kind which no one can anticipate.

(*b*) Before *The Wagon Mound* there was a well-established principle called the 'unusual plaintiff' rule. For example, if X strikes Y a puny blow which might be expected merely to bruise him, but in fact Y has a thin skull and dies from the blow, the law has regarded X as liable for Y's death. The same rule has been applied where the plaintiff is a haemophiliac, i.e. a person with a constitutional tendency to severe bleeding.

The courts have held that this principle is not affected by *The Wagon Mound* and remains as an exception to it. However, the 'unusual plaintiff' rule seems to apply only to disabilities existing before the accident and not to disabilities arising afterwards.

The test of remoteness of damage in tort as laid down in *The Wagon Mound* relies upon the foreseeability of a reasonable man both in respect of culpability and liability to compensate. It appears, therefore, that the law of remoteness of damage is not the same as in the law of contract. In the *Heron II*, 1967 (see p. 712) it will be recalled that the House of Lords decided that a party to a contract is not liable for all foreseeable damage.

Finally, it is perhaps worth noting that *damage which is intended* is never too remote and in this connection there is an inference that a person intends the natural consequences of his or her acts.

ESSENTIAL CASE LAW AND COMMENT

Smith v *Leech Braine & Co Ltd*, 1962 – The thin skull rule survives **(327)**

Martindale v *Duncan*, 1973 – Poverty is within the unusual plaintiff rule **(328)**

Morgan v *T. Wallis*, 1974 – There must be a prior disability **(329)**

Scott v *Shepherd*, 1773 – Intended damage never too remote **(330)**

NOVUS ACTUS INTERVENIENS: A NEW ACT INTERVENING

A loss may be too remote a consequence to be recoverable if the chain of causation is broken by an extraneous act. The scope of this concept is as follows –

(*a*) When the act of a third person intervenes between the original act or omission and the damage the original act or omission is still the direct cause of the damage if the act of the third person might have been expected in the circumstances (see *Scott* v *Shepherd*, 1773) or did not materially cause or contribute to the injury. There is a duty to guard against a *novus actus interveniens*.

ESSENTIAL CASE LAW AND COMMENT

Barnett v *Chelsea and Kensington Hospital Management Committee*, 1968 – An immaterial *novus actus* **(331)**

Robinson v *The Post Office*, 1973 – Complications from an injection **(332)**

Davies v *Liverpool Corporation*, 1949 – Duty to prevent a *novus actus* **(333)**

(*b*) If the act of the third person is such as would not be anticipated by a reasonable man, the chain of causation is broken, and the third party's act and not the initial act or omission will be treated as the cause of the damage.

ESSENTIAL CASE LAW AND COMMENT

Cobb v *Great Western Railway*, 1894 – Where a theft broke the chain of causation **(334)**

(*c*) The *novus actus* may be the act of the plaintiff and in these cases liability will turn on the precise facts.

ESSENTIAL CASE LAW AND COMMENT

Sayers v *Harlow U.D.C.*, 1958 – The new act may be that of the plaintiff **(335)**
McKew v *Holland and Hannen and Cubitts*, 1969 – A fall down the stairs **(336)**

(*d*) In order to establish the liability of the intervenor, it is essential to show that he consciously intended to carry out the act.

ESSENTIAL CASE LAW AND COMMENT

Philco Radio Corporation v *Spurling*, 1949 – The person who does the intervening act must intend it **(337)**

Nervous shock

Damages for illness brought on by nervous shock are not necessarily too remote and may be recoverable where the nervous shock causes physical illness and –

(*a*) the defendant *intended* the shock (see *Wilkinson* v *Downton*, 1897 at p. 728), or
(*b*) where the shock arises from *negligence*, the plaintiff was 'foreseeable'.

Nervous shock will be foreseeable –

(*a*) Where the defendant's negligent act puts the plaintiff in fear of his or her safety.

ESSENTIAL CASE LAW AND COMMENT

Dulieu v *White*, 1901 – Nervous shock: fear for one's own life **(338)**

(*b*) Where the defendant's negligent act threatens or actually injures some person who has a relationship with the plaintiff such as a family relationship. The relationship of rescuer and rescued is included. However the fact that there is a relationship is not enough to allow a successful claim. In addition the plaintiff must have –

(i) seen the accident; or
(ii) although not having seen it suffered shock by a sensible imagining of it from observed surrounding circumstances; or
(iii) seen the victim afterwards.

There also is the requirement that the defendant must owe the plaintiff a duty of care, though such a duty can exist not merely in regard to personal injuries but also to nervous shock following damage to property.

ESSENTIAL CASE LAW AND COMMENT

Chadwick v *British Railways Board*, 1967 – Nervous shock: rescuer and rescued **(339)**
Hinz v *Berry*, 1970 – Where the accident is seen **(340)**
Hambrook v *Stokes*, 1925 – Where the accident is not seen but sensibly imagined **(341)**
McLoughlin v *O'Brian*, 1982 – Where the victim is seen **(342)**
Bourhill v *Young*, 1943 – There must be a duty of care **(343)**

Finally it should be noted that damages for nervous shock may be recovered where the plaintiff has witnessed some awful spectacle even though neither his own life nor that of any third party was put in peril.

ESSENTIAL CASE LAW AND COMMENT

Owens v *Liverpool Corporation*, 1939 – When a coffin was overturned **(344)**

The above rules were developed because of the following problems inherent in actions for nervous shock –

(*a*) the difficulty of proving the degree of suffering involved and the possibility of fraudulent claims; thus, only where a known physical or mental condition is manifest are damages awarded;
(*b*) the difficulty which might arise if the number of possible claims, e.g. from persons not present at the accident, was not limited.

Damage after successive accidents

If a second event, e.g. injury or illness, which is not connected with the tortious accident comes on before the trial and makes the injury worse, damages are reduced to the extent caused by the further injury or illness. If the second event is a tortious accident then no deduction is made.

A defendant who injures a plaintiff *who has already* been injured will be liable only in so far as his tortious act increases or exacerbates the pre-existing injury.

PROVISIONAL DAMAGES

Under the Rules of the Supreme Court there can be an award of provisional damages. Suppose A loses the sight of one eye in an accident caused by B's negligence. There is a risk that he might lose the sight of the other eye. If an award of damages is increased because of this possibility and it does not occur, then the damages were too much. If the sight of the other eye is affected the damages might be too small because the *precise* nature of the injury was not before the court. The judge can now make an award of provisional damages on the basis that the risk will not develop and specify a period during which a 'further award' can be made if it does.

INJUNCTION

An injunction may be granted to prevent the commission, continuance or repetition of an injury, and there is a form of interlocutory injunction called *quia timet* (because he fears) which may be granted, though rarely, even though the injury has not taken place but is merely threatened. As we have seen, injunctions are discretionary remedies and cannot be obtained as of right. Furthermore, an injunction will not be granted where damages would be an adequate remedy. However, it is no defence to say that it will be costly to comply with the injunction, though the court may, as in *Pride of Derby and Derbyshire Angling Association Ltd* v *British Celanese Ltd* [1953] 1 All E.R. 179, where expensive alterations to sewage plant were required to prevent the pollution of a river, grant an injunction and suspend its operation for such time as may seem necessary to enable the defendant to comply with the order.

OTHER REMEDIES

The court may order *specific restitution* of land or goods where the plaintiff has been deprived of possession and a plaintiff may be given an order for an *account* of profits received as a result of a wrongful act. Thus where a company or other business organisation carries on business under a name calculated to deceive the public by confusion with the name of an existing concern, it commits the tort of *passing off* and can be restrained by injunction from doing so. In addition, the existing concern may be given an order for an *account* of profits received by the offending concern as a result of the deception.

ESSENTIAL CASE LAW AND COMMENT

Jobling v *Associated Dairies*, 1980 – Where there is a subsequent non-tortious act **(345)**
Baker v *Willoughby*, 1969 – Where there is a subsequent tortious act **(346)**
Performance Cars Ltd v *Abraham*, 1961 – Where a second accident occurred before the damage from the first was repaired **(347)**

Cessation of liability

Liability in tort may be terminated by *death* (see p. 380), and also by *judgment, waiver, accord and satisfaction* and *lapse of time*.

JUDGMENT

Successive actions cannot be brought by the same person on the same facts and if a competent court gives a final judgment in respect of a right of action that right of action is *merged* into the judgment. Thus in *Fitter* v *Veal* (1701) 12 Mod. Rep. 542, the plaintiff sued the defendant for assault and battery and obtained a judgment for £11. After some years he discovered his injuries were worse than he had thought and he had to have part of his skull removed. It was held that he could not sue for further damages.

However, there are certain exceptional cases, for example, where two separate rights have been infringed. Thus in *Brunsden* v *Humphrey* (1884), 14 Q.B.D. 141, the Court of Appeal held that a cab driver who had brought a successful action for damage to his cab caused by the defendant's negligence was able to bring a further action for personal injuries. One action was for damage to *property*, the other for injury to the *person*.

WAIVER

A person may waive a tort when he forgoes his right to bring an action upon the wrongful act. If, for example, S a second-hand car dealer buys a car from T, a thief, and sells it to B then S will convert the vehicle. If the true owner agrees to settle the matter with S by accepting from S the sale price of the car which S received from B then the true owner cannot sue S in the tort of conversion because he has waived his right.

ACCORD AND SATISFACTION

A person may surrender a right of action in tort by deed or an agreement for consideration.

LAPSE OF TIME

In actions for damages for negligence, nuisance, or breach of duty, e.g. the statutory duty of an employer to fence a dangerous machine, where damages consist of, or include, damages for personal injury, the limitation period is three years (s. 11(1), Limitation Act, 1980). Under s. 2 of the 1980 Act the period in all other actions in tort is six years. However, actions in respect of registered postal packets under s. 30(1) of the Post Office Act, 1969 must be brought within twelve months.

The period of limitation generally begins from the date when the tort was committed, e.g. the date of a trespass to land. However, at one time an action in negligence arose only when the harm was suffered but not, apparently, when it was detected. Thus in *Pirelli General Cable Works Ltd v Oscar Faber & Partners Ltd* [1983] 1 All E.R. 65 the defendants designed a chimney for the plaintiff. It was in the event a negligent design. Cracks were discovered by the plaintiffs in 1977 but evidence showed that they had appeared in 1970. When the plaintiffs sued in 1978 for negligence the House of Lords held that their claim was statute-barred.

The Latent Damage Act, 1986 now applies and the limitation period is either six years from the date on which the cause of action accrued or three years from the earliest date upon which the plaintiff had sufficient knowledge to sue. The Act imposes a 'long-stop' period of 15 years from the negligent act or omission or the occurrence of the damage whether or not the damage was discovered or even discoverable by then. No action can be brought after this time.

The above rules were also rather harsh in personal injury cases where, for example, the plaintiff did not know that he had a claim or the extent of that claim, as where he had contracted a dust disease and was not aware of its onset. Furthermore, if X had been run down by Y's negligent driving, and unknown to X the injuries inflicted on him at the time of the accident caused him to go blind (say) four years after the accident, then X's cause of action in respect of his blindness was barred before he knew it existed, since it was formerly held that once damage had occurred the cause of action accrued and that time began to run against the plaintiff even though he was unaware or mistaken as to the consequences of the damage.

The matter is now covered by the Limitation Act, 1980. The Act applies only to claims for personal injury arising out of negligence, breach of contract or breach of statutory duty. The basic limitation period of three years is retained but time runs from the date of accrual of the cause of action or the 'date of the plaintiff's knowledge if later'. The 'date of the plaintiff's knowledge' is the date on which the plaintiff first had knowledge that his injury was significant and that it was attributable in whole or in part to the act or omission which constitutes the alleged negligence, or breach of duty.

The action may be brought by dependants or on behalf of the estate of a deceased person. Thus actions may be brought within three years of the date of death or of the date on which the personal representatives or dependants, as the case may be, acquired a knowledge of the relevant facts.

If the tort is of a continuing nature, as in the case of nuisance or possibly trespass, an independent cause of action arises on each day during which the tort is committed, and the aggrieved party can recover for such proportion of the injury as lies within the limitation period, even though the wrong was first committed outside the period.

Where the plaintiff is a minor or person suffering from mental disorder, the period of limitation does not run against him until his disability ends, i.e. on becoming 18 or on becoming sane or on death. But once time has started to run, any subsequent disability will not stop it running.

However, a minor was only regarded as being under a disability if he was not in the custody of a parent when the cause of action accrued. If he was in the custody of a parent the parent was expected to commence an action within the limitation period and if he did not the minor's action would be statute-barred. The Act of 1980, s. 8, abolishes that rule so that periods of limitation do not run against a minor whether he is in the custody of a parent or not.

SPECIAL PERIODS OF LIMITATION

The periods of limitation in respect of actions against the estate of a deceased tortfeasor have already been considered on p. 381. However, it should be noted that the Limitation Act, 1980, does not operate to extend the time within which an action must be brought against a deceased tortfeasor's estate. So far as the death of an injured party is concerned, the ordinary six- or three-year periods apply. They run from the accrual of the cause of action as if no death had occurred. As we have seen, personal representatives or dependants may ask for an extension of time under the provisions of the Limitation Act, 1980.

Other special periods of limitation are as follows –

(*a*) Actions arising out of collisions at sea: two years, subject to extension by the court (Maritime Conventions Act, 1911, s. 8).

(*b*) Proceedings against air-carriers: two years (Carriage by Air Act, 1961, s. 1(1)).

(*c*) A joint tortfeasor who wishes to recover a contribution must bring the action within two years from the date on which he admitted liability or judgment was entered against him (Limitation Act, 1980, s. 8).

(*d*) Actions in respect of damage arising from nuclear incidents: thirty years (Nuclear Installations Act, 1965, s. 15).

Public authorities and their officers have no special position and actions against them are governed by the same rules as any other action in tort.

It should also be noted that by s. 32 of the Limitation Act, 1980, the defendant's *fraud* or *negligent concealment* may prevent his pleading that the claim is statute-barred.

> **ESSENTIAL CASE LAW AND COMMENT**
>
> *Beaman* v *A.R.T.S.*, 1949 – Limitation of actions: fraudulent concealment of claim **(348)**

ASSIGNMENT

It is against the rules of public policy to allow the assignment of rights of action in tort, since actions for damages should not become a marketable commodity. However, rights may pass to others by operation of law in the following circumstances –

(*a*) *Death.* Rights and liabilities in tort survive for the benefit or otherwise of the estate, except actions for defamation unless damage to the deceased's estate has resulted.

(*b*) *Bankruptcy.* Rights of action in tort possessed by a debtor which relate to his *property* and which if brought will increase his assets will pass to his trustee in bankruptcy. Actions for *personal torts*, e.g. defamation, remain with the bankrupt.

(*c*) *Subrogation.* An insurance company which compensates an insured person under a policy of insurance can step into his shoes and sue in respect of the injury.

21
The law of torts – specific torts

We shall next examine certain specific torts, beginning with those affecting the person.

Torts affecting the person

TRESPASS TO THE PERSON

This has several aspects:

Assault

An assault is an attempt or offer to apply unlawful force to the person of another. There must be an apparent present ability to carry out the threat, the basis of the wrong being that a person is put in present fear of violence. On general principles, pointing even an unloaded weapon or a model gun at another, who does not know that it is unloaded or a model, would amount to an assault.

It is often said that mere words cannot constitute an assault but this is a doubtful proposition. In *Ansell* v *Thomas* [1974] Crim. L.R. 31 the assault seems to have consisted in words threatening forcible ejectment of a director from the company's premises if he did not leave voluntarily. A threat to use force at some time in the future is not an assault, but it seems that it is enough if the threat is to use force if the person addressed does not immediately do some act. In *Read* v *Coker* (1853) 138 E.R. 1437, it was held that an assault was committed where the defendants threatened to break the plaintiff's neck if he did not leave the premises. Words, however, may prevent an assault coming into being.

As regards the unauthorised taking of a photograph the position is somewhat complicated. It may be that where a flash is used the simple taking of the photograph without more is unlawful, since it is probably a battery (see below) to project light on to another person in such a manner as to cause personal discomfort. Where no flash is used, it is hard to see how, by itself, the taking of a photograph can amount to a battery, an assault or any other trespass.

> ## ESSENTIAL CASE LAW AND COMMENT
> *Turbervell* v *Savage*, 1669 – Words may prevent an assault **(349)**

Battery

Intentionally to bring any material object into contact with the person of another is enough application of force to give rise to a battery. Thus to throw water on a person (*Pursell* v *Horn* (1838) 8 A.&E. 602), or to apply a 'tone-rinse' to the scalp of a customer which was not ordered and caused damaged, i.e. a skin rash, is enough. (*Nash* v *Sheen*, *The Times*, 13 March 1953.) Substantial damages will be awarded when the battery is an affront to personal dignity, e.g. the wrongful taking of a fingerprint. It should, however, be noted that a person who has been detained and charged with or told he will be charged with a recordable offence, e.g. an offence punishable by imprisonment, can have his fingerprints taken without consent (s. 61, Police and Criminal Evidence Act, 1984, referred to hereunder as PACE). Persons who are convicted of a recordable offence but fined rather than imprisoned can be required to attend at a police station for prints to be taken. Failure to do so allows arrest without warrant (s. 27, PACE). The mere jostling which occurs in a crowd does not constitute battery, because there is presumed consent and in any case there is normally no hostility which is also a requirement. Thus in *Wilson* v *Pringle* [1986] 2 All E.R. 440, one schoolboy had intentionally pulled a schoolbag off another boy's shoulder. However, this was only a form of horseplay and in the absence of a hostile intention there was no battery. It should be noted that there may be a battery without an assault, as where a person is attacked from behind.

In considering the defence of *volenti* there has already been some consideration of informed consent in an action for alleged negligence. (See *Sidaway* v *Bethlem Royal Hospital Governors* [1984] 1 All E.R. 1018 at p. 394.) A similar issue was raised in *Freeman* v *Home Office* [1984] 1 All E.R. 1036. The plaintiff was serving a sentence of life imprisonment. He was given drugs by a medical officer employed by the Home Office. He claimed that the drugs were given to discipline and control him and not, as he thought, as medical treatment. He claimed that the medical officer had committed battery upon him and that his consent was negatived because it was not informed. The Court of Appeal decided that since the doctrine of informed consent formed no part of English law, the sole issue was whether on the facts the plaintiff had consented to the administration of the drugs and on that issue the trial judge had found that the plaintiff had so consented. His claim therefore failed.

In more recent times it has been suggested that those who suffer passively from the smoking of others might be able to claim damages for battery. Since spitting at someone is a battery there seems no reason why blowing out poisonous smoke in the vicinity of other people should not also be. In addition a claim for damages for mental illness allegedly caused by sexual abuse has been brought against an alleged abuser and has been allowed to proceed (*Stubbings* v *Webb* [1991] 3 All E.R. 949).

In general there will be some active conduct constituting the assault. However, the courts have accepted that a battery can arise from an omission.

ESSENTIAL CASE LAW AND COMMENT

Fagan v *Metropolitan Police Commissioner*, 1968 – A battery from an omission **(350)**

Defences

There are certain defences to an action brought for assault or for battery –

(*a*) *Self-defence.* This is not merely the defence of oneself but also of those whom one has a legal or moral obligation to protect. It also applies to the protection of property, but no more than reasonable force must be used.

(*b*) *Parental or similar authority.* Moderate chastisement inflicted on children by parents, and school teachers by way of delegation of the parent's authority, is not actionable, but school teachers need a *specific* consent. it is doubtful whether such a consent can in more modern times be *implied* merely because a child is sent to school. This follows from a ruling of the Court of Human Rights that corporal punishment used in schools without parental permission contravenes the Human Rights Convention.

(*c*) *Volenti non fit injuria.* As in the case of the players in a rugby match (see *Simms* v *Leigh R.F.C.*, 1969 at p. 741).

(*d*) *Judicial authority.* This includes the right to inflict proper punishment and to make lawful arrests.

(*e*) *Necessity.* This is not favoured as a defence but may be allowed if the defendant can prove that he committed the battery in order to prevent the happening of a greater harm. Thus in *Leigh* v *Gladstone* (1909) 26 T.L.R. 139, the forcible feeding of a suffragette in prison was held justified by the necessity of preserving her life.

(*f*) *Prosecution in a magistrates' court.* Assault and battery is a crime as well as a civil wrong. If the wrongdoer is prosecuted, and *summary* proceedings are taken and the accused is convicted and punished, or the case is dismissed and the magistrates award a certificate of dismissal, no further action or civil proceedings may be taken in respect of the particular wrong. (Offences against the Person Act, 1861, ss. 44–45.)

It is now clear that trespass to the person is not actionable in itself; the plaintiff must prove intention or negligence though he need not prove damage. It is also settled that where the interference is *unintentional* the plaintiff's only cause of action lies in negligence.

ESSENTIAL CASE LAW AND COMMENT

Fowler v *Lanning*, 1959 – Trespass requires intention or negligence **(351)**

False imprisonment

This is the infliction of unauthorised bodily restraint without lawful justification. It is not necessarily a matter of bars and bolts, but any form of unlawful restraint might turn out to be false imprisonment. The imprisonment must be total, and if certain ways of exit are barred to a prisoner, but he is free to go off in another way, then there is no false imprisonment. If a person is on premises and is not given facilities to leave, then this does constitute false imprisonment, unless the refusal is merely the insistence on a reasonable condition. It is not even essential that the plaintiff should be aware of the fact of his imprisonment, provided it is a fact. *Volenti non fit injuria* is defence to false imprisonment, as where a prison visitor agrees to be locked in a cell with the prisoner.

ESSENTIAL CASE LAW AND COMMENT

Bird v *Jones*, 1845 – Imprisonment must be total **(352)**
Herd v *Weardale Steel Coal and Coke Co*, 1915 – Where refusal to allow a person to leave is reasonable **(353)**
Meering v *Grahame White Aviation Co Ltd*, 1919 – Knowledge of imprisonment is not required **(354)**

Arrest and the tort of trespass to the person

An arrest or other restraint of a person, as by stopping and searching him, will be unlawful and actionable as a trespass in civil law unless the following requirements are met.

ARRESTABLE OFFENCES

The basic rule is that offences are arrestable if they carry a sentence of five years or more (s. 24(1)(b), PACE) or are offences for which the sentence is fixed by law, e.g. murder (s. 24(1)(a), PACE).

A private person may arrest without a warrant anyone who is, or whom he, with reasonable cause, suspects to be, *in the act* of committing an arrestable offence (PACE, s. 24(4)). Where an arrestable offence *has been committed*, any person may arrest without warrant anyone who is, or whom he, with reasonable cause, suspects to be, guilty of the offence (s. 24(5), PACE).

A police constable is protected in respect of arrests made under the authority of a warrant. He may arrest without a warrant in the situations mentioned above. Furthermore he may arrest someone who is or is suspected, on reasonable grounds, to be *about to commit* an arrestable offence, and someone whom he suspects, on reasonable grounds, to be guilty of an arrestable offence even though the offence has *not* been committed (s. 24(7), PACE).

GENERAL POWERS OF ARREST

Section 25 of PACE gives the *police* a new general power of arrest *for any offence* if certain circumstances apply, as where the person arrested will not give his name and address, or the policeman thinks he has given a false one, or to prevent physical harm and damage to property or obstruction of the highway or to protect a child or other vulnerable person.

Section 28 of PACE requires that the person arrested should be told that he is under arrest and the grounds therefor, even if it is obvious, as where a thief is apprehended in the act of theft. However, an arrest made without these formalities is not unlawful if the arresting officer cannot comply with them because of the condition or behaviour of the person arrested.

ESSENTIAL CASE LAW AND COMMENT

Christie v *Leachinsky*, 1947 – An unlawful arrest **(355)**
Wheatley v *Lodge*, 1971 – When arrest is lawful **(356)**

Under s. 32 of PACE a person arrested may be searched for a weapon or evidence relating to the alleged offence. The power of search extends to any premises on which the arrest took place. In addition, s. 1 of PACE gives the police power to stop and search persons. The Act gives the police the power to search any person or vehicle *found in a public place* for stolen or prohibited articles, e.g. a gun, and to detain a person or vehicle for the purpose of such search. A person can be ordered to stop for the purpose of such a search and any stolen or prohibited article found in the course of such a search may be seized.

The matters of cautioning on arrest and procedure to be followed before the person arrested reaches court have already been considered. (See p. 82.)

Remedies available against false imprisonment

The *remedies* available against false imprisonment are self-help, i.e. breaking away, the writ of *habeas corpus* and an action for damages. This prerogative writ of *habeas corpus* is designed to provide a person, who is kept in confinement without legal justification, with a means of obtaining his release. If he can show a *prima facie* case that he might be unlawfully detained, he (or often a friend or relative) will apply to a divisional court of the Queen's Bench Division, though application may be made to any judge of the High Court during vacation times. The person detained applies, through counsel, for the writ to be issued, the facts alleging unlawful detention being set out on an affidavit supporting the application. If the writ is issued the effect is to cause the alleged captor to 'bring the body' of the prisoner before the court which will then decide on the merits of the case whether there are any legal grounds for detention of the prisoner. If not, he is set free by the court.

Torts affecting property

TRESPASS TO LAND

Trespass to land is interference with the possession of land. It is not enough that the plaintiff is the owner; he must also have possession. So where land is leased for a term of years, the lessee is the person entitled to sue in trespass, though the lessor may bring an action if the damage is such as to affect his reversion when the lease ends. However, when a person signs a contract for the purchase of land, he becomes entitled to possession of it, and if a trespass takes place before he actually takes possession, then he can sue in respect of that trespass when he does. His right to sue relates back to the date on which he became entitled to the land under the contract.

Interference with the possession of land may take many forms but it must be direct. For example, an unauthorised entry on land is a trespass. It is trespass to place things on land, e.g. leaving a dead cat in a neighbour's garden. To remain on land after one's authority is terminated constitutes a trespass. So, if a friend invites you into his house for a meal, tires of your company and asks you to leave, then if you refuse you are a trespasser. If you abuse the purpose for which you are allowed to be on land you become a trespasser. In *Hickman* v *Maisey* [1900] 1 Q.B. 752, where the highway was used for making notes of the form of racehorses being tried out on adjoining land, this constituted a trespass, since the proper use of a highway is for passing and re-passing.

While trespass usually takes place above the surface, it may be underneath by means of tunnelling or mining. With regard to trespass in the airspace above land, the position is doubtful, since there is no good authority. It is probably only a trespass if it is either within the area of ordinary user, or if it involves danger or inconvenience.

Section 76 of the Civil Aviation Act, 1982 provides that, subject to the exception of aircraft belonging to, or exclusively employed in the service of Her Majesty, no action lies in respect of trespass or nuisance by reason only of the flight of an aircraft over any property at a height above the ground, which having regard to weather and the other circumstances of the case is reasonable.

ESSENTIAL CASE LAW AND COMMENT

Southport Corporation v *Esso Petroleum Co*, 1954 – Trespass to land must be direct **(357)**

Kelson v *Imperial Tobacco Co*, 1957 – A sign trespasses to airspace **(358)**

Woollerton and Wilson v *Richard Costain (Midlands) Ltd*, 1969 – Crane invades airspace **(359)**

Bernstein v *Skyviews & General*, 1977 – An aerial photograph **(360)**

Subject to the same exception in regard to aircraft in the service of Her Majesty, the owner of an aircraft is liable for all material loss or damage to persons or property caused by that aircraft, whether in flight, taking off, or landing, or by a person in it, or articles falling from it, without proof of negligence or intention, or other cause of action.

Trespass to land or goods will not be unlawful and actionable at civil law if it is by the police who follow the provisions laid down in PACE. Broadly speaking, s. 17(1) of the Act gives the police power to enter premises without a warrant in certain circumstances, e.g. to make an arrest. Section 8 gives the police a power to enter premises to search under a warrant from a J.P. Section 19 gives power to seize articles found on the premises unless they are exempt articles if the officer concerned reasonably believes that it is evidence in relation to an offence which he is investigating or any other offence; and that it is necessary to seize it in order to prevent its 'concealment, loss or destruction'. Section 19(6) states that items exempted from seizure are those subject to legal professional privilege.

REVOCATION OF LICENCES

Problems have arisen where a plaintiff has entered the premises by virtue of a licence, contractual or otherwise, because at one time it was not certain whether this licence could be revoked so as to make the plaintiff a trespasser and permit his ejection.

The common-law view was that, where a person paid for admission to premises, his licence to be on those premises could be revoked at any time, in spite of valuable consideration, so that he could then be ejected as a trespasser, the defendant being liable for breach of contract, but not for assault.

On the other hand, Equity took the view that, if there was an enforceable contract not to revoke, express or implied, as where valuable consideration had been given, the licence could not be revoked so that if the plaintiff had been ejected he could sue for assault; he could not be made a trespasser by a mere attempt at revocation.

The equitable view gave rise to certain problems because it seemed to confuse rights over land with mere contracts, but the matter may now be regarded as settled. The position is that, although a licence for value is contractual in its nature and cannot create a right over land itself (or a right *in rem* which will run with the land and affect third parties), yet, as between the parties to the contract it may be implied, even if it is not expressed, that the licence cannot unreasonably be revoked during the period for which the parties intended it to continue.

ESSENTIAL CASE LAW AND COMMENT

Winter Garden Theatre (London) Ltd v *Millenium Productions Ltd*, 1948 – Revoking a licence **(361)**
Hounslow L.B.C. v *Twickenham Garden Developments*, 1970 – Revoking a licence; a further example **(362)**

EXTRA-JUDICIAL REMEDIES

There are certain extra-judicial remedies available to a person injured by a trespass. For example, *distress damage feasant* is the right to seize chattels which have done damage on land. There is no right to use or sell the chattels but merely to detain until the owner offers compensation. The remedy does not lie against Crown property, and the right to sue in trespass is postponed until the chattel is returned. Livestock may be detained (subject to notice to the owner and police) for compensation supported by a right of sale (s. 7, Animals Act, 1971). These provisions apply only to damage caused by straying animals; they do not give powers of detention in the case of other forms of damage by animals, e.g. damage caused by negligent control where the animal has not in fact strayed.

There is further extra-judicial remedy, often referred to as *self-help*, whereby the person in possession of the land may eject the trespasser, using such force as is reasonably necessary. The trespasser must be asked to depart peacefully and given time in which to quit the land. A trespasser who enters by *force* may be removed immediately and without a previous request to depart.

ESSENTIAL CASE LAW AND COMMENT

Hemmings v *Stoke Poges Golf Club*, 1920 – Ejecting trespassers **(363)**

OTHER REMEDIES

Trespass to land is actionable *per se* (in itself) and it is not necessary for the plaintiff to show actual damage in order to commence his action, although the damages would be nominal in the absence of real loss. Nevertheless it is possible to obtain an injunction without proof of loss. Trespass upon property is not normally a criminal offence. The law does penalise by statute a trespass on particular property, e.g. railway property, and also the law punishes trespass on property for the purpose of committing e.g. theft or rape.

PUBLIC ORDER ACT, 1986

Part V of the Public Order Act, 1986 is now relevant in terms of criminal trespass. Section 39 gives senior police officers power to direct trespassers to leave land. The officer concerned must reasonably believe that two or more persons, having entered land as trespassers, are present with the common purpose of residing there, that reasonable steps have been taken on behalf of the occupier to ask them to leave and either that any of the persons has caused damage to property there or has used threatening, abusive or insulting words or behaviour to the occupier or his family, or that the trespassers have brought at least twelve vehicles on to the land. Failure to comply with a direction is a criminal offence. The Act is aimed mainly at groups of hippies.

SQUATTERS

Apart from these statutory exceptions the criminal law dealt with entering or remaining on property by means of the Statutes of Forcible Entry which were a confusing and archaic set of laws. The fact that trespass is not generally a crime has led to difficulties, particularly in times of acute housing shortage where the civil law is not adequate to deal with the growing activities of 'squatters'. The Criminal Law Act, 1977, s. 6, now creates the offence of using or threatening violence to secure entry to premises on which there is another person who opposes entry. The offence can be committed by a person, notwithstanding he has some interest or right in the premises as where he is a landlord, but the offence cannot be committed by a displaced residential occupier, i.e. a person whose residential occupation of the premises has been interrupted by the occupation of the premises by a trespasser, or someone acting for a displaced residential occupier. Section 7 makes it a summary offence for a trespasser to fail to leave premises when required to do so by a displaced residential occupier. Section 8 makes it an offence for a person who is a trespasser on any premises which he has entered as a trespasser to have with him a weapon of offence. Section 9 makes it an offence to enter or be upon as a trespasser diplomatic or consular premises or the premises or residence of any body or person having diplomatic immunity in respect of its or his premises or residence. Section 10 creates a summary offence of resisting or intentionally obstructing a court officer seeking to execute an order for possession of premises, while s. 11 gives to a constable a power of entry and search for the purpose of exercising a power of arrest under that part of the Act which relates to offences of entering and remaining on property (i.e. Part II). Section 13 abolishes the common law offences of forcible entry and detainer and repeals related statutes.

Wrongful interference with goods

We propose to discuss the tort of wrongful interference by outlining the basic features of it, i.e. the relationship between the plaintiff and the goods, the conduct of the defendant which the plaintiff must prove, and the principle of liability, bearing in mind that the Torts (Interference with Goods) Act, 1977 defines, in s. 1, wrongful interference with goods as including conversion of goods, trespass to goods, negligence or any other tort so far as it results in damage to goods or to an interest in goods.

WRONGFUL INTERFERENCE BY TRESPASS TO GOODS

The relationship between the plaintiff and the goods

Wrongful interference by trespass to goods is a wrong against the possession of goods. Possession in English law is a difficult concept which is considered more fully on p. 496. For the moment it will suffice to say that a person possesses goods when he has some form of *control* over them and has the *intention to exclude* others from possession and to hold the goods on his own behalf.

Possession must exist at the moment when the wrongful interference is alleged to have been committed. Thus a bailee of goods can sue for a wrongful interference to them, but a bailor cannot because, although he is the owner of the goods, he does not possess them at the time. Where there is a *bailment at will*, i.e. one which can be determined at any time, both bailee and bailor have possession so that either can sue for a wrongful interference to the goods. Possession does not necessarily involve an actual grasp of the goods; often a lesser degree of control will suffice.

Difficulties have arisen over the requirement of the intention to exclude others as a necessary ingredient of possession, in regard to things found under or on land.

It has been held that where goods are not attached to land it is necessary to distinguish between a finding in a place over which the occupier has shown a clear intent to control exclusively, and finding in a place to which the finder has access as a matter of course. In the latter case the finder's possessory title takes precedence over that of the occupier.

However, an occupier of land or a building has superior rights to those of a finder in regard to goods in or attached to the land or building.

ESSENTIAL CASE LAW AND COMMENT

The Tubantia, 1924 – Possession and control **(364)**
Parker v *British Airways Board*, 1982 – Finders of property **(365)**
South Staffordshire Water Co v *Sharman*, 1896 – Goods which are
   on or attached to land **(366)**

Although the plaintiff relies on possession and not on ownership or title, the defendant can set up the *jus tertii* (right of a third party), under s. 8(1) of the Torts (Interference with Goods) Act, 1977. Under that section the defendant is entitled to show in accordance with rules of court that a third party has a better right than the plaintiff as respects all or any part of the interest claimed by the plaintiff and any rule of law (sometimes and formerly called *jus tertii*) to the contrary is abolished. Under s. 8(2) rules of court relating to proceedings for wrongful interference require the plaintiff to give particulars of his title; to identify any person who to his knowledge has or claims any interest in the goods; to authorise the defendant to apply for directions as to whether any person should be joined in the action with a view to establishing whether he has a better right than the plaintiff, or has a claim as a result of which the defendant might be doubly liable. If a party refuses to be joined the court may deprive him of any right of action against the defendant for the wrong, either unconditionally or subject to such terms or conditions as the court may specify.

The conduct of the defendant which the plaintiff must prove

In wrongful interference by trespass there must be a *direct* inteference with the goods, and this may consist of moving a chattel or the throwing of something at it. A person who writes with his finger in the dust on the back of a car commits wrongful interference, as does a person who beats another's animals or administers poison to them.

The principle of liability

In wrongful interference by trespass to goods the liability would not now appear to be strict. The defence of inevitable accident would presumably be available to a defendant (*National Coal Board* v *Evans*, 1951, see p. 749) and it is possible that, since *Letang* v *Cooper*, 1964 (see p. 764), the interference with the possession of goods must be intentional. Mere negligence may not suffice. This would follow a similar development in the tort of trespass to the person which began with the decision in *Fowler* v *Lanning*, 1959 (see p. 764).

WRONGFUL INTERFERENCE BY CONVERSION

The relationship between the plaintiff and the goods

It is often said that the right to sue for wrongful interference by conversion depends on ownership, but this is not really true. To be able to sue for wrongful interference the plaintiff must have had either possession or the immediate right to possess at the time the wrong was committed. Mere ownership without one of the above rights is not enough. Nor is the mere right to possess unless it is coupled with ownership.

As in wrongful interference by trespass to goods so in wrongful interference by conversion, the defendant can set up the right of a third party and s. 8(1) and (2) of the 1977 Act apply.

The conduct of the defendant which the plaintiff must prove

In wrongful interference by conversion the defendant must do something which is a complete denial of, or is inconsistent with, the plaintiff's title to the goods; a mere interference with possession is not enough. Furthermore, wrongful interference by conversion need not be a trespass.

Generally the conduct of the defendant must be an act rather than a failure to act. Thus, although the plaintiff may base his case on a demand for the goods followed by a refusal, he must still show a denial of title in the defendant. If, therefore, the defendant can show that he was retaining the goods in the exercise of a lien for (say) repair charges unpaid, the plaintiff will fail in his action. A defendant may also refuse temporarily to give up the goods while he takes steps to check the title of the plaintiff.

The principle of liability

In general, liability in wrongful interference by conversion is strict and it is not necessary for the plaintiff to prove that the defendant had a wrong intention, though sometimes it may be a defence for the defendant to say that he acted honestly. Where the defendant had lost the goods by *negligence* there was no wrongful interference by conversion but the plaintiff may now sue under the provisions of the Torts (Interference with Goods) Act, 1977 for damage to goods caused by negligence.

ESSENTIAL CASE LAW AND COMMENT

Jarvis v *Williams*, 1955 – Conversion: there must be a right of property **(367)**

Fouldes v *Willoughby*, 1841 – Mere interference with possession **(368)**

Oakley v *Lyster*, 1931 – No need for trespass **(369)**

Elvin and Powell Ltd v *Plummer Roddis Ltd*, 1933 – An honest defendant **(370)**

DETENTION OF GOODS

Section 2(1) of the Torts (Interference with Goods) Act, 1977, abolishes the old tort of detinue which was a tort relating to detention of goods. The Act substitutes statutory provisions. Under s. 2(2) the tort of wrongful interference by conversion is substituted for the old action of detinue. Thus mere detention can now amount to conversion. In other words, detinue and conversion are merged.

As regards the form of judgment where goods are detained, s. 3 provides that in proceedings for wrongful interference against a person who is in possession or in control of the goods relief may be given if appropriate in accordance with s. 3(2). Under s. 3(2) the relief is –

(*a*) an order for delivery of the goods, and for payment of any consequential damages, or

(*b*) an order for delivery of the goods, giving the defendant the alternative of paying damages by reference to the value of the goods, together in either alternative with payment of any consequential damages, or

(*c*) damages.

Section 3(2) provides that subject to rules of court relief should be given under only one of paragraphs (*a*), (*b*) and (*c*) above and relief under paragraph (*a*) is at the discretion of the court though the claimant may choose between the others. If it is shown to the satisfaction of the court that an order under (*a*) above has not been complied with the court may revoke the order or the relevant part of it and make an order for payment of damages by reference to the value of the goods.

Where an order is made under (*b*) above the defendant may satisfy the order by returning the goods at any time before execution of judgment, but without prejudice to liability to pay any consequential damages.

REMEDIES

Reference has already been made to the form of judgment where goods are detained. So far as wrongful interference by trespass and by conversion are concerned, the remedy is damages. The value of the goods is usually determined at the date of conversion. When a plaintiff has a claim for conversion he cannot delay the issue of his writ and the duty to mitigate loss operates. If the goods decrease in value between the date of the conversion and the time the court gives judgment, the plaintiff will normally still recover the value at the date of conversion (*Rhodes* v *Moules* [1895] 1 Ch. 236).

Section 5 of the 1977 Act makes it clear that a plaintiff's title to the goods is not extinguished by a judgment for damages but only when the judgment has been paid. The judgment as such does not affect title.

Under s. 6 an allowance is available for an improvement in the goods. For example, where a person in good faith buys a stolen car and improves it he is entitled to an allowance for that improvement, and where a person in good faith buys the car from the improver and is sued in conversion by the true owner, the damages may be reduced to reflect the improvement. Section 7 deals with double liability, providing in particular that where as the result of enforcement of a double liability the claimant is unjustly enriched to any extent he shall be liable to reimburse the wrongdoer to that extent. For example, if a converter of goods pays damages first to a finder of the goods and then to the true owner, the finder is unjustly enriched unless he accounts over to the true owner, which he is required to do, and then the true owner is unjustly enriched and becomes liable to reimburse the converter of the goods.

Special damage for conversion may be awarded. Thus a carpenter whose tools are converted can recover his loss of wages. (*Bodley* v *Reynolds* (1846) 8 Q.B. 779.) Furthermore, in *Hillesden Securities Ltd* v *Ryjack Ltd* [1983] 2 All E.R. 184 the defendant converted a Rolls Royce car which he had hired from the plaintiff. It was held that he remained liable for the hiring charge until he returned it. This was £13,000, although the value of the Rolls Royce at the date of conversion was only £7500.

Finally, s. 2(3), Limitation Act, 1980 provides that once the six-year period of limitation has expired the plaintiff's title to the goods is extinguished. The Act also provides that if there are successive conversions over the same goods, whether by the same person or not, the cause of action is extinguished six years from the first conversion (s. 3(1), Limitation Act, 1980).

RECAPTION

A person who is entitled to the possession of goods of which he has been wrongfully deprived may retake them after a demand for their return but must not use more than reasonable force. It is not clear whether he may enter upon the land of an innocent third party in order to recover the goods. It would seem lawful only after explanation and permission.

REPLEVIN

Goods which have been taken by what is alleged to be unlawful distress, e.g. by a landlord for unpaid rent which is alleged by the tenant to have been paid, may be recovered by the owner giving security to the registrar of the County Court that he will immediately bring an action to determine the legality of the distress. The registrar issues a warrant for the restitution of the goods.

Nuisance

This tort of nuisance is of two types – public and private.

Public nuisance

This is some unlawful act or omission endangering or interfering with the lives, comfort, property, or common rights of the public, e.g. the obstruction of a highway or the keeping of dangerous premises near a highway. A public nuisance is a crime for which the remedy is criminal proceedings brought by the Attorney-General. But it is actionable as a tort at the suit of a private individual if he has suffered peculiar damage over and above that suffered by the public as a whole.

Obstructions to the highway occur daily in our cities and towns, e.g. road repairs and scaffolding. However, these obstructions, being for reasonable purposes, are lawful unless they last for an excessive time. *Dangerous activities* carried on near to the highway may amount to a nuisance. With regard to *projections* on to the highway there is no liability for *things naturally on land*, e.g. trees, unless the person responsible for them knew, or ought to have known, that they were in a dangerous condition, as where a branch of a tree is rotten. However, liability appears to be strict in the case of *artificial projections*. However, where an action is brought for damages for personal injuries arising out of other forms of obstruction on the highway, it appears that fault is essential to liability. Thus in this respect the torts of nuisance and negligence are being drawn together.

ESSENTIAL CASE LAW AND COMMENT

Attorney-General v *Gastonia Coaches*, 1976 – Public nuisance: activities near the highway **(371)**
Castle v *St Augustine's Links Ltd*, 1922 – A golf ball hits a car **(372)**
Tarry v *Ashton*, 1876 – An artificial projection **(373)**
Dymond v *Pearce*, 1972 – Other forms of highway obstruction **(374)**

Private nuisance

This is an unlawful interference with peoples' use of their property or with their health, comfort or convenience, and such interference may vary according to the standard existing in the neighbourhood. It is a wrongful act causing material injury to property or sensible personal discomfort. In this connection injuries to *servitudes* may amount to private nuisance as where the defendant obstructs a right of way, or interferes with the plaintiff's water supply, access of air, light or support.

In considering whether an act or omission is a nuisance, the following points are relevant.

(a) *There need be no direct injury to health.* It is enough that a person has been prevented to an appreciable extent from enjoying the ordinary comforts of life.

(b) *The standard of comfort must be expected to vary with the district.* There is no uniformity of standard between Park Lane and Poplar, although there may be common ground in some matters, e.g. light, since it requires the same amount of light to read in either place. However, where the alleged nuisance has caused *actual damage to property* it is no defence to show that the district concerned is of any particular type.

(c) *A person cannot take advantage of his peculiar sensitivity to noise and smells.* There must be some give and take, and people cannot expect the same amenities in an industrial town as they might enjoy in the country.

(d) *The utility of the alleged nuisance has no bearing on the question.* Pigstyes and breweries may be regarded by the community as very necessary, but if they infringe a person's right to the ordinary comforts of life, they are nuisances. Consent cannot be implied from the fact that the plaintiff came to the premises knowing that the nuisance was in existence. Nor is the fact that the nuisance arises out of the conferment of a public benefit a defence in the ordinary way.

ESSENTIAL CASE LAW AND COMMENT

Bliss v *Hall*, 1838 – Coming to the nuisance **(375)**
Adams v *Ursell*, 1913 – Public benefit **(376)**
Dunton v *Dover District Council*, 1977 – A noisy playground **(377)**

(e) *The modes of annoyance are infinitely various.* They may include such things as bell-ringing, circus performing, the excessive use of the radio, spreading tree roots, opening a sex shop in a residential area (*Laws* v *Florinplace* [1981] 1 All E.R. 659) and many others. It should also be noted that picketing a highway may be actionable as a nuisance and an injunction may be granted to prevent it.

ESSENTIAL CASE LAW AND COMMENT

Christie v *Davey*, 1893 – A versatile amateur musician **(378)**
Hubbard v *Pitt*, 1975 – Picketing the highway **(379)**

(f) *A nuisance may result from the acts of several wrongdoers.* Any one of them may be proceeded against, and he cannot plead in excuse that the nuisance was a joint effort, although he has a right of contribution against joint tortfeasors for the damages which might be assessed against him.

(g) *Duration of the act.* Although the acts complained of in nuisance are usually continuous, e.g. the constant emission of pungent smells from a factory, an act may constitute a nuisance even though it is temporary or instantaneous. The duration of the act complained of has a bearing upon the remedy which is appropriate and the court will not often grant an injunction in respect of a temporary nuisance because damages are an adequate remedy. Furthermore, a temporary nuisance may be too trivial to be actionable.

ESSENTIAL CASE LAW AND COMMENT

British Celanese Ltd v A.H. Hunt (Capacitors) Ltd, 1969 – A temporary nuisance **(380)**

(*h*) *Sometimes malice or evil motive may become the gist of the offence.* Malice or motive may be evidence that the defendant was not using his property in a lawful way.

ESSENTIAL CASE LAW AND COMMENT

Hollywood Silver Fox Farm v Emmett, 1936 – An evil motive **(381)**

(*i*) *It is possible to acquire the right to create a private nuisance by prescription,* that is, by twenty years' continuous operation since the act complained of first constituted a nuisance. There is no corresponding right in respect of a public nuisance. Since a public nuisance is a crime, no length of time will make it legitimate.

Nuisance is primarily a wrong to property, but even where there is no physical damage the court can award compensation for annoyance and discomfort. A claim in private nuisance cannot be based solely upon personal injury, where an action would be in negligence. Claims for personal injuries can be made in public nuisance, though as we have seen in *Dymond v Pearce,* 1972, at p. 773, *fault* in the defendant is generally required which makes the action in nuisance similar to that in negligence.

ESSENTIAL CASE LAW AND COMMENT

Bone v Seale, 1975 – No need for diminution in property values **(382)**

Furthermore, the tort of nuisance refers to the unreasonable use of property and is not a matter of reasonable care (compare negligence). Thus the defendant's use of his property may be offensive and constitute a nuisance no matter how careful he is.

PARTIES TO SUE OR BE SUED

The occupant of the property affected by the nuisance is the person who should bring the action but a landlord may sue if the nuisance is effecting a permanent injury to his property, e.g. where the defendant is erecting a building which infringes the landlord's right to ancient lights.

ESSENTIAL CASE LAW AND COMMENT

Malone v *Laskey*, 1907 – Nuisance: occupier should sue **(383)**

Regarding liability, it is a general rule that the person who creates the nuisance is liable, and this will generally be the occupier. But a landlord may be liable, as a joint tortfeasor with his tenant, (*a*) if he created the nuisance and then leased the property or (*b*) where the nuisance was due to the landlord's authorising the tenant expressly or impliedly to create or continue the nuisance; or (*c*) where the landlord knew or ought to have known of the nuisance before he let the premises.

ESSENTIAL CASE LAW AND COMMENT

Wilchick v *Marks*, 1934 – A landlord who had a right of entry **(384)**
Mint v *Good*, 1951 – A right of entry implied **(385)**
Harris v *James*, 1876 – A landlord authorised the nuisance **(386)**
Smith v *Scott*, 1972 – No authorisation by landlord **(387)**
Brew Bros v *Snax (Ross)*, 1969 – A landlord allowed a nuisance to continue **(388)**

An occupier must abate a nuisance which was on the premises before he took them over, or is placed there afterwards, even by trespassers, provided that the occupier knows or ought to have known of the nuisance. An occupier is also liable for nuisance arising out of the operations of an independent contractor engaged in work on the premises where there is a special danger of nuisance arising from the nature of the works being carried out, e.g. extensive tunnelling operations (and see *Bower* v *Peate*, 1876 at p. 740).

ESSENTIAL CASE LAW AND COMMENT

Sedleigh-Denfield v *O'Callaghan*, 1940 – An occupier must abate a known nuisance **(389)**

REMEDIES

The remedies for nuisance are three in number –

(*a*) The injured party may abate the nuisance, that is, remove it, provided that no unnecessary damage is caused, that no injury arises to an innocent third party, e.g. a tenant, and that, where entry on the defendant's land is necessary, a notice requesting the removal of the nuisance has first been given.

(*b*) He may sue for damages.

(*c*) He may seek an injunction if (i) damages would be an insufficient remedy; and (ii) the nuisance is a continuing nuisance, e.g. smoke frequently emitted from a chimney. Where a continuing actionable nuisance is proved, only in exceptional circumstances should the court award damages in lieu of an injunction.

ESSENTIAL CASE LAW AND COMMENT

Kennaway v *Thompson*, 1980 – Noise from powerboats **(390)**

DEFENCES

Certain defences are available to a person who is charged with committing the nuisance –

(*a*) The injury is trivial. The legal maxim is: *De minimis non curat lex.* (The law does not concern itself with trifles.) Such a case would be an extremely short exposure to fumes from road repairs.

(*b*) The so-called nuisance arose from the lawful use of the land. (*Bradford Corporation* v *Pickles*, 1895, see p. 727.)

(*c*) The nuisance was covered by statutory authority, under the general principles elucidated under the defence of statutory authority.

(*d*) The person committing the alleged nuisance has acquired a prescriptive right through twenty years' use to do what is complained of.

(*e*) The character of the neighbourhood is such that the act, while it might be a nuisance elsewhere, cannot be regarded as such in that particular district.

(*f*) Consent of the plaintiff is a possible defence but consent will not be implied simply because the plaintiff came to the premises knowing that the nuisance was in existence. (*Bliss* v *Hall*, 1838, see p. 773.)

ESSENTIAL CASE LAW AND COMMENT

Sturges v *Bridgman*, 1879 – Nuisance and prescription **(391)**

REMOTENESS OF DAMAGE

For the purpose of deciding problems of remoteness of damage the Privy Council held in *The Wagon Mound (No. 2)*, [1966] 2 All E.R. 709 (see

p. 752), that in a case of nuisance, as of negligence, it is not enough that the damage was a direct result of the nuisance if the injury was not *foreseeable*. Thus in *Lamb* v *Camden London Borough Council* [1981] 2 All E.R. 408 the plaintiffs owned a house which had been let furnished but because of local council work a water main nearby was broken and escaping water severely damaged the house. The tenant left and the house was then unoccupied. While it was empty squatters entered and caused extensive damage before they were evicted. The defendants admitted liability in nuisance and on the issue of the squatters' damage the Court of Appeal held that it was too remote to form part of any damages. (See also *British Celanese* v *Hunt*, 1969 (p. 775) and *Page Motors* v *Epsom and Ewell Borough Council*, 1981, p. 779.)

STATUTORY INTERVENTION

We have been discussing the civil law of nuisance. However, there is also the Environmental Protection Act, 1990. Under s. 80 of that Act an officer of a local authority who is satisfied that a nuisance exists can serve the person responsible for creating it with an abatement notice. Failure to comply is a criminal offence though there is a right of appeal. The section can be used for a wide variety of nuisances from noisy parties to dust from construction or demolition. A complaint is initiated through the environmental health department of the relevant local authority.

Furthermore, since it is uncertain whether the common law has any rules controlling the spread of weeds (see *Giles* v *Walker*, 1890, p. 807) reference should be made to the Weeds Act, 1959. Where any one of five specified weeds is out of control the Minister of Agriculture can call on the occupier of the land concerned to take action to stop them from spreading. The Minister can get the work done himself if the occupier defaults, and prosecute the occupier.

Negligence – generally

In ordinary language negligence may simply mean not done intentionally, e.g. the negligent publication of a libel. But while negligence may be one factor or ingredient in another tort, it is also a specific and independent tort with which we are now concerned.

The tort of negligence has three ingredients and to succeed in an action the plaintiff must show (i) the existence of a duty to take care which was owed to him by the defendant, (ii) breach of such duty by the defendant, and (iii) resulting damage to the plaintiff.

The duty of care – generally

Whether a duty of care exists or not is a question of law for the judge to decide, and it is necessary to know how this is done. The law of contract dominated the legal scene in the nineteenth century and this affected the law of torts. The judges, influenced by the doctrine of privity of contract, used it to establish the existence of a duty of care in negligence in those cases where a contract existed by laying down the principle that, if A is contractually liable to B, he cannot simultaneously be liable to C in tort for the same act or omission.

The House of Lords in *Donoghue* v *Stevenson*, 1932 (see p. 725) dispelled the confusion caused by the application of the doctrine of privity of contract where physical injury is caused to the plaintiff by the defendant's negligent act. As we have seen from the *Donoghue* case the fact that the maker of the ginger beer was liable for its defects in *contract* to the café owner did not prevent him being liable also to *Donoghue* in the *tort of negligence*. In this case also Lord Atkin formulated what has now become the classic test for establishing a duty of care when he said –

You must take reasonable care to avoid acts or omissions which you can reasonably foresee would be likely to injure your neighbour. Who then is my neighbour? The answer seems to be persons who are so closely and directly affected by my act that I ought reasonably to have them in contemplation as being affected when I am directing my mind to the acts or omissions which are called in question.

It will be seen, therefore, that the duty of care is established by putting in the defendant's place a hypothetical 'reasonable man' and deciding whether the reasonable man would have foreseen the likelihood or probability of injury, not its mere possibility. The test is objective not subjective, and the effect of its application is that a person is not liable for every injury which results from his carelessness. There must be a duty of care (see *Bourhill* v *Young*, 1943 at p. 760).

Nevertheless, new duties are established from time to time by case law. As we have seen, Lord Macmillan stated in *Donoghue* v *Stevenson*, 1932 'the categories of negligence are never closed'. However, there is always the requirement of foresight, i.e. the plaintiff must be within the area of foreseeable danger (see *Bourhill* v *Young*, 1943 at p. 760).

Furthermore, there is, in general terms, no liability for failure to act, i.e. for omissions.

ESSENTIAL CASE LAW AND COMMENT

Argy Trading v *Lapid Developments*, 1977 – No liability for omissions **(392)**

RECENT DEVELOPMENTS – THE RETREAT FROM *ANNS*

As regards more recent developments the tendency was to widen liability in negligence to the point where it was more a matter of public policy whether a particular defendant was liable. The view has been, in some cases, that the court can assume objective foresight and then see whether there is anything to prevent the defendant from being liable, e.g. a very wide liability which is currently not insured against may not be imposed as contrary to public policy.

One major development in this direction was the judgment of Lord Reid in *Home Office* v *Dorset Yacht Club Co. Ltd* [1970] 2 All E.R. 294. This was an action by the owner of a yacht which was damaged by runaway Borstal boys who escaped while the three officers in charge of them were, contrary to instructions, in bed. In holding that the Home Office owed a duty of care to the owner of the yacht, Lord Reid made the following general comment regarding duty of care. '*Donoghue* v *Stevenson* may be regarded as a milestone . . . It will require qualification in new circumstances. But I think that the time has come when we can and should say that it ought to apply unless there is some justification or valid explanation for its exclusion.' In other words Lord Reid is saying that the court should lean in favour of finding a duty of care. The House of Lords seems also in this case to have found liability for the officers' failure to act, i.e. an omission but this seems to be confined to negligent failure to exercise statutory powers, in this case powers of control over the boys.

Further moves along these lines came in *Anns* v *London Borough of Merton* [1977] 2 All E.R. 492. In that case, the plaintiffs held a lease of a block of flats built in 1962. Later, considerable settlement caused cracks and the tilting of floors. The plaintiffs blamed the builders and also the local council because, it was alleged, the council had not inspected the flats during building as the bye-laws required, so their shallow foundations were not detected. Their Lordships found that the local authority had a duty of care to the plaintiffs and made general comments on the duty of care. Once again liability arose from a failure to act.

Lord Wilberforce, in particular, took the remarks of Lord Reid (as mentioned) a stage further when he said:

> The position has now been reached that in order to establish that a duty of care arises in a particular situation, it is not necessary to bring the facts of that situation within those of previous situations in which a duty of care has been held to exist. Rather the question has to be approached in two stages.
>
> First, one has to ask whether, as between the alleged wrongdoer and the person who has suffered damage there is a sufficient relationship of proximity or neighbourhood such that, in the reasonable contemplation of the former, carelessness on his part may be likely to cause damage to the latter, in which case a *prima facie* duty of care arises.

Second, if the first question is answered affirmatively, it is necessary to consider whether there are any considerations which ought to negate, or reduce or limit the scope of the duty or the class of person to whom it is owed or the damages to which any breach of it may give rise.

It should be noted, however, that the Privy Council in *Yuen Kun Yeu* v *A.G. of Hong Kong* [1987] 2 All E.R. 705 and the House of Lords in *Curran* v *Northern Ireland Co-Ownership Housing Association* [1987] 2 W.L.R. 1043 pointed out the danger of assuming that the comments of Lord Wilberforce in *Anns* lead to a rule that objective foreseeability of itself automatically leads to a duty of care and that a defendant with objective foresight is therefore liable unless there are reasons, e.g. public policy, why he should not be so.

The movement towards a position where virtually any event can be foreseen leaving the only bar to liability to rest on public policy came to an end in *Murphy* v *Brentwood District Council* [1990] 2 All E.R. 908 when the House of Lords overruled their own decision in *Anns* as the 1966 declaration gives them power to do.

The facts of *Murphy* are similar to those of *Anns*, i.e. a house built on inadequate foundations followed by a claim against the local authority for negligent failure to ensure that the house was built in accordance with the relevant regulations. The House of Lords decided that the local authority was not liable and overruled *Anns*. The judgments of the House of Lords indicate that the problem with *Anns* was not so much what it decided in terms of the liability of the local authority but the broad statements as to the duty of care made by Lord Wilberforce in the case. Their Lordships felt that if the case was left as good law its principles could not be confined to the local authority situation. In fact it had already started to expand professional liability to the point where accountants in particular were unable to get adequate indemnity insurance. In this connection the retreat from *Anns* is to be seen in the *Caparo* case at p. 789 which some think has gone too far the other way.

It would seem that since *Murphy* we are back to a tighter test of liability. A duty of care will be based upon the need for proximity enshrined in Lord Atkin's neighbour test in *Donoghue*.

The duty of care – economic loss

An area of some difficulty, and in which there has been much development, is in the field of economic loss. Is there a duty to avoid causing foreseeable economic loss? The position is as follows –

(*a*) *Careless mis-statements*. These are considered in greater depth at p. 448. However, broadly speaking, a person who makes a careless statement which causes economic loss to a plaintiff within the area of his *foresight* may be liable to compensate that plaintiff for economic loss.

(*b*) *Physical injury – parasitical damages.* Damages for economic loss may be awarded if there is foreseeable physical injury to the plaintiff or his property, though issues of public policy still govern where the line is to be drawn.

ESSENTIAL CASE LAW AND COMMENT

Weller & Co v *Foot and Mouth Disease Research Institute*, 1965 – Where economic loss is irrecoverable **(393)**

S.C.M. (UK) Ltd v *W.J. Whittall & Son Ltd*, 1970 – Where economic loss is not a consequence of physical damage **(394)**

Spartan Steel and Alloys Ltd v *Martin & Co Ltd*, 1972 – Economic loss following from physical damage **(395)**

(*c*) *The Junior Books case.* In *Junior Books Ltd* v *Veitchi Co. Ltd*, 1982 the House of Lords decided that the plaintiffs could recover economic loss which was not parasitical because in that case there was no physical injury to the plaintiff or his property, but merely faulty work.

However, it would be unwise to assume that injury to person or property is now never necessary. There was a very close proximity in terms of foresight of injury between the parties in *Junior Books* and as a matter of public policy it may still be necessary to restrict liability in cases such as *Weller* where liability was potentially endless. There have, in more recent times, been a considerable number of restrictions placed on *Junior Books* almost confining it to its own facts (see below).

ESSENTIAL CASE LAW AND COMMENT

Junior Books Ltd v *Veitchi Co Ltd*, 1982 – A rare recovery of economic loss **(396)**

BREACH OF THE DUTY

If a duty of care is established as a matter of law, whether or not the defendant was in breach of that duty is a matter to be decided by the judge on the facts of the case, though the standard required, i.e. that of acting as a reasonable man, is a *legal standard*.

Here we are concerned with how much care the defendant must take. It is obvious that if motorists did not take out their cars many lives would be saved, and yet it is not negligent to drive a car. Once again the test is to place the 'reasonable man' in the defendant's position. It is an objective test and was thus stated by Baron Alderson in *Blyth* v *Birmingham Waterworks Co* (1856), 11 Ex. 781:

> Negligence is the omission to do something which a reasonable man guided upon those considerations which ordinarily regulate the conduct of human affairs would do, or doing something which a prudent and reasonable man would not do.

The standard required is not that of a particularly conscientious man but that of the average prudent man in the eyes of the court. It has been said that the reasonable man is the man on the Clapham omnibus, but it should not be thought that the average prudent man has a low standard of care. Most of us behave unreasonably from time to time, and if during one of these lapses a person suffers injury, it will be no good our pleading that we are usually reasonable men.

ESSENTIAL CASE LAW AND COMMENT

Daniels v *R. White and Sons Ltd*, 1938 – Duty to take reasonable care **(397)**

Hill v *J. Crowe*, 1977 – A packing case collapses **(398)**

Objective standards – professionals

When a person has undertaken a duty which requires extraordinary skill, he will be expected to use a higher standard of care. For example, one would expect from a builder the degree of skill appropriate to a reasonably competent member of his trade and from an accountant or solicitor also an objective standard of competence. Such a person may, therefore, be negligent even though he does his best.

ESSENTIAL CASE LAW AND COMMENT

Greaves v *Baynham Meikle*, 1974 – An objective standard **(399)**

Medical practitioners

However, in the case of medical practitioners it seems that because allegations of negligence in the medical context are more frequent and serious, a high standard of proof of negligence is required so that an error of clinical judgment does not of itself amount to negligence. Thus in *Whitehouse* v *Jordan* [1981] 1 All E.R. 267 the plaintiff was born with severe brain damage following a difficult birth and sued the defendant, a senior hospital registrar, for damages. The defendant had used forceps to assist delivery of the plaintiff and it was alleged that he pulled too hard and too long. It was held by the

Court of Appeal and later by the House of Lords that if the damage had indeed been caused by the defendant's use of forceps the most that could be said with the benefit of hindsight was that he had made an error of clinical judgment which did not of itself amount to negligence, so that the plaintiff's claim failed.

Advocates

Advocates provide an exception to the above rule because no action lies against them for negligence in conducting a case (see *Rondel* v *Worsley*, 1967 at p. 571) though it does in respect of preparatory work or advice unless it is pre-trial work intimately connected with the trial itself.

Standard set by public policy

In other cases public policy may also require a higher standard of care than the defendant possesses so that again he may be negligent even though he does his best (see *Nettleship* v *Weston*, 1971 at p. 748).

Other special cases

It should be noted that if precautions are taken which would have been reasonable in the case of persons possessed of the usual faculties of sight and hearing, this will be sufficient to absolve a person who does injury to those not possessed of such faculties, so long as he was not aware of their infirmity. However, persons engaged on operations on the *highway* must act reasonably so as not to cause damage to those who are using the highway, including blind people. Furthermore, the court will take into account the importance of the object which the defendant was trying to achieve and whether it was practicable and necessary for the defendant to have taken the precautions which the plaintiff alleged should have been taken.

ESSENTIAL CASE LAW AND COMMENT

Paris v *Stepney Borough Council*, 1951 – Those with infirmities **(400)**

Haley v *L.E.B.*, 1964 – Works on the highway **(401)**

Watt v *Hertfordshire County Council*, 1954 – The importance of the objective **(402)**

Latimer v *A.E.C. Ltd*, 1953 – What could the defendant reasonably do? **(403)**

RESULTING DAMAGE TO THE PLAINTIFF

It is necessary for the plaintiff to show that he has suffered some loss, since negligence is not actionable *per se* (in itself). A breach of contract with no loss will at least give an action for nominal damages but not so in tort. The major problem arising here is the question of remoteness of damage which was dealt with earlier in the chapter. The judge decides the measure of general damages.

RES IPSA LOQUITUR

Although the burden of proof in negligence normally lies on the plaintiff, there is a principle known as *res ipsa loquitur* (the thing speaks for itself), and where the principle applies the court is prepared to lighten his burden. The principle applies wherever it is so unlikely that such an accident would have happened without the negligence of the defendant that the court could find, without further evidence, that it was so caused. It seems also to be a commonsense rule in that there is no point in asking the plaintiff to prove negligence because he has no view of what happened. If two cars collide on a public road, at least the drivers have a view of what happened prior to the crash but when, for example, a barrel falls out of a warehouse on to A he has no view at all of the happenings leading to the impact.

However, two conditions must be satisfied –

(*a*) the thing or activity causing the harm must be wholly under the control of the defendant or his servants; and

(*b*) the accident must be one which would not have happened if proper care had been exercised.

ESSENTIAL CASE LAW AND COMMENT

Easson v *L.N.E. Railway*, 1944 – No exclusive control **(404)**
Roe v *Minister of Health*, 1954 – A defective ampoule **(405)**
Byrne v *Boadle*, 1863 – A falling barrel **(406)**
Scott v *London and St Katherine Docks*, 1865 – Falling bags of sugar **(407)**

It should be noted that just because the principle *res ipsa loquitur* applies, it is not certain that the plaintiff will succeed; the court is not bound to find the defendant negligent. The defendant may be able to prove how the accident happened and that he was not negligent. He may not know how the accident happened but he may be able to prove that it could not have arisen from his negligence. Finally, he may suggest ways in which the accident could have happened without his negligence, and the court may find his explanations convincing. If a tile falls off Y's roof and injures X who is lawfully on the highway below, this would probably be a situation in which *res ipsa loquitur* would apply. But if Y can show that at the time an explosion had occurred nearby and this had probably dislodged the tile, and the court is impressed by this explanation of the event, the burden or proof reverts to X. However, it is not enough to offer purely hypothetical explanations (*Moore* v *R. Fox and Sons* [1956] 1 All E.R. 182), nor is it sufficient to explain how the accident happened unless the explanation also shows that the defendant was not negligent (*Colvilles* v *Devine* [1969] 2 All E.R. 53).

ESSENTIAL CASE LAW AND COMMENT

Pearson v *North-Western Gas Board*, 1968 – Rebutting a presumption of negligence **(408)**

If the defendant successfully rebuts the presumption of *res ipsa loquitur* the plaintiff has to establish his case by positive evidence. He will probably be unable to do this by the very nature and cause of the accident and the chances are that he may lose his claim. If he had had such positive evidence he would probably have adduced it in the first place and not relied on the maxim at all.

CONTRIBUTORY NEGLIGENCE

Sometimes when an accident occurs, both parties have been negligent and this raises the doctrine of *contributory negligence*. At one time a plaintiff guilty of contributory negligence could not recover any damages unless the defendant could, with reasonable care, have avoided the consequences of the plaintiff's contributory want of care. Thus the courts were often concerned to find out who had the last chance of avoiding the accident, and this led to some unsatisfactory decisions.

Now, however, under the Law Reform (Contributory Negligence) Act, 1945, liability is apportionable between plaintiff and defendant. The claim is not defeated but damages may be reduced according to the degree of fault of the plaintiff. A person may contribute to the *damage* he suffers although he is not to *blame* for the accident. Thus failure by a plaintiff to wear a crash helmet on a motor cycle or moped may reduce the damages he obtains on the ground of contributory negligence (*O'Connell* v *Jackson* [1971] 3 All E.R. 129). Similarly, failure by a plaintiff to wear a seat belt in a motor car *may* also reduce damages on the grounds of contributory negligence (*Froom* v *Butcher* [1975] 3 All E.R. 520 (see below)). The defence of contributory negligence also applies to an action brought under the Fatal Accidents Act. Thus a wife whose husband failed to wear a seat belt and was thrown out of the van he was driving and killed had her damages reduced by one-fifth (*Purnell* v *Shields* [1973] R.T.R. 414).

Where a defendant is insured against the injury he has caused, which is often the case, the effect of a finding of contributory negligence is in a sense to punish the plaintiff. There have been suggestions in case law that the rule should be abolished where the defendant is insured since the doctrine merely saves the insurance company money. However, in *Froom* v *Butcher* [1975] 3 All E.R. 520, Lord Denning disapproved of these cases and held that where injuries resulting from a road accident would have been prevented or lessened if a fitted seat belt had been worn, the failure to wear a seat belt amounted to contributory negligence on the part of the plaintiff and damages awarded should therefore be reduced. In consequence Lord Denning has produced an additional definition of contributory negligence so that there are two –

(*a*) to contribute to the accident, which is the old view of contributory negligence; and
(*b*) to contribute to the resulting damage, which is a new concept.

Furthermore in *Froom* Lord Denning laid down a rather precise formula for contributory negligence in order to introduce as much certainty as possible in road traffic cases and reduce the number of trials, by saying that if failure to wear a seat belt by a front-seat passenger or driver would have made no difference, then nothing should be taken off the damages. If it would have prevented the accident altogether the damages should be reduced by 25%, and if the accident would have been less severe the damages should be reduced by 15%, though exemptions would be made, said Lord Denning, for pregnant women and those who were very fat.

Since 1983 it has been a criminal offence for the driver and front-seat passenger not to wear seat belts. The courts may therefore reduce still further the damages where a seat belt is not worn. It is thought unlikely that they will refuse to give damages altogether because the plaintiff is breaking the law, i.e. the defence will probably not be able to raise *ex turpi causa* (see p. 304) as a complete defence.

Since the rules relating to the wearing of seat belts are now extended in many cases to rear-seat passengers no doubt their damages will be reduced if they are injured while not wearing a belt.

It should be mentioned that a young child will seldom, if ever, be guilty of contributory negligence. Furthermore, the contributory negligence of an adult who happened to be with the child is no defence to an action brought by the child.

ESSENTIAL CASE LAW AND COMMENT

Jones v *Lawrence*, 1969 – Contributory negligence and children
  (409)
Oliver v *Birmingham Bus Co*, 1932 – A grandfather's negligence
  (410)

Furthermore, it was held in *Yianni* v *Edwin Evans & Sons* [1981] 3 All E.R. 592 that a house buyer who relies on a valuation of the property he is buying prepared by a building society surveyor is not contributorily negligent because he has not had the property surveyed by another independent surveyor employed by himself.

THE DOCTRINE OF ALTERNATIVE DANGER OR THE 'DILEMMA PRINCIPLE'

It sometimes happens that a person is injured in anticipating negligence. If a passenger jumps off a bus which he believes to be out of control, and breaks his leg in so doing, he is not prejudiced by the fact that the driver later regains control and the anticipated accident is averted. He is not deprived of his remedy. This is sometimes referred to as the *doctrine of alternative danger*, and an act done in the agony of the moment cannot be treated as contributory negligence. Thus in *Jones* v *Boyce* (1816) 1 Starkie 493, in a coach accident, the plaintiff was placed by the negligence of the defendant in a perilous alternative either to jump or not to jump. He jumped off the coach and was injured and it transpired that had he kept his seat he would have escaped. However, he was able to recover from the defendant because he had acted reasonably and in the apprehension of danger.

STATUTORY DUTIES

Sometimes a particular duty of care is laid upon a person by statute, e.g. the duty laid on an employer as to guarding machinery under safety legislation. Such duties are high and very often absolute, though the employer can plead contributory negligence as a defence. In addition, where there is a breach of a statutory duty, it must be shown that the duty is owed to the plaintiff personally and not to the public as a whole.

ESSENTIAL CASE LAW AND COMMENT

Atkinson v *Newcastle Waterworks Co*, 1877 – Where the duty is
  owed to the public **(411)**

A conditional statutory power saying that the person upon whom it is conferred may act cannot be converted into a statutory duty which says he must act. Thus in *East Suffolk Rivers Catchment Board* v *Kent* [1940] 4 All E.R. 527, a river catchment board, which had a power to repair river banks, could not be sued successfully for failing to do so on the grounds that a statutory duty had been breached.

However, where a statute prescribes provision to prevent damage, if an action is brought, the harm resulting from the breach of duty must be of the type contemplated by the statute.

ESSENTIAL CASE LAW AND COMMENT

Gorris v *Scott*, 1874 – Is the damage of the type contemplated?
  (412)

Negligence – product liability

Here we shall consider the liability of a manufacturer for defective goods where in the absence of a contract between the parties liability is based on the common law of negligence and to some extent now on statute law.

PHYSICAL INJURIES

Where the goods are purchased from a retailer, no action can be brought under the Sale of Goods Act by the purchaser against the manufacturer. The doctrine of privity of contract applies (see p. 220) with the result that there is no contract between them into which the warranties and conditions set out in the Act can be implied. However, the purchaser may have an action in negligence against the manufacturer in respect of *physical* injuries caused by defects in the goods. (See *Donoghue* v *Stevenson*, 1932 at p. 725.) The rule arrived at in *Donoghue* v *Stevenson* has been widened since 1932, and now applies to defective chattels generally which cause injuries to purchasers (see *Grant* v *Australian Knitting Mills Ltd* (1936), p. 668). However, although the *Donoghue* case shows that the manufacturer has a duty to take care, evidence may show that he was not in breach of that duty because he took proper precautions.

In addition liability in negligence is not strict as it is under the Sale of Goods Act. The plaintiff must prove negligence in the process of manufacture. However, assistance is given by the plea of *res ipsa loquitur* (the thing speaks for itself). If this plea is accepted by the court the defendant must as we have seen show he was not negligent or explain how the matter could have come about without his negligence. If he fails to do this the plaintiff wins the case.

In certain of the cases mentioned above the question of inspection of the goods was raised. It was an important fact in the decision in *Donoghue* v *Stevenson* (1932) that the bottle was made of dark glass, so that the snail could not be seen on external inspection of the bottle, and that normally no inspection of goods would take place until they reached the consumer. It is not thought that in the developing law of negligence a manufacturer can rely on an inspection revealing the defects in his product, except perhaps in a special case where it is known that an expert inspection normally takes place. If such an inspection does not take place, or fails to find the defect which it should have found, the manufacturer may regard this as a *novus actus interveniens* (a new act intervening) breaking the chain of causation between his negligence and the injury so that the plaintiff's claim will fail.

ECONOMIC LOSS

Product liability in negligence has, up to recent times, been confined to defective chattels which cause *physical* injury to purchasers as in *Donoghue* and *Grant*. The law seemed to have taken a step forward in the *Junior Books* case by extending product liability in negligence to complaints relating to defects in goods which had caused economic loss rather than physical injury. This seems unlikely to develop at the present time for the reasons given in the comment to the case (see p. 783).

CONTRIBUTORY NEGLIGENCE

Even though the plaintiff has managed to prove negligence in the manufacturer the latter may still be able to obtain a reduction in the damages or even defeat the claim by proving that the plaintiff was guilty of contributory negligence as where he contributed to the damage or was even entirely responsible for it by, for example, failing to observe operating instructions or using the product after knowledge that it was defective. As we have seen the Law Reform (Contributory Negligence) Act, 1945 applies. Under it the court may, for example, assess damages at £20,000 but decide that the plaintiff was 50% to blame and reduce the damages to £10,000. In an extreme case the court may decide that the plaintiff was 100% to blame so that he recovers nothing.

THIRD-PARTY PROCEEDINGS

Strict liability under the Act of 1979 can, in effect, be imposed on a manufacturer by means of third- (or fourth-) party proceedings. Thus if the seller is sued by the buyer for breach of an implied condition under the Act, the seller may claim an indemnity from his own supplier which may be the manufacturer. If the retailer has purchased from a wholesaler the retailer may claim an indemnity from the wholesaler who may in turn claim an indemnity from the manufacturer who supplied the goods. In this way the manufacturer can be made to pay for defects affecting the quality or fitness of the goods. *Godley* v *Perry* (1960) provides an example of joinder of parties in a civil action. In connection with third-party proceedings it should be borne in mind that the retailer may be unable to make a successful claim because of a 'reasonable' exclusion clause in the contract between him and his previous suppliers. In addition, the retailer's claim will be ineffective if one or more of the previous suppliers is insolvent.

Statutory product liability – claims against the manufacturer

The Consumer Protection Act, 1987 now provides a statutory basis for a claim against the manufacturer.

PART I OF THE CONSUMER PROTECTION ACT, 1987

This brings into law strict product liability so that the consumer will no longer have to prove negligence when claiming compensation for damage or injury caused by products which are defective or unsafe. Civil liability will arise if damage is caused by a defective product. The Act is by no means a 'cure-all' because the plaintiff will still have to prove that the product *caused* the injury – not always an easy matter.

Damage is described as death, personal injury, or loss of or damage to *private* property. Thus damage to business property is not included. Furthermore, damage to property cannot be recovered unless it exceeds £275. If it does then the whole amount is recoverable, including the first £275. This is to prevent trivial claims for damage to property.

In assessing whether the product is unsafe the court must have regard to any warnings as to its use in advertising and marketing in general, instructions for use, how long ago the goods were supplied, and whether the product was put to what might be described as a reasonable use.

The following may be liable under the Act: the manufacturer of the product; a person who puts his name on the product thus holding himself out to be the manufacturer, i.e. a supermarket 'own brand' which is made for it by another manufacturer; an importer and a supplier if that supplier will not respond to a request to identify the person who supplied the product to him.

It is a defence to show that: (*a*) the product was not supplied in the course of a business; (*b*) the defect did not exist when the product was supplied; (*c*) technical knowledge was such that the defect could not have been known (called the 'development risk defence'). Thus the manufacturers of the drug Thalidomide may well have had a defence under the Act. However, manufacturers pressed for the retention of the development risk defence so as not to inhibit the development of new products.

The Act provides that any attempt to exclude liability by a term of a contract or notice will be ineffective. An injured party has three years in which to commence an action after the injury and discovery of the producer. There is a time bar on claims in any event ten years from when the product was supplied.

The Act does not impose liability on the producer of game or agricultural produce provided it has not undergone an industrial process.

PART II OF THE CONSUMER PROTECTION ACT, 1987

This repeals the Consumer Safety Act, 1978 and the Consumer Safety (Amendment) Act, 1986 and provides a better legal framework to give the public protection from unsafe goods. The main provisions are as follows:

(*a*) A person is guilty of an offence if he supplies any *consumer* goods which fail to comply with the general safety requirement. In general therefore the goods must be ordinarily intended for private use or consumption.

(*b*) The government may make safety regulations for the purpose of defining the general safety requirement set out in (*a*) above.

(*c*) The Department of Trade and Industry may serve upon a supplier a 'prohibition notice' prohibiting him from supplying goods which are considered unsafe or a 'notice to warn' requiring him to publish a warning about the goods at his own expense.

(*d*) A suspension notice may also be served by enforcement authorities, e.g. trading standards officers of local authorities, prohibiting a supplier from supplying specified goods where the authority has reasonable grounds for suspecting that there has been a contravention of the general safety requirement, any safety regulations or any prohibition notice.

Part II is primarily enforced by criminal sanctions. However, the duties laid down in Part II can assist a plaintiff in a civil claim which is why reference has been made to them. A plaintiff injured by goods which infringe the safety requirements of the Act will be able to bring a claim for damages in negligence on the basis that the manufacturer is in breach of his statutory duty under the Act. This will make the plaintiff's claim much easier since he or she will not have to show a duty of care at common law. In this respect the Act is available to those who have no contractual claim against the seller as where they have received the goods as a gift.

Negligence – professional liability

We have considered the scope of a manufacturer's liability for defective products which he puts into circulation and the way in which a consumer can take direct action against a manufacturer in negligence. The law of negligence also applies to the provision of services. In particular we are concerned with the position of those whose work involves giving professional business advice. The law has developed mainly in cases against accountants but the principles apply also to e.g. lawyers and valuers and surveyors.

THE BACKGROUND AND DEVELOPMENTD

Liability for negligent statements is an important area of the law, and the number of claims continues to increase. Negligent *statements* are now a more potent cause of actions at law than negligent *acts*. This state of affairs has had, and will continue to have, a major influence on the cost of indemnity insurance arrangements.

It was not always so. For example, in *Candler* v *Crane Christmas* [1951] 2 K.B. 164 Mr Ogilvie, the owner of a number of companies, was anxious to obtain an investment in them from Mr Candler. The defendants, a firm of accountants, prepared financial statements for Mr Ogilvie, *knowing* that they were to be shown to Mr Candler as a basis for his investment decision. Mr Candler did invest some money but a liquidation followed and he lost it.

He sued the defendants for damages, alleging negligent preparation of the financial statements. It was claimed that the defendants included freehold cottages and leasehold buildings as corporate assets without obtaining ownership evidence.

It was further claimed that the cottages were, in fact, owned by Mr Ogilvie, and that the title deeds were deposited with his bank to secure a personal overdraft. The leasehold buildings, it was alleged, did not belong to the company, but to Mr Ogilvie, and in any case, they had been forfeited, it was said, for non-payment of rent.

To succeed Mr Candler had first to establish, *as a matter of law*, that the defendants owed him a duty of care. If they had indeed been negligent in the preparation of the accounts this could then give rise to liability. The majority of the Court of Appeal decided that there was no duty of care in such circumstances, and so the accountants were not liable to Mr Candler, and would not have been, even if it had been proved that the financial statements were prepared negligently. There was no further appeal.

However, Lord Denning dissented from the majority view, being of the opinion that the accountants did owe a duty to Mr Candler, even though he was not a client. In his judgment, he said:

> I think the law would fail to serve the best interests of the community if it should hold that accountants and auditors owe a duty to no one but their client. There is a great difference between the lawyer and the accountant. The lawyer is never called on to express his personal belief in the truth of his client's case, whereas the accountant, who certifies the accounts of his client, is always called on to express his personal opinion whether the accounts exhibit a true and correct view of his client's affairs, and he is required to do this not so much for the satisfaction of his own client, but more for the guidance of shareholders, investors, revenue authorities and others who may have to rely on the accounts in serious matters of business. In my opinion, accountants owe a duty of care not only to their own clients, but also to all those whom they know will rely on their accounts in the transactions for which those accounts are prepared.

However, although Lord Denning was prepared to widen the liability of accountants to encompass a person who was not a client, he does appear to have restricted that liability to persons who it is *known* will rely on the accounts, as the last sentence of the above extract from his judgment clearly reveals. But he was alone in his view of the case, and the expansion of the liability of accountants (and others) for negligent statements had to wait for more than a decade.

In *Hedley Byrne & Co Ltd v Heller & Partners* (1963) (see p. 652), the House of Lords overruled the majority judgment of the Court of Appeal in *Candler*, and approved the dissenting judgment of Lord Denning.

The decision in *Hedley Byrne* widened the liability of all professionals (including, of course, accountants), but the House of Lords refrained, as a matter of public policy, from imposing the even wider test of *foresight* formulated by Lord Atkin in *Donoghue v Stevenson* (1932) (see p. 725). That case, as we have seen, related to negligence actions for *physical injury* arising from negligent *acts*, e.g. liability for a negligently manufactured product which causes physical injury to a consumer. Liability under that test extended to anyone who might reasonably be foreseen as suffering injury.

THE NEED FOR A SPECIAL RELATIONSHIP – KNOWLEDGE OF VICTIM

Instead the House of Lords decided that in the negligent *statement* cases, there had to be a 'special relationship' between the maker of the statement and the person injured by it. Obviously, this need not be a contractual client relationship. Although their Lordships did not draw up a list of special relationships, comments made by them in their judgments suggest that the duty in regard to a negligent statement would be owed only to those persons whom the maker of the statement *knows* will rely on it, and not beyond that to those whom he might *foresee* relying on it. Thus the test for negligent statements causing monetary loss (knowledge) was narrower than that for negligent acts causing physical injury (foresight), though, in all honesty, it was difficult to see why liability as such should depend upon the nature of the damage.

Indeed, during the decade following *Hedley Byrne* there were a number of judicial decisions which suggested that the foresight test propounded in *Donoghue* v *Stevenson* could be appropriate in the negligent statement situation thus potentially widening liability. This development was of course encouraged by the judgment of Lord Wilberforce in *Anns* v *London Borough of Merton*, 1977 to which we have already referred (see p. 436).

FROM KNOWLEDGE TO FORESIGHT

Lord Wilberforce's view that judges should consider broad principle rather than slavishly follow relevant previous decisions enabled Mr Justice Woolf to break out of the *Hedley Byrne* strait-jacket of 'special relationships' in *J.E.B. Fasteners Ltd* v *Marks, Bloom & Co* [1981] 3 All E.R. 289. In April 1975, the defendants, a firm of accountants, prepared an audited set of accounts for a company called B.G. Fasteners Ltd for the year ended 31 October 1974. The company's stock, which had been bought for some £11,000, was shown as being worth £23,080, that figure being based on the company's own valuation of the net realisable value of the stock.

The accountants nevertheless described the stock in the accounts as being 'valued at lower of cost and net realisable value'. On the basis of the inflated stock figure, the accounts showed a profit of £11.25. If the stock had been shown at cost, with a discount for possible errors, the accounts would have shown a loss of more than £13,000.

The defendant auditors were aware when they prepared the accounts that the company faced liquidity problems, and was looking for outside financial support from, amongst other people, the plaintiffs, J.E.B. Fasteners, who manufactured similar products and were anxious to expand their business.

The accounts which the defendants had prepared were made available by the directors of B.G. to the plaintiffs, who, although they had some reservations about the stock valuation, decided that they would take the company over in June 1975 for a nominal amount, because they would in so doing obtain the services of the company's two directors who had considerable experience in the type of manufacturing which the plaintiffs, J.E.B., carried on.

There were discussions between the plaintiffs and the defendant auditors during the takeover, but the auditors did not inform the plaintiffs that the stock had been put into the accounts at an inflated figure. The merger of the companies was not a financial success, and the plaintiffs brought an action for damages against the defendants.

The plaintiffs alleged that the defendants had prepared the company's accounts negligently, and that they relied on the accounts when buying B.G. Fasteners, and would not have bought the company had they been aware of its true financial position. It was contended on behalf of J.E.B. that an auditor when preparing a set of accounts owes a duty to all persons whom he ought reasonably to have forseen would rely on the accounts. The defendant auditors argued that if a duty of care existed, it could only be to persons who had made a specific request for information.

Woolf, J. decided that the defendant auditors did owe a duty of care to the plaintiffs, but that they were not liable in damages, since their alleged negligence was not the cause of the loss. The overriding reason for the takeover had been to obtain the services of two of B.G.'s directors. On the balance of probabilities, the takeover would have gone ahead even if the accounts had shown the true position.

The judge said that, but for the statement of Lord Wilberforce in *Anns* (as mentioned), Marks, Bloom would not have owed a duty of care to those who took over B.G. because the foresight test could not have been applied, and a 'special relationship' would not have existed (it was admitted that at the time the accounts in question were audited, Marks, Bloom did not know that they would be relied on by the plaintiffs, or even that any takeover was contemplated).

Furthermore, Woolf, J., having found a duty of care, said that following the Wilberforce test in *Anns*, he could find no considerations which he felt ought to exclude it in the circumstances of the J.E.B. case.

As regards the foreseeability issue, the judge said:

As Mr Marks was aware of the financial difficulties of B.G. Fasteners Ltd, and the fact that they were going to need financial support from outside of some sort, I am satisfied that Mr Marks, whom I can treat as being synonymous with the defendants, ought to have realized the accounts could be relied on until the time that a further audit was carried out by the commercial concerns to whom B.G. Fasteners were bound to look for financial assistance. When he audited the accounts, Mr Marks would not know precisely who would provide the financial support, or what form the financial support would take, and he certainly had no reason to know that it would be by way of takeover by the plaintiffs.

However, this was certainly one foreseeable method, and it does not seem to me that it would be right to exclude the duty of care merely because it was not possible to say with precision what machinery would be used to achieve the necessary financial support. Clearly, any form of loan would have been foreseeable, including the raising of money by way of debenture and, while some methods of raising money were more obvious than others, and a takeover was not the most obvious method, it was certainly one method which was within the contemplation of Mr Marks.

The judge went on to decide that the events leading to the takeover of B.G. were therefore foreseeable.

There was an appeal by J.E.B. to the Court of Appeal, which upheld Woolf, J.'s finding that there was a lack of causal connection between J.E.B.'s loss and the auditors' alleged negligence. Thus they were not liable.

However, the Court of Appeal went on to say that it was not necessary in order to decide the appeal to determine the scope of an auditor's liability for professional negligence. Thus Woolf, J.'s ruling on this matter retains some authority, but the law is still a little uncertain and in a state of development.

FURTHER DEVELOPMENTS

Note should be taken of developments in the courts of Scotland, where the law of negligence is the same. The judgment of Lord Stewart in *Twomax Ltd and Goode v Dickson, McFarlane and Robinson* and *Gordon v Dickson, McFarlane and Robinson* (1982) S.C. 113, delivered on 5 March 1982, in the Court of Session, is of interest.

Twomax acquired a controlling shareholding in a private company called Kintyre Knitwear Ltd. Dickson, McFarland and Robinson were the auditors of Kintyre. Messrs Goode and Gordon, the other plaintiffs, bought smaller holdings soon afterwards. All three plaintiffs (or pursuers as they are called in Scotland) said that in purchasing their interests in Kintyre they had relied on accounts prepared by the defendants, especially those for the year ended 31 March 1973 which showed a move away from a previous loss of £12,318 to a profit of £20,346. Subsequently, however, Kintyre went into receivership and then liquidation, and all three plaintiffs lost their entire investment.

The plaintiffs claimed that the accounts were false and misleading, that the auditors had prepared them negligently, and that if they had known the true position, they would not have invested in Kintyre at all.

The profit figure for 1973 was incorrect. The profit of £20,346 should have been £16,779 because of two errors, one of £3200 in the accrual for commission, and another in the understatement of doubtful debts of £367.

Lord Stewart found for the plaintiffs and awarded them the amount of their investment plus interest at 11% from the date of the investment. In reaching this decision, he also accepted the plaintiffs' claim that the accounts for the year ended March 1975 were negligently prepared because they showed a trading loss of £87,727, whereas such a loss could not have occurred in one year and must therefore result from undetected errors in previous years, so that the profit for the year ended 31 March 1973 must have been even more overstated.

Oddly enough, no actual errors could be identified. This suggests, therefore, that it is enough to found a successful claim against an accountant if the plaintiff can show a mere probability that the accounts were wrong together with some evidence of surrounding negligence. It is not, it seems, necessary to show in what particular respects the accounts were wrong.

An aditional point in establishing the negligence of the accountants was that they did not attend stocktaking, even though there was no evidence that the stock was incorrect.

The judge also accepted that it was reasonable to invest in a company by relying solely on the last audited accounts. He also accepted that the auditors did not know the specific intention of the plaintiffs to invest at the time of the audit, but nevertheless held that they were liable. He was impressed by, and used, the J.E.B. foresight test which, he said, applied in this particular case. Although the auditors did not know of the specific intention of the plaintiffs when they did the audit, they were aware that Kintyre needed capital, and that the accounts were normally available to lenders because they were, as the auditors knew, lodged with the company's bank.

The auditors were also aware, apparently, that one of the directors wished to sell his shares. They also knew clean audit certificates were often relied on by lenders and investors as well as shareholders.

FROM FORESIGHT BACK TO KNOWLEDGE

In more recent times the courts have made it clear that mere foresight is not enough. There must be some 'relationship' or 'proximity' or 'neighbourhood' between the parties. This is likely to restrict liability to within reasonable bounds and close the floodgates to a wide variety of claims by plaintiffs *unless they are known to be the users of professional statements and, further, that the professional concerned knows of the use to which they will be put.* Given such a situation a duty of care will exist.

This development was taking place before the *Anns* case was overruled by the decision of the House of Lords in *Murphy* (see p. 437) as the essential case law and comment below shows.

ESSENTIAL CASE LAW AND COMMENT

Caparo Industries plc v *Dickman*, 1990 – Acountants' liability **(413)**
Morgan Crucible Co plc v *Hill Samuel*, 1990 – Accountants'
    liability in a takeover **(414)**

AVOIDING AND EXCLUDING LIABILITY

The most practical suggestion that can be made in terms of avoiding liability is for professionals to follow strictly the recommendations of their professional bodies, e.g. the many financial reporting standards and other published material. If this is done the professional will at least have the advantage of the judgment of McNair, J. in *Bolam* v *Friern Hospital Management Committee* [1957] 2 All E.R. 118. He said in connection with doctors: 'A doctor is not guilty of negligence if he has acted in accordance with a practice accepted as proper by a responsible body of medical men skilled in that particular art . . . merely because there is a body of opinion who would take a contrary view.' The statement is, of course, equally applicable to other professions.

As regards ability to exclude liability by notice under s. 2(2) of the Unfair Contract Terms Act, 1977 (see p. 295), this will work only if the clause is reasonable. It would seem that there are two factors of major importance in deciding the reasonableness or otherwise of limitations or exclusion of liability for professional negligence and these are: (*a*) insurance, and (*b*) the operation of a two-tier service.

As regards insurance, it would seem unreasonable for a professional person to try to exclude totally liability for negligence because that can hardly be regarded as best professional practice. On the other hand, it would probably be reasonable for him to limit his liability to a specified sum. In fact s. 11(4) of the 1977 Act states that if a person seeks to restrict his liability in this way the court must have regard to the resources which he would expect to be available to him for the purposes of meeting the liability and also how far it was possible for him to cover himself by insurance. It is thought, therefore, that a firm which takes out the maximum insurance cover which is reasonable in the circumstances, being one where the cover is not so great that the effect could be greatly to inflate the fees charged by the firm, then to limit liability to that sum would satisfy the requirement of reasonableness. There is judicial support for this argument in a number of cases, particularly *George Mitchell* v *Finney Lock Seeds* (1983) (see p. 682).

As regards a two-tier service, a professional person could offer a full service at a full price and a reduced service at a lower price. Again, it would seem so long as the user of the service is aware that the two-tier service is available and that he is accepting a reduced service at a reduced price without full liability, then the exclusion clause in a lower-tier service ought to be regarded as reasonable.

It is, of course, worth bearing in mind in all of this that a limitation of liability for professional negligence is much more likely to be regarded as reasonable in a contract with a non-consumer, i.e. a business, than it is in a consumer contract. In fact we have already seen in *Smith* v *Eric S. Bush* (1987) (see p. 652) that a disclaimer used by a professional person in a consumer situation was not effective.

It is also worth noting that as regards auditors engaged by a company to carry out a Companies Act audit, s. 310 of the Companies Act, 1985 makes void any provision in a contract of engagement of the auditors which purports to exclude them from liability for negligence or breach of duty, though the company can now pay the premiums on an insurance policy both for auditors and directors.

PROFESSIONAL NEGLIGENCE INSURANCE

Professional indemnity policies are available for a whole range of professional persons and experts, e.g. acountants, solicitors, company directors and insurance brokers. These policies carry an excess clause under which the insured bears the first part of the claim up to a fixed amount. The risk covered is variously described but there is now a tendency to cover 'full civil liability' followed by exclusions from cover of things such as libel. The policies usually cover loss caused to a client (i.e. by breach of contract), and to a non-client (i.e. in the tort of negligence).

Negligence – occupiers' liability

The question of the liability of occupiers of premises to persons suffering injury thereon may be regarded as a further aspect of negligence. The occupier is the person who has *de facto* control of the premises or the possession of them; it is a question of fact in each case and does not depend entirely on title. It should also be noted that occupation may be *shared* between two or more persons, and that an employer may be vicariously liable for the torts of an employee who is acting within the scope of his employment. Thus in *Stone* v *Taffe* [1974] 3 All E.R. 1016, the owner of a hotel was liable when the manager failed to ensure that there was adequate lighting on the premises so that a guest fell and was killed.

ESSENTIAL CASE LAW AND COMMENT

Wheat v *Lacon & Co Ltd*, 1966 – When two persons occupy **(415)**

THE OCCUPIERS' LIABILITY ACT, 1957

A common duty of care is owed to all lawful visitors to premises, 'visitor' being a term which includes anyone to whom the occupier has given, or is deemed to have given, an invitation or permission to use the premises. It includes some persons who enter the premises by right of law, such as inspectors, but not those who cross land in pursuance of a public or private right of way. These are governed by the Occupiers' Liability Act, 1984 (see p. 457).

Implied permission to enter premises is a matter of fact to be decided in the circumstances of each case, and the burden of proof is upon the person who claims implied permission. However, persons who enter upon premises for purposes of business which they believe will be of interest to the occupier, as where they wish to sell him a product, have implied permission to enter even though their presence is distasteful to the occupier.

Under the Act, an occupier of premises owes to all visitors the duty to take such care as, in the circumstances of the case, is necessary to see that the visitor will be reasonably safe in using the premises for the purpose for which he is invited or permitted to be there. If the visitor uses the premises for some other purpose, the occupier does not owe him the same duty; such a person is in effect a trespasser, and liability to him falls to be decided on that basis. (See below.)

Under s. 2(1) of the 1957 Act the occupier may restrict or exclude his liability, by giving adequate warning or by contract. However, this section must be looked at in the light of the Unfair Contract Terms Act, 1977, which states that the common-law duty of care in regard to liability for death or personal injury cannot be excluded in relation to business premises. In addition, liability for other loss or damage occurring on such premises can only be excluded where it is reasonable to do so.

Where the accident has arisen through the defective work of an independent contractor, the occupier can avoid liability by showing that he behaved reasonably in the selection of the contractor.

The defence of *volenti non fit injuria* is available to the occupier, though he must show that the entrant assented to the risk, not that he merely knew of it: the entrant's knowledge is no longer a defence.

The occupier may also raise the defence of *contributory negligence* by the entrant which, though not defeating his claim, may reduce damages.

ESSENTIAL CASE LAW AND COMMENT

Cook v *Broderip*, 1968 – Faulty work of an independent contractor
(416)
Bunker v *Charles Brand*, 1969 – Knowledge is not assent **(417)**

Trespassers

The main case on an occupier's liability to a trespasser was *British Railways Board* v *Herrington* [1972] 1 All E.R. 749 in which the House of Lords was unanimous in deciding that there could be liability to a trespasser. Unfortunately the five judges concerned reached that decision in different ways and the matter was referred to the Law Commission. Eventually Parliament passed the Occupiers' Liability Act, 1984 which now governs the position of trespassers and certain other non-visitors.

Section 1 deals with the duty of an occupier to persons other than his visitors – this includes trespassers and persons entering land without the consent of the owner, but in exercise of a private right of way or public access. In these cases the occupier owes a duty, if he is aware of the danger which exists, or has reasonable grounds to believe that it exists. He must also know, or have reasonable grounds to believe that the non-visitor concerned is in the vicinity of the danger – whether he has lawful authority for being in that vicinity or not. Furthermore, the risk must be one which in all the circumstances of the case it is reasonable to expect the occupier to offer the non-visitor some protection against. It was held, for example, in *Proffit* v *British Railways Board, The Times,* 4 February 1984 that British Rail had no *general* duty to erect or maintain fences sufficient to keep trespassers out.

The duty is to take such care as is reasonable in all the circumstances of the case to see that the non-visitor does not suffer injury because of the danger concerned. The duty may be discharged by giving warning of the danger or taking steps to discourage person from incurring risk. Thus the defence of *volenti* is preserved.

Access to the countryside

Section 2 of the Occupiers' Liability Act, 1984 is designed to encourage access to the countryside. The Unfair Contract Terms Act, 1977 had discouraged landowners with, say, a mountain crag, or potholes on their land, from admitting the public thereto because of the difficulty of excluding liability which might result. Under the 1984 Act they can exclude liability, e.g. by notice, for the dangerous state of the land provided they are prepared to allow the public to come on to it for nothing. So long as the actual letting in of the public is not part of a business, as where access for recreational or educational purposes is charged for, the letting in of the public for nothing will not constitute running a business for the purposes of the 1977 Act.

Children on premises

Dealings with children always demand a high degree of care, whether a person is sued in the capacity of an occupier of premises or not. However, in the case of an occupier of premises, the duty towards children was rather different from the corresponding duty to adults. If, with knowledge of the trespass of children on his land, the occupier made no reasonable attempt to prevent such trespass, e.g. by repairing fences, and a child was injured by something on the land which was especially alluring to children, e.g. turntables, escalators, bright and poisonous berries, then the occupier in general was liable, even though the child was on the face of it a trespasser. The difference owed to child trespassers is no longer so great in view of the broader rules laid down in the Occupiers' Liability Act, 1984. However, it should be noted that what is adequate warning to an adult might not be so to a child. These rules will presumably apply to the warnings which the 1984 Act allows the occupier to give.

ESSENTIAL CASE LAW AND COMMENT

Yachuk v *Oliver Blais & Co Ltd*, 1949 – Negligence liability and children **(418)**

Gough v *National Coal Board*, 1954 – Occupiers' liability and children **(419)**

Mourton v *Poulter*, 1930 – Warning children **(420)**

Pannett v *McGuinness & Co*, 1972 – An alluring bonfire **(421)**

Landlord and tenant

As regards landlord and tenant, s. 4 of the Occupiers' Liability Act, 1957 provided that a landlord would be liable to his tenants' visitors who were injured or whose goods were damaged on the leased premises because of some defect which resulted from his failure to repair. However, s. 4 only applied where the landlord was under an obligation express, implied or statutory to repair, but the Defective Premises Act, 1972 repeals s. 4 and places liability on a landlord who has merely reserved a right to enter and repair. A landlord who does not repair where he has no obligation to do so, nor a power of entry, has no liability, under the Act or at common law.

Thus, now that s. 4 of the 1957 Act is repealed, the landlord's liability is similar to his liability in nuisance. Of course, only an occupier can sue in nuisance but under the Defective Premises Act, 1972, the landlord is liable to all persons who might reasonably be expected to be affected by defects in the state of the premises. This covers not only the tenant, his family and his visitors, but also neighbours, passers-by and trespassers.

Furthermore, under the 1957 Act it became established that a landlord was only liable to his tenants' visitors if he had been notified of the defect by the tenant. However, s. 4(2) of the 1972 Act provides that the duty is owed where the landlord knew or ought to have known of the relevant defect, so notice given by the tenant is no longer essential. Where the lease or tenancy expressly imposes on the tenant a duty to inform the lessor of defects but the tenant fails to do so with the consequence that a third party is injured, then the landlord can still be sued provided it can be shown that he ought to have known of the defect but in this case he will have a right of indemnity against the tenant for what that may be worth.

However, there are still gaps in the law because the duties imposed upon a landlord by s. 4 relate only to the *maintenance* of a property which was satisfactory when let. If an owner knows of a defect – not created by him – in the premises *before he either sells or lets the premises* but does not repair it or warn about it the 1972 Act imposes no liability on him for harm caused after the property is let or sold. Furthermore there is no liability at common law (*Cavalier* v *Pope* [1906] A.C. 428. Affirmed in *McNerny* v *Lambeth Borough Council* (1989) 139 N.L.J. 114).

Where the person injured is the tenant himself the 1972 Act allows a tenant to sue his landlord for breach of his statutory duty but then the lessor would be able to allege contributory negligence in that the tenant failed to notify him of the defect. Where, however, the defect was due to a tenant failing to carry out an obligation expressly imposed on him by the lease or tenancy, the landlord does not owe the tenant any duty, although he would still owe a duty to third parties if they were injured, but in these circumstances could recover an indemnity or contribution from the tenant who would be a joint tortfeasor. There is little a landlord can do to exclude or restrict his liability. Section 6(3) of the 1972 Act renders void any exclusion clause in a lease or tenancy agreement.

Highway authorities

A highway authority is liable for damage which is caused by its *active misfeasance* and, under the Highways Act, 1980, for damage which arises from its failure to repair.

In an action for damages against a highway authority based upon its failure to repair, it is a defence to prove that the authority has in all the circumstances taken reasonable care to ensure that the highway was not dangerous.

ESSENTIAL CASE LAW AND COMMENT

Griffiths v *Liverpool Corporation*, 1966 – Failure to repair a flagstone **(422)**

Defective Premises Act, 1972

This Act brought about three major changes. In the first place a landlord's liability for defects in leased premises was increased. This has already been dealt with in occupiers' liability (see p. 458). Secondly, much of the common-law immunity of a vendor or landlord for negligence was abolished. Thirdly, there is a statutory duty on those concerned with providing dwellings to do the work properly. Section 1 places a duty on builders and developers, sub-contractors, architects and local authorities to see that building contracts are carried out in a workmanlike, or where appropriate, professional manner with proper materials so that the dwelling is fit for habitation. It should be noted that this statutory duty is owed not merely to the immediate client but to everyone who acquires a legal or equitable interest in the dwelling. The liability does not, of course, last for ever. It is subject to the Limitation Act, though s. 1(5) of the 1972 Act provides that a cause of action accrues at the time when the dwelling was completed, but where further work has to be done to put right a fault then the cause of action accrues only when the further work is completed. This means that from that date a plaintiff has six years to start an action or three years where the defect has caused death or personal injury. Section 6(3) of the 1972 Act renders void any term of an agreement which purports to exclude or restrict this statutory duty.

Under s. 1(3) a mere agreement by a client to a particular design or specification being used does not discharge the builder or other persons involved from this statutory duty. Section 2 offers an alternative by providing that no action can be brought where a State-approved scheme has conferred rights on the first sale or letting to those who have or will have an interest in the property in respect of defects in the state of the dwelling. Such schemes can be approved or withdrawn by the Secretary of State by statutory instrument.

The National Housebuilders Registration Council scheme is approved under these arrangements and where an N.H.R.C. scheme is in operation it applies rather than the Act. The advantage of an N.H.R.C. scheme over the Act is that if the builder becomes bankrupt the Council compensates the claimant. Section 3 of the Act sweeps away most of the old common-law immunity from liability for negligence which was formerly enjoyed by sellers of property and lessors of property; they are now liable within the wider rule of *Donoghue* v *Stevenson*, 1932 (see p. 725). Thus under the 1972 Act the maxim *caveat emptor* no longer provides a defence to a claim of negligence against a vendor or lessor in respect of defects in the premises sold or let and this liability extends beyond the immediate purchaser or lessee and can be brought by others who buy or rent the property within the constraints of the Limitation Act, 1980 and s. 1(5) of the 1972 Act. Thus there is now a law against building or letting tumbledown properties.

It should be carefully noted, however, that s. 3 has gaps. The defects have to be caused by works of construction, repair, maintenance or demolition or other works. The section does not apply at all to negligent omissions to repair and the common law provides in general no redress. (See *McNerny* v *Lambeth Borough Council*, 1989 at p. 458.)

Negligence – of employers

Where an employee's case is based on his employer's negligence *at common law*, he will have to prove that his injury was the result of the employer's breach of a duty of care. The employee is assisted in this task because certain specific duties of an employer were laid down by the House of Lords in the leading case of *Wilsons and Clyde Coal Co.* v *English* [1938] A.C. 57, and an employer must take reasonable care to provide –

(a) *proper and safe plant and appliances* for the work;
(b) *a safe system of work* with adequate supervision and instruction;
(c) *safe premises*; and
(d) *a competent staff* of fellow employees.

The employer's duty is a personal one so that he remains liable even though he has delegated the performance of the duty to a competent independent contractor. Thus in *Paine* v *Colne Valley Electricity Supply Co. Ltd* [1938] 4 All E.R. 803, an employer was held liable for injuries to his employee caused by the failure of contractors to install sufficient insulation in an electrical kiosk.

However, in *Davie* v *New Merton Board Mills* [1958] 1 All E.R. 67, the House of Lords decided that an employer was not liable for damage caused by a defective implement purchased from a reputable manufacturer. The employee was thus left to sue the manufacturer and this could prove difficult where the manufacturer had left the country or gone out of business or could not for any other reason be identified. Now the Employer's Liability (Defective Equipment) Act, 1969, provides that an employee who is injured because of a defect in his employer's equipment can recover damages from the employer if he can show that the defect is due to the fault of some person, e.g. the manufacturer, but if no one is at fault damages are not recoverable. Agreements by employees to contract out are void, and rights under the Act are *in addition* to common-law rights. Thus, an injured employee can sue a third party such as a manufacturer if he wishes, e.g. as where the employer is insolvent, though the Employer's Liability (Compulsory Insurance) Act, 1969, requires employers to insure against their liability for personal injury to their employees. The injury must result from equipment provided for the employer's *business*. Thus, domestic servants injured by household equipment would not be covered.

There are numerous statutes which are designed to protect the health, and provide for the welfare and safety of employees. The relevance of such statutes for our present purposes is that where the breach of a statutory duty, e.g. failure to fence a dangerous machine, has caused injury to a worker, he may be able to sue his employer for damages by using the breach of statutory duty to establish the duty of care under the principles already discussed.

ESSENTIAL CASE LAW AND COMMENT

Millard v *Serck Tubes Ltd*, 1969 – A statutory duty of care **(423)**

Torts against business interests

It is a tort knowingly to induce a person to *break his contract* with a third party whereby that party suffers damage. It is also an actionable wrong for two or more persons to combine together (*or conspire*) for the purpose of wilfully causing damage to the plaintiff. There is also an action for *passing off* which occurs where A represents his goods or services to be those of B.

INDUCEMENT OF BREACH OF CONTRACT

If A induces B to break his contract with C, C can sue A.

Trade union activity often involves interference with contract and the position as regards the immunity or otherwise of trade unions in this context has already been considered at p. 193.

ESSENTIAL CASE LAW AND COMMENT

Lumley v *Gye*, 1853 – Inducing a breach of contract **(424)**
Daily Mirror Newspapers v *Gardner*, 1968 – Boycotting a newspaper **(425)**

CONSPIRACY

Where two or more persons act without lawful justification for the purpose of wilfully causing damage to the plaintiff and actual damage results, they commit the tort of conspiracy. The tort was fully considered in *Crofter Hand Woven Harris Tweed Co. Ltd* v *Veitch*, 1942 (see below), where the following principles were laid down –

(*a*) the tort covers acts which would *lawful if done by one person*;
(*b*) the combination will be justified if the predominant motive is self-interest or protection of one's trade rather than injury to the plaintiff;
(*c*) damage to the plaintiff must be proved.

ESSENTIAL CASE LAW AND COMMENT

Crofter Hand Woven Harris Tweed Co Ltd v *Veitch*, 1942 – The principles of conspiracy **(426)**

PASSING OFF

Any person, company or other organisation which carries on or proposes to carry on business under a name calculated to deceive the public by confusion with the name of an existing concern, commits the civil wrong of *passing off* and will be restrained by injunction from doing so. Other examples of passing off are the use of similar wrappings, identification marks, and descriptions. Thus in *Bollinger* v *Costa Brava Wine Co. Ltd* [1959] 3 All E.R. 800, the champagne producers of France objected to the use of the name 'Spanish Champagne' to describe a sparkling wine which was made in Spain and they were granted an injunction to prevent the use of that term. The remedies other than an injunction are an action for damages or for an account of profits.

Defamation

Defamation is the publication of a statement which tends to lower a person in the estimation of right-thinking members of society generally, or which tends to make them shun or avoid that person.

ESSENTIAL CASE LAW AND COMMENT

Byrne v *Deane*, 1937 – What is defamation? **(427)**

In order to constitute a tort the statement must be false and capable of bearing a defamatory meaning. Lord Reid in *Lewis* v *Daily Telegraph Ltd* [1964] A.C. 234 at p. 258 indicated how a trial judge might proceed in deciding whether words in their ordinary and natural meaning are capable of bearing a defamatory meaning.

> What the ordinary man would infer without special knowledge has generally been called the natural and ordinary meaning of the words. But the expression is rather misleading in that it conceals the fact that there are two elements in it. Sometimes it is not necessary to go beyond the words themselves, as where the plaintiff has been called a thief or a murderer. But more often the sting is not so much in the words themselves as in what the ordinary man will infer from them, and that is also regarded as part of their natural and ordinary meaning . . . In this case it is, I think, sufficient to put the test in this way. Ordinary men and women have different temperaments and outlooks. Some are unusually suspicious, and some are unusually naive. One must try to envisage people between these two extremes and see what is the most damaging meaning they would put on the words in question.

In consequence the ordinary and natural meaning of words is to be gathered not only by considering a strictly literal interpretation but also from the inference which would be drawn by the ordinary person who heard or read the words. Statements of *opinion* may be defamatory; defamation is not confined to statements of fact. Thus in *Slazengers Ltd* v *Gibbs (C) & Co.* (1916) 33 T.L.R. 35 the defendants stated during the First World War with Germany that the plaintiffs were a German firm and would, in their opinion, be closed down. This statement of opinion was held to be defamatory of the plaintiffs.

Publication

The essence of the tort is the publication or communication of the falsehood to at least one person other than the person defamed, and other than the author's own husband or wife. Obviously publication to the plaintiff's spouse is defamatory (*Wenman* v *Ash* (1853) 13 C.B. 836). Every successive repetition of the statement is a fresh commission of the tort. Hence a defamatory statement written upon a postcard is published by the sender not only to the ultimate recipient but also to the postal officials through whose hands it may pass, and to every individual who legitimately handles the message, e.g. the secretary of the sender or the receiver. Similarly a libel contained in a newspaper is published by the reporter or author, and by the editor, the printer, the publisher, the proprietor, the wholesaler and the retail seller of that newspaper.

However, mere *mechanical distributors*, e.g. news vendors, booksellers, libraries and the like, are not liable for their acts if they are unaware of the libel. However, if, as in *Viztelly* v *Mudie's Select Library Ltd* [1900] 2 Q.B. 170, the library has overlooked a publisher's circular requesting return of copies of a libellous book, then there is a liability. Persons lending books gratuitously or making gifts of them and tape and record dealers are also protected if unaware of the defamation. There is, of course, no need to consider the liability of the Post Office because it is exempt from any liability in tort in regard to postal packets. Nor is there any need to consider the liability of British Telecommunications because, although the telecommunications service is run under contract, there are excluding terms.

A defendant is not liable when a father opens his son's letter (*Powell* v *Gelstone* [1916] 2 K.B. 615), or the butler opens the unsealed letter of his employer (*Huth* v *Huth* [1915] 3 K.B. 32). However, a correspondent should expect that clerks of the plaintiff, if a business man, might in the ordinary course of business open letters adressed to him at his place of business and not marked 'personal' or 'private', etc., and such a correspondent is responsible for publication of a libel. It should also be noted that marking the communication 'private', 'personal', etc. may not prevent publication in the case of a very busy public figure such as the Prime Minister.

The third person who receives the defamatory statement must be capable of appreciating its significance. A written defamatory statement cannot be published to a blind man except in Braille. It is not publication to repeat a defamatory statement in a foreign language in the presence only of persons who cannot understand the tongue. But if X writes a defamatory statement to Y in (say) German, knowing that Y cannot understand it, X will be responsible for the publication which results from Y's showing it to a linguist for the purpose of translation. In addition, to constitute publication, the person to whom the statement is communicated must understand that it refers to the plaintiff.

WHO MAY BE DEFAMED?

No action lies at civil law for defaming a dead person, no matter how much it may annoy or upset his relatives. There may possibly be a prosecution for criminal libel if the necessary or natural effect of the words used is to render a breach of the peace imminent or probable.

As regards criticism of a trader, it is not defamatory merely to criticise his goods so long as the trader himself is not attacked. To say that a trader is bankrupt or insolvent is defamatory, but to say that he has ceased to be in business is not, for it does not reflect on his reputation (*Ratcliffe* v *Evans* [1892] 2 Q.B. 254). As we have seen, the law of defamation applies to corporations as it does to private individuals (*D. & L. Caterers Ltd.* v *D'Anjou*, 1945 at p. 731).

LIBEL AND SLANDER

The form of publication determines whether the tort committed is libel or slander. *Libel* is defamation in some permanent form; *slander* is a statement of a like kind in transient form. Pictures, effigies, writing and print are clearly libel. Speech is slander, and probably gestures and facial mimicry also. It has been held that a defamatory sound film was a libel, and legislation states that the broadcasting of defamatory matter is libel, whether sound or visual images are transmitted (Defamation Act, 1952, s. 1). (See also Theatres Act, 1968, p. 475.)

ESSENTIAL CASE LAW AND COMMENT

Youssoupoff v *Metro-Goldwyn-Mayer*, 1934 – A film is libel **(428)**

It is necessary to determine whether a tort is libel or slander for two reasons –

(*a*) libel may be a crime as well as a tort;

(*b*) libel is actionable without the plaintiff having to prove special damage, i.e. pecuniary loss, whereas the plaintiff in an action for slander must as a general rule prove such special damage.

Slander is actionable *per se*, i.e. without proof of special damage, in the following cases –

(*a*) Where there is an imputation that the plaintiff has been guilty of a criminal offence punishable with imprisonment, e.g. a statement such as 'I have enough information to put John in gaol'.

(*b*) Where there is an imputation of unchastity to any woman or girl (Slander of Women Act, 1891). This probably includes the case where a woman is alleged to have been the victim of rape and seems to include a false allegation of lesbianism (*Kerr* v *Kennedy* [1942] 1 K.B. 409).

(*c*) Where there is an imputation that the plaintiff is suffering from venereal disease and possibly other contagious diseases, e.g. leprosy or plague, which might cause him to be shunned and avoided. To say that a person *has suffered* from these diseases is not actionable *per se*.

(*d*) Where there have been words calculated to disparage the plaintiff in any office, profession, business or calling, by imputing dishonesty, unfitness or incompetence (Defamation Act, 1952, s. 2). However, it is not necessary for the plaintiff to show e.g. that he has lost his job as a result, but the remark must be one likely to lower his standing in his trade or profession. Presumably, therefore, the old case of *Lumbe* v *Allday* (1831) 1 Cr. & J. 301 is still good law. In that case the court decided that a statement that a clerk employed by a gas company associated with whores was not actionable *per se* because his quality as a clerk would be in no way diminished by his association with prostitutes.

A suggestion, therefore, that a clergyman has been found guilty of immoral conduct, or that a solicitor knows no law is actionable without proof of special damage. Spoken words in a broadcast are now actionable *per se* since they are regarded as libel (Defamation Act, 1952, s. 1).

It is not enough that the words are abusive. Thus to say of A, a bricklayer, that he is a legal ignoramus is not defamatory, though the same words would be defamatory if said of B, a solicitor. Difficulties might arise if the words were said of a chartered accountant who is required to have a knowledge of certain branches of the law.

To resolve problems such as these, two questions must be answered –

(*a*) Are the alleged words capable of bearing a meaning which is defamatory of the plaintiff? (This is a matter of law and is decided by the judge.)

(*b*) If so, in this particular case are the words in fact defamatory of the plaintiff? (This is a matter of fact to be decided by the jury.)

WHAT IS SPECIAL DAMAGE?

Some material loss is required, e.g. refusal of persons to enter into contracts with the plaintiff, or the loss of hospitality from friends who have provided food or drink on former occasions. (*Storey* v *Challands* (1837) 8 C.& P. 234.) Illness resulting from mental suffering is probably special damage. There were some early cases which said that it was not, but the better view is that these would not be followed now.

INNUENDO

Cases may arise where the words are not at first sight defamatory, and only appear as such when the surrounding circumstances have been explained. Again a statement may be ironical, or accompanied by a wink or a gesture, or it may be ambiguous, e.g. the statement that 'X drinks'. In such a case the plaintiff must show that the words contain an innuendo or hidden meaning and that reasonable persons could, and in fact would, interpret the *words* used in a defamatory sense. However, a newspaper article may be defamatory of a person whom readers only identify from their own knowledge of extrinsic facts. The defamation need not arise from words themselves. Evidence is admissible to show that innocent words have a defamatory meaning. The judge decides as a matter of law whether the words are capable of bearing the innuendo alleged by the plaintiff, and the jury decides whether in fact the words do bear that meaning. The meaning sought to be placed upon the words by the innuendo pleaded must be reasonable, and the court will not read into a statement a defamatory sense which is not there on a reasonable interpretation. Furthermore, a plaintiff who claims that the innuendo to be drawn by those with special knowledge of the facts from a publication is libellous is bound to particularise those readers of the publication whom he alleges to have such special knowledge.

ESSENTIAL CASE LAW AND COMMENT

Cassidy v *Daily Mirror Newspapers*, 1929 – Innuendo: at the racecourse **(429)**

Morgan v *Odhams Press*, 1971 – Innocent words may have a defamatory meaning **(430)**

Tolley v *Fry*, 1931 – An amateur golfer defamed **(431)**

Sim v *Stretch*, 1936 – Defamation must appear on a reasonable interpretation **(432)**

Fulham v *Newcastle Chronicle and Journal*, 1977 – Who has special knowledge? **(433)**

Where a plaintiff relies on an innuendo he must prove that the words were published to a specific person who knew *at the time of the publication* of specific facts enabling that person or persons to understand the words in the innuendo sense. Facts which come into existence afterwards do not make a statement defamatory.

ESSENTIAL CASE LAW AND COMMENT

Grappelli v *Derek Block (Holdings) Ltd*, 1981 – Innuendo must arise at the time of publication **(434)**

REFERENCE TO THE PLAINTIFF

If the judge decides that the words are capable of bearing a defamatory meaning, he must then consider whether the words are capable of referring to the plaintiff. This again is a question of law. If he finds the answer to be yes, he must leave to the jury the question: 'Do the words in fact refer to the plaintiff?' This is a simple matter where the plaintiff has been referred to by name, and until recently the rule was that an author used a name at his peril if it turned out that it could reasonably be taken to refer to the plaintiff. Indeed the more obscure the name selected, the greater the chance of success of a plaintiff who bore that name should he sue for libel. It is not uncommon to attach a disclaimer at the beginning of a work of fiction: 'The persons and events described in this book are wholly imaginary', but it is doubtful whether this affects the author's liability.

ESSENTIAL CASE LAW AND COMMENT

Hulton v *Jones*, 1910 – Do the words refer to the plaintiff? **(435)**

The practical restriction on so-called 'gold-digging' actions was the power of the jury to award contemptuous damages of a farthing (when that coin was in existence), but the costs involved in defending an action might well lead a defendant to settle out of court for a substantial sum. The position has been modified by the Defamation Act, 1952, s. 4, which provides for an offer of amends which will be dealt with later.

It sometimes happens that a whole class of persons is the subject of a defamatory statement. Here a member of the class may only sue if he can show that he himself is the person pointed out by the defamatory statement.

ESSENTIAL CASE LAW AND COMMENT

Knupffer v *London Express Newspaper Ltd*, 1944 – A class libel
  fails **(436)**
Schloimovitz v *Clarendon Press*, 1973 – How 'Jew' was defined
  (437)

Words may, of course, be defamatory of the plaintiff without his being mentioned by name, if the statement can be shown to apply to him. (See *Youssoupoff* v *M.G.M.*, 1934 at p. 798.)

The defendant's motives are generally immaterial. The most laudable motives will not by themselves prevent a defamatory statement from being actionable. But where the defendant puts his motives in issue, as where he pleads fair comment or qualified privilege, or relies on s. 4 of the Defamation Act, 1952 (unintentional defamation), the plaintiff may then prove the malice of the defendant, or improper motive, to rebut the defence.

DEFENCES

There are certain special defences which are peculiar to an action for defamation, but these defences do not preclude a defendant from denying in addition that the words are defamatory, or asserting that they do not refer to the plaintiff, or that they were not published.

JUSTIFICATION

There is no burden of proof on the plaintiff to establish that the defendant's statement is untrue; all the plaintiff has to do is to prove publication plus the defamatory nature of the statement. However, as the essence of defamation is a false statement, a defendant may always plead the truth of the statement as a defence in civil proceedings (but not in an action for criminal libel, where the rule is: 'The greater the truth, the greater the libel', since true libels are more likely to influence passions). If the statement is true, no injury is done to the plaintiff's reputation; it is simply reduced to its true level. It does not matter that the statement was made maliciously or even that the defendant did not believe it to be true; so long as it is true the defence of justification is complete.

In the defence of justification the defendant asserts that the statements are 'true both in substance and in fact'. He must show not merely that the words are literally true, but also that there are no significant omissions which would affect the truth of the statement taken as a whole. If, however, the statement is essentially true, an incidental inaccuracy will not deprive the defendant of his right to justify.

ESSENTIAL CASE LAW AND COMMENT

Alexander v *The North Eastern Railway Co*, 1865 – The defence of justification **(438)**

However, that which is proved to be true must tally with that which the defendant's statement is interpreted to mean. Thus in *Wakley* v *Cooke* (1849) 4 Exch. 511 the defendant called the plaintiff 'a libellous journalist'. The defendant proved that the plaintiff had had one judgment against him for libel but the court held that the statement meant that the journalist habitually libelled people and so the defendant had not justified it.

The defence of justification really amounts to a positive charge against the plaintiff, and if it fails the damages may be increased, since the original wrong has been aggravated. The defendant's honest belief that the statement is true is no justification, though it may reduce damages. Nor is it a justification to prove that a quoted statement was made, if the quotation cannot be proved to be true. Suppose a statement is made: 'Mrs A tells me that Dr B has been committing adultery with a woman patient.' It is no justification to show that Mrs A made the statement to the defendant; he must show that Dr B is actually guilty of the conduct alleged.

In connection with this defence, it is important to note s. 5 of the Defamation Act, 1952, which provides that in an action for libel and slander in respect of words containing two or more distinct charges against a plaintiff, a defence of justification shall not fail by reason only that the truth of every charge is not proved if the words not proved to be true do not materially injure the plaintiff's reputation having regard to the truth of the remaining charges.

In connection with justification it should be noted that under s. 8 of the Rehabilitation of Offenders Act, 1974 (see further p. 121) a plaintiff who proves that the defendant has maliciously published details of a spent conviction may recover damages. However, the section does not affect the defences of absolute or qualified privilege and fair comment. Thus an employer will, in the absence of malice, still be protected if he writes a reference which mentions a spent conviction. It was decided in *Herbage* v *Pressdram* [1984] 2 All E.R. 769 by the Court of Appeal that a rehabilitated offender who seeks an interlocutory injunction to prevent publication of his conviction is in the same position as a person against whom a defence of qualified privilege is raised. An injunction will only be granted if there is overwhelming evidence of malice in the publication or some irrelevant, spiteful or improper motive.

FAIR COMMENT ON A MATTER OF PUBLIC INTEREST

Here the defendant must show that the statement alleged to be defamatory is in fact legitimate comment. The defence is designed to cover criticism of matters of public interest in the form of comment upon true, or privileged, statements of fact, such comment being made honestly by a person who did not believe the statements to be untrue and who was not otherwise actuated by malice. The malice element makes the defence similar to that of qualified privilege (see p. 472). The statement must be comment, i.e. the speaker's opinion of a true state of affairs; it must not be an assertion of facts, but a comment on known facts.

ESSENTIAL CASE LAW AND COMMENT

London Artists v *Littler*, 1969 – A comment on the wrong facts **(439)**

Comment is the individual reaction to facts, and the court and the jury require to be satisfied only of the defendant's honesty. The test is: 'Would any honest man, however prejudiced he may be, however exaggerated or obstinate his views, have said that which this criticism has said of what is criticised?' If the answer is 'yes', the comment is fair for the purposes of raising this defence.

The matter upon which the comment is made must be one of legitimate public interest such as the conduct of Parliament, the government, local authorities and other public authorities, or the behaviour of a trade union whose actions affect supplies and services to the public. Further, a matter may become the subject of public interest because the plaintiff has voluntarily submitted himself and his affairs to public criticism. A person who makes a public speech, or publishes a book or presents a play thereby submits the subject matter of such thing for public comment, and cannot complain if the comment is adverse.

It should also be noted that the facts relied on to support a plea of fair comment must be facts existing at the time of the comment and not facts which have occurred some time before the comment was made (*Cohen* v *Daily Telegraph* [1968] 2 All E.R. 407).

It is important to distinguish fair comment from the defence of justification. In fair comment it is not necessary to prove the truth of the comment but merely that the opinion was honestly held; if justification is pleaded in regard to matters of opinion, the defendant must prove not merely that he honestly held the views expressed but that they were correct views. Thus, if we take the following statement – 'X's speech last night was inconsistent with his profession of Liberalism', in a plea of justification the defendant must prove that it was inconsistent, but in a plea of fair comment the defendant need only show that he honestly held this opinion of X's speech.

PRIVILEGE

This defence protects statements made in circumstances where the public interest in securing a free expression of facts or opinion outweighs the private interests of the person about whom the statements are made. Privilege may be absolute – such a statement is never actionable – or qualified, when privilege may be defeated by proof of the defendant's malice.

Absolute privilege

The Bill of Rights, 1689, protects statements in both Houses of Parliament. The Parliamentary Papers Act, 1840, affords a similar protection to reports, papers etc., published by order of either House, e.g. *Hansard* and Government White Papers. The Defamation Act, 1952, s. 9, protects verbatim broadcasts and newspaper reports of Parliamentary proceedings but Parliament itself can fine or imprison those who abuse this privilege. Members of the European Parliament also have immunity for statements made during sessions of the European Parliament *even if it is not actually sitting* (*Wybot* v *Faure, The Times*, 24 July 1986).

With regard to the courts, statements by the judge, members of the jury, counsel, and the parties or witnesses are absolutely privileged, as are Orders of Court. Thus an Order of Court for divorce, including a finding of adultery against a woman, is not actionable even though reversed on appeal. A statement made by a witness is not actionable even though the judge finds it untrue and malicious. The abuse of the above privilege is checked by (*a*) the law of perjury (in the case of untrue statements by witnesses), (*b*) the power of the judge to report improper behaviour on the part of counsel to the Benchers of his Inn, and (*c*) the judge's power to commit persons to prison for contempt of court.

Communications between senior and responsible public officers in the course of their duty are absolutely privileged.

Qualified privilege

Where such privilege exists, a person is entitled to communicate a defamatory statement so long as he does so honestly and reasonably with regard to the words used and the means of publication, and without malice. Qualified privilege has been held to arise in the following cases –

(*a*) Common interest, i.e. where a statement is made by a person who is under a legal or moral duty to communicate it to a person who has a similarly legitimate interest in receiving it. This covers testimonials or references to prospective employers, or to trade protection societies whose function it is to investigate the creditworthiness of persons who are the objects of their enquiry.

ESSENTIAL CASE LAW AND COMMENT

London Association for the Protection of Trade v *Greenlands*, 1916
– A bad report from a trade association **(440)**

(*b*) Statements in protection of one's private interests are privileged.

ESSENTIAL CASE LAW AND COMMENT

Osborn v *Thos Boulter*, 1930 – An allegation of watering the beer
(441)

(*c*) Statements by way of complaint to a proper authority, e.g. petitions to Parliament and complaints to officials of local authorities and professional bodies. It was decided in *Graff* v *Panel on Take-Overs and Mergers, Financial Times*, 11 October 1980 that the Panel had a moral duty to investigate alleged breaches of the Code and that it followed from this that if the Panel had learned of an alleged breach of the Code and had circularised copies of an article – which was the subject of this libel action – in order to establish or to demolish the allegations, the Panel was protected by the defence of qualified privilege.

ESSENTIAL CASE LAW AND COMMENT

Beach v *Freeson*, 1971 – An M.P.'s duty **(442)**

(*d*) Professional confidential communications between solicitor and client on legal advice.

(*e*) Newspaper reports on various public matters. The Defamation Act, 1952, s. 7, confers qualified privilege upon fair and accurate newspaper reports of various matters of public interest and importance. These are of two classes –

(i) Those which are privileged without any explanation or contradiction being issued, e.g. reports of public proceedings of colonial or dominion legislatures, reports of public proceedings of the United Nations Organisation, of the International Court of Justice, or of British courts martial, and fair and accurate copies of and extracts from British public registers and notices.

(ii) Those which are privileged only if the newspaper concerned is prepared, on the plaintiff's request, to publish a reasonable letter or statement in explanation or contradiction of the original report, e.g. semi-judicial findings of the governing bodies of learned societies, professional and trade associations, or authorities controlling games and sports. This also applies to fair and accurate reports of public meetings, meetings of local and public authorities, and the meetings of public companies.

(*f*) Fair and accurate reports of Parliamentary proceedings are the subject of qualified privilege whether contained in a newspaper or not.

ESSENTIAL CASE LAW AND COMMENT

Cook v *Alexander*, 1973 – Privilege and a parliamentary sketch
(443)

(*g*) Fair and accurate reports of public judicial proceedings are privileged. This does not protect reports of proceedings in domestic tribunals, e.g. The Law Society, unless the report is in a newspaper. Such reports will not be privileged if the court has forbidden publication, as is often done in cases affecting children, or if the matter reported is obscene or scandalous. It is also a criminal offence to report indecent matter relating to judicial proceedings. (Judicial Proceedings (Regulation of Reports) Act, 1926; Domestic and Appellate Proceedings (Restriction of Publicity) Act, 1968.)

Qualified privilege may be rebutted by proof of malice or some improper motive, and proof of actual spite or ill will in the publication will defeat it. An improper motive may be inferred from the tone of the statement or from the circumstances attending its publication, and malice may also be inferred from abuse of the privilege, such as the giving of excessive publicity to statements protected by qualified privilege. However, the gross and unreasoning prejudice of the defendant will not defeat the defence of privilege if the defendant honestly believed that what he published was true. But where a person without malice joins with a malicious person in publishing a libel in circumstances of qualified privilege, the person without malice is not liable to the person defamed.

ESSENTIAL CASE LAW AND COMMENT

Horrocks v *Low*, 1972 – Malice cannot be inferred **(444)**
Egger v *Viscount Chelmsford*, 1964 – A judge of Alsatian dogs
  (445)

Where there is a pressing obligation to communicate defamatory matter, a person may communicate it, although he does not believe it to be true, and still claim qualified privilege. Thus an accountant who, on going through the books of a firm, finds evidence that the cashier has embezzled money, may communicate that view to authority and still claim qualified privilege, even though the accountant does not believe that the cashier has, in fact, embezzled the money.

OFFER OF AMENDS

The Defamation Act, 1952 provides that the publisher of 'innocent defamation' may make an offer of amends as defined in the Act (s. 4.). the words shall be treated as published innocently if the words were not defamatory on the face of them, and if the publisher did not know of circumstances by virtue of which they might be understood to be defamatory of the plaintiff, and if reasonable care was exercised in relation to the publication. Given that the above circumstances exist the defendant can apparently make an offer of amends, supported by an affidavit setting out the facts relied on to show that his publication was innocent.

An offer of amends requires the publication of a suitable apology to the party aggrieved and a suitable correction. The offeror must also take steps to notify persons to whom copies have been distributed that the words used are alleged to be defamatory of the party aggrieved. The High Court decides how the offer shall be carried into effect unless the parties have agreed on the matter.

It is a defence in any proceedings for defamation that the defendant's offer (*a*) has been accepted and performed, or (*b*) that it has been refused, after having been made as soon as practicable after the defendant received notice that the words were or might be defamatory of the plaintiff, and that the offer has not been withdrawn.

If the plaintiff rejects the offer because he does not think the publication was innocent, or because the section of the Act has not been complied with, and fails to establish this at the trial, there seems no way of later enforcing the offer of amends.

Consent of the plaintiff to publication

If the plaintiff has agreed to publication, he cannot subsequently sue in respect of that statement. Consent may be given in respect of a particular publication or it may be general.

ESSENTIAL CASE LAW AND COMMENT

Chapman v *Lord Ellesmere*, 1932 – Where the plaintiff is a volunteer **(446)**

THEATRES ACT, 1968

Section 4 of the Theatres Act, 1968 amends the law of defamation (including the law relating to criminal libel) by providing that the publication of words (including pictures, visual images, gestures, and the like) in the public performance of a play shall be treated as publication in permanent form, i.e. libel. Performances given on a domestic occasion in a private dwelling house are exempt (s. 7(1)) and so are rehearsals and performances for broadcast or recording purposes (s. 7(2)) provided such rehearsals and performances are attended only by the persons *directly* connected with the giving of them.

Section 5 of the Act creates an offence of incitement to racial hatred by presenting or directing the public performance of a play though, again, rehearsals and performances attended only by persons directly concerned are exempt. Prosecution under s. 5 is with the consent of the Atorney-General (s. 8).

It is of interest to note also that s. 1 of the Act abolishes the power of the Lord Chamberlain to censor plays.

DAMAGES

Although many slanders are actionable only on proof of special damage to the plaintiff, actual damages awarded by the court will not be confined to the special damage so proved. For example, if as a result of defamation a person loses his or her employment, he or she can prove special damage in this connection, but the actual damages awarded may take in much more than this particular loss. Damages for defamation tend to be high. Juries are often used in such cases, and they are concerned with the *quantum* of damages. The damages awarded for loss of reputation may often be higher than damages awarded for the loss of life. However, damages should be compensatory and not punitive though they may be *aggravated* by mental suffering arising from the defamation, or *mitigated* by a full apology, provocation by the plaintiff, or the plaintiff's bad reputation.

ESSENTIAL CASE LAW AND COMMENT

Davis v *Rubin*, 1967 – Where libel damages are excessive **(447)**

INJUNCTIONS

Apart from damages a defamed person may seek an injunction restraining further publication. Such injunctions are of two kinds –

(*a*) *A perpetual injunction*, which is usually granted at the trial; and

(*b*) *an interim injunction* (or interlocutory injunction), which is granted pending the trial, and may be *quia timet*, that is before the wrong is actually done.

However, publication of an article will not be restrained merely because it is defamatory where the defendant says he intends to justify it or make fair comment on a matter of public interest, or claim privilege and the plaintiff cannot show that the defence(s) concerned will be likely to fail (*Harakas* v *Baltic Mercantile and Shipping Exchange Ltd* [1982] 2 All E.R. 701).

Before concluding the tort of defamation we should notice also the separate tort of *injurious falsehood*. Just as defamation is an attack on a person's reputation, so injurious falsehood is an attack on his or her goods. To say that A's goods are inferior in quality to B's may be an injurious falsehood. To say that A sells inferior goods as goods of superior quality may, on the other hand, be a defamatory statement.

TIME LIMITS FOR CLAIMS

Under s. 57 of the Administration of Justice Act, 1985 (amending the Limitation Act, 1980), the period for bringing claims for libel and slander is reduced from six years to three years from the cause of action, with the ability to apply to the court to sue out of time for one year after becoming aware of the facts, if these were not known within the three-year period.

The rule in *Rylands* v *Fletcher*

This celebrated rule was stated in the case of *Rylands* v *Fletcher*, 1868 –

Where a person for his own purposes brings and keeps on land in his occupation anything likely to do mischief if it escapes, he must keep it in at his peril, and if he fails to do so he is liable for all damage naturally accruing from the escape.

The rule has been held to apply whether the things brought on the land be 'beasts, water, filth or stenches'. The rule also applies to fire. It does not apply to the pollution of beaches by oil because, *inter alia*, the oil does not escape from *land* but from the sea (see *Southport Corporation* v *Esso Petroleum Co.*, 1954 at p. 766).

ESSENTIAL CASE LAW AND COMMENT

Emanuel v *Greater London Council*, 1970 – An escape of fire **(448)**

The duty is an absolute one and does not depend on negligence provided the use of the land is not natural use (see *British Celanese* v *Hunt*, 1969 at p. 775). In the case which gave rise to the rule, the defendant had constructed a reservoir on his land, employing competent workmen for the purpose. Water escaped from the reservoir and percolated through certain old mine shafts, which had been filled with marl and earth, and eventually flooded the plaintiff's mine. The defendant was held liable in that he had collected water on his land, the water not being naturally there, and it had escaped and done damage. Since the defendant employed competent workmen, it follows that the liability is absolute and does not depend on negligence, and in any case the defendant's action was quite innocent as there was no reason why he should know of, or even suspect the existence of, the disused shafts.

In order for the rule to apply, there must be an escape of the thing which inflicts the injury from a place over which the defendant has occupation or control to a place which is outside his occupation or control. It is doubtful to what extent the rule covers personal injury.

ESSENTIAL CASE LAW AND COMMENT

Read v *Lyons*, 1947 – There must be an escape **(449)**

The rule is not confined to wrongs between owners of adjacent land and does not depend on ownership of land but the plaintiff must have some interest in the land (see *Weller* v *Foot and Mouth Disease Research Institute*, 1965 at p. 781). Neither is it confined to the escape of water, but may cover the escape of any offensive or dangerous matter arising out of abnormal use of land provided the defendant has control of it.

ESSENTIAL CASE LAW AND COMMENT

Charing Cross Electricity Supply Co v *Hydraulic Power Co*, 1914 –
   No need for ownership of land **(450)**
Attorney-General v *Corke*, 1933 – An abnormal use of land **(451)**

In general there is no liability under the rule for damage caused by the escape of things naturally on the land, though there may be an action in nuisance or in negligence.

ESSENTIAL CASE LAW AND COMMENT

Giles v *Walker*, 1890 – Escaping thistles **(452)**
Davey v *Harrow Corporation*, 1957 – Escaping tree roots **(453)**

Although *Rylands* v *Fletcher* imposes strict liability, the following defences are still open to the defendant –

(*a*) That the escape was the plaintiff's fault. It should also be noted that there is no reason why the Law Reform (Contributory Negligence) Act, 1945, should not apply where the plaintiff is partly to blame.

(*b*) That it was an Act of God (see *Nichols* v *Marsland*, 1876 at p. 749), though the defence is not often successfully pleaded.

ESSENTIAL CASE LAW AND COMMENT

Greenock Corporation v *Caledonian Railway Co*, 1917 – The
defence of Act of God fails **(454)**

(*c*) That the escape was due to the wrongful act of a stranger.

ESSENTIAL CASE LAW AND COMMENT

Rickards v *Lothian*, 1913 – An act of a stranger **(455)**

(*d*) That the damage was caused by artificial works done for the common benefit of the plaintiff and the defendant.

ESSENTIAL CASE LAW AND COMMENT

Peters v *Prince of Wales Theatre (Birmingham) Ltd*, 1943 –
Property installed for common benefit **(456)**

(*e*) That there was statutory authority for the act of the defendant, provided that the defendant was not negligent. It should be noted that the defence of statutory authority is not available in respect of reservoirs. (Reservoirs Act, 1975, s. 28 and Sch. 2.)

THE RULE IS LIBERALISED

In more recent times the rule has been liberalised. In *Cambridge Water Co v Eastern Counties Leather plc*, *The Times*, 23 October 1991, the High Court held that the storage of organochlorines by firms involved in the tanning industry and based at Sawston, an industrial village, was a natural use of land for the purposes of the rule in *Rylands* v *Fletcher*. Sawston was properly described as an industrial village, said Mr Justice Ian Kennedy, and the creation of employment was clearly for the benefit of that community. Storage in that place was therefore natural use of land. He rejected a claim from the water company in regard to the pollution of a nearby public water supply borehole.

22
The law of property

English law divides property into real property and personal property. Real property includes only freehold interests in land, and personal property comprises all other proprietary rights, whether in land or chattels. This classification is not identical with the obvious distinction between immoveables and moveables, and this is the result of the attitude of early law to the nature of a lease.

The nature of property

Actions in respect of property fall into two kinds: actions *in rem* or real actions, and actions *in personam* or personal actions. An action *in rem* in English law is an action in which a specific thing is recovered; an action *in personam* gives damages only.

It so happened that in early days the courts would allow a real action or *actio realis* only for the specific recovery of land. If an owner was dispossessed of other forms of property, the person who had taken the property had a choice; he could either restore the property taken or pay damages to the rightful owner. Hence land became known as real property or *realty*, and all other forms of property were called personal property or *personalty*. So far the distinction corresponds to that between moveables and immoveables, but this convenient classification was disturbed by the lease for a term of years.

Although a lease of land was an interest in immoveable property, the real action was not available to the dispossessed tenant. Leases did not fit into the feudal system of landholding by tenure but were regarded as personal business arrangements whereby one man allowed another the use of the land for a period in return for a rent.

These transactions were personal contracts and created rights *in personam* between the parties, and not rights *in rem* which could affect feudal status. It was not an uncommon form of investment to buy land and let it out on lease to obtain an income on capital invested, and such transactions were more akin to commercial dealings than to landholding as it was understood in early days. Moreover the system had its advantages, since a lease was immune from feudal burdens and could be bequeathed by will at a time when dispositions by will of other land were still not permitted.

Leaseholds, therefore, come under the heading of personal property or chattels, but because they partake so strongly of the character of land, they are often referred to as *chattels real* to distinguish them from pure personalty, e.g. a watch or a fountain pen. Since the property legislation of 1925 this distinction has lost much of its importance, but it is still true that if in his will a testator says, 'All my personalty to P and all my realty to R', P would get the leaseholds.

Pure personalty itself comprises two different kinds of property known as *choses in possession* and *choses in action*. Choses in possession denote chattels, such as jewellery and furniture, which are tangible objects and can be physically possessed and enjoyed by their owner. Choses in action are intangible forms of property which are incapable of physical possession, and their owner is usually compelled to bring an action if he wishes to enforce his rights over property of this kind. Examples of choses in action are debts, patents, copyrights, trade marks, shares, and negotiable instruments.

Up to now we have been considering the main rights which one has in one's own things. However, it is possible to have rights over the things of another. We have already mentioned the lease, which is the right to possess another's land for a term in return for a rent, but in addition it is possible to become the owner of a *servitude* over the land of another, e.g. a right of way, a right of light, or a right to the support of buildings. A servitude may also be a right to take something from the land of another, e.g. the right to fish or collect firewood. Rights of the first class are called *easements*, and of the second *profits à prendre*. Further, a person may raise a loan on the security of his property either real or personal, and the lender has certain rights over the property so used as a security if the loan is not repaid.

Ownership

Ownership is a term used to express the relationship which exists between a person and certain rights which are vested in him. Ownership is the greatest right or collection of rights – the ultimate right – which a person can have over or in a thing.

For example, X may own a fee simple in Blackacre and may lease the land to Y, so giving up possession. But however long the lease, the ultimate right of ownership is in X, and eventually the right to possess, which he has for the moment forfeited, will return to him or to his estate if he is dead. Z may have a right of way over Blackacre. This is not ownership of Blackacre, but is ownership of a right over it which limits X's enjoyment of the land. B may have lent money to X on the security of the land, so that B is a mortgagee and, therefore, the owner of a right in Blackacre, but this does not constitute ownership of the land; it is a mere encumbrance attached to it, limiting X's enjoyment to the extent of the rights given to B as mortgagee. Nevertheless the supreme right is vested in X, and this right is called ownership of Blackacre.

Ownership is a *de jure* relationship; there is no need to possess the thing. Possession tends to be *de facto*, i.e. evidenced by physical possession, although, as we shall see, physical possession is not necessary in order to have legal possession.

It may be said that in a general sense all rights are capable of ownership, which is of many kinds –

(*a*) *Corporeal*. That is, the ownership of a thing or chose in possession such as a watch or a fountain pen.

(*b*) *Incorporeal*. That is, the ownership of a right only, e.g. the right to recover a debt of £20 from X by an action at law, or the ownership of a chose in action. A share certificate is a chose in action, and ownership of it is incorporeal, for it is ownership of certain rights: the right to dividends as and when declared, the right to vote at meetings, and so on.

(*c*) *Sole ownership*. That is, as where X is the sole owner of Blackacre.

(*d*) *Co-ownership*. That is, as where X and Y are simultaneously owners of Blackacre, as joint tenants or tenants in common. (See further p. 494.)

(*e*) *Legal or equitable ownership*. A grant giving X the fee simple absolute in possession of Blackacre constitutes him the legal owner. But a grant giving X a life interest only constitutes him as equitable owner, whose interest can exist only behind a trust, the legal estate being vested in trustees.

(*f*) *Trust or beneficial ownership*. In the grant set out above giving X a life interest, the trustees hold the legal estate but not beneficially; the beneficial interest is in X and Equity will protect it.

(*g*) *Vested or contingent ownership*. In a grant to X for life with remainder to Y, X and Y have equitable interests and both are vested. Admittedly Y will not become entitled in enjoyment until X dies, but his interest is, nevertheless, vested, and if Y were to die before X the property would descend through Y's estate on X's death.

In a grant to X for life, with remainder to Y if he attains the age of eighteen years, X's interest is equitable and vested, Y's interest is equitable and contingent since he must satisfy the requirement of majority before his interest vests.

Possession

The physical control of a thing by a person is what is normally known as possession, and if the idea of possession had remained wedded to physical control, the position would have been simple enough. But the widening sphere of legal activity made it necessary to attribute to persons who were not actually in physical control some or all of the advantages enjoyed by persons who were.

There are three possible situations at law –

(*a*) A person can have physical control without legal possession, as in the case of a porter carrying a traveller's suitcase in a station.

(*b*) A person can have possession and its advantages without actual physical control, e.g. a person may have books at home which are still in his possession even when he is away on holiday.

(*c*) A person can have both physical control and possession, e.g. a watch in his pocket or a pen in his hand.

Possession, therefore, has acquired a technical legal meaning, and the separation of possession from physical control has given the concept a high degree of flexibility.

The old theory of possession, derived from the Roman Law, relies upon (*a*) *corpus*, i.e. physical control, and (*b*) *animus*, i.e. the intention to exclude others. But although these concepts help in deciding possession, they do not provide the complete answer. In fact English law has never worked out a completely logical and exhaustive definition of possession. The handing over of a key may be sufficient by itself to pass the possession of the contents of a room or box if it provides the effective means of control over the goods.

WRONGFUL INTERFERENCE

In the law of torts, wrongful interference to property is an invasion of possession. The policy of this branch of the law is to compensate the party whose interests have been affected, and in order to enable such persons to recover, the court has contrived to attribute possession to them.

A *bailee* is a person who gets possession of a chattel from another with his consent. A bailment may be at will, i.e. revocable by the bailor at any time, or it may be for a term, i.e. for a fixed period of time, as by hiring a television set for six months. Where a bailment is at will, the bailee, who by definition has possession, can sue a third party for wrongful interference. Since the bailment is revocable at will, the bailor also has an interest worth protecting, and in order that he too may bring an action for wrongful interference, his right to possess is treated as possession itself. Where, on the other hand, the bailment is for a term, only the bailee can bring an action for wrongful interference and not the bailor, although, where the bailee brings the action, he will have to account to the bailor for any damages obtained. If a third person destroys or permanently injures the chattel while it is in the bailee's possession, the bailor may have an action against the third party for injury to his reversionary interest. (*Mears* v *L.S.W. Railway* [1862] 11 C.B. (N.S.) 850.)

Where an employer has temporarily handed a thing to his employee, possession remains with the employer and the employee takes only custody. Thus an employer can sue for wrongful interference for an injury to the goods by a third party.

A person who loses a thing retains his ownership in it, and for the purpose of suing for wrongful interference someone who has taken it, his right to regain possession will suffice. But for the purpose of claiming from an insurance company for loss, he will be regarded as having lost possession, within the terms of the contract, if the thing cannot in fact be found.

Trespass to land by relation is another example of the artificial manipulation of the concept of possession to provide a remedy in trespass to one who needs to be compensated. When a person, with a right to possess, enters in pursuance of that right, he is deemed to have been in possession from the time when his right originally accrued, e.g. from the time when he made the original contract for a purchase or a lease. He can, therefore, sue for any trespass that has been committed between the accrual of the right and the actual entry.

As we have seen, difficulties have arisen over the requirement of the intention to exclude others as a necessary ingredient of possession where property of one sort or another has been found on the land of a person who was not its owner. (See *Parker* v *British Airways Board*, 1982 at p. 769 and *South Staffordshire Water Co.* v *Sharman*, 1896 at p. 770 and the cases noted with it.)

However, it should be noted that *unless an owner* of chattels can be shown to have *abandoned* or *sold* them he remains their owner and has a better title than a finder or a person on whose property they are found.

ESSENTIAL CASE LAW AND COMMENT

Moffat v *Kazana*, 1968 – The rights of an owner **(457)**

ADVERSE POSSESSION

A person may sometimes acquire the ownership of land by adverse possession. This arises from the occupation and use of land without the permission of, or any interference from, the true owner, as where a stranger encloses and cultivates a portion of a neighbour's land or occupies another's house. Under s. 15 of the Limitation Act, 1980 adverse possession for a period of twelve years will give the possessor a title, but such adverse possession must take the form of overt acts which are inconsistent with the title of the owner, and in this case possession is viewed much more strictly than in the others we have been considering above.

ESSENTIAL CASE LAW AND COMMENT

Hayward v *Challoner*, 1967 – The period required **(458)**
Littledale v *Liverpool College*, 1900 – Acts must be inconsistent
  with owner's rights **(459)**

Whether adverse possession necessarily involves inconvenience to the true owner is not clear. In *Wallis's Caton Bay Holiday Camp* v *Shell-Mex & B.P.* [1974] 3 All E.R. 575, the defendants had purchased land for development, though they had no immediate use for it. The plaintiffs used it for twelve years for the purposes of grazing cattle on it and cultivating it. The Court of Appeal held that the plaintiffs had not established a good possessory title because what they had done was of no inconvenience to the defendants who had no immediate use for the land. However, in *Treloar* v *Nute* [1977] 1 All E.R. 230, the plaintiff owned freehold land for which he had no immediate use and which was left derelict. The defendants bought land adjacent and occupied part of the derelict land for a period of twelve years. In holding that the defendants had a good possessory title to that land the Court of Appeal said it was not necessary to import into the definition of adverse possession a requirement that the owner must be inconvenienced or affected by that possession.

This line of reasoning was adopted also in *Buckinghamshire County Council* v *Moran* [1989] 2 All E.R. 225 where the council had acquired a plot of land adjacent to some houses for future use as a road diversion. They had no immediate use for it. Mr Moran (and previous owners) treated it as part of the garden of the Moran residence. It was fenced in and the grass was cut regularly and bulbs planted. This went on for more than twelve years and the Court of Appeal eventually held that Mr Moran had a possesory title to the plot although the council having no immediate use for the plot were not inconvenienced by what had been done.

Where a tenant, during the currency of his tenancy, takes possession of other land belonging to the landlord, the land is presumed to have been taken as part of the holding comprised in the tenancy, and the tenant cannot acquire a good possessory title unless he communicates to his landlord some disclaimer of the landlord's title. Before leaving the topic it should be noted that there are a few limited exceptions where the twelve-year period is increased, e.g to 30 years in the case of acquisition of title by the Crown (s. 15(1), Limitation Act, 1980).

ESSENTIAL CASE LAW AND COMMENT

Smirk v *Lyndale Developments Ltd*, 1974 – Taking possession of a landlord's land **(460)**

Bailment

Bailments are concerned with pure personalty and not with real property. The bailment may or may not originate in a contract.

POSSESSION

An essential feature of a bailment is the transfer of possession to the bailee. There is no precise definition of possession, but the basic features are *control* and *an intention to exclude others*. However, a person can have possession of chattels which he does not know exist (see *South Staffordshire Water Co. v Sharman*, 1896 at p. 770). An employee who receives goods from his employer to take to a third party has mere *custody*; possession remains with the employer and the employee is not a bailee. If a third party hands goods to an employee for his employer the employee obtains possession and is the bailee.

In a bailment for a fixed term the bailee has possession to the exclusion of the bailor, and is, therefore, the only person who can sue a third party for wrongful interference. In a bailment at will, i.e. one which the bailor can terminate at will, the bailor retains either possession or an immediate right to possess and an action for wrongful interference is available to him as well as to the bailee (see also p. 483). A bailee can sue a third party in tort for loss of or damage to the goods even though the bailee is not liable to the bailor for the loss or damage.

ESSENTIAL CASE LAW AND COMMENT

The Winkfield, 1902 – Recovery of damages, bailee in possession
(461)

BAILMENT AND LICENCE

The problem of distinguishing between bailment and licence has arisen mainly in connection with the parking of vehicles. If a vehicle is parked on land, either gratuitously or even on payment of a charge, the transaction may amount to a mere licence and not a bailment which gives rise to duties of care.

ESSENTIAL CASE LAW AND COMMENT

Ashby v Tolhurst, 1937 – Is it a bailment or a licence? **(462)**
Ultzen v Nichols, 1894 – A stolen coat **(463)**
Deyong v Shenburn, 1946 – An actor's clothes **(464)**

FINDERS AND INVOLUNTARY RECIPIENTS

For an act to constitute a bailment, the person who is given possession of goods must be entrusted with them for a particular purpose, e.g. to use and return as in the case of loan or hire, or to take from one place to another as in carriage. A banker is not a bailee of money paid into a customer's account, for his obligation is to return an equivalent sum and not the identical notes and coins. However, a banker is a bailee of property deposited with him for safe custody.

A finder is not a true bailee because he is not entrusted with the goods for a particular purpose. However, if he takes them into his possession he will be liable for loss or damage resulting from his negligence.

ESSENTIAL CASE LAW AND COMMENT

Newman v Bourne & Hollingsworth, 1915 – A finder and bailment
(465)

A person cannot be made a bailee against his will. Where the receipt of the goods is involuntary it is unlikely that the recipient is under any higher duty than to refrain from intentional damage. However, he must not convert the goods, but although liability for conversion is usually strict, an involuntary recipient will only be liable if he acts intentionally or negligently.

ESSENTIAL CASE LAW AND COMMENT

Neuwirth v Over Darwen Industrial Co-operative Society, 1894 –
An involuntary bailee **(466)**

The Unsolicited Goods and Services Acts, 1971 and 1975 are relevant in this connection. The Acts are designed to deal with selling techniques involving the sending of unsolicited goods, thus rendering the recipient an involuntary bailee. The Acts provide for fines to be made on persons making demands for payment for goods they know to be unsolicited. If the demand is accompanied by threats a higher scale of fines applies. Furthermore, unsolicited goods may be kept by the recipient without payment *after a period of thirty days* provided the recipient gives notice to the sender asking that they be collected, or *after six months* even if no notice has been given.

OBLIGATIONS OF THE BAILOR

Where the bailment is gratuitous it has been said that the limit of the liability of the bailor is to communicate to the bailee defects in the article lent *of which he is aware*. However, the principle in *Donoghue v Stevenson*, 1932, see p. 725, may apply to gratuitous bailments so that the bailor would be liable if he had not taken reasonable care to ensure that the goods bailed were not dangerous, even though he had no actual knowledge of a defect in the chattels lent.

When the bailment is for reward there is an implied warranty on the part of the bailor that he has a title to the goods so that the bailee's possession will not be disturbed, and that the goods are fit and suitable for the bailee's purpose. This does not mean that the bailee is liable for all defects but only for those which skill and care can guard against. However, the warranty as to fitness and suitability does not apply where the defect is apparent to the bailee and he does not rely on the skill or judgment of the bailor.

ESSENTIAL CASE LAW AND COMMENT

Hyman v *Nye*, 1881 – Obligations of a bailor **(467)**
Reed v *Dean*, 1949 – A fire on a motor launch **(468)**

OBLIGATIONS OF THE BAILEE

When Lord Holt, in *Coggs* v *Bernard* 1703 (see p. 610), established the liability of the bailee in negligence he laid down different duties of care for different kinds of bailments. Thus, in a bailment for the sole benefit of the bailee, such as a gratuitous loan, the bailee's duty of care was much higher than in a bailment for the benefit of both parties such as a hiring. However, in more recent times there has been disapproval of Lord Holt's different standards of care, and it is now the better view that the standard of care required of a bailee is to take reasonable care in all the circumstances of the case, which equates his duty with that owed by any person in the law relating to negligence, though the burden of disproving negligence is on the bailee.

ESSENTIAL CASE LAW AND COMMENT

Houghland v *R. Low (Luxury Coaches) Ltd*, 1962 – Obligations of a bailee **(469)**
Global Dress Co v *W.H. Boase & Co*, 1966 – Goods stolen from the docks **(470)**

The *main* circumstances which the court is likely to consider when deciding the question of negligence in a bailee are as follows.

The type of bailment

Although some current legal opinion is against a legal distinction between bailment for reward and gratuitous bailment, reward or lack of reward will continue to be an *important circumstance* in the matter of the bailee's negligence. A gratuitous bailee must take the same care of the property bailed as a reasonable man would take of his own property. It is no defence for a bailee to show that he kept the goods with as much care as his own because the test of reasonableness is objective. In a bailment for reward the duty of care tends to be somewhat higher.

ESSENTIAL CASE LAW AND COMMENT

Doorman v *Jenkins*, 1843 – Negligence leading to theft **(471)**
Brabant v *King*, 1895 – Damage to explosives **(472)**

The expertise of the bailee

If the bailee's profession or situation implies a certain expertise he will be liable if he fails to show it.

ESSENTIAL CASE LAW AND COMMENT

Wilson v *Brett*, 1843 – When expertise is required **(473)**

The property bailed

If the goods bailed are, to the knowledge of the bailee, fragile or valuable, a high standard of care will be expected. In addition a bailee may be liable in negligence if he does not give notice to the bailor of a loss or try to recover lost or stolen property.

ESSENTIAL CASE LAW AND COMMENT

Saunders (Mayfair) Furs v *Davies*, 1965 – Valuable goods: the care required **(474)**
Coldman v *Hill*, 1919 – Giving notice of loss **(475)**

A bailee is vicariously liable for the torts of his servants, but a servant who becomes a thief may not be regarded as acting within the scope of his employment. However, in *Morris* v *C. W. Martin & Sons Ltd*, 1965, it was held that a bailee for reward cannot necessarily escape liability for loss of goods stolen by his servant because theft is not necessarily beyond the scope of employment (see further p. 737). The decision in *Morris* represents the better view.

A bailee may attempt to exclude his liability by an exemption clause in the contract of bailment. This matter must now be considered in the light of the rules of construction of contracts and the Unfair Contract Terms Act, 1977 (see pp. 291–302).

DELEGATION BY BAILEE

Whether a bailee can delegate performance of the contract to another depends upon the nature of the bailment and the particular contract which may authorise delegation. Contracts involving the carriage, storage, repair or cleaning of goods often assume personal performance by the bailee. Where there is a delegation, even though unknown to the bailor, the delegate is a bailee and owes a duty of care directly to the bailor.

ESSENTIAL CASE LAW AND COMMENT

Davies v *Collins*, 1945 – Delegation by a bailee **(476)**
Edwards v *Newland*, 1950 – Where a bailee sub-contracts **(477)**
Learoyd Bros v *Pope*, 1966 – Duty of care following delegation
   (478)

ESTOPPEL AND INTERPLEADER

A bailee is estopped at common law from denying the title of his bailor and if the bailor demands the return of the goods it is no defence for the bailee to plead that the bailor is not the owner. However, a bailee may defend an action for non-delivery of the goods –

(*a*) by showing that he has delivered them under an authorisation by the bailor;

(*b*) by showing that he has not got the goods because he has been dispossessed by a person with a better title, as in a bailment of stolen goods which are reclaimed by the owner;

(*c*) if he still retains possession he may allege that a third party has a better title but he must defend the action on behalf of, and with the authority of, the true owner.

ESSENTIAL CASE LAW AND COMMENT

Rogers, Sons & Co v *Lambert & Co*, 1891 – Defence of superior
   title **(479)**

Where adverse claims are made against the bailee by the bailor and a third party, the bailee should take interpleader proceedings under the Rules of the Supreme Court. The effect of this will be to bring the bailor and the third party together in an action which will decide the validity of their claims. The bailee can then hand over the goods to whichever party has established his claims and will not risk liability for wrongful interference.

LIEN

A bailee may, in certain circumstances, have a lien on the goods. The general nature of a lien is described on p. 521.

Land law

Since the Norman Conquest absolute ownership of land has been impossible. William the Conqueror considered himself owner of all land in England and parcelled it out to his barons who became his tenants. In return for this 'honour' the barons had to render to the Crown certain services, of either a military or other public nature, but an exception was made in the case of land held by the Church. The ecclesiastics were not able to provide military services, and special spiritual tenures were introduced.

In order to assist themselves in supplying the services required by the King, the barons began to subgrant part of the land, and a series of tenures sprang up, all persons holding as tenants of the Crown in the last analysis.

It is outside our scope to pursue the rise and fall of the system of tenures, but all land is now held on a single tenure called 'common socage', and all obligations to the Crown have disappeared, except for certain ceremonials preserved because of their antiquity. Even today, however, a person does not own land; he holds an estate in land. The *tenure* answers the question 'How is the land held?' The term *estate* answers the question 'For how long is the land held?'

THE LEGISLATION OF 1925

Before this legislation, which is described below, there were many different ways of holding land, referred to as estates in land. The existence of so many estates in land made the transfer of land most complicated. There might be a large number of legal owners of the same piece of land, and before the land could be conveyed to a purchaser all the interests had to be got in. Other problems arose on intestacy, because the rules for intestate succession were not the same for realty and personalty. In 1925 a thorough reform of land law was undertaken and was eventually achieved by the following statutes: the Law of Property Act, 1925; the Settled Land Act, 1925; the Administration of Estates Act, 1925; the Land Charges Act, 1925; and the Land Registration Act, 1925.

LEGAL ESTATES

The Law of Property Act, 1925 reduced the number of legal estates which can exist over land to two, and the number of legal interests or charges in or over land to five. All other estates, interests and charges in or over land take effect as equitable interests, and can exist only behind a trust, the trustees having the legal fee simple estate.

The difference between a legal estate and a legal interest is that the owner of the legal estate is entitled to the enjoyment of the whole of the property, either in possession or receiving rents, whereas the owner of a legal interest has a limited right in or over the land of another.

The two legal estates possible today are –

(*a*) A *fee simple absolute in possession*; and
(*b*) A *term of years absolute*.

The word *fee* implies that the estate is an estate of inheritance, and the word *simple* shows that the fee is capable of descending to the general class of heirs, and is not restricted to heirs of a particular class. The word *absolute* distinguishes a fee simple which will continue for ever, from a fee which may be determinable. The fee simple must be *in possession*, although this does not imply only physical possession but also the right to receive rents and profits. Even if a landlord has granted a lease he may still have a fee simple in possession because he is entitled to the rent reserved by the lease.

The *term of years absolute* is what is normally understood by a lease. But a term of years includes a term for less than a year, or for a year or years and a fraction of a year, or even a tenancy from year to year. The essential characteristic is that a term of years has a minimum period of certain duration. It seems, therefore, that a lease for life is no longer a legal estate; nor is a tenancy at will or sufference since there is no certainty as to the period of their continuance. A term of years may be absolute notwithstanding that it may be determined by notice, re-entry, or operation of law or other event.

LEGAL INTERESTS AND CHARGES

We have seen that there are, since the 1925 Act, only two possible legal estates: a fee simple absolute in possession and a term of years absolute, but the Law of Property Act, 1925, also lays down a number of legal interests in land. The most important are –

(*a*) An easement, right or privilege for an interest equivalent to either of the above estates. Thus an easement for life would not be a legal interest. (See further p. 500.)
(*b*) A charge by way of legal mortgage.

Equitable interests

All estates, interests or charges over land except those outlined above take effect as equitable interests only and must exist behind a trust. Life interests, for example, are equitable.

The two major trust arrangements over land are called settled land and trusts for sale.

SETTLED LAND

Settlements created after 1925 other than by will require, under the Settled

Land Act, 1925, two deeds to be executed – the vesting deed and the trust instrument. The vesting deed must contain a description of the settled land, a statement that the settled land is vested in the tenant for life upon the trusts for the time being affecting the settled land, the names of the trustees of the settlement, and a statement of any larger powers granted to the tenant for life in addition to his statutory powers.

The trust instrument must contain the appointment of the trustees, the names of the persons entitled to appoint new trustees, a statement of any additional powers conferred by the settlement in extension of the statutory powers, and the trusts of the settlement. Where a settlement is created by will, the will is regarded as the trust instrument, and the personal representatives must execute a vesting instrument, vesting the legal estate in the tenant for life. Thus a purchaser of settled land is only concerned with the vesting deed or assent, since it is from such documents that he derives his title. The trusts can remain secret since the trust instrument need not be produced on sale.

Under the settlement the person obtaining the benefit from the estate is usually an adult with a life interest and he is called the *tenant for life*. It is his function to manage the estate and he has power to sell or exchange the settled land or any part of it with an adjustment of any difference in value in the case of exchange. He may grant leases subject to certain restrictions, but in the absence of a contrary provision in the settlement, he has no power to mortgage or charge the legal estate for his own benefit, although he can mortgage or assign his own beneficial life interest.

He has other powers which he can only exercise with the consent of the settlement trustees or the court, e.g. the power to sell or otherwise dispose of the principal mansion house, the power to cut and sell timber, the power to compromise claims and sell settled chattels. He has the power to make improvements at his own expense, or the cost may be borne by the capital money if he complies with the provisions of the Act. He has also power to select investments for capital money.

The tenant for life is in a strong position, for he is subject to no control in the exercise of his powers except that he must give notice to the trustees of his intention to exercise the most important ones, he must obtain the consent of the trustees or leave of the court in certain cases, and he is in fact himself a trustee for the other beneficiaries. There may be joint tenants for life under a setlement and, where this is so, they must usually agree as to the exercise of their joint powers. The court will exercise a power, e.g. by ordering a sale of property, but only if the joint tenant who does not agree to sell is acting in bad faith (*Barker* v *Addiscott* [1969] 3 All E.R. 685).

It is clear that under a settlement a proper balance must be preserved between the tenant for life and the persons who will be entitled to the land or the proceeds of the land after his death. He is not allowed, therefore, to run down the estate during his lifetime in order to increase his own income, but is only allowed to take from the land the current income and must pass on the estate substantially unimpaired.

TRUSTS FOR SALE

A trust for sale is an immediate binding trust for sale whether or not exercisable at the request or with the consent of any person, and with or without a power at discretion to postpone the sale. Such a trust for sale may be either express or by operation of law. Trusts for sale are governed by the Law of Property Act, 1925, and not by the Settled Land Act, 1925.

An express trust for sale is almost always created by two documents – a conveyance to trustees on trust for sale and a trust instrument. But even where a trust for sale is embodied in a single document, a purchaser of the legal estate is not concerned with the trusts affecting the rents and profits of the land until sale, or with the proceeds of the sale, provided he obtains a receipt for the purchase money signed by at least two trustees or a trust corporation.

There are cases where a trust for sale is imposed by statute. These are –

(*a*) where a person dies intestate,

(*b*) where two or more persons are entitled to land as joint tenants or tenants in common,

(*c*) where trustees lend money on mortgage and the property becomes vested in them free from the right of redemption. (See further p. 510.)

Co-ownership

Two persons may own land simultaneously. In such a case they are either joint tenants or tenants in common. Where they are joint tenants there is no question of a share of the property – each is the owner of the whole. Where there is a tenancy in common, each is regarded as owning an individual share in the property, but that share has not positively been marked out. Tenants in common hold property in undivided shares.

A joint tenancy arises where land is conveyed to two or more persons and no words of severance are used. A tenancy in common arises when there are words of severance. Thus a conveyance 'to A and B' would create a joint tenancy, whilst a conveyance 'to A and B equally' would create a tenancy in common. The right of survivorship or *jus accrescendi* is a distinguishing feature of joint tenancies, and upon the death of one joint tenant, his share in the property passes to the survivors until there is only one person left and he becomes the sole owner of the property. The *jus accrescendi* does not apply to tenancies in common and such a tenant may dispose of his share by will. It will be appreciated also that the conveyance (or a will) may actually state the type of co-ownership, e.g. 'to A and B as joint tenants'.

Both types of co-ownership have advantages and disadvantages. The *jus accrescendi* as applied to joint tenancies prevents too many interests being created in the land, because a joint tenant cannot leave any part of the property by will and so the number of interests decreases. When the land is sold the number of signatures on the conveyance will not be excessive. On the other hand joint tenancies are unfair in that eventual sole ownership depends merely on survival. Where there is a tenancy in common, each tenant can leave his interest by will possibly by dividing it between two or more persons, thus the number of interests increases and on sale many interests must be got in.

The common law preferred the joint tenancy. But Equity preferred the tenancy in common and would in certain circumstances treat persons as tenants in common rather than joint tenants regardless of words of severance. For instance where two persons lend money on mortgage, Equity regards them as tenants in common of the interest in the land subject to the mortgage; also where joint purchasers of land put up the purchase money in unequal shares; and in the case of partnership land, the partners are treated as tenants in common in Equity.

The Law of Property Act, 1925 has combined the best features of both types of co-ownership by providing that where land is owned by two or more persons they, or the first four of them if there are more than four, should be treated as holding the legal estate as trustees and joint tenants, for the benefit of themselves and other co-owners (if any) in Equity. Thus a purchaser of the property is never required to get more than four signatures on the conveyance, and the trusts attach to the purchase money for the benefit of the co-owners. However, the Act does not state what shares the co-owners are to have and this should be dealt with specifically in the conveyance otherwise the court may have to decide in a case of dispute. It does not follow from the provisions of the Act that the co-owners share in Equity equally. The statutory trusts on which the property is held are: to sell the property with power to postpone the sale; and to hold the proceeds of sale, and the rents and profits until sale, for those beneficially entitled under the trust.

It should be noted that although the provisions set out in the above paragraph deal with the problems which formerly arose in conveying land which was in joint ownership, it is still possible to create a joint tenancy in both the land and the proceeds of sale. Where such a joint tenancy exists the *jus accrescendi* will apply to the equitable interests of the joint tenants in the proceeds of sale, unless there has been a severance of the joint tenancy since the creation of the estate. Severance is possible under s. 36(2) of the Law or Property Act, 1925, which provides that –

> where a legal estate (not being settled land) is vested in joint tenants beneficially, and any tenant desires to sever the joint tenancy in Equity, he shall give to the other joint tenants a notice in writing of such desire or do such other acts or things as would, in the case of personal estate, have been effective to sever the tenancy in Equity, and thereupon under the trust for sale affecting the land the net proceeds of sale, and the net rents and profits until sale, shall be held upon the trusts which would have been requisite for giving effect to the beneficial interest if there had been an actual severance.

A notice of severance may be regarded as properly served if sent by post even if it is not received by the addressee. (*Re 88 Berkeley Road, London NW9; Rickwood* v *Turnsek* [1971] 1 All E.R. 254.)

The better view is that severance of a joint tenancy may be effected unilaterally by one party other than by giving notice.

ESSENTIAL CASE LAW AND COMMENT

Re Draper's Conveyance, 1967 – Unilateral severance **(480)**

Before leaving this topic it should be noted that one tenant in common is not entitled to rent from another tenant in common, even though that other occupies the whole of the property (*Jones (A.E.)* v *Jones (F.W.)* [1977] 2 All E.R. 231).

A leasehold or a term of years

The major characteristics of a term of years are that the lessee is given exclusive possession of the land and that the period for which the term is to endure is fixed and definite. It is open to the parties to decide whether their agreement shall be a lease or a licence, though the words used by the parties are not conclusive. If there is no right to exclusive possession then there is a mere licence and not a lease. For example, a guest in a hotel does not normally have a lease, because the proprietor retains general control over the room.

ESSENTIAL CASE LAW AND COMMENT

Shell-Mex and B.P. Ltd v *Manchester Garages Ltd*, 1971 – Is it a lease or a licence? **(481)**

THE DURATION OF LEASES

Leases may be for a fixed period of time, and in this case the commencement and termination of the lease must be ascertainable before the lease takes effect. Thus a lease 'for the life of X' would not come under this heading. A lease may be for an indefinite period in the sense that it is to end when the lessor or lessee gives notice. Even so such an arrangement would operate as a valid lease, since the duration of the term can be made certain by the parties giving notice.

In the absence of agreement, the period of a lease may be determined by reference to the payment of rent. Thus if a person takes possession of the premises with the owner's consent for an indefinite period, but the owner accepts rent paid say weekly, monthly, quarterly or annually, then the term may be based on that period, though from early times there has been a presumption that the payment and acceptance of rent shows an intention to create a yearly tenancy. A yearly tenancy requires half a year's notice to terminate it if there has been no agreement on the matter. Other periodical tenancies, in the absence of agreement, are determined by notice for the full period. Even where there has been a definite term, a periodical tenancy can arise. Where X is granted a lease of 21 years and stays on after the expiration of that term with the owner's consent, then there is a new implied term based on the period of payment of rent.

However, where the tenant is permitted to stay in possession on the understanding that there are to be negotiations for a new lease there is a tenancy at will.

A *tenancy at will* may also arise *by agreement* where a person takes possession of property with the owner's consent, the arrangement being that the term can be brought to an end by either party giving notice. However, the court will look at the transaction in order to ascertain its true nature and will not be put off by ambiguous or wrong terminology.

ESSENTIAL CASE LAW AND COMMENT

Binions v *Evans*, 1972 – What is the true nature of the transaction?
(482)

If there is no agreement as to rent, the tenancy can become a periodical tenancy if the tenant pays and the owner accepts rent paid at given periods of time. A tenancy at will may also arise *by implication* from the conduct of the parties. For example, a prospective purchaser of land who is allowed to take possession before completion occupies the property as a tenant at will until completion.

Where a tenant stays on after the expiration of his term without the consent of the owner, there is a *tenancy by sufferance*. No rent is payable under such a tenancy, but the tenant must compensate the owner by a payment in respect of the use and occupation of the land. This compensation is referred to as *mesne profits*. Such a tenancy can be brought to an end at any time, though it may become a periodical tenancy if the owner accepts a payment of rent at given intervals of time.

It should be noted that the law bases the duration of a periodical tenancy on the intervals of time at which the rent has been paid and accepted, on the ground that this is evidence of the parties' intention. If there is other evidence of intention, then the court will also take this into account, e.g. there may be a prior lease which negatives the intention to create the sort of periodical tenancy which the payment of rent suggests.

CREATION OF LEASES

Leases are normally created by deed. However, where the lease is not to exceed three years, a written or oral lease will suffice, so long as the lease takes effect in possession at once at the best rent obtainable. Where a tenancy is in excess of three years then, if the agreement is not by deed, it will operate at common law as a yearly tenancy if the tenant enters into possession and pays rent on a yearly basis, i.e. by reference to a year, even if the rent is paid in quarterly instalments.

The position in Equity is rather different. In Equity, if a person has entered into an agreement for a lease but has no deed, then, if he has entered and paid rent or carried out repairs, i.e. if there is a sufficient act of part performance, Equity will insist that the owner of the property execute a formal lease by deed. The equitable maxim, 'Equity looks upon that as done which ought to be done', applies.

ESSENTIAL CASE LAW AND COMMENT

Walsh v *Lonsdale*, 1882 – Effect of an agreement for a lease **(483)**

It may seem that the above rule makes an agreement for a lease as effective as a lease by deed, and certainly, as between the parties to the agreement, absence of a deed is not vital.

However, the rights of the tenant under the rule are equitable and not legal rights, and the tenant can be turned out by a third party to whom the landlord sells the legal estate, if the third party purchases the property for value with or without notice of the existence of the lease.

Nevertheless, since the property legislation of 1925, the tenant can register the agreement as an Estate Contract, and, once the agreement is so registered, all subsequent purchasers of the legal estate are deemed to have notice of the lease and are bound to honour it. (See further p. 517.)

A lease which is to commence from the date of the lease is called a lease *in possession*. However, a *reversionary lease* may be created under which the term is to commence at some future date. A restriction is imposed by s. 149(3) of the Law of Property Act, 1925 which provides that the creation of a reversionary lease which is to take effect more than 21 years from the execution of the lease, e.g. a lease signed in 1992 for a term of ten years to run from 2028, is void. This does not affect the granting of a lease with an option to renew in the future.

RIGHTS AND LIABILITIES OF LANDLORD AND TENANT

The rights and liabilities of the parties depend largely upon the lease though a landlord has a special right at common law to distrain for rent, i.e. to move in on the tenant's personal property and remove it for sale to satisfy the amount owing for rent. Where the lease is by deed, the deed will usually fix the rights and liabilities by express clauses which are called covenants. Certain covenants are also implied by law where there is no provision in the lease. The most usual express covenants are covenants to pay rent, covenants regarding repairs and renewals, and a covenant that the tenant will not assign or sub-let without the landlord's consent. In this connection the Landlord and Tenant Act, 1988 imposes a duty upon a landlord to give consent unless he has good reason to withhold it and within a reasonable period. An action for damages arises if consent is not given or is unreasonably withheld.

The main *implied* covenant is that the landlord will not disturb the tenant's quiet enjoyment of the property, or make the use or enjoyment of the land difficult or impossible, i.e. the landlord undertakes not to *derogate from the grant*. As regards furnished houses, the landlord covenants that the property is fit for human habitation. A covenant to keep in repair, whether implied by statute or express, does not impose any liability on a landlord to remedy a latent defect until he becomes aware of it.

ESSENTIAL CASE LAW AND COMMENT

O'Brien v *Robinson*, 1973 – Latent defects **(484)**

The following tenant's covenants are implied by law: a covenant to pay rent, rates and certain taxes, and to repair. The tenant must in general keep the premises wind- and watertight, and must not commit waste, i.e. he must not do deliberate damage to the premises.

Breach of covenant by the tenant can result in forfeiture of the lease. A landlord's covenant to repair can be enforced by specific performance (*Jeune* v *Queen's Cross Properties Ltd* [1973] 3 All E.R. 97). However, since specific performance is a discretionary remedy it is advisable for tenants to rely on doing their own repairs and recouping from the rent for relatively trivial breaches rather than to approach the courts for specific performance.

THE LEASEHOLD REFORM ACT, 1967

This Act (as amended) enables certain tenants to buy the freehold of the property which they are leasing. In order to qualify the tenancy must have been granted for more than 21 years. It must be a tenancy of a house, not a flat, and the tenant must have occupied the house as his only, or main, residence during the past five years, or for periods amounting in total to five years within the past ten years.

A tenant pays the value of the property in the open market but on the assumption that it is subject to a 50-year lease.

Instead of buying the freehold, the tenant can ask for a new lease of 50 years to take effect after the existing lease expires.

Servitudes

Servitudes are rights over the property of another and may be either *easements* or *profits à prendre*.

EASEMENTS

An easement may be defined as a right to use or restrict the use of the land of another person in some way. There are various classes of easement and these include –

    (*a*) rights of way,
    (*b*) rights of light,
    (*c*) rights to abstract water,
    (*d*) rights to the support of buildings.

To be valid an easement must satisfy the following conditions.

There must be a dominant and servient tenement

The land in respect of which, and for the benefit of which, the easement exists is called the dominant tenement, and the land over which the right is exercised is called the servient tenement. A valid easement cannot exist *in gross*, i.e. without reference to the holding of land.

ESSENTIAL CASE LAW AND COMMENT

Hill v *Tupper*, 1863 – No easement 'in gross' **(485)**

The grant of a right of way over his land by a landowner to be exercised by the grantee personally, and without reference to any land capable of deriving benefit from the right of way, is merely a licence and not an easement.

The easement must accommodate the dominant tenement

The easement must confer some benefit on the land itself so as to make it a better and more convenient property; it is not enough that the owner obtains some personal advantage. A right of way over contiguous land generally benefits the dominant tenement, and an easement can exist even where two tenements do not actually adjoin, provided it is clear that the easement benefits the dominant tenement.

The dominant tenement and the servient tenement must not be both owned and occupied by the same person

Thus, if P owns both Blackacre and Whiteacre and habitually walks over Blackacre to reach Whiteacre, he is not exercising a right of way in respect of Blackacre, but merely walking from one part of his land to another. For this rule to apply, P must have simultaneously both ownership and possession of the two properties concerned. It is not enough that he owns the two if they are leased to different tenants, or that he is the tenant of both if they are owned by different owners.

The easement must be capable of forming the subject of a grant

This means that the right must be sufficiently definite. There must be a capable grantor and a capable grantee, and the right must be within the general nature of the rights capable of existing as easements.

ESSENTIAL CASE LAW AND COMMENT

Bass v *Gregory*, 1890 – Is the easement definite enough? **(486)**

An easement is a right to use or restrict the use of a neighbour's land which should not normally involve him in doing any work or spending any money, though the Court of Appeal has recognised an easement of fencing.

ESSENTIAL CASE LAW AND COMMENT

Crow v *Wood*, 1970 – An easement of fencing **(487)**

The categories of easements are not closed and new rights have from time to time been recognised as easements, though in general the courts are still reluctant to extend the categories.

ESSENTIAL CASE LAW AND COMMENT

Re Ellenborough Park, 1956 – Expansion of easements **(488)**
Phipps v *Pears*, 1964 – No easement of property protection **(489)**
Grigsby v *Melville*, 1972 – No easement giving exclusive right of user **(490)**

PROFITS A PRENDRE

A profit *à prendre* is the right to take something of legal value from the land of another, e.g. shooting, fishing, and grazing rights; the right to cut turf or take wood for fuel. The exception is a right to take water from a stream which is treated as an easement because running water cannot be privately owned and is not therefore a thing of legal value.

A profit necessarily involves a servient tenement but there may or may not be a dominant tenement, for a profit can exist *in gross*. A profit may be a several profit, where enjoyment is granted to an individual as is often the case with shooting and fishing rights; or a profit may be in common which may be enjoyed by more than one person, as is often the case with grazing rights and the right to take various materials for use as fuel.

ACQUISITION OF SERVITUDES

Servitudes may be acquired (*a*) by statute, (*b*) by express or implied grant, (*c*) by prescription, (*d*) by equitable estoppel. (See *Crabb* v *Arun District Council*, 1975 at p. 625.)

Easements created by statute are usually in connection with local Acts of Parliament.

When land is sold, a servitude may be expressly reserved in favour of another tenement of the seller, or may be expressly granted in similar circumstances by deed; and under the Law of Property Act, 1925, s. 62, a conveyance, if there is no contrary express intention, operates to convey servitudes appertaining to the land conveyed. (See *Crow* v *Wood*, 1970 at p. 819.)

Where an owner of two plots conveys one of them, then certain easements are implied. These are *easements of necessity*, as where the piece of land would be completely surrounded and inaccessible without a right of way; *intended easements*, which would be necessary to carry out the common intentions of the parties; *ancillary easements*, which would be necessary in view of the right granted, as the grant of the use of water implies the right of way to reach the water. Where part of a tenement is granted, then the grantee acquires easements over the land which are continuous and apparent, are necessary to the reasonable enjoyment of the land granted, and have been and are used by the grantor for the benefit of the part granted. An example of this is a window enjoying light.

ESSENTIAL CASE LAW AND COMMENT

Ward v *Kirkland*, 1966 – An easement for reasonable enjoyment
   (491)

PRESCRIPTION

Prescription may be based on a presumed grant or alternatively may be established by use as of right.

Prescription at common law depended on use since time immemorial, which at law means since 1189. Clearly in most cases it is out of the question to show continuous use for this period, and so the courts were prepared to accept 20 years' continuous use as raising the presumption of a grant. This presumption may be rebutted by showing that at some time since 1189 the right could not have existed, and it follows that an easement of light cannot be claimed by prescription at common law in a building erected since 1189. This serious difficulty was met in part by the presumption of a lost modern grant, and juries were told that if there had been use during living memory or even for 20 years, they might presume a lost grant or deed, and this ultimately become mandatory, even though neither judge nor jury had any belief that such instrument had ever existed.

The position is now clear under the Prescription Act, 1832, which was passed to deal with the difficulties arising under the common law. Under this Act, which supplements the common law, we must distinguish easements other than light from easements of light and easements from profits.

ESSENTIAL CASE LAW AND COMMENT

Tehidy Minerals v *Norman*, 1971 – Lost modern grant **(492)**

Easements other than light

Twenty years' uninterrupted use as of right will establish an easement. Use as of right means *nec vi, nec clam, nec precario*, i.e. without force, stealth, or permission. The law of prescription rests upon the acquiescence of the owner of the servient tenement. Thus he must have knowledge of the exercise of the right claimed. If the owner of the so-called servient tenement can prove that he has given verbal permission, i.e. that the easement is *precario*, then it cannot be claimed. Nevertheless 40 years' similar use will establish the easement, and in this case, if the owner of the servient tenement wishes to prove that the right was exercised by permission, he must produce a written agreement to that effect. To establish a right of way by prescription, periods of use of an original and a substituted way may be added together.

ESSENTIAL CASE LAW AND COMMENT

Diment v *Foot*, 1974 – Where there is no knowledge **(493)**
Davis v *Whitby*, 1974 – Original and substituted ways **(494)**

Easements of light

These can be established by 20 years' use, the defences being that the owner of the servient tenement gave permission and that there is a deed or written agreement to this effect, or that the owner of the servient tenement interrupted the enjoyment of the right for a continuous period of a year by erecting something which blocked the light. Under the Rights of Light Act, 1959 (as amended by the Local Land Charges Act, 1975), it is no longer necessary to erect something of this nature; the owner of the servient land may now register on the local land charges register a statutory notice indicating where he would have put up a screen, and this operates as if the access of light had been restricted for one year. Use as of right is not necessary, and oral consent will not bar the claim even if the claimant has made regular money payments for the use of the right.

The right can only be claimed having regard to the type of room affected. A bedroom does not require the amount of light that other rooms do, and if the claimant has used the bedroom to repair watches for 20 years, he will still only be able to claim that amount of light appropriate to a bedroom. There is no right to receive unlimited light but in *Ough* v *King* [1967] 3 All E.R. 859, the Court of Appeal held that in determining whether there was an infringement of a right to light regard must be had to the nature of the locality and to the higher standard of lighting required in modern times.

However, in *Allen* v *Greenwood* [1979] 2 W.L.R. 187, the Court of Appeal held that the measure of light which can be acquired by prescription can, so far as a greenhouse used for its normal purposes is concerned, include the right to an extraordinary amount of light, and also to the benefits of that light, including the rays of the sun. Nevertheless, there is no claim to a view or a prospect which can be seen from a window.

PROFITS A PRENDRE

The general period for prescription here is 30 years under the Act of 1832, though 20 years is enough if the court is presuming a lost modern grant (see *Tehidy Minerals* v *Norman*, 1971 at p. 821).

If an easement is denied or threatened, it would be necessary to ask the court for an injunction to prevent the owner of the servient tenement from acting contrary to the easement, and its existence would have to be proved under one of the headings given above. The court may then –

(*a*) find the easement not proved; or

(*b*) grant an injunction to restrain the owner of the servient tenement from acting contrary to it; or

(*c*) if the infringement is not serious, award once for all damages, in which case the servient owner will have bought his right to act contrary to the easement.

TERMINATION OR EXTINGUISHMENT OF SERVITUDES

Servitudes may be extinguished by statute, or by express or implied release. At law a deed is necessary for express release, but in Equity an informal release will be effective if it would be inequitable for the dominant owner to claim that the right still exists.

If the dominant owner shows by his conduct an intention to release an easement, it will be extinguished. The demolition of a house to which an easement of light attaches may amount to an implied release, but not if it is intended to replace the house by another building. Mere non-use is not enough, although it may be some evidence of intention to abandon the right (see *Tehidy Minerals* v *Norman*, 1971 at p. 821). There is no fixed time but 20 years' non-use usually constitutes abandonment.

We have already seen that an easement is extinguished when the dominant and servient tenements come into simultaneous ownership and possession of the same person, since a person cannot have an easement over his or her own land.

Restrictive covenants

A restrictive covenant is essentially a contract between two owners of land whereby one agrees to restrict the use of his land for the benefit of the other. We are not concerned here with covenants in leases, which are governed by separate rules already outlined.

Such covenants were not adequately enforced by the common law because the doctrine of privity of contract applied, and as soon as one of the parties to the covenant transferred his land, the covenant was not enforceable by the transferee because he had not been a party to the original contract. However, the common law realised that this was rather too rigid and went so far as to allow a transferee to enforce the benefit of the covenant against the original party to it. Thus if A, the owner of Blackacre, agreed with B, the owner of Whiteacre, that he would not use Blackacre for the purposes of trade, then if B sold Whiteacre to C, C could enforce the covenant against A. However, if A sold Blackacre to D, C could not enforce the covenant against D, because the the common law would not allow D to bear the burden of a covenant he did not make.

Equity takes a different view, and allows C to enforce the sort of covenant outlined above by injunction, if the following conditions are fulfilled –

(*a*) *The covenant must be substantially negative.* Much depends upon the words used in the covenant, and an undertaking which seems *prima facie* to be positive may imply a negative undertaking and this may then be enforced. (See *Tulk* v *Moxhay*, 1848 at p. 618.) A covenant to use a house as a dwelling house implies that it will not be used for other purposes, and would be enforceable in the negative sense. If the covenant requires the covenantor to spend money, it is not a negative covenant.

(*b*) *The covenant must benefit the land.* It is often said that the covenant must 'touch and concern' the land and must not be merely for the personal benefit of the claimant. Restrictive covenants usually endeavour to keep up the residential character of the district and benefit the land by preserving value and amenities as a residential property.

(*c*) *The person claiming the benefit must retain land which can benefit from the covenant taken.* If X owns a piece of land which he splits up into two plots, selling one plot to Y and taking a restrictive covenant in favour of the plot he has retained, then he can enforce the covenant so long as he retains the land to be benefited. If X now sells the plot he had retained, he will not be able to enforce the covenant for the future, although the purchaser from X will be able to do so.

ESSENTIAL CASE LAW AND COMMENT

Kelly v *Barrett*, 1924 – Restrictive covenants: land must benefit
(495)

There is an exception to this rule in the case of *building schemes* involving an estate of houses. Here the covenants are taken by the owner of the land from each person purchasing a house, and although the owner does not retain any of the land, the covenants may be enforced by the purchasers as between themselves. However, a building scheme will not be implied simply because there is a common vendor and the existence of common covenants. It was at one time thought that there must be a defined area and evidence of laying out in lots (*Re Wembley Park Estate Co. Ltd's Transfer* [1968] 1 All E.R. 457). However, in *Re Dolphin's Conveyance* [1970] 2 All E.R. 664, Stamp, J. held that so long as the covenants held in the conveyances were, as a matter of construction, intended to give the purchasers of the parcels mutual rights, this was sufficient to make them enforceable and there was no need, in particular, to consider lotting.

Since restrictive covenants are in general enforceable only in Equity, the question of notice arises. In fact, restrictive covenants created after 1925 are void against a purchaser of the legal estate, even one who has notice of them, unless they are registered as land charges. (See further p. 517.) There is an exception as regards covenants between lessor and lessee. These cannot be registered and will be binding only if known to an assignee of the lease. In practice it is usual for an assignee to inspect the lease. As regards covenants created before 1 January 1926, they bind all persons who acquire the land which is subject to them with the exception of a purchaser for value of the legal estate in the land without notice, actual or constructive, of the covenants.

Under s. 84 of the Law of Property Act, 1925 (as amended by s. 28(1) and Sch. 3 of the Law of Property Act, 1969), the Lands Tribunal has power, on the application of any person interested, to discharge or modify a restrictive covenant.

Whether a covenant runs with the land depends upon the words. In *Roake* v *Chadha* [1983] 3 All E.R. 503 the covenant between plots of land was that no more than one house should be built on each plot. The covenants were expressed to pass *only if specifically assigned*. A plot was sold to the defendant but the covenant was not assigned. He proposed to build more than one house on the plot and the plaintiff, who owned an adjacent plot, tried to enforce the 'one house' covenant. It was held that he could not do so because the covenant had not been specifically assigned as the agreement required.

The transfer of land

It is usual, when a disposition of land is contemplated, to draw up a contract. For a contract of sale to be valid both parties must have contractual capacity, the contract must be legal, there must be clear agreement on all the essential terms, and acceptance of the offer must be unconditional. As we have seen contracts for the sale or other disposition of land are invalid unless they are in writing (Law of Property (Miscellaneous Provisions) Act, 1989. (See further p. 231.)

When a valid contract for sale exists, the purchaser acquires an equitable interest in the property and the vendor is in effect a qualified trustee for him. Thus if the property increases in value between contract and completion, the purchaser is entitled to the increase and similarly he must bear any loss. This is particularly important in cases where property is destroyed by fire between contract and completion, since the purchaser would still have to pay the purchase money, even though he only received a conveyance of the land with the useless buildings on it. It is now provided by s. 47 of the Law of Property Act, 1925 that in such a case the purchaser may become entitled to money payable on an insurance policy maintained by the vendor. However, it it prudent for the purchaser to take out his own insurance in case the vendor has none or his policy is defective. Where, as is usual, the Law Society's Standard Conditions of Sale are used condition 5 expressly states that the seller is under no obligation to the buyer to insure and thus gets rid of s. 47. However, condition 5 imposes an obligation on the seller to transfer the property in the same physical state as it was at the date of the contract (subject to fair wear and tear). If between contract and completion there is a change in the physical state of the property which makes it unusable for the contract purpose the buyer is given an unlimited right to rescind and so is the seller where the damage was uninsurable or where the seller is not able legally to make good the damage.

The vendor has a lien on the property sold to the extent of the unpaid purchase money and may enforce this by an order for sale; this lien may be registered as a general equitable charge. The purchaser has a similar lien in respect of money paid under the contract prior to conveyance.

On a sale of land it is usual to use a standard form of contract prepared by The Law Society since this saves much trouble in drafting. In what is called an open contract for the sale of land the vendor must under s. 23 of the Law of Property Act, 1969 show a title for a least 15 years, beginning with a good 'root of title', i.e. a document dealing with the whole legal and equitable interests in the land. It may be necessary to go back more than 15 years in order to find such a document. The vendor prepares an abstract of title, listing all the relevant documents in connection with its establishment, and he must produce these documents in order to justify the abstract of title he has prepared. It should be noted that all the above matters are attended to by the parties' solicitors.

The Administration of Justice Act, 1985 and the Courts and Legal Services Act, 1990 have removed the monopoly on conveyancing which has been possessed by solicitors for many years. (See further p. 72.)

A contract for the sale of land will normally contain a completion date which is the time by which the transaction must be concluded. The transfer of land involves the following stages –

(*a*) The preparation of the contract.

(*b*) The exchange of contracts between the vendor's and purchaser's solicitors, when the purchaser pays a deposit, usually 10% of the purchase money though deposits of only 5% are sometimes taken.

(*c*) The delivery by the vendor's solicitors of an abstract of title, or as is more usual today, copies of the documents, e.g. previous conveyances, upon which the vendor bases his title.

(*d*) The examination of this title by the purchaser's solicitors and the checking of the abstract against the actual deeds to see that it is correct.

(*e*) After all outstanding queries have been solved, a conveyance is prepared by the purchaser's solicitors which is sent to the vendor's solicitors for approval. The draft conveyance may be exchanged a number of times before agreement is reached. Where the land is registered, a simpler form of transfer deed is used.

(*f*) Just before completion the purchaser's solicitors will make the necessary searches in the Land Charges Register and in the register maintained by the appropriate local authority to see what encumbrances are registered in respect of the property.

(*g*) An appointment is then arranged for completion and the purchaser hands over the money, the vendor handing over the conveyance, which he has signed, together with the title deeds. This brings the transaction to a conclusion. There need not be attendance at an office. Completion is very often carried out by post.

The above procedure refers to unregistered land where the need to examine title is to some extent cumbersome and expensive. The Land Registration Act, 1925 provides that the title to land can be examined by and registered with the State and that this is followed by the issue of a certificate guaranteeing ownership. Where there is a sale of registered land the certificate is handed over and the name of the new owner registered. A transfer, rather than a conveyance, is prepared. This is a more simple procedure than the one outlined above for unregistered land and the legal fees for the transaction are less.

Personal property

We have already mentioned that personal property is divided into two classes – *choses in action* and *choses in possession*, the latter being divided into *chattels real* (i.e. leaseholds) and *chattels personal*. We have already dealt with leaseholds, and the sale of chattels personal has been codified by the Sale of Goods Act, 1979, a full study of which would not be appropriate to a book of this nature. The assignment of choses in action is considered on p. 525.

Mortgages of land

The following types of mortgage are relevant.

LEGAL MORTGAGE OF FREEHOLDS

Under the 1925 legislation the mortgagor (the borrower) does not divest himself of his legal estate, but grants to the mortgagee (the lender) a *demise* (i.e. a lease) for a term of years absolute. Thus, if X owns Blackacre and borrows money on mortgage from Y, he will grant Y a term of usually 3000 years in Blackacre, both agreeing that the term of years will end when the loan is repaid. X will also agree to pay interest on the loan at a stipulated rate.

Alternatively, under the provisions of s. 87 of the Law of Property Act, 1925 it is possible to create a legal mortgage of freeholds by means of a short deed stating that a charge on the land is created. Such a charge does not give a term of years, but the mortgagee has the same rights and powers as if he had received a term of years under a mortgage by demise.

Before 1926 mortgages were created by conveying the freehold to the mortgagee. Since 1925 an attempt to create a mortgage by this method operates as a grant of a mortgage lease of 3000 years, subject to cesser on redemption. (Section 85, Law of Property Act, 1925.)

LEGAL MORTGAGE OF LEASEHOLDS

If X, the owner of a 99-year lease of Blackacre, borrows money on mortgage from Y, he may grant Y a sub-lease of (say) 99 years less ten days, both agreeing that when the loan is repaid the term shall cease. X also agrees to pay interest. Such a term is known as a *mortgage by demise*.

Alternatively a legal mortgage of leaseholds may be created by a charge by way of legal mortgage under s. 87 of the Law of Property Act, 1925, if made by deed. No sub-lease is created but the remedies of the mortgagee are the same as if it had been.

When a person has borrowed money by mortgaging property, he may still be able to borrow further sums, if the amount of the charge is not equal to the full value of the property and there seems to be adequate security for further loans. The owner of freehold land may grant a term of 3000 years plus one day to another mortgagee, whilst the owner of a lease may grant a second sub-lease of (say) 99 years less nine days. Alternatively, a second charge by way of legal mortgage may be created by a further deed.

The only limit to further borrowing on second and subsequent mortgages is that of finding a lender who is prepared to become a second, third or fourth mortgagee.

EQUITABLE MORTGAGE

A mortgagee who receives a mere equitable interest in the land is said to have an equitable mortgage. Thus if the borrower's interest is equitable, e.g. a life interest, then any mortgage of it is necessarily equitable. Such an interest may be mortgaged by lease or charge, as in legal mortgages, or by a deposit of title deeds with the lender, usually accompanied by a memorandum explaining the transaction. Such mortgages must be in writing and signed by the borrower or his agent. (Section 53, Law of Property Act, 1925.)

An informal mortgage of a legal estate or interest creates an equitable mortgage, e.g. an attempt to create a legal mortgage otherwise than by deed.

Where there is a binding agreement to create a legal mortgage, but the formalities necessary to do so have not been carried out, Equity regards the agreement as an equitable mortgage. The agreement can be enforced by specific performance so that the mortgagee can obtain a legal mortgage from the borrower under the rule in *Walsh* v *Lonsdale*, 1882 (see p. 817). Before there is a binding agreement there must be either written evidence of the agreement, signed by the borrower or his agent, or a sufficient act of part performance by the lender.

RIGHTS OF THE MORTGAGOR OR BORROWER

The main right of the mortgagor is the right to redeem (or recover) the land. Originally at common law the land became the property of the lender as soon as the date decided upon for repayment had passed, unless during that time the loan had been repaid. However, Equity regarded a mortgage as essentially a security, and gave the mortgagor the right to redeem the land at any time on payment of the principal sum, plus interest due to the date of payment. What is more important, this rule applied even though the common-law date for repayment had passed. This right, which still exists, is called the *Equity of Redemption*, and there are two important rules connected with it –

(a) *Once a mortgage always a mortgage.* This means that Equity looks at the real purpose of the transaction and does not always have regard to its form. If Equity considers that the transaction is a mortgage, the rules appertaining to mortgages will apply, particularly the right to redeem the property even though the contractual date for repayment has passed, or has not yet arrived. In the latter case, however, the mortgagor must generally give six months' notice of his intention to redeem, or pay six months' interest in lieu, so that the mortgagee may find another investment. However, if the parties contract at arm's length, and there is no evidence of oppression by the mortgagee, the court will endeavour to uphold the principle of sanctity of contract and will enforce any reasonable restriction on the right to redeem.

ESSENTIAL CASE LAW AND COMMENT

Knightsbridge Estates Trust Ltd v *Byrne*, 1939 – Right of redemption postponed **(496)**

(*b*) *There must be no clog on the equity of redemption.* This means that –

(i) the court will not allow postponement of the repayment period for an unreasonable time; and
(ii) the property mortgaged must, when the loan is repaid, be returned to the borrower in the same condition as when it was pledged.

ESSENTIAL CASE LAW AND COMMENT

Noakes v *Rice*, 1902 – No clog on the equity of redemption **(497)**

Nevertheless, particularly in modern times, so long as the parties are at arm's length when the loan is negotiated, Equity will allow a collateral transaction.

It is worth noting that the mortgagor may, where he is in possession of the land, grant leases to third parties subject to any special agreement to the contrary.

ESSENTIAL CASE LAW AND COMMENT

Kreglinger v *New Patagonia Meat*, 1914 – Collateral transaction **(498)**
Cityland and Property v *Dabrah*, 1967 – An unreasonable collateral advantage **(499)**

(*c*) *A term must not amount to an extortionate credit bargain.* Sections 137 to 139 of the Consumer Credit Act, 1974 deal with extortionate credit bargains. The Court may reopen and revise the terms of such bargains to do justice to the borrower.

(*d*) *A term must not be in restraint of trade.* This has already been considered in Chapter 16 where the case of *Esso* v *Harper's Garage*, 1967 (see p. 696) was discussed.

POWERS AND REMEDIES OF THE LEGAL MORTGAGEE

A legal mortgagee (the lender) has the following concurrent powers and remedies.

To take possession

This right does not depend upon default by the mortgagor, but the mortgagee will normally only enter into possession of the property under the term of years granted to him, or under the charge by way of legal mortgage, when he is not being paid the sum due, and when he wishes to pay himself from the proceeds of the property. In addition, the court will grant a possession order where an insurance policy which is the security has been allowed to lapse by the borrower. (*Western Bank* v *Schindler* [1976] 2 All E.R. 393.) This is not a desirable remedy, however, because when the mortgagee takes possession he is strictly accountable to the mortgagor, not only for what he has received but for what he might have received with the exercise of due diligence and proper management.

ESSENTIAL CASE LAW AND COMMENT

White v *City of London Brewery Co*, 1889 – When a mortgagee takes possession **(500)**

If the mortgagee is simply concerned to intercept rents, where the mortgaged property is let and the mortgagor is a landlord, he will do better to appoint a receiver under the Law of Property Act, 1925, s. 109. Most mortgagees who ask for a possession order do so in order to sell with vacant possession. The Administration of Justice Act, 1970, which is concerned, amongst other things, with mortgage possession actions, reinstates the old practice of the Chancery masters by allowing the court to make an order adjourning the proceedings, or suspending or postponing a possession order provided it appears that the mortgagor is likely to be able to pay within a reasonable time any sums due under the mortgage (s. 36). However, the court cannot suspend the execution of an order for possession indefinitely and must specify the period of suspension. (*Royal Trust Co. of Canada* v *Markham* [1975] 3 All E.R. 433.)

The Act applies wherever a mortgage includes a dwelling house even though part may be used for business purposes. Unfortunately, it was held in *Halifax Building Society* v *Clark* [1973] 2 All E.R. 33, that where, as is often the case, the mortgage provided that the whole sum should become payable on default by the mortgagor, the court's power to adjourn or stay execution under s. 36 could only be exercised if it appeared likely that the mortgagor could pay the *whole* sum within a reasonable period. This plainly defeated the intention of the 1970 Act in most cases as the period of the stay envisaged is short, and the likelihood of the mortgagor being able to repay the entire redemption figure remote. Accordingly, s. 8 of the Administration of Justice Act, 1973 now provides that a court may treat as due under the mortgage only those instalments actually in arrear, but shall not exercise the power to postpone the order for possession unless the mortgagor will be able to catch up within a reasonable period. This means that not only must he be able to pay the instalments due month by month but also the arrears within a reasonable time.

It should be noted that where a house is owned by a husband and is mortgaged to secure the loan, the interest of the wife occupying the home overrides the lender's claim under the mortgage and the court may refuse a possession order. (*Williams & Glyn's Bank Ltd* v *Boland*, 1980 (see further p. 519).)

Foreclosure

The mortgagee may obtain a foreclosure order from the court if the mortgagor fails to pay for an unreasonable time. The first order is a *foreclosure order nisi* providing that the debt must be paid within a stated time. If it is not so paid, the order is made *absolute* and the property becomes that of the mortgagee, the mortgagor's equity of redemption being barred, and the property vesting in the mortgagee, free from any right of redemption either in law or Equity. Such orders are seldom used, for it is still open to the court to reopen the foreclosure, i.e. to give the mortgagor a further opportunity to redeem. Section 36 of the Administration of Justice Act, 1970 excluded the power to postpone a foreclosure order because it was considered that the court's power to give the mortgagor time to redeem when granting the decree *nisi* was an adequate remedy. The Payne Committee recommended including actions for foreclosure, and they are now included by the Administration of Justice Act, 1973, s. 8(3). Thus the courts now have power to postpone an order for foreclosure.

Right of sale

Normally this is the most valuable right of the mortgagee. Subject to certain conditions he can, on the default of the mortgagor, sell and convey to a purchaser the whole of the mortgaged property, and recoup himself out of the proceeds. Unless the mortgagee is a building society (Building Societies Act, 1986, Sch. 4), he is not a trustee of the power of sale for the benefit of the mortgagor. However, he must not fraudulently, wilfully or recklessly sacrifice the property of the mortgagor (*Kennedy* v *De Trafford* [1897] A.C. 180) and in addition owes a duty to the mortgagor to take reasonable care to obtain the best price that can be had in the circumstances. (*Cuckmere Brick Co. Ltd* v *Mutual Finance* [1971] 2 All E.R. 633.)

The general rule is that a mortgagee cannot sell to himself or to his nominee. Although a mortgagee is not a trustee of the power of sale and need not get the best possible price (though a building society must) the conflict of interest where he sells to himself is one which Equity generally forbids. However, it is thought that the mortgagee could purchase the property, subject to the mortgage, if he had leave from the court, which is the general rule for trustees who wish to buy the trust property, and provided the mortgagor did not object and possibly also if no other purchaser at an adequate price could be found. It is also probable that a mortgagee could buy the property at an auction since in that event the sale is not directly to himself but through an intermediary, i.e. the auctioneer, and given that there is no collusion between the mortgagee and the auctioneer there would seem to be no good reason why the mortgagee should not buy the property in.

In *Tsi Kwong Lam* v *Wong Chit Sen* [1983] 3 All E.R. 54, the Privy Council decided that a sale by a mortgagee exercising his power of sale to a company in which he had an interest would not necessarily be banned by the law provided the sale was made in good faith and that the mortgagee had taken reasonable precautions to obtain the best price reasonably obtainable at the time, namely by taking expert advice as to the methods of sale and the steps which ought reasonably to be taken to make the sale a success.

To sue for the money owing

The mortgage is a pledge for the repayment of the money, but mortgagors almost invariably give a personal covenant to repay. This is of value should the property be destroyed or lose its value. When the date fixed for redemption is passed, the mortgage money is due and the mortgagee can sue for it. He will rarely do so, for in most cases the other remedies will be more satisfactory.

The right to appoint a receiver

The Law of Property Act, 1925, s. 109, gives the mortgagee the right to appoint a receiver to receive the rents and profits on the mortgagee's behalf in order to pay the money due. The receiver is deemed to be the agent of the mortgagor, who is liable for his acts and defaults unless otherwise provided by the mortgage. The mortgagee thus avoids the disadvantage of strict accountability to which he would be subject if he entered himself.

Remedies of equitable mortgagees

Where the mortgage is equitable and is created by deed, then the mortgagee has virtually the same remedies as have been set out above. Otherwise, if the mortgage is by a mere deposit of title deeds, then the mortgagee must ask the court –

(*a*) for an order to sell; or
(*b*) for an order appointing a receiver.

OTHER RIGHTS OF MORTGAGEES

A mortgagee has other rights and he may, where the mortgage is created by deed, insure the mortgaged property against loss by fire up to two-thirds of its value, and charge the premiums on the property in the same way as the mortgage money.

A mortgagee has a right to the title deeds of the property, and if the mortgage is redeemed by the mortgagor, the mortgagee must return the deeds to him in the absence of notice of a second or subsequent mortgage, in which case the deeds should be handed to the next mortgagee.

There are two other important rights which a mortgagee may exercise in appropriate circumstances – the right to consolidate and the right to tack.

Consolidation

Where a person has two or more mortgages, he may refuse to allow one mortgage to be redeemed unless the other or others are also redeemed. This right is particularly valuable where property might fluctuate in value, and where a mortgagor might redeem one mortgage where the security was more than adequate, leaving the mortgagee with a debt on the other property not properly secured.

Consolidation is only possible if the right to consolidate was reserved in one of the mortgage deeds. The contractual date for redemption must have passed on all mortgages and they must have been created by the same mortgagor, though not necessarily in favour of the same mortgagee. Nevertheless in such cases, where it is proposed to consolidate two mortgages, both the mortgages must have been vested in one person at the same time, as both the equities of redemption were vested in another.

Tacking

The right to tack may bring about a modification of the priority of mortgages. It is now confined to the tacking of further advances. Thus, where a man has lent money on a first mortgage and there are second and third mortgages, if the first morgagee agrees to advance a further sum, he may tack this to his first mortgage and thus get priority over the second and third, which would normally rank before the tacked mortgage. This can now only be done if the intervening mortgagees agree, or if the further advance is made without notice of an intervening mortgage, or if the prior mortgage imposed an obligation to make further advances.

Attornment clause

Many mortgages contain an attornment clause by which the borrower attorns or acknowledges himself as a tenant at will, or from year to year, of the lender at a nominal rent such as a peppercorn. The advantage of such a clause was that it entitled the lender to evict the borrower for failure to pay the mortgage instalments and so obtain possession more speedily. However, changes in the rules of court from 1933 to 1937 made a speedy procedure available to mortgagees as such, and there is now no substantial advantage in an attornment clause.

PRIORITY OF MORTGAGES

The Land Charges Act, 1925 introduced the principle of registering charges on land. The object of searching the Land Charges Register is to discover the rights, if any, of third parties which are enforceable against the land.

It is a general principle that a purchaser or mortgagee of land is deemed to have actual notice of all third-party rights capable of registration and actually registered, whereas he acquires his interest in the land free from third-party rights capable of registration and not registered. There are five separate registers kept in the Land Charges Department of the Land Registry. Search is usually done by filling in an appropriate form and sending it to the Land Charges Superintendent. This results in an *official search certificate.*

Where there is a mortgage of a legal estate with deposit of title deeds, the mortgage ranks from the date of its creation and such a mortgage cannot be registered.

Where there is a mortgage of legal estate without deposit of title deeds, the mortgage ranks from its date of registration as a land charge.

Regarding mortgages of equitable interests, the question of priority is based on the rule in *Dearle* v *Hall* (1828), 3 Russ. 1, and such mortgages rank from the date on which the mortgagee gave notice of his mortgage to the trustees of the equitable interest, though such notice will not postpone a previous mortgage of which the mortgagee giving notice was aware. Equitable mortgages of interests other than equitable interests rank in priority according to the date of creation. Thus, an equitable mortgage created in January 1991, would take priority over one created in May 1993. Legal mortgages take precedence over equitable mortgages, but an equitable mortgagee who obtains a legal interest does not thereby gain priority over an equitable interest of which he has constructive notice. Thus if A obtains an equitable interest in property, e.g. a contract to purchase land, in January 1993, and fails to register it as an estate contract until May 1993, and B, in February 1993, obtains an equitable mortgage over the land which is converted into a legal mortgage in April 1993, at a time when B knows or ought to know that A has an interest, as where A is on the land and carrying out works, then B's mortgage, although legal, will not rank over A's equitable interest. (*McCarthy and Stone* v *Julian S. Hodge & Co.* [1971] 2 All E.R. 973.)

THE LEASEHOLD REFORM ACT, 1967

Where, under the provisions of this Act, a leaseholder buys the freehold, the conveyance automatically discharges the premises from any mortgage even though the lender is not a party to the conveyance (s. 12(1)). However, the leaseholder must apply the money which he is using to buy the freehold, in the first instance, in or towards the payment (or redemption) of the mortgage (s. 12(2)). If the lender raises difficulties the tenant may, in order to protect his interest, pay the money into court (s. 13). The lender (or mortgagee) must accept not less than three months' notice to pay off the whole or part of the principal secured by the mortgage, together with interest to the date of payment regardless of any provisions to the contrary in the mortgage (s. 12(4)).

The court is also given power, under s. 36, to alter the rights of the parties to a mortgage in order to mitigate any financial hardship which may arise as a result of the purchase of a freehold under the provisions of the Act.

If it is desired that a mortgage of the former leasehold interest should be extended to cover the freehold, this may be done by requesting the borrower to execute a deed of substituted security. If a tenant acquires an extended lease a lender is entitled to possession of the documents of title relating to the new lease (s. 14(6)) and should ask for them when the borrower obtains an extended lease. The borrower should also be required to execute a mortgage of the extended lease.

Registration of land charges

The Land Charges Act, 1925 and the Land Registration Act, 1925 introduced the principle of registering charges on land. The object of searching the Land Charges Register is to discover the rights, if any, of third parties which are enforceable against the land. It is a general principle that a purchaser or mortgagee of land is deemed to have actual notice of all third-party rights capable of registration and actually registered, whereas he acquires his interest in the land free from third-party rights capable of registration and not registered.

The injustice to a purchaser of this rule lay in the fact that in practice there is no investigation of the title prior to the formation of the contract. In consequence, if a vendor did not actually disclose to a purchaser that there were charges over the land, then, if the charges were registered, the purchaser was unable to rescind the contract since he was deemed to know that they existed. However, under s. 24 of The Law of Property Act, 1969 the purchaser will be affected *as against his vendor* only by land charges of which he had *actual* knowledge at the time of entering into the contract. If he completes the contract the purchaser remains bound by registered land charges *as against the holder of the charge* whether or not he has actual knowledge of them.

The present system of registration of land charges at the Land Registry is governed by the Land Charges Act, 1972, in the case of unregistered land, and by the Land Registration Act, 1925, in the case of registered land. Prior registration of a land charge does not of itself confer priority; it merely gives notice to everyone dealing with the property so that they will take subject to the charge as purchasers with notice of it. Failure to register a land charge merely means that upon completion of a purchase the charge will be void against the purchaser. Right up to completion the person with the benefit of a land charge can preserve his rights by registering the charge.

The most important search is in the registers of the Land Registry, though local land charges appear in registers kept by local authorities. A common example of a local land charge is road charges, i.e. charges against land which the local authority has in regard to the cost of making up a road which adjoins that land. Search may be in person at some Land Registry offices, of which there are 16 in England and Wales, or may be done by filling in the details on the appropriate form and sending it to the Land Registry in London. This results in an official search certificate.

It is now possible to ask for search by telephone or telex, the applicant receiving a printed result of the search by post. The Land Charges Act, 1972 introduced a number of changes designed to simplify the procedure. These include changes made necessary by computerisation.

The registers are basically registers of names, not properties. Search is therefore under the name of the vendor. Thus a charge affecting Whiteacre, a property situated in Birmingham and owned by John Jones, will be indexed under John Jones, provided he was owner of Whiteacre when the charge was created. Sometimes charges are registered in the name of the property but now that search is by computer this does not give rise to difficulties.

The Land Registration Act, 1988 allows members of the public to go to Land Registry offices in England and Wales and inspect the relevant registers to see who owns land.

The Matrimonial Homes Act, 1967 (see now Matrimonial Homes Act, 1983) created a new type of land charge. It was passed to restore the legal position to what it was before the decision of the House of Lords in *National Provincial Bank Ltd* v *Ainsworth* [1965] 2 All E.R. 472. In that case it was decided that a deserted wife had no special right or 'equity' to continue to occupy the matrimonial home though there had formerly been such a right. The effect of the decision in *Ainsworth*'s case was that a husband who was the owner of the matrimonial home could, having deserted his wife and children, sell or mortgage the house to a third party who would in most cases be able to get an order for possession in order to enforce his rights. In these circumstances the deserted wife and children would have to give up occupation of the matrimonial home and find other accommodation.

The 1983 Act provides that where one spouse owns or is the tenant of the matrimonial home, the other spouse has certain 'rights of occupation' (s. 1(1)) and cannot be evicted without an order of the court. Where a spouse is not in occupation of the matrimonial home he or she has a right, with the leave of the court, to enter and occupy the house. However, the court may order a spouse who is occupying the matrimonial home by reason of the Act to make periodical payments to the other spouse in respect of that occupation. It should be noted that the Act protects husbands as well as wives.

It should be noted that s. 1 of the Matrimonial Homes Act, 1983 provides that either of the spouses may apply to the court for an order prohibiting, suspending, or restricting the exercise by either spouse of the right to occupy the dwelling house or requiring either spouse to permit the exercise by the other of that right.

The Matrimonial Homes Act provides that the rights of occupation provided for in s. 1(1) are a charge on the estate or interest of the other spouse (s. 2(1)), registrable as a new type of land charge (Class F) under the Land Charges Act, 1972. Where the land is registered land a notice or caution must be registered under the Land Registration Act, 1925. A purchaser or mortgagee is deemed to have notice of rights of occupation which have been properly registered. Rights of occupation may be registered on marriage though in most cases registration will not take place unless and until the marriage breaks down.

Where a spouse registers rights of occupation, the house is unlikely subsequently to be an acceptable security for a loan because the rights of occupation represent a prior charge on the property which cannot be sold with vacant possession. However, a spouse who is entitled to rights of occupation may, under s. 6(3) of the Act, agree in writing that any other charge shall rank in priority to his or her charge.

However, even if the spouse's right of occupation is not registered it may still be recognised by the court.

ESSENTIAL CASE LAW AND COMMENT

Williams & Glyn's Bank Ltd v *Boland*, 1980 – An overriding interest **(501)**

Searching applies to encumbrances over unregistered land, but in many parts of the country land registration is compulsory, e.g. in London, Middlesex and Surrey. The system of registration of title to land is similar to registration of title to shares. However, in place of the share register which a company keeps there is a register of land holdings which is maintained by the State and instead of a share certificate there is a land certificate. When the land is transferred the registered owner hands over the land certificate together with a deed of transfer signed by him to the purchaser who then registers these documents with the Registrar who amends the land register and the land certificate and returns the latter to the transferee.

In general terms the State guarantees the accuracy of the register and if there is an error the register will be rectified and an indemnity paid to anyone who suffers loss, e.g. a person does not, in fact, get a good title to the land. The only interests in respect of which title may be registered are legal estates in land, i.e. a fee simple absolute in possession or a term of years absolute. As regards other interests in the land, all registered land is deemed to be subject to overriding interests listed in s. 70 of the Land Registration Act, 1925, whether these are on the register or not. Some of the more important overriding interests are easements and profits which exist over the land, and the interest of a wife in occupying the matrimonial home. (See *Williams & Glyn's Bank Ltd* v *Boland*, 1980, above.) Other interests may be protected by requiring an entry of e.g. a caution on the register. This entitles the person who asks for the caution to be notified by the Registrar of any proposed dealings with the land and to object within a specified period of time. Thus a purchaser under an estate contract could protect himself against further sales of the property in a situation where he had purchased it but had not yet received the land certificate from the registered proprietor.

It is expected that the compulsory registration system will, broadly speaking, be extended to all areas of the country within the next few years.

Mortgages of personal chattels

Just as land can be used as a means of securing debts, so also can personal chattels. There are two principal ways in which this can be done.

(a) *By mortgage.* In this case the borrower retains possession of his goods but transfers their ownership to the lender to secure the loan.

This raises a problem because, since the borrower retains the chattels, he also retains an appearance of wealth, and this may mislead others into giving him credit. Accordingly the Bills of Sale Acts, 1878–82, were passed, and under the statutory provisions, where chattels are retained by the mortgagor, a bill of sale must be made out. Where ownership of the chattel passes to the mortgagee conditionally upon its being reconveyed to the mortgagor on repayment of the loan, the Bill of Sale is called a conditional bill. An absolute Bill of Sale is one which transfers completely the ownership in chattels by way of sale, gift or settlement.

All Bills of Sale must be attested and registered within seven days of execution. Registration is in the Central Office of the Supreme Court. Conditional Bills of Sale must be reregistered every five years if they are still operative.

A conditional Bill of Sale is totally void if it is not registered, whilst an unregistered absolute Bill of Sale is void against the trustee in bankruptcy and judgment creditors of the grantor so that the chattels represented by the Bill are available to pay the grantor's debts. However, an absolute Bill of Sale will not be void for want of registration unless the chattels remain in the sole possession, or apparent possession, of the transferor (or grantor) of the Bill.

ESSENTIAL CASE LAW AND COMMENT

Koppel v *Koppel*, 1966 – What is apparent possession? **(502)**

(b) *By pledge, or 'pawn'.* In this case the lender obtains possession of the goods, the borrower retaining ownership. Thus there is no danger that the borrower will obtain credit on the strength of his possession of the chattels, and the law relating to pledges is mainly concerned to protect the interests of the borrower (or pledger) against dishonest pawnbrokers.

Mortgages of choses in action

It is possible to use a chose in action as security for a loan, and mortgagees frequently take life assurance policies as security, e.g. a bank in the case of an overdraft. However, shares in companies are perhaps the commonest chose in action to be used as security.

Shares may be made subject to a legal mortgage, but here the shares must actually be transferred to the mortgagee so that his name is in fact on the company's share register. An agreement is made out in which the mortgagee agrees to retransfer the shares to the mortgagor when the loan is repaid.

It is also possible to have an equitable mortgage of company shares, and this is in fact the usual method adopted. The share certificate is deposited with the mortgagee, together with a blank transfer signed by the registered holder, the name of the transferee being left blank. The shares are not actually transferred, but the agreement accompanying the transaction allows the mortgagee to sell the shares by completing the form of transfer and registering himself as the legal owner if the mortgagor fails to repay the loan.

Other forms of security

A security is some right or interest in property given to a creditor so that, if the debt is not paid, the creditor can obtain the amount of the debt by exercising certain remedies against the property, rather than by suing the debtor by means of a personal action on his promise to pay. Securities, therefore, create rights over the property of another and since we have already discussed mortgages of land, chattels and choses in action it remains only to consider the lien.

Lien

A lien is a right over the property of another which arises by operation of law and independently of any agreement. It gives a creditor the right (a) to retain possession of the debtor's property until he has paid or settled the debt, or (b) to sell the property in satisfaction of the debt in those cases where the lien is not possessory. Where the parties agree that a lien shall be created, such agreement will effectively create one.

POSSESSORY OR COMMON-LAW LIEN

To exercise this type of lien the creditor must have actual possession of the debtor's property, in which case he can retain it until the debt is paid or settled.

It should be noted that the creditor cannot ask for possession of the debtor's goods in order to exercise a lien.

A common-law lien may be particular or general –

(*a*) *Particular lien.* This gives the possessor the right to retain goods until a debt arising in connection with those goods is paid.

(*b*) *General lien.* This gives the possessor the right to retain goods not only for debts specifically connected with them, but also for all debts due from the owner of the goods however arising.

The law favours particular rather than general liens.

If X sends a clock to R to be repaired at a cost of £5, R may retain the clock under a particular lien until the £5 is paid. If, however, X owed R £10 for the earlier repair of a watch, R cannot retain the clock to enforce payment of £15 unless, as is unlikely, he can claim a general lien.

The following are cases of *particular lien* –

(i) A carrier can retain goods entrusted to him for carriage until his charges are paid.

(ii) An innkeeper has a lien over the property brought into the inn by a guest and also over property sent to him while there, even if it does not belong to him. The lien does not extend to motor cars or other vehicles, or to horses or other animals.

ESSENTIAL CASE LAW AND COMMENT

Robins v *Gray*, 1895 – An innkeeper's lien **(503)**

(iii) A shipowner has a lien on the cargo for freight due.

(iv) In a sale of goods, the unpaid seller has a lien on the goods, if still in his possession, to recover the price.

(v) Where a chattel is bailed in order that work may be done on it or labour and skill expended in connection with it, it may be retained until the charge is paid. Such liens may arise e.g. in favour of a car repairer over the car repaired, by an arbitrator on an award and by an architect over plans he has prepared.

A *general lien* may arise out of contract or custom, and the following classes of persons have a general lien over the property of their customers or clients – factors, bankers, solicitors, stockbrokers, and in some cases insurance brokers.

ESSENTIAL CASE LAW AND COMMENT

Caldwell v *Sumpters*, 1971 – A solicitor's lien **(504)**

In the course of their professional work accountants have at least a particular lien for unpaid fees over any books, files and papers delivered to them by clients and also over any other documents which come into their possession while acting for clients but not the statutory books of a registered company since these are in many cases open to inspection by members and in some cases by the public. (See *Woodworth* v *Conroy* [1976] 1 All E.R. 107.)

Although a common-law lien normally gives no power of sale, there are some exceptional cases in which a right of sale is given by statute. Such a right is given to innkeepers (Innkeepers Act, 1878), unpaid sellers of goods (Sale of Goods Act, 1979) and bailees who accept goods for repair or other treatment for reward (Torts (Interference with Goods) Act, 1977). Briefly, the latter Act provides for the sale of goods accepted for repair or other treatment or for valuation or appraisal or for storage and warehousing provided the bailee gives notice to the bailor specifying the date on or after which he proposes to sell the goods. The period between the notice and the date specifying sale must be such as will afford the bailor a reasonable opportunity of taking delivery of the goods. However, if he does not do so the bailee may sell them but must account to the bailor for the balance of the proceeds of sale after deduction of charges and expenses.

It should also be noted that the High Court has a discretion to order the sale of goods if it is just to do so, e.g. where the goods are perishable.

ESSENTIAL CASE LAW AND COMMENT

Larner v *Fawcett*, 1950 – Power of court to order a sale **(505)**

A common law lien is discharged –

(*a*) by payment of the sum owing;

(*b*) by parting with the possession of the goods or other property upon which the lien is being exercised (but see *Caldwell* v *Sumpters*, 1971 at p. 827.);

(*c*) by an agreement to give credit for the amount due;

(*d*) by accepting an alternative security for the debt owing.

MARITIME LIEN

A maritime lien does not depend on possession. It is a right which attaches to a ship in connection with a maritime liability. It travels with the ship and may be enforced by the arrest and the sale of the ship through the medium of a court having Admiralty jurisdiction. Examples of such liens are –

(*a*) Liens of salvors.

(*b*) The lien of a master for his outgoings.

(*c*) Liens which arise from damage due to collision.

(*d*) Liens of bottomry bond holders. A bottomry bond is a form of security under which a ship and/or its cargo is pledged for the repayment of money borrowed for the purposes of a voyage.

The order of attachment is important and depends on circumstances.

Successive salvage liens attach in inverse order, later ones being preferred to earlier ones, since the earlier lien would be useless if the later salvage had not preserved the ship from loss. Claims for collision damage are treated as of equal rank. Liens for wages, in the absence of salvage liens, have priority over other liens; however, liens for wages earned before a salvage operation are postponed to the lien for salvage, since the value of such a lien has been preserved by the salvage operation.

If a ship which is subject to lien is sold, the purchaser takes it subject to the lien and is responsible for discharging it.

EQUITABLE LIEN

An equitable lien is an equitable right, conferred by law, whereby one person acquires a charge on the property of another until certain claims have been met. It differs from a common-law lien which is founded on possession and does not confer a power of sale. An equitable lien is independent of possession and may be enforced by a judicial sale.

An equitable lien may arise out of an express provision in a contract or from the relationship between parties. Thus a partner has an equitable lien upon the partnership assets for the purpose of ensuring that they are applied, on dissolution, to paying partnership debts. Furthermore, an *unpaid* vendor of land has an equitable lien on the property even after conveyance of ownership to the purchaser, or a third party who has taken it with notice of the lien, under which he may ask the court for an order to sell the property so that he may obtain the purchase money owing to him.

An equitable lien can, like all equitable rights, be extinguished by the owner selling the property to a *bona fide* purchaser for value who has no notice of the lien.

An equitable lien differs from a mortgage. A mortgage, as we have seen, is always created by the act of parties, and an equitable lien may arise by operation of law.

BANKER'S LIEN

At common law a banker has a general possessory lien on all securities, and e.g. bills of exchange, promissory notes and bonds, deposited with him by customers in the ordinary course of business unless there is an agreement, express or implied, to the contrary. The lien does not extend to property or securities deposited for safe custody. However, a customer may deposit a security as collateral for a loan, in which case the banker has rights over it, but the transaction is an equitable mortgage rather than a lien.

A banker's lien gives a right of sale, at least of negotiable securities subject to the lien, because s. 27 of the Bills of Exchange Act, 1882 provides that a person having a possessory lien over a bill is deemed a holder for value to the extent of the lien, and can, therefore, sell and transfer the bill.

Assignments of choses in action

The common law does not recognise assignments of choses in action, but Equity does and so does statute.

ASSIGNMENT BY ACT OF PARTIES

There are four possible categories.

A legal assignment of a legal chose under s. 136 of the Law of Property Act, 1925

To be effective such an assignment, e.g. the goodwill of a business, must be absolute and not partial; must be in writing signed by the assignor; and must be notified in writing to the debtor, generally by the assignee. If the above requirements are complied with, the assignee can sue the debtor without making the assignor a party to the action. Failure to give notice to the debtor means that there is no legal assignment; the debtor can validly pay the assignor, and the assignee is liable to be postponed to a later assignee for value who notifies the debtor. However, it is not necessary for the date of the assignment to be given in the notice of assignment as long as the letter, or other form of written notice, states clearly that there has been an assignment and identifies the assignee. (*Van Lynn Developments Ltd* v *Pelias Construction Co. Ltd* [1968] 3 All E.R. 824.)

Equitable assignments of legal choses

Equitable assignments of equitable choses

The difference between a legal and an equitable chose is historical in that an equitable chose is a right which, before 1875, could only be enforced in the Court of Chancery, e.g. the interest of a beneficiary under a trust fund.

In equitable assignments of legal choses the assignor must be made a party in any action against the debtor, but if the chose is equitable this is not necessary. No particular form is required; all that is necessary is evidence of intention to assign. Notice should be given to the debtor or the trustees, as the case may be, in order to preserve priority as outlined above.

Thus the transfer of a debt by word of mouth, although invalid under statute, may nevertheless be good and enforceable in Equity.

Equitable assignments of mere expectancies

These are mere hopes of future entitlement, e.g. a legacy under the will of a living testator. The rules regarding such assignments are the same as those set out under the previous two sub-headings, but no notice to the debtor can be given because there is none. Value is not needed for assignments within s. 136 of the Law of Property Act, 1925, or for equitable assignments of equitable choses in action. It is probably not needed for an equitable assignment of a legal chose, though the position is not clear. Value is needed for the assignment of mere expectancies; a document by deed is not enough. Value is also needed to support an agreement to assign an equitable chose, but if the assignee lawfully takes delivery of the property assigned, the assignor cannot recover it.

Assignments are said to be 'subject to equities'; the person to whom the right is assigned takes it subject to any right of set off which was available against the original assignor. So if X assigns to Z a debt of £10 due from Y, and X also owes Y £5, then in any action brought by Z for the money, Y can set off the debt of £5. But the assignee is not subject to purely personal claims which would have been available against the assignor, e.g. damages for fraud, though the remedy of rescission is available against the assignee where the assignor obtained the contract by fraud.

Assignments of certain choses in action are governed by special statutes so that the rules outlined above do not apply. In such cases the special statute must be complied with. Examples are –

(a) *Bills of exchange, cheques and promissory notes* – Bills of Exchange Act, 1882.

(b) *Shares in companies* registered under the Companies Act, 1985 and previous Acts – Companies Act, 1985.

(c) *Policies of life assurance* – Policies of Assurance Act, 1867.

Rights of a personal nature under a contract cannot be assigned. If X contracts to write newspaper articles for a certain newspaper, it cannot assign its rights under the contract to another. The right to recover damages in litigation cannot be assigned, for reasons of public policy. Liabilities under a contract cannot be assigned; the party to benefit cannot be compelled by mere notice to accept the performance of another, though a liability can be transferred by a novation (a new contract), if the party to benefit agrees.

ASSIGNMENT BY OPERATION OF LAW

The involuntary assignment of rights and liabilities arises in the case of death and bankruptcy.

Death

The personal representatives of the deceased acquire his rights and liabilities, the latter to the extent of the estate. Contracts of personal service are discharged.

Bankruptcy

The trustee in bankruptcy has vested in him all the rights of the bankrupt, except for actions of a purely personal nature which in no way affect the value of the estate, e.g. actions for defamation. The trustee is liable to the extent of the estate for the bankrupt's liabilities, though the trustee has a right to disclaim onerous or unprofitable contracts.

23
Criminal law – general principles

Crime and civil wrongs distinguished

As we have indicated in Chapter 1 the distinction does not lie in the *nature of the act* itself. For example, if a railway porter is offered a reward to carry A's case and runs off with it, then the porter has committed one crime, that of theft, and two civil wrongs, i.e. the tort of wrongful interference and a breach of his contract with A. Again, a signalman who carelessly fails to operate signals so that a fatal accident occurs will have committed one crime, i.e. manslaughter, if persons are killed, and two civil wrongs, the tort of negligence in respect of those who died and those who are merely injured, and a breach of his contract of service with British Rail in which there is an implied term to take due care. It should also be noted that in this case the right of action in tort and the right of action in contract are vested in different persons.

The distinction does depend on the *legal consequences* which follow the act. If the wrongful act is capable of being followed by what are called criminal proceedings that means that it is regarded as a crime. If it is capable of being followed by civil proceedings that means that it is regarded as a civil wrong. If it is capable of being followed by both it is both a crime and a civil wrong. Criminal and civil proceedings are usually easily distinguishable, they are generally brought in different courts, the procedure is different, the outcome is different and the terminology is different. A major consequence of classifying proceedings as criminal is that the burden of proof is on the Crown.

Terminology and outcome of criminal and civil proceedings

In criminal proceedings a prosecutor prosecutes a defendant. If the prosecution is successful it results in the conviction of the defendant. After the conviction the court may deal with the defendant by giving him a custodial sentence, e.g. prison or detention centre; or a non-custodial sentence, e.g.

probation, or a community service order. In rare cases the court may discharge the defendant without sentence.

As regards *civil proceedings*, a plaintiff *sues* (brings an action against) a defendant. If the plaintiff is successful this leads to the court entering judgment ordering, for example, that the defendant pay a debt owed to the plaintiff or damages. Alternatively, it may require the defendant to transfer property to the plaintiff or to do or not to do something (injunction) or to perform a contract (specific performance). Some of these remedies are legal, others equitable. The matter of remedies for breach of contract and for torts has already been dealt with in detail in the chapters on those topics.

Nulla poena sine lege

This important maxim means that a person should not be made to suffer criminal penalties except for a clear breach of *existing* criminal law, that law being precise and well defined.

The maxim thus prohibits –

(*a*) the introduction of new crimes which operate retrospectively under which a person might be found guilty of a crime for doing an act which was not criminal when he did it;

(*b*) wide interpretation of precedents to include by analogy crimes which do not directly fall within it. Thus the extension of the criminal law in the way, for example, in which the civil law of negligence has been extended (see p. 435) is undesirable;

(*c*) the formulation of criminal laws in wide and vague terms.

The last rule has in general terms been observed in England, with perhaps the major exception of the law of conspiracy under which there has been a tendency to charge persons with criminal conspiracy rather than with specific criminal offences. Thus a conviction might be obtained for conspiracy to do an act even though there were doubts as to whether the act was or ought to be criminal.

Under ss. 1–5 of the Criminal Law Act, 1977, the offence of conspiracy at common law is abolished and the new statutory offence of conspiracy is restricted to agreements to commit criminal offences, though the common-law offences of conspiracy to defraud and conspiracy to corrupt public morals are retained.

ESSENTIAL CASE LAW AND COMMENT

Woolmington v *D.P.P.*, 1935 – Burden of proof in crime **(506)**
Shaw v *D.P.P.*, 1961 – No punishment except for breach of existing law **(507)**

Constituent elements of a criminal offence

The commission of a crime necessarily involves two elements –

(*a*) the *actus reus* (guilty act); and
(*b*) the *mens rea* (guilty mind).

Therefore a guilty act does not make a person guilty of crime unless the mind is guilty and *vice versa*.

The *actus reus*

The defendant's conduct must in general be *voluntary*. If a person is made to act there is no *actus reus*. Sir Matthew Hale says in his treatise on the criminal law entitled *Pleas of the Crown* written in 1682: 'If A takes the hand of B in which is a weapon and therewith kills C, A is guilty of murder but B is excused.' Duress as by threats which cause a person to act is not in fact regarded as involuntary conduct but may be a defence for some crimes (see further p. 555).

In addition if a person acts instinctively in response to some stimulus and in so doing commits a criminal offence he will not be liable. A famous example was given in *Hill* v *Baxter* [1958] 1 All E.R. 193 in connection with a prosecution for dangerous driving where the court said that a person would not be guilty of such an offence if 'the car was temporarily out of control by his being attacked by a swarm of bees'. It will be found, however, that in the case of some statutory offences no voluntary act is required (see further p. 532).

THE ACT MUST BE CAUSATIVE

In order to convict a person of a crime it is necessary to show that the act which he did was the *substantive cause of the crime*. In this connection it should be noted that the accused takes his victim as he finds him so that the abnormal state of the victim's health will not normally excuse a person who by his acts has accelerated the death of such a victim.

ESSENTIAL CASE LAW AND COMMENT

R v *Towers*, 1874 – Need to prove causation **(508)**
R v *Hayward*, 1908 – Accused cannot successfully plead the victim's state of health **(509)**

INTERVENING ACTS AND EVENTS

It may be that between the initial act of the defendant and the criminal event with which he is charged a new act or event occurred and contributed to the criminal event. The defendant will nevertheless be liable unless the intervening event was unforeseeable and would have brought about the consequence on its own.

Sometimes the intervening act is that of the victim but the accused will still be guilty if it was reasonably foreseeable that the victim would act in the way he did as a result of the behaviour of the accused. Finally the intervening act may be the improper medical treatment of an injury inflicted upon the victim by the accused. Here the general rule is that the court will be reluctant to blame doctors and other medical personnel for a death where the condition which they were called upon to treat was brought about by the unlawful act of the accused.

ESSENTIAL CASE LAW AND COMMENT

R v *Curley*, 1909 – Intervening act of victim **(510)**
R v *Smith*, 1959 – Improper medical treatment **(511)**

It should be noted that it is not necesary for the Crown to establish which of the accused's actions caused the death. Thus in *Attorney-General's Reference (No. 4 of 1980)* [1981] 1 W.L.R. 705 the accused pushed his girlfriend downstairs and, believing her to be dead, dragged her upstairs by a rope around her neck, cut her throat, and dismembered and disposed of the body. He was charged with manslaughter and it was held by the Court of Appeal that he could be convicted, provided the jury was satisfied that one of the actions did cause the death, notwithstanding that it was impossible to say which of the culpable acts did so.

Omissions or failure to act

In general terms a mere failure to act cannot lead to criminal liability. However, there may be liability for an omission in the following situations.

MORAL OBLIGATIONS ARISING FROM PARTICULAR RELATIONSHIPS

Sometimes where a person is in a particular relationship with another which is either imposed by law such as parent or child or voluntarily assumed as where A is looking after an old aunt, the relationship may give rise to an obligation to act. Failure to discharge the responsibilities arising from the relationship may result in criminal liability.

ESSENTIAL CASE LAW AND COMMENT

R v *Instan*, 1893 – Liability for omissions **(512)**

CONTRACTUAL DUTIES

A person may incur criminal liability because a contract, e.g. of employment, places upon him a duty to act. The duty is not confined to the other party to the contract but may extend also to third parties.

ESSENTIAL CASE LAW AND COMMENT

R v *Pittwood*, 1902 – A crossing gate is left open **(513)**

PREVIOUS CONDUCT

Where the defendant has by his previous acts created a potentially dangerous situation and later comes to realise this he has a duty to act to prevent the danger.

ESSENTIAL CASE LAW AND COMMENT

R v *Miller*, 1983 – A smoking mattress **(514)**

DUTY TO ACT UNDER STATUTE

Some modern statutes make failure to act a crime. For example s. 170 of the Road Traffic Act, 1988 makes it an offence if those involved in road accidents fail to report the accident to the police within 24 hours or give relevant details to any other person who being at the scene of the accident reasonably requests them.

The *mens rea* – generally

The *actus reus* must be accompanied by an appropriate state of mind which is referred to as *mens rea*. The *mens rea* and the *actus reus* must coincide in order to constitute a crime. (See further p. 534.) Before looking at the different states of mind involved it should be noted that as in the law of torts *motive*, i.e. the reason why the defendant did the act, is irrelevant in regard to his guilt or innocence if his direct intention was to commit the offence.

ESSENTIAL CASE LAW AND COMMENT

Chandler v *D.P.P.*, 1962 – Impeding the operation of an airfield
(515)

The following states of mind are relevant.

DIRECT INTENT

This occurs where there exists in the mind of the defendant *a desire* to commit
the crime, as where A shoots at B foreseeing and desiring and wishing that
B will be killed, or as where A deliberately fails to feed an aged parent in
the hope and expectation of bringing about that parent's death.

OBLIQUE INTENT

Here *the consequence is not desired* as such. The defendant may even hope
that what happened would not happen but has nevertheless gone ahead with
the harmful activity, in what one is tempted to say is a reckless fashion. Indeed
the concepts of oblique intent and recklessness as states of mind are at times
quite close and not readily distinguishable. In homicide cases an oblique intent
will normally result in a conviction for manslaughter and not murder and
the major change brought about by modern case law is that intent is no longer
established by a kind of objective foresight of consequences as is liability in
tort.

ESSENTIAL CASE LAW AND COMMENT

R v *Maloney*, 1985 – Larking with guns **(516)**

RECKLESSNESS

In some crimes it is necessary to find a direct intent. Included here would
be murder and wounding with intent under s. 18 of the Offences Against
the Person Act, 1861. The House of Lords has recently reaffirmed that to
establish an offence under s. 20 it is necessary to prove that the defendant
saw that the consequence of his unlawful act would be to cause some physical
harm to the victim even if of a minor degree. This is oblique intent (see *R*
v *Savage*, *The Times*, 8 November 1991).

   In other cases e.g. criminal damage and rape, intention or recklessness is
enough. So far as manslaughter is concerned either an oblique intent or
recklessness would seem to suffice. The line between oblique intent and
recklessness in the decided cases is as we have seen often very difficult to
draw. Recklesness so far as the earlier cases were concerned was to be decided
subjectively, i.e. the defendant must have appreciated the risk. Objective tests

were to be reserved for the civil law. However, in more recent times the courts have developed an objective test for recklessness though at the moment this test seems to be applied largely in cases involving criminal damage, though a fairly recent case applied it to manslaughter.

ESSENTIAL CASE LAW AND COMMENT

R v *Cunningham*, 1957 – Recklessness: the subjective test **(517)**
R v *Caldwell*, 1981 – Recklessness: the objective test **(518)**

The two tests are therefore available and it seems that the *Cunningham* test survives in cases of rape (see further p. 549) while the *Caldwell* test is to be found in statutory crimes such as criminal damage and sometimes in manslaughter.

NEGLIGENCE

It is extremely rare to find that negligence is a state of mind for a criminal offence. However, the fact that a person has not been negligent can be a defence in some statutory crimes. For example where foreign matter has got into food it is a defence for a person involved in its sale to show that he acted *with due diligence* to prevent the commission of the offence (see s. 21, Food Safety Act, 1990). Thus only persons who are negligent will be successfully prosecuted.

WHERE INTENT IS TRANSFERRED

Provided the defendant has the necessary *mens rea* and commits the intended *actus reus* it does not matter that the victim is not the person he intended to harm. However, the *mens rea* for one offence cannot be transferred to another.

ESSENTIAL CASE LAW AND COMMENT

R v *Latimer*, 1886 – A different victim **(519)**
R v *Pembliton*, 1874 – A different crime **(520)**

MENS REA AND *ACTUS REUS* MUST COINCIDE

There must be a coincidence of these two elements. However, it may be that although at the outset the act did not carry with it the necessary *mens rea* this came later during what the court regards as a continuing act or one transaction.

ESSENTIAL CASE LAW AND COMMENT

Fagan v *Metropolitan Police Commissioner*, 1968 – A car on a
  policeman's foot **(350)**
Thabo Meli v *R*, 1954 – A killing in one transaction **(521)**

Mens rea in statutory offences

The principles applied in regard to *mens rea* where the offence is set out in
a statute are somewhat different from those applied in common-law offences.
The topic may be considered under the headings which follow.

MENS REA IMPLIED

As Lord Reid said in *Sweet* v *Parsley*, 1969 (see p. 836) 'there has for centuries
been a presumption that Parliament did not intend to make criminals of
persons who were in no way blameworthy in what they did. This means that
whenever a section of an Act is silent as to the requirement of *mens rea* there
is a presumption that, in order to give effect to the will of Parliament, we
must read in words appropriate to require *mens rea*.'

ESSENTIAL CASE LAW AND COMMENT

Sweet v *Parsley*, 1969 – Statutory offences: presumption of
  requirement of *mens rea* **(522)**
R v *Tolson*, 1889 – A bigamous wife **(523)**

However, statutes which regulate public conduct and which cannot be
enforced effectively if *mens rea* is required, e.g. pollution of the environment,
are sometimes excepted from the rule that statutory crimes require *mens rea*
by implication.

ESSENTIAL CASE LAW AND COMMENT

Alphacell v *Woodward*, 1972 – Strict liability for pollution **(524)**
Cundy v *Le Cocq*, 1884 – Selling liquor to a drunk **(525)**

PARTICULAR WORDS CONNOTING *MENS REA*

The use of words such as 'maliciously', 'knowingly', 'wilfully', 'permitting'
and 'suffering' in a statute is usually an indication that *mens rea* is required

to establish the offence. However, the absence of such words does not necessarily mean that no *mens rea* is required as we have seen from cases such as *Sweet* v *Parsley*, 1969 at p. 836.

ESSENTIAL CASE LAW AND COMMENT

Gaumont British Distributors Ltd v *Henry*, 1939 – Where a record was not knowingly made **(526)**

R v *Lowe*, 1973 – A charge of wilful neglect **(527)**

Somerset v *Wade*, 1894 – Permitting drunkenness **(528)**

VICARIOUS LIABILITY

If the offence is one which does not require *mens rea* so that it is an *absolute offence* an employer may be liable where an employee commits the offence in the course of his employment. It is no defence for the employer to say that he had no *mens rea* because none is required.

However, if the offence requires *mens rea* as where, for example, it is one involving 'permitting', an employer will not be liable vicariously if it is the employee who does the permitting.

ESSENTIAL CASE LAW AND COMMENT

Griffiths v *Studebakers Ltd*, 1924 – Vicarious liability: an absolute offence **(529)**

James v *Smee*, 1955 – Vicarious liability : where *mens rea* is required **(530)**

If a person carries on a business which requires a licence which is issued subject to the observance of certain conditions, he cannot escape liability by delegating the duty of seeing that those conditions are observed to either an employee or a stranger. However, where the offence requires *knowledge* the holder of the licence will not be liable for the acts of his delegate unless the delegation is of the whole function of the licensee as where he leaves the premises to take a holiday so that the management of the business is in the hands of the delegate.

An employer cannot, it would appear, be liable vicariously for *aiding and abetting* an offence unles he has knowledge of the offence. The knowledge of an employee in regard to such a charge is not imputed to the employer in order to make him liable.

ESSENTIAL CASE LAW AND COMMENT

Vane v *Yiannopoullos*, 1965 – Delegation of duties **(531)**

Ferguson v *Weaving*, 1951 – Aiding and abetting **(532)**

The mental element – corporations

In October 1987 an application was made for leave to apply for judicial review against the decision of the coroner for East Kent made on 18 and 19 September 1987 in the course of an inquest into the deaths of 188 people arising out of the capsize on 6 March 1987 of the *Herald of Free Enterprise* off Zeebrugge (See *ex parte Spooner and Others*; *ex parte de Rohan and Another*, *The Times*, 10 October 1987.)

As we have seen, application can be made to the Queen's Bench Divisional Court for judicial review to correct an alleged defect in a proceeding in a lower court, tribunal or public body. The coroner had decided as a matter of law that –

(*a*) A corporate body could not be guilty of manslaughter.

(*b*) Where the individual acts or omissions of individuals employed by a corporate body or engaged in its management were insufficient to render them guilty of manslaughter, those acts or omissions could not be aggregated in order to make the corporate body guilty.

(*c*) The acts and omissions of the company, Townsend Car Ferries Ltd, were not the direct cause of the deaths.

The applicants, who were seeking to have the coroner's decisions reviewed, relied on three points made against the company in the Sheen Report published in July 1987 following an enquiry under Mr Justice Sheen. These were that –

(*a*) the company had failed to consider seriously a proposal to fit a warning light system on the ferry;

(*b*) five or six previous incidents of ferry doors being left open had not been properly reported and collated by the company; and

(*c*) it lacked any proper system to ensure that the highest standards of safety were observed.

In hearing the application for judicial review, Lord Justice Bingham said that he was prepared tentatively to accept that a corporate body was capable of being found guilty of manslaughter and Mr Justice Mann and Mr Justice Kennedy agreed.

However, the Court refused leave to apply for judicial review. No substantial case had been made against named directors of the company and in any case the Court was always reluctant to intervene in inquests.

So far the proceedings may seem to have been rather ordinary and straightforward but in fact the tentative acceptance of corporate liability for serious crime is far from innocuous. Up to now corporations have been convicted of crimes as follows –

(*a*) those for which no guilty mind (*mens rea*) or even recklessness as to consequences is necessary. Some Acts of Parliament which regulate public conduct cannot be enforced effectively if an intentional or reckless state of mind is required, either in an individual or a corporation, e.g. statutory crimes relating to the pollution of the environment are sometimes excepted from the rule that even statutory crimes require *mens rea*, either expressly or by implication even though no state of mind is mentioned in the statute. An example is provided by *Alphacell* v *Woodward*, 1972 at p. 837.

(*b*) Crimes which require a state of mind. Here, if the appropriate human decision-making organ within the company has the necessary state of mind the company may be found guilty. Examples are to be found in *Director of Public Prosecutions* v *Kent & Sussex Contractors Ltd* [1944] 1 All E.R. 119 where a company was convicted under statutory defence regulations for using a document with *intent* to deceive and for making a false statement, since those managing the company had the necessary state of mind.

Again, in *R* v *ICR Haulage Ltd* [1944] K.B. 551 the company was successfully prosecuted for a *common-law* conspiracy to defraud because of the state of mind of its managing director.

Finally, in *Moore* v *Bresler Ltd* [1944] 2 All E.R. 515 a company was successfully prosecuted for using a document with *intent* to defraud when the acts and state of mind were those of the company secretary and a branch manager, not those of the directors.

The requirements were clearly laid down by Lord Denning in *H.L. Bolton (Engineering) Ltd* v *T.J. Graham & Sons Ltd* [1956] 3 All E.R. 624 where he said:

> A company may in many ways be likened to a human body. It has a brain and nerve centre which controls what it does. It also has hands which hold the tools and act in accordance with directions from the centre. Some of the people in the company are mere servants and agents who are nothing more than hands to do the work and cannot be said to represent the mind or will. Others are directors and managers who represent the directing mind and will of the company and control what it does. The state of mind of these managers is the state of mind of the company and is treated by the law as such.

(*c*) If there is to be a third category of corporate liability it would be based upon the fact that although no single individual is criminally culpable, he or she is nevertheless part of a complex and collective corporate mind which, when aggregated, gives the necessary culpability. These non-culpable people may be regarded by the courts in the future as part of a group lacking, say, a proper system of control and supervision to ensure observance of safety elements which, in a particular case, could lead to a conviction of the organisation involved – the company – for a crime as serious as manslaughter where death of a person or persons has ensued. Since manslaughter is punishable by a fine, which is at the discretion of the court and has no limit, there would be no problem in punishing the corporation.

If such a prosecution were successful, it would bring *Salomon v Salomon*, 1897 (see p. 584) full circle. Since that case people have accepted gradually that it is *companies that do things*, such as make contracts and obtain licences and so on. The last frontier is the corporate doing of a crime where the necessary state of mind is not derived from any particular individual but from all those individuals involved in the failure of the system in general. The admission by the Court in *ex parte Spooner and Others* (above) that a corporate body is capable of being guilty of manslaughter suggests that if appropriate circumstances arise the law will take the final leap in the personification of corporate entities.

It has to be said, however, that the great leap forward has not taken place. The Director of Public Prosecutions decided in 1989 to prosecute in regard to the Zeebrugge disaster. The prosecution collapsed because the Crown was unable to prove that the senior officers involved had any specific duties and responsibilities for certain areas of safety which they had failed to carry out. Since that time some 1000 people have been killed e.g. at work and yet no prosecution of the corporate employer has taken place. The companies concerned have merely been fined following a prosecution under health and safety legislation. The development towards corporate manslaughter has not taken place.

24
Criminal law – specific offences

The intention here is to include only specific offences against the person. These are set out below.

Homicide

Homicide is the unlawful killing of a human being. There are three homicides, i.e. murder, manslaughter and causing death by dangerous driving.

Murder

This is a common-law offence and to constitute it there must be an unlawful killing of a human being under the Queen's peace with malice aforethought the victim dying within a year and a day of the defendant's criminal conduct.

THE *ACTUS REUS*

Since the killing must be of a human being the unlawful killing of an unborn child is not murder. However such killings are covered and made criminal in appropriate circumstances by s. 58 of the Offences Against the Person Act, 1861, s. 1 of the Infant Life (Preservation) Act, 1929 and the Abortion Act, 1967. The detail of these offences is not considered here. The fact that the victim must be 'under the Queen's peace' prevents the killing of the enemy in wartime from being murder. In addition a killing in self-defence may be lawful and so not murder (see further p. 558). Finally the victim must die within a year and a day.

ESSENTIAL CASE LAW AND COMMENT

R v *Dyson*, 1908 – Death within a year and a day **(533)**

THE *MENS REA*

Some consideration has already been given to this (see p. 532). However the *mens rea* for murder is defined as 'malice aforethought'. According to the House of Lords in *Moloney*, 1985 (see p. 832) murder is a crime which requires a specific intent, either direct as where the defendant *desired* the consequences, or oblique as where he foresaw the consequences as *near certain*. Recklessness is not enough. The court must be satisfied of the presence of such an intent either to kill or cause grievous bodily harm.

In this connection it should be noted that the decision in *Moloney*, 1985 confirms that it is enough malice if the intention is not to kill but to cause grievous bodily harm.

Manslaughter

Manslaughter is divided into voluntary manslaughter and involuntary manslaughter.

Voluntary manslaughter

This is murder reduced to manslaughter by the presence under the Homicide Act, 1957 of provocation or diminished responsibility. Once it is shown that one of these partial defences exists the crime ceases to be murder and the fixed penalty of life imprisonment goes, giving the judge a discretion as to sentence.

PROVOCATION – GENERALLY

Section 3 of the Homicide Act, 1957 applies. It provides as follows.

> Where on a charge of murder there is evidence on which the jury can find that the person charged was provoked (whether by things done or by things said or by both together) to lose his self control, the question whether the provocation was enough to make a reasonable man do as he did shall be left to be determined by the jury; and in determining that question the jury shall take into account everything both done and said according to the effect which, in their opinion, it would have on a reasonable man.

WAS THERE PROVOCATION?

Although the issue of provocation is normally raised by the defence the burden of proving that there was *no* provocation is on the prosecution once it is raised. Where therefore the jury has a reasonable doubt about the matter it must be taken that the defendant was provoked. The judge can put the matter to the jury if it is not raised by the defence. The test here is subjective, i.e. was the particular defendant provoked? If the jury find he was not then it is not relevant that a reasonable man would have been.

HOW WOULD A REASONABLE MAN REACT?

The next stage in the test is objective. If the jury decide that the defendant was provoked then they must go on to decide how a *reasonable man with the defendant's characteristics* would have responded to that provocation. The reasonable man test means in effect that the defendant's reaction will normally have to bear some proportion to the provocation.

ESSENTIAL CASE LAW AND COMMENT

R v *Camplin*, 1978 – Taunting a 15-year-old **(534)**

OTHER MATTERS

A relevant provocation can be induced by the defendant himself. In addition there must be a 'sudden and temporary loss of self-control' which means that there must not be a significant 'cooling-off' period between the provocation and the killing.

ESSENTIAL CASE LAW AND COMMENT

R v *Johnson*, 1989 – Where provocation is self-induced **(535)**
R v *Thornton*, 1991 – There must be a sudden and temporary loss of control **(536)**

DIMINISHED RESPONSIBILITY

By reason of s. 2(1) of the Homicide Act, 1957 this defence is available in respect of a murder charge only. The burden of proof is on the defence which must show that the defendant 'was suffering from such abnormality of mind (whether arising from a condition of arrested or retarded development of mind or any inherent causes or induced by disease or injury) as substantially impaired his mental responsibility for his acts and omissions in doing or being a party to the killing'.

The defence is wider than that of insanity (see p. 551) and covers other mental conditions. In fact the defendant may *know* what he is doing and that it is *wrong*. His alleged problem is that he finds it *substantially more difficult to control* his actions than would a normal person, and this difficulty is caused by some *abnormality of his mind*.

It is not correct for a judge to direct the jury that only partial or borderline insanity amounts to diminished responsibility (*R* v *Seers* [1984] 79 Cr. App. R. 261).

A killing arising from drink or drugs is not covered because these conditions do not come within 'disease or injury'. However, where the taking of excessive drink or drugs over a period have, in effect, caused mental disease then the defence has been applied.

ESSENTIAL CASE LAW AND COMMENT

R v *Tandy*, 1987 – Use of alcohol not involuntary **(537)**
R v *Gittins*, 1984 – Where the taking of drink and drugs is a disease **(538)**

Involuntary manslaughter

It is apparent from the case law that involuntary manslaughter is based upon either an unlawful act resulting in death or death resulting from gross (or criminal) negligence or recklessness.

MANSLAUGHTER FROM AN UNLAWFUL ACT

If by an unlawful act done deliberately to the person of another, the circumstances being such that a reasonable person would realise the risk of injury, and that other is killed the killing is manslaughter even though the defendant never foresaw death or the risk of death. The realisation of the risk of some kind of physical harm is enough. An unlawful omission is not enough. There must be an act which is unlawful.

ESSENTIAL CASE LAW AND COMMENT

R v *Church*, 1966 – The unlawful act must create the risk of physical harm **(539)**
R v *Lowe*, 1973 – Unlawful omission not generally enough **(527)**

MANSLAUGHTER BY GROSS NEGLIGENCE OR RECKLESSNESS

To cause death by *any* lack of due care will not amount to manslaughter. A very high degree of negligence is necessary for the establishment of a crime. Whether the appropriate degree of negligence exists is a matter for the jury.

The test according to the Privy Council in *Kong Chuek Kwan* v *The Queen* (1985) 82 Cr. App. R. 18, where there was a collision at sea causing death, is to put the following questions to the jury –

(*a*) Do they find that the defendant's acts created an obvious and serious risk of causing injury? and

(*b*) If such a risk was created do they find that the defendant gave no thought to the possibility of that risk or did he recognise the risk but nevertheless go on to take it?

If the findings on (*a*) and (*b*) above are affirmative then the degree of negligence necessary for crime is established. *R*. v *Caldwell*, 1981 (see p. 834) was applied. It should be noted that in (*a*) above the Privy Council referred to the risk of causing injury not death. Thus risk of injury is all that the law requires.

Causing death by dangerous driving

Under s. 1 of the Road Traffic Act, 1991 the offence of causing death by dangerous driving replaces the offence of causing death by reckless driving in s. 1 of the Road Traffic Act, 1972. It was felt that while the general remarks about criminal recklessness in *Caldwell* had relevance in regard to manslaughter generally they were not entirely suitable in the road traffic situation. In particular it was felt to be *too subjective* so that there was a need to move to an *objective assessment of the standard of driving of the defendant*. The offence of causing death by dangerous driving has two elements as follows.

(*a*) There must be a standard of driving which falls far below that to be expected of a competent and careful driver; and

(*b*) The driving must carry a potential or actual danger of physical injury or serious damage to property.

The standard of driving will be judged objectively taking no account e.g. of inexperience, age or disability – though these will be reflected in the sentence. The requirements of the section would be met where the state of the vehicle was such that a competent and careful driver would not drive it at all. If a driver was in an unfit condition to drive, e.g. by reason of drink or drugs, this would not be a defence if he drove dangerously as defined above.

Violent offences which are not fatal

Under this heading we must consider the following crimes.

Assault and battery

It has already been pointed out in Chapter 21 on the law of specific torts that assault is a threat to apply force immediately to the person of the victim and a battery is the actual application of that force. This distinction also exists in the criminal law.

ASSAULT

The *actus reus* of assault consists of an act which gives the victim reasonable cause to believe that there will be an immediate infliction of violence. Assault requires basic intent and so actual intention or *Caldwell* recklessness is enough.

BATTERY

The *actus reus* consists in the actual application of force however slight to another without that other's consent. As we have seen a battery can consist of an omission (see *Fagan* v *Metropolitan Police Commissioner*, 1968 at p. 736).

The *mens rea* is a basic intent and so once again actual intention or *Caldwell* recklessness will suffice.

DEFENCES

The following defences are available.

CHASTISEMENT

As we have seen reasonable chastisement by a parent is a defence though this is not available to teachers unless they have the parents' permission, since the European Court of Human Rights has decided that corporal punishment in schools without such permission runs contrary to the Convention on Human Rights.

SELF-DEFENCE

This is also called the Private Defence. Where an attack which is e.g. of a violent or indecent nature is made against a person who is put in fear of his life or the safety of his person then that person is entitled to protect himself and repel the attack but must not use more force than is necessary or reasonable in the circumstances. If the defence is accepted it is a complete and not a partial defence because it negates the unlawful nature of the assault carried out in self-defence – in fact there is no *actus reus* and *mens rea*.

Statutory offences against the person

Assault and battery are common-law offences, but the more serious offences against the person are contained in the Offences Against the Person Act, 1861 as follows.

ASSAULT OCCASIONING ACTUAL BODILY HARM

Under s. 47 of the Offences Against the Person Act, 1861 it is an offence punishable with imprisonment for a term not exceeding five years for a person to assault another thereby 'occasioning actual bodily harm'. Actual bodily harm merely means that the victim has suffered some injury. Bruising or abrasions are enough.

The mental state of the defendant is either actual intention or *Cunningham* recklessness (see *R* v *Spratt*, 1991 at p. 844 and *R* v *Parmenter*, 1991 at p. 845).

ESSENTIAL CASE LAW AND COMMENT

D.P.P. v *K*, 1990 – Acid in the hand washer **(540)**

MALICIOUS WOUNDING

Section 20 of the Offences Against the Person Act, 1861 provides as follows –

> Whosoever shall unlawfully and maliciously wound or inflict any grievous bodily harm upon any person either with or without any weapon or instrument shall be guilty of an offence and being convicted thereof shall be liable to imprisonment for five years.

The word 'unlawfully' indicates that acts of genuine self-defence are excluded. As regards the *actus reus* there are two possibilities, i.e. (*a*) wounding and (*b*) inflicting grievous bodily harm. Wounding is fairly straightforward and requires a breaking of the skin, though a graze would be enough. Grievous bodily harm must be some serious harm and where only slight harm is inflicted a prosecution under s. 47 would be more appropriate.

As regards inflicting grievous bodily harm, while one normally thinks of the application of force to the person of the victim the concept does not necessarily require an assault.

ESSENTIAL CASE LAW AND COMMENT

R v *Martin*, 1881 – Inflicting grievous bodily harm: no assault **(541)**

As regards the *mens rea*, intention is required or *Cunningham* recklessness rather than *Caldwell* recklessness, in the sense that the jury must find that the defendant foresaw subjectively that some physical harm to some other person would result from his act.

ESSENTIAL CASE LAW AND COMMENT

R v *Parmenter*, 1991 – Injury to a child **(542)**

CAUSING GRIEVOUS BODILY HARM

Section 18 of the Offences Against The Person Act, 1861 provides as follows –

> Whosoever shall unlawfully and maliciously by any means whatsoever wound or cause grievous bodily harm to any person with intent . . . to do some grievous bodily harm to any person or with intent to resist or prevent the lawful apprehension or detainer of any person shall be guilty of an offence and being convicted thereof shall be liable to imprisonment for life.

The expressions 'wounding' and 'grievous bodily harm' carry the same meanings as they do for the purposes of s. 20. The expression 'cause grievous bodily harm' is used in s. 18 whereas the expression 'inflicted grievous bodily harm' is used in s. 20. It might have been assumed that s. 18 applied to cases of grievous bodily harm caused by any means whereas the expression 'inflicted' in s. 20 meant that it had to be as the result of an assault. However, since it is clear that a s. 20 offence can be committed without an assault the distinction between s. 20 and s. 18 is not really clear. Since a conviction under s. 18 carries a maximum sentence of imprisonment for life it is reserved for the more serious assaults. There are two forms of intent, as follows –

(*a*) an intent to do some grievous bodily harm; or
(*b*) an intent to resist or prevent a lawful detention or arrest.

In both cases the intent must be accompanied by an intention to cause really serious bodily harm as distinct from slight harm. Recklessness even of the *Cunningham* variety is not sufficient *mens rea*. The wounding must be deliberate and without justification and committed with intent. The test of intent is subjective.

ESSENTIAL CASE LAW AND COMMENT

R v *Belfon*, 1976 – Causing grievous bodily harm: recklessness not enough **(543)**

Sexual offences

We shall be concerned here only with the offence of rape. There are of course other sexual offences but because of the developments in both the *actus reus* and the *mens rea* of rape it provides a further opportunity to consider in yet another context these ingredients of crime.

RAPE

Two statutes are relevant. The first is the Sexual Offences Act, 1956 which does not define rape but states merely in s. 1 that it is an offence for a man to rape a woman. However, the second, i.e. the Sexual Offences (Amendment) Act, 1976 goes further. Section 1(1)(a) defines the *actus reus* of rape as follows – A man commits rape if he has unlawful sexual intercourse with a woman who at the time of the intercourse does not consent to it. Section 1(1)(b) defines the *mens rea* necessary for rape as follows – The man must at the time of intercourse *know* that the woman does not consent to it or be *reckless* as to whether she consents to it.

This follows the common law and is a subjective test (see below).

RAPE – THE *ACTUS REUS*

Unlawful sexual intercourse

The phrase 'unlawful sexual intercourse' has meant in the past that the offence could not be committed by a husband upon his wife. A married woman either consented to intercourse with her husband or was deemed, merely by reason of the marriage, to consent. This old rule of the common law has now been eliminated from our law by a decision of the House of Lords (see below).

ESSENTIAL CASE LAW AND COMMENT

R v *R*, 1991 – A husband can rape his wife **(544)**

No degrees of penetration

It is not necessary to constitute the crime of rape that intercourse should be completed by the man ejaculating his semen into the woman. This is expressly stated in s. 44 of the Sexual Offences Act, 1956 which provides: 'Where, on the trial of any offence under this Act, it is necessary to prove sexual intercourse, . . . it shall not be necessary to prove the completion of the intercourse by the emission of seed, but the intercourse shall be deemed complete upon proof of penetration only.' In fact the slightest penetration by the penis into the vagina is enough.

Consent

Lack of consent must be proved by the prosecution. It follows from the definition of rape that if there is consent by the woman it must continue while intercourse is in progress, i.e. through the whole act. If the man realises during the act of intercourse that the woman is no longer consenting or is reckless as to her consent continuing penetration of her is rape.

Apparent consent following threats or intimidation is no consent and a consent which is obtained by deception is not enough to prevent the crime. Indeed s. 1(2) of the Sexual Offences Act, 1956 provides that: 'A man who induces a married woman to have sexual intercourse with him by impersonating her husband commits rape.' Rape would also be committed by intercourse with a sleeping woman.

ESSENTIAL CASE LAW AND COMMENT

R v *Williams*, 1923 – Intercourse by deception **(545)**

RAPE – THE *MENS REA*

Rape requires what we have referred to as a basic intent. Thus a man will be guilty of rape if he knows that the woman is not consenting or if he is reckless in the *Cunningham* and not the *Caldwell* sense as to whether she is consenting or not. The test is subjective.

ESSENTIAL CASE LAW AND COMMENT

D.P.P. v *Morgan*, 1975 – Rape: a subjective test **(546)**

25
Criminal law – age and responsibility: general defences

In this chapter we shall consider the liability of minors in the criminal law, together with the general defences which are available in regard to all prosecutions for crime.

Liability of minors

For the purposes of criminal liability minors are divided into three classes as follows –

(*a*) *Those under ten years.* It is presumed that minors under ten years of age are incapable of any crime and the presumption is irrebuttable (Children and Young Persons Act, 1963, s. 16).

(*b*) *Those between ten and 14 years.* The presumption which is wholly dependent on the common law is that a minor is incapable of forming a guilty intent, but this can be rebutted by proving 'mischievous discretion', i.e. knowledge that what was done was morally wrong. Evidence as to this must be before the court before a conviction can properly be made (*H v Chief Constable of South Wales*, The Times, 5 July 1986). Thus in *York* (1748) Fost. 70, C.C.R., a boy aged ten was convicted of murder on evidence which showed that, after he had killed a five-year-old girl, he concealed the body and then told lies about what had happened.

More recently in *McC v Runeckles*, The Times, 5 May 1984, a girl of 13 was convicted of assault occasioning actual bodily harm contrary to s. 47 of the Offences Against the Person Act, 1861. She stabbed another girl with a broken milk bottle and ran away when police officers arrived. She hid in a garden where she was apprehended. These acts indicated to the court that she knew that what she had done had gone beyond childish mischievousness.

Again in *I v D.P.P.* [1989] Crim. L.R. 498 a boy aged ten took some items from an ambulance which was parked in hospital grounds. He threw a first aid box over a wall and climbed over the wall. He was caught in possession of the box and said to the police: 'It ain't nothing to do with me,

I didn't steal it.' He was convicted of theft and it was held on appeal that there was sufficient evidence that he knew what he was doing so that his conviction was affirmed. The boy had indicated by his words that he knew about theft and that it was wrong.

(c) *Minors of 14 years and over* are fully liable for crimes, but there are certain differences as to procedure and punishment, as we have seen at p. 95.

Insanity

The leading case is *R* v *M'Naghten* (1843) 10 Cl. & Fin. 200. M'Naghten was charged with murder and acquitted on the grounds of insanity. The acquittal became the subject of debate in the House of Lords and it was decided to ask the opinion of the judges on the law governing insanity. The following rules arose.

(a) Every defendant is presumed to be sane until the contrary is proved.

(b) To establish a defence on the ground of insanity, it must be clearly proved that, at the time of the committing of the act, the party accused was labouring under such a defect of reason, from disease of mind, as not to know the nature and quality of the acts he was doing; or, if he did know it, that he did not know he was doing what was wrong. It is a question of the party's knowledge of right and wrong in respect of the act with which he is charged.

The defence is required to show on a balance of probabilities that the defendant is insane. The right to raise the issue of insanity at a trial is a matter for the defence and not the prosecution. However, it was held in *R* v *Dickie* [1984] 3 All E.R. 173 that exceptionally the trial judge may raise it and leave the decision to the jury if the evidence suggests that the accused was insane.

If the defence of insanity is successful the verdict is 'Not guilty by reason of insanity' as provided for by s. 2(1) of the Trial of Lunatics Act, 1883. The judge was then required to order the defendant to be detained in a special hospital, e.g. Broadmoor. This was often a worse form of sentence than might be given for a finding of guilty. For this reason persons who might have pleaded insanity did not do so, pleading guilty instead, and the defence became confined in practical terms to cases of murder. Now the Criminal Procedure (Insanity and Unfitness to Plead) Act, 1991 inserts a new s. 5 into the Criminal Procedure (Insanity) Act, 1964, under which the court can make guardianship or supervision or treatment orders or an order for absolute discharge. However, in the case of murder the court is still bound to make an admission order as before. These orders are also available when a person submits that he is unfit to plead (see below).

Before returning to the defence of insanity it should be noted that the defendant's sanity or mental state is also relevant –

(a) *When he is put up for trial.* Although there may be no doubt that the accused was sane when he did the act with which he is charged, he may be too insane to stand trial or as it is usually put – 'unfit to plead'. If this is found to be so by a jury the orders set out above are available.

(b) *On conviction.* Here the accused's mental condition is relevant to punishment. Under the Mental Health Act, 1983, the court can make a variety of hospital and guardianship orders, though not in the case of murder.

(c) *After sentence.* If the accused is found to be suffering from mental disorder after receiving a sentence of imprisonment he may be transferred to a mental hospital under the Mental Health Act, 1983.

We can now look at the essential ingredients of the defence of insanity.

DISEASE OF THE MIND

The judiciary have never been entirely swayed by the evidence of practitioners in this field of medicine. The matter is they say basically one of *responsibility for the act*. In other words a person may be suffering from a defect of reason due to a disease of the mind and yet be *responsible* in the view of the court for what has been done or not according to the circumstances of the case.

It may be for this reason that the courts have considered as part of the issue of responsibility a variety of mental states which do not truly come within the normal definition of insanity.

ESSENTIAL CASE LAW AND COMMENT

R v *Kemp*, 1956 – a sufferer from arteriosclerosis **(547)**
R v *Hennessy*, 1989 – A sufferer from diabetes **(548)**

DEFECT OF REASON

The disease of the mind must cause a defect of reason so that the defendant (a) did not know the nature and quality of his act or (b) did not know that what he was doing was wrong. This means essentially that to establish the *M'Naghten* defence the defendant must be deprived of reason. The defence does not therefore apply to those who have retained the power of reasoning but who in a moment of forgetfulness, confusion or absent-mindedness have failed to use those powers properly or to the full.

ESSENTIAL CASE LAW AND COMMENT

R v *Clarke*, 1972 – A shoplifter **(549)**

KNOWING THAT THE ACT IS WRONG

It is this branch of the *M'Naghten* defence which has produced difficulty, not the rarely pleaded branch which relates to not knowing what was being done, i.e. failure to understand the physical nature of the act. The problems have arisen in regard to whether, if the act is contrary to law, there might be a successful plea of insanity because the defendant thought the act to be morally right. It would appear that knowledge that the act is *legally* wrong means the defence fails.

ESSENTIAL CASE LAW AND COMMENT

R v *Windle*, 1952 – A fatal dose of aspirin **(550)**

Automatism

As we have seen it is a general rule of the common law that a *voluntary act* is required before liability for a crime can be established in terms of the *actus reus*. In addition it is necessary that the defendant is *conscious of his acts*, otherwise there is no *mens rea*.

Sometimes a defendant will plead automatism as a defence which if established will negative the essential ingredients of the crime and result in an acquittal. The defence of automatism is difficult to establish.

ESSENTIAL CASE LAW AND COMMENT

Hill v *Baxter*, 1958 – A sudden illness while driving **(551)**

DISTINGUISHED FROM INSANITY

Where automatism is induced by a disease of the mind this is insanity and the judge may withdraw the defence of automatism from the jury (*Bratty* v *Attorney-General for Northern Ireland* [1963] A.C. 386).

However, an overdose of insulin in diabetes leading to hypoglycaemia (a medical state with side effects, e.g. double vision, and leading eventually to coma) is not a malfunction of the mind and may be put to a jury as automatism.

ESSENTIAL CASE LAW AND COMMENT

R v *Quick*, 1973 – Defence of automatism admissible **(552)**

WHERE AUTOMATISM IS SELF-INDUCED

A court will not accept the defence of automatism if it is self-induced as by drink or drugs. This is clearly based upon public policy and is considered further below.

In other cases self-induced automatism may be put to the jury as a defence, as where a diabetic does not take sufficient precautions to prevent reduction of blood sugar (see *Moses* v *Winder*, 1980 at p. 850).

ESSENTIAL CASE LAW AND COMMENT

R v *Lipman*, 1969 – Automatism induced by drugs **(553)**

Drunkenness and drugs

Automatism induced voluntarily by drink or drugs could well in fact prevent the defendant from committing a voluntary act or from being conscious of what he was doing. Nevertheless on grounds of public policy it is not normally a complete defence to allege automatism by drink or drugs. It can be partially successful where the crime requires a specific intent which the drink or drugs can negative. However, in offences against the person where the drink/drugs defence is most usually raised this does not result in an acquittal because these crimes are often bolstered up by a similar crime which does not require a specific intent. Thus drink or drugs may reduce murder to manslaughter and wounding with intent to unlawful wounding under ss. 18 and 20 of the Offences Against the Person Act, 1861 respectively but there will still be a conviction for the lesser crime which does not require a specific intent. The jury can be asked to consider drink or drugs as a defence where recklessness is involved.

ESSENTIAL CASE LAW AND COMMENT

D.P.P. v *Majewski*, 1976 – Where no specific intent is required **(554)**
R v *Hardie*, 1984 – Drugs and recklessness **(555)**

The drink/drugs defence is certainly not applicable to rape where the issue before the court is the defendant's intent or recklessness or the issue of the victim's consent or mistake (*R* v *Fotheringham*, *The Times*, 20 July 1988) nor in other situations where the defence of mistake is raised.

ESSENTIAL CASE LAW AND COMMENT

R v *O'Grady*, 1987 – A mistaken self-defence **(556)**

In addition where the defendant takes drink or drugs in order to pluck up courage to commit the offence the drink/drugs defence will not be accepted by the court even as nullifying a specific intent. Thus murder remains murder and is not reduced to manslaughter.

ESSENTIAL CASE LAW AND COMMENT

Attorney-General for Northern Ireland v *Gallagher*, 1963 – Drinking to get Dutch courage **(557)**

DRINK/DRUGS STATES NOT SELF-INDUCED

Here the court will consider the defence of automatism by drink or drugs where the defendant has lost control by drink or drugs administered to him without his knowledge.

ESSENTIAL CASE LAW AND COMMENT

Ross v *H.M. Advocate*, 1991 – Drugs in a can of lager **(558)**

Duress

Duress when raised as a defence may be said to amount to a defence of no voluntary *actus reus*. It may also negative *mens rea* because a person who is made to do an act by threats of a serious nature, e.g. death or serious personal injury, can hardly be said to intend to do the criminal act.

DURESS BY THREATS

Duress is not available as a defence to murder (*R* v *Howe* [1987] 1 All E.R. 771) or attempted murder.

ESSENTIAL CASE LAW AND COMMENT

R v *Gotts*, 1991 – Attempted murder under duress **(559)**

The essential ingredients of duress by threats are as follows –

(*a*) The threats must be serious such as threats of death or serious personal injury. Threats to property are probably not enough.

(*b*) The response of the defendant to those threats must be reasonable. He must have acted as a sober person of reasonable firmness (*R* v *Graham* [1982] 1 All E.R. 801).

(*c*) Where the defence of duress is applicable it must also be shown that the overpowering of the defendant's will was operative at the time when the crime was actually committed by him though this general rule is not always applied.

ESSENTIAL CASE LAW AND COMMENT

R v *Hudson*, 1971 – Duress and perjury **(560)**

(*d*) There is also a duty to neutralise the threat as by informing the police where this is possible having regard to the age of the defendant and the circumstances and risks involved.

MEMBERSHIP OF A GANG

In some recent cases the court has had to consider whether the voluntary joining of a gang of persons by the defendant affects his ability to raise the defence of duress when he is caused to become involved in gang crime by threats from other members of the gang. It would appear that the defence is not available to a person who knows when he voluntarily joins a gang that he might be put under some pressure to commit an offence. It can be available if at the time of joining the defendant failed to appreciate the risk of violence.

ESSENTIAL CASE LAW AND COMMENT

R v *Sharp (David)*, 1987 – The risk of violence was known **(561)**
R v *Shepherd*, 1988 – Risk of violence not appreciated **(562)**

DURESS OF CIRCUMSTANCES

In some recent cases there has been a blurring of the so-called defence of necessity (see p. 557) with that of duress. This form of duress has been referred to as 'duress of circumstances'.

This is probably a more accurate analysis of certain necessity cases. Thus if A who is disqualified from driving drives his son to work because he will otherwise be late and might lose his job because his wife becomes hysterical and threatens to kill herself unless he does so, this situation of 'threat' is called 'duress of circumstances' and can operate as a defence.

ESSENTIAL CASE LAW AND COMMENT

R v *Martin*, 1989 – A threat of suicide **(563)**

DURESS – THE SPECIAL CASE OF A WIFE

Duress is clearly a defence for a wife. Section 47 of the Criminal Justice Act, 1925, which abolished the presumption that a wife who committed a crime in her husband's presence did so under such compulsion as entitled her to an acquittal provides as follows –

> Any presumption of law that an offence committed by a wife in the presence of her husband is committed under the coercion of the husband is hereby abolished, but on a charge against a wife for any offence other than treason or murder it shall be a good defence to prove that the offence was committed in the presence of and under the coercion of the husband.

Necessity

English law does in extreme circumstances recognise a defence of necessity but when it does so it arises from some pressure on the defendant's will from the wrongful threats or violence of another. Equally, however, it can arise from other objective dangers threatening the defendant or others when it is called by the judiciary 'duress of circumstances' (See *R* v *Martin*, 1989 at p. 844).

In the absence of the elements of threat or objective danger where the defence is probably better regarded as duress there is no general defence of necessity in English law.

It is therefore murder to take another's life to save one's own unless it is a case of self-defence (see p. 558).

ESSENTIAL CASE LAW AND COMMENT

R v *Dudley and Stephens*, 1884 – Killing a member of the crew **(564)**

However, situations of genuine necessity not set in a background of duress can be taken into account by the court in the sentence imposed and at an earlier stage, where there is discretion, by the authorities in not bringing a prosecution.

Mistake

It will be appreciated that a normal sane and sober person may make a mistake and it is the effect of such mistakes on criminal liability with which we must now deal.

Suppose that a defendant X saw A apparently attacking B. X believed that A was mugging B and fought A off. It then turned out that A was trying to arrest B who had just mugged an old lady. Can X raise the defence of mistake, i.e. that he believed he was acting to prevent crime (see below)?

The only major problem arising in the case law from attempts to establish the defence of mistake have been as to whether it is enough that the defendant had an honest belief that the facts were as he mistakenly thought them to be or whether that belief must be not only *honest* but also *reasonable*. Since the decision of the House of Lords in *D.P.P.* v *Morgan*, 1975 (see p. 846), an honest belief is sufficient and whether that belief is reasonable is irrelevant. The defence of mistake should therefore be put to the jury in the trial of our defendant X. Indeed his mistake may be both honest and reasonable – not that the latter is relevant in *law*.

However, although the courts do not require as a matter of law that an honest mistake be at the same time reasonable it is unlikely that a jury will accept that the defendant made an honest mistake in circumstances where an ordinary person would not or could not reasonably have made the mistake. So whatever the test it can be said with some confidence that a defendant is unlikely to be acquitted following a pleading of 'honest' mistake in 'unreasonable' circumstances. Finally, and as would be expected, a mistake as to law is no defence.

ESSENTIAL CASE LAW AND COMMENT

R v *Kimber*, 1983 – An indecent assault **(565)**
R v *Bailey*, 1800 – A mistake as to law **(566)**

Self-defence

A person may use such force as is reasonable in all the circumstances in his own defence. What is reasonable force is a matter of fact for the jury but there must be some reciprocity or mutuality between the force being offered and the force used in defence. If A kissed B against her will she may not succeed with self-defence if she stabbed A in the chest with her hatpin! There is no duty to retreat or run away in the face of force. Failure to do so before providing countervailing force is merely a factor to be taken into account when deciding whether (*a*) force was necessary at all and (*b*) if so whether it was reasonable or whether backing off might have solved the problem.

If excessive force is used and death results then the defence fails. Murder is not reduced to manslaughter unless the defendant is regarded as having acted reasonably on the spur of the moment and under stress.

> **ESSENTIAL CASE LAW AND COMMENT**
>
> *R* v *McInnes*, 1971 – Greasers and skinheads: an affray **(567)**

APPREHENDED IMMINENT ATTACK

There is no need for an attack to be taking place. A person can make preparations for self-defence where there is an apprehension of imminent attack.

> **ESSENTIAL CASE LAW AND COMMENT**
>
> *Attorney-General's Reference (No. 2 of 1983)*, 1984 – Fear of a riot **(568)**

Preventing crime

Section 3 of the Criminal Law Act, 1967 provides that 'A person may use such force as is reasonable in the circumstances in the prevention of crime or in effecting or assisting in the lawful arrest of offenders or suspected offenders or of persons unlawfully at large.' This provision would, given reasonable force, cover acts in defence of other persons whether relatives or not. It would also cover defence of property as where reasonable force is used by A against B to prevent B from stealing A's briefcase.

> **ESSENTIAL CASE LAW AND COMMENT**
>
> *R* v *Rose*, 1884 – A son shoots his father **(569)**

Cases and materials

The nature and development of English law

WHERE COMMON LAW AND EQUITY ARE IN CONFLICT EQUITY PREVAILS

1. *The Earl of Oxford's case* (1615) 1 Rep. Ch. 1

Merton College, Oxford, had been granted a lease of Covent Garden for 72 years at £9 a year, and some 50 years later sold the lease to the Earl for £15 a year. Later the college retook possession of part of it, on the ground that a statute of Elizabeth prevented the sale of ecclesiastical and college lands so that the conveyance to the Earl was void. The Earl brought an action to eject the college from the land, and the common law judges found in favour of the college, saying that they were bound by the statute. The Earl filed a Bill in Equity for relief, and Lord Ellesmere granted it, stating that the claim of the college was against all good conscience. This brought law and Equity into open conflict and resulted in the ruling of James I that, where common law and Equity are in conflict, Equity should prevail. (See now s. 49 of the Supreme Court Act, 1981.)

THE COURT MUST APPLY AN ACT OF PARLIAMENT AND CANNOT DECLARE IT ILLEGAL

2. *Cheney v Conn* [1968] 1 All E.R. 779

Cheney objected to his tax assessments under the Finance Act, 1964, on the ground that the government was applying part of the tax collected to the making of nuclear weapons. Cheney alleged that this was contrary to the Geneva Conventions – which had been incorporated into the Geneva Conventions Act, 1957 – and conflicted with international law. *Held* – that even if there was a conflict between the 1964 and 1957 Acts, the 1964 Act gave clear authority to collect the taxes in question and being later in time prevailed. 'It is not for the court to say that a parliamentary enactment, the highest law in this country, is illegal' said the judge.

A STATUTE REMAINS LAW UNTIL REPEALED BY PARLIAMENT

3. *Prince of Hanover* v *Attorney-General* [1957] 1 All E.R. 49

A statute of Anne in 1705 provided for the naturalisation of Princess Sophia, Electress of Hanover, and the issue of her body. The statute was repealed by the British Nationality Act, 1948, s. 34(3), but by s. 12 a person who was a British subject immediately before the commencement of the Act (1 January 1949) became a citizen of the United Kingdom and Colonies. The plaintiff was born in 1914 in Hanover and was lineally descended from the Electress. He now claimed a declaration that he was a British subject immediately before the commencement of the British Nationality Act. It was necessary for him to establish this in order to make a claim on a fund, put up by the Polish Government, to compensate Britons who had lost property in Poland because of nationalisation. It was held at first instance that the statute had not lost its force merely because of its age, but nevertheless, although the statute was unqualified and plain in its meaning, its words taken alone produced an absurd result, since, under the statute, the Kaiser would have been a British subject. Parliament must, therefore, have intended some limitation on the operation of the words used. By referring to the preamble it seemed possible to draw the conclusion that the purpose of the Act was to be effected in the lifetime of Anne, and that after that time its purpose was spent and the plaintiff was not entitled to his declaration. On reaching the Court of Appeal, *it was held* that the appellant was a British subject under the statute of Anne which had remained law until repealed by the 1948 Act, the statute being so clear in its meaning that it was unnecessary to apply rules of interpretation to it. Rules of interpretation were to be used only in case of ambiguity or doubts as to meaning. The decision of the Court of Appeal was affirmed by the House of Lords.

PARLIAMENT MAY SPECIFICALLY ABOLISH OR ALTER STATUTE LAW BY A LATER ENACTMENT. THIS WILL TAKE PLACE BY IMPLICATION IF THE LATER ENACTMENT IS WHOLLY INCONSISTENT WITH THE FORMER

4. *Vauxhall Estates* v *Liverpool Corporation* [1932] 1 K.B. 733

In 1928 the Minister of Health made a Street Improvement Scheme Order for a certain area of Liverpool. The Order required the compulsory purchase of property, and the question of compensation payable to owners arose. Under s. 2 of the Acquisition of Land (Assessment of Compensation) Act, 1919, the plaintiffs would receive £2370, but if s. 46 of the Housing Act, 1925, applied, the plaintiffs would receive £1133. A provision of the Act of 1919 stated that other statutes inconsistent with the 1919 Act were not to have effect. *Held* – the 1925 Act impliedly repealed the 1919 Act. It was inconsistent with it. Compensation was to be assessed under the latest enactment.

COMMENT
It was held in *Re Berry* [1936] 1 Ch. 274 that the court will not construe

a later Act as repealing an earlier Act by implication unless it is *impossible* to make the two Acts, or certain sections of them, stand together, i.e. if a section of the later Act can only be given a sensible meaning, as in *Vauxhall*, if it is treated as impliedly repealing the relevant section of the earlier Act.

LEGAL TEXTS MAY BE A SOURCE OF LAW

5. *Boys* v *Blenkinsop* [1968] Crim. L.R. 513

Mrs Nellie Blenkinsop was charged at Lewes with having 'permitted' her son Donald to drive a car without third-party insurance. The registered owner of the car was the driver's father whose insurance policy did not cover driving by his son. However, it appeared that the son had asked his mother's permission to drive and she had given it and had said she was the owner when asked by a constable. The defence submitted that there was no case to answer because only the registered owner could permit use of the vehicle. The prosecution submitted that this was wrong because Mrs Blenkinsop might have been, if not joint owner, at any rate responsible for care, management or control of the car within *Lloyd* v *Singleton* [1953] 1 All E.R. 291. The prosecuting inspector had asked the justices to refer to *Wilkinson's Road Traffic Offences* (5th ed., 1965, p. 202) which in relation to that case stated: 'A person may "permit" though he is not the owner.' Counsel for the defence objected that unless the justices were referred to the case itself they were not allowed to look at the textbook. The inspector did not have a report of the case with him. The justices dismissed the case and the prosecution appealed to the Divisional Court. The Court allowed the appeal and remitted the case to the justices to continue the hearing of it. Parker, L.C.J., said: 'They are entitled to and should look at the textbook; and if they then feel in doubt they should, of their own motion, send for the authority, and if necessary, adjourn for it to be obtained.'

Other courts and tribunals and legal services

THE COURTS CAN CONTROL THE DEFECTIVE JURISDICTION OF A TRIBUNAL OR ADMINISTRATIVE AUTHORITY BY THE DOCTRINE OF *ULTRA VIRES*

6. *Attorney-General* v *Fulham Corporation* [1921] 1 Ch. 440

The local authority was authorised by the Baths and Wash-houses Acts, 1846–1878 to establish a wash-house where people could come and wash their own clothes. The Corporation decided to run a municipal laundry where people could bring their clothes to be washed by employees of the Corporation. *Held* – that the statutory powers did not cover running a laundry. The action of the authority was, therefore, *ultra vires* and an injunction was granted to prevent the Corporation from running the laundry.

COMMENT

(i) The *ultra vires* principle was used in *Bromley London Borough Council v Greater London Council* [1982] All E.R. 153, where the House of Lords decided that the Labour-controlled GLC had no power under the Transport (London) Act, 1969 to pass resolutions to enforce a 25% cut in London's bus and tube fares. It was also decided that a public authority is under a *fiduciary duty* to hold the balance fairly between the various interests of those who are within its care, i.e. in this case between the ratepayers and the transport users. The effect of the resolutions was to pass on the cost of the reduction to ratepayers. The Labour Party's manifesto, which had advocated a reduction in fares, was no justification. It could not be assumed that all who voted Labour agreed with the whole of the manifesto. A manifesto is not a binding contract between a party and its supporters.

(ii) In *R* v *Lewisham B.C., ex p. Shell UK* [1988] 1 All E.R. 938 the Council passed a resolution to boycott all Shell products where suitable alternatives were available as part of the Council's anti-apartheid policy and on the basis of alleged activities by Shell in South Africa. The court granted Shell a declaration that the resolution was *ultra vires*. The Council had *no power* to put pressure on Shell in this way no matter how reasonable its desire to promote good race relations might be.

THE SUPERVISORY JURISDICTION OF THE HIGH COURT CANNOT NORMALLY BE INVOKED IF OTHER AND MORE APPROPRIATE PROCEDURES FOR APPEAL EXIST

7. *R* v *Brighton Justices, ex parte Robinson* [1973] 1 W.L.R. 69

The defendant was convicted and ordered to pay a fine in her absence for failing to give information about a driver's identity. She applied for *certiorari* on the grounds that she had not received the summons. *Held* –. by the Queen's Bench Divisional Court – that the application would be granted but the court would not be minded to grant *certiorari* in such cases in the future since a statutory procedure existed under s. 24(3) of the Criminal Justice Act, 1967. (See now s. 14(1), Magistrates' Court Act, 1980.)

COMMENT

(i) Section 14(1) provides that the defendant may make a statutory declaration that he did not know of any summons or proceedings until after the trial commenced. The statutory declaration must be served on the clerk to the justices within 14 days of the date when the defendant came to know of the proceedings whereupon the summons and subsequent proceedings are void.

(ii) Judicial review may be granted in exceptional cases. Thus in *R* v *Inspector of Taxes, ex p. Kissane* [1986] 2 All E.R. 37 taxpayers were granted leave to apply for judicial review against the decision of a tax inspector, even though they could have appealed to the Special

Commissioners, because they could not recover costs on an appeal to the Commissioners.

AN APPLICATION FOR JUDICIAL REVIEW WILL NOT BE GRANTED UNLESS THE APPLICANT HAS A SUFFICIENT INTEREST IN THE MATTER TO WHICH THE APPLICATION RELATES

8. *Inland Revenue Commissioners* v *National Federation of Self-Employed and Small Businesses Ltd* [1981] 2 All E.R. 93

The Federation asked for an order of *mandamus* on the Commissioners of Inland Revenue to assess and collect arrears of income tax said to be due from casual employees on national newspapers. The long-standing practice of Fleet Street employers had been to pay the casuals without deduction of tax and for the casuals to supply fake names and addresses when drawing their pay in order to avoid tax. Their true identities were known only to their union which operated a closed shop and controlled all casual employment on the newspapers. *Held* – by the House of Lords – that the Federation could not be granted the order of *mandamus*. The Federation had no *locus standi*. 'The total confidentiality of assessments and of negotiations between individuals and the Revenue is a vital element in the working of the system. As a matter of general principle I would hold that one taxpayer has no sufficient interest in asking the court to investigate the tax affairs of another taxpayer or to complain that the latter has been underassessed or overassessed; indeed there is a strong public interest that he should not. And this principle applies equally to groups of taxpayers: an aggregate of individuals each of whom has no interest cannot of itself have any interest.' (*Per* Lord Wilberforce.)

CERTIORARI IS ALSO AVAILABLE TO CONTROL TRIBUNALS WHICH HAVE ACTED BEYOND THEIR POWERS

9. *R* v *London County Council, ex parte Entertainment Protection Association Ltd* [1931] 2 K.B. 215

The county council granted a new licence, under s. 2 of the Cinematographic Act, 1909, in respect of a cinema called the Streatham Astoria. One of the conditions contained in the Act was that the premises were not to be opened on Sundays, Christmas Day or Good Friday. Subsequent to the grant of the licence, a committee of the council considered an application that the Streatham Astoria be allowed to open on the above-mentioned days. The committee resolved that 'no action be taken for the present in the event of the premises being opened . . . on Sundays, Christmas Day and Good Friday', subject to the applicants paying a sum of money to a selected charity. The Association challenged the ruling of the committee by *certiorari*. *Held* – that the council was usurping its jurisdiction in breaking a condition of the licence, and that this was prohibited by the Act of 1909. *Certiorari* lay to quash the committee's ruling.

A COURT OR OTHER AUTHORITY MUST NOT ACT IF THERE IS BIAS IN THE SENSE OF ANY SUBSTANTIAL PECUNIARY, PERSONAL OR PROPRIETORY INTEREST IN THE DISPUTE BEFORE IT. NATURAL JUSTICE ALSO EMBRACES THE RIGHT TO BE HEARD

10. *Dimes* v *Grand Junction Canal* (1852) 3 H.L.C. 759

Dimes was the Lord of a manor through which the canal passed, and he had been concerned in a case with the proprietors of the canal in which he disputed their title to certain land. Dimes had obtained an order of ejectment, but the canal company approached the Lord Chancellor (Lord Cottenham) to prevent Dimes enforcing the order and to confirm the company's title. The Lord Chancellor granted the relief sought. Dimes now appealed to the House of Lords on the ground that the Lord Chancellor was a shareholder in the company and was therefore biased. *Held* – the Lord Chancellor's order granting the relief must be quashed because, although there was no evidence that his pecuniary interest had influenced him, yet it should not appear that any court had laboured under influences of this nature

> COMMENT
> This case was distinguished in *R* v *Mulvihill* [1990] 1 All E.R. 436 which was an appeal from a conviction in connection with bank robberies. It appeared that the trial judge had 1650 shares in one of them – National Westminster Bank plc. The Court of Appeal would not accept a plea of bias. This was a criminal trial with a jury, which had found M guilty so that the judge was bound to give effect to the verdict of the jury whether he personally agreed with it or not. *Dimes* was a civil matter without a jury the decision being a matter for the judge alone.

11. *R* v *Bingham Justices, ex parte Jowitt,* The Times, 3 July 1974

In announcing the conviction of the defendant for speeding the chairman of the justices said: 'Quite the most unpleasant cases that we have to decide are those where the evidence is a direct conflict between a police officer and a member of the public. My principle in such cases has always been to believe the evidence of the police officer, and therefore we find the case proved.' Mr Jowitt applied to the Divisional Court for *certiorari* and it was *held* that the attitude of the chairman clearly amounted to bias and the conviction was quashed.

> COMMENT
> (i) More recently, in *R* v *Liverpool City Justices, ex parte Topping* [1983] 1 All E.R. 490, a conviction by magistrates was quashed by *certiorari*

on the basis of bias where it was shown that they had gone on to try a case of criminal damage after becoming aware from court computer sheets of T's previous convictions.

(ii) As regards the right to be heard, see *R* v *Wear Valley District Council, ex p. Binks* [1985] 2 All E.R. 699 where B operated a hot-food take-away caravan at a a market under an informal arrangement with the council. She was given notice to quit without reasons or warning. Taylor, J. quashed the Council's decision on the grounds of denial of natural justice. B had a right to be heard and to prior notification and reasons.

(iii) Again in *R* v *Board of Governors of London Oratory School, ex p. R., The Times*, 17 February 1988 the rules of natural justice were applied to an expulsion of a child from school. The child must have an opportunity to state his case and know the nature of the accusations.

RULES OF NATURAL JUSTICE NEED NOT BE APPLIED WHERE MATTERS OF NATIONAL SECURITY ARE INVOLVED

12. *R* v *Secretary of State for Home Department, ex parte Hosenball* [1977] 3 All E.R. 452

Mr Hosenball was an American journalist working in London. He received a letter from the Home Department saying that the Home Secretary had decided to deport him in the interests of national security. The statement said that Mr Hosenball had tried to obtain and, indeed, had obtained, information harmful to the United Kingdom and relating to security arrangements and that that information was prejudicial to the safety of servants of the Crown. Mr Hosenball was given no further particulars amd was told that he could not appeal but might make representations and appear before an independent advisory panel. Mr Hosenball did so but he did not see the panel's report, though the Home Secretary gave it his personal consideration. A deportation order was made under the Immigration Act, 1971, s. 5, and Mr Hosenball applied for an order of *certiorari* to quash the Home Secretary's decision. The Court of Appeal *held* unanimously that the application would be refused. Mr Hosenball had not been given enough information to enable him to meet the charge made against him. However, this was a case in which national security was involved and where the State was in danger even the rules of natural justice must take second place.

In addition, there was no infringement of Article 6 of the Convention for the Protection of Human Rights and Fundamental Freedoms. The European Commission of Human Rights in the case of Mr Philip Agee, whose deportation had been ordered by the Home Secretary at the same time as Mr Hosenball, had considered his application against the United Kingdom under the Convention as manifestly ill-founded. The Commission considered that where the public authorities of a State decided to deport an alien on grounds of security that constituted an Act of State falling within the public sphere and did not constitute a determination of his civil rights or obligations within the meaning of Article 6.

COMMENT
In *R* v *Secretary of State for the Foreign and Commonwealth Office, ex parte The Council of Civil Service Unions, The Times,* 23 November 1984 (and [1984] 3 All E.R. 935) the House of Lords decided that the government, in preventing its employees at Government Communication Headquarters (GCHQ) from joining trade unions, was acting in the interests of national security, and was entitled to act irregularly as regards procedure by not consulting its employees. Procedural propriety must give way to national security, when personal rights taken away by the action of the executive conflict with that security.

THE DECISION OF A TRIBUNAL ACTING IN BREACH OF THE RULES OF NATURAL JUSTICE (OR *ULTRA VIRES*) IS VOID

13. *Ridge* v *Baldwin* [1963] 2 All E.R. 66

Mr Ridge, who was the Chief Constable of Brighton, had been acquitted on a charge of conspiring with other police officers to obstruct the course of justice, though the trial judge, Donovan, J. said that Mr Ridge had not given the necessary professional or moral leadership to the Brighton Police Force. The Brighton Watch Committee subsequently dismissed Mr Ridge from his post as Chief Constable under a power in the Municipal Corporation Act, 1882, giving them a right to dismiss 'any constable whom they think negligent in the discharge of his duty or otherwise unfit for the same'. Ridge was not given a chance to answer the charges or appear before the Watch Committee. *Held* – by the House of Lords – that the action taken, i.e. the dismissal, was void; Mr Ridge should have been heard.

MANDAMUS LIES TO COMPEL THE EXERCISE OF A DISCRETIONARY POWER BUT NOT IN ANY PARTICULAR WAY

14. *R* v *Commissioner of Police of the Metropolis, ex parte Blackburn* [1973] 1 All E.R. 324

Blackburn sought an order of *mandamus* requiring the Commissioner of Police to secure the enforcement of the law against pornography upon various publishers and booksellers, and to reverse his decision that no prosecution should be undertaken without the prior consent of the Director of Public Prosecutions. *Held* – by the Queen's Bench Divisional Court – that although the evidence showed that pornography was widely available, the Commissioner, because of an under-manned force, had to decide an order of priorities to deal with various offences. In these circumstances it was perfectly proper for the Commissioner to seek the Director's advice before embarking on a prosecution, so long as he did not consider himself bound to follow his advice, and, accordingly, the situation in London was not attributable to any breach of legal duty by the Commissioner and the court would not interfere with the legitimate exercise of his discretion in the matter of police powers.

MANDAMUS IS NOT AVAILABLE AGAINST THE CROWN ITSELF BUT IT CAN ISSUE AGAINST A MINISTER

15. *R* v *Secretary of State for Social Services, ex parte Grabaskey*, *The Times*, 15 December 1972

A dentist treating a patient with a broken tooth claimed payment not only for crowning the tooth but also for an amalgam filling. The latter claim was disallowed by the Dental Estimates Board and the Minister dismissed the appeal as unarguable under the proviso to reg. 18 of the National Health Service (Service Committees and Tribunals) Regulations, 1956. *Held* – by the Queen's Bench Divisional Court – that the dentist's case was reasonably arguable and accordingly the Minister had no jurisdiction to dismiss the appeal and *mandamus* would be granted requiring him to refer the matter to two dental referees.

> COMMENT
> In *Padfield* v *Minister of Agriculture, Fisheries and Food* [1968] 1 All E.R. 694 the House of Lords decided that an order of *mandamus* should issue to the Minister of Agriculture, requiring him to refer a complaint by milk producers against the working of a Milk Marketing Board Scheme to a committe of investigation in the exercise of a discretionary power conferred on him by s. 19 of the Agricultural Marketing Act, 1958.

A SIMPLE DECLARATION OF WHAT THE LAW ON A PARTICULAR MATTER IS MAY SOMETIMES BE AN APPROPRIATE REMEDY AGAINST AN ADMINISTRATIVE AUTHORITY OR A MINISTER

16. *Laker Airways* v *Department of Trade* [1977] 2 All E.R. 182

The Civil Aviation Authority granted Laker Airways a licence for ten years from 1973 for a cheap passenger service between the UK and the USA called 'Skytrain'. Laker Airways was then designated as an airline under the Bermuda Agreement of 1946 made between the UK and the USA. Such designation was essential to get 'Skytrain' across the Atlantic. The Civil Aviation Act, 1971, gave the Secretary of State for Trade wide powers to revoke licences without reference to anyone and subject only to questions being asked in Parliament. However, these powers were restricted to time of war or great national emergency or where international relations might be affected. This part of the Act could not, therefore, have been applicable in regard to the revocation of the licence granted to Laker Airways. The Act also gave the Secretary of State power to give policy guidance in regard to civil aviation and it was under this power that the Secretary of State announced in 1976 by a White Paper that future policy would be to license only one UK airline on any given long route. Paragraphs 7 and 8 of the White Paper contained an instruction to the Civil Aviation Authority to revoke the licence for 'Skytrain'. Laker Airways now claimed a declaratory judgment that paras 7 and 8 were *ultra vires* and that the Secretary of State was not entitled to withdraw their licence. Mocatta, J. granted the declaration sought, holding among other things that the power given to the Secretary of State to issue policy guidance did not extend to the revocation of licences in this way. On appeal to the Court of Appeal by the Department of Trade it was held, dismissing the appeal, that Laker Airways were entitled to the declaration sought. The Secretary of State could not lawfully use the procedure of 'guidance' for the revocation of licences.

COMMENT

An example of the use of a declaratory judgment against a minister is to be found in *Congreve* v *Home Office* [1976] 1 All E.R. 697. Mr Congreve on discovering that the price of a TV licence was to be increased shortly bought a new one at the old rate before his old one expired thereby saving about £6. Some 25,000 others did the same. The Home Secretary claimed to revoke the licences under s.1 (4) of the Wireless Telegraphy Act, 1949, under which he had power. Mr C asked for a declaratory judgment that he could not do so. This was granted by the Court of Appeal. Mr C had done nothing unlawful and the revocation was a misuse by the Home Secretary of the powers in the 1949 Act.

WHERE DISCRETIONARY POWERS ARE ENTRUSTED TO THE EXECUTIVE BY STATUTE, THE COURTS MAY EXAMINE THE EXERCISE OF THOSE POWERS IN ORDER TO ENSURE THAT THEY HAVE NOT BEEN EXERCISED MISTAKENLY OR IMPROPERLY

17. *Secretary of State for Education and Science* v *Tameside Metropolitan Borough Council* [1976] 3 All E.R. 665

Tameside, a local education authority, submitted proposals for a comprehensive system of education to the Secretary of State in March 1975. These proposals were approved and Tameside planned to implement them by September 1976. In May 1976, local elections were held and the membership of Tameside changed from a Labour to a Conservative authority. The Conservative council decided not to implement the scheme for comprehensive education fully and on 7 June 1976, notified the Secretary of State of that intention. The Secretary of State was given a supervisory role by s. 68 of the Education Act, 1944. The section provides: 'If the Secretary of State is satisfied, either on complaint by any person or otherwise, that any local education authority or the managers or the governors of any county or voluntary school have acted or are proposing to act unreasonably with respect to the exercise of any power conferred or the performance of any duty imposed by or under this Act, he may, notwithstanding any enactment rendering the exercise of the power or the performance of the duty contingent upon the opinion of the authority or of the authority or of the managers or governors, give such directions as to the exercise of the power or the performance of the duty as appear to him to be expedient.' On 11 June the

Secretary of State replied to Tameside saying that they had acted, or were proposing to act, unreasonably within s. 68 of the 1944 Act and accordingly directed Tameside to implement the 1975 scheme. Tameside refused, so the Secretary of State applied for *mandamus*. The Divisional Court of Queen's Bench granted the order but the Court of Appeal and the House of Lords reversed that decision. Before giving directions under s. 68, the Secretary of State had to be satisfied that Tameside were acting unreasonably, i.e. that their conduct was such that no authority could reasonably engage in it. It had been alleged that there was insufficient time to carry out the necessary selection procedure for entry into grammar school. However, the House of Lords said that there were no grounds for concluding that the authority were acting unreasonably in taking the view that there was sufficient time available to carry out the necessary selection procedure. Although the Secretary of State might legitimately take the view that the authority's proposal to retain the grammar schools and to implement the selection procedure for the two schools where places were available was misguided or wrong, there were no grounds which could justify a conclusion that the proposal was such that no education authority, acting reasonably, would carry it out. It followed that the Secretary of State's direction was *ultra vires* and of no effect.

ADVOCATES AND LITIGATORS ARE NOT LIABLE IN CONTRACT OR TORT FOR NEGLIGENCE IN CONNECTION WITH LITIGATION. THIS IMMUNITY IS, HOWEVER, EXTENDED ONLY TO THE TRIAL ITSELF AND TO ANY PRE-TRIAL WORK WHICH IS INTIMATELY CONNECTED WITH A CASE IN COURT

18. *Rondel* v *Worsley* [1967] 3 All E.R. 993

The appellant was charged with causing grievous bodily harm and was tried and convicted. He was represented at the trial by the respondent barrister. The appellant later issued a writ and statement of claim against the respondent claiming damages for professional negligence in the respondent's presentation of the case and in his dealing with the evidence. The statement was ordered to be struck out by the Master as disclosing no cause of action and this order was upheld by Lawton, J., and the Court of Appeal. On further appeal to the House of Lords it was *held* that the appeal must be dismissed. A barrister's conduct and management of litigation either in court or at an earlier stage could not give rise to a claim for professional negligence. This ruling arose out of public policy in that –

(a) a barrister should be able to carry out *his duty to the court* independently and without fear;

(b) actions against barristers would amount in effect to a retrial of the case in which it was suggested negligence arose; this would prolong litigation contrary to the public interest; and

(c) barristers are obliged to accept any client if a proper fee is paid and cannot refuse clients on any other ground.

Lord Reid, Morris of Borth-y-Gest and Upjohn were of the opinion that public policy did not require the extension of this immunity to the non-litigious aspects of a barrister's work, and along with Lord Pearce thought that a solicitor should be given the same immunity in litigious work which could have been done by a barrister as the latter would have had if engaged.

COMMENT

(i) In *Saif Ali* v *Sydney Mitchell & Co.*, [1978] 3 All E.R. 1033 the majority in the House of Lords were of the opinion that *Rondel* v *Worsley* was concerned only with matters taking place in court which resulted in an outcome unfavourable to the client. So far as the speeches in *Rondel* contained observations as to the extent of barristers' immunity for matters taking place outside court and in barristers' chambers, these, the House of Lords said, had only the status of *obiter dicta*.

(ii) A solicitor acting as an advocate in court enjoys the same immunity said a majority of the House of Lords in the *Saif Ali* case.

CRIMINAL CONDUCT CANNOT BE PREVENTED BY INJUNCTION UNLESS THE ATTORNEY-GENERAL IS PREPARED TO TAKE OR AGREE TO THE TAKING, OF PROCEEDINGS.

19. *Gouriet* v *Union of Post Office Workers* [1977] 3 All E.R. 70

Under ss. 58 and 68 of the Post Office Act, 1953, it is an offence punishable by fine and imprisonment for persons employed by the Post Office wilfully to delay or omit to deliver packets and messages in the course of transmission and for any person to solicit or endeavour to procure another to commit such an offence. The Council of the Union of Post Office Workers called on its members not to handle mail to South Africa for a week because they disapproved of South Africa's policies. The plaintiff, who was the Secretary of the National Association for Freedom, asked the Attorney-General for his consent to act as plaintiff in relator proceedings for an injunction to restrain the Union from soliciting or endeavouring to procure any person wilfully to detain or delay a postal packet in the course of transmission to South Africa. The Attorney-General refused. The plaintiff took the matter to court and eventually the House of Lords decided that proceedings to prevent the infringement of public rights can only be instituted by the consent of the Attorney-General unless an individual has a special interest as where his private rights are threatened. Mr Gouriet had no such interest and was not entitled to the relief sought. Presumably, a company which dealt on a regular basis with South Africa by mail would have had the necessary *locus standi*

Criminal procedure

EXCESSIVE REPORTING OF CRIMINAL PROCEEDINGS: NO NEED TO SHOW PREJUDICE TO ACCUSED

20. *The Eastbourne Herald Case*, *The Times*, 12 June 1973

The *Eastbourne Herald* published an article upon the committal proceedings of a case in which a man was charged with unlawful sexual intercourse. The prosecution of the editor and proprietors which followed was based on the following matters which appeared in the articles –

(a) a headline reading 'New Year's day Bridegroom Bailed'.

(b) a description of the offence charged as being 'serious';

(c) a description of the alleged offender as 'bespectacled and dressed in a dark suit';

(d) a note to the effect that he had been 'married at St Michael's Church on New Year's Day'

(d) a reference to the way in which the prosecuting solicitor had handled the case.

The editor and proprietors were each found guilty by the Eastbourne Magistrates on the five counts relating to these different passages and were each fined a total of £2000 and ordered to pay £37.50 costs. This strange decision stems initially from the fact that liability may be incurred under what is now s. 8(4) of the Magistrates' Court Act, 1980 where a report of committal proceedings contains any details other than those permitted by s. 8(4) and quite irrespective of whether or not the details are potentially prejudicial in nature. All that the prosecution is required to show is –

(a) that the defendent published a report of committal proceedings to which the restrictions apply, and

(b) that the report contained matters for which no specific provision is made in s. 8(4).

Thus in this case it was an offence under the Act to describe unlawful sexual intercourse as a 'serious' offence for s. 8(4) permits of no such qualifying adjective. Equally, it was an offence to describe the defendant as 'bespectacled and dressed in a dark suit' for s. 8(4) only provides for reference to his name, address and occupation. Furthermore, it is not necessary for the prosecution to show that the offending item purported to be an account of what transpired in court, provided only that it is contained within a report of committal proceedings. Thus, in this case the magistrates held that it was an offence under the Act to refer to the fact that the defendant had been married at St Michael's Church on New Year's Day although this piece of background information does not appear to have been adduced as evidence in court.

The law-making process I – the UK Parliament

THE COURTS CANNOT EXAMINE THE PROCEEDINGS OF PARLIAMENT TO SEE WHETHER AN ACT OR DELEGATED LEGISLATION CAN BE REGARDED AS INVALID ON THE GROUNDS THAT IT WAS OBTAINED BY SOME IRREGULARITY OR FRAUD

21. *British Railways Board* v *Pickin* [1974] 1 All E.R. 609

Section 259 of the Bristol and Exeter Railways Act, 1836, provides that if the railway, which it set up, should at any time be abandoned, the land acquired for the track should vest in the adjoining landowners; the same provision was contained in the Act setting up the Yatton to Clevedon line. The British Railways Board, in whom the railways had become vested, closed the line in the early 1960s and took up the tracks in 1969. A private Act of Parliament, the British Railways Act, was passed in 1968 cancelling the effect of s. 259 and vesting the track in the Board; the Act's preamble recited that plans and books of reference had been deposited with Somerset County Council. Pickin, who objected to the closing of the line, purchased a few feet of land adjoining the track in 1969 and sought a declaration that he owned the land as far as the middle of the track, the railway having been abandoned within s. 259. In reply to the Board's defence that the land was vested in them by virtue of s. 18 of the Act of 1968. Pickin pleaded that that Act had contained a false recital in that the requisite documents had not been deposited, that the Board had misled Parliament in obaining the Act *ex parte* (in effect without hearing other views) and that it was ineffective to deprive him of his land. It was *held* – by the House of Lords – that the courts had no power to examine proceedings in Parliament in order to determine whether the passing of an Act was obtained by means of any irregularity or fraud, so that Mr Pickin failed.

> COMMENT
>
> As regards delegated legislation in *R* v *Immigration Appeal Tribunal, ex parte Joyles* [1972] 3 All E.R. 213 it was alleged that some regulations made under the Immigration Appeals Act, 1969 had not been properly laid before Parliament as required by s. 24(2) of the 1969 Act. A Divisional Court of the Queen's Bench relied on letters from the Clerks of the Journal to the Commons and Lords stating that the rules had been duly presented and laid. The Court was not prepared to go further and examine the internal proceedings of Parliament.

DELEGATED LEGISLATION – JUDICIAL CONTROL; THE APPLICATION OF THE DOCTRINE OF *ULTRA VIRES*

22. *Hotel and Catering Industry Training Board* v *Automobile Proprietary Ltd* [1969] 2 All E.R. 582

This was a test case brought by the Board to decide whether the Industrial

Training (Hotel and Catering Board) Order, 1966 made by the Minister of Labour pursuant to powers conferred upon him by the Industrial Training Act, 1964, was *ultra vires* in so far as it purported to extend to any members' clubs. If the order was *ultra vires*, the R.A.C. club in Pall Mall was not liable to pay a levy to the Board by reason of its activities in providing midday and evening meals and board and lodging for reward. The relevant order was made under s. 1(1) of the Act of 1964, which provides that the Minister may 'for the purpose of making better provision for . . . training . . . for employment in any activities of industry or commerce' make an order specifying 'those activities', and establishing a board to exercise the functions of an industrial training board. The 1966 order specified 'the activities' as including the supply of main meals and lodgings for reward by a members' club. Nevertheless this provision was only valid if the activities of members' clubs were activities of 'industry or commerce'. *Held* – by the House of Lords – that the general object of the Act of 1964 was to provide employers in industry and commerce with trained personnel and to finance the training by a levy on employers in the industry, and that it was not intended to allow a levy to be made on private institutions like members' clubs. Although such institutions might pursue activities not unlike those of a hotel keeper, they could not be regarded as within the phrase 'activities of industry or commerce'.

LOCAL AUTHORITY BYE-LAWS CAN BE CHALLENGED IN THE COURTS AS BEING UNREASONABLE

23. *Burnley Borough Council* v *England*, *The Times*, 15 July 1978

In this case it was *held* that a bye-law of the council prohibiting any person from causing any dog belonging to him or in his charge to enter or remain in specified pleasure grounds other than a guide dog in the charge of a blind person was not unreasonable. The council was concerned about the fouling of pleasure grounds by dogs. The court went on to say that a bye-law could be unreasonable if so unjust and oppressive that no reasonable council could have made it – for example a bye-law directed against dog owners with red hair.

INTERPRETATION ACT, 1978: APPLICATION TO STATUTORY INTERPRETATION

24. *Hutton* v *Esher Urban District Council* [1973] 2 All E.R. 1123

The Council proposed to construct a sewer to drain surface water from houses and roads and also to take flood water from a river. The most economical line of the sewer would take it straight through the plaintiff's bungalow which would have to be demolished but might be rebuilt after the sewer had been constructed. The Public Health Act, 1936 empowered the Council to construct a public sewer 'in, on, or over any land not forming part of a street'. The plaintiff argued that the expression 'land' did not include buildings and therefore the Council had no power to demolish his bungalow. However, s. 3 of the Interpretation Act of 1889 (see now s. 5 and Sch. 1 of the Interpretation

Act, 1978) provided that unless a contrary intention appears the expression 'land' includes buildings. It was *held* – by the Court of Appeal – that the Interpretation Act was applicable and 'land' therefore included buildings. In consequence the Council had the power to demolish the plaintiff's bungalow.

JUDICIAL INTERPRETATION OF STATUTES: THE MISCHIEF RULE: A STATUTE IS TO BE CONSTRUED SO AS TO SUPPRESS THE MISCHIEF IN THE COMMON LAW AND ADVANCE THE REMEDY

25. *Gardiner* v *Sevenoaks R.D.C.* (1950) 66 T.L.R. 1091

The local authority served a notice under the Celluloid and Cinematograph Film Act, 1922, on the occupier of a cave where film was stored, requiring him to comply with certain safety regulations. Obviously, the common law had no such rules. The cave was described in the notice as 'premises'. Gardiner, who was the occupier, appealed against the notice on the ground that a cave could not be considered 'premises' for the purposes of the Act. *Held* – whilst it was not possible to lay down that every cave would be 'premises' for all purposes, the Act was a safety Act and was designed to protect persons in the neighbourhood and those working in the place of storage. Therefore, under the 'Mischief Rule' this cave was 'premises' for the purposes of the Act.

> COMMENT
> The mischief rule is very close to the more recent recommendation of the Law Commission for a purposive interpretation of statutes. (See p. 149.)

THE GOLDEN RULE OF INTERPRETATION: EXTENDS THE LITERAL RULE WHERE THE APPLICATION OF THAT RULE LEADS TO AN ABSURD RESULT

26. *Keene* v *Muncaster* [1980] R.T.R. 377

Regulation 115 of the Motor Vehicles (Construction and Use) Regulations, 1973 provides that a motorist may only park a motor vehicle on the road during the hours of darkness with the nearside of the vehicle to the kerb. There is an exception to this if he has the permission of a police officer in uniform to do otherwise. The defendant, a police officer in uniform, parked his vehicle with the offside to the kerb during the hours of darkness. When he was charged with an offence under reg. 115, he claimed that he had given himself permission to park that way. He was convicted by the magistrates and appealed to the Divisional Court of Queen's Bench. *Held* – dismissing the appeal – that under the Golden Rule of interpretation the word 'permission' meant permission had to be requested by one person from another. The permission could not be given by the person whose vehicle was parked with the offside to the kerb.

COMMENT
The Golden Rule of interpretation was considered in *Prince of Hanover* v *A.G.*, 1957 to which reference could usefully be made again at this point (see p. 562).

THE *EJUSDEM GENERIS* RULE

27. *Lane* v *London Electricity Board* [1955] 1 All E.R. 324

The plaintiff was an electrician employed by the defendants to install additional lighting in one of their sub-stations. While inspecting the sub-station, he tripped on the edge of an open duct and fell, sustaining injuries. The plaintiff claimed that the defendants were in breach of their statutory duty under the Electricity (Factories Act) Special Regulations in that the part of the premises where the accident occurred was not adequately lighted to prevent 'danger'. *Held* – it appeared that the word 'danger' in the regulations meant 'danger from shock, burn or other injury'. Danger from tripping was not *ejusdem generis*, since the specific words related to forms of danger resulting from contact with electricity.

COMMENT
This summary is concerned only with the plaintiff's claim under the Regulations. The failure of this claim did not prevent a claim for damages for negligence at common law.

THE *EXPRESSIO UNIUS EST EXCLUSIO ALTERIUS* RULE OF STATUTORY INTERPRETATION: THE EXPRESSION OF ONE THING IMPLIES THE EXCLUSION OF ANOTHER

28. *R* v *Immigration Appeals Adjudicator, ex parte Crew*, *The Times*, 26 November 1982

An Immigration Appeals Tribunal had, in interpreting the Immigration Act, 1971, ruled that a woman who was born in Hong Kong of a Chinese mother and putative English father, was not entitled to a certificate of patriality (a certificate allowing immigration). There was an appeal to the Court of Appeal where the sole question was whether the word 'parent' used in the 1971 Act included the father of an illegitimate child. The father in this case was unknown. It was held that since the definition section in the 1971 Act specifically mentioned the mother alone in the context of an illegitimate child, the Rule *expressio unius est exclusio alterius* served to exclude the father of an illegitimate child for these purposes as a 'parent'. The appeal was dismissed. The Act required patriality to be decided on the basis of the mother alone. The daughter of a Chinese mother was not a patrial.

THE *NOSCITUR A SOCIIS* RULE OF STATUTORY INTERPRETATION: THE MEANING OF A WORD MAY BE GATHERED FROM ITS CONTEXT

29. *Muir v Keay* (1875) L.R. 10 Q.B. 594

Section 6 of the Refreshment Houses Act, 1860 stated that all houses, rooms, shops or buildings, kept open for public refreshment, resort and entertainment during certain hours of the night, must be licensed. The defendant had premises called 'The Café', and certain persons were found there during the night when the café was open. They were being supplied with cigars, coffee and ginger beer which they were seen to consume. The justices convicted the defendant because the premises were not licensed. He appealed to the divisional court by case stated, suggesting that a licence was required only if 'entertainment' in terms e.g. of music or dancing was going on. The divisional court, applying the *noscitur a sociis* rules, *held* – that 'entertainment', because of the context in which it appeared in the Act of 1860, meant matters of bodily comfort and not matters of mental enjoyment such as theatrical or musical performances with which the word 'entertainment' is so often associated in other contexts. The justices were therefore right to convict.

SINCE ITS DECLARATION OF 1966 THE HOUSE OF LORDS IS NOT BOUND BY ITS OWN DECISIONS: APPLICATION OF THE DECLARATION

30. *Schorsch Meier Gmbh v Hennin* [1975] 1 All E.R. 152

The plaintiffs, who carried on business in West Germany, had sold goods to the defendants in England. They had not been paid in full for the goods and DM 3756 remained owing. At the date of the invoice the sterling equivalent of this sum was £452 but between the invoice date and the date of the County Court summons sterling had been devalued so that the value of £452 was only £266. Consequently, the plaintiffs asked for judgement in deutschmarks. The difficulty facing the plaintiffs was that the House of Lords had decided in *Re United Railways of Havana* [1960] 2 All E.R. 332 that an English court could not give judgment for an amount in foreign currency. The plaintiffs challenged this on the grounds that the *Havana* case ran contrary to Article 106 of the EEC Treaty. The County Court judge held that he was bound by the *Havana* case and could only give judgment in sterling. On appeal, however, the Court of Appeal with Lord Denning, M.R., came to a different decision and found for the plaintiffs on two grounds – (*i*) as an English court had since *Beswick v Beswick*, 1967 (see p. 616) the power to order specific performance of a contract to make a money payment there was no longer a justification for the rule in *Havana* that judgment could only be given for a sum of money in sterling; (*ii*) secondly, that the effect of Article 106 of the EEC Treaty was to require the English courts to give judgment in favour of a creditor of a member state in the currency of that state.

31. *Miliangos* v *George Frank (Textiles) Ltd* [1975] 3 All E.R. 801

This case was concerned with a contract for the sale of polyester yarn and in particular the money of payment and the money of account in the contract were in Swiss francs. The Swiss seller, who was unpaid, was allowed in view of the decision in *Schorsch Meier* to claim payment in Swiss francs. Sterling had fallen in value against the Swiss franc and if the new rule in *Schorsch* were to be applied the plaintiff stood to gain £60,000 as opposed to £42,000 under the *Havana* principle. At first instance Bristow, J. *held* that the decision in *Schorsch* had been decided *per incuriam*, the Court of Appeal having been bound by the *Havana* case. Consequently, he felt able to give a judgment only in sterling. From his judgment an appeal was made to the Court of Appeal and his decision was reversed by a court presided over by Lord Denning, who had been in the majority in the Court of Appeal when *Schorsch* was decided. From the judgment of the Court of Appeal a further appeal was made to the House of Lords. Their Lordships quickly reached the conclusion that the *Havana* case had not been overruled, since the only means by which that could have been done was by the House of Lords itself under the declaration of 1966 and, accordingly, the Court of Appeal should have felt bound by the case. It was, however, now open for the House of Lords to re-examine its previous decision in *Havana*. The House of Lords concluded that as the situation regarding currency stability had substantially changed since 1961 when the *Havana* case was decided, there was justification for a departure from that decision under the 1966 declaration. Accordingly, the House refused to follow the *Havana* case and held that an English court may give judgment in a foreign currency. However, the majority of their Lordships were highly critical of the wide interpretation of Article 106 adopted by the Court of Appeal, Switzerland not being a member of the Common Market, and it remains to be seen when the matter comes before the courts again whether that Article is adequate to sustain the view taken in this case.

COMMENT

(i) In *Fitzleet Estates Ltd* v *Cherry (Inspector of Taxes)* [1977] 3 All E.R. 996 which was a case concerned with the tax treatment of interest paid on a loan used to buy property the House of Lords refused to depart from its previous decision in *Chancery Lane Safe Deposit and Offices Co Ltd* [1966] 1 All E.R. 1 and stated that in the absence of a change of circumstances it would not normally depart from a previous decision unless there were serious doubts as to its correctness. So change of circumstances would seem to be the major factor. It will be noted that in the *Miliangos* case the circumstances were very different from those which applied when the *Havana* case was decided. The situation regarding currency stability had changed. Currency values were much more volatile and this justified a departure from the *Havana* case.

(ii) A further example of the use of the 1966 declaration can be seen in *Murphy* v *Brentwood District Council*, 1990 at p. 437 where the House of Lords departed from a previous decision because there were serious doubts as to its correctness.

The law-making process II – case law and the legislative organs of the European Community

PRECEDENT: COURT OF APPEAL CRIMINAL DIVISION: CONSIDERATIONS APPLYING ON A CRIMINAL APPEAL

32. *R* v *Gould* [1968] 1 All E.R. 849

The appellant was convicted of bigamy although when he remarried he believed on reasonable grounds that a decree *nisi* of divorce in respect of his previous marriage had been made absolute which it had not, so that he was still married at the time of the second ceremony. The Court of Criminal Appeal in *R* v *Wheat and Stocks* [1921] 2 K.B. 119 had decided on similar facts that a reasonable belief in the dissolution of a previous marriage was no defence. In this appeal to the Court of Appeal (Criminal Division) the court quashed the conviction *holding* that in spite of the decision in *R* v *Wheat and Stocks*, a defendant's honest belief on reasonable grounds that at the time of his second marriage his former marriage had been dissolved was a good defence to a charge of bigamy. Diplock, L.J., giving the judgment of the court, said that in its criminal jurisdiction the Court of Appeal does not apply the doctrine of *stare decisis* as rigidly as in its civil jurisdiction, and if it is of the opinion that the law has been misapplied or misunderstood it will depart from a previous decision.

COMMENT
In this case a three-judge court expressly overruled *Wheat and Stocks* which was itself a decision of a five-judge Court of Criminal Appeal.

CAUSE OF ACTION AND ISSUE ESTOPPEL DISTINGUISHED

33. *Arnold* v *National Westminster Bank plc* [1990] 1 All E.R. 529

The bank leased premises to the plaintiffs for a term of years. The lease had rent review clauses in it. The reviews were to take place every five years. The review was to give the bank as landlords a 'fair market rent' according to a formula in the lease. At the first review in 1983 the judge who was called upon to interpret the review clause decided that upon its wording he had to give a rent on the basis that there were no review clauses in the lease. This meant a rent which would last until the end of the lease and such a rent would have to be some 20% more than if the fair rent was based on a lease with regular reviews of rent.

The parties went to court again on the 1988 review and that litigation produced this decision. It appeared that following the judge's decision on the 1983 review other cases interpreting similar review clauses decided that the wording meant a fair rent based on a lease with regular rent reviews. The plaintiffs wanted such a decision in regard to the 1988 review. The bank said the court could not give such a decision because the matter had been decided in 1983 and must stand for the whole of the lease in terms of the interpretation of the rent review clause. The Court of Appeal said that the issue could be looked at again in regard to the 1988 review. This was not cause of action estoppel but only issue estoppel and the issue could be litigated again.

COMMENT
It is worth noting that cause of action estoppel would prevent the overruling of the 1983 decision but at least the *issue* which was at the root of the 1983 decision could be looked at again for the future.

SUPREMACY OF EC LAW

34. *Factortame Ltd v Secretary of State for Transport (No. 2)*
[1991] 1 All E.R. 70

The problem in this case was the Merchant Shipping Act, 1988. This requires 75% of directors and shareholders in companies operating fishing vessels in UK waters to be British. This effectively barred certain ships owned by UK companies controlled by Spanish nationals from fishing in British waters. This was alleged to be in conflict with the Treaty of Rome because it deprived Spanish controlled companies and, by implication, their Spanish directors and members of their EC rights under the common fishing policy. The matter was going to take up to two years to sort out. The Spanish would suffer financial loss during that time. They came to the Court and asked for suspension of the operation of the 1988 Act until the final issue had been determined. The House of Lords eventually decided to refer the matter to the European Court which gave an unequivocal answer. It laid it down that Community Law must be fully and uniformly applied in all the member states and that a relevant Community law rendered automatically inapplicable any conflicting provision of national law. It followed that the courts were obliged to grant interim relief in cases of alleged conflict, whereas in this case the only obstacle was a rule of national law. Accordingly, the House of Lords granted interim relief by suspending the relevant provision of the 1988 Act until a final ruling on the issue of conflict could be obtained.

COMMENT
The supremacy of EC Law has been upheld, not only where there is a conflict, but even where there might be. The decision makes a big dent in Parliamentary supremacy to say the least.

Persons and the Crown

DOMICIL OF ORIGIN AND CHOICE: EFFECT ON TAXATION

35. *I.R.C. v Bullock* [1976] 3 All E.R. 353

Mr Bullock was born in Nova Scotia in 1910 and had his domicil of origin there. In 1932 he came to England to join the RAF, intending to go back to Canada when his service was completed. In 1946 he married an Englishwoman and they went on a number of visits to Mr Bullock's father in Canada. In 1959 Mr Bullock retired from the RAF and took up civilian employment in England. In 1961 he was able to retire fully, having become entitled to money from his father's estate on the latter's death. Mr Bullock had always tried to persuade his wife to live in Canada but she would not do so. Even so, Mr Bullock always hoped she would change her mind. In 1966 he made a will subject to Nova Scotia law under which he said that his domicil was Nova Scotia and that he intended to return and remain there if his wife died before him. The Crown claimed that he had acquired a domicil of choice in England and that all his income from Canada was chargeable to income tax. If Mr Bullock was not domiciled in England then tax would be chargeable only on that part of the income from his father's estate which was actually sent to him in England. This was less than all the income. It was *held* – by the Court of Appeal – that the fact that Mr Bullock had established a matrimonial home in England was evidence of his intention, but was not conclusive. On the evidence of his retention of Canadian citizenship and of the terms of a declaration as to domicil in his will, it was impossible not to hold that Mr Bullock had always maintained a firm intention to return to Canada in the event of his surviving his wife, and there was a sufficiently substantial possibility of his surviving his wife to justify regarding the intention to return as a real determination to do so, in that event, rather than a vague hope or aspiration. Accordingly, Mr Bullock could not be said to have formed the intention to acquire an English domicil of choice. Thus he could be taxed only on that part of the Canadian estate which was remitted to England.

DOMICIL: A PERSON WHO ABANDONS A DOMICIL OF CHOICE WITHOUT ACQUIRING ANOTHER REVERTS TO THE DOMICIL OF ORIGIN

36. *Tee* v *Tee* [1973] 3 All E.R. 1105

The parties were married in England in November 1946 when the husband was a domiciled Englishman and the wife was an American citizen. In 1951 they went to the United States and in 1953 the husband became an American citizen and acquired a domicil of choice in that country. In 1960 the husband was posted to Germany by his employers, and in 1965 he left his wife and set up home with a German woman by whom he had two children. Some time during 1966/67 the husband decided to make his permanent home in England but it was not until November 1972 that the husband with his mistress and children actually took up residence in the house he had bought in England in May 1972. The husband had been granted a permit to work in England in 1969. In July 1972, he presented a petition for divorce. The wife challenged the jurisdiction of the English Courrt to hear this petition and the question for the court was whether the husband was domiciled in England in July 1972. *Held* – by the Court of Appeal – that the husband was domiciled in England. He had left the United States in 1960 and the intention not to return there was formed over the period 1966/67. In consequence the two elements necessary to establish the abandonment of a domicil of choice had been proved. When a domicil of choice was lost, the domicil of origin revives; the fact that the husband did not actually take up permanent residence in England until 1972 was immaterial since it is not necessary for the revival of a domicil of origin that residence should also be taken up in that country.

DOMICIL: EVIDENCE OF CHANGE: NATURALISATION: PURCHASE OF BUSINESS

37. *Steiner v Inland Revenue Commissioners* [1973] S.T.C. 547

Steiner was born in the former Austro/Hungarian Empire. He lived in Berlin from 1906 but was driven out of Germany by the Nazis in 1939 and came to England. He acquired a flat in London in 1941 and by the end of 1948 had established a business in England and was naturalised in 1948. From 1948 to 1963 he spent six months of each year in Berlin where he had a property. He was assessed to income tax for the years 1960/61 to 1966/7 on rents on properties in West Berlin, the Special Commissioners holding that he had acquired an English domicil of choice. He appealed. *Held* – by the Court of Appeal – that the appeal would be dismissed; there were no grounds for holding the Special Commissioners' decision to be wrong in law. The Court refused to grant leave to appeal to the House of Lords.

> COMMENT
> (i) If a person is domiciled or resident in England and Wales, tax is charged on the full amount of income arising within a given year wherever made or received. (Income and Corporation Taxes Act, 1988 ss. 334–336.)
> (ii) See also I.R.C. v *Bullock*, 1976 at p. 581 for other examples of evidence of change of domicil, e.g. by a will.

RACIAL DISCRIMINATION: INDUCEMENT TO DISCRIMINATE ON RACIAL GROUNDS

38. *The Commission for Racial Equality v Imperial Society of Teachers of Dancing* [1983] I.C.R. 473

The Society wished to employ a filing clerk. A telephone call was made to a local girls' school to find a suitable applicant. During the course of the phone call it was made clear that a coloured girl would be out of place because there were no other coloured employees. It was held by the Employment Appeal Tribunal that the words 'to induce' in s. 31 of the Race Relations Act, 1976 meant to persuade or to prevail upon or to bring about, and the words used did constitute an attempt to induce the head of careers at the girls' school not to send a coloured girl. In consequence the Society had contravened s. 31.

SEX DISCRIMINATION: FACILITIES AND SERVICES

39. *Gill v El Vino Co Ltd* [1983] 1 All E.R. 398

The plaintiffs, both women, entered a wine bar and stood at the bar and ordered wine. They were refused service under house rules but were told that if they would sit at a table their drinks would be brought to them. The plaintiffs brought an action alleging breach of the 1975 Act. It was *held* – by the Court of Appeal – that applying the simple words of the Act the defendants had failed to provide the plaintiffs with facilities afforded to men and by doing so they had treated women less favourably than men contrary to the 1975 Act.

COMMENT

In *James v Eastleigh Borough Council* [1990] 2 All E.R. 607 the plaintiff and his wife who were both retired and aged 61 went to a leisure centre run by the council. The wife was admitted to the swimming pool free because she was of pensionable age. The plaintiff had to pay because he was not. He brought proceedings alleging discrimination. Eventually the House of Lords ruled that the distinction operated by the council was unlawful direct discrimination on the grounds of sex.

SEX DISCRIMINATION: CREDIT: A REQUIREMENT THAT A WOMAN MUST HAVE HER HUSBAND'S GUARANTEE IS UNLAWFUL

40. *Quinn v Williams Furniture Ltd* [1981] I.C.R. 328

Mrs Quinn wanted to buy certain goods from a shop on hire-purchase terms. She was told by the shop assistant that if she took out a hire-purchase agreement her husband would have to give a guarantee for the credit allowed, but if he took out the agreement she would not be required to give a guarantee of his liability. She bought the goods and took out the agreement herself, her husband acting as guarantor. She then complained that the shop's refusal to give her credit facilities on the same basis as they would to a man in her position was a breach of the Sex Discrimination Act, 1975. The Court of Appeal held that it was. On the facts Mrs Quinn had not been allowed credit facilities in the same way as they would normally be offered to men. Even a suggestion or advice such as this to get her husband's guarantee was unlawful. There did not have to be an outright refusal of credit.

COMMENT

The case shows that credit restrictions based on sex, at one time usual in business, may now infringe the 1975 Act.

A REGISTERED COMPANY HAS A SEPARATE LEGAL ENTITY

41. *Salomon v Salomon & Co* [1897] A.C. 22

Salomon carried on business as a leather merchant and boot manufacturer. In 1892 he formed a limited company to take over the business. The Memorandum of Association was signed by Salomon, his wife, daughter and four sons. Each subscribed for one share. The company paid £38,782 to

Salomon for the business and the mode of payment was to give Salomon £10,000 in debentures, secured by a floating charge, 20,000 shares of £1 each and £8782 in cash. The company fell on hard times and a liquidator was appointed. The debts of the unsecured creditors amount to nearly £8000, and the company's assets were approximately £6000. The unsecured creditors claimed all the remaining assets on the ground that the company was a mere alias or agent for Salomon. *Held* – the company was a separate and distinct person. The debentures were perfectly valid and therefore Salomon was entitled to the remaining assets in part payment of the secured debentures held by him.

LOOKING BEHIND THE CORPORATE MASK

42. *Gilford Motor Company* v *Horne* [1933] Ch. 935

Mr Horne had been employed by Gilford. He had agreed to a restraint of trade in his contract under which he would not approach the company's customers to try to get them to transfer their custom to any similar business which Mr Horne might run himself. Mr Horne left his job with Gilford and set up a similar business using a registered company structure. He then began to send out circulars to the customers of Gilford inviting them to do business with his company. Gilford asked the court for an injunction to stop Mr Horne's activities and he said he was not competing but his company was and that the company had not agreed to a restraint of trade. However, an injunction was granted against both Mr Horne and his company to stop the circularisation of Gilford's customers. The corporate structure could not be used to evade legal responsibilities.

A MEMBER MAY OBTAIN AN INJUNCTION TO RESTRAIN A COMPANY FROM ACTING IN A MANNER INCONSISTENT WITH ITS CONSTITUTION

43. *Jenkin* v *Pharmaceutical Society* [1921] 1 Ch. 392

The defendant society was incorporated by Royal Charter in 1843 for the purpose of advancing chemistry and pharmacy and promoting a uniform system of education of those who should practise the same, and also for the protection of those who carried on the business of chemists or druggists. *Held* – the expenditure of the funds of the society in the formation of an industrial committee, to attempt to regulate hours of work and wages and conditions of work between employers and employee members of the society, was *ultra vires* the charter, because it was a trade union activity which was not contemplated by the Charter of 1843. Further, the expenditure of money on an insurance scheme for members was also not within the powers given in the charter, for it amounted to converting the defendant society into an insurance company. The plaintiff, a member of the society, was entitled to an injunction to restrain the society from implementing the above schemes.

DISCLOSURE OF DOCUMENTS: CROWN OR PUBLIC INTEREST PRIVILEGE

44. *Norwich Pharmacal Co.* v *Commissioners of Customs and Excise* [1973] 2 All E.R. 943

The plaintiffs held the patent of a chemical compound used in animal foods, which they discovered was being infringed by unknown importers. The Commissioners of Customs and Excise were allowing the importation and charging duty thereon, and consequently knew the identity of the importers concerned. The plaintiffs brought proceedings against the Commissioners for infringement of their patent, and for an order that they disclose the identity of the importers. The order was granted by the judge but reversed by the Court of Appeal. On appeal to the House of Lords by the plaintiffs it was *held* – allowing the appeal – that the interests of justice outweighed any public interest in the confidential nature of such information. The Commissioners were under a duty to assist a person wronged by disclosing the identity of the wrongdoer.

45. *Alfred Crompton Amusement Machines* v *Customs and Excise Commissioners (No. 2)* [1973] 2 All E.R. 1169

The appellants had paid purchase tax on the wholesale value of amusement machines for some years on the basis of a formula negotiated with the Commissioners of Customs and Excise. The appellants claimed that the assessments were too high and thereupon the Commissioners investigated the appellants' books and obtained from customers and other sources information bearing on the ascertainment of the wholesale value of the machines. The appellants did not agree with the opinion of the Commissioners as to the way in which the tax should be computed and in subsequent arbitration proceedings Crown privilege was claimed in respect of documents received by the Commissioners from third parties. It was *held* – by the House of Lords – that the considerations for and against disclosure were evenly balanced. In these circumstances it was held that the court ought to uphold the claim to privilege and trust the Executive to mitigate the ill-effects of non-disclosure.

> COMMENT
> It seems that where there is a doubt in regard to disclosure the benefit of the doubt is unfortunately to be allowed in favour of the Executive and against discovery. On considering the issue of Crown privilege their Lordships indicated by way of preface that the title is a misnomer; a more accurate term would be privilege on the ground of 'public interest', since privilege extends beyond cases against the Crown (see p. 200).

Law of contract – making the contract I

OFFER AND UNILATERAL AGREEMENTS

46. *Carlill* v *Carbolic Smoke Ball Co.* [1893] 1 Q.B. 256

The defendants were proprietors of a medical preparation called 'The Carbolic Smoke Ball'. They inserted advertisements in various newspapers in which they offered to pay £100 to any person who contracted influenza after using the ball three times a day for two weeks. They added that they had deposited £1000 at the Alliance Bank, Regent Street, 'to show our sincerity in the matter'. The plaintiff, a lady, used the ball as advertised, and was attacked by influenza during the course of treatment, which in her case extended from 20 November 1891 to 17 January 1892. She now sued for £100 and the following matters arose out of the various defences raised by the company. (*a*) It was suggested that the offer was too vague since no time limit was stipulated in which the user was to contract influenza. The court said that it must surely have been the intention that the ball would protect its user during the period of its use, and since this covered the present case it was not necessary to go further. (*b*) The suggestion was made that the matter was an advertising 'puff' and that there was no intention to create legal relations. Here the court took the view that the deposit of £1000 at the bank was clear evidence of an intention to pay claims. (*c*) It was further suggested that this was an attempt to contract with the whole world and that this was impossible in English law. The court took the view that the advertisement was an offer to the whole world and that, by analogy with the reward cases, it was possible to make an offer of this kind. (*d*) The company also claimed that the plaintiff had not supplied any consideration, but the court took the view that using this inhalant three times a day for two weeks or more was sufficient consideration. It was not necessary to consider its adequacy. (*e*) Finally the defendants suggested that there had been no communication of acceptance but here the court, looking at the reward cases, stated that in contracts of this kind acceptance may be by conduct.

COMMENT

(i) An offer to the public at large can only be made where the contract which eventually comes into being is a unilateral one, i.e. where there is a promise on one side for an act on the other. An offer to the public at large would be made, for example, where there was an advertisement offering a reward for services to be rendered such as finding a lost dog. It is interesting to note that an invitation to treat may be put to the world at large but an offer cannot be unless designed to produce a unilateral contract.

(ii) Most business contracts are bilateral. They are made by an exchange of promises and not, as here, by the exchange of a promise for an act. Nevertheless, *Carlill's* case has occasionally provided a useful legal principle in the field of business law. (See e.g. *The New*

Zealand Shipping Co. Ltd v *A.M. Satterthwaite & Co. Ltd* [1974] 1 All E.R. 1015 at p. 677.)

As regards motive, presumably Mrs Carlill used the ball to prevent influenza and not to recover £100. However, she had seen the offer and her motive was immaterial.

(iii) A deposit of money from which to pay is not essential. In *Wood* v *Lectrik Ltd, The Times*, 13 January 1932 the defendants who were makers of an electric comb had advertised: 'What is your trouble? Is it grey hair? In ten days not a grey hair left. £500 Guarantee.' Mr Wood used the comb as directed but his hair remained grey at the end of ten days of use. All the comb had done was to scratch his scalp. There was no bank deposit by the company but Rowlatt, J. held that there was a contract and awarded Mr Wood the £500.

OFFER AND INVITATION TO TREAT – AUCTION SALES

47. *Harris* v *Nickerson* (1873) L.R. 8 Q.B. 286

The defendant, an auctioneer, advertised in London newspapers that a sale of office furniture would be held at Bury St Edmunds. A broker with a commission to buy furniture came from London to attend the sale. Several conditions were set out in the advertisement, one being: 'The highest bidder to be the buyer.' The lots described as office furniture were not put up for sale but were withdrawn, though the auction itself was held. The broker sued for loss of time in attending the sale. *Held* – he could not recover from the auctioneer. There was no offer since the lots were never put up for sale, and the advertisement was simply an invitation to treat.

COMMENT
(i) A sensible decision, really. The statement, 'I *intend* to auction some office furniture' is not the same as an offer for sale, and in any case there seems to be no way of accepting the 'offer' in advance of the event.

(ii) In *British Car Auctions* v *Wright* [1972] 3 All E.R. 462 the auctioneers sold an unroadworthy vehicle. An attempt to charge them with the offence of 'offering' the car for sale contrary to road traffic legislation failed. The bidder made the offer and not the auctioneer (and see *Partridge* v *Crittenden* 1968 at p. 589).

INVITATION TO TREAT: PRICE INDICATIONS, CIRCULARS ETC.

48. *Pharmaceutical Society of Great Britain* v *Boots Cash Chemists (Southern) Ltd* [1953] 1 Q.B. 401

The defendants' branch at Edgware was adapted to the 'self-service' system. Customers selected their purchases from shelves on which the goods were displayed and put them into a wire basket supplied by the defendants. They then took them to the cash desk where they paid the price. One section of shelves was set out with drugs which were included in the Poisons List referred to in s. 17 of the Pharmacy and Poisons Act, 1933, though they were not dangerous drugs and did not require a doctor's prescription. Section 18 of the Act requires that the sale of such drugs shall take place in the presence of a qualified pharmacist. Every sale of the drugs on the Poisons List was supervised at the cash desk by a qualified pharmacist, who had authority to prevent customers from taking goods out of the shop if he thought fit. One of the duties of the Society was to enforce the provisions of the Act, and the action was brought because the plaintiffs claimed that the defendants were infringing s. 18. *Held* – that the display of goods in this way did not constitute an offer. The contract of sale was not made when a customer selected goods from the shelves, but when the company's servant at the cash desk accepted the offer to buy what had been chosen. There was, therefore, supervision in the sense required by the Act at the appropriate moment of time.

COMMENT

(i) The fact that a price ticket is not regarded as an offer is somewhat archaic, being based, perhaps, on a traditional commercial view that a shop is a place for bargaining and not a place for compulsory sales. However, since there is no bargaining in the United Kingdom in modern times the rule could be a hardship to those purchasers who quite rightly think that the ticket represents the price and not merely an invitation to treat.

(ii) Although a trader can *refuse to sell* at his wrongly advertised price, he commits a criminal offence under s. 20 of the Consumer Protection Act, 1987 for giving a misleading price indication.

(iii) The relevant provisions of the 1933 Act are now in ss. 2 and 3 of the Poisons Act, 1972.

(iv) See also *Esso Petroleum Ltd* v *Customs and Excise Commissioners* [1976] 1 All E.R. 117 where the House of Lords decided that price indications at a petrol filling station were invitations to treat.

49. *Partridge* v *Crittenden* [1968] 2 All E.R. 421

Mr Partridge inserted an advertisement in a publication called *Cage and Aviary Birds* containing the words 'Bramblefinch cocks, bramblefinch hens, 25s. each'. The advertisements appeared under the general heading 'Classified Advertisements' and in no place was there any direct use of the words 'offer for sale'. A Mr Thompson answered the advertisement enclosing a cheque for 25s., and asking that a 'bramblefinch hen' be sent to him. Mr Partridge sent one in a box, the bird wearing a closed ring.

Mr Thompson opened the box in the presence of an RSPCA inspector, Mr Crittenden, and removed the ring without injury to the bird. Mr Crittenden brought a prosecution against Mr Partridge before the Chester magistrates alleging that Mr Partridge had offered for sale a brambling contrary to s. 6(1) of the Protection of Birds Act, 1954, the bird being other than a close-ringed specimen bred in captivity and being of a species which was resident in or visited the British Isles in a wild state.

The justices were satisfied that the bird had not been bred in captivity but had been caught and ringed. A close-ring meant a ring that was completely closed and incapable of being forced or broken except with the intention of damaging it; such a ring was forced over the claws of a bird when it was between three and ten days old, and at that time it was not possible to determine what the eventual girth of the leg would be so that the close-ring soon became difficult to remove. The ease with which the ring was removed in this case indicated that it had been put on at a much later stage and this, together with the fact that the bird had no perching sense, led the justices to convict Mr Partridge.

He appealed to the Divisional Court of the Queen's Bench Division where the conviction was quashed. The court accepted that the bird was a wild bird, but since Mr Partridge had been charged with 'offering for sale' the conviction could not stand. The advertisement constituted in law an invitation to treat, not an offer for sale, and the offence was not, therefore, established. There was of course a completed sale for which Mr Partridge could have been successfully prosecuted but the prosecution in this case had relied on the offence of 'offering for sale' and failed to establish such an offer.

COMMENT

(i) The case shows how concepts of the civil law are sometimes at the root of criminal cases (and see *British Car Auctions* v *Wright*, 1972 at p. 588).

(ii) In *Spencer* v *Harding* (1870) L.R. 5 C.P. 561 the defendants were selling off a business and issued a circular inviting submission of tenders to buy the goods listed. It was held that the circular was merely an invitation to submit offers and not an offer. The defendants need not accept any tender even the highest.

OFFER AND INVITATION TO TREAT – ALLEGED CONTRACTS FOR THE SALE OF LAND

50. *Harvey* v *Facey* [1893] A.C. 552

The plaintiffs sent the following telegram to the defendant: 'Will you sell us Bumper Hall Pen? Telegraph lowest cash price.' The defendant telegraphed in reply: 'Lowest price for Bumper Hall Pen £900.' The plaintiffs then telegraphed: 'We agree to buy Bumper Hall Pen for £900 asked by you. Please send us your title deeds in order that we may get early possession.' The defendant made no reply. The Supreme Court of Jamaica granted the plaintiffs a decree of specific performance of the contract. On appeal the Judicial Committee of the Privy Council *held* that there was no contract. The second telegram was not an offer, but was in the nature of an invitation to treat at a minimum price of £900. The third telegram could not therefore be an acceptance resulting in a contract.

COMMENT

(i) The point was also raised in *Clifton* v *Palumbo* [1944] 2 All E.R. 497 where the owner of a very large estate wrote to the other party to the case as follows: 'I am prepared to offer you or your nominee my Lytham estate for £600,000.' The letter was regarded as an invitation to treat and not an offer. The Court of Appeal said of the letter: 'It is quite possible for persons on a half sheet of notepaper, in the most informal and unorthodox language, to contract to sell the most extensive and most complicated estate that can be imagined. This is quite possible, but, having regard to the habits of the people in this country, it is very unlikely.'

(ii) The matter of invitation to treat and offer in the context of the alleged sale of land produced the most interesting case of *Gibson* v *Manchester City Council* [1979] 1 All E.R. 972. The City Treasurer wrote to Mr Gibson saying that the Council 'may be prepared' to sell the freehold of his council house to him at £2725 less 20%, i.e. £2180. The letter said that Mr G should make a formal application, which he did. Following local government elections three months later the policy of selling council houses was reversed. The Council did not proceed with the sale to Mr Gibson. He claimed that a binding contract existed. The House of Lords said that it did not. The Treasurer's letter was only an invitation to treat. Mr G's application was the offer, but the Council had not accepted it. In the Court of Appeal Lord Denning said that there was an 'agreement in fact' which was enforceable. It was not always necessary, he said, to stick to the strict rules of offer and acceptance in order to produce a binding agreement. The House of Lords would not accept this and Lord Denning's view has not, as yet, found a place in the law.

ACCEPTANCE OF NO EFFECT UNTIL COMMUNICATED TO THE OFFEROR: AGREEMENT MAY BE INFERRED FROM CONDUCT

51. *Brogden* v *Metropolitan Railway* (1877) 2 App. Cas. 666

The plaintiff had been a supplier of coal to the Railway Company for a number of years, though there was no formal agreement between them. Eventually the plaintiff suggested that there ought to be one, and the agents of the parties met and a draft agreement was drawn up by the Railway Company's agent and sent to the plaintiff. The plaintiff inserted several new clauses into the draft, and in particular filled in the name of an arbitrator to settle the parties' differences under the agreement should any arise. He then wrote the word 'Approved' on the draft and returned it to the Railway Company's agent. There was no formal execution, the draft remaining in the agent's desk. However, coal was supplied according to the prices mentioned in the draft, though these were not the market prices, and prices were reviewed from time to time in accordance with the draft. The parties then had a disagreement and the plaintiff refused to supply coal to the Railway Company on the grounds that, since the Railway Company had not accepted the offer contained in the amended draft, there was no binding contract. *Held* –

(a) The draft was not a binding contract because the plaintiff had inserted new terms which the Railway Company had not accepted; but

(b) the parties had indicated by their conduct that they had waived the execution of the formal document and agreed to act on the basis of the draft. There was, therefore, a binding contract arising out of conduct, and its terms were the terms of the draft.

CONDITIONAL ASSENT: ACCEPTANCE MUST BE ABSOLUTE AND UNCONDITIONAL

52. *Winn v Bull* (1877) 7 Ch. D. 29

The defendant had entered into a written agreement with the plaintiff for the lease of a house, the term of the lease and the rent being agreed. However, the written.agreement was expressly made 'subject to the preparation and approval of a formal contract'. It appeared that no other contract was made between the parties. The plaintiff now sued for specific performance of the agreement. *Held* – there was no binding contract between the parties because, although certain covenants are normally implied into leases, it is also true that many and varied express covenants are often agreed between the parties. The words 'subject to contract' indicated that the parties were still in a state of negotiation, and until they entered into a formal contract there was no agreement which the court could enforce.

COMMENT

(i) It should be noted that the court is not bound to accept that the words 'subject to contract' have resulted in a conditional acceptance and therefore no contract. Thus in *Alpenstow Ltd* v *Regalian Properties plc* [1985] 2 All E.R. 545, the parties had been in negotiations regarding the sale of property for some five months. The plaintiffs then sent a letter to the defendants containing quite detailed terms of the contract but said to be subject to contract. The arrangements set out in the letter were accepted by the defendants who then sought specific performance on the contract as a counterclaim in an action brought by the plaintiffs alleging that no contract existed. Nourse, J. refused to give the words 'subject to contract' their usual meaning and he held that a contract existed. His judgment indicates that the circumstances of the case are all-important and in particular that he would not have expected to find the words 'subject to contract' except in the primary stage of a negotiation, and not as in this case, some four to five months on. Nor would he have expected to find them, as he did here, in a detailed and conscientiously drawn document.

(ii) The case of *Filby v Hounsell* [1896] 2 Ch. 737 is also of interest. Property had been offered for sale by auction but had not been sold. An offer was then made to buy the property, stating that if the offer was accepted the purchaser would sign a contract 'on the auction particulars'. This offer was accepted 'subject to contract as agreed'. *Held* – the parties were bound by a contract drafted on the auction particulars, although they had not signed a formal contract.

(iii) The formula 'subject to contract' has been used mainly on correspondence passing between persons engaged in negotiations for the purchase of land. In this field reference should now by made to the provisions of the Law of Property (Miscellaneous Provisions) Act, 1989 (see p. 231). There is no reason why the phrase should not be used wherever the parties wish to make clear that they are in a state of mere negotiation towards a contract and that their statements are not contractual at that stage.

COUNTER-OFFER: IF AN OFFEREE MAKES A COUNTER-OFFER HE CANNOT THEN EFFECTIVELY ACCEPT THE ORIGINAL OFFER: WHAT CONSTITUTES A COUNTER-OFFER: THE OFFEROR CAN ACCEPT A COUNTER-OFFER:

53. *Hyde* v *Wrench* (1840) 3 Beav. 334

The defendant offered to sell his farm for £1000. The plaintiff's agent made an offer of £950 and the defendant asked for a few days for consideration, after which the defendant wrote saying he could not accept it, whereupon the plaintiff wrote purporting to accept the offer of £1000. The defendant did not consider himself bound, and the plaintiff sued for specific performance. *Held* – the plaintiff could not enforce this 'acceptance' because his counter-offer of £950 was an implied rejection of the original offer to sell at £1000.

54. *Stevenson* v *McLean* (1880) 5 Q.B.D. 346

On Saturday the defendant offered to sell to the plaintiffs a quantity of iron at 40s. nett cash per ton open till Monday (close of business). On Monday the plaintiffs telegraphed asking whether the defendant would accept 40s. for delivery over two months, or if not what was the longest limit the defendant would give. The plaintiffs did not necessarily want to take delivery of the goods at once and pay for them. They would have liked to have been able to ask for delivery and pay from time to time over two months as they themselves found buyers for quantities of the iron. The defendant received the telegram at 10.01 am but did not reply, so the plaintiffs, by telegram sent at 1.34 pm, accepted the defendant's original offer. The defendant had already sold the iron to a third party, and informed the plaintiffs of this by a telegram despatched at 1.25 pm arriving at 1.46 pm. The plaintiffs had therefore accepted the offer before the defendant's revocation had been communicated to them. If, however, the plaintiffs' first telegram constituted a counter offer, then it would amount to a rejection of the defendant's original offer. *Held* – the plaintiffs' first telegram was not a counter-offer, but a mere inquiry for different terms which did not amount to a rejection of the defendants original offer, so that the offer was still open when the plaintiffs accepted it. The defendant's offer was not revoked merely by the sale of the iron to another person.

COMMENT
The case shows that a distinction must be drawn between a rejection

by counter-offer and a request for information. A common example of this distinction occurs in business when an offer to sell at a stated price is not regarded as rejected, where, as here, the seller is asked whether he is prepared to give credit or even whether he is prepared to reduce the price.

55. *Butler Machine Tool Co Ltd* v *Ex-Cell-O Corporation (England) Ltd* [1979] 1 All E.R. 965

In this case it appeared that on 23 May 1969 Butler quoted a price for a machine tool of £75,535, delivery to be within ten months of order. The quotation gave terms and conditions which were stated expressly to prevail over any terms and conditions contained in the buyer's order.

One of the terms was a price variation clause which operated if costs increased before delivery. Ex-Cell-O ordered the machine on 27 May 1969, their order stating that the contract was to be on the basis of Ex-Cell-O's terms and conditions as set out in the order. These terms and conditions did not include a price variation clause but did contain additional items to the Butler quotation, including the fact that Ex-Cell-O wanted installation of the machine for £3100 and the date of delivery of ten months was changed to 10–11 months.

Ex-Cell-O's order form contained a tear-off slip which said: 'Acknowledgment: please sign and return to Ex-Cell-O. We accept your order on the terms and conditions stated therein – and undertake to deliver by . . . date . . . signed.' This slip was completed and signed on behalf of Butler and returned with a covering letter to Ex-Cell-O on 5 June 1969.

The machine was ready by September 1970, but Ex-Cell-O could not take delivery until November 1970 because they had to rearrange their production schedule. By the time Ex-Cell-O took delivery, costs had increased and Butler claimed £2892 as due under the price variation clause. Ex-Cell-O refused to regard the variation clause as a term of the contract.

The Court of Appeal, following a traditional analysis, decided that Butler's quotation of 23 May 1969 was an offer and that Ex-Cell-O's order of 27 May 1969 was a counter-offer introducing new terms and that Butler's communication of 5 June 1969 returning the slip was an acceptance of the counter-offer: so the the contract was on Ex-Cell-O's terms and not Butler's, in spite of the statement in Butler's original quotation.

Thus there was no price variation clause in the contract and Ex-Cell-O need not pay the £2892.

COMMENT
(i) Most commonly the parties will exchange terms relating to delivery dates, rights of cancellation, the liability of the supplier for defects, fluctuations in price (as here), and arbitration clauses to settle differences.

(ii) Title retention clauses (where goods are delivered to a buyer with a clause stating that he does not own the goods until he has paid for them) may also be exchanged in this way. For example, in *Sauter Automation* v *Goodman (HC) (Mechanical Services)* (1960) 5 Current Law para. 353 Sauter tendered to supply the control panel of a boiler.

The tender contained a title retention clause. Goodman accepted on the basis of their standard contract which did not contain retention arrangements. Sauter did not formally accept what was in effect a counter-offer by Goodman but they did deliver the panel which was deemed acceptance. Goodman went into liquidation but the court held that Sauter could not recover the panel or the proceeds of its sale. The contract was on Goodman's terms. Goodman's terms did not contain a retention arrangement. Sauter were left to prove in the liquidation of Goodman with little, if any, prospect of getting paid.

EFFECT OF ACCEPTING A TENDER FOR THE SUPPLY OF GOODS OF AN INDEFINITE AMOUNT: THE STANDING OFFER

56. *Great Northern Railway* v *Witham* (1873) L.R.9 C.P.16

The company advertised for tenders for the supply for one year of such stores as they might think fit to order. The defendant submitted a tender in these words: 'I undertake to supply the company for twelve months with such quantities of [certain specified goods] as the company may order from time to time.' The company accepted the tender, and gave orders under it which the defendant carried out. Eventually the defendant refused to carry out an order made by the company under the tender, and this action was brought. *Held* – the defendant was in breach of contract. A tender of this type was a standing offer which was converted into a series of contracts as the company made an order. The defendant might revoke his offer for the remainder of the period covered by the tender, but must supply the goods already ordered by the company.

VAGUE OR INCOMPLETE AGREEMENTS: TREATMENT BY THE COURTS

57. *Hillas & Co. Ltd* v *Arcos Ltd* [1932] All E.R. 494

The plaintiffs had entered into a contract with the defendants under which the defendants were to supply the plaintiffs with '22,000 standards of soft wood (Russian) of fair specification over the season 1930'. The contract also contained an option allowing the plaintiffs to take up 100,000 standards as above during the season 1931. The parties managed to perform the contract throughout the 1930 season without any argument or serious difficulty in spite of the vague words used in connection with the specification of the wood. However, when the plaintiffs exercised their option for 100,000 standards during the season 1931, the defendants refused to supply the wood, saying that the specification was too vague to bind the parties, and the agreement was therefore inchoate as requiring a further agreement as to the precise specification. *Held* – by the House of Lords – that the option to supply 100,000 standards during the 1931 season was valid. There was a certain vagueness about the specification, but there was also a course of dealing between the parties which operated as a guide to the court regarding the difficulties which this vagueness might produce. Since the parties had not experienced serious difficulty in carrying out the 1930 agreement, there was no reason to suppose that the option could not have been carried out without difficulty had the defendants been prepared to go on with it. Judgment was given for the plaintiffs.

COMMENT
In these cases the defendant is trying to avoid damages for failing to perform the contract by saying: 'I would like to perform the contract but I don't know what to do'. If there are e.g. previous dealings then he does know what to do and the defence fails.

58. *Foley* v *Classique Coaches Ltd* [1934] 2 K.B. 1

F owned certain land, part of which he used for the business of supplying petrol. He also owned the adjoining land. The company wished to purchase the adjoining land for use as the headquarters of their charabanc business. F agreed to sell the land to the company on condition that the company would buy all their petrol from him. An agreement was made under which the company agreed to buy its petrol from F 'at a price to be agreed by the parties in writing and from time to time'. It was further agreed that any dispute arising under the agreement should be submitted 'to arbitration in the usual way'. The agreement was acted upon at an agreed price for three years. At this time the company felt it could get petrol at a better price, and the company's solicitor wrote to F repudiating the petrol contract. *Held* – although the parties had not agreed upon a price beyond three years, there was a contract to supply petrol at a reasonable price and of reasonable quality, and although the agreement did not stipulate the future price, but left this to the further agreement of the parties, a method was provided by which the price could be ascertained without such agreement, i.e. by arbitration.

COMMENT
(i) The court awarded the plaintiff damages, a declaration that the agreement was binding, and an injunction restraining the company from buying petrol elsewhere, thus giving the company an enormous incentive to agree a price or go to arbitration as the contract provided. Generally speaking, of course, if the contract is silent as to price, the court is prepared to use s. 8(2) of the Sale of Goods Act, 1979 and imply and ascertain 'a reasonable price'. It would not have been appropriate in *Foley* to use this provision of sale of goods legislation (which in those days was in the 1893 Act) because the contract in *Foley* was not in fact silent as to price.

(ii) A similar problem arose in *F. & S. Sykes (Wessex)* v *Fine-Fare* [1967] 1 Lloyd's Rep. 53. In that case producers of broiler chickens agreed with certain retailers to supply between 30,000 and 80,000 chickens a week during the first year of the agreement and afterwards 'such other figures as might be agreed'. The agreement was to last for not less than five years, and it was agreed that any differences between the parties should be referred to arbitration. Eventually the retailers contended that the agreement was void for uncertainty. *Held* – by the Court of Appeal – it was not, because in default of the further agreement envisaged the number of chickens should be such reasonable number as might be decided by the arbitrator.

59. *Scammell (G.) and Nephew Ltd* v *Ouston* [1941] A.C. 251

Ouston wished to acquire a new motor van for use in his furniture business. Discussions took place with the company's sales manager as a result of which the company sent a quotation for the supply of a suitable van. Eventually Ouston sent an official order making the following stipulation, 'This order is given on the understanding that the balance of the purchase price can be had on hire-purchase terms over a period of two years.' This was in accordance with the discussions between the sales manager and Ouston, which had taken place on the understanding that hire purchase would be available. The company seemed to be content with the arrangement and completed the van. Arrangements were made with a finance company to give hire-purchase facilities, but the actual terms were not agreed at that stage. The appellants also agreed to take Ouston's present van in part exchange, but later stated that they were not satisfied with its condition and asked him to sell it locally. He refused and after much correspondence he issued a writ against the appellants for damages for non-delivery of the van. The appellants' defence was that there was no contract until the hire-purchase terms had been ascertained. *Held* – the defence succeeded; it was not possible to construe a contract from the vague language used by the parties.

COMMENT
If there is evidence of a trade custom, business procedure or previous dealings between the parties, which assists the court in construing the vague parts of an agreement, then the agreement may be enforced. Here there was no such evidence. It should also be noted that the hire-purchase term was essential to the contract which could not be enforced without it.

60. *Nicolene Ltd* v *Simmonds* [1953] 1 All E.R. 882

The plaintiffs alleged that there was a contract for the sale to them of 3000 tons of steel reinforcing bars and that the defendant seller had broken his contract. When the plaintiffs claimed damages the seller set up the defence that, owing to one of the sentences in the letters which constituted the contract, there was no contract at all. The material words were: 'We are in agreement that the usual conditions of acceptance apply.' In fact there were no usual conditions of acceptance so that the words were meaningless but the seller nevertheless suggested that the contract was unenforceable since it was not complete. *Held* – by the Court of Appeal – that the contract was enforceable and that the meaningless clause could be ignored.

In my opinion a distinction must be drawn between a clause which is meaningless and a clause which is yet to be agreed. A clause which is meaningless can often be ignored, whilst still leaving the contract good;

whereas a clause which has yet to be agreed may mean that there is no contract at all, because the parties have not agreed on all the essential terms. . . . In the present case there was nothing yet to be agreed. There was nothing left to further negotiation. All that happened was that the parties agreed that 'the usual conditions of acceptance apply'. That clause was so vague and uncertain as to be incapable of any precise meaning. It is clearly severable from the rest of the contract. It can be rejected without impairing the sense or reasonableness of the contract as a whole, and it should be so rejected. The contract should be held good and the clause ignored. The parties themselves treated the contract as subsisting. They regarded it as creating binding obligations between them; and it would be most unfortunate if the law should say otherwise. You would find defaulters all scanning their contracts to find some meaningless clause on which to ride free. (*Per* Denning, L.J.)

COMMENT

In this case there was no evidence of any usual conditions either in the trade or between the parties as a result of previous dealings. Therefore the expression 'the usual conditions of acceptance apply' had to be regarded as meaningless.

It should also be noted that it was possible to enforce the contract without the meaningless term. (Compare *Scammel* above.)

COMMUNICATION OF ACCEPTANCE

61. *Felthouse* v *Bindley* (1862) 11 C.B. (N.S.) 869

The plaintiff had been engaged in negotiations with his nephew John regarding the purchase of John's horse, and there had been some misunderstanding as to the price. Eventually the plaintiff wrote to his nephew as follows: 'If I hear no more about him I consider the horse is mine at £30 15s.' The nephew did not reply but, wishing to sell the horse to his uncle, he told the defendant, an auctioneer who was selling farm stock for him, not to sell the horse as it had already been sold. The auctioneer inadvertently put the horse up with the rest of the stock and sold it. The plaintiff now sued the auctioneer in conversion, the basis of the claim being that he had made a contract with his nephew and the property in the animal was vested in him (the uncle) at the time of the sale. *Held* – the plaintiff's action failed. Although the nephew intended to sell the horse to his uncle, he had not communicated that intention. There was, therefore, no contract between the parties, and the property in the horse was not vested in the plaintiff at the time of the auction sale.

COMMENT

(i) The rule that silence cannot amount to acceptance does not necessarily mean that words of acceptance have to be spoken or written to the offeror. In a unilateral contract situation such as *Carlill*'s case (see p. 587), an acceptance may be inferred from the way in which the offeree behaves and communication of acceptance may be dispensed with. However, in this case the contract was bilateral so that the conduct of John Felthouse in removing the horse from the sale was not relevant, as it might have been in a unilateral situation. In a bilateral situation the rule against acceptance by silence means only that the offeror is unable to impose on the offeree a stipulation that the offeree will be bound if he merely ignores the offer.

Nevertheless while the general principle laid down in this case, i.e. that an offeree who does not wish to accept an offer should not be put to the trouble of actively refusing it, is quite acceptable the decision is difficult to support on its own facts. John wanted to accept the offer and intended to accept it and his uncle had waived his right to receive an acceptance in his letter – so why no contract?

(ii) It should also be noted that the communication of acceptance must be authorised. In *Powell* v *Lee* (1908) 99 L.T. 284 P offered his services to the managers of a school as headmaster. The secretary to the managers told P that he had been appointed which was true. The secretary had no authority actual or otherwise to do this. The managers later decided to offer the post to another candidate. P's action for breach of contract failed.

WHERE THE MODE OF ACCEPTANCE IS PRESCRIBED: MUST THE OFFEREE COMPLY?

62. *Yates Building Co.* v *R.J. Pulleyn & Sons (York)* (1975) 119 S.J. 370

An option to purchase a certain plot of land was expressed to be exercisable by notice in writing by or on behalf of the intending purchaser to the intending vendor 'such notice to be sent by registered or Recorded Delivery post'. It was *held* – by the Court of Appeal – that the form of posting prescribed was directory rather than mandatory, or alternatively permissive rather than obligatory, and the option was validly exercised by a letter from the purchaser's solicitors to the vendor's solicitors sent by ordinary post and received within the option period.

COMMENT
The fact that the letter arrived within the option shows that there was no prejudice to the offeror.

USE OF TELEPHONE AND TELEX AS A MEANS OF COMMUNICATING ACCEPTANCE

63. *Entores Ltd* v *Miles Far Eastern Corporation* [1955] 2 Q.B. 327

The plaintiffs, who conducted a business in London, made an offer to the defendants' agent in Amsterdam by means of a teleprinter service. The offer was accepted by a message received on the plaintiffs' teleprinter in London. Later the defendants were in breach of contract and the plaintiffs wished to sue them. The defendants had their place of business in New York and in order to commence an action the plaintiffs had to serve notice of writ on the defendants in New York. The Rules of Supreme Court allow service out of the jurisdiction when the contract was made within the jurisdiction. On this point the defendants argued that the contract was made in Holland when it was typed into the teleprinter there, stressing the rule relating to posting. *Held* – where communication is instantaneous, as where the parties are face to face or speaking on the telephone, acceptance must be received by the offeror. The same rule applied to communications of this kind. Therefore the contract was made in London where the acceptance was received.

> COMMENT
>
> (1) The suggestion was made that the doctrine of estoppel may operate in this sort of case so as to bind the offeror, e.g. suppose X telephones his acceptance to Y, and Y does not hear X's voice at the moment of acceptance, as where there is a break in the line or Y simply puts the phone down on his desk for a while without telling X, then Y may be estopped from denying that he heard X's acceptance and may be bound in contract. It is thought that the conversation prior to the acceptance which is not heard must suggest the possibility of an impending acceptance. It should be noted that this estoppel theory amounts to an exception to the rule that silence cannot amount to acceptance.
>
> (ii) The House of Lords approved the *Entores* decision in *Brinkibon* v *Stahag Stahl* [1982] 1 All E.R. 293. The plaintiff wanted leave to serve a writ out of the jurisdiction, as in *Entores*. The message accepting an offer had been sent by telex from London to Vienna. The House of Lords held that the writ could not be served because the contract was made in Vienna and not London.

USE OF THE POST IN OFFER AND ACCEPTANCE

64. *Household Fire Insurance Company* v *Grant* (1879) 4 Ex.D. 216

The defendant handed a written application for shares in the company to the company's agent in Glamorgan. The application stated that the defendant had paid to the company's bankers the sum of £5, being a deposit of 1s. per share on an application for 100 shares, and also agreed to pay 19s. per share within twelve months of the allotment. The agent sent the application to the company in London. The company secretary made out a letter of allotment in favour of the defendant and posted it to him in Swansea. The letter never arrived. Nevertheless the company entered the defendant's name on the share register and credited him with dividends amounting to five shillings. The company then went into liquidation and the liquidator sued for £94 15s., the balance due on the shares allotted. It was *held* by the Court of Appeal that the defendant was liable. Acceptance was complete when the letter of allotment was posted on the ground that, in this sort of case, the Post Office must be deemed the common agent of the parties, and that delivery to the agent constituted acceptance. Bramwell, L.J., in a dissenting judgment, regarded actual communication as essential. If the letter of acceptance does not arrive, an unknown liability is imposed on the offeror. If actual communication is required the status quo is preserved, i.e. the parties have not made a contract.

COMMENT

(i) Not all lawyers would accept the point that the Post Office is the common agent of the parties. Those who do not accept this point would say that the Post Office cannot be an agent for communication since the Post Office and its servants do not know what is in the letter.

(ii) In *Re London and Northern Bank* [1900] 1 Ch. 220 the Court decided that the letter of acceptance must be properly stamped and addressed. If not there is no communication until the letter arrives. The case also decides that the letter must be actually posted and not given to a person to post even a postman. If this happens the acceptance takes place when the person concerned actually posts the letter. This is a matter of evidence. As regards handing a letter of acceptance to a postman this may operate as an acceptance in a country district where the custom of postmen taking letters in this way is better established.

65. *Holwell Securities Ltd* v *Hughes* [1974] 1 All E.R. 161

By an agreement of 19 October 1971 Dr Hughes, a medical practitioner of Wembley, had granted to the plaintiffs an option to purchase his premises in Wembley for £45,000. The agreement provided that the option should be exercisable 'by notice in writing' to Dr Hughes at any time within six months of the date of the agreement. On 14 April 1972, the plaintiffs' solicitors sent to Dr Hughes by ordinary post a written notice exercising the option. That notice was never delivered to Dr Hughes nor left at his address. *Held* – by the Court of Appeal – on a construction of the agreement – that notice in writing had to be given to Dr Hughes in the sense that he had either to have actually received it or to be deemed to have received it under s. 196 of the Law of Property Act, 1925 which provides for service of notices by registered post, or within the Recorded Delivery Service Act, 1962, which applies a similar rule to Recorded Delivery. This was not the case, said Russell, L.J., where the basic principle of the need for communication to the offeror was displaced by the artificial concept of communication by the act of posting: the language of the agreement 'notice . . . to' was inconsistent with the theory that acceptance could be constituted by posting and s. 196 of the Law of Property Act, 1925 also impliedly excluded such a mode of acceptance.

COMMENT

(i) The case illustrates that the rule of acceptance by post does not apply in all situations to which it might logically be applied. As the court said in this case the rule would not be applied where it led to 'manifest inconvenience and absurdity'. In each case, therefore, it is a matter of fact for the court to decide whether the rule should be applied, the test being whether it produces, on balance, a convenient and reasonable result.

(ii) This agreement for an option over land was governed by the Law of Property Act, 1925 and s. 196 deals with the method of serving 'notices' under the Act. It implies that they must be received. So here both the agreement and statute law required actual delivery.

66. *Adams v Lindsell* (1818) 1 B. & A. 681

The defendants were wool dealers in business at St Ives, Huntingdon. By letter dated 2 September they offered to sell wool to the plaintiffs who were wool manufacturers at Bromsgrove, Worcestershire. The defendants' letter asked for a reply 'in course of post' but was misdirected, being addressed to Bromsgrove, Leicestershire. The offer did not reach the plaintiffs until 7 pm on 5 September. The same evening the plaintiffs accepted the offer. This letter reached the defendants on 9 September. If the offer had not been misdirected, the defendants could have expected a reply on 7 September, and accordingly they sold the wool to a third party on 8 September. The plaintiffs now sued for breach of contract. *Held* – where there is a misdirection of the offer, as in this case, the offer is made when it actually reaches the offeree, and not when it would have reached him in the ordinary course of post. The defendants' mistake must be taken against them and for the purposes of this contract the plaintiffs' letter was received 'in course of post'.

COMMENT
The position may be different if the fact of delay is obvious to the offeree so that he is put on notice that the offer has lapsed, e.g. A writes to B offering to sell him certain goods and saying that the offer is open until 30 June. If A misdirects the offer so that it does not reach B until 2 July, it is doubtful whether B could accept it.

REVOCATION OF OFFER: THE EFFECT OF AN OPTION

67. *Routledge v Grant* (1828) 4 Bing. 653

The defendant made an offer to take a lease of the plaintiff's premises: 'a definitive answer to be given within six weeks from 18 March 1825'. On 9 April the defendant withdrew his offer and on 29 April the plaintiff purported to accept it. The Court of Common Pleas held that there was no contract. Best, C.J. *held* that the defendant could withdraw at any moment before acceptance, even though the time limit had expired. The plaintiff could only have held the defendant to his offer throughout the period, if he had bought the option, i.e. given consideration for it.

COMMENT
(i) The consideration need not be adequate. For example let us suppose that on Monday Fred offers to sell Joe his house for £30,000 and Joe says 'Give me until Friday to think it over and I will buy you a pint'. The purchase of the pint for Fred or the promise to buy him a pint is enough to give Joe an enforceable option on the house. Again, in

Mountford v *Scott* [1974] 1 All E.R. 248 the Court of Appeal held that a West Indian who signed an agreement in consideration of £1 giving the plaintiff an option to purchase his house for £10,000 within six months, was bound by the option in spite of the fact that only £1 was given for it.

(ii) The option is really a separate contract to allow time to decide whether to accept the original offer or not. It was thought at one time that, where the option to buy property was not supported by consideration, the offer could be revoked by its sale to another, but in modern law it is necessary for the offeror to communicate the revocation to the offeree either himself, or by means of some reliable person. (See *Stevenson* v *McLean* 1880 at p. 593 where the defendant's offer was not revoked merely by the sale of the iron to another.)

(iii) Before leaving the topic of options, it should be noted that the Law Commission in Working Paper No. 60 entitled 'Firm Offers' and published in 1975 criticised the present position under which a promise to keep an offer open will not be binding on the offeror unless consideration for the promise is given by the offeree (though of course this is not necessary where the option is made in a deed), on the grounds that it is contrary to business practice and also contrary to the law of most foreign countries. The Law Commission make a provisional recommendation that 'an offeror who has promised that he will not revoke his offer for a definite time should be bound by the terms of that promise provided that the promise has been made in the course of business'.

REVOCATION OF AN OFFER MUST BE COMMUNICATED. IT IS NOT EFFECTIVE ON POSTING

68. *Byrne* v *Van Tienhoven* (1880) 5 C.P.D. 344

On 1 October the defendants in Cardiff posted a letter to the plaintiffs in New York offering to sell them tin plate. On 8 October the defendants wrote revoking their offer. On 11 October the plaintiffs received the defendants' offer and immediately telegraphed their acceptance. On 15 October the plaintiffs confirmed their acceptance by letter. On 20 October the defendants' letter of revocation reached the plaintiffs who had by this time entered into a contract to resell the tin plate. *Held* – (a) that revocation of an offer is not effective until it is communicated to the offeree, (b) the mere posting of a letter of revocation is no communication to the person to whom it is sent. The rule is not, therefore, the same as that for acceptance of an offer. Thus the defendants were bound by a contract which came into being on 11 October.

REVOCATION OF OFFER: MAY BE BY A THIRD PARTY IF A REASONABLE PERSON WOULD RELY ON THAT PARTY'S KNOWLEDGE OF THE FACTS

69. *Dickinson* v *Dodds* (1876) 2 Ch.D. 463

The defendant offered to sell certain houses by letter, stating, 'This offer to be left over until Friday 9 am'. On Thursday afternoon the plaintiff was informed by a Mr Berry that the defendant had been negotiating a sale of the property with one Allan. On Thursday evening the plaintiff left a letter of acceptance at the house where the defendant was staying. This letter was never delivered to the defendant. On Friday morning at 7 am Berry, acting as the plaintiff's agent, handed the defendant a duplicate letter of acceptance explaining it to him. However, on the Thursday the defendant had entered into a contract to sell the property to Allan. *Held* – since there was no consideration for the promise to keep the offer open, the defendant was free to revoke his offer at any time. Further Berry's communication of the dealings with Allan indicated that Dodds was no longer minded to sell the property to the plaintiff and was in effect a communication of Dodds' revocation. There was therefore no binding contract between the parties.

COMMENT
The question of whether the person who communicates the revocation is a reliable source and should be relied on is a matter of fact for the court, but it could e.g. be a mutual friend of the offeror and offeree. There is in fact no general statement in this case as to what is reliability or even that it is necessarily required.

LAPSE OF OFFER AFTER A REASONABLE TIME

70. *Ramsgate Victoria Hotel Co.* v *Montefiore* (1866) L.R. 1 Exch. 109

The defendant offered by letter dated 8 June 1864, to take shares in the company sending part-payment of 1 shilling (5p) a share. No reply was made by the company, but on 23 November 1864, they allotted shares to the defendant. The defendant refused to take up the shares. *Held* – his refusal was justified because his offer had lapsed by reason of the company's delay in notifying their acceptance. He also recovered his part-payment.

COMMENT
The question of 'reasonable time' is a matter of fact to be decided by the court on the basis of the subject matter of the contract and the conditions of the market in which the offer is made. Offers to take shares in companies are normally accepted quickly because the price fluctuates in the market. The same would be true of an offer to sell perishable goods. An offer to sell a farm might well not lapse so soon. The form in which the offer is made is also relevant so that an offer by cable could well lapse quickly.

CONDITIONAL OFFER: TERMINATION ON FAILURE OF CONDITION

71. *Financings Ltd* v *Stimson* [1962] 3 All E.R. 386

On 16 March 1961, the defendant saw a motor car on the premises of a dealer and signed a hire-purchase form provided by the plaintiffs (a finance company), this form being supplied by the dealer. The form was to the effect that the agreement was to become binding only when the finance company signed the form. It also carried a statement to the effect that the hirer (the defendant) acknowledged that before he signed the agreement he had examined the goods and had satisfied himself that they were in good order and condition, and that the goods were at the risk of the hirer from the time of purchase by the owners. On 18 March the defendant paid the first instalment and took possession of the car. However, on 20 March, the defendant, being dissatisfied with the car, returned it to the dealer though the finance company were not informed of this. On the night of 24–25 March the car was stolen from the dealer's premises and was recovered badly damaged. On 25 March the finance company signed the agreement accepting the defendant's offer to hire the car. The defendant did not regard himself as bound and refused to pay the instalments. The finance company sold the car, and now sued for damages for the defendant's breach of the hire-purchase agreement. *Held* – the hire purchase agreement was not binding on the defendant because –

(a) he had revoked his offer by returning the car, and the dealer was the agent of the finance company to receive notice;

(b) there was an *implied* condition in the offer that the goods were in substantially the same condition when the offer was accepted as when it was made.

DEATH OF OFFEROR BEFORE ACCEPTANCE

72. *Bradbury* v *Morgan* (1862) 1 H. & C. 249

The defendants were the executors of J. M. Leigh who had entered into a guarantee of his brother's account with the plaintiffs for credit up to £100. The plaintiffs, not knowing of the death of J. M. Leigh, continued to supply goods on credit to the brother, H. J. Leigh. The defendants now refused to pay the plaintiffs in respect of such credit after the death of J. M. Leigh. *Held* – the plaintiffs succeeded, the offer remaining open until the plaintiffs had *knowledge* of the death of J. M. Leigh.

> COMMENT
> This was a continuing guarantee which is in the nature of a standing offer accepted piecemeal whenever further goods are advanced on credit. Where the guarantee is not of this nature, it may be irrevocable. Thus, in *Lloyds* v *Harper* (1880) 16 Ch.D. 290, the defendant, while living, guaranteed his son's dealings as a Lloyds underwriter in consideration of Lloyds admitting the son. It was *held* that, as Lloyds had admitted the son on the strength of the guarantee, the defendant's executors were still liable under it, because it was irrevocable and was not affected by the defendant's death. It continued to apply to defaults committed by the son after the father's death.

DEATH OF OFFEREE BEFORE ACCEPTANCE

73. *Re Cheshire Banking Co., Duff's Executors' Case* (1886) 32 Ch.D. 301

In 1882 the Cheshire and Staffordshire Union Banking Companies amalgamated, and Duff received a circular asking whether he would exchange his shares in the S Bank for shares in the C Bank which took the S Bank over. Duff held 100 £20 shares on which £5 had been paid, but he did not reply to the circular and died shortly afterwards. The option was exercised on behalf of his executors, Muttlebury, Bridges and Watts, and a certificate was made out in their names and an entry made in the register in which they were entered as shareholders, described as 'exectors of William Duff, deceased'. The executors objected to having the share certificates in their names, so the directors of the Cheshire Banking Co. cancelled the certificate and issued a fresh one in the name of William Duff. On 23 October 1884, the company went into liquidation. *Held* – the liquidator acted rightly when he restored the executors' names to the register. The executors wished to enter into a new contract which had not previously existed. They could not make a dead man liable and so could only make themselves personally liable. Their names were improperly removed and must be restored. Although they had a right of indemnity against the estate, they were personally liable for the full amount outstanding on the shares, regardless as to whether the estate was adequate to indemnify them.

COMMENT
This case probably has more to do with the liability of personal representatives in the law of succession than the law of contract. Personal representatives, like receivers, can be personally liable on contracts which they make, subject to a right of indemnity from the estate. The benefit of the contract is held on trust for the estate. This personal liability rule is essential in order to ensure that personal representatives cannot subject the estate to further debt without risk to themselves. There seems to be no direct contract law authority as to the effect of the death of the offeree. In *Reynolds* v *Atherton* (1922) 127 L.T. 189, Warrington, L.J. said: 'The offer having been made to a living person who ceases to be a living person before the offer is accepted, there is no longer an offer at all. The offer is not intended to be made to a dead person, nor to his executors, and the offer ceases to be an offer capable of acceptance.' There is, however, some Canadian authority. In *Re Irvine* [1928] 3 D.L.R. 268 an offeree gave his son a letter of acceptance to post. The son did not post it until after the offeree's death. The Supreme Court of Ontario held that the acceptance was invalid.

OFFER AND ACCEPTANCE NOT ESSENTIAL: THE COLLATERAL CONTRACT

74. *Rayfield* v *Hands* [1958] 2 All E.R. 194

The articles of a private company provided by Art. 11 that: 'Every member who intends to transfer his shares shall inform the directors who will take the said shares . . . at a fair price.' The plaintiff held 725 full-paid shares of £1 each, and he asked the directors to buy them but they refused. *Held* – the directors were bound to take the shares. Having regard to what is now s. 14(1) of the Companies Act, 1985, Art. 11 constituted a binding contract between the directors, as members, and the plaintiff, as a member, in respect of his rights as a member. The word 'will' in the Article did not import an option in the directors. Vaisey, J., did say that the conclusion he had reached in this case may not apply to all companies, but it did apply to a private company, because such a company was an intimate concern closely analogous with a partnership.

> COMMENT
> (i) Although the articles placed the obligation to take shares of members on the directors, Vaisey, J. construed this as an obligation falling upon the directors in their capacity as members. Otherwise the contractual aspect of the provision in the articles would not have applied, since the articles are not a contract between the company and the directors.
> (ii) The leading case is *Clarke* v *Dunraven* [1897] A.C. 59 where it was held that competitors in a regatta had made a contract not only with the club which organised the race but also with each other so that one competitor was able to sue another for damages when his boat was fouled and sank under a rule which said that each competitor was liable 'to pay all damages' that he might cause.

Law of contract – making the contract II

CONSIDERATION NEED NOT BE ADEQUATE SO LONG AS IT HAS SOME ECONOMIC VALUE

75. *Thomas* v *Thomas* (1842) 2 Q.B. 851

The plaintiff's husband had expressed the wish that the plaintiff, if she survived him, should have use of his house. He left a will of which his brothers were executors. The will made no mention of the testator's wish that his wife should be given the house. The executors knew of the testator's wish and agreed to allow the widow to occupy the house on payment of £1 per year for so long as she remained unmarried. The plaintiff remained in possession of the house until the death of one of the executors, Samuel Thomas. The other executor then turned her out. She sued him for breach of contract. It was held that the plaintiff's promise to pay £1 per year was consideration and need not be adequate. The action for breach of contract succeeded.

COMMENT
The rule that consideration need not be adequate allows virtually gratuitous promises to be binding even though not made by deed (and see *Mountford* v *Scott* at p. 603).

76. *Chappell & Co. Ltd* v *Nestlé Ltd* [1959] 2 All E.R. 701

The plaintiffs owned the copyright in a dance tune called 'Rockin' Shoes', and the defendants were using records of this tune as part of an advertising scheme. A record company made the records for Nestlés who advertised them to the public for 1s. 6d. each but required in addition three wrappers from their 6d. bars of chocolate. When they received the wrappers they threw them away. The plaintiffs sued the defendants for infringement of copyright. It appeared that under s. 8 of the Copyright Act of 1956 a person recording musical works for *retail* sale need not get the permission of the holder of the copyright, but had merely to serve him with notice and pay 6¼% of the retail selling price as royalty. The plaintiffs asserted that the defendants were not retailing the goods in the sense of the Act and must therefore get permission to use the musical work. The basis of the plaintiff's case was that retailing meant selling entirely for money, and that as the defendants were selling for money plus wrappers, they needed the plaintiff's consent. The defence was that the sale was for cash because the wrappers were not part of the consideration. The House of Lords by a majority gave judgment for the plaintiffs. The wrappers were part of the consideration since the offer was to supply a record in return, not simply for money, but for the wrappers as well. On the question of adequacy Lord Somervell said: 'It is said that, when received, the wrappers are of no value to the respondents, the Nestlé Co. Ltd. This I would have thought irrelevent. A contracting party can stipulate for what consideration he chooses. A peppercorn does not cease to be good consideration if it is established that the promisee does not like pepper and will throw away the corn.'

COMMENT
(i) There seems to be no doubt that the wrappers could on their own have formed the consideration.

(ii) The statutory licence to copy records sold by retail under s. 8 of the Copyright Act, 1956 was repealed by the Copyright Designs and Patents Act, 1988, Sch. 1, para. 21. Permission to reproduce is now required even by those retailing the records. However, the case remains a classic example of adequacy of consideration.

77. *White* v *Bluett* (1853) 23 L.J. Ex. 36

This action was brought by White who was the executor of Bluett's father's estate. The plaintiff, White, alleged that Bluett had not paid a promissory note given to his father during his lifetime. Bluett admitted that he had given the note to his father, but said that his father had released him from it in return for a promise not to keep on complaining about the fact that he had been disinherited. *Held* – the defence failed and the defendant was liable on the note. The promise not to complain was not sufficient consideration to support his release from the note.

> COMMENT
> This case illustrates the general point that on formation of contract consideration must be capable of expression in terms of value. On its facts, of course, the case is concerned with consideration on discharge of contract, i.e. the promissory note, where the rule is the same. In addition, the decision seems to be based upon the fact that the son had no right to complain of his disinheritance, so he was not giving up anything which he had a right to do. 'The son had no right to complain, for the father might make what distribution of his property he liked; and the son's abstaining from doing what he had no right to do can be of no consideration.' (*Per* Pollock, C.B.)

ADEQUACY OF CONSIDERATION: FORBEARANCE TO SUE CAN SUPPORT A PROMISE

78. *Horton* v *Horton* [1961] 1 Q.B. 215

The parties were husband and wife. In March, 1954, by a separation agreement by deed the husband agreed to pay the wife £30 a month. On the true construction of the deed the husband should have deducted income tax before payment but for nine months he paid the money without deductions. In January 1955, he signed a document, not by deed, agreeing that instead of 'the monthly sum of £30' he would pay such a monthly sum as 'after deduction of income tax should amount to the clear sum of £30'. For over three years he paid this clear sum but then stopped payment. To an action by his wife he pleaded that the later agreement was unsupported by consideration and that the wife could sue only on the earlier deed. The Court of Appeal held that there was consideration to support the later agreement. It was clear that the original deed did not implement the intention of the parties. The wife therefore might have sued to rectify the deed and the later agreement represented a compromise of this possible action. Whether such an action would have succeeded was irrelevant; it sufficed that it had some prospect of success and that the wife believed in it.

ADEQUACY OF CONSIDERATION: THE POSITION IN BAILMENT

79. *Gilchrist Watt and Sanderson Pty* v *York Products Pty* [1970] 1 W.L.R. 1262

Two cases of German clocks were brought by the respondents and shipped to Sydney. The shipowners arranged for the appellant stevedores to unload the ship. The goods were put in the appellants' shed but when the respondents came to collect them one case of clocks was missing. It was admitted that this was due to the appellants' negligence. *Held* – by the Privy Council – that the appellants were liable. Although there was no contract between the parties an obligation to take due care of the goods was created by delivery and voluntary assumption of possession under the sub-bailment.

COMMENT

(i) The matter of consideration and bailment was first raised in *Coggs* v *Bernard* (1703) 2 Ld. Ray. 909 where the defendant had agreed to take several hogsheads of brandy, belonging to the plaintiff, from the cellar of one inn to another. One of the casks was broken and the brandy lost and the plaintiff alleged that this was due to the defendant's carelessness. The defendant denied liability on the grounds that there was no consideration to support the agreement to move the casks. *Held* – the plaintiff's claim succeeded. The case seems to have been decided on the ground that once the relationship of bailor and bailee is established certain duties fall upon the bailee independently of any contract.

(ii) It should be borne in mind, of course, that if a person agrees to take charge of goods gratuitously he could not be sued if he fails to take them into his custody. The duty seen in this case arises only when the goods are in the custody of the gratuitous bailee.

SUFFICIENCY OF CONSIDERATION: PROMISE TO PERFORM OR PERFORMANCE OF AN EXISTING PUBLIC OR CONTRACTUAL DUTY WILL NOT SUPPORT A FURTHER PROMISE: ACTS IN EXCESS OF THE DUTY MAY

80. *Collins* v *Godefroy* (1831) 1 B. & Ad. 950

The plaintiff was subpoenaed to give evidence for the defendant in an action to which the defendant was a party. The plaintiff now sued for the sum of six guineas which he said the defendant had promised him for his attendance. *Held* – the plaintiff's action failed because there was no consideration for the promise. Lord Tenterden said: 'If it be a duty imposed by law upon a party regularly subpoenaed to attend from time to time to give his evidence, then a promise to give him any remuneration for loss of time incurred in such attendance is a promise without consideration.'

81. *Stilk* v *Myrick* (1809) 2 Camp. 317

A sea-captain, being unable to find any substitutes for two sailors who had deserted, promised to divide the wages of the deserters among the rest of the crew if they would work the ship home shorthanded. *Held* – the promise was not enforceable because of absence of consideration. In sailing the ship home the crew had done no more than they were already bound to do. Their original contract obliged them to meet the normal emergencies of the voyage of which minor desertions were one. Compare *Hartley* v *Ponsonby* (1857) 7 E. & B. 872, where a greater remuneration was promised to a seaman to work the ship home when the number of deserters was so great as to render the ship unseaworthy. *Held* – this was a binding promise because the sailor had gone beyond his duty in agreeing to sail an unseaworthy ship. In fact the number of desertions was so great as to discharge the remaining seamen from their original contract, leaving them free to enter into a new bargain.

COMMENT

It must be said that the decision in *Stilk* took a nasty knock in *Williams v Roffey Bros and Nicholls (Contractors) Ltd* [1990] 1 All E.R. 512. The defendants in that case were building contractors. They made a contract to refurbish a block of 27 flats and engaged Mr Williams to carry out carpentry work for £20,000. This turned out to be too low to enable Mr Williams to operate at a profit and after completing some of the flats and receiving interim payments of £16,000 he got into financial difficulties. The defendants, concerned that the job might not be finished on time and that they would in that event have to pay money under a penalty clause in the main contract, made an oral promise to pay Mr Williams a further sum of £10,300 to be paid at the rate of £575 for each flat on which work was completed. Mr Williams was not paid in full for this work and later brought this claim for the additional sum promised. The Court of Appeal *held* that he was entitled to it because where a party to a contract agrees to make an additional payment to secure its performance on time this may provide sufficient consideration contractually to support the extra payment if the agreement to pay is obtained without economic duress or fraud (see further p. 260) and where it ensures the completion of the contract to the paying party's satisfaction and benefit as by avoiding a penalty which was the position here. Apparently *Stilk* survives only where the person making the promise receives no benefit for it. It would seem to have been possible to find benefit in *Stilk* so that it may well be overruled on its own facts though the Court of Appeal would only say that the principle had been 'refined'.

82. *Glasbrook Bros Ltd v Glamorgan County Council* [1925] A.C. 270

In 1921 the Glamorgan police were asked to provide 100 police officers to be billeted on the premises of Glasbrook's colliery near Swansea because it was feared that striking miners were going to prevent safety men going into the mine with the consequence that it would be flooded. The owners of the mine signed a document saying that they would pay not only for the services of the officers but also their travelling expenses. Glasbrook's also undertook to provide them with food and sleeping accommodation. Eventually a bill amounting to £2200 11s. 10d. was rendered to the police authority, by the Glamorgan County Council, for the above services. Glasbrook's refused to pay the bill, alleging that the police were doing no more than was their duty and therefore there was no consideration for Glasbrook's written promise to pay for the protection which they had had. *Held* – by the House of Lords – that Glasbrook's promise was binding on them on the ground that the number of constables provided was in excess of what the local police superintendent thought was necessary and therefore provided consideration over and above the obligation resting on the police to take all steps necessary for protecting property from criminal injury. In the course of his judgment Viscount Cave, L.C. said –

> No doubt there is an absolute unconditional obligation binding the police authorities to take all steps which appear to them to be necessary for keeping the peace, preventing crime, or for protecting property from criminal injury; and the public, who pay for this protection through the rates and taxes, cannot lawfully be called upon to make a further payment for that which is their right. . . . But it has always been recognized that, where individuals desire that services of a special kind which, though not within the obligations of a police authority, can most effectively be rendered by them, should be performed by members of the police force, the police authorities may . . . 'lend' the services of constables for that purpose in consideration of payment. Instances are the lending of constables on the occasions of large gatherings in and ouside private premises, as on the occasions of weddings, athletic or boxing contests or race meetings, and the provision of constables at large railway stations.

COMMENT

(i) This case was applied in *Harris* v *Sheffield United Football Club* [1987] 2 All E.R. 838, where Boreham, J. held that the provision of policemen at a football ground to keep law and order was the provision of special services by the police. The police authority is under a duty to protect persons and property against crime or threatened crime for which no payment is due. However, the police have no public duty to protect persons and property against the mere fear of possible future crime. The claim of the police authority for some £70,000 for police services provided at the defendants' football ground over 15 months was allowed.

(ii) The issue of exceeding a statutory duty was also raised in *Ward* v *Byham* [1956] 2 All E.R. 318. In that case an unmarried mother sued to recover a maintenance allowance by the father of the child. The defence was that, under s. 42 of the National Assistance Act, 1948, the mother of an illegitimate child was bound to maintain it. However, it appeared that in return for the promise of an allowance the mother had promised –

(a) to look after the child well and ensure that it was happy; and
(b) to allow it to decide whether it should live with her or the father.

Held – there was sufficient consideration to support the promise of an allowance because the promises given in (a) and (b) above were in excess of the statutory duty, which was merely to care for the child.

(iii) 'Is a promise to make a child happy adequate consideration?' (Compare *White* v *Bluett*, 1853 at p. 608) This point is not taken in the case and shows the considerable power which judges have to find or not to find contractual obligations.

SUFFICIENCY OF CONSIDERATION: PERFORMANCE OF A CONTRACTUAL DUTY OWED BY X TO Y CAN SUPPORT A PROMISE MADE BY Z TO X

83. *Shadwell* v *Shadwell* (1860) 9 C.B. (N.S.) 159

The plaintiff was engaged to marry a girl named Ellen Nicholl. In 1838 he received a letter from his uncle, Charles Shadwell, in the following terms: 'I am glad to hear of your intended marriage with Ellen Nicholl and, as I promised to assist you at starting, I am happy to tell you that I will pay you one hundred and fifty pounds yearly during my life and until your income derived from your profession of Chancery barrister shall amount to six hundred guineas, of which your own admission will be the only evidence that I shall receive or require.' The plaintiff duly married Ellen Nicholl and his income never exceeded six hundred guineas during the eighteen years his uncle lived after the marriage. The uncle paid twelve annual sums and part of the thirteenth but no more. On his death the plaintiff sued his uncle's executors for the balance of the eighteen instalments to which he suggested he was entitled. *Held* – the plaintiff succeeded even though he was already engaged to Ellen Nicholl when the promise was made. His marriage was sufficient consideration to support his uncle's promise, for, by marrying, the plaintiff had incurred responsibilities and changed his position in life. Further the uncle probably derived some benefit in that his desire to see his nephew settled had been satisfied.

> COMMENT
> (i) In this case the consideration is a little dubious in that it is in part a sentimental benefit to the uncle. This type of consideration, e.g. the 'love and affection' variety, has often been regarded as ineffective to support a contract. Nevertheless, the principle of the case is a good one and makes more sense in a business context. (See *New Zealand Shipping Co. Ltd* v *Satterthwaite*, 1974 at p. 677.)
> (ii) An engagement to marry is no longer binding as a contract, see s. 1, Law Reform (Miscellaneous Provisions) Act, 1970.

PAST CONSIDERATION: WHERE A PARTICULAR ACTIVITY IS UNDERTAKEN WITHOUT ANY PROMISE OF PAYMENT A SUBSEQUENT PROMISE TO PAY IS NOT ACTIONABLE. IF THERE IS A REQUEST TO CARRY OUT THE ACT IN A COMMERCIAL SITUATION WHERE A PROMISE TO PAY CAN BE IMPLIED, THE SUBSEQUENT PROMISE MAY BE ENFORCEABLE

84. *Re McArdle* [1951] Ch. 669

Certain children were entitled under their father's will to a house. However, their mother had a life interest in the property and during her lifetime one of the children and his wife came to live in the house with the mother. The wife carried out certain improvements to the property, and, after she had done so, the children signed a document addressed to her stating: 'In consideration of your carrying out certain alterations and improvements to the property . . . at present occupied by you, the beneficiaries under the Will of William Edward McArdle hereby agree that the executors, the National Provincial Bank Ltd, . . . shall repay to you from the said estate when so distributed the sum of £488 in settlement of the amount spent on such improvements. . . '. On the death of the testator's widow the children refused to authorise payment of the sum of £488, and this action was brought to decide the validity of the claim. *Held* – since the improvements had been carried out before the document was executed, the consideration was past and the promise could not be enforced.

COMMENT
(i) The rule applied also in *Roscorla* v *Thomas* (1842) 3 Q.B. 234 where a horse was sold and the seller *after the sale* gave a warranty as to its quality, i.e. that it was not vicious whereas it was. There was no action on the warranty by the buyer.

(ii) If Mrs McArdle had actually been paid by a cheque she would not have been able to sue upon it under s. 27 of the Bills of Exchange Act, 1882 because her acts were gratuitous and did not create an antecedent (or previous) debt or liability.

85. *Re Casey's Patents*, *Stewart* v *Casey* [1892] 1 Ch. 104

Patents were granted to Stewart and another in respect of an invention concerning appliances and vessels for transporting and storing inflammable liquids. Stewart entered into an arrangement with Casey whereby Casey was to introduce the patents. Casey spent two years 'pushing' the invention and then the joint owners of the patent rights wrote to him as follows: 'In consideration of your services as the practical manager in working both patents we hereby agree to give you one-third share of the patents.' Casey also received the letters patent. Some time later Stewart died and his executors claimed the recovery of the letters patent from Casey, suggesting that he had no interest in them because the consideration for the promise to give him a one-third share was past. *Held* – the previous request to render the services raised an implied promise to pay. The subsequent promise could be regarded as fixing the value of the services so that Casey was entitled to a one-third share of the patent rights.

PRIVITY OF CONTRACT: EFFECT OF THE RULE: REMEDIES (IF ANY) AVAILABLE TO A PERSON NOT IN PRIVITY

86. *Tweddle* v *Atkinson* (1861) 1 B. & S. 393

William Tweddle the plaintiff was married to the daughter of William Guy. In order to provide for the couple, Guy promised the plaintiff's father to pay the plaintiff £200 if the plaintiff's father would pay the plaintiff £100. An agreement was accordingly drawn up containing the above-mentioned promise, and giving William Tweddle the right to sue either promisor for the sums promised. Guy did not make the promised payment during his lifetime and the plaintiff now sued Guy's executor. *Held* – the plaintiff's action failed because he had not given any consideration to Guy in return for the promise to pay £200. The provision in the agreement allowing William Tweddle to sue was of no effect without consideration.

87. *Dunlop* v *Selfridge* [1915] A.C. 847

The appellants were motor tyre manufacturers and sold tyres to Messrs Dew & Co. who were motor accessory dealers. Under the terms of the contract Dew & Co. agreed not to sell the tyres below Dunlop's list price, i.e. £4.05 per tyre, and as Dunlop's agents, to obtain from other traders a similar undertaking. In return for this undertaking Dew & Co. were to receive special discounts, some of which they could, if they wished, pass on to retailers who bought tyres. Selfridge & Co. accepted two orders from customers for Dunlop covers at a lower price. They obtained the covers through Dew & Co. and signed an agreement not to sell or offer the tyres below the list price. For giving this undertaking Dew & Co. gave them part of the discount received by Dew & Co. from Dunlop. It was further agreed that £5 per tyre sold should be paid to Dunlop by way of liquidated damages. Selfridge supplied one of the two tyres ordered below list prices, i.e. at £3.65 per tyre. They did not actually supply the other, but informed the customer that they could only supply it at list price. The appellants claimed an injunction and damages against the respondents for breach of the agreement made with Dew & Co., claiming that Dew & Co. were their agents in the matter. *Held* – there was no contract between the parties. Dunlop could not enforce the contract made between the respondents and Dew & Co. because they had not supplied consideration. Even if Dunlop were undisclosed principals, there was no consideration moving between them and the respondents. The discount received by Selfridge was part of that given by Dunlop to Dew & Co. Since Dew & Co. were not bound to give any part of their discount to retailers the discount received by Selfridge operated only as consideration between themselves and Dew & Co. and could not be claimed by Dunlop as consideration to support a promise not to sell below list price. (See now Resale Prices Act, 1976, s. 26 at p. 315.)

> COMMENT
> It was in this case that the House of Lords adopted the definition of consideration given by Sir Frederick Pollock, i.e.: 'An act or forbearance of one party, *or the promise thereof* is the price for which *the promise* of the other is bought and *the promise* thus given for value is enforceable.'

88. *Jackson* v *Horizon Holidays* [1975] 3 All E.R. 92

Mr Jackson had booked a four-week holiday in an hotel in Ceylon for himself and his family, everything to be 'of the highest standard'. The brochure issued by the defendants described the hotel as enjoying many facilities including a mini golf course, a swimming pool, and beauty and hairdressing salons.

None of these in fact materialised and the food was distasteful. It was *held* that Mr Jackson could sue on the contract not only for his own loss and disappointment but also for that of his family. The decision was based on the fact that Mr Jackson had entered into the contract partly for the benefit of his family. On that basis an award of damages of £1100 was not excessive. In the course of his judgment Lord Denning, M.R. said: 'the case comes within the principle stated by Lush, L.J. in *Lloyd's* v *Harper* [1880] 16 Ch.D. 290 at p. 321: " . . . I consider it to be an established rule of law that where a contract is made with A for the benefit of B, A can sue on the contract for the benefit of B and recover all that B could have recovered if the contract had been made with B himself." ' Speaking of these words, Lord Denning said: 'I think they should be accepted as correct, at any rate so long as the law forbids the third persons themselves to sue for damages. It is the only way in which a just result can be achieved.'

COMMENT

(i) This judgment of Lord Denning has been much critised since it infringes a very old rule of English contract law which states that if A contracts with B in return for B's promise to do something for C, then if B repudiates the contract, C has no enforceable claim, and A is restricted to an action for nominal damages by reason of his having suffered no loss. The judgment in *Jackson* was criticised by the Lords in *Woodar* v *Wimpey* [1980] 1 All E.R. 571 and they assumed that only nominal damages were available in *Beswick* (see below) so that it must be regarded with caution.

The House of Lords said that the *Jackson* case could be justified on the basis that Mr Jackson *actually saw* his family suffering discomfort and disappointment. Their Lordships would not, however, accept that there was a general rule in contract that A could recover damages from B in respect of loss suffered by C.

(ii) If damages are recovered under the ruling given by Lord Denning in *Jackson* the recipient must hand over the relevant shares to the other members of the family and if he does not they can sue him in quasi-contract (see further p. 339).

89. *Beswick* v *Beswick* [1967] 2 All E.R. 1197

A coal merchant agreed to sell the business to his nephew in return for a weekly consultancy fee of £6 10s. payable during his liftime, and after his death an annuity of £5 per week was to be payable to his widow for her lifetime. After the agreement was signed the nephew took over the business and paid his uncle the sum of £6 10s. as agreed. The uncle died on 3 November 1963, and the nephew paid the widow one sum of £5 and then refused to pay her any more. On 30 June 1964, the widow became the admininstratrix of her husband's estate, and on 15 July 1964, she brought an action against the nephew for arrears of the weekly sums and for specific performance of the agreement for the future. She sued in her capacity as administratrix of the estate and also in her personal capacity. Her action failed at first instance and on appeal to the Court of Appeal, [1966] 3 All E.R. 1, it was decided amongst other things that –

(a) specific performance could in a proper case be ordered of a contract to pay money;

(b) 'property' in s. 56(1) of the Law of Property Act, 1925 included a contractual claim not concerned with realty and that therefore a third party could sue on a contract to which he was a stranger. The widow's claim in her personal capacity was therefore good (per Denning, M.R., and Danckwerts, L.J.);

(c) the widow's claim as administratrix was good because she was not suing in her personal capacity but on behalf of her deceased husband who had been a party to the agreement;

(d) that no trust in her favour could be inferred.

There was a further appeal to the House of Lords, though not on the creation of a trust, and there it was *held* that the widow's claim as administratrix succeeded, and that specific performance of a contract to pay money could be granted in a proper case. However, having decided the appeal on these grounds their Lordships went on to say that the widow's personal claim would have failed because s. 56 of the Law of Property Act, 1925 was limited to cases involving realty. The 1925 Act was a consolidating not a codifying measure, so that if it contained words which were capable of more than one construction, effect should be given to the construction which did not alter the law. It was accepted that when the present provision was contained in the Real Property Act, 1845, it had applied only to realty. Although s. 205(1) of the 1925 Act appeared to have extended the provision to personal property, including things in action, it was expressly qualified by the words: 'Unless the context otherwise requires', and it was felt that Parliament had not intended to sweep away the rule of privity by what was in effect a sidewind.

COMMENT

Here the problem of whether or not to award nominal damages to the plaintiff referred to in *Jackson*'s case was overcome because the court awarded specific performance. However, four Law Lords said that if damages had been awarded they would have been nominal only, though Lord Pearce would have awarded substantial damages. Furthermore, it is unlikely that s. 56 does have a very wide application. The sub-section says that a person may take the benefit of an agreement although he is not 'named as a party'. The legislation does not say that he need not *be a party*. There are those who take the view, therefore, that s. 56(1) is designed to cover the situation where there is a covenant over land in favour of, say, 'the owner of Whiteacre', so that the owner of Whiteacre could benefit from the covenant, provided he could be ascertained, even though he was not named in the instrument creating the covenant. If this interpretation is correct then s. 56(1) of the 1925 Act has little effect on the law of contract generally.

PRIVITY OF CONTRACT: EXCEPTIONS IN THE CASE OF BENEFITS AND BURDENS ATTACHING TO LAND

90. *Smith and Snipes Hall Farm Ltd* v *River Douglas Catchment Board* [1949] 2 K.B. 500

In 1938 the defendants entered into an agreement with eleven persons owning land adjoining a certain stream, that, on the landowners paying some part of the cost, the defendants would improve the banks of the stream and maintain the said banks for all time. In 1940 one landowner sold her land to Smith, and in 1944 Smith leased the land to Snipes Hall Farm Ltd. In 1946, because of the defendant's negligence, the banks burst and the adjoining land was flooded. *Held* – the plaintiifs could enforce the covenant given in the agreement of 1938 even though they were strangers to it. The covenants were for the benefit of the land and affected its use and value and could therefore be transferred with it.

91. *Tulk* v *Moxhay* (1848) 2 Ph. 774

The plaintiff was the owner of several plots of land in Leicester Square and in 1808 he sold one of them to a person called Elms. Elms agreed, for himself, his heirs and assigns, 'to keep the Square Garden open as a pleasure ground and uncovered with buildings'. After a number of conveyances, the land was sold to the defendant who claimed a right to build on it. The plaintiff sued for an injunction preventing the development of the land. The defendant, whilst admitting that he purchased the land with notice of the covenant, claimed that he was not bound by it because he had not himself entered into it. *Held* – an injunction to restrain building would be granted because there was a jurisdiction in Equity to prevent, by way of injunction, acts inconsistent with a restrictive covenant on land, so long as the land was acquired with notice of the covenant, and the plaintiff retains land which can benefit from the covenant.

COMMENT
(i) Such notice may now be constructive where the covenant is registered under land charges legislation.

(ii) It was held in *Roake* v *Chadha* [1983] 3 All E.R. 503 that whether a covenant runs with the land depends upon its wording. If the words used in it prevent the benefit of the covenant, in this case that the plot holder of land would not build more than one house on it, passing to a subsequent owner of the land unless specifically assigned to him by the present owner, then the covenant would not run with the land as such but would depend upon assignment.

THE COMMON LAW RULE OF ACCORD AND SATISFACTION: AGREED VARIATIONS IN CONTRACTUAL OBLIGATIONS ARE GENERALLY UNENFORCEABLE WITHOUT CONSIDERATION

92. *Foakes* v *Beer* (1884) 9 App. Cas. 605

Mrs Beer had obtained a judgment against Dr Foakes for debt and costs. Dr Foakes agreed to settle the judgment debt by paying £500 down and £150 per half-year until the whole was paid, and Mrs Beer agreed not to take further action on the judgment. Dr Foakes duly paid the amount of the judgment plus costs. However, judgment debts carry interest by statute, and while Dr Foakes had been paying off the debt, interest amounting to £360 had been accruing on the diminishing balance. In this action Mrs Beer claimed the £360. *Held* – she could do so. Her promise not to take further action on the judgment was not supported by any consideration moving from Dr Foakes. *Pinnel's* case applied.

> COMMENT
> In view of the possible development of Equity envisaged by Lord Denning in the *D. & C. Builders* case, see below, it might be better to restrict the application of this case to situations where the promise has been extorted and not freely given. If this were so, *Foakes'* case would be reconcilable with any development of the equitable rule of promissory estoppel on the lines envisaged by Lord Denning in the *D. & C. Builders* case.

ACCORD AND SATISFACTION: PAYMENT BY CHEQUE IS NOT SUBSTITUTED PERFORMANCE: PROMISSORY ESTOPPEL MAY, IN APPROPRIATE CIRCUMSTANCES, EXTINGUISH AS DISTINCT FROM SUSPEND CONTRACTUAL RIGHTS

93. *D. & C. Builders Ltd* v *Rees* [1965] 3 All E.R. 837

D. & C. Builders, a small company, did work for Rees for which he owed £482 13s. 1d. There was at first no dispute as to the work done but Rees did not pay. In August and October 1964, the plaintiffs wrote for the money and received no reply. On 13 November 1964, the wife of Rees (who was then ill) telephoned the plaintiffs, complained about the work, and said, 'My husband will offer you £300 in settlement. That is all you will get. It is to be in satisfaction.' D. & C. Builders, being in desperate straits and faced with bankruptcy without the money, offered to take the £300 and allow a year to Rees to find the balance. Mrs Rees replied: 'No, we will never have enough money to pay the balance. £300 is better than nothing.' The plaintiffs then said: 'We have no choice but to accept.' Mrs Rees gave the plaintiffs a cheque and insisted on a receipt 'in completion of the account'. The plaintiffs, being worried about their financial position, brought an action for the balance. The defence was bad workmanship and also that there was a binding settlement. The question of settlement was tried as a preliminary issue and the judge, following *Goddard* v *O'Brien* [1880] 9 Q.B.D. 33, decided that a cheque for a smaller amount was a good discharge of the debt, this being the generally accepted view of the law since that date. On appeal it was *held* (*per* the Master of the Rolls, Lord Denning) that *Goddard* v *O'Brien* was wrongly decided. A smaller sum in cash could be no settlement of a larger sum and 'no sensible distinction could be drawn between the payment of a lesser sum by cash and the payment of it by cheque'.

In the course of his judgment Lord Denning said of *High Trees*:

> It is worth noting that the principle may be applied, not only so as to suspend strict legal rights, but also so as to preclude the enforcement of them.
>
> This principle has been applied to cases where a creditor agrees to accept a lesser sum in discharge of a greater. So much so that we can now say that, when a creditor and a debtor enter on a course of negotiation, which leads the debtor to suppose that, on payment of the lesser sum, the creditor will not enforce payment of the balance, and on the faith thereof the debtor pays the lesser sum and the creditor accepts it as satisfaction: then the creditor will not be allowed to enforce payment of the balance when it would be inequitable to do so. . . . But he is not bound unless there has been truly an accord between them.

In the present case there was no true accord. The debtor's wife had held the creditors to ransom, and there was no reason in law or Equity why the plaintiffs should not enforce the full amount of debt.

COMMENT

The case also illustrates the requirements of equality of bargaining power in the negotiation (or as here, the renegotiation) of a contract. (See also *Lloyd's Bank* v *Bundy*, 1974 at p. 658.)

ACCORD AND SATISFACTION: COMPROMISES BETWEEN CREDITORS

94. *Good* v *Cheesman* (1831) 2 B. & Ad. 328

The defendant had accepted two bills of exchange of which the plaintiff was the drawer. After the bills became due and before this action was brought, the plaintiff suggested that the defendant meet his creditors with a view perhaps to an agreement. The meeting was duly held and the defendant entered into an agreement with his creditors whereby the defendant was to pay one-third of his income to a trustee to be named by the creditors, and that this was to be the method by which the defendant's debts were to be paid. It was not clear from the evidence whether the plaintiff attended the meeting, though he certainly did not sign the agreement. There was, however, evidence that the agreement had been in his possession for some time and it was duly stamped before the trial. No trustee was in fact appointed, though the defendant was willing to go on with the agreement. *Held* – the agreement bound the plaintiff and the action on the bills could not be sustained. The consideration, though not supplied to the plaintiff direct, existed in the forbearance of the other creditors. Each was bound in consequence of the agreement of the rest.

COMMENT

(i) The better view is that the basis of this decision is to be found not in the law of contract but in tort, in the sense that once an agreement of this kind has been made it would be a *fraud* on the other creditors for one of their number to sue the debtor separately.

(ii) These arrangements would more usually be made today under the Insolvency Act, 1986. Section 260 of that Act states that such an arrangement binds every creditor if it is approved by a meeting of creditors at which three-quarters in value vote in favour of the arrangement. Therefore, s. 260 really provides an exception to the rule of accord and satisfaction.

ACCORD AND SATISFACTION: PAYMENTS BY THIRD PARTIES

95. *Welby* v *Drake* (1825) 1 C. & P. 557

The plaintiff sued the defendant for the sum of £9 on a debt which had originally been for £18. The defendant's father had paid the plaintiff £9 and the plaintiff had agreed to take that sum in full discharge of the debt. *Held* – the payment of £9 by the defendant's father operated to discharge the debt of £18.

COMMENT

(i) Here again the basis of the decision is that it would be a fraud on the third party to sue the original debtor. 'If the father did pay the smaller sum in satisfaction of this debt, it is a bar to the plaintiff's now recovering against the son; because by suing the son, he commits a fraud on the father, whom he induced to advance his money on the faith of such advance being a discharge of his son from further liability.' (*Per* Lord Tenterden, C.J.)

(ii) Also of course the creditor breaks his contract with the third party.

PROMISSORY ESTOPPEL: VARIATION OF CONTRACTUAL RIGHTS WITHOUT CONSIDERATION: THE APPROACH OF EQUITY: SUSPENSION OF RIGHTS

96. *Central London Property Trust Ltd* v *High Trees House Ltd* [1947] K.B. 130

In 1937 the plaintiffs granted to the defendants a lease of 99 years of a new block of flats at a rent of £2500 per annum. The lease was by deed. During the period of the war the flats were by no means fully let owing to the absence of people from the London area. The defendant company, which was a subsidiary of the plaintiff company, realised that it could not meet the rent out of the profits then being made on the flats, and in 1940 the parties entered into an agreement which reduced the rent to £1250 per annum, this agreement being put into writing but not by deed. The defendants continued to pay the reduced rent from 1941 to the beginning of 1945, by which time the flats were fully let, and they continued to pay the reduced rent thereafter. In September 1945, the receiver of the plaintiff company investigated the matter and asked for arrears of £7916, suggesting that the liability created by the lease still existed, and that the agreement of 1940 was not supported by any consideration. The receiver then brought this friendly action to establish the legal position. He claimed £625, being the difference in rent for the two quarters ending 29 September and 25 December 1945. *Held* – (*a*) A simple contract can in Equity vary a deed (i.e. the lease), though it had not done so here because the simple contract was not supported by consideration. (*b*) As the agreement for the reduction of rent had been acted upon by the defendants, the plaintiffs were estopped in Equity from claiming the full rent from 1941 until early 1945 when the flats were fully let. After that time they were entitled to do so because the second agreement was only operative during the continuance of the conditions which gave rise to it. To this extent the limited claim of the receiver succeeded. If the receiver had sued for the balance of rent from 1941 he would have failed.

97. *Tool Metal Manufacturing Co. Ltd* v *Tungsten Electric Co. Ltd* [1955] 2 All E.R. 657

The appellants were the registered proprietors of British letters patent. In April 1938, they made a contract with the respondents whereby they gave the latter a licence to manufacture 'hard metal alloys' in accordance with the inventions which were the subject of patent. By the contract the respondents agreed to pay 'compensation' to the appellants if in any one month they sold more that a stated quantity of metal alloys.

Compensation was duly paid by the respondents until the outbreak of war in 1939 but thereafter none was paid. It was found as a fact that in 1942 the appellants agreed to suspend the enforcement of compensation payments pending the making of a new contract. In 1944 negotiations for such new contracts were begun but broke down. In 1945 the respondents sued the appellants for breach of contract and the appellants counterclaimed for payment of compensation as from 1 June, 1945. As regards the arguments on the counterclaim, it was eventually *held* by the Court of Appeal that the agreement of 1942 operated in equity to prevent the appellants demanding compensation until they had given reasonable notice to the respondents of their intention to resume their strict legal rights and that such notice had not been given.

In September 1950, the appellants themselves issued a writ against the respondents claiming compensation as from 1 January 1947. The respondents pleaded the equity raised by the agreement of 1942 and argued that reasonable notice of its termination had not been given. When this action reached the House of Lords it was *held* – affirming *Hughes* v *Metropolitan Railway Co.* and the *High Trees* case, that the agreement of 1942 operated in equity to suspend the appellants' legal rights to compensation until reasonable notice to resume them had been given. However, the counterclaim in the first action in 1945 amounted to such notice and since the appellants were not now claiming any compensation as due to them before 1 January 1947, the appellants succeeded in this second action and were awarded £84,000 under the compensation claim.

PROMISSORY ESTOPPEL: THE MEANING OF RELIANCE UPON THE PROMISE

98. *W.J. Alan & Co.* v *El Nasr Export and Import Co.* [1972] 2 All E.R. 127

A contract for the sale of coffee provided for the price expressed in Kenyan shillings to be paid by irrevocable letter of credit. The buyers procured a confirmed letter expressed in sterling and the sellers obtained part payment thereunder. While shipment was in progress sterling was devalued and the sellers claimed such additional sum as would bring the price up to the sterling equivalent of Kenyan shillings at the current rate. Orr, J. *held* that the buyers were liable to pay the additional sum as the currency of account was Kenyan shillings. On appeal by the buyers it was *held* – allowing the appeal – that the sellers by accepting payment in sterling had irrevocably waived their right to be paid in Kenyan currency or had accepted a variation of the sale contract, and that a party who has waived his rights cannot afterwards insist on them if the other party has acted on that belief differently from the way in which he would otherwise have acted; and the other party need not show that he has acted to his detriment. In the course of his judgment Lord Denning, M.R. said:

If one party, by his conduct, leads another to believe that the strict rights arising under the contract will not be insisted on, intending that the other should act on that belief, and he does act on it, then the first party will not afterwards be allowed to insist on the strict legal rights when it would be inequitable for him to do so. . . . There may be no consideration moving from him who benefits by the waiver. There may be no detriment to him acting on it. There may be nothing in writing. Nevertheless, the one who waives his strict rights cannot afterwards insist on them. His strict rights are at any rate suspended so long as the waiver lasts. He may on occasion be able to revert to his strict legal rights for the future by giving reasonable notice in that behalf, or otherwise making it plain by his conduct that he will thereafter insist on them. . . . I know that it has been suggested in some quarters that there must be a detriment. But I can find no support for it in the authorities cited by the judge. The nearest approach to it is the statement by Viscount Simonds in the *Tool Metal* case that the other must have been led 'to alter his position' which was adopted by Lord Hodson in *Emmanuel Ayodeji Ajayi* v *R. T. Briscoe (Nigeria) Ltd.* [1964] 3 All E.R. 556. But that only means that he must have been led to act differently from what he otherwise would have done. And, if you study the cases in which the doctrine has been applied, you will see that all that is required is that one should have '*acted* on the belief induced by the other party'. That is how Lord Cohen put it in the *Tool Metal* case and it is how I would put it myself.

COMMENT
Since as in *High Trees* a tenant who only pays one-half of the rent cannot be said to be 'acting to his detriment' then 'detriment' cannot be a requirement of equitable estoppel. It is a requirement of estoppel at common law.

PROMISSORY ESTOPPEL: DOES NOT OPERATE TO CREATE NEW CONTRACTUAL RIGHTS BUT MERELY TO SUSPEND EXISTING ONES

99. *Combe* v *Combe* [1951] 2 K.B. 215

The parties were married in 1915 and separated in 1939. In February 1943, the wife obtained a decree *nisi* of divorce, and a few days later the husband entered into an agreement under which he was to pay his wife £100 per annum, free of income tax. The decree was made absolute in August 1943. The husband did not make the agreed payments and the wife did not apply to the court for maintenance but chose to rely on the alleged contract. She brought this action for arrears under that contract. Evidence showed that her income was between £700 and £800 per annum and the defendant's was £650 per annum. Byrne, J., at first instance, *held* that, although the wife had not supplied consideration, the agreement was nevertheless enforceable, following the decision in the *High Trees* case (see p. 621) as a promise made to be acted upon and in fact acted upon. *Held* – (a) That the *High Trees* decision was not intended to create new actions where none existed before, and that it had not abolished the requirement of consideration in the formation of simple contracts. In such cases consideration was a cardinal necessity. (b) In the words of Birkett, L.J., the doctrine was 'a shield not a sword', i.e. a defence to an action, not a cause of action. (c) The doctrine applied to the modification of existing agreements by subsequent promises and had no relevance to the formation of a contract. (d) It was not possible to find consideration in the fact that the wife forbore to claim maintenance from the court, since no such contractual undertaking by her could have been binding even if she had given it. Therefore this action by the wife must fail because the agreement was not supported by consideration.

PROMISSORY ESTOPPEL: OTHER APPLICATIONS

100. *Durham Fancy Goods Ltd* v *Michael Jackson (Fancy Goods) Ltd* [1968] 2 All E.R. 987

On 18 September 1967, the plaintiffs drew a bill of exchange on the first defendants in the following form, 'M. Jackson (Fancy Goods) Co.' The bill was signed by Mr Jackson who was the director and company secretary.

The bill was dishonoured and the plaintiffs brought an action against Mr Jackson contending that by signing the form of acceptance he had committed a criminal offence under s. 108 of the Companies Act, 1948 and had made himself personally liable on the bill because he should either have returned the bill with a request that it be re-addressed to Michael Jackson (Fancy Goods) Ltd, or he should have accepted it 'M. Jackson (Fancy Goods) Ltd p.p. Michael Jackson (Fancy Goods) Ltd, Michael Jackson'. It was *held* – by Donaldson, J. – that the misdescription was in breach of s. 108 of the Companies Act, 1948, and that Mr Jackson was personally liable, under the section, to pay the bill. However, since the error was really that of the plaintiffs they were estopped from enforcing Mr Jackson's personal liability. The principle of equity upon which the promissory estoppel cases were based was applicable and barred the plaintiff's claim. That principle was formulated by Lord Cairns in *Hughes v Metropolitan Railway Co.* (1877) 2 App. Cas. 439 at p. 448, and although in his enunciation Lord Cairns assumed a pre-existing contractual relationship between the parties, that was not essential provided that there was a pre-existing legal relationship which could in certain circumstances give rise to liabilities and penalties. Such a relationship was created by s. 108.

COMMENT

(i) A holder other than the plaintiffs might have been able to bring an action against Mr Jackson under s. 108 since such a holder would not have been affected by the equity in that he would not have drawn the bill in an incorrect name. The provisions are now in s. 349, Companies Act, 1985.

(*Note*: s. 108 provided: '(1) every company . . . (c) shall have its name mentioned in legible characters . . . in all bills of exchange . . . purporting to be signed by or on behalf of the company . . . (4) If an officer of the company or any person on his behalf . . . (b) signs . . . on behalf of the company any bill of exchange . . . wherein its name is not mentioned in manner aforesaid . . . he shall be liable to a fine not exceeding £50, and shall further be personally liable to the holder of the bill of exchange . . . for the amount thereof unless it is duly paid by the company.')

(ii) A further application of the doctrine occurred in *Crabb v Arun District Council* [1975] 3 All E.R. 865 where Arun represented to Mr Crabb that he had a right of way across Arun's land which gave access to the public highway. It was *held* – by the Court of Appeal – that Arun could not go back on that promise after Mr Crabb had sold some of his land and had left himself without access to the public highway except by the right of way across Arun's land. He was granted an injuction to enforce the right. When promissory estoppel is used in this situation a plaintiff can raise it and indeed base his action upon it. Thus the expression of Birkett, L.J. in *Combe v Combe*, 1951, that the doctrine is 'a shield not a sword', is not always applicable where estoppel is used in situations other than the variation of contract rights.

CONTRACTUAL INTENTION: DOMESTIC AGREEMENTS BETWEEN HUSBAND AND WIFE ARE IN GENERAL TERMS UNENFORCEABLE

101. *Balfour* v *Balfour* [1919] 2 K.B. 571

The defendant was a civil servant stationed in Ceylon. In November 1915, he came to England on leave with his wife, the plaintiff in the present action. In August 1916, the defendant returned alone to Ceylon because his wife's doctor had advised her that her health would not stand up to a further period of service abroad. Later the husband wrote to his wife suggesting that they should remain apart, and in 1918 the plaintiff obtained a decree *nisi*. In this case the plaintiff alleged that before her husband sailed for Ceylon he had agreed, in consultation with her, that he would give her £30 per month as maintenance, and she now sued because of his failure to abide by the said agreement. The Court of Appeal *held* that there was no enforceable contract because in this sort of situation it must be assumed that the parties did not intend to create legal relations. The provision for a flat payment of £30 per month for an indefinite period with no attempt to take into account changes in the circumstances of the parties did not suggest a binding agreement. Duke, L.J. seems to have based his decision on the fact that the wife had not supplied any consideration.

> COMMENT
> Although this may seem unfair on the wife it should be remembered that if the husband was regarded as contracting to pay a housekeeping allowance, his wife could be sued for inadequate management of the household.

CONTRACTUAL INTENTION: AGREEMENTS BETWEEN HUSBAND AND WIFE DESIGNED TO REGULATE THE TERMS OF THEIR SEPARATION ARE USUALLY REGARDED AS BINDING CONTRACTS

102. *Merritt* v *Merritt* [1970] 2 All E.R. 760

After a husband had formed an attachment for another woman and had left his wife, a meeting was held between the parties on 25 May 1966, in the husband's car. The husband agreed to pay the wife £40 per month maintenance and also wrote out and signed a document stating that in consideration of the wife paying all charges in connection with the matrimonial home until the mortgage repayments had been completed, he would agree to transfer the property to her sole ownership. The wife took the document away with her and had herself paid off the mortgage. The husband did not subsequently transfer the property to his wife and she claimed a declaration that she was the sole beneficial owner and asked for an order that her husband should transfer the property to her forthwith. The husband's defence was that the agreement was a family arrangement not intended to create legal relations. *Held* – by the Court of Appeal –

(*a*) That the agreement, having been made when the parties were not living together in amity, was enforceable. (*Balfour* v *Balfour*, 1919 *distinguished*.)

(*b*) The contention that there was no consideration to support the husband's promise could not be sustained. The payment of the balance of the mortgage was a detriment to the wife and the husband had received the benefit of being relieved of liability to the building society.

Accordingly the wife was entitled to the relief she claimed.

CONTRACTUAL INTENTION: FAMILY AGREEMENTS OTHER THAN THOSE BETWEEN HUSBAND AND WIFE

103. *Simpkins* v *Pays* [1955] 3 All E.R. 10

The defendant and the defendant's granddaughter made an agreement with the plaintiff, who was a paying boarder, that they should submit in the defendant's name a weekly coupon, containing a forecast by each of them, to a Sunday newspaper fashion competition. On one occasion a forecast by the granddaughter was correct and the defendant received a prize of £750. The plaintiff sued for her share of that sum. The defence was that there was no intention to create legal relations but that the transaction was a friendly arrangement binding in honour only. *Held* – there was an intention to create legal relations. Far from being a friendly domestic arrangement, the evidence showed that it was a joint enterprise and that the parties expected to share any prize that was won.

> COMMENT
>
> A family agreement which went the other way was *Julian* v *Furby* (1982) 132 N.L.J. 64. J was an experienced plasterer who helped F, his son-in-law and his wife (J's favourite daughter) to buy, alter, and furnish a house for them. They later quarrelled and J sued for £4440. This included materials supplied and F was prepared to pay for these but not for J's labour which, it was understood, would be free. It was *held* by the Court of Appeal that there was never an intention to create a legal relationship between the parties in regard to the labour which J and F jointly provided in refurbishing the house.

CONTRACTUAL INTENTION: FAMILY AGREEMENTS: EFFECT OF VAGUENESS

104. *Jones* v *Padavatton* [1969] 2 All E.R. 616

In 1962 the plaintiff, Mrs Jones, who lived in Trinidad, made an offer to the defendant Mrs Padavatton, her daughter, to provide maintenance for her at the rate of £42 a month if she would leave her job in Washington in the United States and go to England and read for the Bar. Mrs Padavatton was at that time divorced from her husband having the custody of the child of that marriage. The agreement was an informal one and there was uncertainty as to its exact terms. Nevertheless the daughter came to England in November 1962, bringing the child with her, and began to read for the Bar, her fees and maintenance being paid for by Mrs Jones. In 1964 it appeared that the daughter was experiencing some discomfort in England occupying one room in Acton for which she had to pay £6 17s. 6d. per week. At this stage Mrs Jones offered to buy a large house in London to be occupied partly by the daughter and partly by tenants, the income from rents to go to the daughter in lieu of maintenance. Again there was no written agreement but the house was purchased for £6000 and conveyed to Mrs Jones. The daughter moved into the house in January 1965, and tenants arrived, it still being uncertain what precisely was to happen to the suplus rent income (if any) and what rooms the daughter was to occupy. No money from the rents was received by Mrs Jones and no accounts were submitted to her. In 1967 Mrs Jones claimed possession of the house from her daughter, who had by that time married again, and the daughter counter-claimed for £1655 18s. 9d. said to have been paid in connection with running the house. At the hearing the daughter still had one subject to pass in Part I of the Bar examinations and also the whole of Part II remained to be taken.

Held – by the Court of Appeal –

(a) That the arrangements were throughout family agreements depending upon the good faith of the parties in keeping the promises made and not intended to be rigid binding agreements. Furthermore, the arrangements were far too vague and uncertain to be enforceable as contracts. (*Per* Danckwerts and Fenton Atkinson, L.JJ.)

(b) That although the agreement to maintain while reading for the Bar might have been regarded as creating a legal obligation in the mother to pay (the terms being sufficiently stated and duration for a reasonable time being implied), the daughter could not claim anything in respect of that agreement which must be regarded as having terminated in 1967, five years being a reasonable time in which to complete studies for the Bar. The arrangements in relation to the home were very vague and must be regarded as made without contractual intent. (*Per* Salmon, L.J.)

The mother was therefore entitled to possession of the house and had no liability under the maintenance agreement. The counterclaim by the daughter was left to be settled by the parties.

COMMENT
In this case there was an inference of contractual intent in the mother's promise because it caused Mrs Padavatton to leave one job to study for another, but the vagueness of the arrangement negatived that intent as in *Gould* v *Gould* [1969] 3 All E.R. 728 (see p. 227).

CONTRACTUAL INTENT: GENERALLY BUT NOT ALWAYS ASSUMED IN BUSINESS AGREEMENTS UNLESS EXCLUDED BY THE PARTIES

105. *Kleinwort Benson Ltd* v *Malaysian Mining Corporation, Berhand* [1989] 1 All E.R. 785

In this case the High Court had decided that a letter of comfort (as they are called) stating that it was the policy of Malaysian Mining to ensure that its subsidiary M.M.C. Metals Ltd was 'at all times in a position to meet its liabilities' in regard to a loan made by Kleinworts to M.M.C. had contractual effect. This meant that Kleinworts was entitled to recover from Malaysian the amount owed to it by the insolvent M.M.C. which went into liquidation after the tin market collapsed in 1985. Malaysian appealed to the Court of Appeal which reversed the High Court ruling. The problem has always been to decide whether a letter of comfort of the usual kind contains a legal obligation or only a moral one. In the High Court Mr Justice Hirst decided that there was a legal obligation: the Court of Appeal decided that it was only a moral one. The letter, said the Court of Appeal, stated the policy of Malaysian. It gave no contractual warranty as to the company's future conduct. In these circumstances there was no need to apply the presumption of an intention to create legal relations just because the transaction was in the course of business as laid down in *Edwards* v *Skyways* [1964] (see p. 228).

> COMMENT
> The wording of the letter of comfort must be looked at and if it appears to create a moral obligation only, then it has no contractual force. It is of course no bad thing for those in business to honour moral obligations but as Lord Justice Ralph Gibson said, moral responsibilities are not a matter for the courts.

106. *Jones* v *Vernon's Pools Ltd* [1938] 2 All E.R. 626

The plaintiff said that he had sent to the defendants a football coupon on which the penny points pool was all correct. The defendants denied having received it and relied on a clause printed on every coupon. The said clause provided that the transaction should not 'give rise to any legal relationship . . . or be legally enforceable . . . but . . . binding in honour only'. The court *held* that this clause was a bar to any action in a court of law.

> COMMENT
> This case was followed by the Court of Appeal in *Appleson* v *Littlewood Ltd* [1939] 1 All E.R. 464, where the contract contained a similar clause.

107. *Rose and Frank Co.* v *Crompton (J.R.) & Brothers Ltd* [1925] A.C. 445

In 1913 the plaintiffs, an American firm, entered into an agreement with the defendants, an English company, whereby the plaintiffs were appointed sole agents for the sale in the USA of paper tissues supplied by the defendants.

The contract was for a period of three years with an option to extend that time. The agreement was extended to March 1920, but in 1919 the defendants terminated it without notice. The defendants had received a number of orders for tissues before the termination of the contract, and they refused to execute them. The plaintiffs sued for breach of contract and for non-delivery of the goods actually ordered. The agreement of 1913 contained an 'Honourable Pledge Clause' drafted as follows: 'This arrangement is not entered into nor is this memorandum written as a formal or legal agreement and shall not be subject to legal jurisdiction in the courts of the United States of America or England. . .'. It was *held* by the House of Lords that the 1913 agreement was not binding on the parties, but that in so far as the agreement had been acted upon by the defendants' acceptance of orders, the said orders were binding contracts of sale. Nevertheless the agreement was not binding for the future.

Law of contract – making the contract III

FORMALITIES: CONTRACTS WHICH MUST BE EVIDENCED IN WRITING: GUARANTEE AND INDEMNITY: S. 4, STATUTE OF FRAUDS, 1677

108. *Mountstephen* v *Lakeman* (1871) L.R. 7 Q.B. 196

The defendant was chairman of the Brixham Local Board of Health. The plaintiff, who was a builder and contractor, was employed in 1866 by the Board to construct certain main sewage works in the town. On 19 March 1866, notice was given by the Board to owners of certain homes to connect their house drains with the main sewer within 21 days. Before the expiration of the 21 days Robert Adams, the surveyor of the Board, suggested to the plaintiff that he should make the connections. The plaintiff said he was willing to do the work if the Board would see him paid. On 5 April 1866, i.e. before the expiration of the 21 days, the plaintiff commenced work on the connections. However, before work commenced it appeared that the plaintiff had had an interview with the defendant at which the following conversation took place –

Defendant: 'What objection have you to making the connections?'
Plaintiff: 'I have none, if you or the Board will order the work or become responsible for the payment.'
Defendant: 'Go on Mountstephen and do the work and I will see you paid.'

The plaintiff completed the connections in April and May 1866, and sent an account to the Board on 5 December 1866. The Board disclaimed responsibility on the ground that they had never entered into any agreement with the plaintiff nor authorised any officer of the Board to agree with him for the performance of the work in question. It was *held* – that Lakeman had undertaken a personal liability to pay the plaintiff and had not given a guarantee of the liability of a third party, i.e. the Board. In consequence Lakeman had given an indemnity which did not need to be in writing under

s. 4 of the Statute of Frauds, 1677. The plaintiff was therefore entitled to enforce the oral undertaking given by the defendant.

COMMENT
Section 4 of the Statute of Frauds, 1677 provides that: 'No action shall be brought . . . whereby to charge the defendant upon any special promise to answer for the debt default or miscarriage of another person . . . unless the agreement upon which such action shall be brought or some memorandum or note thereof shall be in writing and signed by the party to be charged therewith or some other person thereunto by him lawfully authorized'. It was *held* in *Birkmyr* v *Darnell* (1704) 1 Salk. 27 that the words 'debt default or miscarriage of *another person'* meant that the section applied only where there was some person other than the surety who was primarily liable.

MINORS: NECESSARIES: THE GENERAL TEST

109. *Nash* v *Inman* [1908] 2 K.B. 1

The plaintiff was a Savile Row tailor and the defendant was a minor undergraduate at Trinity College, Cambridge. The plaintiff sent his agent to Cambridge because he had heard that the defendant was spending money freely, and might be the sort of person who would be interested in high-class clothing. As a result of the agent's visit, the plaintiff supplied the defendant with various articles of clothing to the value of £145 0s. 3d. during the period October 1902 to June 1903. The clothes included eleven fancy waistcoats. The plaintiff now sued the minor for the price of the clothes. Evidence showed that the defendant's father was in a good position, being an architect with a town house and a country house, and it could be said that the clothes supplied were suitable to the defendant's position in life. However, his father proved that the defendant was amply supplied with such clothes when the plaintiff delivered the clothing now in question. *Held* – the plaintiff's claim failed because he had not established that the goods supplied were necessaries.

MINORS: BENEFICIAL CONTRACTS

110. *Roberts* v *Gray* [1913] 1 K.B. 520

The defendant wished to become a professional billiards player and entered into an agreement with the plaintiff, a leading professional, to go on a joint tour. The plaintiff went to some trouble in order to organise the tour, but a dispute arose between the parties and the defendant refused to go. The plaintiff now sued for damages of £6000. *Held* – the contract was for the minor's benefit, being in effect for his instruction as a billiards player. Therefore the plaintiff could sustain an action for damages for breach of contract, and damages of £1500 were awarded.

COMMENT
(i) In *Chaplin* v *Leslie Frewin (Publishers)* [1965] 3 All E.R. 764 the

plaintiff, the minor son of a famous father, made a contract with the defendants under which they were to publish a book written for him, telling his life story and entitled *I Couldn't Smoke the Grass on my Father's Lawn*. The plaintiff sought to avoid the contract on the ground that the book gave an inaccurate picture of his approach to life. *Held* – amongst other things – that the contract was binding if it was for the minor's benefit. The time to determine that question was when the contract was made and at that time it was for the minor's benefit and could not be avoided.

(ii) Although this was not a contract of service it could be regarded as analogous to one, and was for the plaintiff's benefit because although he had a ghost writer the publishing contract could have helped him to make a start as an author. So the court still felt it necessary to use the contract of service analogy and not merely say that the contract was beneficial because it made Mr Chaplin money.

(iii) In *Denmark Productions* v *Boscobel Productions* (1967) 111 Sol. J. 715 Widgery, J. held that a contract by which a minor appoints managers and agents to look after his business affairs is, in modern conditions, necessary if he is to earn his living and rise to fame, and if it is for his benefit it will be upheld by analogy with a contract of service.

(iv) The case of *De Francesco* v *Barnum* (1890) 45 Ch.D. 430 shows that so far as beneficial contracts are concerned the subject matter of the contract is not decisive. Two minors bound themselves in contract to the plaintiff for seven years to be taught stage dancing. The minors agreed that they would not accept any engagements without his consent. They later accepted an engagement with Barnum and the plaintiff sued Barnum for interfering with the contractual relationship between himself and the minors, and also to enforce the apprenticeship deed against the minors and to obtain damages for its breach. The contract was, of course, for the minors' benefit and was *prima facie* binding on them. However, when the court considered the deed in greater detail, it emerged that there were certain onerous terms in it. For example the minors bound themselves not to marry during the apprenticeship; the payment was hardly generous, the plaintiff agreeing to pay them 9d. per night and 6d. for matinee appearances for the first three years, and 1s. per night and 6d. for matinee performances during the remainder of the apprenticeship. The plaintiff did not undertake to maintain them whilst they were unemployed and did not undertake to find them engagements. The minors could also be engaged in performances abroad at a fee of 5s. per week. Further the plaintiff could terminate the contract if he felt that the minors were not suitable for the career of dancer. It appeared from the contract that the minors were at the absolute disposal of the plaintiff. *Held* – the deed was an unreasonable one and was therefore unenforceable against the minors. Barnum could not, therefore, be held liable, since the tort of interference with a contractual relationship presupposes the existence of an enforceable contract.

MINORS: TRADING CONTRACTS ARE NOT BINDING ON A MINOR UNLESS EXCEPTIONALLY THEY ARE ANALOGOUS TO A CONTRACT OF SERVICE

111. *Mercantile Union Guarantee Corporation* v *Ball* [1937] 2 K.B. 498

The purchase on hire-purchase terms of a motor lorry by a minor carrying on a business as a haulage contractor was *held* not to be a contract for necessaries, but a trading contract by which the minor could not be bound.

COMMENT
It would be possible for the owner to recover the lorry without the assistance of s. 3 of the Minors' Contracts Act, 1987 because a hire-purchase contract is a contract of bailment not a sale. Thus, ownership does not pass when the goods are delivered.

MINORS: CONTRACTS BINDING UNLESS REPUDIATED: CONSEQUENCES OF DEFECTIVE CONTRACTS

112. *Steinberg* v *Scala (Leeds) Ltd* [1923] 2 Ch. 452

The plaintiff, Miss Steinberg, purchased shares in the defendant company and paid certain sums of money on application, on allotment and on one call. Being unable to meet future calls, she repudiated the contract whilst still a minor and claimed:

(a) rectification of the Register of Members to remove her name therefrom, thus relieving her from liability on future calls; and
(b) the recovery of the money already paid.

The company agreed to rectify the register but was not prepared to return the money paid.

Held – the claim under (b) above failed because there had not been total failure of consideration. The shares had some value and gave some rights, even though the plaintiff had not received any dividends and the shares had always stood at a discount on the market.

COMMENT
In *Davies* v *Beynon-Harris* (1931) 47 T.L.R. 424 a minor was allowed to avoid a lease of a flat without liability for future rent or damages but was not allowed to recover rent paid. However, in *Goode* v *Harrison* (1821) 5 B. & Ald. 147 a partner who was a minor took no steps to avoid the partnership contract while a minor or afterwards. He was held liable for the debts of the firm incurred after he came of age.

113. *Pearce* v *Brain* [1929] 2 K.B. 310

Pearce, a minor, exchanged his motor cycle for a motor car belonging to Brain. The minor had little use out of the car, and had in fact driven it only

70 miles in all when it broke down because of serious defects in the back axle. Pearce now sued to recover his motor cycle, claiming that the consideration had wholly failed. *Held* – (*a*) That a contract for the exchange of goods, whilst not a sale of goods, is a contract for the supply of goods, and that if the goods are not necessaries, the contract was void if with a minor. (Now not binding unless ratified.) (*b*) The car was not a necessary good and therefore the contract was void. (*c*) Even so the minor could only recover money paid under a void contract, i.e. if the consideration had wholly failed. The court considered that the minor had received a benefit under the contract, albeit small, and that he could not recover the motor cycle.

COMMENT

In *Corpe* v *Overton* (1833) 10 Bing. 252 a minor agreed to enter into a partnership and deposited £100 with the defendant as security for performance of the contract. The minor rescinded the contract before the partnership came into existence. *Held* – he could recover the £100 because he had received no benefit having never been a partner. There had been total failure of consideration.

CONTRACTING WITH PERSONS OF UNSOUND MIND AND DRUNKARDS

114. *Imperial Loan Co* v *Stone* [1892] Q.B. 599

This was an action on a promissory note. The defendant pleaded that at the time of making the note he was insane and that the plaintiff knew he was. The jury found that he was in fact insane but could not agree on the question of whether the plaintiff knew it. The judge entered judgment for the defendant. *Held* – that he was wrong. The defendant in order to succeed must convince the court on both issues.

COMMENT

In *Hart* v *O'Connor* [1985] 2 All E.R. 880 the Privy Council refused to set aside an agreement to sell farmland in New Zealand because although the seller was of unsound mind, his affliction was not apparent. The price paid was not unreasonable. If it had been the Privy Council said that the contract could have been set aside for equitable fraud as an unconscionable bargain.

115. *Matthews* v *Baxter* (1873) L.R. 8 Exch. 132

Matthews agreed to buy houses from Baxter. He was so drunk as not to know what he was doing. Afterwards, when sober, he ratified and confirmed the contract. It was *held* that both parties were bound by it.

COMMENT

A contract with a drunken person must in effect always be voidable by him because presumably the fact that he is drunk will be known to the other party. This is not so in regard to unsoundness of mind which might not be known to the other party.

REGISTERED COMPANIES: THE *ULTRA VIRES* RULE: POSITION AT COMMON LAW

116. *Ashbury Railway Carriage & Iron Co* v *Riche* (1875) L.R. 7 H.L. 653

The company was formed for the purposes (stated in the memorandum of association) of making and selling railway wagons and other railway plant and carrying on the business of mechanical engineers and general contractors. The company bought a concession for the construction of a railway system in Belgium from Antwerp to Tournai and entered into an agreement whereby Messrs Riche were to construct the railway line. Messrs Riche commenced the work and the company paid over certain sums of money in connection with the contract. The Ashbury company later ran into difficulties, and the shareholders wished the directors to take over the contract in a personal capacity and indemnify the shareholders. The directors thereupon repudiated the contract on behalf of the company and Messrs Riche sued for breach of contract. *Held* – the directors were able to repudiate because the contract to construct a railway system was *ultra vires* and void. On a proper construction of the objects, the company had power to supply materials for the construction of railways but had no power to engage in the actual construction of them. Further, the subsequent assent of all the shareholders could not make the contract binding, for a principal cannot ratify the *ultra vires* contracts of his agent. (See now p. 238.)

Law of Contract – Reality of Consent I

MISTAKE: DOCUMENTS MISTAKENLY SIGNED: RELEVANCE OF SIGNER'S NEGLIGENCE

117. *Saunders* v *Anglia Building Society* [1970] 3 All E.R. 961

Mrs Gallie, a widow aged 78 years, signed a document which Lee, her nephew's friend, told her was a deed of gift of her house to her nephew. She did not read the document but believed what Lee had told her. In fact the document was an assignment of her leasehold interest in the house to Lee, and Lee later mortgaged that interest to a building society. In an action by Mrs Gallie against Lee and the building society it was *held* at first instance – (*a*) that the assignment was void and did not confer a title on Lee; (*b*) although Mrs Gallie had been negligent she was not estopped from denying the validity of the deed against the building society for she owed it no duty. The Court of Appeal, in allowing an appeal by the building society, *held* that the plea of *non est factum* was not available to Mrs Gallie. The transaction intended and carried out was the same, i.e. an assignment.

The appeal to the House of Lords was brought by Saunders, the executrix of Mrs Gallie's estate. The House of Lords affirmed the decision of the Court of Appeal but took the opportunity to restate the law relating to the avoidance of documents on the ground of mistake as follows.

(a) The plea of *non est factum* will rarely be available to a person of full capacity who signs a document apparently having legal effect without troubling to read it, i.e. negligently.

(b) A mistake as to the identity of the person in whose favour the document is executed will not normally support a plea of *non est factum* though it may do if the court regards the mistake as fundamental (Lord Reid and Lord Hodson). Neither judge felt that the personality error made by Mrs Gallie was sufficient to support the plea.

(c) The distinction taken in *Howatson* v *Webb* [1908] 1 Ch. 1 that the mistake must be as to the class or character of the document and not merely as to its contents was regarded as illogical. Under the *Howatson* test, if X signed a guarantee for £1000 believing it to be an insurance policy he escaped all liability on the guarantee, but if he signed a guarantee for £10,000 believing it to be a guarantee for £100 he was fully liable for £10,000. Under *Saunders* the document which was in fact signed must be 'fundamentally different', 'radically different', or 'totally different'. The test is more flexible than the character/contents one and yet still restricts the operation of the plea of *non est factum*.

COMMENT

(i) The charge of negligence might be avoided where a person was told he was witnessing a confidential document and had no reason to doubt that he was. Many such documents are witnessed each day and the witnesses would never dream of asking to read them nor would they think themselves negligent because they had not done so. Surely the *Saunders* decision is not intended to turn witnesses into snoopers. Thus the decision in the old case of *Lewis* v *Clay* (1898) 77 L.T. 653 would probably be the same under modern law. In that case Clay was asked by Lord William Neville to witness a confidential document and signed in holes in blotting paper placed over the document by Neville. In fact he was signing two promissory notes and two letters authorising Lewis to pay the amount of the notes to Lord William Neville. The court *held* that the signature of Clay in the circumstances had no more effect than if it had been written for an autograph collector or in an album and he was not bound by the bills of exchange.

(ii) As between the immediate parties to what is always in effect a fraud, there is, of course no difficulty in avoiding the contract or transaction mistakenly entered into. The rules set out above are relevant only where the contract or transaction mistakenly entered into has affected a third party, as where he has taken a bill of exchange bona fide and for value on which the defendant's signature was obtained under circumstances of mistake (*Foster* v *Mackinnon* (1869) L.R. 4 C.P. 704) or has lent money on an interest in land obtained by a fraudulent assignment under circumstances of mistake (*Saunders* v *Anglia Building Society* (1970) see above). The principles set out in *Saunders'* case apply also to those who sign blank forms as well as to those who sign completed documents without reading them (*United Dominions Trust Ltd* v *Western* [1975] 3 All E.R. 1017).

UNILATERAL MISTAKE: INGREDIENTS: A IS MISTAKEN AND B THE OTHER PARTY TO THE CONTRACT KNOWS OR OUGHT TO KNOW HE IS

118. *Higgins (W.) Ltd* v *Northampton Corporation* [1927] 1 Ch. 128

The plaintiff entered into a contract with the corporation for the erection of dwelling houses. The plaintiff made an arithmetical error in arriving at his price, having deducted a certain rather small sum twice over. The corporation sealed the contract, assuming that the price arrived at by the plaintiff was correct. *Held* – the contract was binding on the parties. Rectification of such a contract was not possible because the power of the court to rectify agreements made under mistake is confined to common not unilateral mistake. Here, rectification would only have been granted if fraud or misrepresentation had been present.

> COMMENT
> (i) Since this case was decided the courts have moved away from the idea that rectification of a contract for unilateral mistake is permissible only if there is some form of sharp practice (see *Thomas Bates & Sons Ltd* v *Wyndham's (Lingerie) Ltd* (1981) at p. 645). Even so, rectification would not have been granted in this case because Northampton Corporation were not aware of the plaintiff's error which is still a requirement for rectification.
> (ii) The rule of unilateral mistake does not seem to apply to mistakes as to the value of the contract. If you go into a junk shop and recognise a genuine Georgian silver teapot marked at £10 then your contract of purchase, if made, would be good in law, although it would be obvious that the seller had made a mistake and that the buyer was aware of it. This is the rule of *caveat venditor* (let the seller beware) and applies provided the seller intends to offer the goods at his marked price.

119. *Cundy* v *Lindsay* (1878) 3 App. Cas. 459

The respondents were linen manufacturers in Belfast. A fraudulent person named Blenkarn wrote to the respondents from 37 Wood Street, Cheapside, ordering a quantity of handkerchiefs but signed his letter in such a way that it appeared to come from Messrs Blenkiron, who were a well-known and solvent house doing business at 123 Wood Street. The respondents knew of the existence of Blenkiron but did not know the address. Accordingly the handkerchiefs were sent to 37 Wood Street. Blenkarn then sold them to the appellants, and was later convicted and sentenced for the fraud. The respondents sued the appellants in conversion claiming that the contract they had made with Blenkarn was void for mistake, and that the property had not passed to Blenkarn or to the appellants. *Held* – the respondents succeeded; there was an operative mistake as to the party with whom they were contracting.

> COMMENT
> (i) It is, however, essential that at the time of making the apparent

contract the mistaken party regarded the identity of the other pary as vital and that he intended to deal with some person other that the actual person to whom in fact he addressed the offer, as in *Cundy* v *Lindsay* (1878) (see above). The mistake must be as to *identity*, not *attributes*, e.g. creditworthiness. As between the parties the result is much the same since a mistake as to attributes may made the contract *voidable*, but the difference may vitally affect the interests of third parties. Thus in *King's Norton Metal Co Ltd* v *Edridge, Merrett and Co Ltd* (1897) 14 T.L.R. 98 where the facts were similar to *Cundy*, a fraudulent person called Wallis ordered goods from the plaintiffs using notepaper headed Hallam & Co. The notepaper said that Hallam & Co had agencies abroad and generally represented the company as creditworthy. The plaintiffs sold Hallam & Co some brass rivet wire on credit. The goods were never paid for but Wallis sold the goods on to Edridge Merrett who paid for them and were innocent of the way in which Wallis had obtained them. The plaintiffs sued Edridge Merrett in conversion saying that the contract between them and Hallam/Wallis was void for mistake so that Edridge Merrett did not become owners of the wire because Hallam/Wallis had not. The Court of Appeal *held* that the contract between King's Norton and Edridge was voidable for fraud but not void for mistake. The plaintiffs could not show a confusion of entities. There was no other Hallam or Wallis in their business lives with whom they could have been confused.

(ii) The difference between *Cundy* and *King's Norton* is that in *Cundy* there was another entity to get mixed up with. In *King's Norton* there was no one else to get mixed up with.

UNILATERAL MISTAKE: WHERE THE PARTIES ARE FACE TO FACE

120. *Lewis* v *Avery* [1971] 3 All E.R. 907

Mr Lewis agreed to sell his car to a rogue who called on him after seeing an advertisement. Before the sale took place the rogue talked knowledgeably about the film world giving the impression that he was the actor Richard Green in the 'Robin Hood' serial which was running on TV at the time. He signed a dud cheque for £450 in the name of 'R.A. Green' and was allowed to have the log book and drive the car away late the same night when he produced a film studio pass in the name of 'Green'. *Held* – by the Court of Appeal – that Mr Lewis had effectively contracted to sell the car to the rogue and could not recover it or damages from Mr Averay, a student, who had bought it from the rogue for £200. The contract between Mr Lewis and the rogue was voidable for fraud but not void for unilateral mistake.

COMMENT
It is thought that the contract would be void for mistake in a case such as this if the dishonest person assumed a disguise so that he appeared physically to be the person he said he was.

121. *Ingram and others* v *Little* [1961] 1 Q.B. 31

The plaintiffs, three ladies, were the joint owners of a car. They wished to sell the car and advertised it for sale. A fraudulent person, introducing himself as Hutchinson, offered to buy it. He was taken for a drive in it and during conversation said that his home was at Caterham. Later the rogue offered £700 for the car but this was refused, though a subsequent offer of £717 was one which the plaintiffs were prepared to accept. At this point the rogue produced a cheque book and one of the plaintiffs, who was conducting the negotiations, said that the deal was off and that they would not accept a cheque. The rogue then said that he was P.G.M. Hutchinson, that he had business interests in Guildford, and that he lived at Stanstead House, Stanstead Road, Caterham. One of the plaintiffs checked this information in a telephone directory and, on finding it to be accurate, allowed him to take the car in return for a cheque. The cheque was dishonoured, and in the meantime the rogue had sold the car to the defendants and had disappeared without a trace. The plaintiffs sued for the return of the car, or for its value as damages in conversion, claiming that the contract between themselves and the rogue was void for mistake, and that the property (or ownership) had not passed. At the trial judgment was given for the plaintiffs, Slade, J. finding the contract void. His judgment was *affirmed* by the Court of Appeal, though Devlin, L.J. dissented, saying that the mistake made was as to the creditworthiness of the rogue, not as to his identity, since he was before the plaintiffs when the contract was made. A mistake as to the substance of the rogue would be a mistake as to quality and would not avoid the contract. Devlin, L.J. also suggested that legislation should provide for an apportionment of the loss incurred by two innocent parties who suffer as a result of the fraud of a third.

COMMENT
The distinction drawn in some of these cases are fine ones. It is difficult to distinguish *Ingram* from *Lewis*. As we have seen, the question for the court to answer in these cases is whether or not the offeror at the time of making the offer regarded the identity of the offeree as a matter of vital importance. The general rule seems to be that where the parties are face to face when the contract is made identity will not be vital and the contract voidable only. *Ingram* would appear to be the exceptional case.

UNILATERAL MISTAKE: EFFECT IN EQUITY: REFUSAL OF SPECIFIC PERFORMANCE AND RESCISSION

122. *Webster* v *Cecil* (1861) 30 Beav. 62

The parties had been negotiating for the sale of certain property. Later Cecil offered by letter to sell the property for £1250. Webster was aware that his offer was probably a slip because he knew that Cecil had already refused an offer of £2000, and in fact Cecil wished to offer the property at £2250. Webster accepted the offer and sued for specific performance of the contract. The court refused to grant the decree.

COMMENT

This is not merely a case of mistake as to the value of the contract because here Webster knew that Cecil did not intend to offer the property at £1250. The rule of let the seller beware applies where the seller is mistaken as to the value but a least intends to offer the goods at his marked price.

COMMON MISTAKE: THE RULES OF *RES EXTINCTA* AND *RES SUA*

123. *Couturier* v *Hastie* (1856) 5 H.L.C. 673

Messrs Hastie dispatched a cargo of corn from Salonica and sent the charterparty and bill of lading to their London agents so that the corn might be sold. The London agents employed Couturier to sell the corn and a person named Callander bought it. Unknown to the parties the cargo had become overheated, and had been landed at the nearest port and sold, so that when the contract was made the corn was not really in existence. Callander repudiated the contract and Couturier was sued because he was a *del credere* agent, i.e. an agent who, for an extra commission, undertakes to indemnify his principal against losses arising out of the repudiation of the contract by any third party introduced by him. *Held* – the claim against Couturier failed because the contract presupposed that the goods were in existence when they were sold to Callander.

124. *Cochrane* v *Willis* (1865) L.R. 1 Ch. App. 58

Cochrane was the trustee in bankruptcy of Joseph Willis who was the tenant for life of certain estates in Lancaster. Joseph Willis had been adjudicated bankrupt in Calcutta where he resided. The remainder of the estate was to go to Daniel Willis, the brother of Joseph, on the latter's death, with eventual remainder to Henry Willis, the son of Daniel. Joseph Willis had the right to cut the timber on the estates during his life interest, and the representative of Cochrane in England threatened to cut and sell it for the benefit of Joseph's creditors. Daniel and Henry wished to preserve the timber and so they agreed with Cochrane through his representatives to pay the value of the timber to Cochrane if he would refrain from cutting it. News then reached England that when the above agreement was made Joseph was dead, and therefore the life interest had vested in (i.e. become owned by) Daniel. In this action by the trustee to enforce the agreement it was *held* that Daniel was making a contract to preserve something which was already his and the court found, applying the doctrine of *res sua*, that the agreement was void for an identical or common mistake.

COMMON MISTAKES AS TO QUALITY: NO EFFECT AT COMMON LAW

125. *Bell* v *Lever Bros Ltd* [1932] A.C. 161

Lever Bros had a controlling interest in the Niger Company. Bell was the chairman, and a person called Snelling was the vice-chairman of the Niger Company's Board. Both directors had service contracts which had some time to run. They became redundant as a result of amalgamations and Lever Bros contracted to pay Bell £30,000 and Snelling £20,000 as compensation. These sums were paid over and then it was discovered that Bell and Snelling had committed breaches of duty against the Niger Company during their term of office by making secret profits of £1360 on a cocoa pooling scheme. As directors of the Niger Company, Bell and Snelling attended meetings at which the selling price of cocoa was fixed in advance. Both of them bought and sold on their own account before the prices were made public. They could therefore have been dismissed without compensation. Lever Bros sought to set aside the payments on the ground of mistake. *Held* – the contract was not void because Lever Bros had got what they bargained for, i.e. the cancellation of two service contracts which, though they might have been terminated, were actually in existence when the cancellation agreement was made. The mistake was as to the quality of the two directors and such mistakes do not avoid the contracts. The case is one of common mistake because although Bell and Snelling admitted that they were liable to account to the company for the profit made from office, they convinced the court that they had forgotten their misdemeanour of insider dealing when they made the contract for compensation. They thought they were good directors who were entitled to that compensation.

COMMENT

The case also decided that an employee was not under a duty to disclose to his employer his own misconduct or breaches of duty towards his employer. However, employee/directors do have a duty to disclose their *own* breaches of contract to their companies. This is because their fiduciary position as directors overrides the ordinary employer/employee relationship. However, in the *Bell* case the directors concerned kept the compensation and were not required to disclose their wrongdoings to Lever Bros because they were not directors of Lever Bros but only of Niger. However, a director of, say, company A is under a duty to disclose his wrongdoing, if any, towards company A where he receives his compensation from company A itself. Failure so to disclose will allow the company to claim back a golden handshake of the kind given to Bell and Snelling.

It is worth mentioning that an employee is under a duty to disclose breaches of duty/misconduct of subordinate employees, even though he is not under a duty to disclose to his employer his own misconduct or breaches of duty. This follows from the decision of the Court of Appeal in *Sybron Corporation* v *Rochem Ltd* [1983] 2 All E.R. 707.

126. *Leaf* v *International Galleries* [1950] 1 All E.R. 693

In 1944 the plaintiff bought from the defendants an oil painting of Salisbury Cathedral for £85. A label on the back said that the painting had been exhibited as by Constable. Five years later the plaintiff tried to sell the drawing at Christie's and was told that this was not so. He now sued for rescission of the contract, no claim for damages being made. The following points of interest emerged from the decision of the Court of Appeal. (a) It was possible to restore the status quo by the mere exchange of the drawing and the purchase money so that rescission was not prevented by inability to restore the previous position. (b) The mistake made by the parties in assuming the drawing to be a Constable was a mistake as to quality and did not avoid the contract. (c) The statement that the drawing was by Constable could have been treated as a warranty giving rise to a claim for damages, but it was not possible to award damages because the appeal was based on the plaintiff's right to rescind. (d) The court, therefore, treated the statement as a representation and, finding it to be innocent, refused to rescind the contract because of the passage of time since the purchase.

COMMENT

(i) Although this case was decided after *Solle* v *Butcher* (see below), there was presumably no need for the equitable relief of rescission in regard to the common mistake. After all, Leaf had paid only £85 for the drawing and the court may have regarded the contract as speculation, each party taking a risk as to the authenticity of the drawing.

(ii) Mr Leaf might well have recovered damages if he had sued for these under what is now s. 13 of the Sale of Goods Act, 1979 (sale by description – goods described as by Constable). Mr Leaf asked for leave to amend his claim to include this when the case was in the county court but leave was refused.

COMMON MISTAKE: THE EQUITABLE APPROACH

127. *Cooper* v *Phibbs* (1867) L.R. 2 H.L. 149

Cooper agreed to take a lease of a fishery from Phibbs, his uncle's daughter who became apparent owner of it on her father's death. Unknown to either party the fishery already belonged to Cooper. This arose from a mistake by Cooper's uncle as to how the family land was held. The uncle innocently thought he owned the fishery and before he died told Cooper so, but in fact it was owned by Cooper himself. Cooper now brought this action to set aside the lease and for delivery up of the lease. *Held* – the lease must be set aside on the grounds of common or identical bilateral mistake; however, since equity has the power to give ancillary relief, Phibbs was given a lien on the fishery for the improvements she had made to it during the time she believed it to be hers. This lien could be discharged by Cooper giving Phibbs the value of the improvements.

128. *Solle* v *Butcher* [1950] 1 K.B. 671

Butcher had agreed to lease a flat in Beckenham to Solle at a yearly rental of £250, the lease to run for seven years. Both parties had acted on the assumption that the flat, which had been substantially reconstructed so as to be virtually a new flat, was no longer controlled by the Rent Restriction legislation then in force. If it were so controlled the maximum rent payable would be £140 per annum. Nevertheless Butcher would have been entitled to increase that rent by charging 8% of the cost of repairs and improvements which would bring the figure up to about £250 per annum, the rent actually charged, if he had served a statutory notice on Solle before the new lease was executed. No such notice was in fact served. Actually they both for a time mistakenly thought that the flat was decontrolled when this was not the case. Solle realised the mistake after some two years, and sought to recover the rent he had overpaid and to continue for the balance of the seven years as a statutory tenant at £140 per annum. Butcher counterclaimed for rescission of the lease in equity. It was *held* by a majority of the Court of Appeal that the mistake was one of fact and not of law, i.e. the fact that the flat was not within the provisions of the Rent Acts, and this was a bilateral mistake as to quality which would not invalidate the contract at common law. However, on the counterclaim for rescission, it was held that the lease could be rescinded. In order not to dispossess Solle, the court offered him the following alternatives:

(a) to surrender the lease entirely; or

(b) to remain in possession as a mere licensee until a new lease could be drawn up after Butcher had had time to serve the statutory notice which would allow him to add a sum for repairs to the £140 which would bring the lawful rent up to £250 per annum.

COMMENT

(i) It is impossible to say at the present time what are the limits of this case. Equitable remedies are discretionary and it is not certain whether it applies to a contract for the sale of goods, nor whether it requires some form of sharp practice before it is implemented.

(ii) In *Grist* v *Bailey* [1966] 2 All E.R. 875 a house was sold cheaply because the parties thought that vacant possession could not be obtained as there was a tenant in it who was protected by the Rent Acts and could not be got out. This was not the case and the tenant gave up possession. Even so the plaintiff asked for specific performance while the defendant asked the court to rescind the contract. The contract was set aside on the terms that the defendant would give the plaintiff the opportunity to purchase the property 'at a proper price for vacant possession'. Naturally, perhaps, specific performance was not granted.

(iii) In *Solle* Lord Denning followed *Cooper* v *Phibbs* (above) saying that a contract can be set aside in Equity for common mistake even if the agreement has been partly performed. This distinguishes rescission in mistake from rescission for misrepresentation where part performance prevents rescission (see further p. 653).

RECTIFICATION: EQUITY CAN RECTIFY MISTAKES MADE BY THE PARTIES IN RECORDING THEIR AGREEMENT

129. *Joscelyne* v *Nissen* [1970] 1 All E.R. 1213

The plaintiff, Mr Joscelyne, sought rectification of a written contract made on 18 June 1964, under which he had made over his car hire business to his daughter, Mrs Margaret Nissen. It had been expressly agreed during negotiations that in return for the car hire business Mrs Nissen would pay certain expenses including gas, electricity and coal bills but the agreement on these matters was not expressly incorporated in the written contract. Furthermore, the parties had agreed that no concluded contract was to be regarded as having been made until the signing of a formal written document.

Mrs Nissen failed to pay the bills and the plaintiff brought an action in the Edmonton County Court claiming amongst other things a declaration that Mrs Nissen should pay the gas, electricity and coal bills and alternatively that the written agreement of 18 June 1964 should be rectified to include a provision to that effect. The county court judge allowed the claim for rectification although there was no binding antecedent contract between the parties on the issue of payment of the expenses. The Court of Appeal, after considering different expressions of judicial views upon what was required before a contractual instrument might be rectified by the court, *held* that the law did not require a binding antecedent contract, provided there was some outward expression of agreement between the contracting parties. Rectification could be made even though there was no binding contract until the written agreement which was to be rectified was entered into.

130. *Frederick Rose (London) Ltd* v *William Pim & Co Ltd* [1953] 2 All E.R. 739

The plaintiffs received an order from an Egyptian firm for feveroles (a type of horsebean). The plaintiffs did not know what was meant by feveroles and asked the defendants what they were and whether they could supply them. The defendants said that feveroles were horsebeans and that they could supply them, so the plaintiffs entered into a written agreement to buy horsebeans from the defendants which were then supplied to the Egyptian firm under the order. In fact there were three types of horsebeans: feves, feveroles and fevettes, and the plaintiffs had been supplied with feves, which were less valuable that feveroles. The plaintiffs were sued by the Egyptian firm and now wished to recover the damages they had had to pay from the defendants. In order to do so they had to obtain rectification of the written contract with the defendants in which the goods were described as 'horsebeans'. The word 'horsebeans' had to be rectified to 'feveroles', otherwise the defendants were not in breach. *Held* –

(a) Rectification was not possible because the contract expressed what the parties had agreed to, i.e. to buy and sell horsebeans. Thus the supply of any of the three varieties would have amounted to fulfilment of the contract.

(b) The plaintiffs might have rescinded for misrepresentation but they could not restore the status quo, having sold the beans.

(c) The plaintiffs might have recovered damages for breach of warranty, but the statement that 'feveroles are horsebeans and we can supply them' was oral, and warranties in a contract for the sale of goods of £10 and upwards had in 1953 to be evidenced in writing. This is not the case today.

(d) The defence of mistake was also raised, i.e. both buyer and seller thought that all horsebeans were feveroles. This was an identical bilateral or common mistake, but since it was not a case of *res extincta* or *res sua* it had no effect on the contract.

COMMENT

This case is quite complex on its facts but to put the rule in a simpler context, if A and B orally agreed on the sale of A's drawing of Salisbury Cathedral, thought by A and B to be by John Constable, but in fact by Fred Constable an unknown Victorian artist, and then put that into a written contract, that contract could not be rectified simply because A and B thought that the drawing was by John Constable, because the written contract would be the same as the oral one, as in the above case. The approach is after all logical enough. You cannot sensibly ask the court to make the written agreement conform with the one actually made when it already does!

131. *Thomas Bates & Sons Ltd* v *Wyndham's (Lingerie) Ltd* [1981] 1 All E.R. 1077

The plaintiff granted in 1956 a lease to the defendants with an option for renewal. This lease had a clause under which the rent on renewal was to be agreed by the parties or by arbitration. The option was exercised in 1963 for a seven-year lease, and again in 1970 for a 14-year lease at a rent of £2350 per annum for the first five years and thereafter subject to rent review every five years. This lease, which was drafted by the plaintiffs' managing director, did not contain an arbitration clause. The defendants knew that it did not. At the end of the first five-year period the plaintiffs suggested that a new rent should be agreed. The defendants would not agree and took the view that the rent of £2350 should continue for the whole 14 years unless there was an agreement between the parties to the contrary. Deputy Judge Michael Wheeler QC, sitting in the High Court, ordered rectification and the Court of Appeal affirmed that decision. The clause inserted by the court allowed the rent to be settled by arbitration if the parties did not agree.

COMMENT

At one time it was thought that rectification was available only for a common mistake by both parties. However, as appears from this case, rectification can be given for unilateral mistake. The principles on which it is granted appear in the judgment of Buckley, L.J. who said: 'First, that one party, A, erroneously believed that the document sought to be rectified contained a particular term or provision, or possibly did not contain a particular term or provision, which, mistakenly, it did contain; second that the other party, B, was aware of the omission or the inclusion and that it was due to a mistake on the part of A; third that B has omitted to draw the mistake to the notice of A. And I think there must be a fourth element involved, namely that the mistake must be calculated to benefit B.' The general principle upon which the judgment is based would appear to be one of equitable estoppel.

MUTUAL MISTAKE: EFFECT AT COMMON LAW AND IN EQUITY: THE SENSE OF THE PROMISE

132. *Wood* v *Scarth* (1858) 1 F. & F. 293

The plaintiff was suing for damages for breach of contract alleging that the defendant had entered into an agreement to grant the plaintiff a lease of a public house, but had refused to convey the property. It was shown in evidence that the defendant intended to offer the lease at a rent, and also to include a premium on taking up the lease of £500. The defendant had told his agent to make this clear to the plaintiff, but the agent had not mentioned it. After discussions with the agent the plaintiff wrote to the defendant proposing to take the lease 'on the terms already agreed upon' to which the defendant replied accepting the proposal. There was a mutual or non-identical bilateral mistake. The defendant thought that he was agreeing to lease the premises for a rent plus a premium, and the plaintiff thought he was taking a lease for rental only because he did not know of the premium. The plaintiff had sued for specific performance in 1855, and the court in the exercise of its equitable jurisdiction had decided that specific performance could not be granted in view of the mistake, as to grant it would be unduly hard on the defendant. However, in this action the plaintiff sued at common law for damages, and damages were granted to him on the ground that in mutual or non-identical mistake the court may find the sense of the promise and regard a contract as having been made on these terms. Here it was quite reasonable for the plaintiff to suppose that there was no premium to be paid. Thus a contract came into being on the terms as understood by the plaintiff, and he was entitled to damages for breach of it. The contract clearly identified the agreement made.

> COMMENT
> This case shows that equitable remedies are discretionary and not available as of right as damages at common law are. Also note the benefits of the Judicature Acts, 1873–75. In this case, which pre-dates those Acts, the action for specific performance was brought in Chancery in 1855 and the action at common law for damages in 1858. Common law and equitable remedies could not be granted in one and the same action until the Judicature Acts were passed.

133. *Raffles* v *Wichelhaus* (1864) 2 H.C. 906

The defendants agreed to buy from the plaintiffs 125 bales of cotton to arrive 'ex *Peerless* from Bombay'. There were two ships called *Peerless* sailing from Bombay, one in October and one in December. The defendants thought they were buying the cotton on the ship sailing in October, and the plaintiffs meant to sell the cotton on the ship sailing in December. In fact the plaintiffs had no cotton on the ship sailing in October. The defendants refused to take delivery of the cotton when the second ship arrived and were now sued for breach of contract. *Held* – since there was a mistake as to the subject matter of the contract there was in effect no contract between the parties, or at least no contract which clearly identified the agreement made. The plaintiff's action failed.

Law of contract – reality of consent II

MISREPRESENTATION: EFFECT OF CHANGE OF CIRCUMSTANCES MAKING A STATEMENT UNTRUE

134. *With* v *O'Flanagan* [1936] 1 All E.R. 727

The defendant was a medical practitioner who wished to sell his practice. The plaintiff was interested and in January 1934, the defendant represented to the plaintiff that the income from the practice was £2000 a year. The contract was not signed until May 1934, and in the meantime the defendant had been ill and the practice had been run by various other doctors who substituted for the defendant while he was ill. In consequence the receipts fell to £5 per week, and no mention of this fact was made when the contract was entered into. The plaintiff now claimed rescission of the contract. *Held* – he could do so. The representation made in January was of a continuing nature and induced the contract made in May. The plaintiff had a right to be informed of a change of circumstances, and the defendant's silence amounted to a misrepresentation.

MISREPRESENTATION: STATEMENTS OF INTENTION, OPINION OR BELIEF AS ACTIONABLE STATEMENTS OF FACT

135. *Edgington* v *Fitzmaurice* (1885) 29 Ch. D. 459

The plaintiff was induced to lend money to a company by a representation made by its directors that the money would be used to improve the company's buildings and generally expand the business. In fact the directors intended to use the money to pay off the company's existing debts as the creditors were pressing hard for payment. When the plaintiff discovered that he had been misled, he sued the directors for damages for fraud. The defence was that the statement that they had made was not a statement of a past or present fact but a mere statement of intention which could not be the basis of an action of fraud. *Held* – the directors were liable in deceit. Bowen L.J. said: 'There must be a misstatement of an existing fact: but the state of a man's mind is as much a fact as the state of his digestion. It is true that it is very difficult to prove what the state of a man's mind at a particular time is, but if it can be ascertained, it is as much a fact as anything else. A misrepresentation as to the state of a man's mind is, therefore, a misstatement of fact.'

136. *Smith* v *Land and House Property Corporation* (1884) 28 Ch.D. 7

The plaintiffs put up for sale on 4 August 1882 the Marine Hotel, Walton-on-the-Naze, stating in the particulars that it was let to 'Mr Frederick Fleck (a most desirable tenant) at a rental of £400 for an unexpired term of 27½ years'. The directors of the defendant company sent the Secretary, Mr Lewin, to inspect the property and he reported that Fleck was not doing much business and that the town seemed to be in the last stages of decay. The directors, on receiving this report, directed Mr Lewin to bid up to £5000, and in fact he bought the hotel for £4700. Before completion Fleck became bankrupt and the defendant company refused to complete the purchase, whereupon the plaintiffs sued for specific performance. It was proved that on 1 May 1882 the March quarter's rent was wholly unpaid, that a distress was then threatened, i.e. the landlord was threatening to remove property from the hotel for sale to pay the rent, and that Fleck paid £30 on 6 May, £40 on 13 June, and the remaining £30 shortly before the sale. No part of the June's quarter rent had been paid. The chairman of the defendant company said that the hotel would not have been purchased but for the statement in the particulars that Fleck was a most desirable tenant. *Held* – specific performance would not be granted. The description of Fleck as a most desirable tenant was not a mere expression of opinion, but contained an implied assertion that the vendors knew of no facts leading to the conclusion that he was not. The circumstances relating to the unpaid rent showed that Fleck was not a desirable tenant and there was a misrepresentation. Bowen L.J. said:

> It is material to observe that it is often fallaciously assumed that a statement of opinion cannot involve the statement of a fact. In a case where the facts are equally well known to both parties, what one of them says to the other is frequently nothing but an expression of opinion. The statement of such opinion is in a sense a statement of a fact about the condition of the man's own mind, but only of an irrelevant fact, for it is of no consequence what the opinion is. But if the facts are not equally known to both sides, then a statement of opinion by the one who knows the facts best involves very often a statement of a material fact, for he impliedly states that he knows facts which justify his opinion.

MISREPRESENTATION: MUST INDUCE THE CONTRACT: MATERIALITY

137. *Peek* v *Gurney* (1873) L.R. 6 H.L. 377

Peek purchased shares in a company on the faith of statements appearing in a prospectus issued by the respondents who were directors of the company. Certain statements were false and Peek sued the directors. It appeared that Peek was not an original allottee, but had purchased the shares on the market, though he had relied on the prospectus. *Held* – Peek's action failed because the statements in the prospectus were only intended to mislead the original allottees. Once the statements had induced the public to be original subscribers, their force was spent.

COMMENT
(i) The decision has a somewhat unfortunate effect because at those

times when public issues are over-subscribed it is most likely that persons who did not receive an allotment or an adequate allotment as subscribers will try to purchase further shares within a short time on the Stock Exchange. These people will clearly be relying on the prospectus, but under this decision would have no claim in respect of false statements in it.

(ii) This decision would appear to be quite seriously affected, at least on its own facts, by more recent legislation in the Financial Services Act, 1986. As regards who can sue under an inaccurate prospectus s. 150(1) states: 'any person who has acquired any of the securities in question and suffered loss in respect of them . . .'. This would seem to include all subscribers whether they have relied on the prospectus (or listing particulars) or not. It seems therefore that a subscriber need not be aware of the error or even have seen the listing particulars. The sub-section would also seem to cover subsequent purchasers after the first isssue thus overruling *Peek* v *Gurney* (above), at least on its own facts.

(iii) A claim in tort for damages for negligent misstatement should also be available under *Hedley Byrne* (see P. 652) in that those who publicly advertise a prospectus must surely in the modern context foresee that it will be relied upon by subscribers *and* by those who purchase from subscribers on the stock market for a reasonable time after the issue of the prospectus.

138. *Redgrave* v *Hurd* (1881) 20 Ch.D 1

The plaintiff was a solicitor who wished to take a partner into the business. During negotiations between the plaintiff and Hurd the plaintiff stated that the income of the business was £300 a year. The papers which the plaintiff produced showed that the income was not quite £200 a year, and Hurd asked about the balance. Redgrave then produced further papers which he said showed how the balance was made up, but which only showed a very small amount of income making the total up to about £200. Hurd did not examine these papers in any detail, but agreed to become a partner. Later Hurd discovered the true position and refused to complete the contract. The plaintiff sued for breach and Hurd raised the misrepresentation as a defence, and also counter-claimed for rescission of the contract. *Held* – Hurd had relied on Redgrave's statements regarding the income and the contract could be rescinded. It did not matter that Hurd had the means of discovering their untruth; he was entitled to rely on Redgrave's statement.

COMMENT
Relief is not barred simply because there is an unsuccessful attempt by the person misled to discover the truth where the misrepresentation is fraudulent.

139. *Smith* v *Chadwick* (1884) 9 App. Cas. 187

This action was brought by the plaintiff, who was a steel manufacturer, against Messrs Chadwick, Adamson and Collier, who were accountants and promoters of a company called the Blochairn Iron Co Ltd. The plaintiff claimed £5750 as damages sustained through taking shares in the company which were not worth the price he had paid for them because of certain misrepresentations in the prospectus issued by the defendants. The action was for fraud. Among the misrepresentations alleged by Smith was that the prospectus stated that a Mr J.J. Grieves MP was a director of the company, whereas he had withdrawn his consent the day before the prospectus was issued. *Held* – that the statement regarding Mr Grieves was untrue but was not material to the plaintiff, because the evidence showed that he had never heard of Mr Grieves. His action for damages failed.

MISREPRESENTATION: NEGLIGENT MISREPRESENTATION: PRINCIPAL BUT NOT AGENT LIABLE TO THIRD PARTY FOR AGENT'S NEGLIGENCE

140. *Gosling* v *Anderson*, *The Times*, 8 February 1972

Miss Gosling, a retired schoolmistress, entered into negotiations for the purchase of one of three flats in a house at Minehead owned by Mrs Anderson. Mr Tidbury, who was Mrs Anderson's agent in the negotiations, represented to Miss Gosling by letter that planning permission for a garage to go with the flat had been given. Mrs Anderson knew that this was not so. The purchase of the flat went through on the basis of a contract and a conveyance showing a parking area but not referring to planning permission which was later refused. Miss Gosling now sought damages for misrepresentation under s. 2(1) of the Misrepresentation Act, 1967. *Held* – the facts revealed a negligent representation by Mr Tidbury made without reasonable grounds for believing it to be true. Mrs Anderson was liable for the acts of her agent and must pay damages under the Act of 1967.

COMMENT

(i) This action was against Mrs Anderson who was the other party to the contract. It was decided in *Resolute Maritime Inc and Another* v *Nippon Kaiji Kyokai and Others* [1983] 2 All E.R. 1 that no action is available against an agent such as Mr Tidbury under s. 2(1) of the Misrepresentation Act, 1967. Section 2(1) of the 1967 Act begins: 'Where a person has entered into a contract after a misrepresentation has been made to him by another party thereto . . . ' Thus the sub-section only applies when the representee has entered into a contract after a misrepresentation has been made to him by another party to the contract. Where an agent acting within the scope of his authority makes a representation under s. 2(1), the principal is liable to the third party misled, but not the agent. The agent will be liable to the third party only if he is guilty of fraud, or, under the rule in *Hedley Byrne* v *Heller* (1963) (see p. 652) for negligence at common law. Here the principal will be liable vicariously *along with the agent* for the latter's fraud or negligence if the agent is acting within the scope of his authority.

(ii) As regards proving reasonable grounds, an expert will be expected to verify his statements in a professional way. However, those without relevant technical knowledge will often find that the court will accept a statement as made innocently if the maker of the statement had been induced to purchase the goods himself by the same statement.

Thus in *Humming Bird Motors* v *Hobbs* [1986] R.T.R. 276 H was a young man whom the judge found to be an amateur doing a bit of 'wheeling and dealing' in the motor trade. He bought a car from a dealer who told him that the mileage recorded, 34,900 miles, was correct. H sold the car on to the plaintiffs making the same statement, i.e. that the recorded mileage was, to the best of his knowledge and belief, correct. The plaintiffs discovered that the vehicle had done 80,000 miles and tried to claim damages for negligent misrepresentation. The Court of Appeal decided that H was not negligent; he was an amateur and was merely repeating what he himself believed.

MISREPRESENTATION: FRAUD: DEFINITION AND BURDEN OF PROOF

141. *Derry* v *Peek* (1889) 14 App. Cas. 337

The Plymouth, Devonport and District Tramways Company had power under a special Act of Parliament to run trams by animal power, and with the consent of the Board of Trade (now the Department of Trade and Industry) by mechanical or steam power. Derry and the other appellants were directors of the company and issued a prospectus, inviting the public to apply for shares in it, stating that they had power to run trams by steam power, and claiming that considerable economies would result. The directors had assumed that the permission of the Board of Trade would be granted as a matter of course, but in the event the Board of Trade refused permission except for certain parts of the tramway. As a result the company was wound up and the directors were sued for fraud. The court decided that the directors were not fraudulent but honestly believed the statement in the prospectus to be true. As Lord Herschell said: 'Fraud is proved when it is shown that a false representation had been made (a) knowingly, or (b) without belief in its truth, or (c) recklessly, careless whether it be true or false.'

COMMENT

(i) This case gave rise to the Directors' Liability Act, 1890 which made directors of companies liable to pay compensation for negligent misrepresentation in a prospectus, subject to a number of defences. The latest provisions are in the Financial Services Act, 1986 (see p. 649).

(ii) It will be noticed from this case that the mere fact that no grounds exist for believing a false statement does not of itself constitute fraud. There must also be an element of dishonesty which was not present in this case.

(iii) Fraud is the most difficult of all the forms of misrepresentation to prove. It must be proved beyond a reasonable doubt which is the criminal standard. The civil standard is proof on a balance of probabilities.

MISREPRESENTATION: THE CONTRIBUTION OF THE TORT OF NEGLIGENCE

142. *Hedley Byrne & Co Ltd* v *Heller & Partners Ltd* [1963] 2 All E.R. 575

The appellants were advertising agents and the respondents were merchant bankers. The appellants had a client called Easipower Ltd who was a customer of the respondents. The appellants had contracted to place orders for advertising Easipower's products on television and in newspapers, and since this involved giving Easipower credit, they asked the respondents, who were Easipower's bankers, for a reference as to the creditworthiness of Easipower. The respondents said that Easipower Ltd was respectfully constituted and considered good, although they said in regard to the credit: 'These are bigger figures than we have seen' and also that the reference was 'given in confidence and without responsibility on our part'. Relying on this reply, the appellants placed orders for advertising time and space for Easipower Ltd, and the appellants assumed personal responsibility for payment to the television and newspaper companies concerned. Easipower Ltd went into liquidation and the appellants lost over £17,000 on the advertising contracts. The appellants sued the respondents for the amount of the loss, alleging that the respondents had not informed themselves sufficiently about Easipower Ltd before writing the statement, and were therefore liable in negligence. *Held* – in the present case the respondents' disclaimer was adequate to exclude the assumption by them of the legal duty of care, but, in the absence of the disclaimer, the circumstances would have given rise to a duty of care in spite of the absence of a contract or fiduciary relationship.

COMMENT
(i) The House of Lords stated that the duty of care arose where there was 'a special relationship' requiring care. This arises where the defendant has special knowledge and/or expertise and offers information in the full *knowledge* that it will be relied upon by the plaintiff. (For further developments in professional liability see p. 448.)

(ii) The ease with which the duty to take care placed upon the bank was excluded in this case by the disclaimer was disappointing. However, such a disclaimer of negligence liability would, these days, have to satisfy the test of 'reasonableness' under the Unfair Contract Terms Act, 1977 (see p. 295). It would seem that such a disclaimer would fall short of the reasonable expectations of those in business who naturally and reasonably expect that a bank will have taken proper care before giving a reference of this kind.

(iii) In this connection it was held in *Smith* v *Eric S. Bush* [1987] 3 All E.R. 179 that it was unreasonable to allow a surveyor to rely on a general disclaimer of negligence where he had been asked by a building society to carry out a reasonably careful visual inspection of the property for valuation purposes (paid for by the would-be purchaser) when the valuer knew that the purchaser would be likely to rely on his report and not get another one. The house was purchased but, because of defects, turned out to be unfit for habitation. The surveyors when sued could not escape liability for damages on the basis of disclaimer.

The case suggests that in so far as such disclaimers are still used by professional persons they may not be effective, at least as regards ordinary consumers of professional services.

MISREPRESENTATION: LOSS OF THE RIGHT TO RESCIND

143. *Long* v *Lloyd* [1958] 2 All E.R. 402

The plaintiff and the defendant were haulage contractors. The plaintiff was induced to buy the defendant's lorry by the defendant's misrepresentation as to condition and performance. The defendant advertised a lorry for sale at £850, the advertisement describing the vehicle as being in 'exceptional condition'. The plaintiff telephoned the defendant the same evening when the defendant agreed that his advertisement was a little ambiguous and said that the lorry was 'in first class condition'. The plaintiff saw the lorry at the defendant's premises at Hampton Court on a Saturday. During a trial run on the following Monday the plaintiff found that the speedometer was not working, a spring was missing from the accelerator pedal, and it was difficult to engage top gear. The defendant said there was nothing wrong with the vehicle except what the plaintiff had found. He also said at this stage that the lorry would do eleven miles to the gallon.

The plaintiff purchased the lorry for £750, paying £375 down and agreeing to pay the balance at a later date. He then drove the lorry from Hampton Court to his place of business at Sevenoaks. On the following Wednesday, the plaintiff drove from Sevenoaks to Rochester to pick up a load, and during that journey the dynamo ceased to function, an oil seal was leaking badly, there was a crack in one of the road wheels, and he used eight gallons of petrol on a journey of forty miles. That evening the plaintiff told the defendant of the defects, and the defendant offered to pay half the cost of a reconstructed dynamo, but denied any knowledge of the other defects. The plaintiff accepted the offer and the dynamo was fitted straightaway. On Thursday the lorry was driven by the plaintiff's brother to Middlesbrough, and it broke down on the Friday night. The plaintiff, on learning of this, asked the defendant for his money back, but the defendant would not give it to him. The lorry was subsequently examined and an expert said that it was not roadworthy. The plaintiff sued for rescission. *Held* – at first instance, by Glyn-Jones, J. – that the defendant's statements about the lorry were innocent and not fraudulent because the evidence showed that the lorry had been laid up for a month and it might have deteriorated without the defendant's precise knowledge. The Court of Appeal affirmed this finding of fact and made the following additional points.

(a) The journey to Rochester was not affirmation because the plaintiff was merely testing the vehicle in a working capacity.

(b) However, the acceptance by the plaintiff of the defendant's offer to pay half the cost of the reconstructed dynamo, and the subsequent journey to

Middlesbrough, did amount to affirmation, and rescission could not be granted to the plaintiff.

> COMMENT
> (i) Damages could now be obtained for negligent misrepresentation under the Misrepresentation Act, 1967, s. 2(1), for how could the seller say he had reasonable grounds for believing that the lorry was in exceptional condition or first class condition?
>
> (ii) It seems remarkable that Glyn-Jones, J. did not find fraud. However, fraud must be proved according to the criminal standard, i.e. beyond a reasonable doubt, and not according to the civil standard which is on balance of probabilities. Fraud is therefore difficult to prove and in this case there was presumably a reasonable doubt in the mind of the judge on the issue of fraud.
>
> (iii) The Court of Appeal would not accept that the statement that the lorry was in first class condition was a term of the contract (see further p. 267) but decided that it was only a misrepresentation.

144. *Clarke* v *Dickson* (1858) 27 L.J.Q.B. 223

In 1853 the plaintiff was induced by the misrepresentation of the three defendants, Dickson, Williams and Gibbs, to invest money in what was in effect a partnership to work lead mines in Wales. In 1857 the partnership was in financial difficulty and with the plaintiff's assent it was converted into a limited company and the partnership capital was converted into shares. Shortly afterwards the company commenced winding-up proceedings and the plaintiff, on discovery of the falsity of the representations, asked for rescission of the contract. *Held* – rescission could not be granted because capital in a partnership is not the same as shares in a company. The firm was no longer in existence, having been replaced by the company, and it was not possible to restore the parties to their original positions.

> COMMENT
> It should be noted that in addition to the problem of restoration, third-party rights, i.e. creditors, had accrued on the winding-up of the company and this is a further bar to rescission.

CONTRACTS OF UTMOST GOOD FAITH: INSURANCE: EFFECT OF CONTRACTUAL CLAUSES

145. *Dawsons Ltd* v *Bonnin* [1922] 2 A.C. 413

Dawsons Ltd insured their motor lorry against loss by fire with Bonnin and others, and signed a proposal form which contained the following as Condition 4: 'Material misstatement or concealment of any circumstances by the insured material to assessing the premium herein, or in connection with any claim shall render the policy void.' The policy also contained a clause saying that the 'proposal shall be the basis of the contract and shall be held as incorporated therein'. Actually the proposal form was filled up by an insurance agent, and although he stated the proposer's address correctly as 46 Cadogan Street, Glasgow, he also stated that the vehicle would usually be garaged there, although there was no garage accommodation at the Cadogan Street address and the lorry was garaged elsewhere. Dawsons' secretary, who signed the proposal, overlooked this slip made by the agent. The lorry was destroyed by fire and Dawsons claimed under the policy. *Held* – on appeal, by the House of Lords – the statement was not material within the meaning of Condition 4. However, the basis clause was an independent provision, and since the statement, though not material, was untrue, the policy was void for breach of condition. Viscount Cave said: 'The meaning and effect of the basis clause, taken by itself, is that any untrue statement in the proposal, or any breach of its promissory clauses, shall avoid the policy, and if that be the contract of the parties, the question of materiality has not to be considered.'

COMMENT

(i) The Unfair Contract Terms Act, 1977 does not apply to contracts of insurance. This resulted from a deal between the insurance companies and the government under which the insurance companies agreed to abide by voluntary statements of practice. These have no legal effect but some moral force. If the insurance company follows these statements of practice then certainly in consumer, i.e. non-business, insurance the worst effect of the basis clause (which is what they are called) should be eliminated.

(ii) However, even if we get rid of the basis clause problem, the rules of disclosure of material matters by the person seeking insurance remains a difficulty. It is based upon s. 18(2) of the Marine Insurance Act, 1906. This should not have been used as a basis for *all* insurances. Those seeking marine insurance are well aware of the risks they seek to insure. Those seeking, for example, domestic fire insurance are not. The Law Commission Report entitled *Non-Disclosure and Breach of Warranty* places a heavy burden on insurance companies to phrase their questions so as to elicit the kind and amount of information they want and not to leave it, as at present, to the person seeking insurance to make uninformed guesses as to what might be material to the insurers. The common law has already taken steps in this direction in *Hair* v *Prudential Assurance* [1983] 2 Lloyd's Rep. 667, the court deciding in that case that if a person seeking insurance answered honestly all the questions put to him by the proposal for insurance he should not be required to disclose any other matters. The questions should reveal all material issues.

FIDUCIARY RELATIONSHIPS: THE DUTY TO DISCLOSE

146. *Gordon* v *Gordon* (1819) 3 Swan 400

Two brothers made an agreement for division of the family estates. The elder supposed he was born before the marriage of his parents and was therefore illegitimate. The younger knew that their parents had been married before the birth of the elder brother and the elder brother was therefore legitimate and his father's heir. He did not communicate this information to his elder brother. Nineteen years afterwards the elder brother discovered that he was legitimate and the agreement was set aside following this action brought by him. He would have had no case if at the time of the agreement both brothers had been in honest error as to the date of their parents' marriage.

DURESS: EFFECT UPON CONTRACTS

147. *Welch* v *Cheesman* (1973) 229 E.G. 99

Mrs Welch lived with the defendant, C, for many years in a house which she owned. C was a man given to violence, and after he threatened her Mrs Welch sold the house to him for £300. C died and his widow claimed the house which was worth about £3000. Mrs Welch brought this action to set aside the sale of the house to C on the grounds of duress and she succeeded.

UNDUE INFLUENCE: SITUATIONS IN WHICH PRESUMED: SPECIAL RELATIONSHIPS

148. *Lancashire Loans Ltd* v *Black* [1934] 1 K.B. 380

A daughter married at 18 and went to live with her husband. Her mother was an extravagant woman and was in debt to a firm of moneylenders. When the daughter became of age, her mother persuaded her to raise £2000 on a property in which the daughter had an interest, and this was used to pay off the mother's debt. Twelve months later the mother and daughter signed a joint and several promissory note of £775 at 85% interest in favour of the moneylenders, and the daughter created a further charge on her property in order that the mother might borrow more money. The daughter did not understand the nature of the transaction, and the only advice she received was from a solicitor acting for the mother and the moneylenders. The moneylenders brought this action against the mother and daughter on the note. *Held* – the daughter's defence that she was under the undue influence of her mother succeeded, in spite of the fact that she was of full age and married with her own home.

149. *Allcard* v *Skinner* (1887) 36 Ch.D. 145

In 1868 the plaintiff joined a Protestant institution called the sisterhood of St Mary at the Cross, promising to devote her property to the service of the poor. The defendant Miss Skinner was the Lady Superior of the Sisterhood. In 1871 the plaintiff ceased to be a novice and became a sister in the order, taking her vows of poverty, chastity and obedience. By this time she had left her home and was residing with the sisterhood. The plaintiff remained a sister until 1878 and, in compliance with the vow of poverty, she had by then given property to the value of £7000 to the defendant. The plaintiff left the order in 1879 and became a Roman Catholic. Of the property she had transferred,

£1671 remained in 1885 and the plaintiff sought to recover this sum, claiming that it had been transferred in circumstances of undue influence. *Held* – the gifts had been made under pressure of an unusually persuasive nature, particularly since the plaintiff was prevented from seeking outside advice under a rule of the sisterhood which said, 'Let no sister seek the advice of any extern without the superior's leave.' However, the plaintiff's claim was barred by her delay because, although the influence was removed in 1879, she did not bring her action until 1885.

PRESUMPTION OF UNDUE INFLUENCE: OTHER CATEGORIES

150. *Hodgson* v *Marks* [1970] 3 All E.R. 513

Mrs Hodgson, who was a widow of 83, owned a freehold house in which she lived. In 1959 she took in a Mr Evans as a lodger. She soon came to trust Evans and allowed him to manage her financial affairs. In June 1960, she transferred the house to Evans, her sole reason for so doing being to prevent her nephew from turning Evans out of the house. It was orally agreed between Mrs Hodgson and Evans that the house was to remain hers although held in the name of Evans. Evans later made arrangements to sell the house without the knowledge or consent of Mrs Hodgson. The house was bought by Mr Marks and Mrs Hodgson now asked for a declaration that he was bound to transfer the property back to her. The following questions arose:

(a) whether Evans held the house in trust for Mrs Hodgson. It was *held* – by Ungoed-Thomas, J. – that he did. The absence of written evidence of trust as required by s. 53 of the Law of Property Act, 1925 was not a bar to Mrs Hodgson's claim. The section does not apply to implied trusts of this kind;

(b) whether Evans had exercised undue influence. It was *held* that he had and that a presumption of undue influence was raised. Although the parties were not in the established categories, Evans had a relationship of trust and confidence with Mrs Hodgson of a kind which raised a presumption of undue influence.

However, Mrs Hodgson lost the case because Mr Marks was protected by s. 70 of the Land Registration Act, 1925, which gives rights to a purchaser of property for value in respect of interests in that property of which the purchaser is not aware. In this case Mr Marks bought the house from Mr Evans, the house being in the name of Evans and he had no reason to suppose that Mrs Hodgson had any interest in it.

COMMENT
(i) Mrs Hodgson's appeal to the Court of Appeal in 1971 succeeded and she got her house back, the court holding that in spite of s. 70 a purchaser must pay heed to the possibility of rights in all *occupiers*. Mrs Hodgson was obviously in occupation with Mr Evans and inquiries should have been made by the purchaser as to her rights in the property.

(ii) The application of the presumption in a relationship which was not one of the established ones is also illustrated by *Goldsworthy v Brickell* [1987] 1 All E.R. 853, where a contract to grant a tenancy of a farm advantageous to the defendant in that, for example, it did not allow the landlord, G, to make any rent increases, was set aside. The defendant, B, who had become the tenant, was a neighbour of G's. G was 85 and had come to rely implicitly on the advice of B. Undue influence was presumed although neighbours are not within the established categories where undue influence is generally presumed.

UNCONSCIONABLE BARGAINS: PROTECTION AGAINST IMPROPER PRESSURE AND INEQUALITY OF BARGAINING POWER

151. *Lloyds Bank v Bundy* [1974] 3 All E.R. 757

The defendant and his son's company both banked with the plaintiffs, the defendant having been a customer for many years. The company's affairs deteriorated over a period of years and at the son's suggestion the bank's assistant manager visited the defendant and said that the bank could not continue to support an overdraft for the company unless the defendant entered into a guarantee of the account. The defendant received no independent advice, nor did the bank's assistant manager suggest that he should do so. The defendant charged his house as security for the overdraft and shortly afterwards the company went into receivership. The bank obtained possession of the house from the defendant in the county court, where the assistant branch manager in evidence said that he thought that the defendant had relied upon him implicitly to advise him about the charge.

The defendant appealed to the Court of Appeal in an attempt to set aside the guarantee and the security and it was *held* – allowing the defendant's appeal – that in the particular circumstances a special relationship existed between the defendant and the bank's assistant manager, as agent for the bank, and the bank was in breach of its duty of fiduciary care in procuring the charge which would be set aside for undue influence. The defendant, without any benefit to himself, had signed away his sole remaining asset without taking independent advice.

COMMENT
(i) While the majority of the Court of Appeal (Cairns, L.J. and Sir Eric Sachs) were content to decide that appeal on the conventional ground that a fiduciary relationship existed between the bank and its customer, which is to suggest that a new fiduciary relationship has come into being, Lord Denning took the opportunity to break new ground by deciding that in addition to avoiding the contract on the grounds of fiduciary relationship, Mr Bundy could also have done so on the basis of 'inequality of bargaining power'. Although inequality of bargaining power obviously includes undue influence, Lord Denning made it clear that the principle does not depend on the will of one party being dominated or overcome by the other. This is clear from that part of the

judgment where he says: 'One who is in extreme need may knowingly consent to a most improvident bargain, solely to relieve the straits in which he finds himself.' This approach is, of course, at variance with the traditional view of undue influence which was that it was based on dominance resulting in an inferior party being unable to exercise independent judgment or on a relationship of trust and confidence.

(ii) It should be noted that cases such as this which introduce into the law a requirement that a contract must be fair may eventually develop to the point where adequacy of consideration is required in contract. This is not the case at the present time.

(iii) In *National Westminster Bank plc* v *Morgan* [1983] 3 All E.R. 85 the Court of Appeal set aside a charge over a wife's share in the matrimonial home after she executed it without legal advice in order to secure a loan from the bank to clear a building society mortgage, and after the bank manager had assured her that the charge would not be used to secure her husband's business advances, whereas it did in fact extend to such advances. However, the bank had no intention of using the charge other than to secure the advance to clear the building society mortagage; nor did it.

The above decision, which moved in the direction of saying that banks would have to ensure that all their customers had independent legal advice before taking out a bank mortgage was reversed by the House of Lords in *National Westminster Bank plc* v *Morgan* [1985] 1 All E.R. 821. Undue influence, the House of Lords said, was the use by one person of a power over another person to take a certain course of action generally to his or her disadvantage. A bank manager need not advise independent legal advice in a situation such as this. The manager in this case had stuck to explaining the legal effect of the charge which, though erroneous as to the terms of the charge, correctly represented his intention and that of the bank. The security represented no disadvantage to Mrs Morgan. It was exactly what she wanted to clear the building society loan on her home. The House of Lords also rejected the view that a court would grant relief where there was merely an inequality of bargaining power. Their Lordships rejected that view which was expressed by Lord Denning in *Bundy*. The courts will not, said the House of Lords, protect persons against what they regard as a mistake merely because of inequality of bargaining power. This is a much harder line.

(iv) In *Bundy*, therefore, the Court of Appeal *held* that the bank in not advising the person giving the security to get independent advice exercised undue influence and for this reason set the security aside. In *Morgan* the House of Lords *held* that no presumption of undue influence existed. In *Cornish* v *Midland Bank* [1985] 3 All E.R. 513 the Court of Appeal decided that the proper way to deal with these cases was not through undue influence but by using the law of negligence, though only where the bank had given wrong advice.

In *Cornish* the plaintiff had signed a second mortgage on a farmhouse jointly owned with her husband in order to secure £2000 which her husband had borrowed from the bank. She did so because the bank clerk involved said that the mortgage was like a building society mortgage. It was not because unlike a building society mortgage it covered all future borrowing by the husband. The bank later tried to enforce the security. Eventually the Court of Appeal *held* that the bank was liable in negligence for the wrong advice of its clerk who made a negligent misstatement causing damage, i.e. that £2000 was the borrowing limit when it was not. The mortgage was not set aside for undue influence so that the bank was entitled to the proceeds of the sale of the farmhouse but had to pay the plaintiff £11,231 damages plus interest for negligence. Thus, although it would be good practice for a bank to advise independent advice, it is not necessary for it to do so. The security will be good and there is no presumption of undue influence. However, if an employee of the bank *actually* gives negligent advice or fails to explain the consequences of the charge and/or fails to advise the taking of independent advice (see *Midland Bank plc* v *Perry*, *The Times*, 28 May 1987), the bank will be able to enforce the security but will be liable in damages under the ruling in *Hedley Byrne* v *Heller & Partners* (1963) (see p. 652).

Law of contract – contractual terms

REPRESENTATIONS AND TERMS DISTINGUISHED

152. *Bannerman* v *White* (1861) 10 C.B. (N.S.) 844

The defendant was intending to buy hops from the plaintiff and he asked the plaintiff whether sulphur had been used in the cultivation of the hops, adding that if it had he would not even bother to ask the price, by which he meant he would not make the contract. The plaintiff said that no sulphur had been used, though in fact it had. It was *held* that the plaintiff's assurance that sulphur had not been used was a term of the contract and the defendant was justified in raising the matter as a successful defence to an action for the price.

153. *Oscar Chess Ltd* v *Williams* [1957] 1 All E.R. 325

In May 1955, Williams bought a car from the plaintiffs on hire-purchase terms. The plaintiffs took Williams' Morris car in part exchange. Williams described the car as a 1948 model and produced the registration book, which showed that the car was first registered in April 1948, and that there had been several owners since that time. Williams was allowed £290 on the Morris. Eight months later the plaintiffs discovered that the Morris car was a 1939 model there being no change in appearance in the model between 1939 and 1948. The allowance for a 1939 model was £175 and the plaintiffs sued for £115 damages for breach of warranty that the car was a 1948 model. Evidence showed that some fraudulent person had altered the registration book but he could not be traced, and that Williams honestly believed that the car was a 1948 model. *Held* – the contract might have been set aside in equity for misrepresentation but the delay of eight months defeated this remedy. This mistake was a mistake of quality which did not avoid the contract at common law and in order to obtain damages the plaintiffs must prove a breach of warranty. The court was unable to find that Williams was in a position to give such a warranty, and suggested that the plaintiffs should have taken the engine and chassis number and written to the manufacturers, so using their superior knowledge to protect themselves in the matter. The plaintiffs were not entitled to any redress. Morris, L.J. dissented, holding that the statement that the car was a 1948 model was a fundamental condition.

COMMENT
(i) No doubt Mr Williams would have been liable for innocent and not negligent misrepresentation under the Misrepresentation Act, 1967 for he had reasonable grounds to believe that the car was a 1948 Morris. He was merely repeating an earlier deception made when he bought the vehicle.

(ii) Since the remedy of rescission had been lost by reason of delay the court would not even now grant that remedy or damages at the court's discretion, which the court can do but only if the remedy of rescission is still available. The reluctance of the court to say that statements by non-dealers are contractual terms for breach of which damages can be recovered leads to an unfair result as in this case. After all, Mr Williams obtained £115 more for his Morris than it was worth.

(iii) A contrast is provided by *Dick Bentley Productions Ltd* v *Harold Smith (Motors) Ltd* [1965] 2 All E.R. 65 where a dealer sold a Bentley to a customer, the instruments showing that it had done only 30,000 miles since a replacement engine was fitted when in fact it had done 100,000 miles since that time. The seller was held liable for breach of condition whereas in *Oscar Chess* the seller who was not a dealer was not.

CONDITIONS AND WARRANTIES DISTINGUISHED

154. *Poussard* v *Spiers and Pond* (1876) 1 Q.B.D. 410

Madame Poussard had entered into an agreement to play a part in an opera, the first performance to take place on 28 November 1874. On 23 November Madame Poussard was taken ill and was unable to appear until 4 December. The defendants had hired a substitute, and discovered that the only way in which they could secure a substitute to take Madame Poussard's place was to offer that person the complete engagement. This they had done, and they refused the services of Madame Poussard when she presented herself on 4 December. The plaintiff now sued for breach of contract. *Held* – the failure of Madame Poussard to perform the contract as from the first night was a breach of condition, and the defendants were within their rights in regarding the contract as discharged.

COMMENT
This case merely illustrates the availability of repudiation for serious breach of contract. Madame Poussard was not liable to pay damages

for breach because unlike the defendants in *Gill & Duffus SA* (see p. 264) she could not help the breach, the contract being also frustrated (see p. 327).

155. *Bettini* v *Gye* (1876) 1 Q.B.D. 183

The plaintiff was an opera singer. The defendant was the director of the Royal Italian Opera in London. The plaintiff had agreed to sing in Great Britain in theatres, halls and drawing rooms for a period of time commencing on 30 March 1875, and to be in London for rehearsals six days before the engagement began. The plaintiff was taken ill and arrived on 28 March 1875, but the defendant would not accept the plaintiff's services, treating the contract as discharged. *Held* – the rehearsal clause was subsidiary to the main purpose of the contract, and its breach constituted a breach of warranty only. The defendant had no right to treat the contract as discharged and must compensate the plaintiff, but he had a counterclaim for any damage he had suffered by the plaintiff's late arrival.

> COMMENT
> This case is also concerned with the availability of repudiation and the court decided that the breach was not sufficiently serious. The court suggested that if Gye wanted redress he should cross-claim for damages against Bettini. If and when he did and there is no report suggesting that he did, the matter of Bettini's illness excusing his breach would have had to be raised. Presumably it would have been a defence even though in this case the contract was not discharged by frustration.

INTERMEDIATE OR INNOMINATE TERMS

156. *Cehave NV* v *Bremer Handelsgesellschaft mbH The Hansa Nord* [1975] 3 All E.R. 739

The defendants sold citrus pulp pellets to the plaintiffs. A term of the contract was 'shipment to be made in good condition'. The goods were not delivered all at once but in consignments, and when a particular consignment arrived at Rotterdam the market price of the goods had fallen and it was found that 1260 tons of the goods out of a total consignment of 3293 tons was damaged. The plaintiffs rejected the whole cargo on the grounds that the shipment was not made in good condition. They then claimed the recovery of the price which amounted to £100,000. In the event, a middle man bought the goods at the price of £33,720 and resold them to the plaintiffs at the same price. The plaintiffs then used the pellets for making cattle food as was the original intention. The total result of the transaction, if it had been left that way, was that the plaintiffs had received goods which they had bought for £100,000 for the reduced price of £33,720. The Court of Appeal decided in favour of the sellers. The court *held* that the contractual term 'shipment to be made in good condition' was not a contractual condition but was an intermediate or innominate term. As Lord Denning, M.R. said: 'If a small portion of the whole cargo was not in good condition and arrived a little unsound, it should be met by a price allowance. The buyers should not have the right to reject the whole cargo unless it was serious or substantial.'

COMMENT
This intermediate or innominate term approach was endorsed by the House of Lords in *Reardon Smith Line* v *Hansen-Tangen* [1976] 3 All E.R. 570.

CONTRACTUAL TERMS: TERMS IMPLIED BY CUSTOM

157. *Hutton* v *Warren* (1836) 150 E.R. 517

The plaintiff was the tenant of a farm and the defendant the landlord. At Michaelmas 1833, the defendant gave the plaintiff notice to quit on the Lady Day following. The defendant insisted that the plaintiff should cultivate the land during the period of notice which he did. The plaintiff now asked for a fair allowance for seeds and labour of which he had had no benefit having left the farm before harvest. It was proved that by custom a tenant was bound to farm for the whole of his tenancy and on quitting was entitled to a fair allowance for seeds and labour. *Held* – the plaintiff succeeded.

We are of opinion that this custom was, by implication, imported into the lease. It has long been settled, that in commercial transactions, extrinsic evidence of custom and usage is admissible to annex incidents to written contracts in matters with respect to which they are silent. The same rule has also been applied to contracts in other transactions of life, in which known usages have been established and prevailed; and this has been done upon the principle of presumption that, in such transactions, the parties did not mean to express in writing the whole of the contract by which they intended to be bound, but to contract with reference to those known usages (per Parke B).

COMMENT
Michaelmas Day is 29 September and is a quarter day for payment of rent as well as a Christian feast. Lady Day is 25 March. It is also a quarter day for the payment of rent and is so called because it is a Christian feast.

JUDICIAL IMPLIED TERMS

158. *The Moorcock* (1889) 14 P.D. 64

The appellants in this case were in possession of a wharf and a jetty extending into the River Thames, and the respondent was the owner of the steamship *Moorcock*. In November 1887, the appellants and the respondents agreed that the ship should be discharged and loaded at the wharf and for that purpose should be moored alongside the jetty. Both parties realised that when the tide was out the ship would rest on the river bed. In the event the *Moorcock* sustained damage when she ceased to be waterborne owing to the centre of the vessel settling on a ridge of hard ground beneath the mud. There was no evidence that the appellants had given any warranty that the place was safe for the ship to lie in, but it was *held* – by the Court of Appeal – that there was an implied warranty by the appellants to this effect, for breach of which they were liable in damages. Per Bowen, L.J.:

> Now, an implied warranty, or as it is called, a covenant in law, as distinguished from an express contract or express warranty, really is in all cases founded on the presumed intention of the parties, and upon reason. The implication which the law draws from what must obviously have been the intention of the parties, the law draws with the object of giving efficacy to the transaction and preventing such a failure of consideration as cannot have been within the contemplation of either side; and I believe if one were to take all cases, and they are many, of implied warranties or covenants in law, it will be found that in all of them the law is raising an implication from the presumed intention of the parties with the object of giving to the transaction such efficacy as both parties must have intended that at all events it should have. In business transactions such as this, what the law desires to effect by the implication is to give such business efficacy to the transaction as must have been intended at all events by both parties who are business men; not to impose on one side all the perils of the transaction, or to emancipate one side from all chances of failure, but to make each party promise in law as much, at all events, as it must have been in the contemplation of both parties that he should be responsible for in respect of those perils or chances.

COMMENT

(i) This statement of the law is to the effect that the court cannot imply a term because it is reasonable to do so but only when it is commercially necessary to do so. Lord Denning, particularly, in *Liverpool City Council v Irwin* [1977] (see p. 269) put forward the view that the court could imply a term whenever it was reasonable to do so even if it was not necessary to do so to make the contract work in a commercial sense. This view is still not entirely accepted by the judiciary in general.

(ii) Although the court most often implies covenants or terms which are *positive*, i.e. the party concerned *has to do something*, *negative* covenants can be implied. Thus in *Fraser v Thames Television Ltd* [1983] 2 All E.R. 101 the members of a group called Rock Bottom brought an action alleging that Thames had broken an agreement with them about a TV series, an implied term of which was that Thames would not use the idea for the series, which was based on the history of the group and its subsequent struggles, unless the members of the group were employed as actresses in the series. Hirst, J. implied this negative term on the grounds that it was necessary to give business efficacy to the agreement between the parties.

STATUTORY IMPLIED TERM: SELLER'S RIGHT TO SELL

159. *Rowland* v *Divall* [1923] 2 K.B. 500

In April 1922, the defendant bought an 'Albert' motor car from a man who had stolen it from the true owner. One month later the plaintiff, a dealer, purchased the car from the defendant for £334, repainted it, and sold it for £400 to Colonel Railsdon. In September 1922, the police seized the car from Colonel Railsdon and the plaintiff repaid him the £400. The plaintiff now sued the defendant for £334 on the grounds that there had been a total failure of consideration since the plaintiff had not obtained a title to the car. *Held* – the defendant was in breach of s. 12 of the Sale of Goods Act, which implies conditions and warranties into a sale of goods relating to the seller's right to sell, and there had been a total failure of consideration in spite of the fact that the car had been used by the plaintiff and his purchaser. The plaintiff contracted for the property in the car and not the mere right to possess it. Since he had not obtained the property, he was entitled to recover the sum of £334 and no deductions should be made for the period of use.

COMMENT
(i) Although the court purported to deal with this case as a breach of s. 12(1) of the Act, it would appear that in fact they operated on common-law principles and gave complete restitution of the purchase price because of total failure of consideration arising out of the seller's lack of title. The condition under s. 12(1) had by reason of the plaintiff's use of the car and the passage of time become a warranty when the action was brought, and if the court had been awarding damages for breach of warranty it would have had to reduce the sum of £334 by a sum representing the value to the plaintiff of the use of the vehicle which he had had.

(ii) The drawback to making an allowance to the seller for use is that he gets an allowance for a car which is not his and the owner might sue the buyer in damages for conversion so that he would have to pay an allowance and damages to the true owner in conversion. In other words pay for use twice.

(iii) It is also relevant to say that the court felt an allowance for use should not be made because the plaintiff had paid the price for the car to become its *owner*, and not merely to have *use* of it. So why should he be subject to an allowance for use when that is not what he wanted or bargained for? As Bankes, L.J. said: 'he did not get what he paid for – namely a car to which he would have title.'

160. *Niblett Ltd* v *Confectioners' Materials Co Ltd* [1921] 3 K.B. 387

The defendants agreed to sell to the plaintiffs 3000 cases of condensed milk to be shipped from New York to London. 1000 cases bore labels with the word 'Nissly' on them. This came to the notice of the Nestlé Company and they suggested that this was an infringement of their registered trade mark. The plaintiffs admitted this and gave an undertaking not to sell the milk under the title of 'Nissly'. They tried to dispose of the goods in various ways but eventually discovered that the only way to deal with the goods was to take off the labels and sell the milk without mark or label, thus incurring loss. *Held* – by the Court of Appeal – that the sellers were in breach of the implied condition set out in s. 12(1) of the Sale of Goods Act. A person who can sell goods only by infringing a trade mark has no right to sell, even though he may be the owner of the goods. Atkin, L.J. also found the sellers to be in breach of the warranty under s. 12(2) because the buyer had not enjoyed quiet possession of the goods.

SALE BY DESCRIPTION: S. 13, SALE OF GOODS ACT, 1979 APPLIED

161. *Beale* v *Taylor* [1967] 3 All E.R. 253

The defendant advertised a car for sale as being a 1961 Triumph Herald 1200 and he believed this description to be correct. The plaintiff answered the advertisement and later visited the defendant to inspect the car. During his inspection he noticed, on the rear of the car, a metal disc with the figure 1200 on it. The plaintiff purchased the car, paying the agreed price. However, he later discovered that the car was made up of the rear of a 1961 Triumph Herald 1200 welded to the front of an earlier Triumph Herald 948. The welding was unsatisfactory and the car was unroadworthy. *Held* – by the Court of Appeal – that the plaintiff's claim for damages for breach of the condition implied in the contract by s. 13 of the Sale of Goods Act succeeded. The plaintiff had relied on the advertisement and on the metal disc on the rear and the sale was one by description even though the plaintiff had seen and inspected the vehicle.

COMMENT
It is, however, necessary for the buyer to show that it was the intention of the parties that the description should be relied upon by the buyer. In *Harlingdon Ltd* v *Hull Fine Art Ltd* [1990] 1 All E.R. 737 Hull were a firm of art dealers controlled by Mr Christopher Hull. They were asked to sell two oil paintings described as being by Münter, a German artist of the Impressionist School. Mr Hull had no knowledge of the German Impressionist School. He contacted Harlingdon who were art dealers specialising in that field. Mr Hull told them that the paintings were by Münter. Harlingdon sent an expert to examine the paintings and at this stage Mr Hull made it clear that he was not an expert in the field. Following the inspection Harlingdon bought one of the paintings which turned out to be a forgery. Harlingdon sued for breach of s. 13. It was *held* by the Court of Appeal that the claim failed. Harlingdon had not relied on the description of the painting. They bought it after a proper and expert examination. The 'description' had not therefore become an essential term or condition of the contract.

It should be noted that this matter was not raised in *Leaf* v *International Galleries* (1950) (see p. 641) because Mr Leaf did not claim a breach of s. 13. Presumably if he had done so he would have been required to show that it was the intention of the parties that he should rely on the description that the painting was by John Constable. This will normally be fairly easy to prove where the purchaser is an inexpert consumer. However, it was held in *Cavendish-Woodhouse* v *Manley* (1984) 82 L.G.R. 376 that a seller could show that the sale was not by description by using such phrases as 'Sold as seen' or 'Bought as seen'. Such phrases do not, however, avoid the conditions of fitness and merchantable quality.

SECTION 13 APPLIES TO PACKAGING

162. *Moore & Co* v *Landauer & Co.* [1921] 2 K.B. 519

The plaintiffs entered into a contract to sell the defendants a certain quantity of Australian canned fruit, the goods to be packed in cases containing 30 tins each. The goods were to be shipped 'per S.S. *Toromeo*'. The ship was delayed by strikes at Melbourne and in South Africa, and was very late in arriving at London. When the goods were discharged about one-half of the consignment was packed in cases containing 24 tins only, instead of 30, and the buyers refused to accept them. *Held* – although the method of packing made no difference to the market value of the goods, the sale was by description under s. 13 of the Sale of Goods Act, and the description had not been complied with. Consequently the buyers were entitled to reject the whole consignment.

FITNESS FOR THE PURPOSE: NO NEED TO REVEAL A USUAL PURPOSE BUT A SPECIAL PURPOSE MUST BE DISCLOSED

163. *Priest* v *Last* [1903] 2 K.B. 148

The plaintiff, a draper who had no special knowledge of hot-water bottles, bought such a bottle from the defendant who was a chemist. It was in the ordinary course of the defendant's business to sell hot-water bottles and the plaintiff asked him whether the indiarubber bottle he was shown would stand boiling water. He was told that it would not, but it would stand hot water. The plaintiff did not state the purpose for which the bottle was required. In the event the bottle was filled with hot water and used by the plaintiff's wife for bodily application to relieve cramp. On the fifth time of using, the bottle burst and the wife was severely scalded. Evidence showed that the bottle was not fit for use as a hot-water bottle. *Held* – the plaintiff was entitled to recover the expenses he had incurred in the treatment of his wife's injuries for the defendant's breach of s. 14(3) of the Sale of Goods Act. The circumstances showed that the plaintiff had relied on the defendant's skill and judgment, and although he had not mentioned the purpose for which he required the bottle, he had in fact used it for the usual and obvious purpose.

COMMENT
There was no question of the wife suing the chemist under Sale of Goods legislation because she was not a party to the contract. She could today

have sued the manufacturer or the chemist in *negligence* (see *Dononhue v Stevenson* (1932), p. 725) if she could have proved negligence in either of them. An action against the manufacturers could now be brought under the Consumer Protection Act, 1987 even where negligence cannot be proved (see further p. 446).

164. *Griffiths v Peter Conway Ltd* [1939] 1 All E.R. 685

The defendants who were retail tailors, supplied the plaintiff with a Harris tweed coat which was made to order for her. The plaintiff wore the coat for a short time and then developed dermatitis. She brought this action for damages alleging that the defendants were in breach of s. 14(3) of the Sale of Goods Act because the coat was not fit for the purpose for which it was bought. Evidence showed that the plaintiff had an abnormally sensitive skin and that the coat would not have affected the skin of a normal person. *Held* – the plaintiff failed because s. 14(3) did not apply. The defendants did not know of the plaintiff's abnormality and could not be expected to assume that it existed.

COMMENT
A claim against the manufacturer of the tweed under the Consumer Protection Act, 1987 is not appropriate here. Although the Act does not require negligence to be proved it is necessary to prove causation and the effective cause here was the plaintiff's sensitive skin not the coat.

FITNESS FOR THE PURPOSE: RELIANCE ON THE SELLER'S SKILL AND JUDGMENT READILY INFERRED UNLESS THE SELLER IS KNOWN TO SELL ONLY ONE BRAND OF GOODS

165. *Grant v Australian Knitting Mills Ltd* [1936] A.C. 85

This was an appeal from the High Court of Australia to the Privy Council in England by a Dr Grant of Adelaide, South Australia. Dr Grant bought a pair of long woollen underpants from a retailer, the respondents being the manufacturers. The underpants contained an excess of sulphite which was a chemical used in their manufacture. This chemical should have been eliminated before the product was finished, but a quantity was left in the underpants purchased by Dr Grant. After wearing the pants for a day or two, a rash, which turned out to be dermatitis, appeared on the appellant's ankles and soon became generalised, compelling the appellant to spend many months in hospital. He sued the retailers and the manufacturers for damages. *Held* – (a) The retailers were in breach of the South Australian Sale of Goods Act, 1895 (which is in the same terms as the English Act of 1979). They were liable under s. 14(3) because the article was not fit for the purpose. They were liable under s. 14(2) because the article was not of merchantable quality. (b) The manufacturers were liable in negligence, following *Donoghue v Stevenson* (see p. 725). This was a latent defect which could not have been discovered by a reasonable examination. It should also be noted that the appellant had a perfectly normal skin. (Compare *Griffiths v Peter Conway Ltd* (1939) above.)

COMMENT

(i) Section 13 (sale by description) also applied even though this was a sale of a specific object which was seen by the purchaser. On the issue of reliance Lord Wright said: 'the reliance will be in general inferred from the fact that a buyer goes to the shop in confidence that the tradesman has selected his stock with skill and judgment'.

(ii) This case provides an interesting contrast between the liability of the supplier who was liable although not negligent, Sale of Goods Act liability being *strict*, and the liability of the manufacturer where the plaintiff was put to the extra burden of proving the manfacturer negligent. (But see now Consumer Protection Act, 1987 at p. 446.)

166. *Wren* v *Holt* [1903] 1 K.B. 610

The plaintiff was a builder's labourer at Blackburn, and the defendant was the tenant of a beerhouse in the same town. The beerhouse was a tied house so that the defendant was obliged to sell beer brewed by a firm called Richard Holden Limited. The plaintiff was a regular customer and knew that the beerhouse was a tied house, and that only one type of beer was supplied. The plaintiff became ill and it was established that his illness was caused by arsenical poisoning due to the beer supplied to him. He now sued the tenant. *Held* – there was no claim under s. 14(3) because the plaintiff could not have relied on the defendant's skill and judgment in selecting his stock, because he was bound to supply Holden's beer. However, s. 14(2) applied, and since the beer was not of merchantable quality, the plaintiff was entitled to recover damages.

FITNESS: SECOND-HAND GOODS: WHERE DEFECTS OCCUR FAIRLY QUICKLY AFTER SALE

167. *Crowther* v *Shannon Motor Company* [1975] 1 All E.R. 139

The plaintiff, relying on the skill and judgment of the defendants, bought a second-hand car from them. After being driven for over 2000 miles in the three weeks after the sale the engine seized and had to be replaced. In his evidence the previous owner said that the engine was not fit for use on the road when he sold it to the defendants and on that basis the Court of Appeal *held* that there was a breach of s. 14(3) at the time of resale. The fact that a car does not go for a reasonable time after sale is evidence that the car was not fit for the purpose at the time of sale.

FITNESS AND MERCHANTABLE QUALITY: S. 14(3) CAN OPERATE INDEPENDENTLY

168. *Baldry* v *Marshall* [1925] 1 K.B. 260

The plaintiff was the owner of a Talbot racing car and was anxious to change it for a touring car because his wife refused to ride in the Talbot. The plaintiff wrote to the defendants asking for details of the Bugatti car for which they were agents. The plaintiff knew nothing of the Bugatti range, but asked for a car that would be comfortable and suitable for touring purposes. The defendants' manager said that a Bugatti would be suitable. The plaintiff later inspected a Bugatti chassis and agreed to buy it when a body had been put on it. When the car was delivered it was to all intents and purposes a racing car and not suitable for touring. The plaintiff returned the car, but he had paid £1000 under the contract and now sued for its return on the grounds that the defendants were in breach of s. 14(3) of the Sale of Goods Act, the car not being fit for the purpose. *Held* – the plaintiff had relied on the skill and judgment of the defendants and it was in the course of their business to supply cars. Therefore, there was a breach of s. 14(3).

COMMENT
It will be appreciated that the Bugatti was superbly merchantable!

RESALE PRICE HAS SOME BEARING UPON MERCHANTABILITY

169. *B.S. Brown & Son Ltd* v *Craiks Ltd* [1970] 1 All E.R. 823

Brown and Son ordered a quantity of cloth from Craiks who were manufacturers. Brown's wanted it for making dresses but did not make this purpose known to Craiks who thought the cloth was wanted for industrial use. The price paid by Brown's was 36.25p per yard, which was higher than the normal price for industrial cloth but not substantially so. The cloth was not suitable for making dresses and Brown's cancelled the contract and claimed damages. Both parties were left with substantial quantities of cloth but Craiks had managed to sell some of their stock for 30p per yard. Having failed in the lower court to establish a claim under s. 14(3) since they had not made the purpose known to Craiks, Brown's now sued for damages under s. 14(2). *Held* – by the House of Lords – that the claim failed. The cloth was still commercially saleable for industrial purposes though at a slightly lower price. It was not a necessary requirement of merchantability that there should be no difference between purchase and resale price. If the difference was substantial, however, it might indicate that the goods were not of merchantable quality. The difference in this case was not so material as to justify any such inference.

COMMENT
Even where the goods are not purchased for resale the purchase price may be relevant. Thus the sale of a car with a defective clutch would be sale of unmerchantable goods but if the seller makes an allowance in the price to cover the defect it may not be (*Bartlett* v *Sydney Marcus Ltd* [1965] 2 All E.R. 753).

IMPLIED TERMS RELATING TO FITNESS AND MERCHANTABILITY: ITEMS SUPPLIED WITH THE GOODS

170. *Geddling* v *Marsh* [1920] 1 K.B. 668

The defendants were manufacturers of mineral waters and they supplied the same to the plaintiff who kept a small general store. The bottles were returnable when empty. One of the bottles was defective, and whilst the plaintiff was putting it back into a crate, it burst and injured her. *Held* – even though the bottles were returnable, they were supplied under a contract of sale within s. 14 of the Sale of Goods Act. The fact that the bottles were only bailed to the plaintiff was immaterial. There was an implied warranty of fitness for the purpose for which they were supplied, and the defendant was liable in damages.

COMMENT
Bray, J. was careful to point out that his decision was an interpretation of s. 14 of the Sale of Goods Act only. It does not decide that the liability of a bailor is the same as that of a vendor.

171. *Wilson* v *Rickett, Cockerell & Co Ltd* [1954] 1 Q.B. 598

The plaintiff, a housewife, ordered from the defendants, who were coal merchants, a ton of 'Coalite'. The Coalite was delivered and when part of it was put on a fire in an open grate, it exploded causing damage to the plaintiff's house. In this action the plaintiff claimed damages for breach of s. 14 of the Sale of Goods Act. The County Court judge found that the explosion was not due to the Coalite but to something else, possibly a piece of coal with explosive embedded in it, which had got mixed with the Coalite in transit and had not come from the manufacturers of the Coalite. Therefore, he held that s. 14(3) applied only to the Coalite and dismissed the action since the Coalite itself was fit for the purpose. The Court of Appeal, however, in allowing the appeal, pointed out that fuel of this kind is not sold by the lump but by the bag, and a bag containing explosive materials is, as a unit, not fit for burning. The explosive matter was 'goods supplied under the contract' for the purposes of s. 14 and clearly s. 14(2) applied, because the goods supplied were not of merchantable quality. Damages were awarded to the plaintiff. Regarding the applicability of what is now s. 14(3), the Court of Appeal did not think this applied since the sale was under a trade name, and the plaintiff had not relied on the defendant's skill and judgment in selecting a fuel.

COMMENT
The assumption of no reliance where goods are purchased under a trade name no longer applies under the 1979 Act.

172. *Wormell* v *R.H.M. Agriculture (East) Ltd* [1986] 1 All E.R. 769

Mr Wormell, who was an experienced arable farmer, was unable by reason of cold, wet weather to spray his winter wheat crop to kill wild oats until much later than usual in the spring of 1983. He asked the defendants to recommend the best wild-oat killer which could be used later than normal. The agricultural chemical manager recommended a particular herbicide and Mr Wormell bought £6438 worth of it.

The instructions on the cans stated that it ought not to be applied beyond the recommended stage of crop growth. It was said that damage could occur to crops sprayed after that stage and the herbicide would give the best level of wild-oat control at the latest stage of application consistent with the growth of the crop.

Mr Wormell felt that the need to kill the wild oats was so important that he would risk some damage to the crops by applying the herbicide quite late. From his understanding of the instructions the risk was not that the herbicide would not be effective on the wild oats, but if the spray was used after the recommended time then the crop might be damaged. The herbicide was applied but proved to be largely ineffective.

Mr Wormell claimed damages for breach of contract in respect of the sale of the herbicide. He alleged that it was not of merchantable quality contrary to s. 14(2) of the Sale of Goods Act, nor was it fit for the purpose for which it was supplied, namely to control weeds, and in particular, wild oats, contrary to s. 14(3) of the same Act.

R.H.M. argued that since the herbicide would kill the wild oats, the fact that the instructions caused it to be applied at a time when it was not effective did not make the herbicide itself unmerchantable or unfit for the purpose.

Piers Ashworth QC sitting as a Deputy Judge of the High Court, said that one had to look at how Mr Wormell understood the instructions and how a reasonable user would understand them. Mr Wormell understood the instructions to mean that the herbicide would be effective if it was sprayed at any time, but if sprayed late there was a risk of crop damage. The judge concluded that a reasonable farmer would have understood the instructions in the same way. He thought that the instructions were consequently misleading.

For the purposes of the Sale of Goods Act 'goods' included the container and packaging for the goods and any instructions supplied with them. If the instructions were wrong or misleading the goods would not be of merchantable quality or fit for the purpose for which they were supplied under s. 14(2) and (3). This statement was approved in a 1987 appeal to the Court of Appeal though on the facts the court found the instructions adequate.

COMMENT
It may be that manufacturers look upon instructions for use of the product as merely an aspect of marketing. However, this case shows that there is a legal obligation to give adequate guidance as to how the product is to be used.

RETAILER DOES NOT WARRANT SAFETY OF GOODS USED BY THE BUYER AFTER BUYER KNOWS OF THEIR DEFECTS

173. *Lambert* v *Lewis* [1981] 1 All E.R. 1185

Mr Lewis owned a Land Rover and a trailer. His employee, Mr Larkin, was driving it when the trailer broke away. It collided with a car coming from the opposite direction. Mr Lambert, who was driving that car, was killed and so was his son. His wife and daughter, who were also passengers, survived and then sued Mr Lewis for damages in negligence. He joined the retailer who sold him the towing hitch which had become detached from the trailer and was basically the cause of the collision. The retailer was sued under s. 14 (goods not fit for the purpose nor of merchantable quality). The court found that the towing hitch was badly designed and a securing brass spindle and handle had come off it so that only dirt was keeping the towing pin in position. It had been like that for some months and Mr Lewis had coupled and uncoupled the trailer once or twice a week during that time and knew of the problem.

The plaintiffs succeeded in their action against Mr Lewis. He failed in his claim against the retailer. The House of Lords decided that when a person first buys goods he can rely on s. 14. However, once he discovers that they are defective but continues to use them and so causes injury, he is personally liable for the loss caused. He cannot claim an indemnity under s. 14 from the retailer. The chain of causation is broken by the buyer's continued use of the goods while knowing that they are faulty and may cause injury.

> COMMENT
>
> The above summary does not concern itself with the possible liability of the manfacturers in terms of the design problem. However, a point of interest arises in connection with it. The issue of the manufacturers' liability was taken by an action in negligence. The court refused to construe a collateral contract between Mr Lewis and the manufacturers although he bought the hitch on the strength of the manufacturers' advertising. (Compare *Carlill*, p. 587 where such a contract was rather exceptionally construed.)

SALE BY SAMPLE: WHAT IS A REASONABLE EXAMINATION?

174. *Godley* v *Perry* [1960] 1 All E.R. 36

The first defendant, Perry, was a newsagent who also sold toys, and in particular displayed plastic toy catapults in his window. The plaintiff, who was a boy aged six, bought one for 6d. While using it to fire a stone, the catapult broke and the plaintiff was struck in the eye, either by a piece of the catapult or the stone, and as a result he lost his left eye. The chemist's report given in evidence was that the catapults were made from cheap material unsuitable for the purpose and likely to fracture, and that the moulding of the plastic was poor, the catapults containing internal voids. Perry had purchased the catapults from a wholesaler with whom he had dealt for some time, and this sale was by sample, the defendant's wife examining the sample catapult by pulling the elastic. The wholesaler's supplier was another wholesaler who had imported the catapults from Hong Kong. This sale was also by sample and the sample catapult was again tested by pulling the elastic. In this action the plaintiff alleged that the first defendant was in breach of the conditions implied by s. 14(2) and (3) of the Sale of Goods Act.

The first defendant brought in his supplier as third party, alleging against him a breach of the conditions implied by s. 15(2)(c), and the third party brought in his supplier as fourth party, alleging breach of s. 15(2)(c) against him. *Held* –

(a) The first defendant was in breach of s. 14(2) and (3) because:
 (i) the catapult was not reasonably fit for the purpose for which it was required. The plaintiff relied on the seller's skill or judgment, this being readily inferred where the customer was of tender years (s. 14(3));
 (ii) the catapult was not merchantable (s. 14(2)).

(b) The third and fourth parties were both in breach of s. 15(2)(c) because the catapult had a defect which rendered it unmerchantable, and this defect was not apparent on reasonable examination of the sample. The test applied, i.e. the pulling of the elastic, was all that could be expected of a potential purchaser. The third and fourth parties had done business before, and the third party was entitled to regard without suspicion any sample shown to him and to rely on the fourth party's skill in selecting his goods.

Law of contract – exclusion clauses

EXCLUSION CLAUSES: THE EFFECT OF SIGNING A DOCUMENT CONTAINING SUCH A CLAUSE: EFFECT OF MISREPRESENTATION AS TO CONTENTS

175. *L'Estrange* v *Graucob (F.)* [1934] 2 K.B. 394

The defendant sold to the plaintiff, Miss L'Estrange, who owned a cafe in Llandudno, a cigarette slot machine, inserting in the sales agreement the following clause: 'Any express or implied condition, statement or warranty, statutory or otherwise, is hereby excluded.' The plaintiff signed the agreement but did not read the relevant clause, apparently because she thought it was merely an order form, and she now sued in respect of the unsatisfactory nature of the machine supplied which often jammed and soon became unusable. *Held* – the clause was binding on her, although the defendants made no attempt to read the document to her nor call her attention to the clause. 'Where a document containing contractual terms is signed, then in the absence of fraud, or I will add, misrepresentation, the party signing it is bound, and it is wholly immaterial whether he had read the document or not' (per Scrutton, L.J.).

COMMENT
The ruling in this case would appear to apply even where the party signing cannot understand the document as where the signer cannot read or does not understand the language in which the document is written (*The Luna* [1920] P. 22). This would not, of course, apply if the person relying on the clause *knew* that the other party could not read (*Geir* v *Kujawa* [1971] Lloyd's Rep. 364). It will, of course, be realised that s. 6(3) of the Unfair Contract Terms Act, 1977 would now apply so that the clause could only be effective if reasonable.

176. *Curtis* v *Chemical Cleaning and Dyeing Co* [1951] 1 All E.R. 631

The plaintiff took a wedding dress, with beads and sequins, to the defendant's shop for cleaning. She was asked to sign a receipt which contained the following clause: 'This article is accepted on condition that the company is not liable for any damage howsoever arising.' The plaintiff said in evidence: 'When I was asked to sign the document I asked why? The assistant said I was to accept any responsibility for damage to beads and sequins. I did not read it all before I signed it.' The dress was returned stained, and the plaintiff sued for damages. The company relied on the clause. *Held* – the company could not rely on the clause because the assistant had misrepresented the effect of the document so that the plaintiff was merely running the risk of damage to the beads and sequins.

COMMUNICATION OF EXCLUSION CLAUSES: IN CONTRACTUAL AND NON-CONTRACTUAL DOCUMENTS

177. *Thompson* v *L.M.S. Railway* [1930] 1 K.B. 41

Thompson, who could not read, asked her niece to buy her an excursion ticket to Manchester from Darwin and back, on the front of which was printed the words, 'Excursion. For conditions see back'. On the back was a notice that the ticket was issued subject to the conditions in the company's timetables, which excluded liability for injury however caused. Thompson was injured and claimed damages. *Held* – her action failed. She had constructive notice of the conditions which had, in the court's view, been properly communicated to the ordinary passenger.

> COMMENT
> (i) The railway ticket was regarded as a contractual document. (Contrast *Chapelton* below.)
> (ii) The injuries, which were caused when the train on returning to Darwin at 10 pm did not draw all the way into the station so that the plaintiff fell down a ramp, would not have been the subject of an action at law today because the Unfair Contract Terms Act, 1977 outlaws exclusion clauses relating to death and personal injury. Thus, on its own facts, this case is of historical interest only, though still relevant on the question of constructive notice.

178. *Chapelton* v *Barry Urban District Council* [1940] 1 All E.R. 356

The plaintiff Chapelton wished to hire deck-chairs and went to a pile owned by the defendants, behind which was a notice stating: 'Hire of chairs 2d per session of three hours'. The plaintiff took two chairs, paid for them, and received two tickets which he put into his pocket after merely glancing at them. One of the chairs collapsed and he was injured. A notice on the back of the ticket provided that: 'The council will not be liable for any accident or damage arising from hire of chairs'. The plaintiff sued for damages and the council sought to rely on the clause in the ticket. *Held* – the clause was not binding on Chapelton. The board by the chairs made no attempt to limit the liability, and it was unreasonable to communicate conditions by means of a mere receipt.

COMMENT
The defendants would now have had to face an additional problem, i.e. was the clause reasonable?

EXCLUSION CLAUSE: COMMUNICATION AT OR BEFORE THE CONTRACT ESSENTIAL

179. *Olley* v *Marlborough Court Ltd* [1949] 1 All E.R. 127

A husband and wife arrived at a hotel as guests and paid for a room in advance. They went up to the room allotted to them; on one of the walls was the following notice: 'The proprietors will not hold themselves responsible for articles lost or stolen unless handed to the manageress for safe custody.' The wife closed the self-locking door of the bedroom and took the key downstairs to the reception desk. There was inadequate and therefore negligent staff supervision of the keyboard. A third party took the key and stole certain of the wife's furs. In the ensuing action the defendants sought to rely on the notice as a term of the contract. *Held* – the contract was completed at the reception desk and no subsequent notices could affect the plaintiff's rights.

COMMENT
(i) It was said in *Spurling* v *Bradshaw* [1956] 1 W.L.R. 461 that if the husband and wife had seen the notice on a previous visit to the hotel it would have been binding on them, though this is by no means certain in view of cases such as *Hollier* (see p. 292) which suggest that in consumer transactions previous dealings are not necessarily incorporated unless perhaps the dealings have been frequent.
(ii) A further illustration is provided by *Thornton* v *Shoe Lane Parking Ltd* [1971] 1 All E.R. 686 where the Court of Appeal decided that the conditions exempting the company from certain liabilities on a ticket issued by an automatic barrier at the entrance to a car park were communicated too late. The contract was made when the plaintiff put his car on the place which activated the barrier. This was before the ticket was issued.

EXCLUSION CLAUSE: INEFFECTIVE WHERE THERE IS AN EXPRESS UNDERTAKING RUNNING CONTRARY TO THE CLAUSE

180. *J. Evans & Sons (Portsmouth) Ltd* v *Andrea Merzario Ltd* [1976] 2 All E.R. 930

The plaintiffs imported machines from Italy. They had contracted with the defendants since about 1959 for the transport of these machines. Before the defendants went over to the use of containers the plaintiffs' machines had always been crated and carried under deck. When the defendants went over to containers they orally agreed with the plaintiffs that the plaintiffs' goods would still be carried under deck. However, on a particular occasion a machine being transported for the plaintiffs was carried in a container on deck. At the start of the voyage the ship met a swell which caused the container to fall off the deck and the machine was lost. The contract was expressed to be subject to the printed standard conditions of the forwarding trade which contained an exemption clause excusing the defendants from liability for loss or damage to the goods unless the damage occurred whilst the goods were in their actual custody and by reason of their wilful neglect or default, and even in those circumstances, the clause limited the defendants' liability for loss or damage to a fixed amount. The plaintiffs claimed damages against the defendants for loss of the machine alleging that the exemption clause did not apply. It was *held* by the Court of Appeal that it did not apply. The printed conditions were repugnant to the oral promise for, if they were applicable, they would render that promise illusory. Accordingly, the oral promise was to be treated as overriding the printed conditions and the plaintiffs' claim succeeded, the exemption clause being inapplicable.

COMMENT
The court may also regard these oral promises as collateral contracts (see also p. 607), i.e. in this case a collateral contract to carry the machine under deck, that collateral contract not having an exclusion clause in it.

EXCLUSION CLAUSE: OVERCOMING THE PRIVITY RULE

181. *The New Zealand Shipping Co Ltd* v *A.M. Satterthwaite & Co Ltd* [1974] 1 All E.R. 1015

In this case the makers of an expensive drilling machine entered into a contract for the carriage of the machine by sea to New Zealand. The contract of carriage (the bill of lading) exempted the carriers from full liability for any loss or damage to the machine during carriage and also purported to exempt any servant or agent of the carrier, including independent contractors employed from time to time by the carrier. The machine was damaged by the defendants, who were stevedores, in the course of unloading, and the question to be decided was whether the defendant stevedores, who had been employed by the carrier to unload the machine, could take advantage of the exemption clause in the bill of lading since they were not parties to the contract. It was decided by the Privy Council that they could. The stevedores provided consideration and so became parties to the contract when they unloaded the machine. (*Carlill* v *Carbolic Smoke Ball Co* (1893) (see p. 587) applied.) The performance of services by the stevedores in discharging the cargo was sufficient consideration to constitute a contract, even though they were already under an obligation to the carrier to perform those services because the actual performance of an outstanding contractual obligation was sufficient to support the promise of an exemption from liability given by the makers of the drill to the shippers, who were in effect, third parties to the contract between the carrier and the stevedores. (*Shadwell* v *Shadwell* (1860) at p. 613 applied.)

COMMENT

It is not easy to see when and where the relevant offers and acceptances were made in this case, but as we have already noted, a court can construe a contract from the circumstances without a precise application of the offer and acceptance formula (see *Rayfield* v *Hands* (1958) at p. 607).

AN AMBIGUOUS EXCLUSION CLAUSE IS CONSTRUED AGAINST THE PARTY WHO PUT IT IN THE CONTRACT

182. *Alexander* v *Railway Executive* [1951] 2 All E.R. 442

Alexander was a magician who had been on a tour together with an assistant. He left three trunks at the parcels office at Launceston station, the trunks containing various properties which were used in an 'escape illusion'. The plaintiff paid 5d for each trunk deposited and received a ticket for each one. He then left saying that he would send instructions for their dispatch. Some weeks after the deposit and before the plaintiff had sent instructions for the dispatch of the trunks, the plaintiff's assistant persuaded the clerk in the parcels office to give him access to the trunks, though he was not in possession of the ticket. The assistant took away several of the properties and was later convicted of larceny. The plaintiff sued the defendants for damages for breach of contract, and the defendants pleaded the following term which was contained in the ticket and which stated that the Railway Executive was 'not liable for loss mis-delivery or damage to any articles where the value was in excess of £5 unless at the time of the deposit the true value and nature of the goods was declared by the depositor and an extra charge paid'. No such declaration or payment had been made. *Held* – the plaintiff succeeded because, although sufficient notice had been given constructively to the plaintiff of the term, the term did not protect the defendants because they were guilty of a breach of a fundamental obligation in allowing the trunks to be opened and things to be removed from them by an unauthorised person.

COMMENT

(i) Devlin, J. said that a deliberate delivery to the wrong person did not fall within the meaning of 'mis-delivery', and this may be regarded as the real reason for the decision, as it involved the application of the *contra proferentem* rule.

(ii) Note also that the receipt or ticket for the goods deposited was held to be a contractual document. (Contrast *Chapelton* at p. 675.)

RULES OF CONSTRUCTION: REPUGNANCY AND THE FOUR CORNERS RULE

183. *Pollock* v *Macrae* [1922] S.C. (H.L.) 192

The defendants entered into a contract to build and supply marine engines. The contract had an exclusion clause which was designed to protect them from liability for defective materials and workmanship. The engines supplied under the contract had so many defects that they could not be used. The House of Lords struck out the exclusion clause as repugnant to the main purpose of the contract which was to build and supply workable engines. The plaintiff's claim for damages was allowed to proceed.

184. *Thomas National Transport (Melbourne) Pty Ltd and Pay* v *May and Baker (Australia) Pty Ltd* [1966] 2 Lloyd's Rep. 347

The owners of certain packages containing drugs and chemicals made a contract with carriers under which the packages were to be carried from Melbourne to various places in Australia. The carriers employed a subcontractor to collect the parcels and take them to the carriers' depot in Melbourne. When the subcontractor arrived late at the Melbourne depot it was locked and so he drove the lorry full of packages to his own house and left it in a garage there. This was in accordance with the carriers' instructions to their subcontractors in the event of late arrival at the depot. There was a fire and some of the packages were destroyed. The cause of the fire was unknown. However, the alleged negligence of the carriers consisted in their instruction to the subcontractors to take the goods home. The court said it was unthinkable that valuable goods worth many thousands of pounds should be kept overnight at a driver's house, regardless of any provision for their safety. The owners sued the carriers who pleaded an exemption clause in the contract of carriage. *Held* – by the High Court of Australia – that the plaintiffs succeeded. There had been a fundamental breach of contract. The intention of the parties was that the goods would be taken to the carriers' depot and not to the subcontractor's house, in which case the carriers could not rely on the clause.

> COMMENT
> The decision, which was partly based on fundamental breach of contract (see below), is perhaps better founded on the four corners rule, i.e. the exclusion clause is available only so long as the contract is being performed in accordance with its terms.

EXCLUSION CLAUSES: NO RULE OF FUNDAMENTAL BREACH

185. *Photo Production Ltd* v *Securicor Transport Ltd* [1980] 1 All E.R. 556

The plaintiff company had contracted with the defendant security company for the defendant to provide security services at the plaintiff's factory. A person employed by the defendant lit a fire in the plaintiff's premises while he was carrying out a night patrol. The fire got out of control and burned down the factory. The trial judge was unable to establish from the evidence precisely what the motive was for lighting the fire – it may have been deliberate or merely careless. The defendant relied on an exclusion clause in the contract which read:

> Under no circumstances shall the company (Securicor) be responsible for any injurious act or default by any employee of the company unless such act or default could have been foreseen and avoided by the exercise of due diligence on the part of the company as his employer. . . .

It was accepted that Securicor were not negligent in employing the person who lit the fire. He came to them with good references and there was no reason for them to suppose that he would act as he did. It was *held* by the House of Lords that the exclusion clause applied so that Securicor were not liable. All the judges in the House of Lords were unanimous in the view that there was no rule of law by which exclusion clauses became inapplicable to fundamental breach of contract, which this admittedly was. Although the Unfair Contract Terms Act, 1977 was not in force at the time this action was brought and therefore could not be applied to the facts of this case, the existence of the Act and its relevance was referred to by Lord Wilberforce who said that the doctrine of fundamental breach had been useful in its time as a device for avoiding injustice. He then went on to say:

> But . . . Parliament has taken a hand; it has passed the Unfair Contract Terms Act 1977. This Act applies to consumer contracts and those based on standard terms and enables exception clauses to be applied with regard to what is just and reasonable. It is significant that Parliament refrained from legislating over the whole field of contract. After this Act, in commercial matters generally, when the parties are not of unequal bargaining power, and when risks are normally borne by insurance . . . there is everything to be said . . . for leaving the parties free to apportion the risks as they think fit. . . .

COMMENT

(i) In *Harbutt's Plasticine Ltd* v *Wayne Tank & Pump Co Ltd* [1970] 1 All E.R. 225 Lord Denning accepted that the principle which said that no exclusion clause could excuse a fundamental breach was not a rule of law when the injured party carried on with (or affirmed) the contract. Where this was so rules of construction must be used and the exclusion clause might have to be applied. However, if the injured party elected to repudiate the contract for fundamental breach and, as it were, pushed the contract away, the exclusion clause went with it and could never apply to prevent the injured party from suing for the breach. The same, he said, was true where the consequences were so disastrous (as they were in *Photo Production*) that one could assume that the injured party had elected to repudiate. The *Photo Production* case overrules *Harbutt*, as does s. 9(1) of the Unfair Contract Terms Act, 1977. This provides that if a clause, as a matter of construction, is found to cover the breach and if it satisfies the reasonableness test, it can apply and be relied on by the party in breach, even though the contract has been terminated by express election or assumed election following the disastrous results of the breach.

(ii) The House of Lords also allowed a *Securicor* exemption clause to apply in circumstances of fundamental breach in *Ailsa Craig Fishing Co Ltd* v *Malvern Fishing Co Ltd* [1983] 1 All E.R. 101. In that case the appellants' ship sank while berthed in Aberdeen harbour. It fouled the vessel next to it which was owned by Malvern. The appellants sued Malvern. Securicor were the second defendants. Securicor had a contract with the appellants to protect the ship. The accident happened as a result of a rising tide. At the time the Securicor patrolman had left his post to become involved in New Year celebrations. Although there were arguments by counsel to the contrary, the House of Lords *held* that the exclusion clause covered the circumstances of the case provided the words were given their natural and plain meaning. It therefore applied to limit the liability of Securicor and the appellants failed to recover all their loss.

(iii) The Unfair Contract Terms Act, 1977 gives its strongest protection to those who deal as consumers. The contracts in *Photo Productions* and *Ailsa Craig* were non-consumer contracts where both parties were in business. It by no means follows that in a consumer transaction (see below) the court would have allowed a defendant to rely on a 'Securicor' type of clause. It might well be regarded as unreasonable in that context.

EXCLUSION OF INDUCEMENT LIABILITY: REASONABLENESS

186. *Walker* v *Boyle* [1982] 1 All E.R. 634

The vendor of a house was asked in a pre-contract enquiry whether the boundaries of the land were the subject of any dispute. The vendor asked her husband to deal with the enquiries. He said that there were no disputes. There were, in fact, disputes but the husband did not regard them as valid because he believed that he was in the right and his view could not be contradicted. His answers were nevertheless wrong and misleading. Contracts were later exchanged. These contracts were on the National Conditions of Sale (19th Edition) produced under the aegis of the Law Society. Condition 17(1) excluded liability for misleading replies to preliminary enquiries. The purchaser later heard of the boundary disputes and claimed in the High Court for rescission of the contract and the return of his deposit. Dillon, J. held that condition 17(1) did not satisfy the requirements of reasonableness as set out in s. 3 of the Misrepresentation Act, 1967 (as substituted by s. 8(1) of the Unfair Contract Terms Act, 1977). The plaintiff therefore succeeded.

COMMENT
(i) The National Conditions of Sale have been revised and as regards

misrepresentation, the contract now only attempts a total exclusion of the purchaser's remedies if the misrepresentation is not material or substantial in terms of its effect and is not made recklessly or fraudulently.

(ii) The provisions relating to inducement liability were also applied in *South Western General Property Co Ltd* v *Marton*, *The Times*, 11 May 1982; the court *held* that conditions of sale in an auction catalogue which tried to exclude liability for any representations made, if these were incorrect, were not fair and reasonable. The defendant had relied upon a false statement that some building would be allowed on land which he bought at an auction, even though the facts were that the local authority would be most unlikely to allow any building on the land. The clauses excluding liability for misrepresentation did not apply and the contract could be rescinded.

EXCLUSION CLAUSES AND REASONABLENESS

187. *Mitchell (George) (Chesterhall) Ltd* v *Finney Lock Seeds Ltd* [1983] 1 All E.R. 108

This case is a landmark. It was the last case heard by Lord Denning in the Court of Appeal. In it he gave a review of the development of the law relating to exclusion clauses in his usual clear and concise way. The report is well worth reading in full. Only a summary of the main points can be given here.

George Mitchell ordered 30lb of cabbage seed and Finney supplied it. The seed was defective. The cabbages had no heart; their leaves turned in. The seed cost £192 but Mitchell's loss was some £61,000, i.e. a year's production from the 63 acres planted. Mitchell carried no insurance. When sued Finney defended the claim on the basis of an exclusion clause limiting their liability to the cost of the seed or its replacement. In the High Court Parker, J. found for Mitchell. Finney appealed to the Court of Appeal. The major steps in Lord Denning's judgment appear below

(a) *The issue of communication – was the clause part of the contract?* Lord Denning said that it was. The conditions were usual in the trade. They were in the back of Finney's catalogue. They were on the back of the invoice. 'The inference from the course of dealing would be that the farmers had accepted the conditions as printed – even though they had never read them and did not realize that they contained a limitation on liability. . .'.

(b) *The wording of the clause.* The relevant part of the clause read as follows: 'In the event of any seeds or plants sold or agreed to be sold by us not complying with the express terms of the contract of sale or with any representation made by us or by any duly authorized agent or representative on our behalf prior to, at the time of, or in any such contract, or any seeds, or plants proving defective in varietal purity we will, at our option, replace the defective seeds or plants, free of charge to the buyer or will refund all payments made to us by the buyer in respect of the defective seeds or plants and this shall be the limit of our obligation. We hereby exclude all liability for any loss or damage arising from the use of any seeds or plants supplied by us and for any consequential loss or damage arising out of such use or any failure in the performance of or any defect in any seeds or plants supplied by us for any other loss or damage whatsoever save for, at our option, liability for any such replacement or refund as aforesaid.'

Lord Denning said that the words of the clause did effectively limit Finney's liability. Since the Securicor cases (see *Photo Production* and *Ailsa Craig*, pp. 679–81) words were to be given their natural meaning and not strained. A judge must not proceed in a hostile way towards the wording of exclusion clauses as was, for example, the case with the word 'mis-delivery' in *Alexander* v *Railway Executive* (1951) (see p. 678).

(c) *The test of reasonableness.* Lord Denning then turned to the new test of reasonableness which could be used to strike down an exclusion clause, even though it had been communicated, and in spite of the fact that its wording was appropriate to cover the circumstances. On this he said: 'What is the result of all this? To my mind it heralds a revolution in our approach to exemption clauses; not only where they exclude liability altogether and also where they limit liability; not only in the specific categories in the Unfair Contract Terms Act, 1977, but in other contracts too. . . . We should do away with the multitude of cases on exemption clauses. We should no longer have to harass our students with the study of them. We should set about meeting a new challenge. It is presented by the test of reasonableness.'

(d) *Was the particular clause fair and reasonable?* On this Lord Denning said: 'Our present case is very much on the borderline. There is this to be said in favour of the seed merchant. The price of this cabbage seed was small: £192. The damages claimed are high: £61,000. But there is this to be said on the other side. The clause was not negotiated between persons of equal bargaining power. It was inserted by the seed merchants in their invoices without any negotiation with the farmers. To this I would add that the seed merchants rarely, if ever, invoked the clause. . . . Next, I would point out that the buyers had no opportunity at all of knowing or discovering that the seed was not cabbage seed: whereas the sellers could and should have known that it was the wrong seed altogether. The buyers were not covered by insurance against the risk. Nor could they insure. But as to the seed merchants the judge said [Lord Denning here refers to Parker, J. at first instance]: "I am entirely satisfied that it is possible for seedsmen to insure against this risk . . .". To that I would add this further point. Such a mistake as this could not have happened without serious negligence on the part of the seed merchants themselves or their Dutch suppliers. So serious that it would not be fair to enable them to escape responsibility for it. In all the circumstances I am of the opinion that it would not be fair or reasonable to allow the seed merchants to rely on the clause to limit their liability.'

Oliver and Kerr L.JJ. also dismissed the appeal.

The suppliers asked for leave to appeal to the House of Lords but the Court of Appeal refused. However, the House of Lords granted leave and affirmed the decision of the Court of Appeal in 1983 (see [1983] 2 All E.R. 737).

COMMENT
This is in effect an application of s. 6(3) of the Unfair Contract Terms
Act, 1977. It was actually brought under the Sale of Goods Act, 1979
which contained transitional provisions and s. 55(3) of the 1979 Act plus
para. 11 of Sch. 1 applied to this contract. For contracts made after 31
January 1978 the Unfair Contract Terms Act, 1977, s. 6(3) would apply.

Law of contract – illegality and public policy

PUBLIC POLICY: JUDICIARY: ILLEGAL CONTRACT

188. *Dann* v *Curzon* (1911) 104 L.T. 66

An agreement was made for advertising a play by means of collusive criminal
proceedings brought as a result of a prearranged disturbance at the theatre.
The plaintiffs, who agreed to create the disturbance and did in fact do so,
sued for the remuneration due to them under the agreement. *Held* – the
action failed because it was an agreement to commit a criminal offence and
was therefore against public policy.

189. *Pearce* v *Brooks* (1866) L.R. I. Exch. 213

The plaintiffs hired a carriage to the defendant for a period of twelve months
during which time the defendant was to pay the purchase price by
instalments. The defendant was a prostitute and the carriage, which was of
attractive design, was intended to assist her in obtaining clients. One of the
plaintiffs knew that the defendant was a prostitute but he said that he did
not know that she intended to use the carriage for purposes of prostitution.
The evidence showed to the contrary. The jury found that the plaintiff knew
the purpose for which the carriage was to be used and thereupon the court
held that the plaintiffs' claim for the sum due under the contract failed for
illegality.

COMMENT
The contract would, of course, have been valid if the plaintiffs had not
known of the intended use of the carriage.

190. *Regazzoni* v *K.C. Sethia Ltd* [1958] A.C. 301

The defendants agreed to sell and deliver jute bags to the plaintiff, both
parties knowing and intending that the goods would be shipped from India
to Genoa so that the plaintiff might then send them to South Africa. Both parties
knew that the law of India prohibited the direct or indirect export of goods
from India to South Africa, this law being directed at the policy of apartheid
adopted by South Africa. The defendants did not deliver the jute bags as
agreed and the plaintiff brought this action in an English court, the contract
being governed by English law. *Held* – although the contract was not illegal

in English law, it could not be enforced because it had as its object the violation of the law of a foreign and friendly country in which part of the contract was to be carried out.

COMMENT
In an earlier case, *Foster* v *Driscoll* [1929] 1 K.B. 470, decided on this ground, the court held that a contract to smuggle whisky to the USA during the period of prohibition was illegal and void.

191. *John* v *Mendoza* [1939] 1 K.B. 141

The defendant owed the plaintiff some £852. The defendant was made bankrupt and the plaintiff was intending to prove for his debt in the bankruptcy. The defendant asked him not to do so, but to say that the £852 was a gift whereupon the defendant would pay the plaintiff in full regardless of the sum received by other creditors. In view of the defendant's promise the plaintiff withdrew his proof, but in the event all the other creditors were paid in full and the bankruptcy was annulled. The plaintiff now sued for the debt. *Held* – there was no claim, for the plaintiff abandoned all right to recover on failure to prove in the bankruptcy, and the defendant's promise to pay in full was unenforceable, being an agreement designed to defeat the bankruptcy laws.

192. *Parkinson* v *The College of Ambulance Ltd and Harrison* [1925] 2 K.B. 1

The first defendants were a charitable institution and the second defendant was the secretary, who fraudulently represented to the plaintiff, Colonel Parkinson, that the charity was in a position to obtain some honour (probably a knighthood) for him if he would make a suitable donation to the funds of the charity. The plaintiff paid over the sum of £3000 and said he would pay more if the honour was granted. No honour of any kind was received by the plaintiff and he brought this action to recover the money he had donated to the College. *Held* – the agreement was contrary to public policy and illegal. No relief could be granted to the plaintiff.

193. *Napier* v *National Business Agency Ltd* [1951] 2 All E.R. 264

The defendants engaged the plaintiff to act as their secretary and accountant at a salary of £13 per week plus £6 per week for expenses. Both parties were aware that the plaintiff's expenses could never amount to £6 a week and in fact they never exceeded £1 per week. Income tax was deducted on £13 per week, and £6 per week was paid without deduction of tax as reimbursement of expenses. The plaintiff, having been summarily dismissed, claimed payment of £13 as wages in lieu of notice. *Held* – the agreement was contrary to public policy and illegal. The plaintiff's action failed.

COMMENT
In an earlier case on this point (*Alexander* v *Rayson* [1936] 1 K.B. 169), Mrs Rayson took a lease of a service flat. The rent was £1200 per annum and she signed two forms: under one she agreed to pay £450 for the

lease, under the other £750 for services provided by the plaintiff landlord. His purpose in splitting the transaction was to defraud the rating authorities who assessed the flat for rates on the basis of a rent of £450 p.a. which was all the plaintiff disclosed. This was unknown to the defendant. It was held that the contract was illegal. Mrs Rayson could not be sued for the rent. The service contract was also void.

ILLEGAL CONTRACTS: CONSEQUENCES: IS PERFORMANCE NECESSARILY UNLAWFUL OR NOT? THE *IN PARI DELICTO* RULE: THE MATTER OF REPENTANCE

194. *Bowmakers Ltd* v *Barnet Instruments Ltd* [1944] 2 All E.R. 579

Bowmakers bought machine tools from a person named Smith. This contract was illegal because it contravened an Order made by the Minister of Supply under the Defence Regulations, Smith having no licence to sell machine tools. Bowmakers hired the machine tools to Barnet Instruments under hire-purchase agreements which were also illegal because Bowmaker did not have a licence to sell machine tools. Barnet Instruments failed to keep up the instalments, sold some of the machine tools and refused to give up the others. Bowmakers sued, not on the illegal hire-purchase contracts, but in conversion, and judgment was given for Bowmakers. The Court of Appeal declared the contracts illegal but, since Bowmakers were not suing under the contracts but as owner, their action succeeded. The wrongful sales by Barnet Instruments terminated the hire-purchase contracts.

COMMENT
Although the contract between Smith and Bowmakers was illegal, ownership passed to Bowmakers by reason of delivery. When goods are delivered the person receiving them has some evidence of title by reason of possession and need not necessarily plead a contract. Where, in an illegal situation, the goods have not been delivered there may be difficulty in establishing ownership without relying on the illegal contract. Nevertheless, ownership was established without delivery in *Belvoir Finance Co. Ltd* v *Stapleton* [1970] 3 W.L.R. 530. In this case A (a dealer) sold certain cars to B (a finance company) which let them on hire-purchase to C (a car-hire firm). C did not pay the minimum deposit required by regulation to B; thus the hire-purchase contract was illegal. Later, C's manager, S, sold the cars to innocent purchasers. C did not pay the hire-purchase instalments and B sued S in conversion, the company C having gone into liquidation. It was *held* by the Court of Appeal that B succeeded. They were the owners of the cars and S had converted their property. The decision is of interest since B (the finance company) had never taken delivery of the cars; they were sent direct from A to C as is usual in these transactions. Nevertheless B was accepted as owner although the only means of proving ownership open to B seems to have been the illegal hire-purchase contract with C. This was the only document which showed how B came to acquire ownership

of the cars. On the assumption that this case means what it says, then the rule that there can be no enforcement of illegal contracts loses much of its practical value since the major remedy of claiming the goods back appears to be available equally against a hirer in default, whether the contract is legal or illegal.

195. *Edler* v *Auerbach* [1950] 1 K.B. 359

The defendant leased premises to the plaintiff for use as offices. The lease was contrary to the provisions of the Defence Regulations of 1939, since the premises had previously been used as residential accommodation and should have been let as such. The local authority discovered the illegal use and would not allow it to continue. The plaintiff now sued for rescission of the lease together with rent paid under it. The defendant counterclaimed for rent due and for damage done to the premises, including the removal of a bath. *Held* – the landlord could not enforce the illegal lease but was entitled to damages for the plaintiff's failure to replace the bath.

196. *Hughes* v *Liverpool Victoria Legal Friendly Society* [1916] 2 K.B. 482

John Henry Thomas, a grocer, had orginally taken out five policies on customers who owed him money. It was agreed that Thomas had an insurable interest in the customers because they were his debtors. Thomas let the policies drop and an agent of the defendant company persuaded a Mrs Hughes to take them up, assuring her that she had an insurable interest which she had not. She now brought this action to recover the premiums paid. *Held* – the contract was illegal but the plaintiff could recover the premiums. She had been induced to take up the policies by the fraud of the defendant's agent.

COMMENT
In an earlier case on this point (*Atkinson* v *Denby* (1862) 7 H. & N. 934), the plaintiff was insolvent and wished to compromise with his creditors by paying 25p in the £1. One creditor would not agree unless the plaintiff paid him £50. This sum was paid and was later recovered by the plaintiff who had been forced to defraud his creditors. The money was then available for distribution to creditors generally.

197. *Bigos* v *Bousted* [1951] 1 All E.R. 92

The defendant was anxious to send his wife and daughter abroad for the sake of the daughter's health, but restrictions on currency were in force so that a long stay abroad was impossible. In August 1947, the defendant, in contravention of the Exchange Control Act, 1947, made an agreement under which the plaintiff was to supply £150 of Italian money to be made available at Rapallo, the defendant undertaking to repay the plaintiff with English money in England. As security, the defendant deposited with the plaintiff a share certificate for 140 shares in a company. The wife and daughter went to Italy but were not supplied with currency, and had to return sooner than they would have done. The defendant, thereupon, asked for the return of his share certificate but the plaintiff refused to give it up. This action was brought by the plaintiff to recover the sum of £150 which she insisted she had lent to the defendant. He denied the loan, and counterclaimed for the return of his certificate. In the course of the action the plaintiff abandoned her claim, but the defendant proceeded with his counterclaim saying that, although the contract was illegal, it was still executory so that he might repent and ask the court's assistance. *Held* – the court would not assist him because the fact that the contract had not been carried out was due to frustration by the plaintiff and not the repentance of the defendant. In fact his repentance was really want of power to sin.

198. *Taylor* v *Bowers* (1876) 1 Q.B.D. 291

The plaintiff was under pressure from his creditors and in order to place some of his property out of their reach he assigned certain machinery to a person named Adcock. The plaintiff then called a meeting of his creditors and tried to get them to settle for less than the amount of their debts, representing his assets as not including the machinery. The creditors would not and did not agree to a settlement. The plaintiff now sued to recover his machinery from the defendants who had obtained it from Adcock. *Held* – the plaintiff succeeded because the illegal fraud on the creditors had not been carried out.

199. *Kearley* v *Thomson* (1890) 24 Q.B.D. 742

The plaintiff had a friend who was bankrupt and wished to obtain his discharge. The defendant was likely to oppose the discharge and accordingly the plaintiff paid the defendant £40 in return for which the defendant promised to stay away from the public examination and not to oppose the discharge. The defendant did stay away from the public examination but before an application for discharge had been made the plaintiff brought his action claiming the £40. *Held* – the claim failed because the illegal scheme had been partially effected.

ILLEGAL CONTRACTS: CONSEQUENCES: LAWFUL ON THE FACE OF IT

200. *Fielding and Platt Ltd* v *Najjar* [1969] 2 All E.R. 150

The plaintiffs entered into an agreement with a Lebanese company to make and deliver an aluminium press. Payment was to be made by six promissory notes given at stated intervals by the defendant personally. The defendant, who was the managing director of the Lebanese company, told the plaintiffs that they ought to invoice the goods as part of a rolling mill, his intention being to deceive the Lebanese import authorities into believing that the import of the press was authorised whereas in fact it was not. The first promissory note was dishonoured and the plaintiffs stopped work on the press and cabled a message to the Lebanese company to that effect. The second promissory note was then dishonoured and the plaintiffs sued upon the notes. The case eventually reached the Court of Appeal where it was *held*, that –

(a) since the first note covered work in progress there was no defence based on failure of consideration;

(b) any illegality in connection with the importing of the press was not part of the contract or agreed to by the plaintiffs;

(c) the plaintiffs' claim was not, therefore, affected by illegality;

(d) since the plaintiffs had repudiated the contract before the second note was dishonoured they had no claim for the amount of the note as such but could only sue for damages; the defendant was not liable on the second note.

COMMENT

In an earlier case on this point (*Clay* v *Yates* (1856) 1 H. & B. 73) it was held that a printer who had, without knowledge, printed a book containing libels could recover his charges.

201. *Cowan* v *Milbourn* (1867) L.R. 2 Ex. 230

A person hired a hall to deliver blasphemous lectures and then was refused possession of it. His action claiming possession was refused on the grounds that no relief could be granted by the court where the purpose of the contract was illegal.

202. *Berg* v *Sadler and Moore* [1937] 1 All E.R. 637

The plaintiff was a hairdresser and sold tobacco and cigarettes. He was a member of the Tobacco Trade Association, the Association having as its object the prevention of price cutting. Manufacturers would supply tobacco to traders who agreed not to sell at less than the fixed retail price. The plaintiff sold tobacco at cut prices and was put on the manufacturers' stop list which meant that he could not obtain supplies. The plaintiff made contact with a person named Reece who was a member of the Association and Reece agreed to obtain goods from manfacturers and hand them over to the plaintiff, in return for which Reece was to receive a commission from the plaintiff. One such transaction was carried out. On a later occasion the plaintiff's assistant and a representative of Reece went to the defendant's premises to obtain a supply of cigarettes. The plaintiff's assistant handed over some £72 to Moore, who had some doubt about the matter and said he would send the goods direct to Reece's shop. Thereupon the plaintiff's assistant demanded the return of the money. Moore refused to give it back, and this action was brought to recover it. *Held* – this was an attempt by the plaintiff to obtain goods by false pretences and, since no action arises out of a base cause, the plaintiff's action failed.

PUBLIC POLICY: CONTRACTS TO OUST THE JURISDICTION OF THE COURTS: SEVERANCE

203. *Goodinson* v *Goodinson* [1954] 2 All E.R. 255

A contract made between husband and wife, who had already separated, provided that the husband would pay his wife a weekly sum by way of maintenance in consideration that she would indemnify him against all debts incurred by her, would not pledge his credit, and would not take matrimonial proceedings against him in respect of maintenance. The wife now sued for arrears of maintenance under this agreement. The last promise was admittedly void since its object was to oust the jurisdiction of the courts, but it was *held* that this did not vitiate the rest of the contract; it was not the sole or even the main consideration, and the wife's action for arrears succeeded, this promise being severable.

COMMENT

In a later case on this point (*Re Davstone Estates Ltd* [1969] 2 All E.R. 849) it was decided that a clause in a lease providing that, as regards certain payments to be made by tenants for services to common parts, e.g. staircases, in a block of flats, the certificate of the landlord's surveyor was to be final and conclusive, could be regarded as void.

RESTRAINT OF TRADE AND THE PUBLIC INTEREST

204. *Wyatt v Kreglinger and Fernau* [1933] 1 K.B. 793

In June 1923, the defendants wrote to the plaintiff, who had been in their service for many years, intimating that upon his retirement they proposed to give him an annual pension of £200, subject to the condition that he did not compete against them in the wool trade. The plaintiff's reply was lost and he did not appear ever to have agreed for his part not to engage in the wool trade, but he retired the following September and received the pension until June 1932 when the defendants refused to make any further payments. The plaintiff sued them for breach of contract. The defendants denied any contract existed and also pleaded that if a contract did exist, it was void as being in restraint of trade. The Court of Appeal gave a judgment for the defendants and although there was no unanimity with regard to the *ratio decidendi*, it appeared to two judges that the contract was injurious to the interests of the public, since to restrain the plaintiff from engaging in the wool trade was to deprive the community of services from which it might derive advantage.

COMMENT

The basis of this decision seems to be that if a contract did exist it was supported only by an illegal consideration moving from Wyatt, i.e. an agreement not to engage in the wool trade. If he had been entitled to a pension as part of his original contract of service then no doubt the pension arrangements would have been severed (see p. 312) and enforced.

RESTRAINTS ON EMPLOYEES: TRADE SECRETS

205. *Forster & Sons Ltd v Suggett* (1918) 35 T.L.R. 87

The works manager of the plaintiffs who were mainly engaged in making glass and glass bottles was instructed in certain confidential methods concerning, amongst other things, the correct mixture of gas and air in the furnaces. He agreed that during the five years following the termination of his employment he would not carry on in the United Kingdom, or be interested in, glass-bottle manufacture or any other busines connected with glass-making as conducted by the plaintiffs. It was *held* that the plaintiffs were entitled to protection in this respect and that the restraint was reasonable.

RESTRAINTS ON EMPLOYEES: SOLICITATION OF CUSTOMERS AND CLIENTS

206. *Home Counties Dairies* v *Skilton* [1970] 1 All E.R. 1227

Skilton, a milk roundsman employed by the plaintiffs, agreed, amongst other things, not for one year after leaving his job 'to serve or sell milk or dairy produce' to persons who within six months before leaving his employment were customers of his employers. Skilton left his employment with the plaintiffs in order to work as a roundsman for Westcott Dairies. He then took the same milk round as he had worked when he was with the plaintiffs. *Held* – by the Court of Appeal – that this was a flagrant breach of agreement. The words 'dairy produce' were not too wide. On a proper construction they must be restricted to things normally dealt in by a milkman on his round. 'A further point was taken that the customer restriction would apply to anyone who had been a customer within the last six months of the employment and had during that period ceased so to be, and it was said that the employer could have no legitimate interest in such persons. I think this point is met in the judgment in *G.W. Plowman & Sons Ltd* v *Ash* [1964] 2 All E.R. 10 where it was said that a customer might have left temporarily and that his return was not beyond hope and was therefore a matter of legitimate interest to the employer' (*per* Harman L.J.).

COMMENT

(i) It was held by the Court of Appeal in *John Michael Design* v *Cooke* [1987] 2 All E.R. 332 after referring to *Plowman* v *Ash* that a restraint in a contract of employment preventing an employee (A) from competing with his former employer (B) could be enforced by an injunction even to prevent the former employee from doing business with a customer (C) of his former employer who had made it clear that he would not do business with (B) again. There was always the possibility that (C) would change his mind.

(ii) It is better in these customer/client restraints to restrict the restraint to not soliciting. If in addition the restraint prevents the employee from working in a given area it may fail. Thus in *Office Angels Ltd* v *Rainer-Thomas and O'Connor* [1991] I.R.L.R. 214 the defendants were employed by the plaintiffs at their employment agency in Bow Lane in the City of London. Janette Rainer-Thomas and Elizabeth Ann O'Connor were employed as the manager of the branch and temporaries consultant respectively. The defendants' contracts of employment included a clause which provided that, in order to protect

Office Angels' goodwill, for a six-month period following the termination of employment, office managers and temporaries consultants should not solicit custom from people or companies which had been a client of the company at any time during the period for which the employee was employed by the plaintiffs. In addition, during those six months the relevant employees agreed not to engage in the trade or business of any employment agency within a radius of 3000 metres of the branch or branches of the company at which they had been employed for a period of not less than four weeks during the six months prior to the date of termination of employment, or in the case of a branch or branches in the Greater London area, then within a radius of 1000 metres.

The defendants gave notice and left the plaintiffs' employment on 23 October 1990. On 1 November they became directors and shareholders of a company called Pertempts City Network (London) Ltd which operated an employment agency from Fenchurch Street.

Injunctions preventing the defendants from so operating were granted by the High Court. The defendants appealed to the Court of Appeal. The Court of Appeal allowed the appeal and discharged the injunctions, dismissing all the plaintiffs' claims for relief in the action. While the Court would have been prepared to accept the restraint on the poaching of clients for a period of six months, it was not prepared to accept the area restraint, and for this reason the whole of the clause setting out the restraints failed.

In the main judgment, Sir Christopher Slade said: 'Looking at the matter broadly, a restriction which precludes the defendants, albeit only for a period of six months, from opening an office of an employment agency anywhere in an area of about 1.2 square miles, including most of the City of London, is not an appropriate form of covenant for the protection of the plaintiffs' connection with its clients and is, in any event, wider than is necessary for such protection. The City of London, where there are some 400 employment agencies, is clearly a particularly fertile area for persons carrying on this class of business in view of the many thousands of potential clients and job-seekers who operate in that area. I fully understand the desire of the plaintiffs to preclude the defendants from seeking unfair advantage of the contacts with the 100 or so of the plaintiffs' clients which the defendants had made during their employment by the plaintiffs. In my judgment, however, the restriction imposed by [the clause] placed a disproportionately severe restriction on the defendants' right to compete with the plaintiff after leaving its employment and went further than was reasonable in the interest of the parties.'

(iii) The case represents the modern approach to restraints of trade on ex-employees in regard to the poaching of customers and clients. If the employees agree not to poach clients then it surely does not matter whether they set up in business next door or not. The area restraint does little to protect a client connection and can lead to the unenforceability of the whole restraint clause, as in this case.

RESTRAINTS ON EMPLOYEES: EXCEPTIONALLY FOR LIFE

207. *Fitch* v *Dewes* [1921] 2 A.C. 158

A solicitor at Tamworth employed a person who was successively his articled clerk and managing clerk. In his contract of service, the clerk agreed, if he left the solicitor's employment, never to practise as a solicitor within seven miles of Tamworth Town Hall. *Held* – the agreement was good because during his service the clerk had become acquainted with the details of his employer's clients, and could be restrained even for life from using that knowledge to the detriment of his employer.

> COMMENT
> (i) Although the restraint was for life, it did cover a rather small area in which at the time there were comparatively few people. It is unlikely that such a restraint would be regarded as valid today, particularly in a more densely populated area.
> (ii) The Privy Council stated quite clearly in *Deacons* v *Bridge* [1984] 2 All E.R. 19 that a restraint such as this would only be applied in unusual circumstances. The decision seems confined to its own facts though the statements of principle in the case by the House of Lords are more enduring.

RESTRAINTS ON EMPLOYEES: TAKEN IN A CONTRACT BETWEEN THEIR EMPLOYERS

208. *Kores Manufacturing Co Ltd* v *Kolok Manufacturing Co Ltd* [1958] 2 All E.R. 65

The two companies occupied adjoining premises in Tottenham and both manufactured carbon papers, typewriter ribbons and the like. They made an agreement in which each company agreed that it would not, without the written consent of the other, 'at any time employ any person who during the past five years shall have been a servant of yours'. The plaintiffs' chief chemist sought employment with the defendants, and the plaintiffs were not prepared to consent to this and asked for an injunction to enforce the agreement. *Held* – by the Court of Appeal –

(a) a contract in restraint of trade cannot be enforced unless:
  (i) it is reasonable as between the parties; and
  (ii) it is consistent with the interest of the public;
(b) the mere fact that the parties are dealing on equal terms does not prevent the court from holding that the restraint is unreasonable in the interests of those parties;
(c) the restraint in this case was grossly in excess of what was required to protect the parties and accordingly was unreasonable in the interests of the parties;
(d) the agreement therefore failed to satisfy the first of the two conditions set out in (a) above and was void and unenforceable.

COMMENT

The restrictive agreement which was at the root of *Kores Manufacturing Co* v *Kolok Manufacturing Co Ltd* was not covered by the Restrictive Trade Practices Act which is not concerned with agreements between traders in regard to their employees and was decided on common-law principles. These principles are that the agreement must be reasonable between the parties and reasonable in the public interest. Both of these points arose in *Kores*, the Court of Appeal holding that the agreement was unreasonable as between the parties and also that it was contrary to the public interest, though the *ratio* is based on the fact that the agreement was unreasonable as between the parties.

RESTRAINTS ON VENDORS OF BUSINESSES

209. *British Reinforced Concrete Co* v *Schelff* [1921] 2 Ch. 563

The plaintiffs carried on a large business for the manufacture and sale of B.R.C. Road Reinforcements. The defendant carried on a small business for the sale of 'Loop Road Reinforcements'. The defendant sold his business to the plaintiffs and agreed not to compete with them in the manufacture or sale of road reinforcements in any part of the UK. It was *held* that the covenant was void. All that the defendant transferred was the business of selling the reinforcements called 'Loop'. It was therefore only with regard to that particular variety that it was justifiable to curb his future activities.

COMMENT

It would have been possible to sever the restraint by deleting the part relating to manufacture but the court said that even if this were done it would still be too wide. Not to 'sell any road reinforcement in any part of the UK' was much too wide for what was a very small business.

210. *Nordenfelt* v *Maxim Nordenfelt Guns and Ammunition Co* [1894] A.C. 535

Nordenfelt was a manufacturer of machine guns and other military weapons. He sold the business to a company, giving certain undertakings which restricted his business activities. This company was amalgamated with another company and Nordenfelt was employed by the new concern as managing director. In his contract Nordenfelt agreed that for 25 years he would not manufacture guns or ammunition in any part of the world, and would not compete with the company in any way. *Held* – the covenant regarding the business sold was valid and enforceable, even though it was world-wide, because the business connection was world-wide and it was possible in the circumstances to sever this undertaking from the rest of the agreement (see p. 312). However, the further undertaking not to compete in any way with the company was unreasonable and void.

RESTRAINTS ON EMPLOYEE/SHAREHOLDERS: WHAT IS THE TEST?

211. *Systems Reliability Holdings plc* v *Smith* [1990] I.R.L.R. 377

In 1986 Mr Smith commenced work with a company called Enterprise Computer Systems (E.C.S.). He was a computer engineer engaged upon the reconfiguration of I.B.M. mainframe computers. He became highly skilled in the modification and rebuilding of the latest generation of I.B.M.'s 3090 computer. His skill was instrumental in making E.C.S. a leading company providing computer services. He was dismissed on 1 February 1990.

While he was employed by E.C.S. Mr Smith had purchased shares totalling 1.6% of the holding in the company. After his dismissal Systems Reliability Holdings plc acquired all the shares in E.C.S. and Mr Smith received £247,000 for his 1.6% holding. The share sale agreement had a restrictive covenant. Mr Smith had seen and initialled the agreement in final draft form. The covenant said: 'None of the specifically restricted vendors will during the restricted period directly or indirectly carry on or be engaged or interested . . . in any business which competes with any business carried on at the date of this agreement . . . by the company or any of its subsidiaries.'

Mr Smith was one of the specifically restricted vendors and the restricted period was in effect one of 17 months from the date of the sale. There was a further covenant which provided that: 'None of the vendors will at any time after the date of this agreement disclose or use for his own benefit or that of any other person any confidential information which he now possesses concerning the business or affairs or products of or services supplied by the company or any of the subsidiaries or of any person having dealings with the company or any of its subsidiaries.'

Soon after his dismissal and the share sale Mr Smith set up in business supplying computer services. Systems Reliability asked for an injunction to enforce the restrictive convenant in the share sale agreement.

The High Court *held* that a restrictive covenant imposed upon the defendant as part of the plaintiffs' acquisition of the shares in the company in which he was formerly employed was entirely reasonable and would be enforced against him notwithstanding that his shareholding in the company had amounted to only 1.6% of the total. The present case was a true vendor and purchaser situation in which the defendant had received £247,000 for his 1.6% shareholding. There was no public policy to prevent the defendant taking himself out of competition for what was a comparatively short period of 17 months as required under the agreement which on the evidence was entirely reasonable, or to prevent the imposition of a world-wide restriction which was also reasonable given that the business was completely international. The covenant would therefore be enforced.

COMMENT

As we have seen the courts have traditionally allowed wider restraints on competition to be placed on the vendors of businesses than on employees. In Mr Smith we have a mix of the two and the court applied the wider vendor/purchaser approach.

It must, of course, be significant that Mr Smith got £247,000 for a comparatively small shareholding and it must remain doubtful whether the court would apply the vendor/purchaser test to an employee whose shareholding was merely nominal. Presumably, here the tighter employer/employee test of reasonableness would apply.

The matter is one of some importance because the number of employee/shareholders has increased rapidly over the past few years.

RESTRAINTS ON DISTRIBUTORS OF MERCHANDISE

212. *Esso Petroleum Co Ltd* v *Harper's Garage (Stourport) Ltd* [1967] 1 All E.R. 699

The defendant company owned two garges with attached filling stations, the Mustow Green Garage, Mustow Green, near Kidderminster, and the Corner Garage at Stourport-on-Severn. Each garage was tied to the plaintiff oil company, the one at Mustow Green by a solus supply agreement only with a tie clause binding the dealer to take the products of the plaintiff company at its scheduled prices from time to time. There was also a price-maintenance clause which was no longer enforceable and a 'continuity clause' under which the defendants, if they sold the garage, had to persuade the buyer to enter into another solus agreement with Esso. The defendants also agreed to keep the garage open at all reasonable hours and to give preference to the plaintiff company's oils. The agreement was to remain in force for four years and five months from 1 July 1963, being the unexpired residue of the ten-year tie of a previous owner. At the Corner Garage there was a similar solus agreement for 21 years and a mortgage under which the plaintiffs lent Harpers £7000 to assist them in buying the garage and improving it. The mortgage contained a tie covenant and forbade redemption for 21 years. In August 1964, Harpers offered to pay off the loan but Esso refused to accept it. Harpers then turned over all four pumps at the Corner Garage to VIP, and later sold VIP at Mustow Green. The plaintiff company now asked for an injunction to restrain the defendants from buying or selling fuels other than Esso at the two garages during the subsistence of the agreements. *Held* – by the House of Lords – that the rule of public policy against unreasonable restraints of trade applied to the solus agreements and the mortgage. The shorter period of four years and five months was reasonable so that the tie was valid but the other tie for 21 years in the solus agreement and the mortgage was invalid, so that the injunction asked for by the plaintiffs could not be granted.

COMMENT
The House of Lords appears to have been influenced by the report of the Monopolies Commission on the Supply of Petrol to Retailers in the United Kingdom (Cmnd. 1965, No. 264) which recommended the period of five years.

213. *Cleveland Petroleum Co Ltd* v *Dartstone Ltd* [1969] 1 All E.R. 201

The owner of a garage and filling station at Crawley in Sussex leased the property to Cleveland and they in turn granted an underlease to the County Oak Service Station Ltd. The underlease contained a covenant under which all motor fuels sold were to be those of Cleveland. There was power to assign in the underlease and a number of assignments took place so that eventually Dartstone Ltd became the lessees, having agreed to observe the covenants in the underlease. They then challenged the covenant regarding motor fuels and Cleveland asked for an injunction to enforce it. The injunction was granted. Dealing in the Court of Appeal with *Harper's* case Lord Denning, M.R. said:

> It seems plain to me that in three at least of the speeches of their Lordships a distinction is taken between a man who is already in possession of the land before he ties himself to an oil company and a man who is out of possession and is let into it by an oil company. If an owner in possession ties himself for more than five years to take all his supplies from one company, that is an unreasonable restraint of trade and is invalid. But if a man, who is out of possession, is let into possession by the oil company on the terms that he is to tie himself to that company, such a tie is good.

COMMENT

(i) The essential distinction is, as we have seen, that where the restraint on the use of the land is contained in a conveyance or lease the common-law rules of restraint of trade do not apply. The person who takes over the property under a conveyance or lease has given nothing up. In fact he has acquired rights which he never had before even though subject to some limitations.

(ii) In *Alec Lobb (Garages) Ltd* v *Total Oil GB Ltd* [1985] 1 All E.R. 303 the plaintiff company borrowed from the defendant to develop a site. As part of the loan arrangements, the plaintiff agreed to buy the defendant's petrol for 21 years. Since the company was already in occupation of the garage and filling station when the agreement was made, it was subject to the doctrine of restraint of trade being a *contract* and not a *lease*. The High Court said that 21 years was too long and that the restraint was unenforceable. The Court of Appeal rejected that view and with it the opinion of the Monopolies Commission that it was not in the public interest that a petrol company should tie a petrol filling station for more than five years in the circumstances of this case.

Therefore, the *Lobb* case seems to show that the courts may not be prepared to help the so-called weaker party, i.e. the garage owner, as they were in the past. In the *Lobb* case the Court of Appeal said that each case must depend on its own facts. In fact the longer restriction seems on the facts of the case to have been justified. The loan by Total was a rescue operation greatly benefiting Lobb and enabling it to continue in business. There were also break clauses in the arrangement at the end of seven and 14 years if Lobb wished to use them. In view of the ample consideration offered by Total, the restraint of 21 years was not, according to the Court of Appeal, unreasonable and was therefore valid and enforceable.

INVOLUNTARY RESTRAINTS ON MEMBERS OF TRADE ASSOCIATIONS AND THE PROFESSIONS

214. *Pharmaceutical Society of Great Britain* v *Dickson* [1968] 2 All E.R. 686

The Society passed a resolution to the effect that the opening of new pharmacies should be restricted and be limited to certain specified services, and that the range of services in existing pharmacies should not be extended except as approved by the Society's council. The purpose of the resolution was clearly to stop the development of new fields of trading in conjunction with pharmacy. Mr Dickson, who was a member of the Society and retail director of Boots Pure Drug Company Ltd, brought this action on the grounds that the proposed new rule was *ultra vires* as an unreasonable restraint of trade. A declaration that the resolution was *ultra vires* was made and the Society appealed to the House of Lords where the appeal was dismissed, the following points emerging from the judgment.

(a) Where a professional association passes a resolution regarding the conduct of its members the validity of the resolution is a matter for the courts even if binding in honour only, since failure to observe it is likely to be construed as misconduct and thus become a ground for disciplinary action.

(b) A resolution by a professional association regulating the conduct of its members is *ultra vires* if not sufficiently related to the main objects of the association. The objects of the society in this case did not cover the resolution, being 'to maintain the honour and safeguard and promote the interests of the members in the exercise of the profession of pharmacy'.

(c) A resolution by a professional association regulating the conduct of its members will be void if it is an unreasonable restraint of trade.

Law of contract – discharge of contract

DISCHARGE BY PERFORMANCE: ENTIRE CONTRACTS

215. *Bolton* v *Mahadeva* [1972] 2 All E.R. 1322

Bolton installed a central heating system in the defendant's house. The price agreed was a lump sum of £560. The work was not done properly and it was estimated that it would cost £179 to put the system right. The Court of Appeal decided that the lump-sum payment suggested that the contract was entire and since Bolton had not performed his part of it properly and in full he could not recover anything for what he had done.

COMMENT
The case of *Cutter* v *Powell* (1795) 6 Term Rep. 320 is sometimes used to illustrate the point about entire contracts. The facts of the case were that a seaman agreed to serve on a ship from Jamaica to Liverpool for

the sum of 30 guineas (£31.50 today) to be paid on completion of the voyage. He died when the ship was 19 days short of Liverpool. The court *held* that the contract was entire and his widow was not entitled to anything on behalf of his estate. While the case is valid as an illustration it has been overtaken on its own facts by more recent law. The Merchant Shipping Act, 1970 now provides for the payment of wages for partial performance in such cases and the Law Reform (Frustrated Contracts) Act, 1943 would also have assisted the widow to recover because the seaman had conferred a benefit on the master of the ship prior to his death (which would now frustrate the contract) giving the widow the right to sue the master of the ship for the benefit of the seaman's work up to the time of his death.

DISCHARGE BY PERFORMANCE: EFFECT OF SUBSTANTIAL PERFORMANCE

216. *Hoenig* v *Isaacs* [1952] 2 All E.R. 176

The defendant employed the plaintiff who was an interior decorator and furniture designer to decorate a one-room flat owned by the defendant. The plaintiff was also to provide furniture, including a fitted bookcase, a wardrobe and a bedstead, for the total sum of £750. The terms of the contract regarding payment were as follows: 'Net cash as the work proceeds and the balance on completion'. The defendant made two payments to the plaintiff of £150 each, one payment on 12 April and the other on 19 April. The plaintiff claimed that he had completed the work on 28 August, and asked for the balance, i.e. £450. The defendant asserted that the work done was bad and faulty, but sent the plaintiff a sum of £100 and moved into the flat and used the furniture. The plaintiff now sued for the balance of £350, the defence being that the plaintiff had not performed his contract, or in the alternative that he had done so negligently, unskilfully and in an unworkmanlike manner.

The Official Referee assessed the work that had been done, and found that generally it was properly done except that the wardrobe required replacing and that a bookshelf was too short and this meant that the bookcase would have to be remade. The defendant claimed that the contract was entire and that it must be completely performed before the plaintiff could recover. The Official Referee was of the opinion that there had been substantial performance, and that the defendant was liable for £750 less the cost of putting right the above-mentioned defects, the cost of this being assessed at £55 18s 2d. The court accordingly gave the plaintiff judgment for the sum of £294 1s 10d.

COMMENT
The Official Referee is a judge designated to consider cases referred to him by a court because they involve consideration of documents and accounts to assess what damages should be payable.

DISCHARGE BY PERFORMANCE: PARTIAL PERFORMANCE

217. *Sumpter* v *Hedges* [1898] 1 Q.B. 673

The plaintiff entered into a contract with the defendant under the terms of which the plaintiff was to erect some buildings for the defendant on the defendant's land for a price of £565. The plaintiff did partially erect the buildings up to the value of £333, and the defendant paid him that figure. The plaintiff then told the defendant that he could not finish the job because he had run out of funds. The defendant then completed the work by using materials belonging to the plaintiff which had been left on the site. The plaintiff now sued for work done and materials supplied, and the court gave him judgment for materials supplied, but would not grant him a sum of money by way of a *quantum meruit* (an action for reasonable payment for work done), for the value of the work done prior to his abandonment of the job. The reason given was that, before the plaintiff could sue successfully on a *quantum meruit*, he would have to show that the defendant had voluntarily accepted the work done, and this implied that the defendant must be in a position to refuse the benefit of the work as where a buyer of goods refuses to take delivery. This was not the case here; the defendant had no option but to accept the work done, so his acceptance could not be presumed from conduct. There being no other evidence of the defendant's acceptance of the work, the plaintiff's claim for the work failed.

> COMMENT
> In practice this form of injustice to the builder is avoided because a building contract normally provides for progress payments as various stages of construction are completed, thus making it a divisible agreement.

DISCHARGE BY PERFORMANCE: PERFORMANCE PREVENTED

218. *De Barnardy* v *Harding* (1853) 8 Exch. 822

The plaintiff agreed to act as the defendant's agent for the purpose of preparing and issuing certain advertisements and notices designed to encourage the sale of tickets to see the funeral procession of the Duke of Wellington. The plaintiff was to be paid a commission of 10% upon the proceeds of the tickets actually sold. The plaintiff duly issued the advertisements and notices, but before he began to sell the tickets the defendant withdrew the plaintiff's authority to sell them and in consequence the plaintiff did not sell any tickets and was prevented from earning his commission. The plaintiff now sued upon a *quantum meruit* and his action succeeded.

DISCHARGE BY PERFORMANCE: TIME OF PERFORMANCE: WAIVER

219. *Bowes* v *Shand* (1877) 2 App. Cas. 455

The action was brought for damages for non-acceptance of 600 tons (or 8200 bags) of Madras rice. The sold note stated that the rice was to be shipped during 'the months of March and/or April 1874'. 8150 bags were put on board ship on or before 28 February 1874, and the remaining 50 bags on 2 March 1874. The defendants refused to take delivery because the rice was not shipped in accordance with the terms of the contract. *Held* – the bulk of the cargo was shipped in February and therefore the rice did not answer the description in the contract and the defendants were not bound to accept it.

COMMENT
(i) A buyer can reject in these circumstances even though there is nothing wrong with the goods and he merely wants to reject because the market price has fallen.

(ii) It is of interest to note that the rules about delivery apply to early delivery as well as late delivery. Incidentally the defendants refused to take delivery early because they were not ready with their finance at that time.

220. *Chas Rickards Ltd* v *Oppenhaim* [1950] 1 K.B. 616

The defendant ordered a Rolls-Royce chassis from the plaintiffs, the chassis being delivered in July 1947. The plaintiffs found a coachbuilder prepared to make a body within six or at the most seven months. The specification for the body was agreed in August 1947, so that the work should have been completed in March 1948. The work was not completed by then but the defendant still pressed for delivery. On 29 June 1948, the defendant wrote to the coachbuilder saying that he would not accept delivery after 25 July 1948. The body was not ready by then and the defendant bought another car. The body was completed in October 1948, but the defendant refused to accept delivery and counterclaimed for the value of the chassis which he had purchased. *Held* – time was of the essence of the original contract, but the defendant had waived the question of time by continuing to press for delivery after the due date. However, by his letter of 29 June he had again made time of the essence, and had given reasonable notice in the matter. Judgment was given for the defendant on the claim and counterclaim.

COMMENT
That a waiver of a date of delivery without consideration is binding can be based on promissory estoppel (as in *High Trees* – see p. 621) said Denning, L.J. in *Rickards*, or on s. 11(2) of the Sale of Goods Act, 1979 which states: 'Where a contract of sale is subject to any condition to be fulfilled by the seller, the buyer may waive that condition.' This section was used to justify a waiver without consideration by McCardie, J. in *Hartley* v *Hymans* [1920] 3 K.B. 475.

This is an example of the doctrine of promissory estoppel being used by a plaintiff, i.e. as a sword not a shield, because a seller may tender delivery after the originally agreed date relying on the buyer's promise to accept such delivery by reason of his waiver. If the buyer then refuses to accept the delivery the seller can claim damages and is in essence suing upon the waiver which is unsupported by consideration.

DISCHARGE BY PERFORMANCE: APPROPRIATION OF PAYMENTS

221. *Deeley* v *Lloyds Bank Ltd* [1912] A.C. 756

A customer of the bank had mortgaged his property to the bank to secure an overdraft limited to £2500. He then mortgaged the same property to the appellant for £3500, subject to the bank's mortgage. It is the normal practice of bankers, on receiving notice of a second mortgage, to rule off the customer's account, and not to allow any further withdrawals since these will rank after the second mortgage. In this case the bank did not open a new account but continued the old current account. The customer thereafter paid in sums of money which at a particular date, if they had been appropriated in accordance with the rule in *Clayton*'s case, would have extinguished the bank's mortgage. Even so the customer still owed the bank money, and they sold the property for a price which was enough to satisfy the bank's debt but not that of the appellant. *Held* – the evidence did not exclude the rule in *Clayton*'s case, which applied, so that the bank's morgage had been paid off and the appellant, as second mortgagee, was entitled to the proceeds of the sale.

> COMMENT
> The operation of *Clayton*'s case is normally prevented by the bank stating in the mortgage that it is a continuing security given on a running account varying from day to day and excluding the repayment of the borrower's liability which would otherwise take place as credits are paid in.

DISCHARGE BY FRUSTRATION: CONTRACTS OF PERSONAL SERVICE

222. *Storey* v *Fulham Steel Works* (1907) 24 T.L.R. 89

The plaintiff was employed by the defendant as manager for a period of five years. After he had been working for two years he became ill, and had to have special treatment and a period of convalescence. Six months later he was recovered, but in the meantime the defendant had terminated his employment. The plaintiff now sued for breach of contract, and the defendants pleaded that the plaintiff's period of ill-health operated to discharge the contract. *Held* – the plaintiff's illness and absence from duty did not go the root of the contract, and was not so serious as to allow the termination of the agreement.

223. *Norris* v *Southampton City Council* [1982] I.R.C.R. 141

Mr Norris was employed as a cleaner. He was convicted of assault and reckless driving and was sentenced to a term of imprisonment. His employers wrote dismissing him and Mr Norris complained to an industrial tribunal that his dismissal was unfair. The tribunal held that the contract of employment was frustrated and that the employee was not dismissed and therefore not entitled to compensation. The Employment Appeal Tribunal to which Mr Norris appealed laid down that frustration could only arise where there was no fault by either party. Where there was a fault, such as deliberate conduct leading to an inability to perform the contract, there was not frustration but a repudiatory breach of contract. The employer had the option of whether or not to treat the contract as repudiated and if he chose to dismiss the employee he could do so, regarding the breach as repudiatory. The question then to be decided was whether the dismissal was fair. The case was remitted to the Industrial Tribunal for further consideration of whether there was unfair dismissal on the facts of the case.

DISCHARGE BY FRUSTRATION: GOVERNMENT INTERVENTION

224. *Re Shipton, Anderson & Co and Harrison Bros' Arbitration* [1915] 3 K.B. 676

A contract was made for the sale of wheat lying in a warehouse in Liverpool. Before the seller could deliver the wheat, and before the property in it had passed to the buyer, the government requisitioned the wheat under certain emergency powers available in time of war. *Held* – delivery being impossible by reason of lawful requisition by the government, the seller was excused from performance of the contract.

DISCHARGE BY FRUSTRATION: DESTRUCTION OF SUBJECT MATTER

225. *Taylor* v *Caldwell* (1863) 3 B. & S. 826

The defendant agreed to let the plaintiff have the use of a music hall for the purpose of holding four concerts. Before the first concert was due to be held the hall was destroyed by fire without negligence by any party, and the plaintiff now sued for damages for wasted advertising expenses. *Held* – the contract was impossible of performance and the defendant was not liable.

> COMMENT
> A modern example of the rule is to be found in *Vitol SA* v *Esso Australia*, *The Times*, 1 February 1988, where the buyers of petroleum were discharged from the contract by frustration when the vessel and cargo were destroyed by a missile attack in the Gulf.

DISCHARGE BY FRUSTRATION: NON-OCCURRENCE OF AN EVENT

226. *Krell* v *Henry* [1903] 2 K.B. 740

The plaintiff owned a room overlooking the proposed route of the Coronation procession of Edward VII, and had let it to the defendant for the purpose of viewing the procession. The procession did not take place because of the King's illness and the plaintiff now sued for the agreed fee. *Held* – the fact that the procession had been cancelled discharged the parties from their obligations, since it was no longer possible to achieve the real purpose of the agreement.

227. *Herne Bay Steamboat Co* v *Hutton* [1903] 2 K.B. 683

The plaintiffs agreed to hire a steamboat to the defendant for two days, in order that the defendant might take paying passengers to see the naval review at Spithead on the occasion of Edward VII's Coronation. An official announcement was made cancelling the review, but the fleet was assembled and the boat might have been used for the intended cruise. The defendant did not use the boat, and the plaintiffs employed her on ordinary business. The action was brought to recover the fee of £200 which the defendant had promised to pay for the hire of the boat. *Held* – the contract was not discharged, as the review of the fleet by the Sovereign was not the foundation of the contract. The plaintiffs were awarded the difference between £200 and the profits derived from the use of the boat for ordinary business on the two days in question.

> COMMENT
> It may be thought that it is difficult to reconcile this case with *Krell* (see above). However, whatever the legal niceties may or may not be, there is clearly a difference in fact. To cruise round the fleet assembled at Spithead, even though the figure of the Sovereign (miniscule to the viewer, anyway) would not be present, is clearly more satisfying as the subject matter of a contract than looking through the window at ordinary London traffic.

DISCHARGE BY FRUSTRATION: COMMERCIAL PURPOSE DEFEATED

228. *Jackson* v *Union Marine Insurance Co* (1874) L.R. 10 C.P. 125

The plaintiff was the owner of a ship called *Spirit of the Dawn* which had been chartered to go with all possible dispatch from Liverpool to Newport, and there load a cargo of iron rails for San Francisco. The plaintiff had entered into a contract of insurance with the defendants, in order that he might protect himself against the failure of the ship to carry out the charter. The vessel was stranded in Caernarfon Bay whilst on its way to Newport. It was not refloated for over a month, and could not be fully repaired for some time. The charterers hired another ship and the plaintiff now claimed on the policy of insurance. The insurance company suggested that since the plaintiff might claim against the charterer for breach of contract there was no loss, and the court had to decide whether such a claim was possible. *Held* – the delay consequent upon the stranding of the vessel put an end, in the commercial sense, to the venture, so that the charterer was released from his obligations and was free to hire another ship. Therefore, the plaintiff had no claim against the charterer and could claim the loss of the charter from the defendants.

DISCHARGE BY FRUSTRATION: WHERE FRUSTRATION IS SELF-INDUCED

229. *Maritime National Fish Ltd* v *Ocean Trawlers Ltd* [1935] A.C. 524

The respondents were the owners and the appellants the charterers of a steam trawler, the *St Cuthbert*. The *St Cuthbert* was fitted with, and could only operate with an otter trawl. When the charter-party was renewed on 25 October 1932, both parties knew it was illegal to operate with an otter trawl without a licence from the minister. The appellants operated five trawlers and applied for five licences. The minister granted only three and said that the appellants could choose the names of three trawlers for the licences. The appellants chose three but deliberately excluded the *St Cuthbert* though they could have included it. They were now sued by the owners for the charter fee, and their defence was that the charter-party was frustrated because it would have been illegal to fish with the *St Cuthbert*. It was *held* that the contract was not frustrated, in the sense that the frustrating event was self-induced by the appellants and that therefore they were liable for the hire.

> COMMENT
> An otter trawl is a type of net which can, because of its narrow mesh, pick up small immature fish. Its use is restricted for environmental reasons.

DISCHARGE BY FRUSTRATION: CONTRACTS CONCERNING LAND

230. *Cricklewood Property and Investment Trust Ltd* v *Leighton's Investment Trust Ltd* [1945] A.C. 221

In May 1936, a building lease was granted between the parties for 99 years, but before any building had been erected war broke out in 1939 and government restrictions on building materials and labour meant that the lessees could not erect the buildings as they intended, these buildings being in fact shops. Leighton's sued originally for rent due under the lease and Cricklewood, the builders, said the lease was frustrated. The House of Lords *held* that the doctrine of frustration did not apply because the interruption from 1939 to 1945 was not sufficient in duration to frustrate the lease, and so they did not deal specifically with the general position regarding frustration of leases, basing their judgment on the question of the degree of interrruption. In so far as they did deal with the general position this was *obiter*, but Lord Simon thought that there could be cases in which a lease would be frustrated, and the example that he quoted was a building lease where the land was declared a permanent open space before building took place; here he thought that the fundamental purpose of the transaction would be defeated. Lord Wright took much the same view on the same example. Lord Russell thought frustration could not apply to a lease of real property, and Lord Goddard, C.J. took the same view. Lord Porter expressed no opinion with regard to leases generally and so this case does not finally solve the problem.

COMMENT

(i) Even if the courts were prepared to apply the doctrine of frustration, it would not often apply to leases, particularly long leases. In a lease for 99 years a tenant temporarily deprived of possession as by requisition of the property would hardly ever by put out of possession long enough to satisfy the test of frustration (see below).

(ii) In *National Carriers* v *Panalpina (Northern)* [1981] 1 All E.R. 161 the House of Lords were of the opinion that a lease could be frustrated. The plaintiffs leased a warehouse to the defendants for ten years. The Hull City Council closed the only access road to it because a listed building nearby was in a dangerous condition. The access road was closed for 20 months. The defendants refused to pay the rent for this period. The House of Lords said that they must. A lease could be frustrated, they said, but 20 months out of ten years was not enough to frustrate it in the particular circumstances of this case. Once again, therefore, the decision of the House of Lords on the matter of frustration of leases was *obiter*.

(iii) In *Amalgamated Investment and Property Co Ltd* v *John Walker & Sons Ltd* [1976] 3 All E.R. 509 Buckley, L.J. was prepared to presume that the doctrine of frustration could be applied to contracts for the sale of land, though once again this decision was *obiter* because he did not have to apply the doctrine in this case. Walker sold a warehouse to Amalgamated, both parties believing that the property was suitable and capable of being redeveloped. After the contract was made the Department of the Environment included it in a list of buildings of architectural and historic interest so that the development became more difficult. The Court of Appeal *held* that the contract was not frustrated. The listing merely affected the value of the property and the purchaser always took the risk of this in terms of a listing order or, indeed, compulsory purchase. The contract could be completed according to its terms and specific performance was granted to Walkers. Nor was the contract voidable under *Solle* v *Butcher* (1950) (see p. 642) because the mistake did not exist at the date of the contract.

DISCHARGE BY FRUSTRATION: EFFECT AT COMMON LAW

231. *Chandler* v *Webster* [1904] 1 K.B. 493

The defendant agreed to let the plaintiff have a room for the purpose of viewing the Coronation procession on 26 June 1902 for £141 15s. The contract provided that the money be payable immediately. The procession did not take place because of the illness of the King and the plaintiff, who had paid £100 on account, left the balance unpaid. The plaintiff sued to recover the £100 and the defendant counterclaimed for £41. 15s. It was *held* by the Court of Appeal that the plaintiff's action failed and the defendant's counterclaim succeeded because the obligation to pay rent had fallen due before the frustrating event.

COMMENT

This case is included only to show how important the Law Reform (Frustrated Contracts) Act, 1943 really is!

DISCHARGE BY BREACH: ANTICIPATORY BREACH

232. *Hochster* v *De la Tour* (1853) 2 E. & B. 678

The defendant agreed in April 1852 to engage the plaintiff as a courier for European travel, his duties to commence on 1 June 1852. On 11 May 1852, the defendant wrote to the plaintiff saying that he no longer required his services. The plaintiff commenced an action for breach of contract on 22 May 1852, and the defence was that there was no cause of action until the date due for performance, i.e. 1 June 1852. *Held* – the defendant's express repudiation constituted an actionable breach of contract.

233. *Omnium D' Enterprises and Others* v *Sutherland* [1919] 1 K.B. 618

The defendant was the owner of a steamship and agreed to let her under a charter to the plaintiff for a period of time and to pay the second plaintiffs a commission on the hire payable under the agreement. The defendant later sold the ship to a purchaser, free of all liability under his agreement with the plaintiffs. *Held* – the sale by the defendant was a repudiation of the agreement and the plaintiffs were entitled to damages for breach of the contract.

COMMENT

The charterer would have no claim against the purchaser of the vessel because restrictive covenants do not pass with chattels (which a ship is) but only with land. Compare *Dunlop* v *Selfridge* (1915) (see p. 615) and *Tulk* v *Moxhay* (1848) (see p. 618).

234. *White and Carter (Councils) Ltd* v *McGregor* [1961] 3 All E.R. 1178

The respondent was a garage proprietor on Clydebank and on 26 June 1957, his sales manager, without specific authority, entered into a contract with the appellants whereby the appellants agreed to advertise the respondent's business on litter bins which they supplied to local authorities. The contract was to last for three years from the date of the first advertisement display. Payment was to be by instalments annually in advance, the first instalment being due seven days after the first display. The contract contained a clause that, on failure to pay an instalment or other breach of contract, the whole sum of £196 4s became due. The respondent was quick to repudiate the contract for on 26 June 1957, he wrote to the appellants asking them to cancel the agreement, and at this stage the appellants had not taken any steps towards carrying it out. The appellants refused to cancel the agreement and prepared the advertisement plates which they exhibited on litter bins in

November 1957, and continued to display them during the following three years. Eventually the appellants demanded payment, the respondent refused to pay, and the appellants brought an action against him for the sum due under the contract. *Held* – the appellants were entitled to recover the contract price since, although the respondents had repudiated the contract, the appellants were not obliged to accept the repudiation. The contract survived and the appellants had not completed it. The House of Lords said that there was no duty to mitigate loss until there was a breach which the appellants had accepted and they had not accepted this one.

COMMENT

Although the respondent's agent had no actual authority, he had made a similar contract with the appellants in 1954, and it was not disputed that he had apparent authority to bind his pricipal.

It is worth pointing out that there was in this case no evidence that the appellants could have mitigated their loss. No evidence was produced to show that the demand for advertising space exceeded the supply so it may be that the appellants could not have obtained a new customer for the space on the litter bins intended for the respondent. Thus White and Carter may have had a 'legitimate interest' in continuing with the contract. Perhaps if evidence that mitigation was possible had been produced the House of Lords would have applied the principles of mitigation to the case, or held that White and Carter had no 'legitimate interest' in continuing the agreement. This view is supported by a decision of the Court of Appeal in *Attica Sea Carriers Corporation* v *Ferrostaal Poseidon Bulk Reederei GmbH* [1976] 1 Lloyd's Rep. 250 where the charterer of a ship agreed to execute certain repairs before he redelivered it to the owner and to pay the agreed hire until that time. He did not carry out the repairs but the owner would not take redelivery of the ship until they had been done and later sued for the agreed hire. It was *held* that the owner was not entitled to refuse to accept redelivery and to sue for the agreed hire. The cost of the repairs far exceeded the value which the ship would have if they were done and the owner had therefore no legal interest in insisting on their execution and the payment of the hire. The court held that he should have mitigated his loss by accepting redelivery of the unrepaired ship so that his only remedy was damages and not for the agreed hire.

This line was followed also in the case of *Clea Shipping Corporation* v *Bulk Oil International, The Alaskan Trader* [1984] 1 All E.R. 129. A vessel had been chartered by the plaintiff owners to the defendants, the hire charge having been paid in advance. However, the ship broke down and required expensive repairs. The charterers thereupon gave notice that they intended to end the contract. However, the plaintiffs decided to keep the agreement open and undertook the repairs and then informed the defendants that the vessel was at their disposal. The plaintiffs said they were exercising their right of election conferred upon the innocent party in such circumstances to keep the contract open, thus entitling them to keep the hire money instead of suing for damages.

Lloyd, J. denied the existence of an unfettered right of election for an innocent party to keep the contract running in such circumstances. He found that, in the absence of a 'legitimate interest' in the contract's perpetuation by the party faced with repudiation, the party concerned could, though innocent, be forced to accept damages in lieu of sums falling due under the contract subsequent to the actionable event. This restraint is founded on general equitable principles, to be based on what is reasonable on the facts of each case.

235. *Avery* v *Bowden* (1855) 5 E. & B. 714

The defendants chartered the plaintiff's ship *Lebanon* and agreed to load her with a cargo at Odessa within 45 days. The ship went to Odessa and remained there for most of the 45-day period. The defendant told the captain of the ship that he did not propose to load a cargo and that he would do well to leave, but the captain stayed on at Odessa, hoping that the defendant would change his mind. Before the end of the 45-day period the Crimean War broke out so that performance of the contract would have been illegal as a trading with the enemy. *Held* – the plaintiff might have treated the defendant's refusal to load a cargo as an anticipatory breach of contract but his agent, the captain, had waived that right by staying on at Odessa, and now the contract had been discharged by something which was beyond the control of either party.

> COMMENT
> A modern application of the above rule can be seen in *Fercometal Sarl* v *Mediterranean Shipping Co Ltd* [1988] 2 All E.R. 742. The plaintiffs chartered a ship to the defendants. The charter-party (i.e. the contract) provided that if the ship was not ready to load during the period 3–9 July the defendants could cancel the contract. On 2 July the defendants said that they were not going on with the contract anyway but the plaintiff did not accept that breach and provided the ship, but this was not ready to load until the 12 July and the defendants said again that they would not go on with the contract. The plaintiffs sued for damages and failed. They could have based an action on the first breach but had not done so. Their action on the second 'breach' failed because the ship was not ready to load.

Law of contracts – remedies and limitation of actions

DAMAGES: MUST BE A GENUINE PRE-ESTIMATE OF LOSS

236. *Ford Motor Co (England) Ltd* v *Armstrong* (1915) 31 T.L.R. 267

The defendant was a retailer who received supplies from the plaintiffs. As part of his agreement with the plaintiffs the defendant had undertaken:

(*a*) not to sell any of the plaintiff's cars or spares below list price;

(*b*) not to sell Ford cars to other dealers in the motor trade;

(*c*) not to exhibit any car supplied by the company without their permission.

The defendant also agreed to pay £250 for every breach of the agreement as being the agreed damage which the manufacturer will 'sustain'. The defendant was in breach of the agreement and the plaintiffs sued. It was *held* by the Court of Appeal that the sum of £250 was in the nature of a penalty and not liquidated damages. The same sum was payable for different kinds of breach which were not likely to produce the same loss. Furthermore its size suggested that it was not a genuine pre-estimate of loss.

COMMENT
A contrast is provided by *Dunlop* v *New Garage & Motor Co Ltd* [1915] A.C. 79 where the contract provided that the defendants would have to pay £5 for every tyre sold below the list price. The House of Lords *held* that this was an honest attempt to provide for a breach and was recoverable as liquidated damages. Privity problems did not arise here because the wholesalers were Dunlop's agents.

237. *Cellulose Acetate Silk Co Ltd* v *Widnes Foundry Ltd* [1933] A.C. 20

The Widnes Foundry entered into a contract to erect a plant for the Silk Co by a certain date. It was also agreed that the Widnes Foundry would pay the Silk Co £20 per week for every week they took in erecting the plant beyond the agreed date. In the event the plant was completed 30 weeks late, and the Silk Co claimed for their actual loss which was £5850. *Held* – the Widnes Foundry were only liable to pay £20 per week as agreed.

DAMAGES: THE OBJECT IS TO PUT THE PLAINTIFF IN THE SAME POSITION FINANCIALLY AS IF THE CONTRACT HAD BEEN PROPERLY PERFORMED

238. *Beach* v *Reed Corrugated Cases Ltd* [1956] 2 All E.R. 652

This was an action brought by the plaintiff for wrongful dismissal by the defendants. The plaintiff was the managing director of the company and he had a 15-year contract from 21 December 1950 at a salary of £5000 per annum. His contract was terminated in August 1954 when he was 54 years old and the sum of money that he might have earned would have been £55,000, but the general damages awarded to him were £18,000 after the court had taken into account income tax, including tax on his private investments.

It should be noted that the award of damages itself is not subject to tax.

COMMENT
(i) In a later case and on similar reasoning it was held that what the plaintiff would have paid by way of national insurance contributions must also be deducted (see *Cooper* v *Firth Brown Ltd* [1963] 2 All E.R. 31).

(ii) In *C. & P. Haulage* v *Middleton* [1983] 3 All E.R. 94, C. & P. let Mr Middleton have a licence for six months renewable of premises from which he conducted a business as a self-employed engineer. He lived in a council house and would have used his own garage there, but the council objected. There was a quarrel between the parties and M was evicted from the premises before the licence term expired. This was a breach of contract by C. & P. M stopped a cheque which was payable to C. & P. because of his grievance. They sued him on it. He counter-claimed for damages because of his eviction. In fact the council had let him use his own garage for the remainder of the six months' term. *Held* – by the Court of Appeal – that since he had paid no rent for the premises in which he had worked following his eviction, he was no worse off than if the contract had been properly carried out. It was not the function of the court to put a plaintiff in a better position than he would have been if the contract had not been broken. Only nominal damages were awarded.

(iii) Damages have been awarded for the loss of a chance. This is not prevented by the rule that the plaintiff must not be better off. Thus in *Chaplin* v *Hicks* [1911] 2 K.B. 786 the plaintiff who had won earlier stages of a beauty contest was, by error of the defendant organiser, not invited to the final. Although it was by no means certain that she would have won, the plaintiff was awarded £100 damages.

DAMAGES: FOR MENTAL DISTRESS

239. *Jarvis* v *Swans Tours Ltd* [1973] 1 All E.R. 71

Swans promised the plaintiff a 'Houseparty' holiday in Switzerland. Some of the more important things promised were a welcome party on arrival: afternoon tea and cake, Swiss dinner by candlelight, fondue party, yodeller evening and farewell party. Also the hotel owner was said to speak English.

Among the matters which the plaintiff complained about were that the hotel owner could not speak English. This meant he had no one to talk to since although there were 13 people present during the first week he was on his own for the second week. The cake for tea was potato crisps and dry nutcake. The yodeller evening consisted of a local man who came in his overalls and sang a few songs very quickly. The Court of Appeal *held* that the plaintiff was entitled to an award of £125 damages. (Incidentally the holiday had cost £63.)

DAMAGES: REMOTENESS: LOSS MUST BE PROXIMATE AND NOT TOO REMOTE

240. *Hadley* v *Baxendale* (1845) 9 Exch. 341

The plaintiff was a miller at Gloucester. The driving shaft of the mill being broken, the plaintiff engaged the defendant, a carrier, to take it to the makers at Greenwich so that they might use it in making a new one. The defendant delayed delivery of the shaft beyond a reasonable time, so that the mill was idle for much longer than should have been necessary. The plaintiff now sued in respect of loss of profits during the period of additional delay. The court decided that there were only two possible grounds on which the plaintiff could succeed.

(a) That in the usual course of things the work of the mill would cease altogether for the want of the shaft. This the court rejected because, to take only one reasonable possibility, the plaintiff might have had a spare.

(b) That the special circumstances were fully explained, so that the defendant was made aware of the possible loss. The evidence showed that there had been no such explanation. In fact the only information given to the defendant was that the article to be carried was the broken shaft of a mill, and that the plaintiff was the miller of that mill.

Held – the plaintiff's claim failed, the damage being too remote.

COMMENT
The loss here did not arise *naturally* from the breach because there might have been a spare. The fact that there was no spare was not within the contemplation of the defendant and he had not even been told about it, much less accepted the risk. The defendant did not know that there was no spare nor as a reasonable man ought have known there was not.

241. *The Heron II (Koufos v Czarnikow)* [1967] 3 All E.R. 686

Shipowners carrying sugar from Constanza to Basra delayed delivery at Basra for nine days during which time the market in sugar there fell and the charterers lost more than £4000. It was *held* that they could recover that sum from the shipowners because the very existence of a 'market' for goods implied that prices might fluctuate and a fall in sugar prices was likely or in contemplation.

COMMENT
The existence of a major sugar market at Basra made it within the *contemplation* of the defendants that the plaintiff might sell the sugar and not merely use it in a business.

242. *Horne v Midland Railway Co* (1873) L.R. 8 C.P. 131

The plaintiff had entered into a contract to sell 4595 pairs of boots to the French Army at a price above the market price. The defendants were responsible for a delay in the delivery of boots, and the purchasers refused to accept delivery, regarding time as the essence of the contract. The plaintiff's claim for damages was based on the contract price, namely 4s per pair, but it was held that he could only recover the market price of 2s 9d per pair unless he could show the defendants were aware of the exceptional profit involved, and that they had undertaken to be liable for its loss.

COMMENT
In *Simpson* v *London & North Western Rail Co* (1876) 1 Q.B.D. 274 the

plaintiff entrusted samples of his products to the defendants so that they could deliver them to Newcastle for an agricultural exhibition. The goods were marked 'Must be at Newcastle on Monday certain'. The defendants did not get them to Newcastle on time and were held liable for the plaintiff's prospective loss of profit arising because he could not exhibit at Newcastle. They had agreed to carry the goods knowing of the special instructions of the customer.

243. *Victoria Laundry Ltd* v *Newman Industries Ltd* [1949] 2 K.B. 528

The defendants agreed to deliver a new boiler to the plaintiffs by a certain date but failed to do so, being 22 weeks late, with the result that the plaintiff lost (a) normal business profits during the period of delay, and (b) profits from dyeing contracts which were offered to them during the period. It was *held* that (a) but not (b) were recoverable as damages.

> COMMENT
> The general loss of profit in this case arises naturally from the breach and no further 'contemplation' or 'notice' test need be applied. The loss of profit on the dyeing contracts was not *known* to the defendants nor as reasonable men *ought* they to have had it in *contemplation*.

DAMAGES: THE INJURED PARTY MUST MITIGATE HIS LOSS

244. *Brace* v *Calder* [1895] 2 Q.B. 253

The defendants, a partnership consisting of four members, agreed to employ the plaintiff as manager of a branch of the business for two years. Five months later the partnership was dissolved by the retirement of two of the members and the business was transferred to the other two who offered to employ the plaintiff on the same terms as before but he refused the offer. The dissolution of the partnership constituted a wrongful dimissal of the plaintiff and he brought an action for breach of contract seeking to recover the salary that he would have received had he served the whole period of two years. It was *held* that he was entitled only to nominal damages since it was unreasonable to have rejected the offer of continued employment.

INJUNCTION: OF A NEGATIVE STIPULATION

245. *Warner Brothers Pictures Incorporated* v *Nelson* [1937] 1 K.B. 209

The defendant, the film actress Bette Davis, had entered into a contract in which she agreed to act exclusively for the plaintiffs for twelve months. She was anxious to obtain more money and so she left America, and entered into a contract with a person in England. The plaintiffs now asked for an injunction restraining the defendant from carrying out the English contract. *Held* – an injunction would be granted. The contract contained a negative stipulation not to work for anyone else, and this could be enforced. However, since the contract was an American one, the court limited the operation of the injunction to the area of the court's jurisdiction, and although the contract stipulated that the defendant would not work in any other occupation, the injunction was confined to work on stage or screen.

COMMENT
(i) Even where, as here, there is a negative stipulation, the court will not grant an injunction if the pressure to work for the plaintiffs is so severe as to be for all practical purposes irresistible. In this case it was said that Bette Davis could still earn her living by doing other work.

(ii) The idea that persons such as Bette Davis or others subjected to injunctions of negative stipulations would take other work was challenged by the Court of Appeal in *Warren v Mendy* [1989] 3 All E.R. 103 on the grounds of 'realism and practicality'. The Court of Appeal said that it was unrealistic to suppose that such persons would take up other work, i.e. that boxers would become clerks and actresses secretaries. Thus the making of an injunction of a negative stipulation in this sort of case was in general terms likely to operate as a decree of specific performance. This means that it is in modern law less likely that such injunctions will be granted or that the Warner Brothers case will be followed though it is not overruled.

246. *Whitwood Chemical Co v Hardman* [1891] 2 Ch. 416

The defendant entered into a contract of service with the plaintiffs and agreed to give the whole of his time to them. In fact he occasionally worked for others, and the plaintiffs tried to enforce the undertaking in the service contract by injunction. *Held* – an injunction could not be granted because there was no express negative stipulation. The defendant had merely stated what he would do, and not what he would not do, and to read into the undertaking an agreement not to work for anyone else required the court to imply a negative stipulation from a positive one. No such implication could be made.

COMMENT
It is because of the fact that the granting of an injunction of a negative stipulation is so close to specific performance that it is restricted to cases where the negative stipulation is express.

QUANTUM MERUIT: AS A QUASI-CONTRACTUAL REMEDY

247. *Craven-Ellis v Canons Ltd* [1936] 2 All E.R. 1066

The plaintiff was employed as managing director by the company under a deed which provided for remuneration. The articles provided that directors must have qualification shares, and must obtain these within two months of appointment. The plaintiff and other directors who appointed him never obtained the required number of shares so that the deed was invalid. However, the plaintiff had rendered services, and he now sued on a *quantum meruit* for a reasonable sum by way of remuneration. *Held* – he succeeded on a *quantum meruit*, there being no valid contract.

LIMITATION OF ACTIONS: EFFECT OF FRAUD, CONCEALMENT AND MISTAKE

248. *Lynn* v *Bamber* [1930] 2 K.B. 72

In 1921 the plaintiff purchased some plum trees from the defendant and was given a warranty that the trees were 'Purple Pershores'. In 1928 the plaintiff discovered that the trees were not 'Purple Pershores' and sued for damages. The defendant pleaded that the claim was barred by the current Limitation Act. *Held* – the defendant's fraudulent misrepresentation and fraudulent concealment of the breach of warranty provided a good answer to this plea, so that the plaintiff could recover.

COMMENT
(i) The present jurisdiction is s. 32 of the Limitation Act, 1980.

(ii) In *Peco Arts Inc.* v *Hazlitt Gallery Ltd* [1983] 3 All E.R. 193 the plaintiffs bought from the defendants in November 1970 what purported to be an original drawing in black chalk on paper, *Etude pour le Bain Turc* by J.A.D. Ingres, for the price of $18,000. In 1976 it was revalued by an expert for insurance purposes. No doubts were cast upon its authenticity. However, on a valuation in 1981 it was discovered that the drawing was a reproduction. The plaintiffs claimed rescission and recovery of the purchase price plus interest on the grounds of mutual, common or unilateral mistake of fact. The trial was adjourned on the first day because the parties wished to simplify the issues. After this the only defence was the Limitation Act, 1980, i.e. that the plaintiff's claim was statute barred. It was held that it was not and judgment was given for the plaintiffs. Webster, J. decided that a prudent buyer in the position of the plaintiffs would not normally have obtained an independent authentication but would have relied on the defendant's reputation, as the plaintiffs had done. Further, the plaintiffs were entitled to conclude that the drawing was an original as the valuers who had examined it in 1976 had not questioned its authenticity. There was no lack of diligence on the part of the plaintiffs. Accordingly, the action was not time barred and there would be judgment for the plaintiffs.

(iii) The *Peco* case does not decide what the effect of the mistake was, and to that extent does not go contrary to *Leaf* (see p. 641) and *Bell* (see p. 640). These matters were not contested by the defendants. In *Leaf* the court was deciding how soon an action must be brought for rescission for *innocent misrepresentation*. The issue here was how soon must an action be brought where the plaintiff claimed relief for the consequences of an operative mistake.

Law of contract – employment protection

SEX DISCRIMINATION: DIRECT DISCRIMINATION: LESS FAVOURABLE TREATMENT OF A PERSON ON GROUNDS OF RACE

249. *Johnson* v *Timber Tailors (Midlands)* [1978] I.R.L.R. 146

When the plaintiff, a black Jamaican, applied for a job with the defendants as a wood machinist, the defendants' works manager told him that he would be contacted in a couple of days to let him know whether or not he had been successful. Mr Johnson was not contacted and after a number of unsuccessful attempts to get in touch with the works manager, was told that the vacancy had been filled. Another advertisement for wood machinists appeared in the paper on the same night as Mr Johnson was told that the vacancy had been filled. Nevertheless, Mr Johnson applied again for the job and was told that the vacancy had been filled. About a week later he applied again and was again told that the job had been filled although a further advertisement had appeared for the job on that day. It was held by an Industrial Tribunal that the evidence established that Mr Johnson had been discriminated against on the grounds of race.

> COMMENT
> The other side of the coin is illustrated by *Panesar* v *Nestlé & Co Ltd* [1980] I.C.R. 144 where an orthodox Sikh who naturally wore a beard, which was required by his religion, applied for a job in the defendants' cholocolate factory. He was refused employment because the defendants applied a strict rule under which no beards or excessively long hair were allowed on the grounds of hygiene. The plaintiff made a complaint of indirect discrimination but the defendants said that the rule was justified. The Court of Appeal held that as the defendants had supported their rule with scientific evidence there was in fact no discrimination.

SEX DISCRIMINATION: GENUINE OCCUPATIONAL QUALIFICATION: REQUIREMENT OF DECENCY

250. *Sisley* v *Britannia Security Systems* [1983] I.C.R. 628

The defendants employed women to work in a security control station. The plaintiff applied for a vacant job but was refused employment. It appeared that the women worked twelve hour shifts with rest periods and that beds were provided for their use during such breaks. The women undressed to their underwear during these rest breaks. The plaintiff complained that by advertising for women the defendants were contravening the Sex Discrimination Act, 1975. The defendants pleaded genuine occupational qualification, i.e. that women were required because of the removal of uniform during rest periods was incidental to the employment. The Employment Appeal Tribunal accepted that defence. The defence of preservation of decency was, in the circumstances, a good one. It was reasonably incidental to the women's work that they should remove their clothing during rest periods.

THERE IS NO PRESUMPTION THAT A CONTRACT OF EMPLOYMENT CONTAINS AN IMPLIED TERM THAT SICK PAY WILL BE PROVIDED

251. *Mears* v *Safecar Security* [1982] 2 All E.R. 865

Mr Mears was absent from his employment through sickness for six months out of some 14 months' employment. He then resigned because of ill-health. During the period of his sickness he made no claim for wages and the written statement of his terms of employment under s. 1, EPCA made no mention of sick pay. Indeed, he was told by other employees who visited him while he was sick that the employers did not pay wages during periods when employees were off work through sickness. After resigning Mr Mears applied to an industrial tribunal to determine what particulars regarding sick pay should have been included in the s. 1 statement. The tribunal held that the contract of employment included an implied term under which the employer would pay wages during sickness, subject to deducting any sickness benefit. There was an appeal against that decision by both parties. However, it is the employers' appeal which is of concern here. They alleged that the term relating to sick pay should not be implied at all. The Employment Appeal Tribunal upheld the employers' contention. The industrial tribunal was not right in assuming that a contract of employment must contain an implied term about sick pay. All the facts must be considered and here the implied term was that wages were not paid during sickness.

> COMMENT
> The Employment Appeal Tribunal did not follow an earlier decision, i.e. *Orman* v *Saville Sportswear Ltd* [1960] 3 All E.R. 105, under which it was said that the court could imply a term relating to sick pay and that, indeed, in modern law there seemed to be a presumption in favour of the employee being entitled to sick pay unless and employer could bring evidence to show that this was not the case.

A MAN AND A WOMAN WILL BE REGARDED AS ENGAGED IN 'LIKE WORK' EVEN THOUGH THERE MAY BE SOME DIFFERENCES BETWEEN THE JOBS, BUT NOT IF THESE DIFFERENCES ARE 'MATERIAL'

252. *Capper Pass* v *Lawton* [1976] I.R.L.R. 366

A female cook who worked a 40-hour week preparing lunches for the directors of Capper was paid a lower rate than two male assistant chefs who worked a 45-hour week preparing some 350 meals a day in Cappers' works canteen. The female cook claimed that by reason of the EPA (as amended) she should be paid at the same rate as the assistant chefs since she was employed on work of a broadly similar nature.

It was held by the EAT that if the work done by a female applicant was of a broadly similar nature to that done by a male colleague it should be regarded as being like work for the purposes of the EPA unless there were some practical differences of detail between the two types of job. In this case the EAT decided that the work done by the female cook was broadly similar to the work of the assistant chefs and that the differences of detail were not of practical importance in relation to the terms and conditions of employment. Consequently, the female cook was entitled to be paid at the same rate as her male colleagues.

253. *Navy, Army and Air Force Insitutes* v *Varley* [1977] 1 All E.R. 840

Miss Varley worked as a Grade E clerical worker in the accounts office of NAAFI in Nottingham. NAAFI conceded that her work was like that of Grade E male clerical workers employed in NAAFI's London Office. However, the Grade E workers in Nottingham worked a 37-hour week, while the male Grade E clerical workers in the London office worked a 36½-hour week. Miss Varley applied to an industrial tribunal under the EPA for a declaration that she was less favourably treated as regards hours worked than the male clerical workers in London and that her contract term as to hours be modified so as to reduce it to 36½ hours a week. The industrial tribunal granted that declaration and NAAFI appealed.

It was *held* by the EAT that the variation in hours was genuinely due to a material difference other than the difference of sex. It was due to a real difference in that the male employees worked in London where there was a custom to work shorter hours. Accordingly NAAFI's appeal was allowed and Miss Varley was held not to be entitled to the declaration.

> There is a geographical distinction between the conditions operated by NAAFI in respect of their employees in London and those outside London. That is by no means a unique situation; it is common to the Civil Service and to all sorts of other employment. . . . In other words, the variation between her contract and a man's contract is due really to the fact that she works in Nottingham and he works in London. It seems to us that it is quite plain that that is the difference between her case and his case, namely that she works in Nottingham where this old custom operates and he works in London where the custom of a shorter working week operates. (*Per* Phillips, J.)

SEX DISCRIMINATION: DIRECT DISCRIMINATION: LESS FAVOURABLE TREATMENT OF A PERSON ON GROUNDS OF SEX OR RACE

254. *Coleman* v *Skyrail Oceanic Ltd* (1981) 131 N.L.J. 880

The plaintiff, who was a female booking clerk for Skyrail, a travel agency, was dismissed after she married an employee of a rival agency. Skyrail feared that there might be leaks of information about charter flights and had assumed that her dismissal was not unreasonable since the husband was the breadwinner. The Employment Appeal Tribunal decided that the dimissal was reasonable on the basis that the husband was the breadwinner. However, there was an appeal to the Court of Appeal which decided that those provisions of the Sex Discrimination Act, 1975 which dealt with direct discrimination and dismissal on grounds of sex had been infringed. The assumption that husbands were breadwinners and wives were not, was based on sex and was discriminatory. The plaintiff's injury to her feelings was compensated by an award of £100 damages.

> COMMENT
> The plaintiff was also held to be unfairly dismissed, having received no warning that she would be dismissed on marriage. The additional and discriminatory reason regarding the breadwinner cost the employer a further £100. It was not the totality of the plaintiff's award.

SEXUAL AND RACIAL DISCRIMINATION. INDIRECT DISCRIMINATION: REQUIREMENTS OR CONDITIONS APPLIED TO ALL WORKERS BUT THE ABILITY OF SOME PERSONS TO COMPLY BECAUSE OF SEX OR RACE IS CONSIDERABLY SMALLER AND CANNOT BE JUSTIFIED

255. *Price* v *The Civil Service Commission* [1977] I.R.L.R. 291

The Civil Service required candidates for the position of executive officer to be between 17½ and 28 years. Belinda Price complained that this age bar constituted indirect sex discrimination against women because women between those ages were more likely than men to be temporarily out of the labour market having children or caring for children at home. It was *held* by the Employment Appeal Tribunal that that age bar was indirect discrimination against women. The Court held that the words 'can comply' must not be construed narrowly. It could be said that any female applicant could comply with the condition in the sense that she was not obliged to marry or to have children or to look after them – indeed she may find someone else to look after them or, as a last resort, put them into care. If the legislation was construed in that way it was no doubt right to say that any female applicant could comply with the condition. However, in the view of the Court to construe the legislation in that way appeared to be wholly out of sympathy with the spirit and intention of the Act. A person should not be deemed to be able to do something merely because it was theoretically possible, it was necessary to decide whether it was possible for the person to do so in practice, as distinct from theory.

THE HEALTH AND SAFETY AT WORK ACT 1974 PROVIDES THAT IT SHALL BE THE DUTY OF EVERY EMPLOYER TO CONDUCT HIS UNDERTAKING IN SUCH A WAY AS TO ENSURE, SO FAR AS REASONABLY PRACTICABLE, THAT PERSONS NOT IN HIS EMPLOYMENT WHO MAY BE AFFECTED THEREBY ARE NOT THEREBY EXPOSED TO RISKS TO THEIR HEALTH AND SAFETY

256. *R v Mara*, *The Times*, 13 November 1986

In this case it was alleged that the director of a company was in breach of his duty under the Health and Safety at Work Act where machinery belonging to his cleaning and maintenance company was left at a store which the company was under contract to clean, and the cleaning company agreed that employees of the store could use the machinery for part of the cleaning and one of the employees of the store was electrocuted because of a fault in the cable of one of the machines. The Court of Appeal held that the director concerned was in breach of his duty and dismissed his appeal from the Warwick Crown Court where he had been fined £200. Mr Mara was the director of a small company, Cleaning & Maintenance Ltd (C.M.S.). In December 1983 C.M.S. made a contract with International Stores plc (I.S.) to clean their premises. The work required the use of certain electrical cleaning machines provided by C.M.S. and these were left on the I.S. premises when C.M.S. employees were not there. The machines included a polisher/scrubber.

The cleaning of the loading bay for the store in the morning was inconvenient and it was agreed that its cleaning should be removed from the ambit of the contract and at that time C.M.S. agreed at the request of I.S. that their cleaning machines could be used by I.S. employees for cleaning the loading bay and to Mr Mara's knowledge they were so used.

On 10 November 1984 an employee of I.S. was using a C.M.S. polisher/ scrubber for cleaning the loading bay when he was electrocuted because of the defective condition of the machine's cable.

The legal point was one of construction of the relevant section of the Health and Safety at Work Act which is set out in the headnote to this case. Mr Mara claimed that when the electrocution took place his company, C.M.S. was not conducting its undertaking at all, the only undertaking being conducted was that of I.S. whose employees were using the machine to clean the I.S. premises. The Court of Appeal did not accept this. The undertaking of C.M.S. was the provision of cleaning services. So far as I.S. was concerned the way in which C.M.S. conducted its undertaking was to do the cleaning and also to leave its machines and other equipment on the premises with permission for I.S. employees to use the same with the knowledge that they would use the same. The equipment included an unsafe cable. The failure to remove or replace that cable was clearly a breach by C.M.S. of its duty both to its own employees and also under the Health and Safety at Work Act to the workers of I.S.

COMMENT
This case shows the wide ambit of the Health and Safety at Work Act, 1974. The liability of a director for offences by the company is set out in the 1974 Act which provides that where an offence under any of the provisions of the Act is committed by a body incorporate, then should it be proved to be committed with the consent or connivance of, or to have been attributable to any neglect on the part of any director, manager, secretary, or similar officer of the body corporate, or a person who is purporting to act in such capacity, he as well as the body corporate shall be guilty of that offence and shall be liable to be proceeded against and punished accordingly. It should also be remembered that there is a civil claim for damages for this kind of breach. This case is concerned solely with the criminal offence.

UNFAIR DISMISSAL: IS THE COURT OR TRIBUNAL DEALING WITH AN EMPLOYEE?

257. *Massey* v *Crown Life Insurance Co* [1978] 2 All E.R. 576

Mr Massey was employed by Crown Life as the manager of their Ilford branch from 1971 to 1973, the company paying him wages and deducting tax. In 1973, on the advice of his accountant, Mr Massey registered a business name of J.R. Massey & Associates and with that new name entered into an agreement with Crown Life under which he carried out the same duties as before but as a self-employed person. The Inland Revenue were content that he should change to be taxed under Schedule D as a self-employed person. His employment was terminated and he claimed to have been unfairly dismissed. The Court of Appeal decided that being self-employed he could not be unfairly dismissed.

CONDUCT JUSTIFYING DISMISSAL MAY BE THE WAY IN WHICH AN EMPLOYEE DRESSES

258. *Boychuk* v *H.J. Symons (Holdings) Ltd* [1977] I.R.L.R. 395

Miss B was employed by S Ltd as an accounts audit clerk but her duties involved contact with the public from time to time. Miss B insisted on wearing badges which proclaimed the fact that she was a lesbian and from May 1976 she wore one or other of the following: (a) a lesbian symbol consisting of two circles with crosses (indicating women) joined together; (b) badges with the legends 'Gays against fascism'; and 'Gay power'; (c) a badge with the legend 'Gay switchboard' with a telephone number on it and the words 'Information service for homosexual men and women'; (d) a badge with the word 'Dyke', indicating to the initiated that she was a lesbian.

These were eventually superseded by a white badge with the words 'Lesbians ignite' written in large letters on it. Nothing much had happened in regard to the wearing of the earlier badges but when she began wearing the 'Lesbians ignite' badge there were discussions about it between her and her employer. She was told that she must remove it – which she was not willing to do – and that if she did not she would be dismissed. She would not remove the badge and was dismissed on 16 August 1976 and then made a claim for compensation for unfair dismissal.

No complaint was made regarding the manner of her dismissal in terms e.g. of proper warning. The straight question was whether her employers were entitled to dismiss her because she insisted on wearing the badge. An industrial tribunal had decided that in all the circumstances the dismissal was fair because it was within an employer's discretion to instruct an employee not to wear a particular badge or symbol which could cause offence to customers and fellow employees. Miss B appealed to the Employment Appeal Tribunal which dismissed her appeal and said that her dismissal was fair. The court said that there was no question of Miss B having been dismissed because she was a lesbian or because of anything to do with her private lifte or private behaviour. Such a case would be entirely different and raise different questions. This was only a case where she had been dismissed because of her conduct at work. That, the court said, must be clearly understood.

COMMENT

(i) The decision does not mean that an employer by a foolish or unreasonable judgment of what could be expected to be offensive could impose some unreasonable restriction on an employee. However, the decision does mean that a reasonable employer, who is, after all, ultimately responsible for the interests of the business, is allowed to decide what, upon reflection or mature consideration, could be offensive to customers and fellow employees, and he need not wait to see whether the business would in fact be damaged before he takes steps in the matter.

(ii) In *Kowalski* v *The Berkeley Hotel* [1985] I.R.L.R. 40 the EAT decided that the dismissal of a pastrycook for fighting at work was fair though it was the first time he had done it.

DISMISSAL ON A TRANSFER OF BUSINESS

259. *Meikle v McPhail (Charleston Arms)* [1983] I.R.L.R. 351

After contracting to take over a public house and its employees, the new management decided that economies were essential and dismissed the barmaid. She complained to an industrial tribunal on the grounds of unfair dismissal. Her case was based upon the fact that the 1981 Regulations state that a dismissal is to be treated as unfair if the transfer of a business or a reason connected with it is the reason or principal reason for the dismissal. The pub's new management defended the claim under another provision in the 1981 Regulations which states that a dismissal following a transfer of business is not to be regarded as automatically unfair where there was, as in this case, an economic reason for making changes in the work-force. If there is such a reason, unfairness must be established on grounds other than the mere transfer of the business.

The Employment Appeal Tribunal decided that the reason for dismissal was an economic one under the Regulations and that the management had acted reasonably in the circumstances so that the barmaid's claim failed.

COMMENT
It should be noted that in *Gateway Hotels Ltd* v *Stewart* [1988] I.R.L.R. 287 the Employment Appeal Tribunal decided that on a transfer of business dismissal of employees of the business transferred prior to the transfer at the insistence of the purchaser of the business is not an 'economic' reason within the Regulations so that the dismissals are unfair.

AN EMPLOYEE WHO UNREASONABLY REFUSED AN OFFER OF ALTERNATIVE EMPLOYMENT IS NOT ENTITLED TO A REDUNDANCY PAYMENT

260. *Fuller* v *Stephanie Bowman* [1977] I.R.L.R. 7

F was employed as a secretary at SB's premises which were situated in Mayfair. These premises attracted a very high rent and rates so SB moved their offices to Soho. These premises were situated over a sex shop and F refused the offer of renewed employment at the same salary and she later brought a claim before an industrial tribunal for a redundancy payment. The tribunal decided that the question of unreasonableness was a matter of fact for the tribunal and F's refusal to work over the sex shop was unreasonable so that she was not entitled to a redundancy payment.

COMMENT
(i) It should be noted that in *North East Coast Ship Repairers* v *Secretary of State For Employment* [1978] I.R.L.R. 149 the Employment Appeal Tribunal decided that an apprentice who, having completed the period of his apprenticeship, finds that the firm cannot provide him with work, is not entitled to redundancy payment. This case had relevance for trainees and others completing contracts in order to obtain relevant practical experience.

As regards time limits, the employee must make a written claim to the employer or to an industrial tribunal within six months from the end of the employment. If the employee does not do this an industrial tribunal may extend the time for a further six months, making twelve months in all, but not longer, from the actual date of termination of the employment, provided that it can be shown that it is just and equitable having regard to the reasons put forward by the employee for late application and to all relevant circumstances.

(ii) In *Elliot* v *Richard Stump Ltd* [1987] I.R.L.R. 215 the EAT decided that a redundant employee who is offered alternative employment by an employer who refuses to accept a trial period is unfairly dismissed.

Law of torts

NATURE OF TORT: NOT ALL HARM IS ACTIONABLE

261. *Perera* v *Vandiyar* [1953] 1 All E.R. 1109

The plaintiff was the tenant of a flat in Tooting, and the defendant was the landlord. On 8 October 1952, the landlord cut off the supply of gas and electricity to the flat in order to induce the plaintiff to leave. As a result, the plaintiff was forced to move out of the flat and lived elsewhere until the services were restored on 15 October 1952. The plaintiff claimed damages for breach of implied covenant for quiet enjoyment, and also for eviction. *Held* – the plaintiff was entitled to damages for breach of the implied covenant, but punitive damages on the purported tort of eviction were not recoverable because the defendant had not committed a tort. It had not been necessary for the defendant to trespass on any part of the demised premises in order to cut off the services, and mere intention to evict was not a tort.

> COMMENT
> This kind of conduct by a landlord is now a criminal offence under s. 1, Protection from Eviction Act, 1977. However, there is no civil action for breach of the statutory duty. (*McCall* v *Abelesz* [1976] 1 All E.R. 727.)

262. *Hargreaves* v *Bretherton* [1958] 3 W.L.R. 463

The plaintiff pleaded that the defendant had falsely and maliciously and without just cause or excuse committed perjury as a witness at the plaintiff's trial for certain criminal offences, and that as a result the plaintiff had been convicted and sentenced to eight years' preventive detention. A point of law arose because the plaintiff's action was in effect based on the purported tort of perjury. *Held* – no action lay on this cause, since there was no tort of perjury, and therefore the plaintiff's claim must be struck out.

263. *Roy* v *Prior* [1969] 3 All E.R. 1153

The plaintiff, a doctor, sued the defendant, a solicitor, for damages alleging, amongst other things, that the defendant had caused his arrest and forcible attendance at court to give evidence in a criminal case by saying falsely in court that the plaintiff was evading a witness summons. The action failed. Lord Denning, M.R., saying in the course of his judgment –

> It is settled law that, if a witness knowingly and maliciously tells untruths in the witness box, and as a result an innocent person is imprisoned, nevertheless no action lies against that witness. . . . The reason lies in public

policy. Witnesses must be able to give their evidence without fear of the consequences. They might be deterred from doing so if they were at risk of being sued for what they said. So the law gives a witness the cloak of absolute immunity from suit. This applies not only to statements made by a witness in the box, but also to statements made whilst he is giving his proof to his solicitor beforehand. The reason is because the protection given to the witness in the box would be useless to him if it could be got round by an action against him in respect of his proof. . . .

COMMENT
The Criminal Justice Act, 1988 gives prisoners whose convictions are quashed or pardoned a *right* to monetary compensation from the government. The matter of compensation was formerly a matter for the discretion of the Home Secretary.

NATURE OF TORT: EXPANDING ROLE OF NEGLIGENCE FROM THE ATKINIAN NEIGHBOUR TEST

264. *Donoghue (or M'Alister)* v *Stevenson* [1932] A.C. 562

The appellant's friend purchased a bottle of ginger beer from a retailer in Paisley and gave it to her. The respondents were the manufacturers of the ginger beer. The appellant consumed some of the ginger beer and her friend was replenishing the glass, when, according to the appellant, the decomposed remains of a snail came out of the bottle. The bottle was made of dark glass so that the snail could not be seen until most of the contents had been consumed. The appellant became ill and served a writ on the manufacturers claiming damages. The question before the House of Lords was whether the facts outlined above constituted a cause of action in negligence. The House of Lords *held* by a majority of three to two that they did. It was stated that a manufacturer of products, which are sold in such a form that they are likely to reach the ultimate consumer in the form in which they left the manufacturer with no possibility of intermediate examination, owes a duty to the consumer to take reasonable care to prevent injury. This rule has been broadened in subsequent cases so that the manufacturer is liable more often where defective chattels cause injury. The following important points also arise out of the case.

(a) It was in this case that the House of Lords formulated the test that the duty of care in negligence is based on the foresight of the reasonable man. As Lord Atkin said:

The liability for negligence, whether you style it such or treat it as in other systems as a species of 'culpa' is no doubt based upon a general public sentiment of moral wrongdoing for which the offender must pay. But acts or omissions which any moral code would censure cannot in a practical world be treated so as to give a right to every person injured by them to demand relief. In this way rules of law arise which limit the range of complainants and the extent of their remedy. The rule that you are to love your neighbour becomes in law, you must not injure your neighbour; and the lawyer's question, Who is my neighbour? receives a restricted reply. You must take reasonable care to avoid acts or omissions which you can reasonably foresee would be likely to injure your neighbour. Who, then in law is my neighbour? The answer seems to be – persons who are so closely and directly affected by my act that I ought reasonably to have them in contemplation as being so affected when I am directing my mind to the acts or omissions which are called in question.

(b) Lord Macmillan's remark in his judgment that the categories of negligence are never closed suggests that the tort of negligence is capable of further expansion. That this has been so is revealed by the discussion of later cases at p. 448

(c) The duty of care with regard to chattels as laid down in the case relates to chattels not dangerous in themselves. The duty of care in respect of chattels dangerous in themselves, e.g. explosives, is much higher.

(d) The appellant had no cause of action against the retailer in contract because her friend bought the bottle, so that there was no privity of contract between the retailer and the appellant. Therefore terms relating to fitness for purpose and merchantable quality, now implied into such contracts by the Sale of Goods Act, 1979, did not apply here.

> COMMENT
> A remedy under the Sale of Goods Act could have been given to the appellant if the reasoning of Tucker, J., in *Lockett* v *A. & M. Charles Ltd* [1938] 4 All E.R. 170 had been applied in *Donoghue*. In *Lockett* husband and wife went into a hotel for lunch. The wife ordered whitebait which was not fit for human consumption. She only ate a small amount of the whitebait and was then taken ill. In the subsequent action against the hotel, Tucker. J. held that although the husband ordered the meal there was an assumption in these cases that each party would be, if necessary, personally liable for what he or she consumed. There was therefore a contract between the hotel and the wife into which Sale of Goods Act terms could be implied and she was awarded damages because the whitebait was not fit for the purpose or of merchantable quality. This approach is surprisingly modern in spite of the fact that the case was decided in 1938.

DAMAGE AND LIABILITY: *DAMNUM SINE INJURIA*: EFFECT OF MALICE AND RELEVANCE OF MOTIVE

265. *Best* v *Samuel Fox & Co. Ltd* [1952] 2 All E.R. 394

Best was a workman at the defendants' factory and because of an accident caused by the defendants' negligence he was emasculated and thus rendered incapable of sexual intercourse. Best's claim for damages was successful but his wife also claimed damages for loss of her husband's *consortium* through the defendants' negligence. The House of Lords *held* that her claim failed because the *damnum* was not of a kind recognised by law. 'It is true that a husband is entitled to recover damages for loss of *consortium* against a person who negligently injures his wife, but this exceptional right is an anomaly at the present day. A wife . . . was never regarded as having any proprietary right in her husband. . . .' *per* Lord Morton of Henryton.

COMMENT
Some American jurisdictions allow such a claim. The *Best* case is in no sense anti-female. The House of Lords simply took the view that the right of *consortium* in both parties was an anachronism and took the opportunity to deny the right of *consortium* in the wife. The Law Commissioners recommended giving equal rights to husband and wife by abolishing the husband's right to compensation for loss of his wife's *consortium*. (See Report No. 56 on Personal Injury Litigation – Assessment of Damages (1973).) This has been achieved by s. 2(a), Administration of Justice Act, 1982.

266. *Electrochrome Ltd* v *Welsh Plastics Ltd* [1968] 2 All E.R. 205

A lorry driver employed by the defendants drove the defendants' vehicle into a fire hydrant near to the plaintiff's factory. Water escaped from the damaged hydrant and the supply had to be cut off while repairs were carried out. The plaintiffs lost a day's work at their factory and sued for this loss. However, since they were not the owners of the hydrant it was *held* that no action lay. They had suffered loss but there had been no infringement of their legal rights.

COMMENT
(i) The case is a good example of the reluctance of a court to allow the law of tort to be used to compensate for economic loss, i.e. the mere loss of an opportunity to make a profit, perhaps on the grounds that the law of contract is more concerned with the loss of expectations. Furthermore, the decision in this case can be reached by way of *damnum sine injuria* or by saying that there was no duty of care or, if there was, that the damage was too remote.
(ii) In *Junior Books Ltd* v *Veitchi Co. Ltd*, 1982 (see p. 783), the House of Lords decided that if a plaintiff was in sufficiently close proximity to the defendant he could recover foreseeable economic loss even though there was no physical damage either to a person or to property. It would, however, be unwise to assume that *Junior Books* covers all cases of economic loss, particularly where, as in the *Electrochrome* case, proximity of the plaintiff and defendant does not exist in the *Junior Books* way.

267. *Bradford Corporation* v *Pickles* [1895] A.C. 587

The corporation had statutory power to take water from certain springs. Water reached the springs by percolating (but not in a defined channel) through neighbouring land belonging to Pickles. In order to induce the corporation to buy his land at a high price, Pickles sank a shaft on it, with the result that the water reaching the corporation's reservoir was discoloured and its flow diminished. The corporation asked for an injunction to restrain Pickles from collecting the subterranean water. *Held* – an injunction could not be granted. Pickles had a right to drain from his land subterranean water not running in a defined channel. (This right of a landowner was established by the House of Lords in *Chasemore* v *Richards* (1859) 7 H.L. Cas. 349.) Any malice which he might have had in doing it did not affect that right, since English law knows no doctrine of abuse of rights. No use of property which would be legal if due to a proper motive can become illegal because it is prompted by an improper or malicious motive.

268. *Wilkinson* v *Downton* [1897] 2 Q.B. 57

The defendant as a 'practical joke', called on Mrs Wilkinson and told her that her husband had been seriously injured in an accident and had had both his legs broken. Mrs Wilkinson travelled to see her husband at Leytonstone and, believing the message to be true, sustained nervous shock and in consequence was seriously ill. This action was brought for damages for false and malicious representation. Damages were awarded. The court *held* that intentional physical harm is a tort even though it does not consist of a trespass to the person. Further, whether the act is malicious or by way of a joke is irrelevant.

COMMENT
Although it is often stated that trespass lies only for direct damage, trespass is felt to be the basis of this action and it clearly suggests that the tort of trespass is available for indirect physical damage caused wilfully.

MINORS: LIABILITY AS DEFENDANT

269. *Williams* v *Humphrey*, *The Times*, 20 February 1975

The defendant, a youth of nearly 16, accompanied his friend and the friend's parents to a swimming pool. As part of the general fun the defendant pushed the friend's father, the plaintiff, a middle-aged man, into the shallow end of the pool, merely intending to cause a big splash. The plaintiff's left foot struck the edge of the pool and he sustained severe injuries to his foot and ankle. He underwent five operations and ended up crippled. It was *held* – by Talbot, J. – that the plaintiff had not taken such part in the pool activities that he could be said to have willingly accepted the risk of personal injury and the defendant was guilty of both negligence and trespass to the person. The plaintiff succeeded.

COMMENT
It may be puzzling to the reader why this action was worthwhile in terms of the fact that the defendant would not have had a lot of money in his personal capacity. However, there was a household insurance policy

available. Most modern household insurance policies have a public liability clause which provides cover, sometimes up to £250,000 or more for accidents caused by the householder or his family.

MINORS: LIABILITY OF PARENTS AND OTHERS IN CHARGE OF MINORS: NEGLIGENT CONTROL

270. *Donaldson* v *McNiven* [1952] 1 All E.R. 1213

The defendant lived in a densely populated area of Liverpool and allowed his 13-year-old son to have an air rifle on condition that he did not use it outside the house. The defendant's house had a large cellar and the boy was told to use the rifle there. Without the defendant's knowledge the boy fired the air rifle at some children playing near to the house, injuring the plaintiff, a child of five. *Held* – in the circumstances the precautions taken by the defendant were reasonable and would have been adequate but for his son's disobedience, which could not have been foreseen because the boy was usually obedient. The defendant was not guilty of negligence.

271. *Bebee* v *Sales* (1916) 32 T.L.R. 413

A father allowed his 15-year-old son to retain a shot gun with which he knew he had already caused damage. The father was *held* liable for an injury to another boy's eye.

COMMENT
Cases 270 and 271 were decided on the ordinary principles of negligence at common law. However, since the Air Guns and Shot Guns Act, 1962 (see now Firearms Act, 1968), an action may lie against the parent for breach of statutory duty. The Act makes it a criminal offence to give an air weapon to a person under 14 years, and restricts the use or possession of air weapons by young persons in public places except under supervision. In any case breaches of these statutory duties could be relied upon as evidence of negligence. Furthermore a person injured might now claim compensation from the Criminal Injuries Compensation Board. The age of the child causing the injury is not a bar to a claim against the Board because payments will be made even though the child inflicting the injury is below the age of criminal responsibility. In *Gorely* v *Codd* [1966] 3 All E.R. 891, the plaintiff was injured by a pellet from Codd's air rifle when they were larking about in a field in open country. Codd was 16½ years of age and when the plaintiff sued Codd's father the court found that he had given proper instruction to his son and was not liable at common law. Since the shooting did not occur in a public place there was no breach of the Air Guns and Shot Guns Act, 1962 (see now Firearms Act, 1968).

272. *Carmarthenshire County Council* v *Lewis* [1955] 1 All E.R. 565

A boy aged four years was a pupil at a nursery school run by the appellants who were the local education authority. The boy and another were made ready to go out for a walk with the mistress in charge who left them for a moment in order to get ready herself. She did not return for ten minutes, having treated another child who had cut himself. During her absence the boy got out of the classroom and made his way through an unlocked gate, down a lane, and into a busy highway. He caused the driver of a lorry to swerve into a telegraph pole, as a result of which the driver was killed. His widow brought an action for damages for negligence. *Held* – in the circumstances of the case the mistress was not negligent so the liability of the local authority was not vicarious. However, they were negligent themselves because they had not taken reasonable precautions to keep young children who used the premises from getting out into the highway.

273. Butt v *Cambridgeshire and Isle of Ely County Council* (1969) 119 N.L.J. 118

The plaintiff was a pupil in a class of 37 girls of nine and ten years of age. She lost an eye when another girl in her class waved pointed scissors which the children were using to cut out illustrations. The teacher was giving individual attention to another child. *Held* – by the Court of Appeal – that her claim for damages failed. The teacher was not under a duty to require all work to stop while she was giving individual attention to members of the class. She was not negligent so that there was no vicarious liability in the local authority. The local authority was not liable for its own negligence in that evidence of experienced teachers showed that there was no fault in the system of using pointed scissors.

MENTAL PATIENTS: LIABILITY IN TORT

274. *Morriss v Marsden* [1952] 1 All E.R. 925

The defendant took a room at a hotel in Brighton, and whilst there he violently attacked the plaintiff who was the manager of the hotel. Evidence showed that at the time of the attack the defendant was suffering from a disease of the mind. He knew the nature and quality of his act, but did not know that what he was doing was wrong. The plaintiff sued for damages for assault and battery. *Held* – since the defendant knew the nature and quality of his tortious act, it did not matter that he did not know what he was doing was wrong, and he was liable in tort.

DIPLOMATIC IMMUNITY IN TORT: NATURE OF

275. *Dickinson v Del Solar* [1930] 1 K.B. 376

The plaintiff had been knocked down by a car driven by the defendant's servant. The defendant was the First Secretary of the Peruvian Legation in London. The Head of the Legation directed the defendant not to plead diplomatic privilege, and the defendant entered an appearance in the action. The plaintiff succeeded and the defendant's insurance company refused to indemnify their client, saying, in effect, that his diplomatic immunity was immunity from liability. *Held* – the insurers were liable to indemnify the defendant. Diplomatic agents are not immune from liability for wrongful acts, but are merely immune from suit. This immunity can be waived with the sanction of the sovereign of the state in question, or an official superior of the person concerned. The defendant's act in entering an appearance operated as a waiver of diplomatic privilege, and judgment was properly entered against him.

CORPORATIONS: AS PLAINTIFFS IN TORT

276. *D. & L. Caterers and Jackson* v *D'Anjou* [1945] 1 All E.R. 563

The plaintiffs owned a West End restaurant called the 'Bagatelle'. The defendant made certain statements alleging that the restaurant was operated illegally and obtained its supplies on the black market. *Held* – the statements were defamatory and a limited liability company could sue for slander without proof of special damage. Where the slander related to its trade or business, the law implied the existence of damage to found the action.

CORPORATIONS: AS DEFENDANTS IN TORT

277. *Poulton* v *London and South Western Railway Co* (1867) L.R. 2 Q.B. 534

The plaintiff was arrested by a stationmaster for non-payment of carriage in respect of his horse. The defendants, who were the employers of the stationmaster, had power to detain passengers for non-payment of their own fare, but for no other reason. *Held* – since there was no express authorisation of the arrest by the defendants, the stationmaster was acting outside the scope of his employment and the defendants were not liable.

278. *Campbell* v *Paddington Borough Council* [1911] 1 K.B. 869

The defendants, in accordance with a resolution duly passed, erected a stand in Burwood Place in order that members of the council might view the funeral procession of King Edward VII passing along the Edgware Road. The plaintiff, who occupied certain premises in Burwood Place, often let the premises for the purpose of viewing public processions passing along the Edgware Road. The stand obstructed the view of the funeral procession from the plaintiff's house and she was unable to let the premises for that purpose. *Held* – as the stand constituted a public nuisance, the plaintiff could maintain an action for the special damage which she had sustained through the loss of view. The corporation was properly sued, and the fact that the erection of the stand was probably *ultra vires* did not matter.

COMMENT
The damages in this case must be regarded as parasitical because the law does not recognise a right to a view or prospect and it must be accepted therefore that a plaintiff may recover as part of his damages

for injury to a recognised interest a financial loss related to another interest which would not in itself be protected by the law. (And see also *Spartan Steel and Alloys Ltd* v *Martin & Co Ltd*, 1972, p. 782.)

VICARIOUS LIABILITY: WHO IS A SERVANT? CONTROL AND OTHER TESTS: TRANSFER OF EMPLOYEES

279. *Garrard* v *Southey (A.E.) and Co. and Standard Telephones and Cables Ltd* [1952] 2 Q.B. 174

Two persons employed by electrical contractors were sent to work in a factory on electrical installations. The electrical contractors continued to employ the men, paying their wages, stamping their insurance cards, and retaining the sole right to dismiss them. The electricians worked exclusively at the factory and used the factory canteen. The occupiers of the factory supplied them with all materials, tools and plant, except for certain special tools belonging to the electricians themselves. They were supervised by a foreman employed by the occupiers and they followed the system laid down in the factory. One of the electricians was injured when he fell from a defective trestle owned by some building contractors who were also working in the factory. *Held* – the occupiers of the factory, and not the electrical contractors, owed the injured electrician the common-law duty of a master to his servant (to provide proper plant and equipment) and they were liable to him for breach of that duty.

280. *Mersey Docks and Harbour Board* v *Coggins and Griffiths (Liverpool) Ltd and McFarlane* [1947] A.C. 1.

A firm of stevedores had hired from the Harbour Board the use of a crane together with its driver, Mr Newall, to assist in loading a ship lying in the Liverpool docks. The contract of hire was subject to the Board's regulations, one of which contained the clause: 'The driver provided shall be the servant of the applicants.' The driver of the crane was a skilled man appointed and paid by the Board, and the Board alone had power to dismiss him. The stevedores told the driver what they wanted the crane to lift but had no authority to tell him how to work the crane. MacFarlane, who was a checker employed by the forwarding agents, was noting the number and marks on a case which the crane had picked up when he was trapped because of the negligence of the crane driver in failing to keep the crane still.

The question to be determined was whether in applying the doctrine of vicarious liability the general employers of the crane driver or the hirers were liable for his negligence. The Board contended that, under the terms of the contract between the Board and the stevedores, the stevedores were liable. *Held* – by the House of Lords –

(a) The question of liability was not to be determined by any agreement between the general employers and the hirers, but depended on the circumstances of the case. The test to apply was that of control.

(b) The Board, as the general employers of the crane driver, had not established that the hirers had such control of the crane driver at the time of the accident as to become liable as employers for his negligence. Although the hirers could tell the crane driver where to go and what to carry, they had no authority to tell him how to operate the crane. The Board were, therefore, liable for his negligence.

COMMENT

The answers given by Mr Newall to counsel's questions in this case were highly important. At one point he said: 'I take no orders from anybody.' Commenting on this, Lord Simonds said that it was 'a sturdy answer which meant that he was a skilled man and knew his job and would carry it out in his own way. Yet ultimately he would decline to carry it out in the appellants' way at his peril, for in their hands lay the only sanction the power of dismissal.'

281. *Wright* v *Tyne Improvement Commissioners (Osbeck & Co. Ltd Third Party)* [1968] 1 All E.R. 807

Tyne Improvement Commissioners hired a crane to Osbeck & Co. Ltd, under a written contract whereby the hirers agreed 'to bear the risk of and be responsible for all damage, injury or loss whatsoever, howsoever and whensoever caused arising directly or indirectly out of or in connection with the hiring or use of the said crane'. The plaintiff, who was a docker employed by Osbeck & Co., was injured when a wagon, in which he was standing to receive timber, was negligently moved forward by the capstan driver causing the plaintiff to collide with timber being lowered into the wagon by the crane. The plaintiff and the crane driver did all they could to avoid the accident but failed to do so and it was accepted that the capstan driver, who was employed by the Commissioners, was wholly to blame. Under the doctrine of vicarious liability the Commissioners were also to blame. When the action was tried at Newcastle upon Tyne Assizes, Waller, J. awarded the plaintiff damages of some £2985 against the Commissioners but dimissed a claim by the Commissioners against Osbeck & Co., as hirers of the crane, for an indemnity against the plaintiff's claim by virtue of the clause quoted above. The Commissioners now appealed against the dismissal of the claim for indemnity. *Held* – by the Court of Appeal – that as the accident arose directly, or at least indirectly, out of or in connection with the use of the crane, the indemnity clause entitled the Commissioners to an indemnity against Osbeck & Co. even though the use to which the crane was being put was not a blameworthy cause of the accident.

282. *Cassidy* v *Ministry of Health* [1951] 2 K.B. 343

The plaintiff's left hand was operated on at the defendant's hospital by a whole-time assistant medical officer of the hospital. After the operation the plaintiff's hand and forearm were put in a splint for 14 days. During this time the plaintiff complained of pain but was merely given sedatives by the doctors who attended him. When the splint was removed, it was found that all four fingers of the plaintiff's hand were stiff, and that his hand was virtually useless. Someone – either the doctor, the surgeon, or a nurse – had been negligent, but the plaintiff could not in fact point to which of these it was. The plaintiff sued the defendants for negligence. *Held* – the defendants were liable in spite of their absence of real control over the type of work done by the doctors employed by them. Denning, L.J. stated that only where the patient himself selects and employs the doctor will the hospital authorities escape liability for that doctor's negligence. If the person causing the harm is part of the organisation, the employer is liable.

> COMMENT
> In this case Lord Denning used the doctrine *res ipsa loquitur* (see p. 441) in order to help the plaintiff to establish his case. In other words, he presumed negligence, thus relieving the plaintiff of the burden of actually having to point to a particular employee of the Ministry who was negligent.

283. *Ferguson* v *John Dawson & Partners (Contractors)* [1976] 3 All E.R. 817

The plaintiff who was working 'on the lump' was injured whilst working for the defendants who were contractors. No deductions were made by the defendants for income tax or National Insurance contributions and the plaintiff had been told that he was working 'purely as a lump labour force'. The defendants' site agent was responsible for hiring and dismissing the workmen, including the plaintiff; he told them what to do and moved them from site to site. If tools were required for the work the defendants provided them. The plaintiff was injured when he fell off a roof which had no guard rail and he brought this action against the defendants on the basis that they were liable as his employers for failing to provide a guard rail on the flat roof which was required by construction regulations. It was *held* – by the Court of Appeal – that whatever label was put on the parties' relationship, other factors should be considered, such as the fact that the defendants could dismiss the workmen, including the plaintiff, and tell them what to do and where to do it. Accordingly, the plaintiff was the employee of the defendants who were therefore liable under the construction regulations and must pay the plaintiff damages for breach of that statutory duty.

284. *Lee (Catherine)* v *Lee's Air Farming Ltd* [1960] 3 All E.R. 420

In 1954 the appellant's husband formed the respondent company which carried on the business of crop spraying from the air. In March 1956, Mr Lee was killed while piloting an aircraft during the course of topsoil dressing, and Mrs Lee claimed compensation from the company, as the employer of her husband, under the New Zealand Workers' Compensation Act, 1922. Since Mr Lee owned 2999 of the company's 3000 £1 shares and since he was its governing director, the question arose as to whether the relationship of master and servant could exist between the company and him. He was employed as the company's chief pilot under a provision in the articles at a salary to be arranged by himself. *Held* – Mrs Lee was entitled to compensation because her husband was employed by the company in the sense required by the Act of 1922, and the decision in *Salomon* v *Salomon & Co* was applied.

VICARIOUS LIABILITY: IMPROPER PERFORMANCE OF ACTS WITHIN SCOPE OF EMPLOYMENT

285. *Century Insurance Co. Ltd* v *Northern Ireland Road Transport Board* [1942] A.C. 509

A tanker belonging to the respondents, and driven by one of their employees, was delivering petrol to a garage in Belfast. While the tanker was discharging petrol at the garage, the driver lit a cigarette and threw away the lighted match. The resulting explosion caused considerable damage. The contract under which the petrol was being delivered said that the respondents' employees were to take their orders from a petrol company to which the tankers were hired, a firm named Holmes, Mullin and Dunn, though they were not by virtue of this to be deemed the hirers' employees. The appellants had insured the defendants against liability to third parties, and pleaded that no claim could be made on them because, although the driver was admittedly negligent, he was at the time the servant of the hirers. *Held* – the appellants must pay the third-party claim because the terms of the contract as a whole did not involve a transfer of the employees to Holmes, Mullin and Dunn; therefore, the respondents were liable for the negligence of the driver and were entitled to claim under their insurance.

COMMENT
(i) It would seem that, however improper the manner in which an employee is doing his work, whether negligently or fraudulently, or contrary to express orders, his employer is liable.

(ii) This case was followed in *Harrison* v *Michelin Tyre Company* [1985] 1 All E.R. 918 where the plaintiff, a tool grinder employed by the defendants, was injured at work when standing on a duckboard of his machine talking to a fellow employee. Another employee was pushing a truck along a passage in front of the plaintiff and decided as a joke to suddenly turn it two inches outside the chalk lines of the passageway and push the edge under the plaintiff's duckboard. The duckboard tipped. The plaintiff fell off and suffered injury. In an action against the defendants he claimed that the employee had acted in the course of his employment and that they were vicariously liable. The defendants denied liability saying that the employee had embarked on a frolic of his own. It was held by Comyn, J. that the employers were liable. The test for determining vicarious liability was whether a reasonable man would say either that the employee's act was part and parcel of his employment, even though unauthorised or prohibited, or that it was so divergent as to be plainly alien to it. In this case the employee's act was part and parcel of the employment.

286. *Limpus* v *London General Omnibus Co.* (1862) 1 H. & C. 526

The plaintiff's omnibus was overturned when the driver of the defendants' omnibus drove across it so as to be first at a bus stop to take all the passengers who were waiting. The defendants' driver admitted that the act was intentional, and arose out of bad feeling between the two drivers. The defendants had issued strict instructions to their drivers that they were not to obstruct other omnibuses. *Held* – the defendants were liable. Their driver was acting within the scope of his employment at the time of the collision, and it did not matter that the defendants had expressly forbidden him to act as he did.

COMMENT

As we have seen, the matter to be decided in these cases is whether the employee was doing what he was employed to do. If he is not, then the employer is not liable. Thus in *Beard* v *London General Omnibus Co.* [1900] 2 Q.B. 530 a bus conductor who turned the bus round when the driver was absent and injured the plaintiff whilst he was doing this was held by the Court of Appeal to have been acting outside the course of his employment so that his employers were not liable.

287. *Rose* v *Plenty* [1976] 1 All E.R. 97

Leslie Rose, aged 13, was given to helping Mr Plenty, a milkman, to deliver milk. Co-operative Retail Services Ltd, who employed Mr Plenty, expressly forbade their milkmen to take boys on their floats or to get boys to help them deliver the milk. On one occasion, while helping Mr Plenty, Leslie was sitting in the front of the float when his leg caught under the wheel. The accident was caused partly by Mr Plenty's negligence. It was *held* – by the Court of Appeal (Lord Denning, M.R. and Scarman, L.J.) – that Mr Plenty had been acting in the course of his employment so that his employers were liable to compensate Leslie Rose for his injuries. Lawton, L.J. (dissenting) said that the case of *Twine* v *Bean's Express* (1946) and similar cases were indistinguishable and that in giving Leslie a lift Mr Plenty had acted outside the *scope* of his employment.

COMMENT

There is really very little difference in the facts of *Rose* v *Plenty* and *Twine* other than the fact that Leslie Rose was more than a mere hitchhiker. His presence on the milk-float was connected with the delivery of the milk which was the reason connected with the *scope* of employment and this is why Lord Denning and Scarman, L.J. felt able to distinguish *Twine* and other similar cases.

VICARIOUS LIABILITY: EMPLOYEE MIXING EMPLOYER'S BUSINESS WITH HIS OWN

288. *Britt* v *Galmoye and Nevill* (1928) 44 T.L.R. 294

The first defendant, who had the second defendant in his employment as a van-driver, lent him his private motor car, after the day's work was finished, to take a friend to a theatre. The second defendant by his negligence injured the plaintiff. *Held* – that as the journey was not on the master's business and the master was not in control, he was not liable for his servant's act.

VICARIOUS LIABILITY AT CIVIL LAW FOR CRIMINAL CONDUCT OF EMPLOYEE

289. *Morris* v *C.W. Martin & Sons Ltd* [1965] 2 All E.R. 725

The plaintiff sent a mink stole to a furrier for the purpose of cleaning. The furrier later told the plaintiff by telephone that he did not clean furs himself but intended to send the stole to the defendants, one of the biggest cleaners of fur in the country. The plaintiff knew of Martin & Sons and agreed that the stole be sent to them. Martin & Sons did work only for the fur trade and had issued to the furrier printed conditions which provided that goods belonging to customers were at customer's risk when on the premises of Martin & Sons, and that they should not be responsible for loss or damage however caused, though they would compensate for loss or damage to the goods during the cleaning process by reason of their negligence, but not by reason of any other cause. The furrier knew of these conditions when he handed the stole to the defendants and the defendants knew that it belonged to a customer of the furrier but they did not know that it was Morris. While in the possession of Martin & Sons the fur was stolen by a youth named Morrisey who had been employed by them for a few weeks only, though they had no grounds to suspect that he was dishonest. The plaintiff sued the defendants for conversion or negligence but the County Court Judge felt bound by *Cheshire* v *Bailey* [1905] 1 K.B. 237 and held that the act of Morrisey, who had removed the stole by wrapping it round his body, was beyond the scope of his employment. In the Court of Appeal it was *held* that *Cheshire* v *Bailey*, 1905 had been impliedly overruled by *Lloyd* v *Grace, Smith & Co.* [1912] A.C. 716 (where it was held that a solicitor was liable for the criminal frauds of his managing clerk so long as the clerk was acting in the apparent scope of his authority). The defendants, as sub-bailees, were liable to the plaintiff, and on the matter of the exemption clause the Court of Appeal said that the terms of such a clause must be strictly construed, and since they referred only to goods 'belonging to customers' this could be taken to mean goods belonging to the furrier and not to the furrier's customer, and because of this ambiguity the clause was inapplicable.

COMMENT

(i) The above decision applies only to bailees for reward and only in circumstances where the servant is entrusted with, or put in charge of, the bailor's goods by his master. The mere fact that the servant's employment gave him the opportunity to steal the bailor's goods is not enough. Thus in *Leesh River Tea Co.* v *British India Steam Navigation Co.* [1966] 3 All E.R. 593 a stevedore stole a brass cover plate from the hold of a ship when he was unloading tea and the Court of Appeal held that he was not acting in the course of his employment on the grounds that his job had nothing to do with the cover plate. Perhaps if the plate had been stolen by someone who was sent to clean it, then that person would have been acting within the course of his employment.

(ii) The tortious or criminal act must be committed as part of the employment, i.e. as an act within the scope of the employment. In

Heasmans v *Clarity Cleaning* [1987] I.R.L.R. 286 the Court of Appeal decided that the defendants were not liable when their employee, who was sent to the plaintiffs' premises to clean telephones, made unauthorised telephone calls on them to the value of £1400. He was employed to *clean* telephones, not to *use* them.

VICARIOUS LIABILITY: CASUAL DELEGATION TO 'AGENTS': LIABILITY OF 'PRINCIPAL'

290. *Ormrod* v *Crosville Motor Services Ltd* [1953] 2 All E.R. 753

By an arrangement between the owner of a motor car and his friend, the friend was to drive the car from Birkenhead to Monte Carlo in order that the owner, the friend and the friend's wife might use the car during their holiday in Monte Carlo. The owner of the car was travelling to Monte Carlo in another car as a competitor in the Monte Carlo Rally. Owing to the friend's negligent driving, the car was involved in a collision in which a motor bus was damaged. The question of the liability of the owner of the car for the damage arose. *Held* – the friend was acting as the owner's agent in the matter. The owner had an interest in the arrival of the car at Monte Carlo, and the driving was done for his benefit. Accordingly the owner was vicariously liable for his friend's negligence.

291. *Vandyke* v *Fender* [1970] 2 All E.R. 335

Mr Vandyke and Mr Fender were employed by the same firm and lived 30 miles from the business premises. The employer agreed to supply a car to Mr Fender and to pay him 50p a day for petrol for the journey. The journey could have been made by train but was more convenient by car. Two other employees who lived in the same area were also carried. On one occasion the car loaned to Mr Fender was not available and he was allowed to use a car belonging to the company secretary. While driving this car an accident occurred resulting in an injury to Mr Vandyke who claimed damages from the company. It was *held* that the company was liable because Mr Fender, though not a paid driver, *was driving the car as the company's agent* and they were liable for his negligence. The question then arose as to which of the insurance companies involved should indemnify the company. If the risk was to be borne by the employers' liability insurance it was necessary to show that the accident occurred during and in the course of Mr Vandyke's employment, otherwise the risk would be borne by a road traffic insurance policy of Mr Fender's which covered him while driving someone else's car. It was *held* – by the Court of Appeal – that a man going to or from work as a passenger in a vehicle provided by his employers for that purpose is not in the course of employment unless he is obliged by the terms of his employment to travel in that vehicle. If not then, as here, the liability must be borne by the road traffic insurers and not by the employers' liability insurers.

292. *Nottingham* v *Aldridge; Prudential Assurance Co.* [1971] 2 All E.R. 751

In this case a Post Office trainee was returning to his normal work in his father's van after spending the weekend at his home having attended a training course the previous week. He was carrying another trainee, Nottingham, as a passenger and was entitled to a mileage allowance from the Post Office for himself and his passenger. Nottingham was injured as a result of an accident caused by the defendant's negligent driving. *Held* – by Eveleigh, J. – that the Post Office was not liable because the two trainees were not in the course of employment while travelling to work; *nor was Aldridge the agent of the Post Office for the purposes of the journey.* The vehicle did not belong to the Post Office nor was it provided by them. They had not prescribed the method of travel; admittedly a mileage allowance was payable but travelling expenses of any other kind would have been paid, e.g. bus or train fare. The question of agency was one of fact and on the facts of this case Aldridge was not an agent. The company which had insured the van was therefore liable to indemnify Aldridge in respect of his own liability to Nottingham.

293. *Morgans* v *Launchbury* [1972] 2 All E.R. 606

In this case the family car was registered in the name of the wife though it was used mainly by the husband who worked seven miles from home. The wife had asked her husband not to drive the car home himself if he had been drinking. On one occasion the husband had been drinking heavily and asked a friend, C, to drive him home together with three other passengers. There was an accident caused by the negligent driving of C and the husband and he were killed. The three passengers were injured and sued the wife claiming that she was liable vicariously for the negligence of C, who had been appointed to drive on her behalf by her husband. If the wife was held liable then her insurance company would be liable to the plaintiffs. The House of Lords held that she was not liable. The concept of agency required more than mere permission to use. Use must be at the owner's request or on his instructions.

> COMMENT
> Before 1971 it was not compulsory for road traffic insurance to cover passengers. In fact Mrs Launchbury had an insurance policy which covered passengers but only in respect of accidents which occurred while she or her agent was driving. The plaintiffs would have preferred to get their money from the insurance than to sue the estate of C.

294. *Rambarran* v *Gurrucharran* [1970] 1 All E.R. 749

In this case Rambarran, a chicken farmer in Guyana, owned a car which was used by several of his sons, Rambarran himself being unable to drive. One of his sons, Leslie, damaged Gurrucharran's car by negligently driving the family car. The Privy Council found that Rambarran was not liable for Leslie's negligence because he did not know that Leslie had taken the car since he was away from home at his chicken farm at the time in question. Furthermore, there was no evidence to show what the purpose of Leslie's journey was, but it was clearly not for any business or family purpose. Ownership of the vehicle was not enough in itself to establish liability.

295. *Klein* v *Calnori* [1971] 2 All E.R. 701

The defendant, Calnori, was the manager of a public house at Sunbury-on-Thames. While he was busy at the bar a Mr Freshwater, who knew Calnori, took his car and drove it away without his permission. Later Freshwater telephoned Calnori and told him he had taken his car. Calnori told him to bring it back. On the way back to Sunbury Freshwater collided with Klein's stationary car severely damaging it. Klein alleged that Calnori was liable for this damage because Freshwater was his agent. By asking Freshwater to bring the car back Freshwater was driving it partly for Calnori's purposes. *Held* – by Lyell, J. – Calnori was not liable. If Freshwater had borrowed the car with Calnori's consent then the loan to Freshwater, for his own purposes, would have involved returning it. In these circumstances Calnori would not have been liable for an accident on the return journey. Therefore Calnori's liability could not be greater in circumstances in which the car had been taken without his consent and had been used solely for the taker's purpose.

LIABILITY FOR THE TORTS OF INDEPENDENT CONTRACTORS

296. *Bower* v *Peate* (1876) 1 Q.B.D. 321

The plaintiff and defendant were the respective owners of two adjoining houses, the plaintiff being entitled to the support for his house of the defendant's land. The defendant employed a contractor to pull down his house and to rebuild it after excavating the foundations. The contractor undertook the risk of supporting the plaintiff's house during the work and to make good any damage caused. The plaintiff's house was damaged in the progress of the work because the contractor did not take appropriate steps to support it. *Held* – that the defendant was liable. The fact that the injury would have been prevented if the contractor had provided proper support did not take away the defendant's liability. A person employing a contractor to perform a duty cast upon himself, in this case a duty of support, is responsible for the contractor's negligence in performing it.

297. *Salsbury* v *Woodland* [1969] 3 All E.R. 863

The defendant employed, as an independent contractor, an experienced tree-feller to fell a large tree in his front garden. The contractor was negligent and the tree fell towards the highway bringing down telephone wires on to the highway. A car came along too fast, and the plaintiff, who was a bystander watching the whole operation, was injured when he dived out of the way of the inevitable collision between the car and the wire. *Held* – by the Court of Appeal – the defendant was not liable though the contractor was. There was no special liability in the defendant merely because the contractor was employed to work near, as distinct from on, the highway.

COMMENT

In *Tarry* v *Ashton* (1876) 1 Q.B.D. 314 the defendant employed an independent contractor to carry out repairs to a lamp which, though attached to his house, overhung the highway. The contractor failed to secure the lamp properly and it fell, inuring the plaintiff. It was held that the defendant was liable because it was his duty to make the lamp safe and he was in breach of that duty because the contractor had not secured the lamp properly.

GENERAL DEFENCES: *VOLENTI NON FIT INJURIA*

298. *Simms* v *Leigh Rugby Football Club* [1969] 2 All E.R. 923

The plaintiff was a member of a visiting team playing rugby football on the defendant club's ground when his leg was broken as he was tackled and thrown towards a concrete wall which ran at a distance of 7ft. 3ins. from the touch line. The League's bye-laws prescribed that the distance had to be at least 7ft. *Held* – by Wrangham, J. – that the plaintiff must be taken willingly to have accepted the risks involved in playing on that field. The ground complied with the bye-laws of the Rugby Football League and the defendants were not, therefore, liable under the Occupiers' Liability Act, 1957, or in general negligence by reason of the plaintiff's consent.

COMMENT

(i) In this connection the decision of the Court of Appeal in *Condon* v *Basi* [1985] 2 All E.R. 453 is of interest. In that case the defendant made a late and reckless slide tackle upon the plaintiff resulting in the plaintiff sustaining a broken right leg and the defendant being sent from the field of play. The County Court judge awarded the plaintiff £4900 for damages for the injuries sustained and the Court of Appeal dismissed an appeal against that decision. It was decided by the Court of Appeal that participants in competitive sport owe a duty of care to each other to take all reasonable care having regard to the particular circumstances in which the participants are placed. If one participant injures another he will be liable in negligence for damages at the suit of the injured participant if it is shown that he failed to exercise the degree of care appropriate in all the circumstances or that he acted in a manner to which the injured participant could not have been expected to consent. The law is clearly having to respond to the increasing amount of unnecessary violence in certain sports.

(ii) And of course there may be a criminal prosecution as in *R* v *Lloyd* [1989] Crim L.R. 513 where L was sentenced to 18 months' imprisonment for kicking an opposing rugby player in the face while he was down, fracturing a cheek bone.

299. *Murray* v *Harringay Arena Ltd* [1951] 2 K.B. 529

David Charles Murray, aged six, was taken by his parents to the defendants' ice rink to watch a hockey match. They occupied front seats at the rink, and during the game the boy was hit in the eye by the puck. This action was brought against the defendants for negligence. *Held* – the risk was voluntarily undertaken by the plaintiffs. The defendants had provided protection by means of netting and a wooden barrier which, in the circumstances, was adequate, since further protection would have seriously interfered with the view of the spectators.

COMMENT
As the above case shows it is possible to plead *volenti* against a minor. It is not, however, possible to do so against a person who is mentally disturbed. In *Kirkham* v *Anderton* [1990] 2 W.L.R. 987 a prisoner was remanded in custody. He had suicidal tendencies known to the police which they failed to pass on to the prison authorities. The prisoner killed himself and a claim for negligence was brought against the police authority. The police authority was held liable and the defence of *volenti* failed.

300. *Hall* v *Brooklands Auto-Racing Club* [1933] 1 K.B. 205

The plaintiff paid for admission to the defendants' premises to watch motor-car races. During one of the races a car left the track, as a result of a collison with another car, and crashed through the railings injuring the plaintiff. It was the first time that a car had gone through the railings, and in view of that the precautions taken by the defendants were adequate. In this action by the plaintiff for personal injuries, it was *held* that the danger was not one which the defendants ought to have anticipated, and that the plaintiff must be taken to have agreed to assume the risk of such an accident.

EXCLUSION CLAUSES: CONTRACTUAL ASSENT AND *VOLENTI NON FIT INJURIA*: THE RELATIONSHIP

301. *Burnett* v *British Waterways Board* [1973] 1 W.L.R. 700

Burnett was a lighterman working on his employer's barge. Due to the defendants' negligence a capstan rope parted while the barge was docking, injuring Burnett. At the dock office was a notice stating that persons availed themselves of the dock facilities at their own risk. Burnett had read the notice when he was a young apprentice. The defendants admitted negligence but claimed that Burnett had voluntarily undertaken the risk of injury. *Held* – by the Court of Appeal – that Burnett was an employee sent by his employer and it could not be said that he had freely and voluntarily incurred the risk of negligence on the part of the defendant. In the course of his judgment Lord Denning, M.R. said: 'If there was a contract with Mr Burnett, of course, the Board could rely upon it. But there was no contract with him. He was just one of the men working on the barges. The contract was with the barge owners. . .'.

COMMENT
If the defence of *volenti* succeeds then of course the plaintiff's claim fails.

GENERAL DEFENCES: *VOLENTI*: THE PLAINTIFF MUST KNOW OF THE RISK, THOUGH KNOWLEDGE IS NOT NECESSARILY ASSENT

302. *White* v *Blackmore* [1972] 3 All E.R. 158

The husband of the plaintiff widow was a member of a 'jalopy' racing club. He went to a meeting organised by the defendants as a competitor but stood outside the spectators' ropes close to a stake. The wheel of a car caught on one of the ropes some distance away so that the stake was pulled up sharply and the husband was killed when he was catapulted some 20 feet. The defendants displayed notices warning the public of the danger and stating as a condition of admission that they were absolved from all liabilities for accidents howsoever caused. The widow claimed damages for breach of s. 2 of the Occupiers' Liability Act, 1957 and/or general negligence. *Held* – by the Court of Appeal – (a) that even though the deceased had been negligent in standing where he did, the defence of *volenti* would not succeed as the deceased did not know of the risk that had caused his death; (b) however, the claim would fail as the defendants were entitled to exclude their liability and this they had done by warning notices.

> COMMENT
> It is true that the defendants could effectively exclude their liability under the Occupiers' Liability Act, 1957, by warning notices and without a contract. Section 2(1) of the Act of 1957 provides that an occupier owes 'a common duty of care' to all his visitors but that this can be restricted or excluded 'by agreement or otherwise'. However, as regards the claim in general negligence, it ought not to be possible to exclude liability for negligence unless the plaintiff assents in a contract. But see now Unfair Contract Terms Act, 1977.

303. *Baker* v *James Bros* [1921] 2 K.B. 674

The defendants were wholesale grocers and they employed the plaintiff as a traveller. He was supplied by the defendants with a motor car, the starting gear of which was defective. The plaintiff repeatedly complained about this to the defendants, but nothing was done to remedy the defect. While the plaintiff was on his rounds, the car stopped, and he was injured whilst trying to restart. *Held* – notwithstanding the plaintiff's knowledge of the defect, he had never consented to take upon himself the risk of injury from the continued use of the car. He was not guilty of any contributory negligence and was entitled to recover damages.

304. *Dann* v *Hamilton* [1939] 1 K.B. 509

The plaintiff had been with a party to see the coronation decorations in London. They made the journey in the defendant's car. During the day and evening the defendant had consumed a quantity of intoxicating liquor, but he drove the party back to Staines where they all got out. The plaintiff was at this point a 2d. bus ride from her home but she accepted the defendant's invitation to take her there. During this part of the journey there was an accident caused by the defendant's negligence, and the plaintiff was injured. She now sued in respect of these injuries and the defendant pleaded *volenti non fit injuria*. *Held* – that the defence did not apply and the plaintiff succeeded. She had knowledge of a potential danger, but that did not mean that she assented to it.

COMMENT
(i) The court left open the question where the driver was 'dead drunk' or 'very drunk'. In such a case the maxim might have applied.

(ii) It should be noted that the defence of contibutory negligence was not pleaded in *Dann* although Asquith, J. encouraged counsel for the defence to raise it but he would not be drawn. However, it is now accepted that although *volenti* may not apply in a situation such as *Dann* a plaintiff may be guilty of contributory negligence if he travels as a passenger when he knows the driver has consumed enough alcohol to impair his ability to drive safely, or if he goes drinking with the driver knowing he will be a passenger later when the drink deprives him of his own capacity to appreciate the danger. (So decided in *Owens* v *Brimmell* [1976] 3 All E.R. 765.)

(iii) In *Pitts* v *Hunt, The Times*, 13 April 1990 it was held that a passenger on a motor cycle could not sue the rider whom he had aided and abetted in illegally driving a motor cycle dangerously after they both got drunk together. Further in *Morris* v *Murray, The Times*, 18 September 1990 a plaintiff who knowingly and willingly flew with a pilot who was drunk was not entitled to damages for personal injuries. The defence of *volenti* applied in both cases.

305. *Smith* v *Baker and Sons* [1891] A.C. 325

Smith was employed by Baker and Sons to drill holes in some rock in a railway cutting. A crane, operated by fellow employees, often swung heavy stones over Smith's head while he was working on the rock face. Both Smith and his employers realised that there was a risk the stones might fall, but the crane was nevertheless operated without any warning being given at the moment of jibbing or swinging. Smith was injured by a stone which fell from the crane because of negligent strapping of the load. The House of Lords *held* that Smith had not voluntarily undertaken the risk of his employers' negligence, and that his knowledge of the danger did not prevent his recovering damages.

GENERAL DEFENCES: *VOLENTI*: ACTIONS AGAINST EMPLOYERS BASED ON BREACH OF STATUTORY DUTY

306. *Imperial Chemical Industries Ltd* v *Shatwell* [1964] 2 All E.R. 999

George and James Shatwell were certificated and experienced shot-firers employed by I.C.I. Statutory rules imposed an obligation on them personally (not on their employers) to ensure that certain operations connected with shot-firing should not be done unless all persons in the vicinity had taken cover.

They knew of the risks of premature explosion which had been explained to them; they knew of the prohibition; but on one occasion because a cable they had was too short to reach the shelter, they decided to test without taking cover rather than wait ten minutes for their companion Beswick who had gone to fetch a longer cable. James gave George two wires, and George applied them to the galvanometer terminals. An explosion occurred and both men were injured. At the trial it was found that James was guilty of negligence and breach of statutory duty for which the employers were held vicariously liable, damages being assessed at £1500 on a basis of 50% contributory negligence. The Court of Appeal affirmed, but the House of Lords *reversed*, the decision and *held* that, although James's acts were a contributory cause of the accident to George, the employers were not liable.

(a) They were not themselves in breach of a statutory duty.

(b) They could plead *volenti non fit injuria* to a claim of vicarious liability.

(c) They had shown no negligence. They had instilled the need for caution, made proper provision, and even arranged a scale of remuneration in a way which removed a temptation to take short cuts.

(d) The Shatwell brothers were trained men well aware of the risk involved so the principle of *volenti non fit injuria* applied. Lord Pearce said: 'The defence [of *volenti non fit injuria*] should be available where the employer was not in himself in breach of a statutory duty and was not vicariously in breach of a statutory duty through the neglect of some person of superior rank to the plaintiff and whose commands the plaintiff was bound to obey or who has some special and different duty of care.'

> COMMENT
> If the employers had been compelled to rely on the defence of contributory negligence, they might have escaped liability if only one man were involved and treated as solely responsible, but where two men were involved, as here, they would have been vicariously liable for James's contribution to George's injury and for George's contribution to James's injury so they would have been compelled partially to compensate each man.

GENERAL DEFENCES: *VOLENTI*: THE RESCUE CASES: GENERALLY

307. *Baker v T. E. Hopkins and Son Ltd* [1959] 3 All E.R. 966

The defendants were building contractors and were engaged to clean out a well. Various methods had been used in order to pump out the water, including hand-operated pumps, but eventually a petrol-driven pump was employed. The exhaust from the engine on the pump resulted in a lethal concentration of carbon monoxide forming inside the well. Two of the defendants' employees went down the well to carry on the work of cleaning it and were overcome by the fumes. Baker was a local doctor and, on being told what had happened, he went along to give what assistance he could.

He was lowered down the well on a rope, and on reaching the two men, he realised that they were beyond help. He then gave a prearranged signal to those at the top of the well and started his journey to the surface. Unfortunately the rope became caught on a projection and Dr Baker was himself overcome by fumes and died. His executors claimed damages in respect of Dr Baker's death. *Held* – the defendants were negligent towards their employees in using the petrol-driven pump and the maxim *volenti non fit injuria* did not bar the claim of Dr Baker's executors. Although Dr Baker may have had knowledge of the risk he was running, he did not freely and voluntarily undertake it, but acted under the compulsion of his instincts as a brave man and a doctor.

COMMENT
In an earlier case, *Haynes* v *Harwood* [1935] 1 K.B. 146, a policeman was injured while stopping a runaway horse and van in a crowded street. It was held that he could recover damages. *Volenti* and contributory negligence did not apply.

308. *Cutler* v *United Dairies (London) Ltd* [1933] 2 K.B. 297

The defendants' carman left the defendants' horse and van, two wheels being properly chained, while he delivered milk. The horse, being startled by the noise coming from a river steamer, bolted down the road and into a meadow. It stopped in the meadow and was followed there by the carman who, being in an excited state, began to shout for help. The plaintiff, a spectator, went to the carman's assistance and tried to hold the horse's head. The horse lunged and the plaintiff was injured. In this action by the plaintiff against the defendants for negligence it was *held* that in the circumstances the plaintiff voluntarily and freely assumed the risk. This was not an attempt to stop a runaway horse so that there was no sense of urgency to impel the plaintiff. He therefore knew of the risk and had had time to consider it, and by implication must have agreed to incur it.

COMMENT
Evidence showed that the horse had bolted before and should not have been used on the milk round at all.

309. *Hyett* v *Great Western Railway Co.* [1948] 1 K.B. 345

The plaintiff was employed by a firm of wagon repairers and he was on the defendants' premises with their authority to carry out his duties. While repairing a wagon he saw smoke rising from one of the defendants' wagons in the same siding and went to investigate. The floor of the wagon, which contained paraffin oil, was in flames. The plaintiff was trying to get the drums of paraffin oil out, when one of them exploded and injured him. Evidence showed that the defendants knew that there was a paraffin leakage in the wagon, but had nevertheless allowed it to remain in the siding. *Held* – the plaintiff was entitled to recover damages from the defendants, and the maxim *volenti non fit injuria* did not apply. A man may take reasonable risks in trying to preserve property put in danger by another's negligence.

GENERAL DEFENCES: *VOLENTI*: DUTY TO A RESCUER

310. *Videan v British Transport Commission* [1963] 2 All E.R. 860

A child managed to get on to a railway line and was injured by a trolley. The Court of Appeal *held* that the child's presence was not in the circumstances foreseeable and the defendants did not owe him a duty of care. However, a duty was owed to his father who was injured trying to rescue him.

> COMMENT
> It is difficult to follow the reasoning by which the Court of Appeal held that the defendants ought to have foreseen that a stationmaster would try to rescue a minor on the line (the minor being the son of the stationmaster) yet need not have foreseen the presence of that minor himself.

GENERAL DEFENCES: *VOLENTI*: DEFENCE IRRELEVANT UNLESS THE DEFENDANT HAS COMMITTED A TORT

311. *Wooldridge v Sumner* [1962] 2 All E.R. 978

A competitor of great skill and experience was riding a horse at a horse show when it ran wide at a corner and injured a cameraman who was unfamiliar with horses and who had ignored a steward's request to move outside the competition area. The rider was thrown, but later rode the horse again and it was adjudged supreme champion of its class. The cameraman brought an action for damages, and at the trial was awarded damages on the ground of negligence. *Held* – on appeal, that no negligence had been established because (a) any excessive speed at the corner was not the cause of the accident, and was not negligence but merely an error of judgment; and (b) the judge's finding that the horse would have gone on to a cinder track without harm to the plaintiff if the rider had allowed it to, was an inference from primary facts and unjustified, and in any event an attempt to control the horse did not amount to negligence.

> If, in the course of a game or competition, at a moment when he has not time to think, a participant by mistake takes a wrong measure, he is not to be held guilty of any negligence. . . . A person attending a game or competition takes the risk of any damage caused to him by any act of a participant done in the course of and for the purpose of the game or competition, notwithstanding that such act may involve error of judgment or a lapse of skill, unless the participant's conduct is such as to evince a reckless disregard of the spectator's safety. The spectator takes the risk because such an act involves *no breach of the duty of care* owed by the participant to him. He does not take the risk by virtue of the doctrine expressed or obscured by the maxim *volenti non fit injuria*. . . . The maxim in English law *presupposes a tortious act* by the defendant. The consent that is relevant is not consent to the risk of injury but consent to the lack of reasonable care that may produce that risk. (*Per* Diplock, L.J.)

GENERAL DEFENCES: *VOLENTI*: PUBLIC POLICY: DUTY OF CARE

312. *Nettleship* v *Weston* [1971] 3 All E.R. 581

The plaintiff, a non-professional driving instructor, gave the defendant driving lessons after having first satisfied himself that the car was insured to cover injury to passengers. The defendant was a careful driver but on the third lesson she failed to straighten out after turning left and struck a lamp standard breaking the plaintiff's kneecap. The defendant was convicted of driving without due care and attention. *Held* – by the Court of Appeal – that since the plaintiff had checked on the insurance position he had expressly not consented to run the risk and there was no question of *volenti*. Furthermore, the duty of care owed by a learner-driver was the same as that owed by every driver and the defendant was liable for the damages. A learner-driver owes a duty to his instructor to drive with proper skill and care, the test being the objective one of the careful driver and it is no defence that he was doing his best.

> COMMENT
> (i) Nobody would suggest that a learner-driver can do any more than his best. However, the mere fact of learning to drive a motor car is dangerous, at least in its initial stages, and the risk of injury has to be upon the driver. This facilitates an insurance claim by the injured party. In addition, the application of an objective standard of care facilitates a speedier and cheaper settlement of the many road accident cases. These two points mean that in essence the learner-driver's standard is a matter of public policy.
>
> (ii) A passenger who knows that a driver is under the influence of drink or drugs may, if he is injured, be barred from recovering damages on the grounds of *public policy* since he is aiding and abetting a criminal offence. As Megaw, L.J. said in this case: 'There may in such cases sometimes be an element of aiding and abetting a criminal offence; or, if the facts fall short of aiding and abetting, the passenger's mere assent to benefit from the commission of a criminal offence may involve questions of *turpis causa*.' The phrase *'turpis causa'* denotes something dishonourable or immoral.

GENERAL DEFENCES: INEVITABLE ACCIDENT

313. *Stanley* v *Powell* [1891] 1 Q.B. 86

The defendant was a member of a shooting party, and the plaintiff was employed to carry cartridges and also any game which was shot. The defendant fired at a pheasant, but a shot glanced off an oak tree and injured the plaintiff. *Held* – the plaintiff's claim failed. The defendant's action was neither intentional nor negligent.

314. *National Coal Board* v *Evans (J.E.) & Co. (Cardiff) Ltd and Another* [1951] 2 K.B. 861

Evans & Co. were employed by Glamorgan County Council to carry out certain work on land belonging to the Council. It was necessary to excavate a trench across the land, and Evans & Co. sub-contracted with the second defendants to do this work. An electric cable passed under the land, but the Council, Evans & Co., and the sub-contractors had no knowledge of this and it was not marked on any available map. During the course of the excavation a mechanical digger damaged the cable so that water seeped into it causing an explosion. The electricity supply to the plaintiff's colliery was cut off, and they sued the defendants in trespass and negligence. Donovan, J., at first instance, found that the defendants were not negligent, but were liable in trespass. The Court of Appeal *held* the defendants were entirely free from fault and there was no trespass by them.

GENERAL DEFENCES: ACT OF GOD

315. *Nichols* v *Marsland* (1876) 2 Ex.D. 1

For many years there had existed certain artificial ornamental lakes on the defendant's land, formed by damming up of a natural stream the source of which was at a point higher up. An extraordinary rainfall 'greater and more violent than any within the memory of witnesses' caused the stream and the lakes to swell to such an extent that the artificial banks burst, and the escaping water carried away four bridges belonging to the County Council. Nichols, the county surveyor, sued under the rule in *Rylands* v *Fletcher*. *Held* – the defendant was not liable for this extraordinary act of nature which she could not reasonably have anticipated. The escape of water was owing to the Act of God, and while one is bound to provide against the ordinary operations of nature, one is not bound to provide against miracles.

> COMMENT
> Although *Rylands* v *Fletcher* liability is strict, Act of God is a defence. (See p. 476.)

GENERAL DEFENCES: NECESSITY

316. *Cresswell* v *Sirl* [1948] 1 K.B. 241

The defendant, a farmer's son, was awakened during the night by dogs barking, and on going out found certain ewe sheep in lamb, penned up by the dogs in a corner of a field. The dogs seemed about to attack the sheep and had been chasing them for an hour. A light was turned on the dogs, who then left the sheep and started for the defendant. When they were about 40 yards away, the defendant fired and killed one of the dogs. The owner of the dog sued the defendant for damages. In the County Court, judgment was given for the owner of the dog on the ground that such a killing could be justified only if it took place while the dog was actually attacking the sheep.

In the view of the Court of Appeal, however, the defendant could justify his act by showing that it was necessary to avert immediate danger to property. It was not necessary that the dog should actually be attacking the sheep. This decision is affirmed by s. 9 of the Animals Act, 1971, which now covers the situation. However, the section requires that the person shooting the dog must have had reasonable grounds to believe that there were no other reasonable means of dealing with the problem or ascertaining the owner.

317. *Cope* v *Sharpe (No. 2)* [1912] 1 K.B. 486

The plaintiff was a landowner and he let the shooting rights over part of his land to a tenant. A heath fire broke out on part of the plaintiff's land and the defendant, who was the head gamekeeper of the tenant, set fire to patches of heather between the main fire and a covert in which his master's pheasants were sitting. His object was to prevent the fire spreading. In fact the fire was extinguished independently of what the defendant had done, and the plaintiff now sued the defendant for damages for trespass. *Held* – the defendant was not liable because when he carried out the act it seemed reasonably necessary, and it did not matter that in the event it turned out to be unnecessary.

> COMMENT
> In *Rigby* v *Chief Constable of Northampton* [1985] 2 All E.R. 985, R's shop was burnt out when the police fired a canister of C.S. gas into the building to force out a dangerous psychopath. R's claim in trespass failed on the grounds of the defence of necessity. His claim in negligence succeeded because there was, to the knowledge of the police, no fire-fighting equipment available.

GENERAL DEFENCES: MISTAKE

318. *Beckwith* v *Philby* (1827) 6 B. & C. 635

In this case it was *held* that the mistaken arrest of an innocent man on suspicion of felony by an ordinary citizen is not actionable as false imprisonment, if the felony has been committed, and if there are reasonable grounds for believing that the person arrested is guilty of it.

GENERAL DEFENCES: ACT OF STATE

319. *Buron* v *Denman* (1848) 2 Ech. 167

The captain of a British warship was *held* not liable for trespass when he set fire to the barracoon of a Spaniard slave trader on the West Coast of Africa and released the slaves. The captain had general instructions to suppress the slave trade, and in any case his conduct in this matter was afterwards approved by the Admiralty and the Foreign and Colonial Secretaries. It seems, therefore, that neither the official responsible not the Crown can be sued for injuries inflicted upon others outside the territorial jurisdiction of the Crown, if these are authorised or subsequently ratified by the Crown.

320. *Nissan* v *Attorney-General* [1967] 2 All E.R. 1238

The plaintiff, a British subject, was the tenant of a hotel in Cyprus. In December 1963, the Government of Cyprus accepted an offer that British Forces stationed in Cyprus should give assistance in restoring peace to the island. The British troops occupied the plaintiff's hotel for some months and the plaintiff now sued the Crown for compensation. It was *held* – *inter alia* that the Crown was obliged to pay compensation and that a plea by the Crown of 'Act of State' was no defence as against a Britsh subject.

321. *Johnstone* v *Pedlar* [1921] 2 A.C. 262

Johnstone was the Chief Commissioner of the Dublin Metropolitan Police. He was the defendant in an action in which Pedlar sued for the detention of £124 in cash and a cheque for £4 15s. 6d. Pedlar was convicted of being engaged in the illegal drilling of troops in Ireland, and the above property was found on him at the time of his arrest. Pedlar, who was a naturalised citizen of the United States of America, sued for the return of his property, and the defence was 'Act of State'. A certificate given by the Chief Secretary for Ireland was put in at the trial, certifying that the detention of the property was formally ratified as an Act of State. *Held* – Pedlar was entitled to claim his property, because the defence of 'Act of State' cannot be raised against an alien who is a subject of a friendly nation.

GENERAL DEFENCES: STATUTORY AUTHORITY

322. *Vaughan* v *Taff Vale Railway* (1860) 5 H. & N. 679

The defendants were *held* not liable for fires caused by sparks from engines which they were bound by statute to run and which were constructed with proper care.

COMMENT
(i) By s. 1 of the Railway Fires Acts, 1905 as amended by s. 38 of the Transport Act, 1981, British Rail is under a liability of up to £3000 for damage to crops caused by fire by engines run under statutory authority, though the advent of diesel and electric trains makes the statute somewhat out of date.

(ii) Even if the authority to act is absolute, the damage will not be excused unless it is necessarily incidental. Thus it is not necessary to the processing of sewage that rivers be polluted. (*Pride of Derby and Derbyshire Angling Association* v *British Celanese Ltd* [1952] 1 All E.R. 1326.)

323. *Penny* v *Wimbledon Urban District Council* [1899] 2 Q.B. 72

The defendants, acting under conditional powers conferred upon them by s. 150 of the Public Health Act, 1875, employed a contractor to make up a road in their district. The contractor removed the surface soil and placed it in heaps on the road. The plaintiff, while passing along the road in the dark, fell over one of the heaps, which had been left unlighted and unguarded, and was injured. She now sued for damages. *Held* – she succeeded. Although the Council were operating under statutory powers they must, if they do acts likely to cause danger to the public, see that the work is properly carried out, and take reasonable measures to guard against danger. The Council did not discharge this duty by delegating it to a contractor, and the local authority were liable for negligence.

324. *Marriage* v *East Norfolk Rivers Catchment Board* [1950] 1 K.B. 284

In pursuance of their powers under s. 34 of the Land Drainage Act, 1930, the Catchment Board deposited dredgings taken from the river on the south bank of that river, so raising its height by one to two feet. When the river next flooded, the flood waters instead of escaping over the south bank, as they had always done, ran over the north bank and swept away a bridge leading to a mill owned by the plaintiff. Section 34(3) of the Land Drainage Act, 1930 provided that, in the event of injury to any person by reason of the exercise by a drainage board of any of its powers, the board concerned should make full compensation, disputes being settled by a system of arbitration. The plaintiff had issued a writ for nuisance against the board. *Held* – no action in nuisance lay; the plaintiff's only remedy was to claim compensation under s. 34(3).

REMOTENESS OF DAMAGE: THE FORESIGHT TEST

325. *Overseas Tankship (UK) Ltd* v *Morts Dock and Engineering Co Ltd (The Wagon Mound)* [1961] A.C. 388

The appellants were the charterers of a ship called the *Wagon Mound*. While the ship was taking on furnace oil in Sydney harbour, the appellants' servants negligently allowed oil to spill into the water. The action of the wind and tide carried this oil some 200 yards and over to the respondents' wharf where the business of shipbuilding and repairing was carried on. The servants of the respondents were at this time engaged in repairing a vessel, the *Corrimal*, which was moored alongside the wharf, and for this purpose they were using welding equipment. The manager of the respondents, seeing the oil on the water, suspended welding operations and consulted the wharf manager who told him it was safe to continue work – a decision which was justified, because previous knowledge showed that sparks were not likely to set fire to oil floating on water. Work, therefore, proceeded with safety precautions being taken. However, a piece of molten metal fell from the wharf and set on fire a piece of cotton waste which was floating on the oil. This set the oil alight and the respondents' wharf was badly damaged. The case eventually came before the Judicial Committee of the Privy Council on appeal. *Held* – the appellants were successful in their appeal, the Judicial Committee holding that foreseeability of the actual harm resulting was the proper tort test. On this principle, they held that the damage caused by the fire was too remote, though they would have awarded damages for the fouling of the respondents' slipways by oil, if such a claim had been made, since this was forseeable.

COMMENT

In *Overseas Tankship (UK) Ltd* v *Miller Steamship Property Ltd (The Wagon Mound (No. 2))* [1966] 2 All E.R. 709, the same blaze had caused damage to the respondents' ship (they were the owners of the *Corrimal*). However, the Privy Council had by this time the decision of the House of Lords in *Hughes* v *Lord Advocate*, 1963 (see below) before them. It said that the *precise* nature of the injury suffered need not be foreseeable so long as it was one of a kind that was foreseeable. Therefore the respondents recovered damages in negligence and also nuisance. The Privy Council *held* that in the case of nuisance, as of negligence, it is not enough that the damage was a direct result of the nuisance if the injury was not foreseeable.

326. *Hughes* v *Lord Advocate* [1963] 1 All E.R. 705

Workmen opened a manhole in the street and later left it unattended having placed a tent above it and warning paraffin lamps around it. The plaintiff and another boy, who were aged eight and ten respectively, took one of the lamps and went down the manhole. As they came out the lamp was knocked into the hole and an explosion took place injuring the plaintiff. The explosion was caused in a unique fashion because the paraffin had vaporised (which was unusual) and been ignited by the naked flame of the wick. The defendants argued that although some injury by burning was foreseeable, burning by explosion was not. *Held* – by the House of Lords – that the defendants were liable. 'The cause of this accident was a known source of danger, the lamp, but it behaved in an unpredictable way. . . . This accident was caused by a known source of danger but caused in a way which could not have been foreseen and in my judgment that affords no defence.' (*Per* Lord Reid.) 'The accident was but a variant of the foreseeable. It was, to quote the words of Denning, L.J., in *Roe* v *Minister of Health* [see p. 786] "within the risk created by the negligence". . . . The children's entry into the tent with the ladder, the descent into the hole, the mishandling of the lamp, were all foreseeable. The greater part of the path to injury had thus been trodden, and the mishandled lamp was quite likely at this stage to spill and cause a conflagration. Instead, by some curious chance of combustion, it exploded and no conflagration occurred, it would seem, until after the explosion. There was thus an unexpected manifestation of the apprehended physical dangers. But it would be, I think, too narrow a view to hold that those who created the risk of fire are excused from the liability for the damage by fire because it came by way of explosive combustion. The resulting damage, though severe, was not greater than or different in kind from that which might have been produced had the lamp spilled and caused a more normal conflagration in the hole.' (*Per* Lord Pearce.)

COMMENT

(i) A good illustration of the rule in *Hughes* that the *precise* mechanics of the way in which harm occurs need not be foreseen if it is within the risk caused by the negligence is *Draper* v *Hodder* [1972] 2 All E.R. 210. The defendant owned 30 Jack Russell terriers which he kept on his ungated premises. The dogs could run into a nearby house which was owned by the plaintiff's parents. That house was also ungated. On one occasion the dogs ran into the yard of the nearby house and one or more of them attacked the plaintiff, a three-year-old boy and bit him. His action for damages succeeded. It was foreseeable immediately that the dogs would bowl over and scratch the child. Nevertheless, the fact that one or more of them bit him was within the risk created by the negligence.

(ii) In spite of the more liberal attitude taken to foresight in *Hughes*, some things are still too remote as consequences. For example in *Meah v McCreamer (No. 2)* [1986] 1 All E.R. 943 the plaintiff had been injured in a car accident by reason of the defendant's negligence. The plaintiff alleged that he had suffered a personality change leading to him attacking women. He raped one and indecently assaulted another. The women recovered damages against him and he tried to recover them from the defendant. It was held that the alleged damage was too remote.

REMOTENESS OF DAMAGE: THE UNUSUAL PLAINTIFF RULE

327. *Smith* v *Leech Braine & Co. Ltd* [1962] 2 W.L.R. 148

The plaintiff was the widow of a person employed by the defendants. Mr Smith's work consisted of lowering articles into a galvanizing tank containing molten zinc. On one occasion he was struck on the lip by a piece of molten metal which caused a burn. This resulted in a cancer from which he died three years later. Mr Smith's work had given him a predisposition to cancer and the question arose whether, since the *Wagon Mound*, the so-called 'thin skull rule' had disappeared, so that the plaintiff had to show that the cancer was foreseeable. The Lord Chief Justice, Lord Parker, finding for the plaintiff, said in the course of his judgment: 'I am satisfied that the Judicial Committee of the Privy Council did not have what are called "thin skull" cases in mind. It has always been the common law that a tortfeasor must take his victim as he finds him.'

328. *Martindale* v *Duncan* [1973] 1 W.L.R. 674

The plaintiff's car was damaged in a collision with the defendant's car because of the negligence of the defendant. The plaintiff delayed repairs to his car pending the approval of the defendant's insurers and also of his own. The defendant's insurers wished to seek the advice of independent engineers and did so. About nine weeks after the accident, the defendant's insurers approved the estimate. A few days later the plaintiff's insurers did so and the repairs were started one week afterwards. The District Registrar awarded the plaintiff damages including £220 for loss of use of his vehicle for ten weeks at the rate of £22 per week for hire of a substitute vehicle to cover the period during which he had delayed repairs pending approval of the estimate by the insurers. The defendant had argued that the repairs were not commenced as early as they could have been since the plaintiff was not himself able to pay for the repairs but had to wait to see what the position was as regards payment from an insurance company. On appeal by the defendant it was *held* – by the Court of Appeal – dismissing the appeal – that the plaintiff was not in breach of his duty to mitigate his loss and had acted reasonably in the circumstances.

329. *Morgan* v *T. Wallis* [1974] 1 Ll. Rep. 165

Mr Morgan, a lighterman on the River Thames, sustained back injuries in trying to avoid a wire rope thrown by a stevedore on to a barge where Mr Morgan was working. Liability for his injuries was admitted by the defendants, his employers, because they should have had a better system of working, but the amount of damages was disputed because Mr Morgan unreasonably refused to undergo tests and an operation because he genuinely feared both of these things. The highest estimate by a surgeon of the chances of success of such an operation was 90%. It was *held* – by Browne, J. – that the defendants had proved that Mr Morgan's refusal was unreasonable as to the investigations and that the operation would have been successful on a balance of probabilities. Where there was no prior disability, physical, mental or psychological, a defendant did not have to take a plaintiff as he found him.

REMOTENESS OF DAMAGE: INTENDED DAMAGE NEVER TOO REMOTE: *NOVUS ACTUS INTERVENIENS*: ACT OF A THIRD PARTY EXPECTED

330. *Scott* v *Shepherd* (1773) 2 Wm. Bl. 892

On the evening of a fair-day at Milborne Port, Shepherd threw a lighted squib on to the market stall of one Yates who sold gingerbread. Then one Willis, in order to protect the wares of Yates, threw it away and it landed on the stall of one Ryal. He threw it to another part of the market house where it struck the plaintiff in the face, exploded and put out his eye. *Held* – Shepherd was liable for the injuries to Scott because he intended the initial act and there was no break in the chain of causation. Shepherd should have anticipated that Willis and Ryal would act as they did.

> COMMENT
> The decision in this case is initially difficult to understand because Shepherd did not injure the plaintiff. It would seem that since battery is also a crime the maxim of the criminal law that a person intends the natural consequences of his acts was applied to produce the 'transferred intent' of the type seen in criminal cases.

REMOTENESS OF DAMAGE: *NOVUS ACTUS* NOT MATERIALLY CAUSING OR CONTRIBUTING TO INJURY

331. *Barnett* v *Chelsea and Kensington Hospital Management Committee* [1968] 1 All E.R. 1068

Mr Barnett drank tea which had, unknown to him, been contaminated with arsenic. He attended at the casualty department of a hospital saying that he had been vomiting for some three hours after drinking the tea. The casualty doctor failed to examine him but sent a message that he should report to his own doctor. Some five hours later Mr Barnett died and on his widow's action for damages, it was *held* that the hospital authority owed a duty of care and that the doctor was negligent in failing to examine and admit Mr Barnett and accordingly there had been a breach of that duty. However, on the facts the deceased's condition was such that he must have died despite any medical attention which the hospital could have given so that causation was not established and the widow's claim failed.

332. *Robinson* v *The Post Office*, *The Times*, 26 October 1973

The plaintiff suffered a minor injury for which the defendants, his employers, admitted liability. As a result the plaintiff received an anti-tetanus injection which produced a rare complication of encephalitis, with grave consequences. Ashworth, J. held that the doctor had acted negligently in administering the injection in that he had failed to administer a test dose. However, it appeared that even if such a test had been made the plaintiff would have shown no reaction to it. Thus the doctor's negligence had had no causative effect, since even with the proper precautions the encephalitis would not have been prevented. The defendants appealed and it was *held* – by the Court of Appeal – that the judge's conclusions on the question of the medical negligence were correct and that accordingly the defendant could not rely on that negligence as a *novus actus interveniens*. They were therefore liable for all the plaintiff's disabilities and the contention that these were too remote was to be rejected.

REMOTENESS OF DAMAGE: DUTY TO GUARD AGAINST *NOVUS ACTUS*

333. *Davies* v *Liverpool Corporation* [1949] 2 All E.R. 175

The plaintiff was trying to board a tramcar belonging to the defendants at a request stopping place. An unauthorised person (a passenger) rang the bell, whereupon the car started, throwing the plaintiff off the platform and causing her injury. The conductor was on the upper deck collecting fares. Evidence showed that the car had been standing at the request stop for an appreciable time, and that the conductor had been upstairs for the whole of that time, though it was not a particularly busy period. In this action for negligence brought by the plaintiff, it was *held* that the defendants were liable for the negligent act of the conductor. He should have foreseen that if he was absent from the platform of the car for an appreciable time, some passenger might ring the bell. The act of the passenger did not, therefore, break the chain of causation because it was just that sort of act which the conductor was employed to prevent.

REMOTENESS OF DAMAGE: *NOVUS ACTUS* NOT ANTICIPATED BY DEFENDANT

334. *Cobb* v *Great Western Railway* [1894] A.C. 419

The railway company allowed a railway carriage to become overcrowded, and because of this the plaintiff was hustled and robbed of £89. He now sued the company in respect of his loss. *Held* – this was too remote a consequence of the defendants' negligence. The robbery was a *novus actus interveniens* breaking the chain of causation.

> COMMENT
> In *Stansbie* v *Troman* [1948] 2 K.B. 48 the owner of a house was obliged to leave a painter working alone on the premises. The owner told the painter to shut the front door when he left the house but in fact the painter left the house empty for about two hours in order to obtain some wallpaper and left the door unlocked. It was held that the painter was liable for the loss of jewellery stolen by a third party who entered the house in his absence because this was foreseeable as being just the kind of thing which might happen in the situation. It is difficult to reconcile *Stansbie* with *Cobb* and this leads to the suggestion that *Cobb* may no longer be good law, though it has never been overruled.

REMOTENESS OF DAMAGE: *NOVUS ACTUS* MAY BE THAT OF THE PLAINTIFF

335. *Sayers* v *Harlow U.D.C.* [1958] 2 All E.R. 342

The defendants owned and operated a public lavatory. The plaintiff having paid for admission entered a cubicle. Finding that there was no handle on the inside of the door, and no means of opening the cubicle, the plaintiff had tried for some 10 to 15 minutes to attract attention. Having failed to do so, and wishing to catch a bus to London in the next few minutes, she tried to see if there was a way of climbing out. She placed one foot on the seat of the lavatory and rested her other foot on the toilet roll and fixture, holding the pipe from the cistern with one hand and resting the other hand on the top of the door. She then realised it would be impossible to climb out, and she proceeded to come down, but as she was doing so, the toilet roll rotated owing to her weight on it and she slipped and injured herself. She sued the defendants for negligence. In the County Court the defendants were found negligent, but, as the plaintiff was in no danger on that account, and as she chose to embark on a dangerous act, she must bear the consequences. It was *held* – by the Court of Appeal – that her act was not a *novus actus interveniens*, and the damage was not too remote a consequence of the defendants' negligence. She was 36 years of age, and in her predicament her act was not unreasonable, though if she had been an old lady it might have been. However, the damages recoverable by the plaintiff would be reduced by one-quarter in respect of her share of the responsibility for the damage.

336. *McKew v Holland and Hannen and Cubitts (Scotland) Ltd* [1969] 2 All E.R. 1621

McKew sustained an injury during the course of his employment for which his employers were liable. The injury caused him occasionally and unexpectedly to lose the use of his left leg. On one occasion he left a flat and started to descend some stairs which had no handrail. His leg gave way and he sustained further injury. *Held* – by the House of Lords – that his conduct in trying to descend the stairs was unreasonable and thus broke the chain of causation. The subsequent injury was therefore too remote and the employers were not liable.

REMOTENESS OF DAMAGE: *NOVUS ACTUS*: THE INTERVENER MUST INTEND THE ACT

337. *Philco Radio Corporation v Spurling* [1949] 2 All E.R. 882

Certain packing cases containing inflammable film scrap were delivered in error by the defendants to the plaintiff's premises. No warning as to their contents was given on the cases. The cases were opened by the plaintiffs' servants, and a foreman recognised the contents as inflammable, and gave instructions that the scrap was to be replaced, and that there was to be no smoking in the vicinity. He telephoned the defendants and arranged to have the cases delivered to their proper destination, 150 yards away. Before the cases had been moved, a typist employed by the plaintiffs negligently set light to the scrap with a cigarette, and it exploded causing damage. The defendants pleaded that the proximate cause of the damage was the typist's act and that the chain of causation was broken. *Held* – the defendants were negligent in not ensuring that such dangerous material was properly delivered. The act of the typist did not break the chain of causation; she did not intend to injure her employer, and when she approached the scrap with a cigarette she did so as a joke. Her act was not such a conscious act of violation as to relieve the defendants from liability, and in any case the act formed part of the very risk that was envisaged.

REMOTENESS OF DAMAGE: NERVOUS SHOCK

338. *Dulieu v White* [1901] 2 K.B. 669

The defendant who was driving a van negligently, ran into a public house. The plaintiff, who was pregnant, was in the public house and because of the shock became ill and gave birth to a premature and mentally deficient child. It was *held* that she could recover damages.

339. *Chadwick v British Railways Board* [1967] 1 W.L.R. 912

A serious railway accident was caused by negligence for which the Board was liable. A volunteer rescue worker suffered nervous shock and became psychoneurotic as a result. The plaintiff, as administratrix of his estate, claimed damages for nervous shock. it was *held* that –

(a) damages were recoverable for nervous shock even though the shock was not caused by fear for one's own safety or that of one's children;

(b) in the circumstances injury by shock was foreseeable;

(c) the defendants ought to have foreseen that volunteers might attempt rescue and accordingly owed a duty of care to those who did.

COMMENT

If the plaintiff had merely read of this accident to strangers in his newspaper there would have been no claim for nervous shock if this had resulted.

340. *Hinz* v *Berry* [1970] 1 All E.R. 1074

Mrs Hinz witnessed a car accident in which her husband was killed and her children injured. The accident was caused by the negligent driving of the defendant. As a result of seeing the accident Mrs Hinz, who had been a vigorous and lively woman, became morbid and depressed for years afterwards. *Held* – by the Court of Appeal – she was entitled to damages of £4000 for nervous shock. She was a woman of robust character who would probably have stood up to the strain if she had not *seen* the accident.

Somehow or other the court has to draw a line between sorrow and grief for which damages are not recoverable; and nervous shock and psychiatric illness for which damages are recoverable. The way to do this is to estimate how much the plaintiff would have suffered if, for instance, her husband had been killed in an accident when she was 50 miles away; and compare it with what she is now, having suffered all the shock due to being present at the accident. The evidence shows that she suffered much more by being present. (*Per* Lord Denning, M.R.)

341. *Hambrook* v *Stokes* [1925] 1 K.B. 141

The defendant left his lorry unattended on a sloping street and, because of his negligence in failing to brake the vehicle properly, it began to run away. The plaintiff's wife had just left her children further down the street though they were in fact round a bend and not within her view. However, she saw the lorry moving and suffered shock, which resulted in her death, because she feared for the safety of her children. Her husband brought this action for loss of her services and was *held* entitled to recover damages provided that the shock was brought about by his wife's own experience and not by the accounts of bystanders.

342. *McLoughlin* v *O'Brian* [1981] 1 All E.R. 809

The plaintiff's husband and three children were involved in a road accident caused by the negligence of the defendant. One child was killed and the husband and the other two children were badly injured. At the time of the accident the plaintiff was at home two miles away and was told of the accident by a neighbour and taken to hospital where she saw the injured members of her family and the extent of their injuries and shock, and heard that her daughter had been killed. As a result of hearing and seeing the results of the accident the plaintiff suffered severe and persisting nervous shock and brought this action against the defendant for negligence. It was held by the Court of Appeal that the claim failed. Even though the plaintiff's nervous shock was a reasonable foreseeable consequence of the defendant's negligence, in accordance with precedent and social policy the duty of care owed by a driver of a motor vehicle was limited to persons and owners of property on the road or near it who might be directly affected by the driver's negligent driving and accordingly the defendant did not owe a duty of care to the plaintiff because she had not been in the physical proximity of the accident when it occurred.

The House of Lords, [1982] 2 All E.R. 278, reversed the Court of Appeal and upheld the plaintiff's claim, even though she was two miles from the accident. The argument that this would open the floodgates to many claims by people who had not actually seen the accident, which was a former restriction on claims of this sort, did not deter their Lordships. They all agreed that the plaintiff's nervous shock was a foreseeable event producing an identifiable mental illness. However, that part of the decision in *Hinz* v *Berry* (above) which says that nervous shock does not cover sorrow or grief was upheld.

COMMENT

(i) If the floodgates ever did open they were closed by the Court of Appeal in *Alcock* v *Chief Constable of South Yorkshire*, *The Times*, 6 May 1991. The case was brought following the disaster at Hillsborough football ground at Sheffield where it was alleged that the police let too many people get into the ground causing those in front of them to be crushed against railings and barricades. It was held that only the parents and spouses of the victims could recover damages for nervous shock and then only if they had actually seen the accident by being at the ground or identified bodies afterwards. Parents and spouses who had only seen the disaster by viewing it on a simultaneous TV broadcast could not get damages. The decision was affirmed by the House of Lords. (See *Alcock* v *Chief Constable of South Yorkshire*, *The Times*, 29 November 1991.)

(ii) However, it was held in *Attia* v *British Gas plc* [1987] 3 All E.R. 456 that damages for nervous shock could be recovered where it was caused by damage to property. It need not result from the death or injury of a person. The plaintiff's shock in this case arose when, on returning home, she saw the whole of her house on fire as a result of the defendant's negligence.

REMOTENESS OF DAMAGE: NERVOUS SHOCK: THERE MUST BE A DUTY OF CARE

343. *Hay (or Bourhill)* v *Young* [1943] A.C. 92

The plaintiff, a pregnant Edinburgh fishwife, alighted from a tramcar. While she was removing her fish-basket from the tram, Young, a motor cyclist, driving carelessly but unseen by her, passed the tram and collided with a motor car some 15 yards away. Young was killed. The plaintiff heard the collision, and after Young's body had been removed, she approached the scene of the accident and saw a pool of blood on the road. She suffered a nervous shock and later gave birth to a stillborn child. The House of Lords *held* that her action against Young's personal representative failed, because Young owed no duty of care to persons whom he could not reasonably anticipate would suffer injuries as a result of his conduct on the highway.

344. *Owens* v *Liverpool Corporation* [1939] 2 K.B. 394

A funeral procession was making its way to the cemetery when a negligently driven tram owned by the defendants collided with the hearse and overturned the coffin. Several mourners who were following in a carriage suffered shock and it was *held* by the Court of Appeal that they were entitled to damages.

REMOTENESS OF DAMAGE: SUCCESSIVE ACCIDENTS AND SUPERVENING EVENTS

345. *Jobling* v *Associated Dairies* [1980] 3 All E.R. 769

The plaintiff, an employee in a butcher's shop, suffered a partially disabling accident at work in 1973. In 1976 before the trial in regard to that accident came on, the plaintiff was found to be suffering from a totally disabling but unconnected condition. At the trial in 1979 the judge took no account of the supervening disability. On appeal on amount of damages it was *held* – allowing the appeal that where a plaintiff was subsequently injured by a non-tortious act the tortfeaser's damages were to be reduced by the extent of the plaintiff's further injuries and consequent loss. *Baker* v *Willoughby*, 1969 (below) should not be extended further.

346. *Baker* v *Willoughby* [1969] 3 All E.R. 1528

In September 1964, the plaintiff was involved in an accident on the highway caused by the negligent driving of the defendant, but attributable as to one-quarter to the plaintiff's contributory negligence. The plaintiff received serious injuries to his left leg, but after long hospital treatment he took up employment with a scrap metal merchant. On 29 November 1967, while in the course of his employment, the plaintiff was the innocent victim of an armed robbery receiving gunshot wounds necessitating the immediate amputation of his left leg which was already defective because of the previous accident. The question of the amount of damages for the plaintiff's injuries in the road accident of September 1964 came before the Court for assessment in February 1968. *Held* – by the Court of Appeal – that no consequence of the accident of September 1964 survived the amputation of the plaintiff's left leg and the defendant was liable only for loss suffered by the plaintiff up to 29 November 1967. Damages are compensation for loss arising from a tortious act and cease when by reason of recovery, supervening disease, or further injury there is no continuing loss attributable to that act.

The House of Lords, [1969] 3 All E.R. 1529, reversed the Court of Appeal decision holding that damages are not merely compensation for physical injury but for the loss which the injured person suffers. This loss was not diminished by the supervening event and the second injury was irrelevant. 'The supervening event has not made the appellant less lame nor less disabled nor less deprived of amenities. It has not shortened the period over which he will be suffering. It has made him more lame, more disabled, more deprived of amenities. He should not have less damages through being worse off than he might have expected . . .' (*Per* Lord Pearson, L.J.).

347. *Performance Cars Ltd* v *Abraham* [1961] 3 All E.R. 413

The plaintiffs owned a motor car which was damaged in a collision with a car driven by the defendant. The damage to the plaintiff's car was such that it would necessitate respraying the whole of the lower body. Two weeks before the accident the plaintiff's car had been involved in another collision which had also made respraying of the lower body of the car necessary. The plaintiffs obtained judgment against the driver responsible for the first collision but that judgment was not satisfied and the car had not been resprayed at the time when the second collision took place. The court was asked to decide whether the plaintiffs were entitled to recover as damages from the defendant the cost of respraying the lower body of their car. *Held* – by the Court of Appeal – that the plaintiffs were not entitled to recover the cost of respraying from the defendant because that damage was not the result of his wrongful act.

LIMITATION OF ACTIONS: FRAUDULENT OR NEGLIGENT CONCEALMENT OF CLAIM

348. *Beaman* v *A.R.T.S.* [1949] 1 All E.R. 465

In November 1935, Mrs Beaman, before leaving for Istanbul, deposited with the defendants several packages to be sent to her as soon as she gave notice requesting it. In May 1936, the defendants at her request dispatched one of the packages but afterwards regulations made by the Turkish authorities prevented dispatching of the other packages and Mrs Beaman asked the defendants to keep them in store pending further instructions. Three years later the defendants, who had not received instructions, wrote and asked the plaintiff to insure the contents of the packages. She did not do so but replied saying that she was hoping to return to England. However, the outbreak of war while she was still in Turkey prevented this.

On the entry of Italy into the war in 1940 the defendants, being a company controlled by Italian nationals, had their business taken over by the Custodian of Enemy Property. Wishing to wind up the business as soon as possible, the manager of A.R.T.S. Ltd examined the packages, reported that they were of no value, and gave them to the Salvation Army. No steps were taken to obtain the plaintiff's consent. The plaintiff returned to England in 1946 and commenced proceedings more than six years after the packages were disposed of, claiming damages for conversion. The defendants set up the defence that the action was barred by the Limitation Act. The plaintiff relied

on what is now s. 32 of the Limitation Act, 1980 which provides that where '(a) the action is based on fraud of the defendant . . . or (b) the right of action is concealed by the fraud of any such person . . . the period of limitation shall not begin to run until the plaintiff has discovered the fraud. . .'.
Held –

(a) That the action for conversion was not 'based on fraud' so that what is now s. 32(1)(a) had no application.

(b) The conduct of the defendants constituted a reckless 'concealment by fraud' of the right of action within what is now s. 32(1)(b). Therefore the plaintiff's action was not barred.

> COMMENT
> It appears that it is not necessary to prove a degree of moral turpitude to establish fraud for the purposes of s. 32. Thus in *Kitchen* v *Royal Air Force Association* [1958] 1 W.L.R. 563, solicitors negligently concealed a payment of money on behalf of the plaintiff and this conduct was held to amount to 'fraud' for the purposes of what is now s. 32 even though the court accepted that the solicitors were not dishonest.

The law of torts – specific torts

TRESPASS TO THE PERSON: WORDS MAY PREVENT AN ASSAULT

349. *Turbervell* v *Savage* (1669) 2 Keb. 545

In this old case a man laid his hand menacingly on his sword, but at the same time said, 'If it were not assize time I would not take such language from you.'
Held – this was not an assault because it was assize time, and there was no reason to fear violence.

TRESPASS TO THE PERSON: BATTERY MAY ARISE FROM A FAILURE TO ACT

350. *Fagan* v *Metropolitan Police Commissioner* [1968] 3 All E.R. 442

Fagan was driving his car when he was told by a constable to draw into the kerb. He stopped his car with one wheel on the constable's foot and was slow in restarting the engine and moving the vehicle off. He was convicted of assault on the constable and Quarter Sessions dismissed his appeal. He then appealed to the Queen's Bench Divisional Court where it was *held* – dismissing his appeal – that whether or not the mounting of the wheel on the constable's foot had been intentional the defendant had deliberately allowed it to remain there when asked to move it and that constituted an assault. The decision seems to extend the law because there was no act but merely an omission. Furthermore, there was no intentional application of force but only a failure to withdraw it. A more appropriate charge might have been false imprisonment because the constable could not presumably have moved while the wheel remained on his foot.

COMMENT
This was a criminal prosecution for assault, an expression which is commonly used to mean battery also. In strict civil law terms the trespass to the policeman was a battery.

TRESPASS TO THE PERSON: IS NOT ACTIONABLE IN ITSELF: THE PLAINTIFF MUST PROVE INTENTION OR NEGLIGENCE

351. *Fowler* v *Lanning* [1959] 1 All E.R. 290

By a writ the plaintiff claimed damages for trespass to the person. In his statement of claim he alleged that on 19 November 1957, at Vineyard Farm, Corfe Castle, in the County of Dorset, the defendant shot the plaintiff. By reason of the premises, the plaintiff sustained personal injuries and suffered loss and damage; particulars of the plaintiff's injuries were then set out. The defendant denied the allegations of fact and objected that the statement of claim disclosed no cause of action, because the plaintiff had not alleged that the shooting was either intentional or negligent. *Held* – in an action for trespass to the person, onus of proof of the defendant's intention or negligence lay on the plaintiff and the plaintiff must allege that the shooting was intentional or that the defendant was negligent, stating the facts alleged to constitute the negligence. The plaintiff's statement of claim, therefore, disclosed no cause of action.

COMMENT
If the interference is *unintentional* it was held in *Letang* v *Cooper* [1964] 2 All E.R. 929 that an action must be brought in negligence.

TRESPASS TO THE PERSON: FALSE IMPRISONMENT

352. *Bird* v *Jones* (1845) 7 Q.B. 742

A bridge company enclosed part of the public footway on Hammersmith Bridge, put seats on it for the use of spectators at a regatta on the river, and charged admission. The plaintiff insisted on passing along this part of the footpath, and climbed over the fence without paying the charge. The defendant, who was the clerk of the Bridge Company, stationed two policemen to prevent, and they did prevent, the plaintiff from proceeding forwards along the footway in the direction he wished to go. The plaintiff was at the same time told that he might go back into the carriage way and proceed to the other side of the bridge if he wished. He declined to do so and remained in the enclosure for about half an hour. *Held* – there was no false imprisonment, for the plaintiff was free to go off another way.

353. *Herd* v *Weardale Steel, Coal and Coke Co. Ltd* [1915] A.C. 67

The plaintiff was an employee of the defendant company and at 9.30 am on 30 May 1911, he descended the defendants' mine. In the ordinary way he would have been entitled to be raised at the end of his shift at 4 pm. The plaintiff and two other men were given certain work to do which they believed to be unsafe, and they refused to do it. At about 11 am they, and 29 men acting in sympathy with them, asked the foreman to allow them to ascend the shaft. The foreman, acting on instructions from the management, refused this request. At about 1 pm the cage came down carrying men, and emptied at the bottom of the shaft. The 29 men were refused permission to enter, but some got in and refused to leave the cage, which was left stationary for some 20 minutes. At 1.30 pm permission was given for the men to leave and the plaintiff was brought to the top. He now sued for false imprisonment. *Held* – there was no false imprisonment. There was a collective agreement regarding the use of the cage, and the plaintiff's right to be taken to the surface did not arise under the agreement until 4 pm. The defendants were perfectly willing to let the plaintiff ascend, but were not required in the absence of any emergency to provide him with the means of doing so except in accordance with the agreement.

354. *Meering* v *Grahame White Aviation Co. Ltd* (1919) 122 L.T. 44

The plaintiff, being suspected of stealing a keg of varnish from the defendants, his employers, was asked by two work policemen to accompany them to the Works Office to answer questions. The plaintiff, not realising that he was suspected, assented to the suggestion and even suggested a short cut. He remained in the office for some time during which the works policemen stayed outside the room without his knowledge. The plaintiff later sued for false imprisonment and the question arose as to whether the plaintiff must know that the defendant is restraining his freedom. *Held* – the plaintiff was imprisoned and his knowledge was irrelevant, though knowledge of imprisonment might increase the damages.

TRESPASS TO THE PERSON: UNLAWFUL ARREST

355. *Christie* v *Leachinsky* [1947] A.C. 573

The appellants, without the necessary warrant, arrested the respondent for unlawful possession of a number of bales of cloth. They had reasonable grounds for thinking that the bales were stolen but did not disclose this until later. *Held* – by the House of Lords – that the arrest was unlawful.

356. *Wheatley* v *Lodge* [1971] 1 All E.R. 173

The defendant's car collided with a parked vehicle. A constable saw him about an hour later and smelling alcohol on his breath, cautioned him and said that he was arrested for driving under the influence of drink contrary to what is now the Road Traffic Act, 1988. The defendant was deaf and could not lip read though the constable did not know this. Nevertheless the defendant got into a police car which the constable pointed to and was taken to the police station where he indicated his deafness. From then on the charge and all relevant matters were made clear to him by written and printed matter. On the question of the lawfulness of his arrest it was *held* by the Queen's Bench Divisional Court that the original arrest was valid. A police officer arresting a deaf person had to do what a reasonable person would do in the circumstances and the magistrates were clearly of the opinion that the constable had done so.

> COMMENT
> (i) Presumably on the basis of this decision if a person is arresting someone who cannot speak English he is not obliged to find an interpreter.
> (ii) The Police and Criminal Evidence Act, 1984 confirms the common-law rule that where an arrest is made by seizure of a person, words indicating that the person is under arrest should accompay the seizure (s. 28(1)). However, the common-law rule is modified by requiring that where an arrest is made by a policeman the person arrested must be informed that he is under arrest even though that fact is obvious. The common law also requires that the person arrested be told the reason(s) for the arrest, and s. 23(3) confirms this rule but modifies it where there is an arrest by a constable, requiring that in such a case information regarding the ground for the arrest be furnished, regardless of whether it is obvious (s. 28(4)). The section confirms the common-law rule that there is no requirement to tell a person that he is under arrest or of the ground for arrest if it is not reasonably practicable to do so, as where he has escaped from arrest before the information can be given (s. 28(5)).

TRESPASS TO LAND

357. *Southport Corporation* v *Esso Petroleum Co.* [1954] 2 Q.B. 182

The Esso company's tanker became stranded in the estuary of the River Ribble. The master of the tanker discharged oil in order to refloat the ship. The action of the wind and tide took the oil on to the Corporation's foreshore and caused damage. The Corporation sued in trespass and negligence. Devlin, J., at first instance, thought that trespass would lie, but on appeal to the Court of Appeal, Denning, L.J. contended that there could be no trespass because the injury was not direct, but was caused by the tides and prevailing winds; in trespass the injury must be direct and not consequential. In the House of Lords, [1956] A.C. 218, Lord Tucker agreed with Denning, L.J., though in the House of Lords trespass was not pursued. The appeal was based on negligence and the defendants were *held* not liable.

> COMMENT
> This case illustrates the difficulties of trying to recover for oil pollution damage in negligence or trespass. The action for nuisance has similar difficulties. *Rylands* v *Fletcher* does not apply because, among other things, the oil does not escape from the land but from the sea and the

sea is the equivalent of a public highway. Oil pollution is now dealt with by the Merchant Shipping (Oil Pollution) Act, 1971, which provides a more straightforward method of making claims.

358. *Kelson* v *Imperial Tobacco Co.* [1957] 2 All E.R. 343

The plaintiff was the lessee of a one-storey tobacconist's shop and brought this action against the defendants, seeking an injunction requiring them to remove from the wall above the shop a large advertising sign for cigarettes showing the words 'Players Please'. The sign projected into the airspace above the plaintiff's shop by a distance of some eight inches. The plaintiff claimed that the defendants, by fixing the sign in that position, had trespassed on his air space. *Held* – the invasion of an airspace by a sign of this nature constituted a trespass and, although the plaintiff's injury was small, it was an appropriate case in which to grant an injunction for the removal of the sign.

> COMMENT
> The plaintiff seemed prepared for the sign to remain until he became involved in a dispute with the defendants regarding the quota of cigarettes supplied to him. It was after the dispute that he brought this action, but the court found that the plaintiff's claim was not affected by his acts.

359. *Woollerton and Wilson* v *Richard Costain (Midlands) Ltd* (1969) 119 N.L.J. 1093

In this case the court granted to the owners of a factory and warehouse in Leicester an injunction restraining the defendants from trespassing on and invading airpace over their premises by means of a swinging crane. The injunction was suspended for twelve months to enable the defendants to finish their work, the defendants having offered to pay for the right to continue to trespass and to provide insurance cover for neighbouring properties. It was also *held* that it was no answer to a claim for an injunction for trespass that the trespass did no harm to the plaintiff.

> COMMENT
> There has not been full support from the judiciary on the issue of postponing the injunction. In *John Trenbart Ltd* v *National Westminster Bank Ltd* (1979) 123 S.J. 38, Walton, J. would not postpone the operation of an injunction in similar circumstances and refused to follow *Woollerton* saying it was wrongly decided.

360. *Bernstein* v *Skyviews & General* [1977] 2 All E.R. 902

The plaintiff claimed damages for trespass against a firm which had taken an aerial photograph of his home from about 630 feet, crossing his land in order to do so. It was *held* – by Griffiths, J. – that an owner of land at common law had rights above his land to such height as was necessary for the ordinary use and enjoyment of the land and the structures upon it. The plane was therefore too high to be trespassing. In any case s. 40(1) of the Civil Aviation Act, 1949 (see now Civil Aviation Act, 1982, s. 76) provides a defence to such a claim where the height was reasonable. However the judge did say that constant surveillance from the air with photographing might well be actionable nuisance.

TRESPASS TO LAND: EFFECT OF REVOCATION OF LICENCES

361. *Winter Garden Theatre (London) Ltd* v *Millenium Productions Ltd* [1948] A.C. 173

The respondents were permitted by a contractual licence to use the Winter Garden Theatre, Drury Lane, which belonged to the appellants, for the purpose of producing plays, concerts or ballets in return for a weekly payment of £300. There was no express term in the licence providing that the appellants could revoke it. However, the appellants did revoke it, giving the respondents one month in which to quit the premises, but stating that they were prepared to give fresh notice for a later date if the respondents required further time in which to make other arrangements. The respondents contended that the licence could not be revoked so long as the weekly payments were continued. The appellants claimed that it was revocable on giving reasonable notice. *Held* – on a proper construction of the contract the licence was not intended to be perpetual, but nevertheless could only be determined by reasonable notice. What was reasonable notice depended on the commitments of the licensees and the circumstances of the parties. In this case the notice given by the appellants was reasonable and valid to determine the licence.

> COMMENT
> This case also has a bearing on the ejection of hooligans from soccer and other sports grounds. They may have paid and have a contractual right to enter but as Viscount Simon said in this case: 'the ticket entitles the purchaser to enter and, if he behaves himself, to remain on the premises until the end of the event which he has paid to witness'. This clearly implies that those who do not behave in a reasonable way cease to be licensees and become trespassers and can be evicted.

362. *Hounslow London Borough Council* v *Twickenham Garden Developments* [1970] 3 W.L.R. 538

A building owner granted a licence under a building contract to a builder to enter on his land and do work there. The procedure for terminating the building contract involved an architect giving notice that the work was not being carried out properly. Such a notice was given but the building contractor refused to leave the land and carried on his work. The owner claimed an injunction and damages for trespass. *Held* – by Megarry, J. – in view of the fact that it was not certain whether the architect's notice had been given as a result of following proper procedures the contract had not necessarily been terminated and the builder was not, unless and until that was done, a trespasser. The owner's action failed.

TRESPASS TO LAND: SELF-HELP

363. *Hemmings* v *Stoke Poges Golf Club* [1920] 1 K.B. 720

The plaintiff was employed by the defendants and occupied a cottage belonging to them. Later he left the defendants' service and was called upon to give up possession. On refusal, he and his property were ejected with no more force than was necessary. *Held* – the defendants were not liable for assault or trespass.

> COMMENT
> Since this case concerns the eviction of an employee/occupier, it would seem to be overruled on its facts by s. 8(2) of the Protection From Eviction Act, 1977. Hemmings could now claim damages for breach of that Act. However, the principle behind the decision on the *Hemmings* facts is still relevant in that the occupier of property could eject a person not covered by the 1977 Act, e.g. a squatter, from his property by the use of reasonable force.

WRONGFUL INTERFERENCE WITH GOODS: WHAT IS POSSESSION?

364. *The Tubantia* [1924] P. 78

The plaintiff, who was a marine salvor, was trying to salvage the cargo of the SS *Tubantia* which had been sunk in the North Sea. He had discovered the wreck and marked it with a marker buoy, and his divers were already working in the hold, when the defendant, a rival salvor, appeared on the scene and started to send divers down to salvage the cargo from the wreck. *Held* – whoever was the owner of the property salvaged, the plaintiff was sufficiently in possession of the wreck to found an action in trespass.

CONVERSION: MAY BE BASED ON A POSSESSORY TITLE: FINDERS OF PROPERTY

365. *Parker* v *British Airways Board* [1982] 1 All E.R. 834

The plaintiff was in B.A.'s first class lounge at Heathrow waiting for a flight. He found a gold bracelet on the floor and gave it to an employee of B.A. together with his name and address asking that it be returned to him if not claimed. It was not claimed but B.A. sold it. The plaintiff sued in conversion and the Court of Appeal held that the plaintiff was entitled to the proceeds of sale.

> COMMENT
> This principle was applied in two earlier cases, i.e. *Bridges* v *Hawkesworth* (1851) 21 L.J. Q.B. 75 where the finder of some bank notes which were lying on the floor in the public part of a shop was held entitled to them as against the shopkeeper: and *Hannah* v *Peel* [1945]

K.B. 509, where a soldier billeted in a house found a brooch lying loose in an upstairs room, and he was held entitled to it as against the freeholder of the property who had no knowledge of the brooch until the plaintiff found it.

CONVERSION: POSSESSORY TITLE: GOODS ON OR ATTACHED TO LAND OR BUILDINGS

366. *South Staffordshire Water Co* v *Sharman* [1896] 2 Q.B. 44

The plaintiffs sued the defendant in detinue, claiming possession of two gold rings found by the defendant in the Minster Pool at Lichfield. The plaintiffs were owners of the pool and the defendant was a labourer employed by them to clean it. It was in the course of cleaning the pool that the defendant came across the rings. He refused to hand them to his employers, but gave them to the police for enquiries to be made to find the true owners. No owner was found and the police returned the rings to the defendant who retained them. *Held* – the rings must be given over to the plaintiffs. The plaintiffs were freeholders of the pool, and had the right to forbid anyone coming on the land; they had a right to clean the pool out in any way they chose. They possessed and exercised a practical control over the pool and they had a right to its contents.

COMMENT
It is also worth noting *Elwes* v *Brigg Gas Co* (1886) 33 Ch.D. 562 where it was held that a prehistoric boat found some six feet below the surface of the land belonged to the landowner and not to the finders. Similarly, in *Corporation of London* v *Appleyard* [1963] 2 All E.R. 834, owners of a building site were held entitled against workers of a demolition contractor to banknotes found in a wall safe in an old cellar.

CONVERSION: THE RELATIONSHIP BETWEEN THE PLAINTIFF AND THE GOODS

367. *Jarvis* v *Williams* [1955] 1 All E.R. 108

Jarvis agreed to sell some bathroom fittings to Peterson and at Peterson's request delivered them to Williams. Peterson refused to pay the price and Jarvis agreed to take them back if Peterson would pay for collection. Peterson accepted this offer and Jarvis sent his lorryman, with a letter of authority, to collect the fittings but he was told that he could not take them, so he returned empty-handed. Jarvis claimed against Williams in conversion for the return of the goods. *Held* – on the delivery to Williams the property in the goods passed to Peterson, and the arrangement for re-collection did not re-vest the property in Jarvis. It follows that at the time of collection, Jarvis had no right of property in the goods to sustain an action in conversion.

CONVERSION: THE DEFENDANT'S CONDUCT

368. *Fouldes* v *Willoughby* (1841) 8 M. & W. 540

The plaintiff had put his horses on the defendant's ferry boat and, a dispute having arisen, the defendant asked the plaintiff to take them off. The plaintiff refused so the defendant did so, and since the plaintiff refused to leave the boat, the defendant ferried him across the river. The plaintiff sued in conversion. Maule, J. directed the jury that the putting of the horses ashore was a conversion, but on appeal, the Court of Exchequer *reversed* the decision and found there was no conversion. Lord Abinger, C.B. said:

> In order to constitute a conversion it is necessary either that the party taking the goods should intend some use to be made of them by himself or by those for whom he acts, or that owing to his act, the goods are destroyed or consumed to the prejudice of the lawful owner. The removal of the horses involved not the least denial of the right of the plaintiff to enjoyment or possession of them and was thus no conversion.

369. *Oakley* v *Lyster* [1931] 1 K.B. 148

Oakley, a demolition contractor, agreed to pull down an aerodrome on Salisbury Plain and reinstate the land, a process which involved disposing of 8000 tons of hard core and tar macadam. He thereupon rented three and a half acres of a farm on the opposite side of the road on which to dump it. He sold 4000 tons, but in January 1929, there was still 4000 tons undisposed of when Lyster bought the freehold of the farm. Shortly afterwards Oakley found that some of the hard core was being removed on Lyster's instructions, and Oakley saw him and was told that Lyster had bought the land and all that was on it, and on 9 July 1929, his solicitors wrote to Oakley to this effect and forbade Oakley to remove the hard core otherwise he would become a trespasser on Lyster's land. Correspondence followed but at the trial it was admitted that Oakley was a lawful tenant and owner of the hard core. While the correspondence was continuing, Oakley agreed to sell that 4000 tons to Mr Edney, but in view of Lyster's claim, Edney withdrew and the stuff was undisposed of. The conversion alleged was the removal by Lyster of some of the hard core and the denial of title in the correspondence. *Held* – the defendant was liable in damages for conversion. In the correspondence Lyster was asserting and exercising dominion over the goods inconsistent with the rights of the true owner, Oakley. Nor was it sufficient to allow Oakley to resume dominion over the hard core and remove it. He was entitled to damages of £300 for the loss of the sale to Edney.

CONVERSION: PRINCIPLE OF LIABILITY: WHERE THE DEFENDANT HAS ACTED HONESTLY

370. *Elvin and Powell Ltd* v *Plummer Roddis Ltd* (1933) 50 T.L.R. 158

A fraudulent person ordered a consignment of goods from the plaintiffs in the name of the defendants. He then telephoned the defendants in the plaintiff's name, saying that the goods had been dispatched to them in error and that they would be collected. The fraudulent person then himself collected the goods from the defendants and absconded with them. The plaintiffs now sued the defendants for conversion. *Held* – as involuntary bailees of goods, the defendants had acted reasonably in returning them, as they believed, to the plaintiffs, by a trustworthy messenger. They had not committed conversion.

PUBLIC NUISANCE: OBSTRUCTION OF THE HIGHWAY: DANGEROUS ACTIVITIES NEAR THE HIGHWAY

371. *Attorney-General* v *Gastonia Coaches*, *The Times*, 12 November 1976

G, who were coach operators, owned 22 coaches of which 16 were parked in residential roads adjoining the Gastonia offices. No matter how carefully these coaches were parked they inevitably interfered with the free passage of other traffic. It was *held* – on a public relator action by the Attorney-General – that Gastonia were guilty of a public nuisance and would be restrained from parking the vehicles on the highway. Damages would also be awarded to private litigants who had suffered from the emissions of exhaust gases, excessive noise and obstruction of drives.

> COMMENT
> Reference should also be made to *Campbell* v *Paddington B.C.*, 1911 at p. 731 which is an example of an action by a private person for a public nuisance.

372. *Castle* v *St Augustine's Links Ltd and Another* (1922) 38 T.L.R. 615

On 18 August 1919, the plaintiff was driving a taxicab from Deal to Ramsgate when a ball played by the second defendant, a Mr Chapman, from the thirteenth tee on the golf course, which was parallel with the Sandwich Road, struck the windscreen of the taxicab. In consequence a piece of glass from the screen injured the plaintiff's eye and a few days later he had to have it removed. He then brought this action. *Held* – the plaintiff succeeded. Judgment for £450 damages was given by Sankey, J. The proximity of the hole to the road consituted a public nuisance. Compare *Bolton* v *Stone* [1951] A.C. 650, where cricket balls had been hit out of the ground and into the highway six to ten times in 35 years but had injured nobody. *Held* – no nuisance. See also *Miller* v *Jackson* [1977] 3 W.L.R. 20, where the Court of Appeal held that the public interest, which requires young people to have the benefit of outdoor games, may be held to outweigh the private interest of neighbouring householders who are the victims of sixes landing in their gardens so that it would be impossible to use the garden when cricket was being played. Thus no injunction was granted even though the sportsmen were held to be guilty of both nuisance and negligence.

COMMENT
In *Kennaway* v *Thompson*, 1980 (see p. 779) the Court of Appeal refused
to follow this approach on the matter of an injunction and said in effect
that a court ought not to refuse an injunction if the tort is established
merely because there is benefit to a section of the public.

373. *Tarry* v *Ashton* (1876) 1 Q.B.D. 314

A lamp projected from the defendant's premises over the highway. It fell
and injured the plaintiff who then sued the defendant in respect of his injuries.

The defendant had previously employed an independent contractor, who
was not alleged to be incompetent, to repair the lamp and it was because
of the negligence of that contractor that the lamp fell. Even so the defendant
was *held* liable and the decision suggests that there is strict liability in respect
of injuries caused by artificial projections over the highway.

374. *Dymond* v *Pearce* [1972] 1 All E.R. 1142

A lorry was left parked on a road subject to a 30 m.p.h. speed limit with its
lights on beneath a street lamp. The plaintiff collided with the vehicle and
suffered injury. He sued the defendants alleging negligence and nuisance.
It was *held* – by the Court of Appeal – that the claim in negligence failed
as there was no evidence to show that the driver had not acted reasonably
in the circumstances. The claim in nuisance also failed, for although a nuisance
had been created, the injury suffered resulted solely from the negligence
of the motorcyclist himself. Of more importance than the actual decision are
the comments made in the Court of Appeal regarding the relationship
between negligence and nuisance in terms of fault. See in particular Edmund
Davies, L.J., who said: 'But if an obstruction be created, here too, in my
judgment, fault is essential to liability in the sense that it must appear that
a reasonable man would be bound to realize the likelihood of risk to highway
users resulting from the presence of the obstructing vehicle on the road.'

NUISANCE: UTILITY OR BENEFIT OF ACTIVITY NO DEFENCE: NOR IS COMING TO THE NUISANCE

375. *Bliss* v *Hall* (1838), L.J. C.P. 122

The defendant carried on the trade of a candle-maker in certain premises
near to the dwelling house of the plaintiff and his family. Certain 'noxious
and foul smells' issued from the defendant's premises and the plaintiff sued
him for nuisance. The defence was that, for three years before the plaintiff
occupied the dwelling house in question, the defendant had exercised the
trade complained of in this present establishment. *Held* – this was no answer
to the complaint and judgment was given for the plaintiff.

COMMENT
In *Miller* v *Jackson* [1977] 3 W.L.R. 20 the Court of Appeal decided that
it was no defence to the claim in nuisance that the cricket ground only
became a nuisance when the plaintiff built a house close by it.

376. *Adams* v *Ursell* [1913] 1 Ch. 269

The plaintiff was a veterinary surgeon and he purchased a house in 1907 for £2370. In November 1912, the defendant opened a fried fish shop at premises adjoining the plaintiff's house. Very soon after the commencement of the business, the plaintiff's house was permeated with the odour of fried fish, and the vapour from the stoves filled the rooms 'like fog or steam'. *Held* – an injunction would be granted because the defendant's activities materially interfered with the ordinary comfort of the plaintiff and his family; and it did not matter that the shop was in a large working-class district and therefore supplied a public need.

377. *Dunton* v *Dover District Council*, *The Times*, 31 March 1977

The Council provided a play area for children of a housing estate on grazing land at the rear of the plaintiff's hotel. The playground was not fenced and there was no restriction on the age of the children using it. The plaintiff suffered noise and inconvenience and was awarded £200 damages and a continued injunction against the Council that the playground should only be open between 10 am and 6.30 pm to children under twelve.

NUISANCE: MODES OF ANNOYANCE

378. *Christie* v *Davey* [1893] 1 Ch. 316

The plaintiff was the occupier of a semi-detached house, and she and her daughter gave pianoforte, violin and singing lessons in the house, four days a week for 17 hours in all. There was also practice of music and singing at other times, and occasional musical evenings. The defendant, a woodcarver and a versatile amateur musician, occupied the adjoining portion of the house, and he found the activities of the plaintiff and her family annoying. In addition to writing abusive letters, he retaliated by playing concertinas, horns, flutes, pianos and other musical instruments, blowing whistles, knocking on trays or boards, hammering, shrieking or shouting, so as to annoy the plaintiffs and injure their activities. *Held* – what the plaintiff and her family were doing was not an unreasonable use of the house, and could not be restrained by the adjoining tenant. However, the adjoining tenant was himself restrained from making noises to annoy the plaintiff, the court being satisfied that such noises had been made wilfully for the purpose of annoyance.

379. *Hubbard* v *Pitt* [1975] 3 All E.R. 1

The defendants picketed in the road outside the offices of the plaintiff estate agents to protest against a particular property development. An interlocutory injunction was granted to restrain them from doing so. The Court of Appeal *held* – dismissing their appeal – (*a*) that the original ground for granting the injunction, namely, that street picketing other than in furtherance of a trade dispute was unlawful, was correct; (*b*) that the balance of convenience required an injunction to be issued there being a serious issue to be tried.

COMMENT

As regards what is lawful picketing in a trade dispute, s. 15(1) of the Trade Union and Labour Relations Act, 1974, as amended by s. 16 of the Employment Act, 1980, provides: 'It shall be lawful for a person in contemplation or furtherance of a trade dispute to attend – (a) at or near his own place of work, or (b) if he is an official of a trade union, at or near the place of work of a member of that union whom he is accompanying and whom he represents, for the purpose only of peacefully obtaining or communicating information, or peacefully persuading any person to work or abstain from working.' This provision would not appear to provide a defence if pickets approached and stopped vehicles.

NUISANCE: DURATION OF OFFENDING ACTS

380. *British Celanese Ltd* v *A.H. Hunt (Capacitors) Ltd* [1969] 2 All E.R. 1252

The defendants allowed metal foil to escape from their land and foul the bus bars of overhead electric cables. The plaintiffs lost power and their machines were clogged up and time and material wasted. *Held*, by Lawton, J., that –

(a) The defendants were not liable under *Rylands* v *Fletcher*, because there was no non-natural use of land;

(b) the defendants owed a duty of care to the plaintiffs and could be liable in negligence, the plaintiffs had a proprietary interest in the machines which were damaged and could recover loss flowing from that, pure economic loss was not involved;

(c) the defendants were liable in nuisance, an isolated happening such as this could create an actionable nuisance and the plaintiffs were directly and foreseeably affected.

NUISANCE: EFFECT OF MALICE OR EVIL MOTIVE

381. *Hollywood Silver Fox Farm Ltd* v *Emmett* [1936] 2 K.B. 468

The plaintiffs were breeders of silver foxes and erected a notice board on their land inscribed: 'Hollywood Silver Fox Farm'. The defendant owned a neighbouring field, which he was about to develop as a building estate, and he regarded the notice board as detrimental to such development. He asked the plaintiffs to remove it, and when this request was refused, he sent his son to discharge a 12-bore gun close to the plaintiff's land, with the object of frightening the vixens during breeding. The result of this activity was that certain of the vixens did not mate at all, and others, having whelped, devoured their young. The plaintiff brought this action alleging nuisance, and the defence was that Emmett had a right to shoot as he pleased on his own land. *Held* – an injunction would be granted to restrain Emmett. His evil motive made an otherwise innocent use of land a nuisance.

COMMENT

(i) It seems at first sight difficult to reconcile the above case with *Bradford Corporation* v *Pickles*, (1895), see p. 727. The difference probably is in the fact that *Hollywood Silver Fox Farm* v *Emmett* was an action for nuisance by noise, so that the defendant's motive was relevant in establishing the tort. In *Bradford Corporation* v *Pickles*, the action was really one for interference with a servitude or right over land, and motive was not relevant in establishing the rights of the parties.

(ii) In *Christie* v *Davey*, 1893, see p. 774, also, North, J. took into account the malice of the defendant by saying that the noise was 'made deliberately and maliciously for the purpose of annoying the plaintiff.

NUISANCE: ACT NEED NOT CAUSE ILL-HEALTH OR DIMINISH THE VALUE OF PROPERTY

382. *Bone* v *Seale* [1975] 1 All E.R. 787

Over a period of 12½ years smells coming from a neighbouring pig farm owned by the defendant had caused a nuisance to properties owned by the plaintiff who claimed an injunction restraining the nuisance and damages. The judge found that no diminution in the value of the properties had resulted but granted an injunction and awarded over £6000 damages. The defendants appealed, saying, amongst other things, that the award was too high. It was *held* – by the Court of Appeal allowing the appeal against the award – that by drawing a parallel with loss of sense of smell as a result of personal injury the award was erroneous and £1000 for the plaintiff would be substituted.

NUISANCE: WHO CAN SUE? WHO CAN BE SUED?

383. *Malone* v *Laskey* [1907] 2 K.B. 141

The defendants owned a house which they leased to a firm named Witherby & Co., who sub-let it to the Script Shorthand Company. The plaintiff's husband was employed by the latter company, and was allowed to occupy the house as an emolument of his employment. A flush cistern in the lavatory of the house was unsafe, the wall brackets having been loosened by the vibration of the defendants' electric generator next door. The plaintiff told Witherby & Co. of the situation, and they communicated with the defendants who sent two of their plumbers to repair the cistern gratuitously. The work was carried out in an improper and negligent manner, and four months later the plaintiff was injured when the cistern came loose. The plaintiff sued the defendants (*a*) in nuisance, and (*b*) in negligence. *Held* – there was no claim in nuisance against the defendants. The plaintiff was not their tenant, and in nuisance the tenant is the person to sue, not other persons present on the premises, though such persons may have a claim where the nuisance is a public nuisance. Further, there was no claim in negligence, because the defendants owed no duty of care: firstly, because there was no contractual relationship; secondly, because the defendants did not undertake any duty towards the plaintiff. They were under no obligation to carry out repairs but sent their plumbers merely as a matter of grace. This was a voluntary act and was not in any sense the discharge of a duty. The defendants were not in occupation of the premises and had not invited the plaintiff to occupy them.

COMMENT
The case still represents the law regarding nuisance. Regarding the claim for negligence it was overruled in *Billings* v *Riden* [1958] A.C. 240, where it was held that there may be liability in negligence, where premises are left in a dangerous condition by workmen so that injury results, even though the injured person is not the occupier but is a visitor to the premises.

384. *Wilchick* v *Marks and Silverstone* [1934] 2 K.B. 56
Landlords who had let premises with a defective shutter, and had expressly reserved the right to enter the premises to do repairs, were *held* liable along with their tenant, to a passer-by injured by the shutter.

385. *Mink* v *Good* [1951] 1 K.B. 517
Landlords were *held liable* to the minor plaintiff, who was injured when a wall on the premises, which they had let, collapsed on to the highway. They had not reserved the right to enter to do repairs, but the Court of Appeal stated that such a right must be implied, because the premises were let on weekly tenancies and it was usual to imply a right to enter to do repairs in such tenancies.

386. *Harris* v *James* (1876) 45 L.J.Q.B. 545
A landlord was *held* liable for the nuisance created by his tenant's blasting operations at a quarry because he had let the property for that purpose. The tenant, therefore, inevitably created a nuisance.

COMMENT
In *Tetley* v *Chitty* [1986] 1 All E.R. 663, a local authority granted a seven-year lease to a go-kart club. T and others who were ratepayers living near the track obtained an injunction against the council to prevent the continuance of the nuisance by noise. Damages were an inadequate remedy.

387. *Smith* v *Scott* [1972] 3 All E.R. 645
The local authority had placed in an adjoining house to the plaintiff's a family which it knew was likely to cause a nuisance but on conditions of tenancy which expressly prohibited the commission of such. These tenants had a large and unruly family and their conduct was, in the words of Pennycuick, V.-C., 'Altogether intolerable both in respect of physical damage and noise'. The plaintiff and his wife, an elderly couple, found it impossible to live next door and moved away. Notwithstanding protests on the part of the plaintiff, the local authority took no effective steps to control the unruly family or to evict them. It was *held* by Pennycuick, V.-C., that, whatever the precise tests might be, it was impossible to apply the exception rendering a landlord liable for his tenants' acts in the present case. The exception was not based on cause and probable result apart from express or implied authority. The property had been let on conditions of tenancy which expressly forbade the

commission of a nuisance and it would not be legitimate to say that the local authority had authorised the nuisance.

It should also be noted that the court held that the rule in *Rylands* v *Fletcher* could not be applied and that the rights and liabilities of landowners had already been determined by the law and it was not open to the court to reshape those rights and liabilities by reference to the concept of duty of care. Thus the defendants were not liable in negligence. On the matter of *Rylands* v *Fletcher* liability Pennycuick, V.-C. said:

> The rule in *Rylands* v *Fletcher* was applied in *Attorney-General* v *Corke* [see p. 807] against a defendant who brought caravan dwellers on to his land as licencees but so far as counsel has been able to ascertain the rule has never been sought to be applied against a landlord who lets his property to undesirable tenants and I do not think it can be properly applied in such a case. The person liable under the rule in *Rylands* v *Fletcher* is the owner or controller of the dangerous 'thing', and this is normally the occupier and not the owner of the land. . . . A landlord parts with possession of the demised property in favour of his tenant and could not in any sense known to the law be regarded as controlling the tenant on property still occupied by himself. I should respectfully have thought that *Attorney-General* v *Corke* could equally well have been decided on the basis that the landowner there was in possession of the property and was himself liable in nuisance for the acts of his licencees.

COMMENT

It should be noted that in *O'Leary* v *Islington London Borough Council*, *The Times*, 5 May 1983 it was decided by the Court of Appeal that there was no implied term in a tenancy agreement obliging landlords to enforce a tenant's agreement not to cause nuisance to neighbours who were also their tenants, and the appropriate remedy for aggrieved tenants was to bring an action in tort against the tenant causing the nuisance.

388. *Brew Brothers* v *Snax (Ross)* [1969] 3 W.L.R. 657

In June 1965, the freehold owners of premises leased them for a term of 14 years. The lease contained covenants by the tenants regarding repairs, payment of maintenance expenses and viewing by the landlords. In November 1966, one of the walls of the premises tilted towards the neighbouring premises which belonged to the plaintiff. It was shored up but caused an obstruction for 18 months. It appeared that the reason why the wall had tilted was the seeping of water from certain drains and the removal of a tree by the tenants. The plaintiff sued the landlords and the tenants, and the landlords contended that the responsibility fell entirely on the tenants under the lease. *Held* – by the Court of Appeal –

(a) the tenants were responsible for repairing defects pointed out by the landlords but that the work required on the wall was not within the terms of the lease;

(b) the landlords must be presumed to know the state of the premises and were liable for nuisance in that they allowed the state of affairs to continue;

(c) the tenants were jointly liable in nuisance in that they failed to put the matter right, this liability was quite independent of their duties under the lease.

NUISANCE: ABATEMENT

389. *Sedleigh-Denfield* v *O'Callagan and Others* [1940] A.C. 880

One of the respondents (a college for training foreign missioners) was the owner of property adjoining the appellant's premises in Mill Hill. On the boundary of the property owned by the college there was a ditch and it was admitted that the ditch also belonged to the college. About 1934, when a block of flats was erected on the western side of the appellant's premises, the county council had laid a pipe and grating in the ditch but no permission was obtained and no steps were taken to inform the college authorities of the laying of the pipe. However, the presence of the pipe became known to a member of the college who was responsible for cleaning out the ditch twice a year. The council had not put a guard at the entrance to the pipe to prevent its being blocked by debris. The pipe became blocked and the appellant's garden was flooded. He claimed damages from the college on the ground that the pipe was a nuisance. *Held* – by the House of Lords – the college was liable because it appeared that they should have known about the pipe and realised the risk. Futhermore they had adopted the nuisance by using the pipe to drain their land.

> COMMENT
> This case was applied in *Page Motors* v *Epsom and Ewell Borough Council* (1981) 80 L.G.R. 337 where a site on an industrial estate was leased to a firm for the sale and repair of motor vehicles but was occupied by gypsies who caused a nuisance. The firm claimed damages against the council for the nuisance in the years 1973 until 1978 by which time the authorised gypsy caravans had all left the site. It was held by the Court of Appeal that the council was liable because they had adopted the nuisance by failing to take steps to move the gypsies on. Furthermore, the plaintiffs could recover damages for loss of business. This was a foreseeable result of having a gypsy site nearby.

NUISANCE: THE REMEDY OF INJUNCTION

390. *Kennaway* v *Thompson* [1980] 3 All E.R. 329

The defendants represented a club at which motor-boat racing and water-skiing were carried on. In 1972 the plaintiff moved into a house which she had had built near to the lake on which the above activities were carried out, as they had been since the early 1960s. After the plaintiff moved in the nature of the club's activities increased in frequency and noise because large powerboats took part in international meetings which were preceeded by periods of noisy practice. The plaintiff sought damages for nuisance and an injunction but Mais, J. awarded her damages only – £1000 for the past nuisance and £15,000 in respect of future nuisance, since he regarded it as oppressive to issue an injunction to prevent the club from continuing its activities on the grounds that this was contrary to public interest. The Court of Appeal allowed the plaintiff's appeal and awarded an injunction stating that the public interest should not prevail over the private interest of a person affected by a continuing nuisance, and accordingly the plaintiff was entitled to an injunction under which the club was ordered to curtail its activities, restricting noisy meetings to a limited number of occasions.

NUISANCE: DEFENCES: PRESCRIPTION

391. *Sturges* v *Bridgman* (1879) 11 Ch. D. 852

For more than 20 years the defendant, a confectioner, had used large pestles and mortars in his premises in Wigmore Street. Then the plaintiff, a physician in Wimpole Street, built a consulting room in his garden abutting on the confectioner's premises. The noise and vibration made by the confectioner's activities interfered materially with the plaintiff's practice. He sued for an injunction to prevent the offensive activities and the defence was that the defendant had acquired a prescriptive right to commit the nuisance. *Held* – though it was possible to acquire a right, the defendant had not done so, because the nuisance only arose when the consulting room was built.

NEGLIGENCE: LIABILITY FOR OMISSIONS

392. *Argy Trading Development Co. Ltd* v *Lapid Developments Ltd* [1977] 1 W.L.R. 444

In an under-lease for six years from 19 October 1971 the tenant agreed to insure against fire for the full value of the premises, including two years' rent, and in the event of loss or damage by fire to reinstate the premises. In fact the landlords insured the premises under a block policy covering other property as well and the tenant paid the landlords the appropriate proportion of the premium. In 1973 there was a change in the control of the landlords and the landlords did not renew the block policy but failed to notify the tenant of its cancellation. In 1973, some months after the policy had lapsed, the premises were gutted by fire. Neither party wanted the premises, which were scheduled for redevelopment, to be reinstated. The landlords undertook not to enforce the covenant to reinstate but the tenant wished to recover damages from the landlords on the ground that it had been deprived of the insurance moneys, which it would otherwise have received, by the landlords' failure to continue the insurance or to notify the tenant of its cancellation so that it had no opportunity to take out the policy. It was *held* – by Croom-Johnson, J. – that there was no implied term that the landlords would maintain their block policy or not cancel it without notifying the tenant. Nor was there any equitable estoppel such as was applied in the *High Trees* case, see p. 621, since there was no representation by the landlords intended to affect the legal relations of the parties. There was a special relationship between the parties which might have created a duty of care under the principle of *Hedley Byrne*, see p. 652, but that duty was not to *give* negligent information. The *failure* to give information which amounted to an omission was not within the principle of *Hedley Byrne*.

NEGLIGENCE: ECONOMIC LOSS RECOVERABLE BY WAY OF PARASITICAL DAMAGES

393. *Weller & Co.* v *Foot and Mouth Disease Research Institute* [1965] 3 All E.R. 560

The defendants carried out experiments on their land concerning foot and mouth disease. They imported an African virus which escaped and infected cattle in the vicinity. As a consequence two cattle markets in the area had to be closed and the plaintiffs, who were auctioneers, sued for damages for loss of business. *Held* – by Widgery, J. – that so far as negligence was concerned the defendants owed no duty of care to the plaintiffs who were not cattle owners, and had no proprietary interest in anything which could be damaged by the virus. Furthermore, the defendants owed no absolute duty to the plaintiffs under *Rylands* v *Fletcher*, 1868, because the plaintiffs had no interest in any land to which the virus could have escaped.

> COMMENT
> Had a duty of care been found, the liability in this case would have been endless. The closing of the market no doubt affected also the takings of cafés, car parks, shops, and public houses, amongst others. It would not seem likely that the courts are yet ready to extend liability in this way.

394. *S.C.M. (United Kingdom) Ltd* v *W.J. Whittall & Son Ltd* [1970] 3 All E.R. 245

A workman employed by the defendants who were carrying out construction work near the plaintiffs' factory, cut into an underground electric cable so that the power to the plaintiffs' factory failed. The plaintiffs made typewriters and the lack of power caused molten materials to solidify in their machines which were *physically* damaged. The machines had to be stripped down and reassembled and production was brought to a halt for seven and a half hours. In the Court of Appeal the plaintiffs limited their claim to damages in respect of the physical damage to the machines and the financial loss *directly* resulting from that damage. This enabled the court to decide that the plaintiffs' property had foreseeably been damaged by the defendants' act so that the plaintiffs could recover for damage to the machines and the consequential financial loss flowing from it. Nevertheless the court went on to consider economic loss in the context of negligence and dealt in effect with the position as it might have been if the power cut had stopped production without damaging the machines. The following aspects of the judgments are important: *Per* Lord Denning, M.R. –

In actions of negligence, when the plaintiff has suffered no damage to his person or property, but has only sustained economic loss, the law does not usually permit him to recover that loss. Although the defendants owed the plaintiffs a duty of care, that did not mean that additional economic loss which was not consequent on the material damage suffered by the plaintiffs would also be recoverable; in cases such as *Weller & Co.* v *Foot and Mouth Disease Research Institute*, 1965 (see p. 781), and *Electrochrome Ltd* v *Welsh Plastics Ltd*, 1968 (see p. 727) the plaintiffs did not recover for economic loss because it was too remote to be a head of damage, not because there was no duty owed to the plaintiffs or because the loss suffered in each case was not caused by the negligence of the defendants.

(*Per* Winn, L.J.)

Apart from the special case of imposition of liability for negligently uttered false statements, there is no liability for unintentional negligent infliction of any form of economic loss which is not itself consequential on foreseeable physical injury or damage to property.

COMMENT
The power shut-off lasted for some time and during that time the plaintiffs would normally have processed four more 'melts'; because they had been unable to do so they had lost the profits they would have made on them. However, this was regarded as economic loss not consequent upon the physical damage and therefore what was recoverable was only the loss of profit on the melt which was actually interrupted by the failure of electrical supplies.

395. *Spartan Steel and Alloys Ltd* v *Martin & Co. Ltd* [1972] 3 All E.R. 557

While digging up a road the defendants' employees damaged a cable which the defendants knew supplied the plaintiffs' factory. The cable belonged to the local electricity board and the resulting electrical power failure meant that the plaintiffs' factory was deprived of electricity. The temperature of their furnace dropped and so metal that was in melt had to be poured away. Furthermore, while the cable was being repaired the factory received no electricity so it was unable to function for some 14 hours. The Court of Appeal, however, allowed only the plaintiffs' damages for the spoilt metal and the loss of profit on one 'melt'. They refused to allow the plaintiffs to recover their loss of profit which resulted from the factory being unable to function during the period when there was no electricity. Lord Denning, M.R. chose to base his decision on remoteness of damage rather than the absence of any duty of care to avoid causing economic loss. However, he did make it clear that public policy was involved. In the course of his judgment he said:

At bottom I think the question of recovering economic loss is one of policy. Whenever the courts draw a line to mark out the bounds of duty, they do so as a matter of policy so as to limit the responsibility of the defendant.

Whenever the courts set bounds to the damages recoverable – saying that they are, or are not, too remote – they do it as a matter of policy so as to limit the liability of the defendant.

NEGLIGENCE: ECONOMIC LOSS: INJURY TO PERSON OR PROPERTY NOT ALWAYS ESSENTIAL

396. *Junior Books Ltd* v *Veitchi Co. Ltd* [1982] 3 All E.R. 201

Junior Books (J) owned a building. Veitchi (V) were flooring contractors working under a contract for the main contractor who was doing work on the building. There was no privity of contract between J and V. It was alleged by J that faulty work by V left J with an unserviceable building and high maintenance costs so that J's business became unprofitable. The House of Lords decided in favour of J on the basis that there was a duty of care. V were in breach of a duty owed to J to take reasonable care to avoid acts or omissions, including laying an allegedly defective floor, which they ought to have known would be likely to cause the owners economic loss of profits caused by the high cost of maintaining the allegedly defective floor and, so far as J were required to mitigate the loss by replacing the floor itself, the cost of replacement was the appropriate measure of liability so far as this loss was concerned. The standard of care required is apparently the contractual duty, and so long as the work is up to contract standard, then the defendant in a case such as this cannot be in breach of his duty. Lord Fraser of Tullybelton said:

> Where a building is erected under a contract with a purchaser, then provided the building, or part of it, is not dangerous to persons or to other property and subject to the law against misrepresentation, I can see no reason why the builder should not be free to make with the purchaser whatever contractual arrangements about the quality of the product the purchaser wishes. However jerry-built the product, the purchaser would not be entitled to damages from the builder if it came up to the contractual standards.

COMMENT

The effect of the decision in *Junior Books* was whittled away in *Simaan General Contracting Co.* v *Pilkington Glass Ltd* [1988] 1 All E.R. 345. The plaintiffs (S Ltd) were the main contractors to construct a building in Abu Dhabi for a sheikh. The erection of glass walling together with supplying the glass was sub-contracted to an Italian company (Feal). Feal bought the glass from the defendants (P Ltd). The glass units should have been a uniform shade of green but some were various shades of green and some were red. The sheikh did not pay S Ltd. They chose to sue P Ltd in tort rather than Feal in contract for their loss, i.e. the money the sheikh was withholding. *Held* – by the Court of Appeal – since there was no physical damage this was purely a claim for economic loss and P Ltd had no duty of care. S Ltd's claim failed. Feal would have been liable under the Supply of Goods and Services Act, 1982 (see p. 281) but for some reason were not sued. Economic loss can be recovered in contract.

Dillon, L.J. said of *Junior Books* that it had 'been the subject of so much analysis and discussion that it cannot now be regarded as a useful pointer to any development of the law. It is difficult to see that future citation from *Junior Books* can ever serve any useful purpose.'

NEGLIGENCE: BREACH OF DUTY: BEHAVIOUR AS A REASONABLE MAN

397. *Daniels* v *R. White and Sons Ltd* [1938] 4 All E.R. 258

The plaintiffs, who were husband and wife, sued the first defendants, who were manufacturers of mineral waters, in negligence. The plaintiffs had been injured because a bottle of the first defendants' lemonade, which they had purchased from a public house in Battersea, contained carbolic acid, presumably from the bottle-washing plant. Evidence showed that the manufacturer took all possible care to see that no injurious matter got into the lemonade. It was *held* that the manufacturers were not liable in negligence because the duty was not one to ensure that the goods were in perfect condition but only to take reasonable care to see that no injury was caused to the eventual consumer. This duty had been fulfilled.

398. *Hill* v *J. Crowe (Cases)*, *The Times*, 19 May 1977

The plaintiff was injured when he stood on a packing case whose boards collapsed causing him to fall. It was *held* – by MacKenna, J. – that the case had been badly made and the manufacturers owed a duty of care to the plaintiff. They could not escape liability by showing that they had a good system of work and proper supervision. *Daniels* v *White and Sons* (1938), above, was not followed.

399. *Greaves & Co. (Contractors)* v *Baynham Meikle & Partners* [1974] 3 All E.R. 666

The plaintiff, a builder, was instructed to build a warehouse and sub-contracted its structural design to the defendants who were a firm of consultant structural engineers. B knew, or by reason of the relevant British Standard Code of Practice, ought to have known, that as the warehouse was to carry loaded trucks there was a danger of vibration. The design was competent but inadequate for the purpose of carrying the trucks and it was *held* – by Kilner Brown, J., allowing the plaintiff's claim for breach of duty of care and breach of an implied term of the contract – that the duty of the defendants was not simply to exercise the care and skill of a competent engineer which they had done, but to design a building fit for its purpose in the light of the knowledge which they had as to its proposed use.

400. *Paris* v *Stepney Borough Council* [1951] A.C. 367

The plaintiff was employed by the defendants on vehicle maintenance. He had the use of only one eye and the defendants were aware of this. The plaintiff was endeavouring to remove a bolt from the chassis of a vehicle, and was using a hammer for the purpose, when a chip of metal flew into his good eye so that he became totally blind. The plaintiff claimed damages from his employers for negligence in that he had not been supplied with goggles. The defendants showed in evidence that it was not the usual practice in trades of this nature to supply goggles, at least where the employees were men with two good eyes. The trial judge found for the plaintiff, but the Court of Appeal reversed the decision on the grounds that the plaintiff's disability could be relevant only if it increased the risk, i.e. if a one-eyed man was more likely to get a splinter in his eye than a two-eyed man. Having found that the risk was not increased they allowed the appeal. The House of Lords reversed the judgment of the Court of Appeal, holding that the gravity of the harm likely to be caused would influence a reasonable employer, so that the duty of care to a one-eyed employee required the supply of goggles, and Paris therefore succeeded.

401. *Haley* v *London Electricity Board* [1964] 3 All E.R. 185

The appellant, Haley, a blind man who was on his way to his work as a telephonist, tripped over an obstacle placed by servants of the London Electricity Board near the end of a trench excavated in the pavement of a street in Woolwich. He fell and suffered an injury which rendered him deaf, and brought about his premature retirement from his employment. The guard was sufficient warning for sighted people but was by its nature inadequate to protect or warn the blind. It consisted of a hammer hooked in the railings and resting on the pavement at an angle of 30 degrees, and Haley's white stick, which he was properly using as a guide, did not encounter the obstacle with the result that instead of being warned by it he fell over it. Evidence was given that about one in 500 people were blind and there were 258 registered blind people in Woolwich, many of whom were capable of walking in the streets alone, taking the normal precautions such blind persons were accustomed to take. The House of Lords *held*, reversing the decision of the Court of Appeal, that the London Electricity Board were liable in negligence. Those engaged in operations on the pavement or a highway must act reasonably to prevent danger to passers-by including blind people who must, however, also take reasonable care of themselves. The Board had not fulfilled this duty and were liable in damages for negligence which were assessed at £3000 general damages, and £2250 special damages. Haley's retirement being accelerated by four years.

402. *Watt* v *Hertfordshire County Council* [1954] 2 All E.R. 368

A fireman was injured by a heavy jack which slipped while being carried in a lorry which was going to the scene of an accident. The lorry was not equipped to carry such a heavy jack but it was required to free a woman who had been trapped in the wreckage. No proper vehicle was available and it was *held* that the fire authority was not liable.

403. *Latimer* v *A.E.C. Ltd* [1953] 2 All E.R. 449

A heavy rainstorm flooded a factory and made the floor slippery. The occupiers of the factory did all they could to get rid of the water and make the factory safe, but the plaintiff fell and was injured. He alleged negligence in that the occupiers did not close down the factory. *Held* – the occupiers of the factory were not liable. The risk of injury did not justify the closing down of the factory.

NEGLIGENCE: *RES IPSA LOQUITUR*

404. *Easson* v *L.N.E. Railway Co.* [1944] 1 All E.R. 246

The plaintiff, a boy aged four years, fell through the open door of a corridor train seven miles from its last stopping place. It was *held* that the defendants did not have sufficient control over the doors for *res ipsa loquitur* to apply. In the course of his judgment, Goddard, L.J. said:

> It is impossible to say that the doors of an express corridor train travelling from Edinburgh to London are continuously under the sole control of the railway company . . . passengers are walking up and down the corridors during the journey and get in and out at stopping places. The fact that the door came open could as well have been due to interference by a passenger as to the negligence of the defendants' servants.

405. *Roe* v *Minister of Health* [1954] 2 Q.B. 66

Two patients in a hospital had operations on the same day. Both operations were of a minor character and in each case nupercaine, a spinal anaesthetic, was injected by means of a lumbar puncture. The injections were given by a specialist anaesthetist, assisted by the theatre staff of the hospital. The nupercaine had been contained in sealed glass ampoules, stored in a solution of phenol. After the operations both patients developed symptoms of spastic paraplegia caused by the phenol, which had contaminated the nupercaine by penetrating almost invisible cracks in the ampoules. In the event, both patients became permanently paralysed from the waist down, and they now sued the defendants for negligence. *Held* – the defendants were vicariously liable for the negligence (if any) of those concerned with the operations, but on the standard of medical knowledge in 1947, when the operations took place, those concerned were not negligent. The cracks in the ampoules were not visible on ordinary examination, and could not be reproduced even by deliberate experiment. It was true that in 1954, when the case was brought, phenol used for disinfectant purposes was tinted so that it might be seen on examination, but the case must be decided on medical knowledge at the time when the operations were carried out. It was also suggested that once the accident has been explained, there is no question of *res ipsa loquitur* applying. Nor does the maxim apply when many persons might have been negligent. Denning, L.J. suggested that every surgical operation is attended by risks. Doctors, like the rest of us, have to learn by experience. Further, one must not condemn as negligence that which is only misadventure.

406. *Byrne* v *Boadle* (1863) 2 H. & C. 722

The plaintiff brought an action in negligence alleging that, as he was walking past the defendant's shop, a barrel of flour fell from a window above the shop and injured him. The defendant was a dealer in flour, but there was no evidence that the defendant or any of his servants were engaged in lowering the barrel of flour at the time. The defendant submitted that there was no evidence of negligence to go to the jury, but it was *held* that the occurrence was of itself evidence of negligence sufficient to entitle the jury to find for the plaintiff, even in the absence of an explanation by the defendant.

407. *Scott* v *London and St Katherine Docks Co.* (1865) 3 H. & C. 596

The plaintiff, a Customs officer, proved that when he was passing in front of the defendant's warehouse six bags of sugar fell upon him. It was *held* that the maxim *res ipsa loquitur* applied. In the course of his judgment, Erle, C.J. said: 'where the thing is shown to be under the management of the defendant, or his servants, and the accident is such as, in the ordinary course of things, does not happen if those who have the management use proper care, it affords reasonable evidence, in the absence of explanation by the defendant, that the accident arose from want of care.'

COMMENT
This case was followed in *Ward* v *Tesco Stores* [1976] All E.R. 219, where the Court of Appeal held that an accident which had occurred due to a spillage of yoghurt on a shop floor put an evidential burden upon the defendant shopowners to show that the accident did not occur through any want of care on their part. They were not able to satisfy that burden and the plaintiff succeeded.

408. *Pearson* v *North-Western Gas Board* [1968] 2 All E.R. 669

The plaintiff's husband was killed by an explosion of gas which also destroyed her house. It appeared from the evidence that a gas main had fractured due to a movement of earth caused by a severe frost. When the weather was very cold the defendants had men standing by ready to deal with reports of gas leaks, but unless they received reports there was no way of predicting or preventing a leak which might lead to an explosion. *Held* – by Rees, J. – that assuming the principle of *res ipsa loquitur* applied, the defendants had rebutted the presumption of negligence and the plaintiff's case failed.

CONTRIBUTORY NEGLIGENCE

409. *Jones* v *Lawrence* [1969] 3 All E.R. 267

A boy aged seven years and three months ran out from behind a parked van across a road apparently without looking in order to get to a fun-fair. He was knocked down by Lawrence who was travelling on his motor cycle at 50 miles per hour in a built-up area. The boy's injuries adversely affected his school work and he subsequently failed his eleven-plus examination. In action on his behalf for damages it was *held* by Cumming-Bruce, J. – that –

(a) his conduct was only that to be expected of a seven-year-old child and could not amount to contributory negligence.

(b) the failure to obtain a grammar-school place and the permanent impairing of his powers of concentration affected his job attainment potential and were factors to be taken into account in assessing damages.

410. *Oliver v Birmingham Bus Co.* [1932] 1 K.B. 35

A grandfather was walking with his grandchild aged four, when a bus approached quickly and without warning. The grandfather, being startled, let go the child's hand and the bus struck the child. It was *held* that the damages awarded to the child should not be reduced to take account of the grandfather's negligence.

NEGLIGENCE: ACTIONS BASED ON BREACH OF STATUTORY DUTY

411. *Atkinson v Newcastle and Gateshead Waterworks Co.* (1877) L.R. 2 Ex. D. 441

The plaintiff's timber yard caught fire and was destroyed, there being insufficient water in the mains to put it out. The defendants were required by the Waterworks Clauses Act, 1874, to maintain a certain pressure of water in their water pipes, and the Act provided a penalty of £10 for failure to keep the required pressure and 40s. for each day during which the neglect continued, the sums being payable to aggrieved ratepayers. The plaintiff sued the defendants for loss caused by the fire on the ground that they were in breach of a statutory duty regarding the pressure in the pipes. *Held* – the defendants were not liable. The statute did not disclose a cause of action by individuals for damage of this kind. It was most improbable that the legislature intended the company to be gratuitous insurers against fire of all the buildings in Newcastle.

412. *Gorris v Scott* (1874) L.R. 9 Exch. 125

A statutory order placed a duty on the defendant to supply pens of a specified size in those parts of a ship's deck occupied by animals. The defendant did not supply the pens, and sheep belonging to the plaintiff were swept overboard. The plaintiff claimed damages from the defendant for breach of statutory duty. *Held* – the plaintiff could not recover for his loss under breach of statutory duty, because the object of the statutory order was to prevent the spread of disease, not to prevent animals from being drowned.

COMMENT
A similar point is raised in *Lane v London Electricity Board*, 1955 at p. 577.

NEGLIGENCE: PROFESSIONAL LIABILITY

413. *Caparo Industries plc* v *Dickman and Others* [1990] 2 W.L.R. 358

The facts were, briefly, that Caparo, which already held shares in Fidelity plc, eventually acquired the controlling interest in the company. The group later alleged that certain purchases of Fidelity shares and the final bid were made after relying on Fidelity's accounts, which had been prepared by Touche Ross & Co, the second defendants.

The accounts, Caparo alleged, were inaccurate and misleading in that an apparent pre-tax profit of some £1.3m should in fact have been shown as a loss of £400,000. It was also alleged that, if the supposed true facts had been known, Caparo would not have made a bid at the price it did and might not have made a bid at all.

The Court of Appeal decided that while Touche Ross did not have a duty of care towards members of the public in regard to the Fidelity accounts, it did owe a duty of care to Caparo because Caparo was already a shareholder in Fidelity when it made the final purchase of shares and the bid.

The two main judgments in the House of Lords provide an interesting contrast: Lord Bridge concentrates more on the case law and in particular on the dissenting judgment of Lord Denning in *Candler* v *Crane Christmas* [1951] 1 All E.R. 426, where Lord Denning thought that the defendant accountants should have a duty of care to Candler because they had prepared allegedly negligent financial statements on the basis of which they knew Mr Candler might invest in the company concerned; and the judgment of the House of Lords in *Hedley Byrne & Co Ltd* v *Heller & Partners Ltd* [1963] 2 All E.R. 575, where a bank supplied an allegedly negligent reference as to the creditworthiness of a company called Easipower which they knew would be used by Hedley Byrne as a basis for extending credit to the company, which then went into liquidation.

A salient feature of both those cases, said Lord Bridge, was that the defendant giving advice on information was fully aware of the nature of the transaction the plaintiff was contemplating, knew that the advice or information would be communicated to him, and knew that it was likely that the plaintiff would rely on that advice or information in deciding whether or not to engage in the transaction in contemplation.

The situation was quite different where the statement was put into more or less general circulation and might foreseeably be relied on by strangers for any one of a variety of different purposes which the maker of the statement had no specific reason to anticipate.

Lord Bridge felt that it was one thing to owe a possibly wider duty of care to avoid causing injury to the person or property of others, but quite another to owe a similar duty to avoid causing others to suffer purely economic loss.

His Lordship concluded that auditors of a public company's accounts owed no duty of care to members of the public at large who relied on the accounts in deciding to buy shares in the company. And as a purchaser of additional shares in reliance on the auditors' report, the shareholder stood in no different position from any other investing member of the public to whom the auditor owed no duty.

Lord Oliver was concerned with establishing the purpose of an audit under the Companies Act, 1985. He went on to say that in enacting the statutory provisions Parliament did not have in mind the provision of information for the assistance of purchasers of shares in the market, whether they were already the holders of shares or other securities or people with no previous proprietary interest in the company.

The purpose for which the auditors' certificate was made and published was that of providing those entitled to receive the report with information to enable them to exercise the powers which their respective proprietary rights in the company conferred on them and not for the purposes of individual speculation with a view to profit.

The duty of care was one owed to the shareholders as a body and not to individual shareholders.

COMMENT

The decision represents a further retreat from the judgment of Lord Wilberforce in *Anns* v *Merton London Borough Council* [1977] 2 All E.R. 492. There was a view taken of that judgment that a person should owe a duty of care in negligence to anyone allegedly injured by his conduct, including those suffering economic loss, unless there was any good reason or ground of public policy to prevent the duty being imposed. More recently, and particularly in this case, the courts have shown that there is a real need for proximity and so have gone a long way to reducing the fear of ever increasing potential professional liability.

It now seems that knowledge as to the user of the statement concerned and, seemingly, also as to the purpose or probable purpose for which it will be used, is required to establish the necessary proximity in these cases where allegedly careless misstatements result in economic loss. It seems unlikely that there will now be any further movement towards foresight of the user and use which had begun to show itself in *J.E.B. Fasteners* v *Marks Bloom & Co* [1983] 1 All E.R. 583.

414. *Morgan Crucible Co plc* v *Hill Samuel Bank Ltd and Others*, *Financial Times Law Reports*, 30 October 1990

The crucial events in the case were as follows. On 6 December 1985, Morgan Crucible (M.C.) announced a proposed unsolicited offer to acquire the entire share capital of First Castle Electronics plc (F.C.). When the announcement was made, F.C.'s most recent published financial statements were the reports and audited accounts for the years ended 31 January 1984 and 1985.

On 17 December 1985, M.C. published a formal offer document which was addressed to F.C. shareholders. Morgan Grenfell advised M.C. and Hill Samuel advised F.C. The directors of F.C., acting on its behalf, sent their shareholders a number of circulars. They were also issued as press releases by Hill Samuel and copies were supplied to M.C.'s advisers.

Two days later, a circular was sent out by the directors of F.C., comparing M.C.'s profit record unfavourably with F.C.'s and recommending refusal of the bid. In subsequent circulars reference was made to the published financial statements, and one circular of 31 December 1985 stated that they could be inspected.

An F.C. circular to its shareholders, issued on 24 January 1986, forecast an increase in profits before tax in the year to 31 January 1986 of 38%. A letter from the auditors, Judkins, was included, saying that the profit forecast had been properly compiled. Included also was a letter from Hill Samuel stating that in its opinion the profit forecast had been prepared after due and careful inquiry.

On 29 January, M.C. increased its bid; on 31 January, F.C.'s board sent another letter to shareholders recommending acceptance of that increased bid; on 14 February, the bid was declared unconditional; and on 27 February, a further recommendation to accept the bid was sent by F.C. to its shareholders.

Later, M.C. alleged that the financial statements (audited and unaudited) issued prior to the bid, the profit forecast of 24 January, and the financial material contained in the circulars and recommendation documents were prepared negligently and were misleading. M.C. asserted that if the true facts had been known the bid would not have been made or completed. M.C. issued a writ on 6 May 1987 joining as defendants Hill Samuel, Judkins, and F.C.'s chairman and board. It alleged that the board and the auditors were responsible for circulating the financial statements; that they and Hill Samuel were responsible for the profit forecast; that all of them owed a duty of care to M.C. as a person who could foreseeably rely on them; that the statements and forecasts were negligently prepared; and that M.C. relied on them in making and increasing its offer and thereby suffered heavy loss.

In dealing with the allegations and the House of Lords judgment in *Caparo*, Lord Justice Slade said, first, that in *Caparo* all of the representations relied on had been made before an identified bidder had come forward, whereas in this case some of the representations had been made after a bidder had emerged and indeed because a bid had been made. They were clearly made with an identified bidder in mind, i.e. M.C. M.C. had therefore applied for leave to amend its statement of claim to representations made after the bid and as part of the takeover battle. This could then distinguish M.C.'s case from the situation in *Caparo*.

The issue before the court was whether M.C.'s allegations disclosed a reasonable cause of action. On the assumption that the allegations were true, was there a duty of care to M.C.? The judge went on to say, on the assumed facts, that the defendants could have foreseen that M.C. would or might suffer financial loss if the representations were incorrect; but that foreseeability in itself was not enough for liability to arise – there had to be a sufficient relationship of proximity between the plaintiff and defendant. In addition, it must be just and reasonable to impose liability on the defendant.

The fatal weakness in the *Caparo* case, the judge said, was that the auditors' statement, i.e. the annual accounts, had not been prepared for the purpose for which the plaintiff relied on it. It was therefore arguable that this case could be distinguished from *Caparo*.

On the assumed facts, the directors of F.C., when making the relevant representations, were aware that M.C. would rely on them for the purpose of deciding to make an increased bid and, indeed, intended that they should. M.C. did rely on them for that purpose. It was therefore arguable that there was a sufficient proximity between the directors of F.C. and M.C. to give rise to a duty of care.

For the same reasons, it could be argued that Hill Samuel and Judkins owed M.C. a duty of care in terms of their representations involving the profit forecast and the audited accounts.

Leave was given to amend the statement of claim. M.C.'s amended case should be permitted to go forward to trial.

> COMMENT
> So, some reliance can be placed on financial statements and other representations in a takeover after all. If, during the conduct of a contested takeover and after an identified bidder has emerged, the directors and financial advisers of the target company make express representations with a view to influencing the conduct of the bidder, then they owe him a duty of care not to mislead him negligently as was alleged.

OCCUPIERS' LIABILITY: TWO OR MORE OCCUPIERS

415. *Wheat* v *E. Lacon & Co. Ltd* [1966] 1 All E.R. 582

The manager of a public house was permitted by the owners, Lacon & Co., to take paying visitors who were accommmodated in a part of the premises labelled 'Private'. The plaintiff's husband, while a paying visitor, was killed by a fall from a staircase in the private part of the premises. Lacon & Co. denied liability on the ground that they were not occupiers of the private part of the premises. *Held* – by the House of Lords –

(a) that the defendants retained occupation and control together with the manager;

(b) the deceased was a visitor to whom the defendants owed a common duty of care;

(c) on the facts the staircase, though not lit, was not dangerous if used with proper care.

Wheat's claim therefore failed because there was no breach of the duty of care.

OCCUPIERS' LIABILITY: DEFECTIVE WORK OF AN INDEPENDENT CONTRACTOR

416. *Cook* v *Broderip* (1968) 112 S.J. 193

The owner of a flat employed an apparently competent contractor to put in a new socket. Mrs Cook, who was a cleaner, received an electric shock caused because the socket was faulty. It appeared that the contractor had negligently failed to test the socket for reversed polarity. *Held* – by

O'Connor, J. – that Major Broderip, the owner of the flat, was not vicariously liable for the contractor's negligence and was not in breach of duty under the Occupiers' Liability Act, 1957. Damages of £3081 were awarded against the contractor who was the second defendant.

COMMENT

On the issue of inspection of the work done, the House of Lords stated in *Ferguson* v *Welsh*, *The Times*, 30 October 1987 that it would not ordinarily be reasonable to expect an occupier, having engaged a contractor, whom he believed on reasonable grounds to be competent, to supervise the contractor's activities. If he knew, however, that an unsafe system was being used it might be reasonable for the occupier to take steps to see that things were made safe. If not, he might be liable.

OCCUPIERS' LIABILITY: EFFECT OF PLAINTIFF'S KNOWLEDGE OF DANGER

417. *Bunker* v *Charles Brand & Sons* [1969] 2 All E.R. 59

The plaintiff's employers were engaged as sub-contractors by the defendants who were the main contractors for tunnelling in connection with the Victoria Line. The plaintiff was required to carry out modifications to a digging machine. He had seen the machine *in situ* and was taken to have appreciated the danger in crossing its rollers when in operation. He was injured while attempting to cross the rollers in the course of his work and sued for damages. *Held* – by O'Connor, J. – that the defendants having retained control of the tunnel and the machine were the occupiers. They were not absolved from liability under the Act of 1957 merely because of the plaintiff's knowledge of the danger. Knowledge was not assent. However, the plaintiff's damages were reduced by 50% on the ground of his contributory negligence.

COMMENT

It was held in *Salmon* v *Seafarer Restaurants Ltd* [1983] 3 All E.R. 729 that an occupier owes a duty to firemen attending his premises to put out a fire. A fire occurred in the defendants' fish and chip shop because of the negligence of an employee. The employee failed to turn off a gas heater prior to closing the shop. The plaintiff fireman was injured when attending the fire. The Court said that the defendants were vicariously liable. It was foreseeable that a fireman might be injured following the employee's negligence.

OCCUPIER'S LIABILITY AND NEGLIGENCE LIABILITY: THE SPECIAL CASE OF CHILDREN

418. *Yachuk* v *Oliver Blais & Co. Ltd* [1949] A.C. 386

In this appeal from the Supreme Court of Canada to the Judicial Committee of the Privy Council the facts were as follows: a servant of Oliver Blais & Co.

Ltd had supplied five cents' worth of gasoline in an open lard pail to certain boys, aged nine and seven, who told him that they needed it for their mother's car, which had run out of petrol down the road. In fact they wanted it for a game of Red Indians. The boys dipped a bullrush into the pail and lit it. This set fire to the petrol in the pail and the boy Yachuk was seriously injured. The Judicial Committee *held* that the company was liable for the negligence of its servant in allowing the boys to take away the gasoline. The question of contributory negligence did not arise, because there was no evidence that the minors appreciated the dangerous quality of gasoline. The company was fully responsible even though the boys had resorted to deceit to overcome the supplier's scruples.

419. *Gough v National Coal Board* [1954] 1 Q.B. 191

The defendants were owners of a colliery which included a small railway which was constantly in use. The railway lines were not fenced or guarded, although there were houses on both sides. The public had for a long time been permitted to cross the lines, and children often played on the wagons, although the defendants' servants had been told to keep children off. The plaintiff, a boy aged six and a half, was seriously injured when he jumped off a wagon on which he had been riding. At the trial the boy admitted that he knew he was not supposed to ride on the wagons, and that his father had threatened to punish him if he did. Nevertheless it was *held* that the defendants were liable. The fact that children had for many years played near the railway made them licensees, and although the boy was strictly speaking a trespasser as regards the wagon, he was allured by the slow-moving wagons which the defendants knew were an attraction to children.

420. *Mourton v Poulter* [1930] 2 K.B. 183

The owner of certain land wished to carry out building operations on it, but before he could so do, it was necessary to fell a large elm tree. The land was unfenced, and children of the locality were in the habit of using it as a playground. During the process of felling, a large number of children gathered near the tree, and Poulter, who had been employed to fell the tree, warned the children of the danger likely to arise when the tree came down. He failed to repeat the warning when the tree was about to fall, and the plaintiff, a boy of ten, was crushed by the falling tree. *Held* – the defendant was liable. Even though the children were trespassers, he owed them a duty to give adequate warning.

421. *Pannett v McGuinness & Co.* [1972] 3 All E.R. 137

The defendants were demolishing a warehouse in a heavily populated area near a park where children played. Three workmen were specially appointed to make a bonfire of rubbish and to keep a look-out for children and to see that they came to no harm. The plaintiff, a boy of five, got in while the three men were away and was severely burned. The men had frequently chased children away in the past and in particular the plaintiff on a number of occasions. The contractors contended that the plaintiff was a trespasser, that he had been warned off and that they were under no duty. *Held* – the contractors were in breach of the duty of care owed to the child, their workmen had failed to keep a proper look-out.

COMMENT
Penny v Northampton Borough Council (1974) 72 L.G.R. 733, provides a contrast. In that case a child trespasser was not successful in recovering damages following injury from an aerosol can which exploded when it was thrown into a fire by another child. The accident took place in a discarded rubbish tip some 50 acres in area which resembled a rough field. The children had often been warned off the land by the council's workmen. The court considered the authority had behaved with common sense and humanity and could not have known of the danger on the land so that it had discharged its duty of care. However, in *Harris v Birkenhead Corporation* [1975] 1 All E.R. 1001, a local authority was not successful in showing that it had discharged its duty of care to a child trespasser who had entered a derelict house which the Corporation had purchased under a compulsory purchase order. The child fell from an upstairs window and the authority was held to be the occupier since the previous owner had got out of the premises in view of the order. The authority was fixed with knowledge of the relevant facts and Kilner Brown, J. found for the plaintiff.

HIGHWAYS ACT, 1980: NO DEFENCE UNLESS AUTHORITY HAS DONE WHAT WAS REASONABLY REQUIRED

422. *Griffiths* v *Liverpool Corporation* [1966] 2 All E.R. 1015

The plaintiff tripped and fell on a flagstone which rocked on its centre. In this action against the highway authority for breach of s. 1(1) of the Highways (Miscellaneous Provisions) Act, 1961 (see now Highways Act, 1980), it appeared that a regular system of inspection was desirable but was not carried out because the authority could not get tradesmen to put right faults discovered. The present fault could, however, have been put right by a labourer and no shortage of labourers was alleged. *Held* – by the Court of Appeal – the authority had not brought itself within the statutory defence in s. 1(2) and damages should be awarded.

COMMENT
In *Pridham v Hemel Hempstead Corporation* (1970) 69 L.G.R. 525, the authority proved that it had inspected the footpath of a minor residential road every three months and had kept a complaints book. The Court of Appeal held that this excluded the authority from liability for injury caused by a defect in the footpath.

EMPLOYERS' NEGLIGENCE: EFFECT OF STATUTORY DUTIES OF CARE

423. *Millard* v *Serck Tubes Ltd* [1969] 1 All E.R. 598

The plaintiff operated a power drill during the course of his employment. The drill was fenced, but the guard was not complete in that there was a gap in it through which the operator's hand could be drawn. While the plaintiff's hand was resting on the guard a piece of swarf thrown out from the drill wound itself around the plaintiff's hand and drew it into the drill causing injury to the plaintiff. The defendant employers conceded that the drill had not been properly fenced but contended that they were not liable because the accident itself was unforeseeable. This defence was rejected by the Court of Appeal and the plaintiff succeeded in his claim for damages. Where a defendant has failed to fence dangerous machinery, as here, in breach of s. 14 of the Factories Act, 1961, he cannot escape liability for injury on the grounds that such injury occurred in a way that was not reasonably foreseeable. Thus a plaintiff might succeed when suing on a statutory duty and fail if suing on a common-law one.

TORTS AGAINST BUSINESS INTERESTS: INDUCING A BREACH OF CONTRACT

424. *Lumley* v *Gye* (1853) 2 E. & Bl. 216

The plaintiff, who was the manager of an opera house, made a contract with a *prima donna* Johanna Wagner for her exclusive services for a period of time. Gye induced Johanna Wagner to break her operatic engagement with the plaintiff and sing for him. It was *held* that whatever might have been the origin of the right to sue in such cases as this, it was not now confined to actions by masters for the enticement of their servants but extended to wrongful interference with any contract of personal service.

425. *Daily Mirror Newspapers* v *Gardner* [1968] 2 All E.R. 163

The executive committee of the retailers' federation recommended their members to boycott the *Daily Mirror* for one week after that newspaper had announced that the retailers' discount rate was to be reduced when the price of the newspaper was increased. The newspaper asked for interlocutory injunctions requiring the committee to communicate with their members and withdraw the recommendation on the grounds –

(a) that it was an unlawful interference with the newspaper's contracts with the wholesalers because the wholesalers would not want to take copies of the *Daily Mirror* if the retailers would not take it; and

(b) that it was equivalent to an agreement contrary to the public interest within s. 21(1) of the Restrictive Trades Practices Act, 1956 (see now the Restrictive Trades Practices Act, 1976).

Held – by the Court of Appeal – that a sufficient *prima facie* case had been made out on both grounds and the injunctions would be granted.

CIVIL CONSPIRACY: THE PRINCIPLES ILLUSTRATED

426. *Crofter Hand Woven Harris Tweed Co. Ltd v Veitch* [1942] A.C. 435

Veitch and the other defendants were officials of the Transport and General Workers Union. The dockers at Stornoway on the island of Lewis were all members of the union and so were most of the employees in the spinning mills on the island. The yarn when spun in the mills was woven into tweed cloth by crofters working at home, the woven cloth being finished in the mills. The tweed thus produced was sold by the owners of the mill as Harris Tweed. The Crofter Company also produced tweed cloth but their yarn was not spun on the island but was obtained more cheaply on the mainland. This cloth was sold as Harris Tweed but did not bear the trade mark in the form of a special stamp. The mill owners making the genuine Harris Tweed were being pressed by the union to increase wages but they said that they could not accede to union requests because of the damaging competition of the Crofter Company. Consequently Veitch and others acting in combination placed an embargo on the Crofter Company's imported yarn and exported tweed by instructing dockers at Stornoway to refuse to handle these goods. The dockers obeyed these instructions but were not on strike or in breach of contract. The Crofter Company sought an interdict (or injunction) against the embargo. The House of Lords *held* that the union officials were not liable in conspiracy because their purpose was to benefit the members of the union and the means employed were not unlawful.

DEFAMATION: WHAT IS?

427. *Byrne v Deane* [1937] 1 K.B. 818

The plaintiff was a member of a golf club in which there had been some gaming machines. The defendants, Mr and Mrs Deane, were proprietors of the club. As a result of a complaint being made to the police the machines were removed. Shortly afterwards, the following typewritten lampoon was placed on the wall of the clubhouse near to the place where the machines had stood –

> For many years upon this spot
> You heard the sound of the merry bell
> Those who were rash and those who were not,
> Lost and made a spot of cash
> But he who gave the game away,
> May he Byrne in hell and rue the day.   Diddleramus.

The plaintiff brought this action for libel alleging that the defendants were responsible for exhibiting the lampoon, and that the lampoon was defamatory in that it suggested that he was disloyal to his fellow club members. *Held* – the words were not defamatory because the standard was the view which would be taken by right-thinking members of society, and, in the view of the court, right-thinking persons would not think less of a person who put the law into motion against wrongdoers.

DEFAMATION: LIBEL OR SLANDER: FORM OF PUBLICATION

428. *Youssoupoff* v *Metro-Goldwyn-Mayer Pictures Ltd* (1934) 50 T.L.R. 571

The plaintiff was a member of the Russian royal house. The defendants produced in England a film dealing with the life of Rasputin who had been the adviser of the Tsarina of Russia. The film also dealt with the murder of Rasputin. In the course of the film, a lady (Princess Natasha), who was affectionate towards the murderer of Rasputin, was also represented as having been raped by Rasputin, a man of the worst possible character. The plaintiff was married to a man who was undoubtedly one of the persons concerned in the killing of Rasputin. The plaintiff alleged that because of her marriage reasonable people would think that she was the person who was so raped. The action was for libel. *Held* – the action was properly framed in libel and the plaintiff succeeded.

COMMENT
This case is generally accepted as authority for the view that a defamatory talking film is always libel. However, the rape of Princess Natasha was in the pictorial part of the film and not on the sound track. It is also uncertain whether a plaintiff can sue for a slanderous imputation of rape without proving special damage. The Slander of Women Act, 1891, provides that the 'words spoken and published . . . which impute unchastity or adultery to any woman or girl shall not require special damage to render them actionable'. However, lack of consent, which is essential in rape, may mean that there is no imputation of unchastity.

DEFAMATION: INNUENDO: ILLUSTRATIONS FROM CASE LAW

429. *Cassidy* v *Daily Mirror Newspapers Ltd* [1929] 2 K.B. 331

A man named Cassidy or Corrigan who was well known for his indiscriminate relations with women, allowed a racing photographer to take a photograph of himself and a lady, and said that she was his fiancée and that the photographer might announce his engagement. The photograph was published in the *Daily Mirror* with the following caption: 'Mr M. Corrigan, the race-horse owner, and Miss X whose engagement has been announced.' The plaintiff, Cassidy's lawful wife, who was also known as Mrs Corrigan, sued the newspaper for libel alleging as an innuendo that if Mr Corrigan was unmarried and able to become engaged, she must have been co-habiting with him in circumstances of immorality. *Held* – since there was evidence that certain of her friends thought this to be so, she was entitled to damages.

COMMENT
The case is authority for the view that a person may be liable for a statement which he does not actually know to be defamatory. It does not decide, nor does any other relevant case, that a person who has

taken all possible steps to ensure the accuracy of his statement and could not, by reasonable enquiries, have discovered that his statement was defamatory is or is not liable in defamation.

430. *Morgan v Odhams Press* [1971] 2 All E.R. 1156

In 1965 the *Sun* reported that a kennel girl had been kidnapped by a dog-doping gang. In or about the relevant period various witnesses had seen her in the company of Mr Morgan whose friend she was. The newspaper article made no mention of Mr Morgan's name. Nevertheless he began an action against the newspaper pleading that he had been libelled by innuendo in that persons would think he was involved either in the kidnapping or the dog-doping, or both. *Held* – by the House of Lords – that –

(a) the newspaper article was not, by itself, capable of being so understood;
(b) an article to be defamatory of a person need not contain a 'key or pointer' showing it refers to him. Evidence is admissible to import a defamatory meaning to otherwise innocent words.

431. *Tolley v J.S. Fry & Sons Ltd* [1931] A.C. 333

The plaintiff was a well-known golfer. The defendants published an advertisement without the plaintiff's consent containing his picture and underneath the following words –

The caddy to Tolley said, 'Oh Sir,
Good shot, Sir! That ball, see it go, Sir.
My word, how it flies,
Like a cartet of Fry's,
They're handy, they're good, and priced low, Sir.'

The plaintiff brought an action for libel, alleging an innuendo. It was said that a person reading the advertisement would assume that the plaintiff had been paid for allowing the use of his name in it, and that in consequence he had prostituted his amateur status as a golfer. *Held* – the evidence showed that the advertisement was capable of this construction and the plaintiff was awarded damages.

432. *Sim v Stretch* (1936) 52 T.L.R. 669

The defendant had encouraged the plaintiff's housemaid to leave the plaintiff's employ and re-enter the defendant's. The defendant later sent the following telegram to the plaintiff: 'Edith has resumed her services with us to-day. Please send her possessions and the money you borrowed, also her wages.' The telegram was said to impute that the plaintiff was in financial difficulties and had in consequence borrowed from his housemaid, and that he had been unable to pay her wages, and was a person of no credit. The plaintiff succeeded at first instance and in the Court of Appeal, but the House of Lords reversed the judgment, *holding* that the telegram was incapable of bearing a defamatory meaning. In the words of Lord Atkin: 'It seems to me unreasonable that, when there are a number of good interpretations, the only bad one should be seized upon to give a defamatory sense to the statement.' It was also in this case that Lord Atkin suggested the following test of a 'defamatory' statement: 'Would the words tend to lower the plaintiff in the estimation of right-thinking members of society generally?'

433. *Fulham* v *Newcastle Chronicle and Journal* [1977] 1 W.L.R. 651

In 1962 the plaintiff left the Catholic priesthood. He married in 1964, a child being born 14 months later. In 1973 he was appointed as deputy headmaster of a school in Teeside having previously lived in South Yorkshire. A Newcastle newspaper published by the defendants commented upon his appointment stating that he 'went off very suddenly' from Salford where he had been a priest 'about seven years ago' and had subsequently married. The plaintiff claimed that such statements contained a libellous imputation that he had married while still a priest and had fathered an illegitimate child. The particulars supplied by the plaintiff simply stated his date of marriage and the date of birth of his eldest child. The defendants sought to strike out his claim. It was *held* – by the Court of Appeal – that only those knowing of the dates of the plaintiff's marriage and/or the birth of his child could draw the imputation alleged and that since the defendants' newspaper did not circulate in the area where the plaintiff had been a priest or subsequently lived it was necessary for him to plead particulars of persons receiving the publication having the requisite knowledge and that unless he was able to do so his allegation of innuendo would be struck out.

434. *Grappelli* v *Derek Block (Holdings) Ltd* [1981] 2 All E.R. 272

The plaintiffs, Mr Grappelli and Mr Disley, were jazz musicians with an international reputation. The defendants were their managers and agents. The defendants had, so the plaintiffs alleged, purported to book contracts for them without authority. Then it was said that one of these concerts had been cancelled because Mr Grappelli was seriously ill which was an entirely untrue story. It was said that that was defamatory, not as it stood, but because of an innuendo that people finding out that the plaintiffs were appearing at other concerts on the same dates as those cancelled would think that the plaintiffs had given a false story. It was held by the Court of Appeal that where a plaintiff relies on an innuendo he must prove that the words were published to a specific person who knew *at the time* of the publication of specific facts enabling him to understand the words in the innuendo meaning. Facts which came into existence afterwards did not make the statement defamatory. As Lord Denning said, the statement was not defamatory as it stood, since it is not defamatory of a person to say that he is seriously ill. At the time the statement was made those becoming aware of it would not have access to facts to suggest that it was wrong. Obviously, later on, when concerts were advertised in the *Sunday Times* on the same dates as those which had been cancelled it might have been possible to construe that Mr Grappelli and Mr Disley were not really ill and that the whole story was a put-up job. However, this information had to be available at the time of publication of the defamatory words since, according to Lord Denning, the cause of action arises in defamation when the words are published and they must be seen to be defamatory then, and not later.

DEFAMATION: THE WORDS MUST REFER TO THE PLAINTIFF

435. *E. Hulton & Co.* v *Jones* [1910] A.C. 20

A newspaper published an article descriptive of life in Dieppe in which one Artemus Jones, described as a churchwarden at Peckham, was accused of living with a mistress in France. All persons concerned contended that they were ignorant of the existence of any person of that name, and the writer of the article said that he had invented it. Unfortunately the name so chosen was that of an English barrister and journalist, and the evidence showed that those who knew him thought that the article referred to him. *Held* – the newspaper was responsible for the libel and the plaintiff was awarded damages.

> COMMENT
> (i) In cases of this kind the defence of offer of amends may be available under s. 4 of the Defamation Act, 1952. However, it is by no means certain that it would have been available on the actual facts of this case, because s. 4 applies only where the defendant can show that he and his servants or agents have taken all reasonable care with regard to the publication. On the facts of *Hulton* v *Jones* it seems that the publication was attended by some carelessness.
> (ii) In *Hayward* v *Thompson* [1981] 3 All E.R. 450 the defendants were the editor, a journalist on, and the proprietors and publishers of, a Sunday paper. In one article it was alleged that a wealthy benefactor of the Liberal Party was connected with an alleged murder plot but no name was given. In a later article the paper named the plaintiff reporting that the police wished to interview him in connection with the alleged murder plot which was not, of course, a defamatory allegation that he was involved in it as the first article had been. It was *held* – by the Court of Appeal – that the two articles could be connected. Thus the libel in the first article was of the plaintiff by reason of connection with the second one.

436. *Knupffer* v *London Express Newspaper Ltd* [1944] A.C. 116

The plaintiff was head in the United Kingdom of a Russian refugee organisation, active in France and the United States of America, but having only 24 members in England. An article in the newspaper ascribed Fascism to this 'minute body established in France and the United States of America', but without mentioning the English branch. *Held* – the article was not defamatory of the plaintiff since he was not marked out by it, even assuming that it was defamatory to call someone a Fascist.

437. *Schloimovitz* v *Clarendon Press*, *The Times*, 6 July 1973

The plaintiff by statement of claim alleged that the definitions of the word

'Jew' contained in three dictionaries published by the defendants were derogatory, defamatory and deplorable and sought an injunction restraining the defendants from publishing such definitions, at least without qualification, in any future editions of such dictionaries. *Held* – by Goff, J. – that what was before the court was not whether the definitions were right or wrong or whether they were justly applied to any Jews, but whether in law the plaintiff had a cause of action to restrain the conduct of the defendant. No individual could maintain an action in respect of defamatory matter published about a body of persons unless in its terms, or by reason of the circumstances, it should and must be construed as a reference to him as an individual. There were two questions: (*a*) were the words defamatory? (*b*) did they in fact apply to the plaintiff or were they capable in law of being so regarded? The plaintiff failed to satisfy the latter test and accordingly the defendants were entitled to have the writ and statement of claim struck out. (*Knupffer* applied.)

> COMMENT
> It was decided in *Farringdon* v *Leigh*, *The Times*, 10 December 1987, that it was at least arguable that where defamatory words in a publication referred to an unidentified member or members of a group of persons, each of those persons had a cause of action in libel. In these circumstances an action by members of a team of seven police officers was allowed to proceed to trial where they alleged that certain articles in the *Observer* were defamatory of them in alleging that at least two of them, who were unnamed, had passed confidential information to journalists.

DEFAMATION: DEFENCES: JUSTIFICATION

438. *Alexander* v *The North Eastern Railway Co.* (1865) 6 B. & S. 340

The defendants published the following notice –

> North Eastern Railway. Caution. J. Alexander, manufacturer and general merchant, Trafalgar Street, Leeds, was charged before the magistrates of Darlington on 28th September, for riding on a train from Leeds, for which his ticket was not available, and refusing to pay the proper fair. He was convicted in the penalty of £9 1s., including costs, or three weeks' imprisonment.

In this action for libel, the plaintiff contended that the defence of justification could not lie because, although he had been convicted as stated, the alternative prison sentence was 14 days not three weeks. *Held* – the substitution of three weeks for a fortnight did not make the statement libellous. It could be justified, since the rest of it was true.

DEFAMATION: DEFENCES: FAIR COMMENT

439. *London Artists* v *Littler* [1969] 2 All E.R. 193

In 1965 four of the principal actors and actresses in a play called *The Right*

Honourable Gentleman simultaneously wrote to the defendant, who was the producer of the play, terminating their engagement by four weeks' formal notice. This was, of course, highly unusual and the defendant wrote to the actors and actresses concerned wrongly accusing the plaintiffs, who were their agents, of conspiracy to close down the play. The defendant also communicated the letter to the press. The defendant was now sued for libel. It was *held* – by the Court of Appeal – that he had libelled the plaintiffs because although the subject matter of the allegations was of public interest, i.e. the fate of the play, the defence of fair comment did not apply to the allegation of a plot which was an allegation of fact. The allegation of a plot was defamatory and had not been justified. In fact it seemed that all the actors and actresses involved had their own good and different reasons for leaving the play. There was no evidence of combination.

DEFAMATION: DEFENCES: QUALIFIED PRIVILEGE

440. *London Association for the Protection of Trade* v *Greenlands* [1916] 2 A.C. 15

The respondents were a limited company carrying on business as drapers and general furnishers at Hereford. The appellants were an unincorporated association consisting of about 6300 traders and had, as one of their objects, the making of private inquiries as to the means, respectability and trustworthiness of individuals and firms. A member of the association was about to sell goods to the respondents and he asked the association to report on them, and particularly to say whether the respondents were a good risk for credit of between £20 and £30. In the report submitted, the association declared that the respondents were a fair trade risk for the sum mentioned, but said that they had heavy mortgages charged on their assets, and that the assets barely covered the loans. In fact the mortgages were secured by a charge upon the real and leasehold property only, and all other assets were entirely free from any mortgage whatever, and constituted a large and valuable fund. The respondents were originally the plaintiffs in an action for libel contained in the statement about the mortages, and the statement that they were only good for credit of between £20 and £30. *Held* – the occasion was privileged and thus the respondents had no claim in the absence of malice which they had not proved. Judgment was therefore given for the appellants.

441. *Osborn* v *Thomas Boulter & Son* [1930] 2 K.B. 226

The plaintiff, a publican, wrote a letter to the defendants, his brewers, complaining of the quality of the beer. The defendants sent one of their employees to investigate and report. After receiving the report, Mr Boulter dictated a letter to his typist in which he suggested that the plaintiff had been adding water to the beer, and pointing out the penalties attaching to this if the plaintiff was caught. The plaintiff sued, alleging publication to the typist and certain clerks. *Held* – the occasion was privileged, and since the plaintiff could not prove malice in the defendants, his action failed.

442. *Beach* v *Freeson* [1971] 2 W.L.R. 805

A Member of Parliament wrote to the Law Society complaining of the conduct of a firm of solicitors reported to him by his constituents. He also sent a copy of the letter to the Lord Chancellor. *Held* – by Geoffrey Lane, J. – that both publications were protected by qualified privilege. The privilege arose out of a Member of Parliament's duty to his constituents and the responsibilities of the Law Society and the Lord Chancellor.

443. *Cook* v *Alexander* [1973] 3 W.L.R. 617

The plaintiff sued the defendant for libel in respect of an account of a House of Lords debate which he had written for the *Daily Telegraph*. The debate had been about an approved school where the plaintiff had been a teacher and which had been closed partly because of the plaintiff's revelations as to the system of punishment there. The newspaper had published a précis of each speech on one of the inside pages, but the plaintiff objected to a report written by the defendant which appeared on the back page. In this report, known as 'Parliamentary Sketch', the writer gave his impression of the debate and emphasised the salient aspects of it, but there was a reference to the more detailed account on another page. The plaintiff alleged that the sketch was defamatory of him because it gave great prominence to a speech that was very critical of him and his conduct, while it dismissed in uncomplimentary terms a speech which defended his action. It was *held* – by the Court of Appeal – that such a Parliamentary sketch was protected by qualified privilege. A reporter was entitled to select from a debate those parts which seemed to him to be of public interest and provided that the account as a whole was fair and honest, such a Parliamentary sketch was protected by qualified provilege.

444. *Horrocks* v *Low* [1972] 1 W.L.R. 1625

At a local authority council meeting Low made a speech defamatory of Horrocks who in answer to Low's defence of justification, fair comment and qualified privilege, alleged that Low had been actuated by express malice. *Held* – by the Court of Appeal – that malice could not be inferred. Low held an honest and positive belief in the truth of his statement and had not abused the privileged occasion. '[The defendant] is not to be held malicious merely because he was angry or prejudiced even unreasonably prejudiced, against the plaintiff, so long as he honestly believed what he said to be true. Such is the law as I have always understood it to be.' (*Per* Lord Denning, M.R.)

'What has to be proved is that the defendant was activated by malice in the popular meaning of the word: that is to say, in speaking as he did, he must have been actuated by spite or ill-will against the person defamed or by some indirect or improper motive.' (*Per* Edmund Davis, L.J.)

'When there is . . . [gross and unreasoning] prejudice there will often, perhaps usually, be reckless indifference whether what is said is true or false. But if there is honest belief that it is true, there cannot in any judgment be recklessness whether it be true or false.' (*Per* Stephenson, L.J.)

445. *Egger* v *Viscount Chelmsford* [1964] 3 All E.R. 406

Mrs Egger, a judge of Alsatian dogs, was on the list of judges of the Kennel Club, and Miss Ross, the secretary of a dog club in Northern Ireland, wrote to the Kennel Club asking them to approve of Mrs Egger as a judge of Alsatians at a show. The assistant secretary of the Kennel Club, C.A. Burney, wrote to Miss Ross to say that the committee could not approve the appointment. Mrs Egger brought an action for libel against the ten members of the committee and the assistant secretary on the grounds that the letter reflected on her competence and integrity. There were two long trials at both of which the judge ruled that the occasion was privileged. The jury disagreed the first time, but at the second trial the jury found that the letter was defamatory and that five members of the committee were actuated by malice but three were not. The other two had meanwhile died. The judge gave judgment against all the defendants including the assistant secretary. *Held* – on appeal – the defence of qualified privilege is a defence for the individual who is sued, and not a defence for the publication. It is quite erroneous to say that it is attached to the publication. The three committee members innocent of malice were entitled to protection and were not liable. The assistant secretary also had an independent and individual privilege, and was not responsible or liable for the tort of those members of the committee who had acted with malice. Even in a joint tort, the tort is the separate act of each individual; each is severally answerable for it; and each is severally entitled to his own defence.

DEFAMATION: CONSENT OF THE PLAINTIFF TO PUBLICATION

446. *Chapman* v *Lord Ellesmere and Others* [1932] 2 K.B. 431

The plaintiff was a trainer and one of his horses, after winning a race, was found to be doped. An inquiry was held by the Stewards of the Jockey Club, as a result of which they decided to disqualify the horse for future racing, and to warn the plaintiff off Newmarket Heath. The decision was published in the *Racing Calendar*. The plaintiff contended that the words were defamatory because they implied that he had doped the horse. The defendants, who were the proprietors of the *Racing Calendar*, contended that the words were not defamatory, and meant simply that the plaintiff had been warned off for not protecting the horse against doping. Evidence showed that it was a condition of a trainer's licence that the withdrawal of that licence should appear in the *Racing Calendar*, which was also to be the recognised vehicle of communication for all matters concerning infringement of rules. *Held* – the plaintiff being bound by the terms of his licence, the doctrine of *volenti non fit injuria* applied as regards publication in the *Racing Calendar*, so that the plaintiff had no cause of action.

DEFAMATION: DAMAGES: COMPENSATORY NOT PUNITIVE

447. *Davis* v *Rubin* [1967] 112 Sol. J. 51

The plaintiffs were chartered accountants of good reputation and they wished to buy the lease of business premises. The defendants, who were the landlords, wrote to the holder of the lease saying that they would not accept the plaintiffs if the lease was assigned and referred in a defamatory fashion to the plaintiffs' business and references. The plaintiffs claimed damages in respect of the libel published in the letter, and were awarded £4000 each. The Court of Appeal, allowing the defendants' appeal, said that the damages were 'excessive, extravagant and exorbitant'. There had been publication to one person only and there was no evidence that the plaintiffs' reputation had been diminished in the minds of other persons. A reasonable sum would not have exceeded £1000 each and a new trial was ordered on the issue of damages.

RYLANDS v *FLETCHER*: STRICT LIABILITY: ESCAPE OF FIRE

448. *Emanuel* v *Greater London Council* (1970) 114 Sol. J. 653

A contractor employed by the Ministry of Public Building and Works removed prefabricated bungalows from the Council's land. The contractor lit a fire and negligently allowed sparks to spread to the plaintiff's land where buildings and goods were damaged. The plaintiff claimed against the G.L.C. and it was *held* – by James, J. – that –

(*a*) on the facts the Council remained in occupation of the site;

(*b*) the contractor was not a 'stranger' to the Council since they retained a power of control over his activities; and

(*c*) although the Council had not been negligent and were not vicariously liable for the contractor's negligence since they did not employ him, they were strictly liable under *Rylands* v *Fletcher* for the escape of fire.

RYLANDS v *FLETCHER*: THERE MUST BE AN ESCAPE: WHETHER THE RULE APPLIES TO PERSONAL INJURIES

449. *Read* v *J. Lyons & Co. Ltd* [1947] A.C. 156

The appellant was employed by the Ministry of Supply as an Inspector of Munitions in the respondents' munitions factory. In the course of her employment there she was injured by the explosion of a shell which was in course of manufacture. She did not allege negligence on the part of the defendants, but based her claim on *Rylands* v *Fletcher*. The trial judge found that there was liability under the rule, but the Court of Appeal and the House of Lords reversed this decision, *holding* that the rule did not apply since there had been no escape of the thing that inflicted the injury. In the words of Viscount Simon, L.C. 'Escape for the purpose of applying the proposition in *Rylands* v *Fletcher* means escape from a place which the defendant has occupation of, or control over, to a place which is outside his occupation or control.' It was also suggested *obiter* in this case that the rule in *Rylands* v *Fletcher* does not extend to personal injuries, but only to injury to property.

COMMENT

The *ratio* of the Court of Appeal in *Hale* v *Jennings Bros* [1938] 1 All

E.R. 579 suggests that there may be liability for personal injuries. In that case a stallholder at a fair suffered personal injuries because of the escape of the defendants' chair-o-plane. It was held that she had a good claim under *Rylands* v *Fletcher*.

RYLANDS v *FLETCHER*: DOES NOT DEPEND ON OWNERSHIP OF LAND: COVERS ESCAPES OF A VARIETY OF OFFENSIVE AND DANGEROUS SUBSTANCES

450. *Charing Cross Electricity Supply Co* v *Hydraulic Power Co* [1914] 3 K.B. 772

The defendants' water mains under a public street burst and damaged the plaintiffs' cables which were also laid under the street. *Held* – the defendants were liable under the rule in *Rylands* v *Fletcher*, because the rule was not confined to wrongs between owners of adjacent land and does not depend on ownership of land. Here it could be applied to owners of adjacent chattels.

451. *Attorney-General* v *Corke* [1933] Ch. 89

The defendant was the owner of disused brickfields, and he permitted a number of gypsies to occupy them and live in caravans and tents. The gypsies threw slop water about in the neighbourhood of the fields and accumulated all sorts of filth thereabouts. The court *held* that *Rylands* v *Fletcher* applied, and an injunction was granted against the defendant. While it was not unlawful to license caravan dwellers, it was abnormal use of land, since such persons often have habits of life which are offensive to those persons with fixed homes.

COMMENT
Reference should also be made to *Smith* v *Scott*, 1972 at p. 777.

RYLANDS v *FLETCHER*: NOT APPLICABLE TO ESCAPE OF THINGS NATURALLY ON LAND: OTHER CLAIMS

452. *Giles* v *Walker* (1890) 24 Q.B.D. 656

The defendant wished to redeem certain forest land and ploughed it up. Thistles grew up on the land and thistle-seed was blown in large quantities by the wind from the defendant's land to that of the plaintiff. *Held* – there was no duty as between adjoining occupiers to cut things such as thistles which are the natural growth of the soil; therefore the defendant was not liable. Presumably if a person deliberately set thistles on his land he would be liable under the rule in *Rylands* v *Fletcher*, for it is not usual to cultivate weeds on one's land.

COMMENT
An action for nuisance would probably have succeeded here, because a person is liable for a nuisance on his land (even if he has not caused it) if he lets it continue (but note Weeds Act, 1959, p. 434).

453. *Davey v Harrow Corporation* [1957] 2 All E.R. 305

The roots of the defendants' elm trees spread to the plaintiff's land and caused damage to the plaintiff's property. *Held* – the defendants were liable in nuisance, whether the trees were self-sewn or not. It was no defence to an action for nuisance that the thing causing the nuisance was naturally on the defendants' land, though it might be a defence to liability under the rule in *Rylands* v *Fletcher*.

RYLANDS v *FLETCHER*: DEFENCE OF ACT OF GOD

454. *Greenock Corporation v Caledonian Railway Co* [1917] A.C. 556

The Corporation, in laying out a park, constructed a concrete paddling pool for children in the bed of a stream, thereby altering its course and natural flow. Owing to rainfall of extraordinary violence, the stream overflowed and poured down the street, flooding the railway company's premises. The House of Lords *held* that this was not an Act of God and the Corporation was liable. The House of Lords indicated the restricted range of the defence of Act of God and of the decision in *Nichols* v *Marsland* (1876), at p. 749, distinguishing that case on the grounds that whereas in *Nichols* v *Marsland* the point at issue was the liability for storing water in artificial lakes, the point here was interference with the natural course of a stream, and anyone so interfering must provide even against exceptional rainfall.

RYLANDS v *FLETCHER*: DEFENCE: WRONGFUL ACT OF STRANGER

455. *Rickards v Lothian* [1913] A.C. 263

The defendant was the occupier of business premises and leased part of the second floor to the plaintiff. On the fourth floor was a men's cloakroom with a wash basin. The cloakroom was provided for the use of tenants and persons in their employ. The plaintiff's stock in trade was found one morning seriously damaged by water which had seeped through the ceiling from the wash basin on the fourth floor. Examination showed that the waste pipe had been plugged with various articles such as nails, penholders, string and soap, and the water tap had been turned full on. The defendant's caretaker found the cloakroom in proper order at 10.20 pm the previous evening. *Held* – the defendant was not liable under the rule in *Rylands* v *Fletcher* because the damage had been caused by the act of a stranger.

RYLANDS v *FLETCHER*: DEFENCE: COMMON BENEFIT

456. *Peters v Prince of Wales Theatre (Birmingham) Ltd* [1943] K.B. 73

The defendants leased to the plaintiff a shop in a building which contained a theatre. In the latter there was, to the plaintiff's knowledge, a sprinkler system installed as a precaution against fire and the system extended to the plaintiff's shop. In a thaw, following a severe frost, water poured from the sprinklers in the defendants' rehearsal room into the plaintiff's shop and damaged his stock. The plaintiff claimed damages for negligence, and under *Rylands* v *Fletcher*. *Held* – there was no negligence on the part of the defendants and there was no liability under *Rylands* v *Fletcher*, because the sprinkler had been installed for the common benefit of the plaintiff and defendants.

The law of property

OWNERSHIP AND POSSESSION: RIGHTS OF OWNER PARAMOUNT

457. *Moffat* v *Kazana* [1968] 3 All E.R. 271

The plaintiff hid banknotes in a biscuit tin in the roof of his house. He sold the house to the defendant, one of whose workmen discovered the money. In this action by the plaintiff to recover the money it was *held* – by Wrangham, J. – that the plaintiff succeeded. He had never evinced any intention to pass the title in the money to anyone. Therefore his title was good, not only against the finder, but also against the new owner of the house.

ADVERSE POSSESSION OR SQUATTERS' RIGHTS

458. *Hayward* v *Challoner* [1967] 3 All E.R. 122

The predecessors in title of the plaintiff landowner let land to the rector of a parish at a rent of 10s. a year. The rent was not collected after 1942 and the plaintiff now sued for possession. *Held* – by the Court of Appeal – that a right of action in respect of rent or possession must be held to have accrued when the rent due was first unpaid, and therefore was barred by what is now the Limitation Act, 1980. The rector as a corporation sole had acquired a good squatter's title.

459. *Littledale* v *Liverpool College* [1900] 1 Ch. 19

The plaintiffs had a right of way for agricultural purposes over a strip of grass land belonging to the defendants. The plaintiffs put up gates which they kept locked at each end of the strip, and used the grass for grazing, keeping the hedges of the strip clipped. They now claimed ownership of the land by virtue of adverse possession. *Held* – the plaintiffs' acts could be construed as protecting the right of way, rather than excluding the owner, and were insufficient to establish the plaintiffs title to the land.

460. *Smirk* v *Lyndale Developments Ltd* [1974] 2 All E.R. 8

The plaintiff had a service tenancy of a house owned by the British Railways Board. In 1960 he took effective possession of an adjacent plot of land owned by the Board, though the Board was unaware of his action. The plaintiff did not communicate to the Board at any time that he disclaimed the Board's title. The Board sold the house and the plot to the defendants who granted a new tenancy of the house to Smirk on different terms not including the adjacent plot. The plaintiff claimed a possessory title to that plot. It was *held* – by Pennycuick, V.C. – that the plaintiff did not have a good possessory title to the plot.

BAILMENT: DAMAGE TO GOODS: ACTION BY BAILEE

461. *The Winkfield* [1902] P. 42

This was an Admiralty action arising because a ship called the *Mexican* was negligently struck and sunk by a ship called the *Winkfield*. The *Mexican* was carrying mail from South Africa to England during the Boer War. The Postmaster-General made, among other things, a claim for damages in respect of the estimated value of parcels and letters for which no claim had been made or instructions received from the senders. The Postmaster-General undertook to distribute the amount recovered when the senders were found. An objection was made that the Postmaster-General represented the Crown and was not liable to the senders (see now Crown Proceedings Act, 1947). *Held* – as a bailee in possession the Postmaster-General could recover damages for the loss of the goods irrespective of whether or not he was liable to the bailors.

BAILMENT AND LICENCE DISTINGUISHED

462. *Ashby* v *Tolhurst* [1937] 2 All E.R. 837

The plaintiff drove his car on to a piece of land at Southend owned by the defendants. He paid 1s. to an attendant who was the defendants' servant and was given a ticket. He left the car with the doors locked. When he returned his car had gone, the attendant having allowed a thief, who said he was a friend of the plaintiff, to drive it away. The ticket was called a 'car-park ticket' and contained the words: 'The proprietors do not take any responsibility for the safe custody of any cars or articles therein, nor for any damage to the cars or articles however caused nor for any injuries to any persons, all cars being left in all respects entirely at their owner's risk. Owners are requested to show a ticket when required.' *Held* –

(*a*) The relationship between the parties was that of licensor and licensee, not that of bailor and bailee because there was in no sense a transfer of possession. There was, therefore, no obligation upon the defendants towards the plaintiff in respect of the car.

(*b*) If there was a contract of bailment, the servant delivered possession of the car quite honestly under a mistake and the conditions on the tickets were wide enough to protect the defendants.

(*c*) There could not be implied into the contract a term that the car should not be handed over without production of the ticket.

COMMENT

(i) Where the plaintiff hands over the key, the court may find a transfer of possession and a bailment, but the delivery of the key is not conclusive.

(ii) It was held in *Chappell (Fred) v National Car Parks, The Times,* 22 May 1987, that where a vehicle was parked on NCP land for a fee but there was no barrier, the land was open and no keys to the vehicle were handed over, as the owner locked the vehicle and retained the keys, no bailment of the vehicle took place and NCP were not liable for its theft.

463. *Ultzen v Nicols* [1894] 1 Q.B. 92

A waiter took a customer's overcoat, without being asked to do so, and hung it on a peg behind the customer. The coat was stolen and it was *held* that the restaurant keeper was a bailee of the coat and that there was negligence in supervision on the part of the bailee.

COMMENT

In this case the servant seems to have been regarded as taking possession, but it is unlikely that a bailment will arise if a customer merely hangs his coat on a stand or other device provided by the establishment.

464. *Deyong v Shenburn* [1946] 1 All E.R. 226

An allegation that an actor who left his clothes in a dressing room had constituted the theatre owners bailees of the clothes was not sustained.

BAILMENT: FINDERS AND INVOLUNTARY RECIPIENTS

465. *Newman v Bourne & Hollingsworth* (1915) 31 T.L.R. 209

The plaintiff went into the defendant's shop on a Saturday in order to buy a coat. While trying on coats she took off a diamond brooch and put it on a show case. She left the shop having forgotten the brooch; an assistant found it and handed it to the shopwalker who put it in his desk. By the firm's rules the brooch ought to have been taken to their lost property office. The brooch could not be found on the following Monday. *Held* – there was evidence to support the trial judge's finding that the firm had become bailees and had not exercised proper care.

466. *Neuwirth v Over Darwen Industrial Co-operative Society* (1894) 70 T.L.R. 374

A concert hall was hired for an evening performance. No mention was made of rehearsal but the orchestra rehearsed in the hall during the afternoon without opposition from the proprietors or the keeper of the hall. After the rehearsal Neuwirth left his double-bass fiddle in an ante-room in such a position that when the hall keeper came to turn on the gas in the ante-room he could not do so without first moving the instrument. The fiddle fell and was badly damaged. *Held* – there was no contract of bailment between the parties. The care of musical instruments was outside the scope of the hall keeper's authority and there was no evidence that he had been guilty of negligence in the course of his employment.

COMMENT
Refence should also be made to *Elvin and Powell Ltd* v *Plummer Roddis Ltd*, 1933 at p. 771.

BAILMENT: OBLIGATIONS OF BAILOR

467. *Hyman* v *Nye* (1881) 6 Q.B.D. 685

The plaintiff hired a landau with a pair of horses and a driver for a drive from Brighton to Shoreham and back. The plaintiff was involved in an accident owing to a broken bolt which caused the carriage to upset so that the plaintiff was thrown out of it. *Held* – the trial judge's direction to the jury that the plaintiff must prove negligence was wrong. There was an implied warranty that the carriage was as fit for the purpose for which it was hired as skill and care could make it.

468. *Reed* v *Dean* [1949] 1 K.B. 188

The plaintiffs hired a motor launch called the *Golden Age* from the defendant for a family holiday on the Thames. The plaintiffs set sail at about 7 pm on 22 June 1946, and at about 9 pm, when they were near Sonning, they discovered that a liquid in the bilge by the engine was on fire. They attempted to extinguish the fire but were unable to do so, the fire-fighting equipment with which the launch was supplied being out of order. The plaintiffs had to abandon the launch and suffered personal injuries and loss of belongings. The plaintiffs admitted to a fireman after the accident that they might have spilt some petrol when the tank was refilled. *Held* – the plaintiffs succeeded because there was an implied undertaking by the defendant that the launch was fit for the purpose for which it was hired as reasonable care and skill could make it. Further, as the launch had caught fire due to an unexplained cause, there was a presumption that it was not fit for this purpose. The defendant's failure to provide proper fire-fighting equipment was a breach of the implied warranty of fitness.

BAILMENT: OBLIGATIONS OF BAILEE

469. *Houghland* v *R. Low (Luxury Coaches) Ltd* [1962] 2 All E.R. 159

The defendants supplied a coach for the purposes of an old people's outing to Southampton. On returning the passengers put their luggage into the boot of the coach. During a stop for tea the coach was found to be defective and another one was sent for and the luggage was transferred from the first coach to the relief coach. The removal of the luggage from the first coach was not supervised, but the restacking of the luggage into the new coach was supervised by one of the defendants' employees. When the passengers arrived home a suitcase belonging to the plaintiff was missing and he brought an action against the defendants for its loss. It was *held*, by the Court of Appeal, that whether the action was for negligence or in detinue, the defendants were liable unless they could show that they had not been negligent. On the facts they had failed to prove this and were therefore liable. It was in this case that Ormerod, L.J. made some observations on bailments in general. The County Court judge had found that the bailment was gratuitous and that the defendants were liable only for gross negligence. Dealing with this question, Ormerod, L.J. said:

> For my part I have always found some difficulty in understanding just what was gross negligence, because it appears to me that the standard of care required in a case of bailment or any other type of case is the standard demanded by the circumstances of the particular case. It seems to me to try and put bailment, for instance, into a watertight compartment, such as gratuitous bailment on the one hand and bailment for reward on the other, is to overlook the fact that there might well be an infinite variety of cases which might come into one or other category.

470. *Global Dress Co.* v *W.H. Boase & Co.* [1966] 2 Ll. Rep. 72

B & Co. were master porters and had custody of 30 cases of goods belonging to G & Co. at a Liverpool dock shed. One case was stolen and G & Co. brought an action for damages against B & Co. B & Co. offered evidence of their system of safeguarding the goods and the County Court judge at first instance found the system to be as good as any other in the Liverpool Docks, but notwithstanding this he found B & Co. liable. On appeal to the Court of Appeal it was *held* that if B & Co. could not affirmatively prove that their watchman was not negligent it was of no avail to show that they had an impeccable system, and the appeal should be dismissed. Thus the onus of proving that their servant was not negligent lay upon B & Co.

471. *Doorman* v *Jenkins* (1843) 2 Ad. & El. 256

The plaintiff left the sum of £32 10s. with the defendant, who was a coffee-house keeper, for safe custody and without any reward. The defendant put the money in with his own in a cash box which he kept in the taproom. The taproom was open to the public on a Sunday but the rest of the house was not and the cash was, in fact, stolen on a Sunday. Lord Denman *held* that the loss of the defendant's own money was not enough to prove reasonable care and the court found for the plaintiff.

472. *Brabant* v *King* [1895] A.C. 632

This action was brought against the government of Queensland for damage to certain explosives belonging to the plaintiff which the government as bailees for reward had stored in sheds situated near the water's edge on Brisbane River. The water rose to an exceptional height and the store was flooded. The question of inevitable accident was raised and also the degree of negligence required. The Privy Council *held* that because of the nature of the site the bailees were required to place the goods at such a level as would in all probability ensure their absolute immunity from flood water, and the defendants were held liable. The Privy Council went on to say that in case of deposit for reward the bailees were 'under a level of obligation to exercise the same degree of care, towards the preservation of the goods entrusted to them from injury, which might reasonably be expected from a skilled storekeeper, acquainted with the risks to be apprehended from the character either of the storehouse or of its locality; and the obligations included, not only the duty of taking all reasonable precautions to obviate these risks but the duty of taking all proper measures for the protection of the goods when such risks were imminent or had actually occurred'. Counsel for the government suggested that a bailee was not liable for damage caused by the defects in his warehouse where these defects were known to the bailor, in this case the proximity of the warehouse to the Brisbane River. The Privy Council dismissed this argument on the grounds that it was a dangerous one, not supported by any authority. They said that the bailor could rely on the skill of the bailee in this matter. It will be seen from this decision that a bailee for reward is liable even in the case of uncommon or unexpected danger, unless he uses efforts which are in proportion to the emergency to ward off that danger.

473. *Wilson* v *Brett* (1843) 11 M. & W. 113

Wilson was in process of selling his horse and Brett volunteered to ride the horse in order to show it off to a likely purchaser. Brett rode the horse on to wet and slippery turf and the horse fell and was injured. Brett pleaded that he was not negligent but the court *held* that he had not used the skill he professed to possess when he volunteered to ride the horse and that he was liable.

474. *Saunders (Mayfair) Furs* v *Davies* (1965) 109 S.J. 922

The plaintiffs delivered a valuable fur coat to a shop belonging to the defendants, on sale-or-return terms. The defendants displayed it in their shop window and at 2.30 am one morning the coat was stolen in a smash-and-grab raid. *Held* – that in all the circumstances and because of the valuable nature of the property, the defendants had taken an unreasonable risk and were negligent in leaving the coat on display in the window all night.

475. *Coldman* v *Hill* [1919] 1 K.B. 443

The defendant was a bailee of cows belonging to the plaintiff. Two of these cows were stolen through no fault of the defendant, though he failed to notify the plaintiff and did not inform the police or take any steps to find the cows. The plaintiff now sued him for negligence and it was *held* – by the Court of Appeal – that it was up to the defendant to prove that, even if notice had been given, the cows would not have been recovered. In the circumstances of this case that burden had not been discharged and the defendant was liable.

BAILMENT: DELEGATION BY BAILEE

476. *Davies* v *Collins* [1945] 1 All E.R. 247

An American Army officer sent his uniform to the defendants to be cleaned. It was accepted on the following conditions: 'Whilst every care is exercised in cleaning and dyeing garments, all orders are accepted at owner's risk entirely and we are unable to hold ourselves responsible for damage.' The defendants did not clean the uniform but sub-contracted the work to another firm of cleaners. In the event the uniform was lost and the defendants were *held* liable in damages. The Court of Appeal took the view that the limitation clause operated to exclude the right to sub-contract because it used the words 'every care is exercised', which postulated personal service.

477. *Edwards* v *Newland* [1950] 2 All E.R. 1072

The defendant agreed to store the plaintiff's furniture for reward. Later, without the plaintiff's knowledge, the defendant made arrangements with another company to store the plaintiff's furniture. The third party's warehouse was damaged by a bomb and they asked the defendant to remove the furniture but this was not done immediately because there was a dispute about charges. Eventually the plaintiff removed his furniture but some pieces were missing. *Held* – the plaintiff could recover from the defendant because he had departed from the terms of the contract of bailment by sub-contracting. However, the defendant was not entitled to damages against the third party because the latter, though a bailee, had not, in the circumstances, been negligent.

478. *Learoyd Bros & Co.* v *Pope & Sons* [1966] 2 Ll. Rep. 142

The plaintiffs entered into an agreement with a carrier for the transport of their goods. The carrier sub-contracted the work to the defendants, who were also a firm of carriers, though the plaintiffs had no notice of this arrangement. The lorry was stolen while the defendants' driver was in the wharf office upon arrival at London Docks, and the carrier with whom the plaintiffs had contracted paid some of the plaintiff's loss and the plaintiffs now sued the defendants for the balance. *Held* – that the defendants were bailees to the plaintiffs, notwithstanding the absence of any contract between them, and that the defendants' driver was negligent in leaving the lorry unattended and therefore the defendants were liable for the plaintiff's loss.

BAILMENT: ACTIONS AGAINST BAILEES FOR NON-DELIVERY: DEFENCE OF SUPERIOR TITLES

479. *Rogers, Sons & Co.* v *Lambert & Co.* [1891] 1 Q.B. 318

The plaintiffs had purchased copper from the defendants but did not take delivery of it and left it with the defendants as warehousemen. The plaintiffs then resold the copper to a third person. Some time later the plaintiffs asked for delivery of the copper from the defendants but the defendants refused to deliver on the grounds that the plaintiffs no longer had a title to it. *Held* – this was no defence to an action of detinue. The defendants must show that they were defending the action on behalf, and with the authority of the true owner.

CO-OWNERSHIP: SEVERANCE OF JOINT TENANCY

480. *Re Draper's Conveyance* [1967] 3 All E.R. 853

In 1951 a house was conveyed to a husband and wife in fee simple as joint tenants at law *and* of the proceeds of the trust for sale. In November 1965, the wife was granted a decree *nisi* of divorce and this was made absolute in March 1966. In February 1966, she applied by summons under s. 17 of the Married Women's Property Act, 1882, for an order that the house be sold and in her affidavit asked that the proceeds of sale be distributed equally between her husband and herself. The court made such an order in May 1966, and in August 1966, a further order was made under the Act of 1882 that the former husband give up possession of the house. In spite of the order the former husband remained in possession until January 1967, when a writ of possession was executed. Four days later he died without having made a will. The former wife now applied to the court to determine whether she held the proceeds of any sale absolutely (which would have been the case if she and her former husband had been joint tenants at his death) or for herself and the deceased's estate as tenants in common in equal shares (which would have been the case if there had been severance). *Held* – severance of a joint tenancy in a matrimonial home may be effected by the wife's issue of a summons under s. 17 of the Married Women's Property Act, 1882, and her affidavit in support. The affidavit had stated the former wife's wish for severance and had operated accordingly. Therefore she held any proceeds of sale as trustee for herself and the estate of her former husband as tenants in common in equal shares.

LEASEHOLD: LEASES AND LICENCES DISTINGUISHED

481. *Shell-Mex and B.P. Ltd* v *Manchester Garages Ltd* [1971] 1 All E.R. 841

The plaintiffs by an agreement contained in a document called a licence let the defendants into occupation of a petrol filling station for one year. The parties had some disagreements during this time and at the end of the year the plaintiffs asked the defendants to leave. The defendants refused claiming that the agreement gave them a business tenancy protected by the Landlord and Tenant Act, 1954, Part II, which deal with the method of terminating business tenancies. This method had not been followed by the plaintiffs. *Held* – by the Court of Appeal – that it was open to parties to an agreement to decide whether that agreement should constitute a lease or a licence but the fact that it was called a licence was not conclusive. However, in this case it was a licence because the plaintiffs retained, under the agreement, the right to visit the premises whenever they liked and to exercise general control over the layout, decoration and equipment of the filling station. These rights were inconsistent with the grant of a tenancy.

LEASEHOLD: EXCLUSIVE POSSESSION OF LAND NOT NECESSARILY A TENANCY IN SPITE OF AGREEMENT

482. *Binions* v *Evans* [1972] 2 All E.R. 70

Mr Evans was employed as a chauffeur by the Tredegar Estate which owned a number of houses. His father and grandfather had also worked for the estate. Mr Evans died in 1965 and the trustees of the estate allowed Mrs Evans to continue to reside in a cottage which belonged to the estate, free of rent and rates. In 1968 the trustees made a formal agreement with Mrs Evans, the defendant in this case, who was then aged 76. The agreement purported to create a tenancy at will in order to provide her with a temporary home for the rest of her life free of rent without any rights to assign, sub-let or part with possession. Two years later the trustees sold the cottage and other properties to Mr and Mrs Binions, the plaintiffs, expressly subject to the tenancy of Mrs Evans and because of that tenancy the trustees accepted a lower price. A copy of the trustees' agreement with Mrs Evans was given to the purchasers. Shortly afterwards the purchasers tried to evict Mrs Evans on the ground that her tenancy, being at will, was liable to determination at any time. She refused to vacate and the court was asked to decide whether her occupation was in the nature of a tenancy at will or a mere licence. *Held* – by the Court of Appeal – that the interest of the defendant was not a tenancy at will although it had been so described in the agreement. When the trustees created a right in her favour to live in the cottage for the rest of her life it could not be a tenancy at will liable to be terminated at any time. It was therefore a mere licence though Equity would not permit the plaintiffs to revoke it as long as the defendant was not in breach of the licence. The plaintiffs held on a constructive trust to give effect to the agreement with Mrs Evans.

LEASEHOLDS: EFFECT IN EQUITY OF AGREEMENT FOR A LEASE OTHER THAN BY DEED: PART PERFORMANCE: LIABILITY OF LANDLORD FOR LATENT DEFECTS

483. *Walsh* v *Lonsdale* (1882) 21 Ch.D. 9

The defendant agreed in writing to grant a seven years' lease of a mill to the plaintiff at a rent payable one year in advance. The plaintiff entered into possession without any formal lease having been granted, and he paid his rent quarterly and not in advance. Subsequently the defendant demanded a year's rent in advance, and as the plaintiff refused to pay, the defendant distrained on his property. At common law the plaintiff was a tenant from year to year because no formal lease had been granted, and as such his rent was not payable in advance. The plaintiff argued that the legal remedy of distress was not available to the defendant. *Held* – as the agreement was one of which the court could grant specific performance, and as Equity regarded as done that which ought to be done, the plaintiff held on the same terms as if a lease had been granted. Therefore the distress was valid.

LEASEHOLDS: IMPLIED COVENANTS: INAPPLICABLE TO LATENT DEFECTS

484. *O'Brien* v *Robinson* [1973] 1 All E.R. 583

The plaintiff was the tenant of a flat to which s. 32 of the Housing Act, 1961 (giving an implied covenant to repair) applied. In 1965 the plaintiff had complained about stamping on the ceiling above, but it was found that the landlord was not given notice that the ceiling was defective. In 1968 the ceiling fell and the plaintiff was injured. *Held* – by the House of Lords – that the defendant landlord was not liable for breach of covenant.

> COMMENT
> In *Sheldon* v *West Bromwich Corporation* (1973) 25 P. & C.R. 360, the Court of Appeal held the defendant landlords liable where a water tank in a council house had remained discoloured for some considerable time to the knowledge of the Council. The tank burst and the Council were in breach of their implied convenant under s. 32 of the Housing Act, 1961, to keep the installation for the supply of water in repair. The discolouration of the tank, which the Council knew about, meant that this was not a latent defect.

EASEMENTS: CANNOT EXIST 'IN GROSS' BUT ONLY WITH REFERENCE TO THE HOLDING OF LAND

485. *Hill* v *Tupper* (1863) H. & C. 121

Hill was the lessee of land on the bank of a canal. The land and the canal were owned by the lessor, and Hill was granted the sole and exclusive right of putting pleasure boats on the canal. Later Tupper, without authority, put rival pleasure boats on the canal. Hill now sued Tupper for the breach of a so-called easement granted by the owner of the canal. *Held* – the right to put pleasure boats on the canal was not an interest in property which the law could recogise as attaching to the land. It was in the nature of a contractual licence which could not be enforced against the whole world. Tupper could have been sued by the owner of the canal, or by Hill, as lessee, if he had also been granted a lease of the canal.

EASEMENTS: RIGHT MUST BE DEFINITE ENOUGH TO FORM SUBJECT OF GRANT

486. *Bass* v *Gregory* (1890) 25 Q.B.D. 481

The plaintiffs were the owners of a public house in Nottingham, and the defendant was the owner of some cottages and a yard adjoining the plaintiffs' premises. The plaintiffs claimed to be entitled, by user as of right, to have the cellar of their public house ventilated by means of a hole or shaft cut from the cellar to an old well situated in the yard occupied by the defendant. The plaintiffs claimed an injunction to prevent the defendant from continuing to block the passage of air from the well. *Held* – the right having been established, an injunction would be granted because the access of air to the premises came through a strictly defined channel, and it was possible to establish it as an easement.

> COMMENT
> In *Bryant* v *Lefever* (1879) 4 C.P.D. 172, the plaintiff and defendant occupied adjoining premises, and the plaintiff's complaint was that the defendant, in rebuilding his house, carried up the building beyond its former height and so checked the access of the draught of air to the plaintiff's chimneys. The Court of Appeal held that the right claimed could not exist at law, because it was an attempt to claim special rights over the general current of air which is common to all mankind.

EASEMENTS: NOT NECESSARILY NEGATIVE

487. *Crow* v *Wood* [1970] 3 All E.R. 425

This case arose out of damage done on a farm in Yorkshire by sheep which strayed on to it from an adjoining moor. The owner of the sheep, who was the owner of another farm adjoining the moor, raised, as a defence against an action for trespass, an obligation on the plaintiff to fence her own property to keep the sheep out. It was *held* – by the Court of Appeal – that a duty to fence existed as an easement and that it had passed under s. 62 of the Law of Property Act, 1925, when the defendant purchased his farm, even though his conveyance and previous ones had made no reference to the obligation of other farmers to keep up their fences. However, the right was appurtenant to the land sold and therefore became an easement in favour of the defendant and his successors in title.

EASEMENTS: CATEGORIES CAPABLE OF LIMITED EXPANSION

488. *Re Ellenborough Park* [1956] Ch. 131

Ellenborough Park was a piece of open land near the seafront at Weston-super-Mare. The park and the surrounding land was jointly owned by two persons. The surrounding land was sold for building purposes, and the conveyances granted an easement over the park in favour of the owners of the houses. The owners of the houses undertook to be responsible for some of the maintenance, and the owners of the park agreed not to erect dwelling houses or buildings, other than ornamental buildings, on the park. The park was later sold, and the question of the rights of the owners or occupiers of the houses fronting on to the park to enforce their rights over the park arose.

It was contended that the rights created by the conveyances were not enforceable, because they did not conform to the essential qualities of an easement, and that they gave a right of perambulation which was not a right legally capable of creation. *Held* – the rights granted to the owners of the houses were enforceable as a legal easement.

489. *Phipps* v *Pears* [1964] 2 All E.R. 35

A Mr Field owned two houses, Nos 14 and 16 Market Street, Warwick, and in 1930 he demolished No. 16 and built a new house with a wall adjacent to the existing wall of No. 14. In 1962, No. 14 was demolished uder an order of Warwick Corporation, leaving exposed the wall of No. 16. This wall had never been pointed; indeed it could not have been because it was built hard up against the wall of No. 14. It was not, therefore, weatherproof and the rain got in and froze during the winter causing cracks in the wall. The plaintiff claimed for damage done, claiming an *easement of protection*. It was *held* by the Court of Appeal that there is no such easement. There is a right of support in appropriate cases, No. 16 did not depend on No. 14 for support; the walls, though adjoining, were independent. Lord Denning, M.R., said in the course of his judgment:

> A right to protection from the weather (if it exists) is entirely negative. It is a right to stop your neighbour pulling down his house. Seeing that it is a negative easement, it must be looked at with caution because the law had been very chary of creating any new negative easements. . . . If we were to stop a man pulling down his house, we would put a brake on desirable improvement. If it exposes your house to the weather, that is your misfortune. It is not wrong on his part. . . . The only way for an owner to protect himself is by getting a covenant from his neighbour that he will not pull down his house. . . . Such a covenant would be binding in contract; and it would be enforceable on any successor who took with notice of it, but it would not be binding on one who took without notice.

490. *Grigsby* v *Melville* [1962] 1 W.L.R. 1355

A Mr Holroyd owned two adjoining properties, consisting of a cottage and a shop which had recently been occupied in single occupation by a butcher. Beneath the drawing room of the cottage there was a cellar, the only practical means of access to which was by way of steps from the shop which the butcher had used for storing brine in connection with the business of the shop. In 1962, Holroyd conveyed the cottage to Natinvil Builders Ltd, the predecessor in title of the plaintiff in this case. The conveyance accepted 'such rights and easements or quasi-rights and quasi-easements as may be enjoyed in connection with the . . . adjoining property'. A month later Holroyd conveyed the shop to a Mrs Melville. Mrs Melville, who was a veterinary surgeon, began to use the cellar for storage. The plaintiff acquired the cottage in 1969 but did not realise the situation until 1971 when she heard hammering beneath her drawing room floor. She sought an injunction to prevent Mrs Melville from trespassing there. The defendants claimed that the cellar was excluded from the property conveyed, or alternatively that they enjoyed an easement of storage there equivalent to an estate in fee simple. *Held* – by Brightman,

J. – (a) that the cellar, though not the steps leading to it, formed part of the property conveyed to Natinvil Builders Ltd; (b) that the exclusive right of use claimed was so extensive as probably to be incapable of constituting an easement at law; (c) that in any event on the facts use of the cellar for the purposes of the shop had ceased when the properties were divided, it had never been contemplated that such would be the case in the future and the defendants' claim to an easement failed. This decision was confirmed by the Court of Appeal [1973] 3 All E.R. 455.

EASEMENTS: ACQUISITION: EFFECT OF S. 62, LAW OF PROPERTY ACT, 1925

491. *Ward* v *Kirkland* [1966] 1 All E.R. 609

The wall of a cottage could be repaired only from the yard of the adjoining farm. Before 1928 both properties belonged to a rector and the tenant of the cottage repaired the wall without seeking the permission of the tenant of the farm. In that year the cottage was conveyed to a predecessor in the title of Ward and in 1942 Mrs Kirkland became the tenant of the farm. From 1942 to 1954 work to the wall was done with her permission as tenant and in 1958 she bought the farm. In October 1958, Ward did not make entry on to the farmyard to maintain the wall because Mrs Kirkland would not let him enter as of right. In this action, which was brought to determine, amongst other things, whether Ward was entitled to enter the farmyard to maintain the wall and for an injunction to prevent interference with drains running from the cottage through the farmyard, it was *held* – by Ungoed Thomas, J. –

(a) assuming such a right could exist as an easement it would not be defeated on the ground that it would amount to possession or joint possession of the defendant's property;

(b) although such a right was not created by implication because it was not 'continuous and apparent' yet the advantage having in fact been enjoyed it was transformed into an easement by s. 62 of the Law of Property Act, 1925;

(c) no easement had arisen by prescription because permission had been given between 1942 and 1958;

(d) permission having been granted by the rector to Ward to lay drains from the cottage through the farmyard and Ward having incurred expense in so doing it was assumed that the permission was of indefinite duration and an injunction would be granted to prevent interference with the drains by Mrs Kirkland.

EASEMENTS: ACQUISITION: BY PRESCRIPTION

492. *Tehidy Minerals* v *Norman* [1971] 2 W.L.R. 711

The owners of a number of farms adjoining a down claimed to be entitled to grazing rights over it. The facts of the case were as follows –

(a) the farms and the downs had been owned by one person until 19 Jan 1920;

(*b*) the down had been requisitioned by the government on 6 October 1941;

(*c*) during the period of requisition the owners of surrounding farms had grazed cattle on the down by arrangement with the Ministry concerned;

(*d*) on 31 December 1960, the down was derequisitioned and the association of farmers which had made the arrangements with the Ministry entered into a further arrangement with the owner of the down for the maintenance of certain fences erected by the Ministry and grazing continued but under the control of the association of farmers.

On appeal from a decision of the County Court judge that the farmers were entitled to grazing rights over the down it was *held* by the Court of Appeal that –

(*a*) as there had been no enjoyment of the grazing rights between October 1941 and 31 December 1960, except by permission of the Ministry, the farmers could not claim 30 years' prescription which the Act of 1832 required for a profit to be established by user as of right;

(*b*) despite the extreme unreality of such a presumption it must be presumed that a modern grant, since lost, had been made of grazing rights at some time between 19 January 1920, and 6 October 1921, i.e. 20 years before the requisition; this presumption could not be rebutted by evidence that no such grant had been made but only by evidence – of which there was none – that it could not have been made;

(*c*) the period of 20 years applied to profits as well as to easements for the purposes of the law of lost modern grant although the Act of 1832 provided for different periods in the two cases;

(*d*) only the demonstration of a fixed intention never at any time to assert the right or to attempt to transmit it to anyone else could amount to an abandonment of an easement or profit, thus the acquiescence by the farmers in the arrangement under which the association controlled the grazing for a period of time did not amount to abandonment.

493. *Diment* v *N.H. Foot* [1974] 2 All E.R. 785

A vehicular way across the plaintiff's field was claimed and had been used by the defendant from time to time without dispute between 1936 and 1967. The plaintiff, although the registered owner of the field throughout that period, had never farmed the land herself but had had tenants and during much of the time had lived far away or abroad. Until 1967 the plaintiff knew nothing of the way claimed. *Held* – by Pennycuick, V.-C. – (*a*) the law of prescription rested upon acquiescence for which knowledge was essential; (*b*) the plaintiff had no actual knowledge and knowledge was not to be imputed to her either (*i*) because there was a gateway from the field to a parcel of the defendant's land to which there was no vehicular access; there were a number of possible explanations for it; or (*ii*) because the plaintiff had not shown that her agents did not have knowledge of the use of the way or the means of knowledge. The presumption that long use was known to the owner was rebuttable and in the present case had been rebutted. It did not extend to the knowledge of agents. The burden of proving such knowledge or means of knowledge lay on the defendant and there was no evidence of either in the present case.

COMMENT

Even if the owner of the servient tenement (A) *knows* of the use the right will not arise if A *permits* the use. Thus in *Goldsmith* v *Burrow Construction Co. Ltd*, *The Times*, 31 July 1987, the plaintiffs had used a path over the defendants' land for over 20 years. However, the defendants had a gate across the path and locked it from time to time. The Court of Appeal held that no easement had come into being. The plaintiffs' use depended on the permission of the defendants. They had shown this by locking the gate from time to time.

494. *Davis* v *Whitby* [1974] 1 All E.R. 806

The plaintiff and his predecessors in title had enjoyed a right of way over the defendant's land by a certain route for 15 years and then by another route, substituted by agreement, for a further 18 years. On appeal by the defendant to the Court of Appeal against the decision that a right of way over the substituted route had been established by prescription, it was *held* – by the Court of Appeal – that the appeal should be dismissed. 'When you have a way used for some time and then afterwards a substituted way is used for the same purpose, both uses being as of right, with the apparent consent or acquiescence of those concerned, then the original way and the substituted way should be considered as one.' *Per* Lord Denning, M.R.

RESTRICTIVE COVENANTS: THERE MUST BE LAND WHICH CAN BENEFIT

495. *Kelly* v *Barrett* [1924] 2 Ch. 379

The owner of an estate in Hampstead developed it for building purposes. He made a new road through it, and sold plots of land along the road to a building firm who erected dwelling houses on the land. The purchasers undertook that the houses built should be used as private dwelling houses only. The owner of the estate did not retain any land except the road, which was afterwards taken over and vested in the local authority. A subsequent purchaser of two adjoining houses carried on a nursing and maternity home in them. The tenant for life under the former estate owner's will and one of the original purchasers claimed an injunction to restrain the defendant's activities. *Held* – no injunction could be granted because the agreement was not a valid building scheme, and the vendor's successor did not retain any interest capable of being affected by the restrictions.

MORTGAGES: EQUITY OF REDEMPTION: RESTRAINT ON REDEMPTION ENFORCED IF PARTIES AT ARM'S LENGTH: COLLECTIVE TRANSACTIONS

496. *Knightsbridge Estates Trust Ltd.* v *Byrne* [1939] Ch. 441

The plaintiffs were the owners of a large freehold estate close to Knightsbridge. This estate was mortgaged to a friendly society for a sum of money, which, together with interest, was to be repaid over a period of 40 years in 80 half-yearly instalments. The company wished to redeem the mortgage before the expiration of the term, because it was possible for them to borrow elsewhere at a lower rate of interest. *Held* – the company was not entitled to redeem the mortage before the end of the 40 years because, in the circumstances, the postponement of the right was not unreasonable, since the parties were men of business and equal in bargaining power. A postponement of the right of redemption is not by itself a clog on the equity of redemption; much depends upon the circumstances. Further, the postponement did not offend the rule against perpetuities, which did not apply to mortgages.

497. *Noakes* v *Rice* [1902] A.C. 24

The appellants were a brewery company and the respondent wished to become the purchaser of a public house owned by the company. The respondent borrowed money from the company in order to effect the purchase, and agreed that the company should have the exclusive right to supply the premises with malt liquors during the period of the mortgage and afterwards, whether any money was or was not owed. The respondent subsequently gave notice to the company that he was prepared to pay off the money secured by the mortgage, if the company would release him from the above-mentioned contract. This was refused and the respondent asked the court for relief. *Held* – the covenant was invalid as a clog on the equity of redemption in so far as it purported to tie the public house after payment of the principal money and interest due on the security.

498. *Kreglinger* v *New Patagonia Meat and Cold Storage Co.* [1914] A.C. 25

The appellants were a firm of merchants and wool brokers. The respondents carried on the business of preserving and canning meat, and of boiling down carcasses of sheep and other animals. The appellants advanced money to the respondents, the loan being secured by a charge over all the respondents' property. The appellants agreed not to demand repayment for five years, but the respondents could repay the debt at an earlier period on giving notice. The agreement also contained a provision that the respondents should not sell sheepskins to anyone but the appellants for five years from the date of the agreement, so long as the appellants were willing to purchase the same at an agreed price. The loan was paid off before the expiration of the five years. *Held* – the option of purchasing the sheepskins was not terminated on repayment, but continued for the period of five years. The option was a collateral contract which was not a mortgage and in no way affected the right to redeem the property.

499. *Cityland and Property (Holdings) Ltd* v *Dabrah* [1967] 2 All E.R. 639

A first mortgage of £2900 was granted by the seller of property to a purchaser and was expressed to be repayable in the sum of £4553 for which the property was charged. The £4553 was to be repaid over six years by equal monthly instalments and there was no mention in the mortgage of any interest. The whole of the balance of the £4553 became payable if the borrower defaulted and for this reason Goff, J. *held* that the premium amounting to £1653 was an unreasonable collateral advantage and therefore void under the principle in *Kreglinger*'s case, 1914 (above). The Judge having disallowed the premium was prepared to allow interest at 7% on a day-to-day basis which he thought to be somewhat more than market rates, but in fact it was below market rates. The premium was an interest computation of 9½%, non-reducing over six years and if it had been expressed as such in the mortgage it would appear that the court could not have set it aside since the court can only set aside unreasonable collateral advantages. However, in regard to interest rates, it appears that 'equity does not reform mortage transactions because they are unreasonable', Greene, M.R. in *Knightsbridge Estates Trust Ltd v Byrne*, 1939, see p. 823. But this case was not cited to Goff, J. It would seem that for the future interest in mortgages should be expressed as such and not disguised as premium.

REMEDIES OF LEGAL MORTGAGEE: TAKING POSSESSION: DUTY OF MORTGAGEE

500. *White v City of London Brewery Co.* (1889) 42 Ch.D. 237

The plaintiff had a lease of a public house in Canning Town, and he mortgaged it to the defendants to secure a loan of £900 with interest. One year later, no interest having been paid since the date of the mortgage, the defendants entered into possession of the public house. They later let the premises on a tenancy determinable at three months' notice under which the tenant was to take all his beer from the defendants. Eventually the lease was sold by the defendants, and the plaintiff asked the defendants to account and pay him what should be found due. *Held* – the defendants must account to the plaintiff for the increased rent they might have received if they had let the public house without the restrictive condition regarding the sale of the defendants' beer, since a 'free house' would produce more rent than a 'tied house'.

CHARGES AND ENCUMBRANCES OVER LAND: SPOUSE'S RIGHT OF OCCUPATION

501. *Williams & Glynn's Bank Ltd v Boland* [1980] 3 W.L.R. 138

A husband and wife lived together in the matrimonial home which was owned by the husband and subject to a mortgage with the bank. The husband was registered as the owner for the purposes of the Land Registration Act, 1925. It appeared that his wife had made a substantial contribution of money towards buying the house and that she had, accordingly, equitable rights in it. The husband failed to keep up the mortgage repayments and the bank asked the court for a possession order over the house with a view to selling it. The wife raised objection to the possession order, claiming that her rights and occupation gave her an 'overriding interest' in the home which overrode the bank's claim to possession under s. 70(1) of the Land Registration Act, 1925. Section 70 includes as an overriding interest: 'The rights of every person in actual occupation . . .'. The bank argued that the wife was not in actual occupation and also relied on s. 3 of the 1925 Act which provides that equitable rights, such as the wife had, were not an overriding interest but a 'minor interest' and it was admitted that these would not have defeated the bank's claim. However, the House of Lords *held* that the wife's objection must be sustained and refused the bank an order for possession. The wife was in actual possession just as much as her husband and the fact that he was in occupation did not prejudice her right to be regarded as in occupation also. If she had not been in occupation apparently her equitable rights would have been a minor interest, but since she was also in occupation this fact converted them into an overriding interest.

COMMENT
(i) This decision has caused considerable concern to banks and building societies since the occupation of most houses is shared either with a wife or a mistress or relatives who have made some financial contribution towards the purchase.

(ii) The response of lending institutions has been to ask a spouse (or other relatives who may have rights of occupation) to sign a Deed of Postponement as s. 6(3) of the Matrimonial Homes Act, 1983 allows. This postpones the interest of an occupier to that of the lender.

(iii) Following the decision of the House of Lords in *Abbey National* v *Cann* [1990] 2 W.L.R. 832 the person claiming an overriding interest must occupy the property from the time of purchase. Persons who take up occupation later are excluded. For example John buys a house with some help from his mother in terms of finance. Some time after the purchase John's mother comes to live with John. John's mother cannot claim an overriding interest against a person who e.g. lent John money on mortgage to complete the purchase.

MORTGAGES OF CHATTELS: BILLS OF SALE

502. *Koppel* v *Koppel* [1966] 2 All E.R. 187

Mr Koppel, who was estranged from his wife, invited a Mrs Wide to come to his house and look after his children on a permanent basis. Mrs Wide agreed to do so provided that Mr Koppel transferred the contents of his house to her to compensate for giving up her own home and disposing of her furniture. The transfer was recorded in writing. Later Mrs Koppel sought to levy execution on the contents of the house for her unpaid maintenance which amounted to £114. In proceedings resulting from Mrs Wide's claim to the property, the Registrar of the County Court held that the written transfer of the property to Mrs Wide was void as an unregistered bill of sale. *Held* – by the Court of Appeal – that the contents of the house were not in Mr

Koppel's 'possession or apparent possession' within s. 8 of the Bills of Sale Act, 1878, because –

(a) Mr Koppel had transferred possession to Mrs Wide under the document which was an absolute bill of sale;

(b) the grantor of the bill, Mr Koppel, had therefore neither possession nor apparent possession. He did not have apparent possession because Mrs Wide was living in the house with him and both had apparent possession of the property, not merely Mr Koppel;

(c) Mrs Wide was therefore entitled to the property.

LIEN: INNKEEPERS

503. *Robins & Co.* v *Gray* [1895] 2 Q.B. 501

The plaintiffs dealt in sewing machines and employed a traveller to sell the machines on commission. The plaintiffs' traveller put up at the defendant's inn in April 1894, and stayed there until the end of July 1894. During this time the plaintiffs sent the traveller machines to sell in the neighbourhood. At the end of July, the traveller owed the defendant £4 for board and lodgings, and he failed to pay. The defendant detained certain of the goods sent by the plaintiffs to their traveller, claiming he had a lien on them for the amount of the debt due to him although the defendant knew that the goods were the property of the plaintiffs. *Held* – the defendant was entitled to a lien on the plaintiff's property for the traveller's debt.

LIEN: SOLICITORS

504. *Caldwell* v *Sumpters* [1971] 3 All E.R. 892

The defendants, who were a firm of solicitors, were holding the title deeds to property recently sold by a former client, Mrs Caldwell, who had not paid their charges. They voluntarily released the deeds to another firm which had been instructed to take their place to complete the sale, stating that they did so on the understanding that the deeds would be held to their order until Mrs Caldwell had paid. The second firm of solicitors kept the deeds and refused to accept that understanding. *Held* – by Megarry, J. – Sumpters' lien was lost when they voluntarily parted with possession of the deeds and could not be retained by a one-sided reservation of the kind made. If the agreement of the second firm of solicitors had been obtained the lien would have been preserved as it would also if Sumpters had lost possession by trickery or other wrongdoing. The second firm was under no obligation to accept the reservation or to return the deeds.

COMMENT
The decision of Megarry, J. was reversed by the Court of Appeal (*Caldwell* v *Sumpters* [1972] 1 All E.R. 567), the court holding that Sumpters' lien was not lost when they parted with the deeds since –

(*a*) possession was given up on the clear and express understanding that the deeds were to be held to Sumpters' order; and

(*b*) solicitors as officers of the court could not be allowed to take advantage of this sort of situation even out of regard for any duty owed to a client.

LIEN: POWER OF COURT TO ORDER SALE

505. *Larner* v *Fawcett* [1950] 2 All E.R. 727

The defendant owned a racehorse and made an agreement with a Mr Davis under which it was agreed that Davis would train and race the filly and receive half of any prize money she might win. Davis, unknown to the defendant, agreed to let Larner have the animal to train. Larner did so, and when his charges had reached £125, he discoverd that Fawcett was the true owner. Larner, being unable to recover the cost of training and feeding the filly from Davis, who had no funds, now applied to the court for an order for sale. Fawcett was brought in as defendant. *Held* – by the Court of Appeal – that Larner had a common-law lien for his charges, and although such a lien does not carry with it a power of sale, the power given in the Rules of the Supreme Court to make an order for sale was appropriate here, particularly since the filly was eating a great quantity of food. Fawcett had not made any attempt to get his property back but had clothed Davis with all the indicia of ownership. An order for sale would therefore be made unless Fawcett paid into court the amount of Larner's charges by a given date.

Criminal law – general principles

CRIME AND CIVIL WRONGS DISTINGUISHED: THE BURDEN OF PROOF IN CRIME

506. *Woolmington* v *Director of Public Prosecutions* [1935] A.C. 462

W had been charged with the murder of his wife. He had, on his own admission, shot her but said in his defence that the gun had gone off accidentally. The judge told the jury that so long as the prosecution had shown that the accused had caused the death malice was presumed and that the accused must prove that the killing was an accident. The jury convicted W who appealed to what was then the Court of Criminal Appeal where his conviction was upheld. However, on appeal to the House of Lords his conviction was quashed.

Throughout the web of English Criminal Law one golden thread is always to be seen that it is the duty of the prosecution to prove the prisoner's guilt subject to what I have already said as to the defence of insanity and subject also to any statutory exceptions. If, at the end of and on the whole of the case, there is a reasonable doubt created by the evidence given by either the prosecution or the prisoner, as to whether the prisoner killed the deceased with a malicious intention, the prosecution has not made out the case and the prisoner is entitled to an acquittal. (*Per* Viscount Sankey, L.C.)

NULLA POENA SINE LEGE: THE COMMON LAW OFFENCE OF CONSPIRACY

507. *Shaw* v *Director of Public Prosecutions* [1961] 2 All E.R. 446

S published a booklet called *The Ladies Directory* which contained names and addresses of prostitutes. The entries gave telephone numbers and indicated that they were offering their services for sexual intercourse and some of them for the practice of sexual perversions. S was convicted of conspiracy to corrupt public morals and his appeal eventually reached the House of Lords. His appeal was dismissed and his conviction affirmed. However, Lord Reid, in a strong dissenting judgment, said that in his view there was no such general offence known to the law as conspiracy to corrupt public morals and the court in convicting S of it was creating a new crime on the basis of public mischief which is the criminal law equivalent of public policy. He thought that if the courts had stopped creating new heads of public policy in, for example, the civil law of contract, then they certainly should refrain from doing so in criminal law.

THE REQUIREMENT OF CAUSATION

508. *R* v *Towers* (1874) 12 Cox 530

T had attacked a woman by hitting her and pulling her hair. She was holding a baby of four and a half months. The woman screamed loudly and the baby went black in the face. From then on it had convulsions and died some six months later. Prior to the attack the child had been healthy. T was charged with the murder of the child. He was found not guilty. There was doubt whether a child of such an age could be frightened in the way suggested. The jury took the view that the act of the accused in assaulting the woman was unconnected with the child's death.

509. *R* v *Hayward* (1908) 21 Cox 692

H came home one night in a violent state of excitement. He had said previously that he was going to 'give his wife something' when she returned home. When she arrived there were sounds of quarrelling and soon afterwards the wife ran out of the house followed by H. The wife fell on to the road and H kicked her on her left arm. She died and the medical examination showed that the kick was not the cause of her death. She was in good health apart from thymus gland trouble, on which the medical evidence was that a person with such a condition might die from the combined effects of fright, strong emotion and physical exertion. H was charged with manslaughter at Maidstone Assizes and found guilty. Ridley, J. said that the abnormal state of the deceased's health did not affect the question whether the prisoner knew or did not know of it, if it were proved to the satisfaction of the jury that the death was accelerated by the prisoner's illegal act.

510. *R v Curley* (1909) 2 Cr. App. R. 109

C had been indicted for murder but convicted of manslaughter. He had been heard quarrelling with the woman he lived with. She had been heard shouting in her bedroom. She had said: 'Let me out', 'murder' and 'police'. C was heard to go into her room and the window was opened. The woman later jumped from it. C told a police officer: 'I ran at her to hit her. I didn't quite touch her. Out she jumped.' The court held the accused to be guilty. The jumping out of the window was contributed to by C's unlawful act.

511. *R v Smith* [1959] 2 All E.R. 193

The facts were that the victim of a barrack-room brawl who was stabbed twice with a bayonet was dropped twice by those trying to get him to hospital and given artificial resperation when he got there although he was wounded in the lungs so that this was not advisable. Nevertheless these events were held not to break the chain of causation. However, it must be said that the events in this case, including the death of Private Creed who was the victim, all occurred within a period of some two hours.

> A man is stabbed in the back, his lung is pierced and haemorrhage results; two hours later he dies of haemorrhage from that wound; in the interval there is no time for a careful examination, and the treatment given turns in the light of subsequent knowledge to have been inappropriate and, indeed, harmful. In those circumstances no reasonable jury or court could, properly directed, in our view possibly come to any other conclusion than that the death resulted from the original wound. Accordingly the court dismisses this appeal. (*Per* Lord Parker, C.J.)

> COMMENT
> (i) This case seems to illustrate the usual approach of the court to these causation problems. The case of R v *Jordan* (1956) 40 Cr. App. R. 152 seems to be the odd man out. In that case J had stabbed the victim but it was established that the wound was healing satisfactorily. The victim died after being given an antibiotic to which he was allergic and over-large quantities of liquid intravenously. J's conviction for murder was quashed on appeal.
> (ii) In *R v Malcherek* [1981] 2 All E.R. 422 two victims of assault were placed on life-support machines and in both cases doctors having diagnosed brain death discontinued treatment and disconnected the life-support system. It was held by the Court of Appeal that the original injuries were the continuing operating cause of death. The discontinuance of the treatment did not break the chain of causation between the initial injury and the death.
> (iii) More recently in *R v Cheshire* [1991] 3 All E.R. 670, following an argument in a fish and chip shop C shot his victim in the leg and stomach, seriously wounding him. The victim died two months later following

complications after surgery to assist his breathing. C was convicted of murder even though there was evidence that the leg and stomach wounds were no longer life threatening at the time of his death. The Court of Appeal in dismissing an appeal said that the acts of the accused need not be the sole or even the main cause of the death it being sufficient that his acts contributed significantly to the death.

ACTUS REUS: LIABILITY FOR FAILING TO ACT

512. *R* v *Instan* [1893] 1 Q.B. 450

Instan lived with her 73-year-old aunt. The aunt seemed to be in reasonable health until shortly before her death. During the twelve days prior to her death she had gangrene in her leg and could not look after herself or summon help. That she was in this condition was a matter known only to Instan. It appeared that she had not given her aunt any food nor had she tried to obtain medical or nursing aid. Following the death of her aunt she was accused of manslaughter and convicted. The Court for Crown Cases Reserved (as it then was) affirmed the conviction.

> The prisoner was under a moral obligation to the deceased from which arose a legal duty towards her; that legal duty the prisoner has wilfully and deliberately left unperformed, with the consequence that there has been an acceleration of the death of the deceased owing to the non-performance of that legal duty. It is unnecessary to say more than that upon the evidence this conviction was most properly arrived at. (*Per* Lord Coleridge, C.J.)

ACTUS REUS: CONTRACTUAL DUTIES

513. *R* v *Pittwood* (1902) 19 T.L.R. 37

Pittwood was a gatekeeper employed by a railway company. It was his duty to keep the gate shut whenever a train was passing between 7 am and 7pm. The gate was left open on one afternoon and a hay cart which was crossing the line was struck by a train. A man was killed and another seriously injured. The defendant was charged with manslaughter and was found guilty. Wright, J. said there was gross and criminal negligence as the man was paid to keep the gate shut and protect the public. He added that a man might incur ciminal liability from a duty arising out of contract.

ACTUS REUS: PREVIOUS CONDUCT

514. *R* v *Miller* [1983] 1 All E.R. 978

The defendant who was a vagrant squatter fell asleep after lighting a cigarette. He woke to find his mattress smouldering. He left it as it was and went to sleep in another room. There was a fire and the defendant was charged with arson. He was found guilty and his appeal was dismissed by the House of

Lords. His conviction was justified either on the basis that there was a continuous act or on the basis that the defendant owed a responsibility to try to undo the harm which he had unwittingly done. The House of Lords felt that this latter basis which is really an omission would be easier to explain to juries.

MENS REA: MOTIVE: IRRELEVANT TO GUILT OR INNOCENCE

515. *Chandler* v *Director of Public Prosecutions* [1962] 3 All E.R. 142

In this case the defendants impeded the operation of an airfield at Wethersfield, Essex. Their object was to demonstrate against nuclear armament.

> In the result, I am of opinion that if a person's direct purpose in approaching or entering is to cause obstruction or interference, and such obstruction or interference is found to be a prejudice to the defence dispositions of the State, an offence is thereby committed, and his indirect purposes or his motives in bringing about the obstruction or interference do not alter the nature or content of his offence. . . . Is a man guilty of an offence, it was asked, if he rushed on to an airfield intending to stop an airplane taking off because he knows that a time-bomb has been concealed on board? I should say that he is not, for the reason that his direct purpose is not to bring about an obstruction but to prevent a disaster, the obstruction that he causes being merely a means of securing that end. (*Per* Lord Radcliffe.)

MENS REA: STATES OF MIND

516. *R* v *Maloney* [1985] 1 All E.R. 1025

The defendant and his stepfather had been drinking heavily at a family party. They were part of a united and happy family. In the early hours of the morning they began larking about with shotguns. There was a challenge as to who could load fastest. The defendant was able to load faster and pointed his gun at the stepfather, saying: 'You've lost'. The stepfather said: 'You wouldn't dare pull the trigger'. The defendant did just that and killed the stepfather. It appeared that he did not aim the gun but just pulled the trigger. He was later charged with murder but that was reduced to manslaughter by the House of Lords. The House of Lords felt that the circumstances did not show that the defendant had the intent to kill or cause really serious injury and nothing else would do for the crime of murder. Lord Bridge said:

> I do not believe it is necessary for the judge to do more than invite the jury to consider two questions. First, was death or really serious injury . . . a natural consequence of the defendant's voluntary act? Second, did the defendant *foresee* that consequence as being a natural consequence of his act? The jury should then be told that if they answer Yes to both questions it is a proper inference for them to draw that he intended that consequence.

COMMENT

(i) The matter came before the House of Lords again in *R v Hancock* [1986] 1 All E.R. 641. The defendant, Hancock, and another defendant, Shankland, had thrown items including lumps of concrete from a road-bridge in order to block the road so that a taxi carrying a working miner would not be able to get through and so to some extent break the miners' strike. A lump of concrete hit the windscreen of the taxi and the driver was killed. The defendants were charged with murder and eventually appealed to the House of Lords from their conviction for that offence. Lord Scarman and the other Law Lords were critical of Lord Bridge's approach. His Moloney guidelines required a reference to *probability*. Lord Scarman said: 'They also require an explanation that the greater the probability of a consequence the more likely it is that the consequence was foreseen and that if that consequence was foreseen the greater the probability is that the consequence was also intended.' But he went on to stress that the jury should not be told more except that any inference of intent was for them to make on all the evidence and circumstances of the case and not merely on the judge's directions.

(ii) The matter came before the Court of Appeal again in *R v Nedrick* [1986] 3 All E.R. 1 where the defendant poured paraffin through the letter box of the house of a woman against whom he had a grudge. He set light to it and the woman's child died in the resulting fire. He was convicted of murder the judge bringing in the *Hancock* approach, i.e. that if the defendant knew that it was *highly probable* that his act would result in serious bodily injury to someone inside the house he was guilty of murder. The defendant had admitted starting the fire but said he wanted just to frighten the woman and not to kill anyone. The Court of Appeal substituted a verdict of manslaughter and the Lord Chief Justice had to lay down guidelines as to the direction of juries in this sort of case. He said that the jury should be told that they are not entitled to infer the necessary intent for murder unless they feel sure that death or serious bodily harm was a virtually certain result of the defendant's action (barring some unforeseen intervention) and that the defendant appreciated that fact. This is where the matter currently lies. To equate foresight with intention is now ruled out.

RECKLESSNESS: A SUBJECTIVE TEST

517. *R v Cunningham* [1957] 2 All E.R. 412

C was convicted of unlawfully and maliciously causing to be taken by Sarah Wade a certain noxious thing, namely, coal gas, so as to endanger her life contrary to s. 23 of the Offences Against the Person Act, 1861. C had gone into an empty house and torn away the gas meter in the cellar in order to take the money it contained with the intention of stealing that money. However, coal gas poured out of the pipe he had fractured and percolated into the house next door where it almost asphyxiated the occupant, Sarah Wade. C appealed and his appeal was allowed.

We think it is incorrect to say that the word 'malicious' in a statutory offence merely means wicked. We think the judge was, in effect, telling the jury that if they were satisfied that the appellant acted wickedly – and he had clearly acted wickedly in stealing the gas meter and its contents – they ought to find that he had acted maliciously in causing the gas to be taken by Mrs Wade so as thereby to endanger her life.

In our view it should have been left to the jury to decide whether, even if the appellant did not intend to injure Mrs Wade, he foresaw that the removal of the gas meter might cause injury to someone but nevertheless removed it. We are unable to say that a reasonable jury, properly directed as to the meaning of the word 'maliciously' in the context of s. 23, would without doubt have convicted.

In these circumstances this court has no alternative but to allow the appeal and quash the conviction. (*Per* Byrne, J.)

RECKLESSNESS: AN OBJECTIVE TEST

518. *R* v *Caldwell* [1981] 1 All E.R. 961

Caldwell had done some work for the owner of an hotel and had a quarrel with the owner about this. He got drunk and set fire to the hotel in revenge. The fire was discovered and put out before any serious damage was done and none of the guests was injured. He was charged with criminal damage under the Criminal Damage Act, 1971. It was held incidentally that his self-induced intoxication was no defence but on the issue of recklessness which was part of the charge, i.e. intentionally or recklessly destroying or damaging property, the House of Lords eventually dismissed his appeal. A person is reckless they said if (a) he does an act which in fact creates an obvious risk that property will be destroyed or damaged; and (b) when he does the act he either has not given any thought to the possibility of there being any such risk or has recognised that there was some risk involved and has nonetheless gone on to do it. The test is objective because a person is guilty if he has given no thought at all to the risk when in effect a reasonable person would have done so.

COMMENT
(i) Although the above words were spoken in regard to recklessness for the statutory offence of criminal damage it seems from the general tenor of the judgments in *Caldwell* and another decision of the House of Lords *R* v *Lawrence* [1981] 1 All E.R. 974 (a case of reckless driving) that they might apply to the construction of criminal statutes generally and to recklessness at common law.

(ii) The principles laid down in *Caldwell* and *Lawrence* were applied in another case of criminal damage, i.e. *Elliott* v *C* [1983] 2 All E.R. 1005. C was a 14-year-old schoolgirl who was charged with criminal damage under s. 1(1) of the Criminal Damage Act, 1971 (destroying or damaging property without danger to life). She spent one entire night awake and wandering around. She had entered a toolshed and there poured white spirit on to a carpet and set light to it, destroying the shed. The magistrates found that she did not appreciate just how inflammable the spirit was, and having regard to her extreme state of tiredness, that she did not in fact give any real thought to the risk of fire. In consequence the magistrate acquitted her. It was held by a Divisional Court of Queen's Bench, allowing the prosecutor's appeal, that the correct test was whether a reasonably prudent man would realise the dangers of fire in the circumstances, even though the particular accused might not appreciate them. In other words, it would appear that the test at criminal law has become an objective test of recklessness, at least where criminal damage is concerned.

(iii) The objective standard approach was followed in *R* v *Sangha*, *The Times*, 2 February 1988 where the Court of Appeal said that the test was 'would an ordinary prudent bystander have perceived an obvious risk that property of value and life would be endangered?' Sangha was convicted of *arson* under s. 1(2) of the Criminal Damage Act, 1971 because life was endangered.

TRANSFERRED MALICE

519. *R* v *Latimer* (1886) 17 Q.B.D. 359

Latimer was quarrelling with A in a pub. He struck out at A with his belt. The blow glanced off A and severely injured another person, B. Latimer was found guilty of unlawful and malicious wounding. Lord Coleridge, C.J. said:

We are of opinion that this conviction must be sustained. It is common knowledge that a man who has an unlawful and malicious intent against another, and, in attempting to carry it out, injures a third person, is guilty of what the law deems malice against the person injured, because the offender is doing an unlawful act, and has what the judges call general malice, and that is enough . . . .

520. *R* v *Pembliton* (1874) L.R. 2 C.C.R. 119

Pembliton was fighting outside a pub. He picked up a stone and threw it at the persons he had been fighting. It missed them but broke a window in the pub. It was held that the evidence did not support a conviction for unlawful and malicious damage under the Malicious Damage Act, 1861. There was no intention to break the window.

MENS REA: MUST COINCIDE WITH *ACTUS REUS*

521. *Thabo Meli* v *R* [1954] 1 All E.R. 373

In this case the accused persons planned to kill the victim in a hut and thereafter to roll his body over a cliff so that it would appear that he had died an accidental death. The victim was made unconscious in the hut by the attack and thinking him to be dead, the accused persons rolled him over a cliff. There was evidence that the victim was not in fact killed in the hut but that he died on account of exposure at the bottom of the cliff.

The point of law which was raised in this case can be simply stated. It is said that two acts were necessary and were separable; first, the attack in the hut; and, secondly, the placing of the body outside afterwards. It is said that, while the first act was accompanied by *mens rea*, it was not the cause of death; but that the second act, while it was the cause of death, was not accompanied by *mens rea*; and on that ground it is said that the accused are not guilty of any crime, except perhaps culpable homicide.

It appears to their Lordships impossible to divide up what was really one transaction in this way. There is no doubt that the accused set out to do all these acts in order to achieve their plan and as part of their plan; and it is much too refined a ground of judgment to say that, because they were under a misapprehension at one stage and thought that their guilty purpose had been achieved before in fact it was achieved, therefore they are to escape the penalties of the law. . . . (*Per* Lord Reid.)

The appeal of the accused persons was therefore dismissed.

COMMENT

It is not necessary for the acts to be part of a preconceived plan which went wrong. In *R v Le Brun* [1991] 3 W.L.R. 653 a husband had an argument with his wife in the street and hit her without intending serious harm. She fell unconscious on the highway and he then tried to move her on to the pavement. Her head hit the pavement and she fractured her skull and died. He was acquitted of murder and convicted of manslaughter and his appeal against that conviction was dismissed. The unlawful application of force and the eventual act causing death were part of the same sequence of events. They did not have to be part of a preconceived plan as in *Thabo Meli*.

MENS REA: STATUTORY OFFENCES

522. *Sweet v Parsley* [1969] 1 All E.R. 347

The magistrates had convicted Sweet of being concerned in the management of premises which were used for the purpose of smoking cannabis or cannabis resin, contrary to s. 5(b) of the Dangerous Drugs Act, 1965. The evidence showed that she had no knowledge whatever that the house was being used for the purpose of smoking cannabis or cannabis resin. She visited the premises only occasionally to collect letters and rent and though sometimes she stayed overnight, generally she did not. Section 5 of the 1965 Act provides 'if a person (a) being the occupier of any premises, permits those premises to be used for the purpose of smoking cannabis or cannabis resin or of dealing in cannabis or cannabis resin (whether by sale or otherwise); or (b) is concerned in the management of any premises used for any purposes aforesaid; he shall be guilty of an offence under the Act'. The House of Lords, after holding that in spite of the wording of the Act *mens rea* must be implied, found that there was no *mens rea* in the accused in this case and that therefore her appeal should be allowed and her conviction quashed.

523. *R* v *Tolson* (1889) 23 Q.B.D. 168

Martha Ann Tolson, who married in September 1880, was deserted by her husband in December 1881. She made enquiries and learned from his elder brother that he had been lost at sea in a ship bound for America which sank with all hands. Believing herself to be a widow, she went quite openly through a ceremony of marriage on 10 January 1887, with Y who was fully aware of the circumstances. It was held that she could not be convicted of bigamy under s. 57 of the Offences Against the Person Act, 1861, even though the opening part of that section says: 'Whosoever, being married, shall marry any other person during the life of the former husband or wife . . . shall be guilty of a felony. . .'. She had no *mens rea*. The object of Parliament was not to treat the marriage of widows as an act to be if possible prevented as presumably immoral. Mrs Tolson's conduct was not immoral but perfectly natural and legitimate. A statute may relate to such subject matter and may be so framed as to make an act criminal whether there has been any intention to break the law or not. In other cases a more reasonable construction requires the implication into the statute that a guilty mind is required.

524. *Alphacell* v *Woodward* [1972] 2 All E.R. 475

A Ltd was the owner of paper-making mills. In the course of manufacture effluent passed into two tanks on the banks of a river. Pumps were used to remove the effluent from the tanks but it was inevitable that if the pumps failed the effluent would enter the river and pollute it. As a result of foliage blocking the pump inlets such an overflow occurred and A Ltd was charged with 'causing' polluting matter to enter the river under s. 2(1) of the Rivers (Prevention of Pollution) Act, 1951. It was *held* – by the House of Lords – that they were guilty of that offence even though they had not been negligent. The intervening act of a trespass or Act of God would have been a defence but there was no such trespass or Act of God in this case.

525. *Cundy* v *Le Cocq* (1884) 13 Q.B.D. 207

C, who was a licensed victualler, sold liquor to a person who was drunk though C did not know this. He was, however, convicted of unlawfully selling liquor to a drunken person contrary to s. 13 of the Licensing Act, 1872, which provided that: 'If any licensed person . . . sells any intoxicating liquor to a drunken person he shall be liable to a penalty. . . '. It was *held* – by Stephen, J. – that knowledge of the condition of the person to whom the liquor was sold was not necessary to constitute the offence.

> Against this view we have had quoted the maxim that in every criminal offence there must be a guilty mind; but I do not think that maxim has so wide an application as it is sometimes considered to have. In old time, and as applicable to the common law or to earlier statutes, the maxim may have been of general application; but a difference has arisen owing to the greater precision of modern statutes. It is impossible now, . . . to apply the maxim generally to all statutes, and the substance of all the reported cases is that it is necessary to look at the object of each Act that is under

consideration to see whether and how far knowledge is of the essence of the offence created. Here, as I have already pointed out, the object of this part of the Act is to prevent the sale of intoxicating liquor to drunken persons, and it is perfectly natural to carry that out by throwing on the publican the responsibility of determining whether the person supplied comes within that category. I think, therefore, the conviction was right and must be affirmed.

526. *Gaumont British Distributors Ltd* v *Henry* [1939] 2 K.B. 717

Gaumont British were charged under s. l(a) of the Dramatic and Musical Performers' Protection Act, 1925, with knowingly making a record of a musical work without the written consent of the performers. No consent had actually been given but GB said, and it was accepted, that they had never thought about the question of consent. Nevertheless GB were convicted and appealed. The appeal was allowed.

> I desire to add emphatically that no colour can be obtained from this case, or from the argument, or from any opinion which is present to my mind, that the wholesome and fundamental principle *ignorantia juris neminem excusat* is in any degree to be modified or departed from. . . . I should be very sorry, directly or indirectly, even to appear to add any colour to the suggestion, if it were made – as I do not think it is – that in circumstances of this kind ignorance of the law might excuse. The way in which the topic of the appellants' knowledge came in was solely with reference to the words 'knowingly makes any record without the consent in writing of the performers', and the contention was a contention of fact. According to a true view of the evidence of fact in this case it was incorrect to say that the appellants did knowingly without the consent in writing of the performers that which was done. (*Per* Lord Hewart, C.J.)

527. *R* v *Lowe* [1973] 1 All E.R. 805

Lowe was charged under s. 1 of the Children and Young Persons Act of 1933 as being a person who had the charge of a child and wilfully neglected it in a manner likely to cause it unnecessary suffering or injury to health. L's case was that the child's critical condition arose after he had told the woman he was living with, who was the child's mother, to take the child to a doctor and that she later falsely told him that she had done so. He was convicted and appealed.

> It did not matter what he ought to have realised as the possible consequences of his failure to call a doctor; the sole question was whether his failure to do so was deliberate and thereby occasioned the results referred to in s. 1(1) of the Act of 1933. We are quite satisfied that the conviction on count 2 was justified both on the law and the facts . . .'. (*Per* Phillimore, L.J.)

> COMMENT
> There was another count on the indictment for manslaughter but this was allowed on appeal.

528. *Somerset* v *Wade* [1894] 1 Q.B. 574

Wade was charged with permitting drunkenness under s. 13 of the Licensing Act, 1872 which provides that if any licensed person permits drunkenness, or any violence, quarrelsome or riotous conduct to take place on his premises or sells any intoxicating liquor to any drunken person, he commits an offence. A drunken woman was actually found on Wade's premises but it was accepted that Wade did not know that she was drunk. The charge having been dismissed the prosecutor appealed. The appeal of the prosecutor failed and Wade was not convicted.

> But the word 'suffers' is not distinguishable from 'permits', which is the word used in s. 13, the section now before us. In a case where the defendant does not know that the person who was on his premises was in fact drunk, he cannot be said to permit drunkenness. In the present case the justices have found that the respondent did not know that the woman was drunk and there was evidence to support that finding. (*Per* Mathew, J.)

> COMMENT
> (i) As regards the word 'malicious' it will be recalled that in *R* v *Cunningham*, 1957, *mens rea* was required for an offence which had to be committed 'maliciously'. (See further p. 833.)
> (ii) In the *Somerset* case Mathew, J. was prepared to say that the word 'suffers' was the same as 'permits', i.e. a word requiring *mens rea* in the accused.

VICARIOUS LIABILITY IN CRIME

529. *Griffiths* v *Studebakers Ltd* [1924] 1 K.B. 102

Studebakers were holders of a limited trade licence and were charged with having used on a public road a motor car carrying more than two persons in addition to the driver, which was an offence under the Road Vehicles (Trade Licences) Regulations, 1922. At the time of the alleged offence the car was being driven by a servant of the respondents. He was in the course of his employment because he was giving a trial run to prospective purchasers of the car but by carrying more that two passengers he was infringing the express orders of his employers. The employers were convicted and appealed to the Divisional Court.

> It would be fantastic to suppose that a manufacturer, whether a limited company, a firm, or an individual, would, even if he could, always show cars to prospective purchasers himself; and it would defeat the scheme of this legislation if it were open to an employer, whether a company, or a firm, or an individual, to say that although the car was being used under the limited licence in contravention of the conditions upon which it was granted: 'My hand was not the hand that drove the car.' On these facts there ought to have been a conviction of the respondents and also the driver as aider and abettor. (*Per* Lord Hewart, C.J.)

Thus the conviction of Studebakers was affirmed by the Divisional Court.

530. *James and Son Ltd v Smee* [1955] 1 Q.B. 78

Under the Motor Vehicles (Construction and Use) Regulations in force at the time the alleged offence occurred the braking system of a vehicle or trailer used on the road had to be in efficient working order and further anyone who used or caused or permitted to be used on the road a motor vehicle or trailer where the braking system was not in efficient working order was liable to a fine. James and Son Ltd sent out in the charge of their employee a lorry and trailer the braking system of which was in efficient working order. However, during the course of his rounds the employee had to disconnect the braking system of the trailer and forgot to connect it up again. James and Son were convicted of 'permitting to be used' the trailer in contravention of the regulation then in force. However, their appeal was allowed by the Divisional Court.

> In other words, it is said that in committing the offence of the user in contravention of the regulations he at the same time made his master guilty of the offence of permitting such user. In our opinion this contention is highly artificial and divorced from reality. We prefer the view that before the company can be held guilty of permitting a user in contravention of the regulations it must be proved that some person for whose criminal acts the company is responsible permitted as opposed to committed the offence. There was no such evidence in the present case. (*Per* Parker, J.)

531. *Vane v Yiannopoullos* [1965] A.C. 486

Section 22(1) of the Licensing Act, 1961, which was relevant in this case provided 'If – (a) the holder of a Justices' on-licence knowingly sells or supplies intoxicating liquor to persons to whom he is not permitted by the conditions of the licence to sell or supply it . . . he shall be guilty of an offence'. Y was the licensee of a restaurant and had been granted a Justices' on-licence subject to a condition that intoxicating liquor was to be sold only to those who ordered meals. He employed a waitress and he instructed her to serve drinks only to customers who ordered meals but on one occasion whilst Y was in another part of the restaurant the waitress did serve drinks to two youths who had not in fact ordered a meal. Y did not know of that sale. He was charged with knowingly selling intoxicating liquor on the premises to persons to whom he was not permitted to sell contrary to s. 22(1)(a) of the Act. The magistrates dismissed the information and the prosecutor appealed eventually to the House of Lords. The appeal of the prosecutor was dismissed and there was therefore no conviction of Y.

> So far, however, as the present case is concerned, I feel no doubt that the decision of the Divisional Court was right. There was clearly no ['knowledge'] in the strict sense proved against the licensee: I agree also with the Lord Chief Justice that there was no sufficient evidence of such ['delegation'] on his part of his powers, duties and responsibilities to render him liable on that ground. I would therefore without hesitation dismiss the appeal. (*Per* Lord Evershed.)

532. *Ferguson* v *Weaving* [1951] 1 All E.R. 412

Section 4 of the Licensing Act, 1921, which was relevant in this case, made it an offence for any person, except during permitted hours, to consume intoxicating liquor on any licensed premises. In a large public house of which W was the manager customers were found consuming liquor outside the permitted hours and were convicted of an offence under the section. The evidence did not show that W knew that the liquor was being consumed. It had in fact been supplied to customers by waiters employed by her who had neglected to collect the glasses in time. A charge against W of aiding and abetting the customers' offence was dismissed and the prosecutor appealed. The appeal was dismissed. 'There can be no doubt that this court has more than once laid it down in clear terms that before a person can be convicted of aiding and abetting the commission of an offence he must at least know the essential matters which constitute the offence. . . .' (*Per* Lord Goddard, C.J.)

Criminal law – specific offences

MURDER

533. *R* v *Dyson* [1908] 2 K.B. 454

Dyson was charged with manslaughter it being alleged that injuries which he inflicted on his child in November 1906 had caused its death in March 1908. His conviction was quashed. Lord Alverstone, C.J. said: 'it is still undoubtedly the law of the land that no person can be convicted of manslaughter where the death does not occur within a year and a day after the injury was inflicted. . .'.

> COMMENT
> It should be noted that the 'year and a day rule' applies to all homicides but this case is obviously an authority also for murder. It is an ancient rule coming from the days when medical science could not be precise about causation but it nevertheless applies today.

VOLUNTARY MANSLAUGHTER: PROVOCATION

534. *R* v *Camplin* [1978] 2 All E.R. 168

Paul Camplin was 15 years of age. He went to the house of a Mr K who was in his fifties. While he was there K buggered him in spite of his resistance and after he had finished K laughed at him. Camplin then killed K by splitting his skull with a chapati pan. He pleaded provocation to reduce a charge of murder to manslaughter. In reaching a decision that he was provoked the House of Lords said his age must be taken into account. Lord Diplock said that if the jury think that the same power of self-control is not to be expected in an ordinary average or normal boy of 15 as in an older person the boy's age is relevant to his response. A conviction for manslaughter must stand.

535. *R v Johnson (Christopher)* [1989] 1 W.L.R. 740

Johnson killed his victim in a night club. His own behaviour had been unpleasant, resulting in a girl friend of the victim taunting Johnson calling him a 'white nigger' since he affected a West Indian accent at times. Johnson drew a knife and stabbed the victim because matters were getting more violent and Johnson said he feared that the victim was about to cut him with a glass. A verdict of manslaughter was substituted for one of murder by the Court of Appeal. Watkins, L.J. said that whether or not there were elements in Johnson's conduct which justified the conclusion that he started the trouble and induced others including the victim to act as they did the defence of provocation should nevertheless have been put to the jury and left to them. Since this had not been done the verdict of murder must be set aside.

536. *R v Thornton* (1991) 141 N.L.J. 1223

Mrs Thornton was married in 1988. She realised from the start that her husband was a heavy drinker and jealous and possessive. He was violent in the home assaulting Mrs Thornton. In May 1989 he committed a serious assault which led to charges being brought. In June of that year Mrs Thornton told a workmate that she was going to kill her husband. Later that month after a series of rows with her husband in which he called her a whore Mrs Thornton went to the kitchen to calm down. While in the kitchen she picked up a carving knife and sharpened it. She then went back to her husband who was lying on a sofa. She asked him to come to bed but he would not and said he would kill her when she was asleep. She said she would kill him first. He then suggested sarcastically that she should go ahead. She made a downward movement with the knife expecting he would ward it off but it entered his stomach and killed him. She was charged with and convicted of murder. Her appeal to the Court of Appeal was dismissed. It was held that since provocation can only be put forward as a defence to a charge of murder if it caused a sudden and temporary loss of self-control on the part of the defendant prolonged domestic violence does not of itself amount to provocation unless there is a sudden and temporary loss of self-control by the wife.

COMMENT
Although the decision is in some ways an unfortunate one which does not assist the postion of the battered wife there does in all honesty seem to have been a 'cooling-off' period while the wife was in the kitchen and actually sharpening the knife. Perhaps in cases such as this the cumulative effect of wife beating should be taken into account. In other words, there may be a slow wearing down of the wife's self-control.

DIMINISHED RESPONSIBILITY: USE OF ALCOHOL

537. *R v Tandy*, *The Times*, 23 December 1987

Linda Mary Tandy was an alcoholic who drank nine-tenths of a bottle of vodka over part of a day and then strangled her daugher aged eleven. They had had a good relationship over the years. She was convicted of murder. The defence of diminished responsibility was not available. Her drinking was not involuntary. She had bought the vodka on Monday but had not started to drink it until the Wednesday of the killing. Her first drink was not involuntary even if later drinking was. This amounted to voluntary drinking and could not amount to a disease of the mind as diminished responsibility required.

538. *R v Gittins* [1984] 3 All E.R. 252

Gittins killed his wife and raped and killed his step-daughter while suffering from depression *and* the effects of drinking and drugs. He was charged with murder and convicted. He then appealed to the Court of Appeal. His conviction for murder was reduced to manslaughter on the ground of diminished responsibility. The court was careful to point out that normally the taking of drink or drugs would not amount to diminished responsibility but where other elements were present, such as the mental state of depression in this case which might have been brought on by an extended period of drink and drugs, nevertheless it remained an abnormality of the mind whatever its source and, provided it existed, could be a ground for reducing murder to manslaughter on the grounds of diminished responsibility.

> COMMENT
> Presumably in the absence of a medically certified mental state of depression the defendant would not have had the defence of diminished responsibility merely because he was under the influence of drink and drugs at the time.

INVOLUNTARY MANSLAUGHTER

539. *R v Church* [1966] 1 Q.B. 59

Church had an argument with a woman and had a fight with her. She was knocked unconscious and, having failed to revive her, he threw her in a river. She was in fact alive at the time and died of drowning. He was convicted of manslaughter and appealed. The problem basically was that he had not killed her in the fight and he did not foresee the risk of death when he threw her in the river because he thought wrongly that she was already dead. Nevertheless his conviction for involuntary manslaughter was upheld. The court said that his act was unlawful in the sense that throwing a woman into a river deliberately is unlawful even if the defendant did not intend or foresee that death or serious bodily harm would result. Such an act at least created a risk of physical harm and that was enough.

> COMMENT
> The unlawful act must in general involve the infliction of *physical* as

distinct from *emotional* harm. Thus where in the course of robbing a petrol station the robbers so frighten the attendant that he dies from a heart attack of which neither he nor they knew he was at imminent risk there can be no conviction of manslaughter (see *R* v *Dawson* (1985) 81 Cr. App. R. 150).

STATUTORY OFFENCES AGAINST THE PERSON

540. *Director of Public Prosecutions* v *K* [1990] 1 All E.R. 331

K a 15-year-old schoolboy left a chemistry class to wash his hands following a spillage of acid. He took a test tube of the acid with him and while in the toilet he heard footsteps approaching and panicked. He poured the acid into a hot air drier. He then returned to his class intending to clean out the drier later. Before he could do so the next user of the drier was squirted in the face by the acid and scarred. K was charged under s. 47 of the Offences Against the Person Act, 1861. He was reckless in that he had given no thought to the risk of a subsequent use of the machine before he could clean it. *Caldwell* and *Lawrence* were applied. K was convicted.

> COMMENT
> In *R* v *Spratt* [1991] 1 W.L.R. 1073 the Court of Appeal doubted the above decision. Spratt fired an air pistol from the bedroom window of his flat. Two pellets struck a seven-year-old girl who was playing in the forecourt. He was charged under s. 47 of the 1861 Act. He pleaded guilty on legal advice because although he was unaware of the girl's presence he had given no thought to the risk of his action and was therefore *Caldwell* reckless. Nevertheless he appealed against conviction and the Court of Appeal said *Caldwell* recklessness was not enough for the s. 47 offence. The *mens rea* of every type of offence against the person under the 1861 Act involved intention or recklesness, i.e. taking the risk of harm ensuing *with forsight* that it might happen. *Caldwell* recklessness was not enough, and this even though s. 47 did not use the word 'malice'. The court in *DPP* v *K* had not been referred to *R* v *Cunningham*, 1957 (see p. 833) and the definition of recklessness there. The conviction was quashed. (See also *R* v *Parmenter*, 1991 at p. 845.)

541. *R* v *Martin* (1881) 8 Q.B.D. 54

Just before a theatrical performance came to an end M, intending to terrify people leaving the theatre, put out lights on the staircase which he knew a large number of people would use when leaving the theatre. He then placed an iron bar across an exit door. As a result of his actions several people were hurt as they tried to leave the theatre. M was convicted on a charge of unlawfully and maliciously inflicting grievous bodily harm under s. 20 of the Offences Against the Person Act, 1861. 'The prisoner . . . acted "unlawfully and maliciously", not that he had any personal malice against the particular individuals injured, but in the sense of doing an unlawful act calculated to injure, and by which others were in fact injured. The prisoner was most properly convicted'. (*Per* Lord Coleridge, C.J.)

COMMENT
This would appear to be an early formulation of *Cunningham* recklessness.

542. *R* v *Parmenter* [1991] 2 W.L.R. 408

Parmenter admitted injuring his baby son and was charged amongst other things with inflicting grievous bodily harm contrary to s. 20 of the Offences Against the Person Act, 1861. The Court of Appeal had eventually to decide upon the *mens rea* for the s. 20 offence and the s. 47 offence. They held as follows –

(a) That a direction to the jury on the intent necessary to found a conviction of unlawfully and maliciously inflicting grievous bodily harm contrary to s. 20 should indicate to the jury that it was necessary that the defendant actually foresaw that some physical harm to some other person would result from his act. A direction that it was sufficient that the defendant ought to or should have foreseen the physical harm was a misdirection.

(b) On the suggestion that Parmenter might be convicted on the lesser offence in s. 47 the Court of Appeal said no. The necessary *mens rea* for s. 47 was intention or subjective (or *Cunningham*) recklessness. Since the trial judge's direction had been objective in form Parmenter's conviction on s. 20 was quashed and a s. 47 offence could not be substituted.

R v *Spratt*, 1990 (see p. 844) was applied.

543. *R* v *Belfon* [1976] 3 All E.R. 46

Belfon attacked a man called Paul Horne with a razor causing him serious injury. He was charged under s. 18 of the Offences Against the Person Act, 1861. At his trial the judge directed the jury that intention or *Cunningham* recklessness as to the infliction of grievous bodily harm constituted the *mens rea* for an s. 18 offence. He was convicted and appealed to the Court of Appeal. His conviction was quashed and a conviction for unlawful wounding under s. 20 was substituted. The Court of Appeal laid it down that in directing a jury in relation to an offence under s. 18 the judge should direct the jury that what has to be proved is (a) the wounding; (b) that the wounding was deliberate and without justification; (c) that it was committed with intent to cause really serious bodily harm; and (d) that the test of intent is subjective.

SEXUAL OFFENCES: RAPE

544. *R* v *R* [1991] 4 All E.R. 482

A husband and wife were having matrimonial problems. The wife left her husband and went to live with her parents. She left a note at the matrimonial home saying she was going to petition for a divorce. Some three weeks later the husband forced his way into the house of his wife's parents who were out at the time and attempted to have sexual intercourse with his wife against her will. In the course of doing so he squeezed her neck and therefore assaulted her. He was tried amongst other things for attempted rape. His defence was that he could not in law commit rape or attempted rape upon his wife. Her consent was presumed. He was convicted, the trial judge following an existing rule that rape could take place if the wife had ceased, as in this case, to live with her husband. Nevertheless the husband appealed saying there could be no rape of a wife in the absence of a court order of divorce or separation or a separation agreement.

The House of Lords eventually heard the appeal. They decided that a husband could rape his wife if he had intercourse with her without her consent even if they were not divorced or separated but were co-habiting. It was unacceptable that by marriage a wife submits to sexual intercourse in all circumstances. The Sexual Offences (Amendment) Act, 1976 defines rape as having 'unlawful' intercourse with a woman without her consent but the word 'unlawful' is to be treated as mere surplusage and no longer meaning 'outside marriage' since it is clearly unlawful to have sexual intercourse with any woman without her consent.

COMMENT
It has of course always been possible and still is for a husband to be a secondary party to the rape of his wife by another if he encourages and assists that other to have intercourse with her without her consent and this is so even though the man who actually rapes her is acquitted because he believes the wife is consenting (*R* v *Cogan* [1975] 2 All E.R. 1059). A husband has always been liable to be convicted in law of the crime of buggery on his wife with or without her consent. The law which allows this between consenting adults in private applies only to buggery between men.

545. *R* v *Williams* [1923] 1 K.B. 340

Williams taught singing. He told a 16-year-old female pupil that if she had intercourse with him it would improve her voice. The girl allowed him to have intercourse with her and made no resistance. She believed what he said and in any case was not mature enough to know that he was having sexual intercourse with her. She did not know that that was what they were doing. He was convicted of rape. His appeal was dismissed. Lord Hewart, C.J. said: 'She was persuaded to consent to what he did . . . because she thought it was a surgical operation.' Therefore there was in effect no consent.

546. *Director of Public Prosecutions* v *Morgan* [1975] 2 All E.R. 347

Morgan and his three companions were members of the RAF. Following a drinking session Morgan took the three men home to have sexual intercourse with his wife. He told them she might resist because she was a bit 'kinky' and this was the only way she could get 'turned on'. When they got to Morgan's home Mrs Morgan was in bed asleep. She did not habitually sleep with her husband. She was frog-marched to another bedroom and laid on a double bed; each of her arms was held and her legs were held apart. All three men then had intercourse with her. When they had finished and left the room Morgan had intercourse with her himself. Mrs Morgan immediately left the house and went to a nearby hospital. She said she had done all she could to resist. The three men (not Morgan, who could not commit rape upon his wife in those days) were charged with rape and all four with aiding and abetting the rapes.

The case eventually got to the House of Lords where it was decided:

(a) The crime of rape was committed by having sexual intercourse with a woman with intent to do so without her consent or with reckless indifference as to whether she consented or not. The test of recklessness is subjective and not objective because if the defendant believes the woman is consenting that belief need not be based on *reasonable* grounds.

(b) There could have been no subjective belief in the circumstances of this case that Mrs Morgan was consenting and so the convictions for rape and aiding and abetting rape must stand.

COMMENT
(i) Section 1(1)(b) of the Sexual Offences (Amendment) Act, 1976 which now defines the *mens rea* for rape reflects this judgment.

(ii) It may be that the belief in the woman's consent need not be based on reasonable grounds but a jury is unlikely to acquit a man who says he believed the woman was consenting if the jury do not think he had reasonable grounds for his alleged belief.

Criminal law – age and responsibility: general defences

M'NAGHTEN RULES: DISEASE OF THE MIND

547. *R* v *Kemp* [1956] 3 All E.R. 249

The accused struck his wife with a hammer without, so he said, being conscious of doing so and was charged with causing grievous bodily harm. He was an elderly man of good character who suffered from arteriosclerosis. Medical opinions differed as to the precise effects of this disease on his mind. It was *held* that, whichever medical opinion was accepted, arteriosclerosis was a disease capable of affecting the mind, and was thus a disease of the mind within the M'Naghten Rules, whether or not it was recognised medically as a mental disease.

COMMENT
In *R* v *Sullivan* [1983] 2 All E.R. 673 the House of Lords held that the definition of insanity in *M'Naghten* could apply to a person suffering from epilepsy. Mr Sullivan admitted inflicting grievous bodily harm on a friend of his at a time when he was recovering from a minor epileptic

seizure. His defence was automatism which could have resulted in an acquittal (see further p. 553) but the judge ruled that the defence amounted to one of insanity which would, if successful, have led to Mr Sullivan's immediate detention in a special institution. Mr Sullivan changed his plea to guilty of occasioning actual bodily harm and was convicted and sentenced to probation with medical supervision.

Previously it had been thought that for *M'Naghten* to apply the mind had to be working but not as it should. It seems from this decision that *M'Naghten* applies even if, as in this case, the mind is not working at all.

548. *R v Hennessy* [1989] 1 W.L.R. 287

The defendant was charged with taking a motor vehicle without consent. He suffered from diabetes and had to take insulin every day. He had been having marital and employment problems causing stress and depression and he had not taken his insulin for two or three days before the incident. He claimed that as a result he did not know what he was doing and did not therefore have the necessary *mens rea*. The judge took the view that this was a disease of the mind and he was insane within the *M'Naghten* rules. The defendent changed his plea to guilty and then appealed against the insanity ruling. The Court of Appeal held that the hyperglycaemia caused by the lack of insulin was a disease of the mind within *M'Naghten*. The defence of automatism was not available. The defendant was insane. The trial judge's ruling was correct.

COMMENT
In *R* v *Burgess*, *The Times*, 28 March 1991 a man claimed to have been sleepwalking when he wounded a woman. He said he was suffering from non-insane automatism and lacked the necessary *mens rea* for the offence. The Court of Appeal held that he was insane and that an appeal by him against a verdict of not guilty by reason of insanity failed. He was suffering from insane automatism in spite of the transitory nature of the disorder.

549. *R v Clarke* [1972] 1 All E.R. 219

May Clarke was convicted of theft from the International Stores in Leicester. She had put certain items into her shopping bag and not into the wire basket provided by the store which she presented at the check-out. She suffered from diabetes but did not claim not to have taken her insulin. She had not entirely recovered from 'flu and on the Friday previous to the theft her husband had suffered a broken collar bone and she had become, she said, very depressed and forgetful. In her own words. 'Everything seemed to get on top of me.' She pleaded guilty rather than face a decision that she was not guilty by reason of insanity. She appealed against her conviction on the guilty plea. The Court of Appeal held that her conviction must be quashed. She had been wrongly advised by the assistant recorder that if she did not do so the insanity verdict would be appropriate. It would not have been. The *M'Naghten* rules relating to insanity do not apply to those who retain the powers of reasoning but who in moments of confusion or absent-mindedness fail to use those powers to the full.

550. *R* v *Windle* [1952] 2 Q.B. 826

The defendant gave his wife a large and fatal dose of aspirin. He was admittedly suffering from mental illness but he did admit he had administered the aspirin and said he supposed he would hang for it. His only defence was insanity. He was convicted, the trial judge having ruled that there was no evidence to support such a defence. The defence did not go to the jury. Windle appealed and his appeal failed. Lord Goddard, C.J. said:

> In the opinion of the court there is no doubt that in the *M'Naghten* rules 'wrong' means contrary to law and not 'wrong' according to the opinion of one man or a number of people on the question of whether a particular act might or might not be justified. In the present case it could not be challenged that the appellant knew that what he was doing was contrary to law, and that he realised what punishment the law provided for murder.

ACTUS REUS: AUTOMATISM

551. *Hill* v *Baxter* [1958] 1 All E.R. 42

The defendant had been charged with dangerous driving and failing to conform with a traffic sign under ss. 11 and 49(b) of the Road Traffic Act, 1930, respectively. He said in his defence that he had been unconscious at the time because a sudden illness had overtaken him. The magistrates accepted his defence and dismissed the charges and the prosecutor appealed. The appeal was allowed and the defendant therefore convicted.

> I agree that there may be cases where the circumstances are such that the accused could not really be said to be driving at all. Suppose he had a stroke or an epileptic fit, both instances of what may properly be called acts of God; he might well be in the driver's seat even with his hands on the wheel, but in such a state of unconsciousness that he could not be said to be driving. A blow from a stone or an attack by a swarm of bees I think introduces some conception akin to *novus actus interviens*. In this case, however, I am content to say that the evidence falls far short of what would justify a court holding that this man was in some automatous state. (*Per* Lord Goddard, C.J.)

552. *R* v *Quick* [1973] 3 All E.R. 347

Quick was a nurse employed at a mental hospital. He assaulted a patient and claimed that he could not remember doing so. He was a diabetic and had taken insulin as recommended by his doctor. He then had a small breakfast and no lunch. He had also been drinking before the assault took place. Medical evidence showed that at the time of the assault he was suffering from a deficiency of blood sugar following the insulin injection. The trial judge ruled that this state could only be relied on to support the defence of insanity. Quick changed his plea to guilty and then appealed against his conviction. The Court of Appeal held that the improper functioning of his mind had been caused by an external factor not a disease of the mind. The use of the insulin was that external factor. He was therefore entitled to have the defence of automatism put to the jury and since this had not been done his conviction must be quashed.

COMMENT

(i) All that the Court of Appeal was deciding in this case was that the defence of automatism could and should have been put to the jury after proper argument by counsel. The Court of Appeal does indicate that the defence may not have succeeded because the deficiency of blood sugar might very well have been regarded as self-induced. Those who take insulin should eat regularly afterwards. Quick did not. He had also been advised to take a lump of sugar if he felt an attack coming on. He had not done so. However, the conviction had to be quashed because the jury might have accepted the defence. It is important to know that it is available in these circumstances even though it is by no means certain that it will succeed.

(ii) In *Moses* v *Winder* [1980] Crim. L.R. 232 the defendant had been a diabetic for 20 years. He felt a diabetic attack developing and took a dose of sugar which usually postponed the attacks for about an hour. However, whilst driving home he drove his car on the wrong side of the road, colliding with an oncoming car. He stopped a few minutes later in a daze, examined his car and then drove a further half mile. It was held by a Divisional Court that the defendant was nevertheless guilty of driving without due care and attention. His defence of automatism did not succeed and would rarely succeed without medical evidence. The defendant had not taken sufficient precautions to deal with the threat of a diabetic coma.

553. *R* v *Lipman* [1969] 3 All E.R. 410

L was charged with murder of a girl but convicted of manslaughter. Both he and the girl had taken LSD together in her room and L said that while under the influence of the drug he had an illusion of being attacked by snakes and that he must have killed the girl during this time. The girl had received two severe blows on the head but the immediate cause of her death was asphyxia as a result of having part of a sheet pushed down her mouth. The Court of Appeal affirmed the conviction, saying that when the killing results from the unlawful act of the accused, no specific intent was to be proved to convict of manslaughter and mental states which are self-induced by drink or drugs are no defence to a charge of manslaughter.

DRUNKENNESS AND DRUGS

554. *Director of Public Prosecutions* v *Majewski* [1976] 2 All E.R. 142

There was a disturbance at the Bull public house in Basildon, Essex. Majewski attacked the landlord and two other persons. He also assaulted three police officers. He was charged with assault occasioning actual bodily harm. At his trial he said he did not know what he was doing by reason of drink and drugs.

The case eventually reached the House of Lords which ruled that unless the offence charged required a specific intent a drink/drugs defence was not applicable. Since the assaults charged did not require solely a specific intent (see p. 532) the defendant's submissions as to drink and drugs were no defence and his conviction must be upheld.

555. *R* v *Hardie* [1984] 3 All E.R. 848

Hardie lived with a woman at her flat. The relationship broke down and she insisted that he leave. He was upset and took several tablets of valium, a sedative drug, belonging to the woman. Some hours later he started a fire in the bedroom of the flat while the woman and her daugher were in the sitting room. He was charged with damaging property with intent to endanger life or being reckless as to whether life would be endangered (s. 1 (2), Criminal Damage Act, 1971). The trial judge said in answer to the defence of no *mens rea* that because the valium was voluntarily self-administered it could not negative *mens rea* and was no defence. Hardie was convicted and appealed. The Court of Appeal decided that although self-induced intoxication from alcohol or a dangerous drug was no defence to crimes involving recklessness because the taking of the alcohol or drugs was itself reckless a drug which was merely soporific was different. The jury should have been asked to consider what effect the valium might have had upon the defendant's ability to appreciate the risk. Since they had not been asked to do so the conviction must be quashed.

556. *R* v *O'Grady* [1987] 3 W.L.R. 321

O'Grady and his acquaintances were given to heavy drinking. On the day in question he had drunk at least eight flagons of cider. His companions, Brennan and McCloskey, who had been drinking with him went back to O'Grady's flat. During the night McCloskey attacked O'Grady and in the ensuing fight O'Grady punched McCloskey to death. He put forward self-defence. It seemed from the circumstances that McCloskey's attack was severe but not so severe as to warrant killing him in self-defence. O'Grady asked the court to acquit him because being drunk he had not appreciated the nature of McCloskey's attack. The Court of Appeal heard an appeal by O'Grady against his conviction at his trial of manslaughter. The appeal failed, the Court of Appeal ruling that so far as self-defence is concerned reliance cannot be placed on a mistake as to the nature of the attack induced by voluntary intoxication.

COMMENT
Much depends upon the wording of statutory offences. For example s. 5 of the Criminal Damage Act, 1971 requires that a person causing damage to property has a defence if he believed that the owner of the property would have consented to it. The Act says it is immaterial whether the belief is justified if it is honestly held. This means that the test as to belief is subjective. In addition the section does not go on to say 'if it is honestly held other than because of self-induced intoxication'.

In *Jaggard* v *Dickson* [1980] 3 All E.R. 716 a girl who was drunk broke into a house thinking it was a friend's house which he had said she could use as her own. It was an identical house in the same street but not her friend's. The girl was acquitted of criminal damage because the Divisional Court said if she honestly believed it was her friend's house then the defence in the Act was established even though the honest belief arose from drink. It is doubtful whether there will be much scope to extend this decision into other areas.

557. *Attorney-General for Northern Ireland* v *Gallagher* [1963] A.C. 349

G was convicted of murdering his wife. In his defence he pleaded insanity under the *M'Naghten* rules or, as an alternative, that he was too drunk at the time to form the necessary intent for murder so that he was only guilty of manslaughter. G had shown intention to kill his wife before taking the drink. The case eventually reached the House of Lords where Lord Denning gave a useful summary of the effect of drunkenness when he said.:

> 1. If a man is charged with an offence in which a specific intention is essential (as in murder, though not in manslaughter), then evidence of drunkenness, which renders him incapable of forming that intention is an answer. . . . 2. If a man by drinking brings on a distinct disease of the mind such as *delirium tremens*, so that he is temporarily insane within the M'Naghten Rules, that is to say, he does not at the time know what he is doing or that it is wrong, then he has a defence on the ground of insanity. . . .

However, G's original conviction for murder was upheld becasuse he did not fit the above categories. As Lord Denning said:

> My Lords, I think the law on this point should take a clear stand. If a man, whilst sane and sober, forms an intention to kill and makes preparation for it, knowing it is a wrong thing to do, and then gets himself drunk so as to give himself Dutch courage to do the killing, and whilst drunk carries out his intention, he cannot rely on this self-induced drunkenness as a defence to a charge of murder, nor even as reducing it to manslaughter.

558. *Ross* v *H.M. Advocate*, 1991 S.L.T. 564

This was a trial for attempted murder. The evidence was that on the day of the attempted murder the defendant had been drinking lager from a can. He did not know that five or six tablets of temazepam and a quantity of LSD had been squeezed into the can. The defendant drank the lager. Shortly afterwards the defendant started lunging about with a knife and screaming. He injured various people who were strangers to him. On a charge of attempted murder the defendant said that he had no self-control and therefore no *mens rea*. He was nevertheless convicted. He appealed and his appeal was allowed. He should be acquitted because his absence of self-control was not self-inflicted.

DURESS

559. *R v Gotts* [1991] 2 All E.R. 1

Ben Gotts was charged with the attempted murder of his mother. The mother had left the family home after arguments with the father and gone to a women's aid refuge with two of the younger children. One morning as the mother left the refuge to take one of the children to school Ben then aged 16 armed with a knife supplied by his father ran up behind her and stabbed her. He was charged with attempted murder and wounding with intent. He pleaded duress: that his father had ordered him to kill his mother. The Court of Appeal held that duress was not a defence to attempted murder and his appeal was dismissed. There was no verdict on the count relating to wounding with intent.

560. *R v Hudson* [1971] 2 All E.R. 244

Two girls aged 17 and 19 were the main witnesses for the prosecution on a charge in Manchester of wounding. At the trial they both failed to identify the defendant Wright. He was acquitted as a result of this. The girls were tried for perjury and put in the defence of duress. They had been approached by a group of men who threatened to 'cut them up' if they 'told on' Wright in court. They were nevertheless convicted and appealed. The appeal turned on the trial judge's direction to the jury that duress can only arise where there is a threat of death or serious personal injury at the moment when the crime is committed. The threat here was to do something in the future. The Court of Appeal said that their convictions must be quashed. Lord Parker, C.J. said that the threats in this case were none the less compelling because they could not be executed in the court room if they could be carried out on the streets of Salford the same night.

561. *R v Sharp (David)* [1987] 3 W.L.R. 1

David Sharp was involved in the armed robbery of a post office. He participated in the robbery. He was charged with aiding and abetting murder but he was in fact convicted of manslaughter. He claimed that he had not wished to go on with the robbery but had been forced to because a member of the gang to which he belonged which had masterminded the robbery had held a gun to his head to make him proceed. He appealed because the trial judge rejected the defence of duress. The Court of Appeal dismissed the appeal. The defence of duress was not available where, as here, a person had voluntarily and with knowledge of its nature joined a gang which he knew might put pressure on him to commit an offence.

562. *R v Shepherd* (1988) 86 Cr. App. R. 47

Shepherd and other persons entered retail premises and stole goods. He was charged with burglary. He said that he had participated willingly at first but later lost his nerve but stayed on because a member of the gang threatened him and his family with violence if he did not continue. The trial judge ruled that the defence of duress was not available because he had voluntarily participated in a criminal act. He appealed and the Court of

Appeal held that his conviction must be quashed. The defence of duress was available if at the time he joined the gang he did not contemplate that violence would be used against him if he did not continue to participate.

DURESS OF CIRCUMSTANCES

563. *R* v *Martin* [1989] 1 All E.R. 652

Mr Martin was found guilty of driving whilst disqualified. He appealed on the basis that his wife had suicidal tendencies, and that on the day in question his stepson had overslept and was bound to be late for work and, it was said, at risk of losing his job unless Mr Martin drove him to work. Mr Martin was disqualified from driving but his wife started screaming and beating her head against the wall and threatening suicide unless he drove the stepson to work which he then did. He was stopped and later prosecuted for driving whilst disqualified. His defence was necessity and the Court of Appeal accepted it in this case though referring to the situation as 'duress of circumstances'.

NECESSITY

564. *R* v *Dudley and Stephens* (1884) 14 Q.B.D. 273

A yacht was shipwrecked, and three men and a boy escaped in an open boat. They were adrift for eight days without food when the men killed the boy, who was by then very weak, in order to eat his body and keep themselves alive. They were rescued four days later by a passing ship. They were tried for, and convicted of, murder. It was held that there is no principle of law which entitles a man to take the life of an innocent person to save his own. In any case the death of the the men would not have been inevitable, but only probable. Where the offence committed is not a capital offence, the defence of necessity might result in a mitigation of sentence.

MISTAKE

565. *R* v *Kimber* [1983] 3 All E.R. 316

Kimber sexually assaulted a woman who was a patient in a mental hospital. He was charged with indecent assault. His defence was that he honestly believed that the woman consented. The woman had been diagnosed as schizophrenic. During the indecent act which involved the touching of her private parts she was mumbling all the time giving perhaps to a reasonable person evidence that she was a sick woman. Since the attack took place on the cricket ground near the hospital gardens it might have led a reasonable person to believe that the sickness was mental and throw doubt upon her consent. The Court of Appeal decided that it was enough if the mistake which Kimber made was to honestly believe that she consented. However, his conviction must stand because no reasonable jury properly instructed that an honest belief was sufficient as a defence could have believed that Kimber could or did honestly believe she consented in the circumstances of the case.

566. *R* v *Bailey* (1800) 168 E.R. 651

Bailey, who was the captain of a ship, fired at another ship on the high seas without any justification and wounded one of the sailors on that other ship. He was charged under an Act of Parliament which made such a shooting on the high seas triable and punishable in this country. The following extract from the judgment of the court is relevant:

> It was then insisted that the prisoner could not be found guilty of the offence with which he was charged, because the Act of 39 Geo. 3, c. 37 upon which . . . the prisoner was indicted at this Admiralty Sessions, . . . only received the Royal Assent on 10 May, 1799, and the fact charged in the indictment happened on 27 June in the same year when the prisoner could not know that any such Act existed (his ship the *Langley* being at the time upon the coast of Africa). Lord Eldon told the jury that he was of opinion that he was, in strict law, guilty within the statutes . . . though if the facts laid were proved, though he could not then know that the Act of 39 Geo. 3, c. 37 had passed, and that ignorance of that fact, could in no other wise affect the case, than that it might be the means of recommending him to a merciful consideration elsewhere should he be found guilty. . . .

COMMENT
At the next Admiralty Sessions Bailey was pardoned.

SELF-DEFENCE

567. *R* v *McInnes* [1971] 3 All E.R. 295

McInnes belonged to a group of youths called 'greasers'. There was a fight between a group of 'greasers' and another group of youths called 'skinheads'. It took place at Platt Fields, Manchester. A skinhead jumped on the defendant's back and his response was to stab the skinhead which caused his death. The defendant was convicted of murder. He appealed to the Court of Appeal on two main points.

(a) That the trial judge had said that in self-defence cases it was necessary for the defendant to have retreated as far as he could before using the force in self-defence; and

(b) That even if the force used was unreasonable as it clearly was in this case a jury could be directed to return a verdict of manslaughter.

On these points it was decided that it was not essential that the defendant should have retreated. Whether he did or not was merely one factor in deciding whether the defence of self-defence succeeded or not. Furthermore if the defence failed, as it did here, because of lack of reciprocity then it failed altogether. It was not possible for the jury to return a verdict of manslaughter. The defendant's conviction for murder must stand.

COMMENT

The fact that no retreat is merely a factor to be looked at in terms of a plea of self-defence was affirmed again in *R* v *Bird (Debbie)* [1985] 2 All E.R. 513, where following a house party the defendant hit the victim in the face with a glass after he slapped her while he was pinning her to the wall. She had not shown an unwillingness to fight but the Court of Appeal said this was not absolutely necessary. Incidentally the force used here was totally lacking in reciprocity but the defendant managed to satisfy the court that she did not know she had the glass in her hand and only intended to use her fist.

568. *Attorney-General's Reference (No. 2 of 1983)* [1984] 1 All E.R. 988

The defendant in this case had a shop in an area which had suffered riots and his store had been looted. He was in constant fear of further rioting. He boarded his shop up, bought fire extinguishers and made ten petrol bombs which he kept upstairs to be used to repel rioters. This was an offence under the Explosive Substances Act, 1883. He pleaded self-defence, the problem about that defence being that when he prepared the petrol bombs no attack was taking place. The Court of Appeal held on this point that the defence of self-defence was available to go to a jury at least. A person can make preparations for self-defence where there is an apprehension of imminent attack. The issue of reciprocity was not raised since this was not a trial as such although the defendant did say he did not intend to throw the bombs at people but to throw them on the pavement in front of his shop to keep the rioters away from it.

569. *R* v *Rose* (1884) 15 Cox C.C. 540

John Rose, who was a very powerful man, was killed by his son, a weakly young man aged 22 years. John Rose had frequently threatened to kill his wife, the young man's mother. On this occasion he violently assaulted her, threatened to cut her throat and said he was going to a bedroom to get a knife which the family knew he kept there. He came back with the knife and grabbed his wife and held her in a position which could have been preparatory to cutting her throat. The son got a gun and shot him dead. He was indicted for manslaughter. He was found not guilty. The judge said that homicide was excusable if the fatal blow (or shot in this case) was necessary for the preservation of the life of another.

COMMENT

This case was decided on common-law principles. Today it provides an example of the possible use of s. 3 of the Criminal law Act, 1967.

Glossary of commonly used legal words and phrases

accord and satisfaction A phrase used to indicate that a contract which has not been wholly performed is to be treated as discharged by agreement of the parties (*the accord*), this agreement being supported by consideration (*the satisfaction*).

agent A person who is employed by another (called *the principal*) to put that other into a contractual relationship with a third party.

bailment The transfer by one person to another of possession but not ownership of a tangible asset.

bill of exchange A form of credit under which a seller S who has sold goods to a buyer B will draw up a bill of exchange on B, the bill being payable (say) three months hence. If as is usual B accepts the bill, he will return it to S who may wait three months before presenting it to B for payment, or alternatively get a bank to pay him so that the bank will present the bill for payment at the end of three months. The price paid for the goods or by the bank for the bill will be adjusted to take into account interest during the waiting period of three months.

case stated An appeal from a Magistrates' Court to the Divisional Court of Queen's Bench on a point of criminal law. The magistrates state the facts and the Queen's Bench rules on the correctness or otherwise of the law applied by the magistrates.

caveat emptor 'Let the buyer take care' – this implies that the buyer should watch out for any defects in the goods he is buying since, in the absence of misrepresentation by the seller, he will bear the consequences of anything which he fails to notice.

chattel Personal property consisting of a tangible asset, e.g. a watch.

cheque Essentially, a bill of exchange but always drawn on a bank and payable on demand instead of a fixed or determinable future time.

chose in action An intangible asset such as a claim to money as where A owes money to B. In such a case, the debt is a chose in action. Other forms of property are also included such as copyright in a book.

conveyance A method by which property, in the main land, is transferred or the document by which this is done.

covenant A promise set out in a deed.

demise The grant of a lease of land. According to the context, it can also mean *death*.

devise A gift of real property by will.

estoppel A rule of evidence by which a party may be prevented from proving what is true because he has previously suggested that it was false and another party has relied on that. Thus A and B who are not partners are present together when A asks X for a loan. X knows B but not A. So A says 'Lend me the money, it will be repaid: B is my partner'. B remains silent and X lends A the money which A cannot repay. B is obliged to repay it since partners are jointly and severally liable for the debts of the firm, and B's silence estops him from denying that he is not A's partner.

ex parte An application in judicial proceedings which as an exception is heard in the absence of an opponent.

execution The carrying into effect of a Court order, e.g. for debt by the bailiffs taking the property of the defendant to sell by public auction in order to pay the plaintiff what the court has decided he is entitled to.

indictable offence A crime triable by jury either because the law requires it, as in the case of murder, or at the option of the defendant where the offence is triable either summarily or on indictment.

insurable interest The interest which an insured party must have in the subject matter of the policy.

intestate A person is said to die intestate when the death occurs without leaving a will.

laches Unjustifiable delay in bringing a claim to enforce an equitable right.

legacy A gift of personal property by will.

liquidation A process under which a corporate body such as a registered company is dissolved by an administrative procedure laid down by law.

negotiable instrument Personal property in the form of a document the rights in which can be transferred merely by delivering it to another person or by delivery following endorsement. The most common example is a cheque.

parol contract An agreement made by word of mouth.

personal representatives Executors and administrators being persons who deal with the estate of a deceased person.

pledge The giving-up of possession, but not ownership, of goods as security for the future payment of a debt or other obligation.

probate The official recognition by the Court that executors have authority to deal with the estate under the will of a dead person.

realty Freehold interest in land and buildings.

remainder An equitable interest which becomes effective in possession only when the estate of a previous owner expires. In a gift of property 'to A for life remainder to B', B's interest is in remainder and will become effective in possession on the death of A.

reversion If A owns the freehold of Greenacre and grants B a lease of (say) 25 years in Greenacre, the freehold will return to A or his estate if he is dead when the lease expires. Until then, A's interest in Greenacre is in reversion.

simple contract A contract made orally or in writing but not by deed.

specialty contract A contract made by deed.

surety A person who has given a guarantee or indemnity of a debt.

winding-up The liquidation or dissolution of a company.

General index

ACCORD AND SATISFACTION, 223, 411
ACTE CLAIR, 49
ADMINISTRATIVE INQUIRIES, 55
ADMINISTRATIVE TRIBUNALS—
advantages, 56
conciliation in employment, 363
Council, on tribunals, 56
disadvantages of, 57
Employment Appeal Tribunal, 54
generally, 54
industrial tribunals, 53
judicial control over tribunals, 59
legal aid, 57
legislation relating to, 56
other controls on decision making, 65
Social Security tribunals, 52
valuation and use of land tribunals, 53
ADOPTION—
effect of, 171
generally, 171
ADVERSE POSSESSION, 484
ADVERTISEMENTS—
as invitations to treat, 205
AGENCY, 186
generally, 186
ALIENS, 172, 378
ALIBI, 101
APPEAL—RIGHTS OF, 22
ARBITRATION—
contract arising from, 45
County Court in, 31
High Court in, 36
other arbitrations, 46
ARREST, 86, 418
ASSIGNMENT OF CHOSES IN ACTION—
act of parties by, 525
operation of law by, 414, 526
ATTACHMENT OF EARNINGS, 133

ATTORNEY-GENERAL, 79, 86
AUCTIONS, 204

BAIL, 88
BAILMENT—
bailee, delegation by, 489
bailee, obligations of, 488
bailor, obligations of, 487
estoppel, 490
finders, 486
generally, 187, 485
interpleader, 490
involuntary recipients, 486
licence and, 486
lien and, 490
possession and, 486
BANKRUPTCY COURT, 37
BANKRUPTS, 172
BARRISTERS, 73
BILLS OF EXCHANGE, 219
BYE-LAWS, 142, 145

CANON LAW, 15
CARE PROCEEDINGS, 95
CASE LAW—
advantages, 162
binding force, 155
    exceptions, 159
declaratory precedents, 161
distinguishing, 159
drawbacks, 162
European Court and, 163
law reports, 152
obiter, 154
overruling, 161
precedents—
    generally, 151, 153
    original, 161
persuasive, 160

ratio, 154
res judicata, 161
reversing, 161
CHANCERY DIVISION, 35
CHARGING ORDER, 133
CHARTER CORPORATIONS, 189
CHILDREN, PROTECTION OF, 169
CIRCUIT ADMINISTRATORS, 81
CIVIL PROCEDURE—
acknowledgement of service, 123
counterclaim, 125
defence, 125
discovery, 127
further and better particulars, 125
generally, 122
interrogatories, 128
judgment—enforcing, 132
legal aid, 122
notice—
    to admit, 128
    to produce a document, 129
payment in, 126
pleadings, 126, 127
reply, 125
setting down for trial, 129
statement of claim, 124
striking out, 124
trial, 129
writ, 123
COMMERCIAL COURT, 36
COMMISSIONS FOR LOCAL
    ADMINISTRATION, 66
COMMISSION OF ASSIZE FOR CIVIL
    ACTIONS, 6
COMMISSION OF OYER AND
    TERMINER, 6
COMMON LAW—
defects of, 7
equity, relationship with, 10
generally, 4
COMPANIES COURT, 37
COMPENSATORY AWARDS, 363
CONCILIATION, 33, 46
CONSPIRACY—
civil, 462
criminal, 529
CONTEMPT OF COURT, 112
CONTRACT—GENERALLY—2
acceptance—
    conditional assent, 207
    counter-offer, 207
    generally, 206
    methods of, 210

post, by, 211
accord and satisfaction, 223
classification of contracts, 202
capacity—
    aliens, 172, 378
    corporations, 236
    drunkards, 236
    mental patients, 236
    minors, 233
    unincorporated bodies, 191
collateral contracts, 215
consideration—
    definition, 216
    discharge, on, 223
    executed, 216
    executory, 216
    formation, on, 217
    generally, 216
    past, 219
    privity, doctrine of, 220
    promissory estoppel, 224
    sufficiency, 218
discharge—
    agreement by, 322
    breach by, 331
    frustration by, 327, 362
    lapse of time by, 340
    performance by, 226, 323
duress, 257, 260
employment (see Employment,
    Contract of)
entire contracts, 323
essentials of valid contract, 201
exclusion clauses, 291
executed contracts, 202
executory contracts, 202
formalities—
    absence of writing, 232
    contracts in writing, 230
    deed, contracts by, 203, 230
    evidence in writing, 231
    generally, 230
    memorandum, 231
formation of, 204
fundamental breach, 295
incomplete (or inchoate) agreements,
    208
intention to create legal relations—
    advertisements, 227
    family agreements, 227
    generally, 226
    statutory provisions, 229
misrepresentation—

agents, 253
directors, 252, 254
inducement, 247, 250, 263
meaning of, 247
negligent misstatements, 253
remedies—
  damages, 252
  generally, 251
  rescission, 255
types of, 251
mistake—
  bilateral—
    common, 243, 244
    mutual, 246
  documents mistakenly signed, 242
  unilateral, 242
offer—
  conditional, 214
  death, effect of, 214
  generally, 204
  invitation to treat and, 204–6
  lapse of, 214
  revocation of, 212
  termination of, 212
privity of contract, 220
public policy illegality and—
  judiciary, contribution of, 304, 307
  Parliament, contribution of, 313
  restraint of trade, 308
  severance, 312
  Treaty of Rome, 319
  wagering contracts, 315
rectification, 245
remedies for breach—
  damages—
    assessment of, 335
    classification of, in contract (and
      in tort)—
      aggravated, 404
      contemptuous, 405
      exemplary, 404
      liquidated, 334, 405
      nominal, 405
      ordinary, 403
      special, 403
      unliquidated, 335, 405
    generally, 334
    interest, recovery of, 337
    mitigation of loss, 336
    provisional, 337
    remoteness of damage, 336, 405
  injunction, 338
  quantum meruit, 339

refusal of further performance, 339
rescission, 339
specific performance, 337
simple contracts, 203
specialty contracts, 202
tenders, 208
terms of the contract—
  conditions, 267
  exclusion clauses, 288, 290, 291
  express terms, 263
  implied terms—
    custom, 268
    judicial, 269
    statutory, 270, 282
  innominate terms, 268
  representations and terms, 263
  unfair terms, 295
  warranties, 267
uberrimae fidei, 256
unconscionable bargains, 262
undue influence, 259
unenforceable contracts, 202
void contracts, 202
voidable contracts, 202
CONTRIBUTORY NEGLIGENCE, 442,
  446
CONVERSION, 425
CO-OWNERSHIP, 494
CORONERS' COURTS, 68
CORPORATIONS, 189
COUNTY COURT—
appeal from, 33
arbitration in, 31
generally, 28
jurisdiction, 28
pre-trial review, 32
COURT OF APPEAL—
Civil Division, 39
Criminal Division, 40
precedent, 156
COURT OF PROTECTION, 38
CRIME—
actus reus—
  intervening acts, 531
  must be causative, 530
  omissions, 531
crimes and civil wrongs distinguished,
  2, 3, 528
diminished responsibility, 542
homicide—
  causing death by dangerous driving,
    544
  manslaughter—

involuntary, 543
voluntary, 541
murder, 540
mens rea—
coincidence with *actus reus*, 534
corporations, 537
direct intent, 533
generally, 532
negligence, 534
oblique intent, 533
recklessness, 533
statutory offences in, 535
transferred intent, 534
nulla poena sine lege, 529
provocation, 541
responsibility for criminal acts—
automatism, 553
drunkenness and drugs, 554
duress, 555
insanity, 551
minors, 550
mistake, 557
necessity, 557
preventing crime, 559
self-defence, 558
sexual offences—
rape, 548
statutory offences against the person—
assault occasioning actual bodily
harm, 546
grievous bodily harm, 547
malicious wounding, 546
vicarious liability, 536
violent offences which are not fatal—
assault, 545
battery, 545
defences, 545
CRIMINAL INJURIES COMPENSATION
BOARD, 120
CRIMINAL PROCEDURE—
alibi, 101
arraignment, 102
Attorney-General, 79, 86
bail, 88
children and young persons, 95
committal proceedings—reporting of, 99
Director of Public Prosecutions, 85
fraud—prosecution of, 85
generally, 82
indictment, trial on, 99, 102
legal aid, 92, 99
prosecutor, 83
sentencing, 112

summary trial, 91, 92
summons, 91
warrant, 86
youth courts—
care proceedings, 95
criminal proceedings, 96
CROWN COURT—
Central Criminal Court, 34
constitution, 33
generally, 33
jurisdiction, 34
precedent and, 158
CROWN, THE—
contract liability, 197
generally, 196
privilege, 200
tort liability, 198, 376
CUSTOM—
as source of law, 14

DAMAGES—
administrative law, 64
contract, 334
provisional, 410
tort, 402
DECLARATORY JUDGMENT, 64
DEFAMATION—
amends, offer of, 474
consent to publication, 475
damages, 475
defences—
fair comment, 470
generally, 468
justification, 469
privilege—
absolute, 471
qualified, 472
generally, 463
innuendo, 466
libel, 465
reference to plaintiff, 467
slander, 465
theatres, 475
DEL CREDERE AGENT, 232
DELEGATED LEGISLATION—
advantages, 140
bye-laws of local authorities, 145
disadvantages, 141
generally, 13, 140
Henry VIII clauses, 143
judicial control, 143
ouster clauses, 143
Parliamentary control, 144

types of, 142
DETENTION OF GOODS, 426
DIMINISHED RESPONSIBILITY, 542
DIPLOMATIC IMMUNITY, 378
DIRECTOR OF PUBLIC PROSECUTIONS, 85
DISCHARGE OF CONTRACT, 322
DISCOVERY, 127
DISTRICT REGISTRARS, 80
DIVISIONAL COURTS—
generally, 36
precedent and, 157
DOMESTIC TRIBUNALS, 57
DOMICIL—
choice of, 175
dependent, 173
generally, 173
origin of, 173
residence, and, 175
DUTY SOLICITOR, 21

EASEMENTS, 50
EMPLOYMENT APPEAL TRIBUNAL—
generally, 54
precedent, and, 158
EMPLOYMENT—CONTRACT OF—
discrimination, 342, 347, 365
generally, 342, 345
guarantee payments, 348
health and safety, 352
information, disclosure of by
    employer, 348
insolvency of employer, 352
maternity, 349
notice, minimum periods of, 344
pay, 345, 346
recruitment of employees, 342
redundancy, 358, 365
selection of employees, 342
statutory sick pay, 345
suspension on medical grounds, 349
time off, 352
trade union membership and activities, 354
unfair dismissal, 354
EQUAL PAY, 346
EQUITY—
generally, 7
relationship with common law, 10
ESTOPPEL—
promissory, 224
EUROPEAN COMMUNITY—
Commission, The, 164

Community Law—
introduction of, 163
Council of Ministers, 165
European Parliament, 165
Treaties, The, 166
UK Parliament and, 13
EUROPEAN COURT OF HUMAN RIGHTS, 49
EUROPEAN COURT OF JUSTICE—
court of first instance, 48
generally, 46
procedure, 47
role of, 48
EVIDENCE, 108, 128
EX-OFFICIO MAGISTRATES, 20

FAIR COMMENT, 470
FAIR TRADING, 302, 317
FALSE IMPRISONMENT, 419
FAMILY DIVISION, 36
FATAL ACCIDENTS, 380
FEE SIMPLE, 492
FRUSTRATED CONTRACTS, 327, 362

GARNISHEE ORDER, 133
GAVELKIND, 4
GENERAL EYRE, 4
GENERAL GAOL DELIVERY, 6
GOLDEN RULE, 147

HABEAS CORPUS, 419
HEALTH AND SAFETY EXECUTIVE, 353
HIGH COURT—
generally, 35
precedent and, 157
HOUSE OF LORDS—
constitution, 43
generally, 19
jurisdiction, 43
precedent, 155

INDEPENDENT CONTRACTORS—
torts, liability for, 392
INDUSTRIAL TRIBUNALS, 53
INEVITABLE ACCIDENT, 398
INJUNCTION—
contract in, 338
control of tribunals by, 64
Mareva, 338
tort, in, 410, 476
INJURIA SINE DAMNO, 372
INTEREST ON DEBTS AND
    JUDGMENTS, 337

INTERPRETATION OF STATUTES—
European treaties and instruments, 48
general rules, 145, 146
presumptions, 148
statutory aids, 145

JOINT STOCK COMPANY, 187
JOINT TENANCIES, 494
JOINT TORTFEASORS, 379
JUDGES, *PUISNE*, 35
JUDGES, REMOVAL AND RETIREMENT
   OF, 45
JUDGMENT—
enforcement of, 132
JUDICIAL COMMITTEE OF THE PRIVY
   COUNCIL—
generally, 44
precedent and, 44, 158
JUDICIAL PRECEDENT, 151
JUDICIAL REVIEW, 60
JURISTIC PERSONS, 187
JURY—
advantages of, 105
alternative verdicts, 111
challenge, 106
civil cases, 131
coroner's 68
criminal cases, 131
disadvantages, 105
majority verdicts, 110
membership of, 104
number of jurors, 111
oath, 107
personation, 107
vetting, 106
JUS ACCRESCENDI, 494
JUSTICES OF THE PEACE, 19

LANDLORD AND TENANT, 498
LAND CHARGES—
registration of, 517
LAND—TRANSFER OF, 206
LANDS TRIBUNAL, 53
LAW CENTRES, 78
LAW COMMISSION, 167
LAW MERCHANT, 14
LAW REFORM, 167
LAW REPORTS, 152
LAY MAGISTRATES, 19
LEAPFROG APPEALS, 43
LEASEHOLDS—
creation of, 498
duration of, 496

landlord and tenant—
   rights and liabilities, 498
leasehold reform, 499
rule in *Walsh* v. *Lonsdale*, 498
LEGAL AID AND ADVICE—
civil law, at, 122
criminal cases, in, 99
tribunals, before, 57
LEGAL ESTATES—
fee simple, 491
term of years absolute, 492, 496
LEGAL INTERESTS AND CHARGES, 492
LEGAL OMBUDSMAN, 67
LEGAL PERSONALITY, 187
LEGAL PROFESSION—
barristers—
   briefing, 75
   circuits, 74
   Council of Legal Education, 74
   etiquette, 76
   generally, 73
   negligence by, 75
   Queen's counsel, 75
information and advice from non-
   lawyers, 78
legal executives, 77
solicitors, 76
LEGAL SERVICES, 70
LEGAL TENDER, 325
LEGAL TREATISES, 16
LEGISLATION—
development of, 12
distinguished from case law, 140
enactment of bills, 137
European Community and Parliament,
   13, 166
interpretation of statutes, 145
types of bills, 136
LEX MERCATORIA, 14
LIBEL—
civil, 463
criminal, 469
LICENCE, 421
LIEN—
bankers', 524
equitable, 524
generally, 187
maritime, 523
possessory
   particular, 522
   general, 522
LIMITATION OF ACTIONS—
in contract, 340

in tort, 412, 476
LITERAL RULE, THE, 146
LORD CHANCELLOR, 78

MAGISTRATES' COURTS—
appeals from, 26
civil jurisdiction, 25
clerk, 20
commission areas, 21
committees, 21
criminal jurisdiction, 22
duty solicitor, 21
generally, 19
sentencing, 25
MANDAMUS, 63
MAREVA INJUNCTION, 338
MASTER AND SERVANT, 382
MASTERS OF THE SUPREME COURT, 80
MEMORANDUM IN WRITING, 231
MEMORANDUM OF ASSOCIATION, 188
MENTAL PATIENTS—
contracts of, 236
diminished responsibility, 542
generally, 171
liability in crime, 551
liability in tort, 375
MERCANTILE LAW, 14
MINORS—
contracts of, 233
generally, 168
liability in crime, 550
liability in tort, 374
MISCHIEF RULE, 146
MISREPRESENTATION IN CONTRACT, 247
MISSTATEMENTS—LIABILITY IN TORT, 448
MISTAKE—
in contract, 241
in tort, 399
types of, 242–6
MORTGAGES—
borrower, rights of, 510
choses in action, of, 521
consolidation of, 515
equitable, 510
legal, 509
lender's rights, 511
personal chattels—
bills of sale, 520
pawn, 520
pledge, 520

priority of, 515
redemption, equity of, 510
tacking, 515

NATIONALITY, 176
NATURALIZATION, 176
NATURAL JUSTICE, 61
NATURAL PERSONS, 168
NECESSITY IN TORT, 399
NEGLIGENCE—
alternative danger, 444
breach of duty of care, 438
contributory, 442, 446
damage, 440
defective premises, 459
duty of care, 435, 450
economic loss, 437, 445
employer, of, 460
highway authorities, 459
independent contractor, of, 392
master and servant, 460
misstatements, liability for, 448
occupiers' liability, 455
product liability, 445
remoteness of damage, 405
res ipsa loquitur, 441
statutory duties, 444
statutory product liability, 446
NERVOUS SHOCK, 408
NISI PRIUS, 6
NON EST FACTUM, 242
NOSCITUR A SOCIIS, 148
NOTARY PUBLIC, 78
NOVUS ACTUS INTERVENIENS, 497
NUISANCE—
defences, 433
generally, 428
parties, 432
private, 429
public, 429
remedies, 432
remoteness of damage, 433
statutory intervention, 434

OBITER DICTA, 154
OCCUPIERS' LIABILITY—
access to countryside, 457
children on premises, 457
defective premises, 459
generally, 455
trespassers, 456
visitors, 455

OFFENCES—
indictable, 22
summary, 22
triable either way, 22
OFFICIAL REFEREE, 80
OFFICIAL SOLICITOR, 80
OLD BAILEY, 34
OMBUDSMAN, 65
ORDERS IN COUNCIL, 142
OWNERSHIP, 481

PARLIAMENT—
and European Community, 167
PARLIAMENTARY COMMISSIONER, 66
PARTIES IN TORT, 374
PARTNERSHIP, 194
PASSING OFF, 462
PATENTS COUNTY COURT, 32
PENALTIES, 334
PERSONAL PROPERTY, 508
PIE POWDER, COURTS OF, 14
POSSESSION, 482
adverse, 484
PRECEDENT, 155, 160, 161
PRELIMINARY INVESTIGATION—
into indictable offences, 23
PREROGATIVE ORDERS—
certiorari, 61
generally, 60
grounds for, 61
mandamus, 63
prohibition, 63
PRESIDING JUDGES, 81
PRIMOGENITURE, 4
PRIVATE BILLS, 138
PRIVATE LAW, 1
PRIVILEGE IN CIVIL PROCEEDINGS, 200
PRIVITY OF CONTRACT, 220
PRIVY COUNCIL, JUDICIAL
  COMMITTEE OF, 44
PROBATE, 72
PROHIBITION, 63, 117
PROMISSORY ESTOPPEL, 224
PROPERTY—
assignment of choses in action, 525
co-ownership, 494
equitable interests, 492
estates of freehold, 492
estates in land, 491
fee simple, 492
land charges, 517
leaseholds, 496, 498, 499
legal estates, 491

legal interests and charges, 492
legislation of 1925, 491
lien, 521
mortgages of choses in action, 521
mortgages of land, 509
mortgages of personal chattels, 520
nature of, 480
ownership, 481
possession, 482
restrictive covenants, 505
securities, generally, 521
settled land, 492
settlements, 492
servitudes, 500
trusts for sale, 494
PROSPECTUS, 206
PROTECTION, COURT OF, 38
PUBLIC LAW, 1
PUBLIC ORDER, 182, 423
PUBLIC TRUSTEE, 191

QUANTUM MERUIT, 339
QUASI-CONTRACT—
generally, 339
money had and received, 340
quantum meruit, 339
QUEEN'S BENCH DIVISION, 35
QUEEN'S COUNSEL, 75

RACIAL DISCRIMINATION—
advertisements, 180
charities, 180
Commission for Racial Equality, 181
discriminatory practices, 177, 179
disposal and management of premises,
  179
education in, 178
employment, and, 347
enforcement, 181
exceptions, 180
generally, 177
goods, facilities or services, 178
instructions to discriminate, 180
legal profession in, 179
partnerships, 178
pressure to discriminate, 180
qualifying bodies, 178
trade unions, 178
victimization, 177
RATIO DECIDENDI, 154
RECAPTION, 428
RECORDER, 34
RECTIFICATION OF CONTRACTS, 245

REDUNDANCY, 358, 365
REFORM OF LAW, 167
REGISTERED LAND, 517
REGISTRATION OF LAND CHARGES, 517
REHABILITATION OF OFFENDERS, 121
REMAND, 25, 88
REMOTENESS OF DAMAGE—
in contract, 336
in tort, 405
REPLEVIN, 428
REPORTS, LAW, 152
RESCISSION OF CONTRACT, 339
RESCUE CASES, 397
RESIDENCE, 175
RES IPSA LOQUITUR, 441
RES JUDICATA, 161
RESTITUTION ORDERS, 120
RESTRAINT OF TRADE, 308
RESTRICTIVE AGREEMENTS, 316, 317
RESTRICTIVE COVENANTS, 505
RESTRICTIVE PRACTICES COURT, 38
ROYAL ASSENT, 139
RYLANDS v. *FLETCHER*—
rule in, 476

SALE OF GOODS, 270
SALE OF LAND, 206
SECURITIES—
generally, 521
SELF-HELP, 401, 558
SENTENCING—
community sentences, 116
compensatory awards, 119
generally, 112
restitution orders, 120
types of sentence, 113
SERVITUDES—
acquisition of, 502
easements, 500
extinguishment of, 504
profits, 501, 504
termination of, 504
SETTLED LAND, 492
SEVERANCE, 312
SEX DISCRIMINATION—
advertising, 184
defined, 182
direct, 182
education, in, 183
employment, 342, 347, 365
enforcement, 185
Equal Opportunities Commission, 184

equal pay, 346
housing, goods, facilities and services, 183
indirect, 182
partnerships, 183
qualifying bodies, 183
trade unions, 183
victimization, 184
SMALL CLAIMS COURTS, 31
SOLICITOR GENERAL, 79
SOLICITORS, 76
SPECIFIC PERFORMANCE, 337
SQUATTERS' RIGHTS, 423
STAPLE, COURTS OF, 14
STARE DECISIS, 6
STATUTES—
nature and uses of, 12
STATUTORY AUTHORITY IN TORT, 400
STATUTORY INSTRUMENTS, 140
STIPENDIARY MAGISTRATES, 19
STRICT LIABILITY, 476, 535
SUBPOENA, 10
SUMMARY TRIAL, 91
SUPPLY OF GOODS AND SERVICES, 280
SUPREME COURT OF JUDICATURE, 18
SUSPENDED SENTENCE, 114

TAXING MASTERS, 80
TENANCY AT WILL, 497
TENANT—
rights and liabilities of, 498
TENANT FOR LIFE, 493
TENANTS IN COMMON, 494
TENDER, 325
TORT—
act of State in, 400
against business interests, 461
damage and liability, 372
definition, 2
general defences, 394
limitation of actions, 412
mistake in, 399
motive, 373
nature of, 371
nervous shock, 408
parties in, 374
remoteness of damage in, 405
statutory duties, 444
TRADE UNIONS, 193
TRANSFER OF LAND, 507
TREASURE TROVE, 69

TRESPASS—
to goods, 424
to land, 420
to person, 415
TRIAL, SUMMARY, 91
TRIBUNALS, 46
TRUSTS—
generally, 3, 9
TRUSTS FOR SALE, 492, 494

UBERRIMAE FIDEI, 256
ULTRA VIRES, 59, 237
UNDUE INFLUENCE, 259
UNFAIR CONTRACT TERMS, 295
UNFAIR DISMISSAL, 354
UNINCORPORATED ASSOCIATIONS—
generally, 191
partnerships, 194

trade unions, 193
UNSOLICITED GOODS, 209, 487

VICARIOUS LIABILITY, 382
VOLENTI NON FIT INJURIA, 394

WAGER OF LAW, 8
WRIT—
common law—
drawbacks of, 7
in consimili casu, 8
generally, 123
WRONGFUL INTERFERENCE WITH
GOODS—
generally, 424, 483
remedies, 427

YOUTH COURTS, 27, 95

Courses on which this book is known to be used

AAT
ACCA Level 1
Association of International
Accountants
BA Accounting and Finance
BA Business Studies
BA European Business
BA Estate Management
BA Financial Services
BTEC HND/C
BTEC National
CIB Certificate
CIB Foundation
CGLI

CII
CIMA Stage 1
Licensed Conveyancers Foundation
Course
GCSE
IComA
ICSA
ILEX
Institute of Housing
IPS
Legal Secretaries
LLB (English Legal System)
Pre-LLB
RSA